# HAVE YOU THOUGHT ABOUT
## *Customizing* THIS BOOK?

### THE PRENTICE HALL JUST-IN-TIME PROGRAM IN DECISION SCIENCE

You can combine chapters from this book with chapters from any of the Prentice Hall titles listed on the following page to create a text tailored to your specific course needs. You can add your own material or cases from our extensive case collection. By taking a few minutes to look at what is sitting on your bookshelf and the content available on our Web site, you can create your ideal textbook.

### The Just-In-Time program offers:

➡ **Quality of Material to Choose From**—In addition to the books listed, you also have the option to include any of the cases from Prentice Hall Case Series and/or the Portfolio Custom Case Series which gives you access to cases (and teaching notes where available) from Darden, Harvard, Ivey, NACRA, and Thunderbird. Most cases can be viewed online at our Web site.

➡ **Flexibility**—Choose only that material you want, either from one title or several titles (plus cases) and sequence it in whatever way you wish.

➡ **Instructional Support**—You have access to all instructor's materials that accompany the traditional textbook and desk copies of your JIT book.

➡ **Outside Materials**—There is also the option to include up to 20% of the text from materials outside of Prentice Hall Custom Business Resources.

➡ **Cost Savings**—Students pay only for material you choose. The base price is $5.00, plus $2.00 for case material, plus $.08 per page. The text can be shrink-wrapped with other Pearson textbooks for a 10% discount. Outside material is priced at $.10 per page plus permission fees.

➡ **Quality of Finished Product**—Custom cover and title page—including your name, school, department, course title, and section number. Paperback, perfect bound, black-and-white printed text. Customized table of contents and index. Sequential pagination throughout the text. CD-ROMs can be included with the custom book if applicable.

**Visit our Web site at http://www.prenhall.com/custombusiness**

**and download order forms online.**

# THE PRENTICE HALL
## Just-In-Time program

YOU CAN CUSTOMIZE YOUR TEXTBOOK WITH CHAPTERS FROM ANY OF THE FOLLOWING PRENTICE HALL TITLES:

### BUSINESS STATISTICS

- Berenson/Levine, BASIC BUSINESS STATISTICS, 8/e
- Groebner/Shannon, BUSINESS STATISTICS, 5/e
- Levin/Rubin, STATISTICS FOR MANAGEMENT, 7/e
- Levine, et al., STATISTICS FOR MANAGERS USING MICROSOFT EXCEL, 3/e
- Levine, et al., BUSINESS STATISTICS: A FIRST COURSE, 3/e
- McClave/Benson/Sincich, STATISTICS FOR BUSINESS AND ECONOMICS, 8/e
- Newbold, STATISTICS FOR BUSINESS AND ECONOMICS, 5/e
- Shannon/Groebner, A COURSE IN BUSINESS STATISTICS, 3/e

### PRODUCTION/OPERATIONS MANAGEMENT

- Anupindi, et al., MANAGING BUSINESS PROCESS FLOWS
- Chopra, SUPPLY CHAIN MANAGEMENT
- Foster, MANAGING QUALITY
- Handfield/Nichols, Jr., SUPPLY CHAIN MANAGEMENT
- Haksever/Render/Russell/Murdick, SERVICE MANAGEMENT AND OPERATIONS, 2/e
- Hanna/Newman, INTEGRATED OPERATIONS MANAGEMENT
- Heineke/Meile, GAMES AND EXERCISES IN OPERATIONS MANAGEMENT
- Heizer/Render, OPERATIONS MANAGEMENT, 6/e
- Heizer/Render, PRINCIPLES OF OPERATIONS MANAGEMENT, 4/e
- Krajewski/Ritzman, OPERATIONS MANAGEMENT, 6/e
- Latona/Nathan, CASES AND READINGS IN POM
- Russell/Taylor, OPERATIONS MANAGEMENT, 4/e
- Schmenner, PLANT AND SERVICE TOURS IN OPERATIONS MANAGEMENT, 5/e
- Nicholas, PROJECT MANAGEMENT, 2/e

### MANAGEMENT SCIENCE/OPERATIONS RESEARCH

- Eppen/Gould, INTRODUCTORY MANAGEMENT SCIENCE, 5/e
- Moore/Weatherford, DECISION MODELING WITH MICROSOFT EXCEL, 6/e
- Render/Stair/Hanna, QUANTITATIVE ANALYSIS FOR MANAGEMENT, 8/e
- Render/Stair/Balakrishnan, MANAGERIAL DECISION MODELING WITH SPREADSHEETS
- Render, et al., CASES AND READINGS IN MANAGEMENT SCIENCE
- Taylor, INTRODUCTION TO MANAGEMENT SCIENCE, 7/e

For more information, or to speak to a customer service representative, contact us at 1-800-777-6872.

**www.prenhall.com/custombusiness**

# Managerial Decision Modeling with Spreadsheets

## Barry Render

*Charles Harwood Professor of Management Science*
*Graduate School of Business, Rollins College*

## Ralph M. Stair, Jr.

*Professor of Information and Management Science*
*Florida State University*

## Nagraj (Raju) Balakrishnan

*Professor of Management*
*Clemson University*

**PRENTICE HALL**
Upper Saddle River, New Jersey 07458

**Library of Congress Cataloging-in-Publication Data**

Render, Barry.
    Managerial decision modeling with spreadsheets/Barry Render, Ralph M. Stair, Nagraj Balakrishnan.
        p. cm.
    Includes bibliographical references and index.
    ISBN 0-13-066195-3
        1. Management—Mathematical models. 2. Management science. I. Stair, Ralph M. II. Balakrishnan, Nagraj.
        III. Title.
    HD30.25 .R465 2003
    658.4′032—dc21

                                                                                                    2002019112
                                                                                                    CIP

**Executive Editor:** Tom Tucker
**Editor-in-Chief:** PJ Boardman
**Assistant Editor:** Erika Rusnak
**Editorial Assistant:** Jisun Lee
**Media Project Manager:** Nancy Welcher
**Executive Marketing Manager:** Debbie Clare
**Managing Editor (Production):** Cynthia Regan
**Production Editor:** Kerri M. Limpert
**Production Assistant:** Dianne Falcone
**Permissions Coordinator:** Suzanne Grappi

**Associate Director, Manufacturing:** Vincent Scelta
**Manufacturing Buyer:** Arnold Vila
**Design Manager:** Pat Smythe
**Designer:** Blair Brown
**Manager, Print Production:** Christy Mahon
**Composition:** UG / GGS Information Services, Inc.
**Full-Service Project Management:** UG / GGS
Information Services, Inc.
**Printer/Binder:** RRD-Willard

**Photo Credits**
page 2 AP/Wide World Photos; page 24 SuperStock, Inc.; page 76 George Hall/CORBIS; page 114 AP/Wide
World Photos; page 156 Jim Cummins/CORBIS Stock Market; page 208 SuperStock, Inc.; page 252 © 2001,
Philip Jones–Griffiths courtesy Bechtel Corportation, all rights reserved; page 312 Bob Daemmrich/Stock
Boston; page 364 Cohen/CORBIS SABA Press Photos, Inc.; page 408 Courtesy Reginaldo Manente/Volkswagen,
Resende, Brazil; page 464 Jeff Greenberg/PhotoEdit; page 518 SuperStock, Inc.

Pearson Education LTD.
Pearson Education Australia PTY, Limited
Pearson Education Singapore, Pte. Ltd
Pearson Education North Asia Ltd
Pearson Education, Canada, Ltd
Pearson Educación de Mexico, S.A. de C.V.
Pearson Education–Japan
Pearson Education Malaysia, Pte. Ltd

10 9 8 7 6 5 4 3 2
ISBN 0-13-066195-3

*To Reva Shader*

B. R.


*To Ken Ramsing and Alan Eliason*

R. M. S.


*To Meena, Nitin, and Nandita*

N. B.

# ABOUT THE AUTHORS

**Barry Render** is the Charles Harwood Distinguished Professor of Management Science at the Crummer Graduate School of Business at Rollins College in Winter Park, Florida. He received his M.S. in Operations Research and his Ph.D. in Quantitative Analysis at the University of Cincinnati. He previously taught at George Washington University, the University of New Orleans, Boston University, and George Mason University, where he held the GM Foundation Professorship in Decision Sciences and was Chair of the Decision Science Department. Dr. Render has also worked in the aerospace industry for General Electric, McDonnell Douglas, and NASA.

Professor Render has co-authored ten textbooks with Prentice-Hall, including *Quantitative Analysis for Management, Operations Management, Principles of Operations Management, Service Management, Introduction to Management Science,* and *Cases and Readings in Management Science.* His more than one hundred articles on a variety of management topics have appeared in *Decision Sciences, Production and Operations Management, Interfaces, Information and Management, The Journal of Management Information Systems, Socio-Economic Planning Sciences,* and *Operations Management Review,* among others.

Dr. Render has also been honored as an AACSB Fellow and named as a Senior Fulbright Scholar in 1982 and again in 1993. He was twice vice-president of the Decision Science Institute Southeast Region and served as Software Review Editor for Decision Line from 1989 to 1995. He has also served as Editor of the *New York Times* Operations Management special issues from 1996 to 2001. Finally, Professor Render has been actively involved in consulting for government agencies and for many corporations, including NASA; FBI; the U.S. Navy; Fairfax County, Virginia; and C&P Telephone.

He teaches operations management courses in Rollins College's MBA and Executive MBA programs. In 1995 he was named as that school's Professor of the Year, and in 1996 was selected by Roosevelt University to receive the St. Claire Drake Award for Outstanding Scholarship.

**Ralph Stair** has been Professor of Information and Mangement Science at Florida State University for twenty years, and is currently in the FSU phased retirement program. He received a B.S. in Chemical Engineering from Purdue University and an MBA from Tulane University. Under the guidance of Ken Ramsing and Alan Eliason, he received his Ph.D. in operations management from the University of Oregon.

He has taught at the University of Oregon, the University of Washington, the University of New Orleans, and Florida State University. He has also taught at Florida State University's Study Abroad Program in London. Over the years, his teaching has been concentrated in the areas of information systems, operations research, and operations management.

Dr. Stair is a member of several academic organizations, including Decision Sciences Institute and INFORMS, and he regularly participates at national meetings. He has published numerous articles and books, including *Quantitative Analysis for Management, Introduction to Management Science, Cases and Readings in Management Science, Production and Operations Management, Fundamentals of Information Systems, Principles of Information Systems, Introduction to Information Systems, Computers in Today's World, Principles of Data*

*Processing, Learning to Live with Computers, Programming in BASIC, Essentials of BASIC Programming, Essentials of FORTRAN Programming,* and *Essentials of COBOL Programming.*

Professor Stair splits his time between Florida and Colorado. He enjoys skiing, biking, kayaking, and other outdoor activities.

**Nagraj (Raju) Balakrishnan** is a Professor of Management at Clemson University, where he teaches courses in spreadsheet-based Decision Modeling, Business Statistics, and Operations Management. He holds Bachelor's and Master's degrees in Mechanical Engineering from the University of Madras (India) and the University of Kentucky respectively, and a Ph.D. in Management from Purdue University. He previously taught at Tulane University.

Dr. Balakrishnan's current research focuses on supply chain management, capacity allocation models, and problems related to the interface between manufacturing and marketing. His articles have been published in leading academic journals such as *Decision Sciences, Production and Operations Management, European Journal of Operational Research, Naval Research Logistics, IIE Transactions, Networks,* and *Computers & Operations Research.* He serves on the editorial review boards of *Production and Operations Management* and *Computers & Operations Research.*

Dr. Balakrishnan has won several awards for teaching excellence at Clemson University, including the College of Business Graduate Teaching Excellence Award (twice) and the MBA Teacher of the Year Award. He was also named recipient of the Department of Management's Scholarly Achievement Award in 1997. He is very active in writing research proposals and has authored or co-authored successful grant proposals totaling over $500,000 from the National Science Foundation and other funding agencies.

Dr. Balakrishnan lives in Clemson, SC with his wife Meena, son Nitin, and daughter Nandita. He enjoys traveling and Indian light music, and is an avid racquetball player.

# BRIEF CONTENTS

# CONTENTS

# PREFACE

## OVERVIEW

The first edition of *Managerial Decision Modeling with Spreadsheets* looks to the future with the latest software and pedagogy. In recent years, the use of spreadsheets to teach *decision modeling* (alternatively referred to as *management science, operations research,* or *quantitative analysis*) has become standard practice in many undergraduate and graduate business programs. There are several textbooks that have attempted to discuss spreadsheet-based decision modeling. However, in doing so, some of these textbooks have become too spreadsheet-oriented, focusing more on the Excel commands to use rather than on the underlying decision model. Other textbooks have maintained their algorithmic approach to decision modeling, adding Excel instructions almost as an afterthought. In this textbook, we have tried to achieve the perfect balance between decision modeling and the use of spreadsheets to set up and solve these models. In doing so, this textbook builds on the traditions and strengths of Render and Stair's *Quantitative Analysis for Management*, a recognized and proven leader in this field.

It is important that the textbooks which support decision modeling courses try to combine the student's power to logically model and analyze diverse decision-making scenarios with software-based solution procedures. To facilitate this, *Managerial Decision Modeling with Spreadsheets* focuses on providing the reader with the skills to apply decision models to different kinds of organizational decision-making situations. The discussions are very application-oriented and software-based, with a view toward how a manager can effectively apply the models learned here to improve the decision-making process. The primary target audiences for the textbook are students in undergraduate and graduate level introductory decision modeling courses in business schools. However, the textbook will also be useful to students in other introductory courses in which some of the core decision modeling topics such as linear programming and simulation are covered.

Although the emphasis is on using spreadsheets for decision modeling, the textbook remains, at heart, a *decision modeling* textbook. That is, while we use spreadsheets as a tool to quickly set up and solve decision models, our aim is not to teach how to blindly use a spreadsheet without understanding how and why it works. To accomplish this, we discuss the fundamental concepts, assumptions, and limitations behind each decision modeling technique, show how each decision model works, and illustrate the real-world usefulness of each technique with many applications from both profit and nonprofit organizations.

We have kept the notation, terminology, and equations standard with other textbooks, and have tried to write a textbook that is easy to understand and use. Algebra and a basic knowledge of Excel are the only prerequisites. For your convenience, we have included a brief introduction to Excel as an appendix.

The chapters, supplements, and software packages cover virtually every major topic in the decision modeling field, and are arranged to provide a distinction between techniques that deal with deterministic environments and those that deal with probabilistic environments. Even though we have produced a somewhat smaller textbook that covers only the most important topics, there is still probably more material than most instructors can cover in a typical first course. However, we hope that the resulting flexibility of topic selection is appreciated by instructors who need to tailor their courses to different audiences and curricula.

## OVERALL APPROACH

While writing this textbook, we have tried to adhere to certain themes, as discussed below. First, we have tried to separate the discussion of each decision modeling technique into three distinct issues:

1. formulation or problem setup,

2. model solution, and

3. interpretation of the results and "what-if" analysis.

In this three-step framework, steps 1 and 3 (formulation and interpretation) are where the manager's expertise is called upon ("this is where you earn your big salary since no software package will do this for you"). We therefore emphasize these steps.

Second, we recognize that business students are primarily going to be users of these decision modeling techniques, rather than its developers. Hence, to deal with step 2 (model solution), we have tried to integrate our discussions with software packages so that students can take full advantage of their availability. In this regard, the textbook exploits the wide availability and acceptability of spreadsheet-based software for decision modeling techniques.

Excel is a very important part of what most instructors consider the two main topics in any *basic* decision modeling textbook: Linear Programming and Simulation. However, we recognize that some topics are not best suited for spreadsheet-based software. A case in point is Project Management where Excel is probably not the best choice. In such cases, rather than try to force the topic to suit Excel, we have discussed the use of more practical packages such as Microsoft Project 2000.

Third, although we use software packages as the primary vehicle to deal with step 2, we try to ensure that students focus on *what* they are doing, and *why* they are doing it, rather than just mechanically learning which Excel formula to use or which Excel key to press. To facilitate this, and to avoid the so-called "black box syndrome," we also *briefly* discuss the steps and rationale of the solution process in many cases.

Fourth, we recognize that as an introductory textbook, the material does not need to be (and should not be) too comprehensive. That is, our aim here is to inform students about what is available with regard to decision modeling, and basically pique their interest in the subject material. More detailed instruction can follow, if the student chooses, in advanced elective courses that may use more sophisticated software packages.

Finally, we note that most of the students in decision modeling courses are likely to specialize in *other* functional areas such as finance, marketing, accounting, operations, and human resources. As such, we try to integrate decision modeling techniques with problems drawn from these different areas, so that students can recognize the importance of what they are learning and the potential benefits of using decision modeling in real-world settings. In addition, we have included summaries of selected articles from journals such as *Interfaces* that discuss the actual applications of decision modeling techniques to real-world problems.

It is no secret that unlike courses in functional areas such as finance, marketing, and accounting, decision modeling courses always face an uphill battle in getting students interested and excited about the material. We hope that this textbook will be an ally in this endeavor.

# KEY FEATURES IN THIS TEXTBOOK

There are several key features in this textbook that we hope will enable us to adhere to the themes listed above, and help students to better understand the material. These include the following features:

● *Standard layout and format for creating effective Excel models.* We use a standardized layout and format for creating spreadsheet models for all linear, integer, goal, and nonlinear programming problems. We strongly believe such a consistent approach is more suited to the beginning student of these types of decision models.

● *Pedagogical use of color in the spreadsheets to clarify and illustrate good spreadsheet modeling.* As part of the standardized layout and format for the spreadsheet models, we have used colors in a *consistent* manner so that the various components of the models are easily identifiable. For example, as shown in the following sample screen shot from Chapter 2, cells denoting decision variables are always shown in yellow, the cell denoting the objective function is always shown in green, and the cells denoting left-hand-sides of constraints are always shown in blue.

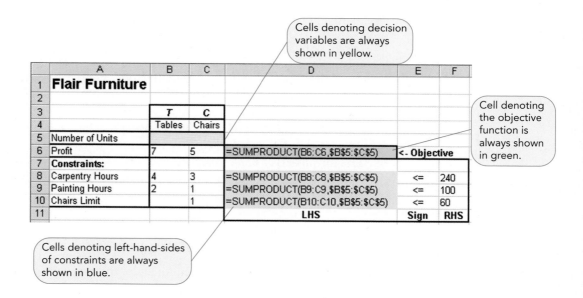

● *Description of the algebraic model and its spreadsheet implementation for all examples.* For each model, we first discuss the algebraic model so that the student can understand the logic and rationale behind the decision model. The spreadsheet implementation then closely follows the algebraic model for ease of understanding.

● *Numerous screen captures of Excel outputs with detailed callouts explaining the important entries.* We have included numerous screen capture shots of the Excel files. Each screen shot has been annotated with detailed callouts explaining the important entries and components of the model. The following sample screen shot from Chapter 2 is a typical example of this feature.

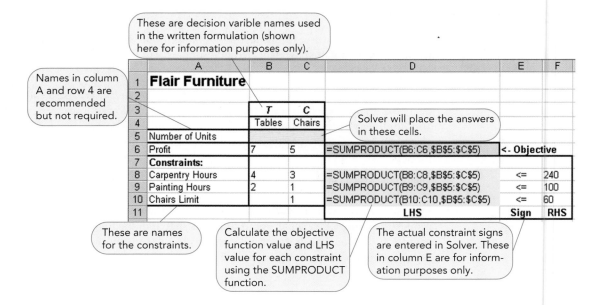

These are decision variable names used in the written formulation (shown here for information purposes only).

Names in column A and row 4 are recommended but not required.

Solver will place the answers in these cells.

These are names for the constraints.

Calculate the objective function value and LHS value for each constraint using the SUMPRODUCT function.

The actual constraint signs are entered in Solver. These in column E are for information purposes only.

- *Ability to teach topics both with and without the use of additional add-ins or software.* We have discussed several topics so that they can be studied either using Excel's standard built-in commands or using additional Excel add-ins or other software. For example, we have discussed how Excel's built-in Data Table procedure can be used to replicate large simulation models. Alternatively, we have also discussed how Crystal Ball 2000 can be used to develop models in a more convenient manner, for students who want to install and use this software. Likewise, we have discussed how Microsoft Project 2000 can be used to effectively manage large projects.

- *Extensive discussion of LP sensitivity analysis using the Solver report.* The discussion of LP sensitivity analysis in this textbook is more comprehensive than any competing textbook.

## ADDITIONAL FEATURES IN THIS TEXTBOOK

This textbook is student oriented and includes the following features that have been proved by Render and Stair's earlier textbooks to be effective aids to the learning process:

- *Decision Modeling in Action* boxes summarize published articles illustrating how real organizations have used decision models to solve problems.

- *Modeling in the Real World* boxes help students apply the steps of the decision modeling approach, first presented in Chapter 1, to every technique discussed in the textbook.

- *History* boxes briefly describe how some decision modeling techniques were developed.

- *Margin notes,* sentences or short paragraphs, are used to make it easier for students to understand important points.

- *Solved problems,* included at the end of chapters, serve as models for students in solving their own homework problems.

- *Self-Tests,* at the end of each chapter, allow students to test their knowledge of important terms and concepts to help them prepare for quizzes and examinations.

- *Discussion questions,* at the end of each chapter, test the student's understanding of concepts.

- *Problems,* included in every chapter, are applications-oriented and test the student's ability to solve exam-type problems. They are graded by three levels of difficulty: (1) introductory (one bullet), (2) moderate (two bullets), and (3) challenging (three bullets).

- *Case studies,* at the end of most chapters, provide challenging managerial applications.

- *Glossaries,* at the end of each chapter, define important terms.

- *Key equations,* which summarize the mathematical equations in a chapter, are listed at the end of each chapter that has equations.

- *End-of-chapter bibliographies* provide a current selection of more advanced textbooks and interesting articles. They include several classic references that give students a flavor of the history and development of the decision modeling field.

- *Companion Web site,* which uses the latest features of the Internet and the World Wide Web (WWW). The Web site, which can be found at www.prenhall.com/render, contains interesting Internet links and numerous additional cases.

- *Microsoft Excel* is the featured software tool for this textbook. Solver (and Premium Solver for Education, an expanded version of Solver) is used extensively in several chapters to solve optimization decision modeling problems. In addition, the textbook has incorporated Crystal Ball and TreePlan into the simulation and decision theory chapters, respectively. These powerful add-ins show students how Excel can be extended to solve simulation and decision theory problems. Further, Excel's Goal Seek has been used to identify parameter values to achieve desired goals (for example, it has been used in Chapter 1 to model a break-even problem).

- *ExcelModules,* a new program from Professor Howard Weiss of Temple University, solves problems and examples in the queuing models (Chapter 9), forecasting models (Chapter 11), and inventory control models (Chapter 12) chapters in the textbook. Students can see the power of this software package in modeling and solving problems in these chapters. ExcelModules is menu driven and easy to use.

- *Microsoft Project* is featured in the project management (Chapter 7) chapter to set up and manage projects. Readers can go to www.microsoft.com to get more information about this popular software.

## FREE SOFTWARE AND DATA FILES ON THE CD-ROM

As a convenience, the following items are conveniently packaged into a CD-ROM and included free to students as part of the textbook:

1. Premium Solver for Education,
2. 140-day student version of Crystal Ball,
3. TreePlan,
4. ExcelModules, and
5. Excel files for all examples discussed in the textbook. For your convenience, the relevant file names are printed on the margins at appropriate places in the textbook.

# SUPPLEMENTS

The supplements reflect the spreadsheet emphasis of the textbook and provide students and instructors with the best teaching and resource package available. Here is a brief list of the supplements available with the textbook.

- *Instructor's Resource CD-ROM.* The Instructor's Resource CD-ROM includes electronic files for the complete Instructor's Solutions Manual and all relevant Excel files, the Test Item File in MS Word, the computerized Test Item File (TestGen EQ), and PowerPoint presentations.

- *Instructor's Solutions Manual.* The Instructor's Solutions Manual, prepared by Raju Balakrishnan, includes all relevant Excel files and solutions for the end-of-chapter exercises and cases. The ISM is available to adopters in electronic form on the Instructor's Resource CD-ROM and can also be downloaded at the text's accompanying Web site.

- *PowerPoint Presentations.* An extensive set of PowerPoint slides, created by Isaac Gottlieb of Rutgers University, is available to adopters in electronic form on the Instructor's Resource CD-ROM and can also be downloaded at the text's accompanying Web site. The slides are oriented toward text learning objectives and build upon key concepts in the text.

- *Test Item File.* The Test Item File, created by Judith McKnew of Clemson University, is available to adopters in print form and on the Instructor's Resource CD-ROM.

- *TestGen-EQ.* New for this edition, the print test item file is designed for use with the TestGen-EQ test-generating software. This computerized package allows instructors to custom design, save, and generate classroom tests. The test program permits instructors to edit, add, or delete questions from the test banks; edit existing graphics and create new graphics; analyze test results; and organize a database of tests and student results. This new software allows for greater flexibility and ease of use. It provides many options for organizing and displaying tests, along with a search and sort feature.

- *Companion Web site* at www.prenhall.com/render. The Web site contains an interactive study guide for students which contains additional review questions written by Judith McNew of Clemson University and additional case studies.

# ACKNOWLEDGMENTS

The Roy E. Crummer School of Business at Rollins College and the Department of Information and Management Sciences at The Florida State University provided support and a conducive environment for the development of this textbook. Raju Balakrishnan would like to thank Professor Terry Leap, Department Chair, and colleagues in the Department of Management at Clemson University who provided support and encouragement during the writing of this textbook.

The authors are thrilled to have partnered with Professor Howard Weiss of Temple University, who did an outstanding job in developing ExcelModules. Professors Jerry Kinard, Mark McKnew, Judith McKnew, F. Bruce Simmons III, Khala Chand Seal, Victor E. Sower, Michael Ballot, Curtis P. McLaughlin, and Zbigniew H. Przasnyski have contributed excellent cases and exercises.

The authors would like to thank Vijay Gupta for checking all of the examples in the book and all of the end-of-chapter problems. The authors also wish to thank Isaac Gottlieb of Rutgers University for creating the PowerPoint presentation and Judith McKnew of Clemson University for writing the Test Item File.

We would also like to express our sincere appreciation to the following reviewers. Their comments on our preliminary chapters helped us greatly in writing this textbook.

Anne Alexander, University of Wyoming
Avi Dechter, California State University—Northridge
Robert Donnelly, Goldey-Beacom College
Isaac Gottlieb, Rutgers University
Susan W. Palocsay, James Madison University
Gary Reeves, University of South Carolina
David A. Schilling, Ohio State University
Sylvia Shafto, College of Notre Dame

There are several people at Prentice Hall who worked very hard to bring the textbook through the publication process. First, we would like to give a special thanks to Tom Tucker, Decision Sciences Executive Editor at Prentice Hall for all his help. His guidance and suggestions have been invaluable in making this textbook a reality. It has been a pleasure to work with him. We would also like to gratefully acknowledge the outstanding help provided by Jisun Lee, Tom's editorial assistant; Kerri Limpert, our top-notch Production Editor, who handled all aspects of the production process; Erika Rusnak, Assistant Editor, who was responsible for putting together all the text supplements; Nancy Welcher, Media Production Manager, who assembled all the nonprint material such as the CD-ROM and the companion Web site; and Debbie Clare, Executive Marketing Manager, who handled the very important marketing component. Thank you all!

Barry Render
407-646-2657 (phone)
brender@rollins.edu(e-mail)

Ralph Stair
rstair@cob.fsu.edu (e-mail)

Raju Balakrishnan
864-656-3769 (phone)
nbalak@clemson.edu (e-mail)

## CHAPTER 1

# INTRODUCTION TO MANAGERIAL DECISION MODELING

### The Management Science Group Is Bullish at Merrill Lynch

Management science groups at corporations can make a huge difference in reducing costs and increasing profits. At Merrill Lynch, the management science group was established in 1986. Its overall mission is to provide high-quality quantitative (or mathematical) analysis, modeling, and decision support. The group analyzes a variety of problems and opportunities related to client services, products, and the marketplace. In the past, this group has helped Merrill Lynch develop asset allocation models, mutual fund portfolio optimization solutions, investment strategy development and research tools, financial planning models, and cross-selling approaches. Currently, there are 20 members of the management science group at Merrill Lynch.

In the late 1990s, Merrill Lynch faced increasing pressure from discount brokers such as Fidelity and Schwab. These discount brokers threatened to severely cut into the business and profits at traditionally full-service firms like Merrill Lynch. Should Merrill Lynch offer discount online trading and face the possibility of alienating its nearly 14,000 financial consultants? With the help of the management science group, Merrill Lynch made the decision to offer a new service, called Integrated Choice. The new offering would allow clients to choose the level of service and advice they wanted. One ad read, "By mouse, by phone, by human being." An important aspect of the new service, Unlimited Advantage, gives clients access to a large array of services for a fixed fee. The new offerings have been a resounding success.

To provide meaningful assistance to Merrill Lynch, the management science group has concentrated on mathematical models that focus on client satisfaction. What are the keys to continued success for the management science group? Although skill and technical expertise in decision modeling are essential, the management science group has identified the following four critical success factors: (1) objective analysis, (2) focus on business impact and implementation, (3) teamwork, and (4) adopting a disciplined consultative approach.[1]

---

[1] R. Nigam et al. "Bullish on Management Science," *OR/MS Today* (June 2000): 48–51.

## 1.1   INTRODUCTION

Just like Merrill Lynch in the preceding application, organizations such as American Airlines, IBM, and AT&T frequently use decision models to help solve complex problems. Although mathematical tools have been in existence for thousands of years, the formal study and application of quantitative (or mathematical) decision modeling techniques to practical decision making is largely a product of the twentieth century. The decision modeling techniques studied here have been applied successfully to an increasingly wide variety of complex problems in business, government, health care, education, and many other areas. Many such successful uses are discussed throughout this textbook.

It isn't enough, though, just to know the mathematical details of how a particular decision modeling technique can be set up and solved. It is equally important to be familiar with the limitations, assumptions, and specific applicability of the model. The correct use of decision modeling techniques usually results in solutions that are timely, accurate, flexible, economical, reliable, easy to understand, and easy to use.

## 1.2   WHAT IS DECISION MODELING?

*Decision modeling is a scientific approach to decision making.*

There are several definitions for *decision modeling*. We define it here as a scientific approach to managerial decision making. Alternatively, we can define it as a representation (usually mathematical) of a practical problem scenario or environment. The resulting model should typically be such that the decision-making process is not affected by personal bias, whim, emotions, and guesswork. Decision modeling is also commonly referred to as *quantitative analysis, management science,* or *operations research.* In this textbook, we prefer the term *decision modeling,* since we will discuss all modeling techniques in a managerial decision-making context.

*The decision modeling process starts with data.*

Any decision modeling process starts with data. Like raw material for a factory, these data are manipulated or processed into information that is valuable to people making decisions. This processing and manipulating of raw data into meaningful information is the heart of decision modeling.

### Quantitative versus Qualitative Data

In dealing with a decision-making problem, managers may have to consider both qualitative and quantitative factors. For example, suppose we are considering several different investment alternatives, such as certificates of deposit (CDs), stock market, and real estate.

### HISTORY   The Origin of Decision Modeling

Decision modeling has been in existence since the beginning of recorded history, but it was Frederick W. Taylor who, in the early 1900s, pioneered the principles of the scientific approach to management. During World War II, many new scientific and quantitative techniques were developed to assist the military. These new developments were so successful that after World War II many companies started using similar techniques in managerial decision making and planning. Today, many organizations employ a staff of operations research or management science personnel or consultants to apply the principles of scientific management to problems and opportunities. The terms *management science, operations research,* and *quantitative analysis* can be used interchangeably, though here we use *decision modeling.*

The origin of many of the techniques discussed in this book can be traced to individuals and organizations that have applied the principles of scientific management first developed by Taylor; they are discussed in *History* boxes scattered throughout the book.

*Both qualitative and quantitative factors must be considered.*

We can use *quantitative* factors such as rates of return, financial ratios, and cash flows in our decision model to guide our ultimate decision. In addition to these factors, however, we may also wish to consider *qualitative* factors such as pending state and federal legislation, new technological breakthroughs, and the outcome of an upcoming election. It can be difficult to quantify these qualitative factors.

Due to the presence (and relative importance) of qualitative factors, the role of quantitative decision modeling in the decision-making process can vary. When there is a lack of qualitative factors, and when the problem, model, and input data remain reasonably stable and steady over time, the results of a decision model can automate the decision-making process. For example, some companies use quantitative inventory models to determine automatically when to order additional new materials and how much to order. In most cases, however, decision modeling will be an aid to the decision-making process. The results of decision modeling should be combined with other (qualitative) information while making decisions in practice.

## Role of Spreadsheets in Decision Modeling

*Spreadsheet packages are capable of handling many decision modeling techniques.*

In keeping with the ever-increasing presence of technology in modern times, computers have become an integral part of the decision modeling process in today's business environments. Until the early 1990s, many of the modeling techniques discussed here required specialized software packages to be solved using a computer. However, spreadsheet packages such as Microsoft Excel have become increasingly capable of setting up and solving most of the decision modeling techniques commonly used in practical situations. For this reason, the current trend in many college courses in decision modeling focuses on spreadsheet-based instruction. In keeping with this trend, we discuss the role and use of spreadsheets (specifically Microsoft Excel) during our study of the different decision modeling techniques presented here.

*Several add-ins for Excel are included in your CD-ROM.*

In addition to discussing the use of some of Excel's built-in functions and procedures (e.g., Goal Seek, Data Table, and Chart Wizard), we also discuss several add-ins for Excel. The Solver add-in comes standard with Excel; others are included in the CD-ROM that accompanies this textbook. Table 1.1 lists these add-ins and indicates the chapter and topic in which each one is discussed and used.

Since a knowledge of basic Excel commands and mechanics will facilitate understanding of the techniques and concepts discussed here, we recommend reading Appendix A, which provides a brief overview of those Excel features most useful in

| TABLE 1.1 | | | |
|---|---|---|---|
| **Excel Add-Ins Included in Your CD-ROM** | **EXCEL ADD-IN** | **USED IN** | **TOPIC** |
| | Premium Solver for Education (enhanced version of the Solver add-in that is included with Microsoft Excel) | Chapters 2–7 | Linear programming, Network flows, Integer programming, Goal programming, Nonlinear programming, and Project Management |
| | Tree Plan | Chapter 8 | Decision theory |
| | Crystal Ball 2000 | Chapter 10 | Simulation |
| | ExcelModules (custom software provided with this textbook) | Chapters 9, 11, and 12 | Queuing Models, Forecasting Models, and Inventory Control Models |

decision modeling, if necessary. In addition, at appropriate places throughout this textbook, we discuss several Excel functions and procedures specific to each decision modeling technique.

## Types of Decision Models

Decision models can be broadly classified into two categories based on the type and nature of the problem environment under consideration: (1) deterministic models and (2) probabilistic models. The following sections define each of these types of models.

*Deterministic means complete certainty.*

**Deterministic Models** *Deterministic models* assume that all the relevant input data are known with certainty; that is, they assume that all the information needed for modeling the decision-making problem environment is available, with fixed and known values. An example of such a model would be the case of Dell Corporation, which makes several different types of PC products (e.g. desktops, laptops), all of which compete for the same resources (e.g., labor, hard disks, chips, working capital). Suppose Dell knows the specific amounts of each resource required to make one unit of each type of PC, and the expected profit contribution per unit of each type of PC. In such an environment, if Dell decides on a specific production plan, it is a simple task to compute the quantity required of each resource to satisfy this production plan. For example, if Dell plans to ship 5,000 units of a specific model and each unit includes two speakers, then Dell will need 10,000 speakers. Likewise, it is easy to compute the total profit that will be realized by this production plan (assuming that Dell can sell all the PCs it makes).

*Resources include labor, raw materials, machine time, and working capital.*

Perhaps the most common and popular deterministic modeling technique is linear programming (LP). In Chapter 2, we first formulate small LP models. Then, we show how these models can be set up and solved using Excel. We extend our discussion of LP in Chapter 3 to more complex problems, which are drawn from a variety of business disciplines. In Chapter 4, we study how the solution to LP models produces, as a by-product, a great deal of information that is useful for managerial interpretation of results. Finally, in Chapters 5 and 6, we study a few extensions to LP models. These include several different network flow models (Chapter 5), and integer, nonlinear, and multi-objective (goal) programming models (Chapter 6).

*The most commonly used deterministic modeling technique is linear programming.*

As we demonstrate during our study of deterministic models, a variety of important managerial decision-making problems can be set up and solved using these techniques. Moreover, it is possible to solve very large models of this type very quickly using available software packages.

*Some input data are unknown in probabilistic models.*

**Probabilistic Models** In contrast to deterministic models, *probabilistic* (also called *stochastic*) models assume that some input data are not known with certainty. That is, they assume that the values of some important variables will not be known *before* decisions are made. It is therefore important to incorporate this "ignorance" into the model. An example of this type of model would be the decision of whether to start a new Internet-based venture. As we have seen during the slump in technology stocks of 2000–2002, the success of such ventures is obviously unsure. However, the investors (e.g. venture capitalists, founders) have to make decisions regarding this venture based on their expectations of future performance. Clearly, such expectations are not guaranteed to occur. In recent years, we have seen several examples of firms that have lived up to their expectations (e.g., EBay) and several that have not (e.g., EToys).

*Probabilistic models use probabilities to incorporate uncertainty.*

Probabilistic modeling techniques incorporate uncertainty by using probabilities on these "random" or unknown variables. Probabilistic modeling techniques discussed in this textbook include decision analysis (Chapter 8), queuing models (Chapter 9), simulation models (Chapter 10), and forecasting (Chapter 11). Two other techniques, project management (Chapter 7) and inventory models (Chapter 12), include aspects of both deterministic and probabilistic modeling.

For each modeling technique, we discuss what kinds of criteria can be used when there is uncertainty and how to use spreadsheets to find optimal decisions. In this context, we use Excel add-ins such as Crystal Ball, TreePlan, and ExcelModules (see Table 1.1).

Since uncertainty plays a vital role in probabilistic models, some knowledge of basic probability and statistical concepts is useful here. Appendix B provides a brief overview of this topic. This should serve as a good refresher while studying these modeling techniques.

## 1.3    STEPS INVOLVED IN DECISION MODELING

*The decision modeling process involves three steps.*

Regardless of the size and complexity of the decision-making problem at hand, the decision modeling process involves three distinct steps: (1) formulation, (2) solution, and (3) interpretation. Figure 1.1 provides a schematic overview of these steps along with the components or parts of each step. We discuss each of these steps in the following sections.

*It is common to iterate between the three steps.*

It is important to note that it is common to have an iterative process between these three steps before the final solution is obtained. For example, testing the solution (see Figure 1.1) might reveal that the model is incomplete or that some of the input data are being measured incorrectly. This means that the formulation needs to be revised. This, in turn, would cause all of the subsequent steps to be changed.

### FIGURE 1.1

**The Decision Modeling Approach**

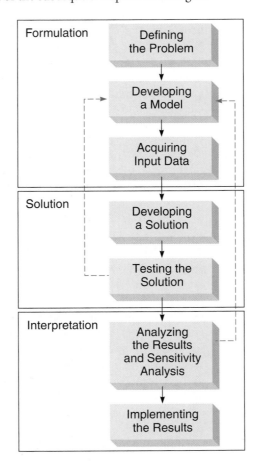

## Step 1: Formulation

*Formulation* is the process by which each aspect of the problem scenario is translated and expressed in terms of a mathematical model. This is perhaps the most important and challenging step in decision modeling, since the results of a poorly formulated problem will almost surely be wrong. It is also in this step that the decision maker's ability to analyze a problem rationally comes into play. Even the most sophisticated software program will not automatically formulate a problem. The aim in formulation is to ensure that the mathematical model completely addresses all the issues relevant to the problem at hand. Formulation can be further classified into three parts: (1) defining a problem, (2) developing a model, and (3) acquiring input data.

*Formulation is the most challenging step in decision modeling.*

**Defining the Problem**   The first part in formulation (and in decision modeling) is to develop a clear, concise statement of the problem. This statement will give direction and meaning to all the parts that follow it.

In many cases, defining the problem is perhaps the most important, and the most difficult, part. It is essential to go beyond just the symptoms of the problem at hand and identify the true causes behind it. One problem may be related to other problems, and solving a problem without regard to its related problems can actually make the situation worse. Thus, it is important to analyze how the solution to one problem affects other problems or the decision-making environment in general. Experience has shown that bad problem definition is a major reason for failure of management science groups to serve their organizations well.

*Defining the problem can be the most important part of formulation.*

When the problem is difficult to quantify, it may be necessary to develop *specific, measurable* objectives. For example, say a problem is defined as inadequate health care delivery in a hospital. The objectives might be to increase the number of beds, reduce the average number of days a patient spends in the hospital, increase the physician-to-patient ratio, and so on. When objectives are used, however, the real problem should be kept in mind. It is important to avoid obtaining specific and measurable objectives that may not solve the real problem.

**Developing a Model**   Once we select the problem to be analyzed, the next part is to develop a decision model. Even though you might not be aware of it, you have been using models most of your life. For example, you may have developed the following model about friendship: Friendship is based on reciprocity, an exchange of favors. Hence, if you need a favor such as a small loan, your model would suggest that you ask a friend.

Of course, there are many other types of models. Architects often make a physical model of a building they plan to construct. Engineers develop scale models of chemical plants, called pilot plants. A schematic model is a picture or drawing of reality. Automobiles, lawn mowers, circuit boards, typewriters, and numerous other devices have schematic models (drawings and pictures) that reveal how these devices work.

*The types of models include physical, scale, schematic, and mathematical models.*

What sets decision modeling apart from other modeling techniques is that the models we develop here are mathematical. A *mathematical model* is a set of mathematical relationships. In most cases, these relationships are expressed as equations and inequalities, as they are in a spreadsheet model that computes sums, averages, or standard deviations.

Although there is considerable flexibility in the development of models, most of the models presented here contain one or more variables and parameters. A *variable*, as the name implies, is a measurable quantity that may vary or is subject to change. Variables can be controllable or uncontrollable. A controllable variable is also called a *decision variable*. An example would be how many inventory items to order. A *parameter* is a measurable quantity that is inherent in the problem, such as the cost of placing an order for more

*A* variable *is a measurable quantity that is subject to change.*

*A* parameter *is a measurable quantity that usually has a known value.*

inventory items. In most cases, variables are unknown quantities, whereas parameters (or input data) are known quantities.

All models should be developed carefully. They should be solvable, realistic, and easy to understand and modify, and the required input data should be obtainable. The model developer has to be careful to include the appropriate amount of detail to be solvable yet realistic.

**Acquiring Input Data**  Once we have developed a model, we must obtain the input data to be used in the model. Obtaining accurate data is essential, since even if the model is a perfect representation of reality, improper data will result in misleading results. This situation is called garbage in, garbage out (GIGO). For larger problems, collecting accurate data can be one of the more difficult aspects of decision modeling.

There are several sources that can be used in collecting data. In some cases, company reports and documents can be used to obtain the necessary data. Another source is interviews with employees or other persons related to the firm. These individuals can sometimes provide excellent information, and their experience and judgment can be invaluable. A production supervisor, for example, might be able to tell you with a great degree of accuracy the amount of time that it takes to manufacture a particular product. Sampling and direct measurement provide other sources of data for the model. You may need to know how many pounds of a raw material are used in producing a new photochemical product. This information can be obtained by going to the plant and actually measuring the amount of raw material that is being used. In other cases, statistical sampling procedures can be used to obtain data.

*Garbage in, garbage out means that improper data will result in misleading results.*

## Step 2: Solution

*In the solution step, we solve the mathematical expressions in the formulation.*

The solution step is when the mathematical expressions resulting from the formulation process are actually solved to identify the optimal solution. Until the mid-1990s, typical courses in decision modeling focused a significant portion of their attention on this step, since it was the most difficult aspect of studying the modeling process. As stated earlier, with the advent of computing technology, the focus today has shifted away from the detailed steps of the solution process and more toward the availability and use of software packages. The solution step can be further classified into two parts: (1) developing a solution and (2) testing the solution.

**Developing a Solution**  Developing a solution involves manipulating the model to arrive at the best (or optimal) solution to the problem. In some cases, this may require that a set of mathematical expressions be solved for the best decision. In other cases, you can use a trial and error method, trying various approaches and picking the one that results in the best decision. For some problems, you may wish to try all possible values for the variables in the model to arrive at the best decision, called complete enumeration. For problems that are quite complex and difficult, you may be able to use an algorithm. An *algorithm* consists of a series of steps or procedures that are repeated until we find the best solution. Regardless of the approach used, the accuracy of the solution depends on the accuracy of the input data, and the decision model itself.

*An* algorithm *is a series of steps that are repeated.*

*The input data and model determine the accuracy of the solution.*

**Testing the Solution**  Before a solution can be analyzed and implemented, it must be tested completely. Since the solution depends on the input data and the model, both require testing. There are several ways to test input data. One is to collect additional data from a different source and use statistical tests to compare these new data with the original data. If there are significant differences, more effort is required to obtain accurate input data. If the data

*Analysts test the data and model before analyzing the results.*

are accurate but the results are inconsistent with the problem, the model itself may not be appropriate. In this case, the model should be checked to make sure that it is logical and represents the real situation.

## Step 3: Interpretation and What-If Analysis

Assuming the formulation is correct and has been successfully implemented and solved, how does a manager use the results? Here again the decision maker's expertise is called upon, since it is up to him or her to recognize the implications of the results that are presented. We discuss this step in two parts: (1) analyzing the results and sensitivity analysis and (2) implementing the results.

**Analyzing the Results and Sensitivity Analysis**  Analyzing the results starts with determining the implications of the solution. In most cases, a solution to a problem will result in some kind of action or change in the way an organization is operating. The implications of these actions or changes must be determined and analyzed before the results are implemented.

*Sensitivity analysis determines how the solutions will change with a different model or input data.*

Because a model is only an approximation of reality, the sensitivity of the solution to changes in the model and input data is an important part of analyzing the results. This type of analysis is called *sensitivity* or *post-optimality analysis*. It determines how much the solution will change if there are changes in the model or the input data. When the optimal solution is very sensitive to changes in the input data and the model specifications, additional testing must be performed to make sure the model and input data are accurate and valid.

The importance of sensitivity analysis cannot be overemphasized. Because input data may not always be accurate or model assumptions may not be completely appropriate, sensitivity analysis can become an important part of decision modeling.

**Implementing the Results**  The final part is to *implement* the results. This can be much more difficult than one might imagine. Even if the optimal solution will result in millions of dollars in additional profits, if managers resist the new solution, the model is of no value. Experience has shown that a large number of decision modeling teams have failed in their efforts because they have failed to implement a good, workable solution properly.

*The solution should be closely monitored even after implementation.*

After the solution has been implemented, it should be closely monitored. Over time, there may be numerous changes that call for modifications of the original solution. A changing economy, fluctuating demand, and model enhancements requested by managers and decision makers are only a few examples of changes that might require the analysis to be modified.

## Decision Modeling in the Real World

The decision modeling approach discussed so far is not just a series of theoretical steps that are seldom used in the real world. These steps, shown in Figure 1.1, are the building blocks of any successful use of decision modeling. As seen in our first **Modeling in the Real World** box (on page 10), the steps of the decision modeling approach can be used to help a large country such as China plan for critical energy needs now and for decades into the future. Throughout this textbook, you will see how this approach is being used to help countries and companies of all sizes save millions of dollars, plan for the future, increase revenues, and provide higher-quality products and services. The Modeling in the Real World boxes in every chapter demonstrate the power and importance of decision modeling in solving real problems for real organizations. Using the steps of decision modeling, however, does not guarantee success. These steps must be applied carefully.

## ⅢⅢ➡ MODELING IN THE REAL WORLD   Planning China's Coal and Electricity Delivery System

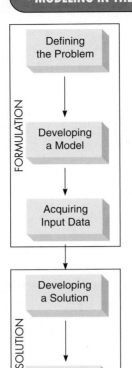

China produces about 1.1 billion tons of coal each year. However, in 1995, demand was estimated to be about 1.6 billion tons. In addition, China faced air pollution problems that could threaten its high gross national product (GNP) growth rate. These problems were identified by the Chinese State Planning Commission and the World Bank as important to the continued growth of the GNP.

To analyze some of the problems associated with the delivery of coal and electricity, the Chinese State Planning Commission developed a comprehensive model, called the Coal Transport Study (CTS) model. The model specified key components in the generation, transmission, and demand for electricity.

In addition to historical data, the model required forecasts of future demand and the potential environmental impact of various energy sources and uses. In addition, specific data concerning the various stages of coal and electricity production were needed.

Instead of developing and reporting one solution, the decision modeling team analyzed 16 different solutions or possibilities. These solutions revealed that the investment in new coal-electricity systems could be as high as $250 billion over a 10 year period. The new system would have to deliver about 2 billion tons of coal.

Assumptions of the model and the solution were carefully tested. About half a year was spent in testing the data, the model, and the solutions. This included running a series of tests on the data and model using known data to make sure that the data and model produced results consistent with the current situation. This testing resulted in fine-tuning the data and model to make them more accurate. After testing, corrections and adjustments were made to make sure that the results were as accurate as possible.

The solutions also resulted in major findings. First, the government should plan on an 8% to 9% growth in power needs. Second, railways will continue to be the dominant transportation system for coal. Next, coal distribution can be greatly increased by increasing the volume and length of coastal and inland waterways. The chance of building and using slurry pipelines was slim. In addition, there were a number of specific findings on how coal should be handled and processed into energy to reduce pollution and negative environmental consequences.

Implementation of the CTS model resulted in a new steam coal-washing procedure, the construction of improved railway systems and a new port, and the use of coal imports. In addition, the planning commission has developed a sophisticated model for strategic-level investment planning. The model will be extended to perform energy planning to the year 2010.

**Source:** M. Kuby et al. "Planning China's Coal and Electricity Delivery System," *Interfaces* 25 (January–February 1995): 41–68.

## 1.4   SPREADSHEET EXAMPLE OF A DECISION MODEL: TAX COMPUTATION

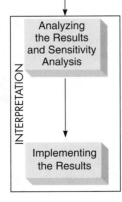

*A decision modeling example.*

Now that we have explained what a decision model is, let us develop a simple model for a real-world situation that we all face each year, namely, paying taxes. Sue and Robert Miller, a newly married couple, will be filing a joint tax return for the first time in 2003. Since both work as independent contractors (Rob is a painter and Sue is an interior decorator), their projected income in 2003 is subject to some variability. However, since their income is not taxed at the source, they know that they have to pay estimated taxes on a quarterly basis, based on their taxable income for 2003. The Millers have the following information available to help in developing their decision model:

- They would like to put away 5% of their total income in a tax deductible retirement account, up to a maximum of $4,000.
- They do not have any income from dividends or capital gains.
- They are entitled to a personal exemption of $3,100 each.
- The standard deduction for joint tax filers is $8,000 in 2003.
- They do not anticipate having any other deductions from their income for tax purposes.
- The tax brackets for 2003 are 15% up to $48,000, and 26% between $48,001 and $115,000. The Millers don't believe the higher tax brackets are relevant for them in 2003. They are sure however that they will have taxable income in the 26% tax bracket.

To help decide the estimated taxes they should pay the tax authorities each quarter, Sue would like to set up a spreadsheet-based decision model. Program 1.1A shows the formulas that we can use to develop this model.

**File: 1-1.xls**

### Excel Notes

- The CD-ROM that accompanies this textbook contains the Excel file for each example problem discussed here. The relevant file name is shown on the margin next to each example.
- In each of our Excel layouts, for clarity, we color-code the cells as follows:
  - input cells, in which we enter the problem data, are shaded yellow.
  - output cells, showing the results of our analysis, are shaded green.

---

**PROGRAM 1.1A**

**Formula View of the Excel Layout for Millers' Tax Computation**

| | A | B | C | D |
|---|---|---|---|---|
| 1 | **Millers' Tax Computation** | | | |
| 2 | | | | |
| 3 | **Problem Parameters** | | | |
| 4 | Retirement Savings % | 0.05 | | |
| 5 | Maximum savings | 4000 | | |
| 6 | Personal exemption per person | 3100 | | |
| 7 | Standard deduction | 8000 | | |
| 8 | Tax brackets | 0.15 | up to | 48000 |
| 9 | | 0.26 | up to | 115000 |
| 10 | | | | |
| 11 | **Input Data** | | | |
| 12 | Sue's income | | | |
| 13 | Rob's income | | | |
| 14 | | | | |
| 15 | **Tax Computation** | | | |
| 16 | Total income | =B12+B13 | | |
| 17 | Retirement savings | =MIN(B4*B16,B5) | | |
| 18 | Personal exemptions | =2*B6 | | |
| 19 | Standard deduction | =B7 | | |
| 20 | Taxable income | =B16-SUM(B17:B19) | | |
| 21 | Tax @ 15% rate | =B8*MIN(B20,D8) | | |
| 22 | Tax @ 26% rate | =B9*(MIN(B20,D9)-D8) | | |
| 23 | Total tax | =B21+B22 | | |
| 24 | Estimated tax per quarter | =B23/4 | | |

This box shows all the *known* input parameters.

This box shows the two input variable cells.

Minimum of 5% of income, or $4,000.

15% tax up to $48,000.

26% tax between $48,001 and $115,000.

Quarterly tax payments.

The known problem data (i.e., constants) are shown in the box labeled Problem Parameters. Rather than use these known constant values directly in the formulas, we recommend that you develop the habit of entering each known value in a cell and then using that cell reference in the formulas. In addition to being more "elegant," this way of modeling has the advantage of making any future changes to these values easy.

Cells B12 and B13 denote the input data, namely, Sue and Rob's projected income for 2003. These entries represent the only two variables in this decision model. Using these variables, the results are now computed in cells B16:B24 and presented in the box labeled Tax Computation.

Cell B16 shows the total income, and cell B17 calculates their tax-deductible contribution to the retirement account. Note that this amount is the smaller value of 5% of their total income, or $4,000. Cells B18 and B19 calculate their personal exemptions and the standard deduction, respectively. Their taxable income is shown in cell B20. The taxes payable at the 15% rate and 26% rates are then calculated in cells B21 and B22, respectively. Finally, the total tax is computed in cell B23, and the estimated quarterly tax is computed in cell B24.

Now that we have developed this decision model, how can the Millers actually use it? Suppose Sue estimates her income in 2003 at $45,000 and Rob's income at $40,000. When we enter these values in cells B12 and B13 respectively, the decision model lets us know that the Millers should pay estimated taxes of $3,022 each quarter. These input values, and the resulting computations, are shown in Program 1.1B. We can use this decision model in a similar fashion with any other projected income values for Sue and Rob Miller.

Observe that the decision model we have developed for the Millers' example does not optimize the decision in any way. That is, the model simply computes the estimated taxes for a given income level. It does not, for example, determine whether these taxes can be reduced in some way by better tax planning. Later in this textbook, we discuss decision models that will not only help compute the implications of a particular specified decision, but also help identify the optimal decision, based on some objective or goal.

**PROGRAM 1.1B**

**Excel Decision Model for Millers' Tax Computation**

| | A | B | C | D |
|---|---|---|---|---|
| 1 | **Millers' Tax Computation** | | | |
| 2 | | | | |
| 3 | **Problem Parameters** | | | |
| 4 | Retirement Savings % | 5.0% | | |
| 5 | Maximum savings | $4,000 | | |
| 6 | Personal exemption per person | $3,100 | | |
| 7 | Standard deduction | $8,000 | | |
| 8 | Tax brackets | 15.0% | up to | $48,000 |
| 9 | | 26.0% | up to | $115,000 |
| 10 | | | | |
| 11 | **Input Data** | | | |
| 12 | Sue's income | $45,000.00 | | |
| 13 | Rob's income | $40,000.00 | | |
| 14 | | | | |
| 15 | **Tax Computation** | | | |
| 16 | Total income | $85,000.00 | | |
| 17 | Retirement savings | $4,000.00 | | |
| 18 | Personal exemptions | $6,200.00 | | |
| 19 | Standard deduction | $8,000.00 | | |
| 20 | Taxable income | $66,800.00 | | |
| 21 | Tax @ 15% rate | $7,200.00 | | |
| 22 | Tax @ 26% rate | $4,888.00 | | |
| 23 | Total tax | $12,088.00 | | |
| 24 | Estimated tax per quarter | $3,022.00 | | |

Projected incomes for 2003.

The Millers should pay $3,022 in taxes each quarter.

**IN ACTION**    The Indispensable Role of Management Science at Reynolds

As the title of this box implies, decision modeling can be indispensable in helping companies such as the Reynolds Metals Company. Headquartered in Richmond, Virginia, Reynolds Metals Company is a Fortune 75 metals producer. Its aluminum operation includes production, mining, and the use of recycled aluminum. Of the company's $6 billion in sales in a recent year, more than 94% was in value-added fabricated products, including aluminum cans, flexible packaging, and a variety of consumer products.

In order to provide a more effective shipping operation, Reynolds decided to use management science to control shipping and reduce transportation costs. The result was the use of an integer programming model (see Chapter 6) that had the minimization of central dispatch freight cost as a primary

objective. Using the annual shipping demand patterns, this decision modeling technique was able to improve on-time delivery of shipments and reduce freight costs by more than $7 million annually. As a company spokesperson said: "The confidence and respect I have for the management science discipline gave me the resolve to stick to the project plan when others doubted it could be done. I am very pleased to report today that the results that were predicted are being achieved. Management science made the difference between success and failure for this venture."

**Source:** W. Moore, J. Warmke, and L. Gorban. "The Indispensable Role of Management Science in Centralizing Freight Operations at Reynolds Metal Company," *Interfaces* 21, 1 (January–February 1991): 107–129.

## 1.5 SPREADSHEET EXAMPLE OF ANOTHER DECISION MODEL: BREAK-EVEN ANALYSIS

*Expenses include fixed and variable costs.*

Let us now develop another decision model—this one to compute the total profit (and associated break-even point) for a firm. We know that the profit is simply the difference between revenues and expenses. In most cases, we can express revenues as the selling price per unit, multiplied by the number of units sold. Likewise, we can express expenses as the sum of the total fixed and variable costs. In turn, the total variable cost is the variable cost per unit, multiplied by the number of units sold. Thus, we can express profit using the following mathematical expression:

$$\text{Profit} = (\text{Selling price per unit}) \times (\text{Number of units}) - \text{Fixed cost} \qquad (1\text{-}1)$$
$$- (\text{Variable cost per unit}) \times (\text{Number of units})$$

We use the Bill Pritchett clock repair shop example to demonstrate the creation of a decision model to calculate profit (and associated break-even point). Bill's company, Pritchett's Precious Time Pieces, buys, sells, and repairs old clocks and clock parts. Bill sells rebuilt springs for a unit price of $10. The fixed cost of the equipment to build the springs is $1,000. The variable cost per unit is $5 for spring material. If we represent the number of springs (units) sold as the variable $X$, we can restate the profit as follows:

$$\text{Profit} = \$10X - \$1,000 - \$5X$$

**File: 1-2.xls**

Program 1.2A shows the formulas used in developing the decision model for Bill Pritchett's example. Cells B4, B5, and B6 show the known problem parameter values, namely, revenue per unit, fixed cost, and variable cost per unit, respectively. Cell B9 is the lone decision variable in the model and represents the number of units sold (i.e., $X$). Using these entries, the total revenue, total variable cost, total cost, and profit are computed in cells B12, B14, B15 and B16, respectively. For example, if we enter a value of 1,000 units for $X$ in cell B9, the profit is calculated as $4,000 in cell B16, as shown in Program 1.2B.

In addition to computing the profit, decision makers are often interested in the *break-even point* (BEP). The BEP is the number of units sold that will result in total revenue

**PROGRAM 1.2A**

**Formula View of the Excel Layout for Pritchett's Precious Time Pieces**

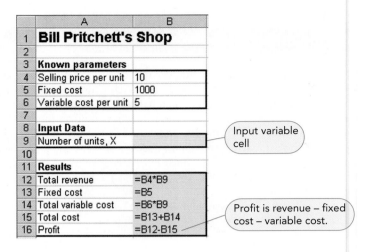

| | A | B |
|---|---|---|
| 1 | **Bill Pritchett's Shop** | |
| 2 | | |
| 3 | **Known parameters** | |
| 4 | Selling price per unit | 10 |
| 5 | Fixed cost | 1000 |
| 6 | Variable cost per unit | 5 |
| 7 | | |
| 8 | **Input Data** | |
| 9 | Number of units, X | |
| 10 | | |
| 11 | **Results** | |
| 12 | Total revenue | =B4*B9 |
| 13 | Fixed cost | =B5 |
| 14 | Total variable cost | =B6*B9 |
| 15 | Total cost | =B13+B14 |
| 16 | Profit | =B12-B15 |

Input variable cell

Profit is revenue − fixed cost − variable cost.

*The BEP results in $0 profit.*

equaling total costs (i.e., profit is $0). We can determine the BEP analytically by setting profit equal to $0 and solving for $X$ in Bill Pritchett's profit expression. That is

$$0 = (\text{Selling price per unit}) \times (\text{Number of units}) - \text{Fixed cost} - (\text{Variable cost per unit}) \times (\text{Number of units})$$

which can be mathematically rewritten as

$$\text{Number of units (BEP)} = \frac{\text{Fixed cost}}{(\text{Selling price per unit} - \text{Variable cost per unit})} \quad (1\text{-}2)$$

For Bill Pritchett's example, we can compute the BEP as $1,000/($10 − $5) = 200 springs. The *BEP in dollars* (which we denote as $BEP_\$$) can then be computed as

$$BEP_\$ = \text{Fixed cost} + \text{Variable cost per unit} \times \text{BEP} \quad (1\text{-}3)$$

For Bill Pritchett's example, we can compute $BEP_\$$ as $1,000 + $5 \times 200 = $2,000.

**PROGRAM 1.2B**

**Excel Decision Model for Pritchett's Precious Time Pieces**

| | A | B |
|---|---|---|
| 1 | **Bill Pritchett's Shop** | |
| 2 | | |
| 3 | **Known parameters:** | |
| 4 | Selling price per unit | $10.00 |
| 5 | Fixed cost | $1,000.00 |
| 6 | Variable cost per unit | $5.00 |
| 7 | | |
| 8 | **Input Data** | |
| 9 | Number of units, X | 1000 |
| 10 | | |
| 11 | **Results** | |
| 12 | Total revenue | $10,000.00 |
| 13 | Fixed cost | $1,000.00 |
| 14 | Total variable cost | $5,000.00 |
| 15 | Total cost | $6,000.00 |
| 16 | Profit | $4,000.00 |

Profit is $4,000 if 1,000 units are sold.

**PROGRAM 1.2C**

**Using Excel's Goal Seek to Compute the Break-Even Point for Pritchett's Precious Time Pieces**

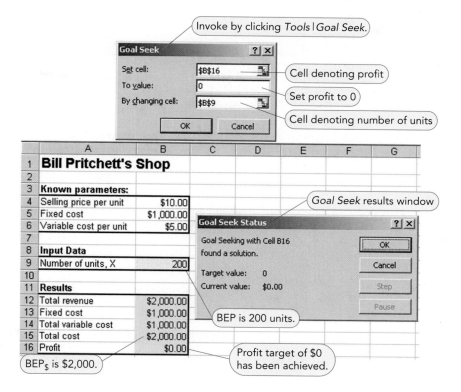

## Using Goal Seek to Find the Break-Even Point

*Excel's Goal Seek can be used to automatically find the BEP.*

While the preceding analytical computations for BEP and BEP$_\$$ are fairly simple, the spreadsheet-based decision model shown in Program 1.2B can be used to automatically calculate these values. To do so, we use a feature in Excel called Goal Seek. This feature allows us to specify a goal or target for a specific cell and the cell that must be automatically manipulated to achieve this target. In our case, we want to manipulate the value of the number of units $X$ (in cell B9 of Program 1.2B) such that the profit (in cell B16 of Program 1.2B) takes on a value of 0. Observe that the formula of profit in cell B16 is a function of the value of $X$ in cell B9 (see Program 1.2A).

Program 1.2C shows how the Goal Seek feature works in Excel. Go to Goal Seek by clicking Tools|Goal Seek on Excel's main menu bar. The window shown in Program 1.2C(a) is displayed. Specify cell B16 as the Set cell with a desired value of 0 for this cell, and cell B9 as the Changing cell. Click OK, the Goal Seek Status window shown in Program 1.2C(b) should display, indicating that the target of $0 profit has been achieved. Cell B9 shows the resulting BEP value of 200 units. The corresponding BEP$_\$$ value of $2,000 is shown in cell B15.

Observe that we can use Goal Seek to compute the sales level needed to obtain any desired profit. For example, see if you can verify that in order to get a profit of $10,000, Bill Pritchett would have to sell 2,200 springs.

## 1.6    POSSIBLE PROBLEMS IN DEVELOPING DECISION MODELS

We present the decision modeling approach as a logical and systematic means of tackling decision-making problems. Even when these steps are followed carefully, however, there are many difficulties that can hurt the chances of implementing solutions to real-world problems. We now look at problems that can happen during each of the steps of the decision modeling approach.

**IDM  IN ACTION**    Better Modeling for Better Pollution Control

It is often difficult to balance economic returns with pollution control. When pollution is a problem, modeling industrial facilities can maintain high profitability while achieving pollution control guidelines and laws. This was the situation in Chile.

Chile is the world's largest producer of copper, producing 2.2 million tons of the metal in 1994. This large copper production represents about 8% of the country's gross domestic product (GDP). Although private businesses operate about 50% of copper mining operations, Chile controls most of the refining. Unfortunately, the production of copper produces solid, liquid, and gas by-products that end up in the environment. As a result, the Chilean government decided to enact pollution and air quality standards for many of the by-products of the copper mining process.

To help meet pollution and air quality standards, a quantitative optimization model was developed. The objective of the

model was to minimize the costs of copper mining while maintaining pollution and air quality standards set by the Chilean government. The model resulted in a number of changes. First, the model solution was substantially different from the cleanup plans that were developed before the model solution. As a result, many of the early cleanup plans were delayed, redone, or scrapped. In addition, some previously developed pollution and air quality cleanup plans were approved because they were consistent with the solution from the model. Furthermore, the model provided critical input to a computerized decision support system to analyze the impact of various copper mining strategies on total costs and pollution control. The result of this optimization model is a cleaner environment at minimal cost.

**Source:** Mondschein et al. "Optimal Investment Policies for Pollution Control in the Copper Industry," *Interfaces* 27 (November–December 1997): 69–87.

## Defining the Problem

*Real-world problems are not easily identifiable.*

In the worlds of business, government, and education, problems are, unfortunately, not easily identified. There are four roadblocks that decision analysts typically face in defining a problem. We use an application, inventory analysis, throughout this section as an example.

**Conflicting Viewpoints**  Analysts may often have to consider conflicting viewpoints in defining the problem. For example, in inventory problems, financial managers usually feel that inventory is too high, since inventory represents cash not available for other investments. In contrast, sales managers often feel that inventory is too low, since high levels of inventory may be needed to fill unexpected orders. If analysts adopt either of these views as the problem definition, they have essentially accepted one manager's perception. They can, therefore, expect resistance from the other manager when the "solution" emerges. So it's important to consider both points of view before stating the problem.

*The problem needs to be examined from several viewpoints.*

**Impact on Other Departments**  Problems do not exist in isolation and are not owned by just one department of a firm. For example, inventory is closely tied with cash flows and various production problems. A change in ordering policy can affect cash flows and upset production schedules to the point that savings on inventory are exceeded by increased financial and production costs. The problem statement should therefore be as broad as possible and include inputs from all concerned departments.

*All inputs must be considered.*

**Beginning Assumptions**  People often have a tendency to state problems in terms of solutions. For example, the statement that inventory is too low implies a solution: that its levels should be raised. The analyst who starts off with this assumption will likely find that inventory should be raised! From an implementation perspective, a "good" solution to the right problem is much better than an "optimal" solution to the wrong problem.

**Solution Outdated**  Even if the problem has been specified correctly at present, it can change during the development of the model. In today's rapidly changing business environment, especially with the amazing pace of technological advances, it is not unusual for problems to change virtually overnight. The analyst who presents solutions to problems that no longer exist can't expect credit for providing timely help.

## Developing a Model

Even with a well-defined problem statement, a decision analyst may have to overcome hurdles while developing decision models for real-world situations. Some are discussed in the following sections.

**Fitting the Textbooks Models**   A manager's perception of a problem will not always match the textbook approach. For example, most textbook inventory models involve minimizing the sum of holding and ordering costs. Some managers view these costs as unimportant; instead, they see the problem in terms of cash flow, turnover, and levels of customer satisfaction. The results of a model based on holding and ordering costs are probably not acceptable to such managers.

*Managers will not use the results of a model they do not understand.*

**Understanding the Model**   Most managers simply will not use the results of a model they do not understand. Complex problems, though, require complex models. One trade-off is to simplify assumptions in order to make the model easier to understand. The model loses some of its reality but gains some management acceptance. For example, a popular simplifying assumption in inventory modeling is that demand is known and constant. This allows analysts to build simple, easy-to-understand models. Demand, however, is rarely known and constant, so the models lack some reality. Introducing probability distributions provides more realism but may put comprehension beyond all but the most mathematically sophisticated managers. In such cases, one approach is for the decision analyst to start with the simple model and make sure that it is completely understood. More complex models can then be introduced slowly as managers gain more confidence in using these models.

## Acquiring Input Data

Gathering the data to be used in the decision modeling approach to problem solving is often no simple task. One-fifth of all firms in a recent study had difficulty with data access.

**Using Accounting Data**   One problem is that most data generated in a firm come from basic accounting reports. The accounting department collects its inventory data, for example, in terms of cash flows and turnover. But decision analysts tackling an inventory problem need to collect data on holding costs and ordering costs. If they ask for such data, they may be shocked to find that the data were simply never collected for those specified costs.

Professor Gene Woolsey tells a story of a young decision analyst sent down to accounting to get "the inventory holding cost per item per day for part 23456/AZ." The accountant asked the young man if he wanted the first-in, first-out figure, the last-in, first-out figure, the lower of cost or market figure, or the "how-we-do-it" figure. The young man replied that the inventory model required only one number. The accountant at the next desk said, "Hell, Joe, give the kid a number." The analyst was given a number and departed.

*The results of a model are only as good as the input data used.*

**Validity of Data**   A lack of "good, clean data" means that whatever data are available must often be distilled and manipulated (we call it "fudging") before being used in a model. Unfortunately, the validity of the results of a model is no better than the validity of the data that go into the model. You cannot blame a manager for resisting a model's "scientific" results when he or she knows that questionable data were used as input.

## Developing a Solution

There are two potential pitfalls that an analyst may have to face while developing solutions to a decision model. These are discussed in the following sections.

**Hard-to-Understand Mathematics**   The first concern in developing solutions is that although the mathematical models we use may be complex and powerful, they may not be completely understood. The aura of mathematics often causes managers to remain silent when they should be critical. The well-known management scientist C. W. Churchman once cautioned that "because mathematics has been so revered a discipline in recent years, it tends to lull the unsuspecting into believing that he who thinks elaborately thinks well."

*Hard-to-understand mathematics and giving only one answer can be problems in developing a solution.*

**The Limitation of Only One Answer**  The second problem is that decision models usually give just one answer to a problem. Most managers would like to have a range of options and not be put in a take-it-or-leave-it position. A more appropriate strategy is for an analyst to present a range of options, indicating the effect that each solution has on the objective function. This gives managers a choice as well as information on how much it will cost to deviate from the optimal solution. It also allows problems to be viewed from a broader perspective, since qualitative factors can also be considered.

### Testing the Solution

The results of decision modeling often take the form of predictions of how things will work in the future if certain changes are made now. To get a preview of how well solutions will really work, managers are often asked how good the solution looks to them. The problem is that complex models tend to give solutions that are not intuitively obvious. And such solutions tend to be rejected by managers. Then the decision analyst must work through the model and the assumptions with the manager in an effort to convince the manager of the validity of the results. In the process of convincing the manager, the analyst will have to review every assumption that went into the model. If there are errors, they may be revealed during this review. In addition, the manager will be casting a critical eye on everything that went into the model, and if he or she can be convinced that the model is valid, there is a good chance that the solution results are also valid.

*Assumptions should be reviewed.*

### Analyzing the Results

Once the solution has been tested, the results must be analyzed in terms of how they will affect the total organization. You should be aware that even small changes in organizations are often difficult to bring about. If the results indicate large changes in organizational policy, the decision analyst can expect resistance. In analyzing the results, the analyst should ascertain who must change and by how much, if the people who must change will be better or worse off, and who has the power to direct the change.

## 1.7    IMPLEMENTATION—NOT JUST THE FINAL STEP

We have just presented some of the many problems that can affect the ultimate acceptance of decision modeling in practice. It should be clear now that implementation isn't just another step that takes place after the modeling process is over. Each one of these steps greatly affects the changes of implementing the results of a decision model.

Even though many business decisions can be made intuitively, based on hunches and experience, there are more and more situations in which decision models can assist. Some managers, however, fear that the use of a formal analytic process will reduce their decision-making power. Others fear that it may expose some previous intuitive decisions as inadequate. Still others just feel uncomfortable about having to reverse their thinking patterns with formal decision making. These managers often argue against the use of decision modeling.

Many action-oriented managers do not like the lengthy formal decision-making process and prefer to get things done quickly. They prefer "quick and dirty" techniques that can yield immediate results. However, once managers see some quick results that have a substantial payoff, the stage is set for convincing them that decision modeling is a beneficial tool.

*Management support and user involvement are important.*

We have known for some time that management support and user involvement are critical to the successful implementation of decision modeling processes. A Swedish study found that only 40% of projects suggested by decision analysts were ever implemented. But 70% of the modeling projects initiated by users, and fully 98% of projects suggested by top managers, were implemented.

## SUMMARY

Decision modeling is a scientific approach to decision making in practical situations faced by managers. Decision models can be broadly classified into two categories based on the type and nature of the problem environment under consideration: (1) deterministic models and (2) probabilistic models. Deterministic models assume that all the relevant input data and parameters are known with certainty. In contrast, probabilistic models assume that some input data are not known with certainty. The decision modeling approach includes three major steps: (1) formulation, (2) solution, and (3) interpretation. It is important to note that

it is common to iterate between these three steps before the final solution is obtained. Spreadsheets are commonly used to develop decision models.

In using the decision modeling approach, however, there can be potential problems such as conflicting viewpoints, disregard of impact of the model on other departments, outdated solutions, misunderstanding of the model, acquiring good input data, and hard-to-understand mathematics. In using decision models, implementation is not the final step. There can be a lack of commitment to the approach and resistance to change.

## GLOSSARY

**Break-Even Point (BEP).** Number of units sold that will result in total revenue equaling total costs (i.e., profit is $0).

**Break-Even Point in Dollars (BEP$_\$$).** Sum of fixed and total variable cost if the number of units sold equals the break-even point.

**Decision Analyst.** An individual who is responsible for developing a decision model.

**Decision Modeling.** A scientific approach that uses quantitative (mathematical) techniques as a tool in managerial decision making. Also known as *quantitative analysis, management science,* and *operations research.*

**Decision Problem.** A statement, which should come from a manager, that indicates a problem to be solved or an objective or goal to be reached.

**Deterministic Model.** Model that assumes that all the relevant input data and parameters are known with certainty.

**Formulation.** Process by which each aspect of the problem scenario is translated and expressed in terms of a mathematical model.

**Goal Seek.** A feature in Excel that allows users to specify a goal or target for a specific cell and automatically manipulate another cell to achieve this target.

**Input Data.** Data that are used in a model in arriving at the final solution.

**Model.** A representation (usually mathematical) of a practical problem scenario or environment.

**Probabilistic Model.** Model that assumes that some input data are not known with certainty.

**Problem Parameter.** A measurable quantity that is inherent in the problem. It typically has a fixed and known value (i.e., a constant).

**Sensitivity Analysis.** Determining how sensitive a solution is to changes in the formulation of a problem.

**Variable.** A measurable quantity that may vary or is subject to change.

## KEY EQUATIONS

(1-1)  Profit = (Selling price per unit) × (Number of units)
  − Fixed cost
  − (Variable cost per unit) × (Number of units)

An equation to determine profit as a function of the selling price per unit, number of units, fixed cost, and variable cost.

(1-2)  Number of units (BEP)

$$= \frac{\text{Fixed cost}}{\text{Selling price per unit} - \text{Variable cost per unit}}$$

An equation to determine the break-even point in units as a function of fixed cost, variable cost, and the selling price per unit.

(1-3)  Break-even point in dollars (BEP$_\$$) =
  Fixed cost + Variable cost per unit × BEP

An equation to determine the break-even point in dollars as a function of fixed cost and variable cost.

**▪▶ SELF-TEST**

- Before taking the self-test, refer back to the learning objectives at the beginning of the chapter, the notes in the margins, and the glossary at the end of the chapter.
- Use the key at the back of the book to correct your answers.
- Restudy pages that correspond to any questions that you answered incorrectly or material you feel uncertain about.

1. In analyzing a problem you should normally study
   a. the qualitative aspects.
   b. the quantitative aspects.
   c. both a and b.
   d. neither a nor b.
2. Decision modeling is
   a. a logical approach to decision making.
   b. a rational approach to decision making.
   c. a scientific approach to decision making.
   d. all of the above.
3. Frederick Winslow Taylor
   a. was a military researcher during World War II.
   b. pioneered the principles of scientific management.
   c. developed the use of the algorithm for decision modeling.
   d. all of the above.
4. The most important and often the most difficult step in the scientific method is
   a. developing a model.
   b. acquiring input data.
   c. defining the problem.
   d. defining a solution.
5. A physical model is an example of
   a. an iconic model.
   b. a schematic model.
   c. a mathematical model.
   d. a stochastic model.
6. An analysis to determine how much a solution would change if there are changes in the model or the input data is called
   a. sensitivity or postoptimality analysis.
   b. schematic or iconic analysis.
   c. futurama conditioning.
   d. both b and c.
7. Decision variables are
   a. controllable.
   b. uncontrollable.
   c. parameters.
   d. constant numerical values associated with any complex problem.
8. Decision models can be classified as
   a. probabilistic and deterministic models.
   b. mathematical and logical models.
   c. simple and complex models.

9. A decision model that assumes all the relevant input data and parameters are known with certainty is a
   a. probabilistic model.
   b. deterministic model.
   c. constant model.
   d. variable model.
10. A decision model that assumes that some input data are not known with certainty is a
    a. probabilistic model.
    b. deterministic model.
    c. constant model.
    d. variable model.
11. The number of units sold that will result in total revenue equaling total costs (i.e., profit is $0) is called the
    a. loss function.
    b. optimal solution.
    c. break-even point.
    d. variable.
12. _____ is the scientific approach to managerial decision making.
13. _____ is the first step in decision modeling.
14. A _____ is a picture, drawing, or chart of reality.
15. A series of steps that are repeated until a solution is found is called a(n) _____.
16. _____ is a representation (usually mathematical) of a practical problem scenario or environment.
17. Decision modeling is also commonly referred to as _____ or _____.
18. Probabilistic models incorporate uncertainty by using _____ on unknown variables.
19. A _____ is a measurable quantity that is inherent in the problem.
20. Decision modeling process involves the following three distinct steps: _____, _____, and _____.

# DISCUSSION QUESTIONS AND PROBLEMS

## Discussion Questions

**1-1**  Define *decision modeling*. What are some of the organizations that support the use of the scientific approach?

**1-2**  What is the difference between deterministic and probabilistic models? Give several examples of each.

**1-3**  What are the differences between quantitative and qualitative factors that may be present in a decision model?

**1-4**  Why might it be difficult to quantify some qualitative factors in developing decision models?

**1-5**  What are the steps involved in the decision modeling process? Give several examples of this process.

**1-6**  Why is it important to have an iterative process between the steps of the decision modeling approach?

**1-7**  Briefly trace the history of decision modeling. What happened to the development of decision modeling during World War II?

**1-8**  What are the different types of models mentioned in this chapter? Give examples of each.

**1-9**  List some sources of input data.

**1-10**  Define a decision variable. Give some examples of variables in a decision model.

**1-11**  What is a problem parameter? Give some examples of parameters in a decision model.

**1-12**  List some advantages of using spreadsheets for decision modeling.

**1-13**  What is implementation, and why is it important?

**1-14**  Describe the use of sensitivity analysis and postoptimality analysis in analyzing the results of decision models.

**1-15**  Managers are quick to claim that decision modelers talk to them in a jargon that does not sound like English. List four terms that might not be understood by a manager. Then explain in nontechnical terms what each term means.

**1-16**  Why do you think many decision modelers don't like to participate in the implementation process? What could be done to change this attitude?

**1-17**  Should people who will be using the results of a new modeling approach become involved in the technical aspects of the problem-solving procedure?

**1-18**  C. W. Churchman once said that "mathematics tends to lull the unsuspecting into believing that he who thinks elaborately thinks well." Do you think that the best decision models are the ones that are most elaborate and complex mathematically? Why?

## Problems

• **1-19**  Tom Johnson Manufacturing intends to increase capacity through the addition of new equipment. Two vendors have presented proposals. The fixed cost for proposal A is $50,000, and for proposal B, $70,000. The variable cost for A is $12, and for B, $10. The revenue generated by each unit is $20.

(a) What is the BEP in units for proposal A?
(b) What is the BEP in units for proposal B?
(c) What is the BEP in dollars for proposal A?
(d) What is the BEP in dollars for proposal B?
(e) If the expected volume is 8,500 units, which alternative should be chosen?
(f) If the expected volume is 15,000 units, which alternative should be chosen?

• **1-20**  If the selling price is $8 per unit, variable cost is $4 per unit, and fixed cost is $50,000, calculate BEP, BEP$_\$$, and the profit at 100,000 units.

⁝ **1-21**  Tom Miller and Jeff Vollmann have opened a copy service on Commonwealth Avenue. They estimate their fixed cost at $12,000 and their variable cost of each copy sold at $0.01. They expect their selling price to average $0.05.

(a) What is their BEP in units?
(b) What is their BEP in dollars?

⁝ **1-22**  Dr. Aleda Roth, a prolific author, is considering starting her own publishing company. She will call it DSI Publishing, Inc. DSI's estimated costs are as follows:

| | |
|---|---|
| Fixed | $250,000 |
| Variable cost per book | $20 |
| Selling price per book | $30 |

(a) How many books must DSI sell to break even?
(b) What is DSI's BEP in dollars?

⁝ **1-23**  In addition to the costs in Problem 1-22, Dr. Roth wants to pay herself a salary of $50,000 per year.

(a) Now what is her BEP in units?
(b) What is her BEP in dollars?

⁝ **1-24**  An electronics firm is currently manufacturing an item that has a variable cost of $0.50 per unit and selling price of $1.00 per unit. Fixed costs are $14,000. Current volume is 30,000 units. The firm can substantially improve the product quality by adding a new piece of equipment at an additional fixed cost of $6,000. Variable cost would increase to $0.60, but volume should jump to 50,000 units due to a higher-quality product. Should the company buy the new equipment?

⁝ **1-25**  The electronics firm in Problem 1-24 is now considering the new equipment and increasing the selling price to $1.10 per unit. With the higher-quality product, the new volume is expected to be 45,000 units. Under these circumstances, should the company purchase the new equipment and increase the selling price?

⁝ **1-26**  Satish Mehra's company is considering producing, in-house, a gear assembly that it now purchases from Memphis Supply, Inc. Memphis Supply charges $4 per unit. Mehra estimates that it will cost $15,000 to set up the process and then $1.82 per unit for labor and materials. Either choice would have the same cost at approximately how many units?

**1-27** Because hula hoops have come back in style, Hoops Unlimited wants to enter the market quickly. It has three choices: (a) refurbish the old equipment at a cost of $600, (b) make major modifications at the cost of $1,100, or (c) purchase new equipment at a net cost of $1,800. If the firm chooses to refurbish the equipment, materials and labor would be $1.10 per hoop. If it chooses to make modifications, materials and labor would be $0.70 per hoop. If it buys new equipment, variable costs are estimated to be $0.40 per hoop.

(a) Which alternative should Hoops Unlimited choose if it thinks it could sell more than 3,000 hula hoops?

(b) Which alternative should the firm use if it thinks the market for hoops would be between 1,600 and 2,400?

**1-28** Zan Azlett and Angela Zesiger have joined forces to start A&Z Lettuce Products, a processor of packaged shredded lettuce for institutional use. Zan has years of food processing experience, and Angela has extensive commercial food preparation experience. The process will consist of opening crates of lettuce and then sorting, washing, slicing, preserving, and finally packaging the prepared lettuce. Together, with help from vendors, they feel they can adequately estimate demand, fixed costs, revenue per five-pound bag of lettuce, and variable cost per five-pound bag of lettuce. They feel that a largely manual process will have monthly fixed costs of $37,500 and variable costs of $1.75 per bag. A more mechanized process will have fixed costs of $75,000 per month with variable costs of $1.25 per five-pound bag. They expect to sell the shredded lettuce for $2.50 per five-pound bag.

(a) What is the BEP for the manual process?

(b) What is the BEP for the mechanized process?

(c) What is the monthly profit/loss of the manual process if they expect to sell 60,000 bags per month?

(d) What is the monthly profit/loss of the mechanized process if they expect to sell 60,000 bags per month?

# BIBLIOGRAPHY

Ackoff, R. L. *Scientific Method: Optimizing Applied Research Decisions.* New York: John Wiley & Sons, Inc., 1962.

Churchman, C. W. "Reliability of Models in the Social Sciences," *Interfaces* 4, 1 (November 1973): 1–12.

———. *The Systems Approach.* New York: Delacort Press, 1968.

Cosares, S. et al. "SONET Toolkit: A Decision Support System for Designing Robust and Cost-Effective Fiber-Optic Networks," *Interfaces* 25 (January 1995): 20–40.

Davis, Joyce. "How to Nurture Creative Sparks," *Fortune* (January 10, 1994): 94. Also see K. MacCrimmon and C. Wagner. "Stimulating Ideas through Creativity Software," *Management Science* (November 1994): 1514–1532.

Dutta, Goutam. "Lessons for Success in OR/MS Practice Gained from Experiences in Indian and U.S. Steel Plants," *Interfaces* 30, 5 (September–October 2000): 23–30.

Epstein, Rafael, Ramiro Morales, Jorge Seron, and Andres Weintraub. "Use of OR Systems in the Chilean Forest Industries," *Interfaces* 29, 1 (January 1999): 7–29.

Geoffrion, Arthur M. and Ramayya Krishnan. "Prospects for Operations Research in the E-Business Era," *Interfaces* 31, 2 (March 2001): 6–36.

Harris, Carl. "Could You Defend Your Model in Court?" *OR/MS Today* (April 1997): 6.

Hueter, Jackie and William Swart. "An Integrated Labor-Management System for Taco Bell," *Interfaces* 28, 1 (January 1998): 75–91.

Keskinocak, Pinar and Sridhar Tayur. "Quantitative Analysis for Internet-Enabled Supply Chains," *Interfaces* 31, 2 (March 2001): 70–89.

Kuby, M. et al. "Planning China's Coal and Electricity Delivery System," *Interfaces* 25 (January 1995): 41–68.

Labe, Russ, Raj Nigam, and Steve Spence. "Management Science at Merrill Lynch Private Client Group," *Interfaces* 29, 2 (March 1999): 1–14.

Moore, William E., Jr., Janice M. Warmke, and Lonny R. Gorban. "The Indispensable Role of Management Science in Centralizing Freight Operation at Reynolds Metals Company," *Interfaces* 21, 1 (January–February 1991): 107–129.

Salveson, Melvin. "The Institute of Management Science: A Prehistory and Commentary," *Interfaces* 27, 3 (May–June 1997): 74–85.

Vazsoni, Andrew. "The Purpose of Mathematical Models Is Insight, Not Numbers," *Decision Line* (January 1998): 20–21.

Venkatakrishnan, C. S. "Optimize Your Career Prospects," *OR/MS Today* (April 1997): 28.

## CHAPTER 2

# LINEAR PROGRAMMING MODELS: GRAPHICAL AND COMPUTER METHODS

After completing this chapter, students will be able to:

1. Understand the basic assumptions and properties of linear programming (LP).

2. Use graphical solution procedures for LP problems with only two variables to understand how LP problems are solved.

3. Understand special situations such as redundancy, infeasibility, unboundedness, and alternate optimal solutions in LP problems.

4. Understand how to set up LP problems on a spreadsheet and solve them using Excel's Solver.

Summary • Glossary • Solved Problems • Self-Test • Discussion Questions and Problems • Case Study: Mexicana Wire Works • Case Study: Golding Landscaping and Plants, Inc. • Internet Case Study • Bibliography

## Using Linear Programming to Select Tenants in a Shopping Mall

Homart Development Company is one of the largest shopping-center developers in the United States. When developing a new center, Homart produces a tentative floor plan, or footprint, for the mall. This plan outlines sizes, shapes, and spaces for large department stores. Leasing agreements are reached with the two or three major department stores that will become anchor stores in the mall. The anchor stores are able to negotiate highly favorable occupancy agreements. Typically, they either pay low rent or receive other concessions. Homart's profits come primarily from the rent paid by the nonanchor tenants—the smaller stores that lease space along the aisles of the mall. The decisions allocating space to potential tenants and establishing the tenant mix are therefore crucial to the success of the investment.

The tenant mix describes the desired stores in the mall by their size, general location, and type of merchandise or service provided. For example, the tenant mix might specify two small jewelry stores in a central section of the mall and a medium-sized shoe store and a large restaurant in one of the side aisles. In the past, Homart developed a plan for tenant mix using "rules of thumb" developed over years of experience in mall development. However, in order to improve its bottom line in an increasingly competitive marketplace, Homart currently treats the tenant-mix problem as a linear programming model.

First, the model assumes that tenants can be classified into different categories according to the type of merchandise or service they provide. Second, the model assumes that for each store type, store sizes can be made into distinct categories. For example, a small jewelry store is said to contain about 700 square feet and a large one about 2,200 square feet. The tenant-mix model is a powerful tool for enhancing Homart's mall planning and leasing activities.[1]

[1] J. Bean et al. "Selecting Tenants in a Shopping Mall," *Interfaces* (March–April 1988): 1–9.

## 2.1    INTRODUCTION

Similar to the resource allocation decision faced by Homart Development Company, management decisions in many organizations involve trying to make the most effective use of resources. Resources typically include machinery, labor, money, time, warehouse space, and raw materials. These resources can be used to manufacture products (e.g., computers, automobiles, furniture, clothing) or provide services (e.g., package delivery, health services, advertising policies, investment decisions).

In all these examples of resource allocation, the manager must sift through several thousands of decision choices or alternatives to identify the best, or optimal, choice. The most widely used decision modeling technique designed to help managers in this process is called *mathematical programming*. The term mathematical programming is somewhat of a misnomer, since the modeling technique requires no advanced mathematical ability (it uses just basic algebra) and has nothing whatsoever to do with computer software programming! In the world of decision modeling, programming refers to setting up and solving a problem mathematically.

*Linear programming helps in resource allocation decisions.*

Within the broad topic of mathematical programming, the most widely used modeling technique designed to help managers in planning and decision making is *linear programming* (LP). We devote this and the next two chapters to illustrating how, why, and where LP works. Then, in Chapter 5, we explore several special LP models called network flow problems. We follow this with a discussion of a few other mathematical programming techniques (i.e., integer programming, goal programming, and nonlinear programming) in Chapter 6.

When developing LP (and other mathematical programming) based decision models, we assume that all the relevant input data and parameters are known with certainty. For this reason, these types of decision modeling techniques are classified as *deterministic* models.

Computers have, of course, played an important role in the advancement and use of LP. Real-world LP problems are too cumbersome to solve by hand or with a calculator, and computers have become an integral part of setting up and solving LP models in today's business environments. As noted in Chapter 1, over the past decade, spreadsheet packages such as Microsoft Excel have become increasingly capable of handling many of the decision modeling techniques (including LP and other mathematical programming models) that are commonly encountered in practical situations. So throughout the chapters on mathematical programming techniques, we discuss the role and use of Microsoft Excel in setting up and solving these models.

*We focus on using Excel to set up and solve LP models.*

## 2.2    DEVELOPMENT OF A LINEAR PROGRAMMING MODEL

Since the mid-twentieth century, LP has been applied extensively to medical, transportation, operations, financial, marketing, accounting, human resources, and agricultural problems. Regardless of the size and complexity of the decision-making problem at hand in

---

## HISTORY    How Linear Programming Started

Linear programming was conceptually developed before World War II by the outstanding Soviet mathematician A. N. Kolmogorov. Another Russian, Leonid Kantorovich, won the Nobel Prize in Economics for advancing the concepts of optimal planning. An early application of linear programming, by Stigler in 1945, was in the area we today call "diet problems."

Major progress in the field, however, took place in 1947 and later when George D. Dantzig developed the solution procedure known as the *simplex algorithm*. Dantzig, then an Air Force mathematician, was assigned to work on logistics problems. He noticed that many problems involving limited resources and more than one demand could be set up in terms of a series of equations and inequalities. Although early LP applications were military in nature, industrial applications rapidly became apparent with the spread of business computers. In 1984, Narendra Karmarkar developed an algorithm that appears to be superior to the simplex method for many very large applications.

these diverse applications, the development of all LP models can be viewed in terms of the three distinct steps first defined in Chapter 1: (1) formulation, (2) solution, and (3) interpretation. We now discuss each with regard to LP models.

*Formulation involves expressing a problem scenario in terms of simple mathematical expressions.*

**Formulation**  Formulation is the process by which each aspect of the problem scenario is translated and expressed in terms of simple mathematical expressions. The aim in LP formulation is to ensure that the set of mathematical equations, taken together, completely addresses all the issues relevant to the problem situation at hand. We demonstrate a few examples of simple LP formulations in this chapter. Then we introduce several more comprehensive formulations in Chapter 3.

*Solution involves solving these mathematical expressions to find values for the variables.*

**Solution**  The solution is where the mathematical expressions resulting from the formulation process are solved to identify an optimal solution. In this textbook, the focus is on solving LP models using spreadsheets. However, we briefly discuss graphical solution procedures for LP models involving only two variables. The graphical solution procedure is useful in that it allows us to provide an intuitive explanation of the procedure used by most software packages to solve LP problems of any size.

**Interpretation and What-If Analysis**  Assuming the formulation is correct and has been successfully implemented and solved using an LP software package, how does a manager use the results? In addition to just providing the solution to the current LP problem, the computer results also allow the manager to evaluate the impact of several different types of what-if questions regarding the problem. We discuss this subject, called *sensitivity analysis*, in Chapter 4.

*Sensitivity analysis allows the manager to answer "what-if" questions regarding the problem's solution.*

In this textbook, our emphasis is on formulation (Chapters 2 and 3) and interpretation (Chapter 4), along with detailed descriptions of how spreadsheets can be used to efficiently set up and solve LP models.

## Properties of a Linear Programming Model

All LP models have the following properties in common:

*First LP property: Problems seek to maximize or minimize an objective.*

1.  All problems seek to maximize or minimize some quantity, usually profit or cost. We refer to this property as the *objective function* of an LP problem. For example, the objective of a typical manufacturer is to maximize profits. In the case of a trucking or railroad distribution system, the objective might be to minimize shipping costs. In any event, this objective must be stated clearly and defined mathematically. It does not matter, by the way, whether profits and cost are measured in cents, dollars, euros, or millions of dollars.

*Second LP property: Constraints limit the degree to which the objective can be obtained.*

2.  LP models usually include restrictions, or *constraints*, that limit the degree to which we can pursue our objective. For example, when we are trying to decide how many units to produce of each product in a firm's product line, we are restricted by the available machinery time. Likewise, in selecting food items for a hospital meal, a dietitian must ensure that minimum daily requirements of vitamins, proteins, and so on are satisfied. We want, therefore, to maximize or minimize a quantity (the objective) subject to limited resources (the constraints).

    LP models usually include a set of constraints known as *nonnegativity* constraints. These constraints ensure that the variables in the model take on only nonnegative values (that is, $\geq 0$). This is logical since negative values of physical quantities are impossible; you simply cannot produce a negative number of chairs or computers.

*Third LP property: There must be alternatives available.*

3.  There must be alternative courses of action from which we can choose. For example, if a company produces three different products, management could use LP to decide how to allocate its limited production resources (of personnel, machinery, and so on) among these products. Should it devote all manufacturing capacity to make only the first prod-

uct, should it produce equal amounts of each product, or should it allocate the resources in some other ratio? If there were no alternative to select from, we would not need LP.

*Fourth LP property: Mathematical relationships are linear.*

4. The objective and constraints in LP problems must be expressed in terms of *linear* equations or inequalities. Linear mathematical relationships just mean that all terms used in the objective function and constraints are of the first degree (i.e., not squared, or to the third or higher power, or appearing more than once). Hence, the equation $2A + 5B = 10$ is a valid linear function, whereas the equation $2A^2 + 5B^3 + 3B = 10$ is not linear because the variable $A$ is squared, variable $B$ is cubed, and the two variables appear as a product in the third term.

*An inequality has a $\leq$ or $\geq$ sign.*

You will see the term *inequality* quite often when we discuss LP problems. By inequalities we mean that not all LP constraints need be of the form $A + B = C$. This particular relationship, called an equation, implies that the sum of term $A$ and term $B$ exactly equals term $C$. In most LP problems, we see inequalities of the form $A + B \leq C$ or $A + B \geq C$. The first of these means that $A$ plus $B$ is less than or equal to $C$. The second means that $A$ plus $B$ is greater than or equal to $C$. This concept provides a lot of flexibility in defining problem limitations.

## Basic Assumptions of a Linear Programming Model

*Four technical requirements are (1) certainty, (2) proportionality, (3) additivity, and (4) divisibility.*

Technically, there are four additional requirements of an LP problem of which you should be aware:

1. We assume that conditions of *certainty* exist. That is, numbers used in the objective function and constraints are known with certainty and do not change during the period being studied.

2. We also assume that *proportionality* exists in the objective function and constraints. This means that if production of 1 unit of a product uses 3 hours of a particular resource, then making 10 units of that product uses 30 hours of the resource.

3. The third assumption deals with *additivity*, meaning that the total of all activities equals the sum of the individual activities. For example, if an objective is to maximize profit = $8 per unit of first product made plus $3 per unit of second product made, and if 1 unit of each product is actually produced, the profit contributions of $8 and $3 must add up to produce a sum of $11.

4. We make the *divisibility* assumption that solutions need not necessarily be in whole numbers (integers). That is, they may take any fractional value. If a fraction of a product cannot be produced (e.g., one-third of a submarine), an integer programming problem exists. We discuss integer programming in more detail in Chapter 6.

## 2.3   FORMULATING A LINEAR PROGRAMMING PROBLEM

*Product mix problems use LP to decide how much of each product to make, given a series of resource restrictions.*

One of the most common LP applications is the *product mix problem*. In many manufacturing firms, two or more products are usually produced using limited resources such a personnel, machines, raw materials, and so on. The profit that the firm seeks to maximize is based on the profit contribution per unit of each product. (Profit contribution, you may recall, is just the selling price per unit minus the variable cost per unit.[2]) The firm would like to determine how many units of each product it should produce so as to maximize overall profit given its limited resources. Let us begin our discussion of LP formulation using a small two-variable example of the Flair Furniture Company.

---

[2] Technically, we maximize total contribution margin, which is the difference between unit selling price and costs that vary in proportion to the quantity of the item produced. Depreciation, fixed general expense, and advertising are excluded from calculations. Problem 2-35 deals with these issues.

## ▐▶ MODELING IN THE REAL WORLD    Setting Crew Schedules at American Airlines

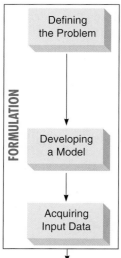

**FORMULATION**

**Defining the Problem**

American Airlines (AA) employs more than 8,300 pilots and 16,200 flight attendants to fly more than 5,000 aircraft. Total cost of American's crews exceed $1.4 billion per year, second only to fuel cost. Scheduling crews is one of AA's biggest and most complex problems. The Federal Aviation Administration (FAA) sets work-time limitations designed to ensure that crew members can fulfill their duties safely. And union contracts specify that crews will be guaranteed pay for some number of hours each day or each trip.

**Developing a Model**

American Airlines Decision Technologies (AA's consulting group) spent 15 labor-years in developing an LP model called TRIP (trip reevaluation and improvement program). The TRIP model builds crew schedules that meet or exceed crews' pay guarantee to the maximum extent possible.

**Acquiring Input Data**

Data and constraints are derived from salary information and union and FAA rules that specify maximum duty lengths, overnight costs, airline schedules, and plane sizes.

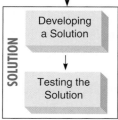

**SOLUTION**

**Developing a Solution**

It takes about 500 hours of mainframe computer time per month to develop crew schedules—these are prepared 40 days prior to the targeted month.

**Testing the Solution**

TRIP results were originally compared with crew assignments constructed manually. Since 1971, the model has been improved with new LP techniques, new constraints, and faster hardware and software. A series of what-if studies have tested TRIP's ability to reach more accurate and optimal solutions.

**INTERPRETATION**

**Analyzing the Results and Sensitivity Analysis**

Each year the LP model improves AA's efficiency and allows the airline to operate with a proportionately smaller work crew. A faster TRIP system now allows sensitivity analysis of the schedule in its first week.

**Implementing the Results**

The model, fully implemented, generates annual savings of more than $20 million. AA has also sold TRIP to 10 other airlines and one railroad.

**Source:** R. Anbil et al. "Recent Advances in Crew Pairing Optimization at American Airlines." *Interfaces* 21, 1 (January–February 1991): 62–74.

## Linear Programming Example: Flair Furniture Company

The Flair Furniture Company produces inexpensive tables and chairs. The production process for each is similar in that both require a certain number of labor hours in the carpentry department and a certain number of labor hours in the painting department. Each table takes 4 hours of carpentry work and 2 hours of painting work. Each chair requires 3 hours in carpentry and 1 hour in painting. During the current production period, 240 hours of carpentry time and 100 hours of painting time are available. The marketing personnel are confident that they can sell all the tables that are made. However, due to an existing inventory of chairs, they want Flair to make no more than 60 new chairs. Each table sold results in a profit contribution of $7, and each chair sold yields a profit contribution of $5.

Flair Furniture's problem is to determine the best possible combination of tables and chairs to manufacture in order to attain the maximum profit. The firm would like this product mix situation formulated as an LP problem.

To provide a structured approach for formulating this problem (and any other LP problem, irrespective of size and complexity), we present a three-step process in the following sections.

### Decision Variables

*Decision variables are the unknown entities in the problem. The problem is solved to find values for decision variables.*

*Decision variables* (or choice variables) represent the unknown entities in the problem. That is, what are we solving for in the problem? For example, in the Flair Furniture problem, there are two unknown entities, namely, the number of tables to be produced and the number of chairs to be produced. Note that all other unknowns in the problem (e.g., the total carpentry hours needed) can be expressed as linear functions of the number of chairs produced and the number of tables produced.

Decision variables are expressed in the problems using alphanumeric symbols. When writing the formulation on paper, it is convenient to express the decision variables using simple names that are easy to understand. For example, the number of tables to be produced can be denoted by names such as $T$, *Tables*, or $X_1$, and the number of chairs to be produced can be denoted by names such as $C$, *Chairs*, or $X_2$.

Throughout this textbook, to the extent possible, we use self-explanatory names to denote the decision variables in our formulations. For example, in Flair Furniture's problem, we use $T$ and $C$ to denote the number of tables and chairs to be produced, respectively.

### Objective Function

*Objective function represents the motivation for solving the problem.*

The objective function states the goal of the problem. That is, why are we trying to solve the problem? An LP model must have a single objective function. In most business-oriented LP models, the objective will be to either maximize profit or minimize cost. The goal in this step is to express the profit (or cost) in terms of the decision variables defined earlier. In Flair Furniture's problem, the total profit can be expressed as

Profit = ($7 profit per table) × (number of tables produced)
+ ($5 profit per chair) × (number of chairs produced)

Using the decision variables $T$ and $C$ defined earlier, the objective function can be written as

Maximize $\$7T + \$5C$

### Constraints

*Constraints represent restrictions on the values the decision variables can take.*

Constraints denote conditions that prevent us from selecting any value we please for the decision variables. An LP model can have as many constraints as necessary for that problem scenario. Each constraint is expressed as a mathematical expression and can be independent of the other constraints in the model.

In Flair Furniture's problem, we note that there are three restrictions on the solution. The first two have to do with the carpentry and painting times available. The third deals with the limit on the number of chairs. With regard to the carpentry and painting times, the constraints must ensure that the amount of the resource (time) required by the production plan is less than or equal to the resource (time) available. For example, in the case of carpentry, the total time used is

(4 hours per table) × (number of tables produced)
+ (3 hours per chair) × (number of chairs produced)

There are 240 carpentry hours available. Using the decision variables $T$ and $C$ defined earlier, this constraint can be stated as

$$4T + 3C \leq 240$$

*The resource constraints put limits on the carpentry labor resource and the painting labor resource mathematically.*

Likewise, the second constraint specifies that painting time used is less than or equal to painting time available. This can be stated as

$$2T + 1C \leq 100$$

Finally, there is the marketing-specified constraint that no more than 60 chairs be produced. This can be expressed as

$$C \leq 60$$

All three constraints represent production capacity restrictions and, of course, affect the total profit. For example, Flair cannot make 70 tables, since the carpentry and painting constraints are both violated if $T = 70$. Likewise, it cannot make 50 tables and 10 chairs, since this would require more than 100 hours of painting time. Hence, we note one more important aspect of LP models: Certain interactions will exist between variables. The more units of one product that a firm produces, the fewer it can make of other products. We show how this concept of interaction affects the optimal solution as we tackle the graphical solution approach in the next section.

*A key principle of LP is that interactions exist between variables.*

Before we consider the graphical solution procedure, there are two other issues we need to address. First, since Flair cannot produce negative quantities of tables or chairs, the nonnegativity constraints must be specified. Mathematically, these can be stated as

$$T \geq 0 \quad \text{(number of tables produced is} \geq 0)$$
$$C \geq 0 \quad \text{(number of chairs produced is} \geq 0)$$

Second, it is possible that the solution to the LP model will result in fractional values for $T$ and $C$. If the production plan in Flair's problem refers to a week's schedule (for example), we can view fractional values as work-in-process inventory that is carried over to the next week. However, in many problems, the values for decision variables must be whole numbers (integers) for the solution to make practical sense. A model in which the variables are restricted to integer values is called an *integer programming* (IP) model. In general, it is considerably harder to solve an IP problem than an LP problem. Further, LP model solutions allow detailed sensitivity analysis (the topic of Chapter 4) to be undertaken, whereas IP model solutions do not. For these reasons, it is quite common to not specify the integer requirement in many LP models. Therefore, we will permit fractional values in our solutions for now. (Chapter 6 discusses IP models in detail.)

## 2.4  GRAPHICAL SOLUTION OF A LINEAR PROGRAMMING PROBLEM WITH TWO VARIABLES

*The graphical method works only when there are two decision variables, but it provides valuable insight into how larger problems are structured.*

A primary advantage of two-variable LP models (such as Flair Furniture's problem) is that their solution can be graphically illustrated using a two-dimensional graph. We recognize that there is very little chance we will encounter LP models with just two variables in real-world situations. As such, these LP models and their graphical solution procedure may be of limited use in practice. It is, nevertheless, worthwhile to spend a little time studying the graphical solution procedure since it is invaluable in providing insights into the properties of solutions to LP models. It also allows us to provide an intuitive explanation of how more complex solution procedures work for larger LP models. For these reasons, we first discuss the solution of Flair's problem using a graphical approach.

## Graphical Representation of Constraints

*Here is a complete mathematical statement of the LP problem.*

The complete LP model for Flair's case can be restated as follows:

$$\text{Maximize profit} = \$7T + \$5C$$

subject to the constraints

| | |
|---|---|
| $4T + 3C \leq 240$ | (carpentry constraint) |
| $2T + 1C \leq 100$ | (painting constraint) |
| $C \leq 60$ | (chairs limit constraint) |
| $T \qquad \geq 0$ | (nonnegativity constraint on tables) |
| $C \geq 0$ | (nonnegativity constraint on chairs) |

To find an optimal solution to this LP problem, we must first identify a set, or region, of feasible solutions. The first step in doing so is to plot each of the problem's constraints on a graph. We can plot either variable on the horizontal ($X$) axis of the graph and the other variable on the vertical ($Y$) axis. In Flair's case, let us plot $T$ (tables) on the $X$-axis and $C$ (chairs) on the $Y$-axis. The nonnegativity constraints imply that we are working only in the first (or positive) quadrant of a graph.

*Nonnegativity constraints mean we are always in the graphical area where T ≥ 0 and C ≥ 0.*

**Carpentry Time Constraint**   To represent the carpentry constraint graphically, we convert the inequality sign ($\leq$) to an equality sign ($=$), and obtain a linear equation—that is, $4T + 3C = 240$.

As you may recall from elementary algebra, the solution of a linear equation in two variables represents a straight line. The easiest way to plot the line is to find any two points that satisfy the equation and then draw a straight line through them. The two easiest points to find are generally the points at which the line intersects the horizontal ($T$) and vertical ($C$) axes.

*Plotting the first constraint involves finding points at which the line intersects the T and C axes.*

If Flair produces no tables (namely $T = 0$), then $4(0) + 3C = 240$, or $C = 80$. Hence, if all the carpentry time available is used to make chairs, 80 chairs could be made. That is, the line representing the carpentry time equation crosses the vertical axis at $C = 80$.

To find the point at which the line crosses the horizontal axis, let us assume that Flair uses all the carpentry time available to make tables—that is, $C = 0$. Then $4T + (3)(0) = 240$, or $T = 60$.

The nonnegativity constraints and the carpentry constraint line are illustrated in Figure 2.1. The line running from the point ($T = 0$, $C = 80$) to the point ($T = 60$, $C = 0$) represents the carpentry time equation.

We know that any combination of tables and chairs represented by points on this line (such as $T = 30$, $C = 40$) will use up all 240 hours of carpentry time.[3] Recall, however, that the actual carpentry constraint was the inequality $4T + 3C \leq 240$. How do we identify all the points on the graph that satisfy this inequality? To do so, we check any possible point in the graph—let's say ($T = 30$, $C = 20$). If we substitute these values in the carpentry constraint, the result is $(4)(30) + (3)(20) = 180$. Since 180 is less than 240, the point ($T = 30$, $C = 20$) satisfies the inequality. Further, note in Figure 2.2 that this point is below the constraint line.

In contrast, let's say the point we select is ($T = 70$, $C = 40$). If we substitute these values in the carpentry constraint, the result is $(4)(70) + (3)(40) = 400$. Since 400 exceeds 240, this point violates the carpentry constraint and is, therefore, an unacceptable production level. Further, note in Figure 2.2 that this point is above the constraint line. As a matter of fact, any point above the constraint line violates that restriction (test this yourself with a few other points), just as any point below the line does not violate the constraint. In Figure 2.2 the shaded region represents all points that satisfy the original inequality carpentry constraint.

*There is a whole region of points that satisfies the first inequality constraint.*

---

[3] Thus, we have plotted the constraint equation in its most binding position, that is, using all of the carpentry resource.

FIGURE 2.1

**Graph of the
Nonnegativity Constraint
and the Carpentry
Constraint Equation**

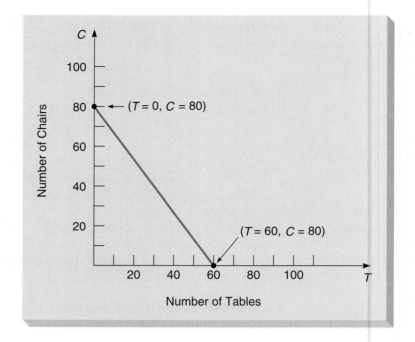

**Painting Time Constraint**  Now that we have identified the points that satisfy the carpentry constraint, we recognize that the final solution must also satisfy all other constraints in the problem. Therefore, let us now add the solution corresponding to the painting time constraint to this graph.

Recall that we expressed this constraint as $2T + 1C \leq 100$. As we did with the carpentry constraint, we start by changing the inequality to an equation and identifying two points on the line specified by the equation $2T + 1C = 100$. When $T = 0$, then $2(0) + 1C = 100$, or $C = 100$. Likewise, when $C = 0$, then $2T + 1(0) = 100$, or $T = 50$.

FIGURE 2.2

**Region That Satisfies the
Carpentry Constraint**

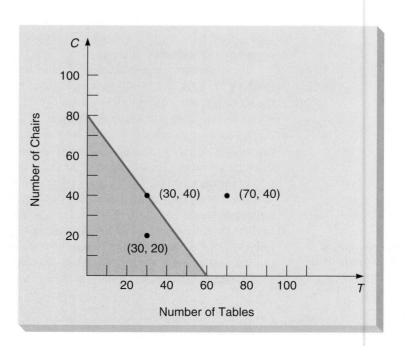

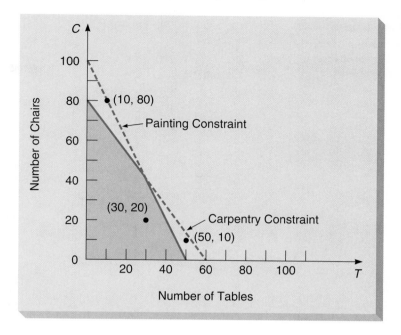

**FIGURE 2.3**

**Region That Satisfies the Carpentry and Painting Constraints**

The line from the point ($T = 0$, $C = 100$) to the point ($T = 50$, $C = 0$) in Figure 2.3 represents all combinations of tables and chairs that use exactly 100 hours of painting time. As with the carpentry constraint, all points on or below this line satisfy the original inequality $2T + 1C \leq 100$.

Looking at Figure 2.3, notice there are some points such as ($T = 30$, $C = 20$) that are below the lines for both the carpentry equation and the painting equation. That is, we have enough carpentry and painting hours available to manufacture 30 tables and 20 chairs. In contrast, there are points, such as ($T = 50$, $C = 10$) and ($T = 10$, $C = 80$), that satisfy one of the two constraints but violate the other. (See if you can verify this statement mathematically.) Since we need the solution to satisfy both the carpentry and painting time constraints, we will consider only those points that satisfy both constraints simultaneously. The region that contains all such points is shaded in Figure 2.3.

**Chairs Limit Constraint**  We have to make sure the final solution requires us to produce no more than 60 chairs ($C \leq 60$). As before, we first convert this inequality to an equation ($C = 60$). This is relatively easy to draw, since this is just a horizontal line that intersects the vertical ($C$) axis at 60. This line is shown in Figure 2.4, and all points below this line satisfy the original inequality ($C \leq 60$).

*In all problems, we are interested in satisfying all constraints at the same time.*

**Feasible Region**  The *feasible region* of an LP problem consists of those points that simultaneously satisfy all constraints in the problem; that is, it is the region where all the problem's constraints overlap.

Consider a point such as ($T = 30$, $C = 20$) in Figure 2.4. This point satisfies all three constraints, as well as the nonnegativity constraints. This point, therefore, represents a *feasible solution* to Flair's problem. In contrast, although the point ($T = 5$, $C = 70$) satisfies both the carpentry and painting time constraints, it violates the maximum chairs constraint. It is, therefore, not a feasible solution. The shaded area in Figure 2.4 represents the feasible region for Flair Furniture's problem. Any point outside the shaded area represents an *infeasible solution* (or production plan).

*The feasible region is the overlapping area of all constraints.*

**FIGURE 2.4**

**Feasible Solution Region
for the Flair Furniture
Company Problem**

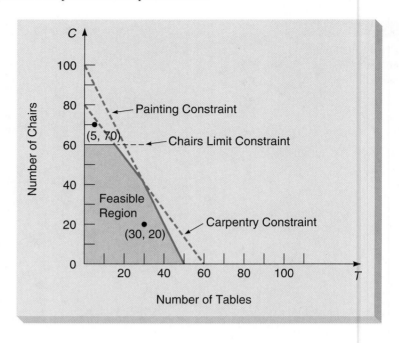

## Isoprofit Line Solution Method

Now that the feasible region has been graphed and identified, we can proceed to find an optimal solution to the problem. An *optimal solution* is the point in the feasible region that produces the highest profit. But there are many, many possible solution points in the region. How do we go about selecting the best one, the one yielding the highest profit?

*The isoprofit method is the
first method we introduce for
finding the optimal solution.*

There are primarily two approaches that we can use to find an optimal solution. The speediest one is called the *isoprofit line* method. In this approach, we let the objective function (i.e., $7T + $5C) guide us toward an optimal point in the feasible region. To do so, we plot the line representing the objective function on the graph, just as we plotted the various constraints. However, note that we do not know what $7T + $5C equals at an optimal solution. In fact, that's what we are trying to find out. Without knowing this value, how do we plot this equation?

To get around this problem, let us first write the objective function as $7T + $5C = Z. We then start the isoprofit line method by selecting any arbitrary value for Z. In selecting this value for Z, the only guideline recommended is to select a value that makes the resulting equation easy to plot. For example, for Flair's problem, we could choose a profit of $210. The objective function can now be written as $7T + $5C = 210.

Clearly, this expression is just the equation of a line. It is known as an isoprofit line and represents all combinations of (T, C) that would yield a total profit of $210. To plot this profit line, we proceed exactly as we did to plot a constraint line. If we let T = 0, then $7(0) + $5C = $210, or C = 42. Likewise, if we let C = 0, then $7T + $5(0) = $210, or T = 30.

The isoprofit line corresponding to Z = $210 is illustrated in Figure 2.5 as the line between (T = 0, C = 42) and (T = 30, C = 0). Observe that if any points on this line lie in the feasible region we identified earlier for Flair's problem, those points represent *feasible production plans* that will yield a profit $210.[4]

---

[4] *Iso* means "equal" or "similar." Thus, an isoprofit line represents a line with all profits the same, in this case $210.

**FIGURE 2.5**

**Isoprofit Line of $210 Plotted for the Flair Furniture Company**

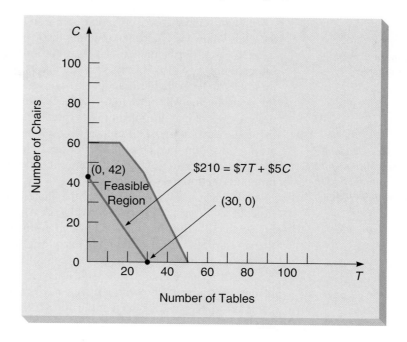

Is $210 the highest profit that Flair can get? To check this, let us graph a different iso-profit line in Figure 2.6, by assuming a higher profit for value $Z$ (e.g., $280). When we set $7T + $5C = $280, we identify two points on this isoprofit line as ($T = 0$, $C = 56$) and ($T = 40$, $C = 0$) using the same approach as before. (See if you can verify these computations.) Again, any combination of tables ($T$) and chairs ($C$) on this isoprofit line yields a total profit of $280. As shown in Figure 2.6, there are points on this isoprofit line that lie in the feasible region for Flair's problem. That is, it is possible for Flair to find a production plan that will yield a profit of $280 (obviously, better than $210).

**FIGURE 2.6**

**Isoprofit Lines of $280 and $350 Plotted for the Flair Furniture Company**

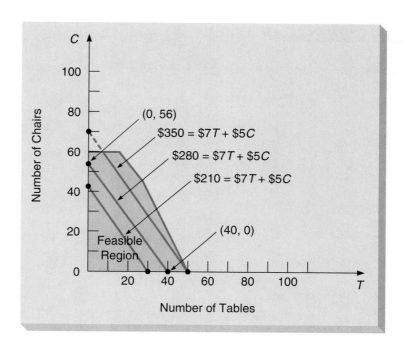

*Isoprofit involves graphing parallel profit lines.*

Likewise, the presence of feasible points on the isoprofit line drawn assuming a profit of $350 (also shown in Figure 2.6) indicates that it is possible for Flair to obtain a profit of $350.

Observe from Figure 2.6 that the isoprofit lines for $280 and $350 are parallel to the isoprofit line for $210. This is a very important point. It implies that as the value we select for Z gets larger (which is desirable in Flair's problem since we want to maximize profits), the isoprofit line will move in a parallel fashion away from the origin. Therefore, we can draw a series of parallel isoprofit lines (by carefully moving a ruler in a plane parallel to the first [$210] profit line). However, as we visualize these parallel lines, we need to ensure that at least one point on each isoprofit line lies in the feasible region. Clearly, the isoprofit line that corresponds to the highest profit but still touches some point of the feasible region pinpoints an optimal solution.

*We draw a series of parallel isoprofit lines until we find the highest isoprofit line, that is, the one with the optimal solution.*

From Figure 2.7, we can see that the highest profit line will be tangential to the shaded feasible region at the point denoted by ④. Any isoprofit line corresponding to a profit higher than that of this line will have no points in the feasible region. For example, note that an isoprofit line corresponding to a profit value of $420 is entirely outside the feasible region (see Figure 2.7). This implies a profit of $420 is not possible for Flair to achieve.

Observe that point ④ defines the intersection of the carpentry and painting time constraint equations. Such points, where two or more constraints intersect, are called *corner points*. From Figure 2.7, note that the other corner points in Flair's problem are, ①, ②, ③, and ⑤.

*The mathematical theory behind LP is that the optimal solution must lie at one of the corner points in the feasible region.*

**Corner Point Property**  The preceding discussion reveals an important property of LP problems, known as the *corner point property*. This property states that an optimal solution to an LP problem will always occur at a corner point of the feasible region.

**Calculating the Solution at an Optimal Corner Point**  Now that we have identified point ④ in Figure 2.7 as an optimal corner point, how do we find the values of T and C, and the profit at that point? Of course, if a graph is perfectly drawn, you can always find point ④ by careful examination of the intersection's coordinates. Otherwise, the algebraic procedure shown here provides more precision.

## FIGURE 2.7

**Optimal Corner Point Solution to the Flair Furniture Company**

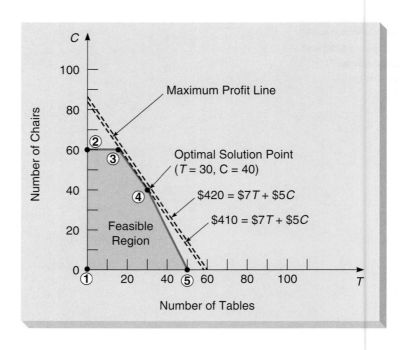

*Solving for corner point ④ requires the use of simultaneous equations, an algebraic technique.*

To find the coordinates of point ④ accurately, we have to solve for the intersection of the two constraint equations—carpentry time and painting time. Recall from your last course in algebra that you can apply the *simultaneous equations* method to the two constraint equations:

$$4T + 3C = 240 \qquad \text{(Carpentry equation)}$$
$$2T + 1C = 100 \qquad \text{(Painting equation)}$$

To solve these equations simultaneously, we need to eliminate one of the variables and solve for the other. One way to do this would be to multiply the second equation by 2 and write it as $4T + 2C = 200$. If we then subtract this equation from the first equation, we get

$$\begin{aligned} 4T + 3C &= 240 \\ -(4T + 2C &= 200) \\ \hline C &= 40 \end{aligned}$$

We can now substitute 40 for $C$ in either of the original equations and solve for $T$. For example, if $C = 40$ in the first equation, then $4T + (3)(40) = 240$, or $T = 30$. That is, point ④ has the coordinates ($T = 30$, $C = 40$). Hence, in order to maximize profit, Flair Furniture should produce 30 tables and 40 chairs. To complete the analysis, we can compute the optimal profit as $\$7(30) + \$5(40) = \$410$.

## Corner Point Solution Method

Since an optimal solution to any LP problem will always occur at a corner point of the feasible region, it is only necessary to find the objective function value at each corner point. Using this principle, the second approach to solving two-variable LP problems graphically employs the *corner point method*. This technique is conceptually much simpler than the isoprofit line approach, but it involves looking at the objective function value at every corner point of the feasible region.

From Figure 2.7, we know that the feasible region for Flair's problem has five corner points, namely, ①, ②, ③, ④, and ⑤. To find the point yielding the maximum profit, we find the coordinates of each corner point and compute their profit level.

*Testing corner points ①, ②, and ⑤ is easy because their T, C coordinates are quickly identified.*

The coordinates of corner points, ①, ②, and ⑤ are easily identifiable from the graph itself. Recall that we calculated the coordinates of point ④ as ($T = 30$, $C = 40$) in the discussion of the isoprofit line method. The coordinates of point ③ can be identified in a similar fashion by simultaneously solving for the intersection of the two constraint equations at that point (i.e., equations $4T + 3C = 240$ and $1C = 60$). It is easy to see that the coordinates are ($T = 15$, $C = 60$).

The profit analysis at each of the five corner points is as follows:

| Point ① | ($T = 0$, $C = 0$) | Profit = $\$7(0) + \$5(0) = \$0$ |
|---|---|---|
| Point ② | ($T = 0$, $C = 80$) | Profit = $\$7(0) + \$5(80) = \$400$ |
| Point ③ | ($T = 15$, $C = 60$) | Profit = $\$7(15) + \$5(60) = \$405$ |
| Point ④ | ($T = 30$, $C = 40$) | Profit = $\$7(30) + \$5(40) = \$410$ |
| Point ⑤ | ($T = 50$, $C = 0$) | Profit = $\$7(50) + \$5(0) = \$350$ |

Note that corner point ④ produces the highest profit of any corner point and is therefore an optimal solution. As expected, this is the same solution we obtained using the isoprofit line method.

Companies often use optimization techniques such as linear programming to allocate limited resources to maximize profits or minimize costs. One of the most important resource allocation problems faced by the United States is dismantling old nuclear weapons and maintaining the safety, security, and reliability of the remaining systems. This is the problem faced by Pantex, a $300 million corporation.

Pantex is responsible for disarming, evaluating, and maintaining the U.S. nuclear stockpile. The company is also responsible for storing critical weapon components that relate to U.S.–Russian nonproliferation agreements. Pantex constantly makes trade-offs in meeting the requirements of disarming some nuclear weapons versus maintaining existing nuclear weapon systems, while effectively allocating limited resources. Like many manufacturers, Pantex must allocate scarce resources among competing demands, all of which are important.

The team charged with solving the resource allocation problem at Pantex developed the Pantex Process Model (PPM). PPM is a sophisticated optimization system capable of analyzing nuclear needs over different time horizons. Since its development, PPM has become the primary tool for analyzing, planning, and scheduling issues at Pantex. PPM also helps to determine future resources. For example, it was used to gain government support for $17 million to modify an existing plant with new buildings and $70 million to construct a new plant.

**Source:** E. Kjeldgaard et al. "Swords into Plowshares: Nuclear Weapon Dismantlement, Evaluation, and Maintenance at Pantex," *Interfaces* 30, (January–February, 2000): 57–82.

## 2.5    A MINIMIZATION LINEAR PROGRAMMING PROBLEM

*Minimization LP problems typically deal with trying to reduce costs.*

Many LP problems involve minimizing an objective such as cost instead of maximizing a profit function. A restaurant, for example, may wish to develop a work schedule to meet staffing needs while minimizing the total number of employees. A manufacturer may seek to distribute its products from several factories to its many regional warehouses in such a way as to minimize total shipping costs. A hospital may want to provide its patients with a daily meal plan that meets certain nutritional standards while minimizing food purchase costs.

Minimization problems that involve only two decision variables can also be solved graphically. To do so, we first set up the feasible solution region and then use either the corner point method or an *isocost* line method (which is analogous to the isoprofit method in maximization problems) to identify a corner point that yields the minimum objective value. Let's take a look at a common LP problem referred to as the *diet problem*. This situation is similar to the one that the hospital faces in feeding its patients at the least cost.

### Holiday Meal Turkey Ranch

The Holiday Meal Turkey Ranch is considering buying two different brands of turkey feed and blending them to provide a good, low-cost diet for its turkeys. Each feed contains, in varying proportions, some or all of the three nutritional ingredients (protein, vitamin, and iron) essential for fattening turkeys. Each pound of brand A contains 5 units of protein, 4 units of vitamin, and $\frac{1}{2}$ unit of iron. Each pound of brand B contains 10 units of protein, 3 units of vitamins, but no iron. The brand A feed costs the ranch 2 cents a pound, and the brand B feed costs 3 cents a pound. The owner of the ranch would like to use LP to determine the lowest-cost diet that meets the minimum monthly intake requirement for each nutritional ingredient. Table 2.1 summarizes the relevant information.

## TABLE 2.1

Holiday Meal Turkey
Ranch Data

| INGREDIENT | COMPOSITION OF EACH POUND OF FEED (OZ) | | MINIMUM MONTHLY REQUIREMENT PER TURKEY (OZ) |
| --- | --- | --- | --- |
| | BRAND A FEED | BRAND B FEED | |
| Protein | 5 | 10 | 90 |
| Vitamin | 4 | 3 | 48 |
| Iron | $\frac{1}{2}$ | 0 | $1\frac{1}{2}$ |
| Cost per pound | 2 cents | 3 cents | |

If we let $A$ denote the number of pounds of brand $A$ feed purchased and $B$ denote the number of pounds of brand B feed purchased, we can proceed to formulate this LP problem as follows:

$$\text{Minimize cost (in cents)} = 2A + 3B$$

*Here is a complete mathematical formulation of the LP problem.*

subject to the constraints

| | | |
| --- | --- | --- |
| $5A + 10B \geq 90$ | | (protein constraint) |
| $4A + \ \ 3B \geq 48$ | | (vitamin constraint) |
| $\frac{1}{2}A \quad\ \ \geq 1\frac{1}{2}$ | | (iron constraint) |
| $A \quad\ \ \geq 0$ | | (nonnegativity constraint on brand A feed) |
| $B \geq 0$ | | (nonnegativity constraint on brand B feed) |

Before solving this problem, note three features that affect its solution. First, the farmer needs to purchase enough brand A feed to meet the minimum standards for iron. Buying only brand B would not be feasible because it lacks iron. Second, as the problem is formulated, we will be solving for the best blend of brands A and B to buy per turkey per month. If the ranch houses 5,000 turkeys in a given month, we can simply multiply the $A$ and $B$ quantities by 5,000 to decide how much feed to order overall. Third, we are now dealing with a series of greater than or equal to constraints. These cause the feasible solution area to be above the constraint lines, a common situation when handling minimization LP problems.

## Graphical Solution of the Holiday Meal Turkey Ranch Problem

*We plot the three constraints to develop a feasible solution region for the minimization problem.*

We first construct the feasible solution region. To do so, we plot each of the three constraint equations as shown in Figure 2.8. Note that in plotting the third constraint, $\frac{1}{2}A \geq 1\frac{1}{2}$, it is more convenient to multiply both sides by 2 and rewrite it as $A \geq 3$. Clearly, this does not change the position of the constraint line in any way.

The feasible region for Holiday Meal's problem is shown by the shaded space in Figure 2.8. Minimization problems are often unbounded outward (i.e., on the right side and on top), but this causes no difficulty in solving them. As long as they are bounded inward (on the left side and the bottom), corner points can be established. Recall that an optimal solution will lie at one of the corner points, just as it did in a maximization problem. In Figure 2.8, the identifiable corner points for Holiday Meal's problem are denoted by, ①, ②, and ③.

*Note that the feasible region of minimization problems is often unbounded (i.e., open outward).*

**FIGURE 2.8**

**Feasible Region for the Holiday Meal Turkey Ranch Problem**

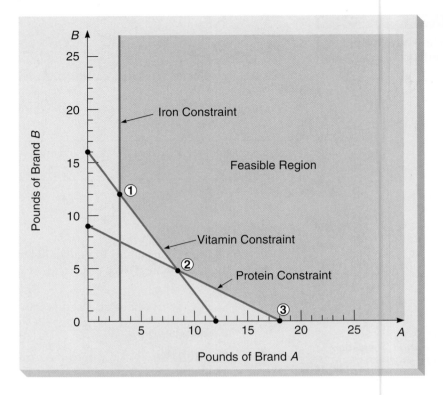

*The isocost line method is analogous to the isoprofit line method we used on maximization problems.*

**Isocost Line Method**  As with the isoprofit lines we used to solve the Flair Furniture maximization problem, we can draw a series of parallel isocost lines to identify Holiday Meal's optimal solution. The lowest isocost line to touch the feasible region pinpoints an optimal corner point.

For example, we start in Figure 2.9 by drawing a 54-cent cost line, or $2A + 3B = 54$. Obviously, there are many points in the feasible region that would yield a lower total cost. We proceed to move our isocost line toward the lower left in a plane parallel to the 54-cent solution line. The last point touched while still in contact with the feasible region is corner point ②, as shown in Figure 2.9.

To find the coordinates of point ② algebraically, we eliminate one of the variables from the two equations that intersect at this point (i.e., $5A + 10B = 90$ and $4A + 3B = 48$), so that we can solve for the other. One way would be to multiply the first equation by 4, the second equation by 5, and subtract the second equation from the first equation as follows:

$$
\begin{aligned}
4(5A + 10B = 90) \text{ implies} & \quad 20A + 40B = 360 \\
-5(4A + 3B = 48) \text{ implies} - & \quad \underline{(20A + 15B = 240)} \\
& \quad \quad 25B = 120
\end{aligned}
$$

or

$$B = 4.8$$

We can substitute $B = 4.8$ into either of the two original equations to solve for $A$. Using the first equation yields $4A + (3)(4.8) = 48$, or $A = 8.4$. The cost at corner point ② is $2A + 3B = (2)(8.4) + (3)(4.8) = 31.2$ cents. That is, Holiday Meal should use 8.4 pounds of brand A feed and 4.8 pounds of brand B feed to make the turkey diet. This will yield a cost of 31.2 cents per turkey. Observe that this solution turns out to have fractional values. In

**FIGURE 2.9**

Graphical Solution to the
Holiday Meal Turkey
Ranch Problem Using
the Isocost Line

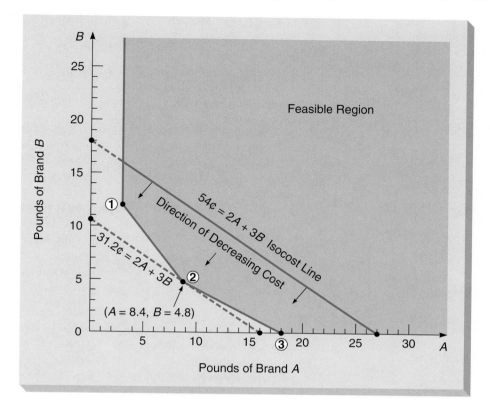

*this case, however, these are perfectly logical since turkey feeds can be measured in fractional quantities.*

*We must solve for the three corner points algebraically.*

**Corner Point Solution Method**  Recall from Figure 2.8 that there are three identifiable corner points—①, ②, and ③—for this problem. For point ① we find the coordinates at the intersection of the vitamin and iron constraints, that is, where the line $A = 3$ crosses the line $4A + 3B = 48$. If we substitute $A = 3$ into the vitamin constraint equation, then $4(3) + 3B = 48$, or $B = 12$. Thus, corner point ① has the coordinates $(A = 3, B = 12)$ and a corresponding cost of $2(3) + 3(12) = 42$ cents.

We have already computed the coordinates of point ② as $(A = 8.4, B = 4.8)$, with a cost of 31.2 cents. Finally, we compute the cost at point ③. This is much easier, as it is evident that ③ has the coordinates $(A = 18, B = 0)$. The cost $2(18) + 3(0) = 36$ cents. Hence, as identified earlier with the isocost method, point ② is the optimal corner point.

## 2.6   SUMMARY OF THE GRAPHICAL SOLUTION METHODS

As shown in the cases of the Flair Furniture Company and the Holiday Meal Turkey Ranch, the graphical methods of solving LP problems involve several steps. Let's review them briefly before moving on:

1. Graph each of the constraint equations.

2. Identify the feasible solution region, that is, the area that satisfies all of the constraints simultaneously.

3. Select one of the two following graphical solution techniques and proceed to solve the problem:

*Corner Point Method*

4. Determine the coordinates of each of the corner points of the feasible region by either visual inspection or the method of simultaneous equations.

5. Compute the profit or cost at each corner point by substituting that point's coordinates into the objective function.

6. Identify an optimal solution as a corner point with the highest profit in a maximization problem or lowest cost in a minimization problem.

*Isoprofit* or *Isocost Method*

4. Select a specific value for the profit or cost, and draw the *isoprofit* or *isocost* line to reveal its slope or angle.

5. If you are dealing with a maximization problem, maintain the same slope, through a series of parallel lines, and move the line up and to the right until it touches the feasible region at only one point. If you have a minimization problem, move down and to the left until it touches only one point in the feasible region.

6. Identify an optimal solution as the coordinates of a point on the feasible region touched by the highest possible *isoprofit* line or the lowest possible *isocost* line.

7. Read the optimal coordinates from the graph or compute their values by using the simultaneous equation method.

8. Compute the optimal profit or cost.

## 2.7  SPECIAL SITUATIONS IN SOLVING LINEAR PROGRAMMING PROBLEMS

In each of the LP problems discussed so far, all the constraints in the model have affected the shape and size of the feasible region. Further, in each case, there has been a unique corner point that we have been able to identify as the optimal corner point. There are, however, some special situations that may be encountered when solving LP problems: (1) redundancy, (2) infeasibility, (3) unboundedness, and (4) alternate optimal solutions.

### Redundancy

*A redundant constraint is one that does not affect the feasible solution region.*

A *redundant* constraint is a constraint that does not affect the feasible region in any way. In other words, there are other constraints in the model that are more restrictive and thereby negate the need to even consider the redundant constraint. The presence of redundant constraints is quite common in large LP models with many variables. However, it is typically impossible to determine if a constraint is redundant just by looking at it.

Let's illustrate a redundant constraint by considering the following LP problem with three constraints:

$$\text{Maximize profit} = 2X + 3Y$$

**FIGURE 2.10**

**Problem with a Redundant Constraint**

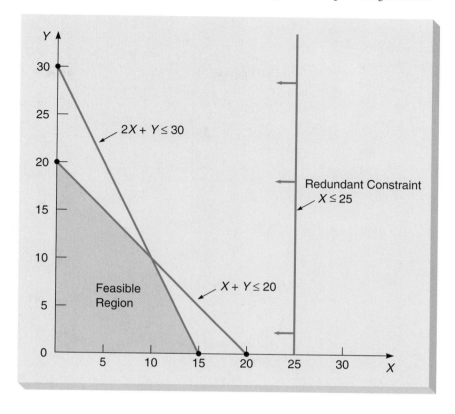

subject to the constraints

$$X + Y \leq 20$$
$$2X + Y \leq 30$$
$$X \leq 25$$
$$X, Y \geq 0$$

From Figure 2.10, we see that the first two constraints are so restrictive that they make the third constraint, $X \leq 25$, redundant. That is, it has no effect on the feasible region and can therefore be eliminated from the model without affecting the feasible region or solution in any way.

## Infeasibility

*Lack of a feasible solution region can occur if constraints conflict with one another. This is called* infeasibility.

*Infeasibility* is a condition that arises when an LP problem has no solution that satisfies all of its constraints; that is, no feasible solution region exists. Such a situation might occur, for example, if the problem has been formulated with conflicting constraints. This, by the way, is a frequent occurrence in real-world, large-scale LP problems that involve hundreds of constraints. For example, the marketing manager may insist that at least 300 tables be produced to meet sales demand (i.e., $T \geq 300$). At the same time, the production manager may insist that no more than 220 tables be produced due to a lumber shortage (i.e., $T \leq 220$). In this case, an infeasible solution region results. When the decision analyst coordinating the LP problem points out this conflict, one manager or the other must revise his or her inputs. Perhaps the production manager could procure more lumber from a new source, or perhaps the sales manager could lower sales demand by substituting a different model table to customers.

**FIGURE 2.11**

**A Problem with No
Feasible Solution**

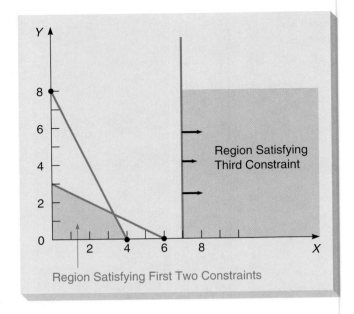

As a further graphic illustration of infeasibility, let us consider an LP problem with the following three constraints:

$$X + 2Y \leq 6$$

$$2X + Y \leq 8$$

$$X \geq 7$$

As seen in Figure 2.11, there is no feasible solution region for this LP problem because of the presence of conflicting constraints.

## Unboundedness

*When the profit in a maximization problem can be infinitely large, the problem is unbounded and is missing one or more constraints.*

Sometimes an LP model will not have a finite solution. This means that in a maximization problem, for example, one or more solution variables—and thus the profit—can be made infinitely large without violating any constraints. In solving such a problem graphically, you will note that the feasible region is open-ended, or *unbounded.*

Let us consider a simple two-variable example to illustrate the situation. A firm has formulated the following LP problem:

$$\text{Maximize profit} = \$3X + \$5Y$$

subject to

$$X \geq 5$$

$$Y \leq 10$$

$$X + 2Y \geq 10$$

$$X, Y \geq 0$$

As shown in Figure 2.12, the feasible region extends infinitely to the right and is therefore unbounded. Further, since this is a maximization problem and the feasible region is unbounded in the direction in which profit increases, the solution itself is unbounded; that

**FIGURE 2.12**

**A Feasible Region That Is Unbounded to the Right**

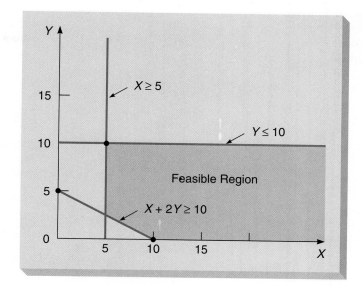

is, the profit can be made to reach infinity. In real-world situations, the occurrence of an unbounded solution usually means the problem has been formulated improperly. It would indeed be wonderful for the company to be able to produce an infinite number of units of $X$ (at a profit of $3 each!), but obviously no firm has infinite resources available or infinite demand.

It is important to note that the presence of an unbounded feasible region does not necessarily mean the solution is also unbounded. To demonstrate this, let us revisit the feasible region for the Holiday Meal Turkey Ranch problem (refer back to Figure 2.8 if necessary). It is clear this feasible region is unbounded. However, since the Holiday Meal problem had a minimization objective, the fact that the feasible region was bounded inward (on the left side and the bottom) allowed us to identify a corner point as the optimal solution.

## Alternate Optimal Solutions

*Multiple optimal solutions are possible in LP problems.*

An LP problem may, on occasion, have more than one optimal solution. Graphically, this is the case when the isoprofit (or isocost) line runs perfectly parallel to a constraint in the problem that lies in the direction in which the isoprofit (or isocost) line is being moved—in other words, when they have the same slope. To illustrate this situation, let us consider the following simple LP problem:

$$\text{Maximize profit} = \$3X + \$2Y$$

subject to

$$6X + 4Y \leq 24$$

$$X \leq 3$$

$$X, Y \geq 0$$

As shown in Figure 2.13, the first isoprofit line of $8 runs parallel to the constraint equation. At a profit level of $12, the isoprofit line will rest directly on top of the first constraint line. This means that any point along the line between corner points ① and ② provides an optimal $X$ and $Y$ combination. Far from causing problems, the presence of more than one optimal solution allows management great flexibility in deciding which solution to select. The profit remains the same at each alternate solution.

**FIGURE 2.13**

**Example of Alternate Optimal Solutions**

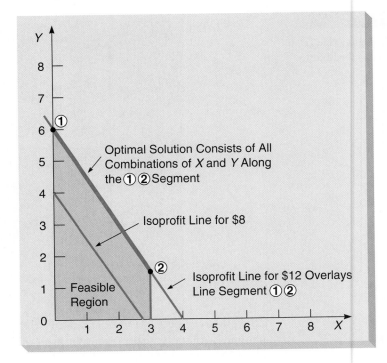

## 2.8 SETTING UP AND SOLVING LINEAR PROGRAMMING PROBLEMS USING EXCEL'S SOLVER

*Excel has a built-in solution tool for solving LP problems.*

Although graphical solution approaches can handle LP models with only two decision variables, more complex solution procedures are necessary to solve larger LP models. Fortunately, such solution procedures exist. (We briefly discuss them in Section 2.10.) However, rather than using these procedures to solve large LP models by hand, the focus here is on using Excel to set up and solve LP problems. Excel and other spreadsheet programs offer users the ability to analyze large LP problems using built-in problem solving tools.

 **IN ACTION** Using LP to Assist AIDS Patients in Italy

Home care for AIDS patients, in the form of nurses, doctors, and social workers, was introduced by law in Italy in 1990. Organizations that provide home-care work with a limited budget must provide a minimum standard of service. A lack of balance between patient needs and available resources can lead to a low level of service, an excessive workload for the medical and social workers, or both.

To produce an optimal schedule for admitting new patients into the home health care system, Italian researchers turned to LP. Using available quantities of each resource as constraints, the objective is to maximize the sum of the number of patients that can be admitted each week. The LP model produces an optimal admissions schedule for a given 12-week planning period.

But to complicate the problem, patients fell into various categories of "dependency," ranging from "self-sufficient" to "permanently in bed" to "hospitalized" to "dead." Patients move with predicted probabilities from one category to another, and different classes are given different weights to express priority. This practical and flexible LP tool for public health has also been extended to support centralized decision making by evaluating the impact of different budget assignments.

**Source:** V. DeAngelis. "Planning Home Assistance for AIDS Patients in the City of Rome, Italy," *Interfaces* 28, 3 (May–June, 1998): 75–83.

There are two main reasons why this book's focus on Excel for setting up and solving LP problems is logical and useful in practice:

■ The use of spreadsheet programs is now very common, and virtually every organization has access to such programs.
■ Since you are likely to be using Excel in many of your other courses, you are probably already familiar with many of its commands. As such, there is no need to learn any specialized software to set up and solve LP problems.

Excel uses an add-in named Solver to find the solution to LP-related problems. The standard version of Solver that is included with Excel can handle problems with up to 200 decision variables and 100 constraints (not including simple constraints such as the non-negativity constraints). Larger versions of Solver are available for commercial use from Frontline Systems Inc., which has developed and marketed this add-in for Excel (and other spreadsheet packages). We use Solver to solve LP problems in Chapters 2–5, and integer and nonlinear programming problems in Chapter 6.

There are several other software packages (e.g., LINDO, GAMS) that are capable of handling very large LP models. Although each program is slightly different in terms of its input and output formats, the approach each takes toward handling LP problems is basically the same. Hence, once you are experienced in dealing with computerized LP procedures, you can easily adjust to minor differences among programs.

## Using Solver to Solve the Flair Furniture Problem

Recall that the decision variables $T$ and $C$ in the Flair Furniture problem denote the number of tables and chairs to make, respectively. The LP formulation for this problem is as follows:

$$\text{Maximize profit} = \$7T + \$5C$$

subject to the constraints

| | |
|---|---|
| $4T + 3C \leq 240$ | (carpentry constraint) |
| $2T + 1C \leq 100$ | (painting constraint) |
| $C \leq 60$ | (chairs limit constraint) |
| $T, C \geq 0$ | (nonnegativity constraints) |

Just as we discussed a three-step process to formulate an LP problem (i.e., decision variables, objective function, and constraints), setting up and solving a problem using Excel's Solver also involves three parts: changing cells, target cell, and constraints. We discuss each of these parts in the following sections.

*There is no prescribed layout for setting up LP problems in Excel.*

In practice, there are no specific guidelines regarding the layout of an LP model in Excel. Depending on your personal preference and expertise, any model that satisfies the basic requirements discussed subsequently will work. However, for purposes of convenience and ease of explanation, we use (to the extent possible) the same layout for all problems in this text. Such a consistent approach is more suited to the beginning student of LP. As you gain experience with spreadsheet modeling of LP problems, we encourage you to try alternate layouts.

*We represent all parameters associated with a decision variable in the same column.*

In our suggested layout, we use a separate column to represent all the parameters (e.g., solution value, profit contribution, constraint coefficients) associated with each decision variable in the problem. The objective function and each constraint in the problem is then modeled on separate rows of the Excel worksheet. Although not required to solve the model, we also add several labels in our spreadsheet to make them as self-explanatory as possible.

### Excel Note

The CD-ROM that accompanies this textbook contains the Excel file for each example problem discussed here. The relevant file name appears in the margin next to each example.

## Changing Cells

*Changing cells are the decision variables in the problem.*

**File: 2-1.xls**

Solver refers to decision variables as changing cells. Each decision variable in the formulation is assigned to a unique cell in the spreadsheet. Although there are no rules regarding the relative positions of these cells, it is typically convenient to use cells that are next to each other.

In the Flair Furniture example, there are two decision variables that need to be assigned to any two cells in the spreadsheet. In Program 2.1A, we use cells B5 and C5 to represent the number of tables to make (*T*) and the number of chairs to make (*C*), respectively.

The initial entries in these two cells can be blank or any value of our choice. At the conclusion of the Solver run, the optimal values of the decision variables will automatically be shown here (if found).

It is possible, and often desirable, to format these cells using any of Excel's formatting features. For example, we can choose to specify how many decimal points to show for these values. Likewise, the cells can be assigned any name (instead of B5 and C5) using the naming option in Excel. Descriptive titles for these cells (such a those shown in Cells A5, B4, and C4 of Program 2.1A) are recommended to make the model as self-explanatory as possible, but they are not required to solve the problem.

### Excel Notes

- In the Excel layouts, for clarity, the changing cells (decision variables) are shaded yellow.
- In the Excel layouts, we show the decision variable names (such as *T* and *C*) used in the written formulation of the model (see cells B3 and C3). These names have no role or relevance in using Solver to solve the model and can therefore be ignored. We show these decision variable names in our models in this textbook so that the equivalence of the written formulation and the Excel layout is clear.

---

**PROGRAM 2.1A**    **Formula View of the Excel Layout for Flair Furniture**

These are decision variable names used in the written formulation (shown here for information purposes only).

Names in column A and row 4 are recommended but not required.

| | A | B | C | D | E | F |
|---|---|---|---|---|---|---|
| 1 | **Flair Furniture** | | | | | |
| 2 | | | | | | |
| 3 | | *T* | *C* | | | |
| 4 | | Tables | Chairs | | | |
| 5 | Number of Units | | | | | |
| 6 | Profit | 7 | 5 | =SUMPRODUCT(B6:C6,$B$5:$C$5) | <- Objective | |
| 7 | **Constraints:** | | | | | |
| 8 | Carpentry Hours | 4 | 3 | =SUMPRODUCT(B8:C8,$B$5:$C$5) | <= | 240 |
| 9 | Painting Hours | 2 | 1 | =SUMPRODUCT(B9:C9,$B$5:$C$5) | <= | 100 |
| 10 | Chairs Limit | | 1 | =SUMPRODUCT(B10:C10,$B$5:$C$5) | <= | 60 |
| 11 | | | | LHS | Sign | RHS |

Solver will place the answers in these cells.

These are names for the constraints.

Calculate the objective function value and LHS value for each constraint using the SUMPRODUCT function.

The actual constraint signs are entered in Solver. These in column E are for information purposes only.

## Target Cell

*The* target cell *is the objective function.*

The objective function, referred to as the target cell by Solver, can now be set up. We select any cell in the spreadsheet (other than the cells allocated to the decision variables). In that cell, we simply enter the formula for the objective function, referring to the two decision variables by their cell references (B5 and C5 in this case). In Program 2.1A, we use cell D6 to represent the objective function. Although we could use the unit profit contribution values ($7 per table and $5 per chair) directly in the formula, it is preferable to make the $7 and $5 entries in some cells in the spreadsheet and refer to them by their cell references in the formula in cell D6. This is a more "elegant" way of setting up the problem and is especially useful if subsequent changes in parameter values are necessary.

In Program 2.1A, we have entered the $7 and $5 in cells B6 and C6 respectively. The formula in cell D6 can therefore be written as

$$=B6*B5 + C6*C5$$

Recall that the "=" at the start of the equation lets Excel know that the entry is a formula. This equation corresponds exactly to the objective function of the Flair Furniture problem. If we had left cells B5 and C5 blank, the result of this formula would be initially shown as 0. As with cells B5 and C5, we can format the target cell (D6) in any manner. For example, since D6 denotes the profit in dollars earned by Flair Furniture, we can format it to show the result as a dollar value.

*Excel's SUMPRODUCT function makes it easy to enter even long expressions.*

If there are several decision variables in the problem, however, formulas such as the one shown here can become somewhat long, and typing them could become quite cumbersome. In such cases, you can use Excel's SUMPRODUCT function to express the equation efficiently. The syntax for the SUMPRODUCT function requires specifying two cell ranges of equal size, separated by a comma.[5] One of the ranges defines the cells containing the profit contributions (cells B6:C6), and the other defines the cells containing the decision variables (cells B5:C5). The SUMPRODUCT function computes the products of the first entries in each range, second entries in each range, and so on. It then sums these products.

Based on the preceding discussion, as shown in Program 2.1A, the objective function for Flair Furniture can be expressed as

$$=SUMPRODUCT(B6:C6,\$B\$5:\$C\$5)$$

Note that this is equivalent to =B6*B5+C6*C5. Also, the $ symbol in the second cell range keeps that cell reference fixed when we copy the formula. This is especially convenient since, as we show next, the formula for each constraint in the model also follows the same structure as the objective function.

---

### Excel Note

In each of our Excel layouts, for clarity, the target cell (objective function) has been shaded green.

---

## Constraints

*Constraints in Solver include three entries: LHS, RHS, and sign.*

Each constraint in the problem must now be set up. To achieve this, let us first separate each constraint into three parts: (1) a *left-hand-side* (LHS) part consisting of every term to the left of the equality or inequality sign, (2) a *right-hand-side* (RHS) part consisting of all terms to the right of the equality or inequality sign, and the (3) equality or inequality sign itself. The RHS in most cases may just be a fixed number, that is, a constant.

---

[5] The SUMPRODUCT function can actually be used with more than two cell ranges. See Excel's help feature for details.

**Creating Cells for Constraint LHS Values**  We now select a unique cell for each LHS in the formulation (one for each constraint) and type in the relevant formula for that constraint. As with the objective function, we refer to the decision variables by their cell references. In Program 2.1A, we use cell D8 to represent the LHS of the carpentry hours constraint. We have entered the coefficients (i.e., 4 and 3) on the LHS of this constraint in cells B8 and C8, respectively. Then, either of the following formulas would be appropriate in cell D8:

$$=B8*B5 + C8*C5$$

or

$$=SUMPRODUCT(B8:C8,\$B\$5:\$C\$5)$$

Here again, the SUMPRODUCT function makes the formula compact in situations in which the LHS has many terms. Note the similarity between the formulas for the objective function in cell D6 (=SUMPRODUCT(B6:C6,$B$5:$C$5)) and the LHS of the carpentry constraint in cell D8 (=SUMPRODUCT(B8:C8,$B$5:$C$5)). In fact, since we have anchored the cell references for the decision variables (B5 and C5) using the $ symbol in cell D6, we can simply copy the formula in cell D6 to cell D8.

*Formula in D9:*
*= SUMPRODUCT*
*(B9:C9,$B$5:$C$5)*

The LHS formula for the painting hours constraint (cell D9) and chairs limit constraint (cell D10) can similarly be copied from cell D6. As you have probably recognized by now, the LHS cell for virtually every constraint in an LP formulation can be created in this fashion.

### Excel Note

In each of our Excel layouts, for clarity, cells denoting LHS formulas of constraints have been shaded blue.

*In Solver, RHS of constraints can also include formulas.*

**Creating Cells for Constraint RHS Values**  When all the LHS formulas have been set up, we can pick unique cells for each RHS in the formulation. Although the Flair Furniture problem has only constants (240, 100, and 60, respectively) for the three constraints, it is perfectly valid in Solver for the RHS to also have a formula like the LHS. In Program 2.1A, we show the three RHS values in cells F8:F10.

**Constraint Type**  In Program 2.1A, we also show the sign ($\leq$, $\geq$, or =) of each constraint between the LHS and RHS cells for that constraint (see cells E8:E10). Although this makes each constraint easier to understand, note that the inclusion of these signs here is for information purposes only. As we show next, the actual sign for each constraint is entered directly in Solver.

## Entering Information in Solver

After all the constraints have been set up, we invoke the Solver Parameters window by clicking Tools|Solver.[6] This window is shown in Program 2.1B.

*Default in Solver is Max.*

**Specifying the Target Cell**  We first enter the relevant cell reference (i.e., cell D6) in the Set Target Cell box. The default is to maximize the target value. (Note that the Max option is already selected.) For a minimization problem, we must click the Min option to specify that the objective function should be minimized. The third option (Value) allows us to specify a

---

[6] If you do not see Solver under the Tools menu in Excel, refer to Appendix A for instructions on how to fix this problem.

**PROGRAM 2.1B**     **Solver Entries for Flair Furniture**

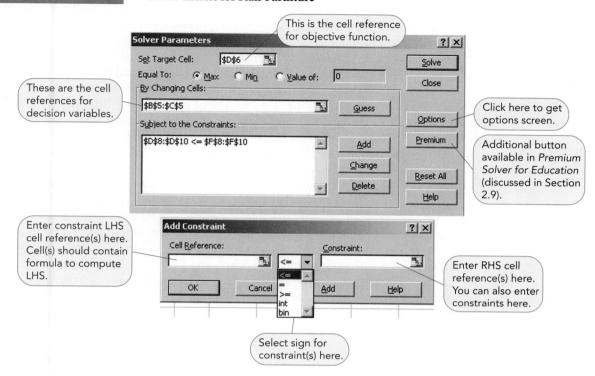

This is the cell reference for objective function.

These are the cell references for decision variables.

Click here to get options screen.

Additional button available in *Premium Solver for Education* (discussed in Section 2.9).

Enter constraint LHS cell reference(s) here. Cell(s) should contain formula to compute LHS.

Enter RHS cell reference(s) here. You can also enter constraints here.

Select sign for constraint(s) here.

value that we want the target cell to achieve, rather than obtain the optimal solution. (We will not use this option in our study of LP and other mathematical programming models.)

*Changing cells can be entered as a block or as individual cell references separated by commas.*

**Specifying the Changing Cells**  We now move the cursor to the box labeled By Changing Cells. We enter the cell references for the decision variables in this box. If the cell references are next to each other, we can simply enter them as one block. For example, we could enter B5:C5 for Flair Furniture's problem. (If you use the mouse or keyboard to highlight cells B5 and C5, Excel will automatically put in the $ anchors, as shown in Program 2.1B.) If the cells are not contiguous (i.e., not next to each other), we can enter the changing cells by placing a comma between noncontiguous cells (or blocks of cells).

Solver includes a button named Guess. We can click this button to get Solver to automatically guess the cell references for the changing cells. This approach is, however, not always reliable, so we recommend that the changing cell references always be entered manually.

*The Add Constraint window is used to enter constraints.*

**Specifying the Constraints**  Next, we use the Add constraints feature to enter the relevant cell references for the LHS and RHS of each constraint. The Add Constraint window (also shown in Program 2.1B) has a box for entering the cell reference of the LHS, a drop-down menu for the sign, and a second box for entering the cell reference of the RHS. The drop-down menu has five choices: "≤," "≥," "=," "Int" (for integer), and "Bin" (for binary). (We discuss the last two choices in Chapter 6.)

We can either add constraints one at a time or add blocks of constraints having the same sign (≤, ≥, or =) at the same time. For instance, we could first add the carpentry constraint by entering D8 in the LHS input box, entering F8 in the RHS input box, and selecting the ≤ sign from the drop-down menu. As noted earlier, the "≤" sign shown in cell E8 is not relevant in Solver, and we must enter the sign of each constraint only using the Add

*Constraints with the same sign can be entered as a block.*

Constraint window. We can now add the painting constraint by entering D9 and F9 in the LHS and RHS input boxes, respectively. Finally, we can add the chairs limit constraint by entering D10 and F10 in the LHS and RHS input boxes, respectively.

Alternatively, since all three constraints have the same sign ($\leq$), we can input cells D8 to D10 in the LHS input box (i.e., enter D8:D10), and correspondingly enter F8:F10 in the RHS input box. We select "$\leq$" as the sign between these LHS and RHS entries. Solver interprets this as taking each entry in the LHS input box and setting it "$\leq$" to the corresponding entry in the RHS input box (i.e., D8 $\leq$ F8, D9 $\leq$ F9, and D10 $\leq$ F10).

Using the latter procedure, note that it is possible to have just three entries in the constraints window: one for all the "$\leq$" constraints in the model, one for all the "$\geq$" constraints in the model, and one for all the "=" constraints in the model. This, of course, requires that the spreadsheet layout be such that the LHS and RHS cells for all constraints having the same sign are in contiguous blocks. However, as we demonstrate in several examples in Chapter 3, this is quite easy to do.

At any point during the constraint input process, we can use the Change or Delete features to modify one or more constraints as necessary. It is important to note that we *cannot* enter the formula for the objective function and the LHS and/or RHS of constraints from within the Solver Parameters window. The formulas must be created in appropriate cells in the spreadsheet before using the Solver Parameters window. Although it is possible to directly enter constants (240, 100, and 60 in our model) in the RHS input box while adding constraints, it is preferable to make the RHS also a cell reference (F8, F9, and F10 in our model).

**Solver Options**  When all constraints have been entered, we are ready to solve the model. However, before clicking the Solve option on the Solver Parameters window, we must first click on the Options button to get the Solver Options window (shown in Program 2.1C). For solving most LP problems, we do not have to change any of the default parameters. However, we must check the boxes titled Assume Non-Negative and Assume Linear Model. Checking the nonnegative box automatically enforces the nonnegativity condition on all the decision variables. Checking the linear model box directs Solver to provide a detailed sensitivity analysis report, which we cover in Chapter 4.

*Check the Assume Non-Negative and Assume Linear Model boxes in Solver's options.*

**PROGRAM 2.1C**

**Solver Options Window**

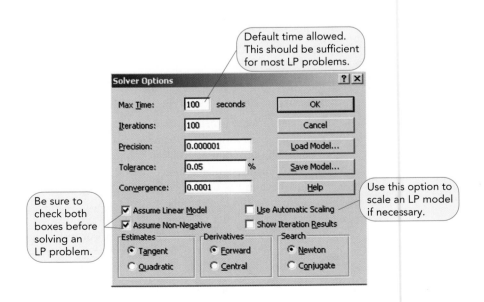

Default time allowed. This should be sufficient for most LP problems.

Be sure to check both boxes before solving an LP problem.

Use this option to scale an LP model if necessary.

Solver also has another option called Use Automatic Scaling (see Program 2.1C). In practice, it is usually a good idea to scale problems in which typical values of the objective function and constraints differ by several orders of magnitude. For instance, a problem with some entries dealing with values in millions and others dealing with fractional values can be considered a poorly scaled model. Due to the effects of a computer's finite precision arithmetic, such poorly scaled models could cause difficulty for Solver, leading to fairly large round-off errors. Checking the automatic scaling box directs Solver to scale models that it detects as poorly scaled and possibly avoid such round-off problems.

**Solving the Model**  When the Solve button is clicked, Solver executes the model and the results are displayed, as shown in Program 2.1D. Before looking at the results, it is important to read the message in the Solver Results window (see Program 2.1D) to verify that Solver did find an optimal solution. In some cases, the message indicates Solver's inability to find an optimal solution (e.g., when the formulation is infeasible or the solution space is unbounded). Table 2.2 shows several different Solver messages that could result when an LP model is solved, the meaning of each message, and a possible cause for each message.

*Solver provides options to obtain different reports.*

The Solver Results window also indicates that there are three reports available: Answer, Sensitivity, and Limits. We discuss the Answer report in the next section and the Sensitivity report in Chapter 4. The Limits report is not useful for our discussion here, and we therefore ignore it. Note that in order to get these reports, we must select them by clicking on the relevant report names to highlight them, before clicking OK on the Solver Results window.

Cells B5 and C5 show the optimal quantities of tables and chairs to make, respectively, and cell D6 shows the optimal profit. Cells D8 and D10 show the LHS values of the three constraints. For example, cell D8 shows the amount of carpentry hours used.

**Excel Layout and Solver Solution for Flair Furniture (Solver Results Window also shown)**

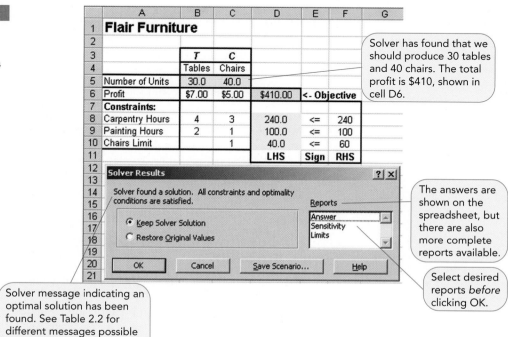

Solver has found that we should produce 30 tables and 40 chairs. The total profit is $410, shown in cell D6.

The answers are shown on the spreadsheet, but there are also more complete reports available.

Select desired reports *before* clicking OK.

Solver message indicating an optimal solution has been found. See Table 2.2 for different messages possible and their implication.

**TABLE 2.2**

Possible Messages in the *Solver Results* Window

| MESSAGE | MEANING | POSSIBLE CAUSE |
|---|---|---|
| Solver found a solution. All constraints and optimality conditions are satisfied. | Ideal message! | *Note:* This does *not* mean the formulation and/or solution is correct. It just means there are no syntax errors in the Excel formulas and Solver entries. |
| Solver could not find a feasible solution. | There is no feasible region. | Incorrect entries in LHS formulas, signs, and/or RHS values of constraints. |
| The Set Cell values do not converge. | Unbounded solution. | Incorrect entries in LHS formulas, signs, and/or RHS values of constraints. |
| Solver encountered an error value in a target or constraint cell. | Formula error in target cell or constraint cells. | Most common cause is division by 0 in some cell. |
| The linearity conditions required by this LP solver are not satisfied. | The "Assume Linear Model" box is checked in Solver's options, but one or more formulas in the model are not linear. | Multiplication or division involving two or more variables in some cell. *Note:* Solver sometimes gives this error message even when the formulas are linear. This occurs especially when both the LHS and RHS of a constraint have formulas. In such cases, try manipulating the constraint algebraically to make the RHS a constant. |

*Answer Report presents the results in a detailed form.*

**Answer Report**  If requested, Solver provides the Answer report in a separate worksheet. The report (shown in Program 2.1E) provides the same information as that discussed previously but in a more organized manner. In addition to indicating the values, it also shows the following:

1. The relevant formula used for each constraint.

*Slack refers to the amount of unused resource in a ≤ constraint.*

2. The *slack*, which is the difference between the RHS and the LHS of the constraint. This denotes the amount of unused resource in a ≤ constraint.

3. Whether the constraint is binding or nonbinding. *Binding* means that all the available resource is fully used in the solution.

The descriptive labels shown in the Name column are directly extracted by Solver based on the information provided in the spreadsheet layout. Solver simply combines labels (if any) to the left of and above a cell to create the name for that cell. Note that these labels can be overwritten manually if necessary. For example, the name Profit for cell D6 (shown in C8 in Program 2.1E) can be overwritten to say Total Profit. Observe that the Excel layout we have used here ensures that all names automatically generated by Solver are logical.

## Using Solver to Solve the Holiday Meal Turkey Ranch Problem

Now that we have studied how to set up and solve a maximization LP problem using Excel's Solver, let us consider a minimization problem—the Holiday Meal Turkey Ranch example. Recall that the decision variables $A$ and $B$ in this problem denote the number of pounds of brand A feed and brand B feed purchased, respectively. The LP formulation for this problem is as follows:

$$\text{Minimize cost (in cents)} = 2A + 3B$$

**PROGRAM 2.1E**     **Solver's Answer Report for Flair Furniture**

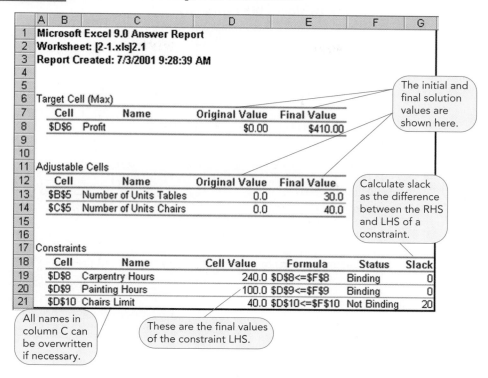

| | A B | C | D | E | F | G |
|---|---|---|---|---|---|---|
| 1 | Microsoft Excel 9.0 Answer Report | | | | | |
| 2 | Worksheet: [2-1.xls]2.1 | | | | | |
| 3 | Report Created: 7/3/2001 9:28:39 AM | | | | | |
| 4 | | | | | | |
| 5 | | | | | | |
| 6 | Target Cell (Max) | | | | | |
| 7 | Cell | Name | Original Value | Final Value | | |
| 8 | $D$6 | Profit | $0.00 | $410.00 | | |
| 9 | | | | | | |
| 10 | | | | | | |
| 11 | Adjustable Cells | | | | | |
| 12 | Cell | Name | Original Value | Final Value | | |
| 13 | $B$5 | Number of Units Tables | 0.0 | 30.0 | | |
| 14 | $C$5 | Number of Units Chairs | 0.0 | 40.0 | | |
| 15 | | | | | | |
| 16 | | | | | | |
| 17 | Constraints | | | | | |
| 18 | Cell | Name | Cell Value | Formula | Status | Slack |
| 19 | $D$8 | Carpentry Hours | 240.0 | $D$8<=$F$8 | Binding | 0 |
| 20 | $D$9 | Painting Hours | 100.0 | $D$9<=$F$9 | Binding | 0 |
| 21 | $D$10 | Chairs Limit | 40.0 | $D$10<=$F$10 | Not Binding | 20 |

*The initial and final solution values are shown here.*

*Calculate slack as the difference between the RHS and LHS of a constraint.*

*All names in column C can be overwritten if necessary.*

*These are the final values of the constraint LHS.*

subject to the constraints

$$5A + 10B \geq 90 \qquad \text{(protein constraint)}$$
$$4A + 3B \geq 48 \qquad \text{(vitamin constraint)}$$
$$\tfrac{1}{2}A \qquad \geq 1\tfrac{1}{2} \qquad \text{(iron constraint)}$$
$$A, \quad B \geq 0 \qquad \text{(nonnegativity constraints)}$$

**File: 2-2.xls**

The formula view of the Excel layout for the Holiday Meal Turkey Ranch LP problem is shown in Program 2.2A. The solution values and the Solver Parameters window are shown

**PROGRAM 2.2A**

**Formula View of the Excel Layout for Holiday Meal**

*Input data and decision variable names shown here are recommended but not required.*

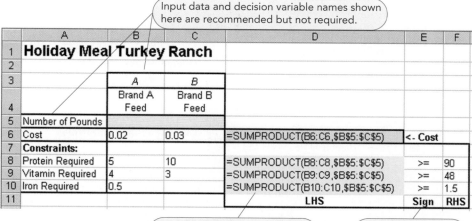

| | A | B | C | D | E | F |
|---|---|---|---|---|---|---|
| 1 | Holiday Meal Turkey Ranch | | | | | |
| 2 | | | | | | |
| 3 | | A | B | | | |
| 4 | | Brand A Feed | Brand B Feed | | | |
| 5 | Number of Pounds | | | | | |
| 6 | Cost | 0.02 | 0.03 | =SUMPRODUCT(B6:C6,$B$5:$C$5) | <- Cost | |
| 7 | Constraints: | | | | | |
| 8 | Protein Required | 5 | 10 | =SUMPRODUCT(B8:C8,$B$5:$C$5) | >= | 90 |
| 9 | Vitamin Required | 4 | 3 | =SUMPRODUCT(B9:C9,$B$5:$C$5) | >= | 48 |
| 10 | Iron Required | 0.5 | | =SUMPRODUCT(B10:C10,$B$5:$C$5) | >= | 1.5 |
| 11 | | | | LHS | Sign | RHS |

*SUMPRODUCT function is used to calculate objective function value and constraint LHS values.*

*Signs are shown here for information purposes only.*

**PROGRAM 2.2B**

**Excel Layout and Solver Entries for Holiday Meal**

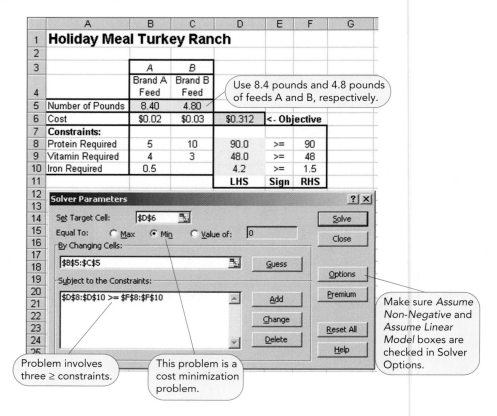

in Program 2.2B. Note that Solver shows the problem as being solved as a Min problem. As with the Flair Furniture example, all problem parameters are entered as entries in different cells of the spreadsheet, and Excel's SUMPRODUCT function is used to compute the objective function as well as the LHS values for all three constraints (corresponding to protein, vitamin, and iron).

**PROGRAM 2.2C**    **Solver's Answer Report for Holiday Meal**

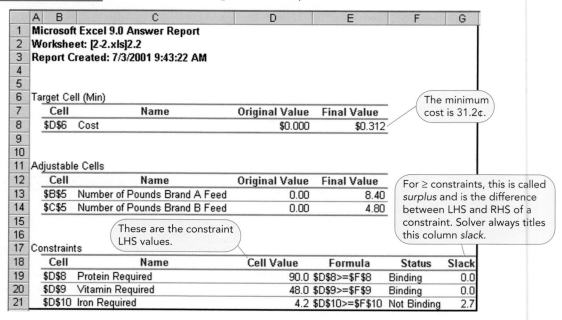

The solved Answer report obtained for this problem is shown in Program 2.2C. As expected, this result is exactly the same as the one we obtained using the graphical approach. Also, since the constraints in this case are of the "≥" type, we refer to the difference between the LHS and RHS of each constraint as the *surplus* rather than as the *slack* (even though Solver refers to this difference in all cases as slack). Just as the slack denotes the amount of a resource that is left unused in a ≤ constraint by the optimal solution, the surplus denotes the extent to which a ≥ constraint is oversatisfied by the optimal solution.

*Surplus refers to the amount of oversatisfaction of a ≥ constraint.*

## 2.9  PREMIUM SOLVER FOR EDUCATION

*Premium Solver includes several additional options.*

Included in your CD-ROM is an enhanced version of the Solver add-in for Excel. This version, called the Premium Solver for Education, is a student version of the powerful Premium Solver software marketed by Frontline Systems Inc. In addition to all the features of the standard Solver that comes with Excel, the Premium Solver for Education includes several options that make it even easier to model and solve LP problems.

As shown in Program 2.3, the initial window for Premium Solver for Education looks exactly like the standard Solver window except for the additional button labeled Premium. In fact, if you wish, you can choose to ignore the enhanced options of Premium Solver for Education by never clicking on the Premium button. Even after clicking the Premium button, you can revert back to the standard mode by clicking the Standard button. (The Premium button toggles the user between the standard and premium modes with the appropriate label showing.)

Clicking on the Premium button gives the user the choice of three different programs to use:

1. *Standard Simplex LP.* Select this procedure for solving all LP problems and integer programming problems (covered in Chapter 6).

2. *Standard Generalized Reduced Gradient (GRG) Nonlinear.* We go over this procedure, which Solver uses to solve nonlinear programs, during our discussion of this topic in Chapter 6.

3. *Standard Evolutionary.* This procedure is based on the principles of a relatively new optimization technique called genetic algorithms. The standard evolutionary procedure in Solver is capable of handling deterministic as well as nondeterministic models. However, unlike the standard simplex and GRG procedures, there is no way of knowing for certain if a given solution is optimal. Genetic algorithms are beyond the scope of this textbook, and we therefore do not discuss this procedure here.

Other enhancements provided in Premium Solver for Education include the following:

- the option to bypass the creation of reports in the Solver Options window (shown in Program 2.3(c)),
- the option to return to the Solver Parameters window after a problem has been solved (shown in Program 2.3(d)),
- the option to present the reports in outline form after a problem has been solved (shown in Program 2.3(d)),
- a feasibility report indicating constraints that may be causing the infeasibility when Solver encounters an infeasible problem, and
- a bounds report indicating constraints that may be the cause when Solver encounters an unbounded problem.

**PROGRAM 2.3**       **Solver Entry Window for Premium Solver for Education**

(a)

**Solver Parameters**     ? ✕

Set Target Cell:    $D$6    🔢      **Solve**

Equal To:    ○ Max    ◉ Min    ○ Value of:    0      **Close**

By Changing Cells:

$B$5:$C$5    🔢     Guess      **Options**

Subject to the Constraints:

$D$8:$D$10 >= $F$8:$F$10     Add     Premium

    Change

    Delete     Reset All

    Help

> Click here to switch to *Premium Solver for Education.*

(b)

**Solver Parameters**     ? ✕

Set Cell:    $D$6    🔢      **Solve**

Equal To:    ○ Max    ◉ Min    ○ Value of:    0      **Close**

By Changing Variable Cells:

$B$5:$C$5    🔢    Guess      **Options**

Subject to the Constraints:      Standard Simplex LP ▼

$D$8:$D$10 >= $F$8:$F$10     Add     Standard

    Change     Reset All

    Delete     Help

> Select *Standard Simplex LP* for Solving all LP and IP problems.

> Click here to revert back to the standard Solver mode.

(c)

**Solver Options**     ? ✕

Max Time:    100   seconds     **OK**

Iterations:    100     Cancel

Precision:    0.000001     Integer Options...

Pivot Tol:    0.000001     Load Model...

Reduced Tol:    0.000001     Save Model...

    Help

☐ Show Iteration Results

☐ Use Automatic Scaling

☑ Assume Non-Negative

☐ Bypass Solver Reports

> Click here to bypass the Solver reports.

(d)

**Solver Results**     ? ✕

Solver found a solution. All constraints and optimality conditions are satisfied.

      Reports

◉ Keep Solver Solution     Answer

○ Restore Original Values     Sensitivity

    Limits

☐ Return to Solver Parameters Dialog     ☐ Outline Reports

**OK**    Cancel    Save Scenario...    Help

## ALGORITHMIC SOLUTION PROCEDURES FOR LINEAR PROGRAMMING PROBLEMS

### Simplex Method

So far, we have looked at examples of LP problems that contain only two decision variables. With only two variables it is possible to use a graphical approach. We plotted the feasible region and then searched for an optimal corner point and corresponding profit or cost. This approach provides a good way to understand the basic concepts of LP. Most real-life LP problems, however, have more than two variables and are thus too large for the simple graphical solution procedure. Problems faced in business and government can have dozens, hundreds, or even thousands of variables. We need a more powerful method than graphing; for this we turn to a procedure called the *simplex method.*

*Recall that the theory of LP states the optimal solution will lie at a corner point of the feasible region. In large LP problems, the feasible region cannot be graphed because it has many dimensions, but the concept is the same.*

How does the simplex method work? The concept is simple and similar to graphical LP in one important respect: In graphical LP we examined each of the corner points; LP theory tells us that an optimal solution lies at one of them. In LP problems containing several variables, we may not be able to graph the feasible region, but an optimal solution will still lie at a corner point of the many-sided, many-dimensional figure (called an *n*-dimensional polyhedron) that represents the area of feasible solutions. The simplex method examines the corner points in a systematic fashion, using basic algebraic concepts. It does so in an iterative manner, that is, repeating the same set of procedures time after time until an optimal solution is reached. Each iteration of the simplex method brings a value for the objective function that is no worse (and usually better) than the current value. Hence, we are progressively moving closer to an optimal solution.

*The simplex method systematically examines corner points, using algebraic steps, until an optimal solution is found.*

In most software packages, including Excel's Solver, the simplex method has been coded in a very efficient manner to exploit the computational capabilities of modern computers. As a result, for most LP problems, the simplex method identifies an optimal corner point after examining just a tiny fraction of the total number of corner points in the feasible region.

### Karmarkar's Algorithm

In 1984, Narendra Karmarkar developed an alternative to the simplex algorithm. The new method, called Karmarkar's algorithm, often takes significantly less computer time to solve very large LP problems.[7]

*Karmarkar's method follows a path of points inside the feasible region.*

Whereas the simplex algorithm finds a solution by moving from one adjacent corner point to the next, following the outside edges of the feasible region, Karmarkar's method follows a path of points on the inside of the feasible region. Karmarkar's method is also unique in its ability to handle an extremely large number of constraints and variables, thereby giving LP users the capacity to solve previously unsolvable problems.

Although it is likely that the simplex method will continue to be used for many LP problems, a newer generation of LP software has been built around Karmarkar's algorithm. Delta Air Lines became the first commercial airline to use this software, called KORBX, which was developed and is sold by AT&T. Delta found that the program was capable of effectively handling the monthly scheduling of 7,000 pilots who fly more than 400 airplanes to 166 cities worldwide. With increased efficiency in allocating limited resources, Delta saves millions of dollars in crew time and related costs.

---

[7] For details, see N. Karmarkar. "A New Polynomial Time Algorithm for Linear Programming," *Combinatorica* 4, 4 (1984): 373–395; or J. N. Hooker. "Karmarkar's Linear Programming Algorithm," *Interfaces* 16, 4 (July–August 1986): 75–90.

## SUMMARY

In this chapter we introduce a mathematical modeling technique called linear programming (LP). Analysts use LP models to find an optimal solution to problems that have a series of constraints binding the objective value. We discuss how to formulate LP models and then show how models with only two decision variables can be solved graphically. The graphical solution approach of this chapter provides a conceptual basis for tackling larger, more complex real-life problems. However, solving LP models with numerous decision variables and constraints requires a solution procedure such as the simplex algorithm.

The simplex algorithm is embedded in Excel's Solver add-in. We describe how LP models can be set up on Excel and solved using Solver. The structured approach presented in this chapter for setting up and solving LP problems with just two variables can be easily adapted to problems of larger size. We address several such problems in Chapter 3.

## GLOSSARY

**Alternate Optimal Solution.** A situation in which more than one optimal solution is possible. It arises when the angle or slope of the objective function is the same as the slope of the constraint.

**Answer Report.** A report created by Solver when it solves an LP model. This report presents the optimal solution in a detailed manner.

**Assume Linear Model.** An option available in Solver that forces it to solve the model as a linear program using the simplex procedure.

**Assume Non-Negative.** An option available in Solver that automatically enforces the nonnegativity constraint.

**Changing Cells.** The cells that represent the decision variables in Solver.

**Constraint.** A restriction (stated in the form of an inequality or an equation) that inhibits (or binds) the value that can be achieved by the objective function.

**Constraint LHS.** The cell that contains the formula for the left-hand side of a constraint in Solver. There is one such cell for each constraint in the problem.

**Constraint RHS.** The cell that contains the value (or formula) for the right-hand side of a constraint in Solver. There is one such cell for each constraint in the problem.

**Corner (or Extreme) Point.** A point that lies on one of the corners of the feasible region. This means that it falls at the intersection of two constraint lines.

**Corner Point Method.** The method of finding the optimal solution to an LP problem by testing the profit or cost level at each corner point of the feasible region. The theory of LP states that the optimal solution must lie at one of the corner points.

**Decision Variables.** The unknown quantities in the problem for which optimal solution values are to be found.

**Feasible Region.** The area satisfying all of the problem's resource restrictions—that is, the region where all constraints overlap. All possible solutions to the problem lie in the feasible region.

**Feasible Solution.** Any point lying in the feasible region. Basically, it is any point that satisfies all of the problem's constraints.

**Inequality.** A mathematical expression containing a greater than or equal to relation ($\geq$) or a less than or equal to relation ($\leq$) between the left-hand-side and the right-hand-side of the expression.

**Infeasible Solution.** Any point lying outside the feasible region. It violates one or more of the stated constraints.

**Infeasibility.** A condition that arises when there is no solution to an LP problem that satisfies all of the constraints.

**Isoprofit (or Isocost) Line.** A straight line representing all non-negative combinations of the decision variables for a particular profit (or cost) level.

**Iterative Procedure.** A process (algorithm) that repeats the same steps over and over.

**Linear Programming (LP).** A mathematical technique used to help management decide how to make the most effective use of an organization's resources.

**Mathematical Programming.** The general category of mathematical modeling and solution techniques used to allocate resources while optimizing a measurable goal; LP is one type of programming model.

**Nonnegativity Constraints.** A set of constraints that requires each decision variable to be nonnegative; that is, each decision variable must be greater than or equal to 0.

**Objective Function.** A mathematical statement of the goal of an organization, stated as an intent to maximize or minimize some important quantity such as profit or cost.

**Product Mix Problem.** A common LP problem involving a decision as to which products a firm should produce given that it faces limited resources.

**Redundancy.** The presence of one or more constraints that do not affect the feasible solution region.

**Simplex Method.** An iterative procedure for solving LP problems.

**Simultaneous Equation Method.** The algebraic means of solving for the intersection point of two or more linear constraint equations.

**Slack.** Difference between the right-hand side and left-hand side of a ≤ constraint. Typically represents the unused resource.

**Solver.** An Excel add-in that allows LP problems to be set up and solved on Excel.

**SUMPRODUCT Function.** An Excel function that allows users to easily model formulas for the objective function and constraints.

**Surplus.** Difference between the left-hand side and right-hand side of a ≥ constraint. Typically represents the level of oversatisfaction of a requirement.

**Target Cell.** The cell that contains the formula for the objective function in Solver.

**Unboundedness.** A condition that exists when the objective value can be made infinitely large (in a maximization problem) or small (in a minimization problem) without violating any of the problem's constraints.

## SOLVED PROBLEMS

### Solved Problem 2-1

Personal Mini Warehouses is planning to expand its successful Orlando business into Tampa. In doing so, the company must determine how many storage rooms of each size to build. Its objective and constraints follow:

$$\text{maximize monthly earnings} = 50X + 20Y$$

subject to

$$2X + 4Y \leq 400 \quad \text{(advertising budget available)}$$
$$100X + 50Y \leq 8{,}000 \quad \text{(square footage required)}$$
$$X \leq 60 \quad \text{(rental limit expected)}$$
$$X, Y \geq 0$$

where

$$X = \text{number of large spaces developed}$$
$$Y = \text{number of small spaces developed}$$

Solve this LP problem using the graphical procedure and Excel.

#### Solution

An evaluation of the five corner points of the accompanying graph indicates that corner point Ⓒ produces the greatest earnings. Refer to Figure 2.14 and the table below.

| CORNER POINT | VALUES OF X, Y | OBJECTIVE FUNCTION VALUE ($) |
|:---:|:---:|:---:|
| Ⓐ | (0, 0) | 0 |
| Ⓑ | (60, 0) | 3,000 |
| Ⓒ | (60, 40) | 3,800 |
| Ⓓ | (40, 80) | 3,600 |
| Ⓔ | (0, 100) | 2,000 |

**File: 2-4.xls**

The Excel layout and Solver entries for this problem are shown in Program 2.4. As expected, the optimal solution is the same as that found using the graphical approach ($X = 60$, $Y = 40$, Earnings = $3,800$).

## FIGURE 2.14

**Graph for Solved Problem 2-1**

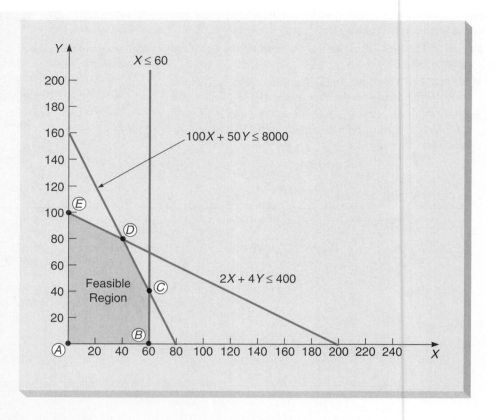

## PROGRAM 2.4

**Excel Layout and Solver Entries for Solved Problem 2-1**

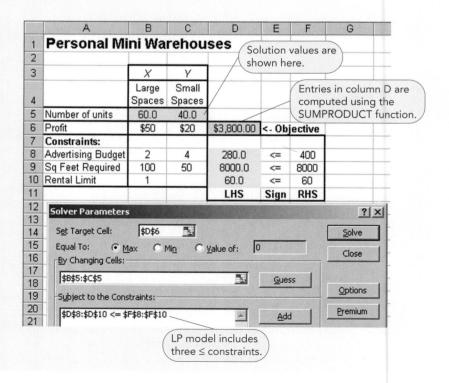

## Solved Problem 2-2

Solve the following LP formulation graphically, using the isocost line approach. Also solve using Excel.

$$\text{minimize costs} = 24X + 28Y$$

$$\text{subject to} \quad 5X + 4Y \leq 2{,}000$$

$$X \qquad \geq 80$$

$$X + Y \geq 300$$

$$Y \geq 100$$

$$X, Y \geq 0$$

### Solution

A graph of the four constraints is shown in Figure 2.15. The arrows indicate the direction of feasibility for each constraint. The second graph illustrates the feasible solution region and plots of two possible objective function cost lines. The first, $10,000, was selected arbitrarily as a starting point. To find the optimal corner point, we need to move the cost line in the direction of the lower cost, that is, down and to the left. The last point where a cost line touches the feasible region as it moves toward the origin is corner point Ⓓ. Thus Ⓓ, which represents $X = 200$, $Y = 100$, and a cost of $7,600, is optimal.

The Excel layout and Solver entries for this problem are shown in Program 2.5. The optimal solution is $X = 200$, $Y = 100$, and a cost of $7,600. As expected, this is the same solution as point Ⓓ in the graph (see Figure 2.15).

**File: 2-5.xls**

---

**FIGURE 2.15**     **Graphs for Solved Problem 2-2**

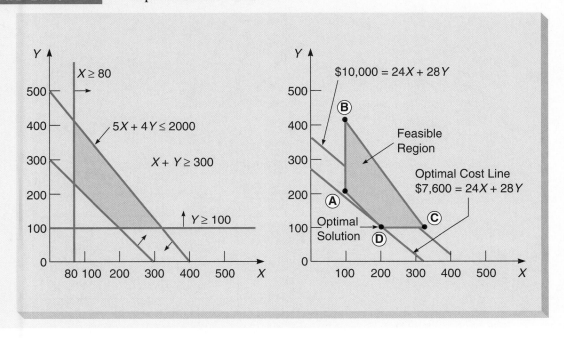

**PROGRAM 2.5**

**Excel Layout and Solver Entries for Solved Problem 2-2**

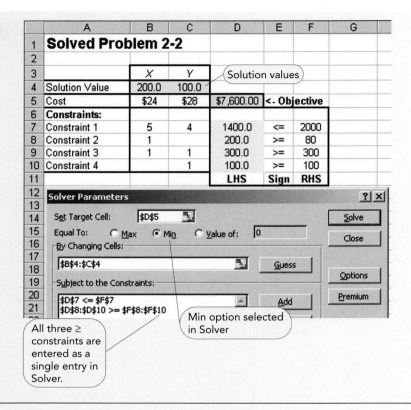

---

**Solved Problem 2-3**

Solve the following problem given these constraints and objective function:

$$\text{maximize profit } = 30X + 40Y$$

$$\text{subject to} \qquad 4X + 2Y \leq 16$$

$$2X - Y \geq 2$$

$$Y \leq 2$$

$$X,Y \geq 0$$

a. Graph the feasible region.
b. Evaluate the objective function at each corner point.
c. Identify the optimal solution.

**Solution**

a. The graph appears in Figure 2.16 with the feasible region shaded.

b.

| CORNER POINT | COORDINATES | PROFIT ($) |
|:---:|:---:|:---:|
| Ⓐ | $X = 1, Y = 0$ | 30 |
| Ⓑ | $X = 4, Y = 0$ | 120 |
| Ⓒ | $X = 3, Y = 2$ | 170 |
| Ⓓ | $X = 2, Y = 2$ | 140 |

c. The optimal profit of $170 is at corner point Ⓒ.

FIGURE 2.16

**Graph for Solved
Problem 2-3**

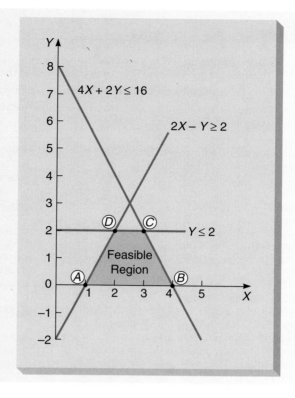

> ⇒ **SELF-TEST**

■ Before taking the self-test, refer back to the learning objectives at the beginning of the chapter, the notes in the margins, and the glossary at the end of the chapter.

■ Use the key at the back of the book to correct your answers.

■ Restudy pages that correspond to any questions that you answered incorrectly or material you feel uncertain about.

1. When using a graphical solution procedure, the region bounded by the set of constraints is called the
   a. solution.
   b. feasible region.
   c. infeasible region.
   d. maximum profit region.
   e. none of the above.

2. The corner-point solution method can only be used to solve maximization problems.
   a. True
   b. False

3. Using the graphical solution procedure to solve a maximization problem requires that we
   a. move the isoprofit line up until it no longer intersects with any constraint equation.
   b. move the isoprofit line down until it no longer intersects with any constraint equation.
   c. apply the method of simultaneous equations to solve for the intersections of constraints.
   d. find the value of the objective functions at the origin.
   e. none of the above.

4. The graphical method of LP can only handle _____ decision variables
   a. one
   b. two
   c. three
   d. none of the above

5. Types of graphical solutions to LP include all but
   a. isoprofit line solution.
   b. the corner-point solution.
   c. the simplex method.
   d. all are solutions to the graphic approach.
   e. none are solutions to the graphic approach.

6. The graphic method of LP uses
   a. objective equations.
   b. constraint equations.
   c. linear equations.
   d. all of the above.
   e. none of the above.

7. Any LP problem can be solved using the graphical solution procedure.
   a. True
   b. False

8. The set of solution points that satisfies all of an LP problem's constraints simultaneously is defined as the feasible region in graphical LP.
   a. True
   b. False

9. An objective function is necessary in a maximization problem but is not required in a minimization problem.
   a. True
   b. False

10. Which of the following is *not* a property of all LP problems?
    a. the presence of restrictions
    b. optimization of some objective
    c. a computer program
    d. alternative courses of action to choose from
    e. usage of only linear equations and inequalities

11. A feasible solution to an LP problem
    a. must satisfy all of the problem's constraints simultaneously.
    b. need not satisfy all of the constraints, only some of them.
    c. must be a corner point of the feasible region.
    d. must give the maximum possible profit.

12. We can specify more than one Target Cell in Solver.
    a. True
    b. False

13. In Excel, we are required to manipulate constraints so that all variables appear on the left-hand side.
    a. True
    b. False

14. We can enter formulas for constraints directly in the Solver input window.
    a. True
    b. False

15. Changing cells in Solver refer to the
    a. decision variables.
    b. left-hand side of a constraint.
    c. right-hand side of a constraint.
    d. objective function.

16. Target cell in Solver refers to the
    a. decision variables.
    b. left-hand side of a constraint.
    c. right-hand side of a constraint.
    d. objective function.

17. To enter decision variables as a block in Solver,
    a. there must be only two decision variables in the problem.
    b. the cells denoting the decision variables must be next to each other.
    c. the decision variables must each be modeled in a separate column.
    d. the problem must have a maximization objective function.

# DISCUSSION QUESTIONS AND PROBLEMS

## Discussion Questions

**2-1** Discuss the similarities and differences between minimization and maximization problems using the graphical solution approaches of LP.

**2-2** It is important to understand the assumptions underlying the use of any quantitative analysis model. What are the assumptions and requirements for an LP model to be formulated and used?

**2-3** It has been said that each LP problem that has a feasible region has an infinite number of solutions. Explain.

**2-4** You have just formulated a maximization LP problem and are preparing to solve it graphically. What criteria should you consider in deciding whether it would be easier to solve the problem by the corner point method or the isoprofit line approach?

**2-5** Under what condition is it possible for an LP problem to have more than one optimal solution?

**2-6** Develop your own set of constraint equations and inequalities and use them to illustrate graphically each of the following conditions:
(a) an unbounded problem
(b) an infeasible problem
(c) a problem containing redundant constraints

**2-7** The production manager of a large Cincinnati manufacturing firm once made the statement, "I would like to use LP, but it's a technique that operates under conditions of certainty. My plant doesn't have that certainty; it's a world of uncertainty. So LP can't be used here." Do you think this statement has any merit? Explain why the manager may have said it.

**2-8** The mathematical relationships that follow were formulated by an operations research analyst at the Smith–Lawton Chemical Company. Which ones are invalid for use in an LP problem, and why?

$$\text{maximize profit} = 4X_1 + 3X_1X_2 + 8X_2 + 5X_3$$

subject to

$$2X_1 + X_2 + 2X_3 \leq 50$$
$$X_1 - 4X_2 \geq 6$$
$$1.5X_1^2 + 6X_2 + 3X_3 \geq 21$$
$$19X_2 - \tfrac{1}{3}X_3 = 17$$
$$5X_1 + 4X_2 + 3\sqrt{X_3} \leq 80$$

**2-9** What is the value of the computer in solving LP problems today?

**2-10** Explain why knowing how to use Excel to set up and solve LP problems may be beneficial to a manager.

**2-11** What are the components of defining a problem on Excel so that it can be solved using Solver?

**2-12** How is the slack (or surplus) calculated for a constraint? How is it interpreted?

**2-13** What is an unbounded solution? How does Solver indicate that a problem solution is unbounded?

## Problems

• **2-14** Consider the following LP problem:

$$\text{maximize profit} = \$1X + \$1Y$$

subject to

$$2X + 1Y \leq 100$$
$$1X + 2Y \leq 100$$
$$X, Y \geq 0$$

What is the optimal solution to this problem? Solve it graphically.

• **2-15** Graph the following LP problem and find the optimal solution.

$$\text{maximize profit} = \$3X + \$2Y$$

subject to

$$2X + 1Y \leq 150$$
$$2X + 3Y \leq 300$$
$$X, Y \geq 0$$

• **2-16** Graphically analyze the following problem:

$$\text{maximize profit} = \$4X + \$6Y$$

subject to

$$1X + 2Y \leq 8$$
$$6X + 4Y \leq 24$$
$$X, Y \geq 0$$

What is the optimal solution?

⋮ **2-17** Solve the following LP problem using the corner point graphical method:

$$\text{maximize profit} = 4X + 4Y$$

subject to

$$3X + 5Y \leq 150$$
$$X - 2Y \leq 10$$
$$5X + 3Y \leq 150$$
$$X, Y \geq 0$$

⋮ **2-18** Consider this LP formulation:

$$\text{minimize cost} = \$1X + \$2Y$$

subject to

$$X + 3Y \geq 90$$
$$8X + 2Y \geq 160$$
$$3X + 2Y \geq 120$$
$$Y \leq 70$$
$$X, Y \geq 0$$

Graphically illustrate the feasible region and apply the isocost line procedure to indicate which corner point produces the optimal solution. What is the cost of this solution?

2-19 Consider the following four LP formulations. Using a graphical approach, determine

    (a) which formulation has more than one optimal solution.

    (b) which formulation is unbounded.

    (c) which formulation is infeasible.

    (d) which formulation has a unique optimal solution.

*Formulation 1*

maximize: $10X + 10Y$

subject to: $2X \qquad \leq 10$

$\qquad 2X + 4Y \leq 16$

$\qquad\qquad 4Y \leq 8$

$\qquad X \qquad \geq 6$

$\qquad X, \quad Y \geq 0$

*Formulation 2*

maximize: $X + Y$

subject to: $X \qquad \leq 1$

$\qquad 2Y \leq 2$

$\qquad X + 2Y \leq 2$

$\qquad X, \quad Y \geq 0$

*Formulation 3*

maximize: $3X + 2Y$

subject to: $X + Y \geq 5$

$\qquad X \qquad \geq 2$

$\qquad\qquad 2Y \geq 8$

$\qquad X, \quad Y \geq 0$

*Formulation 4*

maximize: $3X + 3Y$

subject to: $4X + 6Y \leq 48$

$\qquad 4X + 2Y \leq 12$

$\qquad\qquad 3Y \geq 3$

$\qquad 2X \qquad \geq 2$

$\qquad X, \quad Y \geq 0$

2-20 *(Fertilizer blending)* The Sweet Smell Fertilizer Company markets bags of manure labeled "not less than 60 pounds dry weight." The packaged manure is a combination of compost and sewage wastes. To provide good-quality fertilizer, each bag should contain at least 30 pounds of compost but no more than 40 pounds of sewage. Each pound of compost costs Sweet Smell 5 cents and each pound of sewage costs 4 cents. Use a graphical LP method to determine the least cost blend of compost and sewage in each bag.

2-21 *(Portfolio selection)* The National Credit Union has $250,000 available to invest in a 12-month commitment. The money can be placed in Treasury notes yielding an 8% return or in municipal bonds at an average rate of return of 9%. Credit union regulations require diversification to the extent that at least 50% of the investment be placed in Treasury notes. Because of defaults in such municipalities as Cleveland and New York, it is decided that no more than 40% of the investment be placed in bonds. How much should the National Credit Union invest in each security so as to maximize its return on investment?

2-22 *(Media selection)* The advertising agency promoting the new Breem dishwashing detergent wants to get the best exposure possible for the product within the $100,000 advertising budget ceiling placed upon it. To do so, the agency needs to decide how much of the budget to spend on each of its two most effective media: (1) television spots during the afternoon hours and (2) large ads in the city's Sunday newspaper. Each television spot costs $3,000; each Sunday newspaper ad cost $1,250. The expected exposure, based on industry ratings, is 35,000 viewers for each television commercial and 20,000 readers for each newspaper advertisement. The agency director, Mavis Early, knows from experience that is it important to use both media in order to reach the broadest spectrum of potential Breem customers. She decides that at least 5 but no more than 25 television spots should be ordered, and that at least 10 newspaper ads should be contracted. How many times should each of the two media be used to obtain maximum exposure while staying within the budget? Use the graphical method to solve.

2-23 *(Product mix)* The Electrocomp Corporation manufactures two electrical products: air conditioners and large fans. The assembly process for each is similar in that both require a certain amount of wiring and drilling. Each air conditioner takes 3 hours of wiring and 2 hours of drilling. Each fan must go through 2 hours of wiring and 1 hour of drilling. During the next production period, 240 hours of wiring time are available and up to 140 hours of drilling time can be used. Each air conditioner sold yields a profit of $25. Each fan assembled can be sold for a $15 profit. Formulate and solve this LP product mix situation to find the best combination of air conditioners and fans that yields the highest profit. Use the corner point graphical approach.

2-24 *(Product mix)* Electrocomp's management realizes that it forgot to include two critical constraints (see Problem 2-23). In particular, management decides that to ensure an adequate supply of air conditioners for a contract, at least 20 air conditioners should be manufactured. Because Electrocomp incurred an oversupply of fans the preceding period, management also insists that no more than 80 fans be produced during this production period. Resolve this product mix problem to find the new optimal solution.

2-25 *(Product mix)* The Marriott Tub Company manufactures two lines of bathtubs, called model A and model B. Every tub requires blending a certain amount of steel and zinc; the company has available a total of 25,000 pounds of steel and 6,000 pounds of zinc. Each model A bathtub requires a mixture of 125 pounds of steel and 20 pounds of zinc, and each yields a profit to the firm of $90. Each model B tub produced can be sold for a profit of $70; it in turn requires 100 pounds of steel and 30 pounds of zinc. Find by graphical LP the best product mix of bathtubs.

2-26 *(Product mix)* The Outdoor Furniture Corporation manufactures two products, benches and picnic tables, for use in yards and parks. The firm has two main resources: its carpenters (labor force) and a supply of redwood for use in the furniture. During the next production cycle, 1,200 hours of labor are available under a union agreement. The firm also has a stock of 3,500 feet of good-quality redwood. Each bench that Outdoor Furniture produces requires 4 labor hours and 10 feet of redwood; each picnic table takes 6 labor hours and 35 feet of redwood. Completed benches will yield a profit of $9 each, and tables will result in a profit of $20 each. How many benches and tables should Outdoor Furniture produce to obtain the largest possible profit? Use the graphical LP approach.

**2-27** (*Course planning*) The dean of the Western College of Business must plan the school's course offerings for the fall semester. Student demands make it necessary to offer at least 30 undergraduate and 20 graduate courses in the term. Faculty contracts also dictate that at least 60 courses be offered in total. Each undergraduate course taught costs the college an average of $2,500 in faculty wages, and each graduate course costs $3,000. How many undergraduate and graduate courses should be taught in the fall so that total faculty salaries are kept to a minimum?

**2-28** (*Product mix*) MSA Computer Corporation manufactures two models of minicomputers, the Alpha 4 and the Beta 5. The firm employs five technicians, working 160 hours each per month, on its assembly line. Management insists that full employment (i.e., *all* 160 hours of time) be maintained for each worker during next month's operations. It requires 20 labor hours to assemble each Alpha 4 computer and 25 labor hours to assemble each Beta 5 model. MSA wants to see at least 10 Alpha 4s and at least 15 Beta 5s produced during the production period. Alpha 4s generate a $1,200 profit per unit, and Beta 5s yield $1,800 each. Determine the most profitable number of each model of minicomputer to produce during the coming month. Use the graphical LP approach.

**2-29** (*Agriculture planning*) The seasonal yield of olives in a Piraeus, Greece, vineyard is greatly influenced by a process of branch pruning. If olive trees are pruned every two weeks, output is increased. The pruning process, however, requires considerably more labor than permitting the olives to grow on their own and results in a smaller size olive. It also, though, permits olive trees to be spaced closer together. The yield of 1 barrel of olives by pruning requires 5 hours of labor and 1 acre of land. The production of a barrel of olives by the normal process requires only 2 labor hours but takes 2 acres of land. An olive grower has 250 hours of labor available and a total of 150 acres for growing. Because of the olive size difference, a barrel of olives produced on pruned trees sell for $20, whereas a barrel of regular olives has a market price of $30. The grower has determined that because of uncertain demand, no more than 40 barrels of pruned olives should be produced. Use graphical LP to find

(a) the maximum possible profit.

(b) the best combination of barrels of pruned and regular olives.

(c) the number of acres that the olive grower should devote to each growing process.

**2-30** (*Portfolio selection*) The stock brokerage firm of Blank, Leibowitz, and Weinberger has analyzed and recommended two stocks to an investors' club of college professors. The professors were interested in factors such as short-term growth, intermediate growth, and dividend rates. These data on each stock are as follows:

| | STOCK ($) | |
| --- | --- | --- |
| FACTOR | LOUISIANA GAS AND POWER | TRIMEX INSULATION COMPANY |
| Short-term growth potential, per dollar invested | .36 | .24 |
| Intermediate growth potential (over next three years), per dollar invested | 1.67 | 1.50 |
| Dividend rate potential | 4% | 8% |

Each member of the club has an investment goal of (1) an appreciation of no less than $720 in the short term, (2) an appreciation of at least $5,000 in the next three years, and (3) a dividend income of at least $200 per year. What is the smallest investment that a professor can make to meet these three goals? Solve using the graphical LP approach and using Excel.

**2-31** (*Cargo planning*) **Serendipity**
The three princes of Serendip
Went on a little trip.
They could not carry too much weight:
More than 300 pounds made them hesitate.
They planned to the ounce. When they returned to Ceylon
They discovered that their supplies were just about gone
When, what to their joy, Prince William found
A pile of coconuts on the ground.
"Each will bring 60 rupees," said Prince Richard with a grin
As he almost tripped over a lion skin.
"Look out!" cried Prince Robert with glee
As he spied some more lion skins under a tree.
"These are worth even more—300 rupees each
If we can just carry them all down to the beach."
Each skin weighed fifteen pounds and each coconut, five,
But they carried them all and made it alive.
The boat back to the island was very small
15 cubic feet baggage capacity—that was all.
Each lion skin took up one cubic foot
While eight coconuts the same space took.
With everything stowed they headed to sea
And on the way calculated what their new wealth might be.
"Eureka!" cried Prince Robert, "Our worth is so great

That there's no other way we could return in this state.
Any other skins or nuts that we might have brought
Would now have us poorer. And now I know what—
I'll write my friend Horace in England, for surely
Only he can appreciate our serendipity."

Formulate and solve Serendipity by graphical LP in order to calculate "what their new wealth might be." (The word *serendipity* was coined by the English writer Horace Walpole after a fairy tale titled *The Three Princes of Serendip*. Source of problem is unknown.)

*Problems 2-32 and 2-33 test your ability to formulate LP problems that have more than two variables. They cannot be solved graphically but will give you a chance to set up larger problem.*

**2-32** *(Feed mix blending)* The Feed 'n Ship Ranch fattens cattle for local farmers and ships them to meat markets in Kansas City and Omaha. The owners of the ranch seek to determine the amounts of cattle feed to buy so that minimum nutritional standards are satisfied, and at the same time total feed costs are minimized. The feed mix used can be made up of the three grains that contain the following ingredients per pound of feed:

| | FEED (OZ) | | |
|---|---|---|---|
| INGREDIENT | STOCK X | STOCK Y | STOCK Z |
| A | 3 | 2 | 4 |
| B | 2 | 3 | 1 |
| C | 1 | 0 | 2 |
| D | 6 | 8 | 4 |

The cost per pound of stocks X, Y, and Z are $2, $4, and $2.50, respectively. The minimum requirement per cow per month is 4 pounds of ingredient A, 5 pounds of ingredient B, 1 pound of ingredient C, and 8 pounds of ingredient D.

The ranch faces one additional restriction: it can only obtain 500 pounds of stock Z per month from the feed supplier regardless of its need. Because there are usually 100 cows at the Feed 'n Ship Ranch at any given time, this means that no more than 5 pounds of stock Z can be counted on for use in the feed of each cow per month.

(a) Formulate this as an LP problem.
(b) Solve using Excel.

**2-33** *(Product mix)* The Weinberger Electronics Corporation manufactures four highly technical products that it supplies to aerospace firms that hold NASA contracts. Each of the products must pass through the following departments before they are shipped: wiring, drilling, assembly, and inspection. The time requirement in hours for each unit produced and its

corresponding profit value are summarized in the following table:

| | DEPARTMENT | | | | UNIT |
|---|---|---|---|---|---|
| PRODUCT | WIRING | DRILLING | ASSEMBLY | INSPECTION | PROFIT ($) |
| XJ201 | 0.5 | 0.3 | 0.2 | 0.5 | 9 |
| XM897 | 1.5 | 1 | 4 | 1 | 12 |
| TR29 | 1.5 | 2 | 1 | 0.5 | 15 |
| BR788 | 1 | 3 | 2 | 0.5 | 11 |

The production available in each department each month, and the minimum monthly production requirement to fulfill contracts, are as follows:

| DEPARTMENT | CAPACITY (HOURS) | PRODUCT | MINIMUM PRODUCTION LEVEL |
|---|---|---|---|
| Wiring | 15,000 | XJ201 | 150 |
| Drilling | 17,000 | XM897 | 100 |
| Assembly | 26,000 | TR29 | 300 |
| Inspection | 12,000 | BR788 | 400 |

The production manager has the responsibility of specifying production levels for each product for the coming month. Help him by formulating (i.e., setting up the constraints and objective function) Weinberger's problem. Solve using Excel.

**2-34** *(Product mix)* Androgynous Bicycle Company (ABC) has the hottest new products on the upscale toy market—boys' and girls' bikes in bright fashion colors, with oversized hubs and axles; shell design safety tires; a strong padded frame; chrome-plated chains, brackets and valves; and a nonslip handlebar. Due to the seller's market for high-quality toys for the newest baby boomers, ABC can sell all the bicycles it manufactures at the following prices: boys' bikes—$220, girls' bikes—$175. This is the price payable to ABC at its Orlando plant.

The firm's accountant has determined that direct labor costs will be 45% of the price ABC receives for the boys' model and 40% of the price received for the girls' model. Production costs other than labor, but excluding painting and packaging, are $44 per boys' bicycle and $30 per girls' bicycle. Painting and packaging are $20 per bike, regardless of model.

The Orlando plant's overall production capacity is 390 bicycles per day. Each boy's bike requires 2.5 labor hours to complete and each girl's model, 2.4 hours. ABC currently employs 120 workers, who each put in an 8-hour day. The firm has no desire to hire or fire to affect labor availability, for it believes its stable workforce is one of its biggest assets. Using a graphical approach, determine the best product mix for ABC.

**2-35** *(Product mix)* Modem Corporation of America (MCA) is the world's largest producer of modem communication devices for microcomputers. MCA sold 9,000 of the regular model and 10,400 of the smart ("intelligent") model this September. Its income statement for the month is shown in Table 2.3. Costs presented are typical of prior months and are expected to remain at the same levels in the near future.

The firm is facing several constraints as it prepares its November production plan. First, it has experienced a tremendous demand and has been unable to keep any significant inventory in stock. This situation is not expected to change. Second, the firm is located in a small Iowa town from which additional labor is not readily available. Workers can be shifted from production of one modem to another, however. To produce the 9,000 regular modems in September required 5,000 direct labor hours. The 10,400 intelligent modem absorbed 10,400 direct labor hours. Third, MCA is experiencing a problem affecting the intelligent modem model. Its component supplier is able to guarantee only 8,000 microprocessors for November delivery. Each intelligent modem requires one of these specially made microprocessors. Alternative suppliers are not available on short notice.

MCA wants to plan the optimal mix of the two modem models to produce in November to maximize profits for MCA.

(a) Formulate, using September's data, MCA's problem as a linear program.
(b) Solve the problem graphically.
(c) Discuss the implications of your recommended solution.
(d) Solve using Excel.

### TABLE 2.3

**Table for Problem 2-35
MCA Income Statement
Month Ended
September 30**

|  |  | REGULAR MODEMS | INTELLIGENT MODEMS |
|---|---|---|---|
| Sales |  | $450,000 | $640,000 |
| Less: | Discounts | 10,000 | 15,000 |
|  | Returns | 12,000 | 9,500 |
|  | Warranty replacements | 4,000 | 2,500 |
| Net Sales |  | $424,000 | $613,000 |
| Sales costs |  |  |  |
|  | Direct labor | 60,000 | 76,800 |
|  | Indirect labor | 9,000 | 11,520 |
|  | Materials cost | 90,000 | 128,000 |
|  | Depreciation | 40,000 | 50,800 |
|  | Cost of sales | $199,000 | $267,120 |
| Gross profit |  | $225,000 | $345,880 |
| Selling and general expenses |  |  |  |
|  | General expenses—variable | 30,000 | 35,000 |
|  | General expenses—fixed | 36,000 | 40,000 |
|  | Advertising | 28,000 | 25,000 |
|  | Sales commissions | 31,000 | 60,000 |
|  | Total operating cost | $125,000 | $160,000 |
| Pretax income |  | $100,000 | $185,880 |
| Income taxes (25%) |  | 25,000 | 46,470 |
| Net income |  | $ 75,000 | $139,410 |

# ⫸ CASE STUDY

## Mexicana Wire Works

Ron Garcia felt good about his first week as a management trainee at Mexicana Wire Winding, Inc. He had not yet developed any technical knowledge about the manufacturing process, but he had toured the entire facility, located in the suburbs of Mexico City, and had met many people in various areas of the operation.

Mexicana, a subsidiary of Westover Wire Works, a Texas firm, is a medium-sized producer of wire windings used in making electrical transformers. Carlos Alverez, the production control manager, described the windings to Garcia as being of standardized design. Garcia's tour of the plant, laid out by process type (see Figure 2.17), followed the manufacturing sequence for the windings: drawing, extrusion, winding, inspection, and packaging. After inspection, good product is packaged and sent to finished product storage; defective product is stored separately until it can be reworked.

On March 8, Vivian Espania, Mexicana's general manager, stopped by Garcia's office and asked him to attend a staff meeting at 1:00 P.M.

"Let's get started with the business at hand," Vivian said, opening the meeting. "You all have met Ron Garcia, our new management trainee. Ron studied operations management in his MBA program in southern California, so I think he is competent to help us with a problem we have been discussing for a long time without resolution. I'm sure that each of you on my staff will give Ron your full cooperation."

Vivian turned to José Arroyo, production control manager, "José, why don't you describe the problem we are facing?"

"Well," José said, "business is very good right now. We are booking more orders than we can fill. We will have some new equipment on line within the next several months, which will take care of our capacity problems, but that won't help us in April. I have located some retired employees who used to work in

the drawing department, and I am planning to bring them in as temporary employees in April to increase capacity there. Because we are planning to refinance some of our long-term debt, Vivian wants our profits to look as good as possible in April. I'm having a hard time figuring out which orders to run and which to back-order so that I can make the bottom line look as good as possible. Can you help me with this?"

Garcia was surprised and apprehensive to receive such an important, high-profile assignment so early in his career. Recovering quickly, he said, "Give me your data and let me work with it for a day or two."

### April Orders

| | |
|---|---|
| Product W0075C | 1,400 units |
| Product W0033C | 250 units |
| Product W0005X | 1,510 units |
| Product W0007X | 1,116 units |

*Note:* Vivian Espania has given her word to a key customer that Mexicana will manufacture 600 units of product W0007X and 150 units of product W0075C for him during April.

### Standard Cost

| PRODUCT | MATERIAL | LABOR | OVERHEAD | SELLING PRICE |
|---|---|---|---|---|
| W0075C | $33.00 | $ 9.90 | $23.10 | $100.00 |
| W00033C | 25.00 | 7.50 | 17.50 | 80.00 |
| W0005X | 35.00 | 10.50 | 24.50 | 130.00 |
| W0007X | 75.00 | 11.25 | 63.75 | 175.00 |

---

### FIGURE 2.17

**Mexicana Wire Winding, Inc.**

| Office | Wire drawing | | Finished product storage |
|---|---|---|---|
| Receiving and raw material storage | Packaging | | Rework department |
| | Winding | | |
| | Extrusion | | Rejected product storage |
| | Inspection | | |

**Selecting Operating Data**

Average output per month = 2,400 units

Average machine utilization = 63%

Average percentage of production sent to rework department = 5% (mostly from Winding Department)

Average no. of rejected units awaiting rework = 850 (mostly from Winding Department)

**Bill of Labor (Hours/Unit)**

| PRODUCT | DRAWING | EXTRUSION | WINDING | PACKAGING |
|---------|---------|-----------|---------|-----------|
| W0075C | 1.0 | 1.0 | 1.0 | 1.0 |
| W0033C | 2.0 | 1.0 | 3.0 | 0.0 |
| W0005X | 0.0 | 4.0 | 0.0 | 3.0 |
| W0007X | 1.0 | 1.0 | 0.0 | 2.0 |

### Discussion Questions

1. What recommendations should Ron Garcia make, with what justification? Provide a detailed analysis with charts, graphs, and Excel printouts included.
2. Discuss the need for temporary workers in the drawing department.
3. Discuss the plant layout.

*Source:* Professor Victor E. Sower, Sam Houston State University. This case material is based on an actual situation, with name and data altered for confidentiality.

**Plant Capacity (Hours)**

| DRAWING | EXTRUSION | WINDING | PACKAGING |
|---------|-----------|---------|-----------|
| 4,000 | 4,200 | 2,000 | 2,300 |

*Note:* Inspection capacity is not a problem: Employees can work overtime as necessary to accommodate any schedule.

## ⇒ CASE STUDY

### Golding Landscaping and Plants, Inc.

Kenneth and Patricia Golding spent a career as a husband-and-wife real estate investment partnership in Washington, DC. When they finally retired to a 25-acre farm in northern Virginia's Fairfax County, they became ardent amateur gardeners. Kenneth planted shrubs and fruit trees, and Patricia spent her hours potting all sizes of plants. When the volume of shrubs and plants reached the point that the Goldings began to think of their hobby in a serious vein, they built a greenhouse adjacent to their home and installed heating and watering systems.

By 2001, the Goldings realized their retirement from real estate had really only led to a second career—in the plant and shrub business—and they filed for a Virginia business license. Within a matter of months, they asked their attorney to file incorporation documents and formed the firm Golding Landscaping and Plants, Inc.

Early in the new business's existence, Kenneth Golding recognized the need for a high-quality commercial fertilizer that he could blend himself, both for sale and for his own nursery. His goal was to keep his costs to a minimum while producing a top-notch product that was especially suited to the northern Virginia climate.

Working with chemists at George Mason University, Golding blended "Golding-Grow." It consists of four chemical compounds, C-30, C-92, D-21, and E-11. The cost per pound for each compound is indicated in the following table:

| CHEMICAL COMPOUND | COST PER POUND |
|-------------------|----------------|
| C-30 | $.12 |
| C-92 | .09 |
| D-21 | .11 |
| E-11 | .04 |

The specifications for Golding-Grow are as follows:

a. Chemical E-11 must comprise at least 15% of the blend.
b. C-92 and C-30 must together constitute at least 45% of the blend.
c. D-21 and C-92 can together constitute no more than 30% of the blend.
d. Golding-Grow is packaged and sold in 50-lb bags.

### Discussion Questions

1. Formulate an LP problem to determine what blend of the four chemicals will allow Golding to minimize the cost of a 50-lb bag of the fertilizer.
2. Solve using Excel to find the best solution.

*Source:* J. Heizer and B. Render. *Operations Management* 6/e. Upper Saddle River, NJ: Prentice Hall, Inc. 2001, p.772.

## INTERNET CASE STUDY

See our Internet home page at **www. prenhall.com/render** for this additional case study: Agri Chem Corporation.

# BIBLIOGRAPHY

Bermon, Stuart and Sarah Jean Hood. "Capacity Optimization Planning System (CAPS)," *Interfaces* 29, 5 (September 1999): 31–50.

Eliman, A.A., M. Girgis, and S. Kotob, "A Solution to Post-Crash Debt Entanglements in Kuwait's al-Manakh Stock Market," *Interfaces* 27, 1 (January–February 1997): 89–106.

Ferris, M. C. and A. B. Philpott. "On the Performance of Karmarkar's Algorithm," *Journal of the Operational Research Society,* 39 (March 1988): 257–270.

Fletcher, L. Russell, Henry Alden, Scott P. Holmen, Dean P. Angelides, and Matthew J. Etzenhouser. "Long-Term Forest Ecosystem Planning at Pacific Lumber," *Interfaces* 29, 1 (January 1999): 90–111.

Gass, S. I. *An Illustrated Guide to Linear Programming.* New York: Dover Publications, Inc., 1990.

Gautier, Antoine, Bernard F. Lamond, Daniel Pare, and Francois Rouleau. "The Quebec Ministry of Natural Resources Uses Linear Programming to Understand the Wood-Fiber Market," *Interfaces* 30, 6 (November 2000): 32–48.

Greenberg, H. J. "How to Analyze the Results of Linear Programs—Part 1: Preliminaries." *Interfaces* 23, 4 (July–August 1993): 56–68.

———. "How to Analyze the Results of Linear Programs—Part 3: Infeasibility Diagnosis," *Interfaces* 23, 6 (November–December 1993): 120–139.

Lyon, Peter, R. John Milne, Robert Orzell, and Robert Rice "Matching Assets with Demand in Supply-Chain Management at IBM Microelectronics," *Interfaces* 31, 1 (January 2001): 108–124.

Orden, A. "LP from the '40s to the '90s," *Interfaces* 23, 5 (September–October 1993): 2–12.

Quinn, P., B. Andrews, and H. Parsons. "Allocating Telecommunications Resources at L. L. Bean, Inc.," *Interfaces* 21, 1 (January–February 1991): 75–91.

Saltzman, M. J. "Survey: Mixed Integer Programming," *OR/MS Today* 21, 2 (April 1994): 42–51.

Schindler, S. and T. Semmel. "Station Staffing at Pan American World Airways," *Interfaces* 23, 3 (May–June 1993): 91–98.

Sexton, T. R., S. Sleeper, and R. E. Taggart, Jr. "Improving Pupil Transportation in North Carolina," *Interfaces* 24, 1 (January–February 1994): 87–104.

Zappe, C., W. Webster, and I. Horowitz. "Using Linear Programming to Determine Post-Facto Consistency in Performance Evaluations of Major League Baseball Players," *Interfaces* 23, 6 (November–December 1993): 107–119.

## CHAPTER 3

# LINEAR PROGRAMMING MODELING APPLICATIONS: WITH COMPUTER ANALYSES IN EXCEL

## LEARNING OBJECTIVES

After completing this chapter, students will be able to:

1. Model a wide variety of linear programming (LP) problems.

2. Understand major business application areas for LP problems, including manufacturing, marketing, labor scheduling, blending, transportation, finance, and multiperiod planning.

3. Gain experience in setting up and solving LP problems using Excel's Solver.

## CHAPTER OUTLINE

Summary • Self-Test • Problems • Case Study: Chase Manhattan Bank • Bibliography

## Scheduling Planes at Delta Airlines with Coldstart

It has been said that an airline seat is the most perishable commodity in the world. Each time an airliner takes off with an empty seat, a revenue opportunity is lost forever. For Delta Airlines, which flies more than 2,500 domestic flight legs per day using about 450 aircraft of 10 different models, its scheduling is the very heartbeat of the airline.

One flight leg for Delta might consist of a Boeing 757 jet assigned to fly at 6:21 A.M. from Atlanta to arrive in Boston at 8:45 A.M. Delta's problem, the same as that of every competitor, is to match airplanes such as 747s, 757s, or 767s to flight legs such as Atlanta–Boston, and fill seats with paying passengers. Recent advances in linear programming (LP) algorithms and computer hardware have made it possible to solve optimization problems of this scope for the first time. Delta calls its huge LP model Coldstart and runs the model every day. Delta is the first airline to solve a problem of this scope.

The typical size of a daily Coldstart LP model is about 40,000 constraints and 60,000 variables. The constraints are aircraft availability, balancing arrivals and departures at airports, aircraft maintenance needs, and so on. Coldstart's objective is to minimize a combination of operating costs and lost passenger revenue, called spill costs.

The savings from the model so far have been phenomenal, estimated at $220,000 per day over Delta's earlier schedule planning tool, which was nicknamed Warmstart. Delta expects to save $300 million over the next three years through this use of the LP model.[1]

---

[1] R. Subramanian et al. *Interfaces* 24, 1 (January–February 1994): 104–120; P. R. Horner. *OR/MS Today* 22, 4 (August 1995): 14–15.

## 3.1  INTRODUCTION

The preceding Delta Airlines application is an excellent example of the use of linear programming (LP) to model a large real-world scheduling problem and the cost savings that can result from using such models. Similar examples exist in other managerial decision-making areas such as product mix, labor scheduling, job assignment, production scheduling, marketing research, media selection, shipping and transportation, ingredient mix, and financial portfolio selection. The purpose of this chapter is to show how to use LP to model real-world decision-making problems in some of these areas.

*It is a good idea to always develop the written LP model on paper first before attempting to implement it on Excel.*

For each example discussed, we first briefly describe the development of the written mathematical model and then illustrate its solution using Excel's Solver. Although we use Solver to solve these models, it is critical to understand the logic behind the model before implementing it on the computer. Remember that the solution is only as good as the model itself. If the model is incorrect or incomplete from a logical perspective (even if it is correct from a mathematical perspective), Excel has no way of recognizing the logical error. Too many students, especially those at the early stages of instruction in LP, hit roadblocks when they try to implement an LP problem directly in Excel without conceptualizing the model on paper first. So we highly recommend that, until you become very comfortable with LP formulations (which takes many hours of practice), you sketch out the layout for each problem on paper first. Then, you can translate your written model to the computer.

*We first identify decision variables, and then write linear equations for the objective function and constraints.*

In developing each written mathematical model, we use the approach discussed in Chapter 2. This means first identifying the decision variables and then writing out linear equations for the objective function and each constraint in terms of these decision variables. Although some of the models discussed in this chapter are relatively small numerically, the principles developed here are definitely applicable to larger problems. Moreover, the structured formulation approach used here should provide enough practice in "paraphrasing" LP model formulations and help in developing skills to apply the technique to other, less common applications.

When implementing these models in Excel, to the extent possible, we employ the same layout presented in Chapter 2. That is, all parameters (i.e., the solution value, objective coefficient, and constraint coefficients) associated with a specific decision variable are modeled in the same column. The objective function and each constraint in the problem is shown on separate rows of the worksheet. Later in this chapter (Section 3.8), however, we illustrate an alternate implementation that may be more compact and efficient for some problems. As noted in Chapter 2, we encourage you to try alternate layouts based on your personal preference and expertise with Excel.

### Excel Notes

- The CD-ROM that accompanies this textbook contains the Excel file for each example problem discussed here. The relevant file name is shown in the margin next to each example.
- In each of the Excel layouts, for clarity, changing cells are shaded yellow, the target cell is shaded green, and cells containing the left-hand-side (LHS) formula for each constraint are shaded blue.
- Also, to make the equivalence of the written formulation and the Excel layout clear, the Excel layouts show the decision variable names used in the written formulation of the model. Note that these names have no role in using Solver to solve the model.

## 3.2  MARKETING APPLICATIONS

### Media Selection

Linear programming models have been used in the advertising field as a decision aid in selecting an effective media mix. Sometimes the technique is employed in allocating a fixed

*Media selection problems can be approached with LP from two perspectives. The objective can be to maximize audience exposure or to minimize advertising costs.*

or limited budget across various media, which might include radio or television commercials, newspaper ads, direct mailings, magazine ads, and so on. In other applications, the objective is the maximization of audience exposure. Restrictions on the allowable media mix might arise through contract requirements, limited media availability, or company policy. An example follows.

The Win Big Gambling Club promotes gambling junkets from a large midwestern city to casinos in the Bahamas. The club has budgeted up to $8,000 per week for local advertising. The money is to be allocated among four promotional media: TV spots, newspaper ads, and two types of radio advertisements. Win Big's goal is to reach the largest possible high-potential audience through the various media. The following table presents the number of potential gamblers reached by making use of an advertisement in each of the four media. It also provides the cost per advertisement placed and the maximum number of ads that can be purchased per week.

| MEDIUM | AUDIENCE REACHED PER AD | COST PER AD ($) | MAXIMUM ADS PER WEEK |
|---|---|---|---|
| TV spot (1 minute) | 5,000 | 800 | 12 |
| Daily newspaper (full-page ad) | 8,500 | 925 | 5 |
| Radio spot (30 seconds, prime time) | 2,400 | 290 | 25 |
| Radio spot (1 minute, afternoon) | 2,800 | 380 | 20 |

Win Big's contractual arrangements require that at least five radio spots be placed each week. To ensure a broad-scoped promotional campaign, management also insists that no more than $1,800 be spent on radio advertising every week.

The problem can now be stated mathematically as follows. Let

$T$ = number of 1-minute TV spots taken each week

$N$ = number of full-page daily newspaper ads taken each week

$P$ = number of 30-second prime-time radio spots taken each week

$A$ = number of 1-minute afternoon radio spots taken each week

Objective:

$$\text{maximize audience coverage} = 5{,}000T + 8{,}500N + 2{,}400P + 2{,}800A$$

subject to

$$T \le 12 \qquad \text{(maximum TV spots/week)}$$
$$N \le 5 \qquad \text{(maximum newspaper ads/week)}$$
$$P \le 25 \qquad \text{(maximum 30-second radio spots/week)}$$
$$A \le 20 \qquad \text{(maximum 1-minute radio spots/week)}$$
$$800T + 925N + 290P + 380A \le \$8{,}000 \quad \text{(weekly advertising budget)}$$
$$P + A \ge 5 \qquad \text{(minimum radio spots contracted)}$$
$$290P + 380A \le \$1{,}800 \quad \text{(maximum dollars spent on radio)}$$
$$T, N, P, A \ge 0$$

**File: 3-1.xls**

The formula view of the Excel layout for this problem is shown in Program 3.1A. Observe that in this spreadsheet (as well as in all other spreadsheets discussed in this chapter), the only Excel function we have used to model all formulas is the SUMPRODUCT function (discussed in Section 2.8). We have used this function to compute the objective function value (cell F6) as well as the LHS values for all constraints (cells F8:F14).

**PROGRAM 3.1A**    **Formula View of the Excel Layout for Win Gambling Club**

> These are the decision variable names used in the written LP formulation, shown here for information purposes only.

> The signs are shown here for information only. Actual signs will be entered in Solver.

| | A | B | C | D | E | F | G | H |
|---|---|---|---|---|---|---|---|---|
| 1 | **Win Big Gambling Club** | | | | | | | |
| 2 | | | | | | | | |
| 3 | | T | N | P | A | | | |
| 4 | | TV spots | Newspaper ads | Prime-time radio spots | Afternoon radio spots | | | |
| 5 | Number of Units | | | | | | | |
| 6 | Audience | 5000 | 8500 | 2400 | 2800 | =SUMPRODUCT(B6:E6,$B$5:$E$5) | <- | Objective |
| 7 | Constraints: | | | | | | | |
| 8 | Max TV | 1 | | | | =SUMPRODUCT(B8:E8,$B$5:$E$5) | <= | 12 |
| 9 | Max Newspaper | | 1 | | | =SUMPRODUCT(B9:E9,$B$5:$E$5) | <= | 5 |
| 10 | Max Prime-Time Radio | | | 1 | | =SUMPRODUCT(B10:E10,$B$5:$E$5) | <= | 25 |
| 11 | Max Afternoon Radio | | | | 1 | =SUMPRODUCT(B11:E11,$B$5:$E$5) | <= | 20 |
| 12 | Budget | 800 | 925 | 290 | 380 | =SUMPRODUCT(B12:E12,$B$5:$E$5) | <= | 8000 |
| 13 | Max Radio $ | | | 290 | 380 | =SUMPRODUCT(B13:E13,$B$5:$E$5) | <= | 1800 |
| 14 | Min Radio Spots | | | 1 | 1 | =SUMPRODUCT(B14:E14,$B$5:$E$5) | >= | 5 |
| 15 | | | | | | LHS | Sign | RHS |

> Objective function value (cell F6) and constraint LHS values (cells F8:F14) are computed using the SUMPRODUCT function.

*Formulas for LHS of constraints are modeled using the SUMPRODUCT function in Excel.*

As noted earlier, we have adopted this type of Excel layout for our models in order to make it easier for the beginning student of LP to understand them. Further, an advantage of this layout is the ease with which all the formulas in the spreadsheet can be created. Observe that we have used the $ sign in cell F6 to anchor the cell references for the decision variables (cells B5:E5). This allows us to simply copy this formula to cells F8:F14 to create the corresponding LHS formulas for the constraints.

The entries for the Solver Parameters window for this model, and the resulting solution, are shown in Program 3.1B. The optimal solution is found to be

$$T = 1.97 \quad \text{television spots}$$

$$N = 5.00 \quad \text{newspaper ads}$$

$$P = 6.21 \quad \text{30-second prime time radio spots}$$

$$A = 0.00 \quad \text{1-minute afternoon radio spots}$$

This produces an audience exposure of 67,240 contacts. Observe that this solution turns out to have fractional values. As noted in Chapter 2, since it is considerably harder to solve an integer programming model than an LP model, it is quite common to not specify the integer requirement in many LP models. We discuss problems that require all integer solutions in Chapter 6. In Win Big's problem, since $T$ and $P$ are fractional, the club would probably round them off to 2 and 6, respectively.

## Marketing Research

Linear programming has also been applied to marketing research problems and the area of consumer research. The next example illustrates how statistical pollsters can reach strategy decisions with LP.

Management Sciences Associates (MSA) is a marketing and computer research firm based in Washington, D.C., that handles consumer surveys. One of its clients is a national

**PROGRAM 3.1B**    **Excel Layout and Solver Entries for Win Big Gambling Club**

| | A | B | C | D | E | F | G | H |
|---|---|---|---|---|---|---|---|---|
| 1 | **Win Big Gambling Club** | | | | | | | |
| 2 | | | | | | | | |
| 3 | | T | N | P | A | | | |
| 4 | | TV spots | Newspaper ads | Prime-time radio spots | Afternoon radio spots | | | |
| 5 | Number of Units | 1.97 | 5.00 | 6.21 | 0.00 | | | |
| 6 | Audience | 5000 | 8500 | 2400 | 2800 | 67240.30 | <- Objective | |
| 7 | **Constraints:** | | | | | | | |
| 8 | Max TV | 1 | | | | 1.97 | <= | 12 |
| 9 | Max Newspaper | | 1 | | | 5.00 | <= | 5 |
| 10 | Max Prime-Time Radio | | | 1 | | 6.21 | <= | 25 |
| 11 | Max Afternoon Radio | | | | 1 | 0.00 | <= | 20 |
| 12 | Budget | $800 | $925 | $290 | $380 | $8,000.00 | <= | $8,000 |
| 13 | Max Radio $ | | | $290 | $380 | $1,800.00 | <= | $1,800 |
| 14 | Min Radio Spots | | | 1 | 1 | 6.21 | >= | 5 |
| 15 | | | | | | LHS | Sign | RHS |

Fractional values are allowed in LP solutions.

**Solver Parameters**    ?|×|

Set Target Cell:  $F$6

Equal To:   ⦿ Max   ○ Min   ○ Value of:  0

By Changing Cells:

$B$5:$E$5    Guess

Subject to the Constraints:

$F$14 >= $H$14
$F$8:$F$13 <= $H$8:$H$13

Solve

Close

Options

Premium

Add

All six ≤ constraints are entered as a single entry in Solver.

Make sure *Assume Non-Negative* and *Assume Linear Model* boxes are checked in Solver Options.

press service that periodically conducts political polls on issues of widespread interest. In a survey for the press service, MSA determines that it must fulfill several requirements in order to draw statistically valid conclusions on the sensitive issue of new U.S. immigration laws:

1.  Survey at least 2,300 U.S. households in total.
2.  Survey at least 1,000 households whose heads are 30 years of age or younger.
3.  Survey at least 600 households whose heads are between 31 and 50 years of age.
4.  Ensure that at least 15% of those surveyed live in a state that borders on Mexico.
5.  Ensure that no more than 20% of those surveyed who are 51 years of age or over live in a state that borders on Mexico.

MSA decides that all surveys should be conducted in person. It estimates that the costs of reaching people in each age and region category are as follows:

| | COST PER PERSON SURVEYED ($) | | |
|---|---|---|---|
| **REGION** | **AGE ≤ 30** | **AGE 31–50** | **AGE ≥ 51** |
| State bordering Mexico | $7.50 | $6.80 | $5.50 |
| State not bordering Mexico | $6.90 | $7.25 | $6.10 |

## IN ACTION    LP Modeling in the Forests of Chile

Faced with a series of challenges in making short-term harvesting decisions, Forestal Arauco, a Chilean forestry firm, turned to professors at the University of Chile for LP modeling help. One of the problems in short-term harvesting of trees is to match demand of products—defined by length and diameter—with the supply of standing timber.

The manual system used at the time by foresters led to a significant amount of waste of timber, in which higher diameter logs, suited for export or sawmills, ended up being used for pulp, with a considerable loss in value. An LP model, labeled OPTICORT by the professors, was the logical way to get better schedules.

"The system not only optimized the operational decisions in harvesting but also changed the way managers looked at the problem," said Professor Andres Weintraub. "The model and its concepts became the natural language to discuss the operations. They had to negotiate the parameters, and the model would do the dirty work. The system had to run in a few minutes to allow discussion and negotiation; that was a critical feature for the success of this tool," he added.

The LP program took about two years to develop, and the researchers were careful to observe two cardinal rules: (1) The solution approach had to be comfortable and clear to the user, and (2) The system had to provide answers to the user in a fast development, so the user could see quick improvements.

**Source:** J. Summerour. "Chilean Forestry Firm a 'Model' of Success," *OR/MS Today* (April 1999): 22–23.

MSA's goal is to meet the five sampling requirements at the least possible cost. We let

$B_1$ = number surveyed who are 30 years of age or younger and live in a border state

$B_2$ = number surveyed who are 31–50 years of age and live in a border state

$B_3$ = number surveyed who are 51 years of age or older and live in a border state

$N_1$ = number surveyed who are 30 years of age or younger and do not live in a border state

$N_2$ = number surveyed who are 31–50 years of age and do not live in a border state

$N_3$ = number surveyed who are 51 years of age or older and do not live in a border state

Objective function:

$$\text{minimize total interview costs} = \$7.50B_1 + \$6.80B_2 + \$5.50B_3 \\ + \$6.90N_1 + \$7.25N_2 + \$6.10N_3$$

subject to

$$B_1 + B_2 + B_3 + N_1 + N_2 + N_3 \geq 2{,}300 \quad \text{(total households)}$$
$$B_1 + N_1 \geq 1{,}000 \quad \text{(households 30 years or younger)}$$
$$B_2 + N_2 \geq 600 \quad \text{(households 31–50 in age)}$$
$$B_1 + B_2 + B_3 \geq 0.15(B_1 + B_2 + B_3 + N_1 + N_2 + N_3) \quad \text{(border states)}$$
$$B_3 \leq 0.2(B_3 + N_3) \quad \text{(limit on age group 51+ years who can live in border state)}$$
$$B_1, B_2, B_3, N_1, N_2, N_3 \geq 0$$

The Excel layout and Solver entries for this model are shown in Program 3.2. In implementing this model, we have algebraically modified constraints 4 and 5 to bring all the variables to the left-hand side (LHS) and just leave a constant on the right-hand side (RHS). These are the constraints that ensure that at least 15% of those surveyed live in a state that borders on Mexico and that no more than 20% of those surveyed who are 51 years of age or over live in a state that borders on Mexico, respectively. For example, constraint 4 is presently modeled as

$$B_1 + B_2 + B_3 \geq 0.15(B_1 + B_2 + B_3 + N_1 + N_2 + N_3)$$

This can be rewritten as

$$B_1 + B_2 + B_3 - 0.15(B_1 + B_2 + B_3 + N_1 + N_2 + N_3) \geq 0$$

**File: 3-2.xls**

*Constraints can be algebraically modified to bring all variables to the LHS, if desired.*

**PROGRAM 3.2**

**Excel Layout and Solver Entries for Management Science Associates**

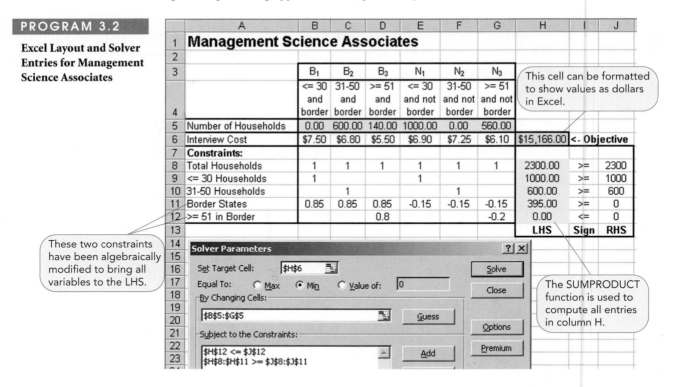

These two constraints have been algebraically modified to bring all variables to the LHS.

This cell can be formatted to show values as dollars in Excel.

The SUMPRODUCT function is used to compute all entries in column H.

which simplifies to

$$0.85B_1 + 0.85B_2 + 0.85B_3 - 0.15N_1 - 0.15N_2 - 0.15N_3 \geq 0$$

Note that such algebraic manipulations are not required to implement this model in Excel. It is perfectly logical to have cell H11 in Program 3.2 represent the formula $(B_1 + B_2 + B_3)$ and cell J11 represent the formula $0.15(B_1 + B_2 + B_3 + N_1 + N_2 + N_3)$. However, we have included such manipulations in our model since it allows us to make the Excel implementation of each constraint consistent. That is, each cell denoting the LHS value of a constraint will have a SUMPRODUCT function involving the decision variables. Likewise, each cell denoting the RHS value of a constraint will have a constant.

The optimal solution to MSA's marketing research problem costs \$15,166 and requires the firm to survey households as follows:

| | |
|---|---|
| State bordering Mexico and head 31–50 years old | = 600 |
| State bordering Mexico and head ≥ 51 years old | = 140 |
| State not bordering Mexico and head ≤ 30 years old | = 1,000 |
| State not bordering Mexico and head ≥ 51 years old | = 560 |

## 3.3  MANUFACTURING APPLICATIONS

### Product Mix

*A popular use of LP is in solving product mix problems.*

A fertile field for the use of LP is in planning for the optimal mix of products to manufacture. A company must meet a myriad of constraints, ranging from financial concerns to sales demands to material contracts to union labor demands. Its primary goal is to generate the largest profit possible. We have already studied a simple version of the product mix problem (Flair Furniture problem) in Chapter 2. Let us now look at a more detailed version of a product mix problem.

Fifth Avenue Industries, a nationally known manufacturer of menswear, produces four varieties of ties. One is an expensive, all-silk tie, one is an all-polyester tie, and two are blends of polyester and cotton. The following table illustrates the cost and availability (per monthly production planning period) of the three materials used in the production process:

| MATERIAL | COST PER YARD ($) | MATERIAL AVAILABLE PER MONTH (YARDS) |
|---|---|---|
| Silk | 21 | 800 |
| Polyester | 6 | 3,000 |
| Cotton | 9 | 1,600 |

The firm has fixed contracts with several major department store chains to supply ties. The contracts require that Fifth Avenue Industries supply a minimum quantity of each tie but allow for a larger demand if Fifth Avenue chooses to meet that demand. (Most of the ties are not shipped with the name Fifth Avenue on their label, incidentally, but with "private stock" labels supplied by the stores.) Table 3.1 summarizes the contract demand for each of the four styles of ties, the selling price per tie, and the fabric requirements of each variety.

Fifth Avenue's goal is to maximize its monthly profit. It must decide upon a policy for product mix. Let

$$S = \text{number of all-silk ties produced per month}$$

$$P = \text{number of polyester ties}$$

$$B_1 = \text{number of blend 1 poly–cotton ties}$$

$$B_2 = \text{number of blend 2 poly–cotton ties}$$

Unlike the Flair Furniture example, in which the unit profit for each product was directly given (e.g., $7 per table and $5 per chair), the unit profits must be first calculated in this example. We illustrate the net profit calculation for all-silk ties ($S$). Each all-silk tie requires 0.125 yards of silk at a cost of $21 per yard, resulting in a material cost of $2.625. The selling price per all-silk tie is $6.70, leaving a net profit of $6.70 − $2.625 = $4.075 per tie. In a similar fashion, we can calculate the net unit profit for all-polyester ties ($P$) to be $3.07, for poly–cotton blend 1 ties ($B_1$) to be $3.56, and for poly–cotton blend 2 ties ($B_2$) to be $4.00. Try to verify these calculations for yourself.

The objective function can now be stated as

$$\text{maximize profit} = \$4.075S + \$3.07P + \$3.56B_1 + \$4.00B_2$$

| TABLE 3.1 | | Data for Fifth Avenue Industries | | | |
|---|---|---|---|---|---|
| VARIETY OF TIE | SELLING PRICE PER TIE ($) | MONTHLY CONTRACT MINIMUM | MONTHLY DEMAND | MATERIAL REQUIRED PER TIE (YARDS) | MATERIAL REQUIREMENTS |
| All silk | 6.70 | 6,000 | 7,000 | 0.125 | 100% silk |
| All polyester | 3.55 | 10,000 | 14,000 | 0.08 | 100% polyester |
| Poly–cotton blend 1 | 4.31 | 13,000 | 16,000 | 0.10 | 50% polyester–50% cotton |
| Poly–cotton blend 2 | 4.81 | 6,000 | 8,500 | 0.10 | 30% polyester–70% cotton |

subject to

$$
\begin{array}{rcll}
0.125S & \le & 800 & \text{(yards of silk)} \\
0.08P + 0.05B_1 + 0.03B_2 & \le & 3{,}000 & \text{(yards of polyester)} \\
0.05B_1 + 0.07B_2 & \le & 1{,}600 & \text{(yards of cotton)} \\
S & \ge & 6{,}000 & \text{(contract minimum for all silk)} \\
S & \le & 7{,}000 & \text{(contract maximum)} \\
P & \ge & 10{,}000 & \text{(contract minimum for all polyester)} \\
P & \le & 14{,}000 & \text{(contract maximum)} \\
B_1 & \ge & 13{,}000 & \text{(contract minimum for blend 1)} \\
B_1 & \le & 16{,}000 & \text{(contract maximum)} \\
B_2 & \ge & 6{,}000 & \text{(contract minimum for blend 2)} \\
B_2 & \le & 8{,}500 & \text{(contract maximum)} \\
S, P, B_1, B_2 & \ge & 0 &
\end{array}
$$

In implementing the model in Excel, we have split the objective function (profit) into two components: a revenue component, and a material cost component. For example, the

**PROGRAM 3.3**      **Excel Layout and Solver Entries for Fifth Avenue Industries**

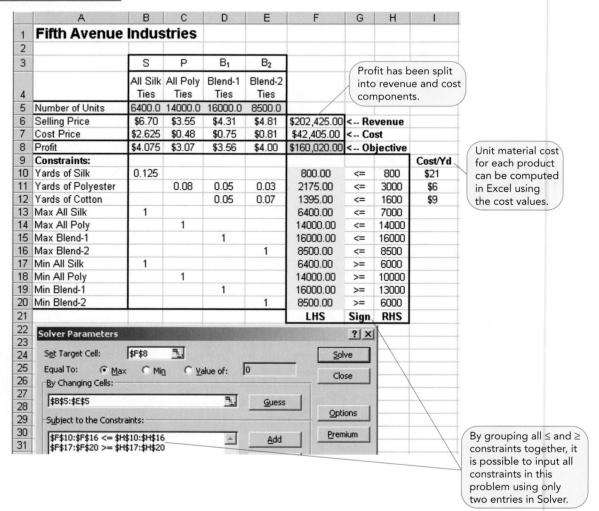

objective coefficient for all-silk ties ($S$) is \$4.075. However, we know that the \$4.075 is obtained by subtracting the revenue (\$6.70) for $S$ from the material cost (\$2.625). Hence, we can rewrite the objective function as follows:

$$\text{Maximize } (\$6.70S + \$3.55P + \$4.31B_1 + \$4.81B_2)$$
$$- (\$2.625S + \$0.48P + \$0.75B_1 + \$0.81B_2)$$

*We can have the Excel layout show as much detail as desired for a problem.*

**File: 3-3.xls**

Whether we model the objective function using the profit coefficients or using the selling price and material cost coefficients, the final solution will be the same. However, in many problems it is convenient, and probably preferable, to have the model show as much detail as possible.

The Excel layout and Solver entries for this model are shown in Program 3.3. Cell F6 defines the revenue component of the objective, and cell F7 defines the cost component of the objective function. Cell F8 (the target cell in Solver) is the difference between cells F6 and F7.

Program 3.3 shows that the optimal solution is to produce 6,400 all-silk ties, 14,000 all-polyester ties, 16,000 poly–cotton blend 1 ties, and 8,500 poly–cotton blend 2 ties. This results in total revenue of \$202,425 and a total material cost of \$42,405, yielding a net profit of \$160,020.

## 3.4    EMPLOYEE SCHEDULING APPLICATIONS

### Labor Planning

Labor planning problems address staffing needs over a specific time period. They are especially useful when managers have some flexibility in assigning workers to jobs that require overlapping or interchangeable talents. Large banks frequently use LP to tackle their labor scheduling.

Hong Kong Bank of Commerce and Industry is a busy bank that has requirements for between 10 and 18 tellers, depending on the time of day. The lunch time, from noon to 2 P.M., is usually heaviest. Table 3.2 indicates the workers needed at various hours that the bank is open.

The bank now employs 12 full-time tellers, but many people are on its roster of available part-time employees. A part-time employee must put in exactly four hours per day but can start anytime between 9 A.M. and 1 P.M. Part-timers are a fairly inexpensive labor pool, since no retirement or lunch benefits are provided for them. Full-timers, on the other hand, work from 9 A.M. to 5 P.M. but are allowed 1 hour for lunch. (Half of the full-timers eat at 11 A.M., the other half at noon.) Full-timers thus provide 35 hours per week of productive labor time.

By corporate policy, the bank limits part-time hours to a maximum of 50% of the day's total requirement. Part-timers earn \$4 per hour (or \$16 per day) on average, and full-timers earn \$50 per day in salary and benefits, on average. The bank would like to set a

| TABLE 3.2 | | |
|---|---|---|
| Hong Kong Bank of Commerce and Industry | **TIME PERIOD** | **NUMBER OF TELLERS REQUIRED** |
| | 9 A.M.–10 A.M. | 10 |
| | 10 A.M.–11 A.M. | 12 |
| | 11 A.M.–NOON | 14 |
| | NOON–1 P.M. | 16 |
| | 1 P.M.–2 P.M. | 18 |
| | 2 P.M.–3 P.M. | 17 |
| | 3 P.M.–4 P.M. | 15 |
| | 4 P.M.–5 P.M. | 10 |

schedule that would minimize its total personnel costs. It will release one or more of its full-time tellers if it is profitable to do so.

We can let

$$F = \text{full-time tellers}$$

$$P_1 = \text{part-timers starting at 9 A.M. (leaving at 1 P.M.)}$$

$$P_2 = \text{part-timers starting at 10 A.M. (leaving at 2 P.M.)}$$

$$P_3 = \text{part-timers starting at 11 A.M. (leaving at 3 P.M.)}$$

$$P_4 = \text{part-timers starting at noon (leaving at 4 P.M.)}$$

$$P_5 = \text{part-timers starting at 1 P.M. (leaving at 5 P.M.)}$$

Objective function:

$$\text{minimize total daily personnel cost} = \$50F + \$16(P_1 + P_2 + P_3 + P_4 + P_5)$$

Constraints:

For each hour, the available labor hours must be at least equal to the required labor hours.

$$
\begin{array}{lll}
F + P_1 & \geq 10 & \text{(9 A.M.–10 A.M. needs)} \\
F + P_1 + P_2 & \geq 12 & \text{(10 A.M.–11 A.M. needs)} \\
\tfrac{1}{2}F + P_1 + P_2 + P_3 & \geq 14 & \text{(11 A.M.–noon needs)} \\
\tfrac{1}{2}F + P_1 + P_2 + P_3 + P_4 & \geq 16 & \text{(noon–1 P.M. needs)} \\
F + P_2 + P_3 + P_4 + P_5 & \geq 18 & \text{(1 P.M.–2 P.M. needs)} \\
F + P_3 + P_4 + P_5 & \geq 17 & \text{(2 P.M.–3 P.M. needs)} \\
F + P_4 + P_5 & \geq 15 & \text{(3 P.M.–4 P.M. needs)} \\
F + P_5 & \geq 10 & \text{(4 P.M.–5 P.M. needs)}
\end{array}
$$

Only 12 full-time tellers are available, so

$$F \leq 12$$

Part-time worker hours cannot exceed 50% of total hours required each day, which is the sum of the tellers needed each hour.

$$4(P_1 + P_2 + P_3 + P_4 + P_5) \leq 0.50(10 + 12 + 14 + 16 + 18 + 17 + 15 + 10)$$

or

$$4P_1 + 4P_2 + 4P_3 + 4P_4 + 4P_5 \leq 56$$

$$F, P_1, P_2, P_3, P_4, P_5 \geq 0$$

**File: 3-4.xls**

The Excel layout and Solver entries for this model, shown in Program 3.4, reveal that the optimal solution is to employ 10 full-time tellers, 7 part-time tellers at 10 A.M., 2 part-time tellers at 11 A.M., and 5 part-time tellers at noon, for a total cost of $724 per day.

It turns out that there are several alternate optimal solutions that Hong Kong Bank can employ. In practice, the sequence in which you present constraints in your model can affect the specific solution that is found. We revisit this example in Chapter 4 (Solved Problem 4-1) to study how we can use Solver's sensitivity reports to detect and identify alternate optimal solutions.

*Alternate optimal solutions are common in many LP applications.*

For this problem, one alternate solution is to employ 10 full-time tellers, 6 part-time tellers at 9 A.M., 1 part-time teller at 10 A.M., 2 part-time tellers at 11 A.M., and 5 part-time tellers at noon. The cost of this policy is also $724.

**PROGRAM 3.4**    **Excel Layout and Solver Entries for Hong Kong Bank**

| | A | B | C | D | E | F | G | H | I | J |
|---|---|---|---|---|---|---|---|---|---|---|
| 1 | **Hong Kong Bank** | | | | | | | | | |
| 2 | | | | | | | | | | |
| 3 | | F | P₁ | P₂ | P₃ | P₄ | P₅ | | | |
| 4 | | Full Time | Part Time @9am | Part Time @10am | Part Time @11am | Part Time @Noon | Part Time @1pm | | | |
| 5 | Number of Tellers | 10.0 | 0.0 | 7.0 | 2.0 | 5.0 | 0.0 | | | |
| 6 | Cost | $50.00 | $16.00 | $16.00 | $16.00 | $16.00 | $16.00 | $724.00 | <- Objective | |
| 7 | **Constraints:** | | | | | | | | | |
| 8 | 9am-10am Needs | 1 | 1 | | | | | 10.0 | >= | 10 |
| 9 | 10am-11am Needs | 1 | 1 | 1 | | | | 17.0 | >= | 12 |
| 10 | 11am-Noon Needs | 0.5 | 1 | 1 | 1 | | | 14.0 | >= | 14 |
| 11 | Noon-1pm Needs | 0.5 | 1 | 1 | 1 | 1 | | 19.0 | >= | 16 |
| 12 | 1pm-2pm Needs | 1 | | 1 | 1 | 1 | 1 | 24.0 | >= | 18 |
| 13 | 2pm-3pm Needs | 1 | | | 1 | 1 | 1 | 17.0 | >= | 17 |
| 14 | 3pm-4pm Needs | 1 | | | | 1 | 1 | 15.0 | >= | 15 |
| 15 | 4pm-5pm Needs | 1 | | | | | 1 | 10.0 | >= | 10 |
| 16 | Max Full Time | 1 | | | | | | 10.0 | <= | 12 |
| 17 | Part Time  Limit | | 4 | 4 | 4 | 4 | 4 | 56.0 | <= | 56 |
| 18 | | | | | | | | LHS | Sign | RHS |

**Solver Parameters**                                    ? ×

Set Target Cell:    $H$6

Equal To:    ○ Max    ● Min    ○ Value of:    0

By Changing Cells:

$B$5:$G$5

Subject to the Constraints:

$H$16:$H$17 <= $J$16:$J$17

$H$8:$H$15 >= $J$8:$J$15

[ Solve ]  [ Close ]  [ Guess ]  [ Options ]  [ Premium ]  [ Add ]

= 0.5 * SUM (J8:J15). This RHS value is set to 50% of the sum of all needs (RHS values of rows 8 to 15).

All ≤ and ≥ constraints are entered as blocks of constraints.

## Assignment Problems

*Assigning people to jobs, jobs to machines, and so on, is an application of LP called the assignment problem.*

Assignment problems involve determining the most efficient assignment of people to jobs, machines to tasks, police cars to city sectors, salespeople to territories, and so on. The objective might be to minimize travel times or costs or to maximize assignment effectiveness.

The assignment problem is an example of a special type of LP problem known as network-flow problems, and we study these types of problems in greater detail in Chapter 5.

## 3.5    FINANCIAL APPLICATIONS

### Portfolio Selection

A problem frequently encountered by managers of banks, mutual funds, investment services, and insurance companies is the selection of specific investments from among a wide variety of alternatives. The manager's overall objective is usually to maximize expected return on investment, given a set of legal, policy, or risk restraints.

*Maximizing return on investment subject to a set of risk constraints is a popular financial application of LP.*

For example, the International City Trust (ICT) invests in short-term trade credits, corporate bonds, gold stocks, and construction loans. To encourage a diversified portfolio, the board of directors has placed limits on the amount that can be committed to any one type of investment. ICT has $5 million available for immediate investment and wishes to do two things: (1) maximize the interest earned on the investments made over the next six months and (2) satisfy the diversification requirements as set by the board of directors. The specifics of the investment possibilities are as follows:

| INVESTMENT | INTEREST EARNED (%) | MAXIMUM INVESTMENT ($ MILLIONS) |
|---|---|---|
| Trade credit | 7 | 1.0 |
| Corporate bonds | 11 | 2.5 |
| Gold stocks | 19 | 1.5 |
| Construction loans | 15 | 1.8 |

In addition, the board specifies that at least 55% of the funds invested must be in gold stocks and construction loans, and that no less than 15% be invested in trade credit.

To formulate ICT's investment decision as an LP problem, we let

$$T = \text{dollars invested in trade credit}$$

$$B = \text{dollars invested in corporate bonds}$$

$$G = \text{dollars invested in gold stocks}$$

$$C = \text{dollars invested in construction loans}$$

Objective:

$$\text{maximize dollars of interest earned} = 0.07T + 0.11B + 0.19G + 0.15C$$

subject to

$$T \leq 1{,}000{,}000$$

$$B \leq 2{,}500{,}000$$

$$G \leq 1{,}500{,}000$$

$$C \leq 1{,}800{,}000$$

$$G + C \geq 0.55(T + B + G + C)$$

$$T \geq 0.15(T + B + G + C)$$

$$T + B + G + C \leq 5{,}000{,}000$$

$$T, B, G, C \geq 0$$

 **IN ACTION**   Using LP for Portfolio Selection at Prudential Securities

Few financial markets have experienced the rapid growth and innovations of the secondary mortgage market in the late twentieth and early twenty-first centuries. This growth has been spurred by federal agencies whose mandate is to make home ownership easier and more affordable by increasing the flow of funds available. Prudential Securities have entered this $1 trillion market for mortgage-backed securities (MBSs) in a huge way, typically trading $5 billion of MBSs per week. These securities, which are mortgage loans pooled by government agencies, are traded in a somewhat complex market by a network of dealers like Prudential.

To reduce investment risk and to value securities properly and quickly for its investors, Prudential has developed and implemented a number of decision models. Its LP model, run hundreds of times per day by Prudential traders, salespeople, and clients, designs an optimal securities portfolio to meet investors' criteria under different interest rate environments. Constraints include the minimum and maximum percentages of a portfolio to invest in any security, the duration of the MBS, and the total amount to be invested. The model helps managers decide how much to invest in each available MBS in order to meet clients' goals.

**Source:** Yosi Ben-Dov, Lakhbir Hayre, and Vincent Pica. "Mortgage Valuation Models at Prudential Securities," *Interfaces*, 22, 1 (January–February 1992): 55–71.

**PROGRAM 3.5**      **Excel Layout and Solver Entries for International City Trust**

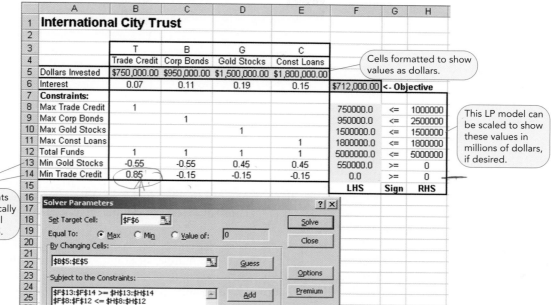

These two constraints have been algebraically modified to bring all variables to the LHS.

Cells formatted to show values as dollars.

This LP model can be scaled to show these values in millions of dollars, if desired.

**File: 3-5.xls**

As in the marketing research problem, before implementing this model on Excel, we have algebraically modified the constraints so that all variables are on the LHS and only a constant is on the RHS. Hence, the constraints dealing with the minimum investments in gold stock and trade credit have been rewritten as follows:

$$-0.55T - 0.55B + 0.45G + 0.45C \geq 0 \qquad \text{Gold stock}$$
$$0.85T - 0.15B - 0.15G - 0.15C \geq 0 \qquad \text{Trade credit}$$

The Excel layout and Solver entries for this model are shown in Program 3.5. The optimal solution is to invest $750,000 in trade credit, $950,000 in corporate bonds, $1,500,000 in gold stocks, and $1,800,000 in construction bonds, earning a total interest of $712,000.

Although we have chosen to implement the decision variables as the amount of dollars invested in each choice, we could have set up the decision variables to represent the amount of dollars invested in *millions*, for example. In such a case, the solution values would be $0.75 in trade credit, $0.95 in corporate bonds, $1.50 in gold stocks, and $1.80 in construction bonds earning a total interest of $0.712.

*Problems with large variability in the magnitudes of parameter and/or variable values should be scaled.*

As noted in Chapter 2, it is usually a good idea in practice to scale problems in which typical values of the objective function and constraints differ by several orders of magnitude. One way to do so would be to click the Use Automatic Scaling option available in Solver, discussed in Chapter 2.

## 3.6    TRANSPORTATION APPLICATIONS

### Truck Loading Problem

The truck loading problem involves deciding which items to load on a truck so as to maximize the value of a load shipped. As an example, we consider Goodman Shipping, an Orlando firm owned by Steven Goodman. One of his trucks, with a capacity of 10,000 pounds, is about to be loaded.[2] Awaiting shipment are the following items:

| ITEM | VALUE ($) | WEIGHT (POUNDS) |
|------|-----------|-----------------|
| 1 | 22,500 | 7,500 |
| 2 | 24,000 | 7,500 |
| 3 | 8,000 | 3,000 |
| 4 | 9,500 | 3,500 |
| 5 | 11,500 | 4,000 |
| 6 | 9,750 | 3,500 |

Each of these six items, we see, has an associated dollar value and weight.

The objective is to maximize the total value of the items loaded onto the truck without exceeding the truck's weight capacity.

*Alternate formulations are possible for some LP problems.*

There are several ways in which this problem can be formulated. For example, we can define the decision variables as the number of pounds of each item that is loaded on the truck. There would be six decision variables (one for each item) in the model. In this case, the value of each item needs to be appropriately scaled for use in the objective function. For example, if the total value of the 7,500 pounds of item 1 is $22,500, the value per pound is then $3 (= 22,500/7,500). Similar calculations can be made for the other items to be shipped.

Alternatively, we can define the six decision variables as the proportion of each item that is loaded on the truck. Under this approach, let $P_i$ be the proportion of each item $i$ loaded on the truck. The LP model can then be formulated as follows:

$$\text{Maximize load value} = \$22{,}500P_1 + \$24{,}000P_2 + \$8{,}000P_3 + \$9{,}500P_4 + \$11{,}500P_5 + \$9{,}750P_6$$

subject to

$$7{,}500P_1 + 7{,}500P_2 + 3{,}000P_3 + 3{,}500P_4 + 4{,}000P_5 + 3{,}500P_6 \le 10{,}000 \text{ lb capacity}$$

$$P_1 \le 1$$
$$P_2 \le 1$$
$$P_3 \le 1$$
$$P_4 \le 1$$
$$P_5 \le 1$$
$$P_6 \le 1$$
$$P_1, P_2, P_3, P_4, P_5, P_6 \ge 0$$

These final six constraints reflect the fact that at most one "unit" (i.e., a proportion of 1) of an item can be loaded onto the truck. In effect, if Goodman can load a *portion* of an item

---

[2] Adapted from an example in S. L. Savage. *What's Best!* Oakland, CA: General Optimization, Inc., and Holden-Day, 1985.

**PROGRAM 3.6A**

**Excel Layout and Solver Entries for Goodman Shipping**

*LP solution permits fractional quantities to be shipped.*

*Solution values show proportion of item loaded on truck.*

| | A | B | C | D | E | F | G | H | I | J |
|---|---|---|---|---|---|---|---|---|---|---|
| 1 | **Goodman Shipping** | | | | | | | | | |
| 2 | | | | | | | | | | |
| 3 | | P₁ | P₂ | P₃ | P₄ | P₅ | P₆ | | | |
| 4 | | Item 1 | Item 2 | Item 3 | Item 4 | Item 5 | Item 6 | | | |
| 5 | Proportion | 0.33 | 1.00 | 0.00 | 0.00 | 0.00 | 0.00 | | | |
| 6 | Load Value | $22,500 | $24,000 | $8,000 | $9,500 | $11,500 | $9,750 | $31,500.00 | <-- Objective | |
| 7 | Constraints: | | | | | | | | | |
| 8 | Capacity | 7500 | 7500 | 3000 | 3500 | 4000 | 3500 | 10000.0 | <= | 10000 |
| 9 | Item 1 Limit | 1 | | | | | | 0.33 | <= | 1 |
| 10 | Item 2 Limit | | 1 | | | | | 1.00 | <= | 1 |
| 11 | Item 3 Limit | | | 1 | | | | 0.00 | <= | 1 |
| 12 | Item 4 Limit | | | | 1 | | | 0.00 | <= | 1 |
| 13 | Item 5 Limit | | | | | 1 | | 0.00 | <= | 1 |
| 14 | Item 6 Limit | | | | | | 1 | 0.00 | <= | 1 |
| 15 | | | | | | | | LHS | Sign | RHS |

**Solver Parameters**  ? X

Set Target Cell: `$H$6`

Equal To: ● Max  ○ Min  ○ Value of: `0`

By Changing Cells:

`$B$5:$G$5`

Subject to the Constraints:

`$H$8:$H$14 <= $J$8:$J$14`

[Buttons: Solve, Close, Guess, Options, Premium, Add]

**File: 3-6.xls**

(e.g., item 1 is a batch of 1,000 folding chairs, not all of which need to be shipped together), the proportions $P_i$ will all have values ranging from 0 (nothing) to 1 (all of that item loaded).

Program 3.6A shows the Excel layout and Solver entries for Goodman Shipping's LP model. The optimal solution yields a total value of $31,500 and requires Goodman to ship a proportion of 0.33 (i.e., 33%) of item 1 and all of item 2.

The answer leads us to an interesting issue that we deal with in detail in Chapter 6. What does Goodman do if fractional values of items cannot be loaded? For example, if luxury cars were the items being loaded, we clearly cannot ship one-third of a Maserati.

If the proportion of item 1 was rounded up to 1.00, the weight of the load would increase to 15,000 pounds. This would violate the 10,000 pounds maximum weight constraint. Therefore, the fraction of item 1 must be rounded down to zero. This would drop the value of the load to 7,500 pounds, leaving 2,500 pounds of the load capacity unused. Because no other item weighs less than 2,500 pounds, the truck cannot be filled up further.

Thus we see that by using regular LP and rounding the fractional weights, the truck would carry only item 2, for a load weight of 7,500 pounds and a load value of $24,000.

As we show in Chapter 6, most LP software packages, including Excel's Solver, are capable of dealing with integer programming problems as well. In fact, using Excel, it turns out that the integer solution to Goodman's problem is to load all of items 3, 4, and 5 for a total weight of 10,000 pounds and load value of $27,250.

Program 3.6B shows an alternate model for Goodman Shipping's problem. The decision variables in this model are the weights in pounds that are shipped, rather than the proportion. The layout for this model is identical to the model shown in Program 3.6A, and you should be able to recognize its written formulation easily. As expected, the solution to this model shows that the maximum load value is $31,500. This load value is achieved by shipping 2,500 pounds (= 0.33 of the 7,500 pounds available) of item 1 and 7,500 (= all of the 7,500 pounds available) of item 2.

**PROGRAM 3.6B**

**Alternate Excel Layout and Solver Entries for Goodman Shipping**

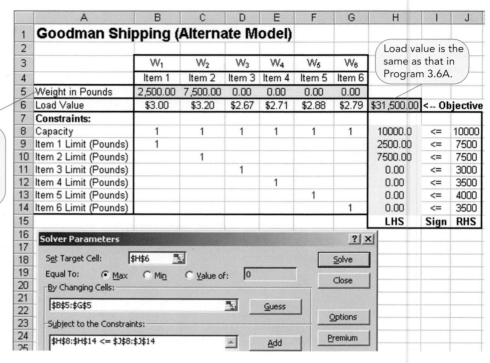

This model shows number of pounds of item loaded on truck.

Load value is the same as that in Program 3.6A.

## Transportation Problem

*Transporting goods from several origins to several destinations efficiently is called the* transportation *problem.*

The transportation or shipping problem involves determining the amount of goods or items to be transported from a number of origins to a number of destinations. The objective usually is to minimize total shipping costs or distances. Constraints in this type of problem deal with capacities or supplies at each origin and requirements or demand at each destination.

Like the assignment problem, the transportation problem is also an example of network-flow problems, which we study in greater detail in Chapter 5.

## 3.7   INGREDIENT BLENDING APPLICATIONS

### Diet Problems

The diet problem, one of the earliest applications of LP, was originally used by hospitals to determine the most economical diet for patients. Known in agricultural applications as the feed mix problem, the diet problem involves specifying a food or feed ingredient combination that satisfies stated nutritional requirements at a minimum cost level.

The Whole Food Nutrition Center uses three bulk grains to blend a natural cereal that it sells by the pound. The store advertises that each 2-ounce serving of the cereal, when taken with ½ cup of whole milk, meets an average adult's minimum daily requirement for protein, riboflavin, phosphorus, and magnesium. The cost of each bulk grain and the protein, riboflavin, phosphorus, and magnesium units per pound of each are shown in Table 3.3.

The minimum adult daily requirement (called the U.S. Recommended Daily Allowance, or USRDA) for protein is 3 units; for riboflavin, 2 units; for phosphorus, 1 unit; and for magnesium, 0.425 unit. Whole Food wants to select the blend of grains that will meet the USRDA at a minimum cost.

| TABLE 3.3 | Whole Food's Natural Cereal Requirements | | | | |
|---|---|---|---|---|---|
| GRAIN | COST PER POUND (CENTS) | PROTEIN (UNITS/LB) | RIBOFLAVIN (UNITS/LB) | PHOSPHORUS (UNITS/LB) | MAGNESIUM (UNITS/LB) |
| A | 33 | 22 | 16 | 8 | 5 |
| B | 47 | 28 | 14 | 7 | 0 |
| C | 38 | 21 | 25 | 9 | 6 |

We let

$$A = \text{pounds of grain } A \text{ in one 2-ounce serving of cereal}$$
$$B = \text{pounds of grain } B \text{ in one 2-ounce serving of cereal}$$
$$C = \text{pounds of grain } C \text{ in one 2-ounce serving of cereal}$$

Objective function:

$$\text{minimize total cost of mixing a 2-ounce serving} = \$0.33A + \$0.47B + \$0.38C$$

subject to

$$
\begin{aligned}
22A + 28B + 21C &\geq 3 &&\text{(protein units)}\\
16A + 14B + 25C &\geq 2 &&\text{(riboflavin units)}\\
8A + 7B + 9C &\geq 1 &&\text{(phosphorus units)}\\
5A + 0B + 6C &\geq 0.425 &&\text{(magnesium units)}\\
A + B + C &= \tfrac{1}{8} &&\text{(total mix is 2 ounces or } \tfrac{1}{8} \text{ pound)}\\
A, B, C &\geq 0
\end{aligned}
$$

**File: 3-7.xls**

Program 3.7 shows the Excel layout and Solver entries for this LP model. The solution to Whole Food Nutrition Center's problem requires mixing together 0.025 lb of grain $A$, 0.050 lb of grain $B$, and 0.050 lb of grain $C$. Another way of stating this solution is in terms of the proportion of the 2-ounce serving of each grain, namely, $\tfrac{2}{5}$ ounce of grain $A$, $\tfrac{4}{5}$ ounce of grain $B$, and $\tfrac{4}{5}$ ounce of grain $C$ in each serving. The cost per serving is $0.05.

## Ingredient Mix and Blending Problems

Diet and feed mix problems are actually special cases of a more general class of LP problems known as *ingredient* or *blending problems*. Blending problems arise when a decision must be made regarding the blending of two or more products to produce one or more products. Resources, in this case, contain one or more essential ingredients that must be blended so that each final product contains specific percentages of each ingredient. The following example deals with an application frequently seen in the petroleum industry, the blending of crude oils to produce refinable gasoline.

*Major oil refineries use LP for blending crude oils to produce gasoline grades.*

The Low Knock Oil Company produces two grades of cut-rate gasoline for industrial distribution. The grades, regular and economy, are produced by refining a blend of two types of crude oil, type $X100$ and type $X220$. Each crude oil differs not only in cost per barrel, but in composition as well. The following table indicates the percentage of crucial ingredients found in each of the crude oils and the cost per barrel for each:

| CRUDE OIL TYPE | INGREDIENT A (%) | INGREDIENT B (%) | COST/BARREL ($) |
|---|---|---|---|
| X100 | 35 | 55 | 30.00 |
| X220 | 60 | 25 | 34.80 |

**PROGRAM 3.7**

**Excel Layout and Solver Entries for Whole Food Nutrition Center**

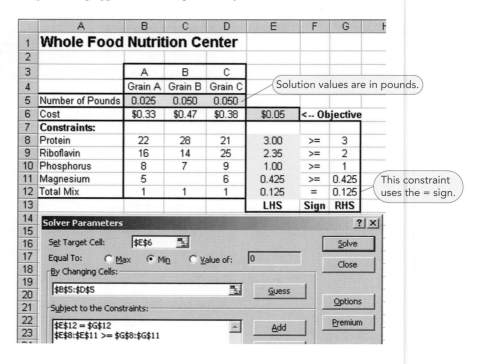

Weekly demand for the regular grade of Low Knock gasoline is at least 25,000 barrels, and demand for the economy grade is at least 32,000 barrels per week. *At least* 45% of each barrel of regular must be ingredient A. *At most* 50% of each barrel of economy should contain ingredient B.

The Low Knock management must decide how many barrels of each type of crude oil to buy each week for blending to satisfy demand at minimum cost. To solve this as an LP problem, the firm lets

$R_1$ = barrels of crude $X100$ blended to produce the refined regular

$E_1$ = barrels of crude $X100$ blended to produce the refined economy

$R_2$ = barrels of crude $X220$ blended to produce the refined regular

$E_2$ = barrels of crude $X220$ blended to produce the refined economy

This problem can be formulated as follows:

Objective:

$$\text{minimize cost} = \$30R_1 + \$30E_1 + \$34.80R_2 + \$34.80E_2$$

subject to

$$R_1 + R_2 \geq 25{,}000 \qquad \text{(demand for regular)}$$
$$E_1 + E_2 \geq 32{,}000 \qquad \text{(demand for economy)}$$

At least 45% of each barrel of regular must be ingredient A.

$$R_1 + R_2 = \text{total amount of crude blended to produce the refined regular gasoline}$$

Thus,

$$0.45(R_1 + R_2) = \text{minimum amount of ingredient A required}$$

But

$$0.35R_1 + 0.60R_2 = \text{amount of ingredient } A \text{ in refined regular gas}$$

So

$$0.35R_1 + 0.60R_2 \geq 0.45R_1 + 0.45R_2$$

or

$$-0.10R_1 + 0.15R_2 \geq 0 \qquad \text{(ingredient } A \text{ in regular constraint)}$$

Similarly, at most 50% of each barrel of economy should be ingredient $B$.

$$E_1 + E_2 = \text{total amount of crude blended to produce the refined economy gasoline}$$

Thus,

$$0.50(E_1 + E_2) = \text{maximum amount of ingredient } B \text{ allowed}$$

But

$$0.55E_1 + 0.25E_2 = \text{amount of ingredient } B \text{ in refined economy gas}$$

So

$$0.55E_1 + 0.25E_2 \leq 0.50E_1 + 0.50E_2$$

or

$$0.05E_1 - 0.25E_2 \leq 0 \qquad \text{(ingredient } B \text{ in economy constraint)}$$

Here is the entire LP formulation:

$$\text{minimize cost} = 30R_1 + 30E_1 + 34.80R_2 + 34.80E_2$$

subject to

$$
\begin{array}{rcrcrcl}
R_1 & & + & & R_2 & & \geq 25{,}000 \\
& E_1 & + & & & E_2 & \geq 32{,}000 \\
-0.10R_1 & & + & & 0.15R_2 & & \geq 0 \\
& 0.05E_1 & & - & & 0.25E_2 & \leq 0 \\
\end{array}
$$
$$R_1, E_1, R_2, E_2 \geq 0$$

Program 3.8 shows the Excel layout and Solver entries for this LP model. The mix will cost Low Knock Oil $1,783,600, and require it to blend the following quantities of crude oil:

**File: 3-8.xls**

$$R_1 = 15{,}000.00 \text{ barrels of } X100 \text{ crude oil into regular}$$

$$E_1 = 26{,}666.67 \text{ barrels of } X100 \text{ crude oil into economy}$$

$$R_2 = 10{,}000.00 \text{ barrels of } X220 \text{ crude oil into regular}$$

$$E_2 = 5{,}333.33 \text{ barrels of } X220 \text{ crude oil into economy}$$

**PROGRAM 3.8**

**Excel Layout and Solver Entries for Low Knock Oil Company**

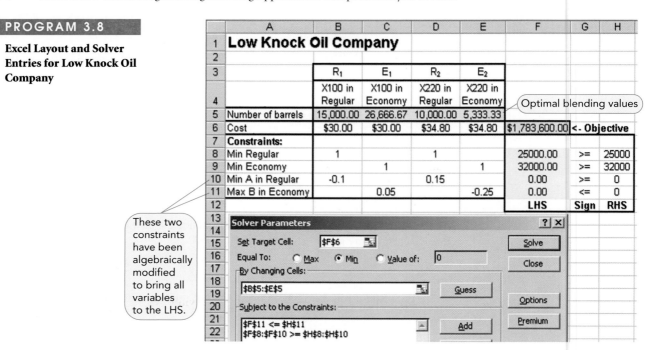

These two constraints have been algebraically modified to bring all variables to the LHS.

## 3.8  MULTIPERIOD APPLICATIONS

*Multiperiod problems are a challenging application of LP.*

Perhaps the most challenging application of LP is in modeling multiperiod scenarios. These are situations in which the decision maker has to determine the optimal decisions for several periods (e.g., weeks, months). What makes these problems especially difficult is that the decision choices in later periods are directly *dependent* on the decisions made in earlier periods. We discuss two examples to illustrate this feature in the following sections. The first example deals with a multiperiod production scheduling problem. The second example involves the establishment of a multiperiod financial sinking fund.

### Production Scheduling

Setting a low-cost production schedule over a period of weeks or months is a difficult and important management problem in most plants. The production manager has to consider many factors: labor capacity, inventory and storage costs, space limitations, product demand, and labor relations. Because most companies produce more than one product, the scheduling process is often quite complex.

Basically, the problem resembles the product mix model for each period in the future. The objective is either to maximize profit or to minimize the total cost (production plus inventory) of carrying out the task.

Production scheduling is amenable to solution by LP because it is a problem that must be solved on a regular basis. When the objective function and constraints for a firm are established, the inputs can easily be changed each month to provide an updated schedule.

*An example of production scheduling: Greenberg Motors*

Greenberg Motors, Inc., manufactures two different electrical motors for sale under contract to Drexel Corp., a well-known producer of small kitchen appliances. Its model GM3A is found in many Drexel food processors, and its model GM3B is used in the assembly of blenders.

Three times each year, the procurement officer at Drexel contracts Irwin Greenberg, the founder of Greenberg Motors, to place a monthly order for each of the coming four

| MODEL | JANUARY | FEBRUARY | MARCH | APRIL |
|-------|---------|----------|-------|-------|
| GM3A | 800 | 700 | 1,000 | 1,100 |
| GM3B | 1,000 | 1,200 | 1,400 | 1,400 |

**TABLE 3.4**

**Four-Month Order Schedule for Electrical Motors**

months. Drexel's demand for motors varies each month based on its own sales forecasts, production capacity, and financial position. Greenberg has just received the January–April order and must begin his own four-month production plan. The demand for motors is shown in Table 3.4.

Production planning at Greenberg Motors must consider four factors:

1. The desirability of producing the same number of each motor each month. This simplifies planning and the scheduling of workers and machines.

2. The necessity to keep down inventory carrying, or holding, costs. This suggests producing in each month only what is needed in that month.

3. Warehouse limitations that cannot be exceeded without great additional storage costs.

4. The company's no-layoff policy, which has been effective in preventing a unionization of the shop. This suggests a minimum production capacity that should be used each month.

Although these four factors often conflict, Greenberg has found that LP is an effective tool in setting up a production schedule that will minimize his total costs of per unit production and monthly holding.

*Double-subscripted variables are often used in LP. Greenberg Motors is more easily formulated with this approach.*

Double-subscripted variables can be used here to develop the LP model. We let

$$P_{A,i} = \text{number of model GM3A motors produced in month } i$$
$$(i = 1, 2, 3, 4 \text{ for January–April})$$

$$P_{B,i} = \text{number of model GM3B motors produced in month } i$$

Production costs are currently $10 per GM3A motor produced and $6 per GM3B unit. A labor agreement going into effect on March 1 will raise each figure by 10%, however. We can write the part of the objective function that deals with production cost as

$$\text{cost of production} = \$10P_{A1} + \$10P_{A2} + \$11P_{A3} + \$11P_{A4} + \$6P_{B1}$$
$$+ \$6P_{B2} + \$6.60P_{B3} + \$6.60P_{B4}$$

To include the inventory carrying costs in the model, we can introduce a second variable. Let

$$I_{A,i} = \text{level of on-hand inventory for GM3A motors at end of month } i$$
$$(i = 1, 2, 3, 4)$$

$$I_{B,i} = \text{level of on-hand inventory for GM3B motors at end of month } i$$

Each GM3A motor held in stock costs $0.18 per month, and each GM3B has a carrying cost of $0.13 per month. Greenberg's accountants allow monthly ending inventories as an acceptable approximation to the average inventory levels during the month. So the carrying cost part of the LP objective function is

$$\text{cost of carrying inventory} = \$0.18I_{A1} + 0.18I_{A2} + 0.18I_{A3} + 0.18I_{A4}$$
$$+ 0.13I_{B1} + 0.13I_{B2} + 0.13I_{B3} + 0.13I_{B4}$$

The total objective function becomes

$$\begin{aligned} \text{minimize total costs} = {} & 10P_{A1} + 10P_{A2} + 11P_{A3} + 11P_{A4} + 6P_{B1} + 6P_{B2} \\ & + 6.6P_{B3} + 6.6P_{B4} + 0.18I_{A1} + 0.18I_{A2} + 0.18I_{A3} + 0.18I_{A4} \\ & + 0.13I_{B1} + 0.13I_{B2} + 0.13I_{B3} + 0.13I_{B4} \end{aligned}$$

*Inventory constraints set the relationship between closing inventory this month, closing inventory last month, this month's production, and sales this month.*

In setting up the constraints, we must recognize the relationship between last month's ending inventory, the current month's production, and the sales to Drexel this month. The inventory at the end of a month is

$$\begin{pmatrix} \text{inventory} \\ \text{at the} \\ \text{end of} \\ \text{this month} \end{pmatrix} = \begin{pmatrix} \text{inventory} \\ \text{at the} \\ \text{end of} \\ \text{last month} \end{pmatrix} + \begin{pmatrix} \text{current} \\ \text{month's} \\ \text{production} \end{pmatrix} - \begin{pmatrix} \text{sales} \\ \text{to Drexel} \\ \text{this month} \end{pmatrix}$$

Suppose that Greenberg is starting the new four-month production cycle with a change in design specifications that left no old motors in stock on January 1. Then, recalling that January's demand for GM3As is 800 and for GM3Bs is 1,000, we can write

$$I_{A1} = 0 + P_{A1} - 800$$

$$I_{B1} = 0 + P_{B1} - 1,000$$

Transposing all unknown variables to the left of the equal sign and multiplying all terms by $-1$, these January constraints can be rewritten as

$$P_{A1} - I_{A1} = 800$$

$$P_{B1} - I_{B1} = 1,000$$

The constraints on demand in February, March, and April follow:

$$\begin{aligned} P_{A2} + I_{A1} - I_{A2} &= \phantom{0,}700 && \text{February GM3A demand} \\ P_{B2} + I_{B1} - I_{B2} &= 1,200 && \text{February GM3B demand} \\ P_{A3} + I_{A2} - I_{A3} &= 1,000 && \text{March GM3A demand} \\ P_{B3} + I_{B2} - I_{B3} &= 1,400 && \text{March GM3B demand} \\ P_{A4} + I_{A3} - I_{A4} &= 1,100 && \text{April GM3A demand} \\ P_{B4} + I_{B3} - I_{B4} &= 1,400 && \text{April GM3B demand} \end{aligned}$$

If Greenberg also wants to have on hand an additional 450 GM3As and 300 GM3Bs at the end of April, we add the constraints

$$I_{A4} = 450$$

$$I_{B4} = 300$$

The constraints discussed address demand; they do not, however, consider warehouse space or labor requirements. First, we note that the storage area for Greenberg Motors can hold a maximum of 3,300 motors of either type (they are similar in size) at any one time. Then

$$I_{A1} + I_{B1} \le 3,300$$

$$I_{A2} + I_{B2} \le 3,300$$

$$I_{A3} + I_{B3} \le 3,300$$

$$I_{A4} + I_{B4} \le 3,300$$

Second, we return to the issue of employment. So that no worker is ever laid off, Greenberg has a base employment level of 2,240 labor hours per month. In a busy period, though, the company can bring two skilled former employees on board (they are now retired) to increase capacity to 2,560 hours per month. Each GM3A motor produced requires 1.3 hours of labor, and each GM3B takes a worker 0.9 hours to assemble.

*Employment constraints are set for each month.*

$$1.3P_{A1} + 0.9P_{B1} \geq 2,240 \quad \text{(January minimum worker hours/month)}$$
$$1.3P_{A1} + 0.9P_{B1} \leq 2,560 \quad \text{(January maximum labor available/month)}$$
$$1.3P_{A2} + 0.9P_{B2} \geq 2,240 \quad \text{(February labor minimum)}$$
$$1.3P_{A2} + 0.9P_{B2} \leq 2,560 \quad \text{(February labor maximum)}$$
$$1.3P_{A3} + 0.9P_{B3} \geq 2,240 \quad \text{(March labor minimum)}$$
$$1.3P_{A3} + 0.9P_{B3} \leq 2,560 \quad \text{(March labor maximum)}$$
$$1.3P_{A4} + 0.9P_{B4} \geq 2,240 \quad \text{(April labor minimum)}$$
$$1.3P_{A4} + 0.9P_{B4} \leq 2,560 \quad \text{(April labor maximum)}$$
$$\text{All variables} \geq 0$$

**File: 3-9.xls**

There are several ways of setting up the Greenberg Motors problem on Excel. The setup shown in Program 3.9A follows the same logic we have used in all problems so far; that is, all parameters associated with a specific decision variable are modeled in the same column. The solution, summarized in Table 3.5, indicates that the four-month total cost is $76,301.61.

For such multiperiod problems, it may often be more convenient to group all the variables for a given month in the same column. Program 3.9B shows an alternate model for the Greenberg Motors problem. Note that in this model, the only decision variables are the production variables. The inventory variables are no longer explicitly stated as decision variables (changing cells in Solver). Rather, they are calculated as simple by-products of the other parameters in the problem. That is, using the standard inventory constraints, the ending inventory each month is calculated as follows:

*Ending inventory is not set as a decision variable in this alternate Excel layout for the Greenberg Motors problem.*

$$\begin{pmatrix} \text{inventory} \\ \text{at the} \\ \text{end of} \\ \text{this month} \end{pmatrix} = \begin{pmatrix} \text{inventory} \\ \text{at the} \\ \text{end of} \\ \text{last month} \end{pmatrix} + \begin{pmatrix} \text{current} \\ \text{month's} \\ \text{production} \end{pmatrix} - \begin{pmatrix} \text{sales} \\ \text{to Drexel} \\ \text{this month} \end{pmatrix}$$

$$\text{Row 8} \quad = \quad \text{Row 5} \quad + \quad \text{Row 6} \quad - \quad \text{Row 7}$$

Since they are no longer decision variables, however, we do need to add constraints to ensure that the ending inventories have nonnegative values. Depending on individual preferences and expertise, we can design other layouts for setting up and solving this problem using Excel.

| TABLE 3.5 | | | | | |
|---|---|---|---|---|---|
| **Solution to Greenberg Motor Problem** | **PRODUCTION SCHEDULE** | **JANUARY** | **FEBRUARY** | **MARCH** | **APRIL** |
| | Units of GM3A produced | 1,277 | 1,138 | 842 | 792 |
| | Units of GM3B produced | 1,000 | 1,200 | 1,400 | 1,700 |
| | Inventory of GM3A carried | 477 | 915 | 758 | 450 |
| | Inventory of GM3B carried | 0 | 0 | 0 | 300 |
| | Labor hours required | 2,560 | 2,560 | 2,355 | 2,560 |

**PROGRAM 3.9A**    **Excel Layout and Solver Entries for Greenberg Motors**

> All entries in column R are computed using the SUMPRODUCT function.

| | A | B | C | D | E | F | G | H | I | J | K | L | M | N | O | P | Q | R | S | T |
|---|---|---|---|---|---|---|---|---|---|---|---|---|---|---|---|---|---|---|---|---|
| 1 | **Greenberg Motors** | | | | | | | | | | | | | | | | | | | |
| 2 | | | | | | | | | | | | | | | | | | | | |
| 3 | | $P_{A1}$ | $I_{A1}$ | $P_{A2}$ | $I_{A2}$ | $P_{A3}$ | $I_{A3}$ | $P_{A4}$ | $I_{A4}$ | $P_{B1}$ | $I_{B1}$ | $P_{B2}$ | $I_{B2}$ | $P_{B3}$ | $I_{B3}$ | $P_{B4}$ | $I_{B4}$ | | | |
| 4 | | GM3A Jan Prod | GM3A Jan Inv | GM3A Feb Prod | GM3A Feb Inv | GM3A Mar Prod | GM3A Mar Inv | GM3A Apr Prod | GM3A Apr Inv | GM3B Jan Prod | GM3B Jan Inv | GM3B Feb Prod | GM3B Feb Inv | GM3B Mar Prod | GM3B Mar Inv | GM3B Apr Prod | GM3B Apr Inv | | | |
| 5 | Number of Units | 1,276.92 | 476.92 | 1,138.46 | 915.38 | 842.31 | 757.69 | 792.31 | 450.00 | 1,000.00 | 0.00 | 1,200.00 | 0.00 | 1,400.00 | 0.00 | 1,700.00 | 300.00 | | | |
| 6 | Cost | $10.00 | $0.18 | $10.00 | $0.18 | $11.00 | $0.18 | $11.00 | $0.18 | $6.00 | $0.13 | $6.00 | $0.13 | $6.60 | $0.13 | $6.60 | $0.13 | $76,301.62 | <- Objective | |
| 7 | Constraints: | | | | | | | | | | | | | | | | | | | |
| 8 | GM3A Jan Demand | 1 | -1 | | | | | | | | | | | | | | | 800.00 | = | 800 |
| 9 | GM3B Jan Demand | | | | | | | | | 1 | -1 | | | | | | | 1000.00 | = | 1000 |
| 10 | GM3A Feb Demand | | 1 | 1 | -1 | | | | | | | | | | | | | 700.00 | = | 700 |
| 11 | GM3B Feb Demand | | | | | | | | | | 1 | 1 | -1 | | | | | 1200.00 | = | 1200 |
| 12 | GM3A Mar Demand | | | | 1 | 1 | -1 | | | | | | | | | | | 1000.00 | = | 1000 |
| 13 | GM3B Mar Demand | | | | | | | | | | | | 1 | 1 | -1 | | | 1400.00 | = | 1400 |
| 14 | GM3A Apr Demand | | | | | | 1 | 1 | -1 | | | | | | | | | 1100.00 | = | 1100 |
| 15 | GM3B Apr Demand | | | | | | | | | | | | | | 1 | 1 | -1 | 1400.00 | = | 1400 |
| 16 | GM3A Apr Inv | | | | | | | | 1 | | | | | | | | | 450.00 | = | 450 |
| 17 | GM3B Apr Inv | | | | | | | | | | | | | | | | 1 | 300.00 | = | 300 |
| 18 | Jan Warehouse Cap | | 1 | | | | | | | | 1 | | | | | | | 476.92 | <= | 3300 |
| 19 | Feb Warehouse Cap | | | | 1 | | | | | | | | 1 | | | | | 915.38 | <= | 3300 |
| 20 | Mar Warehouse Cap | | | | | | 1 | | | | | | | | 1 | | | 757.69 | <= | 3300 |
| 21 | Apr Warehouse Cap | | | | | | | | 1 | | | | | | | | 1 | 750.00 | <= | 3300 |
| 22 | Jan Labor Maximum | 1.3 | | | | | | | | 0.9 | | | | | | | | 2560.00 | <= | 2560 |
| 23 | Feb Labor Maximum | | | 1.3 | | | | | | | | 0.9 | | | | | | 2560.00 | <= | 2560 |
| 24 | Mar Labor Maximum | | | | | 1.3 | | | | | | | | 0.9 | | | | 2355.00 | <= | 2560 |
| 25 | Apr Labor Maximum | | | | | | | 1.3 | | | | | | | | 0.9 | | 2560.00 | <= | 2560 |
| 26 | Jan Labor Minimum | 1.3 | | | | | | | | 0.9 | | | | | | | | 2560.00 | >= | 2240 |
| 27 | Feb Labor Minimum | | | 1.3 | | | | | | | | 0.9 | | | | | | 2560.00 | >= | 2240 |
| 28 | Mar Labor Minimum | | | | | 1.3 | | | | | | | | 0.9 | | | | 2355.00 | >= | 2240 |
| 29 | Apr Labor Minimum | | | | | | | 1.3 | | | | | | | | 0.9 | | 2560.00 | >= | 2240 |
| 30 | | | | | | | | | | | | | | | | | | LHS | Sign | RHS |

**Solver Parameters**

Set Target Cell: $R$6

Equal To:  ○ Max  ● Min  ○ Value of: 0

By Changing Cells:

$B$5:$Q$5

Subject to the Constraints:

$R$18:$R$25 <= $T$18:$T$25
$R$26:$R$29 >= $T$26:$T$29
$R$8:$R$17 = $T$8:$T$17

[Solve] [Close] [Guess] [Options] [Premium] [Add] [Change]

> Solver includes three entries: One for each type of constraints ≤, ≥, and =.

The Greenberg Motors example illustrates a relatively simple production planning problem in that there were only two products being considered. The LP model discussed here can, however, be applied successfully to problems with dozens of products and hundreds of constraints.

## Sinking Fund

Another excellent example of a multiperiod problem is the sinking fund problem. In this case, an investor or firm seeks to establish an investment portfolio using the least possible initial investment that will generate specific amounts of capital at specific time periods in the future.

Consider the example of Larry Fredendall, who is trying to plan for his daughter Susan's college expenses. Based on current projections (it is now the start of year 1),

**PROGRAM 3.9B**    **Alternate Excel Layout and Solver Entries for Greenberg Motors**

Begin inventory in February = Ending inventory in January

Only decision variables are the production quantities.

# Greenberg Motors (Alternate Model)

| | A | B | C | D | E | F | G | H | I | J | K | L |
|---|---|---|---|---|---|---|---|---|---|---|---|---|
| 3 | | P_A1 | P_A2 | P_A3 | P_A4 | P_B1 | P_B2 | P_B3 | P_B4 | | | |
| 4 | | GM3A January | GM3A February | GM3A March | GM3A April | GM3B January | GM3B February | GM3B March | GM3B April | | | |
| 5 | Begin Inventory | 0 | 476.9 | 915.38 | 757.6923 | 0 | 0 | 0 | 0 | | | |
| 6 | Production | 1,276.92 | 1,138.46 | 842.31 | 792.31 | 1,000.00 | 1,200.00 | 1,400.00 | 1,700.00 | | | |
| 7 | Demand | 800 | 700 | 1000 | 1100 | 1000 | 1200 | 1400 | 1400 | | | |
| 8 | Ending Inventory | 476.92 | 915.38 | 757.69 | 450.00 | 0.00 | 0.00 | 0.00 | 300.00 | | | |
| 9 | | | | | | | | | | | | |
| 10 | | Total inv | Sign | Cap | | | Needed | Min (>=) | Max (<=) | | | |
| 11 | Jan Warehouse | 476.9 | <= | 3300 | | Jan Labor | 2560.0 | 2240 | 2560 | | | |
| 12 | Feb Warehouse | 915.4 | <= | 3300 | | Feb Labor | 2,560.0 | 2240 | 2560 | | | |
| 13 | Mar Warehouse | 757.7 | <= | 3300 | | Mar Labor | 2,355.0 | 2240 | 2560 | | | |
| 14 | Apr Warehouse | 750.0 | <= | 3300 | | Apr Labor | 2,560.0 | 2240 | 2560 | | | |
| 15 | | | | | | | | | | | | |
| 16 | | Have | Sign | Need | | | | | | | | |
| 17 | GM3A Apr Inv | 450 | = | 450 | | | | | | | | |
| 18 | GM3B Apr Inv | 300 | = | 300 | | | | | | | | |
| 19 | | | | | | | | | | | | |
| 20 | Prod Cost | $10.00 | $10.00 | $11.00 | $11.00 | $6.00 | $6.00 | $6.60 | $6.60 | $75,794.62 | | |
| 21 | Inv Cost | $0.18 | $0.18 | $0.18 | $0.18 | $0.13 | $0.13 | $0.13 | $0.13 | $507.00 | | |
| 22 | | | | | | | | | Total Cost = | $76,301.62 | | |

**Solver Parameters**

Set Target Cell: $J$22
Equal To: Max / Min
By Changing Cells: $B$6:$I$6
Subject to the Constraints:
$B$11:$B$14 <= $D$11:$D$14
$B$17:$B$18 = $D$17:$D$18
$B$8:$I$8 >= 0
$G$11:$G$14 <= $I$11:$I$14
$G$11:$G$14 >= $H$11:$H$14

Ensure ending inventories are ≥ 0.

Ending inventories are *not* decision variables in this implementation.

Ending inventory = Begin inventory + Production – Demand
Row 8 = Row 5 + Row 6 – Row 7

The SUMPRODUCT function is used to compute cells J20 & J21. Formula in J20 = SUMPRODUCT (B20:I20, B6:I6) formula in cell J21 = SUMPRODUCT (B21:I21, B8:I8)

Total cost is the same as that in Program 3.9A.

Larry anticipates that his financial needs at the start of each of the following years is as follows:

| Year 3 | $20,000 |
|---|---|
| Year 4 | $22,000 |
| Year 5 | $24,000 |
| Year 6 | $26,000 |

Larry has several investment choices (assume these are tax free if used for education) to choose from at the present time, as listed in Table 3.6. Each choice has a fixed known return on investment and a specified maturity date. Assume that each choice is available for investment at the start of every year. Since choices C and D are relatively risky choices, Larry wants no more than 20% of his total investment in those two choices at any point in time.

TABLE 3.6

**Investment Choices for
Larry Fredendall**

| CHOICE | ROI | MATURITY |
|--------|-----|----------|
| A | 5% | 1 year |
| B | 13% | 2 years |
| C | 28% | 3 years |
| D | 40% | 4 years |

Larry wants to establish a sinking fund to meet his requirements. Note that at the start of year 1, the entire initial investment is available for investing in the choices. However, in subsequent years, only the amount maturing from a prior investment is available for investment.

Let us first define the following decision variables. Note that in defining these variables, we need to consider only those investments that will mature by the end of year 5, at the latest, since there is no requirement after 6 years.

$$A_1 = \$ \text{ amount invested in choice } A \text{ at the start of year 1}$$

$$B_1 = \$ \text{ amount invested in choice } B \text{ at the start of year 1}$$

$$C_1 = \$ \text{ amount invested in choice } C \text{ at the start of year 1}$$

$$D_1 = \$ \text{ amount invested in choice } D \text{ at the start of year 1}$$

$$A_2 = \$ \text{ amount invested in choice } A \text{ at the start of year 2}$$

$$B_2 = \$ \text{ amount invested in choice } B \text{ at the start of year 2}$$

$$C_2 = \$ \text{ amount invested in choice } C \text{ at the start of year 2}$$

$$D_2 = \$ \text{ amount invested in choice } D \text{ at the start of year 2}$$

$$A_3 = \$ \text{ amount invested in choice } A \text{ at the start of year 3}$$

$$B_3 = \$ \text{ amount invested in choice } B \text{ at the start of year 3}$$

$$C_3 = \$ \text{ amount invested in choice } C \text{ at the start of year 3}$$

$$A_4 = \$ \text{ amount invested in choice } A \text{ at the start of year 4}$$

$$B_4 = \$ \text{ amount invested in choice } B \text{ at the start of year 4}$$

$$A_5 = \$ \text{ amount invested in choice } A \text{ at the start of year 5}$$

The objective is to minimize the initial investment and can be expressed as

$$\text{Minimize } A_1 + B_1 + C_1 + D_1$$

As in the multiperiod production scheduling problem, we need to recognize the relationship between the investment decisions made in any given year and the investment decisions made in all prior years. Specifically, we need to ensure that the amount used for investment at the start of a given year is restricted to the amount maturing at the end of the previous year *less* any payments made for Susan's education that year. This relationship can be modeled as

*This equation is analogous to the inventory equations in the production scheduling problem.*

Amount invested at start of year $i$  +  Amount paid for education at start of year $i$
= Amounts maturing at the end of year $(i - 1)$

At the start of year 2, the total amount maturing is $1.05A_1$ (investment in choice $A$ in year 1 plus 5% interest). The constraint at the start of year 2 can therefore be written as

$$A_2 + B_2 + C_2 + D_2 = 1.05A_1 \quad \text{(Year 2 cash flow)}$$

*Cash flow constraints*

or

$$1.05A_1 - A_2 - B_2 - C_2 - D_2 = 0$$

Constraints at the start of years 3 through 6 are as follows and also include the amounts payable for Susan's education each year:

$$A_3 + B_3 + C_3 + 20{,}000 = 1.13B_1 + 1.05A_2 \qquad \text{(Year 3 cash flow)}$$

or

$$1.13B_1 + 1.05A_2 - A_3 - B_3 - C_3 = 20{,}000$$

$$A_4 + B_4 + 22{,}000 = 1.28C_1 + 1.13B_2 + 1.05A_3 \qquad \text{(Year 4 cash flow)}$$

or

$$1.28C_1 + 1.13B_2 + 1.05A_3 - A_4 - B_4 = 22{,}000$$

$$A_5 + 24{,}000 = 1.4D_1 + 1.28C_2 + 1.13B_3 + 1.05A_4 \qquad \text{(Year 5 cash flow)}$$

or

$$1.4D_1 + 1.28C_2 + 1.13B_3 + 1.05A_4 - A_5 = 24{,}000$$

$$26{,}000 = 1.4D_2 + 1.28C_3 + 1.13B_4 + 1.05A_5 \qquad \text{(Year 6 cash flow)}$$

or

$$1.4D_2 + 1.28C_3 + 1.13B_4 + 1.05A_5 = 26{,}000$$

These five constraints address the cash flow issues. However, they do not account for Larry's risk preference with regard to investments in choices $C$ and $D$ in any given year. To satisfy these requirements, we need to ensure that total investment in choices $C$ and $D$ in any year is no more than 20% of the total investment in *all* choices that year. In keeping track of these investments, it is important to also account for investments in *prior* years that may have still not matured. At the start of year 1, this constraint can be written as

$$C_1 + D_1 \le 0.2(A_1 + B_1 + C_1 + D_1)$$

or

$$0.8(C_1 + D_1) - 0.2(A_1 + B_1) \le 0 \qquad \text{(Year 1 risk)}$$

*Risk preference constraints*

In writing this constraint at the start of year 2, we must take into account the fact that investments $B_1$, $C_1$, and $D_1$ have still not matured. Therefore,

$$C_1 + D_1 + C_2 + D_2 \le 0.2(B_1 + C_1 + D_1 + A_2 + B_2 + C_2 + D_2)$$

or

$$0.8(C_1 + D_1 + C_2 + D_2) - 0.2(B_1 + A_2 + B_2) \le 0 \qquad \text{(Year 2 risk)}$$

Constraints at the start of years 3 through 5 are as follows. Note that there is no constraint necessary at the start of year 6 since there are no investments that year.

$$C_1 + D_1 + C_2 + D_2 + C_3 \le 0.2(C_1 + D_1 + B_2 + C_2 + D_2 + A_3 + B_3 + C_3)$$

or

$$0.8(C_1 + D_1 + C_2 + D_2 + C_3) - 0.2(B_2 + A_3 + B_3) \le 0 \quad \text{(Year 3 risk)}$$

**PROGRAM 3.10**          **Excel Layout and Solver Entries for Larry Fredendall's Sinking Fund**

Decision variables are arranged on a yearly basis.

| | A | B | C | D | E | F | G | H | I | J | K | L | M | N | O | P | Q | R |
|---|---|---|---|---|---|---|---|---|---|---|---|---|---|---|---|---|---|---|
| 1 | **Larry Fredendall's Sinking Fund** | | | | | | | | | | | | | | | | | |
| 2 | | | | | | | | | | | | | | | | | | |
| 3 | | $A_1$ | $B_1$ | $C_1$ | $D_1$ | $A_2$ | $B_2$ | $C_2$ | $D_2$ | $A_3$ | $B_3$ | $C_3$ | $A_4$ | $B_4$ | $A_5$ | | | |
| 4 | | Inv A Year 1 | Inv B Year 1 | Inv C Year 1 | Inv D Year 1 | Inv A Year 2 | Inv B Year 2 | Inv C Year 2 | Inv D Year 2 | Inv A Year 3 | Inv B Year 3 | Inv C Year 3 | Inv A Year 4 | Inv B Year 4 | Inv A Year 5 | | | |
| 5 | $ Invested | 0.00 | 61,064.11 | 3,804.66 | 8,445.95 | 0.00 | 0.00 | 0.00 | 0.00 | 38,227.50 | 10,774.93 | 0.00 | 0.00 | 23,008.85 | 0.00 | | | |
| 6 | Objective Coefficient | 1 | 1 | 1 | 1 | | | | | | | | | | | $73,314.71 | <- Objective | |
| 7 | **Constraints:** | | | | | | | | | | | | | | | | | |
| 8 | Year 2 Investments | 1.05 | | | | -1 | -1 | -1 | -1 | | | | | | | 0.00 | = | 0 |
| 9 | Year 3 Investments | | 1.13 | | | 1.05 | | | | -1 | -1 | -1 | | | | 20000.00 | = | 20000 |
| 10 | Year 4 Investments | | | 1.28 | | | 1.13 | | | 1.05 | | | -1 | -1 | | 22000.00 | = | 22000 |
| 11 | Year 5 Investments | | | | 1.40 | | | 1.28 | | | 1.13 | | 1.05 | | -1 | 24000.00 | = | 24000 |
| 12 | Year 6 Investments | | | | | | | | 1.40 | | | 1.28 | | 1.13 | 1.05 | 26000.00 | = | 26000 |
| 13 | Year 1 Risk | -0.2 | -0.2 | 0.8 | 0.8 | | | | | | | | | | | -2412.33 | <= | 0 |
| 14 | Year 2 Risk | | -0.2 | 0.8 | 0.8 | -0.2 | -0.2 | 0.8 | 0.8 | | | | | | | -2412.33 | <= | 0 |
| 15 | Year 3 Risk | | | 0.8 | 0.8 | | -0.2 | 0.8 | 0.8 | -0.2 | -0.2 | 0.8 | | | | 0.00 | <= | 0 |
| 16 | Year 4 Risk | | | | 0.8 | | | 0.8 | 0.8 | | -0.2 | 0.8 | -0.2 | -0.2 | | 0.00 | <= | 0 |
| 17 | Year 5 Risk | | | | | | | | 0.8 | | | 0.8 | | -0.2 | -0.2 | -4601.77 | <= | 0 |
| 18 | | | | | | | | | | | | | | | | LHS | Sign | RHS |

All constraints have been algebraically modified to bring all variables to the LHS.

These are the cash requirements each year.

**Solver Parameters**

Set Target Cell: $P$6

Equal To:  ○ Max  ● Min  ○ Value of: 0

By Changing Cells:

$B$5:$O$5

Subject to the Constraints:

$P$13:$P$17 <= $R$13:$R$17
$P$8:$P$12 = $R$8:$R$12

Solve  Close  Guess  Options  Add  Premium

$$D_1 + C_2 + D_2 + C_3 \leq 0.2(D_1 + C_2 + D_2 + B_3 + C_3 + A_4 + B_4)$$

or

$$0.8(D_1 + C_2 + D_2 + C_3) - 0.2(B_3 + A_4 + B_4) \leq 0 \qquad \text{(Year 4 risk)}$$

$$D_2 + C_3 \leq 0.2(D_2 + C_3 + B_4 + A_5)$$

or

$$0.8(D_2 + C_3) - 0.2(B_4 + A_5) \leq 0 \qquad \text{(Year 5 risk)}$$

All variables $\geq 0$

**File: 3-10.xls**

Program 3.10 shows the Excel layout and Solver entries for this model. As with the production scheduling problem, there are several ways in which this model could have been structured, depending on preference and expertise of the analyst.

The optimal solution requires Larry to invest a total of $73,314.71 at the start of year 1, putting $61,064.11 in choice B, $3,804.66 in choice C, and $8,445.95 in choice D. There is no money maturing for investment at the start of year 2. At the start of year 3, using the maturing amounts, Larry should pay off $20,000 for Susan's education, invest $38,227.50 in choice A, and invest $10,774.93 in choice C. At the start of year 4, Larry should use the maturing amounts to pay off $22,000 for Susan's education and invest $23,008.85 in choice B. The investments in place at this time will generate $24,000 at the start of year 5 and $26,000 at the start of year 6, meeting Larry's requirements in those years.

## SUMMARY

This chapter continues the discussion of LP models. To show ways of formulating and solving problems from a variety of disciplines, we examine applications from marketing, manufacturing, employee scheduling, finance, transportation, ingredient blending, and multiperiod planning. We also illustrate how to set up and solve all these models using Excel's Solver add-in.

■ Before taking the self-test, refer back to the learning objectives at the beginning of the chapter, the notes in the margins, and the glossary at the end of the chapter.

■ Use the key at the back of the book to correct your answers.

■ Restudy pages that correspond to any questions that you answered incorrectly or material you feel uncertain about.

1. Linear programming can be used to select effective media mixes, allocate fixed or limited budgets across media, and maximize audience exposure.
   a. True  b. False
2. Blending problems arise when one must decide which of two or more ingredients is to be chosen to produce a product.
   a. True  b. False
3. The only objective functions that are allowed for LP problems are maximizing profits or minimizing costs.
   a. True  b. False
4. When setting up LP models on Excel, you are always required to manipulate constraints so that all variables appear on the left-hand side.
   a. True  b. False
5. Using LP to maximize audience exposure in an advertising campaign is an example of the type of LP application known as
   a. marketing research.
   b. media selection.
   c. portfolio assessment.
   d. media budgeting.
   e. all of the above.
6. The following does not represent a factor a manager might consider when employing LP for a production scheduling
   a. labor capacity
   b. space limitations
   c. product demand
   d. risk assessment
   e. inventory costs
7. Labor planning is a type of LP problem that
   a. is used to address staffing needs over a specific time period.
   b. is useful when there is flexibility in assigning workers to jobs requiring interchangeable talents.
   c. is frequently used by large banks.
   d. might be used to determine teller assignments in banks.
   e. all of the above.

8. When applying LP to diet problems, the objective function is usually designed to
   a. maximize profits from blends of nutrients.
   b. maximize ingredient blends.
   c. minimize production losses.
   d. maximize the number of products to be produced.
   e. minimize the costs of nutrient blends.
9. The diet problem is
   a. also called the feed mix problem in agriculture.
   b. a special case of the ingredient mix problem.
   c. a special case of the blending problem.
   d. all of the above.
10. Determining the most efficient allocation of people, machines, equipment, and so on is characteristic of the LP problem type known as
    a. production scheduling.
    b. labor planning.
    c. assignment.
    d. blending.
    e. none of the above.
11. The selection of specific investments from among a wide variety of alternatives is the type of LP problem known as
    a. the product mix problem.
    b. the investment banker problem.
    c. the portfolio selection problem.
    d. the Wall Street problem.
    e. none of the above.
12. A type of LP problem that is used in marketing is called
    a. the 4P problem.
    b. the Madison Avenue problem.
    c. the marketing research problem.
    d. all of the above.
13. An LP problem in which decisions made in one period affect decisions made in future periods is typically called a
    a. sequential problem.
    b. multiperiod problem.
    c. periodic problem.
    d. none of the above.

## PROBLEMS

• 3-1 (Product mix) Winkler Furniture manufactures two different types of china cabinets, a French Provincial model and a Danish Modern model. Each cabinet produced must go through three departments: carpentry, painting, and finishing. The table at the top of page 106 contains all relevant information concerning production times per cabinet produced and production capacities for each operation per day, along with net

revenue per unit produced. The firm has a contract with an Indiana distributor to produce a minimum of 300 of each cabinet per week (or 60 cabinets per day). Owner Bob Winkler would like to determine a product mix to maximize his daily revenue.

(a) Formulate as an LP problem.
(b) Solve using Excel.

**Table for Problem 3-1**

| CABINET STYLE | CARPENTRY (HOURS/CABINET) | PAINTING (HOURS/CABINET) | FINISHING (HOURS/CABINET) | NET REVENUE/CABINET ($) |
|---|---|---|---|---|
| French Provincial | 3 | $1\frac{1}{2}$ | $\frac{3}{4}$ | 28 |
| Danish Modern | 2 | 1 | $\frac{3}{4}$ | 25 |
| Department capacity (hours) | 360 | 200 | 125 | |

**3-2** *(Investment decision)* The Heinlein and Krampf Brokerage firm has just been instructed by one of its clients to invest $250,000 for her, money obtained recently through the sale of land holdings in Ohio. The client has a good deal of trust in the investment house, but she also has her own ideas about the distribution of the funds being invested. In particular, she requests that the firm select whatever stocks and bonds they believe are well rated, but within the following guidelines:

1. Municipal bonds should constitute at least 20% of the investment.
2. At least 40% of the funds should be placed in a combination of electronics firms, aerospace firms, and drug manufacturers.
3. No more than 50% of the amount invested in municipal bonds should be placed in a high-risk, high-yield nursing home stock.

Subject to these restraints, the client's goal is to maximize projected return on investments. The analysts at Heinlein and Krampf, aware of these guidelines, prepare a list of high-quality stocks and bonds and their corresponding rates of return.

| INVESTMENT | PROJECTED RATE OF RETURN (%) |
|---|---|
| Los Angeles municipal bonds | 5.3 |
| Thompson Electronics, Inc. | 6.8 |
| United Aerospace Corp. | 4.9 |
| Palmer Drugs | 8.4 |
| Happy Days Nursing Homes | 11.8 |

(a) Formulate this portfolio selection problem using LP.
(b) Solve this problem using Excel.

**3-3** *(Restaurant work scheduling)* The famous Y. S. Chang Restaurant is open 24 hours a day. Waiters and busboys report for duty at 3 A.M., 7 A.M., 11 A.M., 3 P.M., 7 P.M., or 11 P.M., and each works an 8-hour shift. The following table shows the minimum number of workers needed during the six period into which the day is divided. Chang's scheduling problem is to determine how many waiters and busboys should report for work at the start of each time period to minimize the total staff required for one day's operation. (*Hint:* Let $X_i$ equal the number of waiters and busboys beginning work in time period $i$, where $i = 1, 2, 3, 4, 5, 6$.)

| PERIOD | TIME | NUMBER OF WAITERS AND BUSBOYS REQUIRED |
|---|---|---|
| 1 | 3 A.M.–7 A.M. | 3 |
| 2 | 7 A.M.–11 A.M. | 12 |
| 3 | 11 A.M.–3 P.M. | 16 |
| 4 | 3 P.M.–7 P.M. | 9 |
| 5 | 7 P.M.–11 P.M. | 11 |
| 6 | 11 P.M.–3 A.M. | 4 |

**3-4** *(Animal feed mix)* The Battery Park Stable feeds and houses the horses used to pull tourist-filled carriages through the streets of Charleston's historic waterfront area. The stable owner, an ex–racehorse trainer, recognizes the need to set a nutritional diet for the horses in his care. At the same time, he would like to keep the overall daily cost of feed to a minimum.

The feed mixes available for the horses' diet are an oat product, a highly enriched grain, and a mineral product. Each of these mixes contains a certain amount of five ingredients needed daily to keep the average horse healthy. The table at the top of page 107 shows these minimum requirements, units of each ingredient per pound of feed mix, and costs for the three mixes.

In addition, the stable owner is aware that an overfed horse is a sluggish worker. Consequently, he determines that 6 pounds of feed per day is the most that any horse needs to function properly. Formulate this problem and solve for the optimal daily mix of the three feeds.

**3-5** *(Media selection)* The advertising director for Diversey Paint and Supply, a chain of four retail stores on Chicago's North Side, is considering two media possibilities. One plan is for a series of half-page ads in the Sunday *Chicago Tribune* newspaper, and the other is for advertising time on Chicago TV. The stores are expanding their lines of do-it-yourself tools, and the advertising director is interested in an exposure level of at least 40% within the city's neighborhoods and 60% in northwest suburban areas.

The TV viewing time under consideration has an exposure rating per spot of 5% in city homes and 3% in the northwest suburbs. The Sunday newspaper has corresponding exposure rates of 4% and 3% per ad. The cost of a half-page *Tribune* advertisement is $925; a television spot costs $2,000.

**Table for Problem 3-4**

| Diet Requirement (Ingredients) | Oat Product (Units/lb) | Enriched Grain (Units/lb) | Mineral Product (Units/lb) | Minimum Daily Requirement (Units) |
|---|---|---|---|---|
| A | 2 | 3 | 1 | 6 |
| B | $\frac{1}{2}$ | 1 | $\frac{1}{2}$ | 2 |
| C | 3 | 5 | 6 | 9 |
| D | 1 | $1\frac{1}{2}$ | 2 | 8 |
| E | $\frac{1}{2}$ | $\frac{1}{2}$ | $1\frac{1}{2}$ | 5 |
| Cost/lb | $0.09 | $0.14 | $0.17 | |

Diversey Paint would like to select the least costly advertising strategy that would meet desired exposure levels.

(a) Formulate using LP.
(b) Solve the problem using Excel.

**3-6** *(Project scheduling)* Capitol Hill Construction Company (CHCC) must complete its current office building renovation as quickly as possible. The first portion of the project consists of six activities, some of which must be finished before others are started. The activities, their precedences, and their estimated times are shown in this table:

| Activity | | Precedence | Time (Days) |
|---|---|---|---|
| Prepare financing options | (A) | — | 2 |
| Prepare preliminary sketches | (B) | — | 3 |
| Outline specifications | (C) | — | 1 |
| Prepare drawings | (D) | A | 4 |
| Write specifications | (E) | C and D | 5 |
| Run off prints | (F) | B | 1 |

Let $X_i$ represent the earliest completion of an activity where $i$ = A, B, C, D, E, F. Formulate and solve CHCC's problem as a linear program.

**3-7** *(Ingredient mix)* Bob Bell's fortieth birthday party promised to be the social event of the year in Cookeville. To prepare, Bob stocked up on the following liquors:

| Liquor | Amount on Hand (Ounces) |
|---|---|
| Bourbon | 52 |
| Brandy | 38 |
| Vodka | 64 |
| Dry vermouth | 24 |
| Sweet vermouth | 36 |

Bob decides to mix four drinks for the party: Chaunceys, Sweet Italians, bourbon on the rocks, and

Russian martinis. A Chauncey consists of $\frac{1}{4}$ bourbon, $\frac{1}{4}$ vodka, $\frac{1}{4}$ brandy, and $\frac{1}{4}$ sweet vermouth. A Sweet Italian contains $\frac{1}{4}$ brandy, $\frac{1}{2}$ sweet vermouth, and $\frac{1}{4}$ dry vermouth. Bourbon on the rocks contains only bourbon. Finally, a Russian martini consists of $\frac{1}{3}$ dry vermouth and $\frac{2}{3}$ vodka. Each drink contains 4 fluid ounces.

Bob's objective is to mix these ingredients in such a way as to make the largest possible number of drinks in advance.

(a) Formulate using LP.
(b) Solve using Excel.

**3-8** *(Pricing and marketing strategy)* The I. Kruger Paint and Wallpaper Store is a large retail distributor of the Supertrex brand of vinyl wall coverings. Kruger will enhance its citywide image in Miami if it can outsell other local stores in total number of rolls of Supertex next year. It is able to estimate the demand function as follows:

> Number of rolls of Supertrex sold
> = 20 × dollars spent on advertising
> + 6.8 × dollars spent on in-store displays
> + 12 × dollars invested in on-hand wallpaper inventory
> − 65,000 × percentage markup taken above wholesale cost of a roll

The store budgets a total of $17,000 for advertising, in-store displays, and on-hand inventory of Supertrex for next year. It decides it must spend at least $3,000 on advertising; in addition, at least 5% of the amount invested in on-hand inventory should be devoted to displays. Markups on Supertrex seen at other local stores range from 20% to 45%. Kruger decides that its markup had best be in this range as well.

(a) Formulate as an LP problem.
(b) Solve the problem using Excel.
(c) What is the difficulty with the answer?
(d) What constraint would you add?

**3-9** *(College meal selection)* Kathy Roniger, campus dietician for a small Idaho college, is responsible for formulating a nutritious meal plan for students. For an evening meal, she feels that the following five meal-content requirements should be met: (1) between 900

**Table for Problem 3-9**

| FOOD ITEM | TABLE OF FOOD VALUES* AND COSTS | | | | | |
| | CALORIES/ POUND | IRON (MG/LB) | FAT (GM/LB) | PROTEIN (GM/LB) | CARBOHYDRATES (GM/LB) | COST/ POUND ($) |
|---|---|---|---|---|---|---|
| Milk | 295 | 0.2 | 16 | 16 | 22 | 0.60 |
| Ground meat | 1216 | 0.2 | 96 | 81 | 0 | 2.35 |
| Chicken | 394 | 4.3 | 9 | 74 | 0 | 1.15 |
| Fish | 358 | 3.2 | 0.5 | 83 | 0 | 2.25 |
| Beans | 128 | 3.2 | 0.8 | 7 | 28 | 0.58 |
| Spinach | 118 | 14.1 | 1.4 | 14 | 19 | 1.17 |
| Potatoes | 279 | 2.2 | 0.5 | 8 | 63 | 0.33 |

*Source:* C. F. Church and H. N. Church. *Bowes and Church's Food Values of Portions Commonly Used*, 12/e. Philadelphia: J.B. Lippincott, 1975.

and 1,500 calories; (2) at least 4 milligrams of iron; (3) no more than 50 grams of fat; (4) at least 26 grams of protein; and (5) no more than 50 grams of carbohydrates. On a particular day, Roniger's food stock includes seven items that can be prepared and served for supper to meet these requirements. The cost per pound for each food item and its contribution to each of the five nutritional requirements are given in the table at the top of the page.

What combination and amounts of food items will provide the nutrition Roniger requires at the least total food cost?

(a) Formulate as an LP problem.
(b) What is the cost per meal?
(c) Is this a well-balanced diet?

**3-10** *(High-tech product mix)* Quitmeyer Electronics Incorporated manufactures the following six microcomputer peripheral devices: internal modems, external modems, graphics circuit boards, floppy disk drives, hard disk drives, and memory expansion boards. Each of these technical products requires time, in minutes, on three types of electronic testing equipment, as shown in the table at the bottom of the page.

The first two test devices are available 120 hours per week. The third (device 3) requires more preventive maintenance and may be used only 100 hours each week. The market for all six computer components is vast, and Quitmeyer Electronics believes that it can sell as many units of each product as it can

manufacture. The table that follows summarizes the revenues and material costs for each product:

| DEVICE | REVENUE PER UNIT SOLD ($) | MATERIAL COST PER UNIT ($) |
|---|---|---|
| Internal modem | 200 | 35 |
| External modem | 120 | 25 |
| Graphics circuit board | 180 | 40 |
| Floppy disk drive | 130 | 45 |
| Hard disk drive | 430 | 170 |
| Memory expansion board | 260 | 60 |

In addition, variable labor costs are $15 per hour for test device 1, $12 per hour for test device 2, and $18 per hour for test device 3. Quitmeyer Electronics wants to maximize its profits.

(a) Formulate this problem as an LP model.
(b) Solve the problem using Excel. What is the best product mix?

**3-11** *(Nuclear plant staffing)* South Central Utilities has just announced the August 1 opening of its second nuclear generator at its Baton Rouge, Louisiana, nuclear power plant. Its personnel department has been directed to determine how many nuclear technicians need to be hired and trained over the remainder of the year.

**Table for Problem 3-10**

| | INTERNAL MODEM | EXTERNAL MODEM | CIRCUIT BOARD | FLOPPY DRIVES | HARD DRIVES | MEMORY BOARDS |
|---|---|---|---|---|---|---|
| Test device 1 | 7 | 3 | 12 | 6 | 18 | 17 |
| Test device 2 | 2 | 5 | 3 | 2 | 15 | 17 |
| Test device 3 | 5 | 1 | 3 | 2 | 9 | 2 |

The plant currently employs 350 fully trained technicians and projects the following personnel needs:

| Month | Personnel Hours Needed |
| --- | --- |
| August | 40,000 |
| September | 45,000 |
| October | 35,000 |
| November | 50,000 |
| December | 45,000 |

By Louisiana law, a reactor employee can actually work no more than 130 hours per month. (Slightly over one hour per day is used for check-in and check-out, record keeping, and daily radiation health scans.) Policy at South Central Utilities also dictates that layoffs are not acceptable in those months when the nuclear plant is overstaffed. So, if more trained employees are available than are needed in any month, each worker is still fully paid, even though he or she is not required to work the 130 hours.

Training new employees is an important and costly procedure. It takes one month of one-on-one classroom instruction before a new technician is permitted to work alone in the reactor facility. Therefore, South Central must hire trainees one month before they are actually needed. Each trainee teams up with a skilled nuclear technician and requires 90 hours of that employee's time, meaning that 90 hours less of the technician's time are available that month for actual reactor work.

Personnel department records indicate a turnover rate of trained technicians at 5% per month. In other words, about 5% of the skilled employees at the start of any month resign by the end of that month. A trained technician earns an average monthly salary of $2,000 (regardless of the number of hours worked, as noted earlier). Trainees are paid $900 during their one month of instruction.

(a) Formulate this staffing problem using LP.
(b) Solve the problem. How many trainees must begin each month?

**3-12** (*Agricultural production planning*) Margaret Young's family owns five parcels of farmland broken into a southeast sector, north sector, northwest sector, west sector, and southwest sector. Young is involved primarily in growing wheat, alfalfa, and barley crops and is currently preparing her production plan for next year. The Pennsylvania Water Authority has just announced its yearly water allotment, with the Young farm receiving 7,400 acre-feet. Each parcel can only tolerate a certain amount of irrigation per growing season, as specified in the following table:

| Parcel | Area (Acres) | Water Irrigation Limit (Acre-Feet) |
| --- | --- | --- |
| Southeast | 2,000 | 3,200 |
| North | 2,300 | 3,400 |
| Northwest | 600 | 800 |
| West | 1,100 | 500 |
| Southwest | 500 | 600 |

Each of Young's crops needs a minimum amount of water per acre, and there is a projected limit on sales of each crop. Crop data follow:

| Crop | Maximum Sales | Water Needed per Acre (Acre-Feet) |
| --- | --- | --- |
| Wheat | 110,000 bushels | 1.6 |
| Alfalfa | 1,800 tons | 2.9 |
| Barley | 2,200 tons | 3.5 |

Young's best estimate is that she can sell wheat at a net profit of $2 per bushel, alfalfa at $40 per ton, and barley at $50 per ton. One acre of land yields an average of 1.5 tons of alfalfa and 2.2 tons of barley. The wheat yield is approximately 50 bushels per acre.

(a) Formulate Young's production plan.
(b) What should the crop plan be, and what profit will it yield?

**3-13** (*Material blending*) Amalgamated Products has just received a contract to construct steel body frames for automobiles that are to be produced at the new Japanese factory in Tennessee. The Japanese auto manufacturer has strict quality control standards for all of its component subcontractors and has informed Amalgamated that each frame must have the following steel content:

| Material | Minimum Percent | Maximum Percent |
| --- | --- | --- |
| Manganese | 2.1 | 3.1 |
| Silicon | 4.3 | 6.3 |
| Carbon | 1.05 | 2.05 |

Amalgamated mixes batches of eight different available materials to produce one ton of steel used in the body frames. The table at the top of page 110 details these materials.

**Table for Problem 3-13**

| MATERIAL AVAILABLE | MANGANESE (%) | SILICON (%) | CARBON (%) | POUNDS AVAILABLE | COST PER POUND |
|---|---|---|---|---|---|
| Alloy 1 | 70.0 | 15.0 | 3.0 | No limit | $0.12 |
| Alloy 2 | 55.0 | 30.0 | 1.0 | 300 | 0.13 |
| Alloy 3 | 12.0 | 26.0 | 0 | No limit | 0.15 |
| Iron 1 | 1.0 | 10.0 | 3.0 | No limit | 0.09 |
| Iron 2 | 5.0 | 2.5 | 0 | No limit | 0.07 |
| Carbide 1 | 0 | 24.0 | 18.0 | 50 | 0.10 |
| Carbide 2 | 0 | 25.0 | 20.0 | 200 | 0.12 |
| Carbide 3 | 0 | 23.0 | 25.0 | 100 | 0.09 |

Formulate and solve the LP model that will indicate how much of each of the eight materials should be blended into a 1-ton load of steel so that Amalgamated meets its requirements while minimizing costs.

**3-14** *(Hospital expansion)* Mt. Sinai Hospital in New Orleans is a large, private, 600-bed facility complete with laboratories, operating rooms, and x-ray equipment. In seeking to increase revenues, Mt. Sinai's administration has decided to make a 90-bed addition on a portion of adjacent land currently used for staff parking. The administrators feel that the labs, operating rooms, and x-ray department are not being fully utilized at present and do not need to be expanded to handle additional patients. The addition of 90 beds, however, involves deciding how many beds should be allocated to the medical staff for medical patients and how many to the surgical staff for surgical patients.

The hospital's accounting and medical records departments have provided the following pertinent information. The average hospital stay for a medical patient is 8 days, and the average medical patient generates $2,280 in revenues. The average surgical patient is in the hospital 5 days and receives a $1,515 bill. The laboratory is capable of handling 15,000 tests per year more than it was handling. The average medical patient requires 3.1 lab tests and the average surgical patient takes 2.6 lab tests. Furthermore, the average medical patient uses one x-ray, whereas the average surgical patient requires two x-rays. If the hospital was expanded by 90 beds, the x-ray department could handle up to 7,000 x-rays without significant additional cost. Finally, the administration estimates that up to 2,800 additional operations could be performed in existing operating room facilities. Medical patients, of course, require no surgery, whereas each surgical patient generally has one surgery performed.

Formulate this problem so as to determine how many medical beds and how many surgical beds should be added to maximize revenues. Assume that the hospital is open 365 days a year. Then solve the problem.

# ⫸ CASE STUDY

## Chase Manhattan Bank

The workload in many areas of bank operations has the characteristics of a nonuniform distribution with respect to time of day. For example, at Chase Manhattan Bank in New York, the number of domestic money transfer requests received from customers, if plotted against time of day, would appear to have the shape of an inverted U curve with the peak around 1 P.M. For efficient use of resources, the personnel available should, therefore, vary correspondingly. Figure 3.1 shows a typical workload curve and corresponding personnel requirements at different hours of the day.

**Figure for Case: Chase Manhattan Bank**

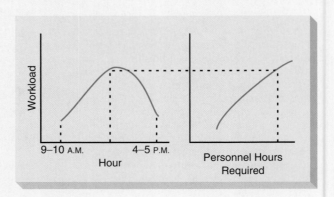

A variable capacity can be achieved effectively by employing part-time personnel. Because part-timers are not entitled to all the fringe benefits, they are often more economical than full-time employees. Other considerations, however, may limit the extent to which part-time people can be hired in a given department. The problem is to find an optimum workforce schedule that would meet personnel requirements at any given time and also be economical.

Some of the factors affecting personnel assignment are listed here:

1. By corporate policy, part-time personnel hours are limited to a maximum of 40% of the day's total requirement.
2. Full-time employees work for 8 hours (1 hour for lunch included) per day. Thus, a full-timer's productive time is 35 hours per week.
3. Part-timers work for at least 4 hours per day but less than 8 hours and are not allowed a lunch break.
4. Fifty percent of the full-timers go to lunch between 11 A.M. and noon and the remaining 50% between noon and 1 P.M.
5. The shift starts at 9 A.M. and ends at 7 P.M. (i.e., overtime is limited to 2 hours). Any work left over at 7 P.M. is considered holdover for the next day.
6. A full-time employee is not allowed to work more than 5 hours overtime per week. He or she is paid at the normal rate for overtime hours—*not* at one and a half times the normal rate applicable to hours in excess of 40 per week. Fringe benefits are not applied to overtime hours.

In addition, the following costs are pertinent:

1. The average cost per full-time personnel hour (fringe benefits included) is $10.11.
2. The average cost per overtime personnel hour for full-timers (straight rate excluding fringe benefits) is $8.08.
3. The average cost per part-time personnel hour is $7.82.

**TABLE 3.7**

**Workforce Requirements**

| TIME PERIOD | NUMBER OF PERSONNEL HOURS REQUIRED |
|---|---|
| 9–10 A.M. | 14 |
| 10–11 | 25 |
| 11–12 | 26 |
| 12–1 P.M. | 38 |
| 1–2 | 55 |
| 2–3 | 60 |
| 3–4 | 51 |
| 4–5 | 29 |
| 5–6 | 14 |
| 6–7 | 9 |

The personnel hours required, by hour of day, are given in Table 3.7.

The bank's goal is to achieve the minimum possible personnel cost subject to meeting or exceeding the hourly workforce requirements as well as the constraints on the workers listed earlier.

**Discussion Questions**

1. What is the minimum-cost schedule for the bank?
2. What are the limitations of the model used to answer question 1?

*Source:* Adapted from Shyam L. Moondra. "An L. P. Model for Work Force Scheduling for Banks," *Journal of Bank Research* (Winter 1976), 299–301.

# BIBLIOGRAPHY

See the Bibliography at the end of Chapter 2.

## CHAPTER 4

# LINEAR PROGRAMMING SENSITIVITY ANALYSIS

## LEARNING OBJECTIVES

After completing this chapter, students will be able to:

1. Understand, using graphs, the impact of changes in objective function coefficients, right-hand side values, and constraint coefficients on the optimal solution of a linear programming problem.

2. Generate answer and sensitivity reports using Excel's Solver.

3. Interpret all parameters of these reports for maximization and minimization problems.

4. Analyze the impact of simultaneous changes in input data values using the 100% rule.

5. Analyze the impact of the addition of a new variable using the pricing-out strategy.

## CHAPTER OUTLINE

Summary • Glossary • Solved Problem • Self-Test • Discussion Questions and Problems • Case Study: Red Brand Canners • Bibliography

### The Right Stuff at NASA

There are many areas at NASA where management science tools such as linear programming (LP) have been successfully applied. With the culture of the U.S. space program changing because of an increasing pressure to develop missions under rigid schedule and budget constraints, NASA has begun to work in an environment of faster-better-cheaper (FBC). After the recent highly publicized Mars failure, NASA now addresses the issue of scarce resources with a technique called sensitivity analysis and a measure of marginal costs called the shadow price.

For example, at the margin, money is sometimes spent on tests that are not justified by this value of information. In other cases, more funds would yield risk reduction benefits that would justify the costs and greatly improve the scientific benefit of a space mission. The landing of Mars Pathfinder was designed to operate for one month but lasted longer than anticipated. The shadow prices of the LP resource constraints in such a case provide valuable insights into the cost-benefit tradeoff.

When NASA looks to a project that is critical to the success of new missions, the costs of losing the project will include marginal values of the delays and loss of data incurred by these future missions. LP doesn't just provide optimal solutions, it provides the ability to conduct sensitivity analysis on these solutions as well.[1]

---

[1] M. E. Pate-Cornell and R. L. Dillon. "The Right Stuff," *OR/MS Today* (February 2000): 36−39.

## 4.1 INTRODUCTION

*We have solved LP models under deterministic assumptions.*

Optimal solutions to linear programming (LP) problems have thus far been found under what are called *deterministic* assumptions. This means that we assume complete certainty in the data and relationships of a problem—namely, prices are fixed, resources' availabilities are known, time needed to produce a unit is exactly set, and so on. But in most real-world situations, conditions are dynamic and changing. How can we handle this apparent discrepancy?

One way to handle this is to revise the formulation and resolve the model each time an input data (or parameter) value changes. It is easy to see that this approach can take a long time to test a series of possible changes. Further, since we may get a different solution each time the model is solved with revised input data values, we can never be sure about the validity and stability (or robustness) of the current solution.

*We examine how sensitive the optimal solution is to changes in profits, resources, or other input parameters.*

An alternate, and preferred, approach is to formulate and solve the LP model assuming that the input data values are, in fact, constant. In other words, we treat the problem as a deterministic situation. However, after solving the model, we analyze the optimal solution to see just how *sensitive* it is to these input data values. That is, after solving an LP problem, we attempt to determine a *range of changes* in input data values that will keep the current corner point as the optimal solution. This is done without resolving the whole LP model. Such analyses are commonly used to examine the effects of changes in two types of input data values: (1) the objective function coefficient for each variable and (2) the right-hand side (RHS) value in each constraint. This task is alternatively called *sensitivity analysis* or *postoptimality analysis*.

*Postoptimality analysis means examining changes after the optimal solution has been reached.*

Changes to input data values typically occur due to two reasons. First, the value may have been estimated incorrectly. For example, a firm may realize during a production problem that it has only 175 pumps in inventory, rather than 200 as specified in the model. Second, management is often interested in getting quick answers to a series of *what-if* questions. For example, what if the profit contribution of a product increases by 10%? What if less money is available for advertising? What if workers can each stay one hour longer every day at $1\frac{1}{2}$-time pay to provide increased production capacity? What if new technology will allow a product to be wired in one-third the time it used to take?

*An important function of sensitivity analysis is to allow managers to experiment with values of the input parameters.*

We first investigate sensitivity analysis using a small two-variable product mix problem involving the High Note Sound Company. Although we are unlikely to encounter two-variable problems in practice, the advantage of studying such models is that we can demonstrate the concepts of sensitivity analysis using a graphical approach. We then discuss how we can use Excel's Solver to generate sensitivity analysis reports for the High Note example. Finally, we discuss this topic using examples with more than two variables involving both maximization and minimization objective functions. These larger problems allow us to illustrate fully the various types of information we can obtain using sensitivity analysis.

*Excel's Solver can be used to generate sensitivity reports.*

## 4.2 SENSITIVITY ANALYSIS USING GRAPHS

The High Note Sound Company manufactures quality compact disc (CD) players and stereo receivers. Each of these products requires a certain amount of skilled craftsmanship, of which there is a limited weekly supply. Let $C$ denote the number of CD players to make, and $R$ denote the number of receivers to make. Using the decision variables, the firm formulates the following LP problem to determine the best product mix:

$$\text{Maximize profit} = \$50C + \$120R$$

subject to

$$2C + 4R \leq 80 \quad \text{(Hours of electricians' time available)}$$
$$3C + R \leq 60 \quad \text{(Hours of audio technicians' time available)}$$
$$C, \quad R \geq 0 \quad \text{(Nonnegativity constraints)}$$

**FIGURE 4.1**

**High Note Sound
Company Graphical
Solution**

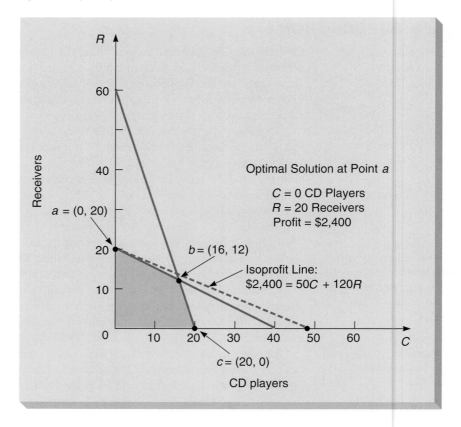

The solution to this problem is illustrated graphically in Figure 4.1. If we assume that all the input data values are deterministic, we can use the isoprofit line approach to identify the optimal corner point. Recall from Chapter 2 that an isoprofit line for a profit of $Z$ represents all combinations of decision variable values that will yield this profit level. It is easy to see in Figure 4.1 that the High Note's isoprofit line is optimal at corner point $a$. At this corner point, the optimal solution is to produce only stereo receivers (20 of them) for a weekly profit of $2,400.

## Changes in an Objective Function Coefficient

*We examine changes in objective function coefficients first.*

In many real-world LP problems, objective function coefficients (OFCs) (usually unit profits or costs) fluctuate periodically, as do most of a firm's expenses. Graphically, this means that while the feasible solution region remains the same, the slope of the isoprofit (or isocost) line will change.

### Impact of a Change in the Profit Contribution of Receivers
What if a technical breakthrough just occurred that raised the unit profit per stereo receiver ($R$) from $120 to $150? Is corner point $a$ still the optimal solution? The answer is definitely yes, as shown in Figure 4.2. In this case, the slope of the isoprofit line accentuates the optimality of the solution at corner point $a$. However, even though the decision variable values did not change, the new optimal objective function value (i.e., the profit) is $3,000 = 0($50) + 20($150).

On the other hand, if a stereo receiver's profit coefficient was overestimated and should only have been $80, the slope of the isoprofit line changes enough to cause a new corner point ($b$) to become optimal. That is, the values of the decision variables change, as does the objective function value. At point $b$, the profit is $1,760 = 16($50) + 12($80).

**Changes in the Receiver
Contribution Coefficient**

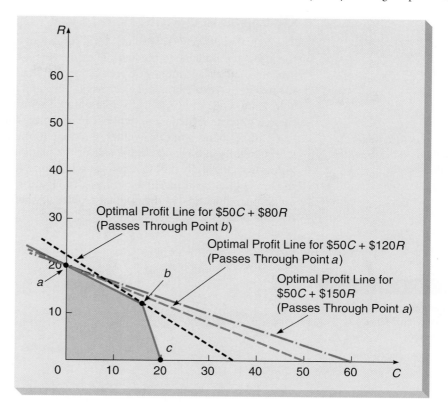

**Impact of a Change in the Profit Contribution of CD Players**  The reason that CD players ($C$) are not being produced in the current optimal solution (corner point $a$) is that they are not profitable enough. It is easy to see that if, for some reason, the unit profit of CD players increases from its current value of $50, the slope of the isoprofit line changes and the optimal solution will eventually move from corner point $a$ to corner point $b$ in Figure 4.2. On the other hand, a decrease in the unit profit of CD players will enhance the desirability of stereo receivers at corner point $a$.

*There is a range for each OFC over which the current solution remains optimal.*

From the preceding discussion, it is apparent that for each OFC, there is a range of possible values for which the *current* optimal corner point solution remains optimal. Any change in an OFC value beyond its relevant range causes a *new* corner point to become the optimal solution.

It is algebraically possible to use the graphical solution procedure to determine the allowable range for each OFC within which the current optimal solution remains optimal. However, we use the information provided in Solver's sensitivity report to discuss this issue further in the next section.

*Changes in OFC values do not affect the size of the feasible region.*

We note again that whenever changes occur in OFCs, the feasible region of the problem (which depends only on the constraints) does not change. Therefore, there is no change in the physical location of each corner point. To summarize, the only things that can occur due to a change in an OFC are (1) if the current optimal corner point continues to remain optimal, the decision variable values do not change, even though the objective function value may change; and (2) if the current corner point is no longer optimal, the values of the decision variables change, as does the objective function value.

## Changes in a Right-Hand Side

The right-hand side (RHS) value of a ≤ constraint can usually be considered to represent the resources available to the firm. These resources could be labor hours or machine time available, or perhaps money or production materials available. In the High Note example, the two resources are hours of electricians' time and hours of audio technicians' time available. Knowledge of how sensitive the optimal solution is to changes in resources such as these is important because of dynamic marketplace conditions.

*Changes in RHS values usually affect the size of the feasible region.*

Unlike changes in OFC values, a change in the RHS value of a nonredundant constraint results in a change in the size of the feasible region. Hence, one or more corner points may physically shift to new locations. Figure 4.3 illustrates two RHS value changes in the hours of electricians' time available. In Figure 4.3(a), there are 100 electricians' hours (as compared with 80 in the original problem), whereas in Figure 4.3(b) there are 60 electricians' hours.

**FIGURE 4.3**

**Changes in the Electricians' Time Resource**

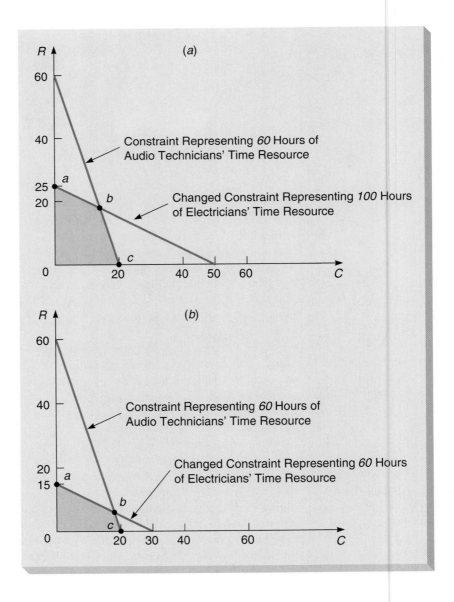

A corner point approach in Figure 4.3(a) indicates that point $a$ is the optimal solution. The values at this point are $C = 0$ CD players, $R = 25$ receivers, and profit = \$3,000. Likewise, a corner point approach in Figure 4.3(b) indicates that point $a$ is once again the optimal solution. However, reducing the available electrician's time to 60 hours has altered the feasible region. This time the optimal solution is $C = 0$ CD players, $R = 15$ receivers, for a profit of \$1,800. That is, even though corner point $a$, which defines the intersection of the *same* two (or more) constraints, is optimal in both cases, its physical location has changed. Hence, the optimal values of the decision variables, and the objective function, have also changed.

*The location of the optimal corner point changes.*

Will corner point $a$ remain optimal (albeit with new values for the decision variables and objective function) no matter how much we change the available electricians' time? The answer is *no*, as discussed next.

**Impact of Increase in Electricians' Available Time**  In Figure 4.3(a), corner points $a$, $b$, and $c$ still exist in the feasible region, even though their locations may have physically shifted when compared with Figure 4.1. As the available electricians' time increases further, we can see that corner points $a$ and $b$ will move closer to each other. Eventually, we will reach a situation in which corner points $a$ and $b$ meet at ($C = 0$, $R = 60$). Any further increase in the available electricians' time will make this constraint redundant; that is, it will no longer affect the feasible region.

*Increasing the RHS of a ≤ constraint will eventually make it a redundant constraint.*

**Impact of Decrease in Electricians' Available Time**  In Figure 4.3(b) also, corner points $a$, $b$, and $c$ still exist in the feasible region, albeit with new coordinates when compared with Figure 4.1. As the available electricians' time decreases further, we can see that corner points $b$ and $c$ will move closer to each other from their current locations. Eventually this constraint will no longer intersect the line representing the audio technicians' time constraint. That is, corner points $b$ and $c$ will no longer be feasible, and the intersection of the electricians' time constraint with the horizontal ($C$) axis will become a new feasible corner point.

*There is a range of values for each RHS for which the current corner points exist.*

From the preceding discussion, it is apparent that for the electricians' time availability (i.e., the constraint RHS value), there is a range of possible values for which the current corner points exist (even if their coordinates have changed). Increasing or decreasing the electricians' time beyond this range causes one or more of the corner points in the current feasible region to no longer exist and new corner points that are currently infeasible to become feasible.

As before, it is algebraically possible to use the graphical solution to determine the range for each RHS within which all corner points of the current feasible region exist. We will, however, use the information provided in Solver's sensitivity report to further discuss this issue in a subsequent section.

## Changes in Constraint Coefficients

*Changes in constraint coefficients affect the shape of the feasible region.*

Although it is not commonly analyzed in practice, we can also study the effect of changes in a third type of input data value, *constraint coefficients* (i.e., the numbers in the left-hand sides [LHS] of constraint equations). Changes in constraint (or *technological*) coefficients often reflect changes in the state of technology. For example, if fewer or more resources are needed to produce a product such as a CD player or stereo receiver, the coefficients in the constraint equations will change. These changes will have no effect on the objective function of an LP problem, but they can produce a significant change in the shape of the feasible solution region, and hence in the optimal profit or cost.

**FIGURE 4.4**    Change in the Constraint Coefficients

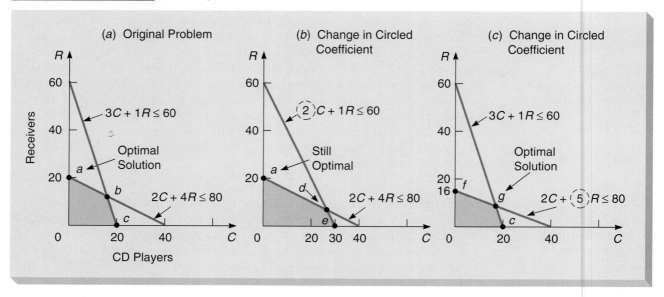

Figure 4.4 illustrates the original High Note Sound Company graphical solution as well as two separate changes in constraint coefficients. In Figure 4.4(a), we see that the optimal solution lies at corner point *a*, which represents $C = 0$, $R = 20$. You should be able to prove to yourself that point *a* remains optimal in Figure 4.4(b) despite a constraint change from $3C + R \leq 60$ to $2C + R \leq 60$. Such a change might take place when the firm discovers that it no longer requires three hours of audio technicians' time to produce a CD player, but only two hours.

In Figure 4.4(c), however, a change in the other constraint changes the shape of the feasible region enough to cause a new corner point (*g*) to become optimal. Before moving on, see if you obtain an optimal objective function value of $1,954 profit at point *g*.

In the real world, changes in constraint coefficients are not as frequent as changes in OFCs and RHS values. The constraint coefficients for High Note, for example, refer to the electrician and audio technician times required per unit—issues that can be regarded as *design* parameters. As such, they are less susceptible to change when compared with OFCs and RHS values. For this reason, we restrict our discussion in the rest of this chapter to the impact of changes in OFCs and RHS values. Solver's sensitivity report also focuses primarily on these two changes.

*Changes in constraint coefficients are not as frequent as changes in RHS and OFC values.*

*Solver's report focuses on changes in RHS and OFC values.*

---

4.3  **SENSITIVITY ANALYSIS USING SOLVER REPORTS**

**File: 4-1.xls**

Program 4.1A shows the Excel implementation and Solver entries for the High Note Sound Company example. For clarity, we use the same Excel layout here as in Chapters 2 and 3. That is, all parameters (i.e., the solution value, objective coefficient, and constraint coefficients) associated with a specific decision variable are listed in the same column, and the objective function and each constraint in the problem are shown on separate rows of the worksheet.

In Program 4.1A, cells B5 and C5 are the Changing Cells that denote the optimal quantities of CD players and receivers to make, respectively. Cell D6 is the Target Cell and shows the total profit. Cells D8 and D9 contain the formulas for the LHS of the two constraints, namely, the total amount of electrician hours used and the total amount of audio technician hours used, respectively.

**PROGRAM 4.1A**

**Excel Layout and Solver
Entries for High Note
Sound Company**

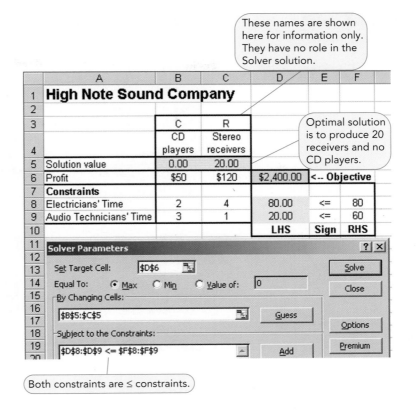

These names are shown here for information only. They have no role in the Solver solution.

Optimal solution is to produce 20 receivers and no CD players.

Both constraints are ≤ constraints.

## Excel Notes

■ The CD-ROM that accompanies this textbook contains the Excel file for each problem in the examples discussed here. The relevant file name is shown in the margin next to each example.

■ In each of our Excel layouts, for clarity, changing cells are shaded yellow, the target cell is shaded green, and cells containing the LHS formula for each constraint are shaded blue.

■ Also, to make the equivalence of the *written* formulation and the Excel layout clear, our Excel layouts show the decision variable names used in the written formulation of the model. Note that these names have no role in using Solver to solve the model.

The Solver solution reveals that it is optimal to produce 20 stereo receivers and no CD players, for a total profit of $2,400.

## Solver Reports

*We must check the Assume Linear Model option to obtain LP sensitivity reports.*

Before solving the LP model, we need to ensure that the Assume Linear Model box has been checked in the Solver Options window (see Program 4.1B). If this box is not checked, Solver does not solve the model as a linear program, and the resulting sensitivity report will look very different from the reports we discuss here. Also, recall that we check the Assume Non-Negative option to enforce the nonnegativity constraints.

*The desired Solver reports must be selected in order for them to be created.*

When Solver finds the optimal solution for a problem, the Solver Results window provides options to obtain three reports: Answer, Sensitivity, and Limits. Note that to obtain the desired reports, we must select them *before* we click OK. In our case, we select the *Answer* and *Sensitivity* reports and then click OK (see Program 4.1B). The *Limits* report is relatively less useful, and we therefore do not discuss it here.

**PROGRAM 4.1B**

**Solver Options and Solver
Results Windows**

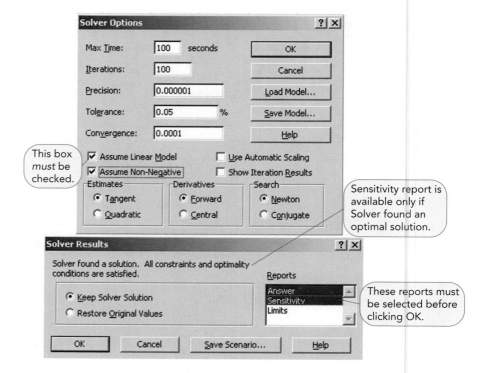

## Answer Report

*Answer Report shows details
of the optimal solution.*

The *Answer Report* for High Note's example is shown in Program 4.1C. We have formatted the values in this report to show a consistent number of decimal points. The report provides essentially the same information as the original Excel layout (see Program 4.1A), but in a more descriptive manner. In addition to showing the original and final (optimal) val-

**PROGRAM 4.1C**        **Solver Answer Report for High Note Sound Company**

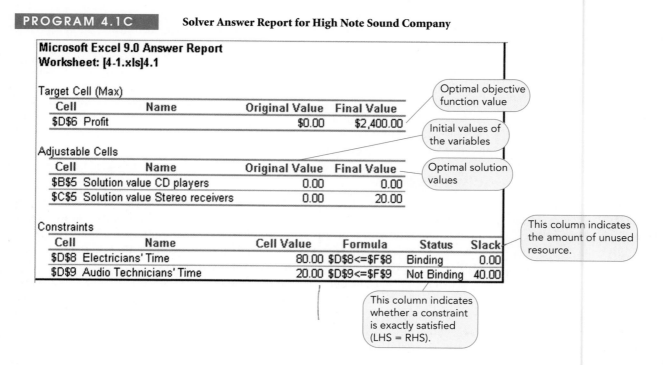

ues for the decision variables and the objective function, the answer report also shows the following:

■ The relevant formula used for each constraint (i.e., the LHS and RHS cell references and the sign relating these entries).

■ The *slack* (difference between the RHS and the LHS of a ≤ constraint), which denotes the amount of unused resource.

■ Whether the constraint is binding or nonbinding. *Binding* means that all the available resource (e.g., electricians' time) is fully used in the solution. *Nonbinding* means that some of the resource has not been fully used up in the final solution.

*Binding means the con-straint is exactly satisfied, and LHS = RHS.*

The descriptive labels shown in the Name column are directly extracted by Solver based on the layout used in setting up the spreadsheet model. Since the layout can vary widely based on the user's preference and expertise, the names extracted by Solver can sometimes be incorrect. In such cases, however, these labels can be directly overwritten to show more meaningful titles. For example, the Excel layout shown in Program 4.1A causes the answer report to name cell D6 as "Profit." If desired, we can rename this cell as "Total Profit" to better reflect its meaning.

*Names in Solver reports can be edited if desired.*

## Sensitivity Report

The *Sensitivity Report* for the High Note example is shown in Program 4.1D. We have formatted these values also to show a consistent number of decimal points. The sensitivity report has two distinct components: (1) a table titled Adjustable Cells and (2) a table titled Constraints. These tables permit us to answer several what-if questions regarding the problem solution.

*The Sensitivity Report has two parts: Adjustable Cells and Constraints.*

It is important to note that while using the information in the sensitivity report to answer these what-if questions, we assume that we are considering a change to only a *single* input data value. That is, the sensitivity information does not always apply to simultaneous changes in several input data values (except under certain special conditions, which are discussed in Section 4.5).

*We are analyzing only one change at a time.*

The *Adjustable Cells* table presents information regarding the impact of changes to the OFCs (i.e., the unit profits of $50 and $120) on the optimal solution. The *Constraints* table

**Solver Sensitivity Report for High Note Sound Company**

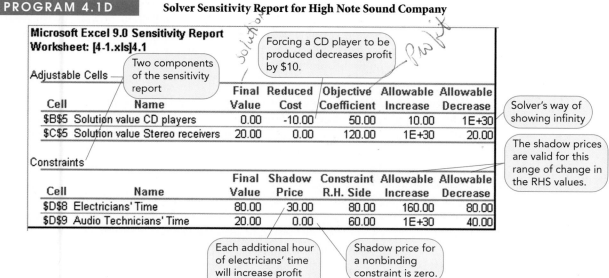

presents information related to the impact of changes in constraint RHS values (i.e., the 80 hours and 60 hours) on the optimal solution. Although different LP software packages may format and present these tables differently, the programs all provide essentially the same information.

## Impact of Changes in a Constraint's Right-Hand Side

*Impact of changes in RHS values is measured by the shadow price.*

Let us first discuss the impact on the optimal solution of a change in the RHS value of a constraint. The primary information to study the impact of such a change is provided by the *shadow price* value for that constraint. This value is shown in the table titled *Constraints* in the sensitivity report (see Program 4.1D).

There are currently 80 hours of electricians' time and 60 hours of audio technicians' time available. The Final Value entries in the table reveal that of these hours, the optimal solution uses all 80 hours of the electricians' time. However, only 20 of the 60 hours of audio technicians' time are used. That is, for High Note, the electricians' time constraint is binding, whereas the audio technicians' time constraint is nonbinding. The 40 unused hours (= 60 − 20) of audio technicians' time are referred to as *slack*. The *Answer Report* shown in Program 4.1C lists this value.

**Change in RHS of a Binding Constraint**  Since electricians' time is a binding constraint, what would happen to High Note's profit if it could acquire additional hours of this resource? Recall from the discussion of the graphical solution of this problem in Section 4.2 that if the RHS value of a nonredundant constraint changes, the size of the feasible region also changes. If the change causes the feasible region to *increase* in size, the optimal objective function value could potentially improve. In contrast, if the change causes the feasible region to *decrease* in size, the optimal objective function value could potentially worsen.

*If the size of the feasible region increases, the optimal objective function value could improve.*

In the High Note example, if the electricians' time increases from the current 80 hours, the feasible region increases in size. The total profit could, therefore, increase. What would be the level of this increase? The answer to this question is given by the entry labeled Shadow Price in the sensitivity report.

*Shadow price is the change in objective function value for a one unit increase in a constraint's RHS value.*

The shadow price can be defined as the change in the optimal objective value for a one unit increase in the RHS value of a constraint. In the case of electrician hours, Program 4.1D shows the shadow price to be $30. This means that for each *additional* hour of electrician time that High Note can obtain, its total profit changes by $30. What is the direction of this change? In this specific case, the change is an increase in profit since the additional electrician time causes the solution to improve.

**Validity Range for the Shadow Price**  Given that High Note's profit increases by $30 for each additional hour of electricians' time, does it mean that High Note can do this indefinitely, essentially earning infinite profit? Clearly, this is illogical. How far can High Note increase its electrician time availability and still earn an extra $30 profit per hour? That is, for what level of increase in the RHS value of the electricians' time constraint is the shadow price of $30 valid?

Recall from our discussion in Section 4.2 that for the electricians' time available, there is a range of possible values for which the current set of corner points exist (even if their coordinates have changed). Increasing or decreasing the RHS value beyond this range causes one or more of the current feasible corner points to no longer exist, or for new corner points that are currently infeasible to become feasible.

The shadow price of $30 is valid as long as the available electricians' time stays in a range within which all current corner points continue to exist. The information to

*The shadow price is valid only as long as the change in the RHS is within the Allowable Increase and Allowable Decrease values.*

compute the upper and lower limits of this range is given by the entries labeled Allowable Increase and Allowable Decrease in the sensitivity report. In High Note's case, these values show that the shadow price of $30 for electricians' time availability is valid for an increase of up to 160 hours from the current value and a decrease of up to 80 hours. That is, the available electrician's time can range from a low of 0 (= 80 − 80) to a high of 240 (= 80 + 160) for the shadow price of $30 to be valid. Note that the allowable decrease implies that for each hour of electricians' time that High Note loses (up to 80 hours), its profit decreases by $30.

**Change in RHS of a Nonbinding Constraint**  We note that as far as audio technicians' time is concerned, we already have 40 unused hours. Clearly, High Note would have no interest at all in acquiring additional hours of this resource. Therefore, the shadow price for audio technicians' time is zero.

*Shadow price of a nonbinding constraint is zero.*

In Program 4.1D, the allowable increase for this RHS value is infinity (shown as 1E+30 in Solver). This is logical since any additional hours of audio technicians' time will only cause the slack in this resource to increase and have no impact on profit.

In contrast, once we lose 40 hours (our current unused portion, or slack) of audio technicians' time, this resource also becomes binding. Any additional loss of this time will clearly have an adverse effect on profit. This is revealed by the value of 40 for the allowable decrease in the RHS of the audio technicians' time constraint. To evaluate the new optimal solution if audio technicians' time decreases by more than 40 hours from its current value, the problem would have to be solved again.

## Impact of Changes in an Objective Function Coefficient (OFC)

Let us now focus on the information provided in the table titled *Adjustable Cells*. For your convenience, we repeat that part of Program 4.1D here as Program 4.1E. Each row in the adjustable cells table contains information regarding a decision variable in the model.

*Reduced cost is the difference between the marginal contribution of a variable and the marginal worth of the resources it uses.*

The Reduced Cost value shows the difference between the marginal contribution of a decision variable to the objective function value (profit in the High Note example) and the marginal worth of the resources it would consume if produced. For instance, CD players are currently not produced in the optimal solution. Assume that for some reason, we insist on producing CD players. Each CD player we produce will force us to divert 2 hours of

**PROGRAM 4.1E**

**Partial Solver Sensitivity Report for High Note Sound Company**

Microsoft Excel 9.0 Sensitivity Report
Worksheet: [4-1.xls]4.1

Adjustable Cells

| Cell | Name | Final Value | Reduced Cost | Objective Coefficient | Allowable Increase | Allowable Decrease |
|------|------|-------------|--------------|----------------------|--------------------|--------------------|
| $B$5 | Solution value CD players | 0.00 | -10.00 | 50.00 | 10.00 | 1E+30 |
| $C$5 | Solution value Stereo receivers | 20.00 | 0.00 | 120.00 | 1E+30 | 20.00 |

CD players must contribute $10 more each to total profit in order to become a viable product.

The current solution remains optimal for this range of change in OFC values.

electricians' time and 3 hours of audio technicians' time away from our other product (stereo receivers).

Based on the preceding discussion of the shadow price, the impact of such a diversion of resources on the objective value can be calculated as

$$= 2 \times \text{shadow price of electricians' time } +$$
$$2 \times \text{shadow price of audio technicians' time}$$

$$= 2 \times \$30 + 2 \times \$0$$

$$= \$60$$

Since the profit contribution of CD players is only $50 per unit, the net impact of producing each CD player will be a *decrease* of $10 in total profit. The result is indicated by the −$10 value for the reduced cost of CD players in the sensitivity report.

Alternatively, if we wish to produce CD players and not have an adverse impact on profit, the reduced cost shows the *minimum* amount by which the OFC for CD players should change (increase in this case) before it becomes a viable product. That is, if High Note can find a way of increasing the selling price of CD players by $10 or, alternatively, decreasing its resource usage so that it costs $10 less per unit to produce, CD players would then become a viable product to produce. This information is also revealed by the $10 under the Allowable Increase column in this table for the OFC of CD players.

*Reduced cost is also the minimum amount by which the OFC of a variable should change in order to affect the optimal solution.*

Not surprisingly, the Allowable Decrease column shows a value of infinity (shown as 1E+30 in Excel) for the OFC of CD players. This is logical since, if CD players are not attractive at a unit profit of $50, they are clearly not going to be attractive at unit profit values lower than $50.

For the case of receivers, we note that each unit requires 4 hours of electrician time and 1 hour of audio technician time. The marginal worth of the resources it consumes per unit can be calculated as

$$= 4 \times \text{shadow price of electricians' time } +$$
$$1 \times \text{shadow price of audio technicians' time}$$

$$= 4 \times \$30 + 1 \times \$0$$

$$= \$120$$

which is equal to a receiver's marginal contribution to the total profit.

**Allowable Ranges for OFCs**  In Figure 4.2, repeated here as Figure 4.5, we saw that as the unit profit contribution of either product changes, the slope of the isoprofit line changes. The size of the feasible region, however, remains the same. That is, the locations of the corner points do not change.

In the case of receivers, as the unit profit increases from the current value of $120, the slope of the profit line in Figure 4.5 changes in a manner that makes corner point *a* an even more attractive optimal point. On the other hand, as the unit profit decreases, the slope of the profit line changes in a manner that makes corner point *b* start to become more and more attractive. At some point, the unit profit of receivers is so low as to make corner point *b* the optimal solution.

*There is an allowable decrease and an allowable increase for each OFC over which the current optimal solution remains optimal.*

The limits to which the profit coefficient of receivers can be changed without affecting the optimality of the current solution (corner point *a*) is revealed by the values in the Allowable Increase and Allowable Decrease columns of the sensitivity report in Program 4.1E.

From the preceding discussion, as expected, the allowable increase in OFC for stereos is infinity. In contrast, the allowable decrease value is only $20. Hence, if the unit profit of

FIGURE 4.5

**Changes in the Receiver
Contribution Coefficient**

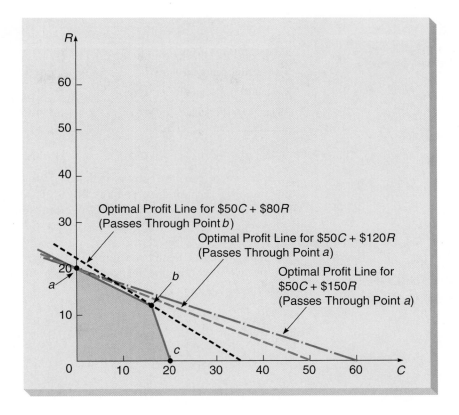

receivers drops to $110 (i.e., a decrease of $10 from the current value of $120), it is still optimal to produce 20 receivers and no CD players. The total profit will, however, drop to $2,200, since each receiver now yields lesser profit ($10 less per unit). However, if the unit profit drops below $100 per receiver (i.e., a decrease of more than $20 from the current $120 profit), the current solution is no longer optimal. The problem would then have to be resolved using Solver to find the new optimal corner point.

## 4.4 SENSITIVITY ANALYSIS FOR A LARGER MAXIMIZATION EXAMPLE

Now that we have explained some of the basic concepts in sensitivity analysis, let us consider a larger production mix example that will allow us to discuss some further issues.

### Anderson Electronics Example

*A larger product mix example.*

Anderson Electronics is considering the production of four potential products: VCRs, stereos, TVs, and DVD players. For the sake of this example, let us assume that the input for all products can be viewed in terms of just three resources: electronic components, nonelectronic components, and assembly time. The composition of the four products in terms of these three inputs is shown in Table 4.1, along with the unit selling prices of the products.

Electronic components can be obtained at $7.00 per unit; nonelectronic components can be obtained at $5.00 per unit; assembly time costs $10.00 per hour. Each resource is available in limited quantities as shown in Table 4.1 on the next page.

**TABLE 4.1**

Data for Anderson
Electronics Example

|  | VCR | STEREO | TV | DVD | SUPPLY |
|---|---|---|---|---|---|
| Electronic components | 3 | 4 | 4 | 3 | 4,700 |
| Nonelectronic components | 2 | 2 | 4 | 3 | 4,500 |
| Assembly time (hours) | 1 | 1 | 3 | 2 | 2,500 |
| Selling price (per unit) | $70 | $80 | $150 | $110 | |

By subtracting the total cost of making a product from its unit selling price, the profit contribution of each product can be easily calculated. For example, the profit contribution of each VCR is $29 (= selling price of $70 less the total cost of $3 × $7 + 2 × $5 + 1 × $10). Using similar calculations, see if you can confirm that the profit contribution of each stereo is $32, each TV is $72, and each DVD player is $54.

Let $V$, $S$, $T$, and $D$ denote the number of VCRs, stereos, TVs, and DVD players to make, respectively. We can then formulate the LP model for this problem as follows:

Maximize $29V + \$32S + \$72T + \$54D$        (Profit)

subject to

$$3V + 4S + 4T + 3D \leq 4{,}700 \quad \text{(Electronic components)}$$
$$2V + 2S + 4T + 3D \leq 4{,}500 \quad \text{(Nonelectronic components)}$$
$$V + S + 3T + 2D \leq 2{,}500 \quad \text{(Assembly time in hours)}$$
$$V, S, T, D \geq 0$$

Programs 4.2A, 4.2B, and 4.2C show the Excel layout and Solver entries, answer report, and sensitivity report, respectively, for Anderson's problem. The results show that Anderson should make 380 stereos, 1060 DVD players, and no VCRs or TVs, for a total profit of $69,400.

**File: 4-2.xls**

## Some Questions We Want Answered

We now ask and answer several questions that will allow us to understand the shadow price, reduced costs, and allowable range information in Anderson Electronics' sensitivity report. Each question is independent of the other questions and assumes that only the change mentioned in that question is being considered.

*Nonelectronic components are a nonbinding constraint.*

**Q:** What is the impact on profit of a change in the supply of nonelectronic components?
**A:** The slack values in the Answer Report (Program 4.2B) indicate that of the potential supply of 4,500 units of nonelectronic components, only 3,940 units are used, leaving 560 units unused. This implies that additional nonelectronic components are of no value to Anderson in terms of contribution to profit; that is, the shadow price is zero.

This shadow price is valid for an unlimited (infinite) increase in the supply of nonelectronic components. Further, Anderson would be willing to give up as much as 560 units of these components with no impact on profit. These values are shown in the Allowable Increase and Allowable Decrease columns in Program 4.2C, respectively, for the supply of nonelectronic components.

*Electronic components are a binding constraint.*

**Q:** What is the impact on profit if we could increase the supply of electronic components by 400 units (to a total of 5,100 units)?
**A:** We first look at the Allowable Increase column for electronic components in Program 4.2C to verify whether the current shadow price is valid for an increase of 400 units in this resource. Since the increase column shows a value of 2,800, the shadow price is valid.

**PROGRAM 4.2A**    **Excel Layout and Solver Entries for Anderson Electronics**

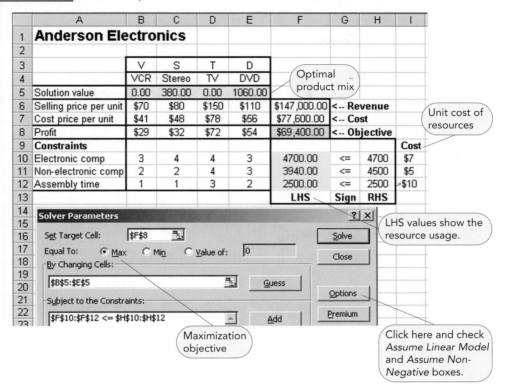

**PROGRAM 4.2B**    **Solver Answer Report for Anderson Electronics**

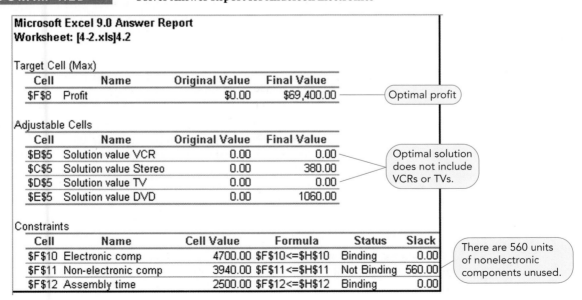

**PROGRAM 4.2C**   **Solver Sensitivity Report for Anderson Electronics**

**Microsoft Excel 9.0 Sensitivity Report**
**Worksheet: [4-2.xls]4.2**

*For changes to OFC values in this range, current solution remains optimal.*

Adjustable Cells

| Cell | Name | Final Value | Reduced Cost | Objective Coefficient | Allowable Increase | Allowable Decrease |
|------|------|-------------|--------------|-----------------------|--------------------|--------------------|
| $B$5 | Solution value VCR | 0.00 | -1.00 | 29.00 | 1.00 | 1E+30 |
| $C$5 | Solution value Stereo | 380.00 | 0.00 | 32.00 | 40.00 | 1.67 |
| $D$5 | Solution value TV | 0.00 | -8.00 | 72.00 | 8.00 | 1E+30 |
| $E$5 | Solution value DVD | 1060.00 | 0.00 | 54.00 | 10.00 | 5.00 |

*Allowable decrease is infinity since product is not attractive even at current OFC value.*

Constraints

| Cell | Name | Final Value | Shadow Price | Constraint R.H. Side | Allowable Increase | Allowable Decrease |
|------|------|-------------|--------------|----------------------|--------------------|--------------------|
| $F$10 | Electronic comp | 4700.00 | 2.00 | 4700.00 | 2800.00 | 950.00 |
| $F$11 | Non-electronic comp | 3940.00 | 0.00 | 4500.00 | 1E+30 | 560.00 |
| $F$12 | Assembly time | 2500.00 | 24.00 | 2500.00 | 466.67 | 1325.00 |

*Since nonelectronic components are nonbinding, shadow price is zero.*

*The allowable increase is infinity since there are already 560 units of slack.*

Next, we look at the shadow price for electronic components, which is $2 per unit. That is, each additional unit of electronic components (up to 2,800 additional units) will allow Anderson to increase its profit by $2. The impact of 400 units will therefore be a net increase in profit by $800. The new profit will be $70,200 (= $69,400 + $800).

It is important to remember that whenever the RHS value of a nonredundant constraint changes, the size of the feasible region changes. Hence, some of the corner points shift locations. In the current situation, since the proposed change is within the allowable change, the current corner point is still *optimal*. That is, the constraints that are binding at present will continue to remain the binding constraints. However, the corner point has shifted from its present location. What are the values of the decision variables at the new location of this corner point? We cannot usually answer this question without resolving the model again.

*Change in RHS value of a binding constraint causes the coordinates of the optimal corner point to change.*

**Q:** In the previous question, what would happen if we could increase the supply of electronic components by 4,000 units (to a total of 8,700 units)?

**A:** From Program 4.2C, we see that the shadow price of $2 per unit is valid only up to 2,800 additional units. This means that the first 2,800 units will cause the total profit to increase by $5,600 (= $2 × 2,800). However, the impact of the last 1,200 units (assuming we are forced to accept all or nothing of the 4,000 units) cannot be analyzed using the current report. The problem would have to be resolved using Solver to measure its impact.

*Changes beyond the allowable increase or decrease cannot be analyzed using the current report.*

It is important to note that the fact the potential additional supply (4,000) of electronic components is beyond the allowable increase value (2,800) does *not* mean Anderson's management cannot implement this change. It just means that the total impact of the change cannot be evaluated from the *current* sensitivity report in Program 4.2C.

**Q:** Refer back to the question about getting an additional 400 units of electronic components. What would happen if the supplier of these 400 units wants $8 per unit (rather than the current cost of $7 per unit)?

**A:** We know that the shadow price of $2 for electronic components represents the increase in total profit from each additional unit of this resource. This value is net after the cost of this additional unit has been taken into account. That is, it is actually beneficial for Anderson to pay a premium of up to $2 per additional unit of electronic components. In the current situation, getting 400 additional units of electronic components would cost Anderson $8 per unit. This represents a premium of $1 per unit over the current rate of $7 per unit. However, it would still be beneficial to get these units, since each additional unit would increase the total profit by $1 (= shadow price of $2, less the premium of $1). The total profit would therefore increase by $400, to a new value of $69,600.

*We must correct the shadow price for any premium that we pay.*

This adjusted value of $1 represents the actual increase in profit and can be referred to as the *adjusted shadow price*.

**Q:** Assume we have an opportunity to get 250 additional hours of assembly time. However, this time will cost us time and a half (i.e., $15 per hour, rather than the current $10 per hour). Should we take it?

*We must calculate the adjusted shadow price here.*

**A:** From Program 4.2C, the shadow price of $24 per hour of assembly time is valid for an increase of up to 466.67 hours. This shadow price, however, assumes the additional time costs only $10 per hour. The $5 per hour premium paid on the additional time therefore results in an increase of only $19 (= $24 − $5) per each additional hour of assembly time obtained.

The net impact on profit of the additional 250 hours of assembly time is an increase of $4,750 (= 250 × $19). Anderson should definitely accept this opportunity.

**Q:** If we force the production of VCRs, what would be the impact on total profit? Alternatively, how profitable must VCRs become before Anderson should consider producing them?

*The impact of forcing VCRs in is shown by the reduced cost.*

**A:** VCRs are currently not being produced, since they are not profitable enough. The reduced cost of −$1 for VCRs (shown in Program 4.2C) implies that the net impact of producing a VCR will be to decrease total profit by $1 (to $69,399). You may recall from our discussion in Section 4.3 that the reduced cost of VCRs shows the difference between its marginal contribution to Anderson's total profit and the marginal worth of resources it would consume if produced. As an exercise, see if you verify that these values are $29 and $30, respectively.

Alternatively, if Anderson can find a way of increasing the selling price of VCRs by $1 (to $71 per unit), VCRs would then become attractive. This information is also seen from the $1 in the Allowable Increase column for the OFC for VCRs.

**Q:** Assume that there is some uncertainty in the price for DVD players. For what range of prices will the current production be optimal? If DVD players sold for $106, what would be Anderson's new total profit?

*Even though the production values do not change, the total profit will decrease.*

**A:** DVD players currently sell for $110, yielding a profit of $54 per unit. The allowable ranges for the OFC of DVD players in Program 4.2C shows that this value can increase by up to $10 (to $64; selling price of $120) or decrease by up to $5 (to $49; selling price of $105) for the current production plan to remain optimal.

If DVD players actually sold for $106, the profit per unit drops to $50. The current values of the decision variables would remain optimal. However, the new total profit would decrease by $4,240 (= $4 per DVD player for 1,060 DVD players) to $65,160.

## Alternate Optimal Solutions

Is the optimal solution identified in Program 4.2A for Anderson Electronics (380 stereos and 1,060 DVD players, for a total profit of $69,400) unique? Are there alternate production mixes that will also yield a profit of $69,400?

Recall that in Chapter 2 (Section 2.8) we show a graphical example of a situation in which a problem with only two variables had alternate optimal solutions (also referred to as multiple optimal solutions). How can we detect a similar condition from the Solver output for problems involving more than two variables?

*Zeros in the Allowable Increase or Allowable Decrease columns for OFC values may indicate alternate optimal solutions.*

In most cases, when the Allowable Increase or Allowable Decrease column for the OFC of a variable has a value of zero in the *Adjustable Cells* table, this indicates the presence of alternate optimal solutions. In Anderson's problem, we see from Program 4.2C that this is not the case.

Note also from Program 4.2C that the reduced costs for both products currently not being produced in the optimal solution (VCRs and TVs) are nonzero. This indicates that if Anderson is forced to produce either of these products, the net impact will be a reduction in total profit (as discussed earlier). That is, there is no solution possible involving products other than stereos and DVD players that will yield a profit as high as the current solution ($69,400). The current optimal solution is therefore, unique.

In Solved Problem 4-1 at the end of this chapter, we discuss how Solver's sensitivity report can be used to detect the presence of alternate optimal solutions for a problem. We also discuss how Solver can be used to identify these alternate optimal solutions.

## 4.5  ANALYZING SIMULTANEOUS CHANGES USING THE 100% RULE

Until now, we have analyzed the impact of a change in just a single parameter value on the optimal solution. That is, when we are studying the impact of one item of the input data (OFC or RHS value), we assume that all other input data in the model stay constant at their current values. What happens when there are *simultaneous* changes in more than one OFC value or more than one RHS value? Is it possible to analyze the impact of such simultaneous changes on the optimal solution with the information provided in the sensitivity report?

The answer is yes, albeit only under a specific condition, as discussed in the following section. It is important to note that the condition is only valid for analyzing simultaneous changes in either OFC values or RHS values, but not a mixture of the two types of input data.

### Simultaneous Changes in Constraint RHS Values

Consider a situation in which Anderson Electronics realizes that its available number of electronic components is actually only 4,200 and, *at the same time*, also finds that it has an opportunity to obtain an additional 200 hours of assembly time. What is the impact of these *simultaneous* changes on the optimal solution? To answer this question, we first use a condition called the *100% rule*. This condition can be stated as follows:

*The 100% rule can be used to check if simultaneous changes in RHS or OFC values can be analyzed using the current sensitivity report.*

$$\sum_{\text{changes}} (\text{Change}/\text{Allowable change}) \leq 1$$

That is, we compute the ratio of each proposed change in a parameter's value to the maximum allowable change in its value, as given in the sensitivity report. The sum of these ratios must not exceed 1 (or 100%) in order for the information given in the current sensitivity report to be valid. If the sum of the ratios does exceed 1, the current information may still be valid; we just cannot guarantee its validity. However, if the ratio does not exceed 1, the information is definitely valid.

To verify this rule for the proposed change in Anderson's problem, consider each change in turn. First, there is a decrease of 500 units (i.e., from 4,700 to 4,200) in the number of electronic components. From the sensitivity report (see Program 4.2C), the allowable decrease in this RHS value is 950. The ratio is therefore

$$500/950 = 0.5263$$

Next, there is an increase of 200 hours (from 2,500 to 2,700) in the assembly time available. From the sensitivity report, the allowable increase for this RHS value is 466.67. This ratio is, therefore,

$$200/466.67 = 0.4285$$

The sum of these ratios is

$$\text{Sum of ratios} = 0.5263 + 0.4285 = 0.9548 < 1$$

*If the sum of ratios does not exceed 1, the information in the sensitivity report is valid.*

Since this sum does not exceed 1, the information provided in the sensitivity report is valid to analyze the impact of these changes. First, the decrease of 500 units in electronic component availability reduces the size of the feasible region and will therefore cause profit to decrease. The magnitude of this decrease is $1,000 (= 500 units of electronic components, at a shadow price of $2 per unit).

In contrast, the additional 200 hours of assembly time will result in a larger feasible region and a net increase in profit of $4,800 (= 200 hours of assembly time, at a shadow price of $24 per hour). The net impact of these simultaneous changes is therefore an increase in profit by $3,800 (= $4,800 − $1,000).

### Simultaneous Changes in OFC Values

The 100% rule can also be used to analyze simultaneous changes in OFC values in a similar manner. For example, what is the impact on the optimal solution if Anderson decides to drop the selling price of DVD players by $3 per unit but, at the same time, increase the selling price of stereos by $8 per unit?

Once again, we calculate the appropriate ratios to verify the 100% rule. For the current solution to remain optimal, the allowable decrease in the OFC for DVD players is $5, while the allowable increase in the OFC for stereos is $40. The sum of ratios is therefore

$$\text{Sum of ratios} = \$3/\$5 + \$8/\$40 = 0.80 < 1$$

Since the sum of ratios does not exceed 1, the current production plan is still optimal. The $3 decrease in profit per DVD player causes total profit to decrease by $3,180 (= $3 × 1,060). However, the $8 increase in the unit profit of each stereo results in an increase of $3,040 (= $8 × 380) in total profit. The net impact is, therefore, a decrease in profit of only $140 to a new value of $69,260.

---

### 4.6   PRICING OUT NEW VARIABLES

*Pricing out analyzes the impact of adding a new variable to the existing LP model.*

The information given in the sensitivity report can also be used to study the impact of the introduction of new decision variables (products, in the Anderson example) in the model. For example, if Anderson's problem is solved again with a new product also included in the model, will we recommend that the new product be made? Or will we recommend that we do not make the new product and continue making the same products (i.e., stereos and DVD players) Anderson is making now?

### Anderson's Proposed New Product

Suppose Anderson Electronics wants to introduce a new product, Home Theater System (HTS), to take advantage of the hot market for that product. The design department estimates that each HTS will require 5 units of electronic components, 4 units of nonelectronic components, and 4 hours of assembly time. The marketing department estimates that it can sell each HTS for $175.

The question now is whether the HTS will be a profitable product for Anderson to produce. That is, is it worthwhile to divert resources from Anderson's existing products to make this new product? Alternatively, we could pose the question as this: What is the minimum price at which Anderson would need to sell each HTS in order to make it a viable product?

The answer to such questions involves a procedure called *pricing out*. Assume that Anderson decides to make a single HTS. Note that the resources required to make this player (5 units of electronic components, 4 units of nonelectronic components, and 4 hours of assembly time) will no longer be available to meet Anderson's existing production plan (380 stereos and 1,060 DVD players for a total profit of $69,400).

**Checking the Validity of the 100% Rule**  Clearly, the loss of these resources is going to reduce the profit that Anderson could have made from its existing products. Using the shadow prices of these resources, we can calculate the exact impact of the loss of these resources. However, we must first use the 100% rule to check if the shadow prices are valid by calculating the ratio of the reduction in each resource's availability to the allowable decrease for that resource (given in Program 4.2C). The resulting calculation is as follows:

$$\text{Sum of ratios} = 5/950 + 4/560 + 4/1,325 = 0.015 < 1$$

*We first calculate the worth of the resources that would be consumed by the new product, if produced.*

**Required Profit Contribution of Each HTS**  Since the total ratio is less than 1, the shadow prices are valid to calculate the impact on profit of using these resources to produce an HTS, rather than the existing products. We can determine this impact as

$$= 5 \times \text{shadow price of electronic components} +$$
$$4 \times \text{shadow price of nonelectronic components} +$$
$$4 \times \text{shadow price of assembly time}$$

$$= 5 \times \$2 + 4 \times \$0 + 4 \times \$24$$

$$= \$106$$

Hence, in order for the HTS to be a viable product, the profit contribution of each HTS has to at least make up this shortfall in profit. That is, the OFC for the HTS must be at least $106 in order for the optimal solution to have a nonzero value for HTS. Otherwise, the optimal solution of Anderson's model with a decision variable for the HTS included will be the same as the current one, with the HTS having a value of zero.

*We then calculate the actual cost of making the new product, if produced.*

The actual cost of the resources used to make one HTS unit can be calculated as

$$= 5 \times \text{unit price of electronic components} +$$
$$4 \times \text{unit price of nonelectronic components} +$$
$$4 \times \text{unit price of assembly time}$$

$$= 5 \times \$7 + 4 \times \$5 + 4 \times \$10$$

$$= \$95$$

**Finding the Minimum Selling Price of Each HTS Unit**  In order to make the HTS a viable product and let it be worthwhile to divert from existing resources to make it, we need one more calculation. We must find the minimum selling price for HTS units. This is calculated as the sum of the cost of making an HTS unit and the marginal worth of resources diverted from existing products. In Anderson's case, this works out to $201 (= $106 + $95). Since Anderson's marketing department estimates it can sell each HTS unit for only $175, this product will not be profitable for Anderson to produce.

What would happen if Anderson *does* include HTS as a variable in its model and solve the expanded formulation again? In this case, from the discussion so far, we can say that the optimal solution will once again recommend producing 380 stereos and 1,060 DVDs for a total profit of $69,400. The HTS will have a final value of zero (just as the VCR and TV in the current solution). What will be the reduced cost of HTS in this revised solution? We have calculated that the minimum selling price required for HTS to be a viable product is $201, while the actual selling price is only $175. Therefore, the reduced cost will be $26, indicating that each HTS unit produced will cause Anderson's profit to decrease by $26.

To verify our conclusions, let us revise the LP model for Anderson Electronics to include the new product, the HTS. The Excel layout and Solver entries for this revised model are shown in Program 4.3A. The sensitivity report for this model is shown in Program 4.3B.

The results show that it continues to be optimal for Anderson to produce 380 stereos and 1,060 DVD players, for a total profit of $69,400. Further, the magnitude of the reduced cost for HTS is $26 (as we had already calculated).

**File: 4-3.xls**

**PROGRAM 4.3A**    **Revised Excel Layout and Solver Entries for Anderson Electronics**

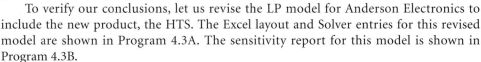

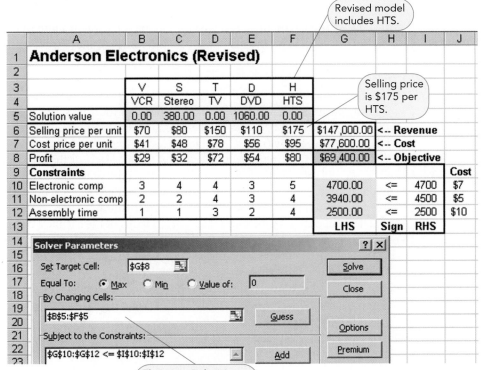

**PROGRAM 4.3B**    **Revised Solver Sensitivity Report for Anderson Electronics**

Microsoft Excel 9.0 Sensitivity Report
Worksheet: [4-3.xls]4.3

*Note that this is same product mix as in Program 4.2C.*

Adjustable Cells

| Cell | Name | Final Value | Reduced Cost | Objective Coefficient | Allowable Increase | Allowable Decrease |
|------|------|-------------|--------------|----------------------|---------------------|---------------------|
| $B$5 | Solution value VCR | 0.00 | -1.00 | 29.00 | 1.00 | 1E+30 |
| $C$5 | Solution value Stereo | 380.00 | 0.00 | 32.00 | 40.00 | 1.67 |
| $D$5 | Solution value TV | 0.00 | -8.00 | 72.00 | 8.00 | 1E+30 |
| $E$5 | Solution value DVD | 1060.00 | 0.00 | 54.00 | 10.00 | 5.00 |
| $F$5 | Solution value HTS | 0.00 | -26.00 | 80.00 | 26.00 | 1E+30 |

*The HTS is not included in the optimal product mix.*

*Reduced cost for HTS is $26.*

Constraints

| Cell | Name | Final Value | Shadow Price | Constraint R.H. Side | Allowable Increase | Allowable Decrease |
|------|------|-------------|--------------|----------------------|---------------------|---------------------|
| $G$10 | Electronic comp | 4700.00 | 2.00 | 4700.00 | 2800.00 | 950.00 |
| $G$11 | Non-electronic comp | 3940.00 | 0.00 | 4500.00 | 1E+30 | 560.00 |
| $G$12 | Assembly time | 2500.00 | 24.00 | 2500.00 | 466.67 | 1325.00 |

*Note that these are the same shadow prices as in Program 4.2C.*

## 4.7    SENSITIVITY ANALYSIS FOR A MINIMIZATION EXAMPLE

*Minimization problems will typically involve some ≥ constraints.*

So far, we have analyzed maximization examples in which all constraints have been of the ≤ type. The analysis is similar for problems with minimization objectives and constraints of the ≥ type. However, we need to be aware that when a solution improves in a minimization problem, the objective value actually decreases rather than increases. We illustrate this with an example.

### Burn-Off Diet Drink Example

Burn-Off, a manufacturer of diet drinks, is planning to introduce a miracle drink that will magically burn the fat away. The drink is made up of four "mystery" ingredients (which we will call ingredients A, B, C, and D). The dosage calls for a person to consume at least three 12-ounce doses per day (i.e., at least 36 ounces per day).

Each of the four ingredients contains different levels of three chemical compounds (which we will call chemicals X, Y, and Z). Health regulations mandate that the dosage consumed per day should contain minimum prescribed levels of chemicals X and Y, and not exceed maximum prescribed levels for the third chemical, Z.

The composition of the four ingredients in terms of the chemical compounds (units per ounce) is shown in Table 4.2, along with the unit cost prices of the ingredients. Burn-Off wants to find the optimal way to mix the ingredients to create the drink, at minimum cost per daily dose.

To formulate this problem, let $A$, $B$, $C$, and $D$ denote the number of ounces of ingredients A, B, C, and D to use, respectively. The problem can then be formulated as follows:

Minimize $4A + 7B + 6C + 3D$          (Daily dose cost in cents)

subject to

$$
\begin{aligned}
A + B + C + D &\geq 36 & \text{(Daily dose requirement)} \\
3A + 4B + 8C + 10D &\geq 280 & \text{(Chemical X requirement)} \\
5A + 3B + 6C + 6D &\geq 200 & \text{(Chemical Y requirement)} \\
10A + 25B + 20C + 40D &\leq 1{,}050 & \text{(Chemical Z max limit)} \\
A, B, C, D &\geq 0
\end{aligned}
$$

**TABLE 4.2**    Data for Diet Drink Example

|  | INGREDIENT A | INGREDIENT B | INGREDIENT C | INGREDIENT D | REQUIREMENT |
|---|---|---|---|---|---|
| Chemical X | 3 | 4 | 8 | 10 | At least 280 units |
| Chemical Y | 5 | 3 | 6 | 6 | At least 200 units |
| Chemical Z | 10 | 25 | 20 | 40 | At most 1,050 units |
| Cost per ounce | 4 cents | 7 cents | 6 cents | 3 cents | |

## Burn-Off's Excel Solution

**File: 4-4.xls**

Programs 4.4A, 4.4B, and 4.4C show the Excel layout and Solver entries, Answer Report, and Sensitivity Report, respectively, for Burn-Off's problem. The Solver output shows that the optimal solution is to use 10.25 ounces of ingredient A, 4.125 ounces of ingredient C, and 21.625 ounces of ingredient D to make the diet drink. No ingredient B is used. The total cost per daily dosage is 130.63 cents (= $1.3063, or $1.31 per day).

*The difference between the LHS and RHS values of a ≥ constraint is called* surplus.

The answer report (Program 4.4B) details the same information but also shows that the constraint for chemical Y is nonbinding. Although the minimum requirement is only 200 units of chemical Y, the final drink actually provides 205.75 units of this chemical. The extra 5.75 units denote the level of oversatisfaction of this requirement. You may recall from Chapter 2 that we refer to this quantity as *surplus*, even though the Solver report always titles this value *slack*.

**PROGRAM 4.4A**    Excel Layout and Solver Entries for Burn-Off Diet Drink

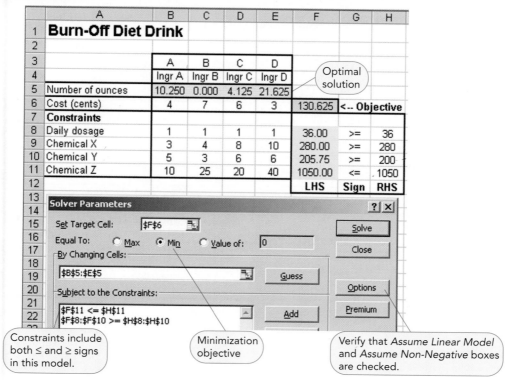

**PROGRAM 4.4B**    Solver Answer Report for Burn-Off Diet Drink

**Microsoft Excel 9.0 Answer Report**
**Worksheet: [4-4.xls]4.4**

Target Cell (Min)

| Cell | Name | Original Value | Final Value |
|------|------|----------------|-------------|
| $F$6 | Cost (cents) | 0.000 | 130.625 |

Optimal cost

Adjustable Cells

| Cell | Name | Original Value | Final Value |
|------|------|----------------|-------------|
| $B$5 | Number of ounces Ingr A | 0.000 | 10.250 |
| $C$5 | Number of ounces Ingr B | 0.000 | 0.000 |
| $D$5 | Number of ounces Ingr C | 0.000 | 4.125 |
| $E$5 | Number of ounces Ingr D | 0.000 | 21.625 |

Ingredient B is *not* used in the optimal mix.

Constraints

| Cell | Name | Cell Value | Formula | Status | Slack |
|------|------|------------|---------|--------|-------|
| $F$11 | Chemical Z | 1050.000 | $F$11<=$H$11 | Binding | 0.000 |
| $F$8 | Daily dosage | 36.000 | $F$8>=$H$8 | Binding | 0.000 |
| $F$9 | Chemical X | 280.000 | $F$9>=$H$9 | Binding | 0.000 |
| $F$10 | Chemical Y | 205.750 | $F$10>=$H$10 | Not Binding | 5.750 |

This is surplus since this is a ≥ constraint.

**PROGRAM 4.4C**    Solver Sensitivity Report for Burn-Off Diet Drink

**Microsoft Excel 9.0 Sensitivity Report**
**Worksheet: [4-4.xls]4.4**

Reduced cost shows increase in total cost if ingredient B is used.

Adjustable Cells

| Cell | Name | Final Value | Reduced Cost | Objective Coefficient | Allowable Increase | Allowable Decrease |
|------|------|-------------|--------------|-----------------------|--------------------|--------------------|
| $B$5 | Number of ounces Ingr A | 10.250 | 0.000 | 4.000 | 3.500 | 2.500 |
| $C$5 | Number of ounces Ingr B | 0.000 | 5.688 | 7.000 | 1E+30 | 5.688 |
| $D$5 | Number of ounces Ingr C | 4.125 | 0.000 | 6.000 | 15.000 | 2.333 |
| $E$5 | Number of ounces Ingr D | 21.625 | 0.000 | 3.000 | 3.800 | 1E+30 |

Constraints

| Cell | Name | Final Value | Shadow Price | Constraint R.H. Side | Allowable Increase | Allowable Decrease |
|------|------|-------------|--------------|----------------------|--------------------|--------------------|
| $F$11 | Chemical Z | 1050.000 | -0.238 | 1050.000 | 47.143 | 346.000 |
| $F$8 | Daily dosage | 36.000 | 3.750 | 36.000 | 16.500 | 1.278 |
| $F$9 | Chemical X | 280.000 | 0.875 | 280.000 | 41.000 | 11.000 |
| $F$10 | Chemical Y | 205.750 | 0.000 | 200.000 | 5.750 | 1E+30 |

Infinity

Shadow price shows decrease in total cost if chemical Z's limit is increased.

## Answering Sensitivity Analysis Questions for Burn-Off

As with the Anderson Electronics example, we use several questions to interpret the information given in the *Sensitivity Report* (Program 4.4C) for Burn-Off.

**Q:** What is the impact on cost if Burn-Off insists on using one ounce of ingredient B to make the drink?

**A:** The reduced cost indicates that each ounce of ingredient B used to make the drink will cause the total cost per daily dosage to increase by 5.688 cents. The new cost will be $130.625 + 5.688 = 136.313$ cents $(= \$1.36)$.

Alternatively, if Burn-Off can find a way of reducing ingredient B's cost per ounce by at least 5.688 cents (to 1.312 cents or less), then it becomes cost-effective to use this ingredient to make the diet drink.

**Q:** There is some uncertainty in the cost of ingredient C. How sensitive is the current optimal solution to this cost?

**A:** The current cost of ingredient C is 6 cents per ounce. The range for the cost coefficient of this ingredient shows an allowable increase of 15 cents and an allowable decrease of 2.333 cents, for the current corner point solution to remain optimal. The cost per ounce of ingredient C could therefore fluctuate between 3.667 cents $(= 6 - 2.333)$ and 21 cents $(= 6 + 15)$ without affecting the current optimal mix.

The total cost will, however, change depending on the actual unit cost of ingredient C. For example, if the cost of ingredient C increases to 10 cents per ounce, the new total cost will be

$$= 130.625 + (4 \text{ cents extra per oz.} \times 4.125 \text{ oz. of C})$$

$$= 130.625 + 16.500 = 147.125 \text{ cents} = \$1.47$$

**Q:** What do the shadow prices for chemical X and chemical Z imply in this problem?

**A:** The shadow price for chemical X is 0.875 cents. Since the constraint for chemical X is a $\geq$ constraint, an increase by one unit in the RHS (from 280 to 281) makes the problem solution even more restrictive. That is, the feasible region becomes smaller. The optimal objective function value could, therefore, worsen. The shadow price indicates that for each additional unit of chemical X required to be present in the drink, the overall cost will increase by 0.875 cents. This value is valid for an increase of up to 41 units and a decrease by 11 units in the requirement for chemical X.

In contrast, the constraint for chemical Z is a $\leq$ constraint. An increase in the RHS of the constraint (from 1,050 to 1,051) will cause the feasible region to become bigger. Hence, the optimal objective function value could possibly improve. The negative value of the shadow price for this constraint indicates that each unit increase in the maximum limit allowed for chemical Z will cause total cost to decrease by 0.238 cents. This value is valid for an increase of up to 47.143 units. Likewise, the total cost will *increase* by 0.238 cents for each unit *decrease* in the maximum limit allowed for chemical Z. This is valid for a decrease of up to 346 units in the maximum limit for chemical Z.

*A negative value for shadow price implies that cost will decrease if RHS value increases.*

**Q:** Burn-Off can decrease the minimum requirement for chemical X by 5 units (from 280 to 275) provided the maximum limit allowed for chemical Z is reduced to 1,000 units (that is, reduced by 50 units). Is this trade-off cost-effective for Burn-Off to implement?

**A:** Since we are dealing with simultaneous changes in RHS values, we first verify if the 100% rule is satisfied. To do so, we take the ratio of each proposed change to its maximum allowable change. The calculations are

*Analyzing simultaneous changes requires the use of the 100% rule.*

$$\text{Sum of ratios} = 5/11 + 50/346 = 0.599 < 1$$

Since the sum of ratio does not exceed 1, we can use the shadow price information in the sensitivity report (Program 4.4C). The reduction of 5 units in the requirement for chemical X will cause the feasible region to increase in size. The total cost will therefore improve (i.e., go down) by 4.375 cents (= 5 units, at a shadow price of 0.875 cents per unit).

In contrast, the reduction of 50 units in the maximum allowable limit for chemical Z makes the feasible region shrink in size. The total cost will therefore be adversely impacted (i.e., go up) by 11.9 cents (= 50 units, at a shadow price of 0.238 cents per unit).

The net impact of this trade-off is therefore an increase in total cost of 7.525 cents (= 11.9 − 4.375). The new cost will be 138.15 cents, or $1.38. Clearly, this trade-off is not cost-effective from Burn-Off's perspective and should be rejected.

## SUMMARY

In this chapter we present the important concept of sensitivity analysis. Sometimes referred to as postoptimality analysis, sensitivity analysis is used by management to answer a series of what if questions about inputs to an LP model. It also tests just how sensitive the optimal solution is to changes in (1) profit or cost coefficients and (2) constraint RHS values.

We first explore sensitivity analysis graphically (i.e., for problems with only two decision variables). We then discuss how to interpret information in the Answer and Sensitivity Reports generated by Solver. We also discussed how the information in these reports can be used to analyze simultaneous changes in model parameter values and determine the potential impact of a new variable in the model.

## GLOSSARY

**Allowable Decrease for an OFC.** The maximum amount by which the OFC of a decision variable can decrease for the current optimal solution to remain optimal.

**Allowable Decrease for a RHS Value.** The maximum amount by which the RHS value of a constraint can decrease for the shadow price to be valid.

**Allowable Increase for an OFC.** The maximum amount by which the OFC of a decision variable can increase for the current optimal solution to remain optimal.

**Allowable Increase for a RHS Value.** The maximum amount by which the RHS value of a constraint can increase for the shadow price to be valid.

**Answer Report.** A report created by Solver when it solves an LP model. This report presents the optimal solution in a detailed manner.

**Objective Function Coefficient (OFC).** The coefficient for a decision variable in the objective function. Typically, this refers to unit profit or unit cost.

**100% Rule.** A rule used to verify the validity of the information in the sensitivity report when dealing with simultaneous changes to more than one RHS value or more than one OFC value.

**Pricing Out.** A procedure by which the shadow price information in the sensitivity report can be used to gauge the impact of the addition of a new variable in the LP model.

**Reduced Cost.** Difference between the marginal contribution to the objective function value from the inclusion of a decision variable and the marginal worth of the resources it consumes. In the case of a decision variable that has an optimal value of zero, it is also the minimum amount by which the OFC of that variable should change before it would have a nonzero optimal value.

**Right-Hand Side (RHS) Value.** The amount of resource available (for a ≤ constraint) or the minimum requirement of some criterion (for a ≥ constraint). Typically expressed as a constant for sensitivity analysis.

**Sensitivity Analysis.** The study of how sensitive an optimal solution is to model assumptions and to data changes. Also referred to as postoptimality analysis.

**Shadow Price.** The magnitude of the change in the objective function value for a unit increase in the RHS of a constraint.

**Slack.** Difference between the RHS and left-hand-side (LHS) of a ≤ constraint. Typically represents the unused resource.

**Surplus.** Difference between the LHS and RHS of a ≥ constraint. Typically represents the level of over-satisfaction of a requirement.

## SOLVED PROBLEM

### Solved Problem 4-1

Let us revisit the Hong Kong Bank of Commerce and Industry example in Chapter 3 (Section 3.4 on page 85). We will use the sensitivity report for this example to illustrate the detection of alternate optimal solutions for an LP problem and the manner in which Excel can be used to identify those alternate optimal solutions. Please reread that example. We repeat just the formulation portion as follows:

For the example, let

$$F = \text{full-time tellers}$$

$$P_1 = \text{part-timers starting at 9 A.M. (leaving at 1 P.M.)}$$

$$P_2 = \text{part-timers starting at 10 A.M. (leaving at 2 P.M.)}$$

$$P_3 = \text{part-timers starting at 11 A.M. (leaving at 3 P.M.)}$$

$$P_4 = \text{part-timers starting at noon (leaving at 4 P.M.)}$$

$$P_5 = \text{part-timers starting at 1 P.M. (leaving at 5 P.M.)}$$

Objective function:

$$\text{minimize total daily personnel cost} = \$50F + \$16(P_1 + P_2 + P_3 + P_4 + P_5)$$

Constraints:

For each hour, the available labor hours must be at least equal to the required labor hours.

$$
\begin{aligned}
F + P_1 &\geq 10 &&(9 \text{ A.M.} - 10 \text{ A.M. needs}) \\
F + P_1 + P_2 &\geq 12 &&(10 \text{ A.M.} - 11 \text{ A.M. needs}) \\
\tfrac{1}{2} F + P_1 + P_2 + P_3 &\geq 14 &&(11 \text{ A.M.} - \text{noon needs}) \\
\tfrac{1}{2} F + P_1 + P_2 + P_3 + P_4 &\geq 16 &&(\text{noon} - 1 \text{ P.M. needs}) \\
F + P_2 + P_3 + P_4 + P_5 &\geq 18 &&(1 \text{ P.M.} - 2 \text{ P.M. needs}) \\
F + P_3 + P_4 + P_5 &\geq 17 &&(2 \text{ P.M.} - 3 \text{ P.M. needs}) \\
F + P_4 + P_5 &\geq 15 &&(3 \text{ P.M.} - 4 \text{ P.M. needs}) \\
F + P_5 &\geq 10 &&(4 \text{ P.M.} - 5 \text{ P.M. needs})
\end{aligned}
$$

Only 12 full-time tellers are available, so

$$F \leq 12$$

Part-time worker hours cannot exceed 50% of total hours required each day, which is the sum of the tellers needed each hour.

$$4(P_1 + P_2 + P_3 + P_4 + P_5) \leq 0.50(10 + 12 + 14 + 16 + 18 + 17 + 15 + 10)$$

or

$$4P_1 + 4P_2 + 4P_3 + 4P_4 + 4P_5 \leq 56$$

$$F, P_1, P_2, P_3, P_4, P_5 \geq 0$$

## Solution

The Excel implementation and Solver entries for this model are shown in Program 4.5A. The Sensitivity Report is shown in Program 4.5B.

**File: 4-5.xls**

Program 4.5A reveals that the optimal solution is to employ 10 full-time tellers, 7 part-time tellers at 10 A.M., 2 part-time tellers at 11 A.M., and 5 part-time tellers at noon, for a total cost of $724 per day.

In Program 4.5B, the shadow price of $-4.333$ for the part time limit of 56 hours (row 17) indicates that each additional hour (over the 56 hour limit) that part-timers are allowed to work will allow the bank to reduce costs by $4.333. This shadow price is valid for a limit of 60 more hours (i.e., up to 116 hours). Note that the shadow price is fractional since we are allowing the solution to include fractional values for the decision variables.

Examining the allowable increase and allowable decrease values for the OFCs, we see that there are several values of zero in these columns. This indicates that there are alternate optimal solutions to this problem.

**PROGRAM 4.5A**    **Excel Layout and Solver Entries for Solved Problem 4-1**

|   | A | B | C | D | E | F | G | H | I | J |
|---|---|---|---|---|---|---|---|---|---|---|
| 1 | **Hong Kong Bank** | | | | | | | | | |
| 2 | | | | | | | | | | |
| 3 | | F | $P_1$ | $P_2$ | $P_3$ | $P_4$ | $P_5$ | | | |
| 4 | | Full Time | Part Time @9am | Part Time @10am | Part Time @11am | Part Time @Noon | Part Time @1pm | Optimal solution | | |
| 5 | Solution value | 10.00 | 0.00 | 7.00 | 2.00 | 5.00 | 0.00 | | | |
| 6 | Cost | $50.00 | $16.00 | $16.00 | $16.00 | $16.00 | $16.00 | $724.00 | <-- Objective | |
| 7 | **Constraints** | | | | | | | | | |
| 8 | 9am-10am Needs | 1 | 1 | | | | | 10.00 | >= | 10 |
| 9 | 10am-11am Needs | 1 | 1 | 1 | | | | 17.00 | >= | 12 |
| 10 | 11am-Noon Needs | 0.5 | 1 | 1 | 1 | | | 14.00 | >= | 14 |
| 11 | Noon-1pm Needs | 0.5 | 1 | 1 | 1 | 1 | | 19.00 | >= | 16 |
| 12 | 1pm-2pm Needs | 1 | | 1 | 1 | 1 | 1 | 24.00 | >= | 18 |
| 13 | 2pm-3pm Needs | 1 | | | 1 | 1 | 1 | 17.00 | >= | 17 |
| 14 | 3pm-4pm Needs | 1 | | | | 1 | 1 | 15.00 | >= | 15 |
| 15 | 4pm-5pm Needs | 1 | | | | | 1 | 10.00 | >= | 10 |
| 16 | Max Full Time | 1 | | | | | | 10.00 | <= | 12 |
| 17 | Part Time  Limit | | 4 | 4 | 4 | 4 | 4 | 56.00 | <= | 56 |
| 18 | | | | | | | | LHS | Sign | RHS |

These define the teller requirements each period.

= 50% of total requirement = 0.5 × SUM (J8:J15)

| Solver Parameters | ? X |
|---|---|
| Se_t Target Cell: $H$6 | Solve |
| Equal To:  ○ Max  ● Min  ○ Value of: 0 | Close |
| By Changing Cells: | |
| $B$5:$G$5 | Guess |
| | Options |
| Subject to the Constraints: | |
| $H$16:$H$17 <= $J$16:$J$17 | Add  Premium |
| $H$8:$H$15 >= $J$8:$J$15 | |

Minimization objective

Likewise, consider the reduced cost for variables $P_1$ and $P_5$. These are zero, even though these variables have values of zero (their lower limit). This implies that, for example, it is possible to force $P_1$ (or $P_5$) to have a nonzero value at optimality and not affect the total cost in any way. This is another indication of the presence of alternate optimal solutions to this problem.

How can we identify these optimal solutions? Sometimes, simply rearranging the order in which the constraints are included in Solver makes Excel identify an alternate optimal solution. There are, however, a couple of ways of *forcing* Excel to identify these alternate optimal solutions. One way would be to include the current objective function as a constraint, as follows:

*We can force Excel to identify these alternate optimal solutions.*

$$50F + 16(P_1 + P_2 + P_3 + P_4 + P_5) = 724$$

Then, the new objective for the problem would be the maximization of the relevant variable ($P_1$ or $P_5$). That is,

$$\text{Max } P_1 \text{ (or } P_5)$$

An alternate approach is to add a constraint forcing the relevant variable ($P_1$ or $P_5$ in this case) to be nonzero. In many cases, even a constraint such as $P_1 \geq 0.001$ will suffice.

**PROGRAM 4.5B**     **Solver Sensitivity Report for Solved Problem 4-1**

Reduced cost of 0 indicates that a solution with part-time tellers at 9 A.M. exists, with no change in optimal objective value.

**Microsoft Excel 9.0 Sensitivity Report**
**Worksheet: [4-5.xls]4.5**

Adjustable Cells

| Cell | Name | Final Value | Reduced Cost | Objective Coefficient | Allowable Increase | Allowable Decrease |
|------|------|------|------|------|------|------|
| $B$5 | Solution value Full Time | 10.00 | 0.00 | 50.00 | 1E+30 | 26.00 |
| $C$5 | Solution value Part Time @9am | 0.00 | 0.00 | 16.00 | 26.00 | 0.00 |
| $D$5 | Solution value Part Time @10am | 7.00 | 0.00 | 16.00 | 0.00 | 25.00 |
| $E$5 | Solution value Part Time @11am | 2.00 | 0.00 | 16.00 | 33.33 | 0.00 |
| $F$5 | Solution value Part Time @Noon | 5.00 | 0.00 | 16.00 | 0.00 | 33.33 |
| $G$5 | Solution value Part Time @1pm | 0.00 | 0.00 | 16.00 | 26.00 | 0.00 |

These 0s indicate that there are alternate optimal solutions.

Constraints

| Cell | Name | Final Value | Shadow Price | Constraint R.H. Side | Allowable Increase | Allowable Decrease |
|------|------|------|------|------|------|------|
| $H$16 | Max Full Time | 10.00 | 0.00 | 12.00 | 1E+30 | 2.00 |
| $H$17 | Part Time Limit | 56.00 | -4.33 | 56.00 | 60.00 | 0.00 |
| $H$8 | 9am-10am Needs | 10.00 | 0.00 | 10.00 | 6.00 | 0.00 |
| $H$9 | 10am-11am Needs | 17.00 | 0.00 | 12.00 | 5.00 | 1E+30 |
| $H$10 | 11am-Noon Needs | 14.00 | 33.33 | 14.00 | 0.00 | 3.00 |
| $H$11 | Noon-1pm Needs | 19.00 | 0.00 | 16.00 | 3.00 | 1E+30 |
| $H$12 | 1pm-2pm Needs | 24.00 | 0.00 | 18.00 | 6.00 | 1E+30 |
| $H$13 | 2pm-3pm Needs | 17.00 | 0.00 | 17.00 | 5.00 | 2.00 |
| $H$14 | 3pm-4pm Needs | 15.00 | 33.33 | 15.00 | 0.00 | 3.00 |
| $H$15 | 4pm-5pm Needs | 10.00 | 0.00 | 10.00 | 3.00 | 0.00 |

By using either of these changes, we can identify alternate solutions for Hong Kong Bank as follows. The cost of both these employment policies is also $724.

1. 10 full-time tellers, 6 part-time tellers at 9 A.M., 1 part-time teller at 10 A.M., 2 part-time tellers at 11 A.M., and 5 part-time tellers at noon.

2. 10 full-time tellers, 7 tellers at 10 A.M., 2 part-time tellers at 11 A.M., 4 part-time tellers at noon, and 1 part-time teller at 1 P.M.

**⫸ SELF-TEST**

■ Before taking the self-test, refer back to the learning objectives at the beginning of the chapter, the notes in the margins, and the glossary at the end of the chapter.

■ Use the key at the back of the book to correct your answers.

■ Restudy pages that correspond to any questions that you answered incorrectly or material you feel uncertain about.

1. The measure that shows the change in the optimal objective function value for a unit increase in a constraint RHS value is the
   a. shadow price.
   b. reduced cost.
   c. allowable increase.
   d. allowable decrease.
2. The measure that compares the marginal contribution of a variable with the marginal worth of the resources it consumes is the
   a. shadow price.
   b. reduced cost.
   c. allowable increase.
   d. allowable decrease.
3. For a nonbinding constraint, the shadow price will always equal zero.
   a. True              b. False
4. The measure that shows the change in the optimal objective function value if a product that is not currently produced is forced to be produced is the
   a. shadow price.
   b. reduced cost.
   c. allowable increase.
   d. allowable decrease.
5. For a constraint, the *Allowable Increase* column in the sensitivity report shows
   a. the allowable increase in the objective value.
   b. the allowable increase in the RHS value of the constraint for which the current optimal corner point remains optimal.
   c. the allowable increase in the shadow price.
6. When analyzing simultaneous changes in parameter values, we need to first verify the 100% rule.
   a. True              b. False
7. If the 100% rule is violated, the information in the sensitivity report is always invalid.
   a. True              b. False
8. If the RHS value of a ≥ constraint increases, the optimal value of a maximization objective function can *never*
   a. increase.         b. decrease.
   c. stay the same.

9. If we wish to increase a constraint RHS value beyond the allowable increase value shown in the sensitivity report, this means
   a. there will no longer be a feasible solution for the problem.
   b. the problem needs to be solved again to get a new sensitivity report.
   c. such a change should never be made.
   d. the shadow price in the report is still valid.
10. The pricing out procedure allows us to
    a. analyze the impact of changes in the selling price of existing products.
    b. analyze the impact of changes in the cost of resources.
    c. analyze the impact of the introduction of a new variable.
    d. analyze simultaneous changes in parameter values.
11. Sensitivity reports can be used to detect the presence of alternate optimal solutions.
    a. True              b. False
12. The reduced cost of a variable that has a value of zero in the current optimal solution will always be nonzero.
    a. True              b. False
13. If the RHS value of a ≤ constraint decreases, the optimal value of a maximization objective function can *never*
    a. increase.
    b. decrease.
    c. stay the same.
14. *Surplus* refers to the
    a. LHS value of a ≥ constraint.
    b. difference between the LHS and RHS values of a ≥ constraint.
    c. difference between the LHS and RHS values of a ≤ constraint.
    d. RHS value of a ≥ constraint.
15. If the objective function coefficient of a variable changes within its allowable range,
    a. the current variable values and the objective value remain the same.
    b. the current variable values remain the same, but the objective value would change.
    c. the current variable values and the objective value will change.

# DISCUSSION QUESTIONS AND PROBLEMS

## Discussion Questions

**4-1** Discuss the role of sensitivity analysis in LP. Under what circumstances is it needed, and under what conditions do you think it is not necessary?

**4-2** Is sensitivity analysis a concept applied to LP only, or should it also be used when analyzing other techniques (e.g., break-even analysis)? Provide examples to prove your point.

**4-3** Explain how a change in resource availability can affect the optimal solution of a problem.

**4-4** Explain how a change in an objective function coefficient can affect the optimal solution of a problem.

**4-5** Are simultaneous changes in input data values logical? Provide examples to prove your point.

**4-6** Explain the 100% rule and its role in analyzing the impact of simultaneous changes in model input data values.

**4-7** How can a firm benefit from using the pricing out procedure?

**4-8** How do we detect the presence of alternate optimal solutions from a Solver Sensitivity Report?

**4-9** Why would a firm find information regarding the shadow price of a resource useful?

## Problems

**4-10** We used a graphical approach to solve the following LP model in Problem 2-14:

Maximize profit $= \$1X + \$1Y$

subject to

$$2X + Y \leq 100$$

$$X + 2Y \leq 100$$

$$X, Y \geq 0$$

Now use the graphical solution to answer the following questions. Each question is independent of the others.

(a) If a technical breakthrough occurred that raised the profit per unit of $X$ to $3, would this affect the optimal corner point? Does it change the optimal objective value?

(b) If the technical breakthrough had raised the profit per unit of $X$ to only $1.25, would this affect the optimal corner point? Does it change the optimal objective value?

(c) If the second constraint is changed form $X + 2Y \leq$ 100 to $X + 4Y \leq 100$, what effect will this have on the optimal corner point and profit? (Use the profit function $1X + 1Y$.)

**4-11** We used a graphical approach to solve the following LP model in Problem 2-15:

Maximize profit $= \$3X + \$2Y$

subject to

$$2X + 1Y \leq 150$$

$$2X + 3Y \leq 300$$

$$X, Y \geq 0$$

Now use the graphical solution to answer the following questions. Each question is independent of the others.

(a) Does the optimal solution change if the profit per unit of $X$ changes to $4.50? What about the optimal profit?

(b) What happens if the profit function changes to $3X + 3Y$?

**4-12** We used a graphical approach to solve the following LP model in Problem 2-16.

Maximize profit $= \$4X + \$6Y$

subject to

$$1X + 2Y \leq 8$$

$$6X + 4Y \leq 24$$

$$X, Y \geq 0$$

Now use the graphical solution to answer the following questions. Each question is independent of the others.

(a) If the first constraint is altered to $X + 3Y \leq 8$, does the feasible region or optimal solution change? If so, how?

(b) If the second constraint is altered to $6X + 4Y \leq 36$, does the feasible region or optimal solution change? If so, how?

**4-13** Consider the Win Big Gambling Club media selection example discussed in Section 3.2 of Chapter 3. Use the Sensitivity Report for this LP model (shown in Program 4.6 on page 146) to answer the following questions. Each question is independent of the others.

(a) What would be the impact if management approves spending $200 more on radio advertising each week?

(b) Would it help Win Big if it can get out of the contractual agreement to place at least five radio spots each week?

(c) The radio station manager agrees to run the afternoon radio spots during some of their more popular programs. He thinks this will increase the audience reached per ad to 3,100. Will this change the optimal solution? Why or why not?

(d) There is some uncertainty in the audience reached per TV spot. For what range of values for this OFC will the current solution remain optimal?

**4-14** Consider the MSA marketing research example discussed in Section 3.3 of Chapter 3. Use the Sensitivity Report for this LP model (shown in Program 4.7) to

**PROGRAM 4.6**

**Solver Sensitivity Report for Problem 4-13**

**Microsoft Excel 9.0 Sensitivity Report**
**Problem 4-13.  Win Big Gambling Club**

Adjustable Cells

| Cell | Name | Final Value | Reduced Cost | Objective Coefficient | Allowable Increase | Allowable Decrease |
|------|------|-------------|--------------|----------------------|--------------------|--------------------|
| $B$5 | Number of Units TV spots | 1.97 | 0.00 | 5000.00 | 1620.69 | 5000.00 |
| $C$5 | Number of Units Newspaper ads | 5.00 | 0.00 | 8500.00 | 1E+30 | 2718.75 |
| $D$5 | Number of Units Prime-time radio spots | 6.21 | 0.00 | 2400.00 | 1E+30 | 263.16 |
| $E$5 | Number of Units Afternoon radio spots | 0.00 | -344.83 | 2800.00 | 344.83 | 1E+30 |

Constraints

| Cell | Name | Final Value | Shadow Price | Constraint R.H. Side | Allowable Increase | Allowable Decrease |
|------|------|-------------|--------------|----------------------|--------------------|--------------------|
| $F$14 | Min Radio Spots | 6.21 | 0.00 | 5.00 | 1.21 | 1E+30 |
| $F$8 | Max TV | 1.97 | 0.00 | 12.00 | 1E+30 | 10.03 |
| $F$9 | Max Newspaper | 5.00 | 2718.75 | 5.00 | 1.70 | 5.00 |
| $F$10 | Max Prime-Time Radio | 6.21 | 0.00 | 25.00 | 1E+30 | 18.79 |
| $F$11 | Max Afternoon Radio | 0.00 | 0.00 | 20.00 | 1E+30 | 20.00 |
| $F$12 | Budget | 8,000.00 | 6.25 | 8000.00 | 8025.00 | 1575.00 |
| $F$13 | Max Radio $ | 1,800.00 | 2.03 | 1800.00 | 1575.00 | 350.00 |

answer the following questions. Each question is independent of the others.

(a) What is the maximum unit cost that will make it worthwhile to include persons 30 years of age or younger who live in a border state in the survey?
(b) What is the impact if MSA wants to increase the sample size to 3,000?
(c) What is the impact if MSA insists on including people 31−50 years of age who do not live in a border state?
(d) What is the impact if we can reduce the minimum 30 or younger persons required to 900 provided we raise the persons 31–50 years of age to 650?

‣ **4-15** Consider the Whole Food Nutrition Center diet problem example discussed in Section 3.7 of Chapter 3. Use the Sensitivity Report for this LP model (shown

in Program 4.8 on page 147) to answer the following questions. Each question is independent of the others.

(a) What is the impact if the daily allowance for protein can be reduced to 2.9 units?
(b) Whole Food believes the unit price of grain A could be 5% overestimated and the unit price of grain B could be 10% underestimated. If these turn out to be true, what is the new optimal solution and optimal total cost?
(c) What is the impact if the reduction in the daily allowance for protein in (a) requires Whole Food to simultaneously increase the daily allowance of riboflavin to 2.20 units?

‣ **4-16** Consider Battery Park Stables' animal feed problem first presented in Chapter 3 as Problem 3-4 on page 106. Use Solver to create the Answer and Sensitivity

**PROGRAM 4.7**

**Solver Sensitivity Report for Problem 4-14**

**Microsoft Excel 9.0 Sensitivity Report**
**Problem 4-14.  MSA Marketing Research**

Adjustable Cells

| Cell | Name | Final Value | Reduced Cost | Objective Coefficient | Allowable Increase | Allowable Decrease |
|------|------|-------------|--------------|----------------------|--------------------|--------------------|
| $B$5 | Number of Households <= 30 and border | 0.00 | 0.60 | 7.50 | 1E+30 | 0.60 |
| $C$5 | Number of Households 31-50 and border | 600.00 | 0.00 | 6.80 | 0.45 | 0.82 |
| $D$5 | Number of Households >= 51 and border | 140.00 | 0.00 | 5.50 | 0.60 | 29.90 |
| $E$5 | Number of Households <= 30 and not border | 1000.00 | 0.00 | 6.90 | 0.60 | 0.92 |
| $F$5 | Number of Households 31-50 and not border | 0.00 | 0.45 | 7.25 | 1E+30 | 0.45 |
| $G$5 | Number of Households >= 51 and not border | 560.00 | 0.00 | 6.10 | 1.03 | 0.60 |

Constraints

| Cell | Name | Final Value | Shadow Price | Constraint R.H. Side | Allowable Increase | Allowable Decrease |
|------|------|-------------|--------------|----------------------|--------------------|--------------------|
| $H$12 | >= 51 in Border | 0.00 | -0.60 | 0.00 | 560.00 | 140.00 |
| $H$8 | Total Households | 2300.00 | 5.98 | 2300.00 | 1E+30 | 700.00 |
| $H$9 | <= 30 Households | 1000.00 | 0.92 | 1000.00 | 700.00 | 1000.00 |
| $H$10 | 31-50 Households | 600.00 | 0.82 | 600.00 | 700.00 | 493.75 |
| $H$11 | Border States | 395.00 | 0.00 | 0.00 | 395.00 | 1E+30 |

**PROGRAM 4.8**

**Solver Sensitivity Report for Problem 4-15**

**Microsoft Excel 9.0 Sensitivity Report**
**Problem 4-15. Whole Food Nutrition Center**

Adjustable Cells

| Cell | Name | Final Value | Reduced Cost | Objective Coefficient | Allowable Increase | Allowable Decrease |
|------|------|-------------|--------------|-----------------------|--------------------|--------------------|
| $B$5 | Number of Pounds Grain A | 0.025 | 0.000 | 0.330 | 0.063 | 1E+30 |
| $C$5 | Number of Pounds Grain B | 0.050 | 0.000 | 0.470 | 1E+30 | 0.190 |
| $D$5 | Number of Pounds Grain C | 0.050 | 0.000 | 0.380 | 1E+30 | 0.073 |

Constraints

| Cell | Name | Final Value | Shadow Price | Constraint R.H. Side | Allowable Increase | Allowable Decrease |
|------|------|-------------|--------------|----------------------|--------------------|--------------------|
| $E$12 | Total Mix | 0.125 | -1.210 | 0.125 | 0.004 | 0.000 |
| $E$8 | Protein | 3.000 | 0.038 | 3.000 | 0.000 | 0.250 |
| $E$9 | Riboflavin | 2.350 | 0.000 | 2.000 | 0.350 | 1E+30 |
| $E$10 | Phosphorus | 1.000 | 0.088 | 1.000 | 0.018 | 0.000 |
| $E$11 | Magnesium | 0.425 | 0.000 | 0.425 | 0.000 | 1E+30 |

Reports for this LP problem. Now answer the following questions using these reports. Each question is independent of the others.

(a) If the price of grain decreases by $0.01 per pound, will the optimal solution change?

(b) Which constraints are binding? Interpret the shadow price for the binding constraints.

(c) What would happen to the total cost if the price of mineral decreased by 20% from its current value?

(d) For what price range of oats is the current solution optimal?

**4-17** Consider Kathy Roniger's diet problem first presented in Chapter 3 as Problem 3-9 on page 107. Use Solver to create the answer and sensitivity reports for this LP problem. Now answer the following questions using these reports. Each question is independent of the others.

(a) Interpret the shadow prices for the carbohydrates and iron constraints.

(b) What would happen to total cost if Kathy insists on using milk in her diet?

(c) What would be the maximum amount Kathy would be willing to pay for beans to make it a cost-effective item for inclusion in her diet?

(d) Is the solution to this problem a unique optimal solution? Justify your answer.

**4-18** Consider Quitmeyer Electronics' product mix problem first presented in Chapter 3 as Problem 3-10 on page 108. Use Solver to create the Answer and Sensitivity Reports for this LP problem. Now answer the following questions using these reports. Each question is independent of the others.

(a) Interpret the reduced costs for the products that are not currently included in the optimal production plan.

(b) Another part of the corporation wants to take 35 hours of time on test device 3. How does this affect Quitmeyer's optimal solution?

(c) Quitmeyer has the opportunity to obtain 20 additional hours on test device 1 at a cost of $25 per hour. Is this deal worthwhile?

(d) Quitmeyer has the opportunity to give up 20 hours of time on device 1 and obtain 40 hours of time on device 2 in return. Is this deal worthwhile? Justify your answer.

**4-19** Consider Margaret Young's farm planning problem first presented in Chapter 3 as Problem 3-12 on page 109. Use Solver to create the Answer and Sensitivity Reports for this LP problem. Now answer the following questions using these reports. Each question is independent of the others.

(a) Is this solution a unique optimal solution? Why or why not?

(b) If there are alternate solutions, use Solver to identify at least one other optimal solution.

(c) Would it help Margaret's total profit if she could increase barley sales by 10%? If so, how?

(d) How would the availability of more water affect Margaret's total profit?

**4-20** Consider the following LP problem, in which $X$ and $Y$ denote the number of units of products $X$ and $Y$ to produce, respectively.

Maximize profit = $4X + $5Y

subject to

| | |
|---|---|
| $X + 2Y \le 10$ | (Labor available in hours) |
| $6X + 6Y \le 36$ | (Material available in pounds) |
| $8X + 4Y \le 40$ | (Storage available in square feet) |
| $X, \quad Y \ge 0$ | |

The Excel Answer and Sensitivity Reports for this problem are shown in Table 4.3 on page 148. Calculate and explain what happens to the optimal solution for each of the following situations. Each question is independent of the other questions.

**TABLE 4.3**

Answer and Sensitivity
Reports for Problem 4-20

| TARGET CELL (MAX) | |
|---|---|
| NAME | FINAL VALUE |
| Profit | 28 |

| ADJUSTABLE CELLS | |
|---|---|
| NAME | FINAL VALUE |
| Product 1 | 2 |
| Product 2 | 4 |

| CONSTRAINTS | | | |
|---|---|---|---|
| NAME | CELL VALUE | STATUS | SLACK |
| Labor | 10 | Binding | 0 |
| Material | 36 | Binding | 0 |
| Storage | 32 | Not Binding | 8 |

| CHANGING CELLS | | | | | |
|---|---|---|---|---|---|
| NAME | FINAL VALUE | REDUCED COST | OBJECTIVE COEFFICIENT | ALLOWABLE INCREASE | ALLOWABLE DECREASE |
| Product 1 | 2 | 0 | 4 | 1.0 | 1.5 |
| Product 2 | 4 | 0 | 5 | 3.0 | 1.0 |

| CONSTRAINTS | | | | | |
|---|---|---|---|---|---|
| NAME | FINAL VALUE | SHADOW PRICE | CONSTRAINT RHS | ALLOWABLE INCREASE | ALLOWABLE DECREASE |
| Labor | 10 | 1.0 | 10 | 2.0 | 2.0 |
| Materials | 36 | 0.5 | 36 | 4.0 | 6.0 |
| Storage | 32 | 0.0 | 40 | 1E+30 | 8.0 |

(a) You acquire 2 additional pounds of material.
(b) You acquire 1.5 additional hours of labor.
(c) You give up 1 hour of labor and get 1.5 pounds of material.
(d) The profit contributions for both products X and Y are changed to $4.75 each.
(e) You decide to introduce a new product that has a profit contribution of $2. Each unit of this product will use 1 hour of labor, 1 pound of material, and 2 square feet of storage space.

⁞ 4-21 Consider the Mt. Sinai Hospital example first presented in Chapter 3 as Problem 3-14 on page 110. Use Solver to create the Answer and Sensitivity Reports for this LP problem. Now answer the following questions using these reports. Each question is independent of the others.

(a) What is the maximum revenue per year, how many medical patients/year are there, and how many surgical patients/year are there? How many medical beds and how many surgical beds of the 90-bed addition should be added?

(b) Are there any empty beds with this optimal solution? If so, how many empty beds are there? Discuss the effect of acquiring more beds if needed.

(c) Are the laboratories being used to their capacity? Is it possible to perform more lab tests/year? If so, how many more? Discuss the effect of acquiring more lab space if needed.

(d) Is the x-ray facility being used to its maximum? Is it possible to do more x-rays/year? If so, how many more? Discuss the effect of acquiring more x-ray facilities if needed.

(e) Is the operating room being used to capacity? Is it possible to do more operations/year? If so, how many more? Discuss the effect of acquiring more operating room if needed. (**Source:** Professor Chris Vertullo.)

⁞ 4-22 The Good-to-Go Suitcase Company makes three kinds of suitcases: (1) Standard, (2) Deluxe, and (3) Luxury styles. Each suitcase goes through four production stages: (1) cutting and coloring, (2) assembly, (3) finishing, and (4) quality and packaging. The total number of hours available in each of these departments is 630, 600, 708, and 135, respectively.

Each Standard suitcase requires 0.7 hours of cutting and coloring, 0.5 hours of assembly, 1 hour of finishing, and 0.1 hours of quality and packaging. The corresponding numbers for each Deluxe suitcase are 1 hour, $\frac{5}{6}$ hours, $\frac{2}{3}$ hours, and 0.25 hours, respectively. Likewise, the corresponding numbers for each Luxury suitcase are 1 hour, $\frac{2}{3}$ hours, 0.9 hours, and 0.4 hours, respectively.

The sales revenue for each type of suitcase is as follows: Standard $36.05, Deluxe $39.50, and Luxury $43.30. The material costs are Standard $6.25, Deluxe $7.50, and Luxury $8.50. The hourly cost of labor for each department is cutting and coloring $10, assembly $6, finishing $9, and quality and packaging $8.

The Excel layout and LP Sensitivity Report of Good-to-Go's problem are shown in Programs 4.9A and 4.9B, respectively. Each of the following questions is independent of the other:

(a) What is the optimal production plan? Which of the resources are scarce?

(b) Suppose Good-to-Go is considering including a polishing process, the cost of which would be added directly to the price. Each Standard suitcase would require 10 minutes of time in this treatment, each Deluxe suitcase would need 15 minutes, and each Luxury suitcase would need 20 minutes. Would the current production plan change as a result of this additional process if 170 hours of polishing time were available? Explain your answer.

(c) Now consider the addition of a waterproofing process where each Standard suitcase would use 1 hour of time in the process, each Deluxe suitcase would need 1.5 hours, and each Luxury suitcase would require 1.75 hours. Would this change the production plan if 900 hours were available? Why or why not? (**Source:** Professors Mark and Judith McKnew, Clemson University.)

4-23 Suppose Good-to-Go (Problem 4-22) is considering the possible introduction of two new products to its line of suitcases: the Compact model (for teenagers) and the Kiddo model (for children). Market research

PROGRAM 4.9A

**Excel Layout for Problem 4-22: Good-to-Go Suitcase Company**

| | A | B | C | D | E | F | G | H |
|---|---|---|---|---|---|---|---|---|
| 1 | **Good-to-Go Suitcase Company** | | | | | | | |
| 2 | | | | | | | | |
| 3 | | Standard | Deluxe | Luxury | | | | |
| 4 | Solution value | 540.00 | 252.00 | 0.00 | | | | |
| 5 | Selling price per unit | $36.05 | $39.50 | $43.30 | $29,421.00 | | | |
| 6 | Material cost per unit | $6.25 | $7.50 | $8.50 | $5,265.00 | | | |
| 7 | Labor cost per unit | $19.80 | $23.00 | $25.30 | $16,488.00 | | | |
| 8 | Profit | $10.00 | $9.00 | $9.50 | $7,668.00 | <-- Objective | | |
| 9 | Constraints | | | | | | | Cost |
| 10 | Cutting & Coloring | 0.70 | 1.00 | 1.00 | 630.00 | <= | 630 | $10 |
| 11 | Assembly | 0.50 | 0.83 | 0.67 | 480.00 | <= | 600 | $6 |
| 12 | Finishing | 1.00 | 0.67 | 0.90 | 708.00 | <= | 708 | $9 |
| 13 | Quality & Packaging | 0.10 | 0.25 | 0.40 | 117.00 | <= | 135 | $8 |
| 14 | | | | | LHS | Sign | RHS | |

PROGRAM 4.9B

**Solver Sensitivity Report for Problem 4-22: Good-to-Go Suitcase Company**

Microsoft Excel 9.0 Sensitivity Report
Problem P4-22. Good-to-Go Suitcase Company

Adjustable Cells

| Cell | Name | Final Value | Reduced Cost | Objective Coefficient | Allowable Increase | Allowable Decrease |
|---|---|---|---|---|---|---|
| $B$4 | Solution value Standard | 540.00 | 0.00 | 10.00 | 3.50 | 2.56 |
| $C$4 | Solution value Deluxe | 252.00 | 0.00 | 9.00 | 5.29 | 1.61 |
| $D$4 | Solution value Luxury | 0.00 | -1.12 | 9.50 | 1.12 | 1E+30 |

Constraints

| Cell | Name | Final Value | Shadow Price | Constraint R.H. Side | Allowable Increase | Allowable Decrease |
|---|---|---|---|---|---|---|
| $E$10 | Cutting & Coloring | 630.00 | 4.38 | 630 | 52.36 | 134.40 |
| $E$11 | Assembly | 480.00 | 0.00 | 600 | 1E+30 | 120.00 |
| $E$12 | Finishing | 708.00 | 6.94 | 708 | 192.00 | 128.00 |
| $E$13 | Quality & Packaging | 117.00 | 0.00 | 135 | 1E+30 | 18.00 |

suggests that Good-to-Go can sell the Compact model for no more than $30, whereas the Kiddo model would go for as much as $37.50 to specialty toy stores. The amount of labor and the cost of raw materials for each possible new product are as follows:

| Cost Category | Compact | Kiddo |
|---|---|---|
| Cutting and coloring (hr) | 0.50 | 1.20 |
| Assembly (hr) | 0.75 | 0.75 |
| Finishing (hr) | 0.75 | 0.50 |
| Quality and packaging (hr) | 0.20 | 0.20 |
| Raw materials ($) | $5.00 | $4.50 |

Use a pricing out strategy to check if either model would be economically attractive to make.

**4-24** The Strollers-to-Go Company makes lightweight umbrella-type strollers for three different groups of children. The TiniTote is designed specifically for newborns who require extra neck support. The ToddleTote is for toddlers up to 30 pounds. Finally, the company also produces a heavy-duty model called TubbyTote, which is designed to carry children up to 60 pounds. The stroller company is in the process of determining its production for each of the three types of strollers for the upcoming planning period.

The marketing department has forecast the following maximum demand for each of the strollers during the planning period: TiniTote 180, TubbyTote 70, and ToddleTote 160. Strollers-to-Go sells TiniTotes for $63.75, TubbyTotes for $82.50, and ToddleTotes for $66.00. As a matter of policy, it wants to produce no less than 50% of the forecast demand for each product. It also wants to keep production of

ToddleTotes to a maximum of 40% of total stroller production.

The production department has estimated that the material costs for TiniTote, TubbyTote, and ToddleTote strollers will be $4, $6, and $5.50 per unit, respectively. The strollers are processed through fabrication, sewing, and assembly workstations. The metal and plastic frames are made in the fabrication station. The fabric seats are cut and stitched together in the sewing station. Finally, the frames are put together with the seats in the assembly station. In the upcoming planning period, there will be 620 hours available in fabrication, where the direct labor cost is $8.25 per hour. The sewing station has 500 hours available, and the direct labor cost is $8.50 per hour. The assembly station has 480 hours available, and the direct labor cost is $8.75 per hour.

The standard processing rate for TiniTotes is 3 hours in fabrication, 2 hours in sewing, and 1 hour in assembly. TubbyTotes require 4 hours in fabrication, 1 hour in sewing and 3 hours in assembly, whereas ToddleTotes require 2 hours in each station.

The Excel layout and LP Sensitivity Report for Strollers-to-Go's problem are shown in Programs 4.10A and 4.10B, respectively. Each of the following questions is independent of the other:

(a) How many strollers of each type should Strollers-to-Go make? What is the profit? Which constraints are binding?
(b) How much labor time is being used in the fabrication, sewing, and assembly areas?
(c) How much would Strollers-to-Go be willing to pay for an additional hour of fabrication time? For an additional hour of sewing time?
(d) Is Strollers-to-Go producing any product at its maximum sales level? Is it producing any product at its minimum level? (**Source:** Professors Mark and Judith McKnew, Clemson University).

**PROGRAM 4.10A**

**Excel Layout for Problem 4-24: Strollers-to-Go Company**

| | A | B | C | D | E | F | G | H |
|---|---|---|---|---|---|---|---|---|
| 1 | **Strollers-to-Go Company** | | | | | | | |
| 2 | | | | | | | | |
| 3 | | TiniTote | TubbyTote | ToddleTote | | | | |
| 4 | Solution value | 100.00 | 35.00 | 90.00 | | | | |
| 5 | Selling price per unit | $63.75 | $82.50 | $66.00 | $15,202.50 | | | |
| 6 | Material cost per unit | $4.00 | $6.00 | $5.50 | $1,105.00 | | | |
| 7 | Labor cost per unit | $50.50 | $67.75 | $51.00 | $12,011.25 | | | |
| 8 | Profit | $9.25 | $8.75 | $9.50 | $2,086.25 | <-- Objective | | |
| 9 | **Constraints** | | | | | | | Cost |
| 10 | Fabrication | 3.0 | 4.0 | 2.0 | 620.00 | <= | 620 | $8.25 |
| 11 | Sewing | 2.0 | 1.0 | 2.0 | 415.00 | <= | 500 | $8.50 |
| 12 | Assembly | 1.0 | 3.0 | 2.0 | 385.00 | <= | 480 | $8.75 |
| 13 | Tinitote demand | 1.0 | | | 100.00 | <= | 180 | |
| 14 | Tubbytote demand | | 1.0 | | 35.00 | <= | 70 | |
| 15 | Toddletote demand | | | 1.0 | 90.00 | <= | 160 | |
| 16 | Toddletote max prod | -0.4 | -0.4 | 0.6 | 0.00 | <= | 0 | |
| 17 | Tinitote min prod | 1.0 | | | 100.00 | >= | 90 | |
| 18 | Tubbytote mon prod | | 1.0 | | 35.00 | >= | 35 | |
| 19 | Toddletote min prod | | | 1.0 | 90.00 | >= | 80 | |
| 20 | | | | | LHS | Sign | RHS | |

**PROGRAM 4.10B**

**Solver Sensitivity Report for Problem 4-24: Strollers-to-Go Company**

**Microsoft Excel 9.0 Sensitivity Report**
**Problem 4-24.  Strollers-to-Go Company**

Adjustable Cells

| Cell | Name | Final Value | Reduced Cost | Objective Coefficient | Allowable Increase | Allowable Decrease |
|---|---|---|---|---|---|---|
| $B$4 | Solution value TiniTote | 100.00 | 0.00 | 9.25 | 5.00 | 3.33 |
| $C$4 | Solution value TubbyTote | 35.00 | 0.00 | 8.75 | 4.10 | 1E+30 |
| $D$4 | Solution value ToddleTote | 90.00 | 0.00 | 9.50 | 1E+30 | 3.33 |

Constraints

| Cell | Name | Final Value | Shadow Price | Constraint R.H. Side | Allowable Increase | Allowable Decrease |
|---|---|---|---|---|---|---|
| $E$10 | Fabrication | 620.00 | 3.60 | 620.00 | 110.50 | 43.33 |
| $E$11 | Sewing | 415.00 | 0.00 | 500.00 | 1E+30 | 85.00 |
| $E$12 | Assembly | 385.00 | 0.00 | 480.00 | 1E+30 | 95.00 |
| $E$13 | Tinitote demand | 100.00 | 0.00 | 180.00 | 1E+30 | 80.00 |
| $E$14 | Tubbytote demand | 35.00 | 0.00 | 70.00 | 1E+30 | 35.00 |
| $E$15 | Toddletote demand | 90.00 | 0.00 | 160.00 | 1E+30 | 70.00 |
| $E$16 | Toddletote max prod | 0.00 | 3.85 | 0.00 | 13.00 | 8.67 |
| $E$17 | Tinitote min prod | 100.00 | 0.00 | 90.00 | 10.00 | 1E+30 |
| $E$18 | Tubbytote mon prod | 35.00 | -4.10 | 35.00 | 8.13 | 35.00 |
| $E$19 | Toddletote min prod | 90.00 | 0.00 | 80.00 | 10.00 | 1E+30 |

**4-25** Consider the Strollers-to-Go production problem (Problem 4-24).

(a) Over what range of costs could the TiniTote materials vary and the current production plan remain optimal? (*Hint*: How are material costs reflected in the problem formulation?)

(b) Suppose that Strollers-to-Go decided to polish each stroller prior to shipping. The process is fast and would require 10, 15, and 12 minutes, respectively for TiniTote, TubbyTote, and ToddleTote strollers. Would this change the current production plan if 48 hours of polishing time were available?

**4-26** Consider the Strollers-to-Go production problem (Problem 4-24).

(a) Suppose that Strollers-to-Go could purchase additional fabrication time at a cost of $10.50 per hour. Should it be interested? Why or why not? What is the most that it would be willing to pay for an additional hour of fabrication time?

(b) Further suppose that it could only purchase fabrication time in multiples of 40 hour bundles. How many should it be willing to purchase then?

**4-27** Suppose that Strollers-to-Go (Problem 4-24) is considering the production of TwinTotes for those families that were doubly blessed. Each TwinTote would require $5.75 in materials, 3.5 hours of fabrication time, 1.75 hours of sewing time, and only 1.5 hours to assemble. Would this product be economically attractive to manufacture if the sales price was $72.00? Why or why not?

# ➡ CASE STUDY

## Red Brand Canners

On Monday, September 13, 2000, Mitchell Gordon, vice president of operations, asked the controller, the sales manager, and the production manager to meet with him to discuss the amount of tomato products to pack that season. The tomato crop, which had been purchased at planting, was beginning to arrive at the cannery, and packing operations would have to be started by the following Monday. Red Brand Canners is a medium-sized company that cans and distributes a variety of fruit and vegetable products under private brands in the western states.

William Cooper, the controller, and Charles Myers, the sales manager, were the first to arrive in Gordon's office. Dan Tucker, the production manager, came in a few minutes later and said

that he had picked up Produce Inspection's latest estimate of the quality of the incoming tomatoes. According to the report, about 20% of the crop was grade A quality, and the remaining portion of the 3-million-pound crop was grade B.

Gordon asked Myers about the demand for tomato products for the coming year. Myers replied that they could sell all of the whole canned tomatoes they could produce. The expected demand for tomato juice and tomato paste, on the other hand, was limited. The sales manager then passed around the latest demand forecast, which is shown in Table 4.4. He reminded the group that the selling prices had been set in light of the long-term marketing strategy of the company and that the potential sales had been forecast at these prices.

| TABLE 4.4 | PRODUCT | SELLING PRICE PER CASE ($) | DEMAND FORECAST (CASES) |
|---|---|---|---|
| **Demand Forecasts** | 24—2½ whole tomatoes | 4.00 | 800,000 |
| | 24—2½ choice peach halves | 5.40 | 10,000 |
| | 24—2½ peach nectar | 4.60 | 5,000 |
| | 24—2½ tomato juice | 4.50 | 50,000 |
| | 24—2½ cooking apples | 4.90 | 15,000 |
| | 24—2½ tomato paste | 3.80 | 80,000 |

Bill Cooper, after looking at Myers's estimates of demand, said that it looked like the company "should do quite well [on the tomato crop] this year." With the new accounting system that had been set up, he had been able to compute the contribution for each product, and according to his analysis the incremental profit on whole tomatoes was greater than the incremental profit on any other tomato product. In May, after Red Brand had signed contracts agreeing to purchase the grower's production at an average delivered price of 6 cents per pound, Cooper had computed the tomato products' contributions (see Table 4.5).

Dan Tucker brought to Cooper's attention that although there was ample production capacity, it was impossible to pro-duce all whole tomatoes because too small a portion of the tomato crop was "grade A" quality. Red Brand used a numeri-cal scale to record the quality of both raw produce and pre-pared products. This scale ran from 0 to 10, the higher number representing better quality. According to this scale, grade A tomatoes averaged nine points per pound and grade B toma-toes averaged five points per pound. Tucker noted that the minimum average input quality was eight points per pound for canned whole tomatoes and six points per pound for juice. Paste could be made entirely from grade B tomatoes. This meant that whole-tomato production was limited to 800,000 pounds.

| TABLE 4.5 | **Product Item Profitability** | | | | | |
|---|---|---|---|---|---|---|
| PRODUCT | 24—2½ WHOLE TOMATOES | 24—2½ CHOICE PEACH HALVES | 24—2½ PEACH NECTAR | 24—2½ TOMATO JUICE | 24—2½ COOKING APPLES | 24—2½ TOMATO PASTE |
| Selling price | $4.00 | $5.40 | $4.60 | $4.50 | $4.90 | $3.80 |
| Variable cost | | | | | | |
| Direct labor | 1.18 | 1.40 | 1.27 | 1.32 | 0.70 | 0.54 |
| Variable overhead | 0.24 | 0.32 | 0.23 | 0.36 | 0.22 | 0.26 |
| Variable selling | 0.40 | 0.30 | 0.40 | 0.85 | 0.28 | 0.38 |
| Packaging material | 0.70 | 0.56 | 0.60 | 0.65 | 0.70 | 0.77 |
| Fruit* | 1.08 | 1.80 | 1.70 | 1.20 | 0.90 | 1.50 |
| Total variable costs | 3.60 | 4.38 | 4.20 | 4.38 | 2.80 | 3.45 |
| Contribution | 0.40 | 1.02 | 0.40 | 0.12 | 1.10 | 0.35 |
| Less allocated overhead | 0.28 | 0.70 | 0.52 | 0.21 | 0.75 | 0.23 |
| Net profit | 0.12 | 0.32 | (0.12) | (0.09) | 0.35 | 0.12 |

*Product usage is as follows:

| Product | Pounds per Case |
|---|---|
| Whole tomatoes | 18 |
| Peach halves | 18 |
| Peach nectar | 17 |
| Tomato juice | 20 |
| Cooking apples | 27 |
| Tomato paste | 25 |

**TABLE 4.6**

**Marginal Analysis of Tomato Products**

$Z$ = cost per pound of grade A tomatoes in cents

$Y$ = cost per pound of grade B tomatoes in cents

$$(600,000 \text{ lb} \times Z) + (2,400,000 \text{ lb} \times Y) = (3,000,000 \text{ lb} \times 6) \tag{1}$$

$$\frac{Z}{9} = \frac{Y}{5} \tag{2}$$

implies $Z$ = 9.32 cents per pound

$Y$ = 5.18 cents per pound

| PRODUCT | CANNED WHOLE TOMATOES | TOMATO JUICE | TOMATO PASTE |
|---|---|---|---|
| Selling price | $4.00 | $4.50 | $3.80 |
| Variable cost (excluding tomato cost) | 2.52 | 3.18 | 1.95 |
|  | $1.48 | $1.32 | $1.85 |
| Tomato cost | 1.49 | 1.24 | 1.30 |
| Marginal profit | ($0.01) | $0.08 | $0.55 |

Gordon stated that this was not a real limitation. He had been recently solicited to purchase 80,000 pounds of grade A tomatoes at 8½ cents per pound and at that time had turned down the offer. He felt, however, that the tomatoes were still available.

Myers, who had been doing some calculations, said that although he agreed that the company "should do quite well this year," it would not be by canning whole tomatoes. It seemed to him that the tomato cost should be allocated on the basis of quality and quantity rather than by quantity only, as Cooper had done. Therefore, he had recomputed the marginal profit on this basis (see Table 4.6) and from his results had concluded that Red Brand should use 2 million pounds of the grade B tomatoes for paste, and the remaining 400,000 pounds of grade B tomatoes and all of the grade A tomatoes for juice. If the demand expectations were realized, a contribution of $48,000 would be made on this year's tomato crop.

### Discussion Questions

1. Structure this problem verbally, including a written description of the constraints and the objective function. What are the decision variables?
2. Develop a mathematical formulation of the LP model for Red Brand's problem.
3. Solve the LP model using Excel and discuss the results.

Use the Answer and Sensitivity Reports for Red Brand's LP model to answer the following questions. Each question is independent of the others.

4. Which constraints are binding?
5. Should Gordon reconsider the offer of 80,000 pounds of grade A tomatoes at 8½ cents per pound? If so, what is its impact on profit?
6. Gordon thinks that Myers, the sales manager, may be underestimating the demand of all tomato products by as much as 5% each. If this belief is in fact true, what would be the impact on the optimal profit?
7. Red Brand Canners' sister concern, Red Label Ketchup Company, has an excess of grade B tomatoes but is severely short of grade A tomatoes. Joan Yu, vice president of operations at Red Label, called Gordon this morning with an offer to make the following trade: 100,000 pounds of grade A tomatoes to Red Label in exchange for 200,000 pounds of grade B tomatoes to Red Brand. Should Gordon accept the trade? Why or why not?

*Source:* "Red Brand Canners," revised with permission of Stanford University, Graduate School of Business, Copyright © 1969 and 1977 by the Board of Trustees of the Leland Stanford Junior University.

# BIBLIOGRAPHY

See the Bibliography at the end of Chapter 2.

## CHAPTER 5

# TRANSPORTATION, ASSIGNMENT, AND NETWORK MODELS

## LEARNING OBJECTIVES

After completing this chapter, students will be able to:

1. Structure special LP network flow models.

2. Set up and solve transportation models using Excel's Solver to determine the minimum cost shipping routes in a network.

3. Extend the basic transportation model to include transshipment points.

4. Set up and solve facility location and other application problems as transportation models.

5. Set up and solve maximal-flow network models using Excel's Solver.

6. Set up and solve shortest-path network models using Excel's Solver.

7. Connect all points of a network while minimizing total distance using the minimal-spanning tree model.

## CHAPTER OUTLINE

Summary • Glossary • Key Equation • Solved Problems • Self-Test • Discussion Questions and Problems • Case Study: Old Oregon Wood Store • Case Study: Custom Vans, Inc. • Case Study: Binder's Beverage • Internet Case Studies • Bibliography

## Scheduling American League Umpires with the Assignment Model

Scheduling umpires in professional baseball is a complex problem that must include a number of criteria. In assigning officials to games, a typical objective is to minimize total travel costs while satisfying a set of constraints such as limiting the number of times an official or crew is exposed to each team, balancing home and away games, and so on. These constraints complicate the problem to such an extent that except for the most trivial cases, the use of a computer-based system is essential.

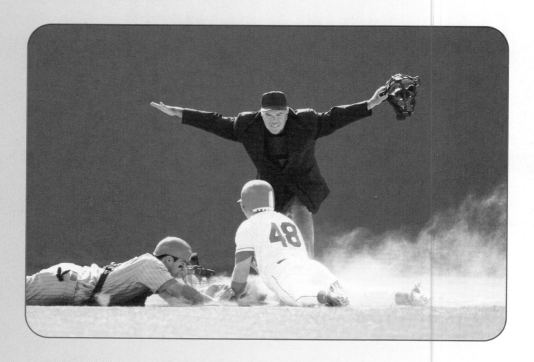

In 2001, the American League is composed of 14 professional baseball teams organized into western (Anaheim, Oakland, Seattle, and Texas), eastern (Baltimore, Boston, New York, Toronto, and Tampa Bay), and central (Chicago, Cleveland, Detroit, Kansas City, and Minnesota) divisions. The game schedule, constructed each winter prior to the start of the baseball season, is a difficult scheduling problem in itself. Consideration must be given to such factors as the number of games played against other teams both within and outside a division, within and outside a league, the split between home games and road trips, travel time, and possible conflicts in cities that have teams in the National League.

The objective of balancing crew assignments relatively evenly and minimizing travel costs are by nature conflicting. Attempting to balance crew assignments necessitates considerable airline travel and equipment moves, and hence increased travel costs.

Using an assignment model as part of a microcomputer-based decision modeling system, the American League was able to reduce travel mileage by about 4% during the first year of use. This not only saved the league thousands of dollars but also improved the crew exposure balance.[1]

---

[1] J. Evans. "Scheduling American League Umpires," *Interfaces* (November–December 1988): 42–51.

## 5.1   INTRODUCTION

Assignment models, such as the one used by the American League in the preceding application, are examples of special linear programming (LP) models, called *network flow models*. Networks consist of nodes (or points) and arcs (or lines) that connect the nodes together. Roadways, telephone systems, and citywide water systems are all examples of networks. In this chapter, we examine six different network flow models: (1) transportation, (2) transshipment, (3) assignment, (4) maximal flow, (5) shortest path, and (6) minimal spanning tree.

### Transportation Model

*Transportation problems deal with distribution of goods from supply points to demand points at minimum cost.*

The *transportation problem* deals with the distribution of goods from several points of supply (called *origins* or *sources*) to a number of points of demand (called *destinations* or *sinks*). Usually, we have a given capacity of goods at each source and a given requirement for the goods at each destination. The most common objective of the transportation problem is to schedule shipments from sources to destinations so that total production and transportation costs are minimized. Occasionally, transportation models can have a maximization objective (e.g., maximize total profit of shipping goods from sources to destinations).

Transportation models can also be used when a firm is trying to decide where to locate a new facility. Before opening a new warehouse, factory, or office, it is good practice to consider a number of alternative sites. Good financial decisions concerning *facility location* also involve minimizing total production and transportation costs for the entire system.

### Transshipment Model

*In transshipment problems, some points can have shipments that arrive as well as leave.*

In the basic transportation problem, shipments either leave a supply point or arrive at a demand point. An extension of the transportation problem is called the *transshipment problem*, in which a point can have shipments that both arrive as well as leave. An example would be a warehouse where shipments arrive from factories and then leave for retail outlets. It may be possible for a firm to achieve cost savings (economies of scale) by consolidating shipments from several factories at the warehouse and then sending them together to retail outlets. This type of approach is the basis for the *hub-and-spoke* system of transportation employed by most major U.S. airlines. For example, most travel on Delta Airlines from the western U.S. to the eastern U.S. (or vice versa) involves a connection through Delta's hub in Atlanta, Georgia.

### Assignment Model

*The assignment problem seeks to find the optimal one-to-one assignment of people to projects, jobs to machines, and so on.*

The *assignment problem* refers to the class of LP problems that involve determining the most efficient assignment of people to projects, salespeople to territories, contracts to bidders, jobs to machines, and so on. The typical objective is to minimize total cost or total time of performing the tasks at hand, although a maximization objective is also possible. An important characteristic of assignment problems is that each job or worker can be assigned to at most one machine or project, and vice versa.

### Maximal-Flow Model

*The maximal-flow problem finds the maximum flow possible through a network.*

Consider a network with a specific starting point (called the *origin*) and a specific ending point (called the *destination*). The arcs in the network have capacities that limit the amounts of flow that can occur on them. These capacities can be different for different arcs. The *maximal-flow problem* finds the maximum flow that can occur from the origin to the destination through this network. This model can be used to determine, for example, the maximum number of vehicles (cars, trucks, and so forth) that can go through a network of roads from one location to another.

### Shortest-Path Model

*The shortest-path problem finds the shortest route from an origin to a destination.*

Consider a network with a specified origin and a specified destination. The arcs in the network are such that there are many paths available to go from the origin to the destination. The *shortest-path problem* finds the shortest path or route through this network from the origin to the destination. For example, this model can be used to find the shortest distance and route from one city to another through a network of roads. The *length* of each arc can be a function of its distance, travel time, travel cost, or any other measure.

### Minimal-Spanning Tree Model

*The minimal-spanning tree problem connects all nodes in a network while minimizing total distance.*

The *minimal-spanning tree problem* determines the path through the network that connects all the points. The most common objective is to minimize total distance of all arcs used in the path. For example, when the points represent houses in a subdivision, the minimal–spanning tree model can be used to determine the best way to connect all of the houses to electrical power, water systems, and so on, in a way that minimizes the total distance or length of power lines or water pipes.

All of the examples used to describe the various network models in this chapter are small and simple compared with real problems to make it easier for you to understand the models. In many cases, these smaller network problems can be solved by inspection or intuition. For larger problems, however, finding a solution can be very difficult and requires the use of computer-based modeling approaches discussed here.

## 5.2 CHARACTERISTICS OF NETWORK FLOW PROBLEMS

*A node is a specific point or location in a network.*

*An arc connects two nodes to each other.*

Figure 5.1 shows a network that has 5 nodes and 10 arcs. Each of the circles (numbered 1 to 5) in the figure is called a *node*. A node can be defined as the location of a specific point on the network. An *arc* can be defined as the line that connects two nodes to each other. For example, the nodes could represent cities on a road network, and the arcs could represent roads connecting these cities.

As shown in Figure 5.1, it is not necessary for an arc to exist between every pair of nodes in a network. A network that does have arcs between all pairs of nodes is called a *fully connected* network. Arcs can be either unidirectional (meaning flow can occur only in one direction, as in a one-way road) or bidirectional (meaning that flow can occur in either direction). From a modeling perspective, it is convenient to represent a bidirectional arc with a pair of unidirectional arcs with opposite flow directions. This concept is illustrated in Figure 5.1 by the pairs of arcs between nodes 1 and 3, nodes 3 and 5, and nodes 2 and 4. Flows between all other pairs of nodes in Figure 5.1 are unidirectional.

*Arcs can be one-way or two-way.*

### FIGURE 5.1

**Example of a Network**
**Note:** Nodes are circles; Arcs are lines.

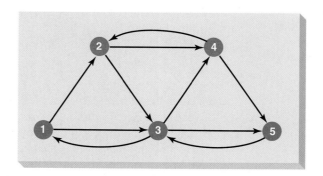

*Nodes can be sources, destinations, or transshipment points.*

Nodes can be classified as sources, destinations, or transshipment points. A source node (or supply point) denotes a location such as a factory that creates goods. A destination node (or demand point) denotes a location such as a retail outlet that consumes goods. A transshipment node denotes a location through which goods pass on their way to or from other locations.

In many practical networks, the same node can be a combination of a source, destination, and transshipment point. For example, in the Delta Airlines case, Atlanta is a source node for those people originating from Atlanta, a destination node for those people terminating in Atlanta, and a transshipment node for those people connecting through Atlanta.

Why are transportation models (and other network flow models) a special case of LP problems? There are several reasons:

1. In all network models, the decision variables represent the amount of flows (or shipments) that occur on the unidirectional arcs in the network. For example, the LP model for the network shown in Figure 5.1 will have 10 decision variables representing the flows on the 10 unidirectional arcs.

2. Second, there will be a *flow balance* constraint written for each node in the network. These flow balance constraints calculate the *net flow* at each node (i.e., the difference between the total flow on all arcs entering a node and the total flow on all arcs leaving the node).

$$\text{Net flow} = (\text{Total flow } in \text{ to node}) - (\text{Total flow } out \text{ of node}) \qquad (5\text{-}1)$$

*The net flow at a node is the difference between the total flow in to the node and the total flow out of the node.*

At source nodes, the total flow *out* of the node will exceed the total flow *in* to the node since goods are created at the node. Hence, the net flow is a negative quantity and represents the amount of goods (flow) created at the source node.

On the other hand, at destination nodes, total flow *out* of the node will be less than the total flow *in* to the node, since goods are consumed at the node. The net flow is therefore a *positive* quantity and represents the amount of goods (flow) consumed at the destination node.

At pure transshipment nodes, goods are neither created nor consumed. The total flow *out* of such a node equals the total flow *in* to the node, and the net flow is therefore zero.

3. The constraint coefficients (i.e., the coefficients in front of decision variables in a constraint) for all flow balance constraints and most other problem-specific constraints in network models equal either 0 or 1. That is, if a decision variable exists in a constraint in a network model, its constraint coefficient is usually 1. This special trait allows network flow models to be solved very quickly using specialized algorithms. However, we use Solver in the same manner as in Chapters 2 and 3 to solve these models here.

*If all supplies and demands are integers, all flows in a network will also be integer values.*

4. If all supplies at the source nodes and all demands at the destination nodes are whole numbers (i.e., integer values), the solution to the LP model will automatically result in integer values for the decision variables, even without specifying the integer condition. This property is especially useful in modeling the assignment and shortest-path models later in this chapter.

## 5.3   TRANSPORTATION MODEL

Let us begin to illustrate the transportation model with an example dealing with the Executive Furniture Corporation. This company manufactures office desks at three locations: Des Moines, Evansville, and Fort Lauderdale. The firm distributes the desks

## ➤MODELING IN THE REAL WORLD      AT&T Solves Network Problems

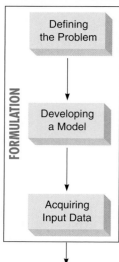

**FORMULATION**

**Defining the Problem**

Serving over 80 million customers in the United States and requiring over 40 thousand miles of cable, AT&T's fiber-optic network is the largest in the industry. Handling about 80 billion calls each year, AT&T defined maintaining network reliability, while maximizing network flow and minimizing network resources, as one of its most important problems.

**Developing a Model**

AT&T developed several comprehensive models to analyze reliability issues. These models investigated two important aspects of network reliability: (1) preventing failures and (2) responding quickly when failures occur. The models included real-time network routing (RTNR), fast automatic restoration (FAS-TAR), and synchronous optical network (SONET).

**Acquiring Input Data**

Over 10 months was spent on collecting a vast amount of data for the models.

**SOLUTION**

**Developing a Solution**

The solution used a network model to find the best way to route voice and data traffic so as to minimize the number of message failures and network resources required. Because of the large size of the problem, a solution was generated for each set of possible traffic demand and failure possibilities.

**Testing the Solution**

AT&T performed testing by comparing the solutions obtained by the new model's approach with the solutions obtained by older planning tools. Improvement expectations of 5% to 10% were established. The company also used computer simulation to test the solution over varying conditions.

**INTERPRETATION**

**Analyzing the Results and Sensitivity Analysis**

To analyze the results, AT&T had to reverse the aggregation steps performed during data collection. Once the disaggregation process was completed, AT&T was able to determine the best routing approach through the vast network. The analysis of the results included an investigation of embedded capacity and spare capacity provided by the solution.

**Implementing the Results**

When implemented, the new approach was able to reduce network resources by more than 30% while maintaining high network reliability. During the study, 99.98% of all calls were successfully completed on the first attempt. The successful implementation also resulted in ideas for changes and improvements, including a full optimization approach that could identify unused capacity and place it into operation.

**Source:** K. Ambs et al. "Optimizing Restoration Capacity at the AT&T Network," *Interfaces* (January–February 2000): 26–44.

---

*Our goal is to select the shipping routes and units to be shipped to minimize total transportation cost.*

through regional warehouses located in Albuquerque, Boston, and Cleveland (see Figure 5.2). An estimate of the monthly production capacity at each factor and an estimate of the number of desks that are needed each month at each of the three warehouses is shown in Figure 5.3.

The firm has found that production costs per desk are identical at each factory, and hence the only relevant costs are those of shipping from each *source* to each *destination*.

## FIGURE 5.2

**Geographical Locations of Executive Furniture's Factories and Warehouses**

These costs, shown in Table 5.1, are assumed to be constant regardless of the volume shipped.[2] The transportation problem can now be described as *how to select the shipping routes to be used and the number of desks shipped on each route so as to minimize total transportation cost.* This, of course, must be done while observing the restrictions regarding factory capacities and warehouse requirements.

We see in Figure 5.3 that the total factory supply available is exactly equal to the total warehouse demand. When this situation of equal demand and supply occurs (something that is rather unusual in real life) a *balanced problem* is said to exist. Later in this section we look at how to deal with unbalanced problems, namely, those in which total destination requirements are greater than or less than total origin capacities.

*Balanced supply and demand occurs when total supply equals total demand.*

## FIGURE 5.3

**Network Model for Executive Furniture's Transportation Problem**

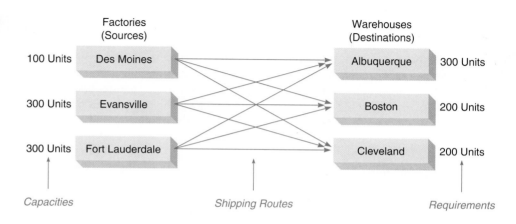

[2] The other assumptions that held for LP problems (see Chapter 2) are still applicable to transportation problems.

| TABLE 5.1 | | | |
|---|---|---|---|
| **Transportation Costs per Desk for Executive Furniture Corporation** | | | |

| TO<br>FROM | ALBUQUERQUE | BOSTON | CLEVELAND |
|---|---|---|---|
| Des Moines | $5 | $4 | $3 |
| Evansville | $3 | $2 | $1 |
| Fort Lauderdale | $9 | $7 | $5 |

## LP Model of Executive Furniture's Transportation Model

Since there are 3 factories (Des Moines, Evansville, and Fort Lauderdale) and 3 warehouses (Albuquerque, Boston, and Cleveland), there are 9 potential shipping routes. We therefore need 9 decision variables to define the number of units that would be shipped from each source (factory) to each destination (warehouse). In general, the number of decision variables in the basic transportation problem is the product of the number of sources times the number of destinations.

Recall (from Section 5.2) that in the transportation model (as well as in other network flow models), decision variables denote the flow between two nodes in the network. Therefore, it is convenient to represent these flows using double-subscripted decision variables. We let the first subscript represent the source (or origin) and the second subscript represent the destination of the flow. Hence, for the Executive Furniture problem, let

*It is convenient to express all network flows using double-subscripted variables.*

$$X_{ij} = \text{number of desks shipped from factory } i \text{ to warehouse } j$$

*where*

$$i = \text{D (for Des Moines), E (for Evansville), or F (for Fort Lauderdale)}$$

$$j = \text{A (for Albuquerque), B (for Boston), or C (for Cleveland)}$$

**Objective Function**  The objective function for this problem seeks to minimize the total transportation cost and can be expressed as

$$\text{Minimize total shipping costs} = 5X_{DA} + 4X_{DB} + 3X_{DC} + 3X_{EA} + 2X_{EB} + 1X_{EC} + 9X_{FA} + 7X_{FB} + 5X_{FC}$$

*We write a flow balance constraint for each node in the network.*

**Constraints**  As discussed earlier, we need to write *flow balance* constraints for each node in the network. Since the Executive Furniture example is a balanced problem, we know that all desks will be shipped from the factories and all demand will be satisfied at the warehouses. The number of desks shipped from each factory will therefore be equal to the number of desks available, and the number of desks received at each warehouse will be equal to the number of desks required.

*We write a supply constraint for each factory.*

**Supply Constraints**  At all factories, the total flow *in* is zero since there are no arcs coming into the node. The net flow at the Des Moines factory (for example) can therefore be expressed as

$$\text{Net flow at Des Moines} = (\text{Total flow } in) - (\text{Total flow } out)$$

$$= (0) - (X_{DA} + X_{DB} + X_{DC})$$

This net flow is equal to the total number of desks available (supply) at Des Moines. Recall (from Section 5.2) that supply is written as a negative quantity in network flow balance constraints. Therefore,

*Supplies are written as negative quantities.*

$$\text{Net flow at Des Moines} = -X_{DA} - X_{DB} - X_{DC} = -100$$
$$\text{(Des Moines capacity)}$$

Likewise, the flow balance constraints at the other factories can be expressed as

$$-X_{EA} - X_{EB} - X_{EC} = -300 \quad \text{(Evansville capacity)}$$
$$-X_{FA} - X_{FB} - X_{FC} = -300 \quad \text{(Fort Lauderdale capacity)}$$

The preceding three constraints are known as *supply constraints*. If we wish, we can multiply each constraint by $-1$ and rewrite as

$$X_{DA} + X_{DB} + X_{DC} = 100 \quad \text{(Des Moines capacity)}$$
$$X_{EA} + X_{EB} + X_{EC} = 300 \quad \text{(Evansville capacity)}$$
$$X_{FA} + X_{FB} + X_{FC} = 300 \quad \text{(Fort Lauderdale capacity)}$$

*We write a demand constraint for each warehouse.*

**Demand Constraints** Now, let us model the constraints (referred to as the *demand constraints*) that represent the warehouse requirements. At all warehouses, the total flow *out* is zero since there are no arcs leaving from the node. The net flow at the Albuquerque warehouse, for example, can therefore be expressed as

$$\text{Net flow at Albuquerque} = (\text{Total flow } in) - (\text{Total flow } out)$$
$$= (X_{DA} + X_{EA} + X_{FA}) - (0)$$

*Net flow at a demand point is written as a positive number.*

This net flow is equal to the total number of desks required (demand) at Albuquerque. Recall (from Section 5.2) that the net flow at a destination node is expressed as a positive number. Therefore,

$$\text{Net flow at Albuquerque} = X_{DA} + X_{EA} + X_{FA} = 300 \quad \text{(Albuquerque demand)}$$

Likewise, the flow balance constraints at the other warehouses can be expressed as

$$X_{DB} + X_{EB} + X_{FB} = 200 \quad \text{(Boston demand)}$$
$$X_{DC} + X_{EC} + X_{FC} = 200 \quad \text{(Cleveland demand)}$$

In general, the number of constraints in the basic transportation problem will be the sum of the number of sources and the number of destinations. There could, however, be other problem-specific constraints that restrict shipments in individual routes. For example, if we wish to ensure that no more than 100 desks are shipped from Evansville to Cleveland, an additional constraint in the model will be $X_{EC} \leq 100$.

## Solving the Transportation Model Using Excel

**File: 5-1.xls**

Program 5.1 shows the Excel setup and Solver entries for Executive Furniture's transportation problem. The supply constraints have been modeled here with negative values for supplies (i.e., the supply constraints have not been multiplied through by $-1$). The Excel layout in Program 5.1 follows the same logic as in Chapter 3. This means that (1) each decision variable is modeled in a separate column of the worksheet and (2) the objective function and left-hand side (LHS) formulas for all constraints are computed using Excel's SUMPRODUCT function.

**PROGRAM 5.1**     **Excel Layout and Solver Entries for Executive Furniture's Transportation Problem**

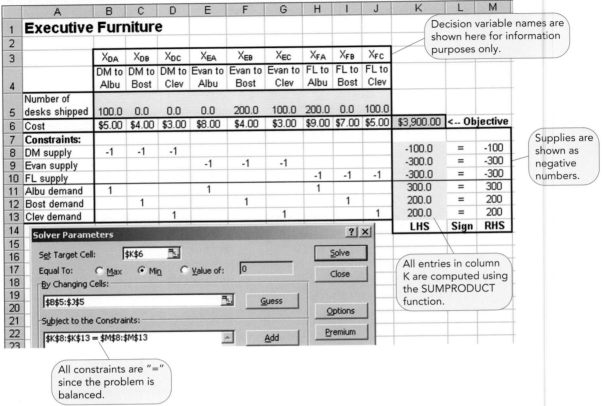

**Excel Notes**

■ The CD-ROM that accompanies this textbook contains the Excel file for each example problem discussed here. The relevant file name is shown on the margin next to each example.

■ In each of our Excel layouts, for clarity, changing cells are shaded yellow, the target cell is shaded green, and cells containing the LHS formula for each constraint are shaded blue.

The optimum solution for Executive Furniture Corporation is to ship 100 desks from Des Moines to Albuquerque, 200 desks from Evansville to Boston, 100 desks from Evansville to Cleveland, 200 desks from Fort Lauderdale to Albuquerque, and 100 desks from Fort Lauderdale to Cleveland. The total shipping cost is $3,900. Observe that since all supplies and demands were integer valued, all shipments turned out to be integer valued as well.

## Alternate Excel Layout for the Model

*The alternate Excel layout for network flow models uses a "tabular" form to model the flows.*

**File: 5-2.xls**

For many network models, the number of arcs (and hence, decision variables) could be quite large. Modeling the problem in Excel using the layout used in Program 5.1 can therefore become quite cumbersome. For this reason, it may be more convenient to model network flow models in Excel in such a way that decision variables are in a *tabular* form, with rows (for example) denoting sources and columns denoting destinations. The formula view of the alternate Excel layout for Executive Furniture's transportation model is shown in Program 5.2A, with the optimal solution shown in Program 5.2B. By adding the row (or column)

**PROGRAM 5.2A**    **Formula View of Alternate Excel Layout for Executive Furniture's Transportation Problem**

Total flow *in* = Sum of all entries in the column

Decision variables are modeled in a table.

Total flow *out* = Sum of all entries in the row

| | A | B | C | D | E | F | G | H | I | J |
|---|---|---|---|---|---|---|---|---|---|---|
| 1 | **Executive Furniture (Alternate Layout)** | | | | | | | | | |
| 2 | | | | | | | | | | |
| 3 | From:   To: | Albuquerque | Boston | Cleveland | Total flow out | | **Flow balance equations:** | | | |
| 4 | Des Moines | | | | =SUM(B4:D4) | | **Location** | **Net flow** | **Sign** | **RHS** |
| 5 | Evansville | | | | =SUM(B5:D5) | | Des Moines | =0-E4 | = | -100 |
| 6 | Fort Lauderdale | | | | =SUM(B6:D6) | | Evansville | =0-E5 | = | -300 |
| 7 | Total flow in | =SUM(B4:B6) | =SUM(C4:C6) | =SUM(D4:D6) | | | Fort Lauderdale | =0-E6 | = | -300 |
| 8 | | | | | | | Albuquerque | =B7 | = | 300 |
| 9 | **Unit costs:** | Albuquerque | Boston | Cleveland | | | Boston | =C7 | = | 200 |
| 10 | Des Moines | 5 | 4 | 3 | | | Cleveland | =D7 | = | 200 |
| 11 | Evansville | 8 | 4 | 3 | | | | | | |
| 12 | Fort Lauderdale | 9 | 7 | 5 | | | | | | |
| 13 | | | | | | | | | | |
| 14 | Total cost = | =SUMPRODUCT(B10:D12,B4:D6) | | | | | | | | |

Supplies are shown as negative numbers.

Demands are shown as positive numbers.

Net flow = Total flow *in* − Total flow *out*

In this table, factories are shown as rows and warehouses are shown as columns. Alternatively, we can show factories as columns and warehouses as rows.

Objective value is SUMPRODUCT of all entries in cost table and decision variable table.

**PROGRAM 5.2B**    **Solver Entries for Alternate Layout of Executive Furniture's Transportation Problem**

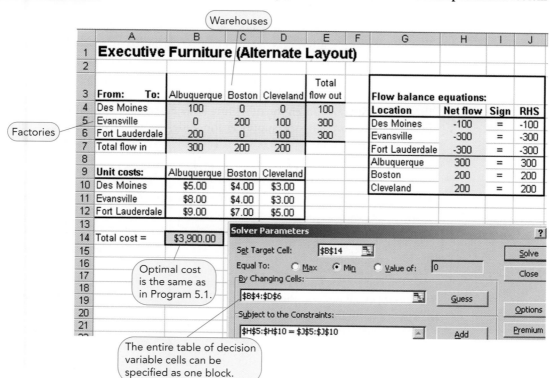

Warehouses

Factories

| | A | B | C | D | E | F | G | H | I | J |
|---|---|---|---|---|---|---|---|---|---|---|
| 1 | **Executive Furniture (Alternate Layout)** | | | | | | | | | |
| 2 | | | | | | | | | | |
| 3 | From:   To: | Albuquerque | Boston | Cleveland | Total flow out | | **Flow balance equations:** | | | |
| 4 | Des Moines | 100 | 0 | 0 | 100 | | **Location** | **Net flow** | **Sign** | **RHS** |
| 5 | Evansville | 0 | 200 | 100 | 300 | | Des Moines | -100 | = | -100 |
| 6 | Fort Lauderdale | 200 | 0 | 100 | 300 | | Evansville | -300 | = | -300 |
| 7 | Total flow in | 300 | 200 | 200 | | | Fort Lauderdale | -300 | = | -300 |
| 8 | | | | | | | Albuquerque | 300 | = | 300 |
| 9 | **Unit costs:** | Albuquerque | Boston | Cleveland | | | Boston | 200 | = | 200 |
| 10 | Des Moines | $5.00 | $4.00 | $3.00 | | | Cleveland | 200 | = | 200 |
| 11 | Evansville | $8.00 | $4.00 | $3.00 | | | | | | |
| 12 | Fort Lauderdale | $9.00 | $7.00 | $5.00 | | | | | | |
| 13 | | | | | | | | | | |
| 14 | Total cost = | $3,900.00 | | | | | | | | |

Optimal cost is the same as in Program 5.1.

**Solver Parameters**

Set Target Cell: $B$14

Equal To:   ○ Max   ● Min   ○ Value of: 0

By Changing Cells:

$B$4:$D$6

Subject to the Constraints:

$H$5:$H$10 = $J$5:$J$10

Solve   Close   Options   Premium   Guess   Add

The entire table of decision variable cells can be specified as one block.

entries, we can easily calculate the appropriate total flows *out* and total flows *in* at each node. It is then possible to model a flow balance constraint for each node by calculating each net flow as the difference between the total flow into the node and the total flow out of the node.

For example, the net flow at Des Moines (cell H5) is computed as $(0 - E4)$, where cell E4 is the sum of cells B4:D4. This net flow is set equal to $-100$ since the supply at Des Moines is 100. Likewise, the net flow at Albuquerque (cell H8) is computed as $(B7 - 0)$, where cell B7 is the sum of cells B4:B6. This net flow is set equal to $+300$, since the demand at Albuquerque is 300.

Note that the optimal solution resulting from this alternate layout, shown in Program 5.2B, is the same as the one shown in Program 5.1.

## Unbalanced Transportation Problems

*The problem is unbalanced if the total supply does not equal the total demand.*

In the Executive Furniture example, the total supply from the three factories equals the total requirements at the three warehouses. All supply and demand constraints could therefore be specified as equalities (i.e., using the "=" sign). But what if the total supply exceeds the total requirement, or vice versa? In these cases, we have an *unbalanced* transportation model, and the supply or demand constraints need to be modified accordingly.

There are two possible scenarios: (1) total supply exceeds the total requirement and (2) total supply is less than the total requirement.

**Total Supply Exceeds the Total Requirement**   If total supply exceeds total requirement, all requirements will be fully satisfied at the destinations, but some of the items at one or more sources will not need to be shipped out. That is, they will remain at the sources. To allow for this possibility, the total flow *out* of each supply node should be permitted to be smaller than the supply at that node. The total flow *in* to the demand nodes will, however, continue to be written with "=" signs.

*If total supply exceeds total demand, the supply constraints are written as inequalities.*

For example, assume the supply and demand values in the Executive Furniture problem are altered so that the total supply at the three factories exceeds the total demand at the three warehouses. Consider the supply at the Des Moines factory. The total flow out of Des Moines (i.e., $X_{DA} + X_{DB} + X_{DC}$) should now be permitted to be smaller than the total supply (i.e., 100). Hence, the constraint would need to be written as

$$X_{DA} + X_{DB} + X_{DC} \leq 100$$

In keeping with our convention of writing flows *out* of nodes with negative constraint coefficients, and expressing the supply at the node as a negative number, we multiply this expression through by $-1$ and rewrite the supply constraint for Des Moines as

$$-X_{DA} - X_{DB} - X_{DC} \geq -100 \qquad \text{(Des Moines capacity)}$$

Likewise, the supply constraints at the Evansville and Fort Lauderdale factories would need to be revised as

$$-X_{EA} - X_{EB} - X_{EC} \geq -300 \qquad \text{(Evansville capacity)}$$
$$-X_{FA} - X_{FB} - X_{FC} \geq -300 \qquad \text{(Fort Lauderdale capacity)}$$

**Total Supply Less Than the Total Requirement**   When total supply is less than total requirement, all items at the sources will be shipped out, but requirements at one or more destinations will remain unsatisfied. To allow for this possibility, the total flow *in* at demand nodes should be permitted to be smaller than the requirement at those nodes. The total flow *out* of supply nodes will, however, continue to be written with "=" signs.

*If total demand exceeds total supply, the demand constraints are written as inequalities.*

For example, assume the supply and demand values in the Executive Furniture problem are altered so that the total supply at the three factories is now *less* than the total demand at the three warehouses. Consider the demand at the Albuquerque warehouse. The

## IN ACTION    Answering Warehousing Questions at San Miguel Corporation

The San Miguel Corporation, based in the Philippines, faces unique distribution challenges. With more than 300 products, including beer, alcoholic drinks, juices, bottled water, feeds, poultry, and meats to be distributed to every corner of Philippine archipelago, shipping and warehousing costs make up a large part of total product cost.

The company grappled with these questions:

■ Which products should be produced in each plant and in which warehouse should they be stored?

■ Which warehouses should be maintained and where should new ones be located?

■ When should warehouses be closed or opened?

■ Which demand centers should each warehouse serve?

Turning to the transportation model of LP, San Miguel was able to answer these questions. The firm used these types of warehouses: company owned and staffed, rented but company staffed, and contracted out (i.e., not company owned or staffed).

San Miguel's Operations Research Department computed that the firm saves $7.5 million annually with optimal beer warehouse configurations over the existing national configurations. In addition, analysis of warehousing for ice cream and other frozen products indicated that the optimal configuration of warehouses, compared with existing setups, produced a $2.17 million savings.

**Source:** Elise del Rosario. "Logistical Nightmare," *OR/MS Today* (April 1999): 44–46.

total flow *in* to Albuquerque (i.e., $X_{DA} + X_{EA} + X_{FA}$) should now be permitted to be smaller than the total demand (i.e., 300). In keeping with our convention of writing flows *in* to nodes with positive constraint coefficients and expressing the demand at the node as a positive number, the demand constraint for this warehouse should therefore be written as

$$X_{DA} + X_{EA} + X_{FA} \leq 300 \qquad \text{(Albuquerque demand)}$$

Likewise, the demand constraints at the Boston and Cleveland warehouses would need to be written as

$$X_{DB} + X_{EB} + X_{FB} \leq 200 \qquad \text{(Boston demand)}$$
$$X_{DC} + X_{EC} + X_{FC} \leq 200 \qquad \text{(Cleveland demand)}$$

### More Than One Optimal Solution

*It is quite common for transportation models to have alternate optimal solutions.*

Just as with regular LP problems, it is possible (and in fact, quite common) for a transportation problem to have multiple optimal solutions. Practically speaking, multiple optimal solutions provide management with greater flexibility in selecting and using resources. Chapter 4 (Section 4.4) indicates that if the allowable increase or allowable decrease for the objective coefficient of a variable has a value of zero (in the Adjustable Cells table of the LP Sensitivity Report), this usually indicates the presence of alternate optimal solutions. In Solved Problem 4-1, we saw how Solver can be used to identify alternate optimal solutions.

### 5.4    FACILITY LOCATION ANALYSIS

*Deciding where to locate a new facility within an overall distribution system is aided by the transportation model.*

The transportation model has proved to be especially useful in helping firms decide where to locate a new factory or warehouse. Since a new location has major financial implications for a firm, several alternative locations must usually be considered and evaluated. Even though a firm may consider a wide variety of subjective factors, including quality of labor supply, presence of labor unions, community attitude, utilities, and recreational and educational facilities, a final decision also involves minimizing total production and shipping costs. This means that each alternative facility location should be analyzed within the framework of one overall distribution system. The new location that will yield the minimum cost for the entire system should be the one recommended. Let us consider the case of the Hardgrave Machine Company.

**TABLE 5.2**

Hardgrave's Demand and Supply Data

| WAREHOUSE | MONTHLY DEMAND (UNITS) | PRODUCTION PLANT | MONTHLY SUPPLY | COST TO PRODUCE ONE UNIT ($) |
|---|---|---|---|---|
| Detroit | 10,000 | Cincinnati | 15,000 | 48 |
| Houston | 12,000 | Kansas City | 6,000 | 50 |
| New York | 15,000 | Pittsburgh | 14,000 | 52 |
| Los Angeles | 9,000 | | 35,000 | |
| | 46,000 | | | |

Supply needed from new plant = 46,000 − 35,000 = 11,000 units per month

| ESTIMATED PRODUCTION COST PER UNIT AT PROPOSED PLANTS | |
|---|---|
| Seattle | $53 |
| Birmingham | $49 |

## Locating a New Factory for Hardgrave Machine Company

The Hardgrave Machine Company produces computer components at its plants in Cincinnati, Kansas City, and Pittsburgh. These plants have not been able to keep up with demand for orders at Hardgrave's four warehouses in Detroit, Houston, New York, and Los Angeles. As a result, the firm has decided to build a new plant to expand its productive capacity. The two sites being considered are Seattle, Washington, and Birmingham, Alabama. Both cities are attractive in terms of labor supply, municipal services, and ease of factory financing.

Table 5.2 presents the production costs and monthly supplies at each of the three existing plants, monthly demands at each of the four warehouses, and estimated production costs at the two proposed plants. Transportation costs from each plant to each warehouse are summarized in Table 5.3.

The important issue now facing Hardgrave is to decide which of the new locations, in combination with the existing plants and warehouses, will yield the lowest cost for the firm. Note that the cost of each individual plant-to-warehouse route is found by adding the shipping costs (in the body of Table 5.3) to the respective unit production costs (from Table 5.2). For example, the total production plus shipping cost of one computer component from Cincinnati to Detroit is $73 (= $25 for shipping plus $48 for production).

To determine which new plant (Seattle or Birmingham) yields the lowest total systemwide cost, we solve two transportation problems: one for each of the two possible combinations.

Programs 5.3A and 5.3B show the resulting optimum solutions with the total cost for each of the two locations. The layout followed in both models is similar to the one shown

*We solve two transportation problems to find the new plant with lowest system cost.*

**File: 5-3.xls**

**TABLE 5.3**

Hardgrave's Shipping Costs

| FROM \ TO | DETROIT | HOUSTON | NEW YORK | LOS ANGELES |
|---|---|---|---|---|
| Cincinnati | $25 | $55 | $40 | $60 |
| Kansas City | 35 | 30 | 50 | 40 |
| Pittsburgh | 36 | 45 | 26 | 66 |
| Seattle | 60 | 38 | 65 | 27 |
| Birmingham | 35 | 30 | 41 | 50 |

**PROGRAM 5.3A**

**Excel Layout and Solver Entries for Hardgrave Machine's Facility Location Problem with a New Facility in Seattle**

The model includes new plant at Seattle.

| | A | B | C | D | E | F | G | H | I | J | K |
|---|---|---|---|---|---|---|---|---|---|---|---|
| 1 | **Facility Location (Seattle)** | | | | | | | | | | |
| 2 | | | | | | | | | | | |
| 3 | **From:    To:** | Detroit | Houston | New York | Los Angeles | Total flow out | | **Flow balance equations:** | | | |
| 4 | Cincinnati | 10000 | 4000 | 1000 | 0 | 15000 | | **Location** | **Net flow** | **Sign** | **RHS** |
| 5 | Kansas City | 0 | 6000 | 0 | 0 | 6000 | | Cincinnati | -15000 | = | -15000 |
| 6 | Pittsburgh | 0 | 0 | 14000 | 0 | 14000 | | Kansas City | -6000 | = | -6000 |
| 7 | Seattle | 0 | 2000 | 0 | 9000 | 11000 | | Pittsburgh | -14000 | = | -14000 |
| 8 | Total flow in | 10000 | 12000 | 15000 | 9000 | | | Seattle | -11000 | = | -11000 |
| 9 | | | | | | | | Detroit | 10000 | = | 10000 |
| 10 | **Unit costs:** | Detroit | Houston | New York | Los Angeles | | | | | | |
| 11 | Cincinnati | $73 | $103 | $88 | $108 | | | Houston | 12000 | = | 12000 |
| 12 | Kansas City | $85 | $80 | $100 | $90 | | | New York | 15000 | = | 15000 |
| 13 | Pittsburgh | $88 | $97 | $78 | $118 | | | Los Angeles | 9000 | = | 9000 |
| 14 | Seattle | $113 | $91 | $118 | $80 | | | | | | |
| 15 | | | | | | | | | | | |
| 16 | Total cost = | $3,704,000 | | | | | | | | | |
| 17 | | | | | | | | | | | |
| 18 | | | | | | | | | | | |
| 19 | | | | | | | | | | | |
| 20 | | | | | | | | | | | |
| 21 | | | | | | | | | | | |

Proposed capacity of Seattle plant

Optimal cost

**Solver Parameters**

Set Target Cell: $B$16

Equal To:  ○ Max  ● Min  ○ Value of:  0

By Changing Cells:

$B$4:$E$7

Subject to the Constraints:

$I$5:$I$12 = $K$5:$K$12

---

**PROGRAM 5.3B**

**Excel Layout and Solver Entries for Hardgrave Machine's Facility Location Problem with a New Facility in Birmingham**

The model includes new plant at Birmingham.

| | A | B | C | D | E | F | G | H | I | J | K |
|---|---|---|---|---|---|---|---|---|---|---|---|
| 1 | **Facility Location (Birmingham)** | | | | | | | | | | |
| 2 | | | | | | | | | | | |
| 3 | **From:    To:** | Detroit | Houston | New York | Los Angeles | Total flow out | | **Flow balance equations:** | | | |
| 4 | Cincinnati | 10000 | 0 | 1000 | 4000 | 15000 | | **Location** | **Net flow** | **Sign** | **RHS** |
| 5 | Kansas City | 0 | 1000 | 0 | 5000 | 6000 | | Cincinnati | -15000 | = | -15000 |
| 6 | Pittsburgh | 0 | 0 | 14000 | 0 | 14000 | | Kansas City | -6000 | = | -6000 |
| 7 | Birmingham | 0 | 11000 | 0 | 0 | 11000 | | Pittsburgh | -14000 | = | -14000 |
| 8 | Total flow in | 10000 | 12000 | 15000 | 9000 | | | Birmingham | -11000 | = | -11000 |
| 9 | | | | | | | | Detroit | 10000 | = | 10000 |
| 10 | **Unit costs:** | Detroit | Houston | New York | Los Angeles | | | | | | |
| 11 | Cincinnati | $73 | $103 | $88 | $108 | | | Houston | 12000 | = | 12000 |
| 12 | Kansas City | $85 | $80 | $100 | $90 | | | New York | 15000 | = | 15000 |
| 13 | Pittsburgh | $88 | $97 | $78 | $118 | | | Los Angeles | 9000 | = | 9000 |
| 14 | Birmingham | $84 | $79 | $90 | $99 | | | | | | |
| 15 | | | | | | | | | | | |
| 16 | Total cost = | $3,741,000 | | | | | | | | | |
| 17 | | | | | | | | | | | |
| 18 | | | | | | | | | | | |
| 19 | | | | | | | | | | | |
| 20 | | | | | | | | | | | |
| 21 | | | | | | | | | | | |

Proposed capacity of plant at Birmingham

Optimal cost

**Solver Parameters**

Set Target Cell: $B$16

Equal To:  ○ Max  ● Min  ○ Value of:  0

By Changing Cells:

$B$4:$E$7

Subject to the Constraints:

$I$5:$I$12 = $K$5:$K$12

in Program 5.2A for the Executive Furniture problem. From these solutions, it appears that Seattle should be selected as the new plant site. Its total cost of $3,704,000 is less than the $3,741,000 cost at Birmingham.

---

## 5.5  TRANSSHIPMENT MODEL

*Transshipment problems include nodes that can have shipments arrive as well as leave.*

In the basic transportation problem, shipments either flow *out* of nodes (sources) or flow *in* to nodes (destinations). That is, it is possible to explicitly distinguish between source nodes and destination nodes for flows. In the more general form of the transportation problem, called the transshipment problem, flows can occur both out of and into the same node in three ways:

1. If the total flow into a node is less than the total flow out from the node, the node then represents a net creator of goods, that is, a supply point. The flow balance equation will therefore have a negative right-hand side (RHS) value.

2. However, if the total flow into a node exceeds the total flow out from the node, the node then represents a net consumer of goods, that is, a demand point. The flow balance equation will therefore have a positive RHS value.

3. Finally, if the total flow into a node is equal to the total flow out from the node, the node then represents a pure transshipment point. The flow balance equation will therefore have a zero RHS value.

### Executive Furniture Corporation Example—Revisited

*Transshipment example: Modified form of the Executive Furniture Problem.*

To study the transshipment problem, let us consider a modified version of the Executive Furniture Corporation example from Section 5.3. As before, we have factories at Des Moines, Evansville, and Fort Lauderdale, and warehouses at Albuquerque, Cleveland, and Boston. Recall that the supply at each factory and demand at each warehouse were shown in Figure 5.3 on page 161.

Now assume that due to a special contract with an Evansville-based shipping company, it is possible for Executive Furniture to ship desks from its Evansville factory to its three warehouses at very low unit shipping costs. These unit costs are so attractive that Executive is considering shipping all the desks produced at its other two factories (Des Moines and Fort Lauderdale) to Evansville, and then using this new shipping company to move desks from Evansville to all its warehouses.

The revised unit shipping costs are shown in Table 5.4. Note that the Evansville factory now shows up both in the "From" and "To" entries since it is possible for this factory to receive desks from other factories and then ship them out to the warehouses. There are therefore two additional shipping routes available: Des Moines to Evansville, and Fort Lauderdale to Evansville.

| TABLE 5.4 | | | | |
|---|---|---|---|---|
| **Revised Transportation Costs per Desk for Executive Furniture Corporation** | **FROM / TO** | **ALBUQUERQUE** | **BOSTON** | **CLEVELAND** | **EVANSVILLE** |
| | Des Moines | $5 | $4 | $3 | $2 |
| | Evansville | $3 | $2 | $1 | — |
| | Fort Lauderdale | $9 | $7 | $5 | $3 |

This data is used in the Transshipment Model.

## LP Model for Executive Furniture's Transshipment Problem

The LP model for this problem follows the same logic and structure as the model for Executive Furniture's transportation problem (see Section 5.3). However, we now have two *additional* decision variables for the two new shipping routes. We define these as follows:

$$X_{DE} = \text{number of desks shipped from Des Moines to Evansville}$$
$$X_{FE} = \text{number of desks shipped from Fort Lauderdale to Evansville}$$

**Objective Function**  The objective function for this transshipment problem, including the two additional decision variables and using the unit costs shown in Table 5.4, can be written as follows:

$$\begin{aligned}\text{Minimize total shipping costs} = {}& 5X_{DA} + 4X_{DB} + 3X_{DC} + 2X_{DE} \\ &+ 3X_{EA} + 2X_{EB} + 1X_{EC} + 9X_{FA} + 7X_{FB} + 5X_{FC} + 3X_{FE}\end{aligned}$$

**Constraints**  Once again, we need to write flow balance constraints for each node in the network. Let us first consider the net flows at the Des Moines and Fort Lauderdale factories. After taking into account the desks shipped from either of these locations to the Evansville factory (rather than directly to the warehouses), the relevant flow balance equations can be written as

$$\begin{aligned}(0) - (X_{DA} + X_{DB} + X_{DC} + X_{DE}) &= -100 \quad \text{(Des Moines capacity)}\\(0) - (X_{FA} + X_{FB} + X_{FC} + X_{FE}) &= -300 \quad \text{(Fort Lauderdale capacity)}\end{aligned}$$

As usual, supplies have been expressed as negative numbers in the RHS. Now, let us model the flow equation at Evansville.

$$\text{Net flow at Evansville} = (\text{Total flow } in) - (\text{Total flow } out)$$
$$= (X_{DE} + X_{FE}) - (X_{EA} + X_{EB} + X_{EC})$$

This net flow is equal to the total number of desks produced, namely, the supply, at Evansville (which would also appear as a negative number in the flow balance constraint). Therefore,

$$\text{Net flow at Evansville} = (X_{DE} + X_{FE}) - (X_{EA} + X_{EB} + X_{EC}) = -300$$

There is no change in the demand constraints that represent the warehouse requirements. So, as discussed in Section 5.2, they are

$$\begin{aligned}X_{DA} + X_{EA} + X_{FA} &= 300 \quad \text{(Albuquerque demand)}\\X_{DB} + X_{EB} + X_{FB} &= 200 \quad \text{(Boston demand)}\\X_{DC} + X_{EC} + X_{FC} &= 200 \quad \text{(Cleveland demand)}\end{aligned}$$

**File: 5-4.xls**

**Excel Solution**  Program 5.4, which uses the tabular layout for representing the network flows, shows the Excel layout and Solver entries for Executive Furniture's transshipment problem. Note that the net flow at Evansville (cell I6) is calculated as (E7 − F5), where cell E7 is the total flow coming into the Evansville factory, and cell F5 represents the total

**PROGRAM 5.4**  **Excel Layout and Solver Entries for Executive Furniture's Transshipment Problem**

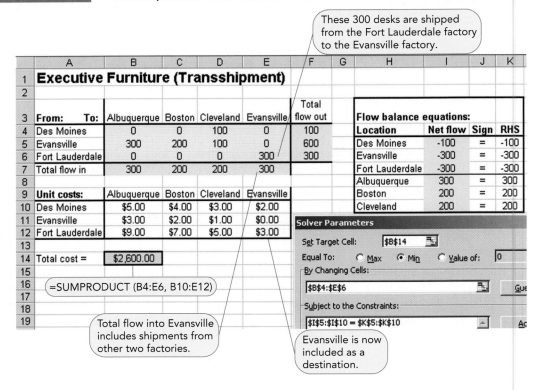

These 300 desks are shipped from the Fort Lauderdale factory to the Evansville factory.

Total flow into Evansville includes shipments from other two factories.

Evansville is now included as a destination.

flow out of Evansville. The difference of 300 is the supply of desks created at the Evansville factory.

In the revised solution, which now has a total transportation cost of $2,600, Executive should ship the 300 desks made at Fort Lauderdale to Evansville and then ship the consolidated load to the warehouses. It continues, though, to be cost beneficial to ship desks made at the Des Moines factory directly to a warehouse.

## IN ACTION    Improving Pupil Transportation

In the early 1990s, North Carolina was spending almost $150 million on transporting students to schools. The state's student transportation system involved some 13,000 buses, 100 school districts, and 700,000 students. In 1989, the General Assembly of the state decided to investigate ways that could be used to save money by developing a better way of transporting students. The General Assembly was committed to funding school districts that transported students efficiently and only reimbursing justifiable expenses for those districts that were not efficient in terms of how they transported students to and from public schools.

The input data to North Carolina's network model included the number of buses used and total operating expenses. Total operating expenses included driver salaries, salaries to other transportation personnel, payments to local governments, fuel costs, parts and repair costs, and other

related costs. These input values were used to compute an efficiency score for the various districts. These efficiency scores were then used to help in allocating funds to the districts. Those districts with an efficiency score of 0.9 or higher received full funding. Converting efficiency scores to funding was originally received with skepticism. After several years, however, more state officials realized the usefulness of the approach. In 1994–1995, the efficiency based funding approach was used alone to determine funding.

The use of efficiency-based funding resulted in the elimination of hundreds of school buses, with savings over a three-year period greater than $25 million.

**Source:** T. Sexton et al. "Improving Pupil Transportation in North Carolina," *Interfaces* 24 (January–February 1994): 87–103.

## 5.6 ASSIGNMENT MODEL

The next model we study is the assignment model. Each assignment model has associated with it a table, or matrix. Generally, the rows denote the people or objects we wish to assign, and the columns denote the tasks or jobs we want them assigned to. The numbers in the table are the costs (or benefits) associated with each particular assignment.

### Fix-It Shop Example

*Assignment example: Fix-It Shop*

As an illustration of the assignment model, let us consider the case of the Fix-It Shop, which has just received three new rush projects to repair: (1) a radio, (2) a toaster oven, and (3) a broken coffee table. Three workers, each with different talents and abilities, are available to do the jobs. The Fix-It Shop owner estimates what it will cost in wages to assign each of the workers to each of the three projects. The costs, which are shown in Table 5.5, differ because the owner believes that each worker will differ in speed and skill on these quite varied jobs.

*The goal is to assign projects to people (one project to one person) so that the total costs are minimized.*

The owner's objective is to assign the three projects to the workers in a way that will result in the lowest total cost to the shop. Note that the assignment of people to projects must be on a one-to-one basis; each project must be assigned to at most one worker only, and vice versa. If the number of rows in an assignment model is equal to the number of columns (such as in the Fix-It example), we refer to this problem as a *balanced* assignment model.

*One way to solve (small) problems is to enumerate all possible outcomes.*

Because the Fix-It Shop problem only consists of three workers and three projects, one easy way to find the best solution is to list all possible assignments and their respective costs. For example, if Adams is assigned to project 1, Brown to project 2, and Cooper to project 3, the total cost will be $11 + $10 + $7 = $28. Table 5.6 summarizes all six assignment options. The table also shows that the least-cost solution would be to assign Cooper to project 1, Brown to project 2, and Adams to project 3, at a total cost of $25.

Obtaining solutions by enumeration works well for small problems but quickly becomes inefficient as assignment problems become larger. For example, a problem involving the assignment of eight workers and eight tasks, which actually is not that large in a

**TABLE 5.5**

**Estimated Project Repair Costs for the Fix-It Shop Assignment Problem**

| PERSON | PROJECT | | |
|---|---|---|---|
| | 1 | 2 | 3 |
| Adams | $11 | $14 | $6 |
| Brown | 8 | 10 | 11 |
| Cooper | 9 | 12 | 7 |

**TABLE 5.6**

**Summary of Fix-It Shop Assignment Alternatives and Costs**

| PROJECT ASSIGNMENT | | | LABOR COSTS ($) | | TOTAL COSTS ($) |
|---|---|---|---|---|---|
| 1 | 2 | 3 | | | |
| Adams | Brown | Cooper | 11 + 10 + 7 | = | 28 |
| Adams | Cooper | Brown | 11 + 12 + 11 | = | 34 |
| Brown | Adams | Cooper | 8 + 14 + 7 | = | 29 |
| Brown | Cooper | Adams | 8 + 12 + 6 | = | 26 |
| Cooper | Adams | Brown | 9 + 14 + 11 | = | 34 |
| Cooper | Brown | Adams | 9 + 10 + 6 | = | 25 |

real-world situation, yields 8! ($= 8 \times 7 \times 6 \times 5 \times 4 \times 3 \times 2 \times 1$) or 40,320 possible solutions! Since it would clearly be impractical to individually examine so many alternatives, a more efficient solution approach is needed.

## Solving Assignment Models

A straightforward approach to solving assignment problems is to model them as LP problems in the same manner as transportation problems. To do so for the Fix-It Shop problem, let us view each worker as a source node in a network with a supply of one unit. Likewise, let us view each project as a destination node in a network with a demand of one unit. The arcs connecting the source nodes to the destination nodes represent the possible assignment of source (worker) to a destination (project). The network model is illustrated in Figure 5.4.

*All supplies and demands in an assignment model equal one unit.*

We see that this model looks identical to a transportation problem with three sources and three destinations. But here, all supplies and demands are equal to one unit each. The objective is to find the least-cost solution for using the one unit supplies at the source nodes to satisfy the one unit demands at the destination nodes. However, we need to also ensure that each worker *uniquely* gets assigned to just one project, and vice versa. That is, the *entire* supply of 1 unit at a source node (worker) should flow to the same destination node (project) indicating the assignment of a worker to a project. How do we ensure this? The answer lies in the special property of network models stated earlier. When all the supplies and demands in a network model are whole numbers (as in this case), it turns out that the resulting solution will automatically have integer-valued flows on the arcs.

*The special integer flow property of network models automatically ensures unique assignments.*

Consider the "flow" out of the source node for Adams in the Fix-It Shop problem. The three arcs (to Projects 1, 2, and 3) denote the assignment of Adams to these projects. Due to the integer property of the resulting network flows, the only possible solutions will have a flow of 1 on one of the three arcs, and a flow of 0 on the other 2 arcs. This is the only way in which a total flow of 1 (equal to the "supply" at the node representing Adams) can flow on these arcs and have integer values. The arc that has a flow of 1 in the optimal solution will indicate the project to which Adams should be assigned. Likewise, arcs that have flows of 1 originating from the other two source nodes will show the optimal assignments for those two workers.

Even without us constraining it to be so, the solution to the assignment model yields a solution in which the optimal values of the decision variables are either 1 (indicating the assignment of a worker to a project) or 0 (indicating that the worker should not be assigned to the project). In fact, there are several situations in which such decision variables, known as *binary* or 0–1 variables must have values of zero or one in the formulation itself. We study these types of problems in more detail in Chapter 6.

**FIGURE 5.4**

**Network Model for Fix-It's Assignment Problem**

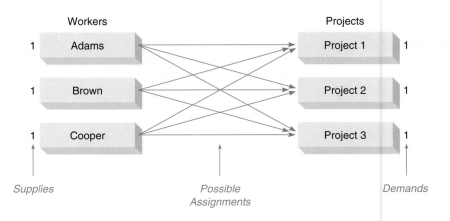

## LP Model for Fix-It Shop's Assignment Problem

We now develop the LP model for Fix-It Shop's problem. Let

$$X_{ij} = \text{"Flow" on arc from node denoting worker } i \text{ to node}$$
denoting project $j$. The solution value will equal 1 if
worker $i$ is assigned to project $j$ and will equal 0 otherwise.

*where*

$$i = \text{A (for Adams), B (for Brown), or C (for Cooper)}$$

$$j = 1 \text{ (for project 1), 2 (for project 2), or 3 (for project 3)}$$

**Objective Function**  The objective is to minimize the total cost of assignment and is expressed as

$$\text{Minimize total assignment costs} = 11X_{A1} + 14X_{A2} + 6X_{A3} + 8X_{B1}$$
$$+ 10X_{B2} + 11X_{B3} + 9X_{C1} + 12X_{C2} + 7X_{C3}$$

*Here again, we write supply constraints and demand constraints.*

**Constraints**  As in the transportation model, we have supply constraints at each of the three source nodes (workers) and demand constraints at each of the three destination nodes (projects). Using the standard convention we have adopted for all flow balance equations, these can be written as

$$
\begin{aligned}
-X_{A1} - X_{A2} - X_{A3} &= -1 & \text{(Adams availability)} \\
-X_{B1} - X_{B2} - X_{B3} &= -1 & \text{(Brown availability)} \\
-X_{C1} - X_{C2} - X_{C3} &= -1 & \text{(Cooper availability)} \\
X_{A1} + X_{B1} + X_{C1} &= 1 & \text{(Project 1 requirement)} \\
X_{A2} + X_{B2} + X_{C2} &= 1 & \text{(Project 2 requirement)} \\
X_{A3} + X_{B3} + X_{C3} &= 1 & \text{(Project 3 requirement)}
\end{aligned}
$$

**File: 5-5.xls**

**Excel Solution**  Program 5.5 shows the Excel layout and Solver entries for Fix-It Shop's assignment problem. The optimal solution identified by the model indicates that Adams should be assigned to project 3, Brown to project 2, and Cooper to project 1, for a total cost of $25.

*Assignment models can sometimes involve a maximization objective.*

**Solving Maximization Assignment Models**  The model discussed here can be very easily modified to solve *maximization* assignment problems, in which the objective coefficients represent profits or benefits rather than costs. The only change needed would be in the statement of the objective function (which would be set to maximize instead of minimize).

**Unbalanced Assignment Problems**  In the Fix-It Shop example, the total number of workers equaled the total number of projects. All supply and demand constraints could therefore be specified as equalities (i.e., using the "=" sign). What if the number of workers exceeds the number of projects, or vice versa? In these cases, we have *unbalanced* assignment models and, just as in the case of unbalanced transportation models, the supply or demand constraints need to be modified accordingly. For example, if the number of workers exceeds the number of projects, the supply constraints would become inequalities and the demand constraints would remain equality constraints. In contrast, if the number of projects exceeds the number of workers, the supply constraints would remain equality constraints and the demand constraints would become inequalities.

**PROGRAM 5.5**    **Excel Layout and Solver Entries for Fix-It Shop's Assignment Problem**

Note that the solution has all integer values.

| | A | B | C | D | E | F | G | H | I | J |
|---|---|---|---|---|---|---|---|---|---|---|
| 1 | **Fix-It Shop** | | | | | | | | | |
| 2 | | | | | | | | | | |
| 3 | From:     To: | Project 1 | Project 2 | Project 3 | Total flow out | | **Flow balance equations:** | | | |
| 4 | Adams | 0.0 | 0.0 | 1.0 | 1 | | Node | Net flow | Sign | RHS |
| 5 | Brown | 0.0 | 1.0 | 0.0 | 1 | | Adams | -1 | = | -1 |
| 6 | Cooper | 1.0 | 0.0 | 0.0 | 1 | | Brown | -1 | = | -1 |
| 7 | Total flow in | 1 | 1 | 1 | | | Cooper | -1 | = | -1 |
| 8 | | | | | | | Project 1 | 1 | = | 1 |
| 9 | **Unit costs:** | Project 1 | Project 2 | Project 3 | | | Project 2 | 1 | = | 1 |
| 10 | Adams | $11.00 | $14.00 | $6.00 | | | Project 3 | 1 | = | 1 |
| 11 | Brown | $8.00 | $10.00 | $11.00 | | | | | | |
| 12 | Cooper | $9.00 | $12.00 | $7.00 | | | | | | |
| 13 | | | | | | | | | | |
| 14 | Total cost = | $25.00 | | | | | | | | |

Workers have supply of 1 unit each.

Projects have demand of 1 unit each.

=SUMPRODUCT (B4:D6, B10:D12)

**Solver Parameters**

Set Target Cell:  |  $B$14

Equal To:   ○ Max   ● Min   ○ Value of:   |0

By Changing Cells:

$B$4:$D$6

Subject to the Constraints:

$H$5:$H$10 = $J$5:$J$10

## 5.7   MAXIMAL-FLOW MODEL

*The maximal-flow model finds the most that can flow through a network.*

The *maximal-flow* model allows us to determine the maximum amount of a material that can flow through a network. It has been used, for example, to find the maximum number of automobiles that can flow through a state highway road system.

### Road Network in Waukesha, Wisconsin

Waukesha, a small town in Wisconsin, is in the process of developing a road system for the downtown area. Bill Blackstone, a city planner, would like to determine the maximum number of cars that can flow through the town from west to east. The road network is shown in Figure 5.5, where the arcs represent the roads.

*Traffic can flow in both directions.*

The numbers by the nodes indicate the maximum number of cars (in hundreds of cars per hour) that can flow (or travel) *from* the various nodes. For example, the number 3 by node 1 (on the road from node 1 to node 2) indicates that 300 cars per hour can travel from node 1 to node 2. Likewise, the numbers 1, 1, and 2 by node 2 indicate that 100, 100, and 200 cars can travel per hour on the roads from node 2 to nodes 1, 4, and 6, respectively. Note that traffic can flow in both directions down a road. A zero (0) means no flow in that direction, or a one-way road.

Unlike the transportation and assignment models, in which there are multiple source nodes and multiple destination nodes, the typical maximal flow model has a single starting node (source) and a single ending node (destination).

### LP Model for Waukesha Road System's Maximal-Flow Problem

*We replace each two-way road (arc) with a pair of one-way roads.*

To model this problem as an LP problem, we first replace each two-way (bidirectional) road in the network with two one-way (unidirectional) roads with flows in opposite directions. Note that some of the unidirectional roads (e.g., the road from node 4 to node 1, the road

**FIGURE 5.5**

Road Network for
Waukesha

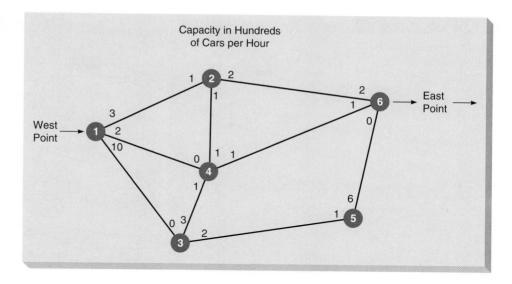

Capacity in Hundreds
of Cars per Hour

*There is a decision variable
associated with each arc in
the network.*

from node 6 to node 5) are not needed since the maximum flow permissible in that direction is zero (i.e., it is a one-way road). The revised network for Waukesha therefore has 15 unidirectional roads (i.e., roads 1→2, 1→3, 1→4, 2→1, 2→4, 2→6, 3→4, 3→5, 4→2, 4→3, 4→6, 5→3, 5→6, 6→2, and 6→4).

As with the transportation and assignment models, the presence of 15 unidirectional arcs in the network implies that there are 15 decision variables in the model—one for each arc (road) in the network. Let

$$X_{ij} = \text{Number of cars that flow (or travel) per hour on road from}$$
$$\text{node } i \text{ to node } j$$

*where*

$$i = 1, 2, 3, 4, 5, \text{ or } 6 \text{ (only roads that actually exist are defined)}$$

$$j = 1, 2, 3, 4, 5, \text{ or } 6 \text{ (only roads that actually exist are defined)}$$

We need to determine the maximum number of cars that can originate at node 1 and terminate at node 6. Hence, node 1 is the source node in this model and node 6 is the destination node. All other nodes (nodes 2 to 5) are transshipment nodes, where flows of cars neither start nor end. However, unlike the transportation and assignment models, there is neither a known quantity of "supply" of cars available at node 1, nor is there a known quantity of "demand" for cars required at node 6. For this reason, we need to slightly modify the network to set up and solve the maximal flow model using LP.

*We add a one-way dummy
road (arc) from the
destination node to the source
node.*

The modification consists of creating a unidirectional *dummy* arc (road) going *from* the destination node (node 6) *to* the source node (node 1). We call this a dummy arc since the arc (road) really does not exist in the network and has been created only for modeling purposes. The capacity of this dummy arc is set at infinity (or any artificially high number such as 1,000 for the Waukesha problem). The modified network is shown in Figure 5.6.

**Objective Function**  Let us consider the objective function first. The objective is to maximize the total number of cars flowing into node 6. Assume there are an unknown number of cars flowing on the dummy road from node 6 to node 1. However, since there is no supply at node 6 (i.e., no cars are created at node 6), the entire number of cars flowing out of node 6 (on road 6→1) must consist of cars that flowed into node 6. Likewise, since there is

FIGURE 5.6

**Modified Road Network for Waukesha**

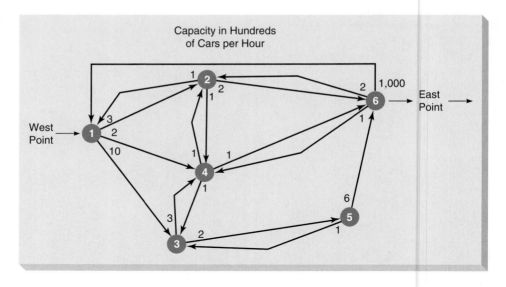

no demand at node 1 (i.e., no cars are consumed at node 1), the entire number of cars on road 6→1 must consist of cars that originally flowed out of node 1 (to nodes 2, 3, and 4).

*The objective is to maximize the flow on the dummy arc.*

These two issues imply that if we maximize the number of cars flowing on the dummy road 6→1, this is equivalent to maximizing the total number of cars flowing out of node 1 as well as the total number of cars flowing into node 6. The objective for the Waukesha problem can therefore be written as

$$\text{Maximize } X_{61}$$

**Constraints**  Since all nodes in the network are transshipment nodes with no supplies or demands, the flow balance equations need to ensure that the net flow (i.e., number of cars) at each node is zero. Hence,

*All net flows are zero.*

$$
\begin{aligned}
(X_{61} + X_{21}) - (X_{12} + X_{13} + X_{14}) &= 0 & &\text{(Net flow at node 1)} \\
(X_{12} + X_{42} + X_{62}) - (X_{21} + X_{24} + X_{26}) &= 0 & &\text{(Net flow at node 2)} \\
(X_{13} + X_{43} + X_{53}) - (X_{34} + X_{35}) &= 0 & &\text{(Net flow at node 3)} \\
(X_{14} + X_{24} + X_{34} + X_{64}) - (X_{42} + X_{43} + X_{46}) &= 0 & &\text{(Net flow at node 4)} \\
(X_{35}) - (X_{53} + X_{56}) &= 0 & &\text{(Net flow at node 5)} \\
(X_{26} + X_{46} + X_{56}) - (X_{61} + X_{62} + X_{64}) &= 0 & &\text{(Net flow at node 6)}
\end{aligned}
$$

Finally, we have capacity constraints on the maximum number of cars that can flow on each road. These are written as

*Capacity constraints limit the flows on the arcs.*

| | | |
|---|---|---|
| $X_{12} \leq 3$ | $X_{13} \leq 10$ | $X_{14} \leq 2$ |
| $X_{21} \leq 1$ | $X_{24} \leq 1$ | $X_{26} \leq 2$ |
| $X_{34} \leq 3$ | $X_{35} \leq 2$ | |
| $X_{42} \leq 1$ | $X_{43} \leq 1$ | $X_{46} \leq 1$ |
| $X_{53} \leq 1$ | $X_{56} \leq 6$ | |
| $X_{61} \leq 1{,}000$ | $X_{62} \leq 2$ | $X_{64} \leq 1$ |

**File: 5-6.xls**

**Excel Solution**  Program 5.6 shows the Excel layout and Solver entries for Waukesha's maximal-flow problem. To be consistent with earlier models, flows on arcs have been modeled here using a tabular layout (cells B4:G9). As noted earlier, a big advantage of the tabular layout is that it greatly simplifies the calculations of the total flows in and total flows out of each node in the network.

## IN ACTION    Traffic-Control System on the Hanshin Expressway

The Hanshin expressway started with a 2.3-kilometer section of road in Osaka City, Japan, in the 1960s. This small stretch of highway was the first urban toll expressway in Osaka City. The traffic flow was approximately 5,000 cars per day. Today, the expressway includes about 200 kilometers of roadway in a system that connects Osaka and Kobe, Japan. The traffic flow in the early 1990s was more than 800,000 vehicles per day, with peak traffic flows that exceeded 1 million cars per day.

As discussed in this chapter, maximizing the flow of traffic through a network involves an investigation of current and future capacity of the various branches in the network. In addition to capacity analysis, Hanshin decided to use an automated traffic control system to maximize the flow of traffic through the existing expressway and to reduce congestion and bottlenecks caused by accidents, and by road maintenance or disabled cars. It was hoped that the control system would also increase income from the expressway.

Hanshin's management investigated the number of accidents and breakdowns on the expressway to help reduce prob-

lems and further increase traffic flow. The traffic control system provides both direct and indirect control. Direct control includes controlling the number of vehicles entering the expressway at the various on-ramps. Indirect control involves providing comprehensive and up-to-the-minute information concerning traffic flows and the general traffic conditions on the expressway. Information on general traffic conditions is obtained using vehicle detectors, TV cameras, ultrasonic detectors, and automatic vehicle identifiers that read information on license plates. The data gathered from these devices give people at home and driving the information they need to determine if they will use the Hanshin expressway.

This application reveals that a solution to a problem involves variety of components, including decision modeling equipment, and other elements, such as providing information to riders.

**Source:** T. Yoshino et al. "The Traffic-Control System on the Hanshin Expressway," *Interfaces* 25 (January–February 1995): 94–108.

---

**PROGRAM 5.6**    **Excel Layout and Solver Entries for Waukesha Road Network's Maximal-Flow Problem**

All values are in 100's of cars per hour.

Only the shaded cells represent roads that actually exist.

|  | A | B | C | D | E | F | G | H | I | J | K | L | M |
|---|---|---|---|---|---|---|---|---|---|---|---|---|---|
| 1 | **Waukesha Road System** | | | | | | | | | | | | |
| 2 | | | | | | | | | | | | | |
| 3 | From: To: | Node 1 | Node 2 | Node 3 | Node 4 | Node 5 | Node 6 | Total flow out | | Flow balance equations: | | | |
| 4 | Node 1 | | 2.0 | 2.0 | 1.0 | | | 5.0 | | Node | Net flow | Sign | RHS |
| 5 | Node 2 | 0.0 | | | 0.0 | | 2.0 | 2.0 | | Node 1 | 0 | = | 0 |
| 6 | Node 3 | 0.0 | | | 0.0 | 2.0 | | 2.0 | | Node 2 | 0 | = | 0 |
| 7 | Node 4 | 0.0 | 0.0 | 0.0 | | | 1.0 | 1.0 | | Node 3 | 0 | = | 0 |
| 8 | Node 5 | | | 0.0 | | | 2.0 | 2.0 | | Node 4 | 0 | = | 0 |
| 9 | Node 6 | 5.0 | 0.0 | | 0.0 | 0.0 | | 5.0 | | Node 5 | 0 | = | 0 |
| 10 | Total flow in | 5.0 | 2.0 | 2.0 | 1.0 | 2.0 | 5.0 | | | Node 6 | 0 | = | 0 |
| 11 | | | | | | | | | | | | | |
| 12 | Flow capacity: | | | | | | | | | | | | |
| 13 | From: To: | Node 1 | Node 2 | Node 3 | Node 4 | Node 5 | Node 6 | | | | | | |
| 14 | Node 1 | | 3 | 10 | 2 | | | | | | | | |
| 15 | Node 2 | 1 | | | 1 | | 2 | | | | | | |
| 16 | Node 3 | 0 | | | 3 | 2 | | | | | | | |
| 17 | Node 4 | 0 | 1 | 1 | | | 1 | | | | | | |
| 18 | Node 5 | | | 1 | | | 6 | | | | | | |
| 19 | Node 6 | 1000 | 2 | | 1 | 0 | | | | | | | |
| 20 | | | | | | | | | | | | | |
| 21 | Maximal flow = | 5.0 | | | | | | | | | | | |

RHS = 0 since all nodes are transshipment nodes.

**Solver Parameters**

Set Target Cell:    $B$21

Equal To:    ⊙ Max    ○ Min    ○ Value of:

By Changing Cells:

$B$5:$B$7,$B$9,$C$4,$C$7,$C$9,$D$4,$D$7:

Subject to the Constraints:

$B$4:$G$9 <= $B$14:$G$19
$K$5:$K$10 = $M$5:$M$10

Table shows road capacities.

Road capacity constraints

=B9

Capacity of dummy road from node 6 to node 1 is set to an artificially high value.

Changing cells that are not contiguous are entered with commas separating them.

*Entries for nonadjacent cells are separated by commas in Solver.*

However, since arcs do not exist from every node to every other node in the network, the decision variables in this model refer only to selected entries in the table. These entries have been shaded *yellow* in Program 5.6.

How do we handle this situation in Solver? There are several simple ways of doing this. First, rather than specify the entire table (cells B4:G9) as the Changing Cells in Solver, we simply enter the shaded cells, as shown in the Changing Cells windows in Program 5.6. Note that we separate entries for nonadjacent cells by commas.

Although this approach is easy, it could be cumbersome, especially if there are too many decision variables in the model. The second (and easier) approach is to specify the entire table (cells B4:G9) as the Changing Cells in Solver. Then, for all roads that do not exist (e.g., road 1→5, road 2→3), we simply set the flow capacity on these roads to 0 (modeled in cells B14:G19 in Program 5.6). To illustrate, we enter 0 in cell F14 to prevent a nonzero flow of cars on road 1→5 (which does not exist). Solved Problem 5-3 at the end of this chapter shows an example of this approach.

*Arc capacities of 0 will prevent flows on arcs.*

Alternatively, we can design an Excel layout for this problem without using the tabular layout for the arc flows. That is, we can use 16 contiguous cells to represent the 16 arc flows for the Waukesha problem. Although this approach creates Changing Cells in Solver only for those arcs that actually exist, computing the total flow in and total flow out at different nodes could be cumbersome. In any case, we encourage you to try different Excel layouts for yourself and pick the one you find most convenient.

The solution shows that 500 cars (recall that all numbers are in hundreds of cars) can flow through the town from west to east. The values of the decision variables indicate the actual car flow on each road. Total flow out (column H) and total flow in (row 10) at each node are also shown. For example, the total flow out of node 1 is 500 cars, split as 200 cars on 1→2, 200 cars on 1→3, and 100 cars on 1→4.

## 5.8  SHORTEST-PATH MODEL

*The shortest-path model finds the path with the minimum distance through a network.*

The *shortest-path model* finds how a person or item can travel from one location to another through a network while minimizing the total distance traveled, time taken, or some other measure. In other words, it finds the shortest path or route from an origin to a series of destinations.

### Ray Design, Inc., Example

Every day, Ray Design, Inc., must transport beds, chairs, and other furniture items from the factory to the warehouse. This involves going through several cities (nodes). Ray would like to find the path with the shortest distance, in miles. The road network is shown in Figure 5.7.

### FIGURE 5.7

**Roads from Ray's Plant to Warehouse**

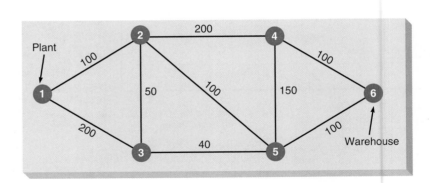

*The shortest-path problem has a unique starting node and a unique ending node.*

*All flows in a shortest-path problem will equal one unit.*

The shortest-path model is another example of a network problem that has a unique starting node (source) and a unique terminating node (destination). If we assume that there is a supply of 1 unit at node 1 (plant) and a demand of 1 unit at node 6 (warehouse), the shortest path model for the Ray Design example is identical to a transshipment problem with a single source node (node 1), a single destination node (node 6), and 4 transshipment nodes (node 2 through node 5).

Since the supply and demand both equal 1 unit, which is a whole number, the solution to the problem will have integer-valued flows on all arcs. Hence, the supply of 1 unit at node 1 will flow in its entirety on either road 1→2 or road 1→3. Further, since the net flow is zero at each of the transshipment nodes (cities), a flow of 1 unit on an incoming arc (road) at any of these cities automatically has to result in a flow of 1 unit on an outgoing road from that city.

## LP Model for Ray Design, Inc.'s Shortest-Path Problem

Since all 9 arcs (roads) in the network are bidirectional, we first replace each one by a pair of unidirectional roads. There are, therefore, 18 decision variables in the model. As usual, let

$X_{ij}$ = "Flow" on road from node $i$ to node $j$. The solution value will equal 1 if travel occurs on the road from node $i$ to node $j$ and will equal 0 otherwise.

*where*

$i$ = 1, 2, 3, 4, 5, or 6 (only roads that actually exist are defined)

$j$ = 1, 2, 3, 4, 5, or 6 (only roads that actually exist are defined)

**Objective Function** The objective is to minimize the distance between node 1 and node 6 and can be expressed as

$$\text{Minimize } 100X_{12} + 200X_{13} + 100X_{21} + 50X_{23} + 200X_{24} + 100X_{25}$$
$$+ 200X_{31} + 50X_{32} + 40X_{35} + 200X_{42} + 150X_{45} + 100X_{46}$$
$$+ 100X_{52} + 40X_{53} + 150X_{54} + 100X_{56} + 100X_{64} + 100X_{65}$$

The optimal value for each variable will be 0 or 1 depending on whether travel occurs on that road. So the objective function is the sum of road distances on which travel (flow) actually occurs.

**Constraints** We write the flow balance constraints at each node as follows:

$$(X_{21} + X_{31}) - (X_{12} + X_{13}) = -1 \text{ (Supply of 1 unit at node 1)}$$
$$(X_{12} + X_{32} + X_{42} + X_{52}) - (X_{21} + X_{23} + X_{24} + X_{25}) = 0 \text{ (Transshipment at node 2)}$$
$$(X_{13} + X_{23} + X_{53}) - (X_{31} + X_{32} + X_{35}) = 0 \text{ (Transshipment at node 3)}$$
$$(X_{24} + X_{54} + X_{64}) - (X_{42} + X_{45} + X_{46}) = 0 \text{ (Transshipment at node 4)}$$
$$(X_{25} + X_{35} + X_{45} + X_{65}) - (X_{52} + X_{53} + X_{54} + X_{56}) = 0 \text{ (Transshipment at node 5)}$$
$$(X_{46} + X_{56}) - (X_{64} + X_{65}) = 1 \text{ (Demand of 1 unit at node 6)}$$

**File: 5-7.xls**

**Excel Solution** Program 5.7 shows the Excel layout and Solver entries for Ray Design, Inc.'s shortest-path problem. Once again, we use the tabular layout to represent arc flows. However, as with the maximal-flow problem, certain arcs do not exist and need to be excluded when specifying entries for the Changing Cells in Solver. This can be achieved by separating noncontiguous cell entries by commas (as shown in Program 5.7).

**PROGRAM 5.7**    **Excel Layout and Solver Entries for Ray Design, Inc.'s Shortest-Path Problem**

> Only the shaded cells represent roads that actually exist.

| | A | B | C | D | E | F | G | H | I | J | K | L | M |
|---|---|---|---|---|---|---|---|---|---|---|---|---|---|
| 1 | **Ray Design, Inc.** | | | | | | | | | | | | |
| 2 | | | | | | | | | | | | | |
| 3 | From:  To: | Node 1 | Node 2 | Node 3 | Node 4 | Node 5 | Node 6 | Total flow out | | Flow balance equations: | | | |
| 4 | Node 1 | | 1.0 | 0.0 | | | | 1.0 | | Node | Net flow | Sign | RHS |
| 5 | Node 2 | 0.0 | | 1.0 | 0.0 | 0.0 | | 1.0 | | Node 1 | -1 | = | -1 |
| 6 | Node 3 | 0.0 | 0.0 | | | 1.0 | | 1.0 | | Node 2 | 0 | = | 0 |
| 7 | Node 4 | | 0.0 | | | 0.0 | 0.0 | 0.0 | | Node 3 | 0 | = | 0 |
| 8 | Node 5 | | 0.0 | 0.0 | 0.0 | | 1.0 | 1.0 | | Node 4 | 0 | = | 0 |
| 9 | Node 6 | | | | 0.0 | 0.0 | | 0.0 | | Node 5 | 0 | = | 0 |
| 10 | Total flow in | 0.0 | 1.0 | 1.0 | 0.0 | 1.0 | 1.0 | | | Node 6 | 1 | = | 1 |
| 11 | | | | | | | | | | | | | |
| 12 | Distances: | | | | | | | | | | | | |
| 13 | From:  To: | Node 1 | Node 2 | Node 3 | Node 4 | Node 5 | Node 6 | | | | | | |
| 14 | Node 1 | | 100 | 200 | | | | | | | | | |
| 15 | Node 2 | 100 | | 50 | 200 | 100 | | | | | | | |
| 16 | Node 3 | 200 | 50 | | | 40 | | | | | | | |
| 17 | Node 4 | | 200 | | | 150 | 100 | | | | | | |
| 18 | Node 5 | | 100 | 40 | 150 | | 100 | | | | | | |
| 19 | Node 6 | | | | 100 | 100 | | | | | | | |
| 20 | | | | | | | | | | | | | |
| 21 | Shorest distance = | 290.0 | | | | | | | | | | | |

> Supply of one unit at node 1

> Demand of one unit at node 6

> =SUMPRODUCT (B4:G9, B14:G19)

**Solver Parameters**

Set Target Cell:  $B$21

Equal To:   ○ Max   ● Min   ○ Value of:

By Changing Cells:

$B$5:$B$6,$C$4,$C$6:$C$8,$D$4:$D$5,$D$8,

Subject to the Constraints:

$K$5:$K$10 = $M$5:$M$10

> Noncontiguous cell entries are separated by commas.

*Arcs with large (infinite) distances will have zero flows.*

Alternatively, the entire table (cells B4:G9) can be specified as the Changing Cells in Solver. However, to prevent items from flowing on roads that do not exist (e.g., 1→4, 1→5), the distance of these roads can be set to infinity (or a very large number) in the corresponding cells in B14:G19. For example, we would enter a distance of infinity for road 1→4 in cell E14. Since the objective is to minimize total distance, no travel will occur on these roads due to their high cost.

The solution shows that the shortest distance from the plant to the warehouse is 290 miles and involves travel through cities 2, 3, and 5.

## IN ACTION    Spanning Tree Analysis of a Telecommunications Network

Network models have been used to solve a variety of problems for many different companies. In telecommunications, there is always a need to connect computer systems and devices together in an efficient and effective manner. Digital Equipment Corporation (DEC) for example, was concerned about how computer systems and devices were connected to a local area network (LAN) using a technology called Ethernet. The DEC net routing department was responsible for this and other network and telecommunications solutions.

Because of a number of technical difficulties, it was important to have an effective way to transport packets of information throughout the LAN. The solution was to use a spanning tree algorithm. The success of this approach can be seen in a poem written by one of the developers:

"I think I shall never see a graph more lovely than a tree.

A tree whose critical property is loop-free connectivity.

A tree that must be sure to span, so packets can reach every LAN.

First the route must be selected, by ID it is elected.

Least-cost paths from the root are traced.

In the tree these paths are placed.

A mesh is made for folks by me, then bridges find a spanning tree."

**Source:** Radia Perlman et al. "Spanning the LAN," *Data Communications* (October 21, 1997): 68.

## 5.9 MINIMAL-SPANNING TREE MODEL

*The minimal-spanning tree model connects nodes at a minimum total distance.*

The *minimal-spanning tree model* can be used to connect all the nodes of a network to each other while minimizing the total distance of all the arcs used for this connection. It has been applied, for example, by telephone companies to connect a number of phones (nodes) together while minimizing the total length of telephone cable (arcs).

### Lauderdale Construction Company Example

Let us consider the Lauderdale Construction Company, which is currently developing a luxurious housing project on Panama City Beach. Melvin Lauderdale, owner and president of Lauderdale Construction, must determine the least expensive way to provide water and power to each house. The network of houses is shown in Figure 5.8.

As seen in Figure 5.8, there are eight houses on the gulf. The distance between each house (in hundreds of feet) is shown on the network. For example, the distance between houses 1 and 2 is 300 feet (shown by the 3 on the arc connecting houses 1 and 2). Now, we can use the minimal-spanning tree model to determine the minimum total length (of water pipes or power cables) needed to connect all the houses.

Unlike the other network flow models studied so far in this chapter, the minimal-spanning tree problem is difficult to formulate as an LP problem using the typical flow balance equations. However, the minimal-spanning tree model is very easy to solve by hand using a simple solution procedure. The procedure is outlined as follows:

### Steps for Solving the Minimal-Spanning Tree Model

*There are four steps in the solution procedure for minimal-spanning tree problems.*

1. Begin by selecting any node in the network.
2. Connect this node to its nearest node.
3. Considering all the connected nodes, find the nearest *unconnected* node, and connect it. If there is a tie and two or more unconnected nodes are equally near, select one arbitrarily. A tie suggests there may be more than one optimal solution.
4. Repeat the third step until all the nodes are connected.

### FIGURE 5.8

**Network for Lauderdale Construction**

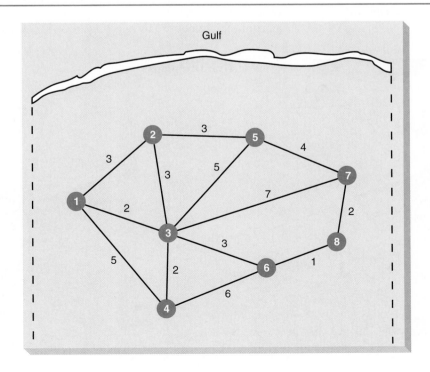

FIGURE 5.9

**First Iteration for Lauderdale Construction**

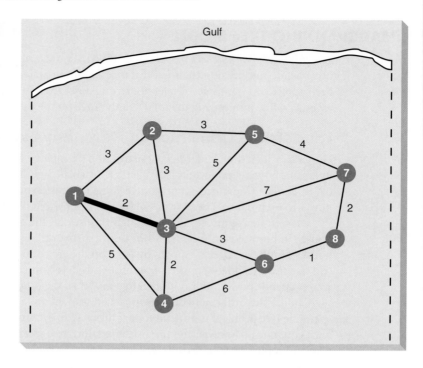

We can now solve the network in Figure 5.8 for Melvin Lauderdale. We start by arbitrarily selecting any node (house). Let's say we select house 1. Since house 3 is the nearest one to house 1 at a distance of 2 (200 feet), we connect these two houses. That is, we select arc 1→3 for inclusion in the spanning tree. This is shown in Figure 5.9.

Next, considering connected houses 1 and 3, we look for the unconnected house that is closest to either house. This turns out to be house 4, which is 200 feet from house 3. We connect houses 3 and 4 by selecting arc 3→4 (see Figure 5.10(a)).

We continue, looking for the nearest unconnected house to houses 1, 3, and 4. This is house 2 or house 6, both at a distance of 300 feet from house 3. We arbitrarily pick house 2 and connect it to house 3 by selecting arc 3→2 (see Figure 5.10(b)).

FIGURE 5.10    **Second and Third Iterations**

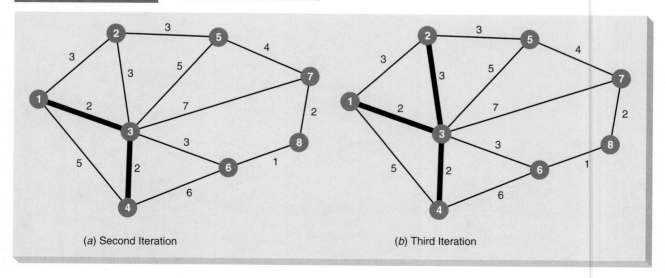

(a) Second Iteration

(b) Third Iteration

**FIGURE 5.11**  **Fourth and Fifth Iterations**

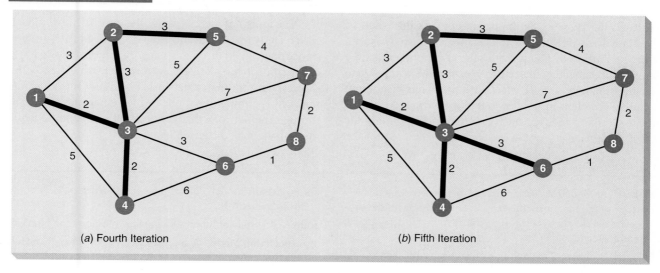

(a) Fourth Iteration

(b) Fifth Iteration

We continue the process. There is another tie for the next iteration with a minimum distance of 300 feet (house 2 to house 5, and house 3 to house 6). Note that we do not consider house 1 to house 2 with a distance of 300 feet at this iteration since both houses are already connected. We arbitrarily select house 5 and connect it to house 2 by selecting arc 2→5 (see Figure 5.11(a)). The next nearest house is house 6, and we connect it to house 3 by selecting arc 3→6 (see Figure 5.11(b)).

At this stage, we have only two unconnected houses left. House 8 is the nearest one to house 6 with a distance of 100 feet, and we connect it using arc 6→8 (see Figure 5.12(a)). Then the remaining house (house 7) is connected to house 8 using arc 8→7 (see Figure 5.12(b)).

Since there are no more unconnected houses, Figure 5.12(b) shows the final solution. Houses 1, 2, 4, and 6 are all connected to house 3. House 2 is connected to house 5. House 6 is connected to house 8, and house 8 is connected to house 7. The total distance is 1,600 feet.

**FIGURE 5.12**  **Sixth and Seventh (Final) Iterations**

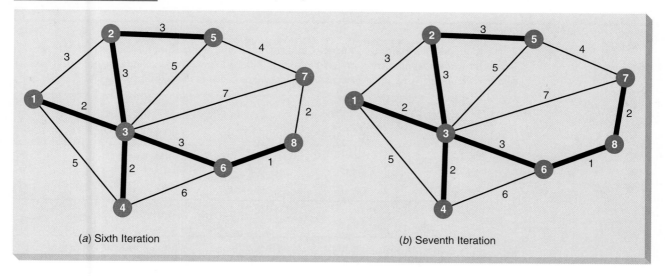

(a) Sixth Iteration

(b) Seventh Iteration

## SUMMARY

This chapter presents six important network flow models. First, we discuss the transportation model, which deals with the distribution of goods from several supply points to a number of demand points. We then extend this discussion to the transshipment model, which includes points that permit goods to both flow in and flow out of them. Next, we discuss the assignment model, which deals with determining the most efficient assignment of issues such as people to projects.

The fourth model covered is the maximal-flow model, which finds the maximum flow of any quantity or substance that can go through a network. This is followed by a discussion of the shortest-path model, which finds the shortest path through a network. Finally, we introduce the minimal-spanning tree model, which determines the path through the network that connects all of the nodes while minimizing total distance.

## GLOSSARY

**Assignment Model.**  A specific class of LP problems that involves determining the most efficient assignment of people to projects, salespeople to territories, contracts to bidders, jobs to machines, and so on.

**Balanced Problem.**  The condition under which total demand (at all destinations) is equal to total supply (at all sources).

**Destination.**  A demand location in a transportation problem.

**Facility Location Analysis.**  An application of the transportation model to help a firm decide where to locate a new factory, warehouse, or other facility.

**Maximal-Flow Model.**  Finds the maximum flow of any quantity or substance through a network.

**Minimal-Spanning Tree Model.**  Determines the path through the network that connects all of the nodes while minimizing total distance.

**Shortest-Path Model.**  Determines the shortest path or route through a network.

**Source.**  An origin or supply location in a transportation problem.

**Transportation Model.**  A specific case of LP involving scheduling shipments from sources to destinations so that total shipping costs are minimized.

**Transshipment Problem.**  An extension of the transportation problem in which some points have both flows in and out of them.

**Unbalanced Problem.**  A situation in which total demand is not equal to total supply.

## KEY EQUATION

(5-1)   Net flow = (Total flow *in* to node) − (Total flow *out* of node)
Flow balance constraint written for each node in the network.

## SOLVED PROBLEMS

### Solved Problem 5-1

Don Yale, president of Hardrock Concrete Company, has plants in three locations and is currently working on three major construction projects, located at different sites. The shipping cost per truckload of concrete, plant capacities, and project requirements are provided in the accompanying table.

| TO<br>FROM | PROJECT A | PROJECT B | PROJECT C | PLANT CAPACITIES |
|---|---|---|---|---|
| Plant 1 | $10 | $4 | $11 | 70 |
| Plant 2 | $12 | $5 | $ 8 | 50 |
| Plant 3 | $ 9 | $7 | $ 6 | 30 |
| Project Requirements | 40 | 50 | 60 | 150 |

Set up and solve Hardrock's problem as a transportation model.

## PROGRAM 5.8   Excel Layout and Solver Entries for Hardrock Concrete Company's Transportation Problem

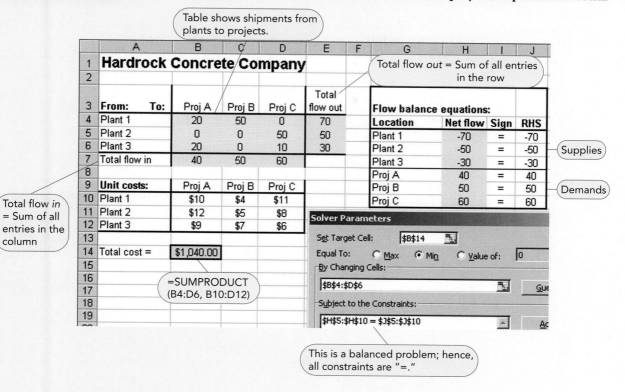

Table shows shipments from plants to projects.

Total flow *out* = Sum of all entries in the row

Total flow *in* = Sum of all entries in the column

=SUMPRODUCT (B4:D6, B10:D12)

This is a balanced problem; hence, all constraints are "=."

### Solution

There are three sources (Plants 1, 2, and 3) and three destinations (Projects A, B, and C). Hence, there are nine decision variables. The Excel layout and solution is shown in Program 5.8. The optimal solution costs $1,040 and involves shipping truckloads of concrete as follows: 20 truckloads from plant 1 to project A, 50 truckloads from plant 1 to project B, 50 truckloads from plant 2 to project C, 20 truckloads from plant 3 to project A, and 10 truckloads from plant 3 to project C.

**File: 5-8.xls**

## Solved Problem 5-2

Prentice Hall, Inc., a publisher headquartered in New Jersey, wants to assign three recently hired college graduates, Jones, Smith, and Wilson, to regional sales districts in Omaha, Dallas, and Miami. But the firm also has an opening in New York and would send one of the three there if it were more economical than a move to Omaha, Dallas, or Miami. It will cost $1,000 to relocate Jones to New York, $800 to relocate Smith there, and $1,500 to move Wilson. What is the optimal assignment of personnel to offices?

| HIREE \ OFFICE | OMAHA | MIAMI | DALLAS |
|---|---|---|---|
| Jones | $800 | $1,100 | $1,200 |
| Smith | $500 | $1,600 | $1,300 |
| Wilson | $500 | $1,000 | $2,300 |

### Solution

Since this is an unbalanced assignment problem with three supply points (hirees) and four demand points (offices), note that the demand constraints should be expressed as inequalities (that is, they should have ≤ signs).

**Excel Layout and Solver Entries for Prentice Hall, Inc.'s Assignment Problem**

Optimal solution has no one assigned to Dallas.

|  | A | B | C | D | E | F | G | H | I | J | K |
|---|---|---|---|---|---|---|---|---|---|---|---|
| 1 | **Prentice-Hall** | | | | | | | | | | |
| 2 | | | | | | | | | | | |
| 3 | Hire:   Office: | Omaha | Miami | Dallas | New York | Total flow out | | **Flow balance equations:** | | | |
| 4 | Jones | 0.0 | 1.0 | 0.0 | 0.0 | 1 | | **Node** | **Net flow** | **Sign** | **RHS** |
| 5 | Smith | 0.0 | 0.0 | 0.0 | 1.0 | 1 | | Jones | -1 | = | -1 |
| 6 | Wilson | 1.0 | 0.0 | 0.0 | 0.0 | 1 | | Smith | -1 | = | -1 |
| 7 | Total flow in | 1 | 1 | 0 | 1 | | | Wilson | -1 | = | -1 |
| 8 | | | | | | | | Omaha | 1 | <= | 1 |
| 9 | **Unit costs:** | Omaha | Miami | Dallas | New York | | | Miami | 0 | <= | 1 |
| 10 | Jones | $800 | $1,100 | $1,200 | $1,000 | | | Dallas | 1 | <= | 1 |
| 11 | Smith | $500 | $1,600 | $1,300 | $800 | | | New York | 1 | <= | 1 |
| 12 | Wilson | $500 | $1,000 | $2,300 | $1,500 | | | | | | |
| 13 | | | | | | | **Solver Parameters** | | | | |
| 14 | Total cost = | $2,400 | | | | | | | | | |
| 15 | | | | | | | Set Target Cell: | $B$14 | | | |
| 16 | | Demand flow balance constraints | | | | | Equal To:   ○ Max   ● Min   ○ Value of:   [0 | | | | |
| 17 | | are ≤ since number of locations | | | | | By Changing Cells: | | | | |
| 18 | | exceeds number of hirees. | | | | | $B$4:$E$6 | | | | |
| 19 | | | | | | | Subject to the Constraints: | | | | |
| 20 | | | | | | | $I$5:$I$7 = $K$5:$K$7 | | | | |
| 21 | | | | | | | $I$8:$I$11 <= $K$8:$K$11 | | | | |

**File: 5-9.xls**

The Excel layout and solution for Prentice Hall's assignment problem is shown in Program 5.9. The optimal solution is to assign Wilson to Omaha, Smith to New York, and Jones to Miami. Nobody is assigned to Dallas. The total cost is $2,400.

### Solved Problem 5-3

PetroChem, an oil refinery located on the Mississippi River south of Baton Rouge, Louisiana, is designing a new plant to produce diesel fuel. Figure 5.13 shows the network of the main processing centers along with the existing rate of flow (in thousands of gallons of fuel). The management at PetroChem would like to determine the maximum amount of fuel that can flow through the plant, from node 1 to node 7.

#### Solution

Node 1 is the source node and node 7 is the destination node. As described in Section 5.7, we introduce a dummy arc from node 7 to node 1 (see Figure 5.14). The capacity of this arc is set at a large number (say, 1,000).

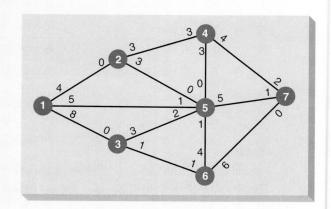

## FIGURE 5.14

**Modified Network for Solved Problem 5-3**

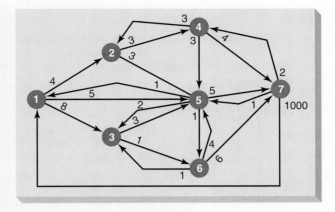

**File: 5-10.xls**

The Excel layout and solution for this problem is shown in Program 5.10. Unlike our earlier example in Program 5.6, the entire table (cells B4:H10) has been specified as the Changing Cells in Solver. However, the capacity of all arcs that do not exist (shown by the non-yellow cells in B4:H10) has been set to zero to prevent any fuel flows on these pipes (arcs).

The optimal solution shows that it is possible to have 10,000 gallons flow from node 1 to node 7 using the existing network.

## PROGRAM 5.10    Excel Layout and Solver Entries for PetroChem's Maximal-Flow Problem

|  | A | B | C | D | E | F | G | H | I |
|---|---|---|---|---|---|---|---|---|---|
| 1 | **PetroChem** | | | Table shows the flow between nodes. | | | Only the shaded cells denote pipes that actually exist. | | |
| 2 | | | | | | | | | |
| 3 | From: To: | Node 1 | Node 2 | Node 3 | Node 4 | Node 5 | Node 6 | Node 7 | Total flow out |
| 4 | Node 1 | 0.0 | 4.0 | 1.0 | 0.0 | 5.0 | 0.0 | 0.0 | 10.0 |
| 5 | Node 2 | 0.0 | 0.0 | 0.0 | 3.0 | 1.0 | 0.0 | 0.0 | 4.0 |
| 6 | Node 3 | 0.0 | 0.0 | 0.0 | 0.0 | 0.0 | 1.0 | 0.0 | 1.0 |
| 7 | Node 4 | 0.0 | 0.0 | 0.0 | 0.0 | 0.0 | 0.0 | 3.0 | 3.0 |
| 8 | Node 5 | 0.0 | 0.0 | 0.0 | 0.0 | 0.0 | 1.0 | 5.0 | 6.0 |
| 9 | Node 6 | 0.0 | 0.0 | 0.0 | 0.0 | 0.0 | 0.0 | 2.0 | 2.0 |
| 10 | Node 7 | 10.0 | 0.0 | 0.0 | 0.0 | 0.0 | 0.0 | 0.0 | 10.0 |
| 11 | Total flow in | 10.0 | 4.0 | 1.0 | 3.0 | 6.0 | 2.0 | 10.0 | |

**Flow balance equations:**

| Node | Net flow | Sign | RHS |
|---|---|---|---|
| Node 1 | 0 | = | 0 |
| Node 2 | 0 | = | 0 |
| Node 3 | 0 | = | 0 |
| Node 4 | 0 | = | 0 |
| Node 5 | 0 | = | 0 |
| Node 6 | 0 | = | 0 |
| Node 7 | 0 | = | 0 |

**Flow capacity:**

|  | From: To: | Node 1 | Node 2 | Node 3 | Node 4 | Node 5 | Node 6 | Node 7 |
|---|---|---|---|---|---|---|---|---|
| 14 | From: To: | Node 1 | Node 2 | Node 3 | Node 4 | Node 5 | Node 6 | Node 7 |
| 15 | Node 1 | 0 | 4 | 8 | 0 | 5 | 0 | 0 |
| 16 | Node 2 | 0 | 0 | 0 | 3 | 3 | 0 | 0 |
| 17 | Node 3 | 0 | 0 | 0 | 0 | 3 | 1 | 0 |
| 18 | Node 4 | 0 | 3 | 0 | 0 | 3 | 0 | 4 |
| 19 | Node 5 | 1 | 0 | 2 | 0 | 0 | 1 | 5 |
| 20 | Node 6 | 0 | 0 | 1 | 0 | 4 | 0 | 6 |
| 21 | Node 7 | **1000** | 0 | 0 | 2 | 1 | 0 | 0 |

| 22 | | |
|---|---|---|
| 23 | Maximal flow = | 10.0 |

**Solver Parameters**

Set Target Cell:  $B$23

Equal To:  ⦿ Max   ○ Min   ○ Value of:

By Changing Cells:

$B$4:$H$10

Subject to the Constraints:

$B$4:$H$10 <= $B$15:$H$21
$L$5:$L$11 = $N$5:$N$11

This is the capacity of dummy pipe from node 7 to node 1.

Capacities of pipes that do not exist are set to zero.

All cells in the table (B4:H10) are specified as changing cells. No flow occurs on pipes that do not exist since their capacities are zero.

## Solved Problem 5-4

**File: 5-11.xls**

The network of Figure 5.15 shows the highways and cities surrounding Leadville, Colorado. Leadville Tom, a bicycle helmet manufacturer, must transport his helmets to a distributor based in Dillon, Colorado. To do this, he must go through several cities. Tom would like to find the shortest way to get from Leadville to Dillon. What do you recommend?

### Solution

We associate a supply of 1 unit at Leadville (node 1) and a demand of 1 unit at Dillon (node 16). The Excel layout and solution for this problem are shown in Program 5.11. As we saw earlier in Program 5.7, the Changing Cell entries in Solver include only those cells that represent actual arcs (shown by the *yellow* shaded cells in B4:G19). Note that it is not possible to denote the entire table as Changing Cells in this example since the number of decision variables will be 256 (= 16 × 16). This exceeds the maximum permissible size of 200 decision variables for the standard version of Solver.

The optimal solution shows that the shortest distance from Leadville to Dillon is 460 miles and involves travel through nodes 3, 7, 11, and 14.

## PROGRAM 5.11    Excel Layout and Solver Entries for Leadville Tom's Shortest-Path Problem

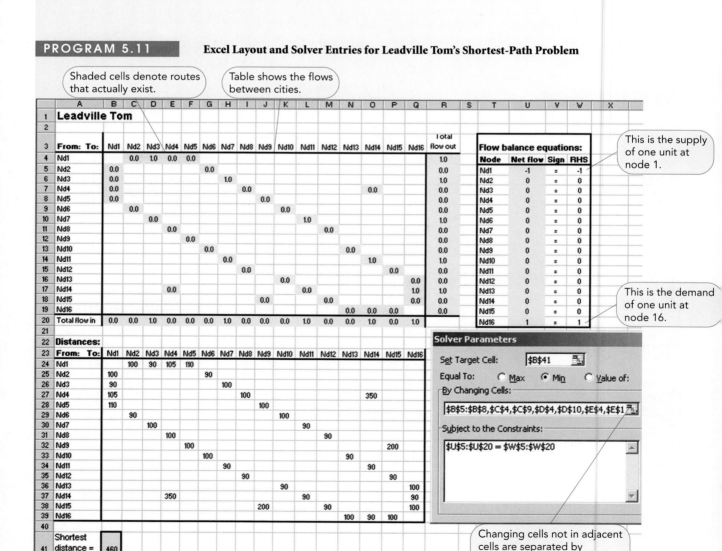

Shaded cells denote routes that actually exist.

Table shows the flows between cities.

This is the supply of one unit at node 1.

This is the demand of one unit at node 16.

Changing cells not in adjacent cells are separated by commas.

FIGURE 5.15

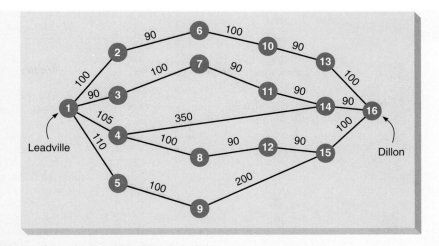

Solved Problem 5-5

Roxie LaMothe, owner of a large horse breeding farm near Orlando, is planning to install a complete water system connecting all of the various stables and barns. The location of the facilities and the distances between them is given in the network shown in Figure 5.16. Roxie must determine the least expensive way to provide water to each facility. What do you recommend?

FIGURE 5.16

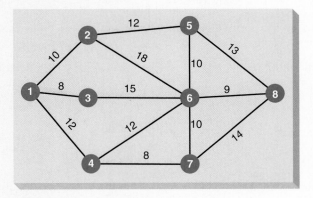

### Solution

This is a typical minimum-spanning tree problem that can be solved by hand. We begin by selecting node 1 and connecting it to the nearest node, which is node 3. Nodes 1 and 2 are the next to be connected, followed by nodes 1 and 4. Now we connect node 4 to node 7 and node 7 to node 6. At this point, the only remaining points to be connected are node 6 to node 8 and node 6 to node 5. The final solution can be seen in Figure 5.17.

FIGURE 5.17

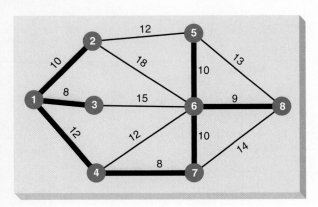

## ⇒ SELF-TEST

- Before taking the self-test, refer back to the learning objectives at the beginning of the chapter, the notes in the margins, and the glossary at the end of the chapter.
- Use the key at the back of the book to correct your answers.
- Restudy pages that correspond to any questions that you answered incorrectly or material you feel uncertain about.

1. Which model is used to connect all points of a network together while minimizing the distance between them?
   a. maximal flow
   b. minimal flow
   c. minimal-spanning tree
   d. shortest route
   e. longest span
2. The first step in solving the minimal-spanning tree model is to
   a. select the node with the highest distance between it and any other node.
   b. select the node with the lowest distance between it and any other node.
   c. select the node that is closest to the origin.
   d. select any arc that connects two nodes.
   e. select any node.
3. Which model involves finding the nearest node to the origin?
   a. maximal flow
   b. minimal flow
   c. maximal-spanning tree
   d. minimal-spanning tree
   e. shortest route
4. The fire chief was not satisfied with the amount of water put on the warehouse fire by pumper 3. With two hydrant connections and a number of different (known) hose capacities due to leakage of repairs, the chief could determine the best combination by several uses of
   a. the minimal-spanning tree model.
   b. the maximal-flow model.
   c. the shortest-route model.
5. The fire chief is on a very tight budget, and the price of gasoline has just gone up again. She wants to minimize the distance traveled by all the fire trucks to each fire hydrant in case of a fire call. She should use
   a. the minimal-spanning tree model.
   b. the maximal-flow model.
   c. the shortest-route model.
6. Tearing up city streets is expensive. The fire chief wants to convince the city council, using the smallest-distance fig-

ures, to put in a new water main connecting eight vital spots downtown. She should use
   a. the minimal-spanning tree model.
   b. the maximal-flow model.
   c. the shortest-route model.
7. The Enfield Company is very concerned about shipping costs when moving its products from its various factories to its regional warehouses. To minimize these costs, it should use
   a. the transportation model.
   b. the assignment model.
   c. the shortest-path model.
   d. the maximal-flow model.
8. A student project has 4 tasks and is to be done by a group of 4 students. Which model is appropriate to use when deciding which student should be responsible for which task?
   a. the transportation model
   b. the assignment model
   c. the shortest-path model
   d. the maximal-flow model
9. _____ is a model that is used to find how a person or item can travel from one location to another while minimizing the total distance traveled.
10. The model that allows us to determine the maximum amount of a material that can flow through a network is called _____.
11. The _____ model can be used to connect all of the points of a network together while minimizing the distance between them.
12. A point or node that has shipments arrive as well as leave is called a
   a. supply node.
   b. demand node.
   c. transshipment node.
   d. dummy node.
13. The net flow at each node is calculated as
   a. total flow in − total flow out.
   b. total flow in + total flow out.
   c. total flow in.
   d. total flow out.

# DISCUSSION QUESTIONS AND PROBLEMS

## Discussion Questions

**5-1** Is the transportation model an example of decision making under certainty or decision making under uncertainty? Why?

**5-2** What is a balanced transportation problem? Describe the approach you would use to solve an unbalanced problem.

**5-3** What is the enumeration approach to solving assignment problems? Is it a practical way to solve a 5 row × 5 column problem? A 7 × 7 problem? Why?

**5-4** What is the minimal-spanning tree model? What types of problems can be solved using this type of model?

**5-5** Give several examples of problems that can be solved using the maximal-flow model.

**5-6** Describe a problem that can be solved by the shortest-route model.

**5-7** What is a flow balance constraint? How is it implemented at each node in a network model?

**5-8** How can we manipulate a maximal-flow network model in order to set it up as a linear program?

**5-9** Why might it be more convenient to set up network models in Excel using a "tabular" form?

**5-10** How can we manipulate a maximal-flow network model in order to specify all arcs between each pair of nodes (i.e., the entire table) as the Changing Cells in Solver?

**5-11** How can we manipulate a shortest-path network model in order to specify all arcs between each pair of nodes (i.e., the entire table) as the Changing Cells in Solver?

## Problems

**5-12** The Arden County, Maryland, superintendent of education is responsible for assigning students to the three high schools in his county. He recognizes the need to bus a certain number of students, for several sectors of the county are beyond walking distance to a school. The superintendent partitions the county into five geographic sectors as he attempts to establish a plan that will minimize the total number of student

miles traveled by bus. He also recognizes that if a student happens to live in a certain sector and is assigned to the high school in that sector, there is no need to bus that student because he or she can walk to school. The three schools are located in sectors, B, C and E.

The table at the bottom of this page reflects the number of high-school-age students living in each sector and the distance in miles from each sector to each school.

Each high school has a capacity of 900 students. Set up the objective function and constraints of this problem using LP so that the total number of student miles traveled by bus is minimized. Then solve the problem.

**5-13** Marc Smith's construction firm currently has three projects under way in various counties in Iowa. Each requires a specific supply of gravel. Three gravel pits are available in Iowa to provide for Smith's needs, but shipping costs differ from location to location. The following table summarizes the problem Smith faces.

| From | Job 1 | Job 2 | Job 3 | Tonnage Allowance |
|---|---|---|---|---|
| Dubuque pit | $9 | $8 | $7 | 1,500 |
| Davenport pit | 7 | 11 | 6 | 1,750 |
| Des Moines pit | 4 | 3 | 12 | 2,750 |
| Job requirements (tons) | 2,000 | 3,000 | 1,000 | 6,000 |

(a) Determine Smith's optimal shipping quantities so as to minimize total transportation costs.

(b) Examining the map, Smith recognizes that Jobs 1 and 2 are very near Des Moines. Rather than shipping gravel directly from the Dubuque and Davenport pits to these job sites, Smith wonders if it would be better for him to consolidate shipping at Des Moines. Given the excellent roads between major cities in Iowa, he believes he can ship gravel between Davenport and Des Moines and between Dubuque and Des Moines for as little as $2 per ton. Set up and solve Smith's problem now with this new information.

**Table for Problem 5-12**

| Sector | School in Sector B | School in Sector C | School in Sector E | Number of Students |
|---|---|---|---|---|
| A | 5 | 8 | 6 | 700 |
| B | 0 | 4 | 12 | 500 |
| C | 4 | 0 | 7 | 100 |
| D | 7 | 2 | 5 | 800 |
| E | 12 | 7 | 0 | 400 |
| | | | | 2,500 |

⋮ **5-14** The Krampf Lines Railway Company specializes in coal handling. On Friday, April 13, Krampf had empty cars at the following towns in the quantities indicated:

| Town | Supply of Cars |
|------|----------------|
| Morgantown | 35 |
| Youngstown | 60 |
| Pittsburgh | 25 |

By Monday, April 16, the following towns will need coal cars as follows:

| Town | Demand for Cars |
|------|-----------------|
| Coal Valley | 30 |
| Coaltown | 45 |
| Coal Junction | 25 |
| Coalsburg | 20 |

Using a railway city-to-city distance chart, the dispatcher constructs a mileage table for the preceding towns. The result is as follows:

| From \ To | Coal Valley | Coaltown | Coal Junction | Coalsburg |
|-----------|-------------|----------|---------------|-----------|
| Morgantown | 50 | 30 | 60 | 70 |
| Youngstown | 20 | 80 | 10 | 90 |
| Pittsburgh | 100 | 40 | 80 | 30 |

Minimizing total miles over which cars are moved to new locations, compute the best shipment of coal cars.

⋮ **5-15** The B. Hall Real Estate Investment Corporation has identified four small apartment buildings in which it would like to invest. Mrs. Hall has approached three savings and loan companies regarding financing. Because Hall has been a good client in the past and has maintained a high credit rating in the community, each savings and loan company is willing to consider providing all or part of the mortgage loan needed on each property. Each loan officer has set differing interest rates on each property (rates are affected by the neighborhood of the apartment building, condition of the property, and desire by the individual savings and loan to finance various-size

buildings), *and* each loan company has placed a maximum credit ceiling on how much it will lend Hall in total. This information is summarized in the table at the bottom of this page.

Each apartment building is equally attractive as an investment to Hall, so she has decided to purchase all buildings possible at the lowest total payment of interest. From which savings and loan companies should she borrow to purchase which buildings? More than one savings and loan can finance the same property.

⋮ **5-16** The J. Mehta Company's production manager is planning for a series of one-month production periods for stainless steel sinks. The demand for the next four months is as follows:

| Month | Demand for Stainless Steel Sinks |
|-------|----------------------------------|
| 1 | 120 |
| 2 | 160 |
| 3 | 240 |
| 4 | 100 |

The Mehta firm can normally produce 100 stainless steel sinks in a month. This is done during regular production hours at a cost of $100 per sink. If demand in any one month cannot be satisfied by regular production, the production manager has three other choices: (1) he can produce up to 50 more sinks per month in overtime but at a cost of $130 per sink; (2) he can purchase a limited number of sinks from a friendly competitor for resale (the maximum number of outside purchases over the four-month period is 450 sinks, at a cost of $150 each); or (3) he can fill the demand from his on-hand inventory. The inventory carrying cost is $10 per sink per month. Back orders are not permitted. Inventory on hand at the beginning of month 1 is 40 sinks. Set up and solve this "production smoothing" problem as a transportation problem to minimize cost.

⋮ **5-17** Ashley's Auto Top Carriers currently maintains plants in Atlanta and Tulsa that supply major distribution centers in Los Angeles and New York. Because of an expanding demand, Ashley has decided to open a third plant and has narrowed the choice to one of two cities—New Orleans or Houston. The pertinent production and distribution costs, as well as the plant

**Table for Problem 5-15**

| Savings and Loan Company | Property (Interest Rates) (%) | | | | Maximum Credit Line ($) |
|--------------------------|---------|----------|-----------|------------|-------------------------|
| | Hill St. | Banks St. | Park Ave. | Drury Lane | |
| First Homestead | 8 | 8 | 10 | 11 | 80,000 |
| Commonwealth | 9 | 10 | 12 | 10 | 100,000 |
| Washington Federal | 9 | 11 | 10 | 9 | 120,000 |
| Loan required to purchase building | $60,000 | $40,000 | $130,000 | $70,000 | |

**Table for Problem 5-17**

| From Plants \ To Distribution Centers | Los Angeles | New York | Normal Production | Unit Production Cost ($) |
|---|---|---|---|---|
| Atlanta (Existing plants) | $8 | $5 | 600 | 6 |
| Tulsa (Existing plants) | $4 | $7 | 900 | 5 |
| New Orleans (Proposed locations) | $5 | $6 | 500 | 4 (*anticipated*) |
| Houston (Proposed locations) | $4 | $6 | 500 | 3 (*anticipated*) |
| Forecast Demand | 800 | 1,200 | 2,000 | |

*Indicates distribution cost (shipping, handling, storage) will be $6 per carrier if sent from Houston to New York*

capacities and distribution demands, are shown in the table at the top of this page. Which of the new possible plants should be opened?

**5-18** Marc Jones, vice-president for operations of HHN, Inc., a manufacturer of cabinets for telephone switches, is constrained from meeting the five-year forecast by limited capacity at the existing three plants. These three plants are Waterloo, Pusan, and Bogota. You, as his able assistant, have been told that because of existing capacity constraints and the expanding world market for HHN cabinets, a new plant is to be added to the existing three plants. The real estate department has advised Mr. Jones that two sites seem particularly good because of a stable political situation and tolerable exchange rate: Dublin, Ireland, and Fontainebleau, France. Mr. Jones suggests that you should be able to take the data in the table at the bottom of this page and determine where the fourth plant should be located on the basis of production costs and transportation costs.

**5-19** Don Levine Corporation is considering adding an additional plant to its three existing facilities in Decatur, Minneapolis, and Carbondale. Both St. Louis and East St. Louis are being considered. Evaluating

**Table for Problem 5-18**

| | Plant Location | | | | |
|---|---|---|---|---|---|
| Market Area | Waterloo | Pusan | Bogota | Fontainebleau | Dublin |
| Canada | | | | | |
| Demand 4,000 | | | | | |
| Production cost | $50 | $30 | $40 | $50 | $45 |
| Transportation cost | 10 | 25 | 20 | 25 | 25 |
| South America | | | | | |
| Demand 5,000 | | | | | |
| Production cost | 50 | 30 | 40 | 50 | 45 |
| Transportation cost | 20 | 25 | 10 | 30 | 30 |
| Pacific Rim | | | | | |
| Demand 10,000 | | | | | |
| Production cost | 50 | 30 | 40 | 50 | 45 |
| Transportation cost | 25 | 10 | 25 | 40 | 40 |
| Europe | | | | | |
| Demand 5,000 | | | | | |
| Production cost | 50 | 30 | 40 | 50 | 45 |
| Transportation cost | 25 | 40 | 30 | 10 | 20 |
| Capacity | 8,000 | 2,000 | 5,000 | 9,000 | 9,000 |

only the transportation costs per unit as shown in the table, which site is best?

| To | FROM EXISTING PLANTS | | | |
|---|---|---|---|---|
| | DECATUR | MINNEAPOLIS | CARBONDALE | DEMAND |
| Blue Earth | $20 | $17 | $21 | 250 |
| Ciro | 25 | 27 | 20 | 200 |
| Des Moines | 22 | 25 | 22 | 350 |
| Capacity | 300 | 200 | 150 | |

| To | FROM PROPOSED PLANTS | |
|---|---|---|
| | EAST ST. LOUIS | ST. LOUIS |
| Blue Earth | $29 | $27 |
| Ciro | 30 | 28 |
| Des Moines | 30 | 31 |
| Capacity | 150 | 150 |

**5-20** Satish Iyer, vice president of operations at Don Levine Corporation (see Problem 5-19), recognizes that unit shipping costs from either of the proposed plants are very high. The reason is that all long-haul carriers in either city already have contracts with other companies. Satish feels confident, however, that he can find short-haul carriers who will ship his product from the proposed plant in East St. Louis to Decatur for only $6 per unit and to Carbondale for only $5 per unit. Set up and solve Don Levine's problem now with this new information.

**5-21** In a job shop operation, four jobs can be performed on any of four machines. The hours required for each job on each machine are presented in the following table. The plant supervisor would like to assign jobs so that total time is minimized. Use the assignment model to find the best solution.

| | MACHINE | | | |
|---|---|---|---|---|
| JOB | W | X | Y | Z |
| A12 | 10 | 14 | 16 | 13 |
| A15 | 12 | 13 | 15 | 12 |
| B2 | 9 | 12 | 12 | 11 |
| B9 | 14 | 16 | 18 | 16 |

**5-22** The Dubuque Sackers, a class D baseball team, face a tough four-game road trip against league rivals in Des Moines, Davenport, Omaha, and Peoria. Manager "Red" Revelle faces the task of scheduling his four starting pitchers for appropriate games. Because the games are to be played back to back in less than one week, Revelle cannot count on any pitcher to start in more than one game.

Revelle knows the strengths and weaknesses not only of his pitchers, but also of his opponents, and he is able to estimate the probability of winning each of the four games with each of the four starting pitchers. Those probabilities are listed in the following table:

| STARTING PITCHER | OPPONENT | | | |
|---|---|---|---|---|
| | DES MOINES | DAVENPORT | OMAHA | PEORIA |
| "Dead-Arm" Jones | 0.60 | 0.80 | 0.50 | 0.40 |
| "Spitball" Baker | 0.70 | 0.40 | 0.80 | 0.30 |
| "Ace" Parker | 0.90 | 0.80 | 0.70 | 0.80 |
| "Gutter" Wilson | 0.50 | 0.30 | 0.40 | 0.20 |

What pitching rotation should manager Revelle set to provide the highest winning probability (i.e., the sum of the probabilities of winning each game) for the Sackers?

(a) Formulate this problem using LP.

(b) Solve the problem.

**5-23** The hospital administrator at St. Charles General must appoint head nurses to four newly established departments: urology, cardiology, orthopedics, and obstetrics. In anticipation of this staffing problem, she had hired four nurses: Hawkins, Condriac, Bardot, and Hoolihan. Believing in the decision modeling approach to problem solving, the administrator has interviewed each nurse, considered his or her background, personality, and talents, and developed a cost scale ranging from 0 to 100 to be used in the assignment. A 0 for Nurse Bardot being assigned to the cardiology unit implies that she would be perfectly suited to that task. A value close to 100, on the other hand, would imply that she is not at all suited to head that unit. The accompanying table gives the complete set of cost figures that the hospital administrator felt represented all possible assignments. Which nurse should be assigned to which unit?

| | DEPARTMENT | | | |
|---|---|---|---|---|
| NURSE | UROLOGY | CARDIOLOGY | ORTHOPEDICS | OBSTETRICS |
| Hawkins | 28 | 18 | 15 | 75 |
| Condriac | 32 | 48 | 23 | 38 |
| Bardot | 51 | 36 | 24 | 36 |
| Hoolihan | 25 | 38 | 55 | 12 |

• **5-24** The Orange Top Cab Company has a taxi waiting at each of four cab stands in Evanston, Illinois. Four customers have called and requested service. The distances, in miles, from the waiting taxis to the customers are given in the following table. Find the optimal assignment of taxis to customers so as to minimize total driving distances to the customers.

|  | CUSTOMER | | | |
|---|---|---|---|---|
| CAB SITE | A | B | C | D |
| Stand 1 | 7 | 3 | 4 | 8 |
| Stand 2 | 5 | 4 | 6 | 5 |
| Stand 3 | 6 | 7 | 9 | 6 |
| Stand 4 | 8 | 6 | 7 | 4 |

• **5-25** The Burlington Police Department has five detective squads available for assignment to five open crime cases. The chief of detectives wishes to assign the squads so that the total time to conclude the cases is minimized. The average number of days, based on past performance, for each squad to complete each case is as follows:

|  | CASE | | | | |
|---|---|---|---|---|---|
| SQUAD | A | B | C | D | E |
| 1 | 14 | 7 | 3 | 7 | 27 |
| 2 | 20 | 7 | 12 | 6 | 30 |
| 3 | 10 | 3 | 4 | 5 | 21 |
| 4 | 8 | 12 | 7 | 12 | 21 |
| 5 | 13 | 25 | 24 | 26 | 8 |

Each squad is composed of different types of specialists and, as noted, whereas one squad may be very effective in certain types of cases, they may be almost useless in others. Solve the problem by using the assignment method.

**5-26** Roscoe Davis, chairman of a college's business department, has decided to use decision modeling to assign professors to courses next semester. As a criterion for judging who should teach each course, Professor Davis reviews the past two years' teaching evaluations (which were filled out by students). Since each of the four professors taught each of the four courses at one time or another during the two-year period, Davis is able to record a course rating for each instructor. These ratings are shown in the following table. Find the best assignment of professors to courses to maximize the overall teaching ratings.

|  | COURSE | | | |
|---|---|---|---|---|
| PROFESSOR | STATISTICS | MANAGEMENT | FINANCE | ECONOMICS |
| Anderson | 90 | 65 | 95 | 40 |
| Sweeney | 70 | 60 | 80 | 75 |
| Williams | 85 | 40 | 80 | 60 |
| McKinney | 55 | 80 | 65 | 55 |

**5-27** Bechtold Construction is in the process of installing power lines to a large housing development. Steve Bechtold wants to minimize the total length of wire used, which will minimize his costs. The housing development is shown as a network in Figure 5.18. Each house has been numbered, and the distance between houses is given in hundreds of feet. What do you recommend?

**5-28** The city of New Berlin is considering making several of its streets one-way. What is the maximum number of cars per hour that can travel from east to west? The network is shown in Figure 5.19 on the next page.

**5-29** Transworld Moving has been hired to move the office furniture and equipment of Cohen Properties to their new headquarters. What route do you recommend? The network of roads is shown in Figure 5.20 on the next page.

**5-30** The director of security wants to connect security video cameras to the main control site from five

**FIGURE 5.18**

**Network for Problem 5-27**

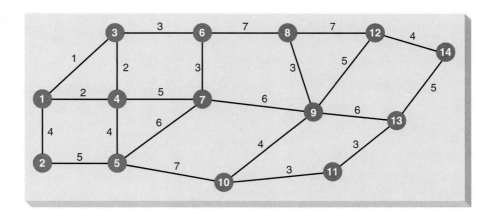

**FIGURE 5.19**

**Network for Problem 5-28**

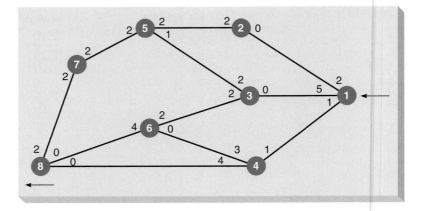

**FIGURE 5.20**

**Network for Problem 5-29**

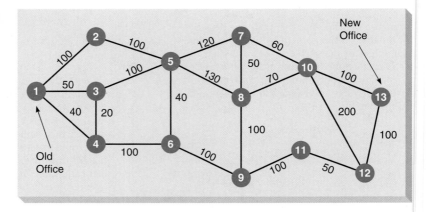

potential trouble locations. Ordinarily, cable would simply be run from each location to the main control site. However, because the environment is potentially explosive, the cable must be run in a special conduit that is continually air purged. This conduit is very expensive but large enough to handle five cables (the maximum that might be needed). Use the minimal-spanning tree model to find a minimum distance

route for the conduit between the locations noted in Figure 5.21. (Note that it makes no difference which one is the main control site.)

**5-31** One of our best customers has had a major plant breakdown and wants us to make as many widgets for him as possible during the next few days, until he gets the necessary repairs done. With our general-purpose equipment there are several ways to make widgets

**FIGURE 5.21**

**Network for Problem 5-30**

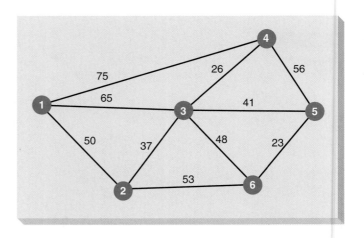

(ignoring costs). Any sequence of activities that takes one from node 1 to node 6 in Figure 5.22, will produce a widget. How many widgets can we produce per day? Quantities given are number of widgets per day.

**5-32** Transworld Moving, like other moving companies, closely follows the impact of road construction to make sure that its routes remain the most efficient. Unfortunately, there has been unexpected road construction due to a lack of planning for road repair around the town of New Haven, represented by node 9 in the network. (See Problem 5-29.) All roads leading to node 9, except the road from node 9 to node 11, can no longer be traveled. Does this have any impact on the route that should be used to ship the office furniture and equipment of Cohen Properties to their new headquarters?

**5-33** The road system around the hotel complex on International Drive (node 1) to Disney World (node 11) in Orlando, Florida, is shown in the network of Figure 5.23. The numbers by the nodes represent the traffic flow in hundreds of cars per hour. What is the maximum flow of cars from the hotel complex to Disney World?

**5-34** A road construction project would increase the road capacity around the outside roads from International Drive to Disney World by 200 cars per hour (see Problem 5-33). The two paths affected would be 1→2→6→9→11 and 1→5→8→10→11. What impact would this have on the total flow of cars? Would the total flow of cars increase by 400 cars per hour?

**5-35** Solve the maximal-flow problem presented in the network of Figure 5.24 on the next page. The numbers in the network represent thousands of gallons per hour as they flow through a chemical processing plant.

**5-36** Two terminals in the chemical processing plant, represented by nodes 6 and 7, require emergency repair (see Problem 5-35). No material can flow into or out of these nodes. What impact does this have on the capacity of the network?

**5-37** Solve the shortest-route problem presented in the network of Figure 5.25 on the next page, going from node 1 to node 16. All numbers represent kilometers between German towns near the Black Forest.

---

**Network for Problem 5-31**

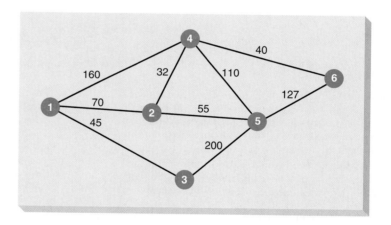

---

**Network for Problem 5-33**

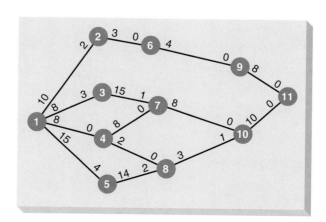

**FIGURE 5.24**

Network for Problem 5-35

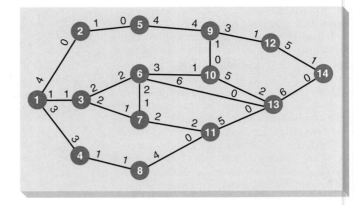

**FIGURE 5.25**

Network for Problem 5-37

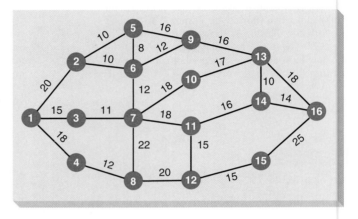

**5-38** Due to bad weather, the roads represented by nodes 7 and 8 have been closed (see Problem 5-37). No traffic can get onto or off of these roads. Describe the impact that this will have (if any) on the shortest route through this network.

**5-39** Grey Construction would like to determine the least expensive way of connecting houses it is building with cable TV. It has identified 11 possible branches or routes that could be used to connect the houses. The cost in hundreds of dollars and the branches are summarized in the table at the bottom of this page. What is the least expensive way to run cable to the houses?

**5-40** Solve the minimal-spanning tree problem in the network shown in Figure 5.26 on the next page. Assume that the numbers in the network represent distance in hundreds of yards.

**Table for Problem 5-39**

| BRANCH | START NODE | END NODE | COST (HUNDREDS OF DOLLARS) |
|--------|-----------|----------|---------------------------|
| Branch 1 | 1 | 2 | 5 |
| Branch 2 | 1 | 3 | 6 |
| Branch 3 | 1 | 4 | 6 |
| Branch 4 | 1 | 5 | 5 |
| Branch 5 | 2 | 6 | 7 |
| Branch 6 | 3 | 7 | 5 |
| Branch 7 | 4 | 7 | 7 |
| Branch 8 | 5 | 8 | 4 |
| Branch 9 | 6 | 7 | 1 |
| Branch 10 | 7 | 9 | 6 |
| Branch 11 | 8 | 9 | 2 |

FIGURE 5.26

Network for Problem 5-40

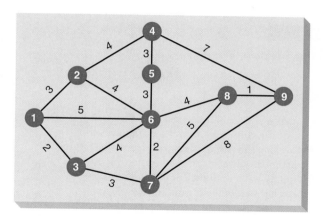

## ⫸ CASE STUDY

### Old Oregon Wood Store

In 2001, George Brown started the Old Oregon Wood Store to manufacture Old Oregon tables. Each table is carefully constructed by hand using the highest-quality oak. Old Oregon tables can support more than 500 pounds, and since the start of the Old Oregon Wood Store, not one table has been returned because of faulty workmanship or structural problems. In addition to being rugged, each table is beautifully finished using a urethane varnish that George developed over 20 years of working with wood-finishing materials.

The manufacturing process consists of four steps: preparation, assembly, finishing, and packaging. Each step is performed by one person. In addition to overseeing the entire operation, George does all of the finishing. Tom Surowski performs the preparation step, which involves cutting and forming the basic components of the tables. Leon Davis is in charge of the assembly, and Cathy Stark performs the packaging.

Although each person is responsible for only one step in the manufacturing process, everyone can perform any one of the steps. It is George's policy that occasionally everyone should complete several tables on his or her own without any help or assistance. A small competition is used to see who can complete an entire table in the least amount of time. George maintains average total and intermediate completion times. The data are shown in Figure 5.27.

It takes Cathy longer than the other employees to construct an Old Oregon table. In addition to being slower than the other employees, Cathy is also unhappy about her current responsibility of packaging, which leaves her idle most of the day. Her first preference is finishing, and her second preference is preparation.

FIGURE 5.27

Manufacturing Time in
Minutes

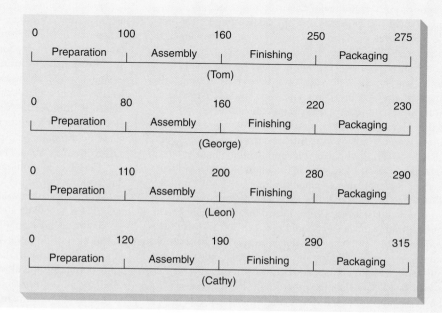

FIGURE 5.28

Randy's Completion Times
in Minutes

| | 110 | | 190 | | 290 | | 300 |
|---|---|---|---|---|---|---|---|
| Preparation | | Assembly | | Finishing | | Packaging | |

In addition to quality, George is concerned with costs and efficiency. When one of the employees misses a day, it causes major scheduling problems. In some cases, George assigns another employee overtime to complete the necessary work. At other times, George simply waits until the employee returns to work to complete his or her step in the manufacturing process. Both solutions cause problems. Overtime is expensive, and waiting causes delays and sometimes stops the entire manufacturing process.

To overcome some of these problems, Randy Lane was hired. Randy's major duties are to perform miscellaneous jobs and to help out if one of the employees is absent. George has given Randy training in all phases of the manufacturing process, and he is pleased with the speed at which Randy has been able to learn how to completely assemble Old Oregon tables. Total and intermediate completion times are given in Figure 5.28.

## Discussion Questions

1. What is the fastest way to manufacture Old Oregon tables using the original crew? How many could be made per day?
2. Would production rates and quantities change significantly if George would allow Randy to perform one of the four functions and make one of the original crew the backup person?
3. What is the fastest time to manufacture a table with the original crew if Cathy is moved to either preparation or finishing?
4. Whoever performs the packaging function is severely underutilized. Can you find a better way of utilizing the four- or five-person crew than either giving each a single job or allowing each to manufacture an entire table? How many tables could be manufactured per day with this scheme?

## ⇒ CASE STUDY

### Custom Vans, Inc.

Custom Vans, Inc., specializes in converting standard vans into campers. Depending on the amount of work and customizing to be done, the customizing could cost less than $1,000 to more than $5,000. In less than four years, Tony Rizzo was able to expand his small operation in Gary, Indiana, to other major outlets in Chicago, Milwaukee, Minneapolis, and Detroit.

Innovation was the major factor in Tony's success in converting a small van shop into one of the largest and most profitable custom van operations in the Midwest. Tony seemed to have a special ability to design and develop unique features and devices that were always in high demand by van owners. An example was Shower-Rific, which was developed by Tony only six months after Custom Vans, Inc., was started. These small showers were completely self-contained, and they could be placed in almost any type of van and in a number of different locations within a van. Shower-Rific was made of fiberglass and contained towel racks, built-in soap and shampoo holders, and a unique plastic door. Each Shower-Rific took 2 gallons of fiberglass and 3 hours of labor to manufacture.

Most of the Shower-Rifics were manufactured in Gary in the same warehouse where Custom Vans, Inc., was founded. The manufacturing plant in Gary could produce 300 Shower-Rifics in a month, but this capacity never seemed to be enough. Custom Van shops in all locations were complaining about not getting enough Shower-Rifics, and because Minneapolis was farther away from Gary than the other locations, Tony was always inclined to ship Shower-Rifics to the other locations before

Minneapolis. This infuriated the manager of Custom Vans at Minneapolis, and after many heated discussions, Tony decided to start another manufacturing plant for Shower-Rifics at Fort Wayne, Indiana. The manufacturing plant at Fort Wayne could produce 150 Shower-Rifics per month.

The manufacturing plant at Fort Wayne was still not able to meet current demand for Shower-Rifics, and Tony knew that the demand for his unique camper shower would grow rapidly in the next year. After consulting with his lawyer and banker, Tony concluded that he should open two new manufacturing plants as soon as possible. Each plant would have the same capacity as the Fort Wayne manufacturing plant. An initial investigation into possible manufacturing locations was made, and Tony decided that the two new plants should be located in Detroit, Michigan; Rockford, Illinois; or Madison, Wisconsin. Tony knew that selecting the best location for the two new manufacturing plants would be difficult. Transportation costs and demands for the various locations should be important considerations.

The Chicago shop was managed by Bill Burch. This Custom Van shop was one of the first established by Tony, and it continued to outperform the other locations. The manufacturing plant at Gary was supplying 200 Shower-Rifics each month, although Bill knew that the demand for the showers in Chicago was 300 units. The transportation cost per unit from Gary was $10, and although the transportation cost from Fort Wayne was double that amount, Bill was always pleading with Tony to get an additional 50 units from the Fort Wayne manufacturer. The two additional manufacturing plants would certainly be able to supply Bill with the additional 100 showers he needed. The transportation costs would, of course, vary, depending on which two locations Tony picked. The transportation cost per shower would be $30 from Detroit, $5 from Rockford, and $10 from Madison.

Wilma Jackson, manager of the Custom Van shop in Milwaukee, was the most upset about not getting an adequate supply of showers. She had a demand for 100 units, and at the present time, she was only getting half of this demand from the Fort Wayne manufacturing plant. She could not understand why Tony didn't ship her all 100 units from Gary. The transportation cost per unit from Gary was only $20, while the transportation cost from Fort Wayne was $30. Wilma was hoping that Tony would select Madison for one of the manufacturing locations. She would be able to get all of the showers needed, and the transportation cost per unit would only be $5. If not Madison, a new plant in Rockford would be able to supply her total needs, but the transportation cost per unit would be twice as much as it would be from Madison. Because the transportation cost per unit from Detroit would be $40, Wilma speculated that even if Detroit became one of the new plants, she would not be getting any units from Detroit.

Custom Vans, Inc., of Minneapolis was managed by Tom Poanski. He was getting 100 showers from the Gary plant. Demand was 150 units. Tom faced the highest transportation costs of all locations. The transportation cost from Gary was $40 per unit. It would cost $10 more if showers were sent from the Fort Wayne location. Tom was hoping that Detroit would not be one of the new plants, as the transportation cost would be $60 per unit. Rockford and Madison would have a cost of $30 and $25, respectively, to ship one shower to Minneapolis.

The Detroit shop's position was similar to Milwaukee's— only getting half of the demand each month. The 100 units that Detroit did receive came directly from the Fort Wayne plant. The transportation cost was only $15 per unit from Fort Wayne, whereas it was $25 from Gary. Dick Lopez, manager of Custom Vans, Inc., of Detroit, placed the probability of having one of the new plants in Detroit fairly high. The factory would be located across town, and the transportation cost would be only $5 per unit. He could get 150 showers from the new plant in Detroit and the other 50 showers from Fort Wayne. Even if Detroit was not selected, the other two locations were not intolerable. Rockford had a transportation cost per unit of $35, and Madison had a transportation cost of $40.

Tony pondered the dilemma of locating the two new plants for several weeks before deciding to call a meeting of all the managers of the van shops. The decision was complicated, but the objective was clear—to minimize total costs. The meeting was held in Gary, and everyone was present except Wilma.

*Tony*: Thank you for coming. As you know, I have decided to open up two new plants at Rockford, Madison, or Detroit. The two locations, of course, will change our shipping practices, and I sincerely hope that they will supply you with the Shower-Rifics that you have been wanting. I know you could have sold more units, and I want you to know that I am sorry for this situation.

*Dick*: Tony, I have given this situation a lot of consideration, and I feel strongly that at least one of the new plants should be located in Detroit. As you know, I am now only getting half of the showers that I need. My brother, Leon, is very interested in running the plant, and I know he would do a good job.

*Tom*: Dick, I am sure that Leon could do a good job, and I know how difficult it has been since the recent layoffs by the auto industry. Nevertheless, we should be considering total costs and not personalities. I believe that the new plants should be located in Madison and Rockford. I am farther away from the other plants than any other shop, and these locations would significantly reduce transportation costs.

*Dick*: That may be true, but there are other factors. Detroit has one of the largest suppliers of fiberglass, and I have checked prices. A new plant in Detroit would be able to purchase fiberglass for $2 per gallon less than any of the other existing or proposed plants.

*Tom*: At Madison, we have an excellent labor force. This is due primarily to the large number of students attending the University of Madison. These students are hard workers, and they will work for $1 less per hour than the other locations that we are considering.

*Bill*: Calm down, you two. It is obvious that we will not be able to satisfy everyone in locating the new plants. Therefore, I would like to suggest that we vote on the two best locations.

*Tony*: I don't think that voting would be a good idea. Wilma was not able to attend, and we should be looking at all of these factors together in some type of logical fashion.

### Discussion Question

Where would you locate the two new plants?

---

**⯈ CASE STUDY**

### Binder's Beverage

Bill Binder's business nearly went under when Colorado almost passed the bottle bill. Binder's Beverage produced soft drinks for many of the large grocery stores in the area. After the bottle bill failed, Binder's Beverage flourished. In a few short years, the company had a major plant in Denver with a warehouse in east Denver. The problem was getting the fin-

ished product to the warehouse. Although Bill was not good with distances, he was good with times. Denver is a big city with numerous roads that could be taken from the plant to the warehouse.

The soft drink plant is located at the corner of North Street and Columbine Street. High Street also intersects North and Columbine Street at the plant. Twenty minutes due north of the

**Street Map for Binder's
Beverage Case**

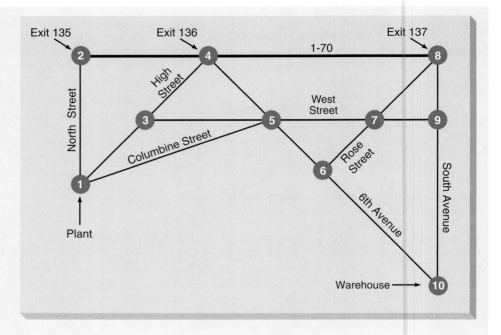

plant on North Street is I-70, the major east-west highway in Denver.

North Street intersects I-70 at Exit 135. It takes five minutes driving east on I-70 to reach Exit 136. This exit connects I-70 with High Street and 6th Avenue. Ten minutes east on I-70 is Exit 137. This exit connects I-70 with Rose Street and South Avenue.

From the plant, it takes 20 minutes on High Street, which goes in a northeast direction, to reach West Street. It takes another 20 minutes on High Street to reach I-70 and Exit 136.

It takes 30 minutes on Columbine Street to reach West Street from the plant. Columbine Street travels east and slightly north.

West Street travels east and west. From High Street, it takes 15 minutes to get to 6th Avenue on West Street. Columbine Street also comes into this intersection. From this intersection, it takes an additional 20 minutes on West Street to get to Rose Street, and another 15 minutes to get to South Avenue.

From Exit 136 on 6th Avenue, it takes 5 minutes to get to West Street. Sixth Avenue continues to Rose Street, requiring 25 minutes. Sixth Avenue then goes directly to the warehouse. From Rose Street, it takes 40 minutes to get to the warehouse on 6th Avenue.

At Exit 137, Rose Street travels southwest. It takes 20 minutes to intersect with West Street, and another 20 minutes to get to 6th Avenue. From Exit 137, South Street goes due south. It takes 10 minutes to get to West Street and another 15 minutes to get to the warehouse.

### Discussion Question

What route do you recommend?

---

## INTERNET CASE STUDIES

See our Internet home page at **www.prenhall.com/render** for these additional case studies: (1) Northwest General Hospital; (2) Andrew Carter, Inc.; and (3) Ranch Development Project.

---

# BIBLIOGRAPHY

Ambs, K. et al. "Optimizing Restoration Capacity at the AT&T Network," *Interfaces* (January–February 2000): 26–44.

Anbil, R., E. Gelman, B. Patty, and R. Tanga. "Recent Advances in Crew-Pairing Optimization at American Airlines," *Interfaces* 21, 1 (January–February 1991): 62–74.

Bentley, Jon. "Faster And Faster And Faster Yet," *UNIX Review*, (June 1997): 59.

Cipra, Barry. "Taking Hard Problems to the Limit: Mathematics," *Science* (March 14, 1997): 15–70.

Current, J. "The Minimum-Covering/Shortest Path Problem," *Decision Sciences* 19 (Summer 1988): 490–503.

del Rosario, Elise. "Logistical Nightmare," *OR/MS* Today (April 1999): 44–46.

Domich, P. D., K. L. Hoffman, R. H. F. Jackson, and M. A. McClain. "Locating Tax Facilities: A Graphics-Based Microcomputer Optimization Model." *Management Science* 37 (August 1991): 960–979.

Glassey, C. Roger and Michael Mizrach. "A Decision Support System for Assigning Classes to Rooms," *Interfaces* 16, 5 (September–October 1986): 92–100.

LeBlanc, Larry J., Dale Randels, Jr., and T. K. Swann. "Heery International's Spreadsheet Optimization Model for Assigning Managers to Construction Projects," *Interfaces* 30, 6 (November 2000): 95–106.

Onal, Hayri et al. "Two Formulations of the Vehicle Routing Problem," *The Logistics and Transportation Review* (June 1996): 117–130.

Perlman, Radia et al. "Spanning the LAN," *Data Communications* (October 21, 1997): 68.

Sancho, N. G. F. "On the Maximum Expected Flow in a Network," *Journal of Operational Research Society* 39 (May 1988): 481–485.

William, Carlton et al. "Solving the Traveling-Salesman Problem with Time Windows Using Tabu Search," *IIE Transactions* (August 1996): 617–629.

Williams, Martyn. "When Does the Shortest Route Between Tokyo and Singapore Include a Stop in New York?" *Data Communications* (December 19, 1997): 45.

## CHAPTER 6

# INTEGER, GOAL, AND NONLINEAR PROGRAMMING MODELS

Summary • Glossary • Key Equation • Solved Problems • Self-Test • Discussion Questions and Problems • Case Study: Schank Marketing Research • Case Study: Oakton River Bridge • Case Study: Puyallup Mall • Bibliography

## Selling Seats at American Airlines Using Integer Programming

American Airlines (AA) describes *yield management* as "selling the right seats to the right customers at the right prices." The role of yield management is to determine how much of each product to put on the shelf (i.e., make available for sale) at a given point in time. American's storefront is the computerized reservations system called SABRE.

The AA yield-management problem is a mixed-integer program that requires data such as passenger demand, cancellations, and other estimates of passenger behavior that are subject to frequent changes. To solve the systemwide yield-management problem would require approximately 250 million decision variables.

To bring this problem down to a manageable size, AA's integer programming model creates three smaller and easier subproblems. The airline looks at

1. overbooking, which is the practice of intentionally selling more reservations for a flight than there are actual seats on the aircraft,

2. discount allocation, which is the process of determining the number of discount fares to offer on a flight, and

3. traffic management, which is the process of controlling reservations by passenger origin and destination to provide the mix of markets that maximizes revenue.

Yield management, much disliked by airline passengers who view it as a way of squeezing the most money out of travelers as possible, has been a big winner of AA and other airlines. Each year, AA estimates that profits increase by several million dollars due to the use of this approach.[1]

---

[1] T. Cook. "SABRE Soars," *OR/MS Today* (June 1998): 26–31; and B. Smith, J. Leimkuheler, and R. Darrow. "Yield Management at American Airlines," *Interfaces* 22, 1 (January–February 1992): 8–31.

## 6.1    INTRODUCTION

Earlier chapters focus on the linear programming (LP) category of mathematical programming models. These LP models had three characteristics:

- the decision variables were allowed to have fractional values,
- there was a unique objective function, and
- all mathematical expressions (objective function and constraints) had to be linear.

This chapter presents a series of other important mathematical models that allow us to relax each of these basic LP conditions. The new models—integer programming, goal programming, and nonlinear programming—are introduced here and then discussed in detail in the remainder of Chapter 6.

### Integer Programming Models

*Integer programming is the extension of LP that solves problems requiring integer solutions.*

*General integer variables can take on any nonnegative integer value.*

*Binary variables must equal either 0 or 1.*

Although fractional values such as $X = 0.33$ and $Y = 109.4$ may be valid for decision variables in many problems, there are a large number of business problems (such as the preceding American Airlines application) that can be solved only if variables have *integer* values. When an airline decides how many flights to operate on a given sector, it can't decide to operate 5.38 flights; it must operate 5, 6 or some other integer amount.

In Sections 6.2 and 6.3, we present two types of integer variables: *general integer* variables and *binary* variables. General integer variables are variables that can take on any nonnegative, integer value that satisfies all the constraints in a model (e.g., 5 submarines, 8 employees, 20 insurance policies). Binary variables are a special type of integer variable that can only take on either of two values: 0 or 1. We present how problems involving both of these types of integer variables can be formulated and solved using Excel's Solver.

Integer programming (IP) problems can also be classified into four types as follows:

1. *Pure IP problems.* These are problems in which all decision variables must have integer solutions.

2. *Mixed IP problems.* These are problems in which some, but not all, decision variables must have integer solutions. The noninteger variables can have fractional optimal values.

3. *Pure binary (or 0–1) IP problems.* These are problems in which all decision variables are of a special type known as binary. These variables must have solution values of either 0 or 1.

4. *Mixed binary IP problems.* These are problems in which some decision variables are binary and other decision variables are either general integer or continuous valued.

### Goal Programming Models

*Goal programming is the extension of LP that permits more than one objective to be stated.*

Another major limitation of LP is that it forces the decision maker to state one objective only. But what if a business has several objectives? Management may indeed want to maximize profit, but it might also want to maximize market share, maintain full employment, and minimize costs. Many of these goals can be conflicting and difficult to quantify. South States Power and Light, for example, wants to build a nuclear power plant in Taft, Louisiana. Its objectives are to maximize power generated, reliability, and safety, and to minimize cost of operating the system and the environmental effects on the community. Goal programming is an extension to LP that can permit multiple objectives such as these. We discuss goal programming in detail in Section 6.5.

## Nonlinear Programming Models

*Nonlinear programming is the case in which objectives or constraints are nonlinear.*

Linear programming can, of course, be applied only to cases in which the constraints and objective function are linear. Yet in many situations this is not the case. The price of various products, for example, may be a function of the number of units produced. As more are made, the price per unit decreases. Hence, an objective function could be as follows:

$$\text{Maximize profit} = 25X - 0.4X^2 + 30Y - 0.5Y^2$$

Because of the squared terms, this is a nonlinear programming problem. We discuss nonlinear programming in detail in Section 6.6.

Now let's examine each of these extensions of LP—integer, goal, and nonlinear programming—one at a time.

## 6.2   MODELS WITH GENERAL INTEGER VARIABLES

*Models with general integer variables are similar to LP models—except that variables must be integer valued.*

A model with general integer variables (which we call an *IP model*) has an objective function and constraints identical to that of LP models. There is no real difference in the basic procedure for formulating an IP model and an LP model.

The only additional requirement in an IP model is that one or more of the decision variables have to take on integer values in the optimal solution. The actual value of this integer variable is, however, limited only by the constraints in the model. That is, values such as 0, 1, 2, 3, and so on are perfectly valid for these variables as long as these values satisfy all constraints in the model.

Let us look at a simple example of an IP problem and see how to formulate it. We then demonstrate how this model can be set up and solved using Excel's Solver.

### Harrison Electric Company

*Example of IP model: Harrison Electric.*

The Harrison Electric Company, located in Chicago's Old Town area, produces two expensive products that are popular with renovators of historic old homes: ornate chandeliers and old-fashioned ceiling fans. Both chandeliers and ceiling fans require a two-step production process involving wiring and assembly time. It takes about 2 hours to wire each chandelier and 3 hours to wire a ceiling fan. Final assembly of each chandelier and fan requires 6 and 5 hours, respectively. The production capability this period is such that only 12 hours of wiring time and 30 hours of assembly time are available. If each chandelier produced nets the firm $600 and each fan $700 in profit, Harrison's production mix decision can be formulated using LP as follows:

$$\text{Maximize profit} = \$600C + \$700F$$

subject to

$$2C + 3F \leq 12 \qquad \text{(wiring hours)}$$
$$6C + 5F \leq 30 \qquad \text{(assembly hours)}$$
$$C, F \geq 0$$

*where*

$$C = \text{number of chandeliers produced}$$

$$F = \text{number of ceiling fans produced}$$

With only two decision variables and two constraints to consider, Harrison's production planner, Wes Wallace, decided to employ the graphical LP approach to generate the optimal solution. The shaded region in Figure 6.1 shows the feasible region for the LP problem. The

**FIGURE 6.1**    **Graph for Harrison Electric's Problem**

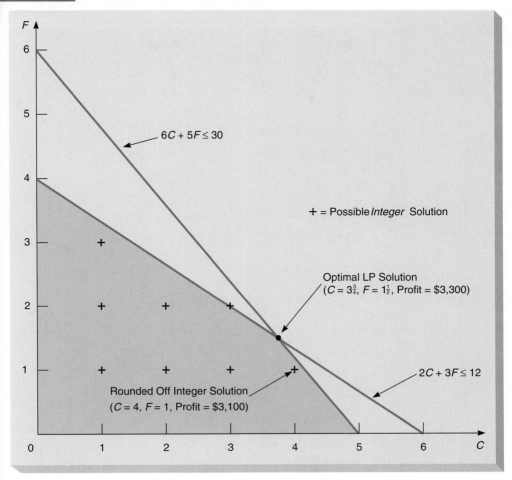

optimal corner point solution turned out to be $C = 3.75$ chandeliers and $F = 1.5$ ceiling fans, for a profit of $3,300 during the production period.

Since Harrison could not produce and sell a fraction of a product, Wes recognized that he was dealing with an IP problem. It seemed to Wes that the simplest approach was to round off the optimal fractional LP solutions for $C$ and $F$ to integer values. Figure 6.1 shows all possible integer solutions for this problem. Unfortunately, rounding can produce two problems. First, the new integer solution may not be in the feasible region and is, hence, not a practical answer. For example, assume we round up the LP solution to $C = 4$ chandeliers and $F = 2$ ceiling fans. As we can see from Figure 6.1, this solution is not feasible. Second, even if we round off to a feasible integer solution such as $C = 4$ and $F = 1$, it may not be the optimal feasible IP solution.

Table 6.1 lists the entire set of integer-valued solutions for Harrison Electric problem. By inspecting the right-hand column, we see that the optimal integer solution is $C = 3$ chandeliers, $F = 2$ ceiling fans, for a total profit = $3,200. The rounded off solution of $C = 4$ and $F = 1$ yields a profit of only $3,100.

We note that the optimal solution $C = 3$ and $F = 2$ is not even a corner point (i.e., a point where two or more constraints intersect) in the LP feasible region. In fact, unlike LP problems, in which the optimal solution is always a corner point of the feasible region, the

*Rounding off is one way to reach integer solution values, but it often does not yield the best solution.*

| TABLE 6.1 | CHANDELIERS (C) | CEILING FANS (F) | PROFIT ($600C + $700F) | |
|-----------|-----------------|------------------|------------------------|---|
| **Integer Solutions to Harrison Electric's Problem** | 0 | 0 | $0 | |
| | 1 | 0 | 600 | |
| | 2 | 0 | 1,200 | |
| | 3 | 0 | 1,800 | |
| | 4 | 0 | 2,400 | |
| | 5 | 0 | 3,000 | |
| | 0 | 1 | 700 | |
| | 1 | 1 | 1,300 | |
| | 2 | 1 | 1,900 | |
| | 3 | 1 | 2,500 | |
| | 4 | 1 | 3,100 | ← *Solution if rounding off is used* |
| | 0 | 2 | 1,400 | |
| | 1 | 2 | 2,000 | |
| | 2 | 2 | 2,600 | |
| | 3 | 2 | 3,200 | ← *Optimal solution to integer programming problem* |
| | 0 | 3 | 2,100 | |
| | 1 | 3 | 2,700 | |
| | 0 | 4 | 2,800 | |

*An important concept to understand is that an IP solution can never be better than the solution to the same LP problem. The integer problem is usually worse in terms of higher cost or lower profit.*

*Although enumeration is feasible for some small integer programming problems, it can be difficult or impossible for large ones.*

optimal solution in an IP model need not be a corner point. As we will discuss subsequently, this is what makes it difficult to solve IP models in practice.

We also note that the integer restriction results in an objective value that is no better (and usually, worse) than the optimal LP solution. The logic behind this occurrence is quite simple. The feasible region for the original LP problem includes *all* IP solution points, in addition to several LP solution points. That is, the optimal IP solution will always be a feasible solution for the LP problem, but *not vice versa*. We call the LP equivalent of an IP problem (i.e., the IP model with the integer requirement deleted) the *relaxed* problem. As a rule, the IP solution can never produce a better objective value than its LP relaxed problem. At best, the two solutions can be equal (if the optimal LP solution turns out to be the integer-valued).

Although it is possible to solve simple IP problems like Harrison Electric's by inspection or enumeration, larger problems cannot be solved in this manner. Fortunately, most LP software packages, including Excel's Solver, are capable of handling models with integer variables.

## Using Solver to Solve Models with General Integer Variables

We can set up Harrison Electric's problem on Excel in exactly the same manner as we have done for several LP examples in Chapters 2 through 4. For clarity, we once again use the same Excel layout here as in those chapters; that is, all parameters (solution value, objective coefficients, and constraint coefficients) associated with a decision variable are modeled in

**▸MODELING IN THE REAL WORLD**     **Scheduling Employees at McDonald's**

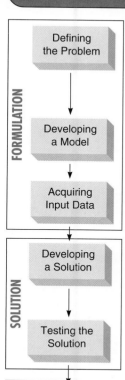

**FORMULATION**

**Defining the Problem**

Each week, the managers of Al Boxley's four McDonald's restaurants in Cumberland, Maryland, were spending more than 8 hours to prepare manually the schedules for 150 employees. This time-consuming activity was complicated by high turnover, movement of employees among restaurants, and constant change in the availability of student workers.

**Developing a Model**

Boxley hired two consultants to develop a PC-based integer programming model.

**Acquiring Input Data**

Boxley prepared the data for each restaurant's three work areas, 150 employees, and 30 possible work shifts needed as input to the integer program.

**SOLUTION**

**Developing a Solution**

The consultants found that the scheduling problem they formulated resulted in 100,000 decision variables and 3,000 constraints. This clearly was too big to be solved very quickly on a PC. So they subdivided the problem into a number of subproblems (in a process called a "decomposition into network flows").

**Testing the Solution**

The model was tested with store managers running the program. Initial schedules were favorably received. The consultants then concentrated efforts on developing user-friendly screens so that inexperienced managers could master the inputs and use the outputs successfully.

**INTERPRETATION**

**Analyzing the Results and Sensitivity Analysis**

Managers found that they could use the model for what-if analysis, to measure the sensitivity of employee schedules to a variety of operating conditions.

**Implementing the Results**

Managers report an 80% to 90% reduction in the time it takes to generate employee schedules. Costs are now kept down by eliminating overstaffing, and employee morale and efficiency are improved.

**Source:** R. R. Love and J. M. Hoey. "Management Science Improves Fast Food Operations," *Interfaces* 20, 2 (March–April 1990): 21–29.

the same column. The objective function and each constraint in the model are shown on separate rows of the worksheet.

### Excel Notes

■ The CD-ROM that accompanies this textbook contains the Excel file for each example problem discussed here. The relevant file name is shown on the margin next to each example.

■ In each of the Excel layouts, for clarity, changing cells are shaded yellow, the target cell is shaded green, and cells containing the left-hand side (LHS) formula for each constraint are shaded blue.

■ Also, to make the equivalence of the *written* formulation and the Excel layout clear, the Excel layouts show the decision variable names used in the written formulation of the model. Note that these names have no role in using Solver to solve the model.

PROGRAM 6.1

**PROGRAM 6.1**

**Excel Layout and Solver
Entries for Harrison
Electric's General Integer
Programming Problem**

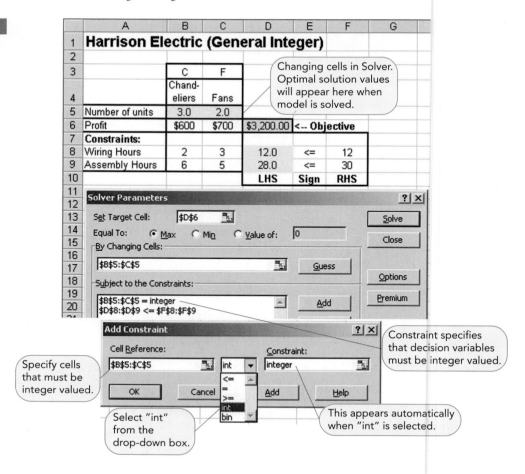

**File: 6-1.xls**

*Integer requirement is
specified as an additional
constraint in Solver.*

*The "int" option is used in
Solver to specify general
integer variables.*

The Excel layout for Harrison Electric's problem is shown in Program 6.1. As usual, we specify the Target Cell (objective function), Changing Cells (decision variables), and constraint LHS and RHS cell references in the Solver Parameters window.

**Specifying the Integer Requirement**  Before we solve the model, we need to specify the integer value requirement for the two decision variables. To enforce this, we use the Add option to include a new constraint. In the LHS entry for the new constraint (see Program 6.1), we enter the cell reference for a decision variable that must be integer valued. If there are several decision variables in the model that must be integer valued, and these are in contiguous cells (i.e., next to each other), we can enter the entire block of cell references in the LHS entry. For Harrison's problem, we enter B5:C5 in this box, which denotes the number of chandeliers and fans to make, respectively.

Next we click on the drop-down box in the Add Constraint window. Recall that this box has five choices: "<=", ">=", "=", "int" (for integer), and "bin" (for binary). Of these, we have so far used only the first three choices. We now click on the choice "int". The word "integer" is displayed automatically in the box for the RHS entry. This indicates to Solver that all variables specified in the LHS box must be integer valued in the optimal solution.

**Solving the IP Model**  We are now ready to solve the IP model. To do so, we verify that the Assume Linear Model and Assume Non-Negative options are enabled in the Solver Options window and then click Solve. The result, shown in Program 6.1 (3 chandeliers and 2 fans, for a profit of $3,200), is identified as the optimal solution.

For small problems like Harrison Electric, and even for problems of slightly larger size, Solver will find the IP solution very quickly. However, the time and computational effort required to solve IP problems grows rapidly with problem size. We now briefly discuss the reason for this phenomenon.

## How Solver Solves IP Models

*Solver uses the branch-and-bound procedure to solve IP problems.*

As shown in Figure 6.1, the optimal solution to an IP model need not be at a corner point of the feasible region. Unfortunately, the simplex method evaluates only corner points as candidates for the optimal solution. In order to use the simplex method to identify an integer-valued optimal point that may *not* be a corner point, we employ a procedure called *branch-and-bound* (B&B). The B&B method is used by most software packages, including Solver, to solve IP models.

Although we do not discuss the details of the B&B procedure in this textbook, we provide a brief description of how it works.[2] Essentially, the B&B procedure uses a "divide and conquer" strategy. Rather than try to search for the optimal IP solution over the entire feasible region at one time, the B&B procedure splits the feasible region progressively into smaller and smaller subregions. It then searches each subregion in turn. Clearly, the best IP solution over all subregions will be the optimal IP solution over the entire feasible region.

In creating each subregion, the B&B procedure makes a corner point of the new region have integer values (at least for one of the variables in the model). This procedure is called *branching*.

*Solving a single IP problem can involve solving several LP problems.*

Finding the optimal solution for each subregion involves the solution of an LP model. Hence, in order to solve a single IP model, we may have to solve several LP models. Clearly, this could become computationally quite burdensome, depending on the number of subregions that need to be created for an IP model. Stopping rules are used to efficiently stop the search process for different subregions.

## Solver Options

Now let us return to Solver's treatment of IP problems. In addition to the Assume Linear Model and Assume Non-Negative options, the Solver Options window includes several other options. These are shown in Program 6.2A for the standard Solver, and in Program 6.2B for Premium Solver for Education. We did not concern ourselves about these options so far since the default values are adequate to solve most, if not all, LP models considered here. However, for IP models, two of the options deserve additional attention.

*The maximum time allowed could become an issue for large IP problems.*

**Maximum Time Allowed**  The Max Time option is set to a default value of 100 seconds. As the number of integer-valued decision variables increases in an IP model, this time limit can be easily exceeded and may need to be extended. In practice, however, it is a good idea to keep the limit at its default value and run the problem. Solver will warn you when the limit is reached and give you the opportunity to allow more time for an IP problem to solve.

*Reducing the tolerance will yield a more accurate IP solution—but could take more time.*

**Tolerance of the Optimal Solution**  The Tolerance option is set at a default value of 5% (or shown as 0.05 in Premium Solver for Education in Program 6.2B). Note that to see this option in Premium Solver for Education, we must select Integer Options in the Solver Options window. A tolerance value of 5% implies that we are willing to accept an IP solution that is within 5% of the true optimal IP solution value. When Solver finds a solution

---

[2] Details of the B&B procedure can be found in B. Render, R. Stair, and M. Hanna. *Quantitative Analysis for Management*, 8/e. Upper Saddle River, NJ: Prentice Hall: 2003.

**PROGRAM 6.2A**

**Options for Integer Programming Problems in Standard Version of Solver**

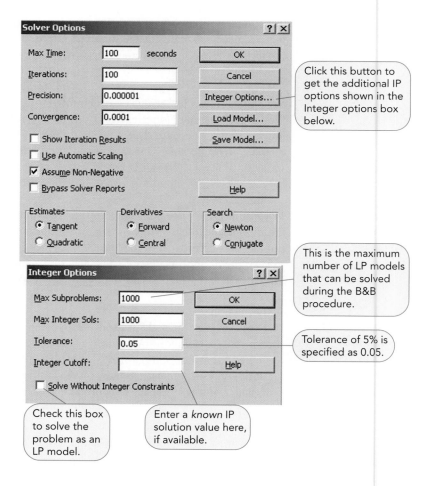

This limit may need to be increased for larger IP problems.

Tolerance specifies how close to the optimal solution the identified IP solution must be in order for Solver to stop.

**PROGRAM 6.2B**

**Options for Integer Programming Problems in Premium Solver for Education**

Click this button to get the additional IP options shown in the Integer options box below.

This is the maximum number of LP models that can be solved during the B&B procedure.

Tolerance of 5% is specified as 0.05.

Check this box to solve the problem as an LP model.

Enter a *known* IP solution value here, if available.

within the allowable tolerance, it stops and presents this as the final solution. In Premium Solver for Education, this is explicitly indicated by the message "Solver found an integer solution within tolerance." If we wish to find the *true* optimal solution, we must set the tolerance to 0%. However, in practice, this may increase the solution time significantly.

*Additional options are available in Premium Solver for Education.*

**Other Options**  Premium Solver for Education has some additional options for IP models (see Program 6.2B). The default value of 1,000 for the Max Subproblems and Max Integer Sols options should be sufficient for most models.

If we already know an integer-valued solution to the model, we can enter that objective value in the Integer Cutoff box. This will prevent Solver from wasting time searching for IP solutions that are worse than the cutoff solution. For example, suppose we know that a feasible integer solution with an objective value of 100 exists for a maximization IP problem. In this case, it is clearly not necessary for the B&B procedure to search for solutions in subregions where even the best noninteger solution has an objective value of less than 100.

Finally, checking the Solve Without Integer Constraints box causes Solver to ignore the integer constraints while solving the model. As discussed earlier, the optimal objective value of an IP model will always be *worse* than that for the corresponding LP model (i.e., lower profit for a maximization problem and higher cost for a minimization problem). Hence, this option allows us to quickly get an idea about the best IP solution that we can find for the problem.

## 6.3  MODELS WITH BINARY VARIABLES

*Binary variables are restricted to values of 0 or 1.*

As discussed earlier, binary variables are restricted to values of 0 or 1. Recall that the assignment model and shortest-path model in Chapter 5 both involve variables that ultimately take on values of either 0 or 1 at optimality. However, in both of those models, we did not have to explicitly specify that the variables were binary. The integer property of network-flow models, along with the supply and demand values of one unit each, automatically ensured that the optimal solution had values of 0 or 1.

In contrast, we now examine a model in which we will explicitly specify that the variables are binary. Binary variables are a powerful modeling tool and are applicable whenever we want to model a decision between exactly two choices. Typical examples include decisions such as introducing a new product (introduce it or not), building a new facility (build it or not), selecting a team (select a specific individual or not), and investing in projects (invest in a specific project or not).

When we are faced with a decision that has exactly two choices, we associate a binary variable with it. With one of the two choices, we associate a value of 1 for the binary variable. A value of 0 for the binary variable is then associated with the other choice. Now, we write the objective function and constraints in a manner that is consistent with this definition of the binary variable.

### Oil Portfolio Selection at Simkin, Simkin, and Steinberg

*Here is an example of stock portfolio analysis with 0–1 programming.*

Let us consider a simple example to illustrate the use of binary variables. The Houston-based investment firm of Simkin, Simkin, and Steinberg specializes in recommending oil stock portfolios for wealthy clients. One such client has made the following specifications:

- At least two Texas oil firms must be in the portfolio.
- No more than one investment can be made in foreign oil companies.
- Exactly one of the two California oil stocks must be purchased.
- If British Petroleum stock is included in the portfolio, then Trans-Texas Oil stock must also be included in the portfolio.

| TABLE 6.2 | COMPANY NAME | EXPECTED ANNUAL RETURN ($1,000's) | COST FOR BLOCK OF SHARES ($1,000's) |
|-----------|--------------|-----------------------------------|-------------------------------------|
| **Oil Investment Opportunities** | Trans-Texas Oil | 50 | 480 |
| | British Petroleum | 80 | 540 |
| | Dutch Shell | 90 | 680 |
| | Houston Drilling | 120 | 1,000 |
| | Lonestar Petroleum (Texas) | 110 | 700 |
| | San Diego Oil | 40 | 510 |
| | California Petro | 75 | 900 |

The client has up to $3 million available for investments and insists on purchasing large blocks of shares of each company in which he invests. Table 6.2 describes the various companies that Simkin is considering. The objective is to maximize annual return on investment subject to the specified constraints.

Note that the decision with regard to each company has to be one of two choices. That is, the investment firm either buys a large block of shares in the oil company or it doesn't buy the oil company's shares. To formulate this problem, let us therefore associate a binary variable with each of the seven oil companies. For each company $i$, we define the binary variable as follows:

$$X_i \begin{cases} = 1 \text{ if a large block of shares in company } i \text{ is purchased} \\ = 0 \text{ if a large block of shares in company } i \text{ is } not \text{ purchased} \end{cases}$$

*where*

$$i = \text{T (Trans-Texas Oil), B (British Petroleum), D (Dutch Shell),}$$
$$\text{H (Houston Drilling), L (Lonestar Petroleum),}$$
$$\text{S (San Diego Oil), or C (California Petro).}$$

We now need to express the objective function and constraints in a manner that is consistent with the previous definition of the binary variables. The objective function can be written as

$$\text{Maximize return on investment} = \$50X_T + \$80X_B + \$90X_D$$
$$+ \$120X_H + \$110X_L + \$40X_S + \$75X_C$$

All costs and revenues are in thousands of dollars. In the previous expression, if $X_T$ has an optimal value of 1 (implying we buy a block of shares in Trans-Texas Oil), this would contribute $50,000 to the total return. In contrast, if $X_T$ has an optimal value of 0 (implying we do *not* buy shares in this company), this would contribute $0 to the total return.

Next, we model the constraints. The constraint regarding the $3 million investment limit can be expressed in a similar manner to that of the objective function. That is,

$$\$480X_T + \$540X_B + \$680X_D + \$1,000X_H + \$700X_L$$
$$+ \$510X_S + \$900X_C \leq \$3,000$$

Again, all figures are in thousands of dollars.

*Binary variables can be used to write different types of constraints.*

Depending on whether the optimal value of a binary variable is 0 or 1, the corresponding investment cost will be calculated in the LHS of the previous expression. The other constraints in the problems are special ones that exploit the binary nature of these variables. These types of constraints are what make the use of binary variables a powerful modeling tool. We discuss these special constraints in the following sections.

*Selecting k out of n choices*

**k Out of n Variables**   The requirement that at least two Texas oil firms must be in the portfolio is an example of a "*k* out of *n* variables" constraint. There are three (i.e., $n = 3$) Texas oil firms ($X_T$, $X_H$, and $X_L$) of which at least two (i.e., $k = 2$) must be selected. We can model this constraint as

$$X_T + X_H + X_L \geq 2$$

*Avoiding incompatible selections*

**Mutually Exclusive Variables**   The condition that no more than one investment can be made in foreign oil companies is an example of a *mutually exclusive* constraint. Note that the inclusion of one foreign oil company means that the other must be excluded. We can model this constraint as

$$X_B + X_D \leq 1$$

The condition regarding the California oil stock is also an example of having mutually exclusive variables. The sign of this constraint is, however, an equality rather than an inequality since Simkin *must* include a California oil stock in the portfolio. That is,

$$X_S + X_C = 1$$

*Enforcing dependencies*

**If-Then (or Linked) Variables**   The condition that if British Petroleum stock is included in the portfolio, then Trans-Texas Oil stock must also be included in the portfolio, is an example of an *if-then* constraint. We can model this relationship as

$$X_B \leq X_T$$

or

$$X_B - X_T \leq 0$$

Note that if $X_B$ equals 0 (i.e., British Petroleum is not included in the portfolio), this constraint allows $X_T$ to equal either 0 or 1. However, if $X_B$ equals 1, then $X_T$ must also equal 1.

The relationship discussed here is a one-way linkage in that Trans-Texas Oil must be included if British Petroleum is included, but not vice versa. If the relationship is two-way (i.e., either include both or include neither), we must then rewrite the constraint as

$$X_B = X_T$$

or

$$X_B - X_T = 0$$

## Solution to the Simkin 0–1 Model

The complete formulation of Simkin's problem is as follows:

$$\text{Maximize return} = \$50X_T + \$80X_B + \$90X_D + \$120X_H$$
$$+ \$110X_L + \$40X_S + \$75X_C$$

subject to

$$\$480X_T + \$540X_B + \$680X_D + \$1{,}000X_H + \$700X_L +$$
$$\$510X_S + \$900X_C \leq \$3{,}000 \quad \text{(Investment limit)}$$

$$X_T + X_H + X_L \quad\quad \geq 2 \quad\quad \text{(Texas)}$$
$$X_B + X_D \quad\quad\quad \leq 1 \quad\quad \text{(Foreign Oil)}$$
$$X_S + X_C \quad\quad\quad = 1 \quad\quad \text{(California)}$$
$$X_B - X_T \quad\quad\quad \leq 0 \quad\quad \text{(Trans-Texas and British Petroleum)}$$

$$\text{All } X_i \in (0, 1)$$

## PROGRAM 6.3

**Excel Layout and Solver Entries for Simkin, Simkin, and Steinberg's Binary Integer Programming Problem**

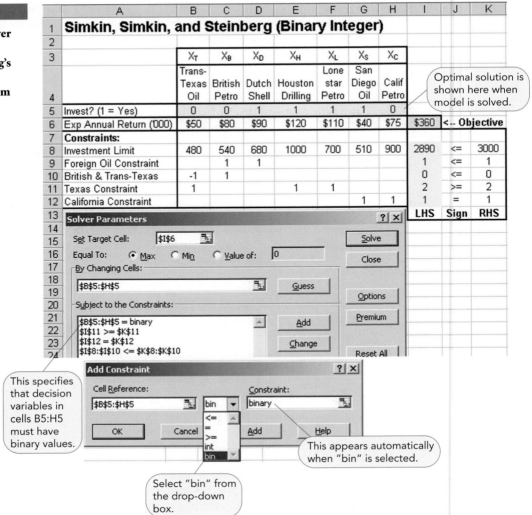

|   | A | B | C | D | E | F | G | H | I | J | K |
|---|---|---|---|---|---|---|---|---|---|---|---|
| 1 | **Simkin, Simkin, and Steinberg (Binary Integer)** | | | | | | | | | | |
| 2 | | | | | | | | | | | |
| 3 | | $X_T$ | $X_B$ | $X_D$ | $X_H$ | $X_L$ | $X_S$ | $X_C$ | | | |
| 4 | | Trans-Texas Oil | British Petro | Dutch Shell | Houston Drilling | Lone star Petro | San Diego Oil | Calif Petro | | | |
| 5 | Invest? (1 = Yes) | 0 | 0 | 1 | 1 | 1 | 1 | 0 | | | |
| 6 | Exp Annual Return ('000) | $50 | $80 | $90 | $120 | $110 | $40 | $75 | $360 | <-- Objective | |
| 7 | **Constraints:** | | | | | | | | | | |
| 8 | Investment Limit | 480 | 540 | 680 | 1000 | 700 | 510 | 900 | 2890 | <= | 3000 |
| 9 | Foreign Oil Constraint | | 1 | 1 | | | | | 1 | <= | 1 |
| 10 | British & Trans-Texas | -1 | 1 | | | | | | 0 | <= | 0 |
| 11 | Texas Constraint | 1 | | | 1 | 1 | | | 2 | >= | 2 |
| 12 | California Constraint | | | | | | 1 | 1 | 1 | = | 1 |
| 13 | | | | | | | | | LHS | Sign | RHS |

Optimal solution is shown here when model is solved.

**Solver Parameters**   ? X

Set Target Cell: $I$6

Equal To:   ⦿ Max   ○ Min   ○ Value of:  0

By Changing Cells:
$B$5:$H$5                Guess

Subject to the Constraints:
$B$5:$H$5 = binary
$I$11 >= $K$11           Add
$I$12 = $K$12
$I$8:$I$10 <= $K$8:$K$10  Change

Solve
Close
Options
Premium
Reset All

This specifies that decision variables in cells B5:H5 must have binary values.

**Add Constraint**   ? X

Cell Reference:           Constraint:
$B$5:$H$5         bin  ▾   binary

    OK      Cancel   =      Add      Help
                     >=
                     int
                     bin ▾

Select "bin" from the drop-down box.

This appears automatically when "bin" is selected.

**File: 6-3.xls**

The Excel layout and Solver entries for Simkin's 0–1 problem are shown in Program 6.3. The specification of the Target Cell, Changing Cells, and constraint LHS and RHS cell references in the Solver Parameters window is similar to that used for LP and general IP models.

## Specifying the Binary Requirement[3]

*The binary requirement is specified as an additional constraint in Solver.*

To specify the binary requirement for all variables, we again use the *Add* option to include a new constraint. In the LHS entry for the new constraint (see Program 6.3), we enter the cell reference for a decision variable that must be binary valued. If there are several decision variables that must be binary valued, we can enter the entire cell range, provided these variables are in contiguous cells. For Simkin's problem, we enter B5:H5 in this box, corresponding to $X_T$ through $X_C$, respectively.

---

[3] For versions of Excel prior to 8.0 in Office 97, the *Bin* option is not available in Solver. To specify that a variable $X$ is binary, you will therefore need to add three constraints: $X \geq 0$, $X \leq 1$, and $X$ = integer.

We then click on the drop-down box in the Add Constraint window, and click on the choice Bin. The word "Binary" automatically is displayed in the box for the RHS entry. This indicates to Solver that all variables specified in the LHS box are binary variables.

Program 6.3 shows that the optimal solution is for Simkin to recommend the client invest in Dutch Shell ($X_D$), Houston Drilling ($X_H$), Lonestar Petroleum ($X_L$), and San Diego Oil ($X_S$). The expected return is $360,000 since the $360 in cell I6 is in units of $1,000.

## 6.4    MIXED INTEGER MODELS: FIXED-CHARGE PROBLEMS

In all LP and general integer models studied so far, we typically deal with situations in which the total cost is directly proportional to the magnitude of the decision variable. For example, if $X$ denotes the number of toasters we will be making, and each toaster costs $10 to make, the total cost of making toasters is written as $10X. Such costs per unit are referred to as *variable* costs.

In many situations, however, there are fixed costs in addition to the per unit variable costs. These costs may include the costs to set up machines for the production run, construction costs to build a new facility, or design costs to develop a new product. Unlike variable costs, these fixed costs are independent of the volume of production. They are incurred whenever the decision to go ahead with a project or production run is taken.

Problems that involve both fixed and variable costs are a classic example of mixed integer programming models. We call such problems *fixed-charge problems*.

*Fixed-charge problems include fixed costs in addition to variable costs.*

We use binary variables to model the fixed cost issue (e.g., whether we will incur the setup cost or not). Either linear or integer variables can be used to deal with the variable costs issue, depending on the nature of these variables. In formulating the model, we need to ensure that whenever the decision variable associated with the variable cost is nonzero, the binary variable associated with the fixed cost takes on a value of 1 (i.e., the fixed cost is also incurred).

To illustrate this type of situation, let us reintroduce the Hardgrave Machine Company example from Section 5.4 of Chapter 5.

### Locating a New Factory for Hardgrave Machine Company

The Hardgrave Machine Company produces computer components at its plants in Cincinnati, Kansas City, and Pittsburgh. These plants have not been able to keep up with demand for orders at Hardgrave's four warehouses in Detroit, Houston, New York and Los Angeles. As a result, the firm has decided to build a new plant to expand its productive capacity. The two sites being considered are Seattle, Washington and Birmingham, Alabama. Both cities are attractive in terms of labor supply, municipal services, and ease of factory financing.

Table 6.3 presents the production costs and capacities for each of the three existing plants, demand at each of the four warehouses, and estimated production costs for the new proposed plants. Transportation costs from each plant to each warehouse are summarized in Table 6.4.

In addition to this information, Hardgrave estimates that the monthly fixed cost of operating the proposed facility in Seattle would be $400,000. The Birmingham plant would be somewhat cheaper due to the cheaper cost of living at that location. Hardgrave therefore estimates that the monthly fixed cost of operating the proposed facility in Birmingham would be $325,000. Note that the fixed costs at *existing* plants need not be considered here since they will be incurred regardless of which new plant Hardgrave decides to open—that is, they are sunk costs.

*Sunk costs are not considered in the optimization model.*

As in Chapter 5, the question facing Hardgrave is this: Which of the new locations will yield the lowest cost in combination with the existing plants and warehouses? Note that the

TABLE 6.3

Hardgrave's Demand and
Supply Data

| WAREHOUSE | MONTHLY DEMAND (UNITS) | PRODUCTION PLANT | MONTHLY SUPPLY | COST TO PRODUCE ONE UNIT ($) |
|---|---|---|---|---|
| Detroit | 10,000 | Cincinnati | 15,000 | 48 |
| Houston | 12,000 | Kansas City | 6,000 | 50 |
| New York | 15,000 | Pittsburgh | 14,000 | 52 |
| Los Angeles | 9,000 | | 35,000 | |
| | 46,000 | | | |

Supply needed from new plant = 46,000 − 35,000 = 11,000 units per month

| ESTIMATED PRODUCTION COST PER UNIT AT PROPOSED PLANTS | |
|---|---|
| Seattle | $53 |
| Birmingham | $49 |

unit cost of shipping from each plant to each warehouse is found by adding the shipping costs (Table 6.4) to the corresponding production costs (Table 6.3). In addition, the solution needs to consider the monthly fixed costs of operating the new facility.

Recall that we handled this problem in Section 5.4 by setting up and solving two separate transportation models (one for each of the two new locations). In what follows, we show how we can use binary variables to model Hardgrave's problem as a single mixed, binary integer programming model.

**Decision Variables**  There are two types of decisions to be made in this problem. The first involves deciding which of the new locations (Seattle or Birmingham) to select for the new plant. The second involves trying to decide the shipment quantities from each plant (including the new plant) to each of the warehouses.

*We use binary variables to model the opening of a plant.*

To model the first decision, we associate a binary variable with each of the two locations. Let

$$Y_S \begin{cases} = 1 \text{ if Seattle is selected for the new plant} \\ = 0 \text{ otherwise} \end{cases}$$

$$Y_B \begin{cases} = 1 \text{ if Birmingham is selected for the new plant} \\ = 0 \text{ otherwise} \end{cases}$$

TABLE 6.4

Hardgrave's Shipping
Costs

| FROM \ TO | DETROIT | HOUSTON | NEW YORK | LOS ANGELES |
|---|---|---|---|---|
| **CINCINNATI** | $25 | $55 | $40 | $60 |
| **KANSAS CITY** | 35 | 30 | 50 | 40 |
| **PITTSBURGH** | 36 | 45 | 26 | 66 |
| **SEATTLE** | 60 | 38 | 65 | 27 |
| **BIRMINGHAM** | 35 | 30 | 41 | 50 |

*We use regular variables (continuous-valued or general integer) to model the shipping quantities.*

To model the shipping quantities, we once again use double-subscripted variables, as discussed in Chapter 5. Note that there will be 20 decision variables (= 5 plants × 4 warehouses) denoting the shipping quantities (one variable for each possible shipping route). Let

$$X_{ij} = \text{Number of units shipped from plant } i \text{ to warehouse } j$$

*where*

$$i = \text{C (Cincinnati), K (Kansas City), P (Pittsburgh),} \\ \text{S (Seattle), or B (Birmingham)}$$

$$j = \text{D (Detroit), H (Houston), N (New York), or} \\ \text{L (Los Angeles)}$$

**Objective Function**  Let us first model the objective function. We want to minimize the total cost of producing and shipping the components and the monthly fixed costs of maintaining the new facility. This can be written as

$$
\begin{aligned}
\text{Minimize Total Costs} = {} & \$73X_{CD} + \$103X_{CH} + \$88X_{CN} + \$108X_{CL} \\
& + \$85X_{KD} + \$80X_{KH} + \$100X_{KN} + \$90X_{KL} \\
& + \$88X_{PD} + \$97X_{PH} + \$78X_{PN} + \$118X_{PL} \\
& + \$113X_{SD} + \$91X_{SH} + \$118X_{SN} + \$80X_{SL} \\
& + \$84X_{BD} + \$79X_{BH} + \$90X_{BN} + \$99X_{BL} \\
& + \$400{,}000Y_S + \$325{,}000Y_B
\end{aligned}
$$

The last two terms in the expression for the objective function represent the fixed costs. Note that these costs will be incurred only if the plant is built at the location (i.e., the variable $Y_i$ has a value of 1).

**Constraints**  We need to write flow balance constraints at each of the plants and warehouses. Recall that at each node, the flow balance constraint ensures that

$$\text{Net flow} = (\text{Total flow } in \text{ to node}) - (\text{Total flow } out \text{ of node}) \qquad \text{(6-1)}$$

At source nodes, the net flow is a negative quantity and represents the amount of goods (flow) created at the source node. In contrast, at destination nodes, the net flow is a positive quantity, and represents the amount of goods (flow) consumed at the source node.

The flow balance constraints at the existing plants (Cincinnati, Kansas City, and Pittsburgh) are straightforward and can be written as

$$
\begin{aligned}
(0) - (X_{CD} + X_{CH} + X_{CN} + X_{CL}) &= -15{,}000 \quad \text{(Cincinnati supply)} \\
(0) - (X_{KD} + X_{KH} + X_{KN} + X_{KL}) &= -6{,}000 \quad \text{(Kansas City supply)} \\
(0) - (X_{PD} + X_{PH} + X_{PN} + X_{PL}) &= -14{,}000 \quad \text{(Pittsburgh supply)}
\end{aligned}
$$

*Supply is available at a plant only if it is opened.*

However, when writing the flow balance constraint for a new plant (Seattle or Birmingham), we need to ensure that a supply is available at that plant *only* if it is actually built. For example, the supply at Seattle is 11,000 units if the new plant is built there and 0 otherwise. We can model this as follows:

$$
\begin{aligned}
(0) - (X_{SD} + X_{SH} + X_{SN} + X_{SL}) &= -11{,}000Y_S \quad \text{(Seattle supply)} \\
(0) - (X_{BD} + X_{BH} + X_{BN} + X_{BL}) &= -11{,}000Y_B \quad \text{(Birmingham supply)}
\end{aligned}
$$

Note that if Seattle is selected for the new plant, $Y_S$ would equal 1. Hence, a supply of 11,000 would be available there. In contrast, if Seattle is not selected for the new plant, $Y_S$ would equal 0. Hence, the supply in the flow balance constraint would become 0; that is, all flows from Seattle would have to equal 0. The flow balance constraint for Birmingham works in a similar manner.

The flow balance constraints at the four existing warehouses (Detroit, Houston, New York, and Los Angeles) can be written as

$$X_{CD} + X_{KD} + X_{PD} + X_{SD} + X_{BD} = 10{,}000 \quad \text{(Detroit demand)}$$
$$X_{CH} + X_{KH} + X_{PH} + X_{SH} + X_{BH} = 12{,}000 \quad \text{(Houston demand)}$$
$$X_{CN} + X_{KN} + X_{PN} + X_{SN} + X_{BN} = 15{,}000 \quad \text{(New York demand)}$$
$$X_{CL} + X_{KL} + X_{PL} + X_{SL} + X_{BL} = 9{,}000 \quad \text{(Los Angeles demand)}$$

*Only one of the two sites can be selected.*

Finally, we need to ensure that exactly one of the two sites is selected for the new plant. This is another example of the mutually exclusive variables discussed in Section 6.3. We can express this as

$$Y_S + Y_B = 1$$

**File: 6-4.xls**

*Total cost includes fixed costs and shipping costs.*

The formula view of the Excel layout for Hardgrave's fixed-charge problem is shown in Program 6.4A. The Solver entries and optimal solution are shown in Program 6.4B.

Referring back to Section 5.4, we see that the cost of shipping was $3,704,000 if the new plant was built in Seattle. This cost was $3,741,000 if the new plant was built at Birmingham. With the fixed costs included, these costs would be

Seattle:       $3,704,000 + $400,000 = $4,104,000
Birmingham:    $3,741,000 + $325,000 = $4,066,000

---

**PROGRAM 6.4A**    **Formula View of Excel Layout for Hardgrave Machine Company's Mixed Integer Programming Problem**

Sum of entries in rows 4–8 gives the total flow *in.*

Sum of entries in columns B–E gives the total flow *out.*

| | A | B | C | D | E | F | G | H | I | J | K |
|---|---|---|---|---|---|---|---|---|---|---|---|
| 1 | **Hardgrave Machine Company (Mixed Integer)** | | | | | | | | | | |
| 2 | | | | | | | | | | | |
| 3 | From: To: | Detroit | Dallas | New York | Los Angeles | Total flow out | | **Flow balance equations:** | | | |
| 4 | Cincinnati | | | | | =SUM(B4:E4) | | Location | Net flow | Sign | RHS |
| 5 | Salt Lake City | | | | | =SUM(B5:E5) | | Cincinnati | =0-F4 | = | -15000 |
| 6 | Pittsburgh | | | | | =SUM(B6:E6) | | Salt Lake City | =0-F5 | = | -6000 |
| 7 | Birmingham | | | | | =SUM(B7:E7) | | Pittsburgh | =0-F6 | = | -14000 |
| 8 | Seattle | | | | | =SUM(B8:E8) | | Birmingham | =0-F7 | = | =-11000*B19 |
| 9 | Total flow in | =SUM(B4:B8) | =SUM(C4:C8) | =SUM(D4:D8) | =SUM(E4:E8) | | | Seattle | =0-F8 | = | =-11000*C19 |
| 10 | | | | | | | | Detroit | =B9 | = | 10000 |
| 11 | Unit costs: | Detroit | Dallas | NY | LA | | | Dallas | =C9 | = | 12000 |
| 12 | Cincinnati | 73 | 103 | 88 | 108 | | | New York | =D9 | = | 15000 |
| 13 | Salt Lake City | 85 | 80 | 100 | 90 | | | Los Angeles | =E9 | = | 9000 |
| 14 | Pittsburgh | 88 | 97 | 78 | 118 | | | | | | |
| 15 | Birmingham | 84 | 79 | 90 | 99 | | | # of new plants | =B19+C19 | = | 1 |
| 16 | Seattle | 113 | 91 | 118 | 80 | | | | | | |
| 17 | | | | | | | | | | | |
| 18 | | Birmingham | Seattle | | | | | | | | |
| 19 | Build? (1 = Yes) | | | | | | | | | | |
| 20 | Fixed Cost | 325000 | 400000 | | | | | | | | |
| 21 | | | | | | | | | | | |
| 22 | Shipping cost = | =SUMPRODUCT(B4:E8,B12:E16) | | | | | | | | | |
| 23 | Fixed Cost = | =SUMPRODUCT(B19:C19,B20:C20) | | | | | | | | | |
| 24 | Total Cost = | =B22+B23 | | | | | | | | | |

This specifies that only one of the two sites must be selected.

RHS = –11,000 if site is selected, = 0 if site is not selected.

Total cost is the sum of shipping cost and fixed cost.

Solver will place the solution values in cells shaded yellow.

PROGRAM 6.4B  **Solver Entries and Solution for Hardgrave Machine Company's Mixed Integer Programming Problem**

That is, Hardgrave should select Birmingham as the site for the new plant. Program 6.4B shows this solution. Note that the shipping quantities in this solution are the same as those obtained in Section 5.4 for the solution with the Birmingham plant (as we saw in Program 5.3B on page 169).

## 6.5  GOAL PROGRAMMING MODELS

*Firms usually have more than one objective.*

In today's business environment, profit maximization or cost minimization are not always the only objectives that a firm sets forth. Often, maximizing total profit is just one of several objectives, including such contradictory objectives as maximizing market share, maintaining full employment, providing quality ecological management, minimizing noise level in the neighborhood, and meeting numerous other noneconomic targets or goals.

Mathematical programming techniques such as LP and IP have the shortcoming that their objective function is measured in one dimension only. It's not possible for LP models to have multiple objectives unless they are all measured in the same units (such as dollars), a highly unusual situation. An important technique that has been developed to supplement LP is called *goal programming*.

*Goal programming permits multiple objectives.*

*Goal programming "satisfices" as opposed to LP, which tries to "optimize." This means coming as close as possible to reaching goals.*

Goal programming is capable of handling decision problems involving multiple goals. A four-decade-old concept, it began with the work of Charnes and Cooper in 1961 and was refined and extended by Ignizio in the 1970s (see the Bibliography).

In typical decision-making situations, the goals set by management can be achieved only at the expense of other goals. It is necessary to establish a hierarchy of importance among these goals so that lower-priority goals are tackled only after higher-priority goals are satisfied. Since it is not always possible to achieve every goal to the extent the decision maker desires, goal programming attempts to reach a satisfactory level of multiple objectives. This, of course, differs from LP, which tries to find the best possible outcome for a *single* objective. Nobel laureate Herbert A. Simon, of Carnegie-Mellon University, states that modern managers may not be able to optimize, but may instead have to "*satisfice*" or "come as close as possible" to reaching goals. This is the case with models such as goal programming.

*The objective function is the main difference between goal programming and LP.*

How, specifically, does goal programming differ from LP? The objective function is the main difference. Instead of trying to maximize or minimize the objective function directly, with goal programming we try to minimize *deviations* between set goals and what we can actually achieve within the given constraints. These deviations are either positive or negative, and not only are they real variables, but they are also the only terms in the objective function. The objective is to minimize these *deviational variables.*

*In goal programming we want to minimize deviational variables, which are the only terms in the objective function.*

## Example of Goal Programming: Harrison Electric Company Revisited

To illustrate the formulation of a goal programming problem, let's look back at the Harrison Electric Company case presented earlier in this chapter as an IP problem. That problem's LP formulation, you recall, was

$$\text{maximize profit} = \$600C + \$700F$$

$$\text{subject to} \qquad 2C + 3F \leq 12 \quad \text{(wiring hours)}$$

$$6C + 5F \leq 30 \quad \text{(assembly hours)}$$

$$C, F \geq 0$$

*where*

$$C = \text{number of chandeliers produced}$$

$$F = \text{number of ceiling fans produced}$$

We saw that if Harrison's management had a single goal, say profit, LP could be used to find the optimal solution. But let's assume that the firm is moving to a new location during a particular production period and feels that maximizing profit is not a realistic goal. Management sets a profit level, which would be satisfactory during the adjustment period, of $3,000. We now have a goal programming problem in which we want to find the production mix that achieves this goal as closely as possible, given the production time constraints. This simple case will provide a good starting point for tackling more complicated goal programs.

We first define two deviational variables:

$$d_1^- = \text{underachievement of the profit target}$$

$$d_1^+ = \text{overachievement of the profit target}$$

Now we can state the Harrison Electric problem as a single-goal programming model:

$$\text{minimize under- or overachievement of profit target} = d_1^- + d_1^+$$

subject to

$$\begin{array}{ll} \$600C + \$700F + d_1^- - d_1^+ = \$3{,}000 & \text{(profit goal constraint)} \\ 2C + \quad 3F \qquad\qquad\qquad\ \ \leq 12 & \text{(wiring hours constraint)} \\ 6C + \quad 5F \qquad\qquad\qquad\ \ \leq 30 & \text{(assembly hours constraint)} \\ \qquad C, F, d_1^-, d_1^+ \geq 0 & \end{array}$$

Note that the first constraint states that the profit made, $\$600C + \$700F$, plus any underachievement of profit minus any overachievement of profit has to equal the target of $\$3,000$. For example, if $C = 3$ chandeliers and $F = 2$ ceiling fans, then $\$3,200$ profit has been made. This exceeds $\$3,000$ by $\$200$, so $d_1^+$ must be equal to 200. Since the profit goal constraint was overachieved, Harrison did not underachieve, and $d_1^-$ will clearly be equal to zero.

*Deviational variables are 0 if a goal is completely obtained.*

If the target profit of $\$3,000$ is exactly achieved, we see that both $d_1^+$ and $d_1^-$ are equal to 0. The objective function will also be minimized at 0. If Harrison's management was only concerned with *underachievement* of the target goal, how would the objective function change? It would be as follows: minimize underachievement $= d_1^-$. This is also a reasonable goal since the firm would probably not be upset with an overachievement of its target.

In general, once all goals and constraints are identified in a problem, management should analyze each goal to see if underachievement or overachievement of that goal is an acceptable situation. If overachievement is acceptable, the appropriate $d^+$ variable can be eliminated from the objective function. If underachievement is okay, the $d^-$ variable should be dropped. If management seeks to attain a goal exactly, both $d^-$ and $d^+$ must appear in the objective function.

## Extension to Equally Important Multiple Goals

Let's now look at the situation in which Harrison's management wants to achieve several goals, each equal in priority.

*Goal 1:* to reach a profit of at least $\$3,000$ during the production period
*Goal 2:* to fully utilize the available wiring department hours
*Goal 3:* to avoid overtime in the assembly department
*Goal 4:* to meet a contract requirement to produce at least seven ceiling fans

*We need a clear definition of deviational variables, such as these.*

The deviational variables can be defined as follows:

$$d_1^- = \text{underachievement of the profit target}$$

$$d_1^+ = \text{overachievement of the profit target}$$

$$d_2^- = \text{idle time in the wiring department (underutilization)}$$

$$d_2^+ = \text{overtime in the wiring department (overutilization)}$$

$$d_3^- = \text{idle time in the assembly department (underutilization)}$$

$$d_3^+ = \text{overtime in the assembly department (overutilization)}$$

$$d_4^- = \text{underachievement of the ceiling fan goal}$$

$$d_4^+ = \text{overachievement of the ceiling fan goal}$$

Management is unconcerned about whether there is overachievement of the profit goal, overtime in the wiring department, idle time in the assembly department, or more than seven ceiling fans are produced: hence $d_1^+$, $d_2^+$, $d_3^-$, and $d_4^+$ can be omitted from the objective function. The new objective function and constraints are:

$$\text{minimize total deviation} = d_1^- + d_2^- + d_3^+ + d_4^-$$

subject to

$$
\begin{aligned}
600C + 700F + d_1^- - d_1^+ &= 3{,}000 && \text{(profit constraint)} \\
2C + 3F + d_2^- - d_2^+ &= 12 && \text{(wiring hours constraint)} \\
6C + 5F + d_3^- - d_3^+ &= 30 && \text{(assembly constraint)} \\
F + d_4^- - d_4^+ &= 7 && \text{(ceiling fan constraint)}
\end{aligned}
$$

$C$, $F$, and all $d_i$ variables $\geq 0$.

To solve this goal programming problem, we can adopt one of two approaches: (1) the weighted goals approach or (2) the prioritized goals approach.

### Weighted Goals

*Weights can be used to distinguish between different goals.*

In this approach, we assign numerical weights to each deviational variable in the objective function. These weights serve as the objective coefficients for the deviational variables. The magnitude of the weight assigned to a specific deviational variable would depend on the relative importance of that variable.

For example, let's assume Harrison's management assigns the following weights to the deviational variables:

| GOAL | WEIGHT |
|---|---|
| Reach a profit of at least $3,000 ($d_1^-$) | 40 |
| Fully use wiring department hours available ($d_2^-$) | 30 |
| Avoid assembly department overtime ($d_3^+$) | 20 |
| Produce at least seven ceiling fans ($d_4^-$) | 10 |

That is, management feels that the goal of getting a profit as much above $3,000 as possible is

- 1.33 times ($= 40/30$) as important as the goal of fully using wiring department hours available,

- 2 times ($= 40/20$) as important as the goal of avoiding assembly department overtime, and

- 4 times ($= 40/10$) as important as the goal of producing at least seven ceiling fans.

We should note here that weighted goals are usually appropriate only if all the goals (and hence, the deviational variables) are being measured in the same units (such as $). Even though it is not the case here, we use Harrison's problem to illustrate the use of weighted goals.

We can now write the objective function for this weighted goal programming problem as

$$\text{Minimize total deviation} = 40d_1^- + 30d_2^- + 20d_3^+ + 10d_4^-$$

*In the weighted goal approach, the problem reduces to a simple LP model.*

The problem now reduces to a simple LP model with a single objective function (i.e., minimize weighted sum of deviational variables). As shown earlier, each goal in the problem has now become a constraint that includes the deviational variables. Setting up this model on Excel and solving it using Solver therefore become rather straightforward tasks.

**File: 6-5.xls**

The Excel layout and Solver entries for Harrison's problem with weighted goals are shown in Program 6.5. The optimal solution is to produce $C = 0$ chandeliers and $F = 6$ ceiling fans. This results in a profit of $4,200 that is $1,200 over the profit goal ($d_1^+ = \$1,200$), uses 6 hours of overtime in the wiring department ($d_2^+ = 6$ hours), needs no overtime in the assembly department ($d_3^+ = 0$ hours), and produces 1 ceiling fan less than the desired target ($d_4^- = 1$). The resulting objective value of 10 is not really relevant here since it is simply a function of the weights assigned to the various deviational variables.

**PROGRAM 6.5**

**Excel Layout and Solver Entries for Harrison Electric's Goal Programming Problem Using Weighted Goals**

> Changing cells include all deviational variables in addition to C and F.

| | A | B | C | D | E | F | G | H | I | J | K | L | M | N |
|---|---|---|---|---|---|---|---|---|---|---|---|---|---|---|
| 1 | **Harrison Electric (Weighted Goals)** | | | | | | | | | | | | | |
| 2 | | | | | | | | | | | | | | |
| 3 | | | C | F | $d_1^-$ | $d_1^+$ | $d_2^-$ | $d_2^+$ | $d_3^-$ | $d_3^+$ | $d_4^-$ | $d_4^+$ | | | |
| 4 | | | Chand-eliers | Fans | Profit Under Goal | Profit Over Goal | Wiring Under Goal | Wiring Over Goal | Asmbly Under Goal | Asmbly Over Goal | Fans Under Goal | Fans Over Goal | | | |
| 5 | Solution value | 0.00 | 6.00 | 0.00 | 1200.00 | 0.00 | 6.00 | 0.00 | 0.00 | 1.00 | 0.00 | | | |
| 6 | Weights | | | 40 | | 30 | | | 20 | 10 | | 10.00 | <-- Objective | |
| 7 | **Constraints:** | | | | | | | | | | | | | |
| 8 | Profit | 600 | 700 | 1 | -1 | | | | | | | 3000 | = | 3000 |
| 9 | Wiring Hours | 2 | 3 | | | 1 | -1 | | | | | 12 | = | 12 |
| 10 | Assembly | 6 | 5 | | | | | 1 | -1 | | | 30 | = | 30 |
| 11 | Fans | | 1 | | | | | | | 1 | -1 | 7 | = | 7 |
| | | | | | | | | | | | | LHS | Sign | RHS |

> The numerical weights for the deviational variables go in this row.

> All goals are expressed as "=" constraints using the deviational variables.

**Solver Parameters**    ? ✕

Set Target Cell: `$L$6`

Equal To: ○ Max  ● Min  ○ Value of: `0`

By Changing Cells:

`$B$5:$K$5`        Guess

Subject to the Constraints:

`$L$8:$L$11 = $N$8:$N$11`        Add

Solve
Close
Options
Premium

## Prioritized or Ranked Goals

*We use priorities when it is difficult to assign weights for deviational variables.*

Solving a goal programming problem by assigning weights to the deviational variables is easy to implement. But in practice, it is typically difficult to come up with precise weights for each goal. For example, how can Harrison's management know for sure whether the profit goal is exactly twice as important as the wiring hours goal? What if the profit is only 1.5 times more important than wiring? This would obviously affect the choice of weights, which in turn, could affect the optimal solution.

*Lower-order goals are considered only after higher-order goals are met.*

To eliminate this difficulty, the alternative approach to solving goal programming problems assigns priorities, rather than weights, to the goals. The idea is that goals can be *ranked* with respect to their importance in management's eyes. Lower-order goals are considered only after higher-order goals are met. Priorities ($P_i$'s) are assigned to each deviational variable—with a ranking that $P_1$ is the most important goal, $P_2$ the next most important, then $P_3$, and so on.

For example, let's assume Harrison's management sets the following priorities to the deviational variables:

| GOAL | PRIORITY |
|---|---|
| Reach a profit of at least \$3,000 ($d_1^-$) | $P_1$ |
| Fully use wiring department hours available ($d_2^-$) | $P_2$ |
| Avoid assembly department overtime ($d_3^+$) | $P_3$ |
| Produce at least seven ceiling fans ($d_4^-$) | $P_4$ |

This means, in effect, that the priority of meeting the profit goal ($P_1$) is infinitely more important than the wiring goal ($P_2$), which is, in turn, infinitely more important than the assembly goal ($P_3$), which is infinitely more important than producing at least seven ceiling fans ($P_4$). The problem is now stated as

$$\text{Minimize total deviation} = P_1(d_1^-) + P_2(d_2^-) + P_3(d_3^+) + P_4(d_4^-)$$

subject to

$$
\begin{aligned}
600C + 700F + d_1^- - d_1^+ &= 3{,}000 \quad \text{(profit constraint)} \\
2C + 3F + d_2^- - d_2^+ &= 12 \quad \text{(wiring hours constraint)} \\
6C + 5F + d_3^- - d_3^+ &= 30 \quad \text{(assembly constraint)} \\
F + d_4^- - d_4^+ &= 7 \quad \text{(ceiling fan constraint)}
\end{aligned}
$$

$C$, $F$, and all $d_i$ variables $\geq 0$

*Solving a model with ranked goals requires us to solve a series of LP models.*

*$P_1$ goals are considered first.*

**Solution Using Solver**  We need to set up and solve a series of LP models in order to find the optimal solution for a goal programming model with ranked goals. In the first of these LP models, we consider only the highest priority ($P_1$) goal, and ignore all other goals ($P_2$–$P_4$). The objective then reduces to the deviational variables with priority $P_1$, namely,

$$\text{Minimize total deviation} = d_1^-$$

**File: 6-6.xls**

Solving this LP model using Solver is a simple task, and Program 6.6A shows the relevant information. The results show that it is possible to fully achieve the first goal (that is, optimal value of $d_1^-$ is zero).

**PROGRAM 6.6A**    **Excel Layout and Solver Entries for Harrison Electric's Goal Programming Problem Considering Only Priority $P_1$ Goals**

$P_1$ goal is to minimize $d_1^-$.

Note that this model considers only priority $P_1$ goals.

Optimal value of 0 implies $P_1$ goal is fully satisfied.

|  | A | B | C | D | E | F | G | H | I | J | K | L | M | N |
|---|---|---|---|---|---|---|---|---|---|---|---|---|---|---|
| 1 | **Harrison Electric (With Priority $P_1$ Goals Only)** | | | | | | | | | | | | | |
| 2 | | | | | | | | | | | | | | |
| 3 | | C | F | $d_1^-$ | $d_1^+$ | $d_2^-$ | $d_2^+$ | $d_3^-$ | $d_3^+$ | $d_4^-$ | $d_4^+$ | | | |
| 4 | | Chand-eliers | Fans | Profit Under Goal | Profit Over Goal | Wiring Under Goal | Wiring Over Goal | Asmbly Under Goal | Asmbly Over Goal | Fans Under Goal | Fans Over Goal | | | |
| 5 | Solution value | 5.00 | 0.00 | 0.00 | 0.00 | 2.00 | 0.00 | 0.00 | 0.00 | 7.00 | 0.00 | | | |
| 6 | Obj Coefficient | | | 1 | | | | | | | | 0.00 | **<-- Objective** | |
| 7 | **Constraints:** | | | | | | | | | | | | | |
| 8 | Profit | 600 | 700 | 1 | -1 | | | | | | | 3000 | = | 3000 |
| 9 | Wiring Hours | 2 | 3 | | | 1 | -1 | | | | | 12 | = | 12 |
| 10 | Assembly | 6 | 5 | | | | | 1 | -1 | | | 30 | = | 30 |
| 11 | Fans | | 1 | | | | | | | 1 | -1 | 7 | = | 7 |
| 12 | | | | | | | | | | | | LHS | Sign | RHS |

Solver Parameters    ? | X

Set Target Cell:    $L$6

Equal To:    ○ Max    ⦿ Min    ○ Value of: 0    **Solve**

By Changing Cells:

$B$5:$K$5    **Guess**    **Close**

Subject to the Constraints:    **Options**

$L$8:$L$11 = $N$8:$N$11    **Add**    **Premium**

Constraints are the four goal equality constraints.

---

*$P_2$ goals are considered next.*

We now consider the goal with the next-highest priority ($P_2$) in the second LP model. However, in setting up this model, we explicitly incorporate the fact that the $P_1$ goal has been fully achieved. To do so, we set the value of $d_1^-$ equal to zero in the model. For the second LP model, the objective function and *additional* constraint are as follows:

$$\text{Minimize total deviation} = d_2^-$$

and

$$d_1^- = 0 \quad (P_1 \text{ goal achieved})$$

Program 6.6B shows the Excel layout and Solver entries for this LP problem. The results show that it is possible to fully achieve the second goal also. That is, the optimal value of $d_2^-$ is also zero.

*$P_3$ goals are now considered.*

Since the first two goals have been fully achieved, we now consider the goal with the next-highest priority ($P_3$) in the third LP model. As before, in setting up this model, we explicitly incorporate the fact that the $P_1$ and $P_2$ goals have been fully achieved. For the third LP model, the objective function and *additional* constraints are as follows:

$$\text{Minimize total deviation} = d_3^+$$

and

$$d_1^- = 0 \quad (P_1 \text{ goal achieved})$$
$$d_2^- = 0 \quad (P_2 \text{ goal achieved})$$

**PROGRAM 6.6B**  **Excel Layout and Solver Entries for Harrison Electric's Goal Programming Problem Considering Only Priority $P_2$ Goals**

($P_2$ goal is to minimize $d_2^-$.)

Note that this model considers only priority $P_2$ goals.

| | A | B | C | D | E | F | G | H | I | J | K | L | M | N |
|---|---|---|---|---|---|---|---|---|---|---|---|---|---|---|
| 1 | **Harrison Electric (With Priority $P_2$ Goals Only)** | | | | | | | | | | | | | |
| 2 | | | | | | | | | | | | | | |
| 3 | | C | F | $d_1^-$ | $d_1^+$ | $d_2^-$ | $d_2^+$ | $d_3^-$ | $d_3^+$ | $d_4^-$ | $d_4^+$ | | | |
| 4 | | Chandeliers | Fans | Profit Under Goal | Profit Over Goal | Wiring Under Goal | Wiring Over Goal | Asmbly Under Goal | Asmbly Over Goal | Fans Under Goal | Fans Over Goal | | | |
| 5 | Solution value | 1.50 | 3.00 | 0.00 | 0.00 | 0.00 | 0.00 | 6.00 | 0.00 | 4.00 | 0.00 | | | |
| 6 | Obj Coefficient | | | | | 1 | | | | | | 0.00 | <-- Objective | |
| 7 | **Constraints:** | | | | | | | | | | | | | |
| 8 | Profit | 600 | 700 | 1 | -1 | | | | | | | 3000 | = | 3000 |
| 9 | Wiring Hours | 2 | 3 | | | 1 | -1 | | | | | 12 | = | 12 |
| 10 | Assembly | 6 | 5 | | | | | 1 | -1 | | | 30 | = | 30 |
| 11 | Fans | | 1 | | | | | | | 1 | -1 | 7 | = | 7 |
| 12 | | | | | | | | | | | | LHS | Sign | RHS |

($P_2$ goal is also fully satisfied.)

**Solver Parameters**  ? ×

Set Target Cell: $L$6

Equal To:  ○ Max  ⦿ Min  ○ Value of:  0

By Changing Cells:

$B$5:$K$5

Subject to the Constraints:

$D$5 = 0
$L$8:$L$11 = $N$8:$N$11

[ Solve ]  [ Close ]  [ Guess ]  [ Options ]  [ Premium ]  [ Add ]

$d_1^-$ set to 0 since $P_1$ goal is fully satisfied.

Program 6.6C shows the Excel layout and Solver entries for this LP problem. The results show that it is possible to fully achieve this goal too, and the optimal value of $d_3^+$ is zero.

*Finally, $P_4$ goals are considered.*

Now that the first three goals have all been fully achieved, we consider the final set of goals (with priority $P_4$). In setting up this model, we explicitly specify that $d_1^-$, $d_2^-$, and $d_3^+$ all have values of 0. In effect, we eliminate these variables. For the final LP model, the objective function and *additional* constraints are as follows:

$$\text{Minimize total deviation} = d_4^-$$

and

$$d_1^- = 0 \quad (P_1 \text{ goal achieved})$$
$$d_2^- = 0 \quad (P_2 \text{ goal achieved})$$
$$d_3^+ = 0 \quad (P_3 \text{ goal achieved})$$

Program 6.6D shows the Excel layout and Solver entries for the final LP problem. The results show that, after fully achieving the first three goals, the best that Harrison can do is to underachieve the ceiling fan goal by 1 unit. That is, the optimal solution for Harrison is to make 6 ceiling fans and 0 chandeliers. This yields a profit of $4,200, uses 18 hours in the wiring department (which is 6 hours over the minimum set), and uses all 30 hours in the assembly department.

*Solutions with weighted goals and ranked goals can be different for the same problem.*

We note that for this specific example, the solution we obtained using prioritized goals was the same as the one obtained using weighted goals. In general, however, this need not be true. Although the weighted goal approach considers all goals simultaneously (and

**Excel Layout and Solver Entries for Harrison Electric's Goal Programming Problem Considering Only Priority $P_3$ Goals**

$P_3$ goal is to minimize $d_3^+$.

Note that only priority $P_3$ goals are considered.

$P_3$ goal is also fully satisfied.

| | A | B | C | D | E | F | G | H | I | J | K | L | M | N |
|---|---|---|---|---|---|---|---|---|---|---|---|---|---|---|
| 1 | **Harrison Electric (With Priority $P_3$ Goals Only)** | | | | | | | | | | | | | |
| 3 | | | C | F | $d_1^-$ | $d_1^+$ | $d_2^-$ | $d_2^+$ | $d_3^-$ | $d_3^+$ | $d_4^-$ | $d_4^+$ | | |
| 4 | | | Chand-eliers | Fans | Profit Under Goal | Profit Over Goal | Wiring Under Goal | Wiring Over Goal | Asmbly Under Goal | Asmbly Over Goal | Fans Under Goal | Fans Over Goal | | |
| 5 | Solution value | | 1.50 | 3.00 | 0.00 | 0.00 | 0.00 | 0.00 | 6.00 | 0.00 | 4.00 | 0.00 | | |
| 6 | Obj Coefficient | | | | | | | | | 1 | | | 0.00 | <-- Objective |
| 7 | **Constraints:** | | | | | | | | | | | | | |
| 8 | Profit | | 600 | 700 | 1 | -1 | | | | | | | 3000 | = | 3000 |
| 9 | Wiring Hours | | 2 | 3 | | | 1 | -1 | | | | | 12 | = | 12 |
| 10 | Assembly | | 6 | 5 | | | | | 1 | -1 | | | 30 | = | 30 |
| 11 | Fans | | | 1 | | | | | | | 1 | -1 | 7 | = | 7 |
| 12 | | | | | | | | | | | | | LHS | Sign | RHS |

Solver Parameters ?|X|

Set Target Cell: $L$6
Equal To: ◯ Max ◉ Min ◯ Value of: 0
By Changing Cells:
$B$5:$K$5
Subject to the Constraints:
$D$5 = 0
$F$5 = 0
$L$8:$L$11 = $N$8:$N$11

Solve / Close / Options / Premium / Add / Change

$d_1^-$ and $d_2^-$ set to 0 since $P_1$ and $P_2$ goals are fully satisfied.

**Excel Layout and Solver Entries for Harrison Electric's Goal Programming Problem Considering Only Priority $P_4$ Goals**

$P_4$ goal is to minimize $d_4^-$.

Note that only priority $P_4$ goals are considered.

$P_4$ goal is under-achieved by 1 unit.

| | A | B | C | D | E | F | G | H | I | J | K | L | M | N |
|---|---|---|---|---|---|---|---|---|---|---|---|---|---|---|
| 1 | **Harrison Electric (With Priority $P_4$ Goals Only)** | | | | | | | | | | | | | |
| 3 | | | C | F | $d_1^-$ | $d_1^+$ | $d_2^-$ | $d_2^+$ | $d_3^-$ | $d_3^+$ | $d_4^-$ | $d_4^+$ | | |
| 4 | | | Chand-eliers | Fans | Profit Under Goal | Profit Over Goal | Wiring Under Goal | Wiring Over Goal | Asmbly Under Goal | Asmbly Over Goal | Fans Under Goal | Fans Over Goal | | |
| 5 | Solution value | | 0.00 | 6.00 | 0.00 | 1200.00 | 0.00 | 6.00 | 0.00 | 0.00 | 1.00 | 0.00 | | |
| 6 | Obj Coefficient | | | | | | | | | | 1 | | 1.00 | <-- Objective |
| 7 | **Constraints:** | | | | | | | | | | | | | |
| 8 | Profit | | 600 | 700 | 1 | -1 | | | | | | | 3000 | = | 3000 |
| 9 | Wiring Hours | | 2 | 3 | | | 1 | -1 | | | | | 12 | = | 12 |
| 10 | Assembly | | 6 | 5 | | | | | 1 | -1 | | | 30 | = | 30 |
| 11 | Fans | | | 1 | | | | | | | 1 | -1 | 7 | = | 7 |
| 12 | | | | | | | | | | | | | LHS | Sign | RHS |

Solver Parameters ?|X|

Set Target Cell: $L$6
Equal To: ◯ Max ◉ Min ◯ Value of: 0
By Changing Cells:
$B$5:$K$5
Subject to the Constraints:
$D$5 = 0
$F$5 = 0
$I$5 = 0
$L$8:$L$11 = $N$8:$N$11

Solve / Close / Options / Premium / Add / Change / Reset All

$d_1^-$, $d_2^-$, and $d_3^+$ set to 0 since $P_1$, $P_2$, and $P_3$ goals are all fully satisfied.

**IN ACTION**    Goal Programming Model for Prison Expenditures in Virginia

Prisons across the United States are overcrowded, and there is need for immediate expansion of their capacity and replacement or renovation of obsolete facilities. This study demonstrates how goal programming was used on the capital allocation problem faced by the Department of Corrections of Virginia.

The expenditure items considered by the Virginia corrections department included new and renovated maximum, medium, and minimum security facilities; community diversion programs; and personnel increases. The goal programming technique forced all prison projects to be completely accepted or rejected.

Model variables defined the construction, renovation, or establishment of a particular type of correctional facility for a specific location or purpose and indicated the people required by the facilities. The goal constraints fell into five categories: additional inmate capacity created by new and renovated correctional facilities; operating and personnel costs associated with each expenditure item; the impact of facility construction and renovation on imprisonment, sentence length, and early releases and parole; the mix of different facility types required by the system; and the personnel requirements resulting from the various capital expenditures for correctional facilities.

The solution results for Virginia were one new maximum security facility for drug, alcohol, and psychiatric treatment activities; one new minimum security facility for youthful offenders; two new regular minimum security facilities; two new community diversion programs in urban areas, renovation of one existing medium security, and one minimum security facility; 250 new correctional officers; four new administrators; 46 new treatment specialist/counselors; and six new medical personnel.

**Source:** R. Russell, B. Taylor, and A. Keown. *Computer Environmental Urban Systems* 11, 4 (1986): 135–146.

depends on the weights assigned), the prioritized goal approach considers each goal in turn. The optimal values for all higher-order goal deviational variables are explicitly specified while considering LP models with lower-order goals as objective functions.

## 6.6    NONLINEAR PROGRAMMING MODELS

Linear, integer, and goal programming all assume that a problem's objective function and constraints are linear. That means that they cannot contain nonlinear terms such as $X^3$, $1/X$, $\log X$, or $5XY$. Yet, in many real-world situations, the objective function and/or one or more constraints may be nonlinear. In this section, we examine three categories of nonlinear programming (NLP) problems and illustrate how Excel's Solver can often be used to solve such problems.

### Nonlinear Objective Function and Linear Constraints

The Great Western Appliance Company sells two models of toaster ovens, the Microtoaster and the Self-Clean Toaster Oven. Let $M$ and $T$ denote the number of microtoasters and toaster ovens produced, respectively. The firm earns a profit of $28 for each Microtoaster regardless of the number sold. Profits for the Self-Clean model, however, increase as more units are sold because of fixed overhead. Profit on this model can be expressed as $21T + 0.25T^2$. Hence the firm's objective function is nonlinear:

*Here is an example of a nonlinear objective function.*

$$\text{Maximize profit} = 28M + 21T + 0.25T^2$$

Great Western's profit is subject to the following two linear constraints on production capacity and sales time available.

$$
\begin{aligned}
M + \quad T &\leq 1{,}000 \quad &\text{(units of production capacity)} \\
0.5M + 0.4T &\leq 500 \quad &\text{(hours of sales time available)} \\
M, T &\geq 0
\end{aligned}
$$

*Quadratic programming contains squared terms in the objective function.*

When an objective function contains squared terms (such as $0.25T^2$) and the problem's constraints are linear, it is called a *quadratic programming* problem. A number of useful problems in the field of portfolio selection fall into this category. Quadratic programs can be solved by a modified version of the simplex method. Although such work is outside the scope of this textbook, it can be found in sources listed in the Bibliography.

**File: 6-7.xls**

**Using Excel's Solver**  We now illustrate how Excel's Solver can be used to solve NLP problems. Program 6.7A shows the formula view of the Excel layout used for Great Western's NLP model.

There are only two decision variables ($M$ and $T$) in the model. These are denoted by cells B5 and C5, respectively, in Program 6.7A. However, the objective function has a third nonlinear term involving $T^2$. We can include this term in our Excel layout in several different ways. For example, we can directly type the formula for the objective function in the Target Cell (E9); that is, the formula in cell E9 can be written as

$$= 28*B5 + 21*C5 + 0.25*C5^2$$

However, if we wish to be consistent with the Excel layouts we have used in our discussions so far, we can implement this model as follows. We create an entry for every linear or nonlinear term involving $M$ and $T$ that exists in the model. In Great Western's case, we need entries for $M$, $T$, and $T^2$. We have created entries for these variable terms in cells B8, C8, and D8, respectively. For clarity, we have shaded these cells *blue* in this (and all other) NLP models. The formulas for these cells are

| | |
|---|---|
| = B5 | (Entry for $M$ in cell B8) |
| = C5 | (Entry for $T$ in cell C8) |
| = C5^2 | (Entry for $T^2$ in cell D8) |

*SUMPRODUCT function is again used to calculate all constraint LHS values and the objective function value.*

The layout for this model now looks similar to all other Excel layouts we have used so far. Hence, we can use the SUMPRODUCT function to model the objective function as well as the constraint left-hand side (LHS) values. Note, however, that only cells B5 and C5 are the Changing Cells in Solver. The entries in row 8 are simply calculated from the final values in cells B5 and C5.

Program 6.7B shows the Solver entries and solution for Great Western's problem. The optimal solution is to make 1,000 toaster ovens and no microtoasters, for a total profit of $271,000.

---

**PROGRAM 6.7A**

**Formula View of Excel Layout for Great Western Appliance's NLP Problem**

| | A | B | C | D | E | F | G |
|---|---|---|---|---|---|---|---|
| 1 | **Great Western Appliance (Nonlinear Programming)** | | | | | | |
| 2 | | | | | | | |
| 3 | | M | T | | *These are the only changing cells.* | | |
| 4 | | Micro Toaster | Toaster Oven | | | | |
| 5 | Number of units | | | | | | |
| 6 | | | | | | | |
| 7 | | M | T | T² | *These cells are functions of the changing cells (decision variables).* | | |
| 8 | Variable terms | =B5 | =C5 | =C5^2 | | | |
| 9 | Profit | 28 | 21 | 0.25 | =SUMPRODUCT(B9:D9,$B$8:$D$8) | <-- Objective | |
| 10 | **Constraints:** | | | | | | |
| 11 | Capacity | 1 | 1 | | =SUMPRODUCT(B11:D11,$B$8:$D$8) | <= | 1000 |
| 12 | Sales time | 0.5 | 0.4 | | =SUMPRODUCT(B12:D12,$B$8:$D$8) | <= | 500 |
| 13 | | | | | LHS | Sign | RHS |

*The SUMPRODUCT function is used to calculate the objective function and all constraint LHS values.*

**PROGRAM 6.7B**

**Solver Entries and Solution for Great Western Appliance's NLP Problem**

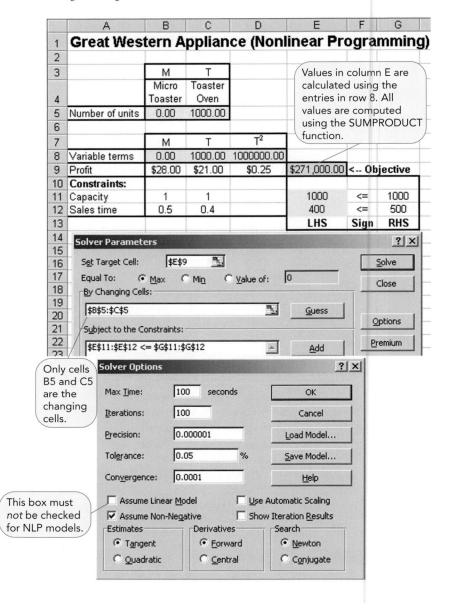

*Assume Linear Model must not be checked in Solver.*

Program 6.7B also shows the options in the standard Solver for solving an NLP problem. Note that the *Assume Linear Model* box is not checked. This is an important issue, since the presence of the $T^2$ term means the model cannot be solved as an LP model (i.e., using the simplex method). For most problems, we can leave all other options at their default values.

The options window in Premium Solver for Education is slightly different, and we illustrate its use in the next example.

## Both Nonlinear Objective Function and Nonlinear Constraints

*An example in which the objective and constraints are both nonlinear.*

The annual profit at a medium-sized (200–400 beds) Hospicare Corporation–owned hospital depends on the number of medical patients admitted (M) and the number of surgical patients admitted (S). The nonlinear objective function for Hospicare is

$$\text{Maximize profit (in \$1,000)} = \$13M + \$6MS + \$5S + \$1/S$$

The corporation identifies three constraints, two of which are also nonlinear, that affect operations:

*An example of two nonlinear constraints*

$$2M^2 + 4S \leq 90 \quad \text{(nursing capacity, in thousands of labor-days)}$$
$$M + S^3 \leq 75 \quad \text{(x-ray capacity, in thousands)}$$
$$8M - 2S \leq 61 \quad \text{(marketing budget required, in thousands of \$)}$$
$$M, S \geq 0$$

**File: 6-8.xls**

To set up Hospicare's problem on Excel and solve it using Solver, we follow the same logic we used in Great Western's problem. Program 6.8 shows the Excel layout and Solver entries for Hospicare's problem. Here again, only cells B5 and C5 are decision variables (i.e., Changing Cells in Solver). In row 8, we have created entries for all terms in the model that are functions of these two decision variables. The relevant formulas are

| | |
|---|---|
| = B5 | (Entry for $M$ in cell B8) |
| = C5 | (Entry for $S$ in cell C8) |
| = B5*C5 | (Entry for $MS$ in cell D8) |
| = 1/C5 | (Entry for $1/S$ in cell E8) |
| = B5^2 | (Entry for $M^2$ in cell F8) |
| = C5^3 | (Entry for $S^3$ in cell G8) |

The rest of the Excel layout is similar to all other layouts we have created so far. To solve this example, however, we have used Premium Solver for Education rather than the standard Solver. Unlike the standard Solver, in which we had to make sure the Assume Linear Model box was not checked, specifying an NLP model is slightly different here.

---

**PROGRAM 6.8**

**Excel Layout and Solver Entries for Hospicare Corporation's NLP Problem**

|  | A | B | C | D | E | F | G | H | I | J |
|---|---|---|---|---|---|---|---|---|---|---|
| 1 | **Hospicare Corp (Nonlinear Programming)** | | | | | | | | | |
| 2 | | | | | | | | | | |
| 3 | | M | S | | | | | | | |
| 4 | | Medical patients | Surgical patients | These are the only two decision variables in the model. | | | | | | |
| 5 | Number of patients (in 1,000's) | 6.066 | 4.100 | | | | | These entries are functions of the Changing Cells. | | |
| 6 | | | | | | | | | | |
| 7 | | M | S | M * S | 1/S | $M^2$ | $S^3$ | | | |
| 8 | Variable terms | 6.066 | 4.100 | 24.873 | 0.244 | 36.799 | 68.934 | | | |
| 9 | Profit (in $1,000) | $13 | $5 | $6 | $1 | | | $248.85 | <-- Objective | |
| 10 | **Constraints:** | | | | | | | | | |
| 11 | Nursing Capacity | | 4 | | | 2 | | 90.00 | <= | 90 |
| 12 | X-ray Capacity | 1 | | | | | 1 | 75.00 | <= | 75 |
| 13 | Marketing Budget | 8 | -2 | | | | | 40.33 | <= | 61 |
| 14 | | | | | | | | **LHS** | **Sign** | **RHS** |

**Solver Parameters**

Set Cell: $H$9

Equal To: ● Max  ○ Min  ○ Value of: 0

By Changing Variable Cells:
$B$5:$C$5

Subject to the Constraints:
$H$11:$H$13 <= $J$11:$J$13

[Solve] [Close] [Guess] [Options] [Add] [Standard]

Standard GRG Nonlinear

The GRG procedure is selected in Premium Solver for Education to handle NLP problems.

Recall from our discussion of LP models that we have always selected Standard Simplex LP as the program Solver should use to solve the model. For NLP models, we should select Standard GRG Nonlinear as the program to use. Program 6.8 shows this selection in the Solver Parameters window.

The optimal solution for Hospicare is to admit 6,066 medical patients and 4,100 surgical patients (note that all values are given in thousands). The total profit earned is $248,850.

## Linear Objective Function and Nonlinear Constraints

Thermolock Corporation produces massive rubber washers and gaskets like the type used to seal joints on the NASA space shuttles. To do so, it combines two ingredients, rubber ($R$) and oil ($O$). The cost of the industrial quality rubber used is $5 per pound and the cost of the high viscosity oil is $7 per pound. Two of the three constraints Thermolock faces are nonlinear. The firm's objective function and constraints are

$$\text{Minimize costs} = \$5R + \$7O$$

subject to

$$3R + 0.25R^2 + 4O + 0.3O^2 \geq 125 \qquad \text{(hardness constraint)}$$
$$13R + R^3 \qquad\qquad\qquad\; \geq 80 \qquad \text{(tensile strength constraint)}$$
$$0.7R + O \qquad\qquad\qquad\; \geq 17 \qquad \text{(elasticity constraint)}$$
$$R, O \qquad\qquad\qquad\qquad \geq 0$$

**File: 6-9.xls**

The Excel layout and Solver entries for Thermolock's problem are shown in Program 6.9. As before, row 8 has entries for all linear and nonlinear terms involving the decision variables in the model. We have used Premium Solver for Education here also to solve the model. Program 6.9 shows that the optimal solution is to use 3.325 pounds of rubber and 14.672 pounds of oil, at a total cost of $119.33.

| PROGRAM 6.9 | **Excel Layout and Solver Entries for Thermolock Gaskets' NLP Problem** |

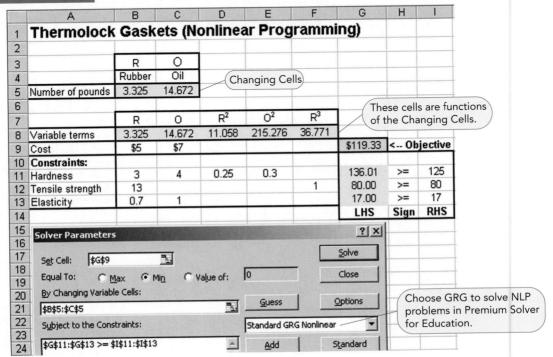

## Computational Procedures for Nonlinear Programming Problems

*We cannot always find an optimal solution to NLP problems.*

We have used Solver to find optimal solutions to all three NLP examples considered in this section. There is, however, no guarantee that computational procedures to solve many NLP problems will yield an optimal solution in a finite number of steps. In addition, there is no general method for solving all NLP problems. Unlike LP problems, NLP problems are inherently harder to solve.

Classical optimization techniques based on calculus can handle some special cases—usually simpler types of problems. Solver uses the *generalized reduced gradient* (GRG) method, sometimes called the steepest ascent (or descent) method. This is an iterative procedure that moves from one feasible solution to the next in improving the value of the objective function. As demonstrated in our discussion, the GRG method can handle problems with both nonlinear constraints and objective function.

But perhaps the best way to deal with nonlinear problems is to try to reduce them into a form that is linear or almost linear. One such approach, called *separable programming*, deals with a class of problems in which the objective and constraints are approximated by linear functions. In this way, the powerful procedures (such as the simplex algorithm) for solving LP problems can again be applied.

In general, however, work in the area of NLP is the least charted and most difficult of all the decision models.

## SUMMARY

This chapter addresses three special types of LP problems. The first, integer programming, examines LP problems that cannot have fractional answers. We note that there are three types of integer programming problems: (1) pure or all-integer programs, (2) mixed problems, in which some solution variables need not be integer, and (3) 0–1 problems, in which some or all variables have values of either 0 or 1. We illustrate how all these models can be set up on Excel and solved using Solver.

The second special type of LP problem studied is goal programming. This extension of LP allows problems to have multiple objective functions, each with its own goal. We show how to model such problems using weighted goals as well as ranked goals. In either case, we use Excel's Solver to obtain optimal solutions.

Finally, we introduce the advanced topic of NLP as a special mathematical programming problem. Excel's Solver can be a useful tool in solving simple NLP models.

## GLOSSARY

**Branch-and-Bound (B&B) Method.** An algorithm used by Solver to solve IP problems. It divides the set of feasible solutions into subregions that are examined systematically.

**Deviational Variables.** Terms that are minimized in a goal programming problem. They are the only terms in the objective function.

**Fixed-Charge Problem.** Problem in which there is a fixed cost in addition to variable costs. Fixed costs need to be modeled using binary (or 0–1) variables.

**General Integer Variables.** Decision variables that are required to be integer valued. Actual value of these variables is restricted only by the constraints in the problem.

**Goal Programming.** A mathematical programming technique that permits decision makers to set and prioritize multiple objective functions.

**GRG Procedure.** Generalized reduced gradient procedure used by Solver to solve NLP problems.

**Integer Programming.** A mathematical programming technique that produces integer solutions to LP problems.

**Mixed Integer Programming.** Problems in which some decision variables must have integer values (either general integer or binary) and other decision variables can have fractional values.

**Nonlinear Programming.** A category of mathematical programming techniques that allow the objective function and/or constraints to be nonlinear.

**Ranked Goals.** Approach in which one ranks goals based on their relative importance to the decision maker. Lower-order goals are considered only after higher-order goals have been optimized. Also known as *prioritized goals*.

**Satisficing.** The process of coming as close as possible to reaching your set of objectives.

**Weighted Goals.** Approach in which one assigns weights to deviational variables based on their relative importance to the decision maker.

**Zero-One Variables.** Decision variables that are required to have integer values of either 0 or 1. Also called *binary variables*.

## KEY EQUATION

(6-1)  Net flow = (Total flow *in* to node) − (Total flow *out* of node)

Flow balance constraint written for each node in network-flow problems.

## SOLVED PROBLEMS

### Solved Problem 6-1

Consider the 0–1 integer programming problem that follows:

$$\text{maximize} \quad 50X_1 + 45X_2 + 48X_3$$

subject to

$$19X_1 + 27X_2 + 34X_3 \leq 80$$

$$22X_1 + 13X_2 + 12X_3 \leq 40$$

$$X_1, X_2, X_3 \text{ must be either 0 or 1}$$

Now reformulate this problem with additional constraints so that no more than two of the three variables can take on a value equal to 1 in the solution. Further, make sure that if $X_1 = 1$, then $X_2 = 1$ also, and vice versa. Then solve the new problem using Excel.

**PROGRAM 6.10**

**Excel Layout and Solver Entries for Solved Problem 6-1**

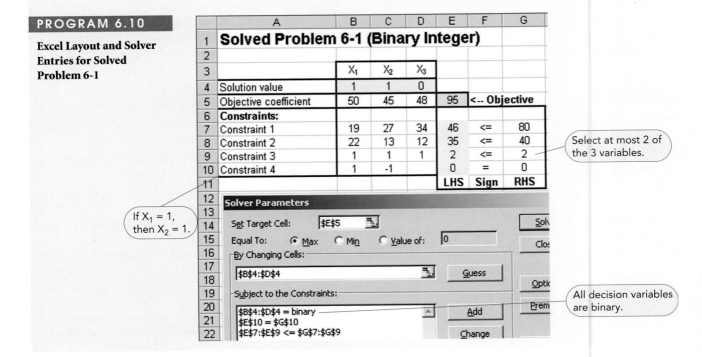

### Solution

We need two new constraints to handle the reformulated problem:

$$X_1 + X_2 + X_3 \leq 2$$

and

$$X_1 - X_2 = 0$$

**File: 6-10.xls**

The Excel layout and Solver entries for this problem are shown in Program 6.10. The optimal solution is $X_1 = 1, X_2 = 1, X_3 = 0$, with an objective value of 95.

## Solved Problem 6-2

Recall the Harrison Electric Company goal programming problem discussed in Section 6.5. Its LP formulation is

$$\text{maximize profit} = \$600C + \$700F$$

subject to

$$
\begin{aligned}
2C + 3F &\leq 12 \quad \text{(wiring hours)}\\
6C + 5F &\leq 30 \quad \text{(assembly hours)}\\
C, F &\quad \geq 0
\end{aligned}
$$

where

$$C = \text{number of chandeliers produced}$$

$$F = \text{number of ceiling fans produced}$$

Reformulate Harrison Electrical as a goal programming model with the following goals:

*Priority 1:* Produce at least 4 chandeliers and 3 ceiling fans.

*Priority 2:* Limit overtime in the assembly department to 10 hours and in the wiring department to 6 hours.

*Priority 3:* Maximize profit.

### Solution

The goal programming problem can be formulated as follows:

$$\text{minimize} = P_1(d_1^- + d_2^-) + P_2(d_3^+ + d_4^+) + P_3(d_5^-)$$

subject to

$$
\begin{aligned}
C + \phantom{xx} d_1^- - d_1^+ &= 4 \\
F + d_2^- - d_2^+ &= 3
\end{aligned}
\Bigg\} Priority\ 1
$$

$$
\begin{aligned}
2C + \phantom{x} 3F + d_3^- - d_3^+ &= 18 \\
6C + \phantom{x} 5F + d_4^- - d_4^+ &= 40
\end{aligned}
\Bigg\} Priority\ 2
$$

$$600C + 700F + d_5^- - d_5^+ = 99{,}999\} \; Priority\ 3$$

$$C, F, \text{ all } d_i \geq 0$$

The target of 99,999 for the priority 3 goal constraint represents an unrealistically high profit. It is just a mathematical trick to use as a target so that we can get as close as possible to the maximum profit.

Note that with regard to the first goal, we must minimize only the underachievement deviational variables $d_1^-$ and $d_2^-$. Likewise, for the priority 2 goal, we must minimize only the overachievement deviational variables $d_3^+$ and $d_4^+$. Finally, for the priority 3 goal, we must minimize only the underachievement deviational variables $d_5^-$.

Programs 6.11A, 6.11B, and 6.11C, respectively, show the Excel layout and Solver entries for this problem when each goal is considered in order of its priority. In each case, optimal values of the deviational

**File: 6-11.xls**

**PROGRAM 6.11A**   Excel Layout and Solver Entries for Solved Problem 6-2 Considering Only Priority $P_1$ Goals

$P_1$ goals are to minimize $d_1^- + d_2^-$.

| | C | F | $d_1^-$ | $d_1^+$ | $d_2^-$ | $d_2^+$ | $d_3^-$ | $d_3^+$ | $d_4^-$ | $d_4^+$ | $d_5^-$ | $d_5^+$ | | | |
|---|---|---|---|---|---|---|---|---|---|---|---|---|---|---|---|
| | Chand-eliers | Fans | Chand Under Goal | Chand Over Goal | Fans Under Goal | Fans Over Goal | Wiring Under Goal | Wiring Over Goal | Asmbly Under Goal | Asmbly Over Goal | Profit Under Goal | Profit Over Goal | | | |
| Solution value | 4.0 | 139.4 | 0.0 | 0.0 | 0.0 | 136.4 | 0.0 | 408.3 | 0.0 | 681.1 | 0.0 | 0.0 | 0.00 | | <-- Objective |
| Obj Coeff | | | 1 | | 1 | | | | | | | | | | |
| Constraints: | | | | | | | | | | | | | | | |
| Chandeliers | 1 | | 1 | -1 | | | | | | | | | 4 | = | 4 |
| Fans | | 1 | | | 1 | -1 | | | | | | | 3 | = | 3 |
| Wiring | 2 | 3 | | | | | 1 | -1 | | | | | 18 | = | 18 |
| Assembly | 6 | 5 | | | | | | | 1 | -1 | | | 40 | = | 40 |
| Profit | 600 | 700 | | | | | | | | | 1 | -1 | 99999 | = | 99999 |
| | | | | | | | | | | | | | LHS | Sign | RHS |

$P_1$ goals are fully satisfied.

**Solver Parameters**

Set Target Cell: $N$6

Equal To:  ○ Max  ⦿ Min  ○ Value of: 0

By Changing Cells:  $B$5:$M$5

Subject to the Constraints:  $N$8:$N$12 = $P$8:$P$12

[Solve] [Close] [Options] [Premium] [Add]

All goals are expressed as "=" constraints using the deviational variables.

Note the artificially high goal for profit.

Decision variables include all deviational variables in addition to C and F.

**PROGRAM 6.11B**   Excel Layout and Solver Entries for Solved Problem 6-2 Considering Only Priority $P_2$ Goals

$P_2$ goals are to minimize $d_3^+ + d_4^+$.

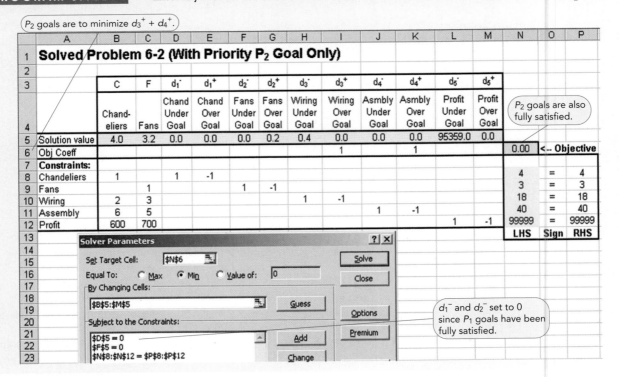

| | C | F | $d_1^-$ | $d_1^+$ | $d_2^-$ | $d_2^+$ | $d_3^-$ | $d_3^+$ | $d_4^-$ | $d_4^+$ | $d_5^-$ | $d_5^+$ | | | |
|---|---|---|---|---|---|---|---|---|---|---|---|---|---|---|---|
| | Chand-eliers | Fans | Chand Under Goal | Chand Over Goal | Fans Under Goal | Fans Over Goal | Wiring Under Goal | Wiring Over Goal | Asmbly Under Goal | Asmbly Over Goal | Profit Under Goal | Profit Over Goal | | | |
| Solution value | 4.0 | 3.2 | 0.0 | 0.0 | 0.0 | 0.2 | 0.4 | 0.0 | 0.0 | 0.0 | 95359.0 | 0.0 | 0.00 | | <-- Objective |
| Obj Coeff | | | | | | | | 1 | | 1 | | | | | |
| Constraints: | | | | | | | | | | | | | | | |
| Chandeliers | 1 | | 1 | -1 | | | | | | | | | 4 | = | 4 |
| Fans | | 1 | | | 1 | -1 | | | | | | | 3 | = | 3 |
| Wiring | 2 | 3 | | | | | 1 | -1 | | | | | 18 | = | 18 |
| Assembly | 6 | 5 | | | | | | | 1 | -1 | | | 40 | = | 40 |
| Profit | 600 | 700 | | | | | | | | | 1 | -1 | 99999 | = | 99999 |
| | | | | | | | | | | | | | LHS | Sign | RHS |

$P_2$ goals are also fully satisfied.

**Solver Parameters**

Set Target Cell: $N$6

Equal To:  ○ Max  ⦿ Min  ○ Value of: 0

By Changing Cells:  $B$5:$M$5

Subject to the Constraints:  $D$5 = 0 ; $F$5 = 0 ; $N$8:$N$12 = $P$8:$P$12

[Solve] [Close] [Options] [Premium] [Add] [Change]

$d_1^-$ and $d_2^-$ set to 0 since $P_1$ goals have been fully satisfied.

variables for a higher-order goal are explicitly specified while solving the problem for a lower-order goal. For example, while solving the problem with the priority 2 goal (Program 6.11B), the optimal values of the priority 1 deviational variables (namely $d_1^- = 0$ and $d_2^- = 0$) from Program 6.11A are explicitly specified.

The optimal solution shown in Program 6.11A considers only the priority 1 goals. As such, restricting overtime in assembly and wiring is not an issue in this problem. The solution therefore uses a large amount of overtime (note values for $d_3^+$ and $d_4^+$ in Program 6.11A).

However, when we now solve the priority 2 goal problem in Program 6.11B, the solution minimizes the use of excessive overtime. As a consequence, the deviational variable for underachieving profit ($d_5^-$) now has a large value (due to the artificially large value of 99,999 we used as the target).

When we now try to minimize this deviational variable in the next problem (Program 6.11C), we obtain the overall optimal solution for this goal programming problem. The optimal solution is $C = 4$, $F = 3.2$, $d_1^- = 0$, $d_2^- = 0$, $d_3^+ = 0$, $d_4^+ = 0$, and $d_5^- = 95,359$. In effect, this means that the maximum profit we can get while achieving our higher-order goals is only \$4,640 (= \$600 × 4.00 + \$700 × 3.20).

---

**PROGRAM 6.11C**    **Excel Layout and Solver Entries for Solved Problem 6-2 Considering Only Priority $P_3$ Goals**

$P_3$ goal is to minimize $d_5^-$.

| | A | B | C | D | E | F | G | H | I | J | K | L | M | N | O | P |
|---|---|---|---|---|---|---|---|---|---|---|---|---|---|---|---|---|
| 1 | **Solved Problem 6-2 (With Priority $P_3$ Goal Only)** | | | | | | | | | | | | | | | |
| 2 | | | | | | | | | | | | | | | | |
| 3 | | | C | F | $d_1^-$ | $d_1^+$ | $d_2^-$ | $d_2^+$ | $d_3^-$ | $d_3^+$ | $d_4^-$ | $d_4^+$ | $d_5^-$ | $d_5^+$ | | | |
| 4 | | | Chand-eliers | Fans | Chand Under Goal | Chand Over Goal | Fans Under Goal | Fans Over Goal | Wiring Under Goal | Wiring Over Goal | Asmbly Under Goal | Asmbly Over Goal | Profit Under Goal | Profit Over Goal | $P_3$ goal is under-achieved. | | |
| 5 | Solution value | | 4.0 | 3.2 | 0.0 | 0.0 | 0.0 | 0.2 | 0.4 | 0.0 | 0.0 | 0.0 | 95359.0 | 0.0 | | | |
| 6 | Obj Coeff | | | | | | | | | | | | 1 | | 95,359.00 | <-- Objective | |
| 7 | **Constraints:** | | | | | | | | | | | | | | | | |
| 8 | Chandeliers | | 1 | | 1 | -1 | | | | | | | | | 4 | = | 4 |
| 9 | Fans | | | 1 | | | 1 | -1 | | | | | | | 3 | = | 3 |
| 10 | Wiring | | 2 | 3 | | | | | 1 | -1 | | | | | 18 | = | 18 |
| 11 | Assembly | | 6 | 5 | | | | | | | 1 | -1 | | | 40 | = | 40 |
| 12 | Profit | | 600 | 700 | | | | | | | | | 1 | -1 | 99999 | = | 99999 |
| 13 | | | | | | | | | | | | | | | LHS | Sign | RHS |

**Solver Parameters**    ? X

Set Target Cell:    $N$6

Equal To:    ◯ Max    ◉ Min    ◯ Value of:    0

By Changing Cells:

$B$5:$M$5

Subject to the Constraints:

$D$5 = 0
$F$5 = 0
$I$5 = 0
$K$5 = 0
$N$8:$N$12 = $P$8:$P$12

[Solve]  [Close]  [Guess]  [Options]  [Premium]  [Add]  [Change]  [Reset All]  [Delete]

$d_1^-$, $d_2^-$, $d_3^+$, and $d_4^+$ set to 0 since $P_1$ and $P_2$ goals are fully achieved.

## ⇒ SELF-TEST

- ■ Before taking the self-test, refer back to the learning objectives at the beginning of the chapter, the notes in the margins, and the glossary at the end of the chapter.
- ■ Use the key at the back of the book to correct your answers.
- ■ Restudy pages that correspond to any questions that you answered incorrectly or material you feel uncertain about.

1. If all of the decision variables require integer solutions, the problem is
   a. a pure IP type of problem.
   b. a simplex method type of problem.
   c. a mixed IP type of problem.
   d. a Gorsky type of problem.

2. The fixed charge problem is an example of a(n)
   a. goal programming problem.
   b. NLP problem.
   c. mixed IP problem.
   d. pure IP problem.

3. In a mixed IP problem
   a. some integers must be even and others must be odd.
   b. some decision variables must require integer results only and some variables must allow for continuous results.
   c. different objectives are mixed together even though they sometimes have relative priorities established.

4. The branch-and-bound method is used by Solver to solve
   a. LP problems.
   b. goal programming problems.
   c. NLP problems.
   d. IP problems.

5. A model containing a linear objective function and linear constraints but requiring that one or more of the decision variables take on an integer value in the final solution is called
   a. an IP problem.
   b. a goal programming problem.
   c. an NLP problem.
   d. a multiple objective LP problem.

6. An IP solution can never produce a greater profit than the LP solution to the same problem.
   a. True                         b. False

7. In goal programming if all the goals are achieved, the value of the objective function will always be zero.
   a. True                         b. False

8. The quantities that are maximized in a goal programming problem are termed deviational variables.
   a. True                         b. False

9. Nobel laureate Herbert A. Simon of Carnegie-Mellon University says that modern managers should always optimize, not satisfice.
   a. True                         b. False

10. The weighted goal approach to setting up and solving a goal programming problem reduces it to a simple LP problem.
    a. True                         b. False

11. The 0–1 integer programming problem
    a. requires the decision variables to have values of 0 or 1.
    b. requires that the constraints all have RHS values of 0 or 1.
    c. requires that the decision variables have coefficients of 0 or 1.
    d. includes the transportation type of problems.

12. Goal programming
    a. requires only that you know whether the goal is direct profit maximization or cost minimization.
    b. allows you to have multiple goals, with or without priorities.
    c. is an algorithm with the goal of a quicker solution to a pure integer programming problem.
    d. is an algorithm with the goal of a quicker solution to a mixed IP problem.

13. Nonlinear programming includes problems
    a. in which the objective function is linear but some constraints are not linear.
    b. in which the constraints are linear but the objective function is not linear.
    c. in which both the objective function and all of the constraints are not linear.
    d. solvable by quadratic programming.
    e. all of the above.

## DISCUSSION QUESTIONS AND PROBLEMS

### Discussion Questions

6-1  Compare the similarities and differences of linear and goal programming.

6-2  Provide your own examples of five applications of IP.

6-3  What is the difference between the three types of IP problems? Which do you think is most common, and why?

6-4  What is meant by "satisficing," and why is the term often used in conjunction with goal programming?

6-5  What are deviational variables? How do they differ from decision variables in traditional LP problems.

6-6  If you were the president of the college you are attending and were employing goal programming to assist in decision making, what might your goals be? What kinds of constraints would you include in your model?

**6-7** What does it mean to rank goals in goal programming? How does this affect the problem's solution?

**6-8** Provide your own examples of problems where (a) the objective is nonlinear and (b) one or more constraints are nonlinear.

**6-9** Explain in your own words why IP problems are more difficult to solve than LP models.

**6-10** Explain the difference between assigning weights to goals and ranking goals.

**6-11** What does the term *quadratic programming* mean?

**6-12** Which of the following are nonlinear programming problems, and why?

(a) maximize profit $= 3X_1 + 5X_2 + 99X_3$
subject to  $X_1 \geq 10$
$X_2 \leq 5$
$X_3 \geq 18$

(b) minimize cost $= 25X_1 + 30X_2 + 8X_1X_2$
subject to  $X_1 \qquad \geq 8$
$X_1 + X_2 \geq 12$
$0.0005X_1 - X_2 = 11$

(c) minimize $Z = P_1d_1^- + P_2d_2^+ + P_3d_3^+$
subject to  $X_1 + X_2 + d_1^- - d_1^+ = 300$
$X_2 + d_2^- - d_2^+ = 200$
$X_1 + \qquad d_3^- - d_3^+ = 100$

(d) maximize profit $= 3X_1 + 4X_2$
subject to  $X_1^2 - 5X_2 \geq 8$
$3X_1 + 4X_2 \geq 12$

(e) minimize cost $= 18X_1 + 5X_2 + X_2^2$
subject to  $4X_1 - 3X_2 \geq 8$
$X_1 + X_2 \geq 18$

Are any of these quadratic programming problems?

## Problems

⋮ **6-13** Student Enterprises sells two sizes of wall posters, a large 3- by 4-foot poster and a smaller 2- by 3-foot poster. The profit earned from the sale of each large poster is $3; each smaller poster earns $2. The firm, although profitable, is not large; it consists of one art student, Jan Meising, at the University of Kentucky. Because of her classroom schedule, Jan has the following weekly constraints: (1) up to three large posters can be sold, (2) up to five smaller posters can be sold, (3) up to 10 hours can be spent on posters during the week, with each large poster requiring 2 hours of work and each small one taking 1 hour. With the semester almost over, Jan plans on taking a three-month summer vacation to England and doesn't want to leave any unfinished posters behind. Find, using Excel, the integer solution that will maximize her profit.

• **6-14** An airline owns an aging fleet of Boeing 727 jet airplanes. It is considering a major purchase of up to 17 new Boeing model 787 and 797 jets. The decision must take into account numerous cost and capability fac-

tors, including the following: (1) the airline can finance up to $400 million in purchases; (2) each Boeing 787 will cost $35 million, and each Boeing 797 will cost $22 million; (3) at least one-third of the planes purchased should be the longer-range 787; (4) the annual maintenance budget is to be no more than $8 million; (5) the annual maintenance cost per 787 is estimated to be $800,000, and it is $500,000 for each 797 purchased; and (6) each 787 can carry 125,000 passengers per year, and each 797 can fly 81,000 passengers annually. Formulate this as an IP problem to maximize the annual passenger-carrying capability. What category of IP problem is this? Solve using Excel.

• **6-15** Innis Construction Company specializes in building moderately priced homes in the Cincinnati, Ohio area. Tom Innis has identified eight potential locations to construct new single-family dwellings, but he cannot put up homes on all of the sites because he has only $300,000 to invest in all projects. The accompanying table shows the cost of constructing homes in each area and the expected profit to be made from the sale of each home. Note that the home-building costs differ considerably due to lot costs, site preparation, and differences in the models to be built. Note also that a fraction of a home cannot be built.

| LOCATION | COST OF BUILDING AT THIS SITE ($) | EXPECTED PROFIT ($) |
|---|---|---|
| Clifton | 60,000 | 5,000 |
| Mt. Auburn | 50,000 | 6,000 |
| Mt. Adams | 82,000 | 10,000 |
| Amberly | 103,000 | 12,000 |
| Norwood | 50,000 | 8,000 |
| Covington | 41,000 | 3,000 |
| Roselawn | 80,000 | 9,000 |
| Eden Park | 69,000 | 10,000 |

(a) Formulate Innis's problem using 0–1 IP.
(b) Solve with Excel.

⋮ **6-16** Stockbroker Susan Shader has made the following recommendations to her client:

| TYPE OF INVESTMENT | COST ($) | EXPECTED RETURN ($) |
|---|---|---|
| Hanover municipal bonds | 500 | 50 |
| Hamilton city bonds | 1,000 | 100 |
| S.E. Power & Light Co. | 350 | 30 |
| Nebraska Electric Service | 490 | 45 |
| Southern Gas and Electric | 700 | 65 |
| Samuels Products Co. | 270 | 20 |
| Nation Builder Paint Co. | 800 | 90 |
| Hammer Head Hotels Co. | 400 | 35 |

The client agrees to this list but provides several conditions: (1) no more than $3,000 can be invested, (2) the money is to be spread among at least five investments, (3) no more than one type of bond can be purchased, and (4) at least two utility stocks and at least two regular stocks must be purchased. Formulate this as a 0–1 IP problem for Ms. Shader to maximize expected return. Solve using Excel.

**6-17** The following IP problem has been developed to help First National Bank decide where, out of 10 possible sites, to locate four new branch offices:

maximize expected returns = $120X_1 + 100X_2 + 110X_3 + 140X_4$
(in thousands) $+ 155X_5 + 128X_6 + 145X_7 + 190X_8$
$+ 170X_9 + 150X_{10}$

subject to

$20X_1 + 30X_2 + 20X_3 + 25X_4 + 30X_5 + 30X_6 + 25X_7 + 20X_8 + 25X_9 + 30X_{10} \leq 110$

$15X_1 + 5X_2 + 20X_3 + 20X_4 + 5X_5 + 5X_6 + 10X_7 + 20X_8 + 5X_9 + 20X_{10} \leq 50$

$X_2 + X_6 + X_7 + X_9 + X_{10} \leq 3$

$X_2 + X_3 + X_5 + X_8 + X_9 \geq 2$

$X_1 + X_3 + X_{10} \geq 1$

$\Sigma X_i \leq 4$

all $X_i = 0$ or $1$

where $X_i$ represents Winter Park, Maitland, Osceola, Downtown, South Orlando, Airport, Winter Garden, Apopka, Lake Mary, Cocoa Beach for $i$ equals 1 to 10, respectively.

(a) Where should the four new sites be located, and what will be the expected return?

(b) If at least one new branch *must* be opened in Maitland or Osceola, will this change the answers? Add the new constraint and rerun.

(c) The expected return at Apopka was overestimated. The correct value is $160,000 per year (i.e., 160). Using the original assumptions (i.e., ignoring (b)), does your answer to part (a) change?

**6-18** Geraldine Shawhan is president of Shawhan File Works, a firm that manufactures two types of metal file cabinets. The demand for her two-drawer model is up to 600 cabinets per week; demand for a three-drawer cabinet is limited to 400 per week. Shawhan File Works has a weekly operating capacity of 1,300 hours, with the two-drawer cabinet taking 1 hour to produce and the three-drawer cabinet requiring 2 hours. Each two-drawer model sold yields a $10 profit, and the profit for the large model is $15. Shawhan has listed the following goals in *order of importance*:

1. Attain a profit as close to $11,000 as possible each week.

2. Avoid underutilization of the firm's production capacity.

3. Sell as many two and three-drawer cabinets as the demand indicates.

Set this up as a goal programming problem.

**6-19** Solve Problem 6-18 using Excel. Are any goals unachieved in this solution? Explain.

**6-20** Harris Segal, marketing director for North-Central Power and Light is about to begin an advertising campaign promoting energy conservation. In trying to budget between television and newspaper advertisements, he sets the following goals and assigns the weights shown.

1. The total advertising budget of $120,000 should not be exceeded. Weight = 100

2. There should be a mix of TV and newspaper ads, with at least 10 TV spots (costing $5,000 each) and at least 20 newspaper ads (costing $2,000 each). Weight = 75 each.

3. The total number of people to read or hear the advertisements should be at least 9 million. Weight = 40 per 100,000 people.

Each television spot reaches approximately 300,000 people. A newspaper advertisement is read by about 150,000 persons. Formulate Segal's goal programming problem to find out how many of each type of ad to place.

**6-21** Solve Problem 6-20 using Excel. How many people, in total, will read or hear the advertisements?

**6-22** Hilliard Electronics produces specially coded computer chips for laser surgery in 64MB, 256MB, and 512MB sizes. (1MB means that the chip holds 1 million bytes of information.) To produce a 64MB chip requires 8 hours of labor, a 256MB chip takes 13 hours, and a 512MB chip requires 16 hours. Hilliard's monthly production capacity is 1,200 hours. Mr. Blank, the firm's sales manager, estimates that the maximum monthly sales of the 64MB, 256MB, and 512MB chips are 40, 50, and 60, respectively. The company has the following goals (ranked in order from most important to least important):

1. Fill an order from the best customer for thirty 64MB chips and thirty-five 256MB chips.

2. Provide sufficient chips to at least equal the sales estimates set by Mr. Blank.

3. Avoid underutilization of the production capacity.

Formulate this problem using goal programming. Solve using Excel.

**6-23** An Oklahoma manufacturer produces two products: speaker telephones ($X_1$) and pushbutton telephones ($X_2$). The following goal programming model has been formulated to find the number of each to produce each day to meet this firm's goals:

minimize $P_1 d_1^- + P_2 d_2^- + P_3 d_3^+ + P_4 d_1^+$

subject to

$2X_1 + 4X_2 + d_1^- - d_1^+ = 80$

$8X_1 + 10X_2 + d_2^- - d_2^+ = 320$

$8X_1 + 6X_2 + d_3^- - d_3^+ = 240$

all $X_i, d_i \geq 0$

Solve this problem using Excel.

**6-24** Major Bill Bligh, director of the Army War College's new six-month attaché training program, is concerned about how the 20 officers taking the course spend their precious time while in his charge. Major Bligh recognizes that there are 168 hours per week and thinks that his students have been using them rather inefficiently. Bligh lets

$X_1$ = number of hours of sleep needed per week

$X_2$ = number of personal hours (eating, personal hygiene, handling laundry, and so on)

$X_3$ = number of hours of class and studying

$X_4$ = number of hours of social time off base (dating, sports, family visits, and so on)

He thinks that students should study 30 hours a week to have time to absorb material. This is his most important goal. Bligh feels that students need at most 7 hours sleep per night on average and that this goal is number 2. He believes that goal number 3 is to provide at least 20 hours per week of social time.

(a) Formulate this as a goal programming problem.
(b) Solve this problem using Excel.

**6-25** Set up and solve the following NLP problem on Excel:

Maximize     $20X_1 + 40X_2 + 31X_3$

subject to

$$X_1 + X_2 + X_3 \leq 15$$

$$X_1^2 + X_2^2 \quad\;\; \leq 49$$

$$2X_1 + \quad\;\; X_3^3 \leq 53$$

$$X_1, X_2, X_3 \geq 0$$

**6-26** Set up and solve the following nonlinear programming problem on Excel:

Maximize     $4X_1 + 2X_2 - 3X_3 + 2X_1X_2 + 8X_3^3$

subject to

$$2X_1 + 4X_2 + 3X_3 \geq 29$$

$$3X_1 + X_2 \qquad\;\; \geq 14$$

$$X_1 + X_2 + X_3 \leq 10$$

$$X_1, X_2, X_3 \geq 0$$

**6-27** Hinkel Rotary Engine, Ltd. produces four- and six-cylinder models of automobile engines. The firm's profit for each four-cylinder engine sold during its quarterly production cycle is $1,800 − $50X_1$, where $X_1$ is the number sold. Hinkel makes $2,400 − $70X_2$ for each of the larger engines sold, with $X_2$ equal to the number of six-cylinder engines sold. There are 5,000 hours of production time available during each production cycle. A four-cylinder engine requires 100 hours of production time, whereas six-cylinder engines take 130 hours to manufacture. Formulate this production problem for Hinkel. Solve using Excel.

**6-28** Motorcross of Wisconsin produces two models of snowmobiles, the XJ6 and the XJ8. In any given production-planning week Motorcross has 40 hours available in its final testing bay. Each XJ6 requires 1 hour to test and each XJ8 takes 2 hours. The revenue (in $1,000s) for the firm is nonlinear and is stated as (no. of XJ6s)(4 − 0.1 no. of XJ6s) + (no. of XJ8s)(5 − 0.2 no. of XJ8s).

(a) Formulate this problem.
(b) Solve using Excel.

## ⇒ CASE STUDY

### Schank Marketing Research

Schank Marketing Research has just signed contracts to conduct studies for four clients. At present, three project managers are free for assignment to the tasks. Although all are capable of handling each assignment, the times and costs to complete the studies depend on the experience and knowledge of each manager. Using his judgment, John Schank, the president, has been able to establish a cost for each possible assignment. These costs, which are really the salaries each manager would draw on each task, are summarized in the following table.

Schank is very hesitant about neglecting NASA, which has been an important customer in the past. (NASA has employed the firm to study the public's attitude toward the Space Shuttle and proposed Space Station). In addition, Schank has promised to try

to provide Ruth a salary of at least $3,000 on his next assignment. From previous contracts, Schank also knows that Gardener does not get along well with the management at CBT Television, so he hopes to avoid assigning her to CBT. Finally, as Hines Corporation is also an old and valued client, Schank feels that it is twice as important to assign a project manager immediately to Hines's task as it is to provide one to General Foundry, a brand-new client. Schank wants to minimize the total costs of all projects while considering each of these goals. He feels that all of these goals are important, but if he had to rank them, he would put his concern about NASA first, his worry about Gardener second, his need to keep Hines Corporation happy third, his promise to Ruth fourth, and his concern about minimizing all costs last.

Each project manager can handle, at most, one new client.

## Discussion Questions

1. If Schank were not concerned about noncost goals, how would he formulate this problem so that it could be solved quantitatively?

2. Develop a formulation that will incorporate all five objectives.

3. Solve using Excel.

| | CLIENT | | | |
|---|---|---|---|---|
| PROJECT MANAGER | HINES CORP. | NASA | GENERAL FOUNDRY | CBT TELEVISION |
| Gardener | $3,200 | $3,000 | $2,800 | $2,900 |
| Ruth | 2,700 | 3,200 | 3,000 | 3,100 |
| Hardgraves | 1,900 | 2,100 | 3,300 | 2,100 |

# ⏭ CASE STUDY

## Oakton River Bridge

The Oakton River had long been considered an impediment to the development of a certain medium-sized metropolitan area in the southeast. Lying to the east of the city, the river made it difficult for people living on its eastern bank to commute to jobs in and around the city and to take advantage of the shopping and cultural attractions that the city had to offer. Similarly, the river inhibited those on its western bank from access to the ocean resorts lying one hour to the east. The bridge over the Oakton River had been built prior to World War II and was grossly inadequate to handle the existing traffic, much less the increased traffic that would accompany the forecasted growth in the area. A congressional delegation from the state prevailed upon the federal government to fund a major portion of a new toll bridge over the Oakton River, and the state legislature appropriated the rest of the needed monies for the project.

Progress in construction of the bridge has been in accordance with what was anticipated at the start of construction. The state highway commission, which will have operational jurisdiction over the bridge, has concluded that opening of the bridge for traffic is likely to take place at the beginning of the next summer, as scheduled. A personnel task force has been established to recruit, train, and schedule the workers needed to operate the toll facility.

The personnel task force is well aware of the budgetary problems facing the state. They have taken as part of their mandate the requirement that personnel costs be kept as low as possible. One particular area of concern is the number of toll collectors that will be needed. The bridge is scheduling three shifts of collectors: shift A from midnight to 8 A.M., shift B from 8 A.M. to 4 P.M., and shift C from 4 P.M. to midnight. Recently, the state employees union negotiated a contract with the state that requires that all toll collectors be permanent, full-time employees. In addition, all collectors must work a five-on, two-off schedule on the same shift. Thus, for example, a worker could be assigned to work Tuesday, Wednesday, Thursday, Friday, and Saturday on shift A, followed by Sunday and Monday off. An employee could not be scheduled to work, say, Tuesday on shift A followed by Wednesday, Thursday, Friday, and Saturday on shift B or on any other mixture of shifts during a five-day block. The employees would choose their assignments in order of their seniority.

The task force has received projections of traffic flow on the bridge by day and hour. These projections are based on extrapolations of existing traffic patterns—the pattern of commuting, shopping, and beach traffic currently experienced with growth projections factored in. Standards data from other state-operated toll facilities have allowed the task force to convert these traffic flows into toll collector requirements, that is, the minimum number of collectors required per shift, per day, to handle the anticipated traffic load. These toll collector requirements are summarized in the following table:

**Minimum Number of Toll Collectors Required Per Shift**

| SHIFT | SUN. | MON. | TUE. | WED. | THU. | FRI. | SAT. |
|---|---|---|---|---|---|---|---|
| A | 8 | 13 | 12 | 12 | 13 | 13 | 15 |
| B | 10 | 10 | 10 | 10 | 10 | 13 | 15 |
| C | 15 | 13 | 13 | 12 | 12 | 13 | 8 |

The numbers in the table include one or two extra collectors per shift to fill in for collectors who call in sick and to provide relief for collectors on their scheduled breaks. Note that each of the eight collectors needed for shift A on Sunday, for example, could have come from any of the A shifts scheduled to begin on Wednesday, Thursday, Friday, Saturday, or Sunday.

## Discussion Questions

1. Determine the minimum number of toll collectors that would have to be hired to meet the requirements expressed in the table.

2. The union had indicated that it might lift its opposition to the mixing of shifts in a five-day block in exchange for additional compensation and benefits. By how much could the numbers of toll collectors required be reduced if this is done?

*Source:* B. Render, R. M. Stair, and I. Greenberg. *Cases and Readings in Management Science,* 2/e. 1990, pp. 55–56. Reprinted by permission of Prentice Hall, Upper Saddle River, New Jersey.

# ⟱➡ CASE STUDY

## Puyallup Mall

Jane Rodney, president of the Rodney Development Company, was trying to decide what types of stores to include in her new shopping center at Puyallup Mall. She had already contracted for a supermarket, a drugstore, and a few other stores that she considered essential. However, she had available an additional 16,000 square feet of floor space yet to allocate. She drew up a list of the 15 types of stores she might consider (see Table 6.5) including the floor space required by each. Rodney did not think she would have any trouble finding occupants for any type of store.

The lease agreements Rodney used in her developments included two types of payment. The store had to pay a certain annual rent, depending on the size and type of store. In addition, Rodney was to receive a small percentage of the store's sales if the sales exceeded a specified minimum amount. The amount of annual rent from each store is shown in the second column of the table. To estimate the profitability of each type of store,

Rodney calculated the present value of all future rent and sales percentage payments. These are given in the third column. Rodney wants to achieve the highest total *present value* over the set of stores she selects. However, she could not simply pick those stores with the highest present values, for there were several restrictions. The first, of course, was that she has available only 16,000 square feet.

In addition, a condition on the financing of the project required that the total annual rent should be at least as much as the annual fixed costs (taxes, management fees, debt service, and so forth). These annual costs were $130,000 for this part of the project. Finally, the total funds available for construction of this part of the project were $700,000, and each type of store required different construction costs depending on the size and type of store (fourth column in the table).

In addition, Rodney had certain requirements in terms of the mix of stores that she considered best. She wanted at least one store from each of the clothing, hardgoods, and miscellaneous

| TABLE 6.5 | | | | |
|---|---|---|---|---|
| **Characteristics of Possible Leases, Puyallup Mall Shopping Center** | | | | |
| TYPE OF STORE | SIZE OF STORE (1000's OF SQ FT) | ANNUAL RENT ($1000's) | PRESENT VALUE ($1000's) | CONSTRUCTION COST ($1000's) |
| Clothing | | | | |
| 1. Men's | 1.0 | $4.4 | $28.1 | $24.6 |
| 2. Women's | 1.6 | 6.1 | 34.6 | 32.0 |
| 3. Variety (both) | 2.0 | 8.3 | 50.0 | 41.4 |
| Restaurants | | | | |
| 4. Fancy restaurant | 3.2 | 24.0 | 162.0 | 124.4 |
| 5. Lunchroom | 1.8 | 19.5 | 77.8 | 64.8 |
| 6. Cocktail lounge | 2.1 | 20.7 | 100.4 | 79.8 |
| 7. Candy and ice cream shop | 1.2 | 7.7 | 45.2 | 38.6 |
| Hardgoods | | | | |
| 8. Hardware store | 2.4 | 19.4 | 80.2 | 66.8 |
| 9. Cutlery and variety | 1.6 | 11.7 | 51.4 | 45.1 |
| 10. Luggage and leather | 2.0 | 15.2 | 62.5 | 54.3 |
| Miscellaneous | | | | |
| 11. Travel agency | 0.6 | 3.9 | 18.0 | 15.0 |
| 12. Tobacco shop | 0.5 | 3.2 | 11.6 | 13.4 |
| 13. Camera store | 1.4 | 11.3 | 50.4 | 42.0 |
| 14. Toys | 2.0 | 16.0 | 73.6 | 63.7 |
| 15. Beauty parlor | 1.0 | 9.6 | 51.2 | 40.0 |

groups, and at least two from the restaurant category. She wanted no more than two from the clothing group. Furthermore, the number of stores in the miscellaneous group should not exceed the total number of stores in the clothing and hardgoods groups combined.

**Discussion Question**

Which tenants should be selected for the mall?

*Source:* Adapted from H. Bierman, C. P. Bonini, and W. H. Hausman. *Quantitative Analysis,* 7/e. (Homewood, IL: Richard D. Irwin, Inc.), pp. 467–468, copyright © 1986.

# BIBLIOGRAPHY

Arntzen, Bruce C. et al. "Global Supply Chain Management at Digital Equipment Corporation," *Interfaces* 25, 1 (January–February 1995): 69–93.

Bertsimas, Dimitris, C. Darnell, and R. Soucy. "Portfolio Construction Through Mixed-Integer Programming at Grantham, Mayo, Van Otterloo and Company," *Interfaces* 29, 1 (January 1999): 49–66.

Bohl, Alan H. "Computer Aided Formulation of Silicon Defoamers for the Paper Industry," *Interfaces* 24, 5 (September–October 1994): 41–48.

Charnes, A. and W. W. Cooper. *Management Models and Industrial Applications of Linear Programming.* New York: Wiley, 1961.

Ignizio, J. P. *Goal Programming and Extensions.* Lexington, MA: D.C. Heath and Company, 1976.

Kuby, Michael et al. "Planning China's Coal and Electricity Delivery System," *Interfaces* 25, 1 (January–February 1995): 41–68.

Montgomery, D. and E. Del Castillo. "A Nonlinear Programming Response to the Dual Response Problem," *Journal of Quality Technology* 25, 3 (1993): 199–204.

Render, B., R. M. Stair, and M. Hanna. *Quantitative Analysis for Management,* 8/e. Upper Saddle River, NJ: Prentice Hall, 2003.

Stowe, J. D. "An Integer Programming Solution for the Optimal Credit Investigation/Credit Granting Sequence," *Financial Management* 14 (Summer 1985): 66–76.

Subramanian, R. et al. "Coldstart: Fleet Assignment at Delta Airlines," *Interfaces* 24, 1 (January–February 1994): 104–120.

Taylor, B. W. "An Integer Nonlinear Goal Programming Model for the Deployment of State Highway Patrol Units," *Management Science* 31, 11 (November 1985): 1335–1347.

Wang, Hongbo. "A Branch and Bound Approach for Sequencing Expansion Projects," *Production and Operations Management* 4, 1 (Winter 1995): 57–75.

Zangwill, W. I. *Nonlinear Programming: A Unified Approach.* Upper Saddle River, NJ: Prentice Hall, 1969.

## CHAPTER 7

# PROJECT MANAGEMENT

## LEARNING OBJECTIVES

After completing this chapter, students will be able to:

1. Understand how to plan, monitor, and control projects using PERT/CPM.

2. Determine earliest start, earliest finish, latest start, latest finish, and slack times for each activity.

3. Understand the impact of variability in activity times.

4. Develop load charts to plan, monitor, and control the use of various resources during the project.

5. Use LP to find the least cost solution to reduce total project time, and solve these LP models using Excel's Solver.

6. Understand the important role of software such as Microsoft Project in project management.

## CHAPTER OUTLINE

### Project Management Provides a Competitive Advantage for Bechtel

Now in its second century, the San Francisco–based Bechtel Group is the world's premier manager of massive construction and engineering projects. Known for billion-dollar projects, Bechtel is famous for its construction feats on the Hoover Dam, the Ted Williams Tunnel project, and the rebuilding of Kuwait's oil and gas infrastructure after the invasion by Iraq.

Even for Bechtel, whose competitive advantage is project management, restoring the 650 blazing oil wells lit by Iraqi sabotage in 1990 was a logistical nightmare. The panorama of destruction in Kuwait was breathtaking, with fire roaring out of the ground from virtually every compass point. Kuwait had no water, electricity, food, or facilities. The country was littered with unexploded mines, bombs, grenades, and shells, and lakes of oil covered its roads.

In Phase 1 of the project, Bechtel devised an unprecedented emergency program to regain control of Kuwait's oil fields and to halt destruction of the environment. Phase 2 focused on rehabilitation. With a major global procurement program, Bechtel specialists tapped the company's network of suppliers and buyers worldwide. At the port of Dubai, 550 miles southeast of Kuwait, the firm established a central transshipment point, deploying 125,000 tons of equipment and supplies. Creating a workforce of 16,000, Bechtel mobilized 742 airplanes and ships and more than 5,800 bulldozers, ambulances, and other pieces of operating equipment from 40 countries on five continents.

Now, more than a decade later, the fires are long out and Kuwait continues shipping oil. Bechtel's more recent projects include (1) building and running a rail line between London and the Channel Tunnel ($7.4 billion); (2) developing an oil pipeline from the Caspian Sea region to Russia ($850 million); (3) expanding the Miami International Airport ($2 billion); and (4) building liquified natural gas plants on the island of Trinidad, West Indies ($1 billion).

When countries seek out firms to manage these massive projects, they go to Bechtel, which, again and again, through outstanding project management, has demonstrated its competitive advantage.[1]

---

[1] Courtesy of Bechtel. This application capsule and portions of Sections 7.1 and 7.2 have been adapted from Jay Heizer and Barry Render. *Operations Management*, 6/e. Upper Saddle River, NJ: Prentice Hall, 2001.

## 7.1   INTRODUCTION

Every organization at one time or another will take on a large and complex project. As noted in the preceding application, the Bechtel project management team had to quickly mobilize an international force of 16,000 workers when it entered Kuwait. Likewise, when Microsoft Corporation set out to develop Windows XP, a program costing hundreds of millions that had hundreds of programmers working on millions of lines of code, immense stakes rode on the project being delivered on time. Other examples of large, expensive projects include the Hubbard Construction Company, which must complete thousands of costly activities while laying a highway in Orlando, and the Avondale Shipyards in New Orleans, which requires tens of thousands of steps in constructing an oceangoing tugboat. Companies in almost every industry worry about how to manage similar large-scale complicated projects effectively.

*Project management techniques can be used to manage large, complex projects.*

Scheduling large projects is a difficult challenge to most managers, especially when the stakes are high. Millions of dollars in cost overruns have been wasted due to poor project planning. Unnecessary delays have occurred due to poor scheduling, and companies have gone bankrupt due to poor controls. How can such problems be solved? The answers lie in a popular decision modeling approach known as *project management*.

### Phases in Project Management

A *project* can be defined as a series of related tasks (or activities) directed toward a major well-defined output. A project can consist of thousands of specific activities, each with its own set of requirements of time, money, and other resources such as labor, raw materials, and machinery. Regardless of the scope and nature of the project, the management of large projects involves the three phases discussed in the following sections (see Figure 7.1). Each phase addresses specific questions regarding the project.

*There are three phases in managing large projects.*

*Project planning is the first phase.*

**Project Planning**   Project planning is the first phase and involves considering issues such as goal setting, defining the project, and team organization. Specific questions that are considered in this phase include the following:

1. What is the goal or objective of the project?
2. What are the various activities (or tasks) that constitute the project?
3. How are these activities linked? That is, what are the precedence relationships between the activities?
4. What is the time required for each activity?
5. What are the other resources (e.g., labor, raw materials, machinery) that are required for each activity?

*Project scheduling is the second phase.*

**Project Scheduling**   The second phase involves developing the specific time schedule for each activity and assigns people, money, and supplies to specific activities. The questions addressed in this phase should be considered soon after the project has been planned but *before* it is actually started. These questions include the following:

1. When will the entire project be completed?
2. What is the schedule (start and finish time) for each activity?
3. What are the critical activities in the project? That is, what are the activities that will delay the entire project if they are late?
4. What are the noncritical activities in the project? That is, what activities can run late without delaying the completion time of the entire project?

**FIGURE 7.1**

**Project Planning, Scheduling, and Controlling**

**Source:** J. Heizer and B. Render. *Operations Management*, 6/e. Upper Saddle River, NJ: Prentice Hall, 2001.

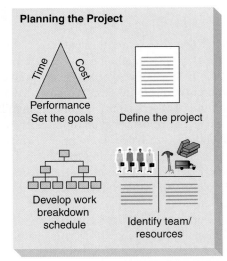

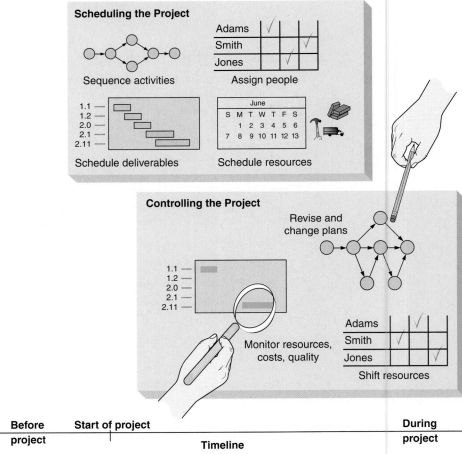

5. By how much can a noncritical activity be delayed without affecting the completion time of the entire project?

6. If we take the variability in activity times into consideration, what is the probability that a project will be completed by a specific deadline?

*Gantt charts are useful for project scheduling.*

One popular project scheduling approach is a *Gantt chart*. Gantt charts are low-cost means of helping managers make sure that (1) all activities are planned for, (2) their order of performance is accounted for, (3) the activity time schedules are recorded, and (4) the overall project time is developed. Gantt charts are easy to construct and understand, and permit managers to plan and track the progress of each activity. For example, Figure 7.2 shows the Gantt chart for a routine servicing of a Delta jetliner during a 60-minute layover. Horizontal bars are drawn for each project activity along a time line.

*For large projects, Gantt charts are used mainly to provide project summaries.*

On simple projects, Gantt charts such as these can be used alone. Gantt charts, though, do not adequately illustrate the interrelationships between the activities and the resources. For this reason, on most large projects Gantt charts are used mainly to provide summaries of a project's status. Projects are planned and scheduled using other network-based approaches discussed in subsequent sections.

*Projects must be monitored and controlled at regular intervals. Project controlling is the third phase.*

**Project Controlling**   Like the control of any management system, the control of large projects involves close monitoring of schedules, resources, and budgets. Control also means using a feedback loop to revise the project plan and having the ability to shift resources to where they are needed most. The questions addressed in this phase should be considered at

## FIGURE 7.2    Gantt Chart of Service Activities for a Commercial Aircraft During a 60-Minute Layover

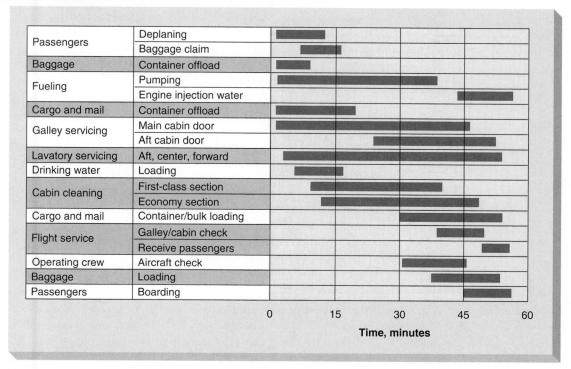

**Source:** J. Heizer and B. Render. *Operations Management*, 6/e. Upper Saddle River, NJ: Prentice Hall, 2001.

regular intervals during the project to ensure that it meets all time and cost schedules. These questions include the following:

1. At any particular date or time, is the project on schedule, behind schedule, or ahead of schedule?

2. At any particular date or time, is the money spent on the project equal to, less than, or greater than the budgeted amount?

3. Are there enough resources available to finish the project on time?

4. If the project is to be finished in a shorter amount of time, what is the best way to accomplish this at the least cost?

In this chapter, we investigate how project management techniques can be used to answer all these questions.

## Use of Software Packages in Project Management

*Software packages automate many of the routine calculations in project management.*

In recent times, managing large and complex projects has become considerably easier due to the availability and capabilities of specialized project management software packages. These programs typically have simple interfaces for entering the project data, and they automate many of the routine calculations required for effective project management. In addition, they are capable of efficiently presenting the status of a project using comprehensive graphs and tables. Some of these programs are Primavera (by Primavera Systems, Inc.), Microsoft Project (by Microsoft Corp.), MacProject (by Apple Computer Corp.), Pertmaster (by Westminster Software, Inc.), VisiSchedule (by Paladin Software Corp.), and Time Line (by Symantec Corp.).

These programs produce a broad variety of reports, including (1) detailed cost breakdowns for each task, (2) total program labor curves, (3) cost distribution tables, (4) functional cost and hour summaries, (5) raw material expenditure forecasts, (6) variance reports, (7) time analysis reports, and (8) work status reports.

Although it is possible to set up spreadsheets to perform many of the routine calculations that are involved, Excel is not the ideal choice for such tasks. So, in this chapter, we illustrate how Microsoft Project 2000 can be used for planning, scheduling, and monitoring projects.

There are, however, some issues that Microsoft Project 2000 does not handle. One such issue is question 4 posed in the section "Project Controlling" (How can we reduce a project's completion time at minimum cost?) We can best answer this question by setting up and solving the problem as a linear programming (LP) model. For this question, we describe using Excel's Solver to solve the LP model.

## 7.2  PROJECT NETWORKS

As noted previously, once the project mission or goal has been clearly specified, the first issues we need to address deal with *project planning*. That is, we need to identify the activities that constitute the project, the precedence relationships between these activities, and the time and other resources required for each *activity*.

### Identifying Activities

*A project can be subdivided into several activities.*

Almost any large project can be subdivided into a series of smaller activities or tasks. Identifying the activities involved in a project and the precedence relationships that may exist between these activities is the responsibility of the project team. In subdividing a project into various activities, however, the project team must be careful to ensure the following:

■ Each activity has clearly identifiable starting and ending points. In other words, we should be able to recognize when an activity has started and when it has ended. For example, if the project goal is to build a house, an activity may be to lay the foundation. It is possible to clearly recognize when we start this activity and when we finish this activity.

■ Each activity is clearly distinguishable from every other activity. That is, we should be able to associate every action we take and every dollar we spend with a specific (and unique) activity. For example, while building a house, we will be able to recognize which actions and expenses are associated with laying the foundation.

*An activity in a project may be a project of its own.*

The number of activities in a project will depend on the nature and scope of the project. It will also depend on the level of detail with which the project manager wants to monitor and control the project. In a typical project, it is common for each activity in a project to be a project of its own. That is, a project may actually be a master project that, in turn, consists of several miniprojects. In practice, it is convenient to develop a work breakdown structure to identify the activities in a project.

---

### ▶ MODELING IN THE REAL WORLD     PERT Helps Change the Face of British Airways

**FORMULATION**

Defining the Problem

British Airways (BA) wanted to rejuvenate its image using international design consultants to help develop a new identity. The "makeover" was to be completed in all areas of BA's public image as quickly as possible.

Developing a Model

Using a computerized project management package—PERTMASTER from Abex Software—a BA team constructed a PERT model of all tasks involved.

Acquiring Input Data

Data were collected from each department involved. Printers were asked to develop time estimates for new company stationery, tickets, timetables, baggage tags; clothing suppliers for uniforms; and Boeing Corp. for all the tasks involved in remaking the inside and outside of BA's jets.

**SOLUTION**

Developing a Solution

All the data were entered into PERTMASTER for a schedule and critical path.

Testing the Solution

The resulting schedule did not please BA management. Boeing could not prepare a huge 747 in time for a December 4 gala launch date. Uniform designs were also going to delay the entire project.

**INTERPRETATION**

Analyzing the Results and Sensitivity Analysis

An analysis of the earliest possible date that all items for a refurbished airplane could be ready (new paint, upholstery, carpets, trim, and so on) revealed that there were just sufficient materials to totally convert a smaller Boeing 737 that was available in the Seattle plant. Critical path analysis also showed that uniforms—the work of British designer Roland Klein—would have to be launched six months later in a separate ceremony.

Implementing the Results

The smaller 737 was outfitted just in time for a brilliant light show in an auditorium specially built in a Heathrow Airport hangar. Ground vehicles were also prepared in time.

**Source:** *Industrial Management and Data Systems* (March–April 1986): 6–7.

**FIGURE 7.3**

**Work Breakdown Structure**

**Source:** J. Heizer and B. Render. *Operations Management*, 6/e. Upper Saddle River, NJ: Prentice Hall, 2001.

| Level | Level ID Number | Activity |
|---|---|---|
| 1 | 1.0 | Develop/launch Windows XP Operating System |
| 2 | 1.1 | Development of GUIs |
| 2 | 1.2 | Ensure compatibility with earlier Windows versions |
| 3 | 1.21 | Compatibility with Windows 98 |
| 3 | 1.22 | Compatibility with Windows NT |
| 3 | 1.23 | Compatibility with Windows 2000 |
| 4 | 1.231 | Ability to import files |

*A work breakdown structure details the activities in a project.*

**Work Breakdown Structure**  A *work breakdown structure* (WBS) defines the project by dividing it into its major subcomponents, which are then subdivided into more detailed subcomponents, and so on. Gross requirements for people, supplies, and equipment are also estimated in this planning phase. The work breakdown structure typically decreases in size from top to bottom and is indented like this:

| Level | |
|---|---|
| 1 | Project |
| 2 | Major tasks in the project |
| 3 | Subtasks in major tasks |
| 4 | Activities to be completed |

This hierarchical framework can be illustrated with the development of Microsoft's operating system, Windows XP. As we see in Figure 7.3, the project, creating a new operating system, is labeled 1.0. The first step is to identify the major tasks in the project (level 2). Two examples would be development of graphic user interfaces (GUIs) (1.1) and creating compatibility with previous versions of Windows (1.2). The major subtasks for 1.2 are creating a team to handle compatibility with Windows 98 (1.21), another for Windows NT (1.22), and another with Windows 2000 (1.23). Then each major subtask is broken down into level 4 activities that need to be done, such as importing files created in Windows 2000 (1.231). There are usually many level 4 activities.

## Identifying Activity Times and Other Resources

*Activity times need to be estimated.*

Once the activities have been identified, the time required and other resources (e.g., money, labor, raw materials) for each activity are determined. In practice, identifying this input data is a complicated task involving a fair amount of expertise and competence on the project leader's part. For example, many individuals will automatically present inflated time estimates, especially if their job is on the line if they fail to complete the activity on time. The project leader has to be able to recognize these types of issues and adjust the time estimates accordingly.

## Project Management Techniques: PERT and CPM

*PERT and CPM are two popular project management techniques.*

When the questions in the project planning phase have been addressed, we move on to the project scheduling phase. The *program evaluation* and *review technique* (PERT) and the *critical path method* (CPM) are two popular decision modeling procedures that help managers answer the questions in this phase, even for large and complex projects. They were developed because there was a critical need for a better way to manage projects (see the History box).

Although some people still view PERT and CPM as separate techniques and refer to them by their original names, the two are similar in their basic approach. The growing practice, therefore, is to refer to PERT and CPM simply as *project management* techniques.

# HISTORY    How PERT and CPM Started

Managers have been planning, scheduling, monitoring, and controlling large-scale projects for hundreds of years, but it has only been in the past 50 years that decision modeling techniques have been applied to major projects. One of the earliest techniques was the *Gantt chart.* This type of chart shows the start and finish times of one or more activities, as shown in the accompanying chart.

In 1958, the Special Projects Office of the U.S. Navy developed the Program Evaluation and Review Technique (PERT) to plan and control the Polaris missile program. This project involved the coordination of thousands of contractors. Today, PERT is still used to monitor countless government contract schedules. At about the same time (1957), the Critical Path Method (CPM) was developed by J. E. Kelly of Remington Rand and M. R. Walker of du Pont. Originally, CPM was used to assist in the building and maintenance of chemical plants at du Pont.

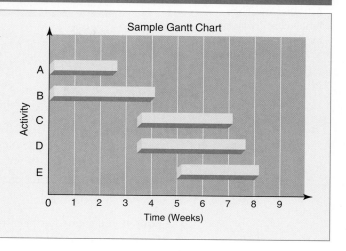

**PERT versus CPM**  The primary difference between PERT and CPM is in the way the time needed for each activity in the project is estimated. In PERT, each activity has three time estimates that are combined to determine the expected activity completion time and its variance. PERT is considered a *probabilistic* technique; it allows us to find the probability that the entire project will be completed by a specific due date.

In contrast, CPM uses a *deterministic* approach. It estimates the completion time of each activity using just a single time estimate. This estimate, called the *normal* or *standard time,* is the time we estimate it will take under typical conditions to complete the activity. In some cases, CPM also associates a second time estimate with each activity. This estimate, called the *crash time,* is the shortest time it would take to finish an activity if additional funds and resources were allocated to the activity.

As noted previously, identifying these time estimates is a complicated task in most real-world projects. In our discussions in this chapter, however, we will assume that the time estimates (single time estimates in CPM and three time estimates in PERT) are available for each activity.

*PERT is a probabilistic technique, whereas CPM is a deterministic technique.*

## Project Management Example: General Foundry, Inc.

General Foundry, Inc., a metal works plant in Milwaukee, has long been trying to avoid the expense of installing air pollution control equipment. The local environmental protection group has recently given the foundry 16 weeks to install a complex air filter system on its main smokestack. General Foundry has been warned that it may be forced to close unless the device is installed in the allotted period. Lester Harky, the managing partner, wants to make sure that installation of the filtering system progresses smoothly and on time.

General Foundry has identified the eight activities that need to be performed in order for the project to be completed. When the project begins, two activities can be simultaneously started: building the internal components for the device (activity A) and the modifications necessary for the floor and roof (activity B). The construction of the collection stack (activity C) can begin when the internal components are completed. Pouring the concrete floor and installation of the frame (activity D) can be started as soon as the internal components are completed and the roof and floor have been modified.

After the collection stack has been constructed, two activities can begin: building the high-temperature burner (activity E) and installing the pollution control system (activity F). The air pollution device can be installed (activity G) after the concrete floor has been

*Activities in the General Foundry project*

TABLE 7.1

**Activities and Their Immediate Predecessors for General Foundry**

| ACTIVITY | DESCRIPTION | IMMEDIATE PREDECESSORS |
|---|---|---|
| A | Build internal components | — |
| B | Modify roof and floor | — |
| C | Construct collection stack | A |
| D | Pour concrete and install frame | A, B |
| E | Build high-temperature burner | C |
| F | Install pollution control system | C |
| G | Install air pollution device | D, E |
| H | Inspect and test | F, G |

poured, the frame has been installed, and the high-temperature burner has been built. Finally, after the control system and pollution device have been installed, the system can be inspected and tested (activity H).

All of these activities and precedence relationships seem rather confusing and complex when they are presented in a descriptive form, as here. It is therefore convenient to list all the activity information in a table, as shown in Table 7.1. We see in the table that activity A is listed as an *immediate predecessor* of activity C. Likewise, both activities D and E must be performed prior to starting activity G.

*It is enough to list only the immediate predecessors for each activity.*

Note that it is enough to list just the *immediate predecessors* for each activity. For example, in Table 7.1, since activity A precedes activity C and activity C precedes activity E, the fact that activity A precedes activity E is *implicit*. This relationship need not be explicitly shown in the activity precedence relationships.

When there are many activities in a project with fairly complicated precedence relationships, it is difficult for an individual to comprehend the complexity of the project from just the tabular information. In such cases, a visual representation of the project, using a *project network*, is convenient and useful. A project network is a diagram of all the activities and the precedence relationships that exist between these activities in a project. We now illustrate how to construct a project network for General Foundry, Inc.

*Networks consist of nodes that are connected by arcs.*

## Drawing the Project Network

There are two approaches for drawing a project network: *activity on node* (AON), and *activity on arc* (AOA). Although both approaches are popular in practice, many of the project management software packages, including Microsoft Project 2000, use AON networks. For this reason, although we illustrate both types of project networks next, we focus on AON networks in all our subsequent discussions in this chapter.

*Two types of project networks—AON and AOA.*

**Activity on Node (AON) Network** Recall from the discussion in Chapter 5 that a network consists of nodes (or points) and arcs (or lines) that connect the nodes together. In an AON approach, we denote each activity by a node. The arcs represent the precedence relationships between the activities.

*Nodes denote activities in an AON network.*

In the General Foundry example, there are two activities (A and B) that do not have any predecessors. We draw separate nodes for each of these activities, as shown in Figure 7.4. Although not required, it is usually convenient to have a unique starting activity for a project. We have therefore included a *dummy activity* called Start in Figure 7.4. This dummy activity does not really exist and takes up zero time and resources. Activity Start is an immediate predecessor for both activities A and B, and serves as the unique starting activity for the entire project.

**FIGURE 7.4**

**Beginning AON Network
for General Foundry**

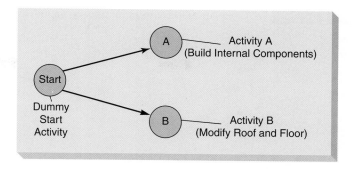

*Arcs denote precedence
relationships.*

We now show the precedence relationships using arcs (shown as the arrow symbols: →). For example, an arrow from activity Start to activity A indicates that Start is a predecessor for activity A. In a similar fashion, we draw an arrow from Start to B.

Next, we add a new node for activity C. Since activity A precedes activity C, we draw an arc from node A to node C (see Figure 7.5). Likewise, we first draw a node to represent activity D. Then, since activities A and B both precede activity D, we draw arcs from A to D, and B to D (see Figure 7.5).

We proceed in this fashion, adding a separate node for each activity and a separate arc for each precedence relationship that exists. The complete AON project network for the General Foundry project example is shown in Figure 7.6.

Drawing a project network properly takes some time and experience. When we first draw a project network, it is not unusual that we place our nodes (activities) in the network in such a fashion that the arcs (precedence relationships) are not simple straight lines. That is, the arcs could be intersecting each other, and even facing in opposite directions. For example, if we had switched the location of the nodes for activities E and F in Figure 7.6, the arcs from F to H and E to G would have intersected. Although such a project network is perfectly valid, it is good practice to have a well-drawn network. One rule that we especially recommend is to place the nodes in such a fashion that all arrows point in the same direction. To achieve this, we suggest that you first get a rough draft version of the network, making sure all the relationships are shown. Then you can redraw the network to make appropriate changes in the location of the nodes.

*It is convenient, but not
required, to have unique
starting and ending activities
in a project.*

As with the unique starting node, it is convenient to have the project network finish with a unique ending node. In the General Foundry example, it turns out that a unique activity, H, is the last activity in the project. We therefore automatically have a unique ending node.

In situations in which a project has multiple ending activities, we include a dummy ending activity. This is an activity that does not exist and takes up zero time or resources.

**FIGURE 7.5**

**Intermediate AON
Network for General
Foundry**

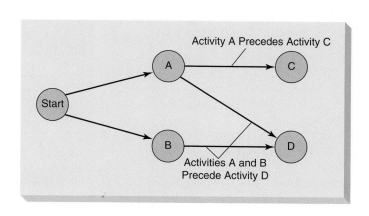

FIGURE 7.6    **Complete AON Network for General Foundry**

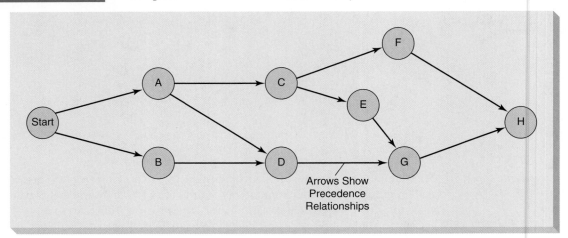

This dummy activity has all the multiple ending activities in the project as immediate predecessors. We illustrate this type of situation in Solved Problem 7-1 at the end of this chapter.

*In AOA networks, arcs denote activities. Nodes denote events.*

**Activity on Arc (AOA) Network**  In an AOA project network, we represent activities by arcs (shown as arrow symbols: →). A node represents an *event*, which marks the start or completion time of an activity. We usually identify an event (node) by a number. The complete AOA project network for General Foundry's problem, shown in Figure 7.7, is drawn as discussed in the following paragraphs.

Activity A starts at event 1 and ends at event 2. Likewise, activity B starts at event 1 and ends at event 3. Activity C, whose only immediate predecessor is activity A, starts at node 2 and ends at node 4. Activity D, however, has two predecessors (i.e., A and B). Hence, we need both activities A and B to end at event 3, so that activity D can start at that event. However, we cannot have multiple activities with common starting and ending nodes in an

**FIGURE 7.7**    **Complete AOA Network (with Dummy Activities) for General Foundry**

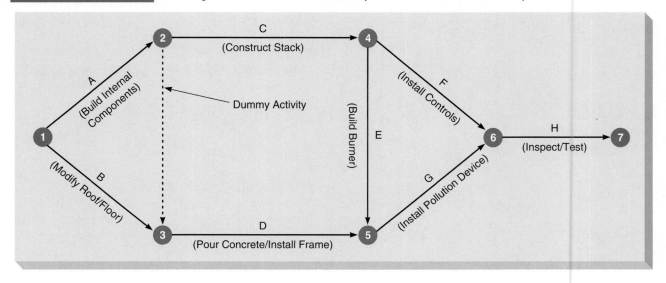

**IN ACTION** Delta's Ground Crew Orchestrates a Smooth Takeoff

Flight 199's three engines screech its arrival as the wide-bodied jet lumbers down Orlando's taxiway with 200 passengers arriving from San Juan. In an hour, the plane is to be airborne again.

But before this jet can depart, there is business to attend to: hundreds of passengers and tons of luggage and cargo to unload and load; hundreds of meals, thousands of gallons of jet fuel, countless soft drinks and bottles of liquor to restock; cabin and rest rooms to clean; toilet holding tanks to drain; and engines, wings, and landing gear to inspect.

The 12-person ground crew knows that a miscue anywhere—a broken cargo loader, lost baggage, misdirected passengers—can mean a late departure and trigger a chain reaction of headaches from Orlando to Dallas to every destination of a connecting flight.

Dennis Dettro, the operations manager for Delta's Orlando International Airport, likes to call the turnaround operation "a well-orchestrated symphony." Like a pit crew awaiting a race car, trained crews are in place for Flight 199 with baggage carts and tractors, hydraulic cargo loaders, a truck to load food and drinks, another to lift the cleanup crew, another to put fuel on, and a fourth to take water off. The "orchestra" usually performs so smoothly that most passengers never suspect the proportions of the effort. Gantt charts and PERT aid Delta and other airlines with the staffing and scheduling that are necessary for this symphony to perform.

**Source:** *New York Times* (January 21, 1997): C1, C20.

---

*Dummy activities may be needed in AOA networks to show all precedence relationships.*

AOA network. To overcome this difficulty, in such cases, we may need to add a dummy arc (activity) to enforce the precedence relationship. The dummy activity, shown in Figure 7.7 as a dashed line, is inserted between events 2 and 3 to make the diagram reflect the precedence between A and D. Remember that the dummy activity does not really exist in the project and takes up zero time.

The remainder of the AOA project network for General Foundry's example is quite simple to draw and should be self-explanatory.

## 7.3 DETERMINING THE PROJECT SCHEDULE

Look back to Figure 7.6 for a moment to see General Foundry's completed AON project network. Once this project network has been drawn to show all the activities and their precedence relationships, the next step is to determine the project schedule. That is, we need to identify the planned starting and ending time for each activity.

*Critical path analysis helps determine the project schedule.*

Let us assume General Foundry estimates the time required for each activity, in weeks, as shown in Table 7.2. The table indicates that the total time for all eight of General Foundry's activities is 25 weeks. However, since several activities can take place simultaneously, it is clear that the total project completion time may be much less than 25 weeks. To find out just how long the project will take, we perform the *critical path analysis* for the network.

*Critical path is the longest path in the network.*

The critical path is the *longest* time path through the network. To find the critical path, we calculate two distinct starting and ending times for each activity. These are defined as follows:

*Earliest start time (EST)* = earliest time at which an activity can start, assuming all predecessors have been completed

*Earliest finish time (EFT)* = earliest time at which an activity can be finished

*Latest start time (LST)* = latest time at which an activity can start so as to not delay the completion time of the entire project

*Latest finish time (LFT)* = latest time by which an activity has to finish so as to not delay the completion time of the entire project

TABLE 7.2

Time Estimates for General
Foundry

| ACTIVITY | DESCRIPTION | TIME (WEEKS) |
|----------|-------------|--------------|
| A | Build internal components | 2 |
| B | Modify roof and floor | 3 |
| C | Construct collection stack | 2 |
| D | Pour concrete and install frame | 4 |
| E | Build high-temperature burner | 4 |
| F | Install pollution control system | 3 |
| G | Install air pollution device | 5 |
| H | Inspect and test | 2 |
| | Total time (Weeks) | 25 |

*We use a two-pass procedure to find the project schedule.*

We use a two-pass process, consisting of a forward pass and a backward pass, to determine these time schedules for each activity. The earliest times (EST and EFT) are determined during the forward pass. The latest times (LST and LFT) are determined during the backward pass.

## Forward Pass

*The* forward pass *identifies all the earliest times.*

To clearly show the activity schedules on the project network, we use the notation shown in Figure 7.8. The EST of an activity is shown in the top left corner of the node denoting that activity. The EFT is shown in the top right corner. The latest times, LST and LFT, are shown in the bottom left and bottom right corners, respectively.

**Earliest Start Time Rule**  Before an activity can start, *all* its immediate predecessors must be finished.

*All predecessor activities must be completed before an activity can begin.*

- If an activity has only a single immediate predecessor, its EST equals the EFT of the predecessor.
- If an activity has multiple immediate predecessors, its EST is the maximum of all EFT values of its predecessors. That is,

$$EST = Max\{EFT \text{ of all immediate predecessors}\} \qquad (7\text{-}1)$$

FIGURE 7.8

Notation Used in Nodes for
Forward and Backward
Pass

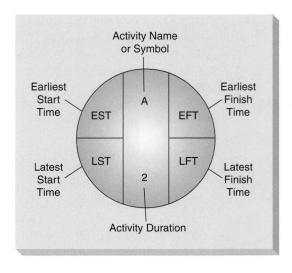

**FIGURE 7.9**    **Earliest Start and Earliest Finish Times for General Foundry**

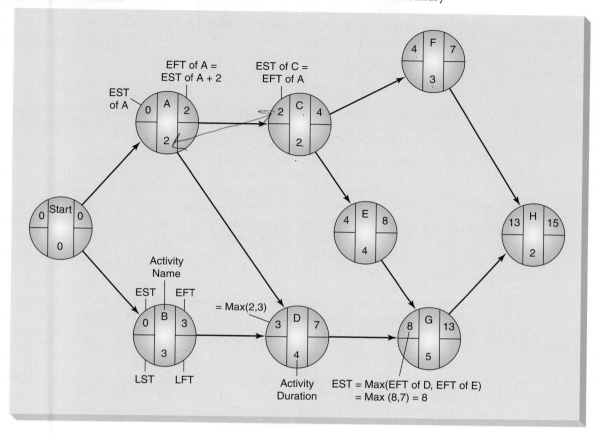

**Earliest Finish Time Rule**   The earliest finish time (EFT) of an activity is the sum of its earliest start time (EST) and its activity time. That is,

$$EFT = EST + \text{Activity time}$$

(7-2)

*EFT = EST + activity time*

Figure 7.9 shows the complete project network for General Foundry's project, along with the EST and EFT values for all activities. In what follows, we describe how these values have been calculated.

Since activity Start has no predecessors, we begin by setting its EST to 0. That is, activity Start can begin at the *end* of week 0, which is the same as the beginning of week 1.[2] If activity Start has an EST of 0, its EFT is also 0, since its activity time is 0.

Next, we consider activities A and B, both of which have only Start as an immediate predecessor. Using the earliest start time rule, the EST for both activities A and B equals zero, which is the EFT of activity Start. Now, using the earliest finish time rule, the EFT for A is 2 (= 0 + 2), and the EFT for B is 3 (= 0 + 3).

---

[2] In writing all earliest and latest times, we need to be consistent. For example, if we specify that the EST value of activity *i* is week 4, do we mean the *beginning* of week 4 or the *end* of week 4? Note that if the value refers to the *beginning* of week 4, it means that week 4 is also available for performing activity *i*. In our discussions, *all* earliest and latest time values correspond to the *end* of a period. That is, if we specify that the EST of activity *i* is week 4, it means that activity *i* starts work only at the beginning of week 5.

EST of an activity =
maximum EFT of all
predecessor activities

Since activity A precedes activity C, the EST of C equals the EFT of A (= 2). The EFT of C is therefore 4 (= 2 + 2).

We now come to activity D. Both activities A and B are immediate predecessors for B. Whereas A has an EFT of 2, activity B has an EFT of 3. Using the earliest finish time rule, we compute the EST of activity D as follows:

$$\text{EST of D} = \text{Max(EFT of A, EFT of B)} = \text{Max}(2, 3) = 3$$

The EFT of D equals 7 (= 3 + 4). Next, both activities E and F have activity C as their only immediate predecessor. Therefore, the EST for both E and F equals 4 (= EFT of C). The EFT of E is 8 (= 4 + 4), and the EFT of F is 7 (= 4 + 3).

Activity G has both activities D and E as predecessors. Using the earliest start time rule, its EST is therefore the maximum of the EFT of D and the EFT of E. Hence, the EST of activity G equals 8 (= maximum of 7 and 8), and its EFT equals 13 (= 8 + 5).

Finally, we come to activity H. Since it also has two predecessors, F and G, the EST of H is the maximum EFT of these two activities. That is, the EST of H equals 13 (= maximum of 13 and 7). This implies that the EFT of H is 15 (= 13 + 2). Since H is the last activity in the project, this also implies that the earliest time in which the entire project can be completed is 15 weeks.

Although the forward pass allows us to determine the earliest project completion time, it does not identify the critical path. In order to identify this path, we need to now conduct the backward pass to determine the LST and LFT values for all activities.

## Backward Pass

The backward pass finds all latest times.

Just as the forward pass began with the first activity in the project, the backward pass begins with the last activity in the project. For each activity, we first determine its LFT value, followed by its LST value. The following two rules are used in this process.

**Latest Finish Time Rule**  This rule is again based on the fact that before an activity can start, all its immediate predecessors must be finished.

■ If an activity is an immediate predecessor for just a single activity, its LFT equals the LST of the activity that immediately follows it.
■ If an activity is an immediate predecessor to more than one activity, its LFT is the minimum of all LST values of all activities that immediately follow it. That is,

$$\text{LFT} = \text{Min\{LST of all immediate following activities\}} \qquad (7\text{-}3)$$

**Latest Start Time Rule**  The latest start time (LST) of an activity is the difference of its latest finish time (LFT) and its activity time. That is,

$$\text{LST} = \text{LFT} - \text{Activity time} \qquad (7\text{-}4)$$

Figure 7.10 shows the complete project network for General Foundry's project, along with LST and LFT values for all activities. In what follows, we analyze how these values were calculated.

*LST = LFT − Activity time*

We begin by assigning an LFT value of 15 weeks for activity H. That is, we specify that the latest finish time for the entire project is the same as its earliest finish time. Using the latest start time rule, the LST of activity H is equal to 13 (= 15 − 2).

Since activity H is the lone succeeding activity for both activities F and G, the LFT for both F and G equals 13. This implies that the LST of G is 8 (= 13 − 5), and the LST of F is 10 (= 13 − 3).

**FIGURE 7.10**        **Latest Start and Latest Finish Times for General Foundry**

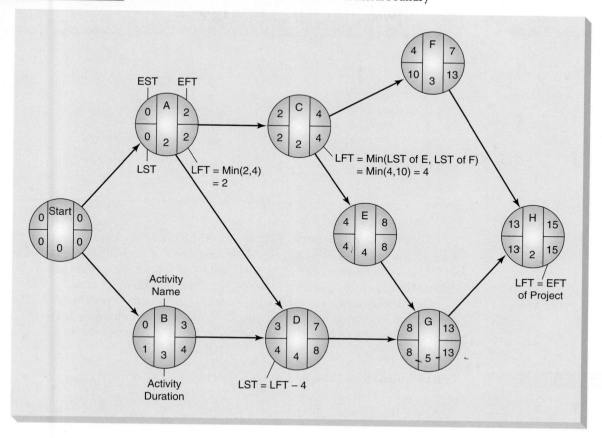

Proceeding in this fashion, the LFT of E is 8 (= LST of G), and its LST is 4 (= 8 − 4). Likewise, the LFT of D is 8 (= LST of G), and its LST is 4 (= 8 − 4).

We now consider activity C, which is an immediate predecessor to two activities: E and F. Using the latest finish time rule, we compute the LFT of activity C as follows:

*LFT of an activity = minimum LST of all activities that follow*

$$\text{LFT of C} = \text{Min(LST of E, LST of F)} = \text{Min}(4, 10) = 4$$

The LST of C is computed as 2 (= 4 − 2). Next, we compute the LFT of B as 4 (= LST of D), and its LST as 1 (= 4 − 3).

We now consider activity A. We compute its LFT as 2 (= minimum of LST of C and LST of D). Hence, the LST of activity A is 0 (= 2 − 2). Finally, both the LFT and LST of activity Start are equal to 0.

## Calculating Slack Time and Identifying the Critical Path(s)

*Slack time is free time for an activity.*

After we have computed the earliest and latest times for all activities, it is a simple matter to find the amount of *slack time*, or free time, that each activity has. Slack is the length of time an activity can be delayed without delaying the entire project. Mathematically,

$$\text{Slack} = \text{LST} - \text{EST} \quad \text{or} \quad \text{Slack} = \text{LFT} - \text{EFT} \qquad (7\text{-}5)$$

| ACTIVITY | EARLIEST START, EST | EARLIEST FINISH, EFT | LATEST START, LST | LATEST FINISH, LFT | SLACK, LST-EST | ON CRITICAL PATH? |
|---|---|---|---|---|---|---|
| A | 0 | 2 | 0 | 2 | 0 | Yes |
| B | 0 | 3 | 1 | 4 | 1 | No |
| C | 2 | 4 | 2 | 4 | 0 | Yes |
| D | 3 | 7 | 4 | 8 | 1 | No |
| E | 4 | 8 | 4 | 8 | 0 | Yes |
| F | 4 | 7 | 10 | 13 | 6 | No |
| G | 8 | 13 | 8 | 13 | 0 | Yes |
| H | 13 | 15 | 13 | 15 | 0 | Yes |

Table 7.3 summarizes the EST, EFT, LST, LFT, and slack time for all of General Foundry's activities. Activity B, for example, has 1 week of slack time since its LST is 1 and its EST is 0 (alternatively, its LFT is 4 and its EFT is 3). This means that activity B can be delayed by up to 1 week, and the whole project can still finish in 15 weeks.

*Critical activities have no slack time.*

On the other hand, activities A, C, E, G and H have *no* slack time. This means that none of them can be delayed without delaying the entire project. Conversely, if Harky wants to reduce the total project time, he will have to reduce the length of one of these activities.

**Critical Path and Slack Times for General Foundry**

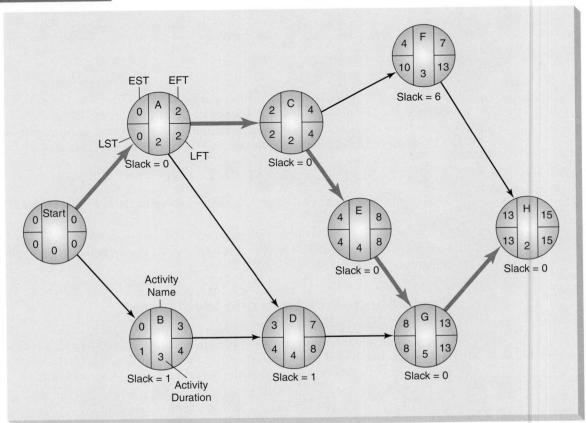

*Critical path is the longest path through the network.*

These activities are called *critical activities* and are said to be on the *critical path*. The critical path is a continuous path through the project network that

- starts at the first activity in the project (Start in our example),
- terminates at the last activity in the project (H in our example), and
- includes only critical activities (i.e., activities with no slack time).

General Foundry's critical path, Start-A-C-E-G-H, is shown in network form in Figure 7.11. The total project completion time of 15 weeks corresponds to the longest path in the network.

*A project can have multiple critical paths.*

**Multiple Critical Paths**   In General Foundry's case, there was just a single critical path. Can a project have multiple critical paths? The answer is yes. For example, what if the time required for activity B had been estimated as 4 weeks, instead of 3 weeks? Due to this change, the earliest and latest times for activities B and D would have to be revised, as shown in Figure 7.12.

Note that in addition to the original critical path (Start-A-C-E-G-H), there is now a second critical path (Start-B-D-G-H). Delaying an activity on either critical path will delay the completion of the entire project.

## Total Slack Time versus Free Slack Time

Let us now refer back to our original project network in Figure 7.11. Consider activities B and D, which have slacks of 1 week each. Does it mean that we can delay *each* activity by 1 week, and still complete the project in 15 weeks? The answer is no, as discussed next.

**FIGURE 7.12**            **Modified Network with Multiple Critical Paths for General Foundry**

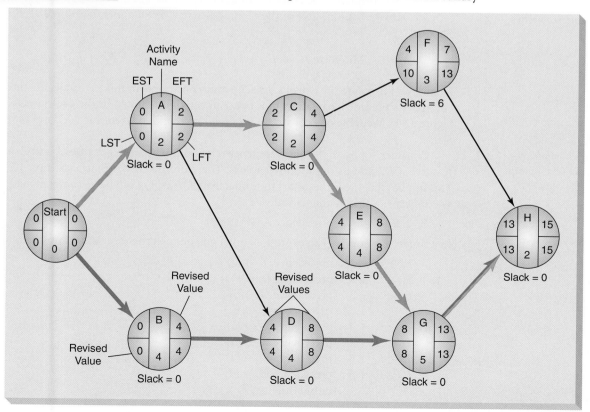

Let's assume that activity B is delayed by 1 week. It has used up its slack of 1 week and now has an EFT of 4. This implies that activity D now has an EST of 4 and an EFT of 8. Note that these are also its LST and LFT values, respectively. That is, activity D also has no slack time now. Essentially, the slack of 1 week that activities B and D had is *shared* between them. Delaying either activity by 1 week causes not only that activity, but also the other activity, to lose its slack. This type of a slack time is referred to as *total slack*. Typically, when two or more noncritical activities appear successively in a path, they share total slack.

*Total slack time is shared among more than one activity.*

In contrast, consider the slack time of 6 weeks in activity F. Delaying this activity decreases only its slack time and does not impact the slack time of any other activity. This type of a slack time is referred to as *free slack*. Typically, if a noncritical activity has critical activities on either side of it in a path, its slack time is free slack.

*Free slack time is associated with a single activity.*

## 7.4   USING LINEAR PROGRAMMING TO IDENTIFY THE CRITICAL PATH

We can also use a linear programming (LP) based approach to determine the earliest and latest times for each activity in a project network. To do so, we solve two LP problems: the first to identify the earliest times and the second to identify the latest times. The only input data required are the activity precedence information (see Figure 7.11) and the activity times. Let us use the General Foundry example to illustrate the LP models.

### Linear Programming Model to Determine the Earliest Times

*The decision variables are the start times.*

As with all the LP models we formulated in Chapters 2–5, we begin by defining the decision variables. For each activity, $i$, we define $E_i$ as its EST. Since there are eight activities in General Foundry's project, there are eight decision variables in the LP model.

Next, we formulate the objective function. Since we are interested in finding the EST for each activity, the objective of the LP model here is to *minimize* the sum of all $E_i$ values. That is,

*Minimization objective*

$$\text{Minimize } E_A + E_B + E_C + E_D + E_E + E_F + E_G + E_H$$

Finally, we formulate the constraints. The only constraints in this LP model are those that enforce the precedence relationships between activities (shown in the project network in Figure 7.11). We write one constraint for each precedence relationship (i.e., arc) in the network.

*Constraints enforce the precedence relationships.*

Consider, for example, the precedence relationship between activities A and C. Activity A starts at $E_A$, and its duration is 2 weeks. Therefore, activity A finishes at time $(E_A + 2)$. This implies that the earliest start time of activity C (i.e., $E_C$) can be *no earlier* than $(E_A + 2)$. We can express this mathematically as

$$E_C \geq E_A + 2 \qquad \text{(precedence A} \to \text{C)}$$

In a similar fashion, we can express all other activity precedence relationships as follows

$$
\begin{array}{ll}
E_D \geq E_A + 2 & \text{(precedence A } \to \text{ D)} \\
E_D \geq E_B + 3 & \text{(precedence B } \to \text{ D)} \\
E_E \geq E_C + 2 & \text{(precedence C } \to \text{ E)} \\
E_F \geq E_C + 2 & \text{(precedence C } \to \text{ F)} \\
E_G \geq E_D + 4 & \text{(precedence D } \to \text{ G)} \\
E_G \geq E_E + 4 & \text{(precedence E } \to \text{ G)} \\
E_H \geq E_F + 3 & \text{(precedence F } \to \text{ H)} \\
E_H \geq E_G + 5 & \text{(precedence G } \to \text{ H)} \\
\text{All } E_i \geq 0 & \text{(nonnegativity)}
\end{array}
$$

**File: 7-1.xls**

*Solver entries are target cell, changing cells, and constraints.*

**Excel Solution**  Program 7.1A shows the formula view of the Excel layout for General Foundry's LP model to determine EST values. This layout follows the same structure and logic we have used in earlier chapters for all LP models. That is, we have modeled all parameters (solution value, objective coefficients, and constraint coefficients) associated with a decision variable in a separate column of the worksheet. We have then computed the objective function and left-hand side (LHS) formulas for all constraints using Excel's SUMPRODUCT function. Finally, we have algebraically modified each constraint so that all variables are in the LHS of the equation. For example, the precedence relationship between activities A and C has been modified as $[E_C - E_A \geq 2]$.

The Solver entries and solution for this LP model are shown in Program 7.1B on page 271. As expected, the EST values for all activities (shown in cells B5:I5) are the same obtained earlier using the two-pass procedure. The EST value of 13 weeks for activity H implies the entire project has an earliest completion time of 15 (= 13 + 2) weeks.

### Excel Notes

■ The CD-ROM that accompanies this textbook contains the Excel file for each example problem discussed here. The relevant file name is shown in the margin next to each example.

■ In each of our Excel layouts, for clarity, changing cells are shaded yellow, the target cell is shaded green, and cells containing the left-hand side (LHS) formula for each constraint are shaded blue. Although these colors are not apparent in the screen captures shown in the textbook, they are seen in the Excel files in your CD-ROM.

■ Also, to make the equivalence of the written formulation and the Excel layout clear, our Excel layouts show the decision variable names used in the written formulation of the model. Note that these names have no role in using Solver to solve the model.

---

**PROGRAM 7.1A**  **Excel Layout to Compute General Foundry's Earliest Starting Times Using Linear Programming**

| | A | B | C | D | E | F | G | H | I | J | K | L |
|---|---|---|---|---|---|---|---|---|---|---|---|---|
| 1 | **General Foundry's EST Calculations** | | | | | | | | | | | |
| 2 | | | | | | | | | | | | |
| 3 | | $E_A$ | $E_B$ | $E_C$ | $E_D$ | $E_E$ | $E_F$ | $E_G$ | $E_H$ | These are the decision variables. | | |
| 4 | | EST A | EST B | EST C | EST D | EST E | EST F | EST G | EST H | | | |
| 5 | Solution value | | | | | | | | | | | |
| 6 | Objective coeff | 1 | 1 | 1 | 1 | 1 | 1 | 1 | 1 | =SUMPRODUCT(B6:I6,$B$5:$I$5) | <-- Objective | |
| 7 | Constraints | | | | | | | | | | | |
| 8 | A --> C | -1 | | 1 | | | | | | =SUMPRODUCT(B8:I8,$B$5:$I$5) | >= | 2 |
| 9 | A --> D | -1 | | | 1 | | | | | =SUMPRODUCT(B9:I9,$B$5:$I$5) | >= | 2 |
| 10 | B --> D | | -1 | | 1 | | | | | =SUMPRODUCT(B10:I10,$B$5:$I$5) | >= | 3 |
| 11 | C --> E | | | -1 | | 1 | | | | =SUMPRODUCT(B11:I11,$B$5:$I$5) | >= | 2 |
| 12 | C --> F | | | -1 | | | 1 | | | =SUMPRODUCT(B12:I12,$B$5:$I$5) | >= | 2 |
| 13 | D --> G | | | | -1 | | | 1 | | =SUMPRODUCT(B13:I13,$B$5:$I$5) | >= | 4 |
| 14 | E --> G | | | | | -1 | | 1 | | =SUMPRODUCT(B14:I14,$B$5:$I$5) | >= | 4 |
| 15 | F --> H | | | | | | -1 | | 1 | =SUMPRODUCT(B15:I15,$B$5:$I$5) | >= | 3 |
| 16 | G --> H | | | | | | | -1 | 1 | =SUMPRODUCT(B16:I16,$B$5:$I$5) | >= | 5 |
| 17 | | | | | | | | | | LHS | Sign | RHS |

Constraints enforce the precedence relationships.

The SUMPRODUCT function is used to compute all LHS values and the objective function.

**PROGRAM 7.1B**

**Solver Entries to Compute General Foundry's Earliest Starting Times Using Linear Programming**

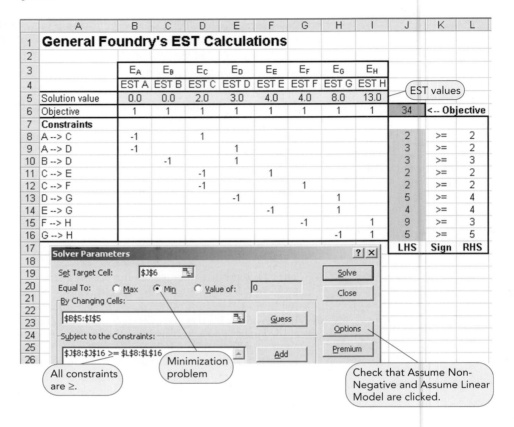

| | A | B | C | D | E | F | G | H | I | J | K | L |
|---|---|---|---|---|---|---|---|---|---|---|---|---|
| 1 | **General Foundry's EST Calculations** | | | | | | | | | | | |
| 2 | | | | | | | | | | | | |
| 3 | | $E_A$ | $E_B$ | $E_C$ | $E_D$ | $E_E$ | $E_F$ | $E_G$ | $E_H$ | | | |
| 4 | | EST A | EST B | EST C | EST D | EST E | EST F | EST G | EST H | | | |
| 5 | Solution value | 0.0 | 0.0 | 2.0 | 3.0 | 4.0 | 4.0 | 8.0 | 13.0 | | | |
| 6 | Objective | 1 | 1 | 1 | 1 | 1 | 1 | 1 | 1 | 34 | <-- Objective | |
| 7 | **Constraints** | | | | | | | | | | | |
| 8 | A --> C | -1 | | 1 | | | | | | 2 | >= | 2 |
| 9 | A --> D | -1 | | | 1 | | | | | 3 | >= | 2 |
| 10 | B --> D | | -1 | | 1 | | | | | 3 | >= | 3 |
| 11 | C --> E | | | -1 | | 1 | | | | 2 | >= | 2 |
| 12 | C --> F | | | -1 | | | 1 | | | 2 | >= | 2 |
| 13 | D --> G | | | | -1 | | | 1 | | 5 | >= | 4 |
| 14 | E --> G | | | | | -1 | | 1 | | 4 | >= | 4 |
| 15 | F --> H | | | | | | -1 | | 1 | 9 | >= | 3 |
| 16 | G --> H | | | | | | | -1 | 1 | 5 | >= | 5 |
| 17 | | | | | | | | | | LHS | Sign | RHS |

*EST values*

Solver Parameters

Set Target Cell:  $J$6

Equal To:  ○ Max  ⦿ Min  ○ Value of:  0

By Changing Cells:

$B$5:$I$5

Subject to the Constraints:

$J$8:$J$16 >= $L$8:$L$16

Solve    Close    Guess    Options    Premium    Add

*Minimization problem*

*All constraints are ≥.*

*Check that Assume Non-Negative and Assume Linear Model are clicked.*

## Linear Programming Model to Determine the Latest Times

*Maximization objective function*

For each activity $i$, we define decision variable $L_i$ as its LST. In this LP model, the objective is to *maximize* the sum of all activity start times since we want to find the *latest* start times. However, we need to ensure that the entire project finishes at its earliest completion time (i.e., in 15 weeks, as computed in Program 7.1B). Hence, in addition to the constraints defining the activity precedence relationships, we also constrain the finish time of the *last activity* in the project. In General Foundry's case, we know that the last activity is H. Hence,

*We need to constrain the project completion time.*

we set the latest finish time of activity H to 15 weeks.

The complete LP model can be written as

$$\text{Maximize } L_A + L_B + L_C + L_D + L_E + L_F + L_G + L_H$$

subject to

$$
\begin{aligned}
L_C &\geq L_A + 2 \quad &&\text{(precedence A} \rightarrow \text{C)} \\
L_D &\geq L_A + 2 \quad &&\text{(precedence A} \rightarrow \text{D)} \\
L_D &\geq L_B + 3 \quad &&\text{(precedence B} \rightarrow \text{D)} \\
L_E &\geq L_C + 2 \quad &&\text{(precedence C} \rightarrow \text{E)} \\
L_F &\geq L_C + 2 \quad &&\text{(precedence C} \rightarrow \text{F)} \\
L_G &\geq L_D + 4 \quad &&\text{(precedence D} \rightarrow \text{G)} \\
L_G &\geq L_E + 4 \quad &&\text{(precedence E} \rightarrow \text{G)} \\
L_H &\geq L_F + 3 \quad &&\text{(precedence F} \rightarrow \text{H)} \\
L_H &\geq L_G + 5 \quad &&\text{(precedence G} \rightarrow \text{H)} \\
L_H + 2 &= 15 \quad &&\text{(latest finish time of H)} \\
\text{All } L_i &\geq 0 \quad &&\text{(nonnegativity)}
\end{aligned}
$$

**PROGRAM 7.2**    **Excel Layout and Solver Entries to Compute General Foundry's Latest Starting Times Using Linear Programming**

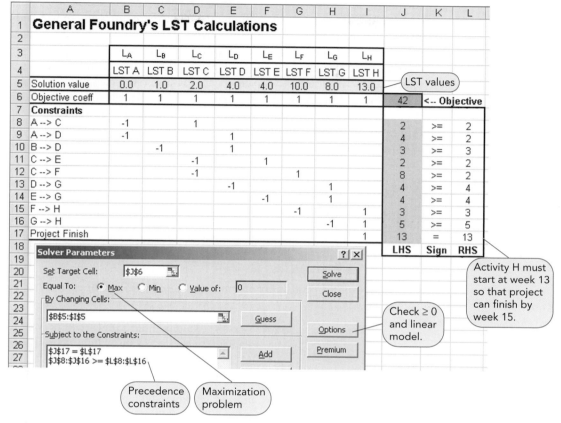

| | A | B | C | D | E | F | G | H | I | J | K | L |
|---|---|---|---|---|---|---|---|---|---|---|---|---|
| 1 | **General Foundry's LST Calculations** | | | | | | | | | | | |
| 2 | | | | | | | | | | | | |
| 3 | | $L_A$ | $L_B$ | $L_C$ | $L_D$ | $L_E$ | $L_F$ | $L_G$ | $L_H$ | | | |
| 4 | | LST A | LST B | LST C | LST D | LST E | LST F | LST G | LST H | | | |
| 5 | Solution value | 0.0 | 1.0 | 2.0 | 4.0 | 4.0 | 10.0 | 8.0 | 13.0 | | LST values | |
| 6 | Objective coeff | 1 | 1 | 1 | 1 | 1 | 1 | 1 | 1 | 42 | <-- Objective | |
| 7 | **Constraints** | | | | | | | | | | | |
| 8 | A --> C | -1 | | 1 | | | | | | 2 | >= | 2 |
| 9 | A --> D | -1 | | | 1 | | | | | 4 | >= | 2 |
| 10 | B --> D | | | -1 | 1 | | | | | 3 | >= | 3 |
| 11 | C --> E | | | -1 | | 1 | | | | 2 | >= | 2 |
| 12 | C --> F | | | -1 | | | 1 | | | 8 | >= | 2 |
| 13 | D --> G | | | | -1 | | | 1 | | 4 | >= | 4 |
| 14 | E --> G | | | | | -1 | | 1 | | 4 | >= | 4 |
| 15 | F --> H | | | | | | -1 | | 1 | 3 | >= | 3 |
| 16 | G --> H | | | | | | | -1 | 1 | 5 | >= | 5 |
| 17 | Project Finish | | | | | | | | 1 | 13 | = | 13 |
| 18 | | | | | | | | | | LHS | Sign | RHS |

*Activity H must start at week 13 so that project can finish by week 15.*

**Solver Parameters**

Set Target Cell: $J$6

Equal To: ● Max  ○ Min  ○ Value of: 0

By Changing Cells:
$B$5:$I$5

Subject to the Constraints:
$J$17 = $L$17
$J$8:$J$16 >= $L$8:$L$16

[ Solve ]  [ Close ]  [ Guess ]  [ Options ]  [ Premium ]  [ Add ]

*Precedence constraints*   *Maximization problem*   *Check ≥ 0 and linear model.*

**File: 7-2.xls**

**Excel Solution**   Program 7.2 shows the Excel layout and Solver entries for this LP model. In this model also, we have algebraically modified each constraint so that all variables are in the LHS.

Here again, as expected, the LST values for all activities (shown in cells B5:I5 in Program 7.2) are the same obtained earlier using the two-pass procedure.

 **IN ACTION**    Project Management and Software Development

Although computers have revolutionized how companies conduct business and allowed some organizations to achieve a long-term competitive advantage in the marketplace, the software that controls these computers is often more expensive than intended and takes longer to develop than expected. In some cases, large software projects are never fully completed. The London Stock Exchange, for example, had an ambitious software project called TAURUS that was intended to improve computer operations at the exchange. The TAURUS project, which cost hundreds of millions of dollars, was never completed. After numerous delays and cost overruns, the project was finally halted. The FLORIDA system, an ambitious software development project for the Department of Health and Rehabilitative Services for the state of Florida, was also delayed, cost more than

expected, and didn't operate as everyone had hoped. Although not all software development projects are delayed or over budget, it has been estimated that more than half of all software projects cost more than 189% of their original projections.

To control large software projects, many companies are now using project management techniques. Ryder Systems, Inc.; American Express Financial Advisors; and United Airlines have all created project management departments for their software and information systems projects. These departments have the authority to monitor large software projects and make changes to deadlines, budgets, and resources used to complete software development efforts.

**Source:** Julia King. "Tough Love Reins in IS Projects," *Computerworld* (June 19, 1995): 1–2.

## 7.5 VARIABILITY IN ACTIVITY TIMES

*Activity times are subject to variability.*

In identifying all earliest and latest times so far, and the associated critical path(s), we have adopted the CPM approach of assuming that all activity times are known and fixed constants. That is, there is no variability in activity times. However, in practice, it is likely that activity completion times vary depending on various factors.

For example, building internal components (activity A) for General Foundry is estimated to finish in 2 weeks. Clearly, factors such as late arrival of raw materials, absence of key personnel, and so on, could delay this activity. Suppose activity A actually ends up taking 3 weeks. Since A is on the critical path, the entire project will now be delayed by 1 week to 16 weeks. If we had anticipated completion of this project in 15 weeks, we would obviously miss our deadline.

Although some activities may be relatively less prone to delays, others could be extremely susceptible to delays. For example, activity B (modify roof and floor) could be heavily dependent on weather conditions. A spell of bad weather could significantly impact its completion time.

The preceding discussion implies that we cannot ignore the impact of variability in activity times when deciding the schedule for a project. The PERT approach to estimating activity times is designed specifically to address this issue.

### Three Time Estimates in PERT

*PERT uses three time estimates for each activity.*

In PERT, we employ a probability distribution based on three time estimates for each activity, as follows:

*Optimistic time (a)* = time an activity will take if everything goes as planned. In estimating this value, there should be only a small probability (say, 1/100) that the activity time will be ≤$a$.

*Pessimistic time (b)* = time an activity will take assuming very unfavorable conditions. In estimating this value, there should also be only a small probability that the activity time will be ≥$b$.

*Most likely time (m)* = most realistic estimate of the time required to complete an activity.

*The beta probability distribution is often used to describe activity times.*

When using PERT, you must often assume that activity time estimates follow the *beta probability distribution* (see Figure 7.13). This continuous distribution has been found to be very appropriate, in many cases, for determining the expected value and variance for activity completion times.

To find the *expected activity time*, $t$, the beta distribution weights the three time estimates as follows:

$$t = (a + 4m + b)/6 \qquad (7\text{-}6)$$

That is, the most likely time ($m$) is given four times the weight as the optimistic time ($a$) and pessimistic time ($b$). The time estimate $t$ computed using Equation 7-6 for each activity is used in the project network to compute all earliest and latest times.

To compute the *dispersion* or *variance of activity completion time*, we use the formula:[3]

$$\text{Variance} = [(b - a)/6]^2 \qquad (7\text{-}7)$$

---

[3] This formula is based on the statistical concept that from one end of the beta distribution to the other is 6 standard deviations (±3 standard deviations from the mean). Since $(b - a)$ is 6 standard deviations, the variance is $[(b - a)/6]^2$.

FIGURE 7.13    **Beta Probability Distribution with Three Time Estimates**

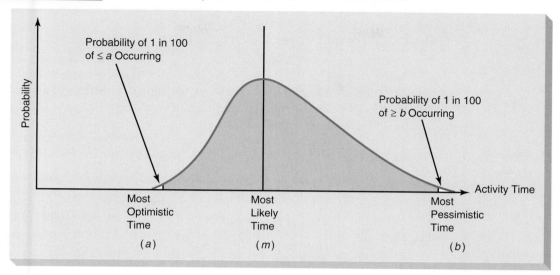

The standard deviation of activity completion time is the square root of the variance. Hence,

$$\text{Standard deviation} = \sqrt{\text{Variance}} = (b - a)/6 \tag{7-8}$$

**File: 7-3.xls**

Let us assume that Lester Harky has estimated the optimistic, most likely, and pessimistic times for each activity in General Foundry's project, as shown in columns C, D, and E, respectively, in Program 7.3. Using these estimates in Equations 7.6 through 7.8, we compute the expected time, variance, and standard deviation for each activity. These values are shown in columns F, G, and H, respectively. Note that expected times shown in column F in

PROGRAM 7.3    **Excel Layout to Compute General Foundry's Expected Times and Variances**

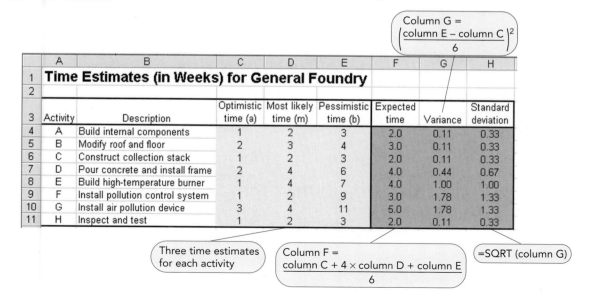

| | A | B | C | D | E | F | G | H |
|---|---|---|---|---|---|---|---|---|
| 1 | **Time Estimates (in Weeks) for General Foundry** | | | | | | | |
| 2 | | | | | | | | |
| 3 | Activity | Description | Optimistic time (a) | Most likely time (m) | Pessimistic time (b) | Expected time | Variance | Standard deviation |
| 4 | A | Build internal components | 1 | 2 | 3 | 2.0 | 0.11 | 0.33 |
| 5 | B | Modify roof and floor | 2 | 3 | 4 | 3.0 | 0.11 | 0.33 |
| 6 | C | Construct collection stack | 1 | 2 | 3 | 2.0 | 0.11 | 0.33 |
| 7 | D | Pour concrete and install frame | 2 | 4 | 6 | 4.0 | 0.44 | 0.67 |
| 8 | E | Build high-temperature burner | 1 | 4 | 7 | 4.0 | 1.00 | 1.00 |
| 9 | F | Install pollution control system | 1 | 2 | 9 | 3.0 | 1.78 | 1.33 |
| 10 | G | Install air pollution device | 3 | 4 | 11 | 5.0 | 1.78 | 1.33 |
| 11 | H | Inspect and test | 1 | 2 | 3 | 2.0 | 0.11 | 0.33 |

Column G = $\left(\dfrac{\text{column E} - \text{column C}}{6}\right)^2$

Three time estimates for each activity

Column F = $\dfrac{\text{column C} + 4 \times \text{column D} + \text{column E}}{6}$

=SQRT (column G)

Program 7.3 are, in fact, the activity times we used in our earlier computation and identification of the critical path.

## Probability of Project Completion

The critical path analysis helped us determine that General Foundry's expected project completion time is 15 weeks. Lester Harky knows, however, that there is significant variation in the time estimates for several activities. Variation in activities that are on the critical path can affect the overall project completion time—possibly delaying it. This is one occurrence that worries Harky considerably.

*We compute the project variance by summing variances of only those activities on the critical path.*

PERT uses the variance of critical path activities to help determine the variance of the overall project. Project variance is computed by summing variances of critical activities:

$$\text{Project variance} = \sum \ (\text{variances of activities on critical path}) \qquad (7\text{-}9)$$

From Program 7.3 we know that the variance of activity A is 0.11, variance of activity C is 0.11, variance of activity E is 1.00, variance of activity G is 1.78, and variance of activity H is 0.11. Hence, the total project variance and project standard deviation may be computed as

$$\text{Project variance} \ (\sigma_p^2) = 0.11 + 0.11 + 1.00 + 1.78 + 0.11 = 3.11$$

*Standard deviation* $= \sqrt{variance}$

which implies

$$\text{Project standard deviation} \ (\sigma_p) = \sqrt{\text{Project variance}} = \sqrt{3.11} = 1.76$$

How can this information be used to help answer questions regarding the probability of finishing the project on time? PERT makes two more assumptions: (1) total project completion times follow a normal probability distribution and (2) activity times are statistically independent. With these assumptions, the bell-shaped normal curve shown in Figure 7.14 can be used to represent project completion dates. This normal curve implies that there is a 50% chance the project completion time will be less than 15 weeks and a 50% chance that it will exceed 15 weeks.

For Harky to find the probability that his project will be finished on or before the 16-week deadline, he needs to determine the appropriate area under the normal curve. The standard normal equation can be applied as follows:

$$Z = (\text{due date} - \text{expected date of completion})/\sigma_p \qquad (7\text{-}10)$$

$$= (16 \text{ weeks} - 15 \text{ weeks})/1.76 \text{ weeks} = 0.57$$

where $Z$ is the number of standard deviations the due date or target date lies from the mean or expected date.

## FIGURE 7.14

**Probability Distribution for Project Completion Times**

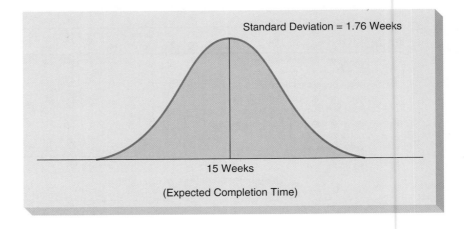

Standard Deviation = 1.76 Weeks

15 Weeks

(Expected Completion Time)

FIGURE 7.15

**Probability of General Foundry Meeting the 16-Week Deadline**

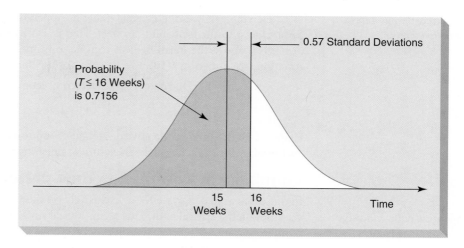

*Computing the probability of project completion.*

Referring to the Normal Table in Appendix C, we find a probability of 0.7156. Thus, there is a 71.6% chance that the pollution control equipment can be put in place in 16 weeks or less. This is shown in Figure 7.15.

## Determining Project Completion Time for a Given Confidence Level

Lester Harky is extremely worried that there is only a 71.6% chance that the pollution control equipment can be put in place in 16 weeks or less. He thinks that it may be possible for him to plead with the environmental group for more time. However, before he approaches the group, he wants to arm himself with sufficient information about the project. Specifically, he wants to find the deadline by which he has a 99% chance of completing the project. He hopes to use his analysis to convince the group to agree to this extended deadline.

Clearly, this due date would be greater than 16 weeks. However, what is the exact value of this new due date? To answer this question, we again use the assumption that General Foundry's project completion time follows a normal probability distribution with a mean of 15 weeks and a standard deviation of 1.76 weeks.

For Harky to find the due date under which the project has a 99% chance of completion, he needs to determine the $Z$ value corresponding to 99%, as shown in Figure 7.16.

FIGURE 7.16

**$Z$-Value for 99% Probability of Project Completion**

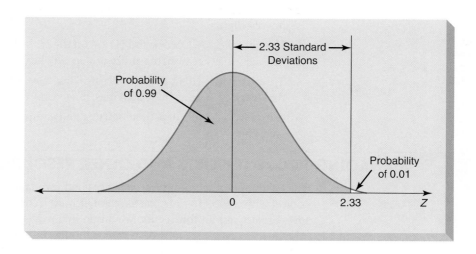

*Computing the due date for a given probability.*

Referring again to the Normal Table in Appendix C, we identify a Z value of 2.33 as being closest to the probability of 0.99. That is, Harky's due date should be 2.33 standard deviations above the mean project completion time. Starting with the standard normal equation (see Equation 7-10), we can solve for the due date and rewrite the equation as

$$\text{Due date} = \text{Expected completion time} + Z \times \sigma_p \qquad (7\text{-}11)$$

$$= 15 + 2.33 \times 1.76 = 19.1 \text{ weeks}$$

Hence, if Harky can get the environmental group to agree to give him a new deadline of 19.1 weeks (or more), he can be 99% sure of finishing the project on time.

### Variability in Completion Time of Noncritical Paths

*Noncritical paths with large variances should also be closely monitored.*

In our discussion so far, we focus exclusively on the variability in the completion times of activities on the critical path. This seems logical since these activities are, by definition, the more important activities in a project network. However, when there is variability in activity times, it is important that we also investigate the variability in the completion times of activities on *noncritical* paths.

Consider, for example, activity D in General Foundry's project. Recall from Table 7.3 on page 268 that this is a noncritical activity, with a slack time of 1 week. We have therefore not considered the variability in D's time in computing the probabilities of project completion times. We observe, however, that D has a variance of 0.44 (see Program 7.3 on page 275). In fact, the pessimistic completion time for D is 6 weeks. This means that if D ends up taking its pessimistic time to finish, the project will not finish in 15 weeks, even though D is not a critical activity.

For this reason, when we find probabilities of project completion times, it may be necessary for us to not focus only on the critical path(s). We may need to also compute these probabilities for noncritical paths, especially those that have relatively large variances. It is possible for a noncritical path to have a smaller probability of completion within a due date, when compared with the critical path. In fact, a different critical path can evolve because of the probabilistic situation.

### What Project Management Has Provided So Far

Project management techniques have thus far been able to provide Lester Harky with several valuable pieces of management information:

1. The project's expected completion date is 15 weeks.
2. There is a 71.6% chance that the equipment will be in place within the 16-week deadline. PERT analysis can easily find the probability of finishing by any date Harky is interested in.
3. Five activities (A, C, E, G, and H) are on the critical path. If any one of these is delayed for any reason, the entire project will be delayed.
4. Three activities (B, D, F) are not critical but have some slack time built in. This means that Harky can delay these activities, if needed.
5. A detailed schedule of activity starting and ending dates have been made available (see Table 7.3).

## 7.6   MANAGING PROJECT COSTS AND OTHER RESOURCES

The techniques discussed so far are very good for planning, scheduling, and monitoring a project with respect to time. We have not, however, considered another very important factor—project *cost*. In this section, we begin by investigating how costs can be planned and scheduled. Then we see how costs can be monitored and controlled.

# Planning and Scheduling Project Costs: Budgeting Process

*The budgeting process determines the budget per period of the project.*

The overall approach in the budgeting process of a project is to determine how much is to be spent every week or month. This is accomplished as follows:

---

## Three Steps of the Budgeting Process

1. Identify all costs associated with each of the activities. Then add these costs together to get one estimated cost or budget for each activity. When dealing with a large project, several activities may be combined into larger *work packages*. A work package is simply a logical collection of activities. Since the General Foundry project is quite small, each activity can be a work package.

2. Convert the budgeted cost per activity into a cost per time period. To do this, assume that the cost of completing any activity is spent at a linear rate over time. Thus, if the budgeted cost for a given activity is $48,000 and the activity's expected time is four weeks, the budgeted cost per week is $12,000 (= $48,000/4 weeks).

3. Using the earliest and latest start times, find out how much money should be spent during each week or month to finish the project by the due date.

---

**Budgeting for General Foundry** Let us apply this budgeting process to the General Foundry problem. Lester Harky has carefully computed the costs associated with each of his eight activities. He has also divided the total budget for each activity by the activity's expected time to determine the weekly budget for the activity. The budget for activity A, for example, is $22,000 (see Table 7.4). Since its expected time ($t$) is 2 weeks, $11,000 is spent each week to complete the activity. Table 7.4 also provides two pieces of data we found earlier: the EST and LST for each activity.

Looking at the total of the budgeted activity costs, we see that the entire project will cost $308,000. Finding the weekly budget will help Harky determine how the project is progressing on a week-to-week basis.

*Weekly budget using EST values*

The weekly budget for the project is developed from the data in Table 7.4. The EST for activity A is 0. Since A takes 2 weeks to complete, its weekly budget of $11,000 should be spent in weeks 1 and 2. For activity B, the EST is 0, the expected completion time is 3 weeks, and the budgeted cost per week is $10,000. Hence, $10,000 should be spent for activity B in each of weeks 1, 2, and 3. Using the EST, we can find the exact weeks during which the

---

**TABLE 7.4**

**Activity Cost for General Foundry**

| ACTIVITY | EARLIEST START TIME, EST | LATEST START TIME, LST | EXPECTED TIME, $t$ | TOTAL BUDGETED COST ($) | BUDGETED COST PER WEEK ($) |
|----------|--------------------------|------------------------|--------------------|-------------------------|----------------------------|
| A | 0 | 0 | 2 | 22,000 | 11,000 |
| B | 0 | 1 | 3 | 30,000 | 10,000 |
| C | 2 | 2 | 2 | 26,000 | 13,000 |
| D | 3 | 4 | 4 | 48,000 | 12,000 |
| E | 4 | 4 | 4 | 56,000 | 14,000 |
| F | 4 | 10 | 3 | 30,000 | 10,000 |
| G | 8 | 8 | 5 | 80,000 | 16,000 |
| H | 13 | 13 | 2 | 16,000 | 8,000 |
| | | | | Total   308,000 | |

**TABLE 7.5**  Budgeted Cost (in Thousands of Dollars) for General Foundry, Using Earliest Start Times

| ACTIVITY | WEEK | | | | | | | | | | | | | | | TOTAL |
|---|---|---|---|---|---|---|---|---|---|---|---|---|---|---|---|---|
| | 1 | 2 | 3 | 4 | 5 | 6 | 7 | 8 | 9 | 10 | 11 | 12 | 13 | 14 | 15 | |
| A | 11 | 11 | | | | | | | | | | | | | | 22 |
| B | 10 | 10 | 10 | | | | | | | | | | | | | 30 |
| C | | | 13 | 13 | | | | | | | | | | | | 26 |
| D | | | | 12 | 12 | 12 | 12 | | | | | | | | | 48 |
| E | | | | | 14 | 14 | 14 | 14 | | | | | | | | 56 |
| F | | | | | 10 | 10 | 10 | | | | | | | | | 30 |
| G | | | | | | | | | 16 | 16 | 16 | 16 | 16 | | | 80 |
| H | | | | | | | | | | | | | | 8 | 8 | 16 |
| | | | | | | | | | | | | | | | | 308 |
| Total per week | 21 | 21 | 23 | 25 | 36 | 36 | 36 | 14 | 16 | 16 | 16 | 16 | 16 | 8 | 8 | |
| Total to date | 21 | 42 | 65 | 90 | 126 | 162 | 198 | 212 | 228 | 244 | 260 | 276 | 292 | 300 | 308 | |

budget for each activity should be spent. These weekly amounts can be summed for all activities to arrive at the weekly budget for the entire project. For example, a total of $21,000 each should be spent during weeks 1 and 2. These weekly totals can then be added to determine the total amount that should be spent to date (total to date). All these computations are shown in Table 7.5.

*Weekly budget using LST values*

Those activities along the critical path must spend their budgets at the times shown in Table 7.5. The activities that are *not* on the critical path, however, can be started at a later date. This concept is embodied in the LST for each activity. Thus, if LST values are used, another budget can be obtained. This budget will delay the expenditure of funds until the last possible moment. The procedures for computing the budget when LST is used are the same as when EST is used. The results of the new computations are shown in Table 7.6.

**TABLE 7.6**  Budgeted Cost (in Thousands of Dollars) for General Foundry, Using Latest Start Times

| ACTIVITY | 1 | 2 | 3 | 4 | 5 | 6 | 7 | 8 | 9 | 10 | 11 | 12 | 13 | 14 | 15 | TOTAL |
|---|---|---|---|---|---|---|---|---|---|---|---|---|---|---|---|---|
| A | 11 | 11 | | | | | | | | | | | | | | 22 |
| B | | 10 | 10 | 10 | | | | | | | | | | | | 30 |
| C | | | 13 | 13 | | | | | | | | | | | | 26 |
| D | | | | | 12 | 12 | 12 | 12 | | | | | | | | 48 |
| E | | | | | 14 | 14 | 14 | 14 | | | | | | | | 56 |
| F | | | | | | | | | | | 10 | 10 | 10 | | | 30 |
| G | | | | | | | | | 16 | 16 | 16 | 16 | 16 | | | 80 |
| H | | | | | | | | | | | | | | 8 | 8 | 16 |
| | | | | | | | | | | | | | | | | 308 |
| Total per week | 11 | 21 | 23 | 23 | 26 | 26 | 26 | 26 | 16 | 16 | 26 | 26 | 26 | 8 | 8 | |
| Total to date | 11 | 32 | 55 | 78 | 104 | 130 | 156 | 182 | 198 | 214 | 240 | 266 | 292 | 300 | 308 | |

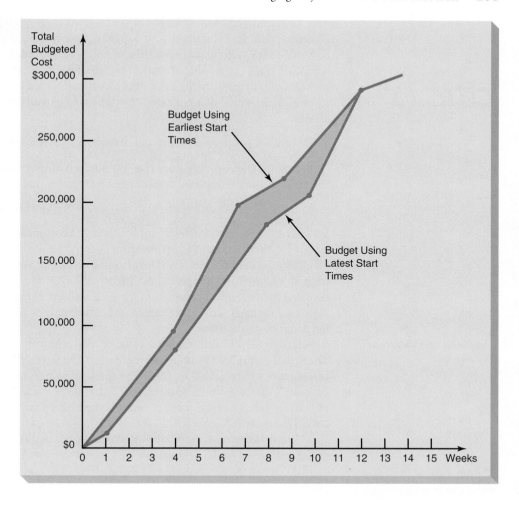

**FIGURE 7.17**

**Budget Ranges for General Foundry**

Compare the budgets given in Tables 7.5 and 7.6. The amount that should be spent to date (total to date) for the budget in Table 7.5 reveals the earliest possible time that funds can be expended. In contrast, the budget in Table 7.6 uses fewer financial resources in the first few weeks since it was prepared using LST values. That is, the budget in Table 7.6 shows the latest possible time that funds can be expended and still finish the project on time. Therefore, Lester Harky can use any budget between these feasible ranges and still complete the air pollution project on time. These two tables form feasible budget ranges.

*The two tables from the feasible budget ranges*

This concept is illustrated in Figure 7.17, which plots the total-to-date budgets for EST and LST.

## Monitoring and Controlling Project Costs

Budgets like the ones shown in Figure 7.17 are normally developed before the project is started. Then, as the project is being completed, funds expended should be monitored and controlled. The purpose of monitoring and controlling project costs is to ensure that the project is progressing on schedule and that cost overruns are kept to a minimum. The status of the entire project should be checked periodically.

*Tracking costs to see if the project is on budget*

Lester Harky wants to know how his air pollution project is going. It is now the end of the sixth week of the 15-week project. Activities A, B, and C have been fully completed. These activities incurred costs of $20,000, $36,000, and $26,000, respectively. Activity D is only 10% complete, and so far the cost expended on it has been $6,000. Activity E is 20% complete, with an incurred cost of $20,000. Activity F is 20% complete, with an incurred cost of $4,000. Activities G and H have not been started. Is the air pollution project on schedule? What is the value of work completed? Are there any cost overruns?

*Computing value of work completed for each activity*

One way to measure the value of the work completed (or the cost-to-date) for an activity is to multiply its total budgeted cost times the percent of completion for that activity.[4] That is,

$$\text{Value of work completed} = (\text{percent of work completed}) \times (\text{total activity budget}) \quad (7\text{-}12)$$

To determine the cost difference (i.e., the amount of overrun or underrun) for an activity, the value of work completed is subtracted from the actual cost. Hence,

$$\text{Cost difference} = \text{Actual cost} - \text{Value of work completed} \quad (7\text{-}13)$$

If a cost difference is negative, it implies there is a cost underrun. In contrast, if the number is positive, there has been a cost overrun.

Table 7.7 summarizes this information for General Foundry's project. The second column shows the total budgeted cost (from Table 7.4 on page 279), and the third column contains the percent of completion for each activity. Using these data, and the actual cost expended for each activity, we can compute the value of work completed and the cost difference for every activity.

*Computing cost underruns and overruns*

Activity D, for example, has a value of work completed of $4,800 (= $48,000 × 10%). The actual cost is $6,000, implying there is a cost overrun of $1,200. The cost difference for all activities can be added to determine the total project overrun or underrun. In General Foundry's case, we can see from Table 7.7 that there is a $12,000 cost overrun at the end of the sixth week. The total value of work completed so far is only $100,000, and the actual cost of the project to date is $112,000.

How do these costs compare with the budgeted costs for week 6? If Harky had decided to use the budget for ESTs (see Table 7.5), we can see that $162,000 should have been spent.

**TABLE 7.7**     Monitoring and Controlling Budgeted Costs for General Foundry

| ACTIVITY | TOTAL BUDGETED COST ($) | PERCENT OF COMPLETION | VALUE OF WORK COMPLETED ($) | ACTUAL COST ($) | ACTIVITY DIFFERENCE ($) |
|---|---|---|---|---|---|
| A | 22,000 | 100 | 22,000 | 20,000 | −2,000 |
| B | 30,000 | 100 | 30,000 | 36,000 | 6,000 |
| C | 26,000 | 100 | 26,000 | 26,000 | 0 |
| D | 48,000 | 10 | 4,800 | 6,000 | 1,200 |
| E | 56,000 | 20 | 11,200 | 20,000 | 8,800 |
| F | 30,000 | 20 | 6,000 | 4,000 | −2,000 |
| G | 80,000 | 0 | 0 | 0 | 0 |
| H | 16,000 | 0 | 0 | 0 | 0 |
| | | Total | 100,000 | 112,000 | 12,000 |

*Overrun*

---

[4] The percent of completion for each activity can be measured in many ways. For example, we might use the ratio of labor hours expended to total labor hours estimated.

## IN ACTION     Costing Projects at Nortel

Many companies, including Nortel, a large telecommunications company, are benefiting from project management. With more than 20,000 active projects worth a total of more than $2 billion, effectively managing projects at Nortel has been challenging. Getting the needed input data, including times and costs, can be difficult.

Like most companies, Nortel used standard accounting practices to monitor and control costs. This typically involves allocating costs to each department. Most projects, however, span multiple departments. This can make it very difficult to get timely cost information. Project managers often get project cost data later than they wanted. Because the cost data are allocated to departments, the data are often not detailed enough to help manage projects and get an accurate picture of true project costs.

To get more accurate cost data for project management, Nortel adopted an activity-based costing (ABC) method often used in manufacturing operations. In addition to standard cost data, each project activity was coded with a project identification number and a regional researched development location number. This greatly improved the ability of project managers to control costs. Because some of the month-end costing processes were simplified, the approach also lowered project costs in most cases. Project managers also were able to get more detailed costing information. Because the cost data were coded for each project, getting timely feedback was also possible. In this case, getting good input data reduced project costs, reduced the time needed to get critical project feedback, and made project management more accurate.

**Source:** Chris Dorey. "The ABCs of R&D at Nortel," *CMA Magazine* (March 1998): 19–22.

Thus, the project is behind schedule and there are cost overruns. Harky needs to move faster on this project to finish on time. He must also control future costs carefully to try to eliminate the current cost overrun of $12,000. To monitor and control costs, the budgeted amount, the value of work completed, and the actual costs should be computed periodically.

### Managing Other Resources

*Other resources can also be planned for and monitored.*

So far, we have focused on monitoring and controlling costs. Although this is clearly an important issue, there may be other resources (e.g., labor, machinery, materials) that also need to be carefully planned for and monitored in order for a project to finish on schedule. For example, activity E (build high-temperature burner) may need some specialized equipment in order to be performed. Likewise, installation of the air pollution device (activity G) may need a specialist to be present. It is therefore important that we be aware of such resource requirements and ensure that the right resources are available at the right time.

Just as we constructed a weekly budget using activity schedules and costs (see Tables 7.5 and 7.6), we can construct weekly requirement charts for any resource. Assume that Lester Harky has estimated the support staff requirement for each of the eight activities in the project, as shown in Table 7.8. That is, during each week that activity A is in progress, Harky needs 4 support staffers to be available.

**TABLE 7.8**

**Support Staff Requirement for General Foundry**

| ACTIVITY | DESCRIPTION | SUPPORT STAFF NEEDED PER WEEK |
|----------|-------------|-------------------------------|
| A | Build internal components | 4 |
| B | Modify roof and floor | 5 |
| C | Construct collection stack | 6 |
| D | Pour concrete and install frame | 4 |
| E | Build high-temperature burner | 3 |
| F | Install pollution control system | 4 |
| G | Install air pollution device | 7 |
| H | Inspect and test | 2 |

| TABLE 7.9 | | | | | | | | Support Staff Required for General Foundry Using Earliest Start Times | | | | | | | | |
|---|---|---|---|---|---|---|---|---|---|---|---|---|---|---|---|---|

| | WEEK | | | | | | | | | | | | | | | |
|---|---|---|---|---|---|---|---|---|---|---|---|---|---|---|---|---|
| ACTIVITY | 1 | 2 | 3 | 4 | 5 | 6 | 7 | 8 | 9 | 10 | 11 | 12 | 13 | 14 | 15 | TOTAL |
| A | 4 | 4 | | | | | | | | | | | | | | 8 |
| B | 5 | 5 | 5 | | | | | | | | | | | | | 15 |
| C | | | 6 | 6 | | | | | | | | | | | | 12 |
| D | | | | 4 | 4 | 4 | 4 | | | | | | | | | 16 |
| E | | | | | 3 | 3 | 3 | 3 | | | | | | | | 12 |
| F | | | | | 4 | 4 | 4 | | | | | | | | | 12 |
| G | | | | | | | | | 7 | 7 | 7 | 7 | 7 | | | 35 |
| H | | | | | | | | | | | | | | 2 | 2 | 4 |
| | | | | | | | | | | | | | | | | 114 |
| Total per week | 9 | 9 | 11 | 10 | 11 | 11 | 11 | 3 | 7 | 7 | 7 | 7 | 7 | 2 | 2 | |
| Total to date | 9 | 18 | 29 | 39 | 50 | 61 | 72 | 75 | 82 | 89 | 96 | 103 | 110 | 112 | 114 | |

Table 7.9 shows the weekly support staff needed for General Foundry's project using EST values. A graph that plots the total resource (such as labor) needed per period (*y*-axis) versus time (*x*-axis) is called a *resource-loading chart*.

## 7.7  PROJECT CRASHING

While managing a project, it is not uncommon for a project manager to be faced with either (or both) of the following situations: (1) the project is behind schedule and (2) the scheduled project completion time has been moved forward. In either situation, some or all of the remaining activities need to be speeded up in order to finish the project by the desired due date. The process by which we shorten the duration of a project in the cheapest manner possible is called *project crashing*.

*Reducing a project's duration is called* crashing.

As mentioned earlier, CPM is a deterministic technique in which each activity has two sets of time. The first is the *normal* or *standard* time that we used in our computation of earliest and latest times. Associated with this normal time is the *normal cost* of the activity, which we used in Section 7.6 to schedule and monitor the cost of the project.

*Crash time is the shortest duration of an activity.*

The second time is the *crash time*, which is defined as the shortest duration required to complete an activity. Associated with this crash time is the *crash cost* of the activity. Usually, we can shorten an activity by adding extra resources (e.g., equipment, people) to it. Hence, it is logical for the crash cost of an activity to be higher than its normal cost.

The amount by which an activity can be shortened (i.e., the difference between its normal time and crash time) depends on the activity in question. We may not be able to shorten some activities at all. For example, if a casting needs to be heat-treated in the furnace for 48 hours, adding more resources does not help shorten the time. In contrast, we may be able to shorten some activities significantly (e.g., frame a house in 3 days instead of 10 days by using three times as many workers).

*We want to find the cheapest way of crashing a project to the desired due date.*

Likewise, the cost of crashing (or shortening) an activity depends on the nature of the activity. Managers are usually interested in speeding up a project at the least additional cost. Hence, in choosing which activities to crash, and by how much, we need to ensure the following:

■ the amount by which an activity is crashed is, in fact, permissible,

■ taken together, the shortened activity durations will enable us to finish the project by the due date, and

■ the total cost of crashing is as small as possible.

In what follows, we first illustrate how to crash a small project using simple calculations that can even be performed by hand. Then, we describe an LP-based approach that can be used to determine the optimal crashing scheme for projects of any size.

## Crashing General Foundry's Project (Hand Calculations)

Suppose that General Foundry has been given only 13 weeks (instead of 16 weeks) to install the new pollution control equipment or face a court-ordered shutdown. As you recall, the length of Lester Harky's critical path was 15 weeks. Which activities should Harky crash, and by how much, in order to meet this 13-week due date? Naturally, Harky is interested in speeding up the project by 2 weeks, at the least additional cost.

Crashing a project using hand calculations involves four steps, as follows:

---

### Four Steps of Project Crashing

1. Compute the crash cost per week (or other time period) for all activities in the network. If crash costs are assumed to be linear over time, the following formula can be used:

$$\text{Crash cost per period} = \frac{(\text{Crash cost} - \text{Normal cost})}{(\text{Normal time} - \text{Crash time})} \tag{7-14}$$

2. Using the current activity times, find the critical path(s) in the project network. Identify the critical activities.

3. If there is only one critical path, then select the activity on this critical path that (a) can still be crashed and (b) has the smallest crash cost per period. Crash this activity by one period.

   If there is more than one critical path, then select one activity from each critical path such that (a) each selected activity can still be crashed and (b) the total crash cost per period of *all* selected activities is the smallest. Crash each activity by one period. Note that the same activity may be common to more than one critical path.

4. Update all activity times. If the desired due date has been reached, stop. If not, return to Step 2.

---

*This assumes crash costs are linear over time.*

General Foundry's normal and crash times, and normal and crash costs, are shown in Table 7.10. Note, for example, that activity B's normal time is 3 weeks (the estimate used in computing the critical path), and its crash time is 1 week. This means that activity B can be shortened by up to 2 weeks if extra resources are provided. The cost of these additional resources is $4,000 (= difference between the crash cost of $34,000 and the normal cost of $30,000). If we assume that the crashing cost is linear over time (i.e., the cost is the same each week), activity B's crash cost per week is $2,000 (= $4,000/2).

| TABLE 7.10 | | TIME (WEEKS) | | COST ($) | | CRASH COST | CRITICAL |
|---|---|---|---|---|---|---|---|
| **Normal and Crash Data for General Foundry** | ACTIVITY | NORMAL | CRASH | NORMAL | CRASH | PER WEEK ($) | PATH? |
| | A | 2 | 1 | 22,000 | 22,750 | 750 | Yes |
| | B | 3 | 1 | 30,000 | 34,000 | 2,000 | No |
| | C | 2 | 1 | 26,000 | 27,000 | 1,000 | Yes |
| | D | 4 | 3 | 48,000 | 49,000 | 1,000 | No |
| | E | 4 | 2 | 56,000 | 58,000 | 1,000 | Yes |
| | F | 3 | 2 | 30,000 | 30,500 | 500 | No |
| | G | 5 | 2 | 80,000 | 84,500 | 1,500 | Yes |
| | H | 2 | 1 | 16,000 | 19,000 | 3,000 | Yes |

This calculation is shown in Figure 7.18. Crash costs for all other activities can be computed in a similar fashion.

Steps 2, 3, and 4 can now be applied to reduce General Foundry's project completion time at a minimum cost. For your convenience, we show the project network for General Foundry again in Figure 7.19.

The current critical path (using normal times) is Start-A-C-E-G-H, in which Start is just a dummy starting activity. Of these critical activities, activity A has the lowest crash cost per week of $750. Harky should therefore crash activity A by 1 week to reduce the project completion time to 14 weeks. The cost is an additional $750. Note that activity A cannot be crashed any further since it has reached its crash limit of 1 week.

*There are now two critical paths.*

At this stage, the original path Start-A-C-E-G-H remains critical with a completion time of 14 weeks. However, a new path Start-B-D-G-H is also critical now, with a completion time of 14 weeks. Hence, any further crashing must be done to both critical paths.

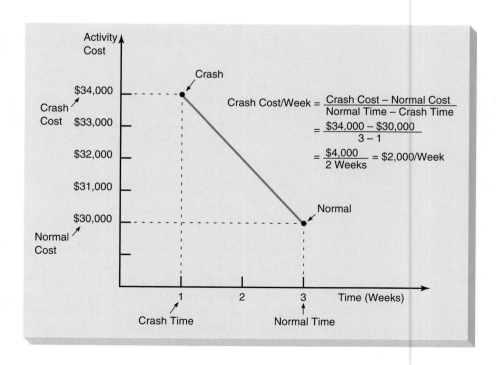

**FIGURE 7.18**

**Crash and Normal Times and Costs for Activity B**

$$\text{Crash Cost/Week} = \frac{\text{Crash Cost} - \text{Normal Cost}}{\text{Normal Time} - \text{Crash Time}}$$

$$= \frac{\$34,000 - \$30,000}{3 - 1}$$

$$= \frac{\$4,000}{2 \text{ Weeks}} = \$2,000/\text{Week}$$

**FIGURE 7.19**  **Critical Path and Slack Times for General Foundry**

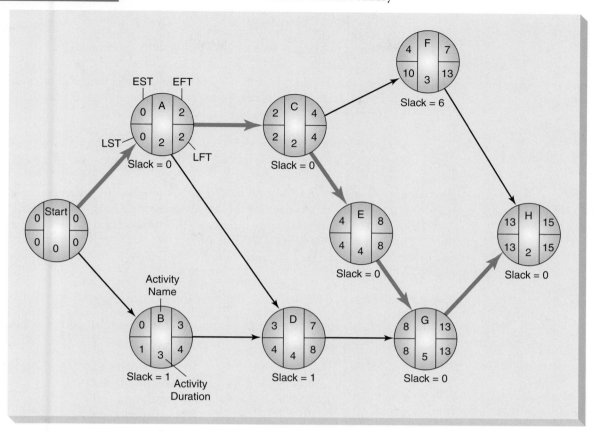

On each of these critical paths, we need to identify one activity that can still be crashed. We also want the total cost of crashing an activity on each path to be the smallest. We might be tempted to simply pick the activities with the smallest crash cost per period in each path. If we do this, we would select activity C from the first path and activity D from the second path. The total crash cost would then be $2,000 (= $1,000 + $1,000).

*Crashing activities common to more than one critical path may be cheaper.*

But we spot that activity G is common to both paths. That is, by crashing activity G, we will simultaneously reduce the completion time of both paths. Even though the $1,500 crash cost for activity G is higher than that for activities C and D, we would still prefer crashing G since the total cost is now only $1,500 (compared with the $2,000 if we crash C and D).

Hence, to crash the project down to 13 weeks, Lester Harky should crash activity A by 1 week, and activity G by 1 week. The total additional cost is $2,250 (= $750 + $1,500).

## Crashing General Foundry's Project Using Linear Programming

Although the preceding crashing procedure is simple for projects involving just a few activities, we can see how it can become extremely cumbersome to use for larger projects. Let us instead examine an LP-based approach that can be applied to projects of any size.

The data needed for General Foundry's LP model are the normal and crash time and cost data (see Table 7.10), and the activity precedence information (see Figure 7.19). We develop the model as follows.

*Decision variables are start times and crash amounts.*

**Decision Variables**  For each activity $i$, we define the following two decision variables:

$$T_i = \text{Time at which activity } i \text{ starts}$$

$$C_i = \text{Number of periods (weeks) by which activity } i \text{ is crashed}$$

*Objective is to minimize total crash cost.*

**Objective Function**  The objective function is to minimize the total cost of crashing the project down to 13 weeks. Using the crash cost per week, computed in Table 7.10, we can express this as

$$\text{Minimize total crash cost} = \$750C_A + \$2{,}000C_B + \$1{,}000C_C$$
$$+ \$1{,}000C_D + \$1{,}000C_E + \$500C_F + \$1{,}500C_G + \$3{,}000C_H$$

*Constraints defining the precedence relationships.*

**Precedence Constraints**  As in the LP models discussed earlier to determine the EST and LST values, these constraints describe the activity precedence relationships in the project (see Figure 7.19). The only difference is that now the duration of activity $i$ can be reduced by $C_i$. That is, if activity A starts at $T_A$, it finishes at $(T_A + 2 - C_A)$. This implies that the start time of activity C (i.e., $T_C$) can be *no earlier* than $(T_A + 2 - C_A)$. We can express this mathematically as

$$T_C \geq T_A + 2 - C_A \qquad \text{(precedence A} \rightarrow \text{C)}$$

In a similar fashion, we can express all other activity precedence relationships as follows:

$$
\begin{array}{ll}
T_D \geq T_A + 2 - C_A & \text{(precedence A} \rightarrow \text{D)} \\
T_D \geq T_B + 3 - C_B & \text{(precedence B} \rightarrow \text{D)} \\
T_E \geq T_C + 2 - C_C & \text{(precedence C} \rightarrow \text{E)} \\
T_F \geq T_C + 2 - C_C & \text{(precedence C} \rightarrow \text{F)} \\
T_G \geq T_D + 4 - C_D & \text{(precedence D} \rightarrow \text{G)} \\
T_G \geq T_E + 4 - C_E & \text{(precedence E} \rightarrow \text{G)} \\
T_H \geq T_F + 3 - C_F & \text{(precedence F} \rightarrow \text{H)} \\
T_H \geq T_G + 5 - C_G & \text{(precedence G} \rightarrow \text{H)} \\
\text{All } T_i \text{ and } C_i \geq 0 & \text{(nonnegativity)}
\end{array}
$$

*Each activity can be crashed only by a finite amount.*

**Crash Time Limit Constraints**  This set of constraints restricts the amount by which each activity can be crashed. Using the crash time limits given in Table 7.10, we can write these constraints as

$$
\begin{array}{lll}
C_A \leq 1 & C_B \leq 2 & C_C \leq 1 \\
C_D \leq 1 & C_E \leq 2 & C_F \leq 1 \\
C_G \leq 3 & C_H \leq 1 &
\end{array}
$$

*Constraint regarding project due date*

**Project Completion Constraint**  Finally, we specify that the project must be completed in 13 weeks or less. Activity H, the last activity in the project, starts at time $T_H$. The normal time for H is 2 weeks, and $C_H$ denotes the number of weeks by which its duration can be crashed. Hence, the actual duration of activity H is $(2 - C_H)$ and its completion time is $(T_H + 2 - C_H)$. We write this constraint as

$$T_H + 2 - C_H \leq 13$$

**File: 7-4.xls**

**Excel Solution**  Program 7.4 shows the Excel layout and Solver entries for General Foundry's project crashing LP model. As usual, we have algebraically modified each constraint so that all variables are in the LHS.

**PROGRAM 7.4**    **Excel Layout and Solver Entries for General Foundry's Crashing Problem**

Activity start times

Crash values

| | $T_A$ | $T_B$ | $T_C$ | $T_D$ | $T_E$ | $T_F$ | $T_G$ | $T_H$ | $C_A$ | $C_B$ | $C_C$ | $C_D$ | $C_E$ | $C_F$ | $C_G$ | $C_H$ | | | |
|---|---|---|---|---|---|---|---|---|---|---|---|---|---|---|---|---|---|---|---|
| | Start Act A | Start Act B | Start Act C | Start Act D | Start Act E | Start Act F | Start Act G | Start Act H | Crash Act A | Crash Act B | Crash Act C | Crash Act D | Crash Act E | Crash Act F | Crash Act G | Crash Act H | | | Total crash cost |
| Solution value | 0.0 | 0.0 | 1.0 | 3.0 | 3.0 | 8.0 | 7.0 | 11.0 | 1.0 | 0.0 | 0.0 | 0.0 | 0.0 | 0.0 | 1.0 | 0.0 | | | |
| Crash Cost | | | | | | | | | $750 | $2,000 | $1,000 | $1,000 | $1,000 | $500 | $1,500 | $3,000 | $2,250 | | |
| **Constraints** | | | | | | | | | | | | | | | | | | | |
| A --> C | -1 | | 1 | | | | | | 1 | | | | | | | | 2 | >= | 2 |
| A --> D | -1 | | | 1 | | | | | 1 | | | | | | | | 4 | >= | 2 |
| B --> D | | -1 | | 1 | | | | | | 1 | | | | | | | 3 | >= | 3 |
| C --> E | | | -1 | | 1 | | | | | | 1 | | | | | | 2 | >= | 2 |
| C --> F | | | -1 | | | 1 | | | | | 1 | | | | | | 7 | >= | 2 |
| D --> G | | | | -1 | | | 1 | | | | | 1 | | | | | 4 | >= | 4 |
| E --> G | | | | | -1 | | 1 | | | | | | 1 | | | | 4 | >= | 4 |
| F --> H | | | | | | -1 | | 1 | | | | | | 1 | | | 3 | >= | 3 |
| G --> H | | | | | | | -1 | 1 | | | | | | | 1 | | 5 | >= | 5 |
| Crash Limit A | | | | | | | | | 1 | | | | | | | | 1 | <= | 1 |
| Crash Limit B | | | | | | | | | | 1 | | | | | | | 0 | <= | 2 |
| Crash Limit C | | | | | | | | | | | 1 | | | | | | 0 | <= | 1 |
| Crash Limit D | | | | | | | | | | | | 1 | | | | | 0 | <= | 1 |
| Crash Limit E | | | | | | | | | | | | | 1 | | | | 0 | <= | 2 |
| Crash Limit F | | | | | | | | | | | | | | 1 | | | 0 | <= | 1 |
| Crash Limit G | | | | | | | | | | | | | | | 1 | | 1 | <= | 3 |
| Crash Limit H | | | | | | | | | | | | | | | | 1 | 0 | <= | 1 |
| Project Finish | | | | | | | | 1 | | | | | | | | -1 | 11 | <= | 11 |
| | | | | | | | | | | | | | | | | | LHS | Sign | RHS |

Minimization objective

The SUMPRODUCT function is used to compute all values in column R.

**Solver Parameters** [?][X]

Set Target Cell: $R$6

Equal To: ○ Max ● Min ○ Value of: 0

By Changing Cells: $B$5:$Q$5

Subject to the Constraints:

$R$17:$R$25 <= $T$17:$T$25
$R$8:$R$16 >= $T$8:$T$16

[ Solve ] [ Close ] [ Guess ] [ Options ] [ Premium ] [ Add ]

Precedence constraints

Crash limit constraints, and project deadline constraint

Check ≥ 0 and linear model.

The results show that the General Foundry project can be crashed to 13 weeks at a cost of $2,250 (cell R6). To do so, activities A (cell J5) and G (cell P5) should be crashed by 1 week each. As expected, this is the same as the result we obtained earlier using hand calculations. Cells B5:I5 show the revised starting times for activities A through H, respectively.

## 7.8  USING MICROSOFT PROJECT TO MANAGE PROJECTS

The analyses discussed so far are effective for managing small projects. However, for managing large complex projects, specialized project management software are preferred. In this section, we provide a brief introduction to a popular example of such specialized software, Microsoft Project 2000.

We should note that at this introductory level, our intent here is not to describe the full capabilities of this program. Rather, we illustrate how it can be used to perform some of the basic calculations in managing projects. We leave it to you to explore the advanced capabilities and functions of Microsoft Project 2000 (or any other project management software) in greater detail, either on your own or as part of an elective course in project management.

*Microsoft Project is useful for project scheduling and control.*

Microsoft Project is extremely useful in drawing project networks (Section 7.2), identifying the project schedule (Section 7.3), and managing project costs and other resources (Section 7.6). It does not, however, perform PERT probability calculations (Section 7.5), or have an LP-based procedure built in for project crashing (Section 7.7).

## Creating a Project Schedule Using Microsoft Project

Let us consider the General Foundry project again. Recall from Section 7.2 that this project has eight activities. The first step is to define the activities and their precedence relationships. To do so, we start Microsoft Project and click File|New to open a blank project. We can now enter the project start date in the summary information that is first presented (see Program 7.5A). Note that dates are referred to by actual calendar dates rather than as day 0, day 1, and so on. For example, we have used July 1, 2002 as our project starting date in Program 7.5A. Microsoft Project will automatically update the project finish date once we have entered all the project information. In Program 7.5A, we have specified the current date as August 12, 2002.

**File: 7-5.mpp**

*First, we define a new project.*

*Next, we enter the activity information.*

| Durations | |
|---|---|
| Activity | Time in Weeks |
| A | 2 |
| B | 3 |
| C | 2 |
| D | 4 |
| E | 4 |
| F | 3 |
| G | 5 |
| H | 2 |

**Entering Activity Information**  After entering the summary information, we now use the window shown in Program 7.5B to enter all activity information. For each activity (or task, as Microsoft Project calls it), we enter its name and duration. Microsoft Project identifies tasks by numbers (e.g., 1, 2) rather than letters. Hence, for convenience, we have shown both the letter (e.g., A, B) and the description of the activity in the Task Name column in Program 7.5B. By default, the duration is measured in days. To specify weeks, we include the letter "*w*" after the duration of each activity. For example, we enter the duration of activity A as 2*w*.

As we enter the activities and durations, the software automatically inserts start and finish dates. Note that all activities have the same start date (i.e., 7/1/02) since we have not yet defined the precedence relationships. Also, as shown in Program 7.5B, if the Gantt Chart option is selected in the View menu, a horizontal bar corresponding to the duration of each activity appears on the right pane of the window.

Observe that Saturdays and Sundays are automatically grayed out in the Gantt chart to reflect the fact that these are nonworking days. In most project management software, we

**PROGRAM 7.5A**

**Project Summary Information in Microsoft Project**

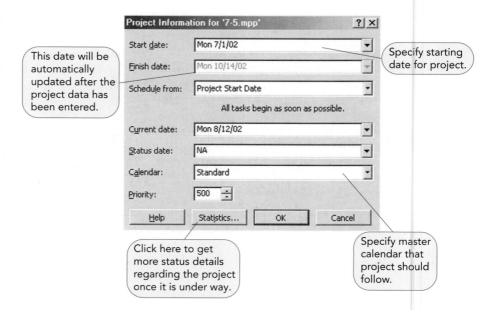

This date will be automatically updated after the project data has been entered.

Specify starting date for project.

Click here to get more status details regarding the project once it is under way.

Specify master calendar that project should follow.

**PROGRAM 7.5B**    **Activity Entry in Microsoft Project for General Foundry**

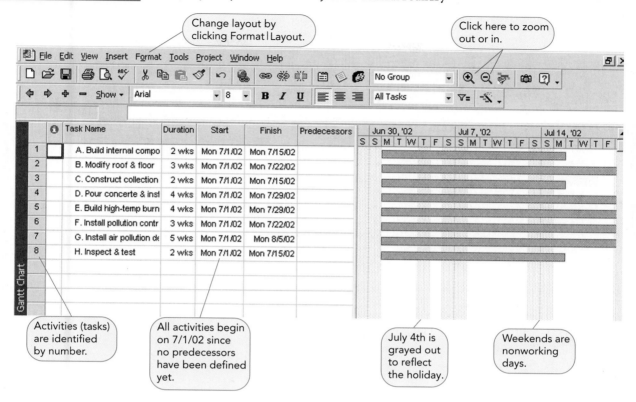

The schedule automatically takes nonworking days into account.

can link the entire project to a master calendar (or alternatively, link each activity to its own specific calendar). Additional nonworking days can be defined using these calendars. For example, we have used Tools|Change Working Time to specify July 4, 2002, as a nonworking day in Program 7.5B. This automatically extends all activity completion times by one day. Since activity A starts on Monday, July 1, 2002, and takes 2 weeks (i.e., 10 working days), its finish time is now Monday, July 15, 2002 (rather than Friday, July 12, 2002).

**Precedences**

| Activity | Predecessors |
|----------|--------------|
| A | — |
| B | — |
| C | A |
| D | A, B |
| E | C |
| F | C |
| G | D, E |
| H | F, G |

**Defining Precedence Relationships**    The next step is to define precedence relationships (or links) between these activities. There are two ways of specifying these links. The first is to enter the relevant activity numbers (e.g., 1, 2) in the Predecessor column, as shown in Program 7.5C for activities C and D. The other approach uses the Link icon. For example, to specify the precedence relationship between activities C and E, we click activity C first, hold the Ctrl key down, and then click activity E. We then click the Link icon, as shown in Program 7.5C. As soon as we define a link, the bars in the Gantt chart are automatically repositioned to reflect the new start and finish times for the linked activities. Further, the link itself is shown as an arrow extending from the predecessor activity.

The project can be viewed either as a Gantt chart or as a network.

**Viewing the Project Schedule**    When all links have been defined, the complete project schedule can be viewed as a Gantt chart, as shown in Program 7.5D. We can also select View|Network Diagram to view the schedule as a project network (shown in Program 7.5E). The critical path is shown in red on the screen (bold in Program 7.5E) in the network diagram. We can click on any of the activities in the project network to view details of the activities. Likewise, we can easily add or remove activities and/or links from the project

**PROGRAM 7.5C**    **Defining Links Between Activities in Microsoft Project**

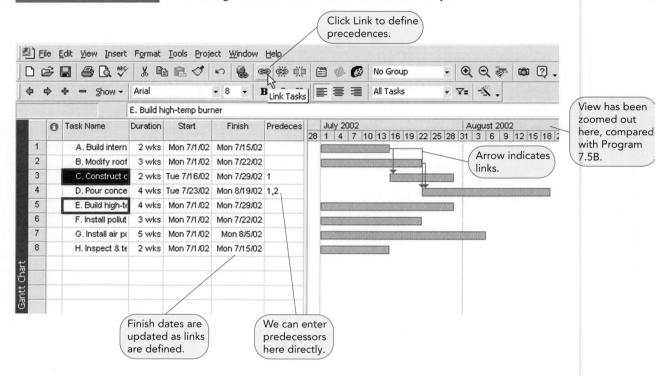

**PROGRAM 7.5D**    **Gantt Chart in Microsoft Project for General Foundry**

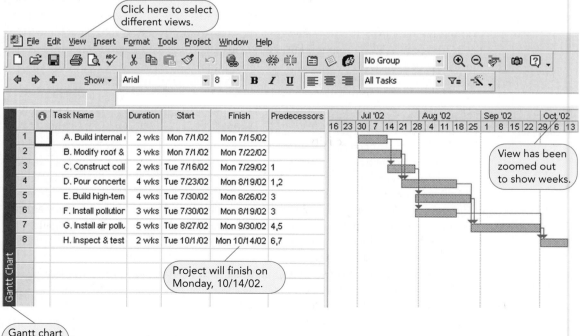

**PROGRAM 7.5E**    **Project Network in Microsoft Project for General Foundry**

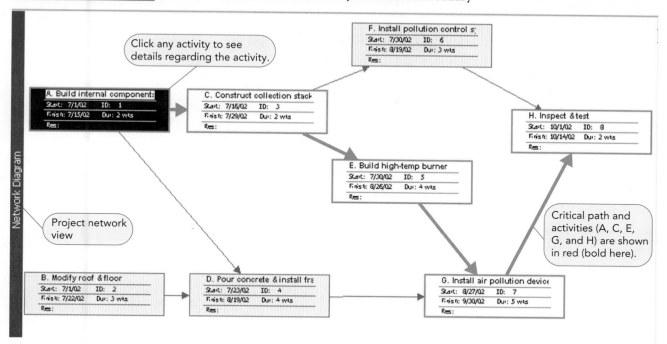

Click any activity to see details regarding the activity.

Project network view

Critical path and activities (A, C, E, G, and H) are shown in red (bold here).

network. Each time we do so, Microsoft Project automatically updates all start dates, finish dates, and the critical path(s). If desired, we can manually change the layout of the network (e.g., reposition activities) by changing the options in Format|Layout.

Programs 7.5D and 7.5E show that if the General Foundry's project starts on July 1, 2002, it can be finished on October 14, 2002. The start and finish dates for all activities are also clearly identified. This schedule takes into account the nonworking days on all weekends, and on July 4. These programs illustrate how the use of specialized project management software can greatly simplify the scheduling procedures discussed in Sections 7.2 to 7.4.

**PERT Analysis**  As mentioned previously, Microsoft Project does not perform the PERT probability calculations discussed in Section 7.5. However, by clicking View|Toolbars|PERT Analysis, we can get Microsoft Project to allow us to enter optimistic, most likely, and pessimistic times for each activity. We can then choose to view Gantt charts based on any of these three times for each activity.

## Tracking Progress and Managing Costs Using Microsoft Project

*The biggest benefit of using software is to track a project.*

Perhaps the biggest advantage of using specialized software to manage projects is that they can track the progress of the project. In this regard, Microsoft Project has many features available to track individual activities in terms of time, cost, resource usage, and so on. In this section, we first illustrate how we can track the progress of a project in terms of time. We then introduce project costs so that we can compute cost overruns or underruns (as we did in Table 7.7 on page 282).

**File: 7-6.mpp**

**Tracking the Time Status of a Project**  An easy way to track the time progress of tasks is to enter the percent of work completed for each task. One way to do so is to double-click on any activity in the Task Name column in Program 7.5D. A window, like the one shown in Program 7.6A, is displayed. Let us now enter the percent of work completed for each task

**PROGRAM 7.6A**

**Updating Activity
Progress in Microsoft
Project**

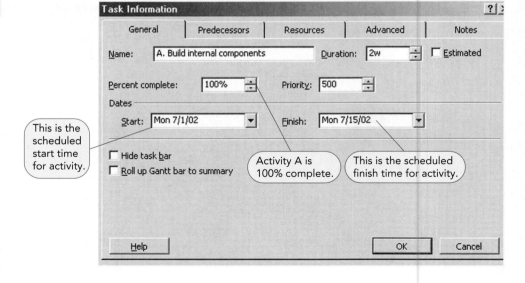

*Revisited Percent Completed*

| Activity | Completed |
|----------|-----------|
| A | 100 |
| B | 100 |
| C | 100 |
| D | 10 |
| E | 20 |
| F | 20 |
| G | 0 |
| H | 0 |

(as we did earlier in Table 7.7). For example, Program 7.6A shows that activity A is 100% complete. We enter the percent completed for all other activities in a similar fashion.

As shown in Program 7.6B, the Gantt chart immediately reflects this updated information by drawing a thick line within each activity's bar. The length of this line is proportional to the percent of that activity's work that has been completed.

How do we know if we are on schedule? Let us assume today is Monday, August 12, 2002 (i.e., the end of the sixth week in the project schedule).[5] Notice that there is a vertical line shown on the Gantt chart corresponding to today's date. Microsoft Project will

**PROGRAM 7.6B**     **Tracking Project Progress in Microsoft Project**

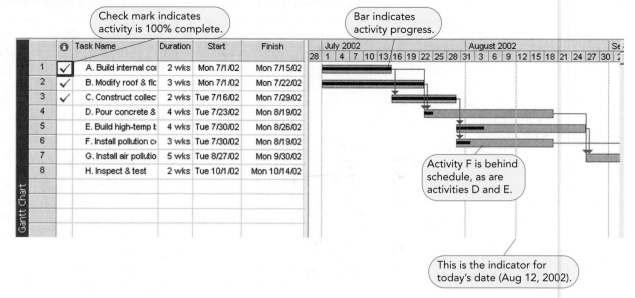

---

[5] Remember that the nonworking day on July 4 has moved all schedules by one day. Therefore, activities end on Mondays rather than on Fridays.

automatically move this line to correspond with the current date. If the project is on schedule, we should see all bars to the *left* of today's line indicate that they have been completed. For example, Program 7.6B shows that activities A, B, and C are on schedule. In contrast, activities D, E, and F appear to be behind schedule. These activities need to be investigated further to determine the reason for the delay. This type of easy *visual* information is what makes such software so useful in practice for project management.

**Tracking the Cost Status of a Project**   Just as we tracked a project's progress with regard to time, we can track its current status with regard to the budget. There are several ways to define the cost of an activity. If the total cost consists of both fixed and variable costs, we need to define the resources used in the project, the unit costs of these resources, and the level of usage for each resource by each activity. We can even specify how resources should be charged to an activity (e.g., prorated basis, full billing upon completion). Microsoft Project uses this information to first calculate the variable cost of each activity based on its level of resource usage. This is then added to the fixed costs to find the total cost for each activity.

*Defining costs for each activity*

In the case of General Foundry's project, since we do not have separate fixed and variable costs available, an easier way to enter activity costs is to click View|Table|Cost. The window shown in Program 7.6C is displayed. We enter the costs (see Table 7.7) in the Fixed Cost column. Microsoft Project automatically shows these values in the Total Cost column. We can now use these total costs to establish a Baseline Cost (or budgeted cost) by clicking Tools|Tracking|Save Baseline. This information is also shown in Program 7.6C.

Once we have entered this cost information, how do we compare our current expenses with the budget? To do so, we first need to turn off the automatic calculation option in Microsoft Project by clicking Tools|Options|Calculation and unchecking the box labeled "Actual costs are always calculated by Microsoft Project." Note that if we do not turn off this option, Microsoft Project assumes that all activities are always working as per the budget.

We now enter the actual costs (from Table 7.7) in the column titled Actual, as shown in Program 7.6D. The Variance column shows the budget overrun or underrun associated with each activity.

*Computing variances in activity budgets*

As noted earlier, our intent here is to provide just a brief introduction to Microsoft Project. This software (and other specialized project management software) has several other features and capabilities that we have not discussed here. For example, we can associate individual resources with specific activities and establish a separate calendar for each

*Revisited Actual Expenses*

| Activity | Expense |
|----------|---------|
| A | $20,000 |
| B | 36,000 |
| C | 26,000 |
| D | 6,000 |
| E | 20,000 |
| F | 4,000 |
| G | 0 |
| H | 0 |

**PROGRAM 7.6C**

**Entering Cost Information in Microsoft Project**

Establish Baseline by clicking Tools|Tracking|Save Baseline.

| | Task Name | Fixed Cost | Fixed Cost Accrual | Total Cost | Baseline |
|---|-----------|-----------|--------------------|-----------|---------|
| 1 | A. Build interna | $22,000.00 | Prorated | $22,000.00 | $22,000.00 |
| 2 | B. Modify roof a | $30,000.00 | Prorated | $30,000.00 | $30,000.00 |
| 3 | C. Construct cc | $26,000.00 | Prorated | $26,000.00 | $26,000.00 |
| 4 | D. Pour concret | $48,000.00 | Prorated | $48,000.00 | $48,000.00 |
| 5 | E. Build high-ter | $56,000.00 | Prorated | $56,000.00 | $56,000.00 |
| 6 | F. Install pollutic | $30,000.00 | Prorated | $30,000.00 | $30,000.00 |
| 7 | G. Install air pol | $80,000.00 | Prorated | $80,000.00 | $80,000.00 |
| 8 | H. Inspect & tes | $16,000.00 | Prorated | $16,000.00 | $16,000.00 |

In this case, we have entered the activity costs as fixed costs.

Total cost = fixed cost, since no variable costs have been defined.

**PROGRAM 7.6D**    **Checking Budget Status in Microsoft Project**

Budgeted costs

| | Task Name | Fixed Cost | Fixed Cost Accrual | Total Cost | Baseline | Variance | Actual | Remaining |
|---|---|---|---|---|---|---|---|---|
| 1 | A. Build internal componen | $22,000.00 | Prorated | $20,000.00 | $22,000.00 | ($2,000.00) | $20,000.00 | $0.00 |
| 2 | B. Modify roof & floor | $30,000.00 | Prorated | $36,000.00 | $30,000.00 | $6,000.00 | $36,000.00 | $0.00 |
| 3 | C. Construct collection sta | $26,000.00 | Prorated | $26,000.00 | $26,000.00 | $0.00 | $26,000.00 | $0.00 |
| 4 | D. Pour concrete & install f | $48,000.00 | Prorated | $49,200.00 | $48,000.00 | $1,200.00 | $6,000.00 | $43,200.00 |
| 5 | E. Build high-temp burner | $56,000.00 | Prorated | $64,800.00 | $56,000.00 | $8,800.00 | $20,000.00 | $44,800.00 |
| 6 | F. Install pollution control s | $30,000.00 | Prorated | $28,000.00 | $30,000.00 | ($2,000.00) | $4,000.00 | $24,000.00 |
| 7 | G. Install air pollution devic | $80,000.00 | Prorated | $80,000.00 | $80,000.00 | $0.00 | $0.00 | $80,000.00 |
| 8 | H. Inspect & test | $16,000.00 | Prorated | $16,000.00 | $16,000.00 | $0.00 | $0.00 | $16,000.00 |

Total cost values are changed to reflect variances.

Cost overruns and underruns. (Negative values indicate underruns).

Current expenses. You must turn off automatic calculations in order to enter information here.

resource. The time schedule of the activity will then be determined based not only on its duration and predecessors, but also on the resource calendars. Likewise, we can track each resource and identify possible conflicts (e.g., the same resource being required by two different activities at the same time). Once again, we encourage you to try these procedures out on your own to understand the full capabilities of specialized project management software.

## SUMMARY

This chapter presents the fundamentals of project management techniques. We discuss two techniques, PERT and CPM, both of which are excellent for controlling large and complex projects.

We first show how to express projects using project networks. Using a two-pass procedure, we can then identify the project schedule and the critical path(s). PERT is probabilistic and allows three time estimates for each activity, which are used to compute the project's expected completion time and variance. We show how to use these parameters to find the probability that the project will be completed by a given date.

We discuss how project management techniques can also be used to plan, schedule, monitor, and control project costs. Using these techniques, we show how to determine whether the project is on schedule at any point in time and whether there are cost overruns or underruns.

Next, we discuss how to crash projects by reducing their completion time through additional resource expenditures. We also illustrate how LP can be used to find the least-cost approach to crashing large projects.

Finally, we provide a brief introduction to Microsoft Project, one of several popular project management software packages currently widely used.

## GLOSSARY

**Activity.** A job or task that consumes time and is a key subpart of the total project.

**Activity on Arc (AOA) Network.** A project network in which arcs denote activities and nodes denote events.

**Activity on Node (AON) Network.** A project network in which nodes denote activities and arcs denote precedence relationships.

**Activity Time Estimate.** Completion time of an activity.

**Backward Pass.** A procedure that moves from the end of the network to the beginning of the network. It is used in determining an activity's LFT and LST.

**Beta Probability Distribution.** Probability distribution that is often used in PERT to compute expected activity completion times and variances.

**CPM.** Critical path method. A deterministic network technique that is similar to PERT but uses only one time estimate. Used for monitoring budgets and project crashing.

**Crashing.** The process of reducing the total time that it takes to complete a project by expending additional funds.

**Critical Path.** The series of activities that have a zero slack. It is the longest time path through the network. A delay for any activity that is on the critical path will delay the completion of the entire project.

**Critical Path Analysis.** An analysis that determines the total project completion time, the critical path for the project, slack, EST, EFT, LST, and LFT for every activity.

**Dummy Activity.** A fictitious activity that consumes no time and is inserted into an AOA project network to display the proper precedence relationships between activities.

**Earliest Finish Time (EFT).** The earliest time that an activity can be finished without violation of precedence requirements.

**Earliest Start Time (EST).** The earliest time that an activity can start without violation of precedence requirements.

**Event.** A point in time that marks the beginning or ending of an activity. Used in AOA networks.

**Expected Activity Time.** The average time that it should take to complete an activity. Expected time = $(a + 4m + b)/6$.

**Forward Pass.** A procedure that moves from the beginning of a network to the end of the network. It is used in determining an activity's EST and EFT.

**Gantt Chart.** An alternative to project networks for showing a project schedule.

**Immediate Predecessor.** An activity that must be completed before another activity can be started.

**Latest Finish Time (LFT).** The latest time that an activity can be finished without delaying the entire project.

**Latest Start Time (LST).** The latest time that an activity can be started without delaying the entire project.

**Most Likely Time ($m$).** The amount of time that you would expect it would take to complete the activity. Used in PERT.

**Optimistic Time ($a$).** The shortest amount of time that could be required to complete the activity. Used in PERT.

**PERT.** Program evaluation and review technique. A network technique that allows three time estimates for each activity in a project.

**Pessimistic Time ($b$).** The greatest amount of time that could be required to complete the activity. Used in PERT.

**Project Network.** A graphical display of a project that shows activities and precedence relationships.

**Slack Time.** The amount of time that an activity can be delayed without delaying the entire project. Slack is equal to the LST minus the EST, or the LFT minus the EFT.

**Variance of Activity Completion Time.** A measure of dispersion of the activity completion time. Variance = $[(b - a)/6]^2$.

# KEY EQUATIONS

(7-1)  EST = Maximum EFT value of all immediate predecessors

Earliest start time.

(7-2)  EFT = EST + Activity Time

Earliest finish time.

(7-3)  LFT = Minimum LST value of all immediate followers

Latest finish time.

(7-4)  LST = LFT − Activity Time

Latest start time.

(7-5)  Slack = LST − EST   or   Slack = LFT − EFT

Slack time in an activity.

(7-6)  $t = (a + 4m + b)/6$

Expected activity completion time.

(7-7)  Variance = $[(b - a)/6]^2$

Activity variance.

(7-8)  Standard deviation = $\sqrt{\text{Variance}}$ = $(b - a)/6$

Activity standard deviation.

(7-9)  Project variance = $\Sigma$ (variances of activities on critical path)

(7-10)  $Z = $ (due date − expected date of completion)$/\sigma_p$

Number of standard deviations the target date lies from the expected date, using the normal distribution.

(7-11)  Due date = Expected date of completion + $Z \times \sigma_p$

Determine due date for given completion probability.

(7-12)  Value of work completed = (percent of work completed) $\times$ (total activity budget)

(7-13)  Activity difference = Actual cost − Value of work completed

(7-14)  Crash cost per period = $\dfrac{(\text{Crash cost} - \text{Normal cost})}{(\text{Normal time} - \text{Crash time})}$

The cost of reducing an activity completion time per time period.

# SOLVED PROBLEMS

### Solved Problem 7-1

To complete the wing assembly for an experimental aircraft, Scott DeWitte has laid out the seven major activities involved. These activities have been labeled A through G in the following table, which also shows their estimated completion times (in weeks) and immediate predecessors. Determine the expected time and variance for each activity.

| ACTIVITY | a | m | b | IMMEDIATE PREDECESSORS |
|----------|---|---|---|------------------------|
| A | 1 | 2 | 3 | — |
| B | 2 | 3 | 4 | — |
| C | 4 | 5 | 6 | A |
| D | 8 | 9 | 10 | B |
| E | 2 | 5 | 8 | C, D |
| F | 4 | 5 | 6 | D |
| G | 1 | 2 | 3 | E |

### Solution

Expected times and variances can be computed using the formulas presented in the chapter. The results are summarized in the following table:

| ACTIVITY | EXPECTED TIME (IN WEEKS) | VARIANCE |
|----------|--------------------------|----------|
| A | 2 | $\frac{1}{9}$ |
| B | 3 | $\frac{1}{9}$ |
| C | 5 | $\frac{1}{9}$ |
| D | 9 | $\frac{1}{9}$ |
| E | 5 | 1 |
| F | 5 | $\frac{1}{9}$ |
| G | 2 | $\frac{1}{9}$ |

### Solved Problem 7-2

Referring to Solved Problem 7-1, now Scott would like to determine the critical path for the entire wing assembly project as well as the expected completion time for the total project. In addition, he would like to determine the earliest and latest start and finish times for all activities.

### Solution

The AON network for Scott DeWitte's project is shown in Figure 7.20. Note that this project has multiple activities (A and B) with no immediate predecessors, and multiple activities (F and G) with no successors. Hence, in addition to a dummy unique starting activity (Start), we have included a dummy unique finishing activity (End) for the project.

**FIGURE 7.20**    **Critical Path for Solved Problem 7-2**

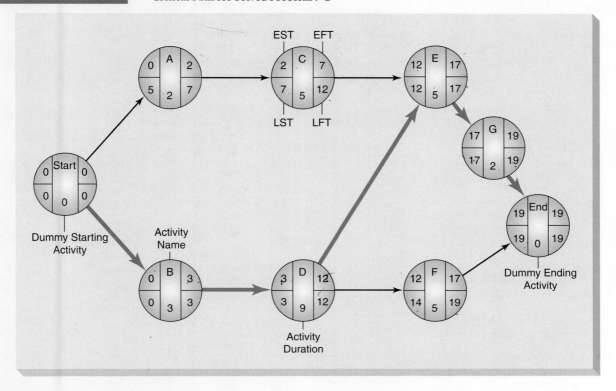

Figure 7.20 shows the earliest and latest times for all activities. The results are also summarized in the following table:

| ACTIVITY | ACTIVITY TIME | | | | |
|----------|-----|-----|-----|-----|-------|
| | EST | EFT | LST | LFT | SLACK |
| A | 0 | 2 | 5 | 7 | 5 |
| B | 0 | 3 | 0 | 3 | 0 |
| C | 2 | 7 | 7 | 12 | 5 |
| D | 3 | 12 | 3 | 12 | 0 |
| E | 12 | 17 | 12 | 17 | 0 |
| F | 12 | 17 | 14 | 19 | 2 |
| G | 17 | 19 | 17 | 19 | 0 |

Expected project length = 19 weeks

Variance of the critical path = 1.333

Standard deviation of the critical path = 1.155 weeks

The activities along the critical path are B, D, E, and G. These activities have zero slack, as shown in the table.

**⫸ SELF-TEST**

■ Before taking the self-test, refer back to the learning objectives at the beginning of the chapter, the notes in the margins, and the glossary at the end of the chapter.

■ Use the key at the back of the book to correct your answers.

■ Restudy pages that correspond to any questions that you answered incorrectly or material you feel uncertain about.

1. Network models such as PERT and CPM are used to
   a. manage complex projects.
   b. save time.
   c. save money.
   d. all of the above.
   e. none of the above.

2. PERT is an acronym for
   a. practical evaluation and research technique.
   b. program evaluation and review technique.
   c. performance elevation and restoration time.
   d. promotion effectiveness and retail trial.
   e. none of the above.

3. In PERT, if the pessimistic time was 14 weeks, the optimistic time was 8 weeks, and the most likely time was 11 weeks,
   a. the variance would be 1 week.
   b. the variance would be 11 weeks.
   c. the expected time would be 6 weeks.
   d. the expected time would be $5\frac{1}{2}$ weeks.
   e. there is not enough information.
   f. none of the above.

4. The critical path is
   a. the least-slack path.
   b. the longest time path through the network.
   c. that series of activities whose delay is most likely to delay the entire project.
   d. one or more paths through a network whose last activity's EFT is the largest for any activity in the project.
   e. all of the above.
   f. none of the above.

5. In PERT, the time estimate $b$ represents
   a. the optimistic time.
   b. the most likely time.
   c. the pessimistic time.
   d. the expected time.
   e. none of the above.

6. In PERT, slack time equals
   a. EST + $t$.
   b. LST − EST.
   c. zero.
   d. EFT − EST.
   e. none of the above.

7. The standard deviation for the PERT project is approximately
   a. the square root of the sum of the variances along the critical path.
   b. the sum of the critical path activity standard deviations.
   c. the square root of the sum of the variances of the project activities.
   d. all of the above.
   e. none of the above.

8. The crash cost per week
   a. is the difference in costs divided by the difference in times (crash and normal).
   b. is considered to be linear in the range between normal and crash.
   c. needs to be determined so that the smallest values on the critical path may be considered for time reduction first.
   d. all of the above.

9. _____ activities are ones that will delay the entire project if they are late or delayed.

10. PERT can use three estimates for activity time. These three estimates are _____, _____, and _____.

11. The probability distribution often used by PERT to describe activity times is the
    a. normal distribution.
    b. exponential distribution.
    c. beta distribution.
    d. uniform distribution.

12. PERT and CPM differ in that
    a. PERT uses dummy activities and CPM does not.
    b. PERT uses three time estimates and CPM uses single-time estimates.
    c. PERT does not allow us to monitor costs and CPM does.
    d. PERT uses AOA networks and CPM uses AON networks.

13. PERT assumes that the completion time of a project follows a
    a. normal distribution.
    b. exponential distribution.
    c. beta distribution.
    d. uniform distribution.

14. If an activity with free slack time of 2 weeks is delayed by 1 week,
    a. the project will be delayed by 1 week.
    b. the slack time of all activities that follow this activity is reduced by 1 week.
    c. no other activity in the project is affected.
    d. the probability of completing the project on time decreases.

15. An AON project network *must* have a unique starting activity (node) and a unique ending activity (node).
    a. True
    b. False

# DISCUSSION QUESTIONS AND PROBLEMS

## Discussion Questions

**7-1** What are some of the questions that can be answered with project management?

**7-2** What are the major differences between PERT and CPM?

**7-3** What is an activity? What is an immediate predecessor?

**7-4** Describe how expected activity times and variances can be computed in a PERT analysis.

**7-5** Briefly discuss what is meant by critical path analysis. What are critical path activities, and why are they important?

**7-6** What are the earliest activity start time and latest activity start time? How are they computed?

**7-7** Describe the meaning of slack and discuss how it can be determined.

**7-8** How can we determine the probability that a project will be completed by a certain date? What assumptions are made in this computation?

**7-9** Briefly describe how project budgets can be monitored.

**7-10** What is crashing, and how is it done by hand?

**7-11** Why is LP useful in project crashing?

## Problems

**7-12** Sid Davidson is the personnel director of Babson and Willcount, a company that specializes in consulting and research. One of the training programs that Sid is considering for the middle-level managers of Babson and Willcount is leadership training. Sid has listed a number of activities that must be completed before a training program of this nature could be conducted. The activities and immediate predecessors appear in the following table:

| ACTIVITY | IMMEDIATE PREDECESSORS |
|----------|------------------------|
| A | — |
| B | — |
| C | — |
| D | B |
| E | A, D |
| F | C |
| G | E, F |

Develop a network for this problem.

**7-13** Sid Davidson (see Problem 7-12) was able to determine the activity times for the leadership training program. He would like to determine the total project completion time and the critical path. The activity times appear in the following table:

| ACTIVITY | TIME (DAYS) |
|----------|-------------|
| A | 2 |
| B | 5 |
| C | 1 |
| D | 10 |
| E | 3 |
| F | 6 |
| G | 8 |
| | 35 |

**7-14** Monohan Machinery specializes in developing weed-harvesting equipment that is used to clear small lakes of weeds. George Monohan, president of Monohan Machinery, is convinced that harvesting weeds is far better than using chemicals to kill weeds. Chemicals cause pollution, and the weeds seem to grow faster after chemicals have been used. George is contemplating the construction of a machine that would harvest weeds on narrow rivers and waterways. The activities that are necessary to build one of these experimental weed-harvesting machines are listed in the following table. Construct a network for these activities.

| ACTIVITY | IMMEDIATE PREDECESSORS |
|----------|------------------------|
| A | — |
| B | — |
| C | A |
| D | A |
| E | B |
| F | B |
| G | C, E |
| H | D, F |

**7-15** After consulting with Butch Radner, George Monohan was able to determine the activity times for constructing the weed-harvesting machine to be used on narrow rivers. George would like to determine EST, EFT, LST, LFT, and slack for each activity. The total project completion time and the critical path should also be determined. (See Problem 7-14 for details). The activity times are shown in the table at the top of page 302:

| ACTIVITY | TIME (WEEKS) |
|----------|--------------|
| A | 6 |
| B | 5 |
| C | 3 |
| D | 2 |
| E | 4 |
| F | 6 |
| G | 10 |
| H | 7 |

**7-16** Zuckerman Wiring and Electric is a company that installs wiring and electrical fixtures in residential construction. John Zuckerman has been concerned with the amount of time that it takes to complete wiring jobs. Some of his workers are very unreliable. A list of activities and their optimistic, their pessimistic, and their most likely completion times in days are given in the following table:

| ACTIVITY | DAYS | | | IMMEDIATE PREDECESSORS |
|----------|---|---|---|------------------------|
| | *a* | *m* | *b* | |
| A | 3 | 6 | 8 | — |
| B | 2 | 4 | 4 | — |
| C | 1 | 2 | 3 | — |
| D | 6 | 7 | 8 | C |
| E | 2 | 4 | 6 | B, D |
| F | 6 | 10 | 14 | A, E |
| G | 1 | 2 | 4 | A, E |
| H | 3 | 6 | 9 | F |
| I | 10 | 11 | 12 | G |
| J | 14 | 16 | 20 | C |
| K | 2 | 8 | 10 | H, I |

Determine the expected completion time and variance for each activity.

**7-17** John Zuckerman would like to determine the total project completion time and the critical path for installing electrical wiring and equipment in residential houses. (See Problem 7-16 for details.) In addition, determine EST, EFT, LST, LFT, and slack for each activity.

**7-18** What is the probability that Zuckerman will finish the project described in Problems 7-16 and 7-17 in 40 days or less?

**7-19** Tom Schriber, director of personnel of Management Resources, Inc., is in the process of designing a program that its customers can use in the job-finding process. Some of the activities include preparing resumés, writing letters, making appointments to see prospective employers, researching companies and industries, and so on. Some of the information on the activities is shown in the following table:

| ACTIVITY | DAYS | | | IMMEDIATE PREDECESSORS |
|----------|---|---|---|------------------------|
| | *a* | *m* | *b* | |
| A | 8 | 10 | 12 | — |
| B | 6 | 7 | 9 | — |
| C | 3 | 3 | 4 | — |
| D | 10 | 20 | 30 | A |
| E | 6 | 7 | 8 | C |
| F | 9 | 10 | 11 | B, D, E |
| G | 6 | 7 | 10 | B, D, E |
| H | 14 | 15 | 16 | F |
| I | 10 | 11 | 13 | F |
| J | 6 | 7 | 8 | G, H |
| K | 4 | 7 | 8 | I, J |
| L | 1 | 2 | 4 | G, H |

(a) Construct a network for this problem.
(b) Determine the expected times and variances for each activity.
(c) Determine EST, EFT, LST, LFT, and slack for each activity.
(d) Determine the critical path and project completion time.
(e) Determine the probability that the project will be finished in 70 days.
(f) Determine the probability that the project will be finished in 80 days.
(g) Determine the probability that the project will be finished in 90 days.

**7-20** Ed Rose was able to determine that the expected project completion time for the construction of a pleasure yacht is 21 months, and the project variance is 4.

(a) What is the probability that the project will be completed in 17 months?
(b) What is the probability that the project will be completed in 20 months?
(c) What is the probability that the project will be completed in 23 months?
(d) What is the probability that the project will be completed in 25 months?

**7-21** The air pollution project discussed in the chapter has progressed over the past several weeks and it is now the end of week 8. Lester Harky would like to know the value of the work completed, the amount of any cost overruns or underruns for the project, and the extent to which the project is ahead of schedule or behind schedule by developing a table like Table 7.7 (see page 282). The revised cost figures appear in the following table:

| Activity | Percent of Completion | Actual Cost ($) |
|----------|------------------------|-----------------|
| A | 100 | 20,000 |
| B | 100 | 36,000 |
| C | 100 | 26,000 |
| D | 100 | 44,000 |
| E | 50 | 25,000 |
| F | 60 | 15,000 |
| G | 10 | 5,000 |
| H | 10 | 1,000 |

**7-22** Fred Ridgeway has been given the responsibility of managing a training and development program. He knows the EST, the LST, and the total costs for each activity. This information is given in the following table:

| Activity | EST | LST | t | Total Cost ($1,000's) |
|----------|-----|-----|---|------------------------|
| A | 0 | 0 | 6 | 10 |
| B | 1 | 4 | 2 | 14 |
| C | 3 | 3 | 7 | 5 |
| D | 4 | 9 | 3 | 6 |
| E | 6 | 6 | 10 | 14 |
| F | 14 | 15 | 11 | 13 |
| G | 12 | 18 | 2 | 4 |
| H | 14 | 14 | 11 | 6 |
| I | 18 | 21 | 6 | 18 |
| J | 18 | 19 | 4 | 12 |
| K | 22 | 22 | 14 | 10 |
| L | 22 | 23 | 8 | 16 |
| M | 18 | 24 | 6 | 18 |

(a) Using ESTs, determine Fred's total monthly budget.
(b) Using LSTs, determine Fred's total monthly budget.

**7-23** General Foundry's project crashing data were shown in Table 7.10 on page 286. Crash this project by hand to 11 weeks. What are the final times for each activity after crashing?

**7-24** Bowman Builders manufactures steel storage sheds for commercial use. Joe Bowman, president of Bowman Builders, is contemplating producing sheds for home use. The activities necessary to build an experimental model and related data are given in the table at the bottom of this page.
(a) What is the project completion date?
(b) Formulate an LP problem to crash this project to 10 weeks.
(c) Set up and solve the LP model using Excel.

**7-25** Software Development Specialists (SDS) is involved with developing software for customers in the banking industry. SDS breaks a large programming project into teams that perform the necessary steps. Team A is responsible for going from general systems design all the way through to actual systems testing. This involves 18 separate activities. Team B is then responsible for the final installation.

To determine cost and time factors, optimistic, most likely, and pessimistic time estimates have been made for all of the 18 activities involved for team A. The first step that this team performs is general systems design. The optimistic, most likely, and pessimistic times are 3 weeks, 4 weeks, and 5 weeks. Following this, a number of activities can begin. Activity 2 is involved with procedures design. Optimistic, most likely, and pessimistic times for completing this activity are 4, 5, and 7 weeks. Activity 3 is developing detailed report designs. Optimistic, most likely, and pessimistic time estimates are 6, 8, and 9 weeks. Activity 4, detailed forms design, has optimistic, most likely, and pessimistic time estimates of 2, 3, and 5 weeks.

The fifth and sixth activities involve writing detailed program specifications and developing file specifications. The three time estimates for activity 5 are 6, 7, and 9 weeks, and the three time estimates for activity 6 are 3, 4, and 5 weeks. Activity 7 is to specify system test data. Before this is done, activity 6, involving file specifications, must be completed. The

**Table for Problem 7-24**

| Activity | Normal Time | Crash Time | Normal Cost ($) | Crash Cost ($) | Immediate Predecessors |
|----------|-------------|------------|-----------------|----------------|------------------------|
| A | 3 | 2 | 1,000 | 1,600 | — |
| B | 2 | 1 | 2,000 | 2,700 | — |
| C | 1 | 1 | 300 | 300 | — |
| D | 7 | 3 | 1,300 | 1,600 | A |
| E | 6 | 3 | 850 | 1,000 | B |
| F | 2 | 1 | 4,000 | 5,000 | C |
| G | 4 | 2 | 1,500 | 2,000 | D, E |

time estimates for activity 7 are 2, 4, and 5 weeks. Activity 8 involves reviewing forms. Before activity 8 can be conducted, detailed forms design must be completed. The time estimates for activity 8 are 3, 4, and 6 weeks. The next activity, activity 9, is reviewing the detailed report design. This requires that the detailed report design, activity 3, be completed first. The time estimates for activity 9 are 1, 2, and 4 weeks, respectively.

Activity 10 involves reviewing procedures design. Time estimates are 1, 3, and 4 weeks. Of course, procedures design must be done before activity 10 can be started. Activity 11 involves the system design checkpoint review. A number of activities must be completed before this is done. These activities include reviewing the forms, reviewing the detailed report design, reviewing the procedures design, writing detailed program specs, and specifying system test data. The optimistic, most likely, and pessimistic time estimates for activity 11 are 3, 4, and 6 weeks. Performing program logic design is activity 12. This can only be started after the system design checkpoint review is completed. The time estimates for activity 12 are 4, 6, and 7 weeks.

Activity 13, coding the programs, is done only after the program logic design is completed. The time estimates for this activity are 6, 8, and 10 weeks. Activity 14 is involved in developing test programs. Activity 13 is the immediate predecessor. Time estimates for activity 14 are 3, 4, and 6 weeks. Developing a system test plan is activity 15. A number of activities must be completed before activity 15 can be started. These activities include specifying system test data, writing detailed program specifications, and reviewing procedure designs, the detailed report design, and forms.

The time estimates for activity 15 are 3, 4, and 5 weeks. Activity 16, creating system test data, has time estimates of 2, 4, and 6 weeks. Activity 15 must be done before activity 16 can be started. Activity 17 is reviewing program test results. The immediate predecessor to activity 17 is to test the programs (activity 14). The three time estimates for activity 17 are 2, 3, and 4 weeks. The final activity is conducting system tests. This is activity 18. Before activity 18 can be started, activities 16 and 17 must be complete. The three time estimates for conducting these system tests are 3, 5, and 6 weeks.

(a) How long will it take for team A to complete its programming assignment?

(b) What would happen if activity 5, writing detailed program specifications, had larger time estimates? Assume that these larger time estimates are 12, 14, and 15.

**7-26** The Bender Construction Co. is involved in constructing municipal buildings and other structures that are used primarily by city and state municipalities. This requires developing legal documents, drafting feasibility studies, obtaining bond ratings, and so forth. Recently, Bender was given a request to submit a proposal for the construction of a municipal building. The first step is to develop legal documents and to perform all steps necessary before the construction contract is signed. This requires more than 20 separate activities that must be completed. These activities, their immediate predecessors, and time requirements are given in Table 7.11 at the top of page 305.

Optimistic (*a*), most likely (*m*), and pessimistic (*b*) time estimates are given for all of the activities described in the table. Using the data, determine the total project completion time for this preliminary step, the critical path, and slack time for all activities involved.

**7-27** Getting a degree from a college or university can be a long and difficult task. Certain courses must be completed before other courses may be taken. Develop a network diagram, in which every activity is a particular course that must be taken for a given degree program. The immediate predecessors will be course prerequisites. Don't forget to include all university, college, and departmental course requirements. Then try to group these courses into semesters or quarters for your particular school. How long do you think it will take you to graduate? Which courses, if not taken in the proper sequence, could delay your graduation?

**7-28** Dream Team Productions was in the final design phases of its new film, *Killer Worms,* to be released next summer. Market Wise, the firm hired to coordinate the release of *Killer Worm* toys, identified 16 activities to be completed before the release of the film.

(a) How many weeks in advance of the film release should Market Wise start its marketing campaign? What are the critical paths? The tasks are as follows:

| Activity | Immediate Predecessors | Optimistic Time | Most Likely Time | Pessimistic Time |
|---|---|---|---|---|
| A | — | 1 | 2 | 4 |
| B | — | 3 | 3.5 | 4 |
| C | — | 10 | 12 | 13 |
| D | — | 4 | 5 | 7 |
| E | — | 2 | 4 | 5 |
| F | A | 6 | 7 | 8 |
| G | B | 2 | 4 | 5.5 |
| H | C | 5 | 7.7 | 9 |
| I | C | 9.9 | 10 | 12 |
| J | C | 2 | 4 | 5 |
| K | D | 2 | 4 | 6 |
| L | E | 2 | 4 | 6 |
| M | F, G, H | 5 | 6 | 6.5 |
| N | J, K, L | 1 | 1.1 | 2 |
| O | I, M | 5 | 7 | 8 |
| P | N | 5 | 7 | 9 |

## TABLE 7.11    Data for Problem 7-26, Bender Construction Company

| ACTIVITY | TIME REQUIRED (WEEKS) | | | DESCRIPTION OF ACTIVITY | IMMEDIATE PREDECESSORS |
|---|---|---|---|---|---|
| | a | m | b | | |
| 1 | 1 | 4 | 5 | Drafting legal documents | — |
| 2 | 2 | 3 | 4 | Preparation of financial statements | — |
| 3 | 3 | 4 | 5 | Draft of history | — |
| 4 | 7 | 8 | 9 | Draft demand portion of feasibility study | — |
| 5 | 4 | 4 | 5 | Review and approval of legal documents | 1 |
| 6 | 1 | 2 | 4 | Review and approval of history | 3 |
| 7 | 4 | 5 | 6 | Review feasibility study | 4 |
| 8 | 1 | 2 | 4 | Draft final financial portion of feasibility study | 7 |
| 9 | 3 | 4 | 4 | Draft facts relevant to the bond transaction | 5 |
| 10 | 1 | 1 | 2 | Review and approval of financial statements | 2 |
| 11 | 18 | 20 | 26 | Firm price received of project | — |
| 12 | 1 | 2 | 3 | Review and completion of financial portion of feasibility study | 8 |
| 13 | 1 | 1 | 2 | Draft statement completed | 6, 9, 10, 11, 12 |
| 14 | 0.10 | 0.14 | 0.16 | All materials sent to bond rating services | 13 |
| 15 | 0.20 | 0.30 | 0.40 | Statement printed and distributed to all interested parties | 14 |
| 16 | 1 | 1 | 2 | Presentation to bond rating services | 14 |
| 17 | 1 | 2 | 3 | Bond rating received | 16 |
| 18 | 3 | 5 | 7 | Marketing of bonds | 15, 17 |
| 19 | 0.10 | 0.10 | 0.20 | Purchase contract executed | 18 |
| 20 | 0.10 | 0.14 | 0.16 | Final statement authorized and completed | 19 |
| 21 | 2 | 3 | 6 | Purchase contract | 19 |
| 22 | 0.10 | 0.10 | 0.20 | Bond proceeds available | 20 |
| 23 | 0 | 0.2 | 0.2 | Sign construction contract | 21, 22 |

(b) If activities I and J were not necessary, what impact would this have on the critical path and the number of weeks needed to complete the marketing campaign?

**7-29** Sager Products has been in the business of manufacturing and marketing toys for toddlers for the past two decades. Jim Sager, president of the firm, is considering the development of a new manufacturing line to allow it to produce high-quality plastic toys at reasonable prices. The development process is long and complex. Jim estimates that there are five phases involved and multiple activities for each phase.

Phase 1 of the development process involves the completion of four activities. These activities have no immediate predecessors. Activity A has an optimistic completion time of 2 weeks, a probable completion time of 3 weeks, and a pessimistic completion time of 4 weeks. Activity B has estimated completion times of 5, 6, and 8 weeks; these represent optimistic, probable, and pessimistic time estimates. Similarly, activity C has estimated completion times of 1 week, 1 week, and 2 weeks; and activity D has expected completion times of 8 weeks, 9 weeks, and 11 weeks.

Phase 2 involves six separate activities. Activity E has activity A as an immediate predecessor. Time estimates are 1 week, 1 week, and 4 weeks. Activity F and activity G both have activity B as their immediate predecessor. For activity F, the time estimates are 3 weeks, 3 weeks, and 4 weeks. For activity G, the time estimates are 1 week, 2 weeks, and 2 weeks. The only immediate predecessor for activity H is activity C. Time estimates for activity H are 5 weeks, 5 weeks, and 6 weeks. Activity D must be performed before activity I and activity J can be started. Activity I has estimated completion times of 9 weeks, 10 weeks, and 11 weeks. Activity J has estimated completion times of 1 week, 2 weeks, and 2 weeks.

Phase 3 is the most difficult and complex of the entire development project. It also consists of six separate activities. Activity K has three time estimates of 2 weeks, 2 weeks, and 3 weeks. The immediate predecessor for this activity is activity E. The immediate predecessor for activity L is activity F. The time estimates for activity L are 3 weeks, 4 weeks, and 6 weeks. Activity M has 2 weeks, 2 weeks, and 4 weeks for the estimates of the optimistic, probable, and pessimistic time estimates. The immediate predecessor for activity M is activity G. Activities N and O both have activity I as their immediate predecessor. Activity N has 8 weeks, 9 weeks, and 11 weeks for its three time estimates. Activity O has 1 week, 1 week, and 3 weeks as its time estimates. Finally, activity P has time estimates of 4 weeks, 4 weeks, and 8 weeks. Activity J is the only immediate predecessor.

Phase 4 involves five activities. Activity Q requires activity K to be completed before it can be started. The three time estimates for activity Q are 6 weeks, 6 weeks, and 7 weeks. Activity R requires that both activity L and activity M be completed first. The three time estimates for activity R are 1, 2, and 4 weeks. Activity S requires activity N to be completed first. Its time estimates are 6 weeks, 6 weeks, and 7 weeks. Activity T requires that activity O be com-

pleted. The time estimates for activity T are 3 weeks, 3 weeks, and 4 weeks. The final activity for phase 4 is activity U. The time estimates for this activity are 1 week, 2 weeks, and 3 weeks. Activity P must be completed before activity U can be started.

Phase 5 is the final phase of the development project. It consists of only two activities. Activity V requires that activity Q and activity R be completed before it can be started. Time estimates for this activity are 9 weeks, 10 weeks, and 11 weeks. Activity W is the final activity of the process. It requires three activities to be completed before it can be started: activities S, T, and U. The estimated completion times for activity W are 2 weeks, 4 weeks, and 5 weeks.

(a) Given this information, determine the expected completion time for the entire process. Also determine those activities along the critical path. Jim hopes that the total project will take less than 40 weeks. Is this likely to occur?

(b) Jim has just determined that activity D has already been completed and that no additional work is required. What is the impact of this change on the activities along the critical path?

(c) What is the impact on the critical path and the total project completion time if both activity D and activity I have been completed?

(d) What would happen if the immediate predecessor activity changed? For example, activity F may have an immediate predecessor of activity A instead of activity B.

---

## ⫸ CASE STUDY

### Haygood Brothers Construction Company

George and Harry Haygood are building contractors who specialize in the construction of private home dwellings, storage warehouses, and small businesses (less than 20,000 sq. ft. of floor space). Both George and Harry entered a carpenter union's apprenticeship program in the early 1990s and, upon completion of the apprenticeship, became skilled craftsmen in 1996. Before going into business for themselves, they worked for several local building contractors in the Detroit area.

Typically, the Haygood Brothers submit competitive bids for the construction of proposed dwellings. Whenever their bids are accepted, various aspects of the construction (e.g., electrical wiring, plumbing, brick laying, painting) are subcontracted. George and Harry, however, perform all carpentry work. In addition, they plan and schedule all construction operations, frequently arrange interim financing, and supervise all construction activities.

The philosophy under which the Haygood Brothers have always operated can be simply stated: "Time is money." Delays in construction increase the costs of interim financing and post-

pone the initiation of their building projects. Consequently, they deal with all bottlenecks promptly and avoid all delays whenever possible. To minimize the time consumed in a construction project, the Haygood Brothers use PERT.

First, all construction activities and events are itemized and properly arranged (in parallel and sequential combinations) in a network. Then time estimates for each activity are made, the expected time for completing each activity is determined, and the critical (longest) path is calculated. Finally, earliest times, latest times, and slack values are computed. Having made these calculations, George and Harry can place their resources in the critical areas to minimize the time of completing the project.

The following are the activities that constitute an upcoming project (home dwelling) of the Haygood Brothers:

1. Arrange financing (A)
2. Let subcontracts (B)
3. Set and pour foundations (C)
4. Plumbing (D)
5. Framing (E)
6. Roofing (F)

## TABLE 7.12

**Haygood Brothers Construction Co.**

| ACTIVITY | IMMEDIATE PREDECESSORS | DAYS | | |
|---|---|---|---|---|
| | | *a* | *m* | *b* |
| A | — | 4 | 5 | 6 |
| B | A | 2 | 5 | 8 |
| C | B | 5 | 7 | 9 |
| D | B | 4 | 5 | 6 |
| E | C | 2 | 4 | 6 |
| F | E | 3 | 5 | 9 |
| G | E | 4 | 5 | 6 |
| H | E | 3 | 4 | 7 |
| I | E | 5 | 7 | 9 |
| J | D, I | 10 | 11 | 12 |
| K | F, G, H, J | 4 | 6 | 8 |
| L | F, G, H, J | 7 | 8 | 9 |
| M | L | 4 | 5 | 10 |
| N | K | 5 | 7 | 9 |
| O | N | 5 | 6 | 7 |
| P | M, O | 2 | 3 | 4 |

7. Electrical wiring (G)
8. Installation of windows and doors (H)
9. Ductwork and insulation (including heating and cooling units) (I)
10. Sheetrock, paneling, and paper hanging (J)
11. Installation of cabinets (K)
12. Bricking (L)
13. Outside trim (M)
14. Inside trim (including fixtures) (N)
15. Painting (O)
16. Flooring (P)

The immediate predecessors and optimistic (*a*), most likely (*m*), and pessimistic (*b*) time estimates are shown in Table 7.12.

### Discussion Questions

1. What is the time length of the critical path? What is the significance of the critical path?
2. Compute the amount of time that the completion of each activity can be delayed without affecting the overall project.
3. The project was begun August 1. What is the probability that the project can be completed by September 30? (Note: Scheduled completion time = 60 days.)

*Source:* Professor Jerry Kinard, Western Carolina University.

---

## ⟹ CASE STUDY

### Family Planning Research Center of Nigeria

Dr. Adinombe Watage, deputy director of the Family Planning Research Center in Nigeria's Over-The-River Province, was assigned the task of organizing and training five teams of field workers to perform educational and outreach activities as part of a large project to demonstrate acceptance of a new method of birth control. These workers already had training in family planning education but must receive specific training regarding the new method of contraception. Two types of materials must also be prepared: (1) those for use in training the workers and (2) those for distribution in the field. Training faculty must be brought in and arrangements made for transportation and accommodations for the participants.

Dr. Watage first called a meeting of this office staff. Together they identified the activities that must be carried out, their necessary sequences, and the time that they would require. Their results are displayed in Table 7.13.

Louis Odaga, the chief clerk, noted that the project had to be completed in 60 days. Whipping out his solar-powered calculator, he added up the time needed. It came to 94 days. "An impossible task, then," he noted. "No," Dr. Watage replied, "some of these tasks can go forward in parallel." "Be careful, though," warned Mr. Oglagadu, the chief nurse, "there aren't that many of us to go around. There are only 10 of us in this office."

"I can check whether we have enough heads and hands once I have tentatively scheduled the activities," Dr. Watage responded. "If the schedule is too tight, I have permission from the Pathminder Fund to spend some funds to speed it up, just so long as I can prove that it can be done at the least cost necessary. Can you help me prove that? Here are the costs for the activities with the elapsed time that we planned and the costs and times if we shorten them to an absolute minimum." Those data are given in Table 7.14.

| TABLE 7.13 | | | | |
|---|---|---|---|---|
| **Family Planning Research Center Activities** | ACTIVITY | MUST FOLLOW | TIME (DAYS) | STAFFING NEEDED |
| | A. Identify faculty and their schedules | — | 5 | 2 |
| | B. Arrange transport to base | — | 7 | 3 |
| | C. Identify and collect training materials | — | 5 | 2 |
| | D. Arrange accommodations | A | 3 | 1 |
| | E. Identify team | A | 7 | 4 |
| | F. Bring in team | B, E | 2 | 1 |
| | G. Transport faculty to base | A, B | 3 | 2 |
| | H. Print program material | C | 10 | 6 |
| | I. Have program materials delivered | H | 7 | 3 |
| | J. Conduct training program | D, F, G, I | 15 | 0 |
| | K. Perform fieldwork training | J | 30 | 0 |

| TABLE 7.14 | | NORMAL | | MINIMUM | | AVERAGE COST |
|---|---|---|---|---|---|---|
| **Family Planning Research Center Costs** | ACTIVITY | TIME | COST ($) | TIME | COST ($) | PER DAY SAVED ($) |
| | A. Identify faculty | 5 | 400 | 2 | 700 | 100 |
| | B. Arrange transport | 7 | 1,000 | 4 | 1,450 | 150 |
| | C. Identify materials | 5 | 400 | 3 | 500 | 50 |
| | D. Make accommodations | 3 | 2,500 | 1 | 3,000 | 250 |
| | E. Identify team | 7 | 400 | 4 | 850 | 150 |
| | F. Bring team in | 2 | 1,000 | 1 | 2,000 | 1,000 |
| | G. Transport faculty | 3 | 1,500 | 2 | 2,000 | 500 |
| | H. Print materials | 10 | 3,000 | 5 | 4,000 | 200 |
| | I. Deliver materials | 7 | 200 | 2 | 600 | 80 |
| | J. Train team | 15 | 5,000 | 10 | 7,000 | 400 |
| | K. Do fieldwork | 30 | 10,000 | 20 | 14,000 | 400 |

## Discussion Questions

1. Some of the tasks in this project can be done in parallel. Prepare a diagram showing the required network of tasks and define the critical path. What is the length of the project without crashing?

2. At this point, can the project be done given the personnel constraint of 10 persons?

3. If the critical path is longer than 60 days, what is the least amount that Dr. Watage can spend and still achieve this schedule objective? How can he prove to Pathminder Foundation that this is the minimum-cost alternative?

*Source:* Professor Curtis P. McLaughlin, Kenan-Flagler Business School, University of North Carolina at Chapel Hill.

## INTERNET CASE STUDIES

See our Internet home page at **www.prenhall.com/render** for these additional case studies: (1) Alpha Beta Gamma Record, (2) Bay Community Hospital, (3) Shale Oil Company, and (4) Southwestern University.

# BIBLIOGRAPHY

Angus, R. B., N. R. Gunderson, and T. P. Cullinano. *Planning, Performing, and Controlling Projects,* 3/e. Upper Saddle River, NJ: Prentice Hall, 2000.

Charoenngam, Chotchai et al. "Cost/Schedule Information System," *Cost Engineering* (September 1997): 29–35.

Dorey, Chris. "The ABCs of R&D at Nortel," *CMA Magazine* (March 1998): 19–22.

Ghattas, R. G. and S. L. McKee. *Practical Project Management.* Upper Saddle River, NJ: Prentice Hall, 2001.

Graham, Robert et al. "Creating an Environment for Successful Projects," *Research Technology Management* (February 1998): 60.

Kolisch, Rainer. "Resource Allocation Capabilities of Commercial Project Management Software Packages," *Interfaces* 29, 4 (July 1999): 19–31.

Mantel, S. J., J. R. Meredith, S. M. Shafer, and M. M. Sutton. *Project Management in Practice.* New York: Wiley, 2000.

Meredith, J. R. and S. J. Mantel. *Project Management: A Managerial Approach,* 4/e. New York: Wiley, 1999.

Murch, Richard. *Project Management: Best Practices for IT Professionals.* Upper Saddle River, NJ: Prentice Hall, 2001.

Roe, Justin. "Bringing Discipline to Project Management," *Harvard Business Review* (April 1998): 153–159.

Sander, Wayne. "The Projects Manager's Guide," *Quality Progress* (January 1998): 109.

Sivathanu, Pillai. "Enhanced PERT for Program Analysis, Control, and Evaluation," *International Journal of Project Management* (February 1993): 39–43.

# DECISION THEORY

After completing this chapter, students will be able to:

1. List the steps of the decision making process.
2. Describe the different types of decision making environments.
3. Make decisions under uncertainty when probability values are not known.
4. Make decisions under risk when probability values are known.
5. Use Excel to set up and solve problems involving decision tables.
6. Develop accurate and useful decision trees.

7. Use TreePlan to set up and analyze decision tree problems with Excel.
8. Revise probability estimates using Bayesian analysis.
9. Understand the importance and use of utility theory in decision making.

Summary • Glossary • Key Equations • Solved Problems • Self-Test • Discussion Questions and Problems • Case Study: Ski Right • Case Study: Blake Electronics • Internet Case Studies • Bibliography

## Decision Theory Helps Solve Airport Ground Delay Problems

One of the most frustrating aspects of air travel is rushing to the airport only to find out that the flight has been delayed. Often triggered by what is called the Ground-Delay Program (GDP), the Federal Aviation Administration (FAA) keeps flights from departing when the air traffic or weather at the destination is unfavorable.

Decisions involving GDP are classic problems in decision theory. At the heart of the problem, there are two decision alternatives: allow the flight to depart or do not allow the flight to depart. In choosing from these alternatives, the decision maker has to consider several unknown future outcomes such as the weather, expected air traffic, and a variety of other factors that could develop at the destination. These factors could delay or prevent a flight from landing safely.

The original GDP system was administered by the FAA. The FAA monitored existing imbalances between demand and capacity at given airports to determine if a ground delay was warranted and justified at other airports that fed into it. Some experts, however, claimed that the FAA lacked current and accurate information. In some cases, the FAA relied on the published airline schedules, which were subject to change and inaccuracies. This resulted in the inefficient use of arrival resources and unnecessary ground delays at some airports. To overcome some of these problems, a decision theory model was developed.

Using decision theory models can improve not only information flow but also performance. Before the initiative, 51% of flights left on time. After it, 66% left on time. In addition to conserving fuel and improving utilization of arrival resources, these types of initiatives can save travelers a tremendous amount of frustration and lost time.[1]

---

[1] K. Chang, et al. "Enhancements to the FAA Ground-Delay Program Under Collaborative Decision Making," *Interfaces* (January–February 2001): 57–76.

## 8.1    INTRODUCTION

*Decision theory is an analytic and systematic way to tackle problems.*

To a great extent, the successes or failures that a person experiences in life depend on the decisions that he or she makes. The development of DOS, followed by Windows and other software, has made Bill Gates the richest person in the world. In contrast, the person who designed the flawed tires at Firestone (which caused so many accidents with Ford Explorers in the late 1990s) is probably not working there anymore. Why and how did these people make their respective decisions? A single decision can make the difference between a successful career and an unsuccessful one. *Decision theory* is an analytic and systematic approach to the study of decision making. In this chapter, we present the decision models useful in helping managers make the best possible decisions.

*A good decision is based on logic.*

What makes the difference between good and bad decisions? In most practical situations, such as in the preceding FAA application, managers have to make decisions without knowing for sure which events will occur in the future. In such cases, a good decision can be defined as one that is based on logic, considers all possible decision alternatives, examines all available information about the future, and applies the decision modeling approach described in this chapter. Occasionally, due to the uncertainty of future events, a good decision could result in an unfavorable outcome. But if a decision is made properly, it is still a good decision.

*A bad decision does not consider all alternatives.*

In contrast, a bad decision is one that is not based on logic, does not use all available information, does not consider all alternatives, and does not employ appropriate decision modeling techniques. If you make a bad decision but are lucky enough that a favorable outcome occurs, you have still made a bad decision. Although occasionally good decisions yield bad results, in the long run, using decision theory will result in successful outcomes.

## 8.2    THE FIVE STEPS IN DECISION THEORY

Whether you are deciding about signing up for next semester's classes, buying a new computer, or building a multimillion-dollar factory, the steps in making a good decision are basically the same:

### Five Steps of Decision Making

1. Clearly define the problem at hand.
2. List *all* possible decision alternatives.
3. Identify the possible future outcomes for each decision alternative.
4. Identify the payoff (usually, profit or cost) for each combination of alternatives and outcomes.
5. Select one of the decision theory modeling techniques discussed in this chapter. Apply the decision model and make your decision.

### Thompson Lumber Company Example

We use the case of Thompson Lumber Company as an example to illustrate the use of the five decision theory steps. John Thompson is the founder and president of Thompson Lumber Company, a profitable firm located in Portland, Oregon.

*The first step is to define the problem.*

**Step 1** John identifies his problem as follows: whether to expand his product line by manufacturing and marketing a new product, backyard storage sheds.

*The second step is to list alternatives.*

**Step 2**  John's second step is to generate the decision alternatives that are available to him. In decision theory, a *decision alternative* is defined as a course of action or a strategy that can be chosen by the decision maker. John decides that his alternatives are to construct (1) a large plant to manufacture the storage sheds, (2) a small plant to manufacture the storage sheds, or (3) no plant at all (i. e., he has the option of not developing the new product line).

One of the biggest mistakes that decision makers make is to leave out some important decision alternatives, like no plant at all. Although a particular alternative may seem to be inappropriate or of little value at this time, it may turn out to be the best choice later.

*The third step is to identify possible outcomes.*

**Step 3**  The third step involves identifying the possible future outcomes of the various alternatives. The criteria for action are established at this time. John determines that there are only two possible outcomes: the market for storage sheds could be favorable, meaning that there is a high demand for the product, or it could be unfavorable, meaning that there is a low demand for the sheds.

A common mistake is to forget about some of the possible outcomes. Optimistic decision makers tend to ignore bad outcomes, whereas pessimistic managers may discount a favorable outcome. If we don't consider all possibilities, we will not be making a logical decision, and the results may be undesirable. In decision theory, outcomes over which the decision maker has little or no control are called *states of nature*.

*The fourth step is to list payoffs.*

**Step 4**  John's next step is to express the payoff resulting from each possible combination of alternatives and outcomes. Since he wants to maximize his profits in this case, he can use profit to evaluate each consequence. Not every decision, of course, can be based on money alone; any appropriate means of measuring benefit is acceptable. In decision theory, we call such *payoffs* or profits *conditional values*.

John has already evaluated the potential profits associated with the various combinations of alternatives and outcomes. With a favorable market, he thinks a large facility would result in a net profit of $200,000 to his firm. This $200,000 is a *conditional value* because John's receiving the money is conditional upon both his building a large factory and having a good market. The conditional value if the market is unfavorable would be a $180,000 net loss. A small plant would result in a net profit of $100,000 in a favorable market, but a net loss of $20,000 would occur if the market were unfavorable. Finally, doing nothing would result in $0 profit in either market.

*During the fourth step, the decision maker can construct decision or payoff tables.*

The easiest way to present these values is by constructing a *decision table*, sometimes called a *payoff table*. A decision table for John's conditional values is shown in Table 8.1. All of the decision alternatives are listed down the left side of the table, and all of the possible outcomes or states of nature are listed across the top. The body of the table contains the actual monetary payoffs.

*The last step is to select and apply a decision theory model.*

**Step 5**  The last step is to select a decision theory model and apply it to the data to help make the decision. The type of decision model available for selection depends on the environment in which we are operating, and the amount of uncertainty and risk involved.

**TABLE 8.1**

**Decision Table with Conditional Values for Thompson Lumber**

| | STATES OF NATURE | |
|---|---|---|
| ALTERNATIVES | FAVORABLE MARKET ($) | UNFAVORABLE MARKET ($) |
| Construct a large plant | 200,000 | −180,000 |
| Construct a small plant | 100,000 | −20,000 |
| Do nothing | 0 | 0 |

*Note:* It is important to include all alternatives, including "do nothing."

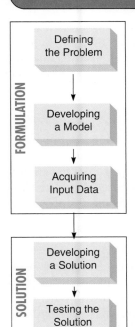

## ⇢ MODELING IN THE REAL WORLD          Using Decision Tree Analysis on R&D Projects

The Canadian subsidiary of ICI discovered a new unpatentable process for anthraquinone (AQ) to reduce paper mill pollution. The company had to decide whether to invest funds in research and development (R&D) for the new process.

A traditional decision tree model was used. Instead of expected monetary values, the model used expected net present value, which converts future monetary flows into today's dollars.

ICI collected both probability and monetary values. The probability data included the probability of a technical success, the probability of a significant market for the new process, and the probability of a commercial success.

The solution was obtained using decision tree analysis like the ones performed in this chapter.

ICI tested the solution by analyzing various risks of the process, including whether the new process could be developed, the market for the new process, the accuracy of the conditional probabilities in the decision tree, and various expenses and monetary flows.

The estimated net present value from decision tree analysis was $3.2 million. If the new project was successful, the net present value could be as high as $25 million.

The decision tree analysis moved this R&D project forward. As a result, it was decided to investigate the process further. After field testing, however, difficulty with pulp mills resulted in the project being canceled.

**Source:** Sidney Hess. "Swinging on the Branch of a Tree: Project Selection Applications," *Interfaces* 23, 6 (November–December 1993): 5–12.

## 8.3   TYPES OF DECISION-MAKING ENVIRONMENTS

The types of decisions people make depend on how much knowledge or information they have about the problem scenario. There are three decision making environments; described in the following sections.

*The consequence of every alternative is known in decision making under certainty.*

***Type 1: Decision Making Under Certainty***   In the environment of *decision making under certainty*, decision makers know for sure (i.e., with certainty) the outcome or consequence of every decision alternative. Naturally, they will select the alternative that will result in the best outcome. The mathematical programming approaches covered in Chapters 2–6 are all examples of decision modeling techniques suited for decision making under certainty.

Let's see how decision making under certainty could affect John Thompson. In this environment, we assume that John knows exactly what will happen in the future. For example, if he knows with certainty that the market for storage sheds will be favorable, what should he do? Look again at John's conditional values in Table 8.1. If the market is going to be favorable, he should build the large plant, which has the highest profit, $200,000.

In real-world cases, however, few managers would be fortunate enough to have complete information and knowledge about the states of nature under consideration. In most situations, managers would either have no information at all about the states of nature, or at best, have probabilistic information about future outcomes. These are the second and third types of decision making environments.

*Probabilities are not unknown in decision making under uncertainty.*

**Type 2: Decision Making Under Uncertainty** In *decision making under uncertainty*, the decision maker has no information at all about the various outcomes or states of nature. That is, he or she does not know the probabilities of the various future outcomes. For example, the probability that Democrats will control Congress 25 years from now is not known. Sometimes it is impossible to assess the probability of success of a new undertaking or product. The various decision models available for decision making under uncertainty are explained in Section 8.4.

*Probabilities are known in decision making under risk.*

**Type 3: Decision Making Under Risk** In *decision making under risk*, the decision maker has some knowledge regarding the probability of occurrence of each outcome or state of nature. We know, for example, that the probability of being dealt a club from a deck of cards is $\frac{1}{4}$. The probability of rolling a 5 on a die is $\frac{1}{6}$. In decision making under risk, the decision maker attempts to identify the alternative that optimizes his or her *expected* profit or cost. Decision theory models for business problems in this environment typically employ one of two criteria: maximization of expected monetary value and minimization of expected opportunity loss. We study decision making under risk in Section 8.5.

---

**IN ACTION** Decision Analysis Helps Allocate Health Care Funds in the United Kingdom

Individuals and companies have often used decision-making techniques to help them invest or allocate funds to various projects. In some cases, decision-making techniques can be used to determine how millions of dollars are to be spent. This same type of analysis can also be used on a larger scale for countries or governments. This was the case in the allocation of health care funds for the United Kingdom.

Over the years, the United States has debated the possible implementation of a comprehensive national health care program. Although this does not seem likely for the United States in the near future, other countries, such as the United Kingdom, have been using some form of national health care system for decades. For the United Kingdom, the question is not whether to have a national health care system, but how funds from such a system are to be allocated.

The United Kingdom's National Health Service (NHS) is funded through general tax revenues. The funds are dispersed to about 105 different local health authorities. The annual funding for the NHS is approximately $35 billion. With such a large sum of national funds going to such an important area,

the decision-making process to justly allocate funds can be difficult indeed.

Starting in the 1970s, a formula, based partly on a standardized mortality ratio, was developed to distribute health funds to the local authorities. This formula, however, failed to take into account social deprivation and general health care needs. As a result, the NHS decided to seek a better way to allocate health care dollars to the local authorities.

A team from York University spent about 4 months developing the original allocation model and another 14 months refining the decision-making model. Using decision theory, the team identified a set of key variables to explain health care needs and usage in the United Kingdom. This resulted in modifications to the decision-making approach regarding health care funds. Many believe that the new model will more fairly and justly allocate the United Kingdom's important national health care funds to those who truly need the assistance.

**Source:** Nancy Bistritz. "Rx for UK Healthcare Woes," *OR/MS Today* (April 1997): 18.

## 8.4 DECISION MAKING UNDER UNCERTAINTY

*Probability data are not available.*

As noted previously, this type of decision making environment exists when a manager cannot assess the probabilities of the different outcomes with confidence, or when virtually no probability data is available. The criteria covered in this section to handle such situations are as follows:

1. Maximax
2. Maximin
3. Equally likely
4. Criterion of realism
5. Minimax regret

The first four criteria can be computed directly from the decision (payoff) table, whereas the minimax regret criterion requires use of the opportunity loss table (which we compute subsequently). Let's look at each of the five criteria and apply them to the Thompson Lumber example. Remember that the decision-making environment assumes that John has no probability information about the two outcomes.

### Maximax Criterion

*Maximax is an optimistic approach.*

The *maximax* criterion selects the alternative that *maxi*mizes the *maxi*mum payoff or consequence over all alternatives. We first locate the maximum payoff for each alternative and then select the alternative with the maximum number. Since this decision criterion locates the alternative with the highest possible gain, it is also called an *optimistic* criterion. In Table 8.2 we see that John's maximax choice is the first alternative, "construct a large plant." The $200,000 payoff is the maximum of the maximum payoffs for each decision alternative.

### Maximin Criterion

*Maximin is a pessimistic approach.*

The *maximin* criterion finds the alternative that *maxi*mizes the *mini*mum payoff or consequence over all alternatives. We first locate the minimum payoff for each alternative and then select the alternative with the maximum number. Since this decision criterion locates the alternative that has the least possible loss, it is also called a *pessimistic* criterion. John's maximin choice, "do nothing," is shown in Table 8.3. The $0 payoff is the maximum of the minimum payoffs for each alternative.

### Equally Likely (Laplace) Criterion

*The equally likely criterion selects the highest average alternative.*

The *equally likely*, also called *Laplace*, criterion finds the decision alternative with the highest average payoff. We first calculate the average payoff for every alternative. Note that the average payoff is simply the sum of all payoffs for an alternative, divided by the number of

**TABLE 8.2**

Thompson's Maximax Decision

| ALTERNATIVES | STATES OF NATURE | | MAXIMUM IN ROW ($) |
|---|---|---|---|
| | FAVORABLE MARKET ($) | UNFAVORABLE MARKET ($) | |
| Construct a large plant | 200,000 | −180,000 | 200,000 Maximax |
| Construct a small plant | 100,000 | −20,000 | 100,000 |
| Do nothing | 0 | 0 | 0 |

| TABLE 8.3 | | STATES OF NATURE | | |
|---|---|---|---|---|
| **Thompson's Maximin Decision** | **ALTERNATIVES** | **FAVORABLE MARKET ($)** | **UNFAVORABLE MARKET ($)** | **MINIMUM IN ROW ($)** |
| | Construct a large plant | 200,000 | −180,000 | −180,000 |
| | Construct a small plant | 100,000 | −20,000 | −20,000 |
| | Do nothing | 0 | 0 | ⓪ ← Maximin |

| TABLE 8.4 | | STATES OF NATURE | | |
|---|---|---|---|---|
| **Thompson's Equally Likely Decision** | **ALTERNATIVES** | **FAVORABLE MARKET ($)** | **UNFAVORABLE MARKET ($)** | **ROW AVERAGE ($)** |
| | Construct a large plant | 200,000 | −180,000 | 10,000 |
| | Construct a small plant | 100,000 | −20,000 | ⟨40,000⟩ ← Equally likely |
| | Do nothing | 0 | 0 | 0 |

outcomes. We then pick the alternative with the maximum average payoff. The Laplace approach assumes that all probabilities of occurrence for the states of nature are equal. That is, each state of nature is equally likely.

The equally likely choice for Thompson Lumber is the second alternative, "construct a small plant." This strategy, as shown in Table 8.4, has the maximum average payoff ($40,000) over all alternatives.

## Criterion of Realism (Hurwicz)

*Criterion of realism uses the weighted average approach.*

Often called the *weighted average*, the *criterion of realism* (or *Hurwicz*) decision criterion is a compromise between an optimistic and a pessimistic decision. To begin with, a *coefficient of realism*, $\alpha$, with a value between 0 and 1 is selected. When $\alpha$ is close to 1, the decision maker is optimistic about the future. When $\alpha$ is close to 0, the decision maker is pessimistic about the future. The advantage of this approach is that it allows the decision maker to build in personal feelings about relative optimism and pessimism. The formula is as follows:

$$\text{Criterion of realism} = \alpha \times (\text{maximum payoff for an alternative}) + \qquad (8\text{-}1)$$
$$(1 - \alpha) \times (\text{minimum payoff for an alternative})$$

If we assume that John sets his coefficient of realism, $\alpha$, to be 0.80, his best decision would be to construct a large plant. As seen in Table 8.5, this alternative has the highest weighted average payoff: $124,000 = (0.80)($200,000) + (0.20)(−$180,000).

## Minimax Regret Criterion

*Minimax regret is based on opportunity loss.*

The final decision criterion that we discuss is based on opportunity loss. *Opportunity loss*, also called *regret*, is the difference between the optimal payoff and the actual payoff received. In other words, it's the amount lost by *not* picking the best alternative. *Minimax regret* finds the alternative that *mini*mizes the *max*imum opportunity loss within each alternative.

**TABLE 8.5**

Thompson's Criterion of Realism Decision (also called Hurwicz criterion)

| | STATES OF NATURE | | |
| ALTERNATIVES | FAVORABLE MARKET ($) | UNFAVORABLE MARKET ($) | CRITERION OF REALISM OR WEIGHTED AVERAGE ($\alpha = 0.8$) $ |
| --- | --- | --- | --- |
| Construct a large plant | 200,000 | −180,000 | (124,000) ← Realism |
| Construct a small plant | 100,000 | −20,000 | 76,000 |
| Do nothing | 0 | 0 | 0 |

To use this criterion, we need to first develop the opportunity loss table. This is done by determining the opportunity loss of not choosing the best alternative for each state of nature. Opportunity loss for any state of nature, or any column, is calculated by subtracting each outcome in the column from the *best* outcome in the same column. In Thompson Lumber's problem, the best outcome for a favorable market is $200,000, as a result of the first alternative, "construct a large plant." We subtract all payoffs in that column from $200,000. Likewise, the best outcome for an unfavorable market is $0, as a result of the third alternative, "do nothing." We now subtract all payoffs in that column from $0. Table 8.6 illustrates these computations and shows John's complete opportunity loss table.

Once this table has been constructed, we first locate the maximum opportunity loss within each alternative. We then pick the alternative with the minimum number. John's minimax regret choice is the second alternative, "construct a small plant." As shown in Table 8.7, the regret of $100,000 is the minimum of the maximum regrets over all alternatives.

**TABLE 8.6**

Opportunity Loss Table for Thompson Lumber

| | STATES OF NATURE | |
| ALTERNATIVES | FAVORABLE MARKET ($) | UNFAVORABLE MARKET ($) |
| --- | --- | --- |
| Construct a large plant | 200,000 − 200,000 = 0 | 0 − (−180,000) = 180,000 |
| Construct a small plant | 200,000 − 100,000 = 100,000 | 0 − (−20,000) = 20,000 |
| Do nothing | 200,000 − 0 = 200,000 | 0 − 0 = 0 |

**TABLE 8.7**

Thompson's Minimax Regret Decision Using Opportunity Loss

| | STATES OF NATURE | | |
| ALTERNATIVES | FAVORABLE MARKET ($) | UNFAVORABLE MARKET ($) | MAXIMUM IN ROW ($) |
| --- | --- | --- | --- |
| Construct a large plant | 0 | 180,000 | 180,000 |
| Construct a small plant | 100,000 | 20,000 | (100,000) ← Minimax |
| Do nothing | 200,000 | 0 | 200,000 |

**File: 8-1.xls**

*Excel worksheets can be created to solve decision making problems under uncertainty.*

# Using Excel to Solve Decision Making Problems Under Uncertainty

As we just demonstrated in the Thompson Lumber example, calculations for the different criteria in decision making under uncertainty are fairly straightforward. In most cases, we can perform these calculations quickly—even by hand. However, if we wish, we can easily construct Excel spreadsheets to calculate these results for us. Program 8.1A shows the relevant formulas for the different decision criteria in the Thompson Lumber example. The results are shown in Program 8.1B.

---

### Excel Notes

■ The CD-ROM that accompanies this textbook contains the Excel file for each example problem discussed here. The relevant file name is shown in the margin next to each example.

■ For clarity, our Excel layouts in this chapter are color coded as follows:
   ■ *input cells*, where we enter the problem data, are shaded yellow.
   ■ *output cells*, where the results are shown, are shaded green.

■ Although these colors are not apparent in the screen captures shown in the textbook, they are seen in the Excel files in your CD-ROM.

---

Note that the number of decision alternatives and number of states of nature would vary from problem to problem. The formulas shown in Program 8.1A can, however, be easily modified to accommodate any changes in these parameters.

**PROGRAM 8.1A**   **Formula View of Excel Layout for Thompson Lumber: Decision Making Under Uncertainty**

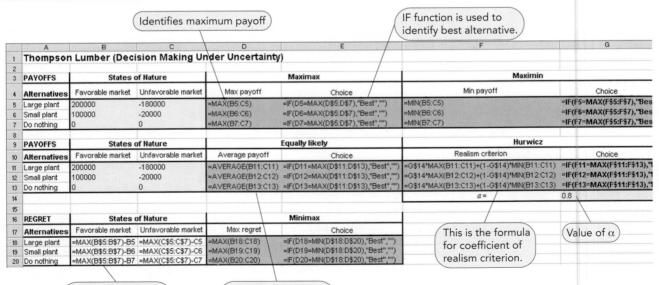

**PROGRAM 8.1B**

**Excel Solution for Thompson Lumber: Decision Making Under Uncertainty**

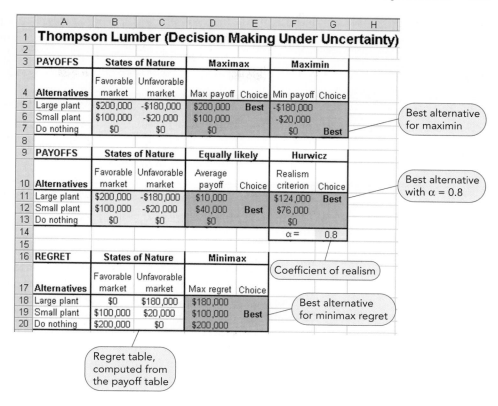

|  | A | B | C | D | E | F | G | H |
|---|---|---|---|---|---|---|---|---|
| 1 | **Thompson Lumber (Decision Making Under Uncertainty)** | | | | | | | |
| 2 | | | | | | | | |
| 3 | **PAYOFFS** | **States of Nature** | | **Maximax** | | **Maximin** | | |
| 4 | **Alternatives** | Favorable market | Unfavorable market | Max payoff | Choice | Min payoff | Choice | |
| 5 | Large plant | $200,000 | -$180,000 | $200,000 | **Best** | -$180,000 | | |
| 6 | Small plant | $100,000 | -$20,000 | $100,000 | | -$20,000 | | |
| 7 | Do nothing | $0 | $0 | $0 | | $0 | **Best** | |
| 8 | | | | | | | | |
| 9 | **PAYOFFS** | **States of Nature** | | **Equally likely** | | **Hurwicz** | | |
| 10 | **Alternatives** | Favorable market | Unfavorable market | Average payoff | Choice | Realism criterion | Choice | |
| 11 | Large plant | $200,000 | -$180,000 | $10,000 | | $124,000 | **Best** | |
| 12 | Small plant | $100,000 | -$20,000 | $40,000 | **Best** | $76,000 | | |
| 13 | Do nothing | $0 | $0 | $0 | | $0 | | |
| 14 | | | | | | $\alpha =$ | 0.8 | |
| 15 | | | | | | | | |
| 16 | **REGRET** | **States of Nature** | | **Minimax** | | | | |
| 17 | **Alternatives** | Favorable market | Unfavorable market | Max regret | Choice | | | |
| 18 | Large plant | $0 | $180,000 | $180,000 | | | | |
| 19 | Small plant | $100,000 | $20,000 | $100,000 | **Best** | | | |
| 20 | Do nothing | $200,000 | $0 | $200,000 | | | | |

Best alternative for maximin

Best alternative with $\alpha = 0.8$

Coefficient of realism

Best alternative for minimax regret

Regret table, computed from the payoff table

## 8.5   DECISION MAKING UNDER RISK

In many real-world situations, it is common for the decision maker to have some idea about the probabilities of occurrence of the different outcomes or states of nature. These probabilities may be based on the decision maker's personal opinions about future events, or on data obtained from market surveys, expert opinions, and so on. As noted previously, when the probability of occurrence of each state of nature can be assessed, the problem environment is called *decision making under risk.*

In this section we consider one of the most popular methods of making decisions under risk: selecting the alternative with the highest expected monetary value. We also look at the concepts of expected opportunity loss and expected value of perfect information.

### Expected Monetary Value

*EMV is the weighted average of possible payoffs for each alternative.*

Given a decision table with conditional values (payoffs) and probability assessments, we can determine the *expected monetary value* (EMV) for each alternative. The EMV for an alternative is computed as the *weighted average* of all possible payoffs for the alternative, where the weights are the probabilities of the different states of nature. That is,

$$
\begin{aligned}
\text{EMV (alternative } i) = & \text{ (payoff of first state of nature)} \\
& \times \text{ (probability of first state of nature)} \\
& + \text{ (payoff of second state of nature)} \\
& \times \text{ (probability of second state of nature)} \\
& + \ldots + \text{ (payoff of last state of nature)} \\
& \times \text{ (probability of last state of nature)}
\end{aligned}
$$

(8-2)

| TABLE 8.8 | Thompson's EMV Decision | | |
|-----------|-------------------------|--|--|

| | STATES OF NATURE | | |
| ALTERNATIVES | FAVORABLE MARKET ($) | UNFAVORABLE MARKET ($) | EMV COMPUTED ($) |
|---|---|---|---|
| Construct a large plant | 200,000 | −180,000 | (0.5)(200,000) + (0.5)(−180,000) = 10,000 |
| Construct a small plant | 100,000 | −20,000 | (0.5)(100,000) + (0.5)(−20,000)  = 40,000 |
| Do nothing | 0 | 0 | (0.5)(0) + (0.5)(0)  =  0 |
| Probabilities | 0.50 | 0.50 | Maximum |

John Thompson believes the probability of a favorable market is the same as the probability of an unfavorable market. That is, each state of nature has a 0.50 probability. Which alternative would give him the greatest EMV? To determine this, John has computed the EMV for each alternative, as shown in Table 8.8. The largest EMV of $40,000 results from the second alternative, "construct a small plant."

Observe that the EMV represents the long-run *average* payoff, although the *actual* payoff from a decision will be one of the payoffs listed in the decision table. The EMV is, however, an acceptable criterion for many business decisions since companies make similar decisions on a repeated basis over time.

## Expected Opportunity Loss

*EOL is the cost of not picking the best solution.*

An alternative approach in decision making under risk is to minimize *expected opportunity loss* (EOL). Recall from Section 8.4 that opportunity loss, also called regret, refers to the difference between the optimal profit or payoff and the actual payoff received. The EOL for an alternative is just the sum of all possible regrets of the alternative, each weighted by the probability of the state of nature for that regret occurring.

$$
\begin{aligned}
\text{EOL (alternative } i) = \;&(\text{regret of first state of nature}) \\
&\times (\text{probability of first state of nature}) \\
+\;&(\text{regret of second state of nature}) \\
&\times (\text{probability of second state of nature}) \\
+\ldots+\;&(\text{regret of last state of nature}) \\
&\times (\text{probability of last state of nature})
\end{aligned}
$$

(8-3)

*EOL will always result in the same decision as the maximum EMV.*

The EOL values for Thompson Lumber's problem are computed as shown in Table 8.9. Using minimum EOL as the decision criterion, the best decision would be the second alternative, "construct a small plant," with an EOL of $60,000. It is important to note that minimum EOL will *always* result in the same decision alternative as maximum EMV.

## Expected Value of Perfect Information

John Thompson has been approached by Scientific Marketing, Inc., a market research firm, with a proposal to help him make the right decision regarding the plant. Scientific claims that its analysis will tell John with *certainty* whether the market will be favorable for his proposed product. In other words, it will change John's problem environment from one of decision making under risk to one of decision making under certainty. This information could prevent John from making an expensive mistake. Scientific would charge Thompson $65,000 for the information.

**TABLE 8.9**    Thompson's EOL Decision

| | STATES OF NATURE | | |
| ALTERNATIVES | FAVORABLE MARKET ($) | UNFAVORABLE MARKET ($) | EOL COMPUTED ($) |
| --- | --- | --- | --- |
| Construct a large plant | 0 | 180,000 | $(0.5)(0) + (0.5)(180,000)$    = 90,000 |
| Construct a small plant | 100,000 | 20,000 | $(0.5)(100,000) + (0.5)(20,000)$ = (60,000) ← |
| Do nothing | 200,000 | 0 | $(0.5)(200,000) + (0.5)(0)$    = 100,000 |
| Probabilities | 0.50 | 0.50 | Minimum |

What should John do? Should he hire Scientific to do the marketing study? Is the information worth $65,000? If not, what is it worth? Although such *perfect information* is usually not available in practice, determining its value can be very useful. It places an upper bound on what we should be willing to spend on *any* information, perfect or otherwise. In this section, we investigate two related terms: the *expected value with perfect information* (EVwPI) and the *expected value of perfect information* (EVPI).

*EVPI places an upper bound on what to pay for information.*

The expected value *with* perfect information is the expected or average return, in the long run, if we have perfect information before a decision has to be made. To calculate this value, we choose the best alternative for each state of nature and multiply its payoff times the probability of occurrence of that state of nature. That is,

$$
\begin{aligned}
\text{EVwPI} = {} & (\text{best payoff for first state of nature}) \\
& \times (\text{probability of first state of nature}) \\
& + (\text{best payoff for second state of nature}) \\
& \times (\text{probability of second state of nature}) \\
& + \ldots + (\text{best payoff for last state of nature}) \\
& \times (\text{probability of last state of nature})
\end{aligned}
\tag{8-4}
$$

*EVPI is the expected value with perfect information minus the maximum EMV.*

We then compute the expected value *of* perfect information (EVPI) as the expected value *with* perfect information (EVwPI) minus the expected value *without* perfect information, namely, the maximum EMV.

$$
\text{EVPI} = \text{EVwPI} - \text{maximum EMV}
\tag{8-5}
$$

By referring back to Table 8.8, we can calculate the EVPI for John as follows:

1. The best outcome for the state of nature "favorable market" is "build a large plant," with a payoff of $200,000. The best outcome for the state of nature "unfavorable market" is "do nothing," with a payoff of $0. Hence, the EVwPI = ($200,000)(0.50) + ($0)(0.50) = $100,000. That is, if we had perfect information, we would expect an *average* payoff of $100,000 if the decision could be repeated many times.

2. The maximum EMV, or the expected value *without* perfect information, is $40,000. Hence, EVPI = EVwPI − maximum EMV = $100,000 − $40,000 = $60,000.

Thus, the most John should pay for perfect information is $60,000. This, of course, is again based on the assumption that the probability of each state of nature is 0.50. It is important to note that the following relationship always holds: EVPI = minimum EOL. Referring back to Thompson's example, we see that EVPI = minimum EOL = $60,000.

File: 8-2.xls

## Using Excel to Solve Decision Making Problems Under Risk

Just as with decision making under uncertainty, calculations for finding the EMV, EOL, and EVPI in decision making under risk are also fairly straightforward. In most small cases, we can perform these calculations quickly even by hand. However, if we wish, we can once again easily construct Excel spreadsheets to calculate these values for us. Program 8.2A shows the relevant formulas to solve the Thompson example. The results are shown in Program 8.2B.

**PROGRAM 8.2A**

**Formula View of Excel Layout for Thompson Lumber: Decision Making Under Risk**

IF function is used to identify best alternative.

| | A | B | C | D | E |
|---|---|---|---|---|---|
| 1 | **Thompson Lumber (Decision Making Under Risk)** | | | | |
| 2 | | | | | |
| 3 | PAYOFFS | States of Nature | | | |
| 4 | Alternatives | Favorable market | Unfavorable market | EMV | Choice |
| 5 | Large plant | 200000 | -180000 | =SUMPRODUCT(B5:C5,B$8:C$8) | =IF(D5=MAX(D$5:D$7),"Best","") |
| 6 | Small plant | 100000 | -20000 | =SUMPRODUCT(B6:C6,B$8:C$8) | =IF(D6=MAX(D$5:D$7),"Best","") |
| 7 | Do nothing | 0 | 0 | =SUMPRODUCT(B7:C7,B$8:C$8) | =IF(D7=MAX(D$5:D$7),"Best","") |
| 8 | Probability | 0.5 | 0.5 | | |
| 9 | Best outcome | =MAX(B5:B7) | =MAX(C5:C7) | | |
| 10 | | | | | |
| 11 | Expected Value WITH Perfect Information  (EVwPI) = | | | | =SUMPRODUCT(B9:C9,B8:C8) |
| 12 | Best Expected Monetary Value (EMV) = | | | | =MAX(D5:D7) |
| 13 | Expected Value OF Perfect Information  (EVPI) = | | | | =E11-E12 |
| 14 | | | | | |
| 15 | REGRET | States of Nature | | | |
| 16 | Alternatives | Favorable market | Unfavorable market | EOL | Choice |
| 17 | Large plant | =MAX(B$5:B$7)-B5 | =MAX(C$5:C$7)-C5 | =SUMPRODUCT(B17:C17,B$20:C$20) | =IF(D17=MIN(D$17:D$19),"Best","") |
| 18 | Small plant | =MAX(B$5:B$7)-B6 | =MAX(C$5:C$7)-C6 | =SUMPRODUCT(B18:C18,B$20:C$20) | =IF(D18=MIN(D$17:D$19),"Best","") |
| 19 | Do nothing | =MAX(B$5:B$7)-B7 | =MAX(C$5:C$7)-C7 | =SUMPRODUCT(B19:C19,B$20:C$20) | =IF(D19=MIN(D$17:D$19),"Best","") |
| 20 | Probability | 0.5 | 0.5 | | |

Best EMV

This is the best payoff for each state of nature, used in calculating regret values and EVwPI.

The SUMPRODUCT formula is used in column D to compute EMV and EOL for each alternative.

EVPI is the difference between EVwPI and best EMV.

**PROGRAM 8.2B**

**Excel Solution for Thompson Lumber: Decision Making Under Risk**

| | A | B | C | D | E | F |
|---|---|---|---|---|---|---|
| 1 | **Thompson Lumber (Decision Making Under Risk)** | | | | | |
| 2 | | | | | | |
| 3 | PAYOFFS | States of Nature | | | | |
| 4 | Alternatives | Favorable market | Unfavorable market | EMV | Choice | |
| 5 | Large plant | $200,000 | -$180,000 | $10,000 | | |
| 6 | Small plant | $100,000 | -$20,000 | $40,000 | Best | |
| 7 | Do nothing | $0 | $0 | $0 | | |
| 8 | Probability | 0.5 | 0.5 | | | |
| 9 | Best outcome | $200,000 | $0 | | | |
| 10 | | | | | | |
| 11 | Expected Value WITH Perfect Information  (EVwPI) = | | | | $100,000 | |
| 12 | Best Expected Monetary Value (EMV) = | | | | $40,000 | |
| 13 | Expected Value OF Perfect Information  (EVPI) = | | | | $60,000 | |
| 14 | | | | | | |
| 15 | REGRET | States of Nature | | | | |
| 16 | Alternatives | Favorable market | Unfavorable market | EOL | Choice | |
| 17 | Large plant | $0 | $180,000 | $90,000 | | |
| 18 | Small plant | $100,000 | $20,000 | $60,000 | Best | |
| 19 | Do nothing | $200,000 | $0 | $100,000 | | |
| 20 | Probability | 0.5 | 0.5 | | | |

Known probability values for each state of nature

Best choice is small plant.

EVPI = minimum EOL

Best choice is small plant.

**IN ACTION**    Using Decision Nodes to Deter the Proliferation of Weapons of Mass Destruction

Weapons of mass destruction (WMD) have put fear in the hearts of people around the world and caused countries to take strong political stands. The production, storage, and use of chemical weapons that can kill or injure the populations of entire cities or regions has been a major concern of all democratic countries. Inspection teams have been used in countries to detect and eliminate these potent weapons. The testing and development of nuclear weapons is another concern. In the spring of 1998, for example, both India and Pakistan tested nuclear devices. Many political leaders were very concerned. Others called for stiff sanctions.

How to handle WMD has been a long-standing political issue in the United States and a concern for national security. In a 1993 speech about national security, President Clinton stated that "one of our most urgent priorities must be attacking the proliferation of weapons of mass destruction—nuclear, chemical, and biological. . . ." To help, the Department of Defense has launched a nonproliferation program based on

four goals: (1) to prevent countries from acquiring WMD, (2) to deter the use of WMD against the United States and its allies, (3) to destroy WMD before they are used, and (4) to develop means to reduce the effectiveness of WMDs.

Decision theory has been employed to help develop sound counterproliferation policies and programs. One decision analysis included a decision tree with nodes to represent each of the possible decisions that can be made by the United States in this effort. These are called the Counterproliferation System Choices. A second set of decisions, called Use Offensive Counterproliferation, is used to determine if the United States should attack a country or group suspected of WMD storage and use. The decision analysis also incorporates sensitivity analysis to determine changes to results based on different assumptions or input data.

**Source:** Stanley Stafira et al. "A Methodology for Evaluating Military Systems in a Counterproliferation Role," *Management Science* (October 1997): 1420–1430.

As with Program 8.1A, note that the number of decision alternatives and number of states of nature would vary from problem to problem. The formulas shown in Program 8.2A can, however, be easily modified to accommodate any changes in these parameters.

## 8.6    DECISION TREES

*Decision trees contain decision nodes and state of nature nodes.*

Any problem that can be presented in a decision table can also be graphically illustrated in a *decision tree*. We illustrate the construction and use of decision trees using the Thompson Lumber example.

A decision tree presents the decision alternatives and states of nature (outcomes) in a sequential manner. All decision trees are similar in that they contain *decision nodes* (or points) and *state of nature nodes* (or points). These nodes are represented using the following symbols:

□ = A *decision* node. Arcs (lines) originating from a decision node denote all decision alternatives available at that node. Of these, the decision maker must select only one alternative.

○ = A *state of nature* (or *chance*) node. Arcs (lines) originating from a chance node denotes all states of nature that could occur at that node. Of these, only one state of nature will occur.

*A decision tree usually begins with a decision node.*

The tree usually begins with a decision node. In Thompson Lumber's case, John has to decide among constructing a large plant, a small plant, or no plant. Then, once this decision is made, one of two possible states of nature (favorable or unfavorable market) will occur. The simple decision tree to represent John's decision is shown in Figure 8.1.

Observe that all alternatives available to John are shown as arcs originating from a decision node (□). Likewise, at each chance node (○), all possible outcomes that could occur if John chooses that decision alternative are shown as arcs. The payoffs resulting from

FIGURE 8.1

**Thompson Lumber's Decision Tree**

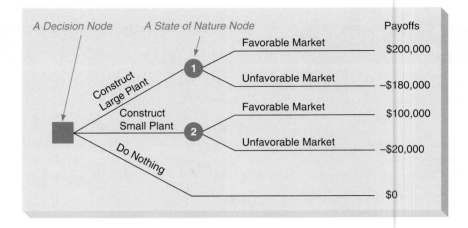

each alternative and state of nature combination are shown at the end of each relevant path in the tree. For example, if John chooses to construct a large plant and market conditions turn out to be favorable, the resulting payoff is $200,000.

## Folding Back a Decision Tree

*We fold back a decision tree to identify the best decision.*

The process by which the tree is analyzed to identify the optimal decision is referred to as *folding back* the decision tree. We start with the payoffs (i.e., the right extreme of the tree) and work our way back to the first decision node. In folding back the decision tree, we use the following two rules:

- At each state of nature (or chance) node, we compute the expected value using the probabilities of all possible outcomes at that node and the payoffs associated with these outcomes.
- At each decision node, we select the alternative that yields the better expected value or payoff. If the expected values or payoffs represent profits, we select the alternative with the largest value. In contrast, if the expected values or payoffs represent costs, we select the alternative with the smallest value.

The complete decision tree for Thompson Lumber is presented in Figure 8.2. For convenience, the probability of each outcome is shown in parentheses next to each state of

FIGURE 8.2

**Completed Decision Tree for Thompson Lumber**

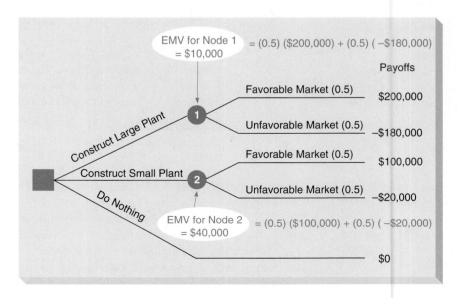

FIGURE 8.3

**Reduced Decision Tree for
Thompson Lumber**

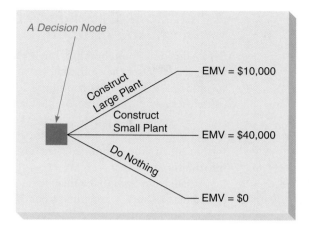

*The EMV is calculated at each
state of nature node.*

nature. The EMV at each state of nature node is then calculated and placed by that node. The EMV at node 1 is $10,000. This represents the arc from the decision node to construct the large plant. The EMV at node 2 (if John decides to construct a small plant) is $40,000. Building no plant has, of course, a payoff of $0.

At this stage, the decision tree for Thompson Lumber has been folded back to just the first decision node and the three alternatives (arcs) originating from it. That is, all state of nature nodes and the outcomes from these nodes have been examined and "collapsed" into the EMVs. The reduced decision tree for Thompson Lumber is shown in Figure 8.3.

*The best alternative is selected
at a decision node.*

Using the rule stated earlier for decision nodes, we now select the alternative with the highest EMV. In this case, it corresponds to the alternative to build a small plant. The resulting EMV is $40,000.

## Decision Trees for Multistage Decision Making Problems

The Thompson Lumber problem discussed so far is a single-stage problem. That is, John has to make an initial decision, which is followed by an outcome. Depending on the decision made and the outcome that occurs, John gets a payoff, and the problem ends there.

In many cases, however, the decision-making scenario is a multistage problem. In such cases, the decision maker must evaluate and make a set of *sequential decisions* up front (i.e., before the first decision is implemented). However, the decisions are actually implemented in a sequential manner, as follows. The problem usually begins with the decision maker

*It is possible for one outcome
(or alternative) to directly
follow another outcome (or
alternative) in a decision tree.*

implementing his or her initial decision. This is then followed by an outcome or state of nature. In some cases, there may be no outcomes for the initial decision. In this case, the decision maker is immediately faced with the second decision. Likewise, it is possible to have one outcome occur directly after another outcome without the decision maker facing a decision in between.

In any case, depending on the initial decision made and the outcome(s) that may have occurred after it, the decision maker now implements his or her next decision. The alternatives for this follow-up decision may be different for different outcomes of the earlier decision. This decision may, in turn, be followed by an outcome. The possible outcomes for this decision may be different from the set of outcomes for the earlier decision. The final payoff is a function of the sequence of decisions and their possible outcomes.

*Multistage decision problems
are analyzed using decision
trees.*

In theory, we can extend such a multistage scenario to a sequence of as many decisions and outcomes as we wish. We will, however, limit our discussion here to problems involving just two stages. For multistage scenarios, decision tables are no longer convenient, and we are forced to analyze the problems using decision trees. Let us discuss this topic by considering an expanded version of the Thompson Lumber problem.

## A Multistage Decision-Making Problem for Thompson Lumber

Before deciding about building a new plant, let's suppose John Thompson has the option of hiring a firm to conduct a market research survey. The firm will charge $10,000 for the survey and will study market conditions for storage sheds. The results of the survey will indicate either favorable or unfavorable market conditions.

John recognizes that such a market survey will not provide him with *perfect* information, but it may help him get a better feel for the states of nature nevertheless. The type of information obtained here is referred to either as *imperfect* information or *sample* information.

*EVPI is an upper bound on the cost of the survey.*

Recall from Section 8.5 that we calculated John's EVPI as $60,000. That is, if the results of the market survey are going to be 100% accurate, John should be willing to pay up to $60,000 for the survey. Since the survey will cost only $10,000, it is at least worth considering further. However, given that it yields only imperfect information, how much is it actually worth? We determine this by extending the decision tree analysis for Thompson Lumber to include the market survey.

## Expanded Decision Tree for Thompson Lumber

John's new decision tree is represented in Figure 8.4. Let's take a careful look at this more complex tree. Note that all possible *outcomes* and *alternatives* are included in their logical sequence. This is one of the strengths of using decision trees in making decisions. The user is forced to examine all possible outcomes, including unfavorable ones. He or she is also forced to make decisions in a logical, sequential manner.

*All outcomes and alternatives must be considered.*

Examining the tree, we see that Thompson's first decision point is whether to conduct the $10,000 market survey. If he chooses not to do the study (the lower part of the tree), he can either construct a large plant, a small plant, or no plant. This is John's second decision point. The market will either be favorable (0.50 probability) or unfavorable (also 0.50 probability) if he builds. The payoffs for each of the possible consequences are listed along the right side. As a matter of fact, the lower portion of John's tree in Figure 8.4 is identical to the simpler decision tree shown in Figure 8.2. Can you see why this is so?

The upper part of Figure 8.4 reflects the decision to conduct the market survey. State of-nature node 1 has two branches. There is a 45% chance that the survey results will indicate a favorable market for storage sheds. We also note that the probability is 0.55 that the survey results will be unfavorable.[2]

*Most of the probabilities are conditional probabilities.*

The rest of the probabilities shown in parentheses in Figure 8.4 are all *conditional probabilities*.[3] For example, 0.78 is the probability of a favorable market for the sheds *given* a favorable result from the market survey. Of course, you would expect to find a high probability of a favorable market given that the research indicated that the market was good. Don't forget, though, there is a chance that John's $10,000 market survey didn't result in perfect or even reliable information. Any market research study is subject to error. In this case, there is a 22% chance that the market for sheds will be unfavorable given that the survey results are positive.

We note that there is a 27% chance that the market for sheds will be favorable given John's survey results are negative. The probability is much higher, 0.73, that the market will actually be unfavorable given that the survey is negative.

---

[2] An explanation of how these two probabilities can be obtained is the topic of Section 8.8. For now, let's assume that Thompson's experience provides them and accept them as reasonable.

[3] The derivation of these probabilities (0.78, 0.22, 0.27, and 0.73) is also discussed in Section 8.8.

FIGURE 8.4 **Larger Decision Tree with Payoffs and Probabilities for Thompson Lumber**

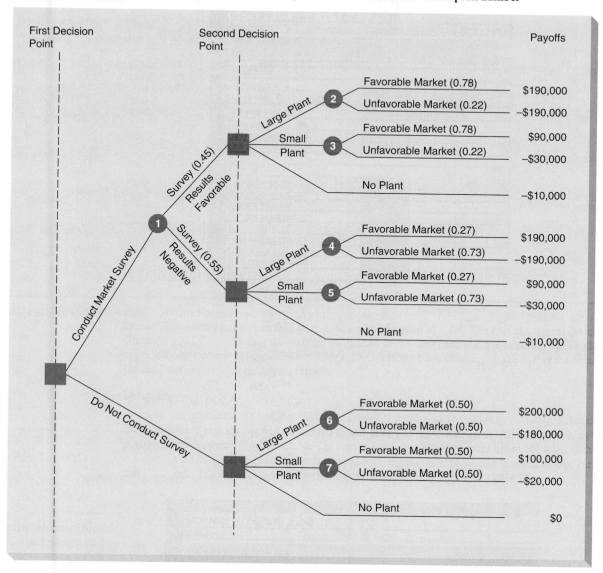

*The cost of the survey has to be subtracted from the original payoffs.*

Finally, when we look to the payoff values in Figure 8.4, we see that $10,000, the cost of the marketing study, had to be subtracted from each of the top 10 tree branches. Thus, a large plant with a favorable market would normally net a $200,000 profit. But because the market study was conducted, this figure is reduced by $10,000 to $190,000. In the unfavorable case, the loss of $180,000 would increase to $190,000. Similarly, conducting the survey and building no plant now results in a loss of $10,000 (i.e., a payoff of −$10,000).

## Folding Back the Expanded Decision Tree for Thompson Lumber

*We start by computing the EMV of each branch.*

With all probabilities and payoffs specified, we can start calculating the expected monetary value of each of the branches. We begin at the end, or right side of the decision tree and work back toward the origin. When we finish, the best decision will be known.

*EMV calculations for favorable survey results are made first.*

1. Given favorable survey results,

$$\text{EMV(node 2)} = \text{EMV(large plant}\,|\,\text{positive survey)}$$

$$= (0.78)(\$190,000) + (0.22)(-\$190,000) = \$106,400$$

$$\text{EMV(node 3)} = \text{EMV(small plant}\,|\,\text{positive survey)}$$

$$= (0.78)(\$90,000) + (0.22)(-\$30,000) = \$63,600$$

The EMV of no plant in this case is −$10,000. Thus, if the survey results are favorable, a large plant should be built.

*EMV calculations for unfavorable survey results are done next.*

2. Given negative survey results,

$$\text{EMV(node 4)} = \text{EMV(large plant}\,|\,\text{negative survey)}$$

$$= (0.27)(\$190,000) + (0.73)(-\$190,000) = -\$87,400$$

$$\text{EMV(node 5)} = \text{EMV(small plant}\,|\,\text{negative survey)}$$

$$= (0.27)(\$90,000) + (0.73)(-\$30,000) = \$2,400$$

The EMV of no plant is again −$10,000 for this branch. Thus, given a negative survey result, John should build a small plant with an expected value of $2,400.

*We continue working backward to the origin, computing EMV values.*

3. Continuing on the upper part of the tree and moving backward, we compute the expected value of conducting the market survey.

$$\text{EMV(node 1)} = \text{EMV(conduct survey)}$$

$$= (0.45)(\$106,400) + (0.55)(\$2,400)$$

$$= \$47,880 + \$1,320 = \$49,200$$

4. If the market survey is *not* conducted,

$$\text{EMV(node 6)} = \text{EMV(large plant)}$$

$$= (0.50)(\$200,000) + (0.50)(-\$180,000)$$

$$= \$10,000$$

$$\text{EMV(node 7)} = \text{EMV(small plant)}$$

$$= (0.50)(\$100,000) + (0.50)(-\$20,000)$$

$$= \$40,000$$

The EMV of no plant is $0.

Thus, building a small plant is the best choice, given that the marketing research is not performed, as we saw earlier.

5. Since the EMV of conducting the survey is $49,200, versus an EMV of $40,000 for not conducting the study, the best choice is to *seek* marketing information. If the survey results are favorable, John should construct a large plant; but if the research is negative, John should construct a small plant.

*Alternatives that are dropped from further consideration are indicated by slash lines (//).*

In Figure 8.5, these expected values are placed on the decision tree. Notice on the tree that a pair of slash lines (//) through a decision branch indicates that a particular alternative is dropped from further consideration. This is because its EMV is lower than the best alternative. After you have solved several decision tree problems, you may find it easier to do all of your computations on the tree diagram.

**FIGURE 8.5**    **Thompson Lumber's Decision Tree with EMVs Shown**

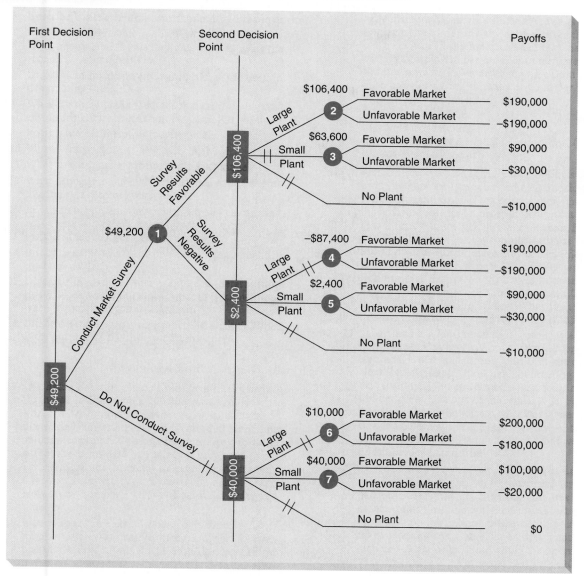

## Expected Value of Sample Information

With the market survey he intends to conduct, John Thompson knows that his best decision will be to build a large plant if the survey is favorable or a small plant if the survey results are unfavorable. But John also realizes that conducting the market research is not free. He would like to know the actual value of doing the survey. One way of measuring the value of market information is to compute the *expected value of sample information* (EVSI), as follows:

*EVSI measures the value of sample information.*

$$\text{EVSI} = \begin{pmatrix} \text{expected value of best} \\ \text{decision } \textit{with } \text{sample} \\ \text{information, assuming} \\ \text{no cost to gather it} \end{pmatrix} - \begin{pmatrix} \text{expected value} \\ \text{of best decision} \\ \textit{without } \text{sample} \\ \text{information} \end{pmatrix} \qquad (8\text{-}6)$$

In John's case, his EMV would be $59,200 *if* he hadn't already subtracted the $10,000 study cost from each payoff. (Do you see why this is so? If not, add $10,000 back into each payoff, as in the original Thompson problem, and recompute the EMV of conducting the market study.) From the lower branch of Figure 8.5, we see that the EMV of not gathering the sample information is $40,000. Thus,

$$\text{EVSI} = \$59{,}200 - \$40{,}000 = \$19{,}200$$

This means that John could have paid up to $19,200 for the market study offered by Scientific and still come out ahead. Since Scientific wants only $10,000, the survey is indeed worthwhile.

## 8.7   USING TREEPLAN TO SOLVE DECISION TREE PROBLEMS WITH EXCEL

*TreePlan: An Excel add-in for solving decision tree problems*

We can use TreePlan, an add-in for Excel, to set up and solve decision tree problems. The TreePlan program consists of a single Excel add-in file, TREEPLAN.XLA, which can be found on the CD-ROM that accompanies this text. You can either run this program directly from the CD-ROM or copy it to your hard disk and run it from there.

### Loading TreePlan

To load and enable TreePlan in Excel, you can use either of the two approaches described in the following sections.

*Two ways of loading TreePlan in Excel*

**Loading Manually**   Each time you run Excel, you will have to load TreePlan manually, like this:

- Open Excel. Click File |Open, and use the browse window to find the TREEPLAN.XLA file (either on your hard disk or on the CD-ROM).
- Open the file. Note that you will not see anything new on your Excel spreadsheet at this time.
- Click Tools in Excel's main menu. You will see an option called Decision Tree.

**Loading Automatically**   You have to load automatically only once, like this:

- Copy the TREEPLAN.XLA file to the hard drive.
- Open Excel. Click Tools|Add-Ins. Then click Browse and use the window to locate the TREEPLAN.XLA file.
- Select the file by clicking on it. Then click OK.
- You will see an option named TreePlan Decision Tree Add-in in the Add-In list. Make sure the box next to this option is checked. Click OK. *Note:* To subsequently prevent TreePlan from loading automatically, click Tools|Add-Ins, and uncheck the box next to this option.
- Click Tools in Excel's main menu. You will see an option called Decision Tree.

### Creating a Decision Tree Using TreePlan

Once you have installed and loaded TreePlan, you can use the following six steps to set up and solve a decision tree problem: (1) starting TreePlan; (2) starting a new tree; (3) adding nodes and branches; (4) changing titles, probabilities, and payoffs; (5) identifying the best decision; and (6) making minor formatting changes. On the next four pages, we illustrate these steps using the original Thompson Lumber problem (i.e., the one without the market survey information included). Recall that the complete decision tree for this problem is shown in Figure 8.2 on page 326.

**PROGRAM 8.3**

**Initial Decision Tree from TreePlan**

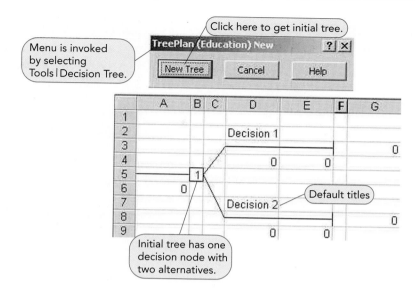

*Select* **Tools|Decision Tree** *in Excel to start TreePlan.*

**Step 1. Starting TreePlan.** Start Excel and open a blank worksheet. Place the cursor in any blank cell (say, cell A1). Select Tools|Decision Tree from Excel's main menu. *Note:* If you don't see Decision Tree as a choice in the Tools menu, you will have to install TreePlan, as discussed in the preceding section.

**Step 2. Starting a new tree.** Select New Tree. As shown in Program 8.3, this will create an initial decision tree with a single decision node (in cell B5, if the cursor was placed in cell A1). Two alternatives (named Decision 1 and Decision 2, respectively) are automatically created at this node.

*The TreePlan menu that appears depends on the location of the cursor.*

**Step 3. Adding nodes and branches.** We now modify the basic decision tree in Program 8.3 to reflect our full decision problem. To do so, we use TreePlan menus. To bring up a TreePlan menu, we either select Tools|Decision Tree or press the Control (Ctrl) and T keys at the same time. The actual TreePlan menu that is displayed each time depends on the location of the cursor when we bring up the menu, as follows:

- If the cursor is at a node in the tree (such as cell B5 in Program 8.3), the menu shown in Program 8.4(a) is displayed.
- If the cursor is at a terminal point in the tree (such as cells F3 and F8 in Program 8.3), the menu shown in Program 8.4(b) is displayed.
- If the cursor is at any other location in the spreadsheet, the menu shown in Program 8.4(c) is displayed.

*Solving the Thompson Lumber Example Using TreePlan*

For the Thompson Example, we begin by placing the cursor in cell B5 and bringing up the menu in Program 8.4(a). We then select Add Branch and click OK to get the third decision branch (named Decision 3).

Next, we move the cursor to the end of the branch for Decision 1 (i.e., to cell F3) and bring up the menu in Program 8.4(b). We first select Change to Event Node. (TreePlan refers to state of nature nodes as event nodes.) Then we select Two under Branches to add two state of nature arcs to this decision node. When we click OK, TreePlan creates two arcs, named Event 4 and Event 5, respectively. Since these are states of nature, we need to associate probability values to each event. TreePlan

*TreePlan refers to chance nodes as event nodes.*

**PROGRAM 8.4**

**TreePlan Menus**

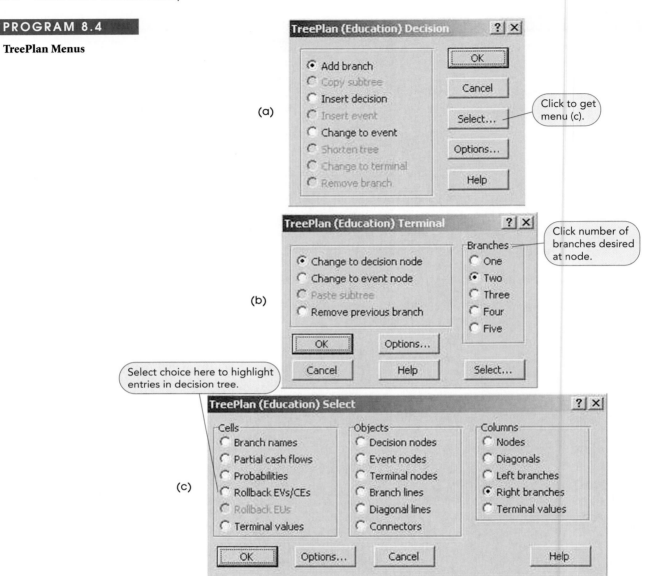

(a)

(b)

(c)

automatically assigns equal probability values by default. In this case, since there are two events, the default value assigned is 0.5.

We now move the cursor to the end of the branch for Decision 2 and repeat the preceding step to create Event 6 and Event 7. The structure of the decision tree, shown in Program 8.5, is now similar to the tree in Figure 8.2.

Step 4. Changing titles, probabilities, and payoffs. We can change the default titles for all arcs in the decision tree to reflect the Thompson problem. For example, we can replace "Decision 1" (in cell D4 of Program 8.5) with "Large Plant." Likewise, we can replace "Event 4" (in cell H2 of Program 8.5) with "Fav Market." The changes are shown in Program 8.6 on page 336.

We can also change the default probability values on the event arcs to the correct values, if needed. In Thompson's case, it turns out the actual event probabilities (0.5) are the same as the default probabilities.

**File: 8-5.xls**

*Titles can be changed in TreePlan, if desired.*

**File: 8-6.xls**

**PROGRAM 8.5**

**Completed Decision Tree
Using TreePlan for
Thompson Lumber**

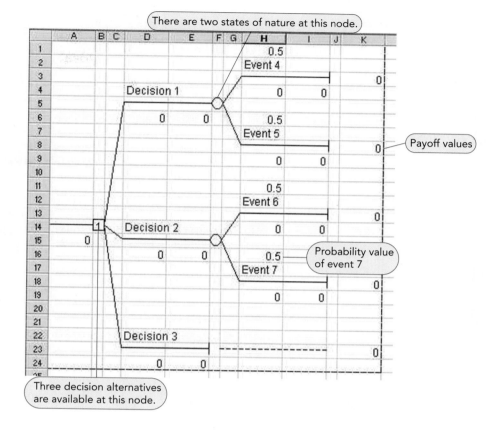

*Two ways of entering payoffs
in TreePlan*

Finally, we enter the payoffs. TreePlan allows us to enter these values in one of two ways:

■ We can directly enter the payoffs at the end of each path in the decision tree. That is, we can enter the appropriate payoff values in cells K3, K8, K13, K18, and K23, as shown in Program 8.6.

■ Allow TreePlan to compute the payoffs. Each time we create an arc (decision alternative or state of nature) in TreePlan, it assigns a default payoff of zero to that branch. We can edit these payoffs (or costs) for all alternatives and states of nature. For example, we leave cell D6 at $0 (default value) since there is no cost specified to build a large plant. However, we change the entry in cell H4 to $200,000 to reflect the payoff if the market turns out to be favorable. TreePlan adds these entries (in cells D6 and H4) automatically and reports it as the payoff in cell K3. We can do likewise for all other payoffs in John's tree.

*TreePlan writes formulas in
the appropriate cells as the
tree is created.*

Step 5. Identifying the best decision. TreePlan automatically writes formulas into the appropriate cells as the tree is created and structured. For example, TreePlan writes the following formula in cell E6 (which computes the EMV of building a large plant) of Program 8.6:

$$=\text{IF}(\text{ABS}(1-\text{SUM}(H1,H6))<=0.00001,\text{SUM}(H1*I4,H6*I9),\text{NA}())$$

The ABS part of the formula verifies that the sum of probabilities of all states of nature at a given chance node equals one. The second part (SUM) computes the EMV using the appropriate payoffs and probability values. The EMVs are shown next to the chance nodes. For example, cell E6 shows the EMV of $10,000 for the large plant.

**PROGRAM 8.6**

**Solved Decision Tree Using TreePlan for Thompson Lumber**

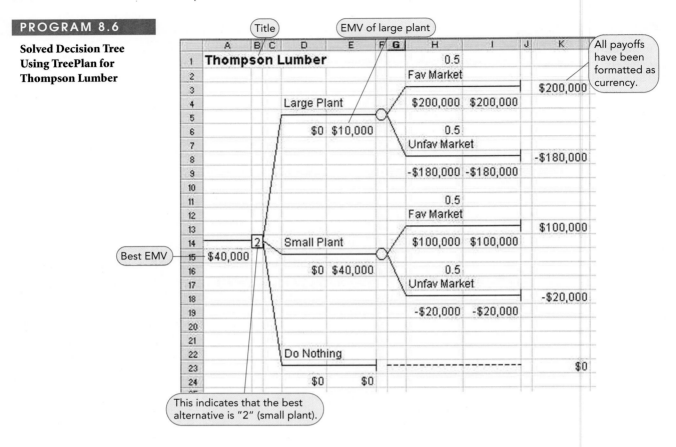

Once all expected values have been computed, TreePlan then selects the optimal decision alternative at each decision node. The selection is indicated within that node. For example, the "2" in the decision node in cell B14 indicates that the second alternative (i.e., build a small plant) is the best choice for Thompson Lumber. The best EMV of $40,000 is shown next to this decision node (in cell A15).

If the payoffs denote costs, we can click on Options in any of the TreePlan menus (see Program 8.4) to change the selection criterion from maximizing profits to minimizing costs. In this case, TreePlan will select the decision alternative with the smallest expected costs.

Step 6. Making minor formatting changes. If desired, we can add titles, format payoffs to be shown as dollar values, change number of decimals shown, and make other cosmetic changes to the tree as shown in Program 8.6. Appendix A illustrates how to make such formatting changes.

As a practice exercise, see if you can develop a decision tree using TreePlan to include the market survey (as shown in Figure 8.4). The calculations and results should be similar to that shown in Figure 8.5.

## 8.8    ESTIMATING PROBABILITY VALUES USING BAYESIAN ANALYSIS

There are many ways of getting probability data for a problem such as Thompson's. The numbers (e.g., 0.78, 0.22, 0.27, 0.73 in Figure 8.4) can be assessed by a manager based on experience and intuition. They can be derived from historical data, or they can be computed from other available data using Bayes' theorem. We discuss this last option in this section.

*Bayes' theorem allows decision makers to revise probability values.*

The Bayes' theorem approach recognizes that a decision maker does not know with certainty what state of nature will occur. It allows the manager to revise his or her initial or prior probability assessments. The revised probabilities are called *posterior probabilities*. (Before continuing, you may wish to review Bayes' theorem in Appendix B.)

## Calculating Revised Probabilities

In the Thompson Lumber case solved in Section 8.6, we made the assumption that the following four conditional probabilities were known:

$$P(\text{favorable market(FM)} \mid \text{survey results positive}) = 0.78$$

$$P(\text{unfavorable market(UM)} \mid \text{survey results positive}) = 0.22$$

$$P(\text{favorable market(FM)} \mid \text{survey results negative}) = 0.27$$

$$P(\text{unfavorable market(UM)} \mid \text{survey results negative}) = 0.73$$

We now show how John Thompson was able to derive these values with Bayes' theorem.

From discussions with market research specialists at the local university, John knows that special surveys such as his can either be positive (i.e., predict a favorable market) or be negative (i.e., predict an unfavorable market). The experts have told John that, statistically, of all new products with a *favorable market* (FM), market surveys were positive and predicted success correctly 70% of the time. Thirty percent of the time the surveys falsely predicted negative results or an *unfavorable market* (UM). On the other hand, when there was actually an unfavorable market for a new product, 80% of the surveys correctly predicted negative results. The surveys incorrectly predicted positive results the remaining 20% of the time. These conditional probabilities are summarized in Table 8.10. They are an indication of the accuracy of the survey that John is thinking of undertaking.

*Prior probabilities are estimates before the market survey.*

Recall that without any market survey information, John's best estimates of a favorable and unfavorable market are

$$P(\text{FM}) = 0.50$$

$$P(\text{UM}) = 0.50$$

These are referred to as the *prior probabilities*.

We are now ready to compute Thompson's revised or posterior probabilities. These desired probabilities are the reverse of the probabilities in Table 8.10. We need the probability of a favorable or unfavorable market given a positive or negative result from the market study. The general form of Bayes' theorem is

$$P(A \mid B) = \frac{P(B \mid A) \cdot P(A)}{P(B \mid A) \cdot P(A) + P(B \mid \overline{A}) \cdot P(\overline{A})} \tag{8-7}$$

**TABLE 8.10**    **Market Survey Reliability in Predicting Actual States of Nature**

| | ACTUAL STATES OF NATURE | |
| --- | --- | --- |
| RESULT OF SURVEY | FAVORABLE MARKET (FM) | UNFAVORABLE MARKET (UM) |
| Positive (predicts favorable market for product) | $P(\text{survey positive} \mid \text{FM}) = 0.70$ | $P(\text{survey positive} \mid \text{UM}) = 0.20$ |
| Negative (predicts unfavorable market for product) | $P(\text{survey negative} \mid \text{FM}) = 0.30$ | $P(\text{survey negative} \mid \text{UM}) = 0.80$ |

*where*

$$A, B = \text{any two events}$$

$$\overline{A} = \text{complement of } A$$

*Conditional probabilities are determined using the prior probabilities and the market survey.*

Substituting the appropriate numbers into this equation, we obtain the conditional probabilities, given that the market survey is positive:

$P(\text{FM} \mid \text{survey positive})$

$$= \frac{P(\text{survey positive} \mid \text{FM}) \cdot P(\text{FM})}{P(\text{survey positive} \mid \text{FM}) \cdot P(\text{FM}) + P(\text{survey positive} \mid \text{UM}) \cdot P(\text{UM})}$$

$$= \frac{(0.70)(0.50)}{(0.70)(0.50) + (0.20)(0.50)} = \frac{0.35}{0.45} = 0.78$$

$P(\text{UM} \mid \text{survey positive})$

$$= \frac{P(\text{survey positive} \mid \text{UM}) \cdot P(\text{UM})}{P(\text{survey positive} \mid \text{UM}) \cdot P(\text{UM}) + P(\text{survey positive} \mid \text{FM}) \cdot P(\text{FM})}$$

$$= \frac{(0.20)(0.50)}{(0.20)(0.50) + (0.70)(0.50)} = \frac{0.10}{0.45} = 0.22$$

*Calculating conditional probabilities using a probability table.*

An alternative method for these calculations is to use a probability table, as shown in Table 8.11.

The conditional probabilities, given the market survey is negative, are

$P(\text{FM} \mid \text{survey negative})$

$$= \frac{P(\text{survey negative} \mid \text{FM}) \cdot P(\text{FM})}{P(\text{survey negative} \mid \text{FM}) \cdot P(\text{FM}) + P(\text{survey negative} \mid \text{UM}) \cdot P(\text{UM})}$$

$$= \frac{(0.30)(0.50)}{(0.30)(0.50) + (0.80)(0.50)} = \frac{0.15}{0.55} = 0.27$$

$P(\text{UM} \mid \text{survey negative})$

$$= \frac{P(\text{survey negative} \mid \text{UM}) \cdot P(\text{UM})}{P(\text{survey negative} \mid \text{UM}) \cdot P(\text{UM}) + P(\text{survey negative} \mid \text{FM}) \cdot P(\text{FM})}$$

$$= \frac{(0.80)(0.50)}{(0.80)(0.50) + (0.30)(0.50)} = \frac{0.40}{0.55} = 0.73$$

These computations could have been performed in a table instead, as in Table 8.12.

**TABLE 8.11**    **Probability Revisions Given a Positive Survey**

| STATE OF NATURE | CONDITIONAL PROBABILITY $P(\text{SURVEY POSITIVE} \mid \text{STATE OF NATURE})$ | PRIOR PROBABILITY | JOINT PROBABILITY | POSTERIOR PROBABILITY $P\left(\dfrac{\text{STATE OF NATURE}}{}\bigg| \dfrac{\text{SURVEY POSITIVE}}{}\right)$ |
|---|---|---|---|---|
| FM | 0.70 | × 0.50 | = 0.35 | 0.35/0.45 = 0.78 |
| UM | 0.20 | × 0.50 | = 0.10 | 0.10/0.45 = 0.22 |
|  |  | $P(\text{survey results positive}) = 0.45$ |  | 1.00 |

**TABLE 8.12**    Probability Revisions Given a Negative Survey

| STATE OF NATURE | CONDITIONAL PROBABILITY $P$(SURVEY NEGATIVE ⎮ STATE OF NATURE) | PRIOR PROBABILITY | JOINT PROBABILITY | POSTERIOR PROBABILITY $P\left(\dfrac{\text{STATE OF NATURE}}{}\bigg\vert\dfrac{\text{SURVEY NEGATIVE}}{}\right)$ |
|---|---|---|---|---|
| FM | 0.30 | × 0.50 | = 0.15 | 0.15/0.55 = 0.27 |
| UM | 0.80 | × 0.50 | = 0.40 | 0.40/0.55 = 0.73 |
|  |  | $P$(survey results negative) = 0.55 |  | 1.00 |

*New probabilities provide valuable information.*

The posterior probabilities now provide John Thompson with estimates for each state of nature if the survey results are positive or negative. As you know, John's *prior probability* of success without a market survey was only 0.50. Now he is aware that the probability of successfully marketing storage sheds will be 0.78 if his survey shows positive results. His chances of success drop to 27% if the survey report is negative. This is valuable management information, as we saw in the earlier decision tree analysis.

## Potential Problems in Using Survey Results

In many decision-making problems, survey results or pilot studies are done before an actual decision (e.g., building a new plant or taking a particular course of action) is made. As discussed earlier in this section, Bayes' analysis is used to help determine the correct conditional probabilities that are needed to solve these types of decision theory problems. In computing these conditional probabilities, we need to have data about the surveys and their accuracies. If a decision to build a plant or to take another course of action is actually made, we can determine the accuracy of our surveys. Unfortunately, we cannot get data about those situations in which the decision was not to build a plant or not to take some course of action. Thus, when we use survey results, we are basing our probabilities only on those cases in which a decision to build a plant or take some course of action is actually made. This means that conditional probability information is not quite as accurate as we would like. Even so, calculating conditional probabilities helps to refine the decision-making process and, in general, to make better decisions.

## 8.9    UTILITY THEORY

*EMV is not always the best approach.*

So far we have used EMV to make decisions. In practice, however, using EMV could lead to bad decisions in some cases. For example, suppose that you are the lucky holder of a lottery ticket. Five minutes from now a fair coin could be flipped, and if it comes up tails, you would win $5 million. If it comes up heads, you would win nothing. Just a moment ago a wealthy person offered you $2 million for your ticket. Let's assume that you have no doubts about the validity of the offer. The person will give you a certified check for the full amount, and you are absolutely sure the check would be good.

A decision tree is shown in Figure 8.6. EMV indicates that you should hold on to your ticket, but what would you do? Just think, $2 million for *sure* instead of a 50% chance at nothing. Suppose you were greedy enough to hold on to the ticket, and then lost. How would you explain that to your friends? Wouldn't $2 million be enough to be comfortable for a while?

Most people would sell for $2 million. Most of us, in fact, would probably be willing to settle for a lot less. Just how low we would go is, of course, a matter of personal preference. People have different feelings about seeking or avoiding risk. EMV is not a good way to make these types of decisions.

FIGURE 8.6

**Your Decision Tree for the
Lottery Ticket**

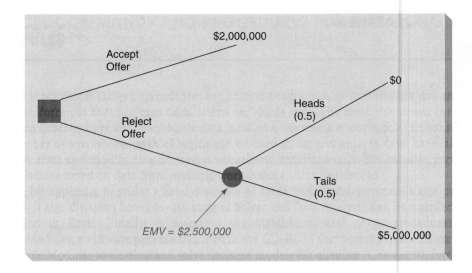

One way to incorporate your own attitudes toward risk is through *utility theory*. In the next section we explore first how to measure utility and then how to use utility measures in decision making.

## Measuring Utility and Constructing a Utility Curve

**Utility assessment** *assigns the worst outcome a utility of 0 and the best outcome, 1.*

*Utility assessment* begins by assigning the worst outcome a utility of 0 and the best outcome a utility of 1. All other outcomes will have a utility value between 0 and 1. In determining the utilities of all outcomes, other than the best or worst outcome, a *standard gamble* is considered. This gamble is shown in Figure 8.7.

In Figure 8.7, $p$ is the probability of obtaining the best outcome, and $(1 - p)$ is the probability of obtaining the worst outcome. Assessing the utility of any other outcome involves determining the probability, $p$, that makes you indifferent between alternative 1, which is the gamble between the best and worst outcomes, and alternative 2, which is obtaining the other outcome for sure. When you are indifferent between alternatives 1 and 2, the expected utilities for these two alternatives must be equal. This relationship is shown as

*When you are indifferent, the expected utilities are equal.*

expected utility of alternative 2 = expected utility of alternative 1

utility of other outcome = $(p)$(utility of *best* outcome, which is 1)
  $+ (1 - p)$(utility of the *worst* outcome, which is 0)

utility of other outcome = $(p)(1) + (1 - p)(0) = p$     (8-8)

FIGURE 8.7

**Standard Gamble for
Utility Assessment**

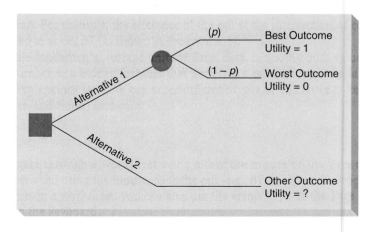

Now all you have to do is to determine the value of the probability ($p$) that makes you indifferent between alternatives 1 and 2. In setting the probability, you should be aware that utility assessment is completely subjective. It's a value set by the decision maker that can't be measured on an objective scale. Let's look at an example.

*A utility curve plots utility values versus monetary values.*

**Jane Dickson's Utility Curve**  Jane Dickson would like to construct a utility curve revealing her preference for money between $0 and $10,000. A *utility curve* is a graph that plots utility value versus monetary value. She can either invest her money in a bank savings account or she can invest the same money in a real estate deal.

If the money is invested in the bank, in three years Jane would have $5,000. If she invested in the real estate, after three years she could either have nothing or $10,000. Jane, however, is very conservative. Unless there is an 80% chance of getting $10,000 from the real estate deal, Jane would prefer to have her money in the bank, where it is safe. What Jane has done here is to assess her utility for $5,000. When there is an 80% chance (this means that $p$ is 0.8) of getting $10,000, Jane is indifferent between putting her money in real estate or putting it in the bank. Jane's utility for $5,000 is thus equal to 0.8, which is the same as the value for $p$. This utility assessment is shown in Figure 8.8.

Other utility values can be assessed in the same way. For example, what is Jane's utility for $7,000? What value of $p$ would make Jane indifferent between $7,000 and the gamble that would result in either $10,000 or $0? For Jane, there must be a 90% chance of getting the $10,000. Otherwise, she would prefer the $7,000 for sure. Thus, her utility for $7,000 is 0.90. Jane's utility for $3,000 can be determined in the same way. If there was a 50% chance of obtaining the $10,000, Jane would be indifferent between having $3,000 for sure and taking the gamble of either winning the $10,000 or getting nothing. Thus, the utility of $3,000 for Jane is 0.5. Of course, this process can be continued until Jane has assessed her utility for as many monetary values as she wants. These assessments, however, are enough to get an idea of Jane's feelings toward risk. In fact, we can

*Once utility values have been determined, a utility curve can be constructed.*

plot these points in a *utility curve*, as is done in Figure 8.9. In the figure, the assessed utility points of $3,000, $5,000, and $7,000 are shown by dots, and the rest of the curve is eyeballed in.

Jane's utility curve is typical of a *risk avoider*. A risk avoider is a decision maker who gets less utility or pleasure from a greater risk and tends to avoid situations in which high losses might occur. As monetary value increases on her utility curve, the utility increases at a slower rate.

**FIGURE 8.8**

**Utility of $5,000 for Jane Dixon**

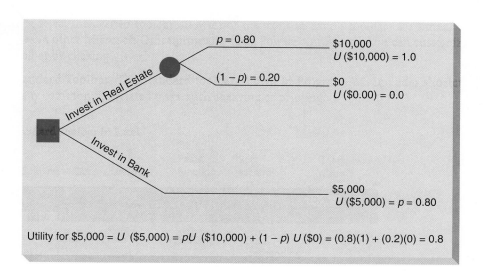

Utility for $5,000 = $U$ ($5,000) = $pU$ ($10,000) + $(1 - p)$ $U$ ($0) = (0.8)(1) + (0.2)(0) = 0.8

FIGURE 8.9

**Utility Curve for Jane Dickson**

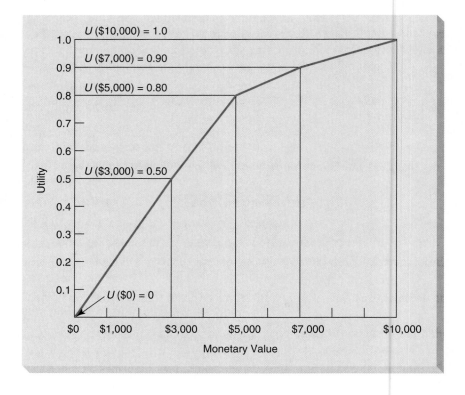

The shape of a person's utility curve depends on many factors.

Figure 8.10 illustrates that a person who is a *risk seeker* has an opposite-shaped utility curve. This decision maker gets more utility from a greater risk and higher potential payoff. As monetary value increases on his or her utility curve, the utility increases at an increasing rate. A person who is *indifferent* to risk has a utility curve that is a straight line. The shape of a person's utility curve depends on the specific decision being considered, the person's psychological frame of mind, and how the person feels about the future. It may well be that you have one utility curve for some situations you face and completely different curves for others.

FIGURE 8.10

**Preferences for Risk**

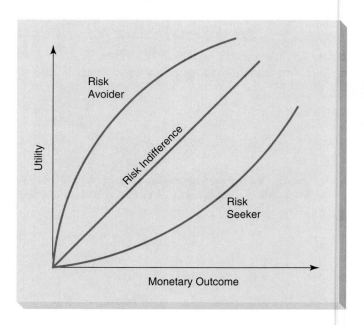

**IN ACTION**    Using Utility and Decision Trees in Hip Replacement

Should you or a family member undergo a somewhat dangerous surgery for an illness, or is it better to manage the illness medically by drugs? Should a health care firm put a new drug on its list of approved medicines? What medical procedures should the government reimburse? Individuals and institutions face medical treatment decision problems from a variety of perspectives. For example, the decision an individual patient faces is driven by the medical treatment that best describes the patient's attitudes about risk (utility) and quality of life over the rest of his or her life.

One common application of utility theory decision tree modeling in medicine is the total hip replacement surgery for patients with severe arthritis of the hip. Over 120,000 hip replacements are performed per year in North America. Although this surgery is mostly successful, the treatment decision for an individual patient can be difficult. Although surgery offers the potential of increased quality of life, it also carries the risk of death.

A decision tree analysis helps define all of the time-sequenced outcomes that can occur in dealing with arthritis of the hip. Conservative management by medicine is a surgical alternative, but the disease is degenerative and a worsening condition is inevitable. A successful surgery, which restores full function, is likely, but uncertainty exists even then. First, infection can cause the new prosthetic hip to fail. Or the new hip may fail over time due to breakage or malfunction. Both cases require a revision surgery, whose risks are greater than the first surgery. Decision trees and utility theory help patients first assess their personal risk levels and then allow them to compute life expectancy based on sex and race.

**Source:** G. Hazen, J. Pellissier, and J. Sounderpandian. "Stochastic Tree Models in Medical Decision Making," *Interfaces* (July–August 1998): 64–80.

## Utility as a Decision-Making Criterion

*Utility values replace monetary values.*

After a utility curve has been determined, the utility values from the curve are used in making decisions. Monetary outcomes or values are replaced with the appropriate utility values and then decision analysis is performed as usual. Let's look at an example in which a decision tree is used and expected utility values are computed in selecting the best alternative.

**Mark Simkin Example**    Mark Simkin loves to gamble. He decides to play a game that involves tossing thumbtacks in the air. If the point on the thumbtack is facing up after it lands, Mark wins $10,000. If the point on the thumbtack is down, Mark loses $10,000. Should Mark play the game (alternative 1) or should he not play the game (alternative 2)?

Alternatives 1 and 2 are displayed in the tree shown in Figure 8.11. As can be seen, alternative 1 is to play the game. Mark believes that there is a 45% chance of winning $10,000 and a 55% chance of suffering the $10,000 loss. Alternative 2 is not to gamble. What should Mark do? Of course, this depends on Mark's utility for money. As stated pre-

**FIGURE 8.11**

**Decision Facing Mark Simkin**

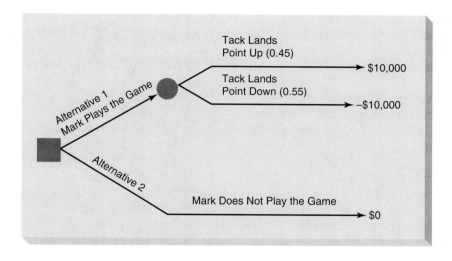

**Utility Curve for Mark Simkin**

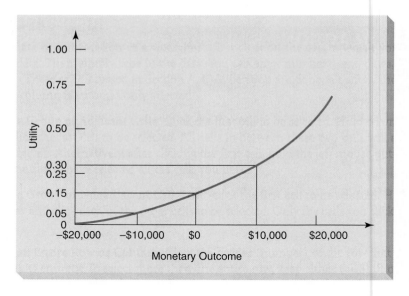

*Mark's objective is to maximize expected utility.*

viously, he likes to gamble. Using the procedure just outlined, Mark was able to construct a utility curve showing his preference for money. This curve is shown in Figure 8.12.

We see that Mark's utility for −$10,000 is 0.05, his utility for not playing ($0) is 0.15, and his utility for $10,000 is 0.30. These values can now be used in the decision tree. Mark's objective is to maximize his expected utility, which can be done as follows:

**Step 1**

$$U(-\$10,000) = 0.05$$

$$U(\$0) = 0.15$$

$$U(\$10,000) = 0.30$$

**Step 2**  Replace monetary values with utility values. Refer to Figure 8.13. Here are the utilities for alternatives 1 and 2:

$$E(\text{alternative 1: play the game}) = (0.45)(0.30) + (0.55)(0.05)$$

$$= 0.135 + 0.027 = 0.1625$$

$$E(\text{alternative 2: don't play the game}) = 0.15$$

**Using Expected Utilities in Decision Making**

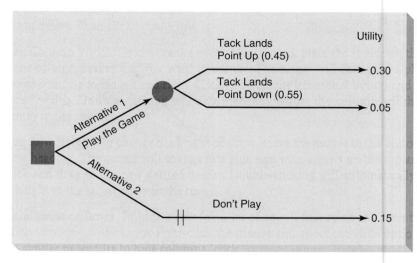

Therefore, alternative 1 is the best strategy using utility as the decision criterion. If EMV had been used, alternative 2 would have been the best strategy. The utility curve is a risk-seeker utility curve, and the choice of playing the game certainly reflects this preference for risk.

## SUMMARY

This chapter introduces the topic of decision theory, which is an analytic and systematic approach to study decision making. We first indicate the steps involved in making decisions in three different environments: (1) decision making under certainty, (2) decision making under uncertainty, and (3) decision making under risk. For decision problems under uncertainty, we identify the best alternatives using criteria such as maximax, maximin, equally likely, criterion of realism, and minimax regret. For decision problems under risk, we discuss the computation and use of the expected monetary value (EMV), expected opportunity loss (EOL), and expected value of perfect

information (EVPI). We also illustrate the use of Excel to solve decision theory problems.

Decision trees are used for larger decision problems in which decisions must be made in sequence. In this case we compute the expected value of sample information (EVSI). Bayesian analysis is used to revise or update probability values. We also discuss how decision trees can be set up and solved using TreePlan, an Excel add-in.

When it is inappropriate to use monetary values, utility theory can be used to assign a utility value to each decision payoff. In such cases, we compute expected utilities and select the alternative with the highest utility value.

## GLOSSARY

**Coefficient of Realism ($\alpha$).** A number from 0 to 1. When $\alpha$ is close to 1, the decision criterion is optimistic. When $\alpha$ is close to zero, the decision criterion is pessimistic.

**Conditional Value or Payoff.** A consequence or payoff, normally expressed in a monetary value, which occurs as a result of a particular alternative and state of nature.

**Decision Alternative.** A course of action or a strategy that can be chosen by a decision maker.

**Decision Making under Certainty.** A decision-making environment in which the future outcomes or states of nature are known.

**Decision Making under Risk.** A decision-making environment in which several outcomes or states of nature can occur as a result of a decision or alternative. Probabilities of the outcomes or states of nature are known.

**Decision Making under Uncertainty.** A decision-making environment in which several outcomes or states of nature can occur. Probabilities of these outcomes, however, are not known.

**Decision Table.** A table in which decision alternatives are listed down the rows and states of nature are listed across the column. The body of the table contains the payoffs.

**Equally Likely.** A decision criterion that places an equal weight on all states of nature.

**Expected Monetary Value (EMV).** The average or expected monetary outcome of a decision if it can be repeated many times. This is determined by multiplying the monetary outcomes by their respective probabilities. The results are then added to arrive at the EMV.

**Expected Opportunity Loss (EOL).** The average or expected regret of a decision.

**Expected Value of Perfect Information (EVPI).** The average or expected value of information if it were completely accurate.

**Expected Value with Perfect Information (EVwPI).** The average or expected value of the decision if you knew what would happen ahead of time.

**Maximax.** An optimistic decision-making criterion. This is the alternative with the highest possible return.

**Maximin.** A pessimistic decision-making criterion that maximizes the minimum outcome. It is the best of the worst possible outcomes.

**Minimax Regret.** A decision criterion that minimizes the maximum opportunity loss.

**Opportunity Loss.** The amount you would lose by not picking the best alternative. For any state of nature, this is the difference between the consequences of any alternative and the best possible alternative. Also called *regret*.

**Sequential Decisions.** Decisions in which the outcome of one decision influences other decisions.

**State of Nature.** An outcome or occurrence over which the decision maker has little or no control.

**Risk Avoider.** Person who avoids risk. As the monetary value increases on the utility curve, the utility increases at a decreasing rate. This decision maker gets less utility for a greater risk and higher potential returns.

**Risk Seeker.** Person who seeks risk. As the monetary value increases on the utility curve, the utility increases at an increasing rate. This decision maker gets more pleasure for a greater risk and higher potential returns.

**Utility Assessment.** The process of determining the utility of various outcomes. This is normally done using a standard gamble between any sure outcome and a gamble between the worst and best outcomes.

**Utility Curve.** A graph or curve that illustrates the relationship between utility and monetary values. When this curve has been constructed, utility values from the curve can be used in the decision making process.

**Utility Theory.** A theory that allows decision makers to incorporate their risk preference and other factors into the decision making process.

## KEY EQUATIONS

**(8-1)**  Criterion of realism = $\alpha \times$ (maximum payoff for an alternative) + $(1 - \alpha) \times$ (minimum payoff for an alternative)

Computes the payoffs for the coefficient of realism criterion.

**(8-2)**  EMV (alternative $i$) = (payoff of first state of nature) $\times$ (probability of first state of nature) + (payoff of second state of nature) $\times$ (probability of second state of nature) + . . . + (payoff of last state of nature) $\times$ (probability of last state of nature)

Computes the expected monetary value.

**(8-3)**  EOL (alternative $i$) = (regret of first state of nature) $\times$ (probability of first state of nature) + (regret of second state of nature) $\times$ (probability of second state of nature) + . . . + (regret of last state of nature) $\times$ (probability of last state of nature)

Computes the expected opportunity loss.

**(8-4)**  EVwPI = (best payoff for first state of nature) $\times$ (probability of first state of nature) + (best payoff for second state of nature) $\times$ (probability of second state of nature) + . . . +

(best payoff for last state of nature) $\times$ (probability of last state of nature)

Computes the expected value with perfect information.

**(8-5)**  EVPI = EVwPI − maximum EMV

Computes the expected value of perfect information.

**(8-6)**  Expected value of sample information (EVSI)

$$= \begin{pmatrix} \text{expected value of the best} \\ \text{decision } with \text{ sample} \\ \text{information, assuming} \\ \text{no cost to gather it} \end{pmatrix} - \begin{pmatrix} \text{expected value of} \\ \text{the best decision} \\ without \text{ sample} \\ \text{information} \end{pmatrix}$$

**(8-7)**  $P(A \mid B) = \dfrac{P(B \mid A) \cdot P(A)}{P(B \mid A) \cdot P(A) + P(B \mid \overline{A}) \cdot P(\overline{A})}$

Bayes' theorem—it yields the conditional value of event $A$ given that event $B$ has occurred.

**(8-8)**  Utility of other outcome = $(p)(1) + (1 - p)(0) = p$

Determines the utility of an intermediate outcome.

## SOLVED PROBLEMS

### Solved Problem 8-1

Cal Bender and Becky Addison have known each other since high school. Two years ago they entered the same university and today they are taking undergraduate courses in the business school. Both hope to graduate with degrees in finance. In an attempt to make extra money and to use some of the knowledge gained from their business courses, Cal and Becky have decided to look into the possibility of starting a small company that would provide word processing services to students who needed term papers or other reports prepared in a professional manner. Using a systems approach, Cal and Becky have identified three strategies. Strategy 1 is to invest in a fairly expensive microcomputer system with a high-quality laser printer. In a favorable market, they should be able to obtain a net profit of $10,000 over the next two years. If the market is unfavorable, they can lose $8,000. Strategy 2 is to purchase a less expensive system. With a favorable market, they could get a return during the next two years of $8,000. With an unfavorable market, they would incur a loss of $4,000. Their final strategy, strategy 3, is to do nothing. Cal is basically a risk taker, whereas Becky tries to avoid risk.

a. What type of decision procedure should Cal use? What would Cal's decision be?
b. What type of decision maker is Becky? What decision would Becky make?
c. If Cal and Becky were indifferent to risk, what type of decision approach should they use? What would you recommend if this were the case?

### Solution

The problem is one of decision making under uncertainty. Before answering the specific questions, a decision table should be developed showing the alternatives, states of nature, and related consequences.

| ALTERNATIVE | FAVORABLE MARKET ($) | UNFAVORABLE MARKET ($) |
|---|---|---|
| Strategy 1 | 10,000 | −8,000 |
| Strategy 2 | 8,000 | −4,000 |
| Strategy 3 | 0 | 0 |

a. Since Cal is a risk taker, he should use the maximax decision criteria. This approach selects the row that has the highest or maximum value. The $10,000 value, which is the maximum value from the table, is in row 1. Thus Cal's decision is to select strategy 1, which is an optimistic decision approach.
b. Becky should use the maximin decision criteria. The minimum or worst outcome for each row, or strategy, is identified. These outcomes are −$8,000 for strategy 1, −$4,000 for strategy 2, and $0 for strategy 3. The maximum of these values is selected. Thus, Becky would select strategy 3, which reflects a pessimistic decision approach.
c. If Cal and Becky are indifferent to risk, they should use the equally likely approach. This approach selects the alternative that maximizes the row averages. The row average for strategy 1 is $1,000 [$1,000 = ($10,000 − $8,000)/2]. The row average for strategy 2 is $2,000, and the row average for strategy 3 is $0. Thus, using the equally likely approach, the decision is to select strategy 2, which maximizes the row averages.

## Solved Problem 8-2

Maria Rojas is considering the possibility of opening a small dress shop on Fairbanks Avenue, a few blocks from the university. She has located a good mall that attracts students. Her options are to open a small shop, a medium-sized shop, or no shop at all. The market for a dress shop can be good, average, or bad. The probabilities for these three possibilities are 0.2 for a good market, 0.5 for an average market, and 0.3 for a bad market. The net profit or loss for the medium-sized and small shops for the various market conditions are given in the table at the top of the next page. Building no shop at all yields no loss and no gain. What do you recommend?

| ALTERNATIVE | GOOD MARKET ($) | AVERAGE MARKET ($) | BAD MARKET ($) |
|---|---|---|---|
| Small shop | 75,000 | 25,000 | −40,000 |
| Medium-sized shop | 100,000 | 35,000 | −60,000 |
| No shop | 0 | 0 | 0 |

## Solution

The problem can be solved by developing a payoff table that contains all alternatives, states of nature, and probability values. The EMV for each alternative is also computed. See the following table:

| ALTERNATIVE | STATES OF NATURE | | | |
|---|---|---|---|---|
| | GOOD MARKET ($) | AVERAGE MARKET ($) | BAD MARKET ($) | EMV ($) |
| Small shop | 75,000 | 25,000 | −40,000 | 15,500 |
| Medium-sized shop | 100,000 | 35,000 | −60,000 | 19,500 |
| No shop | 0 | 0 | 0 | 0 |
| Probabilities | 0.20 | 0.50 | 0.30 | |

$$\text{EMV(small shop)} = (0.2)(\$75,000) + (0.5)(\$25,000) \\ + (0.3)(-\$40,000) = \$15,500$$

$$\text{EMV(medium-sized shop)} = (0.2)(\$100,000) + (0.5)(\$35,000) \\ + (0.3)(-\$60,000) = \$19,500$$

$$\text{EMV(no shop)} = (0.2)(\$0) + (0.5)(\$0) + (0.3)(\$0) = \$0$$

As can be seen, the best decision is to build the medium-sized shop. The EMV for this alternative is $19,500.

## Solved Problem 8-3

Monica Britt has enjoyed sailing small boats since she was 7 years old, when her mother started sailing with her. Today Monica is considering the possibility of starting a company to produce small sailboats for the recreational market. Unlike other mass-produced sailboats, however, these boats will be made specifically for children between the ages of 10 and 15. The boats will be of the highest quality and extremely stable, and the sail size will be reduced to prevent problems of capsizing.

Because of the expense involved in developing the initial molds and acquiring the necessary equipment to produce fiberglass sailboats for young children, Monica has decided to conduct a pilot study to make sure that the market for the sailboats will be adequate. She estimates that the pilot study will cost her $10,000. Furthermore, the pilot study can be either successful or not successful. Her basic decisions are to build a large manufacturing facility, a small manufacturing facility, or no facility at all. With a favorable market, Monica can expect to make $90,000 from the large facility or $60,000 from the smaller facility. If the market is unfavorable, however, Monica estimates that she would lose $30,000 with a large facility, whereas she would lose only $20,000 with the small facility. Monica estimates that the probability of a favorable market given a successful pilot study is 0.8. The probability of an unfavorable market given an unsuccessful pilot study result is estimated to be 0.9. Monica feels that there is a 50–50 chance that the pilot study will be successful. Of course, Monica could bypass the pilot study and simply make the decision as to whether to build a large plant, small plant, or no facility at all. Without doing any testing in a pilot study, she estimates that the probability of a successful market is 0.6. What do you recommend?

### Solution

Before Monica starts to solve this problem, she should develop a decision tree that shows all alternatives, states of nature, probability values, and economic consequences. This decision tree is shown in Figure 8.14.

Once the decision tree has been developed, Monica can solve the problem by computing expected monetary values starting at the endpoints of the decision tree. The final solution is shown on the revised decision tree in Figure 8.15. The optimal solution is to *not* conduct the study but to construct the large plant directly. The expected monetary value is $42,000.

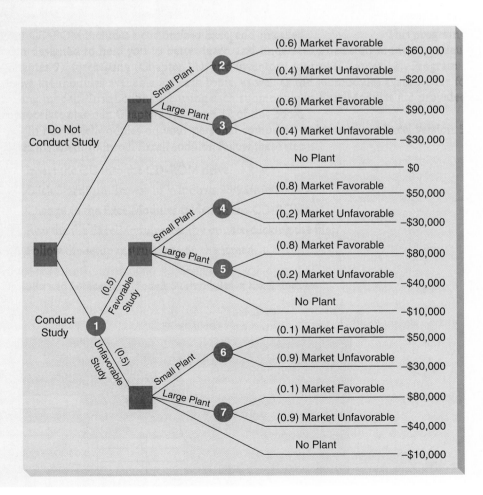

### FIGURE 8.14

**Complete Decision Tree for Solved Problem 8-3**

**FIGURE 8.15**    Revised Decision Tree for Solved Problem 8-3

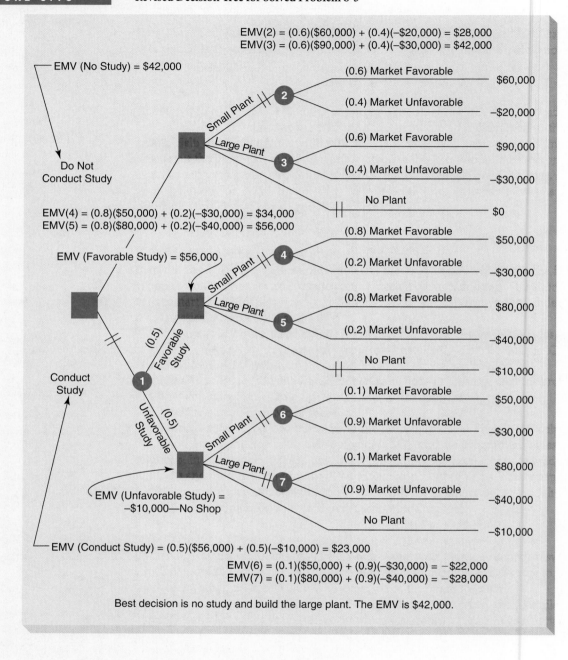

EMV(2) = (0.6)($60,000) + (0.4)(−$20,000) = $28,000
EMV(3) = (0.6)($90,000) + (0.4)(−$30,000) = $42,000

EMV (No Study) = $42,000

Do Not
Conduct Study

Small Plant

2    (0.6) Market Favorable    $60,000
     (0.4) Market Unfavorable   −$20,000

Large Plant

3    (0.6) Market Favorable    $90,000
     (0.4) Market Unfavorable   −$30,000

No Plant    $0

EMV(4) = (0.8)($50,000) + (0.2)(−$30,000) = $34,000
EMV(5) = (0.8)($80,000) + (0.2)(−$40,000) = $56,000

EMV (Favorable Study) = $56,000

Small Plant

4    (0.8) Market Favorable    $50,000
     (0.2) Market Unfavorable   −$30,000

Large Plant

5    (0.8) Market Favorable    $80,000
     (0.2) Market Unfavorable   −$40,000

No Plant    −$10,000

(0.5) Favorable Study

Conduct
Study

1

Unfavorable Study (0.5)

(0.1) Market Favorable    $50,000
6    (0.9) Market Unfavorable   −$30,000

Small Plant

Large Plant

7    (0.1) Market Favorable    $80,000
     (0.9) Market Unfavorable   −$40,000

No Plant    −$10,000

EMV (Unfavorable Study) =
−$10,000—No Shop

EMV (Conduct Study) = (0.5)($56,000) + (0.5)(−$10,000) = $23,000

EMV(6) = (0.1)($50,000) + (0.9)(−$30,000) = −$22,000
EMV(7) = (0.1)($80,000) + (0.9)(−$40,000) = −$28,000

Best decision is no study and build the large plant. The EMV is $42,000.

## Solved Problem 8-4

Developing a small driving range for golfers of all abilities has long been a desire of John Jenkins. John, however, believes that the chance of a successful driving range is only about 40%. A friend of John's has suggested that he conduct a survey in the community to get a better feeling of the demand for such a facility. There is a 0.9 probability that the research will be favorable if the driving range facility will be successful. Furthermore, it is estimated that there is a 0.8 probability that the marketing research will be unfavorable if indeed the facility will be unsuccessful. John would like to determine the chances of a successful driving range given a favorable result from the marketing survey.

### Solution

This problem requires the use of Bayes' theorem. Before we start to solve the problem, we will define the following terms:

$$P(SF) = \text{probability of successful driving range facility}$$

$$P(UF) = \text{probability of unsuccessful driving range facility}$$

$$P(RF \mid SF) = \text{probability that the research will be favorable given a successful driving range facility}$$

$$P(RU \mid SF) = \text{probability that the research will be unfavorable given a successful driving range facility}$$

$$P(RU \mid UF) = \text{probability that the research will be unfavorable given an unsuccessful driving range facility}$$

$$P(RF \mid UF) = \text{probability that the research will be favorable given an unsuccessful driving range facility}$$

Now, we can summarize what we know:

$$P(SF) = 0.4$$

$$P(RF \mid SF) = 0.9$$

$$P(RU \mid UF) = 0.8$$

From this information we can compute three additional probabilities that we need to solve the problem:

$$P(UF) = 1 - P(SF) = 1 - 0.4 = 0.6$$

$$P(RU \mid SF) = 1 - P(RF \mid SF) = 1 - 0.9 = 0.1$$

$$P(RF \mid UF) = 1 - P(RU \mid UF) = 1 - 0.8 = 0.2$$

Now we can put these values into Bayes' theorem to compute the desired probability:

$$P(SF \mid RF) = \frac{P(RF \mid SF) \cdot P(SF)}{P(RF \mid SF) \cdot P(SF) + P(RF \mid UF) \cdot P(UF)}$$

$$= \frac{(0.9)(0.4)}{(0.9)(0.4) + (0.2)(0.6)}$$

$$= \frac{0.36}{(0.36 + 0.12)} = \frac{0.36}{0.48} = 0.75$$

In addition to using formulas to solve John's problem, it is possible to perform all calculations in a table:

**Revised Probabilities Given a Favorable Research Result**

| STATES OF NATURE | CONDITIONAL PROBABILITY | | PRIOR PROBABILITY | | JOINT PROBABILITY | POSTERIOR PROBABILITY |
|---|---|---|---|---|---|---|
| Favorable market | 0.9 | × | 0.4 | = | 0.36 | 0.36/0.48 = 0.75 |
| Unfavorable market | 0.2 | × | 0.6 | = | 0.12 | 0.12/0.48 = 0.25 |
| | | | | | 0.48 | |

As you can see from the table, the results are the same. The probability of a successful driving range given a favorable research result is 0.36/0.48 or 0.75.

## Solved Problem 8-5

Like many students before her, Anne Martin is facing a difficult and important career decision. While at school, Anne worked for a local accounting firm. She did a good job and the firm has given her a standing offer to work for them for $30,000. She can take as much time as she wants to make her decision. There are, however, two other companies that are interested in her. Barnes Accounting has given her an offer of $32,000. Unfortunately, Barnes has given her only two weeks to make a decision. The company that Anne would really like to work for is Ketchum Accounting Services. This company, she feels, may make her an offer of $28,000. Unfortunately, Anne is quite uncertain about whether Ketchum will offer her the position. Thus, Anne has to make a difficult decision. Should she accept the offer from Barnes for $32,000, or should she wait and hope to get the offer from Ketchum? If she waits and doesn't get the offer from Ketchum, she can always go back to her old job for $30,000. The worst situation would be her old job, whereas the best situation would be the job with Ketchum. For Anne to be indifferent between taking the job with Barnes and the gamble of waiting and trying to get a job with Ketchum, the probability of landing the job at Ketchum would have to be 0.6. Given this information, what utility should Anne place on the three jobs?

### Solution

The problem facing Anne Martin is one of determining utility values. We begin by assigning a utility value of 1 to the best situation, which is obtaining a job from Ketchum. We also assign a utility value of 0 to the worst outcome in this situation, which is keeping the old job. Furthermore, the problem states that the probability for Anne to be indifferent between taking the job with Barnes and taking the gamble of waiting and trying to get the job with Ketchum is 0.6. This indifference situation can be shown in Figure 8.16.

Given the information and diagram, Anne can proceed to determine her indifference point. This point is where the utility ($U$) for getting the job with Barnes is equal to the gamble of getting the job with Ketchum, with a 0.6 probability, and her old job, with a 0.4 probability. The appropriate calculations are

$$U(\text{Ketchum}) = 1.0$$

$$U(\text{old job}) = 0$$

$$U(\text{Barnes}) = (0.6)U(\text{Ketchum}) + (0.4)U(\text{old job})$$

$$= (0.6)(1) + (0.4)(0) = 0.6$$

**FIGURE 8.16**

**Decision Facing Anne Martin (Solved Problem 8-5)**

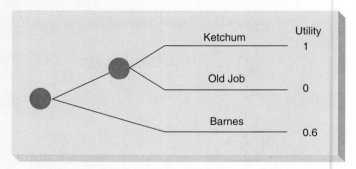

■ Before taking the self-test, refer back to the learning objectives at the beginning of the chapter, the notes in the margins, and the glossary at the end of the chapter.

■ Use the key at the back of the book to correct your answers.

■ Restudy pages that correspond to any questions that you answered incorrectly or material you feel uncertain about.

1. Which of the following is not a type of decision making?
   a. decision making under chance
   b. decision making under risk
   c. decision making under certainty
   d. decision making under uncertainty

2. A payoff table
   a. lists states of nature on one axis and alternatives on the other axis.
   b. is also called a decision table.
   c. is a matrix (table) of conditional values.
   d. all of the above.

3. Which of these models is valid under conditions of uncertainty?
   a. maximax
   b. maximin
   c. equally likely
   d. minimax regret
   e. all of the above

4. Probabilities are needed under conditions of
   a. certainty.
   b. risk.
   c. uncertainty.
   d. both a and c.

5. The minimum EOL is
   a. the minimum expected opportunity loss.
   b. the minimum regret.
   c. equivalent to the EVPI.
   d. the alternative to select.
   e. all of the above.

6. The sum of the products of the probabilities of mutually exclusive and exhaustive states of nature and the conditional values of those same states of nature is called the
   a. EOL.
   b. EMV.
   c. EVPI.

7. EVPI is
   a. the expected value with perfect information.
   b. equal to maximum EOL.
   c. equal to expected value with perfect information minus maximum EMV.

8. An α value is needed to indicate the decision maker's optimism when using the
   a. maximax.
   b. equally likely.
   c. criterion of realism.
   d. minimax regret.

9. The decision model that utilizes the opportunity loss table is the
   a. maximax.
   b. maximin.
   c. equally likely.
   d. criterion of realism.
   e. minimax regret.

10. In calculating the expected monetary value on decision trees
    a. all probabilities and payoffs should be specified first.
    b. you begin at the right-hand side of each route and travel backward.
    c. the EMV at each decision node should be the highest of the choices from the succeeding branches.
    d. you assume a constantly increasing utility for constantly increasing amounts of money.
    e. all of the above.

11. Constantly increasing utility for constantly increasing amounts of money
    a. is an attribute of a person who is risk indifferent.
    b. would eliminate your desire to gamble and also your desire to buy life insurance.
    c. is a fundamental assumption to EMV analysis.
    d. all of the above.
    e. none of the above.

12. A utility curve
    a. can be used in the decision-making process.
    b. shows utility increasing at an increasing rate when the monetary value increases for a risk seeker.
    c. shows utility increasing at a decreasing rate when the monetary value increases for a risk avoider.
    d. all of the above.

13. _____ are typically used when a sequence of decisions needs to be made.

14. The revised probabilities computed using Bayesian analysis are called _____.

15. In utility theory, _____ is used to determine utility values for various decision outcomes.

# DISCUSSION QUESTIONS AND PROBLEMS

## Discussion Questions

**8-1** Give an example of a good decision that you made that resulted in a bad outcome. Also give an example of a bad decision that you made that had a good outcome. Why was each decision good or bad?

**8-2** Describe what is involved in the decision process.

**8-3** What is an alternative? What is a state of nature?

**8-4** Discuss the differences between decision making under certainty, decision making under risk, and decision making under uncertainty.

**8-5** State the meanings of EMV and EVPI.

**8-6** Under what conditions is a decision tree preferable to a decision table?

**8-7** What is the difference between prior and posterior probabilities?

**8-8** What is the purpose of Bayesian analysis? Describe how you would use Bayesian analysis in the decision-making process.

**8-9** What is the purpose of utility theory?

**8-10** Briefly discuss how a utility function can be assessed. What is a standard gamble, and how is it used in determining utility values?

**8-11** How is a utility curve used in selecting the best decision for a particular problem?

**8-12** What is risk seeker? What is a risk avoider? How does the utility curve for these types of decision makers differ?

## Problems

• **8-13** Kenneth Brown is the principal owner of Brown Oil, Inc. After quitting his university teaching job, Ken has been able to increase his annual salary by a factor of over 100. At the present time, Ken is forced to consider purchasing some more equipment for Brown Oil because of competition. His alternatives are shown in the following table:

| EQUIPMENT | FAVORABLE MARKET ($) | UNFAVORABLE MARKET ($) |
|---|---|---|
| Sub 100 | 300,000 | −200,000 |
| Oiler J | 250,000 | −100,000 |
| Texan | 75,000 | −18,000 |

For example, if Ken purchases a Sub 100 and there is a favorable market, he will realize a profit of $300,000. On the other hand, if the market is unfavorable, Ken will suffer a loss of $200,000. But Ken has always been a very optimistic decision maker.

(a) What type of decision is Ken facing?
(b) What decision criterion should he use?
(c) What alternative is best?

• **8-14** Although Ken Brown (discussed in Problem 8-13) is the principal owner of Brown Oil, his brother Bob is credited with making the company a financial success.

Bob is vice president of finance. Bob attributes his success to his pessimistic attitude about business and the oil industry. Given the information from Problem 8-13, it is likely that Bob will arrive at a different decision. What decision criterion should Bob use, and what alternative will he select?

• **8-15** The *Lubricant* is an expensive oil newsletter to which many oil giants subscribe, including Ken Brown. In the last issue, the letter described how the demand for oil products would be extremely high. Apparently, the American consumer will continue to use oil products even if the price of these products doubles. Indeed, one of the articles in the *Lubricant* states that the chance of a favorable market for oil products was 70%, whereas the chance of an unfavorable market was only 30%. Ken would like to use these probabilities in determining the best decision. (See Problem 8-13 for details.)

(a) What decision model should be used?
(b) What is the optimal decision?

⁞ **8-16** Janet Kim, president of Kim Manufacturing, Inc., is considering whether to build more manufacturing plants in Wisconsin. Her decision is summarized in the following table:

| ALTERNATIVES | FAVORABLE MARKET ($) | UNFAVORABLE MARKET ($) |
|---|---|---|
| Build a large plant | 400,000 | −300,000 |
| Build a small plant | 80,000 | −10,000 |
| Don't build | 0 | 0 |
| Probabilities | 0.4 | 0.6 |

(a) Construct an opportunity loss table.
(b) Determine EOL and the best strategy.
(c) What is the expected value of perfect information?

⁞ **8-17** Helen Murvis, hospital administrator for Portland General Hospital, is trying to determine whether to build a large wing onto the existing hospital, a small wing, or no wing at all. If the population of Portland continues to grow, a large wing could return $150,000 to the hospital each year. If the small wing was built, it would return $60,000 to the hospital each year if the population continues to grow. If the population of Portland remains the same, the hospital would encounter a loss of $85,000 if the large wing was built. Furthermore, a loss of $45,000 would be realized if the small wing was constructed and the population remains the same. Unfortunately, Helen does not have any information about the future population of Portland.

(a) What type of decision problem is this?
(b) Construct a decision table.
(c) Using the equally likely criterion, determine the best alternative.

**8-18** Hardie Lord, Helen Murvis's boss, is not convinced that Helen used the correct decision technique. (Refer to Problem 8-17.) Hardie believes that Helen should use a coefficient of realism of 0.75 in determining the best alternative. Hardie thinks of himself as a realist.

(a) Develop a decision table for this problem.
(b) Using the criterion of realism, what is the best decision?
(c) Did Hardie's decision technique result in a decision that was different from Helen's?

**8-19** Megley Cheese Company is a small manufacturer of several different cheese products. One of the products is a cheese spread that is sold to retail outlets. Jason Megley must decide how many cases of cheese spread to manufacture each month. The probability that the demand will be six cases is 0.1, for 7 cases is 0.3, for 8 cases is 0.5, and for 9 cases is 0.1. The cost of every case is $45, and the price that Jason gets for each case is $95. Unfortunately, any cases not sold by the end of the month are of no value, due to spoilage. How many cases of cheese should Jason manufacture each month?

**8-20** Even though independent gasoline stations have been having a difficult time, Susan Solomon has been thinking about starting her own independent gasoline station. Susan's problem is to decide how large her station should be. The annual returns will depend on both the size of her station and a number of marketing factors related to the oil industry and demand for gasoline. After a careful analysis, Susan developed the following table:

| SIZE OF FIRST STATION | GOOD MARKET ($) | FAIR MARKET ($) | POOR MARKET ($) |
|---|---|---|---|
| Small | 50,000 | 20,000 | −10,000 |
| Medium | 80,000 | 30,000 | −20,000 |
| Large | 100,000 | 30,000 | −40,000 |
| Very large | 300,000 | 25,000 | −160,000 |

For example, if Susan constructs a small station and the market is good, she will realize a profit of $50,000.

(a) What is the maximax decision?
(b) What is the maximin decision?
(c) What is the equally likely decision?
(d) What is the criterion of realism decision? Use an α value of 0.8.
(e) Develop an opportunity loss table.
(f) What is the minimax regret decision?

**8-21** Dorothy Stanyard has three major routes to take to work. She can take Tennessee Street the entire way, she can take several back streets to work, or she can use the expressway. The traffic patterns are, however, very complex. Under good conditions, Tennessee Street is the fastest route. When Tennessee is congested, one of the other routes is usually preferable. Over the past two months, Dorothy has tried each route several times under different traffic conditions. This information

is summarized in minutes of travel time to work in the following table:

| | NO TRAFFIC CONGESTION (MINUTES) | MILD TRAFFIC CONGESTION (MINUTES) | SEVERE TRAFFIC CONGESTION (MINUTES) |
|---|---|---|---|
| Tennessee Street | 15 | 30 | 45 |
| Back roads | 20 | 25 | 35 |
| Expressway | 30 | 30 | 30 |

In the past 60 days, Dorothy encountered severe traffic congestion 10 days and mild traffic congestion 20 days. Assume that the past 60 days are typical of traffic conditions.

(a) Develop a decision table for this decision.
(b) What route should Dorothy take?
(c) Dorothy is about to buy a radio for her car that would tell her the exact traffic conditions before she started to work each morning. How much time in minutes on the average would Dorothy save by buying the radio?

**8-22** A group of medical professionals is considering constructing a private clinic. If the medical demand is high (i.e., there is a favorable market for the clinic), the physicians could realize a net profit of $100,000. If the market is not favorable, they could lose $40,000. Of course, they don't have to proceed at all, in which case there is no cost. In the absence of any market data, the best the physicians can guess is that there is a 50–50 chance the clinic will be successful.

Construct a decision tree to help analyze this problem. What should the medical professionals do?

**8-23** The physicians in Problem 8-22 have been approached by a market research firm that offers to perform a study of the market at a fee of $5,000. The market researchers claim their experience enables them to use Bayes' theorem to make the following statements of probability:

probability of a favorable market given a favorable study = 0.82

probability of an unfavorable market given a favorable study = 0.18

probability of a favorable market given an unfavorable study = 0.11

probability of an unfavorable market given an unfavorable study = 0.89

probability of a favorable research study = 0.55

probability of an unfavorable research study = 0.45

(a) Develop a new decision tree for the medical professionals to reflect the options now open with the market study.
(b) Use the EMV approach to recommend a strategy.
(c) What is the expected value of sample information? How much might the physicians be willing to pay for a market study?

**8-24** Jerry Young is thinking about opening a bicycle shop in his hometown. Jerry loves to take his own bike on 50-mile trips with his friends, but he believes that any small business should be started only if there is a good chance of making a profit. Jerry can open a small shop, a large shop, or no shop at all. Because there will be a five-year lease on the building that Jerry is thinking about using, he wants to make sure that he makes the correct decision. Jerry is also thinking about hiring his old marketing professor to conduct a marketing research study. If the study is conducted, the results could be either favorable or unfavorable. Develop a decision tree for Jerry.

**8-25** Jerry Young (of Problem 8-24) has done some analysis about the profitability of the bicycle shop. If Jerry builds the large bicycle shop, he will earn $60,000 if the market is favorable, but he will lose $40,000 if the market is unfavorable. The small shop will return a $30,000 profit in a favorable market and a $10,000 loss in an unfavorable market. At the present time, he believes that there is a 50–50 chance that the market will be favorable. His old marketing professor will charge him $5,000 for the marketing research. It is estimated that there is a 0.6 probability that the survey will be favorable. Furthermore, there is a 0.9 probability that the market will be favorable given a favorable outcome from the study. However, the marketing professor has warned Jerry that there is only a probability of 0.12 of a favorable market if the marketing research results are not favorable. Jerry is confused. What should he do?

**8-26** Before the marketing research was done, Peter Martin believed that there was a 50–50 chance that his brother's food store would be a success. The research team determined that there is a 0.8 probability that the marketing research will be favorable given a successful food store. Moreover, there is a 0.7 probability that the marketing research will be unfavorable given an unsuccessful food store. This information is based on past experience.

(a) If the marketing research is favorable, what is Peter's revised probability of a successful food store for his brother?

(b) If the marketing research is unfavorable, what is Peter's revised probability of a successful food store for his brother?

**8-27** Kuality Komponents buys on–off switches from two suppliers. The quality of the switches from the suppliers is as follows:

| PERCENT DEFECTIVE | PROBABILITY FOR SUPPLIER A | PROBABILITY FOR SUPPLIER B |
|---|---|---|
| 1 | 0.70 | 0.30 |
| 3 | 0.20 | 0.40 |
| 5 | 0.10 | 0.30 |

For example, the probability of getting a batch of switches that are 1% defective from supplier A is 0.70. Since Kuality Komponents orders 10,000 switches per order, this would mean that there is a 0.7 probability of getting 100 defective switches out of the 10,000 switches if supplier A is used to fill the order. A defective switch can be repaired for 50 cents. Although the quality of supplier B is lower, it will sell an order of 10,000 switches for $37 less than supplier A.

(a) Develop a decision tree.

(b) Which supplier should Kuality Komponents use?

(c) For how much less would supplier B have to sell an order of 10,000 switches than supplier A for Kuality Komponents to be indifferent between the two suppliers?

**8-28** Jim Sellers is thinking about producing a new type of electric razor for men. If the market is favorable, he would get a return of $100,000, but if the market for this new type of razor is unfavorable, he would lose $60,000. Since Ron Bush is a good friend of Jim Sellers, Jim is considering the possibility of using Bush Marketing Research to gather additional information about the market for the razor. Bush has suggested that Jim either use a survey or a pilot study to test the market. The survey would be a sophisticated questionnaire administered to a test market. It will cost $5,000. Another alternative is to run a pilot study. This would involve producing a limited number of the new razors and trying to sell them in two cities that are typical of American cities. The pilot study is more accurate but is also more expensive. It will cost $20,000. Ron Bush has suggested that it would be a good idea for Jim to conduct either the survey or the pilot before Jim makes the decision concerning whether to produce the new razor. But Jim is not sure if the value of the survey or the pilot is worth the cost.

Jim estimates that the probability of a successful market without performing a survey or pilot study is 0.5. Furthermore, the probability of a favorable survey result given a favorable market for razors is 0.7, and the probability of a favorable survey result given an unsuccessful market for razors is 0.2. In addition, the probability of an unfavorable pilot study given an unfavorable market is 0.9, and the probability of an unsuccessful pilot study result given a favorable market for razors is 0.2.

(a) Draw the decision tree for this problem without the probability values.

(b) Compute the revised probabilities needed to complete the decision, and place these values in the decision tree.

(c) What is the best decision for Jim? Use EMV as the decision criterion.

**8-29** The Jamis Corporation is involved with waste management. During the past 10 years it has become one of the largest waste disposal companies in the Midwest, serving primarily Wisconsin, Illinois, and Michigan. Bob Jamis, president of the company, is considering the possibility of establishing a waste treatment plant in Mississippi. From past experience. Bob believes that a small plant in Northern Mississippi would yield a $500,000 profit regardless of the market for the facility. The success of a medium-sized waste treatment plant would depend on the market. With a low demand for waste treatment, Bob expects a $200,000 return. A medium demand would yield a $700,000 return in Bob's estimation, and a high demand would return $800,000. Although a large facility is much riskier, the potential return is much greater. With a high demand for waste treatment in Mississippi, the large facility should return a million dollars. With a medium demand, the large facility will return only $400,000. Bob estimates that the large facility would be a big loser if there is a low demand for waste treatment. He estimates that he would lose approximately $200,000 with a large treatment facility if demand was indeed low. Looking at the economic conditions for the upper part of the state of Mississippi and using his experience in the field, Bob estimates that the probability of a low demand for treatment plants is 0.15. The probability for a medium-demand facility is approximately 0.40, and the probability of a high demand for a waste treatment facility is 0.45.

Because of the large potential investment and the possibility of a loss, Bob has decided to hire a market research team that is based in Jackson, Mississippi. This team will perform a survey to get a better feeling for the probability of a low, medium, or high demand for a waste treatment facility. The cost of the survey is $50,000. To help Bob determine whether to go ahead with the survey, the marketing research firm has provided Bob with the following information:

$P$ (survey results | possible outcomes)

| POSSIBLE OUTCOME | SURVEY RESULTS | | |
|---|---|---|---|
| | LOW SURVEY RESULTS | MEDIUM SURVEY RESULTS | HIGH SURVEY RESULTS |
| Low demand | 0.7 | 0.2 | 0.1 |
| Medium demand | 0.4 | 0.5 | 0.1 |
| High demand | 0.1 | 0.3 | 0.6 |

As you see, the survey could result in three possible outcomes. Low survey results mean that a low demand is likely. In a similar fashion, medium survey results or high survey results would mean a medium or a high demand, respectively. What should Bob do?

**8-30** Jim Sellers has been able to estimate his ability for a number of different values. He would like to use these utility values in making the decision in Problem 8-28. The utility values are $U(-\$80,000) = 0$, $U(-\$65,000) = 0.5$, $U(-\$60,000) = 0.55$, $U(-\$20,000) = 0.7$, $U(-\$5,000) = 0.8$, $U(\$0) = 0.81$, $U(\$80,000) = 0.9$, $U(\$95,000) = 0.95$, and $U(\$100,000) = 1$. Solve Problem 8-28 again using utility values. Is Jim a risk avoider?

**8-31** In Problem 8-23, you helped the medical professionals analyze their decision using EMV as the decision criterion. This group has also assessed their utility for money: $U(-\$45,000) = 0$, $U(-\$40,000) = 0.1$, $U(-\$5,000) = 0.7$, $U(\$0) = 0.9$, $U(\$95,000) = 0.99$,

and $U(\$100,000) = 1$. Use expected utility as the decision criterion, and determine the best decision for the medical professionals. Are the medical professionals risk seekers or risk avoiders?

**8-32** In this chapter a decision tree was developed for John Thompson. (See Figure 8.4 for the complete decision tree analysis.) After completing the analysis John was not completely sure that he is indifferent to risk. After going through a number of standard gambles, John was able to assess his utility for money. Here are some of the utility assessments: $U(-\$190,000) = 0$, $U(-\$180,000) = 0.05$, $U(-\$30,000) = 0.10$, $U(-\$20,000) = 0.15$, $U(-\$10,000) = 0.2$, $U(\$0) = 0.3$, $U(\$90,000) = 0.5$, $U(\$100,000) = 0.6$, $U(\$190,000) = 0.95$, and $U(\$200,000) = 1.0$. If John maximizes his expected utility, does his decision change?

**8-33** In the past few years, the traffic problems in Lynn McKell's hometown have gotten worse. Now, Broad Street is congested about half the time. The normal travel to work for Lynn is only 15 minutes when Broad Street is used and there is no congestion. With congestion, however, it takes Lynn 40 minutes to get to work. If Lynn decides to take the expressway, it will take 30 minutes regardless of the traffic conditions. Lynn's utility for travel time is: $U(15 \text{ minutes}) = 0.9$, $U(30 \text{ minutes}) = 0.7$, and $U(40 \text{ minutes}) = 0.2$.

(a) Which route will minimize Lynn's expected travel time?
(b) Which route will maximize Lynn's utility?
(c) When it comes to travel time, is Lynn a risk seeker or a risk avoider?

**8-34** Jack Belkin considers himself an expert when it comes to fine foods and beverage, and Jack is proud to tell his out-of-town friends that the best restaurant that he has encountered, Old Tavern, is located in his hometown. Big Burger, a national franchise, is the worst restaurant he has ever been to. Unfortunately, Jack's kids love the french fries at Big Burger, and when his family is deciding where to eat, his kids always say, "Let's flip a coin to see if we go to Big Burger or Old Tavern." Jack hates Big Burger, but his kids hate Old Tavern. Jack's wife always has a compromise. She wants to go to Ralph's Diner instead of flipping a coin. But Jack is totally indifferent to these two alternatives. Once when Jack and his wife were alone, his wife suggested that they flip a coin to see if they would go to Old Tavern or Ralph's Diner. (Jack's wife does not like the rich food at Old Tavern.) When Jack demurred at this gamble, his wife proposed that they simply go to the Vacation Inn Restaurant, which is slightly more expensive than Ralph's Diner. Again, Jack was totally indifferent to this choice. Determine Jack's utility for restaurants.

**8-35** Jack Belkin's kids love to play games while riding in the car, and this outing was no exception. (See Problem 8-34 for some additional details.) The entire family was about 50 miles from home, and Jack was looking forward to eating at the Vacation Inn Restaurant, which was a compromise restaurant choice. His oldest kid said, "Let's make a bet. If we see three red Volkswagens between here and home, we will eat at Big Burger. Otherwise, we will go to Old Tavern." Jack believes that the probability of seeing three red Volkswagens is very low—about 0.20. Should Jack take his kids' bet, or should he tell them that they are eating at Vacation Inn Restaurant and that is final?

**8-36** After driving down the road and seeing one red Volkswagen, Jack Belkin had second thoughts about his probability assessment. (Refer to Problem 8-35.) In Problem 8-35, Jack estimated that the probability of seeing three red Volkswagens before the family got home was 0.20. How sensitive is Jack's decision in Problem 8-35 to his probability assessment? What probability would make him indifferent between the bet his kids proposed and eating at Vacation Inn Restaurant?

**8-37** Sue Reynolds has to decide if she should get information (at a cost of $20,000) to invest in a retail store. If she gets the information, there is a 0.6 probability that the information will be favorable and a 0.4 probability that the information will not be favorable. If the information is favorable, there is a 0.9 probability that the store will be a success. If the information is not favorable, the probability of a successful store is only 0.2. Without any information, Sue estimates that the probability of a successful store will be 0.6. A successful store will give a return of $100,000. If the store is built but is not successful, Sue will see a loss of $80,000. Of course, she could always decide not to build the retail store.

(a) What do you recommend?

(b) What impact would a 0.7 probability of obtaining favorable information have on Sue's decision? The probability of obtaining unfavorable information would be 0.3.

(c) Sue believes that the probabilities of a successful and an unsuccessful retail store given favorable

information might be 0.8 and 0.2, respectively, instead of 0.9 and 0.1 respectively. What impact, if any, would this have on Sue's decision and the best EMV?

(d) Sue had to pay $20,000 to get information. Would her decision change if the cost of the information increased to $30,000?

(e) Using the data in this problem and the following utility table, compute the expected utility. Is this the curve of a risk seeker or a risk avoider?

| MONETARY VALUE | UTILITY |
|---|---|
| $100,000 | 1 |
| $80,000 | 0.4 |
| $0 | 0.2 |
| −$20,000 | 0.1 |
| −$80,000 | 0.05 |
| −$100,000 | 0 |

(f) Compute the expected utility given the following utility table. Does this utility table represent a risk seeker or a risk avoider?

| MONETARY VALUE | UTILITY |
|---|---|
| $100,000 | 1 |
| $80,000 | 0.9 |
| $0 | 0.8 |
| −$20,000 | 0.6 |
| −$80,000 | 0.4 |
| −$100,000 | 0 |

---

## ⇒ CASE STUDY

### Ski Right

After retiring as a physician, Bob Guthrie became an avid downhill skier on the steep slopes of the Utah Rocky Mountains. As an amateur inventor, Bob was always looking for something new. With the recent deaths of several celebrity skiers, Bob knew he could use his creative mind to make skiing safer and his bank account larger. He knew that many deaths on the slopes were caused by head injuries. Although ski helmets have been on the market for some time, most skiers considered them boring and basically ugly. As a physician, Bob knew that some type of new ski helmet was the answer.

Bob's biggest challenge was to invent a helmet that was attractive, safe, and fun to wear. Multiple colors, using the latest fashion designs would be a must. After years of skiing, Bob knew that many skiers believed that how you looked on the slopes was more important than how you skied. His helmets would have to

look good and fit in with current fashion trends. But attractive helmets were not enough. Bob had to make the helmets fun and useful. The name of the new ski helmet, Ski Right, was sure to be a winner. If Bob could come up with a good idea, he believed that there was a 20% chance that the market for the Ski Right helmet would be excellent. The chance of a good market should be 40%. Bob also knew that the market for his helmet could be only average (30% chance) or even poor (10% chance).

The idea of how to make ski helmets fun and useful came to Bob on a gondola ride to the top of a mountain. A busy executive on the gondola ride was on his cell phone trying to complete a complicated merger. When the executive got off of the gondola, he dropped the phone and it was crushed by the gondola mechanism. Bob decided that his new ski helmet would have a built-in cell phone and an AM/FM Stereo radio. All of the electronics could be operated by a control pad worn on a skier's arm or leg.

Bob decided to try a small pilot project for Ski Right. He enjoyed being retired and didn't want a failure to cause him to go back to work. After some research, Bob found Progressive Products (PP). The company was willing to be a partner in developing the Ski Right and sharing any profits. If the market was excellent, Bob would net $5,000. With a good market, Bob would net $2,000. An average market would result in a loss of $2,000, and a poor market would mean Bob would be out $5,000.

Another option for Bob was to have Leadville Barts (LB) make the helmet. The company had extensive experience in making bicycle helmets. Progressive would then take the helmets made by Leadville Barts and do the rest. Bob had a greater risk. He estimated that he could lose $10,000 in a poor market or $4,000 in an average market. A good market for Ski Right would result in a $6,000 profit for Bob, and an excellent market would mean a $12,000 profit.

A third option for Bob was to use TalRad (TR), a radio company in Tallahassee, Florida. TalRad had extensive experience in making military radios. Leadville Barts could make the helmets, and Progressive Products could do the rest. Again, Bob would be taking on greater risk. A poor market would mean a $15,000 loss, and an average market would mean a $10,000 loss. A good market would result in a net profit of $7,000 for Bob. An excellent market would return $13,000.

Bob could also have Celestial Cellular (CC) develop the cell phones. Thus, another option was to have Celestial make the phones and have Progressive do the rest of the production and distribution. Because the cell phone was the most expensive component of the helmet, Bob could lose $30,000 in a poor market. He could lose $20,000 in an average market. If the market was good or excellent, Bob would see a net profit of $10,000 or $30,000, respectively.

Bob's final option was to forget about Progressive Products entirely. He could use Leadville Barts to make the helmets, Celestial Cellular to make the phones, and TadRad to make the AM/FM stereo radios. Bob could then hire some friends to assemble everything and market the finished Ski Right helmets. With this final alternative, Bob could realize a net profit of $55,000 in an excellent market. Even if the market was just good, Bob would net $20,000. An average market, however, would mean a loss of $35,000. If the market was poor, Bob would lose $60,000.

### Discussion Questions

1. What do you recommend?
2. What is the opportunity loss for this problem?
3. Compute the expected value of perfect information.
4. Was Bob completely logical in how he approached this decision problem?

---

## ⇒ CASE STUDY

### Blake Electronics

In 1969, Steve Blake founded Blake Electronics in Long Beach, California, to manufacture resistors, capacitors, inductors, and other electronic components. During the Vietnam War, Steve was a radio operator, and it was during this time that he became proficient at repairing radios and other communications equipment. Steve viewed his four-year experience with the army with mixed feelings. He hated army life, but this experience gave him the confidence and the initiative to start his own electronics firm.

Over the years, Steve kept the business relatively unchanged. By 1980, total annual sales were in excess of $2 million. In 1984, Steve's son, Jim, joined the company after finishing high school and two years of courses in electronics at Long Beach Community College. Jim was always aggressive in high school athletics, and he became even more aggressive as general sales manager of Blake Electronics. This aggressiveness bothered Steve, who was more conservative. Jim would make deals to supply companies with electronic components before he bothered to find out if Blake Electronics had the ability or capacity to produce the components. On several occasions this behavior caused the company some embarrassing moments when Blake Electronics was unable to produce the electronic components for companies with which Jim had made deals.

In 1988, Jim started to go after government contracts for electronic components. By 1990, total annual sales had increased to more than $10 million, and the number of employees exceeded 200. Many of these employees were electronic specialists and graduates of electrical engineering programs from top colleges and universities. But Jim's tendency to stretch Blake Electronics to contracts continued as well, and by 1997, Blake Electronics had a reputation with government agencies as a company that could not deliver what it promised. Almost overnight, government contracts stopped, and Blake Electronics was left with an idle workforce and unused manufacturing equipment. This high overhead started to melt away profits, and in 1999, Blake Electronics was faced with the possibility of sustaining a loss for the first time in its history.

In 2001, Steve decided to look at the possibility of manufacturing electronic components for home use. Although this was a totally new market for Blake Electronics, Steve was convinced that this was the only way to keep Blake Electronics from dipping into the red. The research team at Blake Electronics was given the task of developing new electronic devices for home use. The first idea from the research team was the Master Control Center. The basic components for this system are shown in Figure 8.17.

The heart of the system is the master control box. This unit, which would have a retail price of $250, has two rows of five buttons. Each button controls one light or appliance and can be set as either a switch or a rheostat. When set as a switch, a light finger touch on the bottom either turns a light or appliance on or

## FIGURE 8.17

**Master Control Center**

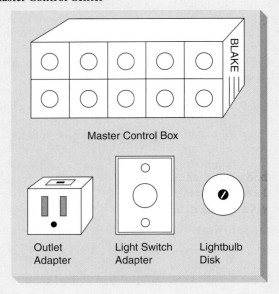

Master Control Box

Outlet Adapter

Light Switch Adapter

Lightbulb Disk

## TABLE 8.13

**Success Figures for MAI**

| OUTCOME | SURVEY RESULTS | | |
| --- | --- | --- | --- |
| | FAVORABLE | UNFAVORABLE | TOTAL |
| Successful venture | 35 | 20 | 55 |
| Unsuccessful venture | 15 | 30 | 45 |

off. When set as a rheostat, a finger touching the bottom controls the intensity of the light. Leaving your finger on the button makes the light go through a complete cycle ranging from off to bright and back to off again.

To allow for maximum flexibility, each master control box is powered by two D-sized batteries that can last up to a year, depending on usage. In addition, the research team has developed three versions of the master control box—versions A, B, and C. If a family wants to control more than 10 lights or appliances, another master control box can be purchased.

The lightbulb disk, which would have a retail price of $2.50, is controlled by the master control box and is used to control the intensity of any light. A different disk is available for each button position for all three master control boxes. By inserting the lightbulb disk between the lightbulb and the socket, the appropriate button on the master control box can completely control the intensity of the light. If a standard light switch is used, it must be on at all times for the master control box to work.

One disadvantage of using a standard light switch is that only the master control box can be used to control the particular light. To avoid this problem, the research team developed a special light switch adapter that would sell for $15. When this device is installed either the master control box or the light switch adapter can be used to control the light.

When used to control appliances other than lights, the master control box must be used in conjunction with one or more outlet adapters. The adapters are plugged into a standard wall outlet, and the appliance is then plugged into the adapter. Each outlet adapter has a switch on top that allows the appliance to be controlled from the master control box or the outlet adapter. The price of each outlet adapter would be $25.

The research team estimated that it would cost $500,000 to develop the equipment and procedures needed to manufacture the master control box and accessories. If successful, this venture could increase sales by approximately $2 million. But will the master control boxes be a successful venture? With a 60% chance of success estimated by the research team, Steve has serious doubts about trying to market the master control boxes even though he liked the basic idea. Because of his reservations, Steve decided to send requests for proposals (RFPs) for additional marketing research to 30 marketing research companies in southern California.

The first RFP to come back was from a small company called Marketing Associates, Inc. (MAI), which would charge $100,000 for the survey. According to its proposal, MAI has been in business for about three years and has conducted about 100 marketing research projects. MAI's major strengths appeared to be individual attention to each account, experienced staff, and fast work. Steve was particularly interested in one part of the proposal, which revealed MAI's success record with previous accounts. This is shown in Table 8.13.

The only other proposal to be returned was by a branch office of Iverstine and Kinard, one of the largest marketing research firms in the country. The cost for a complete survey would be $300,000. Although the proposal did not contain the same success record as MAI, the proposal from Iverstine and Kinard did contain some interesting information. The chance of getting a favorable survey result, given a successful venture, was 90%. On the other hand, the chance of getting an unfavorable survey result, given an unsuccessful venture, was 80%. Thus, it appeared to Steve that Iverstine and Kinard would be able to predict the success or failure of the master control boxes with a great amount of certainty.

Steve pondered the situation. Unfortunately, both marketing research teams gave different types of information in their proposals. Steve concluded that there would be no way that the two proposals could be compared unless he got additional information from Iverstine and Kinard. Furthermore, Steve wasn't sure what he would do with the information, and if it would be worth the expense of hiring one of the marketing research firms.

### Discussion Questions

1. Does Steve need additional information from Iverstine and Kinard?
2. What would you recommend?

## INTERNET CASE STUDIES

See our Internet home page at **www.prenhall.com/render** for these additional case studies: (1) Starting Right Corporation; (2) Drink-at-Home Inc.; (3) Ruth Jones' Heart By-Pass Operation; and (4) Toledo Leather Company.

# BIBLIOGRAPHY

Ahlbrecht, Martin et al. "An Empirical Study on Intertemporal Decision Making under Risk," *Management Science* (June 1997): 813–826.

Bistritz, Nancy. "Rx for UK Healthcare Woes," *OR/MS Today* (April 1997): 18.

Borison, Adam. "Oglethorpe Power Corporation Decides about Investing in a Major Transmission System," *Interfaces* 25, 2 (March 1995): 25–36.

Brown, R. "Do Managers Find Decision Theory Useful?" *Harvard Business Review* (May–June 1970): 78–89.

Brown, R. V. "The State of the Art of Decision Analysis: A Personal Perspective," *Interfaces* 22, 6 (November–December 1992): 5–14.

Derfler, Frank. "Use These Decision Trees and Our Questionnaire to Find the Best Way to Reduce Your Total Cost of Ownership," *PC Magazine* (May 5, 1998): 231.

Hammond, J. S., R. L. Kenney, and H. Raiffa. "The Hidden Traps in Decision Making," *Harvard Business Review* (September–October 1998): 47–60.

Jbuedj, Coden. "Decision Making Under Conditions of Uncertainty: A Wakeup Call for the Financial Planning Profession," *Journal of Financial Planning* (October 1997): 84.

Lane, M. S., A. H. Mansour, and J. L. Harpell. "Operations Research Techniques: A Longitudinal Update 1973–1988," *Interfaces* 23, 2 (March–April 1993): 63–68.

Lev, B. "Airline Operations Research," *Interfaces* 20, 3 (May–June 1990): 100–102.

McDonald, John. "Decision Trees Clarify Novel Technology Applications," *Oil and Gas Journal* (February 24, 1997): 69–74.

Miller, Craig. "A Systematic Approach to Tax Controversy Management," *Tax Executive* (May 15, 1998): 231–233.

Perdue, Robert K., William J. McAllister, Peter V. King, and Bruce G. Berkey. "Valuation of R and D Projects Using Options Pricing and Decision Analysis Models," *Interfaces* 29, 6 (November 1999): 57–74.

Raiffa, H. *Decision Analysis.* Reading, MA: Addison-Wesley Publishing Co., Inc., 1968.

Schlaifer, R. *Analysis of Decisions under Uncertainty.* New York: McGraw-Hill Book Company, 1969.

Strait, Scott. "Decision Analysis Approach to Competitive Situations with a Pure Infinite Regress," *Decision Sciences* (September 1994): 853–864.

Stafira, Stanley et al. "A Methodology for Evaluating Military Systems in a Counterproliferation Role," *Management Science* (October 1997): 1420–1430.

Stone, Lawrence D. "Search for the SS *Central America*: Mathematical Treasure Hunting," *Interfaces* 21, 1 (January–February 1992): 32–54.

Sullivan, Gerald and Kenneth Fordyce. "IBM Burlington's Logistics Management System," *Interfaces* 20, 1 (January–February 1990): 43–64.

# QUEUING MODELS

After completing this chapter, students will be able to:

1. Discuss the trade-off curves for cost of waiting time and cost of service.

2. Understand the three parts of a queuing system: the arrival population, the queue itself, and the service facility.

3. Describe the basic queuing system configurations.

4. Understand the assumptions of the common queuing models dealt with in this chapter.

5. Use Excel to analyze a variety of operating characteristics of queuing systems.

6. Understand more complex queuing systems.

Summary • Glossary • Key Equations • Solved Problems • Self-Test • Discussion Questions and Problems • Case Study: New England Castings • Case Study: Winter Park Hotel • Internet Case Study • Bibliography

### Shortening the Arrest to Arraignment Time in New York City's Police Department

On March 23, 1990, the *New York Times* ran a front-page story about a woman who spent 45 hours in prearraignment detention in that city under the headline "Trapped in the terror of New York's holding pens." Indeed, people arrested in New York City at that time averaged a 40-hour wait (some more than 70 hours) prior to arraignment. These people were held in crowded, noisy, stressful, unhealthy, and often dangerous holding facilities. In effect, they were denied a speedy court appearance. That same year, the New York Supreme Court ruled that the city was to attempt to arraign in 24 hours or to release the prisoner.

The arrest-to-arraignment (ATA) process, which has the general characteristics of a large queuing system, involves the following steps: arrest a suspected criminal, transport to a police precinct, search/fingerprint, paperwork for arrest, transport to a central booking facility, additional paperwork, process fingerprints, a bail interview, transport to either a courthouse or outlying precinct, check for a criminal record, and finally, have an assistant district attorney draw up a complaint document.

To solve the very complex problem of improving this system, the city hired Queues Enforth Department, Inc., a Massachusetts consulting firm. Their decision model of the ATA process included single- and multiple-server queuing models. The modeling approach successfully reduced the average ATA time to 24 hours and resulted in an annual cost savings of $9.5 million for the city and state.[1]

---

[1] R. C. Larson, M. F. Colan, and M. C. Shell. "Improving the New York Arrest-to-Arraignment System," *Interfaces* 23, 1 (January–February 1993): 76–96.

## 9.1  INTRODUCTION

The study of *queues*,[2] also called *waiting lines*, is one of the oldest and most widely used decision modeling techniques. Queues are an everyday occurrence, affecting people shopping for groceries, buying gasoline, making a bank deposit, or waiting on the telephone for the first available airline reservation person to answer. Queues can also take the form of machines waiting to be repaired, prisoners to be processed in the New York City jail system, or airplanes lined up on a runway for permission to take off.

In this chapter, we discuss how analytical models of queues can help managers evaluate the cost of effectiveness of service systems. We begin with a look at queuing system costs. Then, we describe the characteristics of queues and the underlying mathematical assumptions used to develop queuing decision models. Next, we discuss several different queuing systems and provide examples of how they are analyzed and used. Although we show the equations needed to compute the operating performance characteristics of these queuing systems, we use Excel worksheets (included on your CD-ROM) to actually calculate these values in each case. Finally, we briefly discuss more complex queuing models and how these can be analyzed in practical situations.

## 9.2  QUEUING SYSTEM COSTS

*One of the goals of queuing analysis is finding the best level of service for an organization.*

Most queuing problems are centered on the question of finding the ideal level of services that a firm should provide. Supermarkets must decide how many cash register checkout positions should be opened. Gasoline stations must decide how many pumps should be available. Manufacturing plants must determine the optimal number of mechanics to have on duty each shift to repair machines that break down. Banks must decide how many teller windows to keep open to serve customers during various hours of the day. In most cases, this level of service is an option over which management has control. An extra teller, for example, can be borrowed from another chore or can be hired and trained quickly if demand warrants it. This may not always be the case, though. A plant may not be able to locate or hire skilled mechanics to repair sophisticated electronic machinery.

When an organization does have control, its objective is usually to find a happy medium between two extremes. On the one hand, a firm can retain a large staff and provide many service facilities. This may result in excellent customer service, with seldom more than one or two customers in a queue. Customers are kept happy with the quick response and appreciate the convenience. This can, however, become very expensive.

The other extreme is to have the minimum possible number of checkout lines, pumps, or teller windows open. This keeps the service cost down but may result in customer dissatisfaction. How many times would you return to a large discount department store that had

---

**HISTORY**    How Queuing Models Began

Queuing theory had its beginning in the research work of a Danish engineer named A. K. Erlang. In 1909 Erlang experimented with fluctuating demand in telephone traffic. Eight years later he published a report addressing the delays in auto-matic dialing equipment. At the end of World War II, Erlang's early work was extended to more general problems and to business applications of waiting lines.

---

[2] The word *queue* is pronounced like the letter Q, that is "kew."

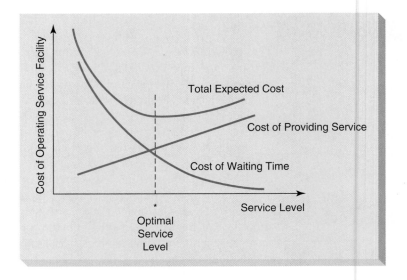

*Managers must deal with the
trade-off between the cost of
providing good service and
the cost of customer waiting
time. The latter may be hard
to quantify.*

*Total expected cost is the sum
of service plus waiting costs.*

only one cash register open during the day you shop? As the average length of the queue increases and poor service results, customers and goodwill may be lost.

Most managers recognize the trade-off that must take place between the cost of providing good service and the cost of customer waiting time. They want queues that are short enough so that customers don't become unhappy and either storm out without buying or buy but never return. But they are willing to allow some waiting in line if this wait is balanced by a significant savings in *service costs.*

One means of evaluating a service facility is thus to look at a total expected cost, a concept illustrated in Figure 9.1. Total expected cost is the sum of expected *waiting costs* and expected costs of providing service.

Service costs are seen to increase as a firm attempts to raise its level of service. For example, if three teams of stevedores, instead of two, are employed to unload a cargo ship, service costs are increased by the additional price of wages. As service improves in speed, however, the cost of time spent waiting in lines decreases. This waiting cost may reflect lost productivity of workers while their tools or machines are awaiting repairs or may simply be an estimate of the costs of customers lost because of poor service and long queues.

**Three Rivers Shipping Company Example**   As an illustration of a queuing system, let's look at the case of the Three Rivers Shipping Company. Three Rivers runs a huge docking facility located on the Ohio River near Pittsburgh. Approximately five ships arrive to unload their cargoes of steel and ore during every 12-hour work shift. Each hour that a ship sits idle in line waiting to be unloaded costs the firm a great deal of money, about $1,000 per hour. From experience, management estimates that if one team of stevedores is on duty to handle the unloading work, each ship will wait an average of 7 hours to be unloaded. If two teams are working, the average waiting time drops to 4 hours; for three teams, it is 3 hours; and for four teams of stevedores, only 2 hours. But each additional team of stevedores is also an expensive proposition, due to union contracts.

*The goal is to find the service
level that minimizes total
expected cost.*

Three Rivers' superintendent would like to determine the optimal number of teams of stevedores to have on duty each shift. The objective is to minimize total expected costs. This analysis is summarized in Table 9.1. To minimize the sum of service costs and waiting costs, the firm makes the decision to employ two teams of stevedores each shift.

## ⇒ MODELING IN THE REAL WORLD    New Haven Fire Department

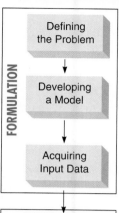

**FORMULATION**

Defining the Problem

Developing a Model

Acquiring Input Data

**SOLUTION**

Developing a Solution

Testing the Solution

**INTERPRETATION**

Analyzing the Results and Sensitivity Analysis

Implementing the Results

Facing severe budget restrictions, the city of New Haven, Connecticut, decided to investigate whether its fire department could close one or more firehouses with an acceptable small risk to public safety.

Two consultants, Arthur Swersey (from Yale) and Louis Goldring, developed a series of hour-by-hour queuing models that estimated the average time a person calling would have to wait for emergency service. The models were based on Poisson arrivals and exponential service times.

A grid map of the city of New Haven was developed to measure travel times/distances. Consultants also collected data on utilization of each of the 10 engine companies and five truck companies. 1990 emergency medical equipment and fire alarm data were employed.

Two alternative configurations for closing/merging firehouses that appeared to be reasonable and feasible were developed.

Using a mathematical probability analysis of fires occuring in each census tract area, the solutions were tested. They predicted the average emergency travel time to reach each of New Haven's 28 census tracts. One plan showed a response rate more than a half-minute faster than the other.

The Fire Department analyzed the trade-offs of the various plans and submitted them to public hearings and to the Board of Aldermen for a vote.

On Sept. 27, 1991, New Haven Fire Chief Earl D. Geyer announced the implementation of the selected plan and its projected savings of $1.4 million/year, 10% of the department's budget.

**Source:** A. J. Swersey, L. Goldring, and E. D. Geyer. "Improving Fire Department Productivity," *Interfaces* 23, 1 (January–February 1993): 109–129.

## TABLE 9.1    Three Rivers Shipping Company Waiting Line Cost Analysis

| | NUMBER OF TEAMS OF STEVEDORES WORKING | | | |
|---|---|---|---|---|
| | 1 | 2 | 3 | 4 |
| (a) Average number of ships arriving per shift | 5 | 5 | 5 | 5 |
| (b) Average time each ship waits to be unloaded (hours) | 7 | 4 | 3 | 2 |
| (c) Total ship hours lost per shift ($a \times b$) | 35 | 20 | 15 | 10 |
| (d) Estimated cost per hour of idle ship time | $1,000 | $1,000 | $1,000 | $1,000 |
| (e) Value of ship's lost time or waiting cost ($c \times d$) | $35,000 | $20,000 | $15,000 | $10,000 |
| (f) Stevedore team salary,* or service cost | $6,000 | $12,000 | $18,000 | $24,000 |
| (g) Total expected cost ($e + f$) | $41,000 | ($32,000) | $33,000 | $34,000 |

→ Optimal cost

*Stevedore team salaries are computed as the number of people in a typical team (assumed to be 50), times the number of hours each person works per day (12 hours), times an hourly salary of $10 per hour. If two teams are employed, the rate is just doubled.

## 9.3  CHARACTERISTICS OF A QUEUING SYSTEM

In this section we look at the three parts of a queuing system: (1) the arrivals or inputs to the system (sometimes referred to as the *calling population*), (2) the queue or the waiting line itself, and (3) the service facility. These three components have certain characteristics that we must examine before we can develop mathematical *queuing models*.

### Arrival Characteristics

The input source that generates arrivals or customers for the service system has major characteristics. It is important to consider (1) the *size* of the arrival population, (2) the *pattern* of arrivals (or the *arrival distribution*) at the queuing system, and (3) the *behavior* of the arrivals.

*Unlimited (or infinite) arrival populations are assumed for most queuing models.*

**Size of the *Arrival Population***  *Population* sizes are considered to be either *unlimited* (essentially *infinite*) or *limited* (*finite*). When the number of customers or arrivals on hand at any given moment is just a small portion of potential arrivals, the arrival population is considered unlimited. For practical purposes, examples of unlimited populations include cars arriving at a highway tollbooth, shoppers arriving at a supermarket, or students arriving to register for classes at a large university. Most queuing models assume such an infinite arrival population. When this is not the case, modeling becomes much more complex. An example of a finite population is a shop with only eight machines that might break down and require service.

*Arrivals are random when they are independent of one another and cannot be predicted exactly.*

**Arrival Distribution**  Customers either arrive at a service facility according to some known schedule (e.g., one patient every 15 minutes or one student for advising every half hour) or else they arrive *randomly*. Arrivals are considered random when they are independent of one another and their occurrence cannot be predicted exactly. Frequently in queuing problems, the number of arrivals per unit of time can be estimated by a probability distribution known as the *Poisson distribution*. For any given arrival rate, such as two customers per hour, or four trucks per minute, a discrete Poisson distribution can be established by using the following formula[3]:

$$P(X) = \frac{e^{-\lambda}\lambda^X}{X!} \quad \text{for } X = 0, 1, 2, \dots$$

(9-1)

*where*

*The Poisson probability distribution is used in many queuing models to represent arrival patterns.*

$X$ = number of arrivals per unit of time (e.g., hour)

$P(X)$ = probability of exactly $X$ arrivals

$\lambda$ = average arrival *rate* (i.e., average number of arrivals per unit of time)

$e$ = 2.7183 (known as the exponential constant)

These values are easy to compute with the help of a calculator or Excel. Figure 9.2 illustrates the shape of the Poisson distribution for $\lambda = 2$ and $\lambda = 4$. This means that if the average arrival rate is $\lambda = 2$ customers per hour, the probability of 0 customers arriving in any random hour is about 13.5%, probability of 1 customer is about 27%, 2 customers about 27%, 3 customers about 18%, 4 customers about 9%, and so on. The chances that 9 or more will arrive are virtually zero.

---

[3] The term $X!$, called $X$ *factorial*, is defined as $(X)(X - 1)(X - 2) \dots (3)(2)(1)$. For example, 5! = (5)(4)(3)(2)(1) = 120. By definition, 0! = 1.

**FIGURE 9.2**      **Two Examples of the Poisson Distribution for Arrival Times**

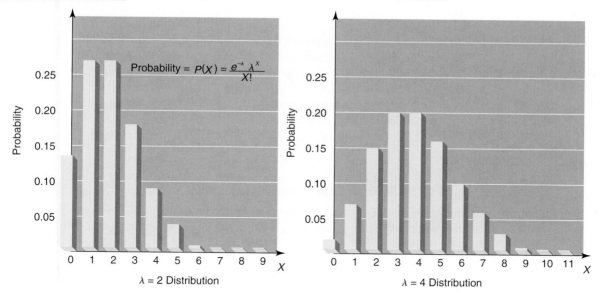

$$\text{Probability} = P(X) = \frac{e^{-\lambda}\lambda^{x}}{X!}$$

$\lambda = 2$ Distribution

$\lambda = 4$ Distribution

Arrivals, of course, are not always Poisson. They may follow some other probability distribution and should be examined periodically to make certain that they are well approximated by Poisson before that distribution is applied. This usually involves observing arrivals, plotting the data, and applying statistical measures of goodness of fit, a topic discussed in more advanced texts.

**Behavior of the Arrivals**  Most queuing models assume that an arriving customer is a patient customer. Patient customers are people or machines that wait in the queue until they are served and do not switch between lines. Unfortunately, life and decision models are complicated by the fact that people have been known to balk or renege. *Balking* refers to customers who refuse to join a queue because it is too long to suit their needs or interests. *Reneging* customers are those who enter the queue but then become impatient and leave without completing their transaction. Actually, both of these situations just serve to accentuate the need for queuing models. How many times have you seen a shopper with a basket full of groceries, including perishables such as milk, frozen food, or meats, simply abandon the shopping cart before checking out because the queue was too long? This expensive occurrence for the store makes managers acutely aware of the importance of service-level decisions.

*Balking refers to customers who do not join a queue. Reneging customers join a queue, but leave before being served.*

## Queue Characteristics

The queue itself is the second component of a queuing system. The *length* of a *queue* can be either *limited* (finite) or *unlimited* (infinite). A queue is said to be limited when it cannot increase to an infinite length due to physical or other restrictions. For example, the queue at a bank's drive-up window may be limited to 10 cars due to space limitations. Or, the number of people waiting for service in an airline's phone reservation system may be limited to 30 due to the number of telephone lines available. In contrast, a queue is defined as unlimited when its size is unrestricted, as in the case of the tollbooth serving arriving automobiles. In all the analytic queuing models we discuss in this chapter we assume that queue lengths are *unlimited*.

*The models in this chapter assume unlimited queue length.*

*Most queuing models use the first-in, first-out rule. This is obviously not appropriate in all service systems, especially those dealing with emergencies.*

A second waiting line characteristic deals with *queue discipline*. This refers to the rule by which customers in the line are to receive service. Most systems use a queue discipline known as the *first-in, first-out* rule (FIFO). However, in places such as a hospital emergency room or an express checkout line at a supermarket, various assigned priorities may preempt FIFO. Patients who are critically injured will move ahead in treatment priority over patients with broken fingers or noses. Shoppers with fewer than 10 items may be allowed to enter the express checkout queue but are then treated as first-come, first-served. Computer programming runs are another example of queuing systems that operate under priority scheduling. In many large companies, when computer-produced paychecks are due out on a specific date, the payroll program has highest priority over other runs.[4]

## Service Facility Characteristics

The third part of any queuing system is the service facility itself. It is important to examine two basic properties: (1) the configuration of the service facility and (2) the pattern of service times.

*Number of service channels in a queuing system is the number of servers.*

**Service Facility Configurations**  Service facilities are usually classified in terms of their number of servers (or channels), and number of phases (or service stops) that must be made. A *single-server system* is typified by the drive-in bank that has only one open teller, or by the type of drive-through fast-food restaurant that has become so popular in the United States. If, on the other hand, the bank had several tellers on duty and each customer waited in one common line for the first available teller, we would have a *multiple-server system* at work. Many banks today are multiple-server service systems, as are most post offices and many airline ticket counters.

*Single-phase means the customer receives service at only one station before leaving the system.*

*Multiphase implies two or more stops before leaving the system.*

A *single-phase system* is one in which the customer receives service from only one station and then exits the system. A fast-food restaurant in which the person who takes your order also brings you the food and takes your money is a single-phase system. So is a driver's license agency in which the person taking your application also grades your test and collects the license fee. But if a fast-food restaurant requires you to place your order at one station, pay at a second, and pick up the food at a third service stop, it becomes a *multiphase system*. Similarly, if the driver's license agency is large or busy, you will probably have to wait in line to complete the application (the first service stop), then queue again to have the test graded (the second service stop), and finally go to a third service counter to pay the fee. To help you relate the concepts of channels and phases, Figure 9.3 presents four possible service facility configurations.

## Service Time Distribution

*Service times often follow the exponential distribution.*

Service patterns are like arrival patterns in that they can be either constant or random. If the service time is constant, it takes the same amount of time to take care of each customer. This is the case, for example, in a machine-performed service operation such as an automatic car wash. More often, however, service times are randomly distributed. Even in many such cases, it turns out we can assume that random service times are described by the *exponential probability distribution*. For any given service rate, such as two customers per

---

[4] The term FIFS (*first in, first served*) is often used in place of FIFO. Another discipline, LIFS (*last in, first served*), is common when material is stacked or piled and the items on top are used first.

**FIGURE 9.3**    **Four Basic Queuing System Configurations**

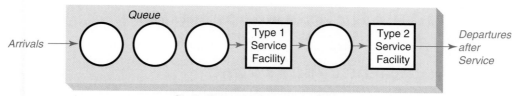

Single-Server, Single-Phase System

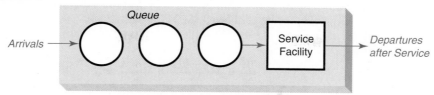

Single-Server, Multiphase System

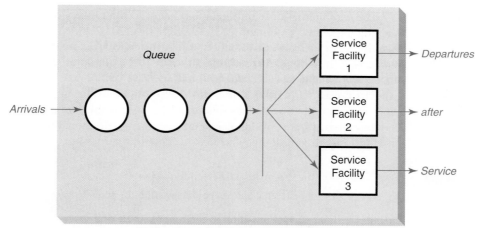

Multiple-Server, Single-Phase System

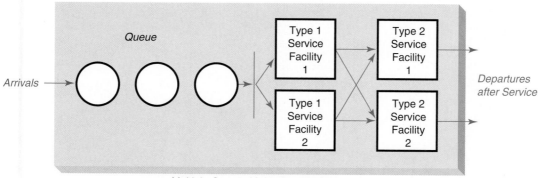

Multiple-Server, Multiphase System

hour, or four trucks per minute, an exponential distribution can be established using the formula:

$$P(t) = e^{-\mu t} \quad \text{for } t \geq 0 \tag{9-2}$$

*where*

$t$ = service time

$P(t)$ = probability that service time will be *greater* than $t$

$\mu$ = average service *rate* (i.e., average number of customers served per unit of time)

$e$ = 2.7183 (exponential constant)

Figure 9.4 illustrates that if service times follow an exponential distribution, the probability of any very long service time is low. For example, when the average service *rate* is 3 customers per hour (i.e., the average service *time* is 20 minutes per customer), seldom if ever will a customer require more than 1.5 hours (= 90 minutes). Likewise, if the average service rate is one customer per hour (i.e., $\mu = 1$), the probability of the customer spending more than 3 hours (= 180 minutes) in service is quite low.

*It is important to confirm that the queuing assumptions of Poisson arrivals and exponential services are valid before applying the model.*

The exponential distribution is important to the process of building mathematical queuing models because many of the models' theoretical underpinnings are based on the assumption of Poisson arrivals and exponential services. Before they are applied, however, the decision modeler can and should observe, collect, and plot service time data to determine if they fit the exponential distribution.

The Poisson and exponential probability distributions are directly related to each other. If the number of arrivals follows a Poisson distribution, it turns out that the time between successive arrivals follows an exponential distribution. Processes that follow these distributions are commonly referred to as *Markovian* processes.

**FIGURE 9.4**    **Two Examples of the Exponential Distribution for Service Times**

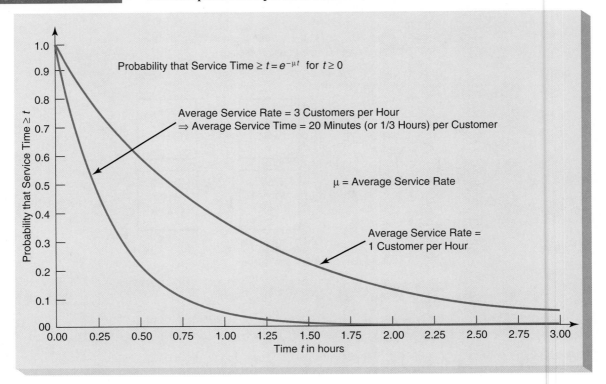

## Measuring the Queue's Performance

Queuing models can help a manager obtain many performance measures (also known as *operating characteristics*) of a waiting line system. We list here some of the measures commonly used in practice. For each performance measure, we also list the standard notation that is used.

*Here is a listing of the key operating characteristics of a queuing system.*

- $\rho$ = *Utilization factor* of the system (i.e., probability that all servers are busy)
- $L_q$ = Average length (i.e., number of customers) of the queue
- $L$ = Average number of customers in the system (i.e., the number in the queue plus the number being served)
- $W_q$ = Average time that each customer spends in the queue
- $W$ = Average time that each customer spends in the system (i.e., time spent waiting plus time spent being served)
- $P_0$ = Probability that there are no customers in the system (i.e., the probability that the service facility will be idle)
- $P_n$ = Probability that there are exactly $n$ customers in the system

## Kendall's Notation for Queuing Systems

*Kendall's notation is used to classify queuing systems.*

In queuing theory we commonly use a three-symbol notation, known as *Kendall's notation*, to classify the wide variety of queuing models that are possible in practice. The three-symbol notation is as follows:

$$A/B/s$$

*where*

$A$     denotes the arrival probability distribution. Typical choices are $M$ (Markovian) for a Poisson distribution, $D$ for a constant or deterministic distribution, or $G$ for a general distribution with known mean and variance.

$B$     denotes the service time probability distribution. Typical choices are $M$ for exponential service times, $D$ for constant or deterministic service times, or $G$ for general service times with known mean and variance.

$s$     denotes the number of servers (or channels)

Using the Kendall notation, we would denote a single-server queuing system with Poisson arrival and exponential service time distributions as an M/M/1 *system*. If this system had two servers, we would then classify it as an M/M/2 system.

*Kendall's three-symbol notation is sometimes extended to include five symbols.*

    The Kendall notation has sometimes been extended to include five symbols. The first three symbols are the same as just discussed. The fourth symbol denotes the maximum allowable length of the queue. It is used in systems in which the queue length is finite. The fifth symbol denotes the size of the arrival population. It is used in systems in which the size of the arrival population is finite. By default, if these two symbols are omitted, their values are assumed to be infinity. Hence, the M/M/1 notation discussed previously corresponds to an M/M/1/∞/∞ queuing system.

## Variety of Queuing Models Studied Here

*We study five commonly used queuing models here.*

Although there is a wide variety of queuing models that can be applied in practice, we introduce you to five of the most widely used models in this chapter. These are outlined in Table 9.2 and examples of each follow in the next few sections. More complex models are

| TABLE 9.2 | | | | | | | Queuing Models Described in This Chapter |
| --- | --- | --- | --- | --- | --- | --- | --- |

| NAME (KENDALL'S NOTATION IN PARENTHESES) | EXAMPLE | NUMBER OF SERVERS | NUMBER OF PHASES | ARRIVAL RATE PATTERN | SERVICE TIME PATTERN | POPULATION SIZE | QUEUE DISCIPLINE |
| --- | --- | --- | --- | --- | --- | --- | --- |
| Simple system (M/M/1) | Information counter at department store | Single | Single | Poisson | Exponential | Unlimited | FIFO |
| Multiple-server (M/M/s) | Airline ticket counter | Multiple | Single | Poisson | Exponential | Unlimited | FIFO |
| Constant service (M/D/1) | Automated car wash | Single | Single | Poisson | Constant | Unlimited | FIFO |
| General service (M/G/1) | Auto repair shop | Single | Single | Poisson | General | Unlimited | FIFO |
| Limited population (M/M/s/∞/N) | Shop with only a dozen machines that might break | Multiple | Single | Poisson | Exponential | Limited | FIFO |

described in queuing theory textbooks[5] or can be developed through the use of computer simulation (which is the focus of Chapter 10). Note that all of the five queuing models listed in Table 9.2 have five characteristics in common. They all assume the following:

1. Arrivals that follow the Poisson probability distribution.
2. FIFO queue discipline.
3. A single-phase service facility.
4. Infinite queue length. That is, the fourth symbol in Kendall's notation is ∞.
5. Service systems that operate under steady, ongoing conditions. This means that both arrival rates and service rates remain stable during the analysis.

## 9.4 SINGLE-SERVER QUEUING SYSTEM WITH POISSON ARRIVALS AND EXPONENTIAL SERVICE TIMES (M/M/1 MODEL)

In this section we present a decision model to determine the operating characteristics of an M/M/1 queuing system. After these numeric measures have been computed, we then add in cost data and begin to make decisions that balance desirable service levels with waiting line costs.

### Assumptions of the M/M/1 Queuing Model

The single-server, single-phase model we consider here is one of the most widely used and simplest queuing models. It assumes that seven conditions exist:

*These seven assumptions must be met if the single-server, single-phase model is to be applied.*

1. Arrivals are served on a FIFO basis.
2. Every arrival waits to be served regardless of the length of the line; that is, there is no balking or reneging.

---

[5] See, for example, B. D. Bunday. *An Introduction to Queuing Theory*. New York: Halsted Press, 1996; or C. H. Ng. *Queuing Modeling Fundamentals*. New York: Wiley, 1996.

3. Arrivals are independent of preceding arrivals, but the average number of arrivals (the arrival rate) does not change over time.

4. Arrivals are described by a Poisson probability distribution and come from an infinite or very large population.

5. Service times also vary from one customer to the next and are independent of one another, but their average rate is known.

6. Service times occur according to the exponential probability distribution.

7. The average service rate is greater than the average arrival rate; that is, $\mu > \lambda$. If this condition does not hold (and $\mu \leq \lambda$), the queue length will grow indefinitely since the service facility does not have the capacity to handle the arriving customers (on average).

When these seven conditions are met, we can develop equations that define the system's *operating characteristics*. The mathematics used to derive each equation is rather complex and outside the scope of this textbook, so we will just present the resulting equations here.

*We use Excel templates to calculate operating characteristics for our queuing models.*

Although we could calculate the operating characteristic equations for *all* the queuing systems discussed in this chapter by hand, it can be quite cumbersome to do so. An easier approach is to develop Excel worksheets for these formulas and use them for all calculations. Therefore, we adopt this approach in our discussions in this chapter.

## Operating Characteristic Equations for an M/M/1 Queuing System

We let

$$\lambda = \text{average number of arrivals per time period (e.g., per hour)}$$

$$\mu = \text{average number of people or items served per time period}$$

*$\lambda$ and $\mu$ must be defined for the same time period.*

It is very important that we define both $\lambda$ and $\mu$ for the *same time period*. That is, if $\lambda$ denotes the number of units arriving *per hour*, then $\mu$ must denote the number of units served *per hour*. As noted earlier, it is necessary for the average service rate to be greater than the average arrival rate (i.e., $\mu > \lambda$). The operating characteristic equations for the M/M/1 queuing system are as follows:

1. Average server utilization in the system:

$$\rho = \lambda/\mu \qquad \text{(9-3)}$$

 **IN ACTION** L.L. Bean Turns to Queuing Theory

L.L. Bean faced severe problems. It was the peak selling season, and the service level to incoming calls was simply unacceptable. Widely known as a high-quality outdoor goods retailer, about 65% of L.L. Bean's sales volume is generated through telephone orders via its toll-free service centers located in Maine.

Here is how bad the situation was: During certain periods, 80% of the calls received a busy signal, and those that did not often had to wait up to 10 minutes before speaking with a sales agent. L.L. Bean estimated that it lost $10 million in profit because of the way it allocated telemarketing resources. Keeping customers waiting "in line" (on the phone) was costing $25,000 per day. On exceptionally busy days, the total orders lost because of queue problems approached $500,000 in gross revenues.

Developing queuing models similar to those presented here, L.L. Bean was able to set the number of phone lines and the number of agents to have on duty for each half-hour of every day of the season. Within a year, use of the model resulted in 24% more calls answered, 17% more orders taken, and 16% more revenues. It also meant 81% fewer abandoned callers and 84% faster answering time. The percentage of calls spending less than 20 seconds in the queue increased from 25% to 77%. Queuing theory changed the way L.L. Bean thinks about telecommunications.

**Source:** Phil Quinn, Bruce Andrews, and Henry Parsons. "Allocating Telecommunication Resources at L.L. Bean, Inc.," *Interfaces* 21, 1 (January–February 1991): 75–91.

*These seven queuing equations for the single-server, single-phase model describe the important operating characteristics of the service system.*

2. Average number of customers or units waiting in line for service:

$$L_q = \frac{\lambda^2}{\mu(\mu - \lambda)}$$ 

(9-4)

3. Average number of customers or units in the system:

$$L = L_q + \lambda/\mu$$ 

(9-5)

4. Average time a customer or unit spends waiting in line for service:

$$W_q = L_q/\lambda = \frac{\lambda}{\mu(\mu - \lambda)}$$ 

(9-6)

5. Average time a customer or unit spends in the system (namely, in the queue or being served):

$$W = W_q + 1/\mu$$ 

(9-7)

6. Probability that there are zero customers or units in the system:

$$P_0 = 1 - \lambda/\mu$$ 

(9-8)

7. Probability that there are *n* customers or units in the system:

$$P_n = (\lambda/\mu)^n P_0$$ 

(9-9)

## Arnold's Muffler Shop Example

We now apply these formulas to the queuing problem faced by Arnold's Muffler Shop in New Orleans. Arnold's mechanic, Reid Blank, is able to install new mufflers at an average rate of 3 per hour, or about 1 every 20 minutes. Customers needing this service arrive at the shop on the average of 2 per hour. Larry Arnold, the shop owner, studied queuing models in an MBA program and feels that all seven of the conditions for a single-server queuing model are met. He proceeds to calculate the numerical values of the operating characteristics of his queuing system.

## Using ExcelModules for Queuing Model Computations

---

### Excel Note

*ExcelModules includes worksheets for all the queuing models discussed in this chapter.*

- ■ The CD-ROM that accompanies this textbook contains a set of Excel worksheets, bundled together in a software package called ExcelModules. The procedure for installing and running this program, as well as a brief description of its contents, is given in Appendix A.

- ■ The CD-ROM also contains the Excel file for each example problem discussed here. The relevant file name is shown in the margin next to each example.

- ■ For clarity, all worksheets for queuing models in ExcelModules are color coded as follows:

    *input cells*, where we enter the problem data, are shaded yellow.

    *output cells*, where the results are shown, are shaded green.

- ■ Although these colors are not apparent in the screen captures shown in the textbook, they are seen in the Excel files in your CD-ROM.

---

When we run the ExcelModules program, we see a menu option titled ExcelModules in the main menu bar of Excel. We click on ExcelModules, and then click on Queuing Models. The choices shown in Program 9.1A are displayed. From these choices, we select the appropriate queuing model.

When *any* of the queuing models is selected in ExcelModules, we are first presented with an option to specify a title for the problem (see Program 9.1B). The default title is Problem Title.

*To analyze M/M/1 systems, we use the M/M/s worksheet in ExcelModules and set s = 1.*

**File: 9-2.xls**

**Operating Characteristics for Arnold Muffler Shop's Case** The M/M/1 queuing model has been included in ExcelModules as a special case of the *M/M/s* model with *s* = 1. Hence, to analyze Arnold's problem using ExcelModules, we first select the choice labeled Exponential Service Times (M/M/s) as shown in Program 9.1A. When we click OK after entering the problem title, we get the screen shown in Program 9.2A. Each queuing worksheet in ExcelModules includes one or more messages specific to that model. It is important to note and follow the messages. For example, the M/M/s worksheet includes the following two messages:

1. Both λ and μ must be RATES and use the same time unit. For example, given a service time such as 10 minutes per customer, convert it to a service rate such as 6 per hour.

2. The total service rate (rate × servers) must be greater than the arrival rate.

---

**PROGRAM 9.1A**

**Queuing Models Submenu in ExcelModules**

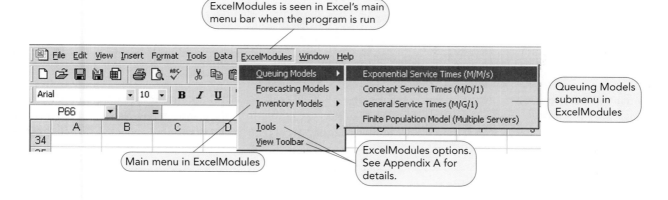

---

**PROGRAM 9.1B**

**Input Window for Optional Problem Title**

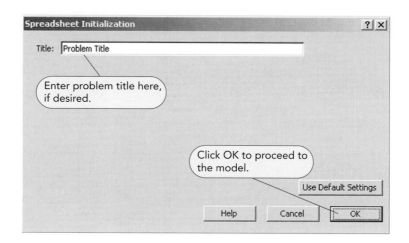

## PROGRAM 9.2A — M/M/s Worksheet in ExcelModules

Default title

Queuing model being used

Important messages to be followed

| | A | B | C | D | E | F |
|---|---|---|---|---|---|---|
| 1 | **Problem Title** | | | | | |
| 2 | Queuing Model | M/M/s (Exponential Service Times) | | | | |
| 3 | | | | | | |
| 4 | 1. Both λ and μ must be RATES, and use the same time unit. For example, given a service time such as 10 minutes | | | | | |
| 5 | per customer, convert it to a service rate such as 6 per hour. | | | | | |
| 6 | 2. The total service rate (rate x servers) must be greater than the arrival rate. | | | | | |
| 7 | | | | | | |
| 8 | Input Data | | | Operating Characteristics | | |
| 9 | Arrival rate (λ) | | | Average server utilization (ρ) | #VALUE! | |
| 10 | Service rate (μ) | | | Average number of customers in the queue (L_q) | #N/A | |
| 11 | Number of servers (s) | | | Average number of customers in the system (L) | #N/A | |
| 12 | | | | Average waiting time in the queue (W_q) | #N/A | |
| 13 | | | | Average time in the system (W) | #N/A | |
| 14 | | | | Probability (% of time) system is empty (P_0) | #N/A | |
| 15 | | | | | | |
| 16 | ERROR. The total service rate (rate x servers) must be greater than the arrival rate. | | | | | |
| 17 | | | | | | |
| 18 | Probabilities | | | | | |
| 19 | Number of Units | Probability | Cumulative Probability | | | |
| 20 | 0 | #N/A | #N/A | | | |
| 21 | 1 | #VALUE! | #N/A | | | |
| 22 | 2 | #VALUE! | #N/A | | | |
| 23 | 3 | #VALUE! | #N/A | | | |
| 24 | 4 | #VALUE! | #N/A | | | |
| 25 | 5 | #VALUE! | #N/A | | | |
| 36 | 16 | #VALUE! | #N/A | | | |
| 37 | 17 | #VALUE! | #N/A | | | |
| 38 | 18 | #VALUE! | #N/A | | | |
| 39 | 19 | #VALUE! | #N/A | | | |
| 40 | 20 | #VALUE! | #N/A | | | |

Input values

Output values

This message is displayed only when total service rate is not greater than the arrival rate.

Hidden rows. See CD-ROM for full file.

Table shows probabilities of 0 through 20 units in the system.

**Important:** *The total service rate must exceed the arrival rate.*

If the total service rate (μ × s) does *not* exceed the arrival rate (λ), the worksheet will automatically print an error message in row 16. This message is seen in Program 9.2A since the values of λ, μ, and number of servers (s) have not been input yet and have defaulted to zero values.

## Excel Notes

■ The worksheets in ExcelModules contain formulas to compute the operating characteristics for different queuing models. The default values of zero for input data such as λ and μ cause the results of these formulas to initially appear as #N/A, #VALUE!, or #DIV/0! (see Program 9.2A). However, as soon as we enter valid values for these input data, the worksheets will display the formula results.

■ Once ExcelModules has been used to create an Excel worksheet for a particular queuing model (such as M/M/s), the resulting worksheet can be used to compute the operating characteristics with several different input parameter values. For example, we can enter different input values in cells B9:B11 of Program 9.2A and compute the resulting operating characteristic values without having to create a *new* M/M/s worksheet each time.

In Larry Arnold's case, the arrival rate (λ) is 2 cars per hour. The service rate (μ) is 3 mufflers per hour. We therefore enter these values in cells B9 and B10, respectively, as shown in Program 9.2B. The number of servers (cell B11) equals 1 here since there is only one mechanic.

**PROGRAM 9.2B**   **Operating Characteristics with $\mu = 3$ for Arnold's Muffler Shop M/M/1 Queuing System**

M/M/s with $s = 1$ is the
M/M/1 model.

Problem title

|    | A | B | C | D | E | F |
|----|---|---|---|---|---|---|
| 1 | Arnold's Muffler Shop | | | | | |
| 2 | Queuing Model | M/M/s (Exponential Service Times) | | | | |
| 3 | | | | | | |
| 4 | 1. Both λ and μ must be RATES, and use the same time unit. For example, given a service time such as 10 minutes | | | | | |
| 5 | per customer, convert it to a service rate such as 6 per hour. | | | | | |
| 6 | 2. The total service rate (rate x servers) must be greater than the arrival rate. | | | | | |
| 7 | | | | | | |
| 8 | Input Data | | | Operating Characteristics | | |
| 9 | Arrival rate (λ) | 2 | | Average server utilization (ρ) | 0.6667 | |
| 10 | Service rate (μ) | 3 | | Average number of customers in the queue (Lq) | 1.3333 | |
| 11 | Number of servers (s) | 1 | | Average number of customers in the system (L) | 2.0000 | |
| 12 | | | | Average waiting time in the queue (Wq) | 0.6667 | |
| 13 | | | | Average time in the system (W) | 1.0000 | |
| 14 | | | | Probability (% of time) system is empty (P0) | 0.3333 | |
| 15 | | | | | | |
| 16 | | | | | | |
| 17 | | | | | | |
| 18 | Probabilities | | | | | |
| 19 | Number of Units | Probability | Cumulative Probability | | | |
| 20 | 0 | 0.3333 | 0.3333 | | | |
| 21 | 1 | 0.2222 | 0.5556 | | | |
| 22 | 2 | 0.1481 | 0.7037 | | | |
| 23 | 3 | 0.0988 | 0.8025 | | | |
| 24 | 4 | 0.0658 | 0.8683 | | | |
| 25 | 5 | 0.0439 | 0.9122 | | | |
| 36 | 16 | 0.0005 | 0.9990 | | | |
| 37 | 17 | 0.0003 | 0.9993 | | | |
| 38 | 18 | 0.0002 | 0.9995 | | | |
| 39 | 19 | 0.0002 | 0.9997 | | | |
| 40 | 20 | 0.0001 | 0.9998 | | | |

*Annotations:* 2 cars per hour — One mechanic — 3 mufflers per hour — Mechanic is busy 67% of the time. — = 60 minutes — 0.67 hours = 40 minutes — This is the probability that there are ≤4 cars in the system.

The worksheet now displays the operating characteristics of this queuing system in cells E9:E14. In addition, the worksheet computes the probability that there are exactly $n$ customers in the system, for $n = 0$ through 20. Cumulative probabilities (i.e., the probability that there are $n$ or *fewer* customers) are also calculated. These values are shown in cells A19:C40.

*Results for Arnold's Muffler Shop problem*

The results show that there are, on average, 2 cars in the system (i.e., $L = 2$), and each car spends an average of one hour in the system (i.e., $W = 1$ hour). The corresponding values for the waiting line alone (not including the server) are $L_q = 1.33$ cars, and $W_q = 0.667$ hours (or 40 minutes). The mechanic (server) is busy 67% of the time (i.e., the utilization factor $\rho = 0.67$). Since there is only one mechanic, this implies that an arriving car has a 33% chance of not having to wait ($P_0 = 0.33$).

**Introducing Costs into the Model**  Now that the operating characteristics of the queuing system have been computed, Arnold decides to do an economic analysis of their impact. The queuing model was valuable in predicting potential waiting times, queue lengths, idle times, and so on. But it did not identify optimal decisions or consider cost factors. As stated earlier, the solution to a queuing problem may require a manager to make a trade-off between the increased cost of providing better service and the decreased waiting costs derived from providing that service.

*Conducting an economic analysis is the next step. It permits cost factors to be included.*

*Customer waiting time is often considered the most important factor.*

Arnold estimates that the cost of customer waiting time, in terms of customer dissatisfaction and lost goodwill, is $10 per hour spent in his shop. Observe that this time includes the time a customer's car is waiting in the queue for service as well as the time when the car is actually being serviced. The only cost of providing service that Arnold can identify is the salary of Reid Blank, the mechanic, who is paid $12 per hour.

*Waiting costs plus service costs equal total cost.*

The total cost, defined as the sum of the waiting cost and the service cost, is calculated as follows:

$$\text{Total cost} = C_w \times L + C_s \times s \tag{9-10}$$

*where*

$$C_w = \text{customer waiting cost per unit time period}$$

$$L = \text{average number of customers in the system}$$

$$C_s = \text{cost of providing service per server per unit time period}$$

$$s = \text{number of servers in the queuing system}$$

In Arnold's case, $C_w = \$10$ per hour, $L = 2$ (see Program 9.2B), $C_s = \$12$ per hour, and $s = 1$ (since there is only one mechanic). Hence, Arnold computes his total cost as ($10)(2) + ($12)(1) = $32 per hour.

### Increasing the Service Rate

Now comes a decision. Arnold finds out through the muffler business grapevine that the Rusty Muffler, a crosstown competitor, employs a mechanic named Jimmy Smith who can efficiently install new mufflers at the rate of 4 per hour. Larry Arnold contacts Smith and inquires as to his interest in switching employers. Smith says that he would consider leaving the Rusty Muffler but only if he were paid a $15 per hour salary. Arnold, being a crafty businessman, decides that it may be worthwhile to fire Blank and replace him with the speedier but more expensive Smith.

He first recomputes all the operating characteristics using a new service rate ($\mu$) of 4 mufflers per hour. The arrival rate ($\lambda$) remains at 2 cars per hour. The revised characteristic values if Smith is employed are shown in Program 9.2C.

It is quite evident that Smith's higher speed (4 mufflers per hour compared to Blank's 3 mufflers per hour) will result in considerably shorter queues and waiting times. For example, a customer would now spend an average of 0.5 hours in the system (i.e., $W = 0.5$) and 0.25 hours waiting in the queue ($W_q = 0.25$) as opposed to 1 hour in the system and 0.67 hours in the queue with Blank as the mechanic. The average number of customers in the system ($L$) decreases from 2 units to 1 unit.

*Here is a comparison for total costs using the two different mechanics.*

Arnold revises his economic analysis with the new information. The revised values are $C_w = \$10$ per hour, $L = 1$ (see Program 9.2C), $C_s = \$15$ per hour, and $s = 1$ (since there is still only one mechanic). Hence, Arnold's revised total cost with Smith as the mechanic is ($10)(1) + ($15)(1) = $25 per hour. Since total costs with Blank as the mechanic was $32 per hour, Arnold may very well decide to hire Smith and reduce costs by $7 per hour (or $56 per 8-hour day).

---

### 9.5  MULTIPLE-SERVER QUEUING SYSTEM WITH POISSON ARRIVALS AND EXPONENTIAL SERVICE TIMES (M/M/s MODEL)

The next logical step is to look at a multiple-server queuing system, in which two or more servers are available to handle arriving customers. Let us still assume that customers awaiting service form one single line and then proceed to the first available server. An

**PROGRAM 9.2C**   **Revised Operating Characteristics with $\mu = 4$ for Arnold's Muffler Shop M/M/1 Queuing System**

|   | A | B | C | D | E | F |
|---|---|---|---|---|---|---|
| 1 | **Arnold's Muffler Shop** | | | | | |
| 2 | Queuing Model | M/M/s (Exponential Service Times) | | | | |
| 3 | | | | | | |
| 4 | 1. Both λ and μ must be RATES, and use the same time unit. For example, given a service time such as 10 minutes | | | | | |
| 5 | per customer, convert it to a service rate such as 6 per hour. | | | | | |
| 6 | 2. The total service rate (rate x servers) must be greater than the arrival rate. | | | | | |
| 7 | | | | | | |
| 8 | Input Data | | | Operating Characteristics | | |
| 9 | Arrival rate (λ) | 2 | | Average server utilization (ρ) | 0.5000 | |
| 10 | Service rate (μ) | 4 | | Average number of customers in the queue (L_q) | 0.5000 | |
| 11 | Number of servers (s) | 1 | | Average number of customers in the system (L) | 1.0000 | |
| 12 | | | | Average waiting time in the queue (W_q) | 0.2500 | |
| 13 | | | New service rate | Average time in the system (W) | 0.5000 | |
| 14 | | | | Probability (% of time) system is empty (P_0) | 0.5000 | |
| 15 | | | | | | |
| 16 | | | | | = 30 minutes | 0.25 hours = |
| 17 | | | | | | 15 minutes |
| 18 | Probabilities | | | | | |
| 19 | Number of Units | Probability | Cumulative Probability | | | |
| 20 | 0 | 0.5000 | 0.5000 | | | |
| 21 | 1 | 0.2500 | 0.7500 | | | |
| 22 | 2 | 0.1250 | 0.8750 | | | |
| 23 | 3 | 0.0625 | 0.9375 | | | |
| 24 | 4 | 0.0313 | 0.9688 | | | |
| 25 | 5 | 0.0156 | 0.9844 | | | |
| 36 | 16 | 0.0000 | 1.0000 | | | |
| 37 | 17 | 0.0000 | 1.0000 | | | |
| 38 | 18 | 0.0000 | 1.0000 | | | |
| 39 | 19 | 0.0000 | 1.0000 | | | |
| 40 | 20 | 0.0000 | 1.0000 | | | |

---

## IN ACTION   Using Queuing Models in a Hospital Eye Clinic

The hospital outpatient eye clinic at the United Kingdom's Royal Preston Hospital is not unlike clinics at hospitals throughout the world: It is regularly overbooked, overrun, and has excessive patient waiting times. Even though its Patient Charter states no one should wait to be seen for more than 30 minutes past their appointment time, patients, on average, waited over 50 minutes.

Many problems in hospital clinics can be explained as a vicious circle of events: (1) appointments staff overbook every clinic session because of the large patient volume; (2) this means patients wait in long queues; (3) doctors are overburdened; and (4) when a doctor is ill, the staff spends much time canceling and rescheduling appointments.

To break out of this circle, the clinic at Royal Preston needed to reduce patient waiting times. This was done by applying computer-driven queuing models and attempting to reduce the patient time variability. The hospital used queuing software to specifically address the 30-minute statistic in the Patient Charter. Researchers assumed that (1) each patient arrived on time, (2) the service distribution was known from past history, (3) 12% of patients missed their appointments, and (4) one-third of the patients queued for a second consultation.

Making a list of 13 recommendations (many nonquantitative) to the clinic, researchers returned two years later to find that most of their suggestions were followed (or at least seriously attempted), yet performance of the clinic had shown no dramatic improvement. Patient waiting times were still quite long, the clinic was still overbooked, and appointments sometimes had to be canceled. The conclusion: Even though models can often help *understand* a problem, some problems, like those in the outpatient clinic, are messy and hard to fix.

**Source:** J. C. Bennett and D. J. Worthington. "An Example of a Good but Partially Successful OR Engagement: Improving Outpatient Clinic Operations," *Interfaces* (September–October 1998) 56–69.

example of such a multiple-server, single-phase waiting line is found in many banks or post offices today. A common line is formed, and the customer at the head of the line proceeds to the first free teller or clerk. (Refer back to Figure 9.3 on page 371 for a typical multiple-server configuration.)

*The multiple-server model also assumes Poisson arrivals and exponential services.*

The multiple-server system presented here again assumes that arrivals follow a Poisson probability distribution and that service times are distributed exponentially. Service is first come, first served, and all servers are assumed to perform at the same rate. Other assumptions listed earlier for the single-server model apply as well.

## Operating Characteristic Equations for an M/M/s Queuing System

We let

$\lambda$ = average number of arrivals per time period (e.g., per hour)

$\mu$ = average number of customers served per time period *per server*

$s$ = number of servers

As with the M/M/1 system, it is very important that we define both $\lambda$ and $\mu$ for the *same time period*. It is also important to note that the service rate $\mu$ is defined *per server*. That is, if there are 2 servers and each server is capable of handling 3 customers per hour, $\mu$ is defined as 3 per hour, *not* 6 per hour (= 2 × 3). Finally, as noted earlier, it is necessary for the average total service rate to be greater than the average arrival rate (that is, $s\mu > \lambda$).

The operating characteristic equations for the M/M/s queuing system are as follows:

1. Average server utilization in the system:

$$\rho = \lambda/(s\mu) \tag{9-11}$$

2. Probability that there are zero customers or units in the system:

$$P_0 = \frac{1}{\left[\displaystyle\sum_{k=0}^{s-1} \frac{1}{k!}\left(\frac{\lambda}{\mu}\right)^k\right] + \frac{1}{s!}\left(\frac{\lambda}{\mu}\right)^s \frac{s\mu}{(s\mu - \lambda)}} \tag{9-12}$$

3. Average number of customers or units waiting in line for service:

$$L_q = \frac{(\lambda/\mu)^s \lambda\mu}{(s-1)!\,(s\mu - \lambda)^2}\,P_0 \tag{9-13}$$

4. Average number of customers or units in the system:

$$L = L_q + \lambda/\mu \tag{9-14}$$

5. Average time a customer or unit spends waiting in line for service:

$$W_q = L_q/\lambda \tag{9-15}$$

6. Average time a customer or unit spends in the system:

$$W = W_q + 1/\mu \tag{9-16}$$

7. Probability that there are $n$ customers or units in the system:

$$P_n = \frac{(\lambda/\mu)^n}{n!} P_0 \quad \text{for } n \leq s \tag{9-17}$$

$$P_n = \frac{(\lambda/\mu)^n}{s! \, s^{(n-s)}} P_0 \quad \text{for } n > s \tag{9-18}$$

These equations are more complex than the ones used in the single-server model. Yet they are used in exactly the same fashion and provide the same type of information as the simpler M/M/1 model.

## Arnold's Muffler Shop Revisited

For an application of the multiple-server queuing model, let us return to the Arnold Muffler Shop problem. Earlier, Larry Arnold examined two options. He could retain his current mechanic, Reid Blank, at a total system cost of $32 per hour; or he could fire Blank and hire a slightly more expensive but faster worker named Jimmy Smith. With Smith on board, system costs could be reduced to $25 per hour.

*The muffler shop considers opening a second muffler service channel that operates at the same speed as the first one.*

A third option is now explored. Arnold finds that at minimal after-tax cost he can open a second garage bay in which mufflers can be installed. Instead of firing his first mechanic, Blank, he would hire a second worker. The new mechanic would be expected to install mufflers at the same rate as Blank ($\mu = 3$ per hour). Customers, who would still arrive at the rate of $\lambda = 2$ per hour, would wait in a single line until one of the two mechanics becomes available. To find out how this option compares with the old single-server queuing system, Arnold computes the operating characteristics for the M/M/2 system.

**File: 9-3.xls**

*In the M/M/s model, the service rate $\mu$ is per server.*

**Excel Solution for Arnold Muffler Shop's with Two Mechanics**   Once again, we select the choice titled Exponential Service Times (M/M/s) in the Queuing Models submenu (see Program 9.1A of ExcelModules. After entering the optional title, we enter the input data as shown in Program 9.3. For Arnold's problem, observe that the arrival rate ($\lambda$) is 2 cars per hour. The service rate ($\mu$) is 3 mufflers per hour *per mechanic*. We enter these values in cells B9 and B10, respectively, as shown in Program 9.3. The number of servers (cell B11) is 2 since there are now two mechanics.

*Dramatically lower waiting time results from opening the second service bay.*

The worksheet now displays the operating characteristics of this queuing system in cells E9:E14. Probabilities of having a specific number of units in the system are shown in cells A19:C40. Arnold first compares these results with the earlier results. The information is summarized in Table 9.3. The increased service from opening a second bay has a dramatic effect on almost all results. In particular, time spent waiting in line ($W_q$) drops from 40 minutes with one mechanic (Blank) or 15 minutes with Smith down to only 2.5 minutes! Similarly, the average number of cars in the system ($L$) falls to 0.75.[6] But does this mean that a second bay should be opened?

---

[6] Note that adding a second mechanic cuts queue waiting time and length by more than half, that is, the relationship between number of servers and queue characteristics is *nonlinear*. This is because of the random arrival and service processes. When there is only one mechanic and two customers arrive within a minute of each other, the second will have a long wait. The fact that the mechanic may have been idle for 30 minutes before they both arrive does not change the average waiting time. Thus, single-server models often have high wait times relative to multiple-server models.

**PROGRAM 9.3**    **Revised Operating Characteristics for Arnold's Muffler Shop M/M/2 Queuing System**

M/M/s with s = 2 is the
M/M/2 model.

| | A | B | C | D | E | F |
|---|---|---|---|---|---|---|
| 1 | **Arnold's Muffler Shop** | | | | | |
| 2 | Queuing Model | M/M/s (Exponential Service Times) | | | | |
| 3 | | | | | | |
| 4 | 1. Both λ and μ must be RATES, and use the same time unit. For example, given a service time such as 10 minutes | | | | | |
| 5 | per customer, convert it to a service rate such as 6 per hour. | | | | | |
| 6 | 2. The total service rate (rate x servers) must be greater than the arrival rate. | | | | | |
| 7 | | | | | | |
| 8 | Input Data | | | Operating Characteristics | | |
| 9 | Arrival rate (λ) | 2 | | Average server utilization (ρ) | 0.3333 | |
| 10 | Service rate (μ) | 3 | | Average number of customers in the queue (Lq) | 0.0833 | |
| 11 | Number of servers (s) | 2 | | Average number of customers in the system (L) | 0.7500 | |
| 12 | | | | Average waiting time in the queue (Wq) | 0.0417 | |
| 13 | | | | Average time in the system (W) | 0.3750 | |
| 14 | | | | Probability (% of time) system is empty (P0) | 0.5000 | |
| 15 | | | | | | |
| 16 | | | | | | |
| 17 | | | | | | |
| 18 | Probabilities | | | | | |
| 19 | Number of Units | Probability | Cumulative Probability | | | |
| 20 | 0 | 0.5000 | 0.5000 | | | |
| 21 | 1 | 0.3333 | 0.8333 | | | |
| 22 | 2 | 0.1111 | 0.9444 | | | |
| 23 | 3 | 0.0370 | 0.9815 | | | |
| 24 | 4 | 0.0123 | 0.9938 | | | |
| 25 | 5 | 0.0041 | 0.9979 | | | |
| 36 | 16 | 0.0000 | 1.0000 | | | |
| 37 | 17 | 0.0000 | 1.0000 | | | |
| 38 | 18 | 0.0000 | 1.0000 | | | |
| 39 | 19 | 0.0000 | 1.0000 | | | |
| 40 | 20 | 0.0000 | 1.0000 | | | |

Servers are busy
only 33.3% of the
time.

Two mechanics on duty

Equal service rate for both
mechanics. Rate shown is
*per mechanic.*

0.0417 hours
= 2.5 minutes

Hidden rows.
See CD-ROM
for full file.

## Economic Analysis

*Economic analysis with two bays.*

To complete his economic analysis, Arnold assumes that the second mechanic would be paid the same as the current one, Blank, namely, $12 per hour. The relevant values are $C_w$ = $10 per hour, $L$ = 0.75 (see Program 9.3), $C_s$ = $12 per hour, and $s$ = 2 (since there are two mechanics). The total cost is, therefore, ($10)(0.75) + ($12)(2) = $31.50 per hour.

**TABLE 9.3**    **Effect of Service Level on Arnold's Operating Characteristics**

| | LEVEL OF SERVICE | | |
|---|---|---|---|
| **OPERATING CHARACTERISTIC** | **ONE MECHANIC (REID BLANK)** $\mu = 3$ | **TWO MECHANICS** $\mu = 3$ FOR EACH | **ONE FAST MECHANIC (JIMMY SMITH)** $\mu = 4$ |
| Probability that the system is empty ($P_0$) | 0.33 | 0.50 | 0.50 |
| Average number of cars in the system ($L$) | 2 cars | 0.75 cars | 1 car |
| Average time spent in the system ($W$) | 60 minutes | 22.5 minutes | 30 minutes |
| Average number of cars in the queue ($L_q$) | 1.33 cars | 0.083 cars | 0.50 cars |
| Average time spent in the queue ($W_q$) | 40 minutes | 2.5 minutes | 15 minutes |

As you recall, total cost with just Blank as mechanic was found to be $32 per hour. Cost with just Smith was $25 per hour. Although opening a second bay would be likely to have a positive effect on customer goodwill and hence lower the cost of waiting time (i.e., lower $C_w$), it means an increase in the total cost of providing service. Look back to Figure 9.1 and you will see that such trade-offs are the basis of queuing theory. Arnold's decision is to replace his present worker with the speedier Smith and not to open a second service bay.

## SINGLE-SERVER QUEUING SYSTEM WITH POISSON ARRIVALS AND CONSTANT SERVICE TIMES (M/D/1 MODEL)

*Constant service rates speed the process compared to exponentially distributed service times with the same value of $\mu$.*

When customers or equipment are processed according to a fixed cycle, as in the case of an automatic car wash or an amusement park ride, constant service rates are appropriate. Because constant rates are certain, the values for $L_q$, $W_q$, $L$, and $W$ are always less than they would be in the models discussed previously, which have variable service times. As a matter of fact, both the average queue length and the average waiting time in the queue are *halved* with the constant service rate model.

### Operating Characteristic Equations for an M/D/1 Queuing System

We let

$$\lambda = \text{average number of arrivals per time period (e.g., per hour)}$$

$$\mu = \text{constant number of people or items served per time period}$$

The operating characteristic equations follow.

1. Average server utilization in the system:

$$\rho = \lambda/\mu \tag{9-19}$$

2. Average number of customers or units waiting in line for service:

$$L_q = \frac{\lambda^2}{2\mu(\mu - \lambda)} \tag{9-20}$$

3. The average number of customers or units in the system:

$$L = L_q + \lambda/\mu \tag{9-21}$$

4. Average time a customer or unit spends waiting in line for service:

$$W_q = L_q/\lambda = \frac{\lambda}{2\mu(\mu - \lambda)} \tag{9-22}$$

5. The average time a customer or unit spends in the system (namely, in the queue or being served):

$$W = W_q + 1/\mu \tag{9-23}$$

6. The probability that there are zero customers or units in the system:

$$P_0 = 1 - \lambda/\mu \tag{9-24}$$

## Garcia-Golding Recycling, Inc.

Garcia-Golding Recycling, Inc., collects and compacts aluminum cans and glass bottles in New York City. Their truck drivers, who arrive to unload these materials for recycling, currently wait an average of 15 minutes before emptying their loads. The cost of the driver and truck time wasted while in queue is valued at $60 per hour. A new automated compactor can be purchased that will process truckloads at a constant rate of 12 trucks per hour (i.e., 5 minutes per truck). Trucks arrive according to a Poisson distribution at an average rate of 8 per hour. If the new compactor is put in use, its cost will be amortized at a rate of $3 per truck unloaded.

**File: 9-4.xls**

**Excel Solution for Garcia-Golding's Problem** We select the choice titled Constant Service Times (M/D/1) in the Queuing Models submenu (see Program 9.1A on page 377) of ExcelModules. After entering the optional title, we enter the input data as shown in the screen in Program 9.4. For Garcia-Golding's problem, the arrival rate ($\lambda$) is 8 trucks per hour. The constant service rate ($\mu$) is 12 trucks per hour. We enter these values in cells B9 and B10, respectively. The worksheet now displays the operating characteristics of this queuing system in cells E9:E14.

*Cost analysis for the recycling example*

## Economic Analysis

The *current* system makes drivers wait an average of 15 minutes before emptying their trucks. The waiting cost per trip is

$$\text{Current waiting cost per trip} = (0.25 \text{ hours waiting}) \times (\$60/\text{hour})$$

$$= \$15 \text{ per trip}$$

As seen in Program 9.4, the average waiting time in the queue ($W_q$) with the new automated compactor is only 0.0833 hours, or 5 minutes. Therefore, the revised waiting cost per trip is

$$\text{Revised waiting cost per trip} = (0.0833 \text{ hours waiting}) \times (\$60/\text{hour})$$

$$= \$5 \text{ per trip}$$

$$\text{Savings with new equipment} = \$15 - \$5 = \$10 \text{ per trip}$$

$$\text{Amortized cost of equipment} = \$3 \text{ per trip}$$

$$\text{Hence, net savings} = \$10 - \$3 = \$7 \text{ per trip}$$

### PROGRAM 9.4

**Operating Characteristics for Garcia-Golding Recycling M/D/1 Queuing System**

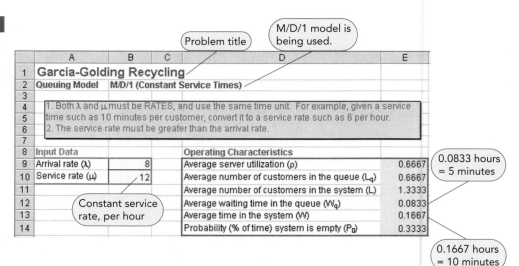

Problem title

M/D/1 model is being used.

| | A | B | C | D | E |
|---|---|---|---|---|---|
| 1 | Garcia-Golding Recycling | | | | |
| 2 | Queuing Model | M/D/1 (Constant Service Times) | | | |
| 3 | | | | | |
| 4 | 1. Both λ and μ must be RATES, and use the same time unit. For example, given a service | | | | |
| 5 | time such as 10 minutes per customer, convert it to a service rate such as 6 per hour. | | | | |
| 6 | 2. The service rate must be greater than the arrival rate. | | | | |
| 7 | | | | | |
| 8 | Input Data | | | Operating Characteristics | |
| 9 | Arrival rate (λ) | 8 | | Average server utilization (ρ) | 0.6667 |
| 10 | Service rate (μ) | 12 | | Average number of customers in the queue (Lq) | 0.6667 |
| 11 | | | | Average number of customers in the system (L) | 1.3333 |
| 12 | | | | Average waiting time in the queue (Wq) | 0.0833 |
| 13 | | | | Average time in the system (W) | 0.1667 |
| 14 | | | | Probability (% of time) system is empty (P0) | 0.3333 |

Constant service rate, per hour

0.0833 hours = 5 minutes

0.1667 hours = 10 minutes

## 9.7  SINGLE-SERVER QUEUING SYSTEM WITH POISSON ARRIVALS AND GENERAL SERVICE TIMES (M/G/1 MODEL)

*General service time models assume arbitrary distributions for service times.*

So far, we have studied systems in which service times are either exponentially distributed or constant. In many cases, however, service times could follow some arbitrary distribution with a mean $\mu$ and a standard deviation $\sigma$. In such cases, we refer to the model as a *general* service time model. Real-world examples of general service times include (1) time required to service vehicles at an auto repair shop (e.g., an oil change service) and (2) time required by a store clerk to complete a sales transaction.

The single-server system presented here assumes that arrivals follow a Poisson probability distribution. As in earlier models, we also assume (1) service is first-come, first-served; (2) there is no balking or reneging, and (3) the average service rate is greater than the average arrival rate.

### Operating Characteristic Equations for an M/G/1 Queuing System

We let

$$\lambda = \text{average number of arrivals per time period (e.g., per hour)}$$

$$\mu = \text{average number of people or items served per time period}$$

$$\sigma = \text{standard deviation of service time}$$

The operating characteristic equations follow.

1. Average server utilization in the system:

$$\rho = \lambda/\mu \tag{9-25}$$

2. Average number of customers or units waiting in line for service:

$$L_q = \frac{\lambda^2\sigma^2 + (\lambda/\mu)^2}{2(1 - (\lambda/\mu))} \tag{9-26}$$

3. Average number of customers or units in the system:

$$L = L_q + \lambda/\mu \tag{9-27}$$

4. Average time a customer or unit spends waiting in line for service:

$$W_q = L_q/\lambda \tag{9-28}$$

5. Average time a customer or unit spends in the system:

$$W = W_q + 1/\mu \tag{9-29}$$

6. Probability that there are zero customers or units in the system:

$$P_0 = 1 - \lambda/\mu \tag{9-30}$$

### Meetings with Professor Crino

*Example of a general service time model*

Professor Michael Crino advises all Honors students at Central College. During the pre-registration period, students meet with Professor Crino to decide courses for the following semester and to discuss any other issues they may be concerned about. Rather than have students set up specific appointments to see him, Professor Crino prefers setting aside 2 hours each day during the preregistration period and having students drop in on an informal basis. This approach, he believes, makes students feel more at ease with him.

Based on his experience, Professor Crino thinks that students arrive at an average rate of 1 every 12 minutes (or 5 per hour) to see him. He also thinks the Poisson distribution is appropriate to model the arrival process. Advising meetings last an average of 10 minutes; that is, Professor Crino's service rate is 6 per hour. However, since some students have concerns that they wish to discuss with Professor Crino, the length of these meetings varies. Professor Crino estimates that the standard deviation of the service time (i.e., the meeting length) is 5 minutes.

**File: 9-5.xls**

*λ and μ are rates and must be for the same time unit. The standard deviation, σ, must also be for this same time unit.*

**Excel Solution for Professor Crino's Problem**   We select the choice titled General Service Times (M/G/1) in the Queuing Models submenu (see Program 9.1A on page 377) of ExcelModules. After entering the optional title, we enter the input data in the screen shown in Program 9.5A. For Professor Crino's problem, the mean arrival rate ($\lambda$) is 5 students per hour. The mean service rate ($\mu$) is 6 students per hour. Observe that $\mu$ must exceed $\lambda$, and both must be for the same time period (per hour, in this case). The standard deviation ($\sigma$) of the service time is 5 minutes. However, since $\lambda$ and $\mu$ are expressed per hour, we also express $\sigma$ in hours and write it as 0.0833 hours (= 5 minutes).

We enter the values $\lambda$, $\mu$, and $\sigma$ in cells B9, B10, and B11, respectively, as shown in Program 9.5A. The worksheet now displays the operating characteristics of this queuing system in cells E9:E14.

The results indicate that, on average, Professor Crino is busy during 83.3% of his advising period. There are 2.60 students waiting to see him on average, and each student waits an average of 0.52 hours (or approximately 31 minutes).

## Using Excel's Goal Seek to Identify Required Model Parameters

Looking at the results in Program 9.5A, Professor Crino realizes that making students wait an average of 31 minutes is unacceptable. Ideally, he would like to speed these meetings up so that students wait no more than 15 minutes (or 0.25 hours) on average. He realizes that he has little control over the standard deviation of the service time. However, by insisting that students come prepared (e.g., decide which courses they want to take) for these meetings, Professor Crino thinks he can decrease the average meeting length. The question is this: What should be the average meeting length that will enable Professor Crino to meet his goal of a 15-minute average waiting time?

*Excel's Goal Seek procedure allows us to find the required value of a queue parameter to achieve a stated goal.*

One way to solve this problem is to plug in different values for the service rate $\mu$ in cell B10 of Program 9.5A and keep track of the $W_q$ value in cell E12 until it drops below 0.25. An alternate, and preferred, approach is to use a procedure in Excel called Goal Seek to automate the search process for the value of $\mu$. Assume we designate a cell as the Changing Cell in a spreadsheet model. Also assume a different cell (which we designate as the Target Cell) is a function of the value in the changing cell. That is, the Target Cell contains a formula that involves the Changing Cell. The Goal Seek procedure allows us to try to find the value in the Changing Cell that will make the Target Cell achieve a specified value.

In our model, the Changing Cell is the service rate $\lambda$ (cell B10). The Target Cell is the average waiting time $W_q$ (cell E12). We want the Target Cell to achieve a value of 15 minutes (which we specify as 0.25 hours since $\mu$ and $\lambda$ are per hour). After bringing up the General Service Times (M/G/1) worksheet in ExcelModules (see Program 9.5A), we invoke the Goal Seek procedure by clicking Tools|Goal Seek in Excel's main menu bar. The window shown in Program 9.5B is now displayed.

We specify cell E12 as the target, set its value to 0.25, and identify cell B10 as the Changing Cell. When we click OK, we get the windows shown in Program 9.5C. The results indicate that if Professor Crino can increase his service rate to 6.92 students per hour, the

**PROGRAM 9.5A**  **Operating Characteristics for Professor Crino's Problem M/G/1 Queuing System**

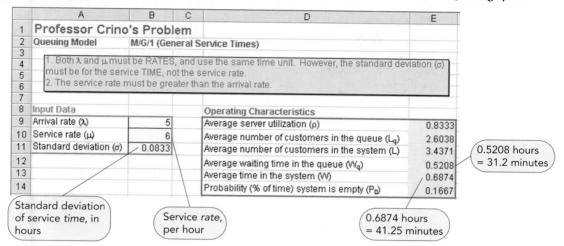

|   | A | B | C | D | E |
|---|---|---|---|---|---|
| 1 | Professor Crino's Problem | | | | |
| 2 | Queuing Model | M/G/1 (General Service Times) | | | |
| 3 | | | | | |
| 4 | 1. Both λ and μ must be RATES, and use the same time unit. However, the standard deviation (σ) | | | | |
| 5 | must be for the service TIME, not the service rate. | | | | |
| 6 | 2. The service rate must be greater than the arrival rate. | | | | |
| 7 | | | | | |
| 8 | Input Data | | | Operating Characteristics | |
| 9 | Arrival rate (λ) | 5 | | Average server utilization (ρ) | 0.8333 |
| 10 | Service rate (μ) | 6 | | Average number of customers in the queue (Lq) | 2.6038 |
| 11 | Standard deviation (σ) | 0.0833 | | Average number of customers in the system (L) | 3.4371 |
| 12 | | | | Average waiting time in the queue (Wq) | 0.5208 |
| 13 | | | | Average time in the system (W) | 0.6874 |
| 14 | | | | Probability (% of time) system is empty (P0) | 0.1667 |

0.5208 hours = 31.2 minutes

Standard deviation of service *time*, in hours

Service *rate*, per hour

0.6874 hours = 41.25 minutes

**PROGRAM 9.5B**

**Goal Seek Input Window in Excel**

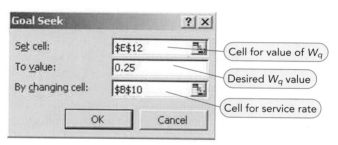

Goal Seek  ? X

Set cell:  $E$12 — Cell for value of $W_q$

To value:  0.25 — Desired $W_q$ value

By changing cell:  $B$10 — Cell for service rate

OK    Cancel

**PROGRAM 9.5C**  **Goal Seek Status Window and Revised Operating Characteristics for Professor Crino's Problem: M/G/1 Queuing System**

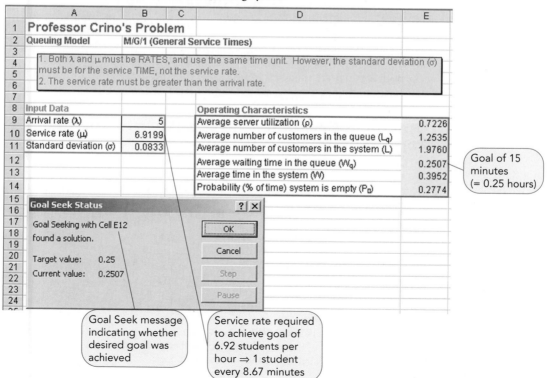

|   | A | B | C | D | E |
|---|---|---|---|---|---|
| 1 | Professor Crino's Problem | | | | |
| 2 | Queuing Model | M/G/1 (General Service Times) | | | |
| 3 | | | | | |
| 4 | 1. Both λ and μ must be RATES, and use the same time unit. However, the standard deviation (σ) | | | | |
| 5 | must be for the service TIME, not the service rate. | | | | |
| 6 | 2. The service rate must be greater than the arrival rate. | | | | |
| 7 | | | | | |
| 8 | Input Data | | | Operating Characteristics | |
| 9 | Arrival rate (λ) | 5 | | Average server utilization (ρ) | 0.7226 |
| 10 | Service rate (μ) | 6.9199 | | Average number of customers in the queue (Lq) | 1.2535 |
| 11 | Standard deviation (σ) | 0.0833 | | Average number of customers in the system (L) | 1.9760 |
| 12 | | | | Average waiting time in the queue (Wq) | 0.2507 |
| 13 | | | | Average time in the system (W) | 0.3952 |
| 14 | | | | Probability (% of time) system is empty (P0) | 0.2774 |

Goal of 15 minutes (= 0.25 hours)

Goal Seek Status  ? X

Goal Seeking with Cell E12 found a solution.

Target value:    0.25
Current value:   0.2507

OK    Cancel    Step    Pause

Goal Seek message indicating whether desired goal was achieved

Service rate required to achieve goal of 6.92 students per hour ⇒ 1 student every 8.67 minutes

average waiting time drops to around 15 minutes. That is, Professor Crino needs to reduce his average meeting length to approximately 8.67 minutes (= 6.92 students per 60 minutes).

We can use Goal Seek in any of the queuing models discussed here to determine the value of an input parameter (e.g., $\mu$ or $\lambda$) that would make an operating characteristic reach a desired value. For example, we could have used it in the M/M/1 worksheet (Section 9.4) to find the value of $\mu$ that would allow Arnold to offer his customers a guarantee of having to wait no more than 5 minutes (or 0.0833 hours). The answer turns out to be 6 mufflers per hour. See if you can verify this using Goal Seek and the Exponential Service Times (M/M/s) worksheet in ExcelModules.

## 9.8 MULTIPLE-SERVER QUEUING SYSTEM WITH POISSON ARRIVALS, EXPONENTIAL SERVICE TIMES, AND FINITE POPULATION SIZE (M/M/s/∞/N MODEL)

When there is a limited population of potential customers for a service facility, we need to consider a different queuing model. This model would be used, for example, if we were considering equipment repairs in a factory that has five machines, if we were in charge of maintenance for a fleet of 10 commuter airplanes, or if we ran a hospital ward that has 20 beds. The limited population model permits any number of servers to be considered.

*In the finite population model, the arrival rate is dependent on the length of the queue.*

The reason this model differs from the earlier queuing models is that there is now a dependent relationship between the length of the queue and the arrival rate. To illustrate this situation, assume your factory has five machines. If all five are broken and awaiting repair, the arrival rate drops to zero. In general, as the waiting time becomes longer in a limited population queuing system, the arrival rate of customers drops lower.

In this section, we describe a finite arrival population model that has the following assumptions:

1. There are $s$ servers with *identical* service time distributions.
2. The population of units seeking service is finite, of size $N$.[7]

*Arrival rate $\lambda$ is per customer or unit.*

3. The arrival distribution of *each customer* in the population follows a Poisson distribution with a mean rate of $\lambda$.
4. Service times are exponentially distributed with a mean rate of $\mu$.
5. Both $\lambda$ and $\mu$ are specified for the same time period.
6. Customers are served on a first-come, first-served basis.

### Operating Characteristic Equations for the Finite Population Queuing System

We let

$$\lambda = \text{average number of arrivals per time period (e.g., per hour)}$$

$$\mu = \text{average number of people or items served per time period}$$

$$s = \text{number of servers}$$

$$N = \text{size of the population}$$

---

[7] Although there is no definite number that we can use to divide finite from infinite arrival populations, the general rule of thumb is this: If the number in the queue is a significant proportion of the arrival population, we should use a finite queuing model.

The operating characteristic equations follow.

1. Probability that there are zero customers or units in the system:

$$P_0 = \frac{1}{\sum_{n=0}^{s-1} \frac{N!}{(N-n)!\,n!}\left(\frac{\lambda}{\mu}\right)^n + \sum_{n=s}^{N} \frac{N!}{(N-n)!\,s!\,s^{n-s}}\left(\frac{\lambda}{\mu}\right)^n} \tag{9-31}$$

2. Probability that there are exactly $n$ customers in the system:

$$P_n = \frac{N!}{(N-n)!\,n!}\left(\frac{\lambda}{\mu}\right)^n P_0, \qquad \text{if } 0 \le n \le s \tag{9-32}$$

$$P_n = \frac{N!}{(N-n)!\,s!\,s^{n-s}}\left(\frac{\lambda}{\mu}\right)^n P_0, \quad \text{if } s < n \le N \tag{9-33}$$

$$P_n = 0, \qquad \text{if } n > N \tag{9-34}$$

3. Average number of customers or units in line waiting for service:

$$L_q = \sum_{n=s}^{N} (n-s)P_n \tag{9-35}$$

4. Average number of customers or units in the system:

$$L = \sum_{n=0}^{s-1} nP_n + L_q + s\left(1 - \sum_{n=0}^{s-1} P_n\right) \tag{9-36}$$

5. Average time a customer or unit spends in the queue waiting for service:

$$W_q = \frac{L_q}{\lambda(N-L)} \tag{9-37}$$

6. Average time a customer or unit spends in the system:

$$W = \frac{L}{\lambda(N-L)} \tag{9-38}$$

## Department of Commerce Example

*Example of a finite population model.*

The U.S. Department of Commerce (DOC) in Washington, DC, uses five high-speed print-ers to print all documents. Past records indicate that each of these printers needs repair after about 20 hours of use. Breakdowns have been found to be Poisson distributed. The one technician on duty can repair a printer in an average of 2 hours, following an exponen-tial distribution.

**File: 9-6.xls**

**Excel Solution for DOC's Problem** We select the choice titled Finite Population Model (Multiple Servers) in the Queuing Models submenu (see Program 9.1A) of ExcelModules. After entering the optional title, we get the screen shown in Program 9.6A. For DOC's prob-lem, the arrival rate ($\lambda$) for *each printer* is 1/20 = 0.05 per hour. The mean service rate ($\mu$) is 1 every two hours, or 0.50 printers per hour. As before, both $\mu$ and $\lambda$ are expressed for the same time period (per hour, in this case). The number of servers ($s$) is 1, since there is only one tech-nician on duty. Finally, the population size ($N$) is 5, since there are five printers at the DOC.

**PROGRAM 9.6A**     Operating Characteristics for the Department of Commerce's Problem: M/M/1 Queuing System with Finite Population

| | A | B | C | D | E |
|---|---|---|---|---|---|
| 1 | **Department of Commerce** | | | | |
| 2 | Queuing Model | **M/M/s with a finite population** | | | |
| 3 | | | | | |
| 4 | 1. Both λ and μ must be RATES, and use the same time unit. | | | | |
| 5 | 2. The arrival rate is for each member of the population. For example, if each member of the | | | | |
| 6 | population goes for service once every 20 minutes, then enter λ = 3 (per hour). | | | | |
| 7 | | | | | |
| 8 | Input Data | | | Operating Characteristics | |
| 9 | Arrival rate per customer (λ) | 0.05 | | Average server utilization (ρ) | 0.4360 |
| 10 | Service rate (μ) | 0.5 | | Average number of customers in the queue (L_q) | 0.2035 |
| 11 | Number of servers (s) | 1 | | Average number of customers in the system (L) | 0.6395 |
| 12 | Population size (N) | 5 | | Average waiting time in the queue (W_q) | 0.9333 |
| 13 | | | | Average time in the system (W) | 2.9333 |
| 14 | | | | Probability (% of time) system is empty (P_0) | 0.5640 |
| 15 | | | | Effective arrival rate | 0.2180 |
| 16 | | | | | |
| 17 | Probabilities | | | | |
| 18 | Number of Units | Probability | Cumulative Probability | Number waiting | Arrival rate(n) |
| 19 | 0 | 0.5640 | 0.5640 | 0 | 0.25 |
| 20 | 1 | 0.2820 | 0.8459 | 0 | 0.2 |
| 21 | 2 | 0.1128 | 0.9587 | 1 | 0.15 |
| 22 | 3 | 0.0338 | 0.9926 | 2 | 0.1 |
| 23 | 4 | 0.0068 | 0.9993 | 3 | 0.05 |
| 24 | 5 | 0.0007 | 1.0000 | 4 | 0 |
| 25 | 6 | | | | |
| 26 | 7 | | | | |
| 27 | 8 | | | | |
| 28 | 9 | | | | |
| 29 | 10 | | | | |
| 48 | 29 | | | | |
| 49 | 30 | | | | |
| 50 | 31 | | | | |

Annotations: 1 technician · 5 printers · 0.9333 hours = 56 minutes · 2.9333 hours = 176 minutes · Calculation space used by worksheet · Hidden rows. See CD-ROM for full file. · Probabilities for n > 5 are not shown since there are only 5 printers.

We enter the values of λ, μ, s, and N in cells B9, B10, B11, and B12, respectively, as shown in Program 9.6A. The worksheet now displays the operating characteristics of this queuing system in cells E9:E15. Probability values $(P_n)$ are shown in cells A18:C50.

The results indicate that there are 0.64 printers on average in the system. If printer downtime is estimated at $120 per hour, and the technician is paid $25 per hour, we can compute the total cost per hour as

*Total cost computation*

$$\text{Total cost} = (\text{average number of printers down}) \times (\text{cost of downtime hour}) + \text{cost of technician hour}$$

$$= (0.64)(\$120) + \$25 = \$101.80 \text{ per hour}$$

The office manager is willing to consider hiring a second printer technician provided it is cost-effective. To check this, we compute the DOC queue's operating characteristics again. However, the number of servers this time (cell B11) is 2. The results are shown in Program 9.6B.

**PROGRAM 9.6B**    **Revised Operating Characteristics for the Department of Commerce's Problem: M/M/2 Queuing System with Finite Population**

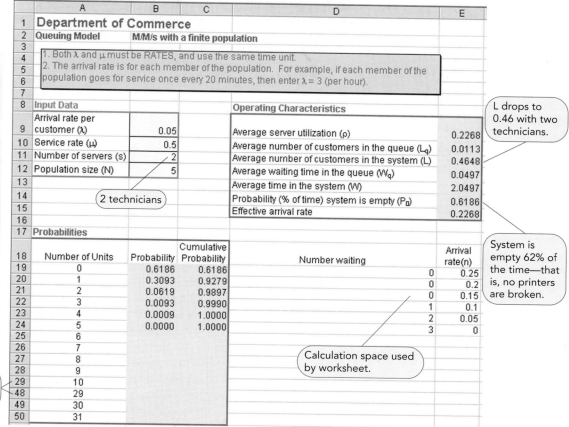

|   | A | B | C | D | E |
|---|---|---|---|---|---|
| 1 | **Department of Commerce** | | | | |
| 2 | Queuing Model | M/M/s with a finite population | | | |
| 3 | | | | | |
| 4 | 1. Both λ and μ must be RATES, and use the same time unit. | | | | |
| 5 | 2. The arrival rate is for each member of the population. For example, if each member of the | | | | |
| 6 | population goes for service once every 20 minutes, then enter λ = 3 (per hour). | | | | |
| 7 | | | | | |
| 8 | Input Data | | | Operating Characteristics | |
| 9 | Arrival rate per customer (λ) | 0.05 | | Average server utilization (ρ) | 0.2268 |
| 10 | Service rate (μ) | 0.5 | | Average number of customers in the queue ($L_q$) | 0.0113 |
| 11 | Number of servers (s) | 2 | | Average number of customers in the system (L) | 0.4648 |
| 12 | Population size (N) | 5 | | Average waiting time in the queue ($W_q$) | 0.0497 |
| 13 | | | | Average time in the system (W) | 2.0497 |
| 14 | | | | Probability (% of time) system is empty ($P_0$) | 0.6186 |
| 15 | | | | Effective arrival rate | 0.2268 |
| 16 | | | | | |
| 17 | Probabilities | | | | |
| 18 | Number of Units | Probability | Cumulative Probability | Number waiting | Arrival rate(n) |
| 19 | 0 | 0.6186 | 0.6186 | 0 | 0.25 |
| 20 | 1 | 0.3093 | 0.9279 | 0 | 0.2 |
| 21 | 2 | 0.0619 | 0.9897 | 0 | 0.15 |
| 22 | 3 | 0.0093 | 0.9990 | 1 | 0.1 |
| 23 | 4 | 0.0009 | 1.0000 | 2 | 0.05 |
| 24 | 5 | 0.0000 | 1.0000 | 3 | 0 |
| 25 | 6 | | | | |
| 26 | 7 | | | | |
| 27 | 8 | | | | |
| 28 | 9 | | | | |
| 29 | 10 | | | | |
| 48 | 29 | | | | |
| 49 | 30 | | | | |
| 50 | 31 | | | | |

*L drops to 0.46 with two technicians.*

*2 technicians*

*System is empty 62% of the time—that is, no printers are broken.*

*Calculation space used by worksheet.*

*Hidden rows. See CD-ROM for full file.*

Program 9.6B indicates that there are now only 0.46 printers on average in the system. We can compute the revised total cost per hour as

*Total cost with two technicians.*

$$\text{Total cost} = (\text{average number of printers down}) \times (\text{cost of downtime hour})$$
$$+ (\text{cost of technician hour}) \times (\text{number of technicians})$$

$$= (0.46)(\$120) + (\$25)(2) = \$105.20 \text{ per hour}$$

Since the total cost is higher in this case ($105.20 versus $101.80 per hour), the office manager should not hire a second technician.

## 9.9    MORE COMPLEX QUEUING SYSTEMS

Many queuing systems that occur in real-world situations have characteristics like those of Arnold's Muffler Shop, Garcia-Golding Recycling, Inc., Professor Crino's advising meetings, or the Department of Commerce examples. This is true when the situation calls for issues such as: (1) single- or multiple-servers, (2) Poisson arrivals, (3) exponential, constant, or arbitrary service times, (4) a finite or infinite arrival population, (5) no balking or reneging, and (6) first-in, first-out service.

Often, however, *variations* of this specific case are present in an analysis. Arrival times, for example, may not be Poisson distributed. A college registration system in which seniors have first choice of courses and hours over all other students is an example of a first-come, first-served model with a preemptive priority queue discipline. A physical examination for military recruits is an example of a multiphase system—one that differs from the single-phase models discussed in this chapter. Recruits first line up to have blood drawn at one station, then wait to take an eye exam at the next station, talk to a psychiatrist at the third, and are examined by a doctor for medical problems at the fourth. At each phase, the recruits must enter another queue and wait their turn.

*More sophisticated models exist to handle variations of basic assumptions, but when even these do not apply we can turn to computer simulation, the topic of Chapter 10.*

Analytical models to handle these cases have been developed by operations researchers. The mathematical expressions for the operating characteristics are somewhat more complex than the ones covered in this chapter.[8] Many real-world queuing applications are, in fact, too complex to be modeled analytically at all. When this happens, decision modelers usually turn to *computer simulation*, the topic of Chapter 10.

## SUMMARY

Queuing systems are an important part of the business world. This chapter describes several common queuing situations and presents decision models for analyzing systems that follow certain assumptions: (1) the queuing system involves just a single phase of service, (2) arrivals are Poisson distributed, (3) arrivals are treated on a first-in, first-out basis and do not balk or renege, (4) service times follow the exponential distribution, an arbitrary distribution, or are constant, and (5) the average service rate is faster than the average arrival rate.

The models illustrated in this chapter are for single-server, single-phase and multiple-server, single-phase problems. We show how to compute a series of operating characteristics in each case using Excel worksheets and then study total expected costs. Total cost is the sum of the cost of providing service plus the cost of waiting time.

Key operating characteristics for a system are (1) utilization rate, (2) percent idle time, (3) average time spent waiting in the system, and in the queue, (4) average number of customers in the system and in the queue, and (5) probabilities of various numbers of customers in the system.

We emphasize that a variety of queuing situations exist that do not meet all of the assumptions of the traditional models. In these cases we need to use more complex mathematical models or turn to a technique called computer simulation. The application of simulation to problems of inventory control, queuing systems, and other decision modeling situations is the topic discussed in Chapter 10.

## GLOSSARY

**Arbitrary Distribution.** A probability distribution that is sometimes used to describe random service times in a queuing system.

**Arrival Population.** The population from which arrivals at the queuing system come. Also known as the *calling population.*

**Balking.** The case in which arriving customers refuse to join the waiting line.

**Exponential Probability Distribution.** A probability distribution that is often used to describe random service times in a queuing system.

**FIFO.** Denotes first-in, first-out. A queue discipline in which the customers are served in the strict order of arrival.

**Goal Seek.** A procedure in Excel that can be used to identify the value of a queuing system parameter required to achieve a desired value of an operating characteristic.

**Limited or Finite Population.** A case in which the number of customers in the system is a significant proportion of the calling population.

**Limited Queue Length.** A waiting line that cannot increase beyond a specific size.

**M/D/1.** Kendall's notation for the constant service time model.

**M/G/1.** Kendall's notation for the arbitrary service time model.

**M/M/1.** Kendall's notation for the single-server model with Poisson arrivals and exponential service times.

---

[8] Often, the qualitative results of queuing models are as useful as the quantitative results. Results show that it is inherently more efficient to pool resources, use central dispatching, and provide single multiple-server systems rather than multiple single-server systems.

**M/M/s.** Kendall's notation for the multiple-server queuing model (with *s* servers), Poisson arrivals, and exponential service times.

**Multiphase System.** A system in which service is received from more than one station, one after the other.

**Multiple-Server Queuing System.** A system that has more than one service facility, all fed by the same single queue.

**Operating Characteristics.** Descriptive characteristics of a queuing system, including the average number of customers in a line and in the system, the average waiting times in a line and in the system, and percent idle time.

**Poisson Distribution.** A probability distribution that is often used to describe random arrivals in a queue.

**Queue Discipline.** The rule by which customers in a line receive service.

**Queuing Model.** A mathematical model that studies the performance of waiting lines or queues.

**Reneging.** The case in which customers enter a queue but then leave before being served.

**Service Cost.** The cost of providing a particular level of service.

**Simulation.** A technique for representing queuing models that are complex and difficult to model analytically.

**Single-Phase System.** A queuing system in which service is received at only one station.

**Single-Server Queuing System.** A system with one service facility fed by one queue. Servers are also referred to as *channels*.

**Unlimited or Infinite Population.** A calling population that is very large relative to the number of customers currently in the system.

**Unlimited Queue Length.** A queue that can increase to an infinite size.

**Utilization Factor ($\rho$).** The proportion of time that the service facility is in use.

**Waiting Cost.** The cost to the firm of having customers or units waiting in line to be served.

**Waiting Line or Queue.** One or more customers or units waiting to be served.

## KEY EQUATIONS

$\lambda$ = average number of arrivals per time period (e.g., per hour)

$\mu$ = average number of people or items served per time period

**(9-1)** $P(X) = (e^{-\lambda}\lambda^X)/X!$   for $X = 0, 1, 2, \ldots$

Poisson probability distribution used in describing arrivals.

**(9-2)** $P(\text{service time} > t) = e^{-\mu t}$   for $t \geq 0$

Exponential probability distribution used in describing service times.

*Equations 9-3 through 9-9 describe the operating characteristics in a single-server queuing system that has Poisson arrivals and exponential service times.*

**(9-3)** $\rho = \lambda/\mu$

Average server utilization in the system.

**(9-4)** $L_q = \dfrac{\lambda^2}{\mu(\mu - \lambda)}$

Average number of customers or units waiting in line for service.

**(9-5)** $L = L_q + \lambda/\mu$

The average number of customers or units in the system.

**(9-6)** $W_q = L_q/\lambda = \dfrac{\lambda}{\mu(\mu - \lambda)}$

Average time a customer or unit spends waiting in line for service.

**(9-7)** $W = W_q + 1/\mu$

Average time a customer or unit spends in the system.

**(9-8)** $P_0 = 1 - \lambda/\mu$

The probability that there are zero customers or units in the system.

**(9-9)** $P_n = (\lambda/\mu)^n P_0$

The probability that there are *n* customers or units in the system.

**(9-10)** Total cost $= C_w \times L + C_s \times s$

Total cost is the sum of waiting cost and service cost.

*Equations 9-11 through 9-18 describe the operating characteristics in a multiple-server queuing system that has Poisson arrivals and exponential service times.*

**(9-11)** $\rho = \lambda/(s\mu)$

Average server utilization in the system.

**(9-12)** $P_0 = \dfrac{1}{\left[\displaystyle\sum_{k=0}^{s-1} \dfrac{1}{k!}\left(\dfrac{\lambda}{\mu}\right)^k\right] + \dfrac{1}{s!}\left(\dfrac{\lambda}{\mu}\right)^s \dfrac{s\mu}{(s\mu - \lambda)}}$

Probability that there are zero customers or units in the system.

**(9-13)** $L_q = \dfrac{(\lambda/\mu)^s \lambda\mu}{(s-1)!(s\mu - \lambda)} P_0$

Average number of customers or units waiting in line for service.

**(9-14)** $L = L_q + \lambda/\mu$

The average number of customers or units in the system.

**(9-15)** $W_q = L_q/\lambda$

Average time a customer or unit spends waiting in line for service.

**(9-16)** $W = W_q + 1/\mu$

Average time a customer or unit spends in the system.

**(9-17)** $P_n = \dfrac{(\lambda/\mu)^n}{n!} P_0 \quad \text{for } n \leq s$

**(9-18)** $P_n = \dfrac{(\lambda/\mu)^n}{s!\, s^{(n-s)}} P_0 \quad \text{for } n > s$

Probability that there are $n$ customers or units in the system.

*Equations 9-19 through 9-24 describe the operating characteristics in a multiple-server queuing system that has Poisson arrivals and constant service times.*

**(9-19)** $\rho = \lambda/\mu$

Average server utilization in the system.

**(9-20)** $L_q = \dfrac{\lambda^2}{2\mu(\mu - \lambda)}$

Average number of customers or units waiting in line for service.

**(9-21)** $L = L_q + \lambda/\mu$

The average number of customers or units in the system.

**(9-22)** $W_q = L_q/\lambda = \dfrac{\lambda}{2\mu(\mu - \lambda)}$

Average time a customer or unit spends waiting in line for service.

**(9-23)** $W = W_q + 1/\mu$

Average time a customer or unit spends in the system.

**(9-24)** $P_0 = 1 - \lambda/\mu$

Probability that there are zero customers or units in the system.

*Equations 9-25 through 9-30 describe the operating characteristics in a single-server queuing system that has Poisson arrivals and general service times.*

**(9-25)** $\rho = \lambda/\mu$

Average server utilization in the system.

**(9-26)** $L_q = \dfrac{\lambda^2 \sigma^2 + (\lambda/\mu)^2}{2(1 - (\lambda/\mu))}$

Average number of customers or units waiting in line for service.

**(9-27)** $L = L_q + \lambda/\mu$

The average number of customers or units in the system.

**(9-28)** $W_q = L_q/\lambda$

Average time a customer or unit spends waiting in line for service.

**(9-29)** $W = W_q + 1/\mu$

Average time a customer or unit spends in the system.

**(9-30)** $P_0 = 1 - \lambda/\mu$

The probability that there are zero customers or units in the system.

*Equations 9-31 through 9-38 describe the operating characteristics in a multiple-server queuing system that has Poisson arrivals, exponential service times, and a finite population of size* N.

**(9-31)** $P_0 = \dfrac{1}{\displaystyle\sum_{n=0}^{s-1} \dfrac{N!}{(N-n)!\, n!}\left(\dfrac{\lambda}{\mu}\right)^n + \sum_{n=s}^{N} \dfrac{N!}{(N-n)!\, s!\, s^{n-s}}\left(\dfrac{\lambda}{\mu}\right)^n}$

The probability that there are zero customers or units in the system.

**(9-32)** $P_n = \dfrac{N!}{(N-n)!\, n!}\left(\dfrac{\lambda}{\mu}\right)^n P_0, \qquad \text{if } 0 \leq n \leq s$

**(9-33)** $P_n = \dfrac{N!}{(N-n)!\, s!\, s^{n-s}}\left(\dfrac{\lambda}{\mu}\right)^n P_0, \quad \text{if } s < n \leq N$

**(9-34)** $P_n = 0, \qquad\qquad\qquad\qquad \text{if } n > N$

Probability that there are exactly $n$ customers in the system.

**(9-35)** $L_q = \displaystyle\sum_{n=s}^{N} (n - s) P_n$

Average number of customers or units waiting in line for service.

**(9-36)** $L = \displaystyle\sum_{n=0}^{s-1} n P_n + L_q + s\left(1 - \sum_{n=0}^{s-1} P_n\right)$

Average number of customers or units in the system.

$$(9\text{-}37) \quad W_q = \frac{L_q}{\lambda(N - L)}$$

Average time a customer or unit spends waiting in line for service.

$$(9\text{-}38) \quad W = \frac{L}{\lambda(N - L)}$$

Average time a customer or unit spends in the system.

# SOLVED PROBLEMS

## Solved Problem 9-1

The Maitland Furniture store gets an average of 50 customers per shift. The manager of Maitland wants to calculate whether she should hire 1, 2, 3, or 4 salespeople. She has determined that average waiting times will be 7 minutes with one salesperson, 4 minutes with two salespeople, 3 minutes with three salespeople, and 2 minutes with four salespeople. She has estimated the cost per minute that customers wait at $1. The cost per salesperson per shift (including fringe benefits) is $70.

How many salespeople should be hired?

### Solution

The manager's calculations are as follows:

| | NUMBER OF SALESPEOPLE | | | |
|---|---|---|---|---|
| | 1 | 2 | 3 | 4 |
| (a) Average number of customers per shift | 50 | 50 | 50 | 50 |
| (b) Average waiting time per customer (minutes) | 7 | 4 | 3 | 2 |
| (c) Total waiting time per shift (a × b) (minutes) | 350 | 200 | 150 | 100 |
| (d) Cost per minute of waiting time (estimated) | $1.00 | $1.00 | $1.00 | $1.00 |
| (e) Value of lost time (c × d) per shift | $350 | $200 | $150 | $100 |
| (f) Salary cost per shift | $ 70 | $140 | $210 | $280 |
| (g) Total cost per shift | $420 | $340 | $360 | $380 |

Because the minimum total cost per shift relates to two salespeople, the manager's optimum strategy is to hire two salespeople.

## Solved Problem 9-2

Marty Schatz owns and manages a chili dog and soft drink store near the campus. Although Marty can service 30 customers per hour on the average ($\mu$), he only gets 20 customers per hour ($\lambda$). Because Marty could wait on 50% more customers than actually visit his store, it doesn't make sense to him that he should have any waiting lines.

Marty hires you to examine the situation and to determine some characteristics of his queue. After looking into the problem, you make the seven assumptions listed in Section 9.4. What are your findings?

### Solution

For this problem, we use the Exponential Service Times (M/M/s) queuing worksheet in ExcelModules. The arrival rate ($\lambda$) is 20 customers per hour, service rate ($\mu$) is 30 customers per hour, and there is one server. We enter these values in cells B9, B10, and B11 respectively, as shown in Program 9.7.

The operating characteristics of this queuing system are displayed in cells E9:E14. The probabilities that there are exactly $n$ customers in the system, for $n = 0$ through 20, are shown in cells A19:C40.

**PROGRAM 9.7**    **Operating Characteristics for Solved Problem 9-2: M/M/1 Queuing System**

|    | A | B | C | D | E | F |
|----|---|---|---|---|---|---|
| 1 | Solved Problem 9-2 | | | | | |
| 2 | Queuing Model | M/M/s (Exponential Service Times) | | — M/M/s with s = 1 | | |
| 3 | | | | | | |
| 4 | 1. Both λ and μ must be RATES, and use the same time unit.  For example, given a service time such as 10 minutes | | | | | |
| 5 | per customer, convert it to a service rate such as 6 per hour. | | | | | |
| 6 | 2. The total service rate (rate x servers) must be greater than the arrival rate. | | | | | |
| 7 | | | | | | |
| 8 | Input Data | | | Operating Characteristics | | 0.0667 hours |
| 9 | Arrival rate (λ) | 20 | | Average server utilization (ρ) | 0.6667 | = 4 minutes |
| 10 | Service rate (μ) | 30 | | Average number of customers in the queue (Lq) | 1.3333 | |
| 11 | Number of servers (s) | 1 | | Average number of customers in the system (L) | 2.0000 | |
| 12 | | | | Average waiting time in the queue (Wq) | 0.0667 | |
| 13 | | 1 server | | Average time in the system (W) | 0.1000 | |
| 14 | | | | Probability (% of time) system is empty (P0) | 0.3333 | |
| 15 | | | | | | = 6 minutes |
| 16 | | | | | | |
| 17 | | | | | | |
| 18 | Probabilities | | | | | |
| 19 | Number of Units | Probability | Cumulative Probability | | | |
| 20 | 0 | 0.3333 | 0.3333 | | | |
| 21 | 1 | 0.2222 | 0.5556 | | | |
| 22 | 2 | 0.1481 | 0.7037 | | | |
| 23 | 3 | 0.0988 | 0.8025 | | | |
| 24 | 4 | 0.0658 | 0.8683 | | | |
| 25 | 5 | 0.0439 | 0.9122 | | | |
| 36 | 16 | 0.0005 | 0.9990 | | | |
| 37 | 17 | 0.0003 | 0.9993 | | | |
| 38 | 18 | 0.0002 | 0.9995 | | | |
| 39 | 19 | 0.0002 | 0.9997 | | | |
| 40 | 20 | 0.0001 | 0.9998 | | | |

Hidden rows. See CD-ROM for full file.

**Solved Problem 9-3**

Refer to Solved Problem 9-2. Marty agreed that these figures seemed to represent his approximate business situation. You are quite surprised at the length of the lines and elicit from him an estimated value of the customer's waiting time (in the queue, not being waited on) at 10 cents per minute. During the 12 hours that he is open he gets $(12 \times 20) = 240$ customers. The average customer is in a queue 4 minutes, so the total customer waiting time is $(240 \times 4 \text{ minutes}) = 960$ minutes. The value of 960 minutes is $(\$0.10)(960 \text{ minutes}) = \$96$. You tell Marty that not only is 10 cents per minute quite conservative, but he could probably save most of that $96 of customer ill will if he hired another salesclerk. After much haggling, Marty agrees to provide you with all the chili dogs you can eat during a week-long period in exchange for your analysis of the results of having two clerks wait on the customers.

Assuming that Marty hires one additional salesclerk whose service rate equals Marty's rate, complete the analysis.

**Solution**

We once again use the Exponential Service Times (M/M/s) queuing worksheet in ExcelModules. The arrival rate ($\lambda$) is 20 customers per hour and the service rate ($\mu$) is 30 customers per hour. There are, however, two servers now. We enter these values in cells B9, B10, and B11 respectively, as shown in Program 9.8.

The operating characteristics of this queuing system are displayed in cells E9:E14. The probabilities that there are exactly *n* customers in the system, for *n* = 0 through 20, are shown in cells A19:C40.

You now have (240 customers) × (0.0042 hours) = 1 hour total customer waiting time per day. The total cost of 1 hour of customer waiting time is (60 minutes) × ($0.10 per minute) = $6.

**PROGRAM 9.8**    **Operating Characteristics for Solved Problem 9-3: M/M/2 Queuing System**

| | A | B | C | D | E | F |
|---|---|---|---|---|---|---|
| 1 | Solved Problem 9-3 | | | | | |
| 2 | Queuing Model | M/M/s (Exponential Service Times) | | | | |
| 3 | | | | | | |
| 4 | 1. Both λ and μ must be RATES, and use the same time unit. For example, given a service time such as 10 minutes | | | | | |
| 5 | per customer, convert it to a service rate such as 6 per hour. | | | | | |
| 6 | 2. The total service rate (rate x servers) must be greater than the arrival rate. | | | | | |
| 7 | | | | | | |
| 8 | Input Data | | | Operating Characteristics | | |
| 9 | Arrival rate (λ) | 20 | | Average server utilization (ρ) | 0.3333 | |
| 10 | Service rate (μ) | 30 | | Average number of customers in the queue (Lq) | 0.0833 | |
| 11 | Number of servers (s) | 2 | | Average number of customers in the system (L) | 0.7500 | |
| 12 | | | | Average waiting time in the queue (Wq) | 0.0042 | |
| 13 | | 2 servers | | Average time in the system (W) | 0.0375 | |
| 14 | | | | Probability (% of time) system is empty (P0) | 0.5000 | |
| 15 | | | | | | |
| 16 | | | | | | |
| 17 | | | | | | |
| 18 | Probabilities | | | | | |
| 19 | Number of Units | Probability | Cumulative Probability | | | |
| 20 | 0 | 0.5000 | 0.5000 | | | |
| 21 | 1 | 0.3333 | 0.8333 | | | |
| 22 | 2 | 0.1111 | 0.9444 | | | |
| 23 | 3 | 0.0370 | 0.9815 | | | |
| 24 | 4 | 0.0123 | 0.9938 | | | |
| 25 | 5 | 0.0041 | 0.9979 | | | |
| 36 | 16 | 0.0000 | 1.0000 | | | |
| 37 | 17 | 0.0000 | 1.0000 | | | |
| 38 | 18 | 0.0000 | 1.0000 | | | |
| 39 | 19 | 0.0000 | 1.0000 | | | |
| 40 | 20 | 0.0000 | 1.0000 | | | |

Wq drops from 0.0667 hours to 0.0042 hours (= 0.25 minutes) with two servers.

Hidden rows. See CD-ROM for full file.

You are ready to point out to Marty that the hiring of one additional clerk will save $96 − $6 = $90 of customer ill will per 12-hour shift. Marty responds that the hiring should also reduce the number of people who look at the line and leave as well as those who get tired of waiting in line and leave. You tell Marty that you are ready for two chili dogs, extra hot.

**⫸ SELF-TEST**

- ■ Before taking the self-test, refer back to the learning objectives at the beginning of the chapter, the notes in the margins, and the glossary at the end of the chapter.
- ■ Use the key at the back of the book to correct your answers.
- ■ Restudy pages that correspond to any questions that you answered incorrectly or material you feel uncertain about.

1. Most systems use the queue discipline known as the first-in, first-out rule.
   **a.** True          **b.** False
2. Before using exponential distributions to build queuing models, the decision analyst should determine if the service-time data fit the distribution.
   **a.** True          **b.** False
3. In a multiserver single-phase queuing system, the arrival will pass through at least two different service facilities.
   **a.** True          **b.** False
4. Which of the following is *not* an assumption in common queuing mathematical models?
   **a.** arrivals come from an infinite or very large population
   **b.** arrivals are Poisson distributed
   **c.** arrivals are treated on a first-in, first-out basis and do not balk or renege
   **d.** service times follow the exponential distribution
   **e.** the average arrival rate is faster than the average service rate
5. Which of the following is *not* a key operating characteristic for a queuing system?
   **a.** utilization rate
   **b.** percent idle time
   **c.** average time spent waiting in the system and in the queue
   **d.** average number of customers in the system and in the queue
   **e.** none of the above
6. Three parts of a queuing system are
   **a.** the inputs, the queue, and the service facility.
   **b.** the arrival population, the queue, and the service facility.
   **c.** the arrival population, the waiting line, and the service facility.
   **d.** all of the above.
7. The utilization factor for a system is defined as
   **a.** mean number of people served divided by the mean number of arrivals per time period.
   **b.** the average time a customer spends waiting in a queue.
   **c.** proportion of the time the service facilities are in use.
   **d.** the percent idle time.
   **e.** none of the above.

8. If everything else remains constant, including the mean arrival rate and service rate, except that the service time becomes constant instead of exponential,
   **a.** the average queue length will be halved.
   **b.** the average waiting time will be doubled.
   **c.** the average queue length will increase.
   **d.** none of the above.
9. A queuing system with one server, Poisson arrivals, and arbitrary service times is denoted by the following Kendall's notation:
   **a.** M/M/1
   **b.** M/G/1
   **c.** G/G/1
   **d.** M/D/1
10. The case in which a customer joins a queue but then leaves before being served is called
    **a.** balking.
    **b.** reneging.
    **c.** first-in, first-out.
    **d.** finite queue length.
11. The total cost of a queuing system is typically calculated as the
    **a.** waiting cost.
    **b.** service cost.
    **c.** sum of waiting cost and service cost.
    **d.** difference of the waiting cost and service cost.
12. In the standard queuing model, we assume that the queue discipline is _____.
13. The service *time* in the basic queuing model is assumed to be _____.
14. When managers find standard queuing formulas inadequate or the mathematics unsolvable, the often resort to _____ to obtain their solutions.
15. In the basic queuing model, the number of arrivals is assumed to be _____.

# DISCUSSION QUESTIONS AND PROBLEMS

## Discussion Questions

**9-1** What is the queuing problem? What are the components in a queuing system?

**9-2** What are the assumptions underlying common queuing models?

**9-3** Describe the important operating characteristics of a queuing system.

**9-4** Why must the service rate be greater than the arrival rate in a single-server queuing system?

**9-5** Briefly describe three situations in which the FIFO discipline rule is not applicable in queuing analysis.

**9-6** Provide examples of four situations in which there is a limited, or finite, waiting line.

**9-7** What are the components of the following systems? Draw and explain the configuration of each.
(a) Barbershop
(b) Car wash
(c) Laundromat
(d) Small grocery store

**9-8** Do doctor's offices generally have random arrival rates for patients? Are service times random? Under what circumstances might service times be constant?

**9-9** Do you think the Poisson distribution, which assumes independent arrivals, is a good estimation of arrival rates in the following queuing systems? Defend your position in each case.
(a) Cafeteria in your school
(b) Barbershop
(c) Hardware store
(d) Dentist's office
(e) College class
(f) Movie theater

## Problems

**9-10** The Golding Discount Department Store has approximately 300 customers shopping in its store between 9 A.M. and 5 P.M. on Saturdays. In deciding how many cash registers to keep open each Saturday, Golding's manager considers two factors: customer waiting time (and the associated waiting cost) and the service costs of employing additional checkout clerks. Checkout clerks are paid an average of $4 per hour. When only one is on duty, the waiting time per customer is about 10 minutes (or $\frac{1}{6}$ of an hour); when two clerks are on duty, the average checkout time is 6 minutes per person; 4 minutes when three clerks are working; and 3 minutes when four clerks are on duty.

Golding's management has conducted customer satisfaction surveys and has been able to estimate that the store suffers approximately $5 in lost sales and goodwill for every *hour* of customer time spent waiting in checkout lines. Using the information provided, determine the optimal number of clerks to have on duty each Saturday to minimize the store's total expected cost.

**9-11** The Rockwell Electronics Corporation retains a service crew to repair machine breakdowns that occur on an average of $\lambda = 3$ per day (approximately Poisson in nature). The crew can service an average of $\mu = 8$ machines per day, with a repair time distribution that resembles the exponential distribution.
(a) What is the utilization rate of this service system?
(b) What is the average downtime for a machine that is broken?
(c) How many machines are waiting to be serviced at any given time?
(d) What is the probability that more than one machine is in the system? What is the probability that more than two are broken and waiting to be repaired or being serviced? More than three? More than four?

**9-12** From historical data, Harry's Car Wash estimates that dirty cars arrive at the rate of 10 per hour all day Saturday. With a crew working the wash line, Harry figures that cars can be cleaned at the rate of one every 5 minutes. One car at a time is cleaned in this example of a single-server waiting line.

Assuming Poisson arrivals and exponential service times, find the
(a) average number of cars in line.
(b) average time a car waits before it is washed.
(c) average time a car spends in the service system.
(d) utilization rate of the car wash.
(e) probabiliby that no cars are in the system.

**9-13** Mike Dreskin manages a large Los Angeles movie theater complex called Cinema I, II, III, and IV. Each of the four auditoriums plays a different film; the schedule is set so that starting times are staggered to avoid the large crowds that would occur if all four movies started at the same time. The theater has a single ticket booth and a cashier who can maintain an average service rate of 280 movie patrons per hour. Service times are assumed to follow an exponential distribution. Arrivals on a typically active day are Poisson distributed and average 210 per hour.

To determine the efficiency of the current ticket operation, Mike wishes to examine several queue operating characteristics.
(a) Find the average number of moviegoers waiting in line to purchase a ticket.
(b) What percentage of the time is the cashier busy?
(c) What is the average time that a customer spends in the system?
(d) What is the average time spent waiting in line to get to the ticket window?
(e) What is the probability that there are more than two people in the system? More than three people? More than four?

**9-14** A university cafeteria line in the student center is a self-serve facility in which students select the food items they want and then form a single line to pay the cashier. Students arrive at a rate of about four per minute according to a Poisson distribution. The single cashier ringing up sales takes about 12 seconds per customer, following an exponential distribution.
(a) What is the probability that there are more than two students in the system? More than three students? More than four?
(b) What is the probability that the system is empty?
(c) How long will the average student have to wait before reaching the cashier?
(d) What is the expected number of students in the queue?
(e) What is the average number in the system?
(f) If a second cashier is added (who works at the same pace), how will the operating characteristics computed in parts (b), (c), (d), and (e) change? Assume that customers wait in a single line and go to the first available cashier.

**9-15** The wheat harvesting season in the American Midwest is short, and most farmers deliver their truckloads of wheat to a giant central storage bin within a two-week span. Because of this, wheat-filled trucks waiting to unload and return to the fields have been known to back up for a block at the receiving bin. The central bin is owned cooperatively, and it is to every farmer's benefit to make the unloading/storage process as efficient as possible. The cost of grain deterioration caused by unloading delays and the cost of truck rental and idle driver time are significant concerns to the cooperative members. Although farmers have difficulty quantifying crop damage, it is easy to assign a waiting and unloading cost for truck and driver of $18 per hour. The storage bin is open and operated 16 hours per day, 7 days per week, during the harvest season and is capable of unloading 35 trucks per hour according to an exponential distribution. Full trucks arrive all day long (during the hours the bin is open) at a rate of about 30 per hour, following a Poisson pattern.

To help the cooperative get a handle on the problem of lost time while trucks are waiting in line or unloading at the bin, find the

(a) average number of trucks in the unloading system.
(b) average time per truck in the system.
(c) utilization rate for the bin area.
(d) probability that there are more than three trucks in the system at any given time.
(e) total daily cost to the farmers of having their trucks tied up in the unloading process.
(f) The cooperative, as mentioned, uses the storage bin only two weeks per year. Farmers estimate that enlarging the bin would cut unloading costs by 50% next year. It will cost $9,000 to do so during the off-season. Would it be worth the cooperative's while to enlarge the storage area?

**9-16** Ashley's Department Store in Kansas City maintains a successful catalog sales department in which a clerk takes orders by telephone. If the clerk is occupied on one line, incoming phone calls to the catalog department are answered automatically by a recording machine and asked to wait. As soon as the clerk is free, the party that has waited the longest is transferred and answered first. Calls come in at a rate of about 12 per hour. The clerk is capable of taking an order in an average of 4 minutes. Calls tend to follow a Poisson distribution, and service times tend to be exponential. The clerk is paid $5 per hour, but because of lost goodwill and sales, Ashley's loses about $25 per hour of customer time spent waiting for the clerk to take an order.

(a) What is the average time that catalog customers must wait before their calls are transferred to the order clerk?
(b) What is the average number of callers waiting to place an order?
(c) Ashley is considering adding a second clerk to take calls. The store would pay that person the same $5 per hour. Should it hire another clerk? Explain.

**9-17** Sal's International Barbershop is a popular haircutting and styling salon near the campus of the University of New Orleans. Four barbers work full-time and spend an average of 15 minutes on each customer. Customers arrive all day long at an average rate of 12 per hour. When they enter, they take a number to wait for the first available barber. Arrivals tend to follow the Poisson distribution, and service times are exponentially distributed.

(a) What is the probability that the shop is empty?
(b) What is the average number of customers in the barbershop?
(c) What is the average time spent in the shop?
(d) What is the average time that a customer spends waiting to be called to the barber chair?
(e) What is the average number waiting to be served?
(f) What is the shop's utilization factor?
(g) Sal's is thinking of adding a fifth barber. How will this affect the utilization rate?

**9-18** The medical director of a large emergency clinic faces a problem of providing treatment for patients who arrive at different rates during the day. There are four doctors available to treat patients when needed. If not needed, they can be assigned to other responsibilities (e.g., lab tests, reports, x-ray diagnoses) or else rescheduled to work at other hours.

It is important to provide quick and responsive treatment, and the medical director feels that, on average, patients should not have to sit in the waiting area for more than 5 minutes before being seen by a doctor. Patients are treated on a first-come, first-served basis and see the first available doctor after waiting in the queue. The arrival pattern for a typical day is as follows:

| TIME | ARRIVAL RATE (PATIENTS/HOUR) |
| --- | --- |
| 9 A.M.–3 P.M. | 6 |
| 3 P.M.–8 P.M. | 4 |
| 8 P.M.–midnight | 12 |

These arrivals follow a Poisson distribution, and treatment times, 12 minutes on the average, follow the exponential pattern.

How many doctors should be on duty during each period to maintain the level of patient care expected?

**9-19** Juhn and Sons Wholesale Fruit Distributors employ one worker whose job it is to load fruit on outgoing company trucks. Trucks arrive at the loading gate at an average of 24 per day, or 3 per hour, according to a Poisson distribution. The worker loads them at a rate of 4 per hour, following approximately the exponential distribution in service times.

Determine the operating characteristics of this loading gate problem. What is the probability that there will be more than three trucks either being loaded or waiting? Discuss the result of your queuing model computation.

**9-20** Juhn believes that adding a second fruit loader will substantially improve the firm's efficiency. He estimates that a two-person crew, still acting like a single-server system, at the loading gate will double the loading rate from 4 trucks per hour to 8 trucks per hour. Analyze the effect on the queue of such a change and compare the results with those found in Problem 9-19.

**9-21** Truck drivers working for Juhn and Sons (see Problems 9-19 and 9-20) are paid a salary of $10 per hour on average. Fruit loaders receive about $6 per hour. Truck drivers waiting in the queue or at the loading gate are drawing a salary but are productively idle and unable to generate revenue during that time. What would be the *hourly* cost savings to the firm associated with employing two loaders instead of one?

**9-22** Juhn and Sons Wholesale Fruit Distributors (of Problem 9-19) are considering building a second platform or gate to speed the process of loading their fruit trucks. This, they think, will be even more efficient than simply hiring another loader to help out the first platform (as in Problem 9-20).

Assume that workers at each platform will be able to load 4 trucks per hour each and that trucks will continue to arrive at the rate of 3 per hour. Then apply the preceding equations to find the waiting line's new operating conditions. Is this new approach indeed speedier than the other two considered?

**9-23** Customers arrive at an automated coffee vending machine at a rate of 4 per minute, following a Poisson distribution. The coffee machine dispenses a cup of coffee at a constant rate of 10 seconds.

(a) What is the average number of people waiting in line?

(b) What is the average number in the system?

(c) How long does the average person wait in line before receiving service?

**9-24** Customers arrive at Rao's insurance agency at an average rate of 1 per hour. Arrivals can be assumed to follow the Poisson distribution. Anand Rao, the insurance agent, estimates that he spends an average of 30 minutes with each customer. The standard deviation of service time is 15 minutes, and the service time distribution is arbitrary. Calculate the operating characteristics of the queuing system at Rao's agency. What is the probability that an arriving customer will have to wait for service?

**9-25** Refer again to Rao's agency in Problem 9-24. If Rao wants to ensure that his customers wait an average of around 10 minutes, what should be his mean service time? Assume the standard deviation of service time remains at 15 minutes.

**9-26** Chuck's convenience store has only one gas pump. Cars pull up to the pump at the rate of 1 car of every 8 minutes. Depending on the speed at which the customer works, the pumping time varies. Chuck estimates that the pump is occupied for an average of 5 minutes, with a standard deviation of 1 minute. Calculate Chuck's operating characteristics. Comment on the values obtained. What, if any, would you recommend Chuck should do?

**9-27** Get Connected, Inc. operates several Internet kiosks in Atlanta, Georgia. Customers can access the Web at these kiosks, paying $2 for 30 minutes, or a fraction thereof. The kiosks are typically open for 10 hours each day and are always full.

Due to the rough usage these PCs receive, they break down frequently. Get Connected has a central repair facility to fix these PCs. PCs arrive at the facility at an average rate of 0.9 per day. Repair times take an average of 1 day, with a standard deviation of 0.5 days.

Calculate the operating characteristics of this queuing system. How much is it worth to Get Connected to increase the average service rate to 1.25 PCs per day?

**9-28** One mechanic services five drilling machines for a steel plate manufacturer. Machines break down on an average of once every six working days, and breakdowns tend to follow a Poisson distribution. The mechanic can handle an average of one repair job per day. Repairs follow an exponential distribution.

(a) How many machines are waiting for service, on average?

(b) How many are currently being served?

(c) How many drills are in running order, on average?

(d) What is the average waiting time in the queue?

(e) What is the average wait in the system?

**9-29** A technician monitors a group of five computers that run an automated manufacturing facility. It takes an average of 15 minutes (exponentially distributed) to adjust a computer that develops a problem. The computers run for an average of 85 minutes (Poisson distributed) without requiring adjustments. What is the

(a) average number of computers waiting for adjustment?

(b) average number of computers not in working order?

(c) probability the system is empty?

(d) average time in the queue?

(e) average time in the system?

**9-30** The typical subway station in Washington, DC, has six turnstiles, each of which can be controlled by the station manager to be used for either entrance or exit control—but never for both. The manager must decide at different times of the day just how many turnstiles to use for entering passengers and how many to be set up to allow exiting passengers.

At the Washington College Station, passengers enter the station at a rate of about 84 per minute between the hours of 7 and 9 A.M. Passengers exiting trains at the stop reach the exit turnstile area at a rate of about 48 per minute during the same morning rush hours. Each turnstile can allow an average of 30 passengers per minute to enter or exit. Arrival and service times have been thought to follow Poisson and exponential distributions, respectively. Assume riders form a common queue at both entry and exit turnstile areas and proceed to the first empty turnstile.

The Washington College Station manager does not want the average passenger at his station to have to wait in a turnstile line for more than 6 seconds, nor does he want more than eight people in any queue at any average time.

(a) How many turnstiles should be opened in each direction every morning?
(b) Discuss the assumptions underlying the solution of this problem using queuing theory.

---

## ⮕ CASE STUDY

### New England Castings

For more than 75 years, New England Castings, Inc., has manufactured wood stoves for home use. In recent years, with increasing energy prices, George Mathison, president of New England Castings, has seen sales triple. This dramatic increase in sales has made it even more difficult for George to maintain quality in all the wood stoves and related products.

Unlike other companies manufacturing wood stoves, New England Castings is *only* in the business of making stoves and stove-related products. Their major products are the Warmglo I, the Warmglo II, the Warmglo III, and the Warmglo IV. The Warmglo I is the smallest wood stove, with a heat output of 30,000 Btu, and the Warmglo IV is the largest, with a heat output of 60,000 Btu. In addition, New England Castings, Inc., produces a large array of products that have been designed to be used with one of their four stoves. These products include warming shelves, surface thermometers, stovepipes, adaptors, stove gloves, trivets, mitten racks, andirons, chimneys, and heat shields. New England Castings also publishes a newsletter and several paperback books on stove installation, stove operation, stove maintenance, and wood sources. It is George's belief that their wide assortment of products is a major contributor to the sales increases.

The Warmglo III outsells all the other stoves by a wide margin. The heat output and available accessories are ideal for the typical home. The Warmglo III also has a number of outstanding features that make it one of the most attractive and heat-efficient stoves on the market. Each Warmglo III also has a thermostatically controlled primary air intake valve that allows the stove to adjust itself automatically to produce the correct heat output for varying weather conditions. A secondary air opening is used to increase the heat output in case of very cold weather. The internal stove parts produce a horizontal flame path for more efficient burning, and the output gases are forced to take an S-shaped path through the stove. The S-shaped path allows more complete combustion of the gases and better heat transfer from the fire and gases through the cast iron to the area to be heated. These features, along with the accessories, resulted in expanding sales and prompted George to build a new factory to manufacture Warmglo III stoves. An overview diagram of the factory is shown in Figure 9.5.

The new foundry uses the latest equipment, including a new Disamatic that helps in manufacturing stove parts. Regardless of new equipment or procedures, casting operations have remained basically unchanged for hundreds of years. To begin with, a wooden pattern is made for every cast-iron piece in

| FIGURE 9.5 | Overview of Factory |

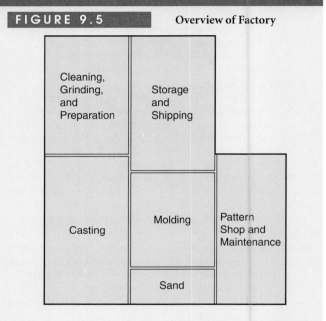

the stove. The wooden pattern is an exact duplication of the cast-iron piece that is to be manufactured. New England Castings has all of its patterns made by Precision Patterns, Inc., and these patterns are stored in the pattern shop and maintenance room. Then a specially formulated sand is molded around the wooden pattern. There can be two or more sand molds for each pattern. Mixing the sand and making the molds are done in the molding room. When the wooden pattern is removed, the resulting sand molds form a negative image of the desired casting. Next, the molds are transported to the casting room, where molten iron is poured into the molds and allowed to cool. When the iron has solidified, the molds are moved into the cleaning, grinding, and preparation room. The molds are dumped into large vibrators that shake most of the sand from the casting. The rough castings are then subjected to both sandblasting to remove the rest of the sand and grinding to finish some of the surfaces of the castings. The castings are then painted with a special heat-resistant paint, assembled into workable stoves, and inspected for manufacturing defects that may have gone undetected thus far. Finally, the finished stoves are moved to storage and shipping, where they are packaged and shipped to the appropriate locations.

At present, the pattern shop and the maintenance department are located in the same room. One large counter is used by both maintenance personnel to get tools and parts and by sand molders that need various patterns for the molding operation. Pete Nawler and Bob Bryan, who work behind the counter, are able to service a total of 10 people per hour (or about 5 per hour each). On the average, 4 people from maintenance and 3 people from the molding department arrive at the counter per hour. People from the molding department and from maintenance arrive randomly, and to be served they form a single line. Pete and Bob have always had a policy of first-come, first-served. Because of the location of the pattern shop and maintenance department, it takes about 3 minutes for a person from the maintenance department to walk to the pattern and maintenance room, and it takes about 1 minute for a person to walk from the molding department to the pattern and maintenance room.

After observing the operation of the pattern shop and maintenance room for several weeks, George decided to make some changes to the layout of the factory. An overview of these changes is shown in Figure 9.6.

Separating the maintenance shop from the pattern shop had a number of advantages. It would take people from the maintenance department only 1 minute instead of 3 to get to the new maintenance department. Using time and motion studies, George was also able to determine that improving the layout of the maintenance department would allow Bob to serve 6 people from the maintenance department per hour, and improving the layout of the pattern department would allow Pete to serve 7 people from the molding shop per hour.

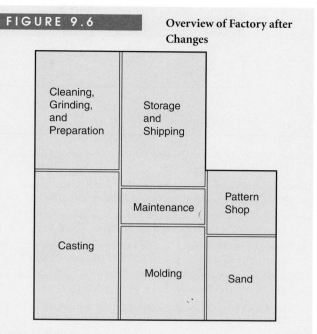

**FIGURE 9.6**    **Overview of Factory after Changes**

## Discussion Questions

1. How much time would the new layout save?
2. If maintenance personnel were paid $9.50 per hour and molding personnel were paid $11.75 per hour, how much could be saved per hour with the new factory layout?

---

# ⫸ CASE STUDY

## Winter Park Hotel

Donna Shader, manager of the Winter Park Hotel, is considering how to restructure the front desk to reach an optimum level of staff efficiency and guest service. At present, the hotel has five clerks on duty, each with a separate waiting line, during the peak check-in time of 3:00 P.M. to 5:00 P.M. Observation of arrivals during this time show that an average of 90 guests arrive each hour (although there is no upward limit on the number that could arrive at any given time). It takes an average of 3 minutes for the front-desk clerk to register each guest.

Ms. Shader is considering three plans for improving guest service by reducing the length of time guests spend waiting in line. The first proposal would designate one employee as a quick-service clerk for guests registering under corporate accounts, a market segment that fills about 30% of all occupied rooms. Because corporate guests are preregistered, their registration takes just 2 minutes. With these guests separated from the rest of the clientele, the average time for registering a typical guest would climb to 3.4 minutes. Under plan 1, noncorporate guests would choose any of the remaining four lines.

The second plan is to implement a single-line system. All guests could form a single waiting line to be served by whichever of five clerks became available. This option would require sufficient lobby space for what could be a substantial queue.

The use of an automatic teller machine (ATM) for check-ins is the basis of the third proposal. This ATM would provide approximately the same service rate as would a clerk. Given that initial use of this technology might be minimal, Shader estimated that 20% of customers, primarily frequent guests, would be willing to use the machines. (This might be a conservative estimate if the guests perceive direct benefits from using the ATM, as bank customers do. Citibank reports that some 95% of its Manhattan customers use its ATMs.) Ms. Shader would set up a single queue for customers who prefer human check-in clerks. This would be served by the five clerks, although Shader is hopeful that the machine will allow a reduction to four.

## Discussion Questions

1. Determine the average amount of time that a guest spends checking in. How would this change under each of the stated options?
2. Which option do you recommend?

## INTERNET CASE STUDY

See our Internet home page at **www.prenhall.com/render** for this
additional case study: Pantry Shopper.

## BIBLIOGRAPHY

Cooper, R. B. *Introduction to Queuing Theory*, 2/e. New York: Elsevier—
North Holland, 1980.

Grassmann, Winfried, K. "Finding the Right Number of Servers in Real-
World Queuing Systems," *Interfaces* 18, 2 (March–April 1988): 94–104.

Haksever, C., B. Render, and R. Russell. *Service Management and
Operations*, 2/e. Upper Saddle River, NJ: Prentice Hall, 2000.

Ho, C. and H. Lau. "Minimizing Total Cost in Scheduling Outpatient
Appointments," *Management Science* 38, 12 (December 1992): 17-50.

Kaplan, Edward H. "A Public Housing Queue with Reneging and Task-
Specific Servers," *Decision Sciences* 19 (1988): 383–391.

Katz, K., B. Larson and R. Larson. "Prescription for the Waiting-in-Line
Blues," *Sloan Management Review* (Winter 1991): 44–53.

Mandelbaum, A. and M. I. Reiman. "On Pooling Queuing Networks,"
*Management Science* 44, 7 (July 1998): 971–981.

Prabhu, N. U. *Foundations of Queuing Theory*. Klewer Academic
Publishers, 1997.

Quinn, Phil, Bruce Andrews, and Henry Parsons. "Allocating
Telecommunications Resources at L.L. Bean, Inc.," *Interfaces* 21, 1
(January–February 1991): 75–91.

Solomon, S. *Simulation of Waiting Lines*. Upper Saddle River, NJ: Prentice
Hall, 1983.

Swersey, Arthur J. et al. "Improving Fire Department Productivity,"
*Interfaces* 23, 1 (January–February 1993): 109–129.

Whitt, W. "Predicting Queuing Delays," *Management Science* 45, 6 (June
1999): 870–888.

Worthington, D. J. "Queuing Models for Hospital Waiting Lists," *Journal
of the Operational Research Society* 38, 5 (May 1987): 413–422.

# SIMULATION MODELING

### Simulating Volkswagen's Supply Chain

Volkswagen (VW) of America imports, markets, and distributes Volkswagens and Audis in the United States from its parent company in Germany. As part of a reengineering effort, VW developed a computer simulation model, using ProModel software, to analyze how to save money in its huge supply chain.

Since the early 1900s, vehicle distribution in the United States has followed the system introduced by Ford Motor. This structure, in which manufacturers view auto dealers as their primary customers, is so old that its original performance intentions are rarely examined. Dealers and auto manufacturers are loosely coupled, with each managing their own inventory costs. Like other manufacturers, VW encourages dealers to carry as much stock as possible but understands that too much inventory could force a dealer out of business. Dealers recognize the threatening inventory costs but know that if they don't purchase enough cars, VW may restrict supply or appoint additional dealers. The average VW dealer sells 30 cars per month and stocks fewer than 100 in inventory.

To better the chances of a customer getting his or her first choice of car, to be able to deliver that car in 48 hours, and to be able to reduce total system (dealers and VW) costs for transportation, financing and storage, VW considered a new strategy: pooling vehicles in regional depots. Rather than opening these centers and observing how well the concept worked, VW focused on simulating the flow of cars from plants to dealers. The model showed that there would be significant savings by opening its distribution centers. VW managers also learned that supply-chain performance must be viewed from the system level.[1]

---

[1] Karabakal, N., A. Gunal, and W. Ritchie. "Supply-Chain Analysis at Volkswagen of America," *Interfaces* (July–August 2000): 46–55.

## 10.1 INTRODUCTION

We are all aware to some extent of the importance of simulation models in our world. Boeing Corporation and Airbus Industries, for example, commonly build simulation models of their proposed jet aircraft and then test the aerodynamic properties of the models. Your local civil defense organization may carry out rescue and evacuation practices as it simulates the natural disaster conditions of a hurricane or tornado. The U.S. Army simulates enemy attacks and defense strategies in war games played on a computer. Business students take courses that use management games to simulate realistic competitive business situations. And thousands of organizations such as Volkswagen of America develop simulation models to assist in making decisions involving their supply chain, inventory control, maintenance scheduling, plant layout, investments, and sales forecasting. Simulation is one of the most widely used decision modeling tools. Various surveys of the largest U.S. corporations reveal that over half use simulation in corporate planning.

Simulation sounds like it may be the solution to all management problems. This is, unfortunately, by no means true. Yet we think you may find it one of the most flexible and fascinating of the decision modeling techniques in your studies. Let's begin our discussion of simulation with a simple definition.

### What Is Simulation?

*Simulate means to duplicate the features of a real system. The idea is to imitate a real-world situation with a mathematical model that does not affect operations.*

To *simulate* is to try to duplicate the features, appearance, and characteristics of a real system. In this chapter we show how to simulate a business or management system by building a *mathematical model* that comes as close as possible to representing the reality of the system. We won't build any *physical* models, as might be used in airplane wind tunnel simulation tests. But just as physical model airplanes are tested and modified under experimental conditions, our mathematical models need to be experimented with to estimate the effects of various actions. The idea behind simulation is to imitate a real-world situation mathematically, then to study its properties and operating characteristics, and finally, to draw conclusions and make action decisions based on the results of the simulation. In this way, the real-life system is not touched until the advantages and disadvantages of what may be a major policy decision are first measured on the system's model.

To use simulation, a manager should (1) define a problem, (2) introduce the variables associated with the problem, (3) construct a numerical model, (4) set up possible courses of action for testing, (5) run the experiment, (6) consider the results (possibly deciding to modify the model or change data inputs), and (7) decide what course of action to take. These steps are illustrated in Figure 10.1.

The problems tackled by simulation can range from very simple to extremely complex, from bank teller lines to an analysis of the U.S. economy. Although very small simulations can be conducted by hand, effective use of this technique requires some automated means of calculation, namely, a computer. Even large-scale models, simulating perhaps years of business decisions, can be handled in a reasonable amount of time by computer. Though simulation is one of the oldest decision modeling tools (see the History box on page 410), it was not until the introduction of computers in the mid 1940s and early 1950s that it became a practical means of solving management and military problems.

We begin this chapter with a presentation of the advantages and disadvantages of simulation. We then explain the Monte Carlo method and present several sample simulations. We also briefly discuss other simulation models besides the Monte Carlo approach.

For each simulation model, we show how Excel can be used to set up and solve the problem. In this regard, we discuss two approaches. In the first approach, we show how Excel's standard built-in functions can be used for simulation. This approach is adequate for many applications and is especially useful if you are operating in a computer environment

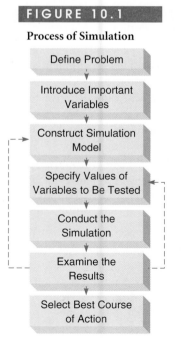

**FIGURE 10.1**

**Process of Simulation**

Define Problem

Introduce Important Variables

Construct Simulation Model

Specify Values of Variables to Be Tested

Conduct the Simulation

Examine the Results

Select Best Course of Action

## HISTORY    Simulation

The history of simulation goes back 5,000 years to Chinese war games, called *weich'i*, and continues through 1780, when the Prussians used the games to help train their army. Since then, all major military powers have used war games to test out military strategies under simulated environments.

From military or operational gaming, a new concept, *Monte Carlo simulation*, was developed as a decision modeling technique by the great mathematician John von Neumann during World War II. Working with neutrons at the Los Alamos Scientific Laboratory, von Neumann used simulation to solve physics problems that were too complex or expensive to analyze by hand or by physical model. The random nature of the neutrons suggested the use of a roulette wheel in dealing with probabilities. Because of the gaming nature, von Neumann called it the Monte Carlo model of studying laws of chance.

With the advent and common use of business computers in the 1950s, simulation grew as a management tool. Specialized computer languages were developed in the 1960s (GPSS and SIMSCRIPT) to handle large-scale problems more effectively. In the 1980s, prewritten simulation programs to handle situations ranging from queuing to inventory were developed. They have such names as ProModel, Xcell, SLAM, Witness and MAP/1.

where the installation of additional software is not preferred or possible. There are, however, several add-ins available that make setting up and solving simulation models on Excel even easier. Therefore, in our second approach, we illustrate the use of one of the more powerful Excel add-ins for simulation, Crystal Ball 2000. A student version of this package (valid for 140 days from date of installation) is included in your CD-ROM.

## 10.2   ADVANTAGES AND DISADVANTAGES OF SIMULATION

Simulation is a tool that has become widely accepted by managers for several reasons:

*These seven advantages of simulation make it one of the most widely used decision modeling techniques in corporate America.*

1. It is relatively straightforward and flexible. Properly implemented, a simulation model can be made flexible enough to easily accommodate several changes to the problem scenario.

2. It can be used to analyze large and complex real-world situations that cannot be solved by conventional decision models. For example, it may not be possible to build and solve a purely mathematical model of a city government system that incorporates important economic, social, environmental, and political factors. But simulation has been used successfully to model urban systems, hospitals, educational systems, national and state economies, and even world food systems.

3. Simulation allows what-if types of questions. With a simulation model, a manager can try out several policy decisions within a matter of minutes.

4. Simulations do not interfere with the real-world system. It may be too disruptive, for example, to experiment with new policies or ideas in a hospital, school, or manufacturing plant. With simulation, experiments are done with the model, not on the system itself.

5. Simulation allows us to study the interactive effects of individual components or variables to determine which ones are important. In any given problem scenario, not all inputs are equally important. We can use simulation to selectively vary each input (or combination of inputs) to identify the ones that most affect the results.

6. "Time compression" is possible with simulation. The effect of ordering, advertising, or other policies over many months or years can be obtained by a computer simulation model in a short time.

7. Simulation allows for the inclusion of real-world complications that most decision models cannot permit. For example, some of the queuing models discussed in Chapter 9 require exponential or Poisson distributions; the PERT analysis covered in Chapter 8 requires normal distributions. But simulation can use any probability distribution that the user defines.

*The four disadvantages of simulation are cost, its trial-and-error nature, the need to generate answers to tests, and uniqueness.*

The main disadvantages of simulation are as follows:

1. Good simulation models can be very expensive. It is often a long, complicated process to develop a model. A corporate planning model, for example, can take months or even years to develop.

2. Simulation does not generate optimal solutions to problems, as do other decision modeling techniques such as linear programming or integer programming. It is a trial-and-error approach that can produce different solutions in repeated runs.

3. Managers must generate all of the conditions and constraints for solutions that they want to examine. The simulation model does not produce answers by itself.

4. Each simulation model is unique. Its solutions and inferences are not usually transferable to other problems.

---

## ⟫⟫ MODELING IN THE REAL WORLD · U.S. Postal Service Simulates Automation

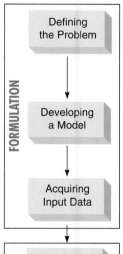

**FORMULATION**
- Defining the Problem
- Developing a Model
- Acquiring Input Data

**SOLUTION**
- Developing a Solution
- Testing the Solution

**INTERPRETATION**
- Analyzing the Results and Sensitivity Analysis
- Implementing the Results

The U.S. Postal Service (USPS) recognizes that automation technology is the only way to handle increases in mail volume, stay price competitive, and satisfy service goals. To do so, it needs to evaluate automation options: (1) on other automated or semiautomated equipment, (2) on the workforce, (3) on facilities, and (4) on other costs of operation.

Kenan Systems Corporation was hired to develop a national simulation model called META (model for evaluating technology alternatives) to quantify the effects of different automation strategies. The initial version of META took three months to develop.

Data needed were collected from the USPS technology resource and delivery services departments. They included a nationwide survey that measured 3,200 of the 150,000 city carrier routes.

Users specify inputs for the quantity and type of mail to be processed, the people/equipment used to sort the mail, the flow of mail, and unit costs. META models how the entire nationwide mail system will function with these scenarios or inputs. META is not an optimization model, but allows users to examine changes in output that result from modifying inputs.

META's simulations were submitted to a three-month period of testing and validation to ensure that scenarios run produced reliable outputs. Hundreds of META scenarios were run.

USPS uses META to analyze the effect of rate discounts, technology changes or advances, and changes to current processing operations.

The U.S. Postal Service estimates savings starting in 1995 at 100,000 work years annually, which translates into more than $4 billion. The simulation model also ensures that future technologies will be implemented in a timely and cost-effective manner.

**Sources:** M. E. Cebry, A. H. DeSilva, and F. J. DiLisio, "Management Science is Automating Postal Operations," *Interfaces* 22, 1 (January–February 1992): 110–130 and M. D. Lasky and C. T. Balbach, "Special Delivery," *OR/MS Today* 23, 6 (December 1996): 38–41.

## 10.3 MONTE CARLO SIMULATION

*The Monte Carlo method can be used with variables that are probabilistic.*

When a system contains elements that exhibit chance in their behavior, the *Monte Carlo* method of simulation may be applied. The basis of Monte Carlo simulation is experimentation on the chance (or *probabilistic*) elements through random sampling. The technique breaks down into the following simple steps. This section examines each of these steps in turn.

---

### Steps of Monte Carlo Simulation

1. Set up a probability distribution for each variable in the model that is subject to chance.
2. Using random numbers, simulate values from the probability distribution for each variable in Step 1.
3. Repeat the process for a series of *replications* or *trials*.

---

### Step 1. Establish a Probability Distribution for Each Variable

*Variables we may want to simulate abound in business problems because very little in life is certain.*

The basic idea in Monte Carlo simulation is to generate values for the variables in the model being studied. There are many variables in real-world systems that are probabilistic in nature and that we might want to simulate. A few of these variables are as follows:

- Product demand
- Lead time for orders to arrive
- Time between machine breakdowns
- Time between arrivals at a service facility
- Service time
- Time to complete a project activity
- Number of employees absent from work each day
- Stock market performance

There are several ways by which we can establish a *probability distribution* for a given variable. One common way is to examine the historical outcomes of that variable. The probability, or relative frequency, for each possible outcome of the variable is found by dividing the frequency of observation by the total number of observations.

**Harry's Auto Tire Shop Example**  Consider, for example, the monthly demand for radial tires at Harry's Auto Tire shop over the past 60 months. The data are shown in the first two columns of Table 10.1. If we assume that past demand rates will hold in the future, we can

**TABLE 10.1**

**Historical Monthly Demand for Radial Tires at Harry's Auto Tire**

| DEMAND FOR TIRES | FREQUENCY | PROBABILITY |
|---|---|---|
| 300 | 3 | 3/60 = 0.05 |
| 320 | 6 | 6/60 = 0.10 |
| 340 | 12 | 12/60 = 0.20 |
| 360 | 18 | 18/60 = 0.30 |
| 380 | 15 | 15/60 = 0.25 |
| 400 | 6 | 6/60 = 0.10 |
| | 60 | 60/60 = 1.00 |

*To establish a probability distribution for tires, we assume that historical demand is a good indicator of future outcomes.*

*Managerial estimates can also be used to identify probability distributions for variables.*

convert these data to a probability distribution. To do so, we divide each demand frequency by the total number of months, 60. This is illustrated in the third column of Table 10.1.

In addition to using historical data to estimate probabilities, managerial estimates, based on judgment and experience, can often be used to create a probability distribution for a variable. For example, a sample of sales, machine breakdowns, or service rates can be used to create probability distributions for those variables. The distributions themselves can either be empirical, as in Table 10.1, or based on commonly known distributions such as the normal, binomial, Poisson, or exponential patterns.

## Step 2: Simulate Values from the Probability Distributions

Now that we have identified the probability distribution for Harry's monthly demand of tires (see Table 10.1), how do we simulate the demand for a *specific* month? In simulating this demand for any given month, we need to ensure the following:

- The actual demand value is 300, 320, 340, 360, 380, or 400.
- There is a 5% chance that monthly demand is 300, 10% chance that it is 320, 20% chance that it is 340, 30% chance that it is 360, 25% chance that it is 380, and 10% chance that it is 400.

*Probabilities reflect long-term behavior.*

These probability values, however, reflect only the long-term behavior. That is, if we simulate tire demand for many months (several hundred, or better yet, several thousand), the demand will be 300 for exactly 5% of those months, 320 for exactly 10% of those months, and so on. Based on our knowledge of probability distributions, we can also use these probability values to compute Harry's expected value (or average) of monthly demand ($D_i$) as follows:

$$\text{Expected monthly demand} = \Sigma(\text{demand } D_i) \times (\text{probability of } D_i)$$

$$= (300)(0.05) + (320)(0.10) + (340)(0.20)$$
$$+ (360)(0.30) + (380)(0.25) + (400)(0.10)$$

$$= 358 \text{ tires}$$

*Simulated results can differ from analytical results in a short simulation.*

In the short term, however, the occurrence of demand may be quite different from these probability values. For example, if we simulate demand for just five months, it is entirely possible (and logical) for the demand to be 320 tires per month for *all* five months. The average demand for these five months would then be 320 tires per month, which is quite different from the expected value of 358 tires per month we just calculated. Hence, what we need is a procedure that will do the following:

- Generate, in the *short term*, random demand values that do not exhibit any specific pattern. The expected value need not necessarily equal 358 tires per month.
- Generate, in the *long term*, random demand values that conform exactly to the required probability distribution. The expected value must equal 358 tires per month.

**Random Numbers**  In simulation, we use *random numbers* to achieve the preceding objectives. Basically, a random number is a number that has been selected by a totally random process. For example, assume we want to generate an integer valued random number from the set 0, 1, 2, . . . , 97, 98, 99. One way to do this would be as follows:

1. Take 100 identical balls. Mark each one with a unique number between 00 and 99. Put all balls in a large bowl, and mix thoroughly.
2. Select *one* ball from the bowl. Write down the number.
3. Replace the ball in the bowl and mix again. Go back to step 2.

**TABLE 10.2**

**Table of Random Numbers**

| 52 | 06 | 50 | 88 | 53 | 30 | 10 | 47 | 99 | 37 | 66 | 91 | 35 | 32 | 00 | 84 | 57 | 07 |
| 37 | 63 | 28 | 02 | 74 | 35 | 24 | 03 | 29 | 60 | 74 | 85 | 90 | 73 | 59 | 55 | 17 | 60 |
| 82 | 57 | 68 | 28 | 05 | 94 | 03 | 11 | 27 | 79 | 90 | 87 | 92 | 41 | 09 | 25 | 36 | 77 |
| 69 | 02 | 36 | 49 | 71 | 99 | 32 | 10 | 75 | 21 | 95 | 90 | 94 | 38 | 97 | 71 | 72 | 49 |
| 98 | 94 | 90 | 36 | 06 | 78 | 23 | 67 | 89 | 85 | 29 | 21 | 25 | 73 | 69 | 34 | 85 | 76 |
| 96 | 52 | 62 | 87 | 49 | 56 | 59 | 23 | 78 | 71 | 72 | 90 | 57 | 01 | 98 | 57 | 31 | 95 |
| 33 | 69 | 27 | 21 | 11 | 60 | 95 | 89 | 68 | 48 | 17 | 89 | 34 | 09 | 93 | 50 | 44 | 51 |
| 50 | 33 | 50 | 95 | 13 | 44 | 34 | 62 | 64 | 39 | 55 | 29 | 30 | 64 | 49 | 44 | 30 | 16 |
| 88 | 32 | 18 | 50 | 62 | 57 | 34 | 56 | 62 | 31 | 15 | 40 | 90 | 34 | 51 | 95 | 26 | 14 |
| 90 | 30 | 36 | 24 | 69 | 82 | 51 | 74 | 30 | 35 | 36 | 85 | 01 | 55 | 92 | 64 | 09 | 85 |
| 50 | 48 | 61 | 18 | 85 | 23 | 08 | 54 | 17 | 12 | 80 | 69 | 24 | 84 | 92 | 16 | 49 | 59 |
| 27 | 88 | 21 | 62 | 69 | 64 | 48 | 31 | 12 | 73 | 02 | 68 | 00 | 16 | 16 | 46 | 13 | 85 |
| 45 | 14 | 46 | 32 | 13 | 49 | 66 | 62 | 74 | 41 | 86 | 98 | 92 | 98 | 84 | 54 | 33 | 40 |
| 81 | 02 | 01 | 78 | 82 | 74 | 97 | 37 | 45 | 31 | 94 | 99 | 42 | 49 | 27 | 64 | 89 | 42 |
| 66 | 83 | 14 | 74 | 27 | 76 | 03 | 33 | 11 | 97 | 59 | 81 | 72 | 00 | 64 | 61 | 13 | 52 |
| 74 | 05 | 81 | 82 | 93 | 09 | 96 | 33 | 52 | 78 | 13 | 06 | 28 | 30 | 94 | 23 | 37 | 39 |
| 30 | 34 | 87 | 01 | 74 | 11 | 46 | 82 | 59 | 94 | 25 | 34 | 32 | 23 | 17 | 01 | 58 | 73 |
| 59 | 55 | 72 | 33 | 62 | 13 | 74 | 68 | 22 | 44 | 42 | 09 | 32 | 46 | 71 | 79 | 45 | 89 |
| 67 | 09 | 80 | 98 | 99 | 25 | 77 | 50 | 03 | 32 | 36 | 63 | 65 | 75 | 94 | 19 | 95 | 88 |
| 60 | 77 | 46 | 63 | 71 | 69 | 44 | 22 | 03 | 85 | 14 | 48 | 69 | 13 | 30 | 50 | 33 | 24 |
| 60 | 08 | 19 | 29 | 36 | 72 | 30 | 27 | 50 | 64 | 85 | 72 | 75 | 29 | 87 | 05 | 75 | 01 |
| 80 | 45 | 86 | 99 | 02 | 34 | 87 | 08 | 86 | 84 | 49 | 76 | 24 | 08 | 01 | 86 | 29 | 11 |
| 53 | 84 | 49 | 63 | 26 | 65 | 72 | 84 | 85 | 63 | 26 | 02 | 75 | 26 | 92 | 62 | 40 | 67 |
| 69 | 84 | 12 | 94 | 51 | 36 | 17 | 02 | 15 | 29 | 16 | 52 | 56 | 43 | 26 | 22 | 08 | 62 |
| 37 | 77 | 13 | 10 | 02 | 18 | 31 | 19 | 32 | 85 | 31 | 94 | 81 | 43 | 31 | 58 | 33 | 51 |

**Source:** Excerpted from *A Million Random Digits with 100,000 Normal Deviates* (New York: Free Press, 1955), p. 7, with permission of the Rand Corporation.

*There are several ways to pick random numbers—tables (such as Table 10.2), a roulette wheel, and so on.*

Instead of balls in a bowl, we could have used the spin of a roulette wheel that has 100 slots to accomplish this task. Another commonly used means is to choose numbers from a table of random digits such as Table 10.2.[2] Let us see how we can use the random numbers in Table 10.2 to simulate demands in Harry's tire shop example.

**Using Random Numbers to Simulate Demand in Harry's Tire Shop**  We begin by converting the probability distribution in Table 10.1 to a *cumulative probability* distribution. As shown in Table 10.3, the cumulative probability for each demand level is the sum of the probability of that demand, and all demands *less than* that demand level. For example, the cumulative probability for a demand of 340 tires is the sum of the probabilities for 300, 320, or 340 tires. Obviously, the cumulative probability for a demand of 400 tires (the maximum demand) is 1.

*Cumulative probabilities are found by summing all the previous probabilities up to the current demand.*

---

[2] Such tables are commonly available. The random numbers in these tables are generated using computer software (which we discuss later in this chapter).

| DEMAND FOR TIRES | PROBABILITY | CUMULATIVE PROBABILITY |
|---|---|---|
| 300 | 0.05 | 0.05 |
| 320 | 0.10 | 0.05 + 0.10 = 0.15 |
| 340 | 0.20 | 0.15 + 0.20 = 0.35 |
| 360 | 0.30 | 0.35 + 0.30 = 0.65 |
| 380 | 0.25 | 0.65 + 0.25 = 0.90 |
| 400 | 0.10 | 0.90 + 0.10 = 1.00 |

*We create a random number interval for each value of the variable.*

We now use these cumulative probabilities to help assign random numbers. Observe that the random numbers in Table 10.2 are two-digit numbers ranging from 00 to 99. That is, there are 100 different random numbers possible. We create *random number intervals* by assigning these 100 random numbers to represent the different possible demand values. Since there is a 5% probability that demand is 300 tires, we assign 5% of the random numbers to denote this level of demand. That is, we want to assign 5 of the 100 possible random numbers (between 00 and 99) to a demand of 300 tires. For example, we could assign the first five random numbers possible (i.e., 00, 01, 02, 03, and 04) to denote a demand of 300 tires. Every time one of these random numbers is drawn, the simulated demand that month would be 300 tires. Likewise, since there is a 10% chance that demand is 320 tires, we could let the next ten random numbers (i.e., 05 to 14) represent that demand—and so on for the other demand levels. The complete random number intervals for Harry's tire shop example are shown in Table 10.4.

*We simulate values by comparing the random numbers against the random number intervals.*

To simulate demand using these random number intervals, we now select random numbers from Table 10.2. Assume we start with the random number at the top row of the first column and proceed along that row. The first random number is 52 (which is between 35 and 64). This implies the simulated demand is 360 tires in month 1. The second number is 06 (which is between 05 and 14). This implies the simulated demand is 320 tires in month 2, and so on.

## Step 3: Repeat the Process for a Series of Trials

As noted earlier, it would be very risky to draw any hard and fast conclusion regarding a simulation model from only a few simulation trials. For example, although the expected demand is 358 tires per month in Harry's example, it is likely that we will get different values for the average from a short simulation (of just a few months). Hence, we need to run the simulation model for several thousand trials (also referred to as *replications*) in order to gather meaningful results.

*A simulation process must be repeated numerous times to get meaningful results.*

| DEMAND FOR TIRES | PROBABILITY | CUMULATIVE PROBABILITY | RANDOM NUMBER INTERVAL |
|---|---|---|---|
| 300 | 0.05 | 0.05 | 00 to 04 |
| 320 | 0.10 | 0.15 | 05 to 14 |
| 340 | 0.20 | 0.35 | 15 to 34 |
| 360 | 0.30 | 0.65 | 35 to 64 |
| 380 | 0.25 | 0.90 | 65 to 89 |
| 400 | 0.10 | 1.00 | 90 to 99 |

Miami's Jackson Memorial Hospital, Florida's largest with 1,576 inpatient beds, is also one of the United States' finest. In June 1996, it received the highest accreditation score of any public sector hospital in the country. Jackson's Department of Management Systems Engineering is constantly seeking ways of increasing hospital efficiency, and the construction of new operating rooms (ORs) prompted the development of a simulation of the existing 31 ORs.

The OR boundary includes the Holding Area and the Recovery Area, all of which were experiencing problems due to ineffective scheduling of OR services. A simulation study, modeled using the ARENA software package, sought to maximize the current use of OR rooms and staff. Inputs to the model included (1) the amount of time a patient waits in holding, (2) the specific process the patient undergoes, (3) the staff schedule, (4) room availability, and (5) time of day.

The first hurdle that the research team had to deal with at Jackson was the vast amount of records to scour so as to extract information for the probabilistic simulation model. The second hurdle was the *quality* of the data. A thorough analysis of the records determined which were good and which had to be discarded. In the end, Jackson's carefully screened databases led to a good set of model inputs. The simulation model then successfully developed five measures of OR performance: (1) number of procedures a day, (2) average case time, (3) staff utilization, (4) room utilization, and (5) average waiting time in the holding area.

**Source:** M. A. Centeno et al. "Challenges of Simulating Hospital Facilities," *Proceedings of the 12th Annual Conference of the Production and Operations Management Society.* Orlando, FL, March 2001.

## 10.4  ROLE OF COMPUTERS IN SIMULATION

Although it is possible to simulate small examples by hand, it is easier and much more convenient to conduct most simulation exercises using a computer. Three of the primary reasons for this follow:

*Software packages have built-in procedures for simulating from several different probability distributions.*

1. Although it is relatively easy to generate random values by hand from simple probability distributions (e.g., in Harry's tire example), it is quite cumbersome to do so when dealing with more complicated probability distributions. In fact, simulating by hand—even from common distributions such as the normal, Poisson, and binomial—is cumbersome. Most computer software packages have built-in procedures for generation of random numbers. Using these *random number generators*, it is quite easy to simulate values from many probability distributions using a software package.

2. In order for the simulation results to be valid and useful, it is necessary to replicate the process hundreds (or even thousands) of times. Doing this by hand is laborious and time-consuming. In contrast, it is possible to simulate thousands of trials for a model in just a matter of seconds using most software packages.

*Software packages allow us to easily replicate the model and keep track of several output measures.*

3. During the simulation process, depending on the complexity and scope of the model, we may need to keep track of several input parameters as well as output statistics. Here again, doing so by hand could become very cumbersome. Software packages, on the other hand, can be used to easily track as many measures as required in any simulation model.

### Types of Simulation Software Packages

There are three types of software packages that are available to help set up and run simulation models on computers, as discussed in the following sections.

*The use of simulation has been broadened by the availability of computing technology.*

**General-Purpose Programming Languages**  These include standard programming languages such as Visual Basic, C++, and FORTRAN. The main advantage of these languages is that an experienced programmer can use them to develop simulation models for many diverse situations. The big disadvantage, however, is that the models are not easily portable.

That is, the simulation model developed for one problem or situation may not be easily transferable to a different situation.

*Special purpose simulation languages have several advantages over general purpose languages.*

**Special-Purpose Simulation Languages and Programs** These include languages such as GPSS/H, Simscript II.5, SLAM II, GASP, and programs such as Extend, MicroSaint, BuildSim, AweSim, ProModel, and Xcell. Using such special-purpose languages and programs has three advantages when compared with general-purpose languages: (1) they require less programming time for large simulations, (2) they are usually more efficient and easier to check for errors, and (3) they have built-in procedures to automate many of the tasks in simulation modeling.

**Spreadsheet Models** The built-in ability to generate random numbers and use them to select values from several probability distributions makes spreadsheets excellent tools for conducting simulations. Spreadsheets are also very powerful for quickly tabulating results and presenting them using graphs. In keeping with the focus of this textbook, we use Excel (and Excel add-ins) in the remainder of this chapter to develop several simulation models.

*We focus on building simulation models using Excel in this chapter.*

## Random Generation from Probability Distributions Using Excel

In what follows, we define a few commonly used probability distributions in simulation models, and Excel's built-in commands for generating random values from these distributions.

*Excel's RAND function generates random numbers.*

**Generating Random Numbers in Excel** Excel uses the *RAND* function to generate random numbers. The format for using this function is

$$=\text{RAND}()$$

Note that the "=" sign before the RAND function implies that the cell entry is a formula. Also, there is no argument within the parentheses; that is, the left parenthesis is immediately followed by the right parenthesis.

If we enter =RAND() in any cell of a spreadsheet, it will return a random value between 0 and 1 (actually, between 0 and 0.9999 . . . ), *each time you press the calculate key* (F9 key). The RAND function can be used either by itself in a cell, or as part of a formula. For example, if we wish to generate a random number between 0 and 4.9999 . . . , the appropriate formula to use would simply be

$$=5*\text{RAND}()$$

*Uniform distributions can either be discrete or continuous.*

**Uniform Distribution** Assume we want to model a variable that follows a uniform distribution between $a$ and $b$. That is, all values between $a$ and $b$ are equally likely. If the variable is allowed to take on fractional values between $a$ and $b$, we refer to this as a *continuous uniform distribution*. In contrast, if only integer values are allowed between $a$ and $b$ (inclusive), we refer to this as a *discrete uniform distribution*.

For continuous uniform distributions, we use the following formula:

$$=a+(b-a)*\text{RAND}()$$

For example, if $a = 3$ and $b = 9$, we know that =(9−3)*RAND() will generate a random value between 0 and 5.9999. . . . If we add this to 3, we will get a random value between 3 and 8.999 . . . (which, for all practical purposes, is 9).

For discrete uniform distributions, there are two different formulas we can use in Excel. First, we can extend the preceding formula by including Excel's INT function. Note

*Two ways of simulating from a discrete uniform distribution.*

that we need to add 1 to the $(b - a)$ term since the INT function always rounds down (i.e., it just drops the fractional part from the value). The resulting formula is

$$=INT(a+(b-a+1)*(RAND()))$$

Alternatively, we can use a built-in function in Excel called *RANDBETWEEN* to generate random values from discrete uniform distributions between *a* and *b*. The format for this function is

$$=RANDBETWEEN(a,b)$$

**Normal Distribution** The normal distribution is probably one of the more commonly used distributions in simulation models. The normal distribution is always identified by two parameters: mean $\mu$ and standard deviation $\sigma$ (or variance $\sigma^2$). To simulate a random value from a normal distribution with mean $\mu$ and standard deviation $\sigma$, we use the following formula in Excel:

*Excel's NORMINV function can be used to simulate from a normal distribution.*

$$=NORMINV(RAND(),\mu,\sigma)$$

For example, the formula =NORMINV(RAND(),30,5) will generate a random value from a normal distribution with a mean of 30 and a standard deviation of 5. If we repeat this process several thousand times, 50% of the values will be below 30 and 50% will be above 30, 68.26% will be between 25 and 35 (=mean $\pm$ 1 standard deviation), and so on.

*Excel's LN function can be used to simulate from an exponential distribution.*

**Exponential Distribution** As we saw in Chapter 9, the exponential distribution is commonly used in analyzing queuing systems. To simulate a random value from an exponential distribution with mean $\mu$ (i.e., the average time between successive occurrences is $\mu$), we use the following formula in Excel:

$$=-\mu*LN(RAND())$$

*Excel's IF function can be used to select from two possible outcomes.*

**General Discrete Distribution with Two Outcomes** Assume that the number of females in a population is 45%. This implies that if we draw a random individual from this population, the probability the individual will be female is 45%. The probability the individual will be male is 55%. To simulate these random draws in Excel, we use the IF function as follows:

$$=IF(RAND()<0.45, \text{``Female''}, \text{``Male''})$$

Note that the quotes are needed in the IF function since Female and Male are both text characters. If we used numerical codes (e.g., 1=Female, 2=Male) instead, the formula would be

$$=IF(RAND()<0.45,1,2)$$

*Random numbers can actually be assigned in many different ways—as long as they represent the correct proportion of the outcomes.*

Since RAND() has a 45% chance of returning a value between 0 and 0.45 (which implies it has a 55% chance of returning a value between 0.45 and 0.999 . . . ), the above formula is logical. Note that we could have set up the IF function such that *any* 45% of values between 0 and 1 denotes female, and the other 55% denotes male. For example, we could have expressed the formula as follows:

$$=IF(RAND()<0.55, \text{``Male''}, \text{``Female''})$$

If we replicate the simulation enough times, the female to male split will be the same regardless of how the IF function is set up (i.e., the long-term result will be 45% female and 55% male).

*Probability of Demand for Radial Tires*

| Demand | Probability |
|--------|-------------|
| 300 | 0.05 |
| 320 | 0.10 |
| 340 | 0.20 |
| 360 | 0.30 |
| 380 | 0.25 |
| 400 | 0.10 |

**General Discrete Distribution with More Than Two Outcomes**  Let us now reconsider the demand for tires in Harry's auto shop example (Table 10.1 is repeated in the margin for your convenience.) The demand is one of six values, namely, 300, 320, 340, 360, 380, or 400. Unlike the discrete uniform distribution, however, the probability of demand being each value is not the same. We refer to such distributions as *general discrete distributions*.

We want to use Excel to simulate demands randomly from this distribution, just as we did manually in Table 10.4 (on page 415) using random number intervals. To do so, we can use *nested* IF functions (i.e., IF statements within IF statements) to model the distribution. However, it is more convenient to use Excel's VLOOKUP, HLOOKUP, or LOOKUP functions to randomly select values from this type of probability distribution. In our discussion here, we illustrate the use of the *VLOOKUP* function.

---

### Excel Notes

■  The CD-ROM that accompanies this textbook contains the Excel file for each example problem discussed here. The relevant file name is shown in the margin next to each example.

■  For clarity, our simulation worksheets are color coded as follows:
   *input cells*, where we enter known data, are shaded yellow.
   *simulation cells*, which show simulated values, are shaded blue.
   *output cells*, where the results are shown, are shaded green.

■  Although these colors are not apparent in the screen captures shown in the textbook, they are seen in the Excel files in your CD-ROM.

■  When you open any of the Excel files for the examples in this chapter, Excel will automatically recalculate all random numbers in the model (if the calculation option in Excel is set to Automatic). This, in turn, will cause all simulated values in the worksheet to change. Hence, the values you see in the Excel file will not be the same as those shown in the screen captures included in the textbook.

■  *Tip:* After creating a simulation model, if you wish to save your results in such a way that the values do *not* change each time you open the Excel file, you can use the Paste Values feature in Excel (see Appendix A for details). Copy the cells showing the results and use Paste Values to save your answers as values rather than as formulas. Remember, however, that any cell overwritten in this manner will no longer contain the formula. Alternatively, you can set the calculation option in Excel to Manual.

---

*Excel's VLOOKUP function can be used to simulate from a general discrete distribution.*

**File: 10-1.xls**

*We use random number intervals in this simulation.*

The Excel layout showing the formulas for setting up a VLOOKUP function is shown in Program 10.1A. We begin by arranging all the demand values in *ascending* order in a column (say, column C). Titles, like the ones shown in row 1, are optional. We then list the probability of each demand in another column (say, column D). In Program 10.1A, we have shown the demand values in cells C2:C7 and the probabilities in cells D2:D7.

Just as we did in Table 10.4, we now create the *random number intervals*. The only difference is that instead of using two-digit random numbers from 00 to 99, we use continuous-valued random numbers from 0.00 to 0.9999. The formulas to compute the random number intervals for Harry's tire example are shown in cells A2:B7 of Program 10.1A. The actual values are shown in Program 10.1B. Note that the lower limit numbers in cells A2:A7 are identical to the ones we developed in Table 10.4. (The upper limit numbers are slightly different since we used discrete random numbers in Table 10.4 and we are using continuous-valued random numbers here.) It is very important to note that we have specified the random number intervals in columns *preceding* (i.e., to the left of) the column with the demand values. For example, since the demands are shown in column C in Program 10.1B, we have placed the random number intervals in columns A and B.

**PROGRAM 10.1A**

**Excel Layout and Formulas for VLOOKUP Function**

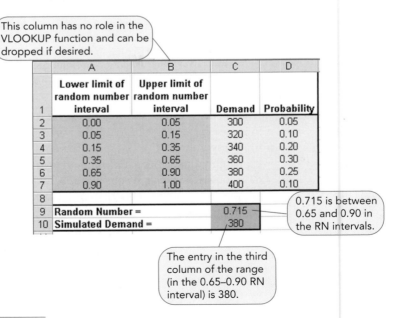

| | A | B | C | D |
|---|---|---|---|---|
| 1 | **Lower limit of random number interval** | **Upper limit of random number interval** | **Demand** | **Probability** |
| 2 | 0 | =A2+D2 | 300 | 0.05 |
| 3 | =B2 | =A3+D3 | 320 | 0.1 |
| 4 | =B3 | =A4+D4 | 340 | 0.2 |
| 5 | =B4 | =A5+D5 | 360 | 0.3 |
| 6 | =B5 | =A6+D6 | 380 | 0.25 |
| 7 | =B6 | =A7+D7 | 400 | 0.1 |
| 8 | | | | |
| 9 | **Random Number =** | | =RAND() | |
| 10 | **Simulated Demand =** | | =VLOOKUP(C9,A2:C7,3) | |

*Entries in these two columns are known values.*

*RAND() function generates a random number between 0 and 1.*

*Random number*

*The first column in the range must contain lower limits of RN intervals.*

*This is the column number in the range that contains the variable values.*

*The first column in the VLOOKUP range must contain the lower limits of the random number intervals.*

The format for the VLOOKUP function is

$$=\text{VLOOKUP}(\text{RAND}(),\text{A2:C7},3)$$

The first column in the range A2:C7 must contain the lower limits of the random number intervals (column A in Program 10.1B). Excel takes the value generated by the RAND() function and proceeds down this column until the RAND() value exceeds the lower limit. It then moves to the third column (specified by the "3" in the arguments for the VLOOKUP function) in the range A2:C7 and selects the value there. In our case, the third column (column C) has the demand value that we wish to simulate.[3]

**PROGRAM 10.1B**

**Simulation Using a VLOOKUP Function**

*This column has no role in the VLOOKUP function and can be dropped if desired.*

| | A | B | C | D |
|---|---|---|---|---|
| 1 | **Lower limit of random number interval** | **Upper limit of random number interval** | **Demand** | **Probability** |
| 2 | 0.00 | 0.05 | 300 | 0.05 |
| 3 | 0.05 | 0.15 | 320 | 0.10 |
| 4 | 0.15 | 0.35 | 340 | 0.20 |
| 5 | 0.35 | 0.65 | 360 | 0.30 |
| 6 | 0.65 | 0.90 | 380 | 0.25 |
| 7 | 0.90 | 1.00 | 400 | 0.10 |
| 8 | | | | |
| 9 | **Random Number =** | | 0.715 | |
| 10 | **Simulated Demand =** | | 380 | |

*0.715 is between 0.65 and 0.90 in the RN intervals.*

*The entry in the third column of the range (in the 0.65–0.90 RN interval) is 380.*

---

[3] Note that the upper limit of the random number interval (column B) played no role in the VLOOKUP function. In fact, it is not necessary to even show this column, and we can safely delete it. However, we recommend that you include it since it makes it easier to understand the simulation. We show this column in all our models.

## TABLE 10.5

**Simulation from Various Probability Distributions Using Excel's Built-In Functions**

| TO SIMULATE | USE BUILT-IN EXCEL FORMULA |
|---|---|
| **Random Number** | =RAND() |
| **Continuous Uniform Distribution** Between $a$ and $b$ | =$a$+($b$−$a$)*RAND() |
| **Discrete Uniform Distribution** Between $a$ and $b$ | =INT($a$+($b$−$a$ + 1)*RAND()) |
| **Discrete Uniform Distribution** Between $a$ and $b$ | =RANDBETWEEN($a$,$b$) |
| **Normal Distribution** Mean = $\mu$; Standard deviation = $\sigma$ | =NORMINV(RAND(),$\mu$,$\sigma$) |
| **Exponential Distribution** Mean = $\mu$ | =−$\mu$*LN(RAND()) |
| **General Discrete Distribution** **Two outcomes only**. $A$ and $B$. Probability of outcome $A = p$ | =IF(RAND()<$p$, $A$, $B$) |
| **General Discrete Distribution** **More than two outcomes** *Range* = Cell range containing probability and variable values. First column must contain the lower limits of the random number intervals. *Column* = Column number in the range which contains the variable values. | =VLOOKUP(RAND(), *Range*, *Column*) |

The values of this simulation are shown in Program 10.1B. Using the preceding logic, if the random number is 0.715 (shown in cell C9), the VLOOKUP function returns a demand of 380 (shown in cell C10).[4]

*Summary of Excel's built-in functions used in simulation.*

Table 10.5 presents a summary of the Excel formulas we have presented so far. In what follows, we describe two simulation models that use some of these formulas for their implementation.

## 10.5  USING SIMULATION TO COMPUTE EXPECTED PROFIT

*Table 10.1 Revisited*

| Demand | Probability |
|---|---|
| 300 | 0.05 |
| 320 | 0.10 |
| 340 | 0.20 |
| 360 | 0.30 |
| 380 | 0.25 |
| 400 | 0.10 |

*Demand, selling price, and profit margin are all probabilistic.*

Let us begin our discussion of simulation using Harry's auto tire example. Recall from Table 10.1 that Harry's monthly demand of auto tires is 300, 320, 340, 360, 380, or 400, with specific probabilities for each value. Assume the following additional information is known regarding Harry's operating environment:

■ The average selling price of tires each month varies, based on competitors' prices and other market conditions. Harry estimates that his average selling price per tire in a month follows a discrete uniform distribution between $60 and $80 (in increments of $1).

■ The average profit margin per tire each month also varies based on market conditions. Using past data, Harry estimates that his profit margin per tire follows a continuous uniform distribution between 20% and 30%.

■ Harry estimates that his fixed operating cost is $2,000 per month.

Using this information, let us simulate and calculate Harry's *average profit* per month from the sale of auto tires.

---

[4] For this example, we show the value of the random number separately in cell C9 and use this number in cell C10. Note that the RAND() function could have been directly embedded in the VLOOKUP formula itself. Except for the simulation model discussed in Section 10.5, we do not show the random number values separately in our discussions.

**IN ACTION**    Using Simulation at Mexico's Largest Truck Manufacturer

The manufacturing world has gone global. To remain competitive, firms have made strategic and cultural alliances. Mexico is the United States' third-largest trading partner ($27 billion), after Canada and Japan. Trading breakthroughs, such as the North American Economic Community (NAEC), have fundamental implications for industries in the United States and Mexico, including the truck manufacturer Vilpac headquartered in Mexicali, Mexico.

Vilpac developed a comprehensive simulation model for the analysis and design of its manufacturing operation using SIMNET II (a network-based simulation language on an IBM 3090 supercomputer). The idea was to allow manufacturing engineers to experiment with alternative systems and strategies to seek the best overall factory performance.

Ninety-five machines and 1,900 parts were included in the model, which performed a wide variety of experiments. SIMNET II was used to study the effects of policies on (1) the flexibility of the factory to adapt to change in the demand and product mix, (2) the factory's responsiveness to customer orders, (3) product quality, and (4) total cost. Benefits of the simulation approach included a 260% increase in production, a 70% decrease in work-in-process, and an increase in market share.

**Source:** J. P. Nuno et al. "Mexico's Vilpac Truck Company Uses a CIM Implementation to Become a World Class Manufacturer," *Interfaces* 23, 1 (January–February 1993): 59–75.

**File: 10-2.xls**

FIGURE 10.2

**Flowchart for Harry's Auto Tire Simulation Model**

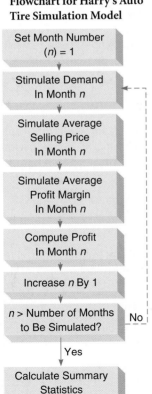

## Setting Up the Model

The logic of the simulation process to answer this question is presented in Figure 10.2. Such *flow diagrams* or *flowcharts* are useful to understand the coding procedures for simulation.

Let us now take the flowchart in Figure 10.2 and translate it into a simulation model using Excel. The formula view of the Excel layout for Harry's problem is presented in Program 10.2A. All titles, like the ones shown in rows 1 and 3, are optional. The spreadsheet is organized as follows:

■ Column A shows the month number.

■ Column B shows the random number used to simulate the demand that month. For this model alone, we show the actual value of the random number used to simulate each variable value.

■ The random number in column B is used in a VLOOKUP function to simulate the monthly demand in column C. The data (random number intervals, demands, and probabilities) of the VLOOKUP function are shown in cells I4:L9.

■ In column D, we simulate the average selling price per tire using the *RANDBETWEEN* function (with $a = 60$ and $b = 80$). The formula is: *=RANDBETWEEN(60,80)*

■ Column E shows the random number used to simulate the average profit margin per tire.

■ The random number in column E is used in column F to simulate the average profit margin per tire. For this, we use the continuous uniform distribution formula, with $a = 0.20$ and $b = 0.30$. The formula is: *=0.2+(0.3−0.2)RAND()*

■ Using all the simulated values, Harry's monthly profit is calculated in column G as

$$\text{Profit} = (\text{Demand for tires}) \times (\text{average selling price per tire})$$
$$\times (\text{average profit margin per tire}) - (\text{monthly fixed cost})$$

Cell G4, for example, shows the profit in month 1. Clearly, due to the presence of random numbers, this value will change each time the simulation is replicated (i.e., it will change each time the F9 key is pressed in Excel). Hence, it would be incorrect to estimate Harry's profit based on just this one month.

**PROGRAM 10.2A**  **Excel Layout and Formulas for Harry's Auto Tire Shop**

Use the VLOOKUP function to simulate from a general discrete distribution.

Use the RANDBETWEEN function to simulate from a discrete uniform distribution.

Continuous uniform distribution between 0.2 and 0.3

| | A | B | C | D | E | F | G | H | I | J | K | L |
|---|---|---|---|---|---|---|---|---|---|---|---|---|
| 1 | **Harry's Auto Tire Shop** | | | | | | | | | | | |
| 2 | | | | | | | | | | **Demand Distribution** | | |
| 3 | Month | Random number 1 | Demand | Selling price | Random number 2 | Margin | Profit | | RN interval lower limit | RN interval upper limit | Demand | Proba-bility |
| 4 | 1 | =RAND() | =VLOOKUP(B4,$I$4:$K$9,3) | =RANDBETWEEN(60,80) | =RAND() | =0.2+(0.3-0.2)*E4 | =C4*D4*F4-2000 | | 0 | =I4+L4 | 300 | 0.05 |
| 5 | 2 | =RAND() | =VLOOKUP(B5,$I$4:$K$9,3) | =RANDBETWEEN(60,80) | =RAND() | =0.2+(0.3-0.2)*E5 | =C5*D5*F5-2000 | | =J4 | =I5+L5 | 320 | 0.1 |
| 6 | 3 | =RAND() | =VLOOKUP(B6,$I$4:$K$9,3) | =RANDBETWEEN(60,80) | =RAND() | =0.2+(0.3-0.2)*E6 | =C6*D6*F6-2000 | | =J5 | =I6+L6 | 340 | 0.2 |
| 7 | 4 | =RAND() | =VLOOKUP(B7,$I$4:$K$9,3) | =RANDBETWEEN(60,80) | =RAND() | =0.2+(0.3-0.2)*E7 | =C7*D7*F7-2000 | | =J6 | =I7+L7 | 360 | 0.3 |
| 8 | 5 | =RAND() | =VLOOKUP(B8,$I$4:$K$9,3) | =RANDBETWEEN(60,80) | =RAND() | =0.2+(0.3-0.2)*E8 | =C8*D8*F8-2000 | | =J7 | =I8+L8 | 380 | 0.25 |
| 9 | 6 | =RAND() | =VLOOKUP(B9,$I$4:$K$9,3) | =RANDBETWEEN(60,80) | =RAND() | =0.2+(0.3-0.2)*E9 | =C9*D9*F9-2000 | | =J8 | =I9+L9 | 400 | 0.1 |
| 10 | 7 | =RAND() | =VLOOKUP(B10,$I$4:$K$9,3) | =RANDBETWEEN(60,80) | =RAND() | =0.2+(0.3-0.2)*E10 | =C10*D10*F10-2000 | | | | | |
| 11 | 8 | =RAND() | =VLOOKUP(B11,$I$4:$K$9,3) | =RANDBETWEEN(60,80) | =RAND() | =0.2+(0.3-0.2)*E11 | =C11*D11*F11-2000 | | | | | |
| 12 | 9 | =RAND() | =VLOOKUP(B12,$I$4:$K$9,3) | =RANDBETWEEN(60,80) | =RAND() | =0.2+(0.3-0.2)*E12 | =C12*D12*F12-2000 | | | | | |
| 13 | 10 | =RAND() | =VLOOKUP(B13,$I$4:$K$9,3) | =RANDBETWEEN(60,80) | =RAND() | =0.2+(0.3-0.2)*E13 | =C13*D13*F13-2000 | | | | | |
| 14 | 11 | =RAND() | =VLOOKUP(B14,$I$4:$K$9,3) | =RANDBETWEEN(60,80) | =RAND() | =0.2+(0.3-0.2)*E14 | =C14*D14*F14-2000 | | | | | |
| 15 | 12 | =RAND() | =VLOOKUP(B15,$I$4:$K$9,3) | =RANDBETWEEN(60,80) | =RAND() | =0.2+(0.3-0.2)*E15 | =C15*D15*F15-2000 | | | | | |
| 16 | 13 | =RAND() | =VLOOKUP(B16,$I$4:$K$9,3) | =RANDBETWEEN(60,80) | =RAND() | =0.2+(0.3-0.2)*E16 | =C16*D16*F16-2000 | | | | | |
| 17 | 14 | =RAND() | =VLOOKUP(B17,$I$4:$K$9,3) | =RANDBETWEEN(60,80) | =RAND() | =0.2+(0.3-0.2)*E17 | =C17*D17*F17-2000 | | | | | |
| 18 | 15 | =RAND() | =VLOOKUP(B18,$I$4:$K$9,3) | =RANDBETWEEN(60,80) | =RAND() | =0.2+(0.3-0.2)*E18 | =C18*D18*F18-2000 | | | | | |
| 194 | 191 | =RAND() | =VLOOKUP(B194,$I$4:$K$9,3) | =RANDBETWEEN(60,80) | =RAND() | =0.2+(0.3-0.2)*E194 | =C194*D194*F194-2000 | | | | | |
| 195 | 192 | =RAND() | =VLOOKUP(B195,$I$4:$K$9,3) | =RANDBETWEEN(60,80) | =RAND() | =0.2+(0.3-0.2)*E195 | =C195*D195*F195-2000 | | | | | |
| 196 | 193 | =RAND() | =VLOOKUP(B196,$I$4:$K$9,3) | =RANDBETWEEN(60,80) | =RAND() | =0.2+(0.3-0.2)*E196 | =C196*D196*F196-2000 | | | | | |
| 197 | 194 | =RAND() | =VLOOKUP(B197,$I$4:$K$9,3) | =RANDBETWEEN(60,80) | =RAND() | =0.2+(0.3-0.2)*E197 | =C197*D197*F197-2000 | | | | | |
| 198 | 195 | =RAND() | =VLOOKUP(B198,$I$4:$K$9,3) | =RANDBETWEEN(60,80) | =RAND() | =0.2+(0.3-0.2)*E198 | =C198*D198*F198-2000 | | | | | |
| 199 | 196 | =RAND() | =VLOOKUP(B199,$I$4:$K$9,3) | =RANDBETWEEN(60,80) | =RAND() | =0.2+(0.3-0.2)*E199 | =C199*D199*F199-2000 | | | | | |
| 200 | 197 | =RAND() | =VLOOKUP(B200,$I$4:$K$9,3) | =RANDBETWEEN(60,80) | =RAND() | =0.2+(0.3-0.2)*E200 | =C200*D200*F200-2000 | | | | | |
| 201 | 198 | =RAND() | =VLOOKUP(B201,$I$4:$K$9,3) | =RANDBETWEEN(60,80) | =RAND() | =0.2+(0.3-0.2)*E201 | =C201*D201*F201-2000 | | | | | |
| 202 | 199 | =RAND() | =VLOOKUP(B202,$I$4:$K$9,3) | =RANDBETWEEN(60,80) | =RAND() | =0.2+(0.3-0.2)*E202 | =C202*D202*F202-2000 | | | | | |
| 203 | 200 | =RAND() | =VLOOKUP(B203,$I$4:$K$9,3) | =RANDBETWEEN(60,80) | =RAND() | =0.2+(0.3-0.2)*E203 | =C203*D203*F203-2000 | | | | | |
| 204 | | | | | | Average Profit = | =AVERAGE(G4:G203) | | | | | |
| 205 | | | | | | Standard Deviation of Profit = | =STDEV(G4:G203) | | | | | |
| 206 | | | | | | Number of months with Profit >= 4000 = | =COUNTIF(G4:G203,">=4000") | | | | | |
| 207 | | | | | | Probability that Profit >= 4000 = | =G206/COUNT(G4:G203) | | | | | |

Parameters for the VLOOKUP function in column C

Random number, used in column F to simulate profit margin

This counts number of months with profit >$4,000.

Rows 19 to 193 have been hidden here. See CD-ROM file for full model.

Random number, used in column C to simulate demand

## Replicating the Model

To calculate Harry's *average* monthly profit, we need to replicate the simulation model several thousand times. However, for illustration purposes, we use only 200 replications of Harry's simulation model here.[5] We then compute the average based on these 200 profit values. Note that, in practice, 200 replications are not enough for the model to give consistent results. That is, an average based on just 200 replications will be different every time we run the simulation model.

*For small models, we can simply copy the model several times.*

In problems (such as this one) in which the simulation model consists of just a single row, the easiest way to perform 200 replications is to copy all *formulas* and *values* in that row 200 times. In Program 10.2A, for example, we have copied all entries in row 4 to rows 5 through 203. *Note*: Some of the rows in Program 10.2A (and a few other screen captures in this chapter) are hidden for brevity. See the CD-ROM for the full files.

---

[5] Note that there is nothing magical about our choice of 200 for the number of replications. We have selected it only for convenience and to make our spreadsheets concise. In practice, you should replicate your model as many times as convenient.

## Analyzing the Results

The values resulting from the formulas in Program 10.2A are shown in Program 10.2B. Due to the use of random numbers (shown in columns B and E) in the formulas, we see that the values of the simulated variables are different in each row (replication). Cells G4 to G203 show the monthly profit for 200 replications (months). We can now calculate the following statistics. (Values in your CD-ROM file may be different since Excel generates new random numbers each time the file is opened.)

Average monthly profit (cell G204) = $4,277.89

Standard deviation of monthly profit (cell G205) = $1024.88

*The simulation results can be used to compute several output measures.*

We can also calculate several other measures of performance. For example, suppose Harry estimates that in order to survive, he needs to get a monthly profit of at least $4,000 from his shop. What is the probability that Harry will get this level of profit? To answer this question, we first count the number of months (of the 200 months) in which Harry's profit exceeds $4,000. As shown in cell G206 of Program 10.2A, Excel's COUNTIF function can be used to do this. Then, we divide this count by 200 to get the probability value (cell

**PROGRAM 10.2B**        **Results for the Simulation Model of Harry's Auto Tire Shop**

Random number used to simulate profit margin

Random number used to simulate demand

| | A | B | C | D | E | F | G | H | I | J | K | L |
|---|---|---|---|---|---|---|---|---|---|---|---|---|
| 1 | Harry's Auto Tire Shop | | | | | | | | | | | |
| 2 | | | | | | | | | | Demand Distribution | | |
| 3 | Month | Random number 1 | Demand | Selling price | Random number 2 | Margin | Profit | | RN interval lower limit | RN interval upper limit | Demand | Probability |
| 4 | 1 | 0.215 | 340 | $62.00 | 0.150 | 21.50% | $2,531.82 | | 0.00 | 0.05 | 300 | 0.05 |
| 5 | 2 | 0.477 | 360 | $65.00 | 0.375 | 23.75% | $3,557.77 | | 0.05 | 0.15 | 320 | 0.10 |
| 6 | 3 | 0.309 | 340 | $70.00 | 0.583 | 25.83% | $4,147.69 | | 0.15 | 0.35 | 340 | 0.20 |
| 7 | 4 | 0.018 | 300 | $72.00 | 0.448 | 24.48% | $3,288.40 | | 0.35 | 0.65 | 360 | 0.30 |
| 8 | 5 | 0.817 | 380 | $70.00 | 0.550 | 25.50% | $4,782.26 | | 0.65 | 0.90 | 380 | 0.25 |
| 9 | 6 | 0.482 | 360 | $71.00 | 0.788 | 27.88% | $5,126.56 | | 0.90 | 1.00 | 400 | 0.10 |
| 10 | 7 | 0.628 | 360 | $80.00 | 0.692 | 26.92% | $5,752.12 | | | | | |
| 11 | 8 | 0.802 | 380 | $61.00 | 0.426 | 24.26% | $3,622.92 | | | | | |
| 12 | 9 | 0.788 | 380 | $71.00 | 0.404 | 24.04% | $4,485.97 | | | | | |
| 13 | 10 | 0.247 | 340 | $80.00 | 0.800 | 28.00% | $5,615.38 | | | | | |
| 14 | 11 | 0.724 | 380 | $75.00 | 0.231 | 22.31% | $4,357.30 | | | | | |
| 15 | 12 | 0.868 | 380 | $78.00 | 0.265 | 22.65% | $4,712.84 | | | | | |
| 16 | 13 | 0.569 | 360 | $69.00 | 0.342 | 23.42% | $3,818.00 | | | | | |
| 17 | 14 | 0.310 | 340 | $75.00 | 0.929 | 29.29% | $5,468.60 | | | | | |
| 18 | 15 | 0.323 | 340 | $66.00 | 0.933 | 29.33% | $4,581.45 | | | | | |
| 194 | 191 | 0.106 | 320 | $78.00 | 0.058 | 20.58% | $3,137.08 | | | | | |
| 195 | 192 | 0.278 | 340 | $67.00 | 0.582 | 25.82% | $3,881.12 | | | | | |
| 196 | 193 | 0.636 | 360 | $61.00 | 0.477 | 24.77% | $3,440.26 | | | | | |
| 197 | 194 | 0.895 | 380 | $78.00 | 0.782 | 27.82% | $6,244.76 | | | | | |
| 198 | 195 | 0.478 | 360 | $72.00 | 0.912 | 29.12% | $5,547.62 | | | | | |
| 199 | 196 | 0.824 | 380 | $62.00 | 0.861 | 28.61% | $4,739.41 | | | | | |
| 200 | 197 | 0.777 | 380 | $78.00 | 0.356 | 23.56% | $4,982.68 | | | | | |
| 201 | 198 | 0.073 | 320 | $66.00 | 0.855 | 28.55% | $4,029.89 | | | | | |
| 202 | 199 | 0.494 | 360 | $63.00 | 0.763 | 27.63% | $4,266.35 | | | | | |
| 203 | 200 | 0.231 | 340 | $61.00 | 0.079 | 20.79% | $2,311.72 | | | | | |
| 204 | | | | | | Average Profit = | $4,277.89 | | | | | |
| 205 | | | | | | Standard Deviation of Profit = | $1,024.88 | | | | | |
| 206 | | | | | Number of months with Profit >= 4000 = | | 118 | | | | | |
| 207 | | | | | Probability that Profit >= 4000 = | | 59.00% | | | | | |

Hidden rows

Output measures

118 of 200 months is a 59% chance.

G207). Program 10.2B shows that Harry has a 59% chance of getting a monthly profit in excess of $4,000. Here again, the values when you open your CD-ROM file may be different since Excel generates new random numbers, and we are using only 200 replications.

Now suppose Harry estimates that if his profit is below $3,000 in any month, he is in danger of having to shut his business down. Using an approach similar to the one discussed here, see if you can calculate the probability of this event.

Since each replication in Harry's tire example was modeled on just a single row, we could easily perform 200 replications by copying this row 200 times. However, in cases in which the model for each replication itself uses several rows, this could be cumbersome to do. For such situations, we use Excel's Data Table to perform replications. We illustrate this feature in the next section using an inventory problem.

## 10.6  USING SIMULATION FOR AN INVENTORY PROBLEM

*Question in inventory problems: (1) how much to order and (2) when to order.*

There are usually two main questions in most inventory problems: (1) how much to order and (2) when to order. Under specific assumptions, it is possible to develop precise analytical models to answer these questions.[6]

In many real-world inventory situations, though, several inventory parameters are random variables. For example, the demand for an item could be random, implying that the rate at which its inventory is depleted is uncertain. Likewise, the time between when we place an order for an item with our supplier and when we receive it (known as the *lead time*) could be random. This implies that we may run out of inventory for the item before we receive the next consignment, causing a *stockout*.

*Simulation is useful when demand and lead time are probabilistic.*

Although it may be possible for us to express the behavior of parameters like demand and lead time using probability distributions, developing analytical models becomes extremely difficult. In such situations, the best means to answer the kind of inventory questions noted here is simulation.

In Solved Problem 10-1 at the end of this chapter, we simulate a fairly simple inventory problem in which only the demand is random. In what follows here, we illustrate a more comprehensive inventory problem in which both the demand and lead time are random variables.

### Simkin Hardware Store

Barry Simkin's Hardware store sells the Ace model electric drill. Daily demand for the drill is relatively low but subject to some variability. Over the past 300 days, Simkin has observed the demand frequency shown in column 2 of Table 10.6. He converts this historical frequency into a probability distribution for the variable daily demand (column 3).

*Lead time is the time between order placement and order receipt.*

When Simkin places an order to replenish his inventory of drills, the time between when he places an order and when it is received (i.e., the lead time) is a probabilistic variable. Based on the past 100 orders, Simkin has found that lead time follows a discrete uniform distribution between 1 and 3 days. He currently has 7 Ace electric drills in stock, and there are no orders due.

Simkin wants to identify the *order quantity*, $Q$, and *reorder point*, $R$, that will help him reduce his total monthly costs. The order quantity is the fixed size of each order that is placed. If the inventory level at the end of a day is at or below the reorder point, an order is placed. The total cost includes the following components:

*Components of total cost*

■ A fixed ordering cost that is incurred each time an order is placed

■ A holding cost for each drill held in inventory from one period to the next

■ A stockout cost for each drill that is not available to satisfy demand

---

[6] We discuss some of these models in Chapter 12.

| TABLE 10.6 | DEMAND FOR DRILLS | FREQUENCY | PROBABILITY |
|---|---|---|---|
| **Distribution of Daily Demand for Ace Electric Drills** | 0 | 15 | 15/300 = 0.05 |
| | 1 | 30 | 30/300 = 0.10 |
| | 2 | 60 | 60/300 = 0.20 |
| | 3 | 120 | 120/300 = 0.40 |
| | 4 | 45 | 45/300 = 0.15 |
| | 5 | 30 | 30/300 = 0.10 |
| | | 300 | 300/300 = 1.00 |

Simkin estimates that the fixed cost of placing an order with his Ace drill supplier is $20. The cost of holding a drill in stock is $0.50 per drill per month. Assuming the shop operates 25 days each month on average, this translates to a holding cost of $0.02 per drill per day. Each time Simkin is unable to satisfy a demand (i.e., he has a stockout), the customer buys the drill elsewhere, and Simkin loses the sale. He estimates that the cost of a stockout is $8 per drill.

*Two decision variables: order quantity* (Q) *and reorder point* (R).

Note that there are two decision variables (order quantity, $Q$, and reorder point, $R$) and two probabilistic components (demand and lead time) in Simkin's inventory problem. Using simulation, we can try different $(Q, R)$ combinations to see which combination yields the lowest total cost. As an illustration, let us first examine a policy that has $Q = 10$ and $R = 5$; that is, each time the inventory at the end of a day drops to 5 or less, we place an order for 10 drills with the supplier.

## Setting Up the Model

**File: 10-3A.xls**

*To run several "what-if?" scenarios using the same model, it is good to make parameter values cell references in all formulas.*

*Here is how we simulated the inventory example.*

The Excel layout for Simkin's problem is shown in Program 10.3A. Wherever necessary, we have shown the Excel formula used in a column. Recall that in Harry's tire problem in Section 10.4, each replication of the model consisted of entries in just a single row (corresponding to a single month). In Simkin's problem, however, each replication of the model consists of simulations for 25 days (i.e., one business month).

In Program 10.3A, all input parameters for the simulation model (e.g., the order quantity, reorder point, lead time range, all unit costs) are shown in separate cells (in column S). All formulas in the model use these cell references, rather than the values directly. This is a good practice to follow, especially if we want to use the simulation model to run several "what-if?" scenarios using different values for these parameters. The model in Program 10.3A is organized as follows:

■ Column A shows the day number (1 to 25).

■ Column B shows the inventory at the start of a day. On day 1, this equals 7 (given). On all other days, the beginning inventory equals the ending inventory of the previous day. For example, cell B5 = cell G4, cell B6 = cell G5, and so on.

■ Column C shows the units received (if any) that day from a prior order. Since there are no outstanding orders on day 1, cell C4 shows a value of 0. The formula for the remaining cells in this column uses Excel's COUNTIF function. In column L (discussed shortly), we simulate the arrival day for each order that is placed. We use the COUNTIF formula to check the number of times the current day number matches these arrival day numbers. The formula used to calculate the number of units arriving each day is then as follows:

Units received = (Number of orders due that day) × (Order size)

**PROGRAM 10.3A**   Excel Layout and Results for Simkin's Hardware Store

Callouts:
- Beginning inventory = ending inventory on previous day
- Simulated using a VLOOKUP function
- Place order if value in column I ≤ Reorder point.
- Parameters for the VLOOKUP function in column E

**Simkin's Hardware Store**

| Day | Begin Inv | Units Rec | Avail Inv | Dem-and | Demand Filled | End Inv | Stock out | End Inv + Order | Place order? | Lead time | Arrive on day | Inv cost | Stock out cost | Order cost |
|---|---|---|---|---|---|---|---|---|---|---|---|---|---|---|
| 1 | 7 | 0 | 7 | 2 | 2 | 5 | 0 | 5 | 1 | 3 | 5 | $0.10 | $0 | $20 |
| 2 | 5 | 0 | 5 | 5 | 5 | 0 | 0 | 10 | 0 | 0 | 0 | $0.00 | $0 | $0 |
| 3 | 0 | 0 | 0 | 2 | 0 | 0 | 2 | 10 | 0 | 0 | 0 | $0.00 | $16 | $0 |
| 4 | 0 | 0 | 0 | 3 | 0 | 0 | 3 | 10 | 0 | 0 | 0 | $0.00 | $24 | $0 |
| 5 | 0 | 10 | 10 | 2 | 2 | 8 | 0 | 8 | 0 | 0 | 0 | $0.16 | $0 | $0 |
| 6 | 8 | 0 | 8 | 3 | 3 | 5 | 0 | 5 | 1 | 3 | 10 | $0.10 | $0 | $20 |
| 7 | 5 | 0 | 5 | 3 | 3 | 2 | 0 | 12 | 0 | 0 | 0 | $0.04 | $0 | $0 |
| 8 | 2 | 0 | 2 | 2 | 2 | 0 | 0 | 10 | 0 | 0 | 0 | $0.00 | $0 | $0 |
| 9 | 0 | 0 | 0 | 3 | 0 | 0 | 3 | 10 | 0 | 0 | 0 | $0.00 | $24 | $0 |
| 10 | 0 | 10 | 10 | 3 | 3 | 7 | 0 | 7 | 0 | 0 | 0 | $0.14 | $0 | $0 |
| 11 | 7 | 0 | 7 | 4 | 4 | 3 | 0 | 3 | 1 | 1 | 13 | $0.06 | $0 | $20 |
| 12 | 3 | 0 | 3 | 3 | 3 | 0 | 0 | 10 | 0 | 0 | 0 | $0.00 | $0 | $0 |
| 13 | 0 | 10 | 10 | 3 | 3 | 7 | 0 | 7 | 0 | 0 | 0 | $0.14 | $0 | $0 |
| 14 | 7 | 0 | 7 | 2 | 2 | 5 | 0 | 5 | 1 | 2 | 17 | $0.10 | $0 | $20 |
| 15 | 5 | 0 | 5 | 0 | 0 | 5 | 0 | 15 | 0 | 0 | 0 | $0.10 | $0 | $0 |
| 16 | 5 | 0 | 5 | 3 | 3 | 2 | 0 | 12 | 0 | 0 | 0 | $0.04 | $0 | $0 |
| 17 | 2 | 10 | 12 | 2 | 2 | 10 | 0 | 10 | 0 | 0 | 0 | $0.20 | $0 | $0 |
| 18 | 10 | 0 | 10 | 3 | 3 | 7 | 0 | 7 | 0 | 0 | 0 | $0.14 | $0 | $0 |
| 19 | 7 | 0 | 7 | 3 | 3 | 4 | 0 | 4 | 1 | 3 | 23 | $0.08 | $0 | $20 |
| 20 | 4 | 0 | 4 | 5 | 4 | 0 | 1 | 10 | 0 | 0 | 0 | $0.00 | $8 | $0 |
| 21 | 0 | 0 | 0 | 3 | 0 | 0 | 3 | 10 | 0 | 0 | 0 | $0.00 | $24 | $0 |
| 22 | 0 | 0 | 0 | 3 | 0 | 0 | 3 | 10 | 0 | 0 | 0 | $0.00 | $24 | $0 |
| 23 | 0 | 10 | 10 | 2 | 2 | 8 | 0 | 8 | 0 | 0 | 0 | $0.16 | $0 | $0 |
| 24 | 8 | 0 | 8 | 4 | 4 | 4 | 0 | 4 | 1 | 1 | 26 | $0.08 | $0 | $20 |
| 25 | 4 | 0 | 4 | 5 | 4 | 0 | 1 | 10 | 0 | 0 | 0 | $0.00 | $8 | $0 |
| | | | | | | | | | | Total = | | $1.64 | $128 | $120 |
| | | | | | | | | | | Total monthly cost = | | | | $249.64 |

**Demand Distribution**

| RN interval lower limit | RN interval upper limit | Demand | Probability |
|---|---|---|---|
| 0 | 0.05 | 0 | 0.05 |
| 0.05 | 0.15 | 1 | 0.10 |
| 0.15 | 0.35 | 2 | 0.20 |
| 0.35 | 0.75 | 3 | 0.40 |
| 0.75 | 0.90 | 4 | 0.15 |
| 0.90 | 1.00 | 5 | 0.10 |

| Order Quantity, Q | 10 |
|---|---|
| Reorder Point, R | 5 |

| Min Leadtime | 1 |
|---|---|
| Max Leadtime | 3 |

| Inv Cost (per unit per day) | $0.02 |
|---|---|

| Stockout cost (per unit) | $8 |
|---|---|

| Order cost (per order) | $20 |
|---|---|

Callouts:
- Simulate for 25 days.
- Q units are received on a day, if a shipment is due.
- Lead time is simulated using a RANDBETWEEN function.
- Total cost of inventory, stockout, and ordering per month
- Input values for the model

For example, the formula in cell C5 is

$$=\text{COUNTIF}(\$L\$4:L4,A5)*\$S\$11$$

*Using a $ sign anchors cell references while copying formulas.*

The COUNTIF portion of the formula checks to see how many orders are due for arrival on day 2 (specified by cell A5). This number is then multiplied by the order quantity, Q, specified in cell S11. Note that the use of $ signs to anchor cell references in this formula allows us to directly copy it to cells C6:C28.

■ The total *available* inventory each day, shown in column D, is then the sum of the values in columns B and C. This is

$$\text{Column D} = \text{Column B} + \text{Column C}$$

*Demand is simulated using a VLOOKUP function.*

■ Column E shows the demand each day. These values are simulated from a general discrete probability distribution, shown in Table 10.6, using Excel's VLOOKUP function. The parameters (random number intervals, demands and probabilities) of the VLOOKUP function are shown in cells Q4:T9. Hence, the formula in cells E4:E28 is

$$=\text{VLOOKUP}(\text{RAND}(),\$Q\$4:\$S\$9,3)$$

■ Column F shows the actual demand filled. If demand is less than or equal to the available inventory, the entire demand is satisfied. In contrast, if demand exceeds the available inventory, then only the demand up to the inventory level is satisfied. We can use Excel's MIN function to model this as follows:

$$\text{Demand satisfied} = \text{MIN(Available inventory, Demand)}$$

or

$$\text{Column F} = \text{MIN(Column D, Column E)}$$

*If demand is less than available inventory, there is some ending inventory.*

■ Column G calculates the ending inventory. If demand is less than available inventory, there is some ending inventory. However, if demand is greater than or equal to available inventory, the ending inventory is zero. We can use Excel's MAX function to model this as follows:

$$\text{Ending inventory} = \text{MAX(Available inventory} - \text{Demand, 0)}$$

or

$$\text{Column G} = \text{MAX(Column D} - \text{Column E, 0)}$$

*A stockout occurs when demand exceeds available inventory.*

■ We now calculate the stockout (or lost sales) in column H. If demand exceeds the available inventory, there is a stockout. However, if demand is less than or equal to available inventory, there is no stockout. Once again, we can use the MAX function to model this as follows:

$$\text{Stockout} = \text{MAX(Demand} - \text{Available inventory, 0)}$$

or

$$\text{Column H} = \text{MAX(Column E} - \text{Column D, 0)}$$

*We need to check for outstanding orders before placing a new order.*

■ If the ending inventory is at or below the reorder point, an order needs to be placed with the supplier. Before doing so, however, we need to verify that there are no outstanding orders. That is, if an order has already been placed on an earlier day and has not yet been received (due to the delivery lead time), a duplicate order should not be placed. Hence, in column I, we calculate the *apparent* ending inventory; that is, we track the *actual* ending inventory (also shown in column G), as well as any orders that have already been placed. The logic behind the formula in column I is as follows:

$$\text{Apparent inventory at end of period } t = \text{Apparent inventory}$$
$$\text{at end of period } (t - 1) - \text{Demand satisfied in period } t$$
$$+ \text{Order size, if an order was placed at the end of period } (t - 1)$$

For example, the formula in cell I5 is

$$\text{=I4}-\text{F5}+\text{IF(J4=1,\$S\$11,0)}$$

■ If the apparent inventory at the end of any day is at or below the reorder point (cell S12), an order is to be placed that day. We denote this event in column J using an IF function (1 implies place an order, 0 implies don't place an order). For example, the formula in cell J5 is

$$\text{=IF(I5<=\$S\$12,1,0)}$$

*Lead time is simulated using a RANDBETWEEN function.*

■ If an order is placed, the delivery lead time for this order is simulated in column K using a RANDBETWEEN function (between 1 and 3). For example, the formula in cell K5 is

$$\text{=IF(J5=1,RANDBETWEEN(\$S\$14,\$S\$15),0)}$$

■ Finally, in column L, we calculate the arrival day of this order as follows:

$$\text{Arrive on day} = \text{Current day} + \text{Lead time} + 1$$

For example, the formula in cell L5 is

$$=\text{IF}(J5=1,A5+K5+1,0)$$

Note that this formula includes a "+1" since the order is actually placed at the end of the current day (or equivalently, the start of the next day).

## Computation of Costs

Columns M, N, and O show the cost computations for Simkin's inventory model each day of the month. The relevant formulas are as follows:

*Computation of the three cost components*

Column M:  Inventory Cost = $0.02*Ending inventory (in column G)

Column N:  Shortage Cost = $8*Shortage (in Column H)

Column O:  Order Cost = $20 (if order is placed; in Column J)

The totals for each cost component for the entire month are shown in row 29 (cells M29:O29). The overall total is shown in cell O30. For instance, the replication in Program 10.3A shows an inventory cost of $1.64 (cell M29), stockout (or shortage) cost of $128 (cell N29), and order cost of $120 (cell O29). The total cost in cell O30 is, therefore, $249.64.

## Replicating the Model Using Data Table

To compute Simkin's average monthly cost, we need to replicate the model several thousand times. Each time, due to the presence of random variables, values in the spreadsheet will change. Hence, the total cost in cell O30 will change.

*The Data Table feature in Excel is a convenient way of replicating a large model several times.*

If we wish to replicate the model *N* times, it is *theoretically* possible to copy the entire simulation model (in cells A4:O30) *N* times. From a practical perspective, however, this is extremely cumbersome since it makes the resulting spreadsheet model too large and unwieldy. Hence, we want a procedure that will automatically replicate the model *N* times and report the total cost value computed in cell O30 each time.

To do so, we can use an Excel feature called Data Table. The primary use of data tables in Excel is to plug in different values for a variable in a formula and compute the result each time. For example, if the formula is $(2a + 5)$, we can set up a Data Table to plug in several values for *a* and report the result of the formula each time. A Data Table can involve either one or two variables. In a one-variable table, the formula has only one variable for which different values need to be plugged in. In a two-variable table, the formula has two variables, such as $(2a + 3b + 5)$, each with its own set of values to be plugged in. The Data Table tries every combination of values for the two variables (*a* and *b*) and reports the result of the formula each time.

## One-Variable Data Table

*We use one-variable data tables to replicate a model with a given set of parameter values.*

For Simkin's inventory problem, we use a one-variable Data Table. In our simulation model, we don't really have a "variable" and a "formula" to use in the Data Table. So, as explained next, we make the Data Table plug in *N* values for a dummy variable in a dummy formula (both of which have nothing to do with the simulation model), and report the "result" in cell O30 each time. In effect, this is like making Excel automatically recompute the model *N* times. Note that each time the model is recomputed, all random numbers change. The result is a new replication of the simulation model and a new value for the total cost in cell O30.

We illustrate a one-variable Data Table for Simkin's simulation model in Program 10.3B. The procedure is as follows:

*This is how we set up a one-variable Data Table.*

1. We first use cells in an empty column in the spreadsheet to represent the N values of the *dummy* variable. If we wish, we can leave these cells blank since they have no real role to play in the simulation model. However, it is convenient to fill these cells with numbers from 1 to N, to indicate we are performing N replications. In Program 10.3B, we have entered numbers 1 to 200 in cells V4:V203, corresponding to the 200 replications we want to run for this model. (Here again, we have chosen 200 replications just for convenience.) If we wish, we can title these numbers as *Replications* (as shown in cell V3).

2. In cell W4 (i.e., adjacent to the *first* cell in the range V4:203), we specify the cell reference for the cell we want replicated 200 times. In our problem, this corresponds to cell O30. Hence, the formula in a cell W4 would be "=O30." We can title this column as *Total cost* if we wish (as shown in cell W3). We leave the rest of the cells in column W (i.e., cells W5:W203) blank. The Data Table will fill in these cells when we run it.

## PROGRAM 10.3B  One-Variable Data Table for Simkin's Hardware Store

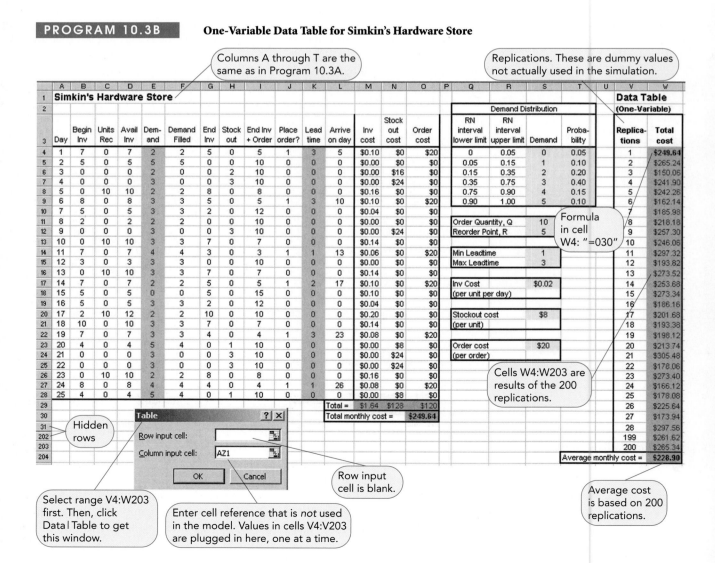

3. We now use the mouse or keyboard to select the range V4:W203. *After* selecting this range, we choose Data\Table. The window titled Table, shown in Program 10.3B, is now seen.

4. We leave the row input cell entry blank and enter some arbitrary cell reference (such as AZ1) as the column input cell. We need to make sure the selected cell (AZ1, in this case) has nothing to do with the simulation model. In effect, we are telling the Data Table that cell AZ1 contains our dummy formula.

5. Finally, we click OK to run the Data Table. The Data Table now takes the 200 entries in cells V4:V203, plugs them in one at a time in cell AZ1, and reports the value of cell O30 in cells W4:W203. As noted earlier, even though the variable values in cells V4:V203 and the formula in cell AZ1 are dummies, Excel generates new random numbers for each replication. The simulation values, and the total cost value in cell O30, are therefore different for each replication.

## Analyzing the Results

*We can conduct statistical analyses on the replicated values.*

We now have 200 simulated values of the total monthly cost (cell O30) in cells W4:W203. The details (e.g., the daily demands, lead times) of these 200 replications are not shown. Entries in the data tables can be formatted (e.g., as currency) if necessary. We can now use these 200 values to conduct statistical analyses, as before. For example, if $Q = 10$ and $R = 5$, Program 10.3B indicates that Simkin's average monthly total cost of inventory, stockout, and ordering is $228.90 (in cell W204).

As an exercise, see if you can set up a Data Table to calculate Simkin's average demand fill rate per month. That is, what percentage of monthly demand received does Simkin satisfy on average? Hint: The fill rate for each replication is the ratio of demand satisfied (sum of entries in column F) to demand received (sum of entries in column E).

---

### Excel Notes

1. It is usually a good idea to change the calculation feature in Excel to Manual or Automatic except tables (Tools\Option\Calculation) when using Data Table. Otherwise, Excel will recalculate the entire Data Table each time you make *any* change in the spreadsheet. Depending on the size of the simulation model and the table, this could be time-consuming.

2. For the same reason, it is a good idea to set up each simulation model on a separate Excel file, rather than on different sheets of the same file.

3. If you change to the calculation feature, remember that Excel will recalculate values only when you press the F9 key. Also, the Data Table will initially show the same result value for all replications. You need to press F9 to get the final values.

---

## Two-Variable Data Table

In our simulation model so far, we have assumed a fixed order quantity, $Q$, of 10, and a fixed reorder point, $R$, of 5. Now suppose Simkin wants to keep $R$ fixed at 5 units but wants to try different order quantities such as 8, 10, 12, and 14. One approach to run this extended simulation would be to run the model (see Program 10.3A) and one-variable Data Table (Program 10.3B) four times—once with each value of $Q$. We can then compute the average cost in each case to determine which value of $Q$ is best.

*We use a two-variable Data Table when we want to try several values for an input parameter in the model.*

However, as noted earlier, a two-variable Data Table that allows us to plug in values for two variables at a time is also available. Let us use this alternate approach for Simkin's simulation model. The first variable in the Data Table is again a dummy variable corresponding to the $N$ replications we want to run (as discussed for the one-variable Data Table).

**PROGRAM 10.3C**    **Two-Variable Data Table for Simkin's Hardware Store**

Columns A through T are the same as in Program 10.3A.

Formula in cell V4: "=O30"

Possible values of Q

**Simkin's Hardware Store**

| Day | Begin Inv | Units Rec | Avail Inv | Dem-and | Demand Filled | End Inv | Stock out | End Inv + Order | Place order? | Lead time | Arrive on day | Inv cost | Stock out cost | Order cost |
|---|---|---|---|---|---|---|---|---|---|---|---|---|---|---|
| 1 | 7 | 0 | 7 | 2 | 2 | 5 | 0 | 5 | 1 | 2 | 4 | $0.10 | $0 | $20 |
| 2 | 5 | 0 | 5 | 5 | 5 | 0 | 0 | 10 | 0 | 0 | 0 | $0.00 | $0 | $0 |
| 3 | 0 | 0 | 0 | 3 | 0 | 0 | 3 | 10 | 0 | 0 | 0 | $0.00 | $24 | $0 |
| 4 | 0 | 10 | 10 | 4 | 4 | 6 | 0 | 6 | 0 | 0 | 0 | $0.12 | $0 | $0 |
| 5 | 6 | 0 | 6 | 1 | 1 | 5 | 0 | 5 | 1 | 3 | 9 | $0.10 | $0 | $20 |
| 6 | 5 | 0 | 5 | 5 | 5 | 0 | 0 | 10 | 0 | 0 | 0 | $0.00 | $0 | $0 |
| 7 | 0 | 0 | 0 | 0 | 0 | 0 | 0 | 10 | 0 | 0 | 0 | $0.00 | $0 | $0 |
| 8 | 0 | 0 | 0 | 3 | 0 | 0 | 3 | 10 | 0 | 0 | 0 | $0.00 | $24 | $0 |
| 9 | 0 | 10 | 10 | 2 | 2 | 8 | 0 | 8 | 0 | 0 | 0 | $0.16 | $0 | $0 |
| 10 | 8 | 0 | 8 | 3 | 3 | 5 | 0 | 5 | 1 | 3 | 14 | $0.10 | $0 | $20 |
| 11 | 5 | 0 | 5 | 3 | 3 | 2 | 0 | 12 | 0 | 0 | 0 | $0.04 | $0 | $0 |
| 12 | 2 | 0 | 2 | 3 | 2 | 0 | 1 | 10 | 0 | 0 | 0 | $0.00 | $8 | $0 |
| 13 | 0 | 0 | 0 | 3 | 0 | 0 | 3 | 10 | 0 | 0 | 0 | $0.00 | $24 | $0 |
| 14 | 0 | 10 | 10 | 2 | 2 | 8 | 0 | 8 | 0 | 0 | 0 | $0.16 | $0 | $0 |
| 15 | 8 | 0 | 8 | 4 | 4 | 4 | 0 | 4 | 1 | 3 | 19 | $0.08 | $0 | $20 |
| 16 | 4 | 0 | 4 | 3 | 3 | 1 | 0 | 11 | 0 | 0 | 0 | $0.02 | $0 | $0 |
| 17 | 1 | 0 | 1 | 2 | 1 | 0 | 1 | 10 | 0 | 0 | 0 | $0.00 | $8 | $0 |
| 18 | 0 | 0 | 0 | 2 | 0 | 0 | 2 | 10 | 0 | 0 | 0 | $0.00 | $16 | $0 |
| 19 | 0 | 10 | 10 | 4 | 4 | 6 | 0 | 6 | 0 | 0 | 0 | $0.12 | $0 | $0 |
| 20 | 6 | 0 | 6 | 4 | 4 | 2 | 0 | 2 | 1 | 2 | 23 | $0.04 | $0 | $20 |
| 21 | 2 | 0 | 2 | 1 | 1 | 1 | 0 | 11 | 0 | 0 | 0 | $0.02 | $0 | $0 |
| 22 | 1 | 0 | 1 | 2 | 1 | 0 | 1 | 10 | 0 | 0 | 0 | $0.00 | $8 | $0 |
| 23 | 0 | 10 | 10 | 4 | 4 | 6 | 0 | 6 | 0 | 0 | 0 | $0.12 | $0 | $0 |
| 24 | 6 | 0 | 6 | 5 | 5 | 1 | 0 | 1 | 1 | 2 | 27 | $0.02 | $0 | $20 |
| 25 | 1 | 0 | 1 | 3 | 1 | 0 | 2 | 10 | 0 | 0 | 0 | $0.00 | $16 | $0 |

Total = $1.20  $128  $120
Total monthly cost = $249.20

**Demand Distribution**

| RN interval lower limit | RN interval upper limit | Demand | Probability |
|---|---|---|---|
| 0 | 0.05 | 0 | 0.05 |
| 0.05 | 0.15 | 1 | 0.10 |
| 0.15 | 0.35 | 2 | 0.20 |
| 0.35 | 0.75 | 3 | 0.40 |
| 0.75 | 0.90 | 4 | 0.15 |
| 0.90 | 1.00 | 5 | 0.10 |

| | |
|---|---|
| Order Quantity | 10 |
| Reorder Point | 5 |

| | |
|---|---|
| Min Leadtime | 1 |
| Max Leadtime | 3 |

| | |
|---|---|
| Inv Cost (per unit per day) | $0.02 |

| | |
|---|---|
| Stockout cost (per unit) | $8 |

| | |
|---|---|
| Order cost (per order) | $20 |

200 replicated values of cost for each value of Q

**Data Table (Two-Variable)**

| Replication | Order Quantity, Q | | | |
|---|---|---|---|---|
| $249.20 | 8 | 10 | 12 | 14 |
| 1 | $233.40 | $233.48 | $174.54 | $155.02 |
| 2 | $253.04 | $213.76 | $209.90 | $111.40 |
| 3 | $301.08 | $281.36 | $253.66 | $194.72 |
| 4 | $285.34 | $281.52 | $222.10 | $158.86 |
| 5 | $229.36 | $245.52 | $150.86 | $142.78 |
| 6 | $341.18 | $206.26 | $190.52 | $151.00 |
| 7 | $245.36 | $154.20 | $126.94 | $119.94 |
| 8 | $177.52 | $249.56 | $118.50 | $230.18 |
| 9 | $345.00 | $277.56 | $202.40 | $198.68 |
| 10 | $285.16 | $229.36 | $206.06 | $126.88 |
| 11 | $273.40 | $170.52 | $230.02 | $250.18 |
| 12 | $333.30 | $213.74 | $233.98 | $130.88 |
| 13 | $249.48 | $185.94 | $230.10 | $163.20 |
| 14 | $265.64 | $193.80 | $181.96 | $127.12 |
| 15 | $305.22 | $229.72 | $221.78 | $138.64 |
| 16 | $317.36 | $162.24 | $225.74 | $210.56 |
| 17 | $297.10 | $249.56 | $118.82 | $123.72 |
| 18 | $245.72 | $233.46 | $222.00 | $166.68 |
| 19 | $217.88 | $229.58 | $166.34 | $159.10 |
| 20 | $321.16 | $201.86 | $190.20 | $266.04 |
| 21 | $229.40 | $233.54 | $269.70 | $254.12 |
| 22 | $201.74 | $238.16 | $238.20 | $218.16 |
| 23 | $253.50 | $233.46 | $186.06 | $174.72 |
| 24 | $261.14 | $257.42 | $237.68 | $139.24 |
| 25 | $245.18 | $257.38 | $190.24 | $134.48 |
| 26 | $249.70 | $245.58 | $154.50 | $206.30 |
| 27 | $205.42 | $269.58 | $190.68 | $174.36 |
| 199 | $373.14 | $177.96 | $194.40 | $147.06 |
| 200 | $245.34 | $241.76 | $174.44 | $194.40 |
| Avg = | $262.53 | $222.15 | $197.17 | $176.56 |

Averages are based on 200 replications for each value of Q.

**Table** [? X]

Row input cell: S11

Column input cell: AZ1

OK    Cancel

Hidden rows

Any cell that is *not* used in the model.

Row input cell shows the cell where values in W4:Z4 need to be plugged in.

**File: 10-3B.xls**

*This is how we set up a two-variable Data Table.*

However, the second variable is a real variable used in the simulation model. It denotes the value of Q, which is shown in cell S11 of Program 10.3B. For each value of Q, we use the Data Table to run N replications.

We illustrate a two-variable Data Table for Simkin's simulation model in Program 10.3C. As before, we have chosen to run 200 replications for convenience. The procedure is as follows:

1. As with the one-variable table, we first use cells in an empty column in the spreadsheet to represent the N values of the dummy variable (number of replications). In Program 10.3C, we have entered the numbers 1 through 200 in cells V5:V204.

2. Next, we enter the different values for Q (i.e., 8, 10, 12, and 14) in cells W4:Z4.

3. In cell V4, we specify the cell reference for the cell we want replicated 200 times (i.e., cell O30). Note that this is different from what we did for the one-variable Data Table, in which we entered this formula adjacent to the number 1 in column V. We leave the cells W5:Z204 in the Data Table blank. The table will fill in these cells when we run it.

4. We now use the mouse or keyboard to select the range V4:Z204. *After* selecting this range, we choose Data|Table. The window titled *Table*, shown in Program 10.3C, is now seen.

5. We enter cell S11 (denoting the order quantity, *Q*) as the row input cell. As with the one-variable data table, we enter an *unused* cell reference (such as AZ1) as the column input cell.

6. Finally, we click *OK* to run the procedure. For each value of *Q* in cells W4:Z4, Data Table now takes the 200 entries in cells V5:V204, plugs them in one at a time in cell AZ1, and reports the value of cell O30 in cells W5:Z204. As before, due to the use of random numbers, the total cost value will be different for each replication.

## Analyzing the Results

For each value of the order quantity, we now have 200 simulated values of the total monthly cost (cell O30) in cells W5:Z204. As with the one-variable data table, details (e.g., the daily demands, lead times) of each replication are not shown.

*We can conduct statistical analyses of the results.*

We can now use these values to compute various statistical measures of performance. For example, the average monthly total cost for each order quantity (shown in row 205 of Program 10.3C) indicates that Simkin's lowest cost of $176.56 per month is obtained when he uses an order quantity of 14 units.

Here again, we can compute other statistical measures for each order quantity. In each case, we can set up a two-variable data table. The row input cell will denote the cell that we wish to vary (such as cell S11), and the column input cell will denote some obscure cell that is unused in the model.

As an exercise, see if you can extend the one-variable Data Table you set up earlier for Simkin's monthly fill rate to a two-variable table that considers the four order quantities (8, 10, 12, and 14). *Hint:* The highest fill rate should be obtained when *Q* = 14 and should be around 88% (based on 200 replications).

*Solved Problem 10-2 describes the simulation of a queuing system.*

So far, we have developed two simulation models using Excel's built-in functions to generate random values from probability distributions. We have also used one-variable and two-variable Data Tables to easily replicate these simulation models. In Solved Problem 10-2 at the end of this chapter, we develop another simulation model using Excel's built-in functions and replicate it using the Data Table feature. This model simulates the queuing system at a service facility.

---

## IN ACTION  Simulating Taco Bell's Restaurant Operation

Determining how many employees to schedule each 15 minutes to perform each function in a Taco Bell restaurant is a complex and vexing problem. So Taco Bell, the $5 billion giant with 6,500 U.S. and foreign locations, decided to build a simulation model. It selected MODSIM as its software to develop a new labor-management system called LMS.

To develop and use a simulation model, Taco Bell had to collect quite a bit of data. Almost everything that takes place in a restaurant, from customer arrival patterns to the time it takes to wrap a taco, had to be translated into reliable, accurate data. Just as an example, analysts had to conduct time studies and data analysis for every task that is part of preparing every item

on the menu. To the researcher's surprise, the hours devoted to collecting data greatly exceeded those it took to actually build the LMS model.

Inputs to LMS include staffing, such as number of people and positions. Outputs are performance measures, such as mean time in the system, mean time at the counter, people utilization and equipment utilization. The model paid off. More than $53 million in labor costs were saved in LMS's first four years of use.

**Sources:** J. Hueter and W. Swart. "An Integrated Labor-Management System for Taco Bell," *Interfaces* 28, 1 (January–February 1998): 75–91 and L. Pringle. "Productivity Engine," *OR/MS Today* 27, 3 (June 2000): 30.

There are, however, several add-in programs available that make it even easier to develop and replicate simulation models using Excel. Hence, in the next two sections, we discuss the use of one of the more powerful Excel add-ins for simulation, Crystal Ball 2000.

 ## USING CRYSTAL BALL TO SIMULATE AN INVENTORY PROBLEM

*Crystal Ball, found on your CD-ROM, is an Excel add-in used for simulation.*

Crystal Ball 2000, an add-in for Excel, is published by Decisioneering Inc. As noted earlier, a student version of this package (valid for 140 days from date of installation) is included in your CD-ROM.

### Reasons for Using Add-In Programs

Here are some of the reasons why using an add-in program is useful in simulation modeling:

*These three advantages of add-ins make them useful tools for developing simulation models on spreadsheets.*

1. They have built-in functions to simulate not only from the probability distributions discussed so far, but also from many other distributions that are commonly encountered in practice (e.g., binomial, triangular, lognormal). Further, many of these formulas are simple and easy to use. For example, to simulate a random value from a normal distribution with mean $\mu$ and standard deviation $\sigma$, we use the following formula in Crystal Ball:

$$=CB.NORMAL(\mu,\sigma)$$

2. They have built-in procedures that make it very easy to replicate the simulation several hundred (or even several thousand) times.

3. They have built-in procedures that make it easy to collect information on various output measures. These measures can also be displayed graphically if desired.

To illustrate the use of Crystal Ball, let us revisit the Simkin Hardware Store inventory problem. Recall from Section 10.6 that Simkin is trying to find the order quantity, $Q$, and reorder point, $R$, that will minimize his total monthly costs. The total cost includes the following components: ordering cost, holding cost, and stockout cost.

We should note that our intent here is to only provide a brief introduction to Crystal Ball and not to describe every aspect or capability of this add-in program. Once you have completed this section and the next, however, you should have sufficient knowledge about Crystal Ball to explore some of its other options and procedures. Many of these are self-explanatory, and we strongly encourage you to try these out on your own.

### Simulation of Simkin's Hardware Store Using Crystal Ball

*Simkin's Hardware store example revisited.*

Let us begin by simulating Simkin's problem for an inventory policy with order quantity $(Q) = 10$ and reorder point $(R) = 5$. In setting up this simulation model, the two main differences from the procedure we used in Section 10.6 are the manner in which we (1) simulate random values from the probability distributions and (2) replicate the model. Rather than using Excel's built-in functions and the Data Table feature, we use functions and procedures provided by Crystal Ball for these tasks.

**Starting Crystal Ball**  The instructions for installing Crystal Ball on your personal computer can be found on your CD-ROM.[7] After you have installed the program, you can start it (and Excel) by clicking on Crystal Ball in the Windows Start menu.

---

[7] Basically, you need to run the file named Setup.exe in the Crystal Ball directory in your CD-ROM. See the Readme.doc file in the same directory for detailed instructions.

**PROGRAM 10.4A**    **Excel Layout and Results Using Crystal Ball for Simkin's Hardware Store**

Crystal Ball toolbar. Place cursor over each icon to see what that icon does.

Crystal Ball menus

Formula in column E to simulate demand

File  Edit  View  Insert  Format  Tools  Data  Window  Cell  Run  CBTools  Help

Arial     11

E4    =    =CB.Custom($Q$4:$R$9)

# Simkin's Hardware Store (Using *Crystal Ball*)

| Day | Begin Inv | Units Rec | Avail Inv | Dem-and | Demand Filled | End Inv | Stock out | End Inv + Order | Place order? | Lead time | Arrive on day | Inv cost | Stockout cost | Order cost | | Demand | Probability |
|---|---|---|---|---|---|---|---|---|---|---|---|---|---|---|---|---|---|
| | | | | | | | | | | | | | | | | **Demand Distribution** | |
| 1 | 7 | 0 | 7 | 4 | 4 | 3 | 0 | 3 | 1 | 1 | 3 | $0.06 | $0 | $20 | | 0 | 0.05 |
| 2 | 3 | 0 | 3 | 3 | 3 | 0 | 0 | 10 | 0 | 0 | 0 | $0.00 | $0 | $0 | | 1 | 0.10 |
| 3 | 0 | 10 | 10 | 2 | 2 | 8 | 0 | 8 | 0 | 0 | 0 | $0.16 | $0 | $0 | | 2 | 0.20 |
| 4 | 8 | 0 | 8 | 3 | 3 | 5 | 0 | 5 | 1 | 3 | 8 | $0.10 | $0 | $20 | | 3 | 0.40 |
| 5 | 5 | 0 | 5 | 2 | 2 | 3 | 0 | 13 | 0 | 0 | 0 | $0.06 | $0 | $0 | | 4 | 0.15 |
| 6 | 3 | 0 | 3 | 3 | 3 | 0 | 0 | 10 | 0 | 0 | 0 | $0.00 | $0 | $0 | | 5 | 0.10 |
| 7 | 0 | 0 | 0 | 3 | 0 | 0 | 3 | 10 | 0 | 0 | 0 | $0.00 | $24 | $0 | | | |
| 8 | 0 | 10 | 10 | 3 | 3 | 7 | 0 | 7 | 0 | 0 | 0 | $0.14 | $0 | $0 | | Order Quantity, Q | 10 |
| 9 | 7 | 0 | 7 | 5 | 5 | 2 | 0 | 2 | 1 | 1 | 11 | $0.04 | $0 | $20 | | Reorder Point, R | 5 |
| 10 | 2 | 0 | 2 | 4 | 2 | 0 | 2 | 10 | 0 | 0 | 0 | $0.00 | $16 | $0 | | | |
| 11 | 0 | 10 | 10 | 5 | 5 | 5 | 0 | 5 | 1 | 1 | 13 | $0.10 | $0 | $20 | | Min Leadtime | 1 |
| 12 | 5 | 0 | 5 | 5 | 5 | 0 | 0 | 10 | 0 | 0 | 0 | $0.00 | $0 | $0 | | Max Leadtime | 3 |
| 13 | 0 | 10 | 10 | 4 | 4 | 6 | 0 | 6 | 0 | 0 | 0 | $0.12 | $0 | $0 | | | |
| 14 | 6 | 0 | 6 | 1 | 1 | 5 | 0 | 5 | 1 | 2 | 17 | $0.10 | $0 | $20 | | Inv Cost | $0.02 |
| 15 | 5 | 0 | 5 | 3 | 3 | 2 | 0 | 12 | 0 | 0 | 0 | $0.04 | $0 | $0 | | (per unit per day) | |
| 16 | 2 | 0 | 2 | 3 | 2 | 0 | 1 | 10 | 0 | 0 | 0 | $0.00 | $8 | $0 | | | |
| 17 | 0 | 10 | 10 | 5 | 5 | 5 | 0 | 5 | 1 | 3 | 21 | $0.10 | $0 | $20 | | Stockout cost | $8 |
| 18 | 5 | 0 | 5 | 3 | 3 | 2 | 0 | 12 | 0 | 0 | 0 | $0.04 | $0 | $0 | | (per unit) | |
| 19 | 2 | 0 | 2 | 2 | 2 | 0 | 0 | 10 | 0 | 0 | 0 | $0.00 | $0 | $0 | | | |
| 20 | 0 | 0 | 0 | 1 | 0 | 0 | 1 | 10 | 0 | 0 | 0 | $0.00 | $8 | $0 | | Order cost | $20 |
| 21 | 0 | 10 | 10 | 2 | 2 | 8 | 0 | 8 | 0 | 0 | 0 | $0.16 | $0 | $0 | | (per order) | |
| 22 | 8 | 0 | 8 | 4 | 4 | 4 | 0 | 4 | 1 | 3 | 26 | $0.08 | $0 | $20 | | | |
| 23 | 4 | 0 | 4 | 3 | 3 | 1 | 0 | 11 | 0 | 0 | 0 | $0.02 | $0 | $0 | | | |
| 24 | 1 | 0 | 1 | 4 | 1 | 0 | 3 | 10 | 0 | 0 | 0 | $0.00 | $24 | $0 | | | |
| 25 | 0 | 0 | 0 | 4 | 0 | 0 | 4 | 10 | 0 | 0 | 0 | $0.00 | $32 | $0 | | | |
| | | | | | | | | | | | Total = | $1.32 | $112 | $140 | | | |
| | | | | | | | | | | | Total monthly cost = | | | $253.32 | | | |

Demand parameters

Simulate 25 days.

This is output measure that we want to replicate.

Alternatively, you can use the following procedure to automatically load Crystal Ball each time you start Excel:

■ Open Excel. Click Tools|Add-Ins.

■ You will see an option named Crystal Ball in the Add-Ins list. Make sure the box next to this option is checked. Click OK.

*Crystal Ball menus and toolbar are seen when the program is run.*

Once Crystal Ball has been enabled in Excel, you will see menus titled Cell, Run, and CBTools displayed in the main menu bar. In addition, you will see the Crystal Ball toolbar (shown in Program 10.4A).

**File: 10-4.xls**

**Excel Layout Using Crystal Ball for Simkin's Hardware Store**  The Excel layout shown in Program 10.4A is similar to the one we developed in Program 10.3A for this problem. (Refer back to Section 10.6 if necessary for a quick refresher on this model.) The only

| TABLE 10.7 | | |
|---|---|---|
| **Simulating from Various Probability Distributions Using Crystal Ball** | **TO SIMULATE FROM** | **CRYSTAL BALL FORMULA** |
| | **Continuous Uniform Distribution** Between $a$ and $b$ | $=$CB.Uniform$(a,b)$ |
| | **Normal Distribution** Mean $= \mu$; Standard deviation $= \sigma$ | $=$CB.Normal$(\mu,\sigma)$ |
| | **General Discrete Distribution** *Range* = Cell range containing variable values (in first column) and their probabilities (in second column). | $=$CB.Custom$(Range)$ |
| | **Binomial Distribution** Probability of success $= p$ Number of trials $= n$ | $=$CB.Binomial$(p,n)$ |
| | **Exponential Distribution** Mean $= \mu$ | $=$CB.Exponential$(\mu)$ |
| | **Poisson Distribution** Mean $= \lambda$ | $=$CB.Poisson$(\lambda)$ |
| | **Triangular Distribution** Minimum value $= a$ Most likely value $= b$ Maximum value $= c$ | $=$CB.Triangular$(a,b,c)$ |

*We use the CB.Custom function to simulate demand here.*

difference is in column E, in which we simulate the demand each day. Recall that we simulate these values in Program 10.3A using Excel's *VLOOKUP* function. In Program 10.4A, however, we use a function called CB.Custom that is available in Crystal Ball to simulate from general discrete distributions. Table 10.7 presents a summary of the functions available in Crystal Ball to generate random values from several common probability distributions.[8,9]

Note that while specifying the parameters (demand values and probabilities) for Crystal Ball's custom distribution function, the values for the variable are defined in the first column, and the corresponding probabilities are defined in the adjacent column (see cells Q4:R9 in Program 10.4A). The formula for demand in cells E4:E28 is[10]

$$=\text{CB.Custom}(\$Q\$4{:}\$R\$9)$$

## Replicating the Model

We want to replicate Simkin's simulation model several thousand times and keep track of the total monthly cost (cell O30) each time. To do this in Crystal Ball, we use two steps described in the following sections.

---

[8] You can see a listing of all the functions available in Crystal Ball by clicking $f_x$ in Excel's standard toolbar and selecting Crystal Ball in the function category.

[9] Instead of using the formulas shown in Table 10.7 to define probability distributions in Crystal Ball, we could have used the Cell|Define Assumption menu option. Using this option opens up a graphical template of all the probability distributions available, from which we select the distribution we want. We have, however, chosen to use the formulas here since we find them more convenient.

[10] To see the simulated value for a variable change each time the model is recomputed, uncheck the Set to Distribution Mean box under Cell|Cell Preferences. Otherwise, Crystal Ball will *always* show the mean of the distribution for the variable.

*Output measures are called forecasts in Crystal Ball.*

**Defining Output Measures** First, we define the cells that we want to replicate and track. This is done as follows:

- Select cell O30. This cell *must* contain the formula for the output measure we want to track.
- Click Cells|Define Forecast (or click the Define Forecast icon on the Crystal Ball toolbar). The window shown in Program 10.4B is displayed.
- If desired, specify the name and units of the output measure as shown in Program 10.4B. Click OK.

*We can track several forecasts at the same time.*

If necessary, we can repeat this procedure several times to track more than one output measure (forecast). For example, suppose Simkin also wants to track his monthly fill rate (i.e., monthly demand satisfied divided by demand received). In this case, we would set up a cell with the formula for the fill rate and then define that cell also as a forecast cell.

**Running the Model Several Times** Once all output measures have been defined, we click Run|Run Preferences (or click the Run Preferences icon on the Crystal Ball toolbar). The window shown in Program 10.4C is displayed. We now enter the number of trials (replications) desired and click OK. Note that since Crystal Ball is not going to show each replication's actual cost in the spreadsheet (unlike in the Data Table in Section 10.6), we do not have to be concerned about the Excel file getting too large. Hence, we can ask for as many replications as we wish. For our discussion here, let us simulate the model 3,000 times. All other options in the window can be left at their defaults.

*The results can be viewed in either graphical or tabular form.*

To now run the model, we click Run|Run (or click the Run icon on the Crystal Ball toolbar). Crystal Ball runs the model for the specified number of replications, keeping track of cell O30 (and any other cells that we may have specified) for each replication. When finished, the output of the simulation is presented. This output can be viewed either in graphical form (as in Program 10.4D(a)), or in tabular form (as in Program 10.4D(b)). We click View to select from the different choices.

**Defining a Forecast Cell in Crystal Ball**

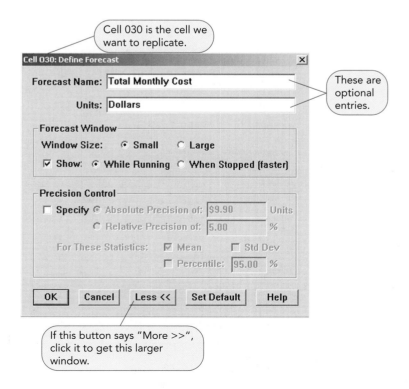

**PROGRAM 10.4C**

**Setting Run Preferences in Crystal Ball**

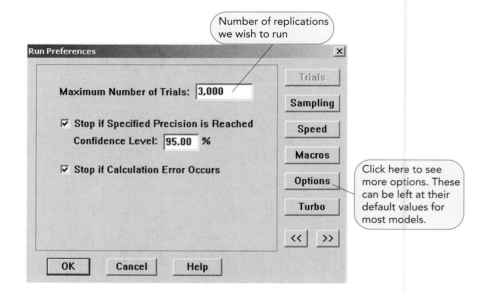

**PROGRAM 10.4D**    **Graphical and Tabular Results from Crystal Ball for Simkin's Hardware Store**

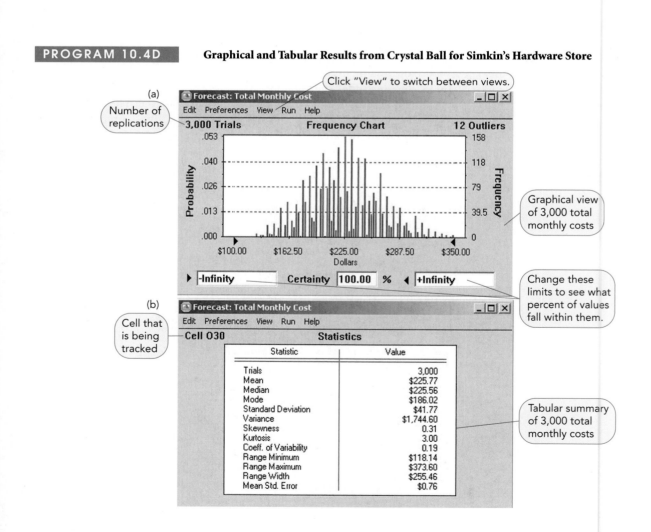

Program 10.4D(b) indicates that if $Q = 10$ and $R = 5$, Simkin's average monthly total cost of inventory, stockout, and ordering is $225.77. Note that this cost is a more precise estimate than the average cost of $228.90 we computed in Section 10.6. Can you see why?

As an exercise, see if you can set up Crystal Ball to run 3,000 replications and compute Simkin's average fill rate per month with $Q = 10$. *Hint:* The answer should be around 82%.

## Using a Decision Table in Crystal Ball

*We use a Decision Table in Crystal Ball to try several values automatically for a parameter in the model.*

The model discussed so far allows us to determine Simkin's average monthly cost for an inventory policy with $Q = 10$, and $R = 5$. Recall that we use a two-variable Data Table in Section 10.6 to get Excel to try different values automatically for the order quantity, $Q$. In a similar fashion, we can use a feature called Decision Table in Crystal Ball to try different values for an input parameter.

In Simkin's problem, we want to try out 4 different values (8, 10, 12, and 14) for the order quantity, $Q$: that is, we want the simulation model to automatically plug in these values one at a time in cell S11 of Program 10.4A and run 3,000 replications each time. To do so, we set up and run the Decision Table procedure in Crystal Ball as follows:

1. As before, define cell O30 as the forecast cell using Cell|Define Forecast.
2. Select cell S11 (cell in which we want the values to be plugged in).
3. Select Cell|Define Decision. The window shown in Program 10.4E is displayed. Enter the lower and upper limits for the order quantity. Specify a discrete step size of 2 since we want to analyze only $Q$ values of 8, 10, 12, and 14. Click OK.
4. Select CBTools|Decision Table. The window shown in Program 10.4F is displayed. Make sure the appropriate forecast cell (O30 in this case) is shown as the target cell. Click Next.
5. The window shown in Program 10.4G now is displayed. Select the decision variable cell (S11) and click the button marked ">>." Click Next.
6. The window shown in Program 10.4H is displayed. Make sure the appropriate number of values is shown for cell S11 (4 choices in this case). Enter the desired number of replication (3,000) and click Start.

**Defining a Decision Variable Cell in Crystal Ball**

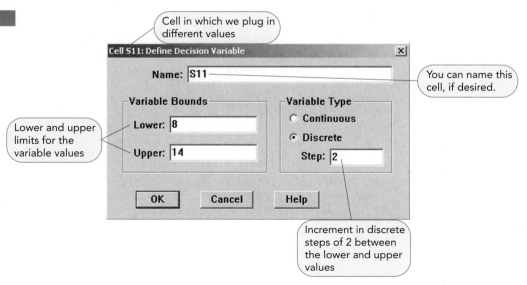

**PROGRAM 10.4F**

**Setting Up a Decision
Table in Crystal Ball—
Step 1 of 3**

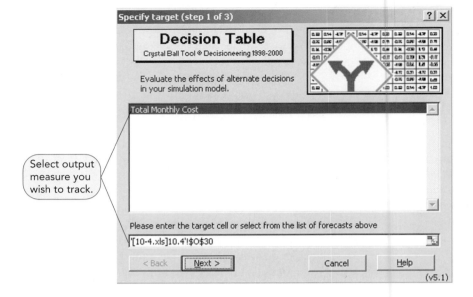

When we click the Start button, the Decision Table plugs in each value of $Q$ in cell S11 (see Program 10.4A) and runs 3,000 replications in each case. The results are displayed in a separate workbook and are shown in Program 10.4I. We can click on any of these cost values (cells B2:E2 of Program 10.4I), and select the charts shown (Trend, Overlay, or Forecast) to see details of the simulation for a specific value of $Q$. For example, Program 10.4I shows the forecast frequency chart obtained for the cost in cell B2, which corresponds to a $Q$ value of 8 in cell S11.

Comparing the average values in Program 10.4I, it appears that Simkin's best choice would be to set $Q = 14$ (based, at least, on 3,000 replications). The resulting average total cost is \$175.96 per month.

**PROGRAM 10.4G**

**Setting Up a Decision
Table in Crystal Ball—
Step 2 of 3**

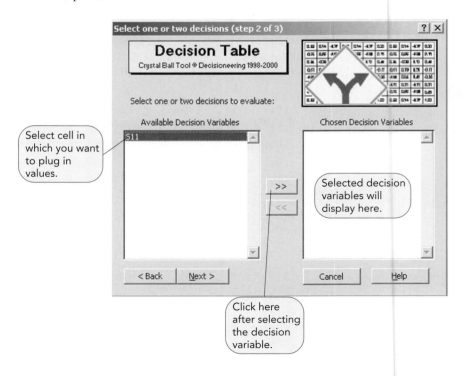

## PROGRAM 10.4H

**Setting Up a Decision Table in Crystal Ball— Step 3 of 3**

Verify that number of values shown here is consistent with definition in Program 10.4E.

**Specify options (step 3 of 3)**

**Decision Table**
Crystal Ball Tool ◆ Decisioneering 1998-2000

**Simulation Control**

Test [4] values for S11

Run each simulation for [3000] trials (maximum)

Number of replications for each value

**While Running**
- ○ Show forecasts as defined
- ● Show only target forecast
- ○ Hide all forecasts

[< Back] [Start] [Cancel] [Help]

Click here to run the simulation.

## PROGRAM 10.4I

**Results from Decision Table in Crystal Ball for Simkin's Hardware Store**

Place cursor on any average value and select type of chart desired.

Click "View" to switch between different views.

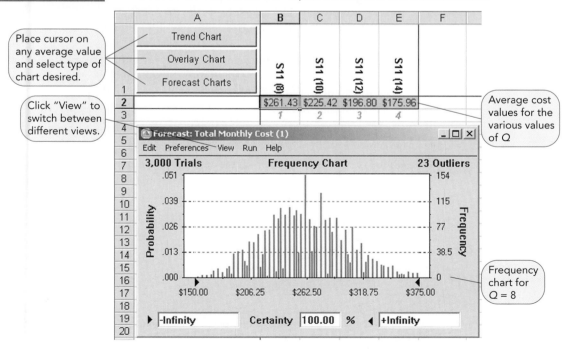

|  | A | B | C | D | E | F |
|---|---|---|---|---|---|---|
|  | Trend Chart | S11 (8) | S11 (10) | S11 (12) | S11 (14) |  |
|  | Overlay Chart |  |  |  |  |  |
|  | Forecast Charts |  |  |  |  |  |
| 2 |  | $261.43 | $225.42 | $196.80 | $175.96 |  |
| 3 |  | 1 | 2 | 3 | 4 |  |

Average cost values for the various values of Q

**Forecast: Total Monthly Cost (1)**

Edit  Preferences  View  Run  Help

3,000 Trials          Frequency Chart          23 Outliers

.051 — 154
.039 — 115
.026 — 77
.013 — 38.5
.000 — 0

$150.00    $206.25    $262.50    $318.75    $375.00

Probability / Frequency

Frequency chart for Q = 8

▶ -Infinity    Certainty [100.00] %    ◀ +Infinity

## 10.8   USING CRYSTAL BALL TO FIND THE BEST RESERVATION POLICY

In this section, we use Crystal Ball to simulate another problem in which the owner of a limousine service wants to find the optimal number of reservations she should accept for a trip.

### Judith's Airport Limousine Service

*Another simulation example using Crystal Ball*

Judith McKnew is always on the lookout for entrepreneurial opportunities. Living in Six Mile, South Carolina, she recognizes that the nearest airport is 50 miles away. Judith estimates that, on average, there are about 45 people from Six Mile (and its vicinity) who need rides to, or from, the airport each day. To help them, Judith is considering leasing a 10-passenger van and offering a limousine service between Six Mile and the airport. There would be four trips per day: a morning trip and an evening trip to the airport, and a morning trip and an evening trip from the airport.

After researching the issue carefully, Judith sets some operating guidelines for her problem and estimates the following parameters for each trip:

- Reservations can be made for a trip up to 12 hours in advance, by paying a nonrefundable $10 deposit. Judith will accept reservations up to her reservation limit (which this simulation model will help her decide).

- The ticket price is $35 per passenger per trip. Passengers with reservations must pay the $25 balance at the start of the trip.

*Number of reservations is probabilistic.*

- The number of reservations requested each trip follows a discrete uniform distribution between 7 and 14. Judith will, of course, reject a reservation request if she has reached her reservation limit.

*Number of show-ups is also probabilistic.*

- The probability that a person with a reservation shows up for the trip is 0.80. In other words, 20% of people with reservations do not show up. Anyone who does not show up forfeits the $10 deposit.

- If the number of passengers who show up exceeds 10 (the passenger capacity of the van), alternate arrangements must be made to get these extra people to the airport. This will cost Judith $75 per person. That is, Judith will lose $40 (= $75 − $35) per overbooked person.

*Finally, the number of walk-ups is also probabilistic.*

- The number of walk-up passengers (i.e., passengers without reservations) for a trip has the following general discrete distribution: probability of zero walk-ups is 0.30, probability of one walk-up is 0.45, and probability of two walk-ups is 0.25. Judith does not anticipate that there will ever be more than 2 walk-ups per trip.

- Walk-up passengers pay $50 per trip. Judith, however, does not have to make alternate arrangements for these passengers if her van is full.

- The total cost per trip (to or from the airport) to Judith is $100. Note that due to the possibility of walk-up passengers on the return trip, Judith has to make a trip to the airport even if she has no passengers on that trip.

Judith wants to find out how many reservations she should accept in order to maximize her average profit per trip. Specifically, she is considering accepting 10, 11, 12, 13, or 14 reservations.[11]

---

[11] The problem being considered here is a simplified version of the *yield management* problem faced by airlines and hotels. A description of this topic can be found in B. C. Smith, J. F. Leimkuhler, and R. M. Darrow. "Yield Management at American Airlines," *Interfaces* (January 1992), 22, 1, 8–31.

**PROGRAM 10.5A**   **Excel Layout and Results Using Crystal Ball for Judith's Limousine Service**

*Crystal Ball menus*

*CB.Binomial function is used to simulate cell C4.*

*Crystal Ball toolbar*

C4    =CB.Binomial(D10,B4)

| | A | B | C | D | E | F | G | H | I | J |
|---|---|---|---|---|---|---|---|---|---|---|
| 1 | **Judith's Limousine Service (Using *Crystal Ball*)** | | | | | | | | | |
| 2 | | | | | | | | | | |
| 3 | Reservations requested | Reservations accepted | Number show up | Number overbook | Seats remaining | Number walk-up | Walk-up accepted | Revenue | Cost | Profit |
| 4 | 13 | 12 | 11 | 1 | 0 | 2 | 0 | $395 | $175 | $220 |
| 5 | | | | | | | | | | |
| 6 | Judith's reservation limit | | | 12 | (Want to try values of 10, 11, 12, 13, and 14 in cell D6) | | | | | |
| 7 | Van's passenger capacity | | | 10 | | | | | | |
| 8 | Minimum reservation request = | | | 7 | | | | | | |
| 9 | Maximum reservation request = | | | 14 | | | | | | |
| 10 | Probability passenger shows up | | | 0.80 | | | | | | |
| 11 | Reservation deposit amount = | | | $10 | | | | | | |
| 12 | Balance of ticket price = | | | $25 | | | | | | |
| 13 | Walk-up ticket price = | | | $50 | | | | | | |
| 14 | Cost per overbooked passenger = | | | $75 | | | | | | |
| 15 | Fixed cost per trip = | | | $100 | | | | | | |
| 16 | | | | | | | | | | |
| 17 | Distribution of number of walk-ups | | | Number | Probability | | | | | |
| 18 | | | | 0 | 0.30 | | | | | |
| 19 | | | | 1 | 0.45 | | | | | |
| 20 | | | | 2 | 0.25 | | | | | |

*Simulated using a RANDBETWEEN function*

*Input values for the model*

*Profit per trip. This is the cell we wish to track.*

*Range for custom distribution of walk-ups, simulated in cell F4.*

**File: 10-5.xls**

*This is how we set up Judith's problem.*

## Setting Up the Model

Each replication in Judith's problem corresponds to a trip. The Excel layout for this problem, shown in Program 10.5A, is organized as follows:

■ Cell A4 shows the number of reservations requested for a trip. This is simulated from a discrete uniform distribution using the RANDBETWEEN function with parameters $a = 7$ (specified in cell D8) and $b = 14$ (specified in cell D9). The formula in cell A4 is

$$=RANDBETWEEN(D8,D9)$$

■ In cell B4, the number of reservations accepted by Judith is set as the *smaller* of the number of reservations requested (cell A4), and Judith's reservation limit (specified in cell D6). The formula in cell C4 is

$$=MIN(A4,D6)$$

*Number of people showing up is simulated using Crystal Ball's CB.Binomial function.*

■ Cell C4 simulates the number of passengers with reservations who actually show up for the trip. To do so, we recognize that this number follows a *binomial distribution* with parameters $p = 0.8$ (specified in cell D10), and $n$ = number of reservations accepted (cell B4). Hence, the formula in cell C4 is[12]

$$=CB.Binomial(D10,B4)$$

■ If the number of passengers showing up (cell C4) exceeds the van's passenger capacity (specified in cell D7), we have overbooked passengers. Otherwise, we have no over-booked passengers. In cell D4, we calculate the number of overbooked passengers using the MAX function as follows:

$$=MAX(C4-D7,0)$$

■ Likewise, if the van capacity exceeds the number of passengers showing up, we have some seats remaining. Otherwise, we are full. In cell E4, we calculate this number as follows:

$$=MAX(D7-C4,0)$$

*The CB.Custom function is used here to simulate number of walk-ups.*

■ Next, in cell F4, we simulate the number of walk-up passengers using Crystal Ball's custom distribution function (refer back to Table 10.7 on page 436 for details if necessary). The range of values and probabilities has been specified in cells D18:E20 in Program 10.4A. The formula in cell E4 is

$$=CB.Custom(D10:E20)$$

■ The number of walk-ups who can be accommodated in the van is obviously limited by the seats remaining (cell E4). Hence, in cell G4, we calculate the number of walk-ups accepted using a MIN function as follows:

$$=MIN(F4,E4)$$

■ The total revenue and cost for the trip are now calculated in cells H4 and I4, respectively, as

Revenue = \$10 (Reservations accepted) × \$25 (Number of people who show up)
    + \$50 (Walk-ups accepted)

= B4*D11+C4*D12+G4*D13

Cost = \$75 (Number overbooked) + \$100

= D4*D14+D15

■ Finally, in cell J4, we calculate the profit as (Revenue − Cost).

## Replicating the Model

For illustration purposes, let us first use Crystal Ball to run 3,000 replications of Judith's simulation model for a reservation limit of 12. We then use a Decision Table in Crystal Ball to extend this model to consider the other reservation limits.

---

[12] If you are modeling this problem without Crystal Ball, simulating from a binomial distribution is difficult. In this case, you can first use an IF function for each passenger to check if he or she shows up. Then, count the ones who show up to get the total number.

**Replications with Reservation Limit = 12**  As with the simulation model for Simkin's Hardware Store, we use the following steps:

1. Select cell J4, which contains the formula for the output measure (i.e., profit) that we want to track.

*Define the forecast cell that we want to track.*

2. Click Cells|Define Forecast (or click the Define Forecast icon on the Crystal Ball toolbar). If desired, specify the name and units of the output measure in the window that is displayed (refer back to Program 10.4B on page 437 for a sample view of this window). Click OK.

3. Click Run|Run Preferences (or click the Run Preferences icon on the Crystal Ball toolbar). Specify the number of replications (3,000 in this case) desired in the window that appears (see Program 10.4C on page 438 for a sample view of this window). Click OK.

*Output can be viewed graphically or as a table.*

4. To run the model, click Run|Run (or click the Run icon on the Crystal Ball toolbar). Crystal Ball runs the model for the specified number of replications, keeping track of cell J4. The output is shown in both graphical and tabular forms in Program 10.5B.

The results in Program 10.5B indicate that Judith's average profit (based on 3,000 replications) is $228 per trip. The range extends from a minimum of $45 to a maximum of $320.

**PROGRAM 10.5B**    **Graphical and Tabular Results from Crystal Ball for Judith's Limousine Service**

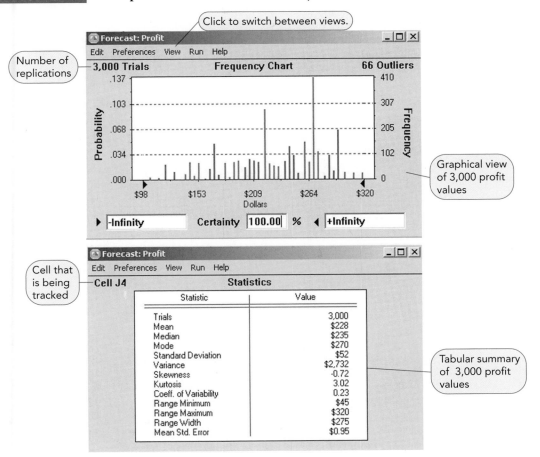

*We use a Decision Table to test different values for the reservation limit.*

**Replications with Many Reservation Limits Using a Decision Table**  In Judith's problem, we want to try out 5 different values (10, 11, 12, 13, and 14) for the reservation limit. To do so using Decision Table in Crystal Ball, we use the following steps just as we did in Section 10.7 for Simkin's inventory problem.

■ Using Cell|Define Forecast to define cell J4 as the forecast cell.

■ Select cell D6 (cell in which we want the reservation limit values to be plugged in). Click Cell|Define Decision. In the window that is displayed (see Program 10.4E on page 439 for a sample view of this window), enter a lower value of 10 and an upper value of 14. The discrete step size is 1 since we want to study all reservations limits between 10 and 14. Click OK.

■ Click CBTools|Decision Table. Make sure the appropriate forecast cell (cell J4 in Judith's problem) is shown as the target cell in the window that is displayed. Click Next.

■ Select the decision variable (D6) and click the button marked ">>" in the window that is displayed. Click Next.

■ In the final window (refer back to Program 10.4H on page 441 for a sample view of this window), make sure the appropriate number of values is shown for cell D6 (5 choices in Judith's problem). Enter the desired number of replications for each choice (3,000). Click Start.

When we click the Start button, the Decision Table plugs in each value (i.e., 10 to 14) of the decision variable (reservation limit) in cell D6 (see Program 10.5A) and runs 3,000 replications in each case. The results, shown in Program 10.5C, are displayed in a separate workbook. We can click on any of these profit values (cells B2:F2 of Program 10.5C), and

*We can see details for any of the simulation runs.*

select the charts shown to see details for that simulation. For example, Program 10.5C shows the frequency chart obtained for Profit (3), which corresponds to a reservation limit of 12 in cell D6.

---

**PROGRAM 10.5C**  **Results from Decision Table in Crystal Ball for Judith's Limousine Service**

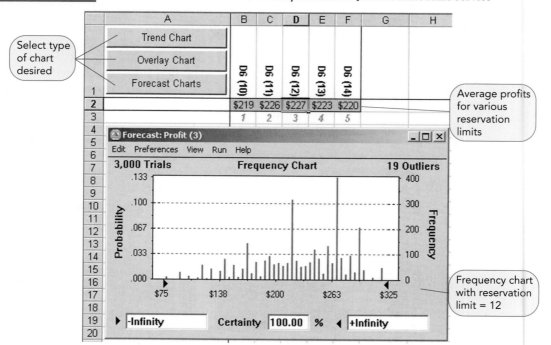

Comparing the profit values in Program 10.5C, it appears that Judith's best choice would be to accept 12 reservations per trip (based on 3,000 replications). The resulting average profit is $227 per trip.

As an exercise, see if you can set up a Decision Table in Crystal Ball to determine the reservation limit that will give Judith the highest *load factor*. The load factor is defined as the number of passengers traveling (i.e., =C4−D4+G4) on a trip, divided by the capacity of the van (cell D7). *Hint:* Although your answers will vary depending on the number of replications, the load factor should typically increase with the reservation limit. The load factor with a reservation limit of 14 should be around 88%.

As noted earlier, our intent here is to provide just a brief introduction to Crystal Ball. As you navigate the various menus in the package (some of which are discussed here), you may notice several other choices and options. Once again, we encourage you to try these procedures out on your own.

## 10.9  OTHER TYPES OF SIMULATION MODELS

Simulation models are often broken into three categories. The first, the Monte Carlo method discussed in this chapter, uses the concepts of probability distribution and random numbers to evaluate system responses to various policies. The other two categories are operational gaming and systems simulation. Although in theory the three methods are distinctly different, the growth of computerized simulation has tended to create a common basis in procedures and blur these differences.[13]

### Operational Gaming

*Operational gaming* refers to simulation involving two or more competing players. The best examples are military games and business games. Both allow participants to match their management and decision-making skills in hypothetical situations of conflict.

*Business simulation games are popular educational tools in many colleges.*

Military games are used worldwide to train a nation's top military officers, to test offensive and defensive strategies, and to examine the effectiveness of equipment and armies. Business games, first developed by the firm Booz, Allen, and Hamilton in the 1950s, are popular with both executives and business students. They provide an opportunity to test business skills and decision-making ability in a competitive environment. The person or team that performs best in the simulated environment is rewarded by knowing that his or her company has been most successful in earning the largest profit, grabbing a high market share, or perhaps increasing the firm's trading value on the stock exchange.

During each period of competition, be it a week, month, or quarter, teams respond to market conditions by coding their latest management decisions with respect to inventory, production, financing, investment, marketing, and research. The competitive business environment is simulated using a computer, and a new printout summarizing current market conditions is presented to players. This allows teams to simulate years of operating conditions in a matter of days, weeks, or a semester.

---

[13] Theoretically, random numbers are used only in Monte Carlo simulation. However, in some complex gaming or systems simulation problems in which relationships cannot be defined exactly, it may be necessary to use the probability concepts of the Monte Carlo method.

**FIGURE 10.3**

**Inputs and Outputs of a
Typical Economic System
Simulation**

| Inputs | Model | Outputs |
|---|---|---|
| Income Tax Levels → | Econometric Model (in Series of Mathematical Equations) | → Gross National Product |
| Corporate Tax Rates → | | → Inflation Rates |
| Interest Rates → | | → Unemployment Rates |
| Government Spending → | | → Monetary Supplies |
| Foreign Trade Policy → | | → Population Growth Rates |

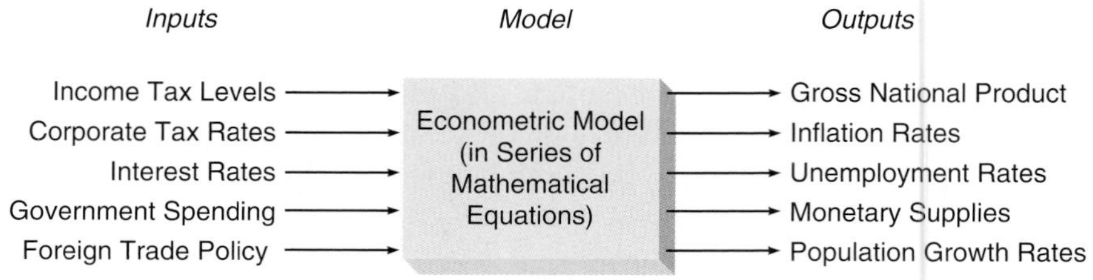

## Systems Simulation

*Systems simulation* is similar to business gaming in that it allows users to test various managerial policies and decisions to evaluate their effect on the operating environment. This variation of simulation models the dynamics of large systems. Such systems include corporate operations,[14] the national economy, a hospital, or a city government system.

In a corporate operating system, sales, production levels, marketing policies, investments, union contracts, utility rates, financing, and other factors are all related in a series of mathematical equations that are examined by simulation. In a simulation of an urban government, systems simulation could be employed to evaluate the impact of tax increases, capital expenditures for roads and buildings, housing availability, new garbage routes, immigration and out-migration, locations of new schools or senior citizen centers, birth and death rates, and many more vital issues. Simulations of *economic systems*, often called *econometric* models, are used by government agencies, bankers, and large organizations to predict inflation rates, domestic and foreign money supplies, and unemployment levels. Inputs and outputs of a typical economic system simulation are illustrated in Figure 10.3.

*Econometric models are huge simulations involving thousands of regression equations tied together by economic factors. They use what-if questions to test out various policies.*

The value of systems simulation lies in its allowance of what-if questions to test the effects of various policies. A corporate planning group, for example, can change the value of any input, such as an advertising budget, and examine the impact on sales, market share, or short-term costs. Simulation can also be used to evaluate different research and development projects or to determine long-range planning horizons.

## SUMMARY

This chapter discusses the concept and approach of simulation as a problem-solving tool. Simulation involves building a mathematical model that attempts to describe a real-world situation. The model's goal is to incorporate important variables and their interrelationships in such a way that we can study the impact of managerial changes upon the total system. The approach has many advantages over other decision modeling techniques and is especially useful when a problem is too complex or difficult to solve by other means.

The Monte Carlo method of simulation uses random numbers to generate random variable values from probability distributions. The simulation procedure is conducted for many time periods to evaluate the long-term impact of each policy value being studied.

We first illustrate how to set up Monte Carlo simulations using Excel's built-in functions. We also show how Excel's Data Table could be used to run several replications of simulation models and try different values for an input variable. Then, we show how Crystal Ball, an Excel add-in for simulation, can be used to develop and run simulation models. The major advantages of using add-ins are (1) the availability of easy formulas for many common probability distributions, (2) the ability to quickly set up and run many replications of the model, and (3) the ability to easily collect statistical information on many different output measures.

We conclude this chapter with a brief discussion of operational gaming and systems simulation, two other categories of simulations.

---

[14] This is sometimes referred to as *industrial dynamics*, a term coined by Jay Forrester. Forrester's goal was to find a way "to show how policies, decisions, structure, and delays are interrelated to influence growth and stability" in industrial systems. See J. W. Forrester. *Industrial Dynamics*. Cambridge, MA: The MIT Press, 1961.

# GLOSSARY

**Crystal Ball.** An add-in for Excel that simplifies the implementation and solution of simulation models.

**Data Table.** A feature in Excel that allows simulation models to be replicated several times. Two-variable data tables can be used to try different values for a decision variable in the simulation model.

**Decision Table.** A feature in Crystal Ball used to automatically try different values for a decision variable in the simulation model.

**Flow Diagram or Flowchart.** A graphical means of presenting the logic of a simulation model. It is a tool that helps in writing a simulation computer program.

**General Discrete Probability Distribution.** A distribution in which a variable can take on one of several discrete values, each with its own probability.

**Monte Carlo Simulation.** Simulations that experiment with probabilistic elements of a system by generating random numbers to create values for those elements.

**NORMINV.** An Excel function that can be used to randomly generate values from normal probability distributions.

**Operational Gaming.** The use of simulation in competitive situations such as military games and business or management games.

**RAND.** An Excel function that generates a random number between 0 and 1 each time it is computed.

**RANDBETWEEN.** An Excel function that can be used to randomly generate values from discrete uniform probability distributions.

**Random Number.** A number (typically between zero and one in most computer programs) whose value is selected completely at random.

**Replication.** A single run of a simulation model. Also known as a *trial*.

**Simulation.** A technique that involves building a mathematical model to represent a real-world situation. The model is then experimented with to estimate the effects of various actions and decisions.

**Systems Simulation.** Simulation models dealing with the dynamics of large organizational or governmental systems.

**VLOOKUP.** An Excel function that can be used to randomly generate values from general discrete probability distributions.

# SOLVED PROBLEMS

### Solved Problem 10-1

Higgins Plumbing and Heating maintains a stock of 30-gallon hot water heaters that it sells to homeowners and installs for them. Owner Jerry Higgins likes the idea of having a large supply on hand to meet customer demand, but he also recognizes that it is expensive to do so. He examines hot water heater sales over the past 50 weeks and notes the following:

| HOT WATER HEATER SALES PER WEEK | NUMBER OF WEEKS THIS NUMBER WAS SOLD |
|:---:|:---:|
| 4 | 6 |
| 5 | 5 |
| 6 | 9 |
| 7 | 12 |
| 8 | 8 |
| 9 | 7 |
| 10 | 3 |
| | Total 50 |

a. Simulate Higgins' weekly sales over a four-year (208-week) period. Compute his average weekly sales.

b. Now use the probability distribution for sales to determine the expected value of sales. Explain any differences between this value and the average value computed in part (a).

c. Assume Higgins maintains a constant supply of 8 hot water heaters in any given week. Set up a simulation model to determine how many weeks he will have a stockout over a four-year period. Replicate your model 200 times using a Data Table to determine the probability that Higgins will have more than 40 weeks with stockouts over the four-year period.

**File: 10-6.xls**

## Solution

The Excel layout to answer all questions is presented in Program 10.6. The spreadsheet is organized as follows:

- Column A shows the week number.
- Column B shows a random number generated using the RAND function.
- The random number column in column B is used in a VLOOKUP function to simulate the weekly sales in column C. The parameters (random number intervals, sales, and probabilities) for the VLOOKUP function are shown in cells F4:I10.
- In column D, we calculate the occurrence of a stockout using an IF function (1 = stockout, 0 = no stockout).

a. Average sales over the 208-week period is the average of values in cells C4:C211. This value, shown in cell H13 in Program 10.6, is 6.69 units per week. Note that this value may vary slightly in your file due to the use of random numbers in the formula for sales.

b. Using expected values,

$$E(\text{heater sales}) = 0.12 \times 4 + 0.10 \times 5 + 0.18 \times 6 + 0.24 \times 7$$
$$+ 0.16 \times 8 + 0.14 \times 9 + 0.06 \times 10$$

$$= 6.88 \text{ heaters}$$

**PROGRAM 10.6**  **Excel Layout and Results for Solved Problem 10-1**

Range for VLOOKUP function to simulate sales

| | A | B | C | D | E | F | G | H | I | J | K | L |
|---|---|---|---|---|---|---|---|---|---|---|---|---|
| 1 | Solved Problem 10-1 | | | | | | | | | | Data Table | |
| 2 | | | | | | | Sales Distribution | | | | (One-Variable) | |
| 3 | Week | Random number | Sales | Stockout? (1 = Yes) | | RN interval lower limit | RN interval upper limit | Sales | Probabilty | | Replica tions | No. of stockouts |
| 4 | 1 | 0.772 | 8 | 0 | | 0.00 | 0.12 | 4 | 0.12 | | 1 | 32 |
| 5 | 2 | 0.111 | 4 | 0 | | 0.12 | 0.22 | 5 | 0.10 | | 2 | 45 |
| 6 | 3 | 0.321 | 6 | 0 | | 0.22 | 0.40 | 6 | 0.18 | | 3 | 46 |
| 7 | 4 | 0.898 | 9 | 1 | | 0.40 | 0.64 | 7 | 0.24 | | 4 | 49 |
| 8 | 5 | 0.200 | 5 | 0 | | 0.64 | 0.80 | 8 | 0.16 | | 5 | 42 |
| 9 | 6 | 0.075 | 4 | 0 | | 0.80 | 0.94 | 9 | 0.14 | | 6 | 48 |
| 10 | 7 | 0.255 | 6 | 0 | | 0.94 | 1.00 | 10 | 0.06 | | 7 | 37 |
| 11 | 8 | 0.522 | 7 | 0 | | | | | | | 8 | 40 |
| 12 | 9 | 0.303 | 6 | 0 | | (a) | | | | | 9 | 49 |
| 13 | 10 | 0.558 | 7 | 0 | | Average sales = | | 6.69 | | | 10 | 49 |
| 14 | 11 | 0.729 | 8 | 0 | | | | | | | 11 | 49 |
| 15 | 12 | 0.482 | 7 | 0 | | Expected sales = | | 6.88 | | | 12 | 44 |
| 16 | 13 | 0.173 | 5 | 0 | | | | | | | 13 | 33 |
| 17 | 14 | 0.021 | 4 | 0 | | (b) | | | | | 14 | 38 |
| 18 | 15 | 0.509 | 7 | 0 | | Number of stockouts = | | 32 | | | 15 | 48 |
| 19 | 16 | 0.211 | 5 | 0 | | | | | | | 16 | 43 |
| 20 | 17 | 0.274 | 6 | 0 | | ">40 stockout" weeks = | | 122 | | | 17 | 48 |
| 21 | 18 | 0.144 | 5 | 0 | | | | | | | 18 | 35 |
| 22 | 19 | 0.206 | 5 | 0 | | | | | | | 19 | 32 |
| 23 | 20 | 0.831 | 9 | 1 | | | | | | | 20 | 40 |
| 200 | 197 | 0.316 | 6 | 0 | | | | | | | 197 | 33 |
| 201 | 198 | 0.493 | 7 | 0 | | | | | | | 198 | 36 |
| 202 | 199 | 0.048 | 4 | 0 | | | | | | | 199 | 43 |
| 203 | 200 | 0.607 | 7 | 0 | | | | | | | 200 | 40 |
| 204 | 201 | 0.216 | 5 | 0 | | | | | | | | |
| 205 | 202 | 0.093 | 4 | 0 | | | | | | | | |
| 206 | 203 | 0.042 | 4 | 0 | | | | | | | | |
| 207 | 204 | 0.417 | 7 | 0 | | | | | | | | |
| 208 | 205 | 0.884 | 9 | 1 | | | | | | | | |
| 209 | 206 | 0.941 | 10 | 1 | | | | | | | | |
| 210 | 207 | 0.107 | 4 | 0 | | | | | | | | |
| 211 | 208 | 0.512 | 7 | 0 | | | | | | | | |

Hidden rows

COUNTIF function is used to count no. of weeks with >40 stockouts.

200 replications done here.

One-variable Data Table to replicate number of stockouts

We can compute this value using the following formula:

$$=SUMPRODUCT(H4:H10,I4:I10)$$

This value is shown in cell H15 in Program 10.6.

The simulated average (6.69 in Program 10.6) is based on weekly demands for just 208 weeks. Hence, although this value is close to the expected value of 6.88, the two values need not necessarily be the same. With a longer simulation, the two values will become even closer.

c. We can use the 208 stockout indicators in cells D4:D211 to determine the number of stockouts over the 208-week period. This value, shown in cell H18 in Program 10.6, is determined using the formula:

$$=SUM(D4:D211)$$

We now set up a one-variable Data Table to run 200 replications of the value in cell H18. The Data Table is shown in columns K and L in Program 10.6. We now use Excel's COUNTIF function on the 200 replicated values in column L to count the number of four-year periods in which there were more than 40 weeks with stockouts. The formula is

$$=COUNTIF(L4:L203,">40")$$

The value, shown in cell H20 in Program 10.6, is 122 (which corresponds to a probability of $122/200 = 0.61$). Again, your value could be different since we are replicating this simulation model only 200 times here.

## Solved Problem 10-2

The manager of Denton Savings and Loan is attempting to determine how many teller windows need to be open at the bank each day. As a general policy, the manager wishes to offer service such that (1) the average customer waiting time does not exceed 2 minutes and (2) the average queue length is 2 or fewer customers. Given the existing service level, as shown in the following data, does the bank meet these criteria? The manager estimates that the bank gets 150 customers each day. Use 300 replications of your model to answer this question (3,000 replications if using Crystal Ball).

| SERVICE TIME IN MINUTES | PROBABILITY | TIME BETWEEN SUCCESSIVE ARRIVALS IN MINUTES | PROBABILITY |
|---|---|---|---|
| 1 | 0.25 | 0 | 0.10 |
| 2 | 0.20 | 1 | 0.15 |
| 3 | 0.40 | 2 | 0.10 |
| 4 | 0.15 | 3 | 0.35 |
| | | 4 | 0.25 |
| | | 5 | 0.05 |

## Solution

This problem simulates a queuing system in which both the arrival times of customers and the service times at the facility follow general discrete distributions. Note that in this model, we need to keep track of the passage of time to record the specific arrival and departure times of customers. We refer to such models, in which events (e.g., customer arrivals and departures) occur at discrete points in time, as *discrete-event simulation models.*

Each replication of this model corresponds to a day's operation at the bank (i.e., the arrival and service of 150 customers). The Excel layout for this problem is presented in Program 10.7. Observe that we have included customer number "0" with zero values for all columns to *initialize* the simulation clock

**File: 10-7.xls**

**PROGRAM 10.7**    **Excel Layout and Results for Solved Problem 10-2**

Simulated using a VLOOKUP function

= Start time + service time

Length of queue, including current customer

| Custo-mer # | Time between arrivals | Arrival time | Start service | Service time | End service | Wait time | Queue length | | RN interval lower limit | RN interval upper limit | Time | Proba-bility | | | Replica tions | Average wait time | Average queue length |
|---|---|---|---|---|---|---|---|---|---|---|---|---|---|---|---|---|---|
| | | | | | | | | | | | | | | | | | |

**Data Table** =M19
(One-Variable)

| Custo-mer # | Time between arrivals | Arrival time | Start service | Service time | End service | Wait time | Queue length |
|---|---|---|---|---|---|---|---|
| 0 | 0 | 0 | 0 | 0 | 0 | 0 | 0 |
| 1 | 3 | 3 | 3 | 1 | 4 | 0 | 0 |
| 2 | 2 | 5 | 5 | 3 | 8 | 0 | 0 |
| 3 | 4 | 9 | 9 | 1 | 10 | 0 | 0 |
| 4 | 3 | 12 | 12 | 2 | 14 | 0 | 0 |
| 5 | 0 | 12 | 14 | 4 | 18 | 2 | 1 |
| 6 | 2 | 14 | 18 | 2 | 20 | 4 | 1 |
| 7 | 1 | 15 | 20 | 2 | 22 | 5 | 2 |
| 8 | 3 | 18 | 22 | 3 | 25 | 4 | 2 |
| 9 | 5 | 23 | 25 | 1 | 26 | 2 | 1 |
| 10 | 3 | 26 | 26 | 2 | 28 | 0 | 0 |
| 11 | 4 | 30 | 30 | 3 | 33 | 0 | 0 |
| 12 | 1 | 31 | 33 | 2 | 35 | 2 | 1 |
| 13 | 3 | 34 | 35 | 4 | 39 | 1 | 1 |
| 14 | 1 | 35 | 39 | 4 | 43 | 4 | 1 |
| 15 | 4 | 39 | 43 | 4 | 47 | 4 | 1 |
| 16 | 5 | 44 | 47 | 4 | 51 | 3 | 1 |
| 17 | 4 | 48 | 51 | 1 | 52 | 3 | 1 |
| 18 | 0 | 48 | 52 | 3 | 55 | 4 | 2 |
| 19 | 3 | 51 | 55 | 1 | 56 | 4 | 2 |
| 20 | 0 | 51 | 56 | 3 | 59 | 5 | 3 |
| 146 | 4 | 381 | 381 | 2 | 383 | 0 | 0 |
| 147 | 1 | 382 | 383 | 2 | 385 | 1 | 1 |
| 148 | 3 | 385 | 385 | 3 | 388 | 0 | 0 |
| 149 | 0 | 385 | 388 | 3 | 391 | 3 | 1 |
| 150 | 2 | 387 | 391 | 2 | 393 | 4 | 2 |

**Arrival Distribution**

| RN interval lower limit | RN interval upper limit | Time | Probability |
|---|---|---|---|
| 0.00 | 0.10 | 0 | 0.10 |
| 0.10 | 0.25 | 1 | 0.15 |
| 0.25 | 0.35 | 2 | 0.10 |
| 0.35 | 0.70 | 3 | 0.35 |
| 0.70 | 0.95 | 4 | 0.25 |
| 0.95 | 1.00 | 5 | 0.05 |

=M20

**Service Time Distribution**

| | | | |
|---|---|---|---|
| 0.00 | 0.25 | 1 | 0.25 |
| 0.25 | 0.45 | 2 | 0.20 |
| 0.45 | 0.85 | 3 | 0.40 |
| 0.85 | 1.00 | 4 | 0.15 |

| | |
|---|---|
| Average wait time = | 4.34 minutes |
| Average queue length = | 2.04 customers |

Output measures

| Replica tions | Average wait time | Average queue length |
|---|---|---|
| 1 | 4.34 | 2.04 |
| 2 | 2.83 | 1.26 |
| 3 | 8.13 | 3.44 |
| 4 | 1.87 | 1.06 |
| 5 | 4.90 | 2.10 |
| 6 | 8.61 | 3.65 |
| 7 | 2.88 | 1.41 |
| 8 | 17.52 | 6.93 |
| 9 | 3.79 | 1.78 |
| 10 | 7.65 | 3.31 |
| 11 | 4.03 | 1.87 |
| 12 | 5.84 | 2.59 |
| 13 | 3.29 | 1.57 |
| 14 | 7.41 | 3.33 |
| 15 | 1.81 | 0.91 |
| 16 | 3.89 | 1.75 |
| 17 | 6.41 | 2.74 |
| 18 | 3.82 | 1.85 |
| 19 | 2.58 | 1.26 |
| 20 | 3.84 | 1.73 |
| 21 | 4.77 | 2.06 |
| 147 | 1.56 | 0.85 |
| 148 | 5.85 | 2.56 |
| 149 | 4.01 | 1.87 |
| 150 | 2.37 | 1.15 |
| 151 | 3.33 | 1.53 |
| 152 | 1.13 | 0.64 |
| 297 | 2.77 | 1.30 |
| 298 | 6.45 | 2.79 |
| 299 | 6.52 | 2.73 |
| 300 | 8.39 | 3.59 |
| Average | 5.12 | 2.25 |

Hidden rows

= Start time – arrival time

One-variable Data Table to run 300 replications of output measures

Averages based on 300 replications

that keeps track of the passage of time. This is a good practice in all discrete-event simulation models. Rows 5 through 154 in the spreadsheet are organized as follows:

■ Column A shows the customer number (1 through 150).

■ Column B shows the time between arrivals of successive customers, simulated using a VLOOKUP function. The parameters (random number intervals, sales, and probabilities) for this VLOOKUP function are shown in cells J6:M11. The formula in cells B5:B154 is

=VLOOKUP(RAND(),$J$6:$L$11,3)

■ In column C, we calculate the arrival time of the current customer as the sum of the arrival time of the previous customer and the time between arrivals (column B). This type of computation is an example of a simulation clock, which is used to record time in a simulation model. For example, the formula in cell C5 is

=C4+B5

■ The time this customer actually starts service is calculated in column D as the maximum of the arrival time and the time the previous customer finishes service. For example, the formula in cell D5 is

$$=MAX(C5,F4)$$

■ Column E shows the service time for this customer, simulated using a VLOOKUP function. The parameters of this VLOOKUP function are shown in cells J14:M17. The formula in cells E5:E154 is

$$=VLOOKUP(RAND(),\$J\$14:\$L\$17,3)$$

■ The time at which this customer ends service is shown in column F as the sum of the start time (shown in column D) and the service time (shown in column E).

■ In column G, we calculate the wait time of this customer as the difference between the customer's start time (shown in column D) and arrival time (shown in column C).

■ Finally, in column H, we calculate the queue length using Excel's MATCH function. The MATCH function is used to determine how many customers (up to the current customer) have start times that are smaller than the arrival time of the current customer. Clearly, all customers (including the current one) who do not meet this criterion are in the queue. For example, the formula in cell I5 is

$$=A5-MATCH(C5,\$D\$5:D5,1)$$

Using the 150 wait time and queue length values in cells G5:H154, we determine the following two measures for the 150 customers each day: (1) average wait time per customer (shown in cell M19), and (2) average queue length (shown in cell M20).

The values in cells M19 and M20 represent just one replication of the model. To determine more precise values for these averages, we now replicate both measures 300 times each. The one-variable Data Table to do so is shown in columns P through R in Program 10.7.

Observe that a single one-variable Data Table can be used to replicate more than one output value at the same time. The procedure is as follows:

1. We enter numbers 1 to 300 in cells P4:P303, corresponding to the 300 replications we want to run for this model.
2. In cell Q4, we specify the cell reference for the average waiting time of each replication (i.e., cell M19). Then, in cell R4, we specify the cell reference for the average queue length of each replication (i.e., cell M20).
3. We now use the mouse or keyboard to select the range P4:R303 (i.e., all three columns), and run the one-variable Data Table as usual.

The Data Table for this problem is also shown in Program 10.7. The average waiting time per customer and the average queue length (both based on 300 replications) are shown in cells Q304 and R304, respectively.

Based on the values in Program 10.7, it seems that the system does not meet the manager's goal of making customers wait no more than 2 minutes on average. The average waiting time of 5.12 minutes per customer is more than double the desired target. The average queue length of 2.25 customers is, however, close to the manager's desired target. The manager should, perhaps, focus on initiating training programs to improve the average service rate of his tellers.

## ⟫ SELF-TEST

■ Before taking the self-test, refer back to the learning objectives at the beginning of the chapter, the notes in the margins, and the glossary at the end of the chapter.

■ Use the key at the back of the book to correct your answers.

■ Restudy pages that correspond to any questions that you answered incorrectly or material you feel uncertain about.

1. Simulation is a technique usually reserved for studying only the simplest and most straightforward of problems.
   **a.** True          **b.** False
2. A simulation model is designed to arrive at a single specific numerical answer to a given problem.
   **a.** True          **b.** False
3. Simulation typically requires a familiarity with statistics to evaluate the results.
   **a.** True          **b.** False
4. Simulation is best thought of as a technique to
   **a.** give concrete numerical answers.
   **b.** increase understanding of a problem.
   **c.** provide rapid solutions to relatively simple problems.
   **d.** provide optimal solutions to complex problems.
5. Specialized computer languages have been developed that allow one to readily simulate specific types of problems.
   **a.** True          **b.** False
6. Simulation is perhaps the only technique that can be applied to the study of virtually *any* problem.
   **a.** True          **b.** False
7. The seven steps we should perform when using simulation to analyze a problem are
   **a.** _____,
   **b.** _____,
   **c.** _____,
   **d.** _____,
   **e.** _____,
   **f.** _____,
   **g.** _____.
8. Advantages of simulation include
   **a.** _____,
   **b.** _____,
   **c.** _____,
   **d.** _____,
   **e.** _____,
   **f.** _____,
   **g.** _____.
9. Disadvantages of simulation include
   **a.** _____,
   **b.** _____,
   **c.** _____,
   **d.** _____.
10. When simulating the Monte Carlo experiment, the average simulated demand over the long run should approximate the
    **a.** real demand.
    **b.** expected demand.
    **c.** sampled demand.
    **d.** daily demand.
11. The idea behind simulation is to
    **a.** imitate a real-world situation.
    **b.** study the properties and operating characteristics of a real-world situation.
    **c.** draw conclusions and make action decisions based on simulation results.
    **d.** all of the above.
12. Special-purpose simulation languages include
    **a.** C++.
    **b.** Visual Basic.
    **c.** GPSS/H.
    **d.** FORTRAN.
    **e.** all of the above.
13. In a Monte Carlo simulation, a variable that we might want to simulate is
    **a.** lead time for inventory orders to arrive.
    **b.** times between machine breakdowns.
    **c.** time between arrivals at a service facility.
    **d.** number of employees absent from work each day.
    **e.** all of the above.
14. To simulate from a general discrete distribution in Excel, we use a
    **a.** COUNTIF function.
    **b.** NORMINV function.
    **c.** VLOOKUP function.
    **d.** Data Table.
15. It is enough to simulate a problem 100 times in order to calculate the average value of an output measure.
    **a.** True          **b.** False
16. To run several applications of a large simulation model in Excel, we use the
    **a.** IF function.
    **b.** NORMINV function.
    **c.** VLOOKUP function.
    **d.** Data Table.
17. To try different values automatically of a decision variable in Crystal Ball, we use a
    **a.** Data Table.
    **b.** Decision Table.
    **c.** VLOOKUP function.
    **d.** COUNTIF function.
18. To generate the value of a variable randomly in a simulation model, its probability distribution must be known.
    **a.** True          **b.** False

# DISCUSSION QUESTIONS AND PROBLEMS

## Discussion Questions

**10-1** What are the advantages and limitations of simulation models?

**10-2** Why might a manager be forced to use simulation instead of an analytical model in dealing with a problem of

(a) inventory ordering policy?
(b) ships docking in a port to unload?
(c) bank teller service windows?
(d) the U.S. economy?

**10-3** What types of management problems can be solved more easily by decision modeling techniques other than simulation?

**10-4** What are the major steps in the simulation process?

**10-5** What is Monte Carlo simulation? What principles underlie its use, and what steps are followed in applying it?

**10-6** Why is a computer necessary in conducting a real-world simulation?

**10-7** What is operational gaming? What is systems simulation? Give examples of how each may be applied.

**10-8** Do you think the application of simulation will increase strongly in the next 10 years? Why or why not?

**10-9** Would the average output value in a simulation problem change appreciably if a longer period were simulated? Why or why not?

**10-10** How might drawing a flow diagram help in developing a simulation model?

**10-11** List the advantages of using an Excel add-in program rather than using Excel's built-in functions to develop a simulation model.

**10-12** Discuss the differences between a two-variable Data Table and a one-variable Data Table.

**10-13** Do you think we can use Excel's Solver to solve simulation models? Why or why not?

## Problems

### Note

All of the following problems should be simulated using Excel and replicated either using Data Table or Crystal Ball. In all the problems, we have indicated the number of replications you should use simply as *N*. Your instructor may specify the actual value of *N* that he or she wants you to use. If not, we recommend that you try to replicate each simulation model as many times as is convenient. If you are using a Data Table, 200 to 300 replications should be appropriate to keep the Excel file reasonably small (even though the average values may vary from simulation to simulation). However, if you are using Crystal Ball, you should try 3,000 or more replications.

• **10-14** Clark Property Management is responsible for the maintenance, rental, and day-to-day operation of several large apartment complexes on the east side of

New Orleans. George Clark is especially concerned about the cost projections for replacing air conditioner compressors. He would like to simulate the number of compressor failures each month. Using data from similar apartment buildings he manages in a New Orleans suburb, Clark establishes a table of relative frequency of failures during a month as follows:

| NUMBER OF AIR CONDITIONER COMPRESSOR FAILURES | PROBABILITY (RELATIVE FREQUENCY) |
|---|---|
| 0 | 0.06 |
| 1 | 0.13 |
| 2 | 0.25 |
| 3 | 0.28 |
| 4 | 0.20 |
| 5 | 0.07 |
| 6 | 0.01 |

Simulate Clark's monthly compressor failures for a period of 300 months. Compute the average number of failures per month. Explain any difference between this value and the expected value of failures computed using the probability distribution.

⁝ **10-15** Vincent Maruggi, an MBA student at Northern Massachusetts University, has been having problems balancing his checkbook. His monthly income is derived from a graduate research assistantship; however, he also makes extra money in most months by tutoring undergraduates in their decision modeling course. His chances of various income levels are shown here:

| MONTHLY INCOME* ($) | PROBABILITY |
|---|---|
| 350 | 0.40 |
| 400 | 0.20 |
| 450 | 0.30 |
| 500 | 0.10 |

*Assume that this income is received at the beginning of each month.

Maruggi's expenditures also vary from month to month, and he estimates that they will follow this distribution:

| MONTHLY EXPENSES ($) | PROBABILITY |
|---|---|
| 300 | 0.10 |
| 400 | 0.45 |
| 500 | 0.30 |
| 600 | 0.15 |

Maruggi begins his final year with $600 in his checking account. Simulate an entire year (12 months) and identify Maruggi's (a) ending balance at the end of the year and (b) probability that he will have a negative balance in any month. Replicate your model *N* times and discuss Maruggi's financial picture based on the average values for these two measures.

**10-16** The Brennan Aircraft Division of TLN Enterprises operates a large number of computerized plotting machines. For the most part, the plotting devices are used to create line drawings of complex wing airfoils and fuselage part dimensions. The engineers operating the automated plotters are called loft lines engineers.

   The computerized plotters consist of a minicomputer system connected to a 4- by 5-foot flat table with a series of ink pens suspended above it. When a sheet of clear plastic or paper is properly placed on the table, the computer directs a series of horizontal and vertical pen movements until the desired figure is drawn.

   The plotting machines are highly reliable, with the exception of the four sophisticated ink pens that are built in. The pens constantly clog and jam in a raised or lowered position. When this occurs, the plotter is unusable.

   Currently, Brennan Aircraft replaces each pen as it fails. The service manager has, however, proposed replacing all four pens every time one fails. This should cut down the frequency of plotter failures. At present, it takes one hour to replace one pen. All four pens could be replaced in two hours. The total cost of a plotter being unusable is $50 per hour. Each pen costs $8.

   If only one pen is replaced each time a clog or jam occurs, the following breakdown data are thought to be valid:

| HOURS BETWEEN PLOTTER FAILURES IF ONE PEN IS REPLACED DURING A REPAIR | PROBABILITY |
|---|---|
| 10 | 0.05 |
| 20 | 0.15 |
| 30 | 0.15 |
| 40 | 0.20 |
| 50 | 0.20 |
| 60 | 0.15 |
| 70 | 0.10 |

Based on the service manager's estimates, if all four pens are replaced each time one pen fails, the probability distribution between failures is as follows:

| HOURS BETWEEN PLOTTER FAILURES IF ALL FOUR PENS ARE REPLACED DURING A REPAIR | PROBABILITY |
|---|---|
| 100 | 0.15 |
| 110 | 0.25 |
| 120 | 0.35 |
| 130 | 0.20 |
| 140 | 0.05 |

(a) Simulate Brennan Aircraft's problem and determine the best policy. Use *N* replications. Should the firm replace one pen or all four pens on a plotter each time a failure occurs?

(b) Develop a second approach to solving this problem, this time without simulation. Compare the results. How does it affect Brennan's policy decision using simulation?

**10-17** Dr. Mark Greenberg practices dentistry in Topeka, Kansas. Greenberg tries hard to schedule appointments so that patients do not have to wait beyond their appointment time. His October 20 schedule is shown in the following table.

| SCHEDULED APPOINTMENT AND TIME | | EXPECTED TIME NEEDED |
|---|---|---|
| Adams | 9:30 A.M. | 15 |
| Brown | 9:45 A.M. | 20 |
| Crawford | 10:15 A.M. | 15 |
| Dannon | 10:30 A.M. | 10 |
| Erving | 10:45 A.M. | 30 |
| Fink | 11:15 A.M. | 15 |
| Graham | 11:30 A.M. | 20 |
| Hinkel | 11:45 A.M. | 15 |

Unfortunately, not every patient arrives exactly on schedule, and expected times to examine patients are just that—*expected*. Some examinations take longer than expected, and some take less time.

   Greenberg's experience dictates the following:

(a) 20% of the patients will be 20 minutes early.
(b) 10% of the patients will be 10 minutes early.
(c) 40% of the patients will be on time.
(d) 25% of the patients will be 10 minutes late.
(e) 5% of the patients will be 20 minutes late.

He further estimates that
(a) 15% of the time he will finish in 20% less time than expected.
(b) 50% of the time he will finish in the expected time.

(c) 25% of the time he will finish in 20% more time than expected.

(d) 10% of the time he will finish in 40% more time than expected.

Dr. Greenberg has to leave at 12:15 P.M. on October 20 to catch a flight to a dental convention in New York. Assuming that he is ready to start his workday at 9:30 A.M. and that patients are treated in order of their scheduled exam (even if one late patient arrives after an early one), will he be able to make the flight? Comment on this simulation. Use $N$ replications.

**10-18** The Pelnor Corporation is the nation's largest manufacturer of industrial-size washing machines. A main ingredient in the production process is 8- by 10-foot sheets of stainless steel. The steel is used for both interior washer drums and outer casings.

Steel is purchased weekly on a contractual basis from the Smith-Layton Foundry, which, because of limited availability and lot sizing, can ship either 8,000 or 11,000 square feet of stainless steel each week. When Pelnor's weekly order is placed, there is a 45% chance that 8,000 square feet will arrive and a 55% chance of receiving the larger size order.

Pelnor uses the stainless steel on a stochastic (nonconstant) basis. The probabilities of demand each week follow:

| STEEL NEEDED PER WEEK (SQ FT) | PROBABILITY |
|---|---|
| 6,000 | 0.05 |
| 7,000 | 0.15 |
| 8,000 | 0.20 |
| 9,000 | 0.30 |
| 10,000 | 0.20 |
| 11,000 | 0.10 |

Pelnor has a capacity to store no more than 25,000 square feet of steel at any time. Because of the contract, orders *must* be placed each week regardless of the on-hand supply.

(a) Simulate stainless steel order arrivals and use for 52 weeks. (Begin the first week with a starting inventory of 5,000 stainless steel.) If an end-of-week inventory is ever negative, assume that back orders are permitted and fill the demand from the next arriving order.

(b) Should Pelnor add more storage area? If so, how much? If not, comment on the system. Use $N$ replications of your model in (a) to answer these questions.

**10-19** Milwaukee's General Hospital has an emergency room that is divided into six departments: (1) the initial exam station, to treat minor problems or make diagnoses; (2) an x-ray department; (3) an operating room; (4) a cast-fitting room; (5) an observation room for recovery and general observation before

final diagnoses or release; and (6) an out-processing department where clerks check patients out and arrange for payment or insurance forms.

The probabilities that a patient will go from one department to another are presented in the following table:

| FROM | TO | PROBABILITY |
|---|---|---|
| Initial exam at emergency room entrance | X-ray department | 0.45 |
| | Operating room | 0.15 |
| | Observation room | 0.10 |
| | Out-processing clerk | 0.30 |
| X-ray department | Operating room | 0.10 |
| | Cast-fitting room | 0.25 |
| | Observation room | 0.35 |
| | Out-processing clerk | 0.30 |
| Operating room | Cast-fitting room | 0.25 |
| | Observation room | 0.70 |
| | Out-processing clerk | 0.05 |
| Cast-fitting room | Observation room | 0.55 |
| | X-ray department | 0.05 |
| | Out-processing clerk | 0.40 |
| Observation room | Operating room | 0.15 |
| | X-ray department | 0.15 |
| | Out-processing clerk | 0.70 |

(a) Simulate the trail followed by 200 emergency room patients. Proceed one patient at a time from each one's entry at the initial exam station until he or she leaves through out-processing. You should be aware that a patient can enter the same department more than once.

(b) Using your simulation data, what are the chances that a patient enters the x-ray department twice?

**10-20** Management of the First Syracuse Bank is concerned over a loss of customers at its main office downtown. One solution that has been proposed is to add one or more drive-through teller stations to make it easier for customers in cars to obtain quick service without parking. Chris Carlson, the bank president, thinks the bank should only risk the cost of installing one drive-through. He is informed by his staff that the cost (amortized over a 20-year period) of building a drive-through is $12,000 per year. It also costs $16,000 per year in wages and benefits to staff each new teller window.

The director of management analysis, Beth Shader, believes that the following two factors encourage the immediate construction of two drive-through stations, however. According to a recent article in *Banking Research* magazine, customers who wait in long lines for drive-through teller service will cost banks an average of $1 per minute in loss of goodwill. Also, adding a second drive-through will cost an additional $16,000 in staffing, but amortized construction costs can be cut to a total of $20,000 per year if two drive-throughs are installed together instead of one at a time. To complete her analysis, Shader collected one month's arrival and service rates at a competing downtown bank's drive-through stations. These data are shown as observation analyses 1 and 2 in the following tables.

(a) Simulate a one-hour time period, from 1 to 2 P.M., for a single-teller drive-through. Replicate the model *N* times.

(b) Simulate a one-hour time period, from 1 to 2 P.M., for a two-teller system. Replicate the model *N* times.

(c) Conduct a cost analysis of the two options. Assume that the bank is open 7 hours per day and 200 days per year. Use the averages computed in parts (a) and (b).

### Observation Analysis 1: Interarrival Times for 1,000 Observations

| TIME BETWEEN ARRIVALS (MINUTES) | NUMBER OF OCCURRENCES |
|---|---|
| 1 | 200 |
| 2 | 250 |
| 3 | 300 |
| 4 | 150 |
| 5 | 100 |

### Observation Analysis 2: Customer Service Time for 1,000 Customers

| SERVICE TIME (MINUTES) | NUMBER OF OCCURRENCES |
|---|---|
| 1 | 100 |
| 2 | 150 |
| 3 | 350 |
| 4 | 150 |
| 5 | 150 |
| 6 | 100 |

**10-21** The Alfredo Fragrance Company produces only one product, a perfume called Hint of Elegance. Hint of Elegance consists of two secret ingredients blended into an exclusive fragrance which is marketed in Zurich. An economic expression referred to as the Cobb–Douglas function describes the production of Hint of Elegance as follows:

$$X = \sqrt{(\text{ingredient 1})(\text{ingredient 2})}$$

where *X* is the amount of perfume produced.

The company operates at a level where ingredient 1 is set daily at 25 units and ingredient 2 at 36 units. Although the price Alfredo pays for ingredient 1 is fixed at $50 per unit, the cost of ingredient 2 and the selling price for the final perfume are both probabilistic. The sales price for Hint of Elegance follows this distribution:

| SALES PRICE ($) | PROBABILITY |
|---|---|
| 300 | 0.2 |
| 350 | 0.5 |
| 400 | 0.3 |

The cost for ingredient 2 is discrete uniformly distributed between $35 and $45 (in increments of $1). Simulate the firm's profits for a month (30 days). Use *N* replications of your model to compute the average monthly profit.

**10-22** Julia Walters owns and operates one of the largest Mercedes-Benz auto dealerships in Washington, DC. In the past 36 months her sales of this luxury car have ranged from a low of 6 new cars to a high of 12 new cars, as reflected in the following table:

| SALES OF NEW CARS PER MONTH | FREQUENCY |
|---|---|
| 6 | 3 |
| 7 | 4 |
| 8 | 6 |
| 9 | 12 |
| 10 | 9 |
| 11 | 1 |
| 12 | 1 |
| | Total 36 months |

Walters believes that sales will continue during the next 24 months at about the same historical rates and that delivery times will also continue to follow this pace (stated in probability form):

| DELIVERY TIME (MONTHS) | PROBABILITY |
|---|---|
| 1 | 0.44 |
| 2 | 0.33 |
| 3 | 0.16 |
| 4 | 0.07 |
| | 1.00 |

Walters's current policy is to order 14 cars at a time (two full truckloads, with 7 autos on each truck) and to place a new order whenever the stock on hand reaches 12 autos. What are the results of this policy when simulated over the next two years? Use *N* replications. Assume a beginning inventory of 14 cars.

• **10-23** Referring to Problem 10-22, Julia Walters establishes the following relevant costs: (1) the carrying cost per Mercedes per month is $600, (2) the cost of a lost sale averages $4,350, and (3) the cost of placing an order is $570. What is the total inventory cost of the policy simulated ($Q = 14$, ROP = 12) in Problem 10-22? Use $N$ replications of your model.

**10-24** Julia Walters (see Problems 10-22 and 10-23) wishes to try several new inventory policies. Set up a two-variable Data Table (or a Decision Table in Crystal Ball) with $N$ replications to identify the best policy from $Q = 12$, 14, 16, 18, or 20. Set $R = 12$ in each case.

**10-25** Janis Miller is considering building a 300-seat theater in a popular tourist destination. After studying the market, Janis has drawn the following conclusions:

■ There will be one show every night

■ The theater will make a profit of $2.00 on each occupied seat, and a loss of $0.50 on each unoccupied seat.

■ The probability that it rains on any given night is 0.30.

■ The number of customers on a dry night is normally distributed with a mean of 275, and a standard deviation of 30.

■ The number of customers on a rainy night is normally distributed with a mean of 250, and a standard deviation of 45.

Set up Janis's problem in Excel and simulate demand for one month (30 days). Use Excel's INT function to convert all simulated demands to integers. Replicate your model $N$ times and calculate Janis's average monthly profit.

**10-26** The Clemson Police Department makes annual door-to-door solicitations for funds. Residents of each visited house are asked to contribute either $15 (and receive a free family portrait package) or $25 (and receive two free family portrait packages). An analysis from previous years' solicitations indicates that

■ only 80% of the homes visited have the man or woman of the house at home.

■ when someone is home, there is only a 40% chance that he or she will make a donation.

■ of the people making donations, there is a 55% chance they will contribute $15, and a 43% chance they will contribute $25. Occasionally (2% chance), a person makes a donation in excess of $25. Such distributions follow a discrete uniform distribution between $30 and $50 (in increments of $1).

The police chief plans to visit 30 houses tomorrow. Set up a simulation model on Excel, and replicate it $N$ times to determine the probability that the chief will receive more than $250 in donations from these 30 houses.

**10-27** The owner of Dwayne's Concrete Service notes that the number of jobs each month follows a discrete uniform distribution between 10 and 16. The probability that a specific job will be for a residential driveway is 70%, and the probability that it will be for a commercial project is 30%. Revenues for residential driveways follow a normal distribution with a mean of $500 and a standard deviation of $50. Commercial projects, although more lucrative, also have larger variability. Dwayne estimates revenues here follow a normal distribution with a mean of $1,500 and a standard deviation of $400. Set up a simulation model for Dwayne's problem, and replicate it $N$ times to calculate the average value of revenue each month.

**10-28** Ann sells hot dogs at the local peewee league baseball games. For the upcoming championship game, Ann has to decide how many hot dogs to order (170, 190, or 210), at a cost of $0.25 each. Ann sells hot dogs for $1 each. However, any unsold hot dogs must be thrown away.

If the game is interesting, Ann thinks that fewer people will visit her stand. In such a case, Ann estimates that demand will be normally distributed with a mean of 140 and a standard deviation of 20. However, if the game is a blowout, she expects more people to visit the stand. Demand in this case will be normally distributed with a mean of 190 and a standard deviation of 15. Based on her familiarity with the two teams, she estimates that there is only a 40% chance the game will be a blowout.

Set up a simulation model and replicate it $N$ times for each order size to determine Ann's (a) expected profit and (b) expected percentage of unsold hot dogs. What do you recommend Ann should do?

---

## ⇒ CASE STUDY

### Alabama Airlines

Alabama Airlines opened its doors in June 2000 as a commuter service with its headquarters and only hub located in Birmingham. A product of airline deregulation, Alabama Air joined the growing number of successful short-haul, point-to-point airlines, including Lone Star, Comair, Atlantic Southeast, Skywest, and Business Express.

Alabama Air was started and managed by two former pilots, David Douglas (who had been with the defunct Eastern Airlines) and Michael Hanna (formerly with Pan Am). It acquired a fleet of 12 used prop-jet planes and the airport gates vacated by Delta Airlines' 1999 downsizing.

With business growing quickly, Douglas turned his attention to Alabama Air's toll-free reservations system. Between

## TABLE 10.8

**Incoming Call Distribution**

| TIME BETWEEN CALLS (MINUTES) | PROBABILITY |
|:---:|:---:|
| 1 | 0.11 |
| 2 | 0.21 |
| 3 | 0.22 |
| 4 | 0.20 |
| 5 | 0.16 |
| 6 | 0.10 |

## TABLE 10.10

**Incoming Call Distribution**

| TIME BETWEEN CALLS (MINUTES) | PROBABILITY |
|:---:|:---:|
| 1 | 0.22 |
| 2 | 0.25 |
| 3 | 0.19 |
| 4 | 0.15 |
| 5 | 0.12 |
| 6 | 0.07 |

midnight and 6:00 A.M., only one telephone reservations agent had been on duty. The time between incoming calls during this period is distributed as shown in Table 10.8. Douglas carefully observed and timed the agent and estimated that the time taken to process passenger inquiries is distributed as shown in Table 10.9.

## TABLE 10.9

**Service Time Distribution**

| TIME TO PROCESS CUSTOMER ENQUIRIES (MINUTES) | PROBABILITY |
|:---:|:---:|
| 1 | 0.20 |
| 2 | 0.19 |
| 3 | 0.18 |
| 4 | 0.17 |
| 5 | 0.13 |
| 6 | 0.10 |
| 7 | 0.03 |

All customers calling Alabama Air go on hold and are served in the order of the calls unless the reservations agent is available for immediate service. Douglas is deciding whether a second agent should be on duty to cope with customer demand. To maintain customer satisfaction, Alabama Air does not want a customer on hold for more than 3 to 4 minutes and also wants to maintain a "high" operator utilization.

Further, the airline is planning a new TV advertising campaign. As a result, it expects an increase in toll-free line phone inquiries. Based on similar campaigns in the past, the incoming call distribution from midnight to 6 A.M. is expected to be as shown in Table 10.10. (The same service time distribution will apply.)

### Discussion Questions

1. What would you advise Alabama Air to do for the current reservation system based on the original call distribution? Create a simulation model to investigate the scenario. Describe the model carefully and justify the duration of the simulation, assumptions, and measures of performance.

2. What are your recommendations regarding operator utilization and customer satisfaction if the airline proceeds with the advertising campaign?

*Source:* Professor Zbigniew H. Przasnyski, Loyola Marymount University.

---

## ⇒ CASE STUDY

### Abjar Transport Company

In 2001, Samir Khaldoun, after receiving an MBA degree from a leading university in the United States, returned to Jeddah, Saudi Arabia, where his family has extensive business holdings. Samir's first assignment was to stabilize and develop a newly formed, family-owned transport company—Abjar Transport.

An immediate problem facing Samir was the determination of the number of trucks needed to handle the forecasted freight volume. Heretofore, trucks were added to the fleet on an "as-needed" basis without comprehensive capacity planning. This approach created problems of driver recruitment, truck service

and maintenance, and excessive demurrage (i.e., port fees) because of delays at unloading docks and retention of cargo containers.

Samir forecasts that Abjar's freight volume should average 160,000 tons per month with a standard deviation of 30,000 tons. Freight is unloaded on a uniform basis throughout the month. Based on past experience, the amount handled per month is assumed to be normally distributed.

After extensive investigation, Samir concluded that the fleet should be standardized to 40-foot Mercedes 2624 2 × 4 tractor-trailer rigs, which are suitable for carrying two 20-foot containers, one 30-foot container, or one 40-foot container. Cargo capacity is approximately 60 tons per rig. Each tractor-trailer unit is estimated to cost 240,000 riyals. Moreover, they must meet Saudi Arabian specifications—double cooling fans, oversized radiators, and special high-temperature tires. Historical evidence suggests that these Mercedes rigs will operate 96% of the time.

Approximately 25% of the freight handled by these tractor-trailer rigs is containerized in container lengths of 20, 30, and 40 feet. (The balance of the freight—75%—is not containerized.) The 20-foot containers hold approximately 20 tons of cargo, the 30-foot containers hold 45 tons, and the 40-foot containers hold 60 tons of freight. Approximately 60% of the containerized freight is shipped in 40-foot units, 20% is shipped in 30-foot units, and 20% is transported in 20-foot units.

Abjar Transport picks up freight at the dock and delivers it directly to customers, or warehouses it for later delivery. Based on his study of truck routing and scheduling patterns, Samir concluded that each rig should pick up freight at the dock three times each day.

### Discussion Question

How many tractor-trailer rigs should make up the Abjar Transport fleet?

---

## INTERNET CASE STUDIES

See our Internet home page at **www.prenhall.com/render** for these additional case studies: (1) Biales Waste Disposal, GmbH, and (2) Buffalo Alkali and Plastics.

---

# BIBLIOGRAPHY

Abdou, G., and S. P. Dutta. "A Systematic Simulation Approach for the Design of JIT Manufacturing Systems," *Journal of Operations Management* 11, 3 (September 1993): 25–38.

Banks, Jerry, John S. Carson, Barry L. Nelson, and David M. Nicol. *Discrete-Event System Simulation*, 3/e. Upper Saddle River, NJ: Prentice Hall, 2001.

Banks, J. and V. Norman. "Justifying Simulation in Today's Manufacturing Environment," *IIE Solutions* (November 1995): 16–18.

———. "Second Look at Simulation Software," *OR/MS Today* 23, 4 (August 1996): 55–57.

Brennan, J. E., B. L. Golden, and H. K. Rappoport. "Go with the Flow: Improving Red Cross Bloodmobiles Using Simulation Analysis," *Interfaces* 22, 5 (September–October 1992): 1–13.

Buchanan, E., and R. Keeler, "Simulating Health Expenditures Under Alternative Insurance Plans," *Management Science* (September 1991): 1069–1088.

Centeno, M. A. et al. "Challenges of Simulating Hospital Facilities," *Proceedings of the 12th Annual Conference of the Production and Operations Management Society.* Orlando, FL (March 2001).

Evans, J. R. and D. L. Olson. *Introduction to Simulation and Risk Analysis.* Upper Saddle River, NJ: Prentice Hall, 1998.

Fishman, George S. *Monte Carlo: Concepts, Algorithms, and Applications.* Springer-Verlag, New York, 1996.

Grossman, Thomas A., Jr. "Teachers' Forum: Spreadsheet Modeling and Simulation Improves Understanding of Queues," *Interfaces* 29, 3 (May 1999): 88–103.

Hartvigsen, David. *SimQuick: Process Simulation with Excel-Updated Version.* Upper Saddle River, NJ: Prentice Hall, 2001.

Karabakal, N., A. Gunal, and W. Ritchie. "Supply-Chain Analysis at Volkswagen of America," *Interfaces* (July–August 2000): 46–55.

Lev, B. "Simulation of Manufacturing Systems," *Interfaces* 20, 3 (May–June 1990): 99–100.

Pegden, C. D., R. E. Shannon, and R. P. Sadowski. *Introduction to Simulation Using SIMAN*, New York: McGraw-Hill, 1995.

Premachandra, I. M. and Liliana Gonzalez. "A Simulation Model Solved the Problem of Scheduling Drilling Rigs at Clyde Dam," *Interfaces* 26, 2 (March 1996): 80–91.

Samuelson, Douglas A. "Predictive Dialing for Outbound Telephone Call Centers," *Interfaces* 29, 5 (September 1999): 66–81.

Winston, Wayne L. *Simulation Modeling Using @Risk.* Pacific Grove, CA: Duxbury, 2001.

# FORECASTING MODELS

After completing this chapter, students will be able to:

1. Understand and know when to use various types of forecasting models.

2. Compute a variety of forecasting error measures.

3. Understand Delphi and other qualitative forecasting techniques.

4. Compute moving averages, weighted moving averages, and exponential smoothing time-series models.

5. Identify and analyze trends and seasonality in time-series data.

6. Decompose time-series data.

7. Identify variables and use them in a causal linear regression model.

8. Use Excel to analyze a variety of forecasting models.

## CHAPTER OUTLINE

Summary • Glossary • Key Equations • Solved Problems • Self-Test • Discussion Questions and Problems • Case Study: North–South Airline • Case Study: Forecasting Football Game Attendance at Southwestern University • Internet Case Studies • Bibliography

### Forecasting at Disney World

When Disney Chairman Michael Eisner receives a daily report from his main theme parks in Orlando, Florida, the report contains only two numbers: the forecast of yesterday's attendance at the parks (Magic Kingdom, Epcot, Animal Kingdom, Disney-MGM Studios, Fort Wilderness, and Blizzard Beach) and the actual attendance. An error close to zero (using Mean Absolute Percent Error [MAPE] as the measure) is expected. Eisner takes his forecasts very seriously.

The forecasting team at Disney World doesn't just do a daily prediction, however, and Eisner is not its only customer. It also provides daily, weekly, monthly, annual, and five-year forecasts to the labor management, maintenance, operations, finance, and park scheduling departments. It uses judgmental models, econometric models, moving average models, and regression analysis. The team's forecast of annual volume, conducted in 1999 for the year 2000, resulted in a MAPE of zero.

With 20% of Disney World's customers coming from outside the United States, its econometric model includes such variables as consumer confidence and the gross domestic product of seven countries. Disney also surveys one million people each year to examine their future travel plans and their experiences at the parks. This helps forecast not only attendance but behavior at each ride (how long people will wait and how many times they will ride). Inputs to the monthly forecasting model include airline specials, speeches by the Chair of the Federal Reserve, and Wall Street trends. Disney even monitors 3,000 school districts inside and outside the United States for holiday/vacation schedules.[1]

---

[1] J. Newkirk and M. Haskell. "Forecasting in the Service Sector," presentation at the *12th Annual Meeting of the Production and Operations Management Society* (April 1, 2001), Orlando, FL.

## 11.1  INTRODUCTION

Every day, managers make decisions without knowing exactly what will happen in the future. Inventory is ordered, though no one knows what sales will be, new equipment is purchased though no one knows the demand for products, and investments are made though no one knows what profits will be. Managers are always trying to reduce this uncertainty and to make better estimates of what will happen in the future. As in the preceding application at Disney World, accomplishing this is the main purpose of forecasting.

There are many ways to forecast the future. In numerous firms (especially smaller ones), the entire process is subjective, involving seat-of-the-pants methods, intuition, and years of experience. There are also many *quantitative* forecasting models, such as moving averages, exponential smoothing, trend analysis, seasonality analysis, decomposition models, and causal regression analysis.

*No single method is superior—whatever works best should be used.*

There is seldom a single superior forecasting method. One firm may find regression models effective, another firm may use several quantitative models, and a third may combine both quantitative and subjective techniques. Whatever tool works best for a firm is the one that should be used. In this chapter, we discuss several different forecasting models that are commonly used in practice. For each model, we show the equations needed to compute the forecasts and provide examples of how they are analyzed.

Regardless of the model used to make the forecast, the same eight overall procedures that follow are used. These steps present a systematic way of initiating, designing, and implementing a forecast system.

*List of steps for forecasting*

### Eight Steps to Forecasting

1. Determine the use of the forecast—what objective are we trying to obtain?
2. Select the items or quantities that are to be forecasted.
3. Determine the time horizon of the forecast: Is it 1 to 30 days (short time horizon), one month to one year (medium time horizon), or more than one year (long time horizon)?
4. Select the forecasting model or models.
5. Gather the data needed to make the forecast.
6. Validate the forecasting model.
7. Make the forecast.
8. Implement the results.

When the forecasting model is to be used to generate forecasts regularly over time, data must be collected routinely, and the actual computations must be repeated. In this day of technology and computers, however, forecast calculations are seldom preformed by hand. Computers and forecasting software packages simplify these tasks to a great extent. Numerous statistical programs such as SAS, SPSS, and Minitab are readily available to handle various forecasting models. However, in keeping with the spreadsheet focus of this textbook, we use Excel worksheets (included in your CD-ROM) to actually calculate the forecast values for each model. Several other spreadsheet-based forecasting software programs (such as Crystal Ball Predictor® by Decisioneering, Inc. and StatPro™ by Palisade Corporation) are also commonly used in practice.

## 11.2  TYPES OF FORECASTS

*The three categories of models are time series, causal, and qualitative.*

The forecasting models we consider here can be classified into one of three categories. These categories, shown in Figure 11.1, are qualitative models, time-series models, and causal models. Although we provide a brief description of a few qualitative models in Section 11.3, the focus of this chapter is on time-series and causal models.

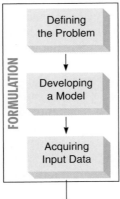

**IIII➡ MODELING IN THE REAL WORLD**   Forecasting at Tupperware International

**FORMULATION**

Defining the Problem

To drive production at each of Tupperware's 15 plants in the United States, Latin America, Africa, Europe, and Asia, the firm needs accurate forecasts of demand for its products.

Developing a Model

A variety of statistical models are used, including moving averages, exponential smoothing, and regression analysis. Decision modeling is also employed in the process.

Acquiring Input Data

At world headquarters in Orlando, Florida, huge databases are maintained that map the sales of each product, the test market results of each *new* product (since 20% of the firm's sales come from products less than two years old), and where each product falls in its own life cycle.

**SOLUTION**

Developing a Solution

Each of Tupperware's 50 profit centers worldwide develops computerized monthly, quarterly, and 12-month sales projections. These are aggregated by region and then globally.

Testing the Solution

Reviews of these forecasts take place in sales, marketing, finance, and production departments.

**INTERPRETATION**

Analyzing the Results and Sensitivity Analysis

Participating managers analyze forecasts with Tupperware's version of a "jury of executive opinion."

Implementing the Results

Forecasts are used to schedule materials, equipment, and personnel at each plant.

**Source:** Interviews by the authors with Tupperware executives.

## Qualitative Models

*Qualitative models incorporate subjective factors.*

*Qualitative models* attempt to incorporate judgmental or subjective factors into the forecasting model. Opinions by experts, individual experiences and judgments, and other subjective factors may be considered. Qualitative models are especially useful when subjective factors are expected to be very important or when accurate quantitative data are difficult to obtain. Qualitative models are also useful for long-term forecasting.

## Time-Series Models

*Time-series models assume the past is an indication of the future.*

Whereas qualitative models rely on judgmental or subjective data, *time-series models* rely on quantitative data. Time-series models attempt to predict the future by using historical data. These models make the assumption that what happens in the future is a function of what has happened in the past. In other words, time-series models look at what has happened over a period of time and use a series of past data to make a forecast. Thus, if we are forecasting weekly sales for lawn mowers, we use the past weekly sales for lawn mowers in making the forecast. The time-series models we examine in this chapter are (1) moving averages, (2) weighted moving averages, (3) exponential smoothing, (4) linear trend analysis, (5) seasonality analysis, and (6) multiplicative decomposition.

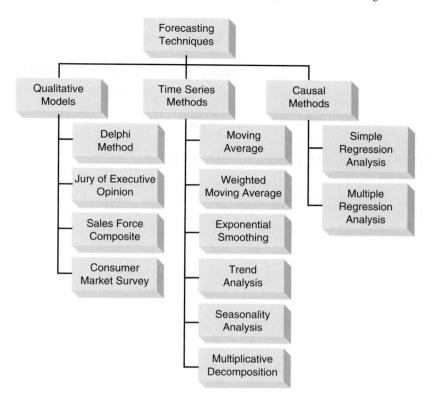

**FIGURE 11.1**

**Forecasting Models
Discussed**

## Causal Models

*Causal models incorporate factors that influence the quantity being forecasted.*

As with time-series models, *causal models* also rely on quantitative data. Causal models incorporate the variables or factors that might influence the quantity being forecasted into the forecasting model. For example, daily sales of a cola drink might depend on the season, the average temperature, the average humidity, whether it is a weekend or a weekday, and so on. Thus, a causal model would attempt to include factors for temperature, humidity, season, day of the week, and so on. Causal models can also include past sales data as time-series models do.

## 11.3  QUALITATIVE FORECASTING MODELS

Here is a brief overview of four different qualitative forecasting techniques commonly used in practice:

*Overview of four qualitative or judgmental approaches: Delphi, jury of executive opinion, sales force composite, and consumer market survey.*

1. *Delphi method.* This iterative group process allows experts, who may be located in different places, to make forecasts. There are three different types of participants in the Delphi process: decision makers, staff personnel, and respondents. The *decision-making group* usually consists of 5–10 experts who will be making the actual forecast. The *staff personnel* assist the decision makers by preparing, distributing, collecting, and summarizing a series of questionnaires and survey results. The *respondents* are a group of people whose judgments are valued and are being sought. This group provides inputs to the decision makers before the forecast is made.

2. *Jury of executive opinion.* This method takes the opinions of a small group of high-level managers, often in combination with statistical models, and results in a group estimate of demand.

3. *Sales force composite.* In this approach, each salesperson estimates what sales will be in his or her region; these forecasts are reviewed to ensure that they are realistic and are then combined at the district and national levels to reach an overall forecast.

4. *Consumer market survey.* This method solicits input from customers or potential customers regarding their future purchasing plans. It can help not only in preparing a forecast but also in improving product design and planning for new products.

## 11.4 MEASURING FORECAST ERROR

The overall accuracy of a forecasting model can be determined by comparing the forecasted values with the actual or observed values. If $F_t$ denotes the forecast in period $t$ and $A_t$ denotes the actual value in period $t$, the *forecast error* (or deviation) is defined as

$$\text{Forecast error} = \text{Actual value} - \text{Forecast value}$$

$$= A_t - F_t \tag{11-1}$$

*The forecast error tells us how well the model performed against itself using past data.*

There are several measures commonly used in practice to calculate the overall forecast error. These measures can be used to compare different forecasting models, as well as to monitor forecasts to ensure they are performing well. Three of the most popular measures are covered in the following sections.

**Mean Absolute Deviation**   *Mean absolute deviation* (MAD) is computed as the average of the *absolute* values of the individual forecast errors. That is, if we have forecasted and actual values for $T$ periods, the MAD is calculated as

$$\text{MAD} = \sum_{t=1}^{T} \left| \text{forecast error} \right| / T = \sum_{t=1}^{T} \left| A_t - F_t \right| / T \tag{11-2}$$

**Mean Squared Error**   The *mean squared error* (MSE) is computed as the average of the *squared* values of the individual forecast errors. That is, if we have forecasted and actual values for $T$ periods, the MSE is calculated as

$$\text{MSE} = \sum_{t=1}^{T} \left| \text{forecast error} \right|^2 / T = \sum_{t=1}^{T} (A_t - F_t)^2 / T \tag{11-3}$$

*MSE accentuates large deviations.*

A drawback of using the MSE is that it tends to accentuate large deviations due to the squared term. For example, if the forecast error for period 1 is twice as large as the error for period 2, the squared error in period 1 is four times as large as that for period 2. Hence, using MSE as the measure of forecast error typically indicates that we prefer to have several smaller deviations rather than even one large deviation.

*MAPE expresses the error as a percentage of the actual values.*

**Mean Absolute Percent Error**   A problem with both the MAD and MSE is that their values depend on the magnitude of the item being forecast. If the forecast item is measured in thousands, the MAD and MSE values can be very large. To avoid this problem, we can use the *mean absolute percent error* (MAPE). This is computed as the average of the absolute difference between the forecasted and actual values, expressed as a percentage of the actual values. That is, if we have forecasted and actual values for $T$ periods, the MAPE is calculated as

$$\text{MAPE} = 100 \sum_{t=1}^{T} \left[ \left| A_t - F_t \right| / A_t \right] / T \tag{11-4}$$

The MAPE is perhaps the easiest measure to interpret. For example, a result that the MAPE is 2% is a clear statement that is not dependent on issues such as the magnitude of the input data. For this reason, although we calculate all three measures in our analyses, we focus primarily on the MAPE in our discussions.

## 11.5    BASIC TIME-SERIES FORECASTING MODELS

A time series is based on a sequence of evenly spaced (e.g., weekly, monthly, quarterly) data points. Examples include weekly sales of Dell personal computers, quarterly earnings reports of Cisco Systems stock, daily shipments of Energizer batteries, and annual U.S. consumer price indices. Forecasting time-series data implies that future values are predicted *only* from past values. Other variables, no matter how potentially valuable, are ignored.

### Components of a Time Series

*Four components of a time series are trend, seasonality, cycles, and random variations.*

We can view a long-term time series (i.e., data for over one year) as being made up of four distinct components. Analyzing a time series means breaking down the data to identify these four components and then projecting them forward. The process of identifying the four components is referred to as *decomposition*. The four components are as follows:

1. *Trend.* This is the upward or downward movement of the data over time. For example, prices for many consumer goods exhibit an upward trend over time due to the presence of inflation. Although it is possible for the relationship between time and the data to have any form (linear or nonlinear), we focus only on linear trend relationships in this chapter.

2. *Seasonality.* This is the pattern of demand fluctuations that occurs every year above or below the average demand. That is, the same seasonal pattern repeats itself every year over the time horizon. For example, lawn mower sales are always above average each year in spring and below average in winter.

3. *Cycles.* Just as seasonality is the pattern that occurs each year, cycles are patterns that occur over several years. Cycles are usually tied into the business cycle. For example, the economies of most countries experience cycles of high growth followed by a period of relatively low growth or even recession.

4. *Random variations.* These are "blips" in the data caused by chance and unusual situations. They follow no discernible pattern. For this reason, we cannot really capture this component and use it to forecast future values.

Figure 11.2 shows a time series and its components.

There are two general forms of time-series models in statistics. The most widely used is a *multiplicative model*, which assumes that the forecasted value is the product of the four components. It is stated as

*Multiplicative model*

$$\text{Forecast} = \text{Trend} \times \text{Seasonality} \times \text{Cycles} \times \text{Random} \tag{11-5}$$

We study the multiplicative model in Section 11.7. An *additive model* that adds the components together to provide an estimate is also available. It is stated as

*Additive model*

$$\text{Forecast} = \text{Trend} + \text{Seasonality} + \text{Cycles} + \text{Random} \tag{11-6}$$

As noted earlier, the random variations follow no discernible pattern. In most real-world models, forecasters assume these variations are averaged out over time. They then concentrate on only the seasonal component and a component that is a combination of the trend and cyclical factors.

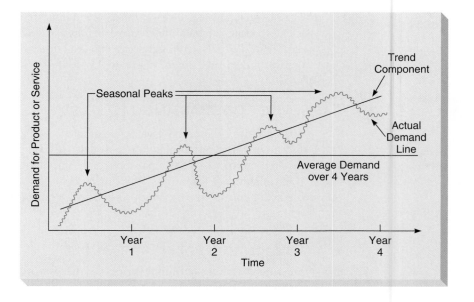

## Stationary and Nonstationary Time-Series Data

**Stationary data** *have no*
*trend.*

Time-series *data* are said to be *stationary* if there is no significant upward or downward movement (or trend) in the data over time. That is, the average value for the time-series data remains constant over the time horizon considered in the model. Stationary time-series data are typically encountered when the time horizon is short term (1–30 days) or medium term (one month to one year). For time horizons that are long term (one year or greater), time-series data tend to typically exhibit some trend. In such cases, we refer to the data as *nonstationary*.

*Nonstationary data exhibit*
*trend.*

In the remainder of this section, we discuss three popular forecasting models used for stationary time-series data: (1) moving averages, (2) weighted moving averages, and (3) exponential smoothing. Although we show the equations needed to compute the forecasts for each model, we use Excel worksheets (included in your CD-ROM) to actually calculate these values.

## Moving Averages

*Moving averages* are useful if we can assume the item we are trying to forecast will stay fairly steady over time. We calculate a three-period moving average by summing the actual value of the item for the past three periods and dividing the total by 3. This three-period moving average serves as the forecast for the next period. With each passing period, the most recent period's actual value is added to the sum of the previous two periods' data, and the earliest period is dropped. This tends to smooth out short-term irregularities in the time series.

**Moving averages smooth out**
**variations when forecasting**
**demands are fairly steady.**

The moving average for the preceding $k$ periods (where $k$ can be any integer $\geq 2$) serves as the forecast for the following period. Mathematically, the $k$-period moving average can be expressed as

$$k\text{-period moving average} = \sum(\text{Actual value in previous } k \text{ periods})/k \qquad (11\text{-}7)$$

**Wallace Garden Supply Example**   Monthly sales of storage sheds at Wallace Garden Supply are shown in the middle column of Table 11.1. A three-month moving average is shown on the right most column. As discussed next, we can also use the ExcelModules program to calculate these moving averages.

**TABLE 11.1**

Three-Month Moving
Averages Forecast for
Wallace Garden Supply

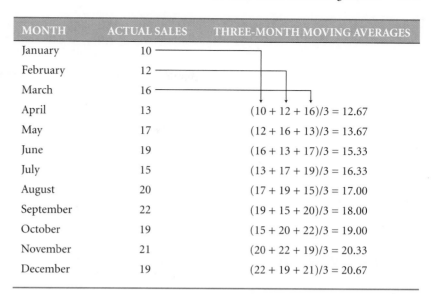

| MONTH | ACTUAL SALES | THREE-MONTH MOVING AVERAGES |
|---|---|---|
| January | 10 | |
| February | 12 | |
| March | 16 | |
| April | 13 | $(10 + 12 + 16)/3 = 12.67$ |
| May | 17 | $(12 + 16 + 13)/3 = 13.67$ |
| June | 19 | $(16 + 13 + 17)/3 = 15.33$ |
| July | 15 | $(13 + 17 + 19)/3 = 16.33$ |
| August | 20 | $(17 + 19 + 15)/3 = 17.00$ |
| September | 22 | $(19 + 15 + 20)/3 = 18.00$ |
| October | 19 | $(15 + 20 + 22)/3 = 19.00$ |
| November | 21 | $(20 + 22 + 19)/3 = 20.33$ |
| December | 19 | $(22 + 19 + 21)/3 = 20.67$ |

## Using ExcelModules for Forecasting Model Computations

### Excel Note

- The CD-ROM that accompanies this textbook contains a set of Excel worksheets, bundled together in a software package called ExcelModules. The procedure for installing and running this program, as well as a brief description of its contents, is given in Appendix A.

- The CD-ROM also contains the Excel file for each example problem discussed here. The relevant file name is shown in the margin next to each example.

- For clarity, all worksheets for forecasting models in ExcelModules are color coded as follows:

  *input cells*, where we enter the problem data, are shaded yellow.

  *output cells* showing forecasts and measures of forecast error are shaded green.

- Although these colors are not apparent in the screen captures shown in the textbook, they are seen in the Excel files in your CD-ROM.

---

 **IN ACTION**  Forecasting Customer Demand at Taco Bell

Like most quick service restaurants, Taco Bell understands the quantitative trade-off between labor and speed of service. More than 50% of the $5 billion company's daily sales come from the 3-hour lunch period. Customers don't like to wait more than 3 minutes for service, so it is critical that proper staffing is in place at all times.

Taco Bell tested a series of forecasting models to predict demand in specific 15-minute intervals during each day of the week. The company's goal was to find the technique that minimized the average squared deviation between actual and predicted data. Because company computers only stored 6 weeks of transaction data, exponential smoothing was not considered. Results indicated that a 6-week moving average was best.

Building this forecasting methodology into each of Taco Bell's 6,500 stores' computers, the model makes weekly projections of customer transactions. These in turn are used by store managers to schedule staff, who begin in 15-minute increments, not one-hour blocks as in other industries. The forecasting model has been so successful that Taco Bell has documented more than $50 million in labor cost savings, while increasing customer service, in its first four years of use.

**Sources:** J. Hueter and W. Swart. "An Integrated Labor-Management System for Taco Bell," *Interfaces* 28, 1 (January–February 1998): 75–91 and L. Pringle. "Productivity Engine," *OR/MS Today* 27, 3 (June 2000): 30.

When we run the ExcelModules program, we see a menu option titled ExcelModules in the main menu bar of Excel. We click on ExcelModules, and then click on Forecasting Models. The choices shown in Program 11.1A are displayed. From these choices, we select the appropriate forecasting model.

When *any* of the forecasting models is selected in ExcelModules, we are first presented with a window that allows us to specify several options. Some of these options are common for all models, whereas others are specific to the forecasting model selected. For example, Program 11.1B shows the Options window when we select the Moving Averages forecasting model. The options here include the following:

1. Title of the problem. Default value is *Problem Title*.

2. Number of past periods for which we have data regarding the item (e.g., demand, sales) being forecast. Default value is *3*.

**File: 11-2.xls**

---

**PROGRAM 11.1A**    **Forecasting Models Submenu in ExcelModules**

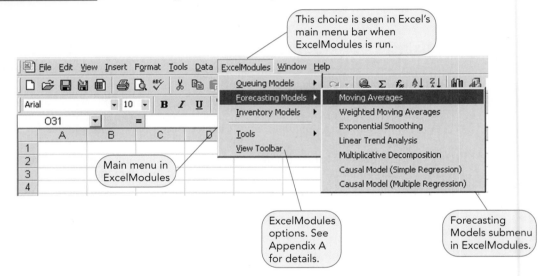

---

**PROGRAM 11.1B**

**Sample Options Window for Forecasting Models in ExcelModules**

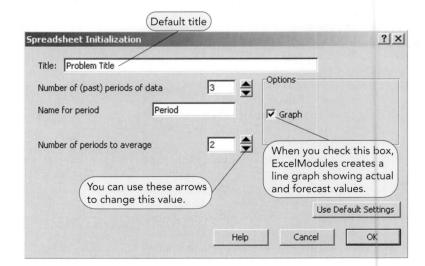

3. Name for the period (e.g., Week, Month). Default value is *Period*.

4. Number of periods to average (i.e., the value of $k$ in Equation 11-7). Default value is *2*.

5. Graph. Checking this box results in line graphs of the actual and forecast values.

**Using ExcelModules for Moving Averages.**  We first show, in Program 11.2A, the options we select for the Wallace Garden Supply example.

When we click OK on this screen, we get the screen shown in Program 11.2B. We now enter the actual shed sales for the 12 months (see Table 11.1) in cells B7:B18.

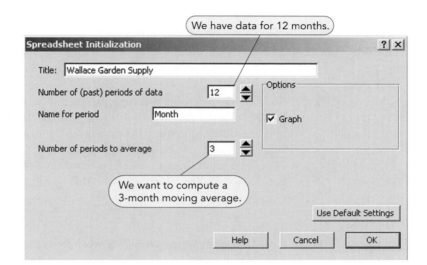

## PROGRAM 11.2A

**Options Window for Moving Averages Worksheet in ExcelModules**

*We have data for 12 months.*

*We want to compute a 3-month moving average.*

## PROGRAM 11.2B    **Moving Averages Model for Wallace Garden Supply**

*Average of 3 previous months*
$$= \frac{10 + 12 + 16}{3} = 12.667$$

| | A | B | C | D | E | F | G | H |
|---|---|---|---|---|---|---|---|---|
| 1 | **Wallace Garden Supply** | | | | | | | |
| 2 | **Forecasting** | | 3 period moving average | | | | | |
| 3 | Enter the data in the cells shaded YELLOW. | | | | | | | |
| 4 | | | | | | | | |
| 5 | Input Data | | | Forecast Error Analysis | | | | |
| 6 | Period | Actual Value | | Forecast | Error | Absolute error | Squared error | Absolute % error |
| 7 | Month 1 | 10 | | | | | | |
| 8 | Month 2 | 12 | | | | | | |
| 9 | Month 3 | 16 | | | | | | |
| 10 | Month 4 | 13 | | 12.667 | 0.333 | 0.333 | 0.111 | 2.56% |
| 11 | Month 5 | 17 | | 13.667 | 3.333 | 3.333 | 11.111 | 19.61% |
| 12 | Month 6 | 19 | | 15.333 | 3.667 | 3.667 | 13.444 | 19.30% |
| 13 | Month 7 | 15 | | 16.333 | -1.333 | 1.333 | 1.778 | 8.89% |
| 14 | Month 8 | 20 | | 17.000 | 3.000 | 3.000 | 9.000 | 15.00% |
| 15 | Month 9 | 22 | | 18.000 | 4.000 | 4.000 | 16.000 | 18.18% |
| 16 | Month 10 | 19 | | 19.000 | 0.000 | 0.000 | 0.000 | 0.00% |
| 17 | Month 11 | 21 | | 20.333 | 0.667 | 0.667 | 0.444 | 3.17% |
| 18 | Month 12 | 19 | | 20.667 | -1.667 | 1.667 | 2.778 | 8.77% |
| 19 | | | | **Average** | | **2.000** | **6.074** | **10.61%** |
| 20 | **Next period** | **19.667** | | | | **MAD** | **MSE** | **MAPE** |

*Forecast value for month 13*

*Input data for past 12 months*

*Measures of forecast error*

### Excel Notes

■ The worksheets in ExcelModules contain formulas to compute the forecasts and forecast errors for different forecasting models. The default values of zero for the input data cause the results of these formulas to initially appear as #N/A, #VALUE!, or #DIV/0!. However, as soon as we enter valid values for the input data, the worksheets will display the formula results.

■ Once ExcelModules has been used to create the Excel worksheet for a particular forecasting model (such as moving averages), the resulting worksheet can be used to compute the forecasts with several different input data. For example, we can enter different input data in cells B7:B18 of Program 11.2B and compute the results without having to create a new moving averages worksheet each time.

The worksheet now displays the 3-month moving averages (shown in cells D10:D18), and the forecast for the next month (i.e., January of the next year), shown in cell B20. In addition, the following measures of forecast error are also calculated and reported: MAD (cell F19), MSE (cell G19), and MAPE (cell H19).

The output indicates that a 3-month moving average model results in a MAPE of 10.61%. The forecast for the next period is 19.667 storage sheds. The line graph (if checked in the options in Program 11.2A) is shown in a separate worksheet. We show the graph for the Wallace Garden Supply example in Program 11.2C.

**PROGRAM 11.2C**    **Plot of 3-Period Moving Averages Forecast for Wallace Garden Supply**

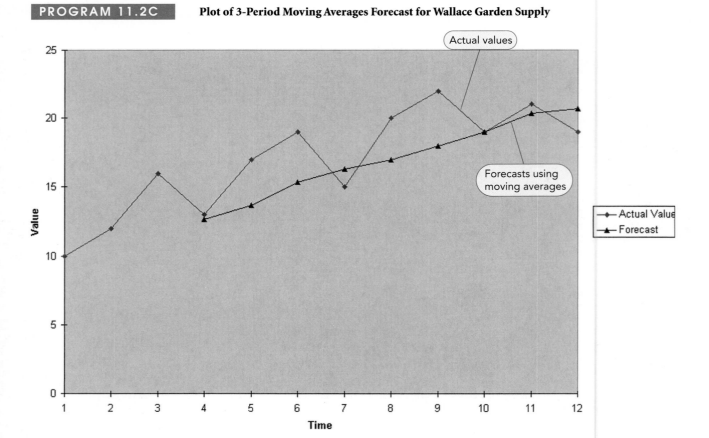

## Interpreting Forecast Errors

*Forecast error measures permit comparison of different models.*

As noted earlier, the measures of forecast error allow us to compare different forecasting models to see which one provides the best forecast. For example, instead of a 3-month moving average, we can try a 4-month moving average for this example. See if you can repeat the procedure described in Programs 11.2A and 11.2B for a 4-month moving average. You should see that the MAPE with $k = 4$ is 14.22%. This implies that, at least in this example, the 3-month moving average model provides a better forecast than the 4-month model. We can try other values for $k$ in a similar fashion.

## Weighted Moving Averages

In the regular moving average approach, all the input data are assumed to be equally important. For example, in a three-period model, data for all three previous periods are given equal importance, and a simple average of the three values is computed. In a few cases, however, data for some periods (e.g., recent periods) may be more important than data for other periods (e.g., earlier periods). This is especially true if there is a trend or pattern in the data. In such cases, we can use weights to place more emphasis on some periods and less emphasis on others.

*Weights can be used to put more emphasis on recent periods.*

The choice of weights is somewhat arbitrary because there is no set formula to determine them. As such, deciding which weights to use requires some experience and a bit of luck. For example, if the latest period is weighted too heavily, the model might reflect a large unusual change in the forecast value too quickly.

Mathematically, the $k$-period *weighted moving average*, which serves the forecast for the next period, can be expressed as

$$k\text{-period weighted moving average} = \frac{\sum_{i=1}^{k} (\text{weight for period } i)(\text{actual value in period } i)}{\sum_{i=1}^{k} (\text{weights})} \tag{11-8}$$

**Wallace Garden Supply Revisited—Part I**   Instead of using a 3-month moving average, assume Wallace Garden Supply would like to forecast sales of storage sheds by weighting the past three months as follows:

| PERIOD | WEIGHT APPLIED |
|---|---|
| Last month | 3 |
| Two months ago | 2 |
| Three months ago | 1 |
| Sum of weights | 6 |

The results of Wallace Garden Supply weighted average forecast using these weights are shown in Table 11.2. Let us now see how we can also use ExcelModules to compute these weighted moving averages.

**Using *ExcelModules* for Weighted Moving Averages**   We select the Weighted Moving Averages option from the Forecasting Models submenu in ExcelModules (see Program 11.1A). The window shown in Program 11.3A is displayed. The option entries in this

**File: 11-3.xls**

TABLE 11.2

**Three-Month Weighted Moving Averages Forecast for Wallace Garden Supply**

| MONTH | ACTUAL SALES | WEIGHTED MOVING AVERAGES |
|---|---|---|
| January | 10 | |
| February | 12 | |
| March | 16 | |
| April | 13 | $(1 \times 10 + 2 \times 12 + 3 \times 16)/6 = 13.67$ |
| May | 17 | $(1 \times 12 + 2 \times 16 + 3 \times 13)/6 = 13.83$ |
| June | 19 | $(1 \times 16 + 2 \times 13 + 3 \times 17)/6 = 15.50$ |
| July | 15 | $(1 \times 13 + 2 \times 17 + 3 \times 19)/6 = 17.33$ |
| August | 20 | $(1 \times 17 + 2 \times 19 + 3 \times 15)/6 = 16.67$ |
| September | 22 | $(1 \times 19 + 2 \times 15 + 3 \times 20)/6 = 18.17$ |
| October | 19 | $(1 \times 15 + 2 \times 20 + 3 \times 22)/6 = 20.17$ |
| November | 21 | $(1 \times 20 + 2 \times 22 + 3 \times 19)/6 = 20.17$ |
| December | 19 | $(1 \times 22 + 2 \times 19 + 3 \times 21)/6 = 20.50$ |

*Weights usually add up to 1.*

window are similar to that for the moving averages (see Program 11.2A). The only additional choice is the box labeled Weights sum to 1. Although not required (e.g., the sum of weights in the Wallace Garden Supply example is 6), it is common practice to assign weights to various periods such that they sum to one. Our specific entries for Wallace Garden Supply's problem are shown in Program 11.3A.

When we click OK on this screen, we get the screen shown in Program 11.3B. We now enter the actual shed sales for the 12 months (see Table 11.2) in cells B7:B18, and the weights for the past 3 months in cells C7:C9.

The worksheet now displays the 3-month weighted moving averages (shown in cells E10:E18) and the forecast for the next month (i.e., January of the next year), shown in cell B20. In addition, the following measures of forecast error are also calculated and reported: MAD (cell G19), MSE (cell H19), and MAPE (cell I19). The line graph, if asked for, is shown on a separate worksheet.

In this particular example, you can see that weighting the latest month more heavily actually provides a less accurate forecast. That is, the MAPE value is now 12.20%, compared with a MAPE value of only 10.61% for the 3-month simple moving average.

**Options Window for Weighted Moving Averages Worksheet in ExcelModules**

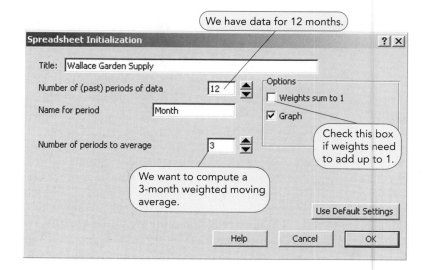

**PROGRAM 11.3B**    **Weighted Moving Averages Model for Wallace Garden Supply**

|   | A | B | C | D | E | F | G | H | I |
|---|---|---|---|---|---|---|---|---|---|
| 1 | **Wallace Garden Supply** | | | | | | | | |
| 2 | Forecasting | | 3 period weighted moving average | | | | | | |
| 3 | Enter the data in the cells shaded YELLOW. | | | | | | | | |
| 4 | | | | | | | | | |
| 5 | Input Data | | | | Forecast Error Analysis | | | | |
| 6 | Period | Actual value | Weights | | Forecast | Error | Absolute error | Squared error | Absolute % error |
| 7 | Month 1 | 10 | 1 | | | | | | |
| 8 | Month 2 | 12 | 2 | | | | | | |
| 9 | Month 3 | 16 | 3 | | | | | | |
| 10 | Month 4 | 13 | | | 13.667 | -0.667 | 0.667 | 0.444 | 5.13% |
| 11 | Month 5 | 17 | | | 13.833 | 3.167 | 3.167 | 10.028 | 18.63% |
| 12 | Month 6 | 19 | | | 15.500 | 3.500 | 3.500 | 12.250 | 18.42% |
| 13 | Month 7 | 15 | | | 17.333 | -2.333 | 2.333 | 5.444 | 15.56% |
| 14 | Month 8 | 20 | | | 16.667 | 3.333 | 3.333 | 11.111 | 16.67% |
| 15 | Month 9 | 22 | | | 18.167 | 3.833 | 3.833 | 14.694 | 17.42% |
| 16 | Month 10 | 19 | | | 20.167 | -1.167 | 1.167 | 1.361 | 6.14% |
| 17 | Month 11 | 21 | | | 20.167 | 0.833 | 0.833 | 0.694 | 3.97% |
| 18 | Month 12 | 19 | | | 20.500 | -1.500 | 1.500 | 2.250 | 7.89% |
| 19 | | | | | **Average** | | 2.259 | 6.475 | 12.20% |
| 20 | **Next period** | **19.667** | | | | | MAD | MSE | MAPE |

Weighted average of the 3 previous months =
$$\frac{3 \times 16 + 2 \times 12 + 1 \times 10}{6} = 13.667$$

Weights for the 3 previous months

Measures of forecast error

**Using Solver to Determine Optimal Weights** As noted earlier, the choice of weights is somewhat arbitrary because there is no set formula to determine them. However, for a specified value of *k* (i.e., number of periods to use in computing the weighted moving average), we can use Excel's Solver to find the optimal weights to use in the forecasting model.

Recall that we used Solver to solve linear, integer, and nonlinear programming problems in Chapters 2 through 6. Setting up a problem on Solver requires three components:

- *Changing Cells.* These are the cells denoting the decision variables for which we are trying to identify optimal values.

- *Target Cell.* This is the cell containing the formula for the measure we are trying to either maximize or minimize.

- *Constraints.* These are one or more restrictions on the values that the decision variables are allowed to take.

In our case, the decision variables are the weights to be used in computing the weighted moving average. Hence, we specify cells C7:C9 as our Changing Cells. The objective is to minimize some measure of forecast error, such a MAD, MSE, or MAPE. Let us assume we want to minimize the MAPE here. Cell I19 is, therefore, the Target Cell.

If we want to specify that the weights must add up to 1, we must include it as a constraint in the model. The only other constraint is the nonnegativity constraint on the decision variables (weights). Recall that we can easily enforce this constraint by checking the Assume Non-negative box in Solver's options. It is important to note that the Assume Linear Model option should *not* be checked in solving this problem since the formula for the objective function (MAPE in this case) is *nonlinear*.

*The problem is a nonlinear program.*

Program 11.3C shows the Solver entries and results for the Wallace Garden Supply problem. For illustration purposes, we have chosen to include the constraint that the sum of weights must equal 1. The formula to model this constraint is shown in Program 11.3C.

**PROGRAM 11.3C**    **Optimal Weights Using Solver for Wallace Garden Supply**

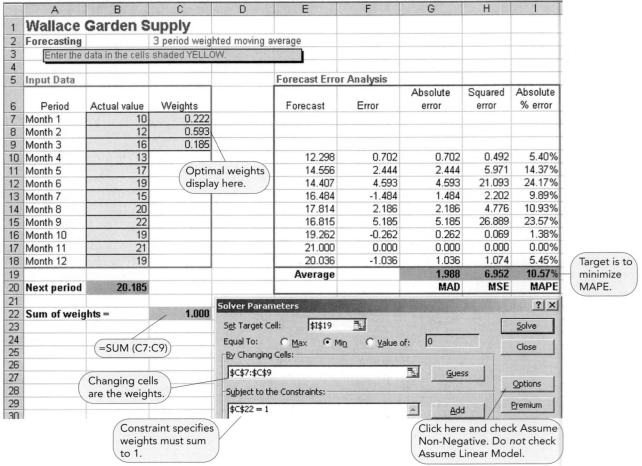

The results indicate that the MAPE decreases to 10.57% when weights of 0.185, 0.593, and 0.222 are associated with the latest period, the period before that, and two periods before that, respectively. Observe that the MSE actually increased from 6.475 in Program 11.3B to 6.952 in Program 11.3C. That is, the weights that minimize the MAPE need not necessarily minimize the MSE value also.

*The same weights need not minimize both MAPE and MSE.*

## Exponential Smoothing

Both moving averages and weighted moving averages are effective in smoothing out sudden fluctuations in the demand pattern in order to provide stable estimates. In fact, increasing the size of $k$ (number of periods averaged) smoothes out fluctuations even better. However, doing so requires us to keep extensive records of past data.

*Exponential smoothing is also a type of moving averages model.*

An alternate forecasting approach that is also a type of moving average technique, but requires little record keeping of past data, is called *exponential smoothing*. Let $F_t$ denote the forecast in period $t$ and $A_t$ denote the actual value in period $t$. The basic exponential smoothing formula is as follows:

$$\text{Forecast for period } (t + 1) = \text{forecast for period } t$$
$$+ \alpha \text{ (actual value in period } t - \text{forecast for period } t)$$

or

$$F_{t+1} = F_t + \alpha(A_t - F_t) \qquad (11\text{-}9)$$

where $\alpha$ is a weight (called a *smoothing constant*) that has a value between 0 and 1, inclusive. It is generally in the range from 0.1 to 0.3. The forecast for a period is equal to the forecast for the previous period, adjusted by a fraction (specified by $\alpha$) of the forecast error in the previous period. Observe that in Equation 11-9, $F_t$ can be written as

$$F_t = F_{t-1} + \alpha(A_{t-1} - F_{t-1})$$

Likewise, $F_{t-1}$ can be expressed in terms of $F_{t-2}$ and $A_{t-2}$, and so on. Substituting for $F_t$, $F_{t-1}$, $F_{t-2}$, and so on in Equation 11-9, we can show that

$$F_{t+1} = \alpha A_t + \alpha(1-\alpha)A_{t-1} + \alpha(1-\alpha)^2 A_{t-2} + \alpha(1-\alpha)^3 A_{t-3} + \ldots \qquad (11\text{-}10)$$

That is, the forecast in period $t + 1$ is just a weighted average of the actual values in period $t$, $t-1$, $t-2$, and so on. Observe that the weight associated with a period's actual value decreases exponentially over time. For this reason, the term *exponential smoothing* is used to describe the technique.

*The smoothing constant, $\alpha$, allows managers to assign weight to recent data.*

The actual value of $\alpha$ can be changed to give more weight to recent periods (when $\alpha$ is high), or more weight to past periods (when $\alpha$ is low). For example, when $\alpha = 1$, the forecast in period $t + 1$ is equal to the actual value in period $t$. That is, the entire new forecast is based just on the most recent period. When $\alpha = 0.5$, it can be shown mathematically that the new forecast is based almost entirely on values in just the past three periods. When $\alpha = 0.1$, the forecast places relatively little weight on recent periods and takes many periods of values into account.

**Wallace Garden Supply Revisited—Part II**  Suppose Wallace Garden Supply would like to forecast sales of storage sheds using an exponential smoothing model. Assume the forecast for sales of storage sheds in January equals the actual sales that month (i.e., 10 sheds). The exponential smoothing forecast calculations are shown in Table 11.3 for $\alpha = 0.1$ and $\alpha = 0.9$. Next, we show how we can use ExcelModules to do these calculations.

**TABLE 11.3**

Exponential Smoothing Forecasts for Wallace Garden Supply ($\alpha = 0.1$ and $\alpha = 0.9$)

| MONTH | ACTUAL SALES | FORECAST ($\alpha = 0.1$) | $\alpha = 0.9$ |
|---|---|---|---|
| January | 10 | 10.0 | 10.0 |
| February | 12 | $10.0 + 0.1(10 - 10.0) = 10.0$ | 10.0 |
| March | 16 | $10.0 + 0.1(12 - 10.0) = 10.2$ | 11.8 |
| April | 13 | $10.2 + 0.1(16 - 10.2) = 10.8$ | 15.6 |
| May | 17 | $10.8 + 0.1(13 - 10.8) = 11.0$ | 13.3 |
| June | 19 | $11.0 + 0.1(17 - 11.0) = 11.6$ | 16.6 |
| July | 15 | $11.6 + 0.1(19 - 11.6) = 12.3$ | 18.8 |
| August | 20 | $12.3 + 0.1(15 - 12.3) = 12.6$ | 15.4 |
| September | 22 | $12.6 + 0.1(20 - 12.6) = 13.4$ | 19.5 |
| October | 19 | $13.4 + 0.1(22 - 13.4) = 14.2$ | 21.7 |
| November | 21 | $14.2 + 0.1(19 - 14.2) = 14.7$ | 19.3 |
| December | 19 | $14.7 + 0.1(21 - 14.7) = 15.3$ | 20.8 |

**PROGRAM 11.4A**

**Options Window for
Exponential Smoothing
Worksheet in
ExcelModules**

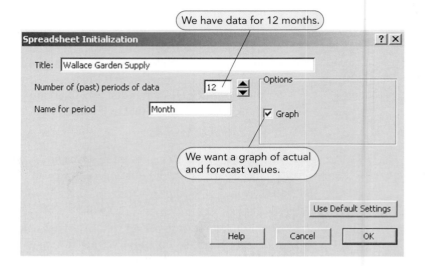

**Using ExcelModules for Exponential Smoothing** We select the Exponential Smoothing option from the Forecasting Models submenu in ExcelModules (see Program 11.1A). The window shown in Program 11.4A is displayed. The option entries in this window are similar to that for the moving averages (as we saw in Program 11.2A).

When we click OK on this screen, we get the screen shown in Program 11.4B. We now enter the actual shed sales for the 12 months (see Table 11.3) in cells B7:B18 and the value of $\alpha$ in cell B20. We use $\alpha = 0.1$ for this sample computer run.

**File: 11-4.xls**

**PROGRAM 11.4B**

**Exponential Smoothing Model for Wallace Garden Supply Using a Smoothing Constant of $\alpha = 0.1$**

| | A | B | C | D | E | F | G | H |
|---|---|---|---|---|---|---|---|---|
| 1 | **Wallace Garden Supply** | | | | | | | |
| 2 | **Forecasting** | | Exponential smoothing | | | | | |
| 3 | Enter the data in the cells shaded YELLOW. | | | | | | | |
| 4 | | | | | | | | |
| 5 | **Input Data** | | | Forecast Error Analysis | | | | |
| 6 | Period | Actual value | | Forecast | Error | Absolute error | Squared error | Absolute % error |
| 7 | Month 1 | 10 | | 10.000 | | | | |
| 8 | Month 2 | 12 | | 10.000 | 2.000 | 2.000 | 4.000 | 16.67% |
| 9 | Month 3 | 16 | | 10.200 | 5.800 | 5.800 | 33.640 | 36.25% |
| 10 | Month 4 | 13 | | 10.780 | 2.220 | 2.220 | 4.928 | 17.08% |
| 11 | Month 5 | 17 | | 11.002 | 5.998 | 5.998 | 35.976 | 35.28% |
| 12 | Month 6 | 19 | | 11.602 | 7.398 | 7.398 | 54.733 | 38.94% |
| 13 | Month 7 | 15 | | 12.342 | 2.658 | 2.658 | 7.067 | 17.72% |
| 14 | Month 8 | 20 | | 12.607 | 7.393 | 7.393 | 54.650 | 36.96% |
| 15 | Month 9 | 22 | | 13.347 | 8.653 | 8.653 | 74.879 | 39.33% |
| 16 | Month 10 | 19 | | 14.212 | 4.788 | 4.788 | 22.925 | 25.20% |
| 17 | Month 11 | 21 | | 14.691 | 6.309 | 6.309 | 39.806 | 30.04% |
| 18 | Month 12 | 19 | | 15.322 | 3.678 | 3.678 | 13.529 | 19.36% |
| 19 | | | | **Average** | | 5.172 | 31.467 | 28.44% |
| 20 | **Alpha** | 0.1 | | | | **MAD** | **MSE** | **MAPE** |
| 21 | | | | | | | | |
| 22 | **Next period** | **15.690** | | | | | | |

Assumed forecast for month 1

Value of the smoothing constant

MAPE is 28.44%.

Forecast for month 13

The worksheet now displays the exponential smoothing forecasts (shown in cells D7:D18), and the forecast for the next month (i.e., January of the next year), shown in cell B22. In addition, the following measures of forecast error are also calculated and reported: MAD (cell F19), MSE (cell G19), and MAPE (cell H19). The line graph, if asked for, is shown on a separate worksheet.

With $\alpha = 0.1$, the MAPE turns out to be 28.44%. Note that all error values here have been computed using months 2 through 12, compared to earlier cases (see Programs 11.2B and 11.3B) where only months 4 through 12 were used.

See if you can repeat the exponential smoothing calculations for $\alpha = 0.9$, and obtain a MAPE of 17.18%.

**Using Solver to Determine the Optimal Value of $\alpha$**   Just as we used Solver to find the optimal weights in the weighted moving average technique, we can use it to find the optimal smoothing constant in the exponential smoothing technique. The lone Changing Cell here is the value of $\alpha$ (cell B20, as shown in Program 11.4C). The Target Cell is the measure of forecast error (i.e., MAD, MSE, or MAPE) that we want to minimize. In Program 11.4C, we have chosen to minimize the MAPE (cell H19). The only constraint (other than the non-negativity constraint) is that the value of $\alpha$ must be less than or equal to 1.

*This nonlinear program has only one constraint.*

**PROGRAM 11.4C**      **Optimal Smoothing Constant Using Solver for Wallace Garden Supply**

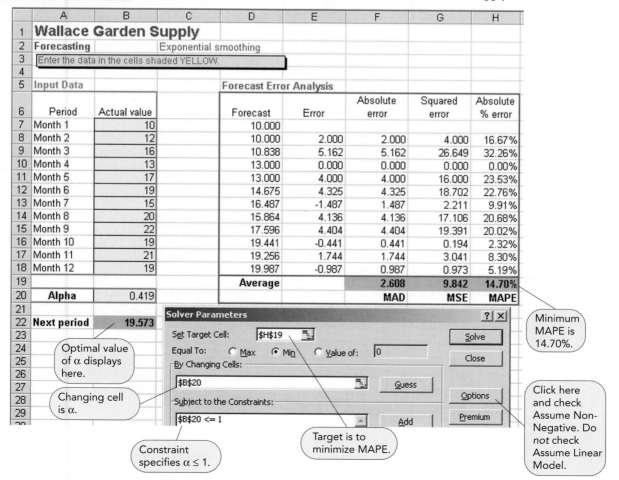

**IN ACTION** Forecasting Spare Parts at American Airlines

To support the operation of its fleet of more than 400 aircraft, American Airlines maintains a vast inventory of spare repairable (rotatable) aircraft parts. Its PC-based forecasting system, the Rotatables Allocation and Planning System (RAPS), provides demand forecasts for spare parts, helps allocate these parts to airports, and computes the availability of each spare part. With 5,000 different kinds of parts, ranging from landing gear to wing flaps to coffeemakers to altimeters, meeting demand for each part at each station can be extremely difficult—and expensive. The average price of a rotatable part is about $5,000, with some parts (such as avionics computers) costing well over $500,000 each.

Before developing RAPS, American used only time-series methods to forecast the demand for spare parts. The time-series approach was slow to respond to even moderate changes in aircraft utilizations, let alone major fleet expansions. RAPS, instead, uses linear regression to establish a relationship between monthly part removals and various functions of monthly flying hours. Correlation coefficients and statistical significance tests are used to find the best regressions, which now take only one hour instead of the days that the old system needed.

The results? Using RAPS, American says that it had a one-time savings of $7 million and recurring annual savings of nearly $1 million.

**Source:** Mark J. Tedone. "Repairable Part Management," *Interfaces* 19, 4 (July–August 1989): 61–68.

Program 11.4C shows the Solver entries and results for the Wallace Garden Supply problem. The optimal value of $\alpha$ turns out to be 0.419, yielding a MAPE value of 14.70%. Compare this with a MAPE of 28.44% when $\alpha = 0.1$, and a MAPE of 17.18% when $\alpha = 0.9$.

The value of the MSE is 9.842 when $\alpha = 0.419$. However, the minimum value of the MSE is 8.547 and is obtained when $\alpha = 0.646$. (See if you can verify this for yourself using Solver.) That is, the same value of $\alpha$ need not necessarily minimize both the MAPE and MSE measures.

## 11.6 TREND AND SEASONALITY IN TIME-SERIES DATA

Although moving average models do smooth out fluctuations in the time series, they are not very good at picking up trends in the data. Likewise, they are not very good at detecting seasonal variations in the data. In this section, we therefore discuss how trend and seasonal variations can be detected and analyzed in time-series data. Here again, although we show the equations needed to compute the forecasts for each model, we use worksheets (included in ExcelModules) to actually calculate these values.

*Linear trend analysis fits a straight line to time-series data.*

### Linear Trend Analysis

The *trend analysis* technique fits a trend equation (or curve) to a series of historical data points. It then projects the curve into the future for medium- and long-term forecasts. There are several mathematical trend equations that can be developed (e.g., linear, exponential, or quadratic equations). However, in this section, we discuss only linear trends. In other words, the mathematical trend equation we develop will be a straight line.

**TABLE 11.4**

**Sales of Electrical Generators at Midwestern Manufacturing**

| YEAR | SALES |
|------|-------|
| 1995 | 74 |
| 1996 | 79 |
| 1997 | 80 |
| 1998 | 90 |
| 1999 | 105 |
| 2000 | 142 |
| 2001 | 122 |

**Midwestern Manufacturing Company Example** Let us consider the case of Midwestern Manufacturing Company. The firm's demand for electrical generators over the period 1995–2001 is shown in Table 11.4.

The goal here is to identify a straight line that describes the relationship between demand for electrical generators, and time. The variable to be predicted (demand, in this case) is called the *dependent* variable, and is denoted by $Y$. The variable used in the prediction (time, in this case) is called the *independent* variable, and is denoted by $X$.

## Scatter Diagram

*A scatter diagram helps obtain ideas about a relationship.*

To get a quick idea if any relationship exists between two variables, a *scatter diagram* should be plotted on a two-dimensional graph. The independent variable (e.g., time) is usually measured on the horizontal ($X$) axis, and the dependent variable (e.g., demand) is usually measured on the vertical ($Y$) axis.

**File: 11-5.xls**

**Scatter Diagrams Using Excel** Although we can draw a scatter diagram using ExcelModules (discussed shortly), we can also use Excel's built-in charting capabilities to draw such diagrams. The input data for Midwestern Manufacturing's problem is shown in Program 11.5A.

The Excel steps for creating a scatter plot are as follows:

1. Enter the time period and generator demand data in two columns (preferably adjacent), as shown in Program 11.5A.

2. Start Excel's Chart Wizard either by clicking Insert|Chart or by clicking the Chart Wizard icon on Excel's main menu bar. See Program 11.5A for illustration.

3. *Step 1* of 4: Select X-Y (Scatter), as shown in Program 11.5A. Click *Next*.

**PROGRAM 11.5A**    **Using Excel's Chart Wizard to Draw a Scatter Diagram—Step 1 of 4**

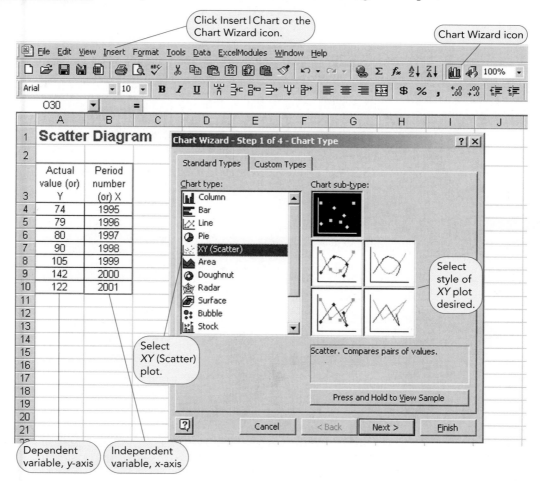

**PROGRAM 11.5B**

**Using Excel's Chart Wizard to Draw a Scatter Diagram—Step 2 of 4**

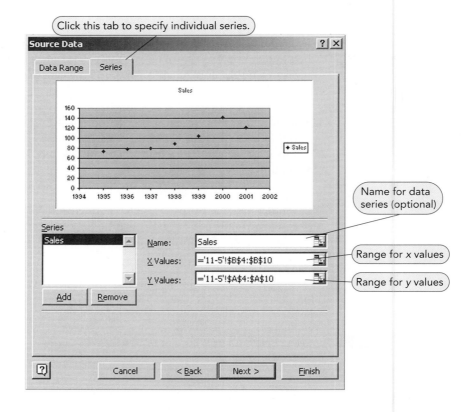

4. *Step 2* of 4: Select the appropriate data range (A4:B10 in our case). Click the *Column* box since the data are arranged in columns. Excel automatically puts the variable in the first column on the *X*-axis, and the second variable on the *Y*-axis. To swap these (if necessary, as in our case), click the tab named *Series* and make the necessary modifications. Add a name for the series, if desired. Click *Next*. See Program 11.5B for illustration.

5. *Step 3* of 4: Enter titles for the chart, *Y*-axis, and *X*-axis, if desired. Click *Next*. See Program 11.5C for illustration.

**PROGRAM 11.5C**

**Using Excel's Chart Wizard to Draw a Scatter Diagram—Step 3 of 4**

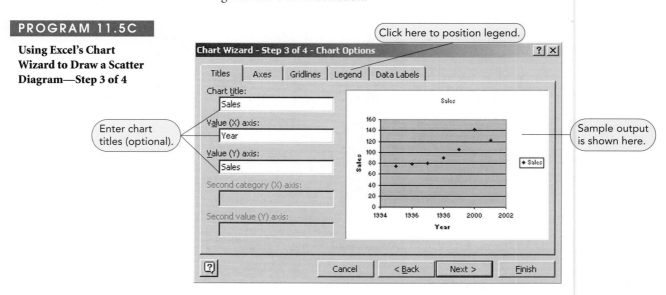

**PROGRAM 11.5D**

**Using Excel's Chart Wizard to Draw a Scatter Diagram—Step 4 of 4**

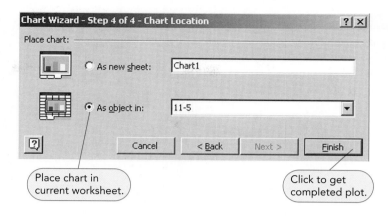

Place chart in current worksheet.

Click to get completed plot.

6. *Step 4* of 4: Decide where you want the chart to be placed (either in a new sheet or as an object in the same sheet). Click *Finish*. See Program 11.5D for illustration.

7. The plot shown in Program 11.5E now is displayed.

It appears from the plot in Program 11.5E that it may be reasonable to approximate the relationship between time and demand for generators in Midwestern Manufacturing's problem by a linear trend line.

## Least Squares Procedure for Linear Regression

*The least squares method finds a straight line that minimizes the sum of the vertical differences from the line to each of the data points.*

To develop the *linear* trend line by a precise statistical method, the *least squares procedure* can be applied. This approach results in a straight line that minimizes the sum of the squares of the vertical differences from the line to each of the actual observations. That is, it minimizes the sum of the squared errors. Figure 11.3 illustrates the least squares approach.[2]

**PROGRAM 11.5E**

**Scatter Diagram for Midwestern Manufacturing**

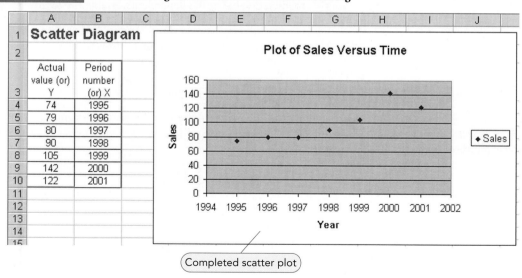

Completed scatter plot

---

[2] See a statistics textbook such as D. F. Groebner, P. W. Shannon, P. C. Fry, and K. D. Smith. *Business Statistics*, 5/e. Upper Saddle River, NJ: Prentice Hall, 2001, for more details on the least squares procedure.

**FIGURE 11.3**

**Least Squares Method for Finding the Best-Fitting Straight Line**

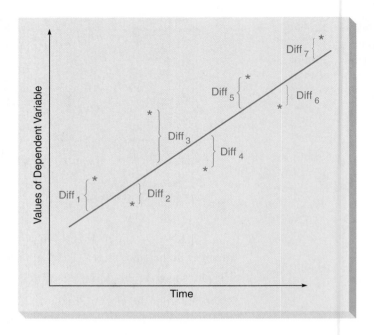

The least squares line is described in terms of its $Y$-intercept (i.e., the height at which it intersects the $Y$-axis) and its slope (i.e., the angle of the line). The line can be expressed by the following equation:

$$\hat{Y} = a + bX \tag{11-11}$$

*where*

$\hat{Y}$ = predicted value of the dependent variable (generator demand). Pronounced "$Y$-hat."

$X$ = value of the independent variable (time)

$a$ = $Y$-axis intercept

$b$ = slope of the regression line

*We need to solve for the Y-intercept and the slope to find the equation of the least squares line.*

The slope of the regression line is interpreted as the average change in $Y$ for a one-unit increase in the value of $X$. Statisticians have developed the following equations that we can use to find the values of $a$ and $b$:

$$b = \frac{[\sum XY - n\overline{X}\overline{Y}]}{[\sum X^2 - n\overline{X}^2]} \tag{11-12}$$

and

$$a = \overline{Y} - b\overline{X} \tag{11-13}$$

*where*

$\overline{X}$ = average of the values of the $X$'s

$\overline{Y}$ = average of the values of the $Y$'s

$n$ = number of data points or observations (7 in this case)

**PROGRAM 11.6A**

**Options Window for
Linear Trend Analysis
Worksheet in
ExcelModules**

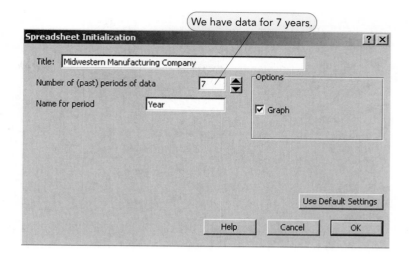

**File: 11-6.xls**

**Transforming Time Variables**  With a series of data over time, we can make the computations easier by transforming the values of time (*X*) to simpler numbers. Thus, in the case of Midwestern Manufacturing's data, we can designate 1995 as year 1, 1996 as year 2, and so on.

**Using ExcelModules for Linear Trend Analysis**  For this, we select the Linear Trend Analysis option from the Forecasting Models submenu in ExcelModules (see Program 11.1A on page 472). The window shown in Program 11.6A is displayed. The option entries in this window are similar to that for the moving averages (as we saw in Program 11.2A on page 473). Note that if we check Graph in the options shown in Program 11.2A, ExcelModules will automatically draw a scatter diagram as part of the output.

When we click OK on this screen, we get the screen shown in Program 11.6B. We now enter the actual generators sold for 1995 to 2001 (see Table 11.4 on page 482) in cells

**PROGRAM 11.6B**    **Linear Trend Analysis Model for Midwestern Manufacturing Company**

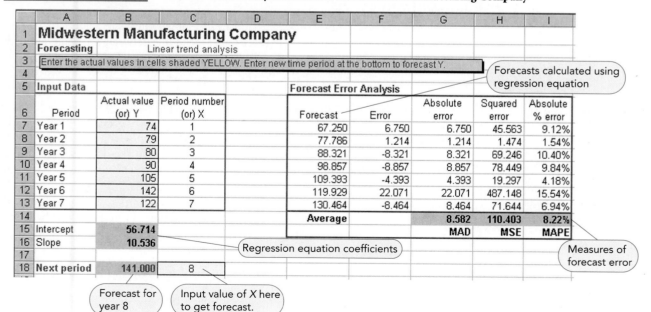

**PROGRAM 11.6C**    **Plot of Linear Trend Analysis Forecast for Midwestern Manufacturing Company**

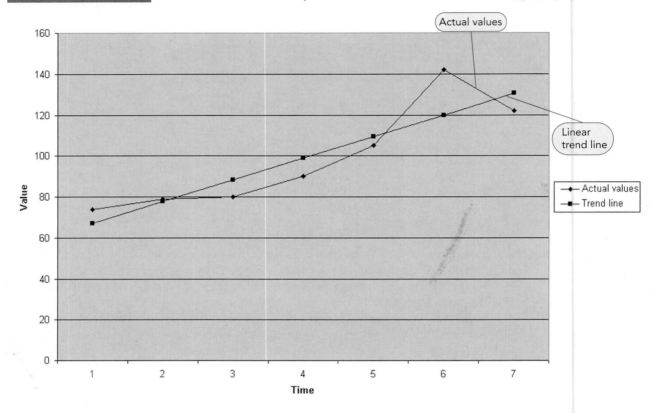

B7:B13 (*Y* values). The corresponding time periods (*X*) are automatically input by ExcelModules in cells C7:C13. We also enter the time period for the forecast needed (*X* = 8) in cell C18.

The worksheet now reports the values of *a* and *b* (shown in cells B15 and B16, respectively, in Program 11.6B) for the least squares linear trend line between time and demand. In Midwestern Manufacturing's case, the relationship between time and demand is

$$\text{Demand} = 56.714 + 10.536 \times \text{Time}$$

Using this equation, demand forecasts for 1995 through 2001 are displayed in cells E7:E13. The forecast for 2002 (i.e., time *X* = 8) is shown in cell B18. In addition, the following measures of forecast error are also calculated and reported: MAD (cell G14), MSE (cell H14), and MAPE (cell I14). The scatter diagram, if asked for, is shown on a separate worksheet, along with the least squares linear trend line. We show this plot in Program 11.6C.

*We can draw and compare plots of actual versus forecast values.*

To check the validity of this trend line model, we can compare the plot of actual demand values and the trend line (shown in Program 11.6C). In Midwestern Manufacturing's case, we may wish to be cautious and try to understand the 2000–2001 swings in demand.

## Exponential Smoothing with Trend Adjustment

Recall the exponential smoothing model in Section 11.5. As with any moving average technique, simple exponential smoothing fails to respond to trends. A more complex exponential smoothing that adjusts for trend can, at this point, be considered. The idea is to compute a simple exponential smoothing forecast and then adjust for positive or negative lag in trend. The formula used is

$$\text{Forecast including trend in period } t \ (FIT_t) = \tag{11-14}$$
$$\text{New forecast } (F_t) + \text{Trend correction } (T_t)$$

To smooth out the trend, the equation for the trend correction uses a smoothing constant, β, in the same way the simple exponential model uses α. The trend correction $T_t$ is computed as

$$T_t = (1 - \beta)T_{t-1} + \beta(F_t - F_{t-1}) \tag{11-15}$$

*β's responsiveness is like that of α—a low β gives less weight to more recent trends, while a high β gives higher weight.*

The value of β resembles the α constant in that a high β is more responsive to recent changes in trend. Values of β can be found by a trial-and-error approach, with the MAD used as a measure of comparison.

Simple exponential smoothing is often referred to as *first-order smoothing*, and trend-adjusted smoothing is called *second-order* or *double smoothing*. Other advanced exponential smoothing models are also in use; they include seasonal-adjusted and triple smoothing, but these are beyond the scope of this book.[3]

## Seasonality Analysis

Time-series forecasting such as that in the example of Midwestern Manufacturing involves looking at the *trend* of data over a series of time observations. Sometimes, however, recurring variations at certain periods (i.e., months) of the year make a *seasonal* adjustment in the time-series forecast necessary. Demand for coal and oil fuel, for example, usually peaks during cold winter months. Demand for golfing equipment or sunscreen may be highest in summer.

*Seasonal variations occur annually.*

Analyzing time-series data in monthly or quarterly terms usually makes it easy to spot seasonal patterns. A seasonal *index*, which can be defined as the ratio of the average value of the item in a season to the overall annual average value, can then be computed for each season.

There are several methods available to compute seasonal indices. One such method, which bases these indices on the *average* value of the item over all periods (e.g., months, quarters), is illustrated in the following example.

**File: 11-7.xls**

**Eichler Supplies Example**   Monthly demands of a brand of telephone answering machines at Eichler Supplies are shown in cells C3:C26 of Program 11.7, for the two most recent years.

To compute the monthly seasonal indices using the average demand value over the two years, we can create an Excel worksheet as follows:

1.  *Column D.* Compute the average monthly demand using all the available data. In Eichler's case, this is calculated by taking the average of the demand values for the 24 months.

2.  *Column E.* Compute the seasonal ratio for each month by dividing the actual demand each month by the average demand; that is, column E = column C / column D. For example, the seasonal ratio for January of year 1 is 80/94 = 0.851.

3.  *Column F.* Observe that since we have two years of time-series data, we have two seasonal ratios for each month. For example, January has ratios of 0.851 and 1.064, as shown in cells E3 and E15, respectively. We compute the seasonal *index* for January as

---

[3] For more detail, see G. E. P. Box, G. M. Jenkins, and G. C. Reinsel. *Time Series Analysis: Forecasting and Control*, 3/e. Upper Saddle River, NJ: Prentice Hall, 1994.

**PROGRAM 11.7**

**Computation of Seasonal Indices for Eichler Supplies**

Average of seasonal ratios for each month

$$= \frac{0.851 + 1.064}{2}$$

| | A | B | C | D | E | F |
|---|---|---|---|---|---|---|
| 1 | **Eichler Supplies** | | | | | |
| 2 | Year | Month | Demand | Average Demand | Ratio | Seasonal Index |
| 3 | 1 | January | 80 | 94 | 0.851 | 0.957 |
| 4 | | February | 75 | 94 | 0.798 | 0.851 |
| 5 | | March | 80 | 94 | 0.851 | 0.904 |
| 6 | | April | 90 | 94 | 0.957 | 1.064 |
| 7 | | May | 115 | 94 | 1.223 | 1.309 |
| 8 | | June | 110 | 94 | 1.170 | 1.223 |
| 9 | | July | 100 | 94 | 1.064 | 1.117 |
| 10 | | August | 90 | 94 | 0.957 | 1.064 |
| 11 | | September | 85 | 94 | 0.904 | 0.957 |
| 12 | | October | 75 | 94 | 0.798 | 0.851 |
| 13 | | November | 75 | 94 | 0.798 | 0.851 |
| 14 | | December | 80 | 94 | 0.851 | 0.851 |
| 15 | 2 | January | 100 | 94 | 1.064 | |
| 16 | | February | 85 | 94 | 0.904 | |
| 17 | | March | 90 | 94 | 0.957 | |
| 18 | | April | 110 | 94 | 1.170 | |
| 19 | | May | 131 | 94 | 1.394 | |
| 20 | | June | 120 | 94 | 1.277 | |
| 21 | | July | 110 | 94 | 1.170 | |
| 22 | | August | 110 | 94 | 1.170 | |
| 23 | | September | 95 | 94 | 1.011 | |
| 24 | | October | 85 | 94 | 0.904 | |
| 25 | | November | 85 | 94 | 0.904 | |
| 26 | | December | 80 | 94 | 0.851 | |

Average demand for all 24 months

$$\text{Ratio} = \frac{\text{Demand}}{\text{Average Demand}}$$

the average of these two ratios. Hence, the seasonal index for January is equal to $(0.851 + 1.064)/2 = 0.957$. Similar computations for all 12 months of the year are shown in column F of Program 11.7.

A seasonal index with value below 1 indicates demand is below average that month, and an index with value above 1 indicates demand is above average that month. Using these seasonal indices, we can adjust the monthly demand for any future month appropriately. For example, if we expect the third year's average demand for answering machines to be 100 units per month, we would forecast January's monthly demand as $100 \times 0.957 = 96$ units, which is below average. Likewise, we would forecast May's monthly demand as $100 \times 1.309 = 131$ units, which is above average.

## 11.7  MULTIPLICATIVE DECOMPOSITION OF A TIME SERIES

*Decomposition breaks down a time series into its components.*

Now that we have analyzed both trend and seasonality, we can combine both of these issues to decompose time-series data. Recall from Section 11.5 that a time series is composed of four components, namely, trend, seasonality, cycles, and random. In this section, we discuss a multiplicative decomposition model that breaks down a time series into two components: (1) seasonal component and (2) a combination of the trend and cycle component (we refer to this combined component simply as *trend*). As discussed earlier, it is not possible to discern the random component. The forecast is calculated as the product of the composite trend and seasonality components.

TABLE 11.5

Sales of Grand Pianos at
Sawyer Piano House

| | 1997 | 1998 | 1999 | 2000 | 2001 |
|---|---|---|---|---|---|
| Quarter 1 | 4 | 6 | 10 | 12 | 18 |
| Quarter 2 | 2 | 4 | 3 | 9 | 10 |
| Quarter 3 | 1 | 4 | 5 | 7 | 13 |
| Quarter 4 | 5 | 14 | 16 | 22 | 35 |

## Sawyer Piano House Example

Sandy Sawyer's family has been in the piano business for three generations. The Sawyers stock and sell a wide range of pianos, from console pianos to grand pianos. Sandy's father, who currently runs the business, forecasts sales for different types of pianos each year using his experience. Although his forecasts have been reasonably good, Sandy (who has recently completed her undergraduate degree in management) is highly skeptical of such a seat-of-the-pants approach. She feels confident that she can develop a quantitative model that will do a much better job of forecasting piano sales.

To convince her father that she is correct, Sandy decides to develop a model to forecast sales for grand pianos. She hopes to show him how good the model could be in capturing patterns in past sales. For this purpose, she collects sales data for the past five years, broken down by quarters each year. That is, she collects data for the past 20 quarters, as shown in Table 11.5. Since piano sales are seasonal and there has been an upward trend in sales each year, Sandy believes a decomposition model would be appropriate here. More specifically, she decides to use a multiplicative decomposition model.

Although the computations for decomposing a time series using a multiplicative model are fairly simple, we illustrate them using an Excel worksheet included for this purpose in ExcelModules.

## Using ExcelModules for Multiplicative Decomposition

We select the Multiplicative Decomposition option from the Forecasting Models submenu in ExcelModules (see Program 11.1A). The window shown in Program 11.8A is displayed. We specify the number of periods for which we have past data (20, in Sandy's example), the name for the period (Quarter, since we have quarterly data), and number of seasons each

**File: 11-8.xls**

PROGRAM 11.8A

**Options Window for
Multiplicative
Decomposition Worksheet
in ExcelModules**

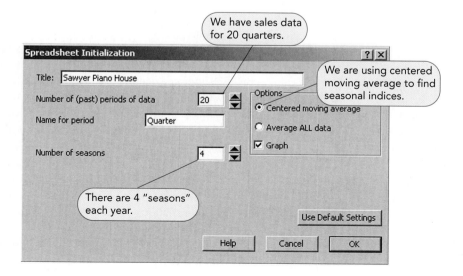

year (4, in Sandy's example). In addition, we see an option for the procedure to use in computing the seasonal indices.

The option named *Average ALL Data* uses the procedure discussed in Section 11.6 to compute the seasonal indices. In Sandy's example, this implies that we would first compute the average sales for all 20 quarters for which we have data. We would then divide the sales each quarter by the average sales to compute that quarter's seasonal ratio. Note that this will yield five ratios for each quarter (one for each year). Finally, we would average the five ratios for each quarter to compute that quarter's seasonal index.

*The centered moving average approach helps smooth out fluctuations in the data.*

The option named *Centered Moving Average* uses a slightly more complicated procedure to compute the seasonal indices. Recall from Section 11.5 that moving averages smooth out fluctuations in the time series. Hence, using this option could help us obtain more precise estimates of the seasonal indices. In what follows, we illustrate this procedure for computing seasonal indices, using Sandy's example.

When we click OK on the screen in Program 11.8A, we get the screen shown in Program 11.8B. We now enter the actual pianos sold during the past 20 quarters (see Table 11.5) in cells B7:B26. The corresponding time periods (i.e., the *X* variable values) are automatically specified in cells C7:C26 by the worksheet.

The worksheet now displays the results shown in Program 11.8B. The calculations are as follows:

*The seasonal indices are computed first.*

1. *Computation of the seasonal indices. Columns D–G.*

   ■ In column D, we first smooth out fluctuations in each quarter's sales data by computing the moving average sales for *k* quarters, centered on that quarter. Since there are four seasons (quarters) in Sandy's time-series data, we use $k = 4$ here. Then, in cell D9 (for example), we compute the average sales for four quarters, where these four quarters are centered on the third quarter of year 1 (i.e., quarter number 3). *Note:* In cases in which *k* is even (such as here, in which $k = 4$), it is not possible to directly center *k* quarters of data around a quarter. We therefore modify the computations as follows (e.g., when $k = 4$):

   $$\text{Centered average for quarter } t = [0.5 \times \text{sales in quarter } t-2$$
   $$+ \text{ sales in quarter } t-1 + \text{sales in quarter } t$$
   $$+ \text{ sales in quarter } t+1 + 0.5 \times \text{sales in quarter } t+2]/4$$

   ■ Next, we compute the seasonal ratio for each quarter by dividing the actual sales (column B) in that quarter by its centered average (column D). That is, column E = column B / column D.

   ■ The seasonal ratios for each quarter (five for each quarter in Sandy's case) are collected in cells B33:E37. The seasonal index for each quarter is computed as the average of all the ratios for that quarter. These seasonal indices are shown in cells B38:E38 and repeated in column F next to the appropriate quarter each year.

*The time-series data are then deseasonalized.*

   ■ Finally, in column G, we compute the unseasonalized sales in each quarter as the actual sales (column B) in that quarter divided by the seasonal index (column F) for that quarter. That is, column G = column B / column F.

*The linear trend equation is computed.*

2. *Computation of the trend equation.* Now that we have the unseasonalized sales data, we can analyze the trend. Since the purpose of the linear trend equation is to minimize the least squares error (as shown in Section 11.6), it is important to remove the seasonal effects from the data before we develop the trend line. Otherwise, the presence of seasonal variations can severely affect the linear trend equation.

Using the unseasonalized sales in column G as the dependent variable (*Y*) and the time period number in column C as the independent variable (*X*), we compute the linear trend equation. The resulting *Y*-intercept (*a*) and slope (*b*) for this straight

**PROGRAM 11.8B**    **Multiplicative Decomposition Model for Sawyer Piano House**

$$= \frac{\text{Actual value}}{\text{Centered moving average}} \qquad = \frac{\text{Actual value}}{\text{Seasonal index}}$$

| | A | B | C | D | E | F | G | H | I | J | K | L | M |
|---|---|---|---|---|---|---|---|---|---|---|---|---|---|
| 1 | Sawyer Piano House | | | | | | | | | | | | |
| 2 | Forecasting | | | Multiplicative decomposition | | | | | | | | | |
| 3 | 4 seasons | | Enter the actual values in the cells shaded YELLOW. Do not change the time period numbers! | | | | | | | | | | |
| 4 | | | | | | | | | | | | | |
| 5 | Input Data | | | Seasonal Index Computation | | | | Forecast Error analysis | | | | | |
| 6 | Period | Actual value (Y) | Time period (X) | Centered average | Seasonal ratio | Seasonal index | Unseasonalized value | Unseasonalized Forecast | Seasonalized Forecast | Error | Absolute error | Squared error | Absolute % error |
| 7 | Quarter 1 | 4 | 1 | | | 1.239 | 3.227 | 0.658 | 0.815 | 3.185 | 3.185 | 10.144 | 79.62% |
| 8 | Quarter 2 | 2 | 2 | | | 0.596 | 3.353 | 1.680 | 1.002 | 0.998 | 0.998 | 0.996 | 49.89% |
| 9 | Quarter 3 | 1 | 3 | 3.250 | 0.308 | 0.485 | 2.061 | 2.703 | 1.311 | -0.311 | 0.311 | 0.097 | 31.13% |
| 10 | Quarter 4 | 5 | 4 | 3.750 | 1.333 | 1.577 | 3.170 | 3.725 | 5.876 | -0.876 | 0.876 | 0.768 | 17.53% |
| 11 | Quarter 5 | 6 | 5 | 4.375 | 1.371 | 1.239 | 4.841 | 4.748 | 5.884 | 0.116 | 0.116 | 0.013 | 1.93% |
| 12 | Quarter 6 | 4 | 6 | 5.875 | 0.681 | 0.596 | 6.706 | 5.770 | 3.442 | 0.558 | 0.558 | 0.311 | 13.95% |
| 13 | Quarter 7 | 4 | 7 | 7.500 | 0.533 | 0.485 | 8.244 | 6.793 | 3.296 | 0.704 | 0.704 | 0.496 | 17.60% |
| 14 | Quarter 8 | 14 | 8 | 7.875 | 1.778 | 1.577 | 8.875 | 7.816 | 12.328 | 1.672 | 1.672 | 2.795 | 11.94% |
| 15 | Quarter 9 | 10 | 9 | 7.875 | 1.270 | 1.239 | 8.069 | 8.838 | 10.954 | -0.954 | 0.954 | 0.910 | 9.54% |
| 16 | Quarter 10 | 3 | 10 | 8.250 | 0.364 | 0.596 | 5.029 | 9.861 | 5.882 | -2.882 | 2.882 | 8.305 | 96.06% |
| 17 | Quarter 11 | 5 | 11 | 8.750 | 0.571 | 0.485 | 10.305 | 10.883 | 5.280 | -0.280 | 0.280 | 0.079 | 5.61% |
| 18 | Quarter 12 | 16 | 12 | 9.750 | 1.641 | 1.577 | 10.143 | 11.906 | 18.780 | -2.780 | 2.780 | 7.730 | 17.38% |
| 19 | Quarter 13 | 12 | 13 | 10.750 | 1.116 | 1.239 | 9.682 | 12.928 | 16.023 | -4.023 | 4.023 | 16.186 | 33.53% |
| 20 | Quarter 14 | 9 | 14 | 11.750 | 0.766 | 0.596 | 15.088 | 13.951 | 8.322 | 0.678 | 0.678 | 0.460 | 7.54% |
| 21 | Quarter 15 | 7 | 15 | 13.250 | 0.528 | 0.485 | 14.427 | 14.973 | 7.265 | -0.265 | 0.265 | 0.070 | 3.78% |
| 22 | Quarter 16 | 22 | 16 | 14.125 | 1.558 | 1.577 | 13.947 | 15.996 | 25.232 | -3.232 | 3.232 | 10.447 | 14.69% |
| 23 | Quarter 17 | 18 | 17 | 15.000 | 1.200 | 1.239 | 14.523 | 17.019 | 21.093 | -3.093 | 3.093 | 9.564 | 17.18% |
| 24 | Quarter 18 | 10 | 18 | 17.375 | 0.576 | 0.596 | 16.765 | 18.041 | 10.761 | -0.761 | 0.761 | 0.580 | 7.61% |
| 25 | Quarter 19 | 13 | 19 | | | 0.485 | 26.794 | 19.064 | 9.249 | 3.751 | 3.751 | 14.067 | 28.85% |
| 26 | Quarter 20 | 35 | 20 | | | 1.577 | 22.188 | 20.086 | 31.684 | 3.316 | 3.316 | 10.994 | 9.47% |
| 27 | | | | | | | | | Average | | 1.722 | 4.751 | 23.74% |
| 28 | | | | | | Intercept | -0.365 | | | | MAD | MSE | MAPE |
| 29 | | | | | | Slope | 1.023 | | | | | | |

Input data for 20 quarters.

Regression (trend line) parameters

Measures of forecast error

| | A | B | C | D | E |
|---|---|---|---|---|---|
| 30 | | | | | |
| 31 | Seasonal Ratios | | | | |
| 32 | | Season 1 | Season 2 | Season 3 | Season 4 |
| 33 | | | | 0.308 | 1.333 |
| 34 | | 1.371 | 0.681 | 0.533 | 1.778 |
| 35 | | 1.270 | 0.364 | 0.571 | 1.641 |
| 36 | | 1.116 | 0.766 | 0.528 | 1.558 |
| 37 | | 1.200 | 0.576 | | |
| 38 | Average | 1.239 | 0.596 | 0.485 | 1.577 |
| 39 | | | | | |
| 40 | Forecasts for future periods | | | | |
| 41 | Period | Unseasonalized forecast | Seasonal index | Seasonalized forecast | |
| 42 | 21.000 | 21.109 | 1.239 | **26.162** | |
| 43 | 22.000 | 22.131 | 0.596 | **13.201** | |
| 44 | 23.000 | 23.154 | 0.485 | **11.234** | |
| 45 | 24.000 | 24.176 | 1.577 | **38.136** | |

Seasonal ratios in column E have been collected here.

Seasonal indices, also shown in column F

Forecast using trend equation

Forecasts multiplied by seasonal index

line are shown in cells G28 and G29, respectively. In Sandy's case, the linear trend equation is

$$\text{Sales} = -0.365 + 1.023 \times \text{Quarter number}$$

3. *Computation of forecast. Columns H and I.*

*The forecasts are now computed.*

- In column H, we use the trend equation to compute the unseasonalized forecast for each quarter. For example, for the fourth quarter of year 2 (i.e., quarter number 8), this value is computed in cell H14 as $[-0.365 + 1.023 \times 8] = 7.816$. These values are also computed for the next year (i.e., quarters 21 to 24) in cells B42:B45.

*Forecasts are seasonalized.*

- The unseasonalized forecasts are multiplied by the appropriate seasonal indices to get the seasonalized forecast for each quarter in column I. That is, column I = column H × column F. Cells D42:D45 show the seasonal forecasts for quarter numbers 21 to 24.

*Finally, measures of forecast error are computed.*

4. *Computation of forecast error measures. Columns J through M.* As with all the other forecasting models in ExcelModules discussed so far, we compute the forecast error (i.e., actual value − forecast value) in column J, the absolute error in column K, the squared error in column L, and the absolute percentage error in column M for each quarter. We then use these error values to compute the MAD (cell K27), MSE (cell L27), and MAPE (cell M27) values.

**PROGRAM 11.8C**   **Plot of Multiplicative Decomposition Forecast for Sawyer Piano House**

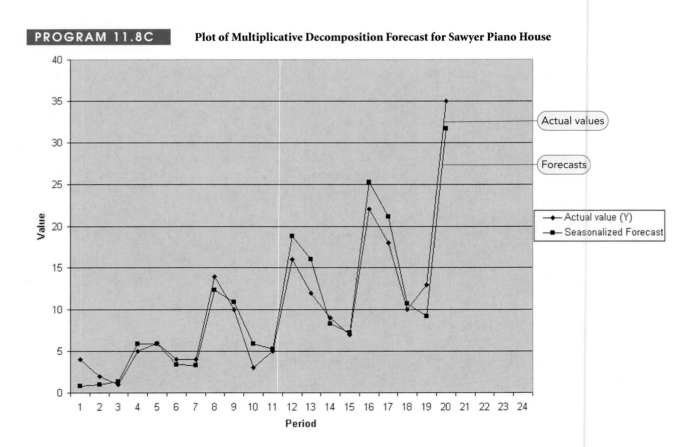

**Using Plots to Check the Validity of the Model** How good is Sandy's multiplicative decomposition model in predicting piano sales? One approach, of course, is to use the measures of forecasting error we have computed as indicators. As discussed earlier, however, these measures are difficult to interpret by themselves and are better suited for purposes of comparing different models. An alternative approach is to draw line plots of the actual and forecast values (columns B and I, respectively, in Program 11.8B) against the quarter number. These line plots are automatically drawn by ExcelModules and presented on a separate worksheet. The graph is shown in Program 11.8C.

*Line plots of the actual and forecast values are used to check the validity of the model.*

The line plots show that there are a few quarters (e.g., quarters 1, 10, 13, 19, and 20) in which there are sizable errors in the forecast. Overall, however, Sandy's decomposition model seems to do a good job of replicating the pattern of piano sales over the past few years. There is no consistent under- or overforecast seen, and the forecast errors appear to be randomly distributed.

Using this analysis as evidence, it looks like Sandy will be able to convince her father that such quantitative forecasting decision models are the way to go in the future!

## 11.8  CAUSAL FORECASTING MODELS

Consider an apparel firm that wishes to forecast the sales of its line of swimwear. It is likely that sales are related to factors such as the average daily temperature, whether schools are in session or not, the price charged, competitors' prices, and advertising budgets. The purpose of *causal forecasting models* is to develop a mathematical relationship between one or more of these factors, and the variable being forecast (swimwear sales, in this case).

*The dependent variable is the item we are trying to forecast, and the independent variable(s) is an item (or items) we think might have a causal effect on the dependent variable.*

In this causal model, swimwear sales is called the *dependent* (or predicted) variable. The variables used to forecast swimwear sales are called *independent* (or predictor) variables. The goal of the causal forecasting model is to develop the best statistical relationship between the dependent variable and the independent variables. The most common model used in practice is *regression analysis.*

There are several types of regression equations that can be developed (e.g., linear, quadratic, cubic, logarithmic). In this section, however, we discuss only linear regression models. Recall that we use linear regression in Sections 11.6 and 11.7 to develop linear trend lines. In those cases, the independent variable is time (or period number).

**IN ACTION**   Multiple Regression Modeling at Canada's TransAlta Utilities

TransAlta Utilities (TAU) is a $1.6 billion energy company operating in Canada, New Zealand, Australia, Argentina, and the United States. Headquartered in Alberta, Canada, TAU is that country's largest publicly owned utility. It serves 340,000 customers in Alberta through 57 customer-service facilities, each of which is staffed by 5–20 customer service linemen. The 270 linemen's jobs are to handle new connections and repairs, and to patrol power lines and check substations. This existing system was not the result of some optimal central planning but was put in place incrementally as the company grew.

With help from the University of Alberta, TAU wanted to develop a causal model to decide how many linemen should be best assigned to each facility. The research team decided to build a multiple regression model with only three independent variables. The hardest part of the task was to select variables that were easy to quantify based on available data. In the end,

the explanatory variables were number of urban customers, number of rural customers, and the geographic size of a service area. The implicit assumptions in this model are that the time spent on customers is proportional to the number of customers and the time spent on facilities (line patrol and substation checks) and travel are proportional to the size of the service region. By definition, the unexplained time in the model accounts for time that is not explained by the three variables (e.g., meetings, breaks, unproductive time).

Not only did the results of the model please TAU managers, but the savings of the project (which included optimizing the number of facilities and their locations) is $4 million per year.

**Source:** E. Erkut, T. Myroon, and K. Strangway. "TransAlta Redesigns its Service-Delivery Network," *Interfaces* (March–April, 2000: 54–69).

In causal forecasting models, when we try to predict the dependent variable using just a single independent variable, the model is called a *simple* regression model. When we use more than one independent variable to forecast the dependent variable, the model is called a *multiple* regression model. We illustrate both types of models in the following sections using simple examples. As with all models so far in this chapter, although we present a few key equations, we perform the actual calculations using worksheets provided in ExcelModules.

## Example of a Causal Simple Regression Model: Forecasting Dividends

Caught up in the euphoria of the stock market in the late 1990s, Richard Wheeler had invested a significant portion of his retirement funds in technology stocks. Reality struck in 2001, and Richard is now seriously looking for ways to salvage what's left of his portfolio. He plans to invest in more traditional "brick-and-mortar" firms, rather than the "dot-coms." Richard considers himself a shrewd investor (at least, he did until the year 2000!) Since he is nearing retirement, he wants to invest in companies that make sizable dividend payouts each year. Based on his investing knowledge and experience, he believes that the dividend payout is a function of earnings per share (EPS).

Richard is thinking about investing in Blue Star Manufacturing Company, which makes central air conditioning units. The company has been in business for over 50 years and Richard believes it is very stable. Using the Internet, Richard has been able to find the EPS and dividend per share paid by Blue Star for each of the past 10 years, as shown in Table 11.6.

*The least squares procedure can be used here.*

Richard wants to establish a mathematical relationship that will help predict dividend, based on EPS. Just as we did with the least squares method for trend projection, we can let $Y$ represent the dependent variable that we want to forecast (dividends, in this case). But unlike the trend models, the independent variable, $X$, is not time. Instead, it is the EPS each year.

*We can use a scatter diagram to check the relationship.*

As a first step toward developing this mathematical relationship, we should draw a scatter diagram between dividend and EPS. (Refer back to Section 11.6 on page 482 to see how this diagram can be drawn using Excel's Chart Wizard if necessary.) We will, in fact, draw such a diagram using ExcelModules shortly. For now, let us proceed under the assumption that the scatter diagram reveals a linear relationship between dividend and EPS. That is, the mathematical equation denotes a straight line.

| TABLE 11.6 | | |
| --- | --- | --- |
| **Blue Star Data for the Simple Regression Model: 1992–2001** | | |

| YEAR | EARNINGS PER SHARE | DIVIDEND PER SHARE |
| --- | --- | --- |
| 1992 | $1.59 | $0.39 |
| 1993 | $0.95 | $0.24 |
| 1994 | $1.14 | $0.29 |
| 1995 | $1.19 | $0.26 |
| 1996 | $0.76 | $0.15 |
| 1997 | $1.29 | $0.49 |
| 1998 | $0.97 | $0.21 |
| 1999 | $1.23 | $0.37 |
| 2000 | $1.14 | $0.29 |
| 2001 | $0.82 | $0.19 |

*We determine* a *and* b *(the Y-intercept and slope) using the least squares formulas.*

Least squares regression analysis can now be used to establish the equation of this straight line. The same basic model discussed in Section 11.5 applies. That is,

$$\hat{Y} = a + bX$$

*where*

$\hat{Y}$ = predicted value of the dependent variable (dividend here)

$X$ = value of the independent variable (EPS here)

$a$ = Y-axis intercept

$b$ = slope of the regression line

We next discuss how to use ExcelModules to develop this regression equation, the forecasts, and the measures of forecast error.

**File: 11-9.xls**

**Using ExcelModules for Causal Simple Regression Models**  We select the Causal Model (Simple Regression) option from the Forecasting Models submenu in ExcelModules (see Program 11.1A). The window shown in Program 11.9A is displayed. The option entries in this window are similar to that for earlier procedures. If we check the graph option, ExcelModules draws the scatter plot as part of the results.

When we click OK on this screen, we get the screen shown in Program 11.9B. We now enter the dividend values (dependent variable, *Y*) for the past 10 years in cells B7:B16 and the corresponding EPS values (independent variable, *X*) in cells C7:C16.

The worksheet now computes and displays the regression equation. For Richard's example, the Y-intercept (*a*) is shown in cell B18, and the slope (*b*) is shown in cell B19. The causal simple regression model is

$$\text{Dividend} = -0.101 + 0.351 \times \text{EPS}$$

The EPS values for years 1 through 10 are now plugged into the regression equation to compute the dividend forecast each year. These forecasts are shown in cells E7:E16. The following measures of forecast error are then calculated and reported: MAD (cell G17), MSE (cell H17), and MAPE (cell I17). Finally, if Richard estimates that Blue Star's EPS next year will be $1.05 (entered in cell C21), the model forecasts a dividend payout of $0.27 per share (shown in cell B21).

**Options Window for Causal Model (Simple Regression) Worksheet in ExcelModules**

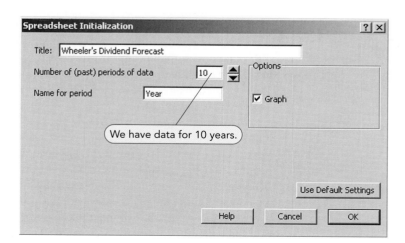

| PROGRAM 11.9B | Causal Model (Simple Regression) for Richard Wheeler's Dividend Problem |

| | A | B | C | D | E | F | G | H | I |
|---|---|---|---|---|---|---|---|---|---|
| 1 | **Wheeler's Dividend Forecast** | | | | | | | | |
| 2 | Forecasting | Causal regression analysis | | | | | | | |
| 3 | Enter the (Y,X) pairs in cells shaded YELLOW. Enter new value of X at the bottom to forecast Y. | | | | | | | | |
| 4 | | | | | | | | | |
| 5 | Input Data | | | | Forecast Error Analysis | | | | |
| 6 | Period | Dep Variable (or) (Y) | Indep Variable (or) (X) | | Forecast | Error | Absolute error | Squared error | Absolute % error |
| 7 | Year 1 | 0.39 | 1.59 | | 0.457 | -0.067 | 0.067 | 0.004 | 17.18% |
| 8 | Year 2 | 0.24 | 0.95 | | 0.233 | 0.007 | 0.007 | 0.000 | 3.09% |
| 9 | Year 3 | 0.29 | 1.14 | | 0.299 | -0.009 | 0.009 | 0.000 | 3.18% |
| 10 | Year 4 | 0.26 | 1.19 | | 0.317 | -0.057 | 0.057 | 0.003 | 21.83% |
| 11 | Year 5 | 0.15 | 0.76 | | 0.166 | -0.016 | 0.016 | 0.000 | 10.65% |
| 12 | Year 6 | 0.49 | 1.29 | | 0.352 | 0.138 | 0.138 | 0.019 | 28.20% |
| 13 | Year 7 | 0.21 | 0.97 | | 0.240 | -0.030 | 0.030 | 0.001 | 14.10% |
| 14 | Year 8 | 0.37 | 1.23 | | 0.331 | 0.039 | 0.039 | 0.002 | 10.60% |
| 15 | Year 9 | 0.29 | 1.14 | | 0.299 | -0.009 | 0.009 | 0.000 | 3.18% |
| 16 | Year 10 | 0.19 | 0.82 | | 0.187 | 0.003 | 0.003 | 0.000 | 1.57% |
| 17 | | | | | Average | | 0.038 | 0.003 | 11.36% |
| 18 | Intercept | -0.101 | | | | | MAD | MSE | MAPE |
| 19 | Slope | 0.351 | | Regression coefficients | | | | | |
| 20 | | | | | | | SE | 0.061 | |
| 21 | Forecast | 0.268 | 1.05 | | | | Correlation | 0.831 | |
| 22 | | | | | | | r-squared | 0.690 | |

Measures of forecast error

Forecast of dividend for next year

Estimate of EPS for next year

69% of variation in dividends is explained by EPS.

Standard error of the regression estimate

*One weakness of regression is that we need to know the values of the independent variable.*

This final computation of future dividends illustrates a central weakness of causal forecasting methods such as regression. We see that even after a regression equation has been computed, it is necessary to provide an estimate of the independent variable (EPS) before forecasting the dependent variable (dividend) for the next time period. Although not a problem in many cases, you can imagine the difficulty of estimating future values of some common independent variables such as the unemployment rate, gross national product, and consumer price index.

**Regression Plots**  To get an idea about the validity and accuracy of the causal simple regression model, we can use the scatter diagram of dividend versus EPS. Recall that we can also draw and interpret such scatter diagrams in linear trend analysis (see Program 11.6C on page 488 for an example). The plot for Richard's example is shown in Program 11.9C, along with the linear regression line to see how well the model fits the data. From this plot, it appears that there is, in fact, a linear relationship between dividend and EPS. However, there seems to be a few sizable differences between the actual values and the fitted line (forecast values).

An alternative approach is to draw line plots of the actual and forecast values (columns B and E, respectively, in Program 11.9B) against the observation number. If the graph option is checked in Program 11.9A, ExcelModules draws these line plots also (in addition to the scatter diagram) and presents them on a separate worksheet. The line plots for Richard's example, shown in Program 11.9D, indicate that the causal model he has developed does replicate the pattern of dividends paid each year. However, these plots also confirm the presence of a few sizable forecast errors. Richard may therefore want to consider including other independent variables in his causal model.

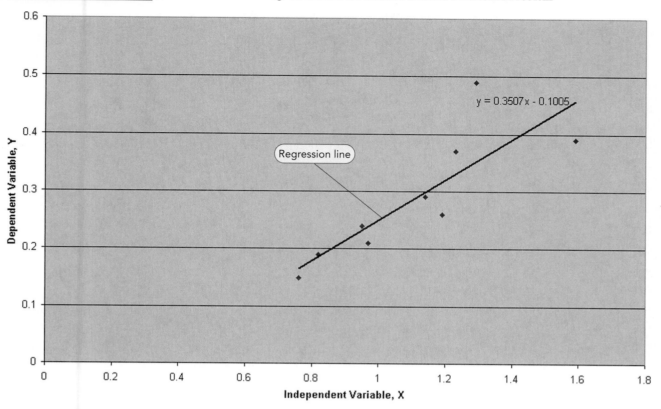

**PROGRAM 11.9C**  **Scatter Plot with Regression Line for Richard Wheeler's Dividend Problem**

Regression line

$y = 0.3507x - 0.1005$

Dependent Variable, Y

Independent Variable, X

**PROGRAM 11.9D**  **Plot of Causal Model (Simple Regression) Forecast for Richard Wheeler's Dividend Problem**

Actual values

Forecast values

Value

Period

Year 1  Year 2  Year 3  Year 4  Year 5  Year 6  Year 7  Year 8  Year 9  Year 10

◆ Actual
■ Forecast

**Standard Error of the Regression Estimate**   The dividend forecast of $0.27 for next year in Richard's example is called a *point estimate* of *Y*. The point estimate is actually the mean, or expected value, of a distribution of possible values of dividends, for a given value of EPS.

*The standard error is useful in creating confidence intervals around the regression line.*

Another way of measuring the accuracy of the regression estimates is to compute the *standard error of the* regression *estimate*, $S_{Y.X}$, also known as the *standard deviation of the regression*. The standard error can be used in setting up prediction intervals around the point estimate.[4] The expression for computing the standard error is

$$S_{Y.X} = \sqrt{\Sigma(Y_i - \hat{Y}_i)^2/(n-2)} \tag{11-16}$$

*where*

$Y_i$ = actual value of the dependent variable for the $i^{\text{th}}$ data point

$\hat{Y}_i$ = regression value of dependent variable for the $i^{\text{th}}$ data point

$n$ = the number of data points

ExcelModules automatically computes and shows the standard error. The value for Richard's example, shown in cell H20 of Program 11.9B, is 0.061. That is, the standard deviation of the distribution of dividend values around the regression line, for a given value of EPS, is $0.061.

**Correlation Coefficient**   The regression equation is one way of expressing the nature of the relationship between two variables.[5] The equation shows how one variable relates to the value and changes in another variable.

*The correlation coefficient helps measure the strength of the linear relationship.*

Another way to evaluate the relationship between two variables is to compute the *coefficient of correlation*. This measure expresses the degree or strength of the linear relationship. It is usually denoted by *r* and can be any number between and including +1 and −1. Figure 11.4 illustrates what different values of *r* might look like.

The rather cumbersome equation for *r* is

$$r = \frac{[n \, \Sigma \, XY - \Sigma \, X \, \Sigma \, Y]}{\sqrt{[n \, \Sigma \, X^2 - (\Sigma \, X)^2][n \, \Sigma \, Y^2 - (\Sigma \, Y)^2]}} \tag{11-17}$$

ExcelModules also calculates and reports the value of the coefficient of correlation. In Richard's example, the *r* value (shown in cell H21 of Program 11.9B) of 0.831 helps to confirm the closeness of the linear relationship between dividend and EPS.

*The coefficient of determination tells us how much of the variation in Y is explained by the independent variable (X).*

Although the coefficient of correlation is a commonly used measure to describe the linear relationship between two variables, another measure does exist: the *coefficient of determination*. This is simply the square of the coefficient of correlation and is denoted by $R^2$. The value of $R^2$ will always be a positive number in the range $0 \le R^2 \le 1$. The coefficient of determination is the percent of variation in the dependent variable (*Y*) that is explained

---

[4] When the sample size is large ($n > 30$), the prediction interval for an individual value of *Y* can be computed using normal (*Z*) tables. When the number of observations is small, the *t*-distribution is appropriate. For details, see any forecasting or statistics textbook, such as J. E. Hanke and A. G. Reitsch. *Business Forecasting*, 7/e. Upper Saddle River, NJ: Prentice Hall, 2003.

[5] Regression lines are not always cause-and-effect relationships. In general, they describe the relationship between movement of variables.

**FIGURE 11.4**

**Four Values of the Correlation Coefficient**

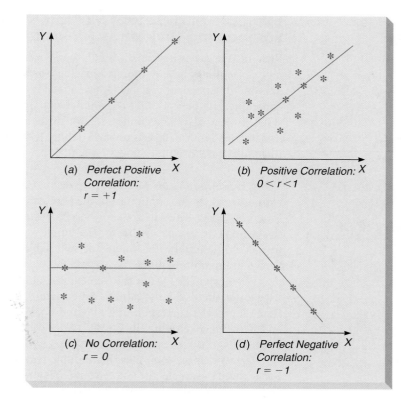

(a) *Perfect Positive Correlation:* $r = +1$

(b) *Positive Correlation:* $0 < r < 1$

(c) *No Correlation:* $r = 0$

(d) *Perfect Negative Correlation:* $r = -1$

by the regression equation. In Richard's case, the value of $R^2$ is 0.69 (shown in cell H22 in Program 11.9B), indicating that 69% of the total variation in dividends is explained by the EPS. As noted earlier, Richard may therefore want to consider including other independent variables in his causal model.

## Multiple Regression Analysis

*Adding another independent variable turns a simple regression model into a multiple regression model.*

*Multiple regression* is a practical extension of the simple regression model covered in the preceding section. It allows us to build a model with several independent variables. The general form of the least squares multiple regression equation is

$$\hat{Y} = a + b_1 X_1 + b_2 X_2 + \ldots + b_p X_p$$

(11-18)

*where*

$a = Y$-axis intercept

$b_i =$ slope of the regression for the $i^{\text{th}}$ independent variable ($X_i$)

$p =$ number of independent variables in the model

The mathematics of multiple regression becomes quite complex, and the equations vary depending on the number of independent variables. We therefore refer you to a statistics text for details on this procedure. There is, however, a worksheet included in ExcelModules to handle causal multiple regression models. In what follows, we illustrate causal multiple regression models using an expanded version of Richard Wheeler's dividend forecasting example.

## Example of a Causal Multiple Regression Model: Forecasting Dividends (Revisited)

Richard Wheeler is not satisfied with the $R^2$ value of 0.69 for his causal simple regression model. He thinks he can forecast Blue Star's dividend payouts more precisely by including a second independent variable in his regression model. Using his investing knowledge and experience, he believes that the annualized growth rate of the gross domestic product (GDP) would also be a good predictor of dividend payouts. Using the Internet, he has updated his input data, as shown in Table 11.7. Let us now use ExcelModules to develop Richard's causal multiple regression model.

**File: 11-10.xls**

**Using *ExcelModules* for Multiple Regression Causal Models**  We select the Causal Model (Multiple Regression) option from the Forecasting Models submenu in ExcelModules (see Program 11.1A). The window shown in Program 11.10A is displayed. The option entries in this window are similar to that for the simple regression model, with the additional choice to specify the number of independent variables. The entries for Richard's problem are shown in Program 11.10A.

When we click OK on this screen, we get the screen shown in Program 11.10B. We now enter the dividend values (dependent variable, $Y$) for the past 10 years in cells B8:B17, and the corresponding EPS and GDP growth values (independent variable $X_1$ and $X_2$, respectively) in cells C8:D17. After we enter all these values, we click the button marked Regress.

The worksheet computes the multiple regression equation and displays the results.[6] For Richard's example, the $Y$-intercept ($a$) is shown in cell B20, and the slopes ($b_1$ for EPS and $b_2$ for GDP growth) are shown in cells C21 and D21, respectively. The causal regression model is

*The forecasts are made by filling in the values of the two independent variables, EPS and GDP growth, in the regression equation.*

$$\text{Dividend} = -0.122 + 0.327 \times \text{EPS} + 0.013 \times \text{GDP Growth}$$

The EPS and GDP growth values for years 1 through 10 are now plugged into the regression equation to compute the dividend forecast each year. These forecasts are shown in cells

**TABLE 11.7**

**Blue Star Data for the Multiple Regression Model: 1992–2001**

| YEAR | EARNINGS PER SHARE | DIVIDEND PER SHARE | GDP GROWTH % |
|---|---|---|---|
| 1992 | $1.59 | $0.39 | 4.02 |
| 1993 | $0.95 | $0.24 | 2.57 |
| 1994 | $1.14 | $0.29 | 4.09 |
| 1995 | $1.19 | $0.26 | 2.16 |
| 1996 | $0.76 | $0.15 | 4.08 |
| 1997 | $1.29 | $0.49 | 4.31 |
| 1998 | $0.97 | $0.21 | 4.62 |
| 1999 | $1.23 | $0.37 | 4.99 |
| 2000 | $1.14 | $0.29 | 3.43 |
| 2001 | $0.82 | $0.19 | 1.24 |

[6] The multiple regression worksheet in ExcelModules uses Excel's Data Analysis add-in to perform the regression calculations. Hence, we are required to have Data Analysis installed and enabled for this worksheet to work. Please see Appendix A for details.

**PROGRAM 11.10A**

**Options Window for Causal Model (Multiple Regression) Worksheet in ExcelModules**

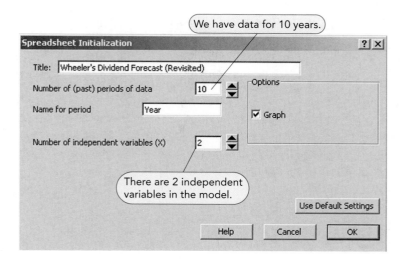

We have data for 10 years.

There are 2 independent variables in the model.

F8:F17. The following measures of forecast error are calculated and reported: MAD (cell H18), MSE (cell I18), and MAPE (cell J18). If the graph option is checked in Program 11.10A, the program plots line plots of the actual and forecast values against the observation number on a graph and shows them on a separate worksheet. We present the graph for Richard's example in Program 11.10C.

**PROGRAM 11.10B**    **Causal Model (Multiple Regression) for Richard Wheeler's Dividend Problem**

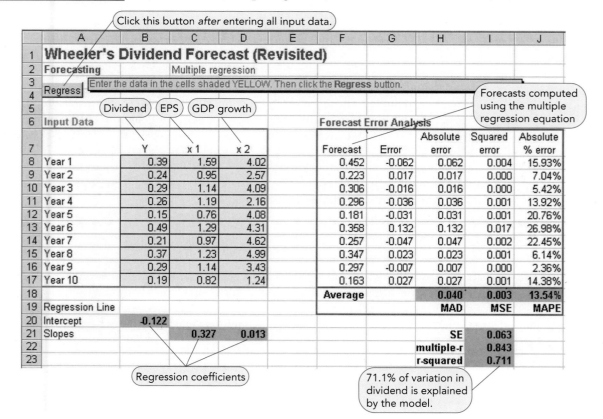

Click this button *after* entering all input data.

|  | A | B | C | D | E | F | G | H | I | J |
|---|---|---|---|---|---|---|---|---|---|---|
| 1 | **Wheeler's Dividend Forecast (Revisited)** | | | | | | | | | |
| 2 | Forecasting | | Multiple regression | | | | | | | |
| 3 | Regress | Enter the data in the cells shaded YELLOW. Then click the **Regress** button. | | | | | | | | |
| 4 | | | | | | | | | | |
| 5 | | Dividend | EPS | GDP growth | | | | | | |
| 6 | Input Data | | | | | Forecast Error Analysis | | | | |
| 7 | | Y | x 1 | x 2 | | Forecast | Error | Absolute error | Squared error | Absolute % error |
| 8 | Year 1 | 0.39 | 1.59 | 4.02 | | 0.452 | -0.062 | 0.062 | 0.004 | 15.93% |
| 9 | Year 2 | 0.24 | 0.95 | 2.57 | | 0.223 | 0.017 | 0.017 | 0.000 | 7.04% |
| 10 | Year 3 | 0.29 | 1.14 | 4.09 | | 0.306 | -0.016 | 0.016 | 0.000 | 5.42% |
| 11 | Year 4 | 0.26 | 1.19 | 2.16 | | 0.296 | -0.036 | 0.036 | 0.001 | 13.92% |
| 12 | Year 5 | 0.15 | 0.76 | 4.08 | | 0.181 | -0.031 | 0.031 | 0.001 | 20.76% |
| 13 | Year 6 | 0.49 | 1.29 | 4.31 | | 0.358 | 0.132 | 0.132 | 0.017 | 26.98% |
| 14 | Year 7 | 0.21 | 0.97 | 4.62 | | 0.257 | -0.047 | 0.047 | 0.002 | 22.45% |
| 15 | Year 8 | 0.37 | 1.23 | 4.99 | | 0.347 | 0.023 | 0.023 | 0.001 | 6.14% |
| 16 | Year 9 | 0.29 | 1.14 | 3.43 | | 0.297 | -0.007 | 0.007 | 0.000 | 2.36% |
| 17 | Year 10 | 0.19 | 0.82 | 1.24 | | 0.163 | 0.027 | 0.027 | 0.001 | 14.38% |
| 18 | | | | | | **Average** | | **0.040** | **0.003** | **13.54%** |
| 19 | Regression Line | | | | | | | **MAD** | **MSE** | **MAPE** |
| 20 | Intercept | -0.122 | | | | | | | | |
| 21 | Slopes | | 0.327 | 0.013 | | | | **SE** | **0.063** | |
| 22 | | | | | | | | **multiple-r** | **0.843** | |
| 23 | | | | | | | | **r-squared** | **0.711** | |

Forecasts computed using the multiple regression equation

Regression coefficients

71.1% of variation in dividend is explained by the model.

**PROGRAM 11.10C**    **Plot of Causal Model (Multiple Regression) Forecast for Richard Wheeler's Dividend Problem**

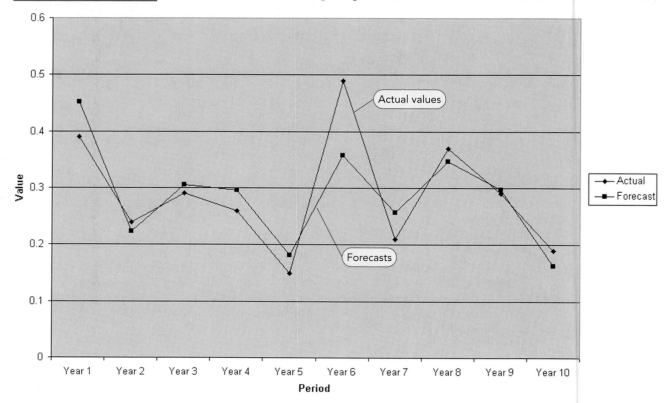

**Analyzing the Results**  Is this multiple regression model better than Richard's simple regression model? The line plots in Program 11.10C do not show any real improvement over the plots for the simple regression model (see Program 11.9D on page 499). Further, the $R^2$ value increased only marginally from 69% to 71.1%. These issues raise some concerns about the usefulness of adding GDP growth as a second independent variable in the causal model.[7] At this stage, Richard should perhaps stop relying on his own expertise in developing a causal forecasting model, and seek professional advice from an investment counselor!

# SUMMARY

Forecasts are a critical part of a manager's function. Demand forecasts drive the production, capacity, and scheduling systems in a firm and affect the financial, marketing, and personnel planning functions.

This chapter introduces three types of forecasting models: judgmental, time series, and causal. Four qualitative models are discussed for judgmental forecasting: Delphi method, jury of executive opinion, sales force

---

[7] We are *not* concluding here that GDP growth is a poor predictor of dividends. Rather, we are stating that GDP growth adds little incremental value once EPS has already been included in the model. Refer to a statistics book for the correct interpretation of results in multiple regression models.

composite, and consumer market survey. We then develop moving averages, weighted moving averages, exponential smoothing, trend projection, seasonality, and multiplicative decomposition models for time-series data. Finally, we illustrate a popular causal model, regression analysis. In addition, we discuss the use of scatter diagrams and provide an analysis of forecasting accuracy. The forecast measure discussed includes mean absolute deviation (MAD), mean squared error (MSE), and the mean absolute percent error (MAPE).

As we demonstrate in this chapter, no forecasting method is perfect under all conditions. Even when management has found a satisfactory approach, it must still monitor and control its forecasts to make sure that errors do not get out of hand. Forecasting can be a very challenging but rewarding part of managing.

## GLOSSARY

**Additive Model.** Forecasted value is the sum of the four components, namely, trend, seasonality, cycles, and random.

**Causal Models.** Models that forecast using variables and factors, in addition to time.

**Correlation Coefficient.** A measure of the strength of the linear relationship between two variables.

**Cycles.** Patterns that occur over several years. Cycles are usually tied into the business cycle.

**Decision-Making Group.** A group of experts in a Delphi technique who have the responsibility of making the forecast.

**Delphi.** A judgmental forecasting technique that uses decision makers, staff personnel, and respondents to determine a forecast.

**Exponential Smoothing.** A forecasting technique that is a combination of the last forecast and the last actual value.

**Forecast Error.** Difference between the actual and forecast values.

**Least Squares.** A procedure used in trend projection and regression analysis to minimize the squared distances between the estimated straight line and the actual values.

**Mean Absolute Deviation (MAD).** The average of the absolute forecast errors.

**Mean Absolute Percent Error (MAPE).** The average of the absolute forecast errors as a percentage of the actual values.

**Mean Squared Error (MSE).** The average of the squared forecast errors.

**Moving Average** A forecasting technique that averages past values in computing the forecast.

**Multiplicative Model.** Forecasted value is the product of the four components, namely, trend, seasonality, cycles, and random.

**Qualitative Models.** Models that forecast using judgments, experience, and qualitative and subjective data.

**Random Variations.** "Blips" in the data caused by chance and unusual situations. They follow no discernible pattern.

**Regression Analysis.** A forecasting procedure that uses the least squares approach on one or more independent variables to develop a forecasting model.

**Scatter Diagrams.** Diagrams of the variable to be forecasted or predicted, plotted against another variable such as time.

**Seasonality.** The pattern of demand fluctuations above or below the trend line that occurs every year.

**Smoothing Constant.** A value between 0 and 1 that is used in an exponential smoothing forecast.

**Standard Error of the Estimate.** A measure of the accuracy of regression estimates.

**Stationary Data.** A time-series data in which there is no significant upward or downward movement (or trend) over time.

**Time-Series Models.** Models that forecast using historical data.

**Trend.** This is the upward or downward movement of the data over time.

**Weighted Moving Average.** A moving average forecasting method that places different weights on past values.

## KEY EQUATIONS

**(11-1)** Forecast error = $A_t - F_t$

where $A_t$ = actual value and $F_t$ = forecasted value.

**(11-2)** $\text{MAD} = \sum_{t=1}^{T} |A_t - F_t| / T$

Equation for computing the mean absolute deviation.

**(11-3)** $\text{MSE} = \sum_{t=1}^{T} (A_t - F_t)^2 / T$

Equation for computing the mean squared error.

**(11-4)** $\text{MAPE} = \sum_{t=1}^{T} [|A_t - F_t|/A_t]/T$

Equation for computing the mean absolute percent error.

**(11-5)** Forecast = Trend × Seasonality × Cycles × Random

Multiplicative decomposition model.

**(11-6)** Forecast = Trend + Seasonality + Cycles + Random

Additive decomposition model.

**(11-7)** $k$-period moving average = $\sum$(Actual value in previous $k$ periods) / $k$

Equation for computing a $k$-period moving average forecast.

**(11-8)** $k$-period weighted moving average

$$= \frac{\sum_{i=1}^{k} (\text{weight for period } i)(\text{actual value in period } i)}{\sum_{i=1}^{k} (\text{weights})}$$

Equation for computing a $k$-period weighted moving average forecast.

**(11-9)** Forecast for period $(t + 1)$ = forecast for period $t$ + $\alpha$(actual value in period $t$ – forecast for period $t$)

Equation for computing an exponential smoothing forecast.

**(11-10)** $F_{t+1} = \alpha A_t + \alpha(1 - \alpha)A_{t-1} + \alpha(1 - \alpha)^2 A_{t-2}$
$$+ \alpha(1 - \alpha)^3 A_{t-3} + \ldots$$

Expanded equation for an exponential smoothing forecast.

**(11-11)** $\hat{Y} = a + bX$

Least squares straight line used in trend analysis and causal forecasting.

**(11-12)** $b = [\sum XY - n\overline{X}\overline{Y}] / [\sum X^2 - n\overline{X}^2]$

Equation to compute the slope, $b$, of a linear regression line.

**(11-13)** $a = \overline{Y} - b\overline{X}$

Equation to compute the $Y$-intercept, $a$, of a linear regression line.

**(11-14)** Forecast including trend in period $t$ ($FIT_t$)
= New forecast ($F_t$) + Trend correction ($T_t$)

Equation for exponential smoothing with trend adjustment.

**(11-15)** $T_t = (1 - \beta)T_{t-1} + \beta(F_t - F_{t-1})$

Equation to compute the trend correction.

**(11-16)** $S_{Y.X} = \sqrt{\sum(Y_i - \hat{Y})^2 /(n - 2)}$

Equation to compute the standard error of the regression estimate.

**(11-17)** $r = \dfrac{[n \sum XY - \sum X \sum Y]}{\sqrt{[n \sum X^2 - (\sum X)^2][n \sum Y^2 - (\sum Y)^2]}}$

Equation to compute the correlation coefficient.

**(11-18)** $\hat{Y} = a + b_1 X_1 + b_2 X_2 + \ldots + b_p X_p$

Least squares equation used in multiple regression.

# SOLVED PROBLEMS

## Solved Problem 11-1

Demand for outpatient surgery at Washington General Hospital has increased steadily in the past few years, as seen in the following table:

| YEAR | OUTPATIENT SURGERIES PERFORMED |
|------|-------------------------------|
| 1 | 45 |
| 2 | 50 |
| 3 | 52 |
| 4 | 56 |
| 5 | 58 |
| 6 | |

The director of medical services predicted six years ago that demand in year 1 would be 42 surgeries. Using exponential smoothing with a weight of $\alpha = 0.20$, develop forecasts for years 2 through 6. What is the MAD?

**PROGRAM 11.11**     **Exponential Smoothing Model for Solved Problem 11-1**

| | A | B | C | D | E | F | G | H |
|---|---|---|---|---|---|---|---|---|
| 1 | **Solved Problem 11-1** | | | | | | | |
| 2 | Forecasting | | Exponential smoothing | | | | | |
| 3 | Enter the data in the cells shaded YELLOW. | | | | | | | |
| 4 | | | | | | | | |
| 5 | Input Data | | | Forecast Error Analysis | | | Given forecast for year 1 | |
| 6 | Period | Actual value | | Forecast | Error | Absolute error | Squared error | Absolute % error |
| 7 | Year 1 | 45 | | 42.000 | | | | |
| 8 | Year 2 | 50 | | 42.600 | 7.400 | 7.400 | 54.760 | 14.80% |
| 9 | Year 3 | 52 | | 44.080 | 7.920 | 7.920 | 62.726 | 15.23% |
| 10 | Year 4 | 56 | | 45.664 | 10.336 | 10.336 | 106.833 | 18.46% |
| 11 | Year 5 | 58 | | 47.731 | 10.269 | 10.269 | 105.448 | 17.70% |
| 12 | | | | Average | | 8.981 | 82.442 | 16.55% |
| 13 | **Alpha** | 0.2 | | | | MAD | MSE | MAPE |
| 14 | | | | | | | | |
| 15 | **Next period** | **49.785** | | Value of the smoothing constant | | | | |

### Solution

**File: 11-11.xls**

To solve this problem, we use the *Forecasting Models | Exponential Smoothing* choice in ExcelModules. Program 11.11 shows the computations. The input entries are shown in cells B7:B11, and the α value is shown in cell B13.

The MAD is calculated to be 8.98 (cell F12). The rounded off forecast for year 6 is 50 (cell B15).

---

### Solved Problem 11-2

Room registrations in the Toronto Towers Plaza Hotel have been recorded for the past nine years. Management would like to determine the mathematical trend of guest registration in order to project future occupancy. This estimate would help the hotel determine whether a future expansion will be needed. Given the following time-series data, develop a regression equation relating registrations to time. Then forecast year 11's registrations. Room registrations are in thousands:

> Year 1: 17
>
> Year 2: 16
>
> Year 3: 16
>
> Year 4: 21
>
> Year 5: 20
>
> Year 6: 20
>
> Year 7: 23
>
> Year 8: 25
>
> Year 9: 24

### Solution

**File: 11-12.xls**

To solve this problem, we use the *Forecasting Models | Linear Trend Analysis* choice in ExcelModules. Program 11.12 shows the computations. The input entries are shown in cells B7:B15. The period values are automatically entered by ExcelModules in cells C7:C15.

The regression equation is Registrants = 14.556 + 1.133 × Year number. The MAPE is calculated to be 5.88% (cell I16). The projected registration for year 11 is 27,022 guests (cell B20).

**PROGRAM 11.12**   **Trend Analysis Model for Solved Problem 11-2**

| | A | B | C | D | E | F | G | H | I |
|---|---|---|---|---|---|---|---|---|---|
| 1 | **Solved Problem 11-2** | | | | | | | | |
| 2 | Forecasting | | Linear trend analysis | | | | | | |
| 3 | Enter the actual values in cells shaded YELLOW. Enter new time period at the bottom to forecast Y. | | | | | | | | |
| 4 | | | | | | | | | |
| 5 | Input Data | | | | Forecast Error Analysis | | | | |
| 6 | Period | Actual value (or) Y | Period number (or) X | | Forecast | Error | Absolute error | Squared error | Absolute % error |
| 7 | Year 1 | 17 | 1 | | 15.689 | 1.311 | 1.311 | 1.719 | 7.71% |
| 8 | Year 2 | 16 | 2 | | 16.822 | -0.822 | 0.822 | 0.676 | 5.14% |
| 9 | Year 3 | 16 | 3 | | 17.956 | -1.956 | 1.956 | 3.824 | 12.22% |
| 10 | Year 4 | 21 | 4 | | 19.089 | 1.911 | 1.911 | 3.652 | 9.10% |
| 11 | Year 5 | 20 | 5 | | 20.222 | -0.222 | 0.222 | 0.049 | 1.11% |
| 12 | Year 6 | 20 | 6 | | 21.356 | -1.356 | 1.356 | 1.838 | 6.78% |
| 13 | Year 7 | 23 | 7 | | 22.489 | 0.511 | 0.511 | 0.261 | 2.22% |
| 14 | Year 8 | 25 | 8 | | 23.622 | 1.378 | 1.378 | 1.898 | 5.51% |
| 15 | Year 9 | 24 | 9 | | 24.756 | -0.756 | 0.756 | 0.571 | 3.15% |
| 16 | | | | | **Average** | | **1.136** | **1.610** | **5.88%** |
| 17 | Intercept | **14.556** | Regression coefficients | | | | MAD | MSE | MAPE |
| 18 | Slope | **1.133** | | | | | | | |
| 19 | | | | | | | | | |
| 20 | Next period | **27.022** | 11 | | | | | | |

Forecast for next year 11, in thousands

## Solved Problem 11-3

Quarterly demand for Jaguar XJ8's at a New York auto dealership is forecast with the equation

$$\hat{Y} = 10 + 3X$$

*where*

$X$ = quarters:  quarter I of last year  = 0

quarter II of last year  = 1

quarter III of last year = 2

quarter IV of last year = 3

quarter I of this year  = 4 and so on

and

$$\hat{Y} = \text{quarterly demand}$$

The demand for luxury sedans is seasonal, and the indices for quarters I, II, III, and IV are 0.80, 1.00, 1.30, and 0.90, respectively. Forecast the demand for each quarter of next year. Then seasonalize each forecast to adjust for quarterly variations.

### Solution

Quarter II of this year is coded $x = 5$; quarter III of this year, $x = 6$; and quarter IV of this year, $x = 7$. Hence, quarter I of next year is coded $x = 8$; quarter II, $x = 9$; and so on.

$\hat{Y}$ (next year quarter I) = 10 + (3)(8)  = 34    Adjusted forecast = (0.80)(34) = 27.2

$\hat{Y}$ (next year quarter II) = 10 + (3)(9)  = 37    Adjusted forecast = (1.00)(37) = 37

$\hat{Y}$ (next year quarter III) = 10 + (3)(10) = 40    Adjusted forecast = (1.30)(40) = 52

$\hat{Y}$ (next year quarter IV) = 10 + (3)(11) = 43    Adjusted forecast = (0.90)(43) = 38.7

## SELF-TEST

- Before taking the self-test, refer back to the learning objectives at the beginning of the chapter, the notes in the margins, and the glossary at the end of the chapter.
- Use the key at the back of the book to correct your answers.
- Restudy pages that correspond to any questions that you answered incorrectly or material you feel uncertain about.

1. Qualitative forecasting models include
   a. sales force composite.
   b. Delphi.
   c. consumer market survey.
   d. all of the above.
   e. none of the above.

2. A forecast that projects company's sales is a(n)
   a. economic forecast.
   b. technological forecast.
   c. demand forecast.
   d. none of the above.

3. The method that considers several variables that are related to the variable being predicted is
   a. exponential smoothing.
   b. causal forecasting.
   c. weighted moving average.
   d. all of the above.
   e. none of the above.

4. Exponential smoothing is an example of a causal model.
   a. True                b. False

5. A time-series model incorporates the various factors that might influence the quantity being forecast.
   a. True                b. False

6. In a multiplicative decomposition model, the forecast is calculated as _____.

7. Decomposing a time series refers to breaking down past data into the components of
   a. constants and variations.
   b. trend, seasonality, cycles, and random variations.
   c. strategic, tactical, and operational variations.
   d. long-term, short-term, and medium-term variations.
   e. none of the above.

8. In exponential smoothing, when the smoothing constant is high, more weight is placed on the more recent data.
   a. True                b. False

9. Three popular measures of forecast accuracy are
   a. total error, average error, and mean error.
   b. average error, median error, and maximum error.
   c. median error, minimum error, and maximum absolute error.
   d. mean absolute error, mean squared error, and mean absolute percent error.
   e. none of the above.

10. The value of $\alpha$ that minimizes the MAD in exponential smoothing can be computed in Excel using
    a. Goal Seek.
    b. Solver.
    c. ExcelModules.
    d. the SUMPRODUCT function.

11. Unfortunately, regression analysis can only be used to develop a forecast based on a single independent variable.
    a. True                b. False

12. A fundamental weakness of causal forecasting methods is that we must first forecast the value of the independent variable and *then* apply that value in the forecast of the dependent variable.
    a. True                b. False

13. With regard to a regression-based forecast, the *standard error of the estimate* gives a measure of
    a. the overall accuracy of the forecast.
    b. the time period for which the forecast is valid.
    c. the time required to derive the forecast equation.
    d. the maximum error of the forecast.
    e. none of the above.

14. One method of choosing among various smoothing constants when using exponential smoothing is to evaluate the MAPE for each smoothing constant, and choose the smoothing constant that provides the minimum MAPE.
    a. True                b. False

15. No single forecast methodology is appropriate under all conditions.
    a. True                b. False

16. The difference between a *dependent* and an *independent* variable is that _____.

17. Quantitative forecasting methods include
    a. _____,
    b. _____,
    c. _____,
    d. _____,
    e. _____.

18. A time-series variable typically has the four components:
    a. _____
    b. _____
    c. _____
    d. _____

19. Time-series data that show no significant upward or downward movement (or trend) over time are called
    a. immovable.
    b. constant.
    c. stationary.
    d. non-stationary.

20. The main difference between simple and multiple regression is _____.

21. The difference between a *moving average* model and an *exponential smoothing* model is that _____.

22. The purpose of drawing a scatter diagram is to _____.

# DISCUSSION QUESTIONS AND PROBLEMS

## Discussion Questions

**11-1**   Describe briefly the steps used to develop a forecasting system.

**11-2**   What is a time-series forecasting model?

**11-3**   What is the difference between a causal model and a time-series model?

**11-4**   What is a qualitative forecasting model, and when is it appropriate?

**11-5**   What is the meaning of least squares in a regression model?

**11-6**   What are some of the problems and drawbacks of the moving average forecasting model?

**11-7**   What effect does the value of the smoothing constant have on the weight given to the past forecast and the past observed value?

**11-8**   Describe briefly the Delphi technique.

**11-9**   What is MAPE, and why is it important in the selection and use of forecasting models?

**11-10**   Describe how you can use plots to determine if a forecasting model is valid.

**11-11**   What is a correlation coefficient? Why is it useful?

**11-12**   Explain how Solver can be used to identify the optimal weights in the weighted moving average model.

## Problems

• **11-13**   John Smith has developed the following forecasting model:

$$\hat{Y} = 36 + 4.3X$$

*where*

$\hat{Y}$ = demand for K10 air conditioners

$X$ = the outside temperature (°F)

(a)  Forecast the demand for K10 when the temperature is 70°F.
(b)  What is the demand for a temperature of 80°F?
(c)  What is the demand for a temperature of 90°F?

‣ **11-14**   Data collected on the yearly demand for 50-pound bags of fertilizer at Wallace Garden Supply are shown in the following table. Develop a three-year moving average to forecast sales. Then estimate demand again with a weighted moving average in which sales in the most recent year are given a weight of 2 and sales in the other two years are each given a weight of 1. Which method do you think is best?

| Year | Demand for Fertilizer (1,000's of Bags) | Year | Demand for Fertilizer (1,000's of Bags) |
|---|---|---|---|
| 1 | 4 | 7 | 7 |
| 2 | 6 | 8 | 9 |
| 3 | 4 | 9 | 12 |
| 4 | 5 | 10 | 14 |
| 5 | 10 | 11 | 15 |
| 6 | 8 | | |

• **11-15**   Develop a two- and a four-year moving average for the demand for fertilizer in Problem 11-14.

‣ **11-16**   In Problems 11-14 and 11-15, four different forecasts were developed for the demand for fertilizer: a two-year moving average, a three-year moving average, a weighted moving average, and a four-year moving average. Which one would you use? Explain your answer.

‣ **11-17**   Use exponential smoothing with a smoothing constant of 0.3 to forecast the demand for fertilizer given in Problem 11-14. Assume that last period's forecast for year 1 is 5,000 bags to begin the procedure. Would you prefer to use the exponential smoothing model or the weighted average model developed in Problem 11-14? Explain your answer.

• **11-18**   Sales of Cool-Man air conditioners have grown steadily during the past five years, as shown in the following table:

| Year | Sales |
|---|---|
| 1 | 450 |
| 2 | 495 |
| 3 | 518 |
| 4 | 563 |
| 5 | 584 |
| 6 | ? |

The sales manager had predicted, before the business started, that year 1's sales would be 410 air conditioners. Using exponential smoothing with a weight of $\alpha = 0.30$, develop forecasts for years 2 through 6.

• **11-19**   Using smoothing constants of 0.6 and 0.9, develop a forecast for the sales of Cool-Man air conditioners (see Problem 11-18).

‣ **11-20**   What effect did the smoothing constant have on the forecast for Cool-Man air conditioners? (See Problems 11-18 and 11-19.) Which smoothing constant gives the most accurate forecast?

• **11-21** Use a three-year moving average forecasting model to forecast sales of Cool-Man air conditioners. (See Problem 11-18.)

• **11-22** Using the trend projection method, develop a forecasting model for the sales of Cool-Man air conditioners. (See Problem 11-18.)

• **11-23** Would you use exponential smoothing with a smoothing constant of 0.3, a three-year moving average, or a trend to predict the sales of Cool-Man air conditioners? Refer to Problems 11-18, 11-21, and 11-22.

⁞ **11-24** The operations manager of a musical instrument distributor feels that demand for bass drums may be related to the number of television appearances by the popular rock group Green Shades during the preceding month. The manager has collected the data shown in the following table:

| DEMAND FOR BASS DRUMS | GREEN SHADES TV APPEARANCES |
|---|---|
| 3 | 3 |
| 6 | 4 |
| 7 | 7 |
| 5 | 6 |
| 10 | 8 |
| 8 | 5 |

(a) Graph these data to see whether a linear equation might describe the relationship between the group's television shows and bass drum sales.
(b) Use the least squares regression method to derive a forecasting equation.
(c) What is your estimate for bass drum sales if the Green Shades performed on TV nine times last month?

⁞ **11-25** Sales of industrial vacuum cleaners at R. Lowenthal Supply Co. over the past 13 months are as follows:

| SALES (1000's) | MONTH | SALES (1000's) | MONTH |
|---|---|---|---|
| 11 | January | 14 | August |
| 14 | February | 17 | September |
| 16 | March | 12 | October |
| 10 | April | 14 | November |
| 15 | May | 16 | December |
| 17 | June | 11 | January |
| 11 | July | | |

(a) Using a moving average with three periods, determine the demand for vacuum cleaners for next February.
(b) Using a weighted moving average with three periods, determine the demand for vacuum cleaners for February. Use 3, 2, and 1 for the weights of the most recent, second most recent, and third most recent periods, respectively. For example, if you were forecasting the demand for February, November would have a weight of 1, December would have a weight of 2, and January would have a weight of 3.
(c) Evaluate the accuracy of each of these methods.
(d) What other factors might R. Lowenthal consider in forecasting sales?

⁞ **11-26** Passenger miles flown on Northeast Airlines, a commuter firm serving the Boston hub, are as follows for the past 12 weeks:

| WEEK | ACTUAL PASSENGER MILES (1,000's) |
|---|---|
| 1 | 17 |
| 2 | 21 |
| 3 | 19 |
| 4 | 23 |
| 5 | 18 |
| 6 | 16 |
| 7 | 20 |
| 8 | 18 |
| 9 | 22 |
| 10 | 20 |
| 11 | 15 |
| 12 | 22 |

(a) Assuming an initial forecast for week 1 of 17,000 miles, use exponential smoothing to compute miles for weeks 2 through 12. Use $\alpha = 0.2$.
(b) What is the MAPE for this model?

⁞ **11-27** Emergency calls to Winter Park, Florida's 911 system for the past 24 weeks are as follows:

| WEEK | CALLS | WEEK | CALLS | WEEK | CALLS |
|---|---|---|---|---|---|
| 1 | 50 | 9 | 35 | 17 | 55 |
| 2 | 35 | 10 | 20 | 18 | 40 |
| 3 | 25 | 11 | 15 | 19 | 35 |
| 4 | 40 | 12 | 40 | 20 | 60 |
| 5 | 45 | 13 | 55 | 21 | 75 |
| 6 | 35 | 14 | 35 | 22 | 50 |
| 7 | 20 | 15 | 25 | 23 | 40 |
| 8 | 30 | 16 | 55 | 24 | 65 |

(a) Compute the exponentially smoothed forecast of calls for each week. Assume an initial forecast of 50 calls in the first week and use $\alpha = 0.1$. What is the forecast for the 25th week?

(b) Reforecast each period using $\alpha = 0.6$.

(c) Actual calls during the 25th week were 85. Which smoothing constant provides a superior forecast?

**11-28** Using the 911 call data in Problem 11-27, forecast calls for weeks 2 through 25 using $\alpha = 0.9$. Which $\alpha$ is best? (Again, assume that actual calls in week 25 were 85 and use an initial forecast of 50 calls.)

**11-29** Consulting income at Kate Walsh Associates for the period February–July has been as follows:

| Month | Income ($1,000's) |
|---|---|
| February | 70.0 |
| March | 68.5 |
| April | 64.8 |
| May | 71.7 |
| June | 71.3 |
| July | 72.8 |

Use exponential smoothing to forecast August's income. Assume that the initial forecast for February is $65,000. The smoothing constant selected is $\alpha = 0.1$.

**11-30** Resolve Problem 11-29 with $\alpha = 0.3$. Using MAPE, which smoothing constants provide a better forecast?

**11-31** The accountant at O. H. Hall Coal Distributors, Inc., notes that the demand for coal seems to be tied to an index of weather severity developed by the National Weather Service. That is, when weather was extremely cold in the United States over the past five years (and hence the index was high), coal sales were high. The accountant proposes that one good forecast of next year's coal demand could be made by developing a regression equation and then consulting the *Farmer's Almanac* to see how severe next year's winter will be.

(a) Derive a least squares regression and compute the coefficient of correlation for the data in the following table.

(b) Also compute the standard error of the estimate.

| Coal Sales (Millions of Tons) Y | Weather Index X |
|---|---|
| 4 | 2 |
| 1 | 1 |
| 4 | 4 |
| 6 | 5 |
| 5 | 3 |

**11-32** Bus and subway ridership in Washington, DC, during the summer months is believed to be heavily tied to the number of tourists visiting the city. During the past 12 years, the following data have been obtained:

| Year | Number of Tourists (1,000,000's) | Ridership (100,000's) |
|---|---|---|
| 1 | 7 | 15 |
| 2 | 2 | 10 |
| 3 | 6 | 13 |
| 4 | 4 | 15 |
| 5 | 14 | 25 |
| 6 | 15 | 27 |
| 7 | 16 | 24 |
| 8 | 12 | 20 |
| 9 | 14 | 27 |
| 10 | 20 | 44 |
| 11 | 15 | 34 |
| 12 | 7 | 17 |

(a) Plot these data and decide if a linear model is reasonable.

(b) Develop a regression relationship.

(c) What is the expected ridership if 10 million tourists visit the city?

(d) If there are no tourists at all, explain the predicted ridership.

**11-33** Jerilyn Ross, a New York City psychologist, specializes in treating patients who are phobic and afraid to leave their homes. The following table indicates how many patients Dr. Ross has seen each year for the past ten years. It also indicates what the robbery rate was in New York City during the same year.

| Year | Number of Patients | Crime Rate (Robberies Per 1,000 Population) |
|---|---|---|
| 1 | 36 | 58.3 |
| 2 | 33 | 61.6 |
| 3 | 40 | 73.4 |
| 4 | 41 | 75.7 |
| 5 | 40 | 81.1 |
| 6 | 55 | 89.0 |
| 7 | 60 | 101.1 |
| 8 | 54 | 94.8 |
| 9 | 58 | 103.3 |
| 10 | 61 | 116.2 |

Using trend analysis, how many patients do you think Dr. Ross will see in years 11, 12, and 13? How well does the model fit the data?

**11-34** Using the data in Problem 11-33, apply linear regression to study the relationship between the crime rate and Dr. Ross's patient load. If the robbery rate increases to 131.2 in year 11, how many phobic patients will Dr. Ross treat? If the crime rate drops to 90.6, what is the patient projection?

**11-35** Management of Davis's Department Store has used time-series extrapolation to forecast retail sales for the next four quarters. The sales estimates are $100,000, $120,000, $140,000, and $160,000 for the respective quarters. Seasonal indices for the four quarters have been found to be 1.30, 0.90, 0.70, and 1.15, respectively. Compute a seasonalized or adjusted sales forecast.

**11-36** In the past, Judy Holmes's tire dealership sold an average of 1,000 radials each year. In the past two years, 200 and 250, respectively, were sold in fall, 300 and 350 in winter, 150 and 165 in spring, and 285 and 300 in summer. With a major expansion planned, Ms. Holmes projects sales next year to increase to 1,200 radials. What will the demand be each season?

**11-37** Thirteen students entered the undergraduate business program at Rollins College two years ago. The following table indicates what their grade-point averages (GPAs) were after being in the program for two years and what each student scored on the SAT math exam when he or she was in high school. Is there a meaningful relationship between grades and SAT math scores? If a student scores a 350 on the SAT, what do you think his or her GPA will be? What about a student who scores 800?

| STUDENT | SAT MATH SCORE | GPA | STUDENT | SAT MATH SCORE | GPA |
|---------|------|------|---------|------|------|
| A | 421 | 2.90 | H | 481 | 2.53 |
| B | 377 | 2.93 | I | 729 | 3.22 |
| C | 585 | 3.00 | J | 501 | 1.99 |
| D | 690 | 3.45 | K | 613 | 2.75 |
| E | 608 | 3.66 | L | 709 | 3.90 |
| F | 390 | 2.88 | M | 366 | 1.60 |
| G | 415 | 2.15 | | | |

**11-38** Smith Savings and Loan (S&L) is proud of its long tradition in Apopka, Florida. Begun by Laurie Shader-Smith twelve years after World War II, the S&L has bucked the trend of financial and liquidity problems that have plagued the industry since 1988. Deposits have increased slowly but surely over the years, despite recessions in 1967, 1972, and 1987. Ms. Shader-Smith believes it necessary to have a strategic plan for her firm, including a one-year

forecast of deposits. She examines the past deposit data and also peruses Florida's gross state product (GSP) over the same 44 years. (GSP is analogous to gross national product [GNP], but on the state level.)

(a) Using exponential smoothing with $\alpha = 0.6$, trend analysis, and finally, linear regression, discuss which forecasting model fits best for Shader-Smith's strategic plan. Justify why one model should be selected over another.

(b) Examine the data carefully. Can you make a case for excluding a portion of the information? Why? Would that change your choice of model?

| YEAR | DEPOSITS | GSP | YEAR | DEPOSITS | GSP |
|------|----------|-----|------|----------|-----|
| 1958 | 0.25 | 0.4 | 1980 | 6.2 | 2.5 |
| 1959 | 0.24 | 0.4 | 1981 | 4.1 | 2.8 |
| 1960 | 0.24 | 0.5 | 1982 | 4.5 | 2.9 |
| 1961 | 0.26 | 0.7 | 1983 | 6.1 | 3.4 |
| 1962 | 0.25 | 0.9 | 1984 | 7.7 | 3.8 |
| 1963 | 0.30 | 1.0 | 1985 | 10.1 | 4.1 |
| 1964 | 0.31 | 1.4 | 1986 | 15.2 | 4.0 |
| 1965 | 0.32 | 1.7 | 1987 | 18.1 | 4.0 |
| 1966 | 0.24 | 1.3 | 1988 | 24.1 | 3.9 |
| 1967 | 0.26 | 1.2 | 1989 | 25.6 | 3.8 |
| 1968 | 0.25 | 1.1 | 1990 | 30.3 | 3.8 |
| 1969 | 0.33 | 0.9 | 1991 | 36.0 | 3.7 |
| 1970 | 0.50 | 1.2 | 1992 | 31.1 | 4.1 |
| 1971 | 0.95 | 1.2 | 1993 | 31.7 | 4.1 |
| 1972 | 1.7 | 1.2 | 1994 | 38.5 | 4.0 |
| 1973 | 2.3 | 1.6 | 1995 | 47.9 | 4.5 |
| 1974 | 2.8 | 1.5 | 1996 | 49.1 | 4.6 |
| 1975 | 2.8 | 1.6 | 1997 | 55.8 | 4.5 |
| 1976 | 2.7 | 1.7 | 1998 | 70.1 | 4.6 |
| 1977 | 3.9 | 1.9 | 1999 | 70.9 | 4.6 |
| 1978 | 4.9 | 1.9 | 2000 | 79.1 | 4.7 |
| 1979 | 5.3 | 2.3 | 2001 | 94.0 | 5.0 |

*Note*: Deposits in millions of dollars, GSP in billions of dollars.

**11-39** In addition to his day job as an engineer, Luis Garcia runs a small ethnic grocery store in Easley, South Carolina. The shop stocks food items from southeast Asian countries and caters to the large population of people from this region who live in Easley and surrounding areas. Luis wants to develop a quantitative model to forecast sales. His sales data for the past 16 quarters are as follows:

| QUARTER | 1998 | 1999 | 2000 | 2001 |
|---------|------|------|------|------|
| Quarter 1 | 48.6 | 49.5 | 54.7 | 57.0 |
| Quarter 2 | 54.2 | 56.0 | 59.9 | 63.9 |
| Quarter 3 | 59.8 | 63.5 | 65.0 | 68.6 |
| Quarter 4 | 79.8 | 85.5 | 89.0 | 94.2 |

| MONTH | 1998 | 1999 | 2000 | 2001 |
|-------|------|------|------|------|
| January | 54,525 | 52,978 | 52,066 | 51,141 |
| February | 58,142 | 58,145 | 61,921 | 62,647 |
| March | 18,362 | 19,756 | 23,249 | 23,278 |
| April | 25,429 | 25,975 | 27,083 | 26,150 |
| May | 22,322 | 23,720 | 25,072 | 27,445 |
| June | 14,617 | 13,376 | 15,598 | 16,579 |
| July | 15,534 | 16,609 | 14,807 | 18,261 |
| August | 15,108 | 18,359 | 18,969 | 18,627 |
| September | 15,408 | 18,124 | 20,202 | 22,084 |
| October | 53,918 | 56,279 | 56,149 | 56,868 |
| November | 83,188 | 83,298 | 82,176 | 84,064 |
| December | 72,913 | 74,194 | 75,539 | 76,531 |

Develop a multiplicative decomposition model for Luis's sales data. Use the model to forecast revenues for 2002. Comment on the validity of your model.

**11-40** The Fowler Martial Arts Academy trains young boys and girls in self-defense. Joan Fowler, the owner of the academy, notes that monthly revenue is higher when schools are in session but quite low when school is out (since many children are away on vacation or at summer camps). She has researched revenues for the past four years and obtained the following information:

Decompose Joan's time-series data using a multiplicative model. Use the model to forecast revenues for 2002. Comment on the validity of your model.

## ➡ CASE STUDY

### North–South Airline

In January 2002, Northern Airlines merged with Southeast Airlines to create the fourth largest U.S. carrier. The new North–South Airline inherited both an aging fleet of Boeing 727–300 aircraft and Stephen Ruth. Ruth was a tough former secretary of the navy who stepped in as new president and chairman of the board.

Ruth's first concern in creating a financially solid company was maintenance costs. It was commonly surmised in the airline industry that maintenance costs rise with the age of the aircraft. He quickly noticed that historically there had been a significant difference in the reported B727–300 maintenance costs (from ATA Form 41's) both in the airframe and engine areas between

Northern Airlines and Southeast Airlines, with Southeast having the newer fleet.

On February 12, 2002, Peg Young, vice-president for operations and maintenance, was called into Ruth's office and asked to study the issue. Specifically, Ruth wanted to know whether the average fleet age was correlated to direct airframe maintenance costs, and whether there was a relationship between average fleet age and direct engine maintenance costs. Young was to report back by February 26 with the answer, along with quantitative and graphical descriptions of the relationship.

Young's first step was to have her staff construct the average age of Northern and Southeast B727–300 fleets, by quarter, since the introduction of that aircraft to service by each airline in late

**North-South Airline Data for Boeing 727-300 Jets**

| | NORTHERN AIRLINE DATA | | | | SOUTHEAST AIRLINE DATA | | |
|------|-----------------------------|---------------------------|--------------------------|---|------------------------------|-------------------------|-------------------------|
| YEAR | AIRFRAME COST PER AIRCRAFT | ENGINE COST PER AIRCRAFT | AVERAGE AGE (HOURS) | | AIRFRAME COST PER AIRCRAFT | ENGINE COST PER AIRCRAFT | AVERAGE AGE (HOURS) |
| 1995 | $51.80 | $43.49 | 6,512 | | $13.29 | $18.86 | 5,107 |
| 1996 | 54.92 | 38.58 | 8,404 | | 25.15 | 31.55 | 8,145 |
| 1997 | 69.70 | 51.48 | 11,077 | | 32.18 | 40.43 | 7,360 |
| 1998 | 68.90 | 58.72 | 11,717 | | 31.78 | 22.10 | 5,773 |
| 1999 | 63.72 | 45.47 | 13,275 | | 25.34 | 19.69 | 7,150 |
| 2000 | 84.73 | 50.26 | 15,215 | | 32.78 | 32.58 | 9,364 |
| 2001 | 78.74 | 79.60 | 18,390 | | 35.56 | 38.07 | 8,259 |

1994 and early 1995. The average age of each fleet was calculated by first multiplying the total number of calendar days each aircraft had been in service at the pertinent point in time by the average daily utilization of the respective fleet to total fleet hours flown. The total fleet hours flown was then divided by the number of aircraft in service at that time, giving the age of the "average" aircraft in the fleet.

The average utilization was found by taking the actual total fleet hours flown at September 30, 2001, from Northern and Southeast data, and dividing by the total days in service for all aircraft at that time. The average utilization for Southeast was 8.3 hours per day, and the average utilization for Northern was 8.7 hours per day. Because the available cost data were calculated for each yearly period ending at the end of the first quarter, average fleet age was calculated at the same points in time. The fleet data are shown in the table at the bottom of page 514. Airframe cost data and engine cost data are both shown paired with fleet average age in that table.

### Discussion Question

Prepare Peg Young's response to Stephen Ruth.

*Note: Dates and names of airlines and individuals have been changed in this case to maintain confidentiality. The data and issues described here are actual.*

---

## ➠ CASE STUDY

### Forecasting Football Game Attendance at Southwestern University

Southwestern University (SWU), a large state college in Stephenville, Texas, 30 miles southwest of the Dallas/Fort Worth metroplex, enrolls close to 20,000 students. In a typical town–gown relationship, the school is a dominant force in the small city, with more students during fall and spring than permanent residents.

A longtime football powerhouse, SWU is a member of the Big Eleven conference and is usually in the top 20 in college football rankings. To bolster its chances of reaching the elusive and long-desired number-one ranking, in 1997 SWU hired the legendary Bo Pitterno as its head coach. Although the number-one ranking remained out of reach, attendance at the five Saturday home games each year increased. Prior to Pitterno's arrival, attendance generally averaged 25,000 to 29,000 per game. Season ticket sales bumped up by 10,000 just with the announcement of the new coach's arrival. Stephenville and SWU were ready to move to the big time!

The immediate issue facing SWU, however, was not NCAA ranking. It was capacity. The existing SWU stadium, built in 1953, has seating for 54,000 fans. The following table indicates attendance at each game for the past six years.

**Southwestern University Football Game Attendance, 1997–2002**

| GAME | 1997 ATTENDEES | 1997 OPPONENT | 1998 ATTENDEES | 1998 OPPONENT | 1999 ATTENDEES | 1999 OPPONENT |
|------|-----------|----------|-----------|----------|-----------|----------|
| 1 | 34,200 | Baylor | 36,100 | Oklahoma | 35,900 | TCU |
| 2* | 39,800 | Texas | 40,200 | Nebraska | 46,500 | Texas Tech |
| 3 | 38,200 | LSU | 39,100 | UCLA | 43,100 | Alaska |
| 4** | 26,900 | Arkansas | 25,300 | Nevada | 27,900 | Arizona |
| 5 | 35,100 | USC | 36,200 | Ohio State | 39,200 | Rice |

| GAME | 2000 ATTENDEES | 2000 OPPONENT | 2001 ATTENDEES | 2001 OPPONENT | 2002 ATTENDEES | 2002 OPPONENT |
|------|-----------|----------|-----------|----------|-----------|----------|
| 1 | 41,900 | Arkansas | 42,500 | Indiana | 46,900 | LSU |
| 2* | 46,100 | Missouri | 48,200 | North Texas | 50,100 | Texas |
| 3 | 43,900 | Florida | 44,200 | Texas A&M | 45,900 | Prairie View A&M |
| 4** | 30,100 | Miami | 33,900 | Southern | 36,300 | Montana |
| 5 | 40,500 | Duke | 47,800 | Oklahoma | 49,900 | Arizona State |

*Source:* Heizer, Jay and Barry Render. *Operations Management*, 6/e. Upper Saddle River: Prentice Hall, 2001, p. 126.

*Homecoming games

**During the fourth week of each season, Stephenville hosted a hugely popular southwestern crafts festival. This event brought tens of thousands of tourists to the town, especially on weekends, and had an obvious negative impact on game attendance.

One of Pitterno's demands upon joining SWU had been a stadium expansion, or possibly even a new stadium. With attendance increasing, SWU administrators began to face the issue head-on. Pitterno had wanted dormitories solely for his athletes in the stadium as an additional feature of any expansion.

SWU's president, Dr. Marty Starr, decided it was time for his vice president of development to forecast when the existing stadium would "max out." He also sought a revenue projection, assuming an average ticket price of $20 in 2003 and a 5% increase each year in future prices.

### Discussion Questions

1. Develop a forecasting model, justifying its selection over other techniques, and project attendance through 2004.
2. What revenues are to be expected in 2003 and 2004?
3. Discuss the school's options.

---

## INTERNET CASE STUDIES

See our Internet home page at www.prenhall.com/render for these additional case studies: (1) Akron Zoological Park;
(2) Kwik Lube; and
(3) Human Resources, Inc.

---

# BIBLIOGRAPHY

Clements, Dale W. and Richard A. Reid. "Analytical MS/OR Tools Applied to a Plant Closure," *Interfaces* 24, 2 (March–April 1994): 1–43.

De Lurgio, S. A. *Forecasting Principles and Applications.* New York: Irwin-McGraw-Hill, 1998.

Diebold, F. X. *Elements of Forecasting.* Cincinnati: South-Western College Publishing, 1998.

Gardner, E. S. "Exponential Smoothing: The State of the Art," *Journal of Forecasting* 4, 1 (March 1985): 1–28.

Georgoff, D. M. and R. G. Murdick. "Manager's Guide to Forecasting," *Harvard Business Review* 64, 1 (January–February 1986): 110–120.

Hanke, J. E. and A. G. Reitsch. *Business Forecasting*, 6/e. Upper Saddle River, NJ: Prentice Hall, 1998.

Heizer, J., and B. Render. *Operations Management*, 6/e. Upper Saddle River, NJ: Prentice Hall, 2001.

Herbig, P., J. Milewicz, and J. E. Golden. "Forecasting: Who, What, When, and How," *The Journal of Business Forecasting* 12, 2 (Summer 1993): 16–22.

Li, X. "An Intelligent Business Forecaster for Strategic Business Planning," *Journal of Forecasting* 18, 3 (May 1999): 181–205.

Murdick, R., and D. M. Georgoff. "Forecasting: A Systems Approach," *Technological Forecasting and Social Change* 44 (1993): 1–16.

Niemera, M. P. *Forecasting Financial and Economic Cycles.* New York: John Wiley & Sons, 1994.

Wilson, J. H., and D. Allison-Koerber. "Combining Subjective and Objective Forecasts Improves Results," *The Journal of Business Forecasting* 11, 3 (Fall 1992): 1–10.

Yurkiewicz, J. "Forecasting That Fits," *OR/MS Today* 25, 1 (February 1998): 42–55.

———. "Forecasting 2000," *OR/MS Today* 27, 1 (February 2000): 58–65.

## CHAPTER 12

# INVENTORY CONTROL MODELS

## LEARNING OBJECTIVES

After completing this chapter, students will be able to:

1. Understand the importance of inventory control.

2. Use the Economic Order Quantity (EOQ) model to determine how much to order.

3. Compute the reorder point (ROP) in determining when to order more inventory.

4. Use the EOQ with non-instantaneous receipt model to determine how much to order or produce.

5. Handle EOQ problems that allow quantity discounts.

6. Understand the use of safety stock with known and unknown stockout costs.

7. Understand the importance of ABC inventory analysis.

8. Use Excel to analyze a variety of inventory control models.

## CHAPTER OUTLINE

Summary • Glossary • Key Equations • Solved Problems • Self-Test • Discussion Questions and Problems • Case Study: Sturdivant Sound Systems • Case Study: Martin-Pullin Bicycle Corporation • Internet Case Studies • Bibliography

### Inventory Modeling at Teradyne

Teradyne, a huge manufacturer of electronic testing equipment for semiconductor plants worldwide, recently asked Wharton's Business School to evaluate its global inventory parts system. Teradyne's system is complex because it stocks over 10,000 parts of a wide variety in price (from a few dollars to $10,000) because its customers are dispersed all over the world, and because customers demand immediate response when a part is needed.

The professors selected two basic inventory models they felt could be used to improve the current inventory system effectively. An important consideration in using basic inventory models is their simplicity, which improved the professors' communication with Teradyne executives. In the field of modeling, it is very important for managers who depend on the models to thoroughly understand the underlying processes and the model's limitations.

Input data to the inventory models included actual planned inventory levels, holding costs, observed demand rates, and estimated lead times. The outputs included service levels and a prediction of the expected number of late part shipments. The first inventory model showed that Teradyne could reduce late shipments by over 90% with just 3% increase in inventory investment. The second model showed that the company could reduce inventory by 37%, while improving customer service levels by 4%.[1]

[1] M. A. Cohen, Y. Zheng, and Y. Wang. "Identifying Opportunities for Improving Teradyne's Service Parts Logistics System," *Interfaces* (July–August 1999): 1–18.

## 12.1   INTRODUCTION

Inventory is one of the most expensive and important assets to many companies, representing as much as 50% of total invested capital. Managers have long recognized that good inventory control is crucial. On one hand, a firm like Teradyne Corporation can try to reduce costs by reducing on-hand inventory levels. On the other hand, customers become dissatisfied when frequent inventory outages, called *stockouts*, occur. Thus, companies must make the balance between low and high inventory levels. As you would expect, cost minimization is the major factor in obtaining this delicate balance.

*Inventory is any stored resource that is used to satisfy a current or future need.*

Inventory is any stored resource that is used to satisfy a current or a future need. Raw materials, work-in-process, and finished goods are examples of inventory. Inventory levels for finished goods are a direct function of demand. When we determine the demand for completed clothes dryers, for example, it is possible to use this information to determine how much sheet metal, paint, electric motors, switches, and other raw materials and work-in-process are needed to produce the finished product.

All organizations have some type of inventory planning and control system. A bank has methods to control its inventory of cash. A hospital has methods to control blood supplies and other important items. State and federal governments, schools, and virtually every manufacturing and production organization are concerned with inventory planning and control. Studying how organizations control their inventory is equivalent to studying how they achieve their objectives by supplying goods and services to their customers. Inventory is the common thread that ties all the functions and departments of the organization together.

Figure 12.1 illustrates the basic components of an inventory planning and control system. The *planning* phase involves primarily what inventory is to be stocked and how it is to be acquired (whether it is to be manufactured or purchased). This information is then used in *forecasting* demand for the inventory and in *controlling* inventory levels. The feedback loop in Figure 12.1 provides a way of revising the plan and forecast based on experiences and observation.

Through inventory planning, an organization determines what goods and/or services are to be produced. In cases of physical products, the organization must also determine whether to produce these goods or to purchase them from another manufacturer. When this has been determined, the next step is to forecast the demand. As discussed in Chapter 11, there are many mathematical techniques that can be used in forecasting demand for a particular product. The emphasis in this chapter is on inventory control, that is, how to maintain adequate inventory levels within an organization.

In this chapter, we discuss several different inventory control models that are commonly used in practice. For each model, we provide examples of how they are analyzed. Although we show the equations needed to compute the relevant parameters for each model, we use Excel worksheets (included in your CD-ROM) to actually calculate these values.

### FIGURE 12.1

**Inventory Planning and Control**

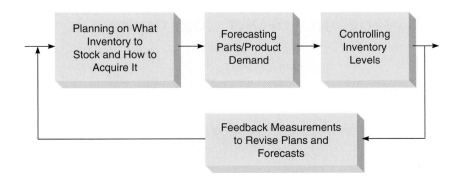

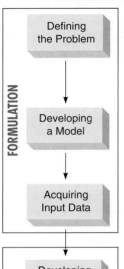

In making products for different markets, manufacturing companies often produce basic products and materials that can be used in a variety of end products. Hewlett-Packard, a leading manufacturer of printers, wanted to explore ways of reducing material and inventory costs for its Deskjet line of printers. One specific problem is that different power supplies are required in different countries.

The inventory model investigates inventory and material requirements as they relate to different markets. An inventory and materials flow diagram was developed that showed how each Deskjet printer was to be manufactured for various countries requiring different power supplies.

The input data consisted of inventory requirements, costs, and product versions. A different Deskjet version is needed for the U.S. market, European markets, and Far East markets. The data included estimated demand in weeks of supply, replenishment lead times, and various cost data.

The solution resulted in tighter inventory control and a change in how the printer was manufactured. The power supply was to be one of the last components installed in each Deskjet during the manufacturing process.

Testing was done by selecting one of the markets and performing a number of tests over a two-month period. The tests included material shortages, downtime profiles, service levels, and various inventory flows.

The results revealed that an inventory cost savings of 18% could be achieved using the inventory model.

As a result of the inventory model, Hewlett-Packard decided to redesign how its Deskjet printers are manufactured to reduce inventory costs in meeting a global market for its printers.

**Source:** H. Lee et al. "Hewlett-Packard Gains Control of Inventory and Service Through Design for Localization," *Interfaces* 23, 4 (July–August 1993): 1–11.

## 12.2 IMPORTANCE OF INVENTORY CONTROL

Inventory control serves several important functions and adds a great deal of flexibility to the operation of the firm. Five main uses of inventory are as follows:

*Five main uses of inventory.*

1. The decoupling function
2. Storing resources
3. Irregular supply and demand
4. Quantity discounts
5. Avoiding stockouts and shortages

## Decoupling Function

*Inventory can act as a buffer.*

One of the major functions of inventory is to decouple manufacturing processes within the organization. If you did not store inventory, there could be many delays and inefficiencies. For example, when one manufacturing activity has to be completed before a second activity can be started, it could stop the entire process. If, however, you have some stored inventory between processes, it could act as a buffer.

## Storing Resources

*Resources can be stored in work-in-process.*

Agricultural and seafood products often have definite seasons over which they can be harvested or caught, but the demand for these products is somewhat constant during the year. In these and similar cases, inventory can be used to store these resources.

In a manufacturing process, raw materials can be stored by themselves, as work-in-process, or as finished products. Thus, if your company makes lawn mowers, you might obtain lawn mower tires from another manufacturer. If you have 400 finished lawn mowers and 300 tires in inventory, you actually have 1,900 tires stored in inventory. Three hundred tires are stored by themselves, and 1,600 (= 4 tires per lawn mower × 400 lawn mowers) tires are stored in the finished lawn mowers. In the same sense, labor can be stored in inventory. If you have 500 subassemblies and it takes 50 hours of labor to produce each assembly, you actually have 25,000 labor hours stored in inventory in the subassemblies. In general, any resource, physical or otherwise, can be stored in inventory.

## Irregular Supply and Demand

*Inventory helps when there is irregular supply or demand.*

When the supply or demand for an inventory item is irregular, storing certain amounts in inventory can be important. If the greatest demand for Diet-Delight beverage is during the summer, you will have to make sure that there is enough supply to meet this irregular demand. This might require that you produce more of the soft drink in the winter than is actually needed to meet the winter demand. The inventory levels of Diet-Delight will gradually build up over the winter, but this inventory will be needed in the summer. The same is true for irregular *supplies*.

## Quantity Discounts

*Purchasing in large quantities may lower unit costs.*

Another use of inventory is to take advantage of quantity discounts. Many suppliers offer discounts for large orders. For example, an electric jigsaw might normally cost $10 per unit. If you order 300 or more saws at one time, your supplier may lower the cost to $8.75. Purchasing in larger quantities can substantially reduce the cost of products. There are, however, some disadvantages of buying in larger quantities. You will have higher storage costs and higher costs due to spoilage, damaged stock, theft, insurance, and so on. Furthermore, by investing in more inventory, you will have less cash to invest elsewhere.

## Avoiding Stockouts and Shortages

*Inventory can help avoid stockouts.*

Another important function of inventory is to avoid shortages or stockouts. If you are repeatedly out of stock, customers are likely to go elsewhere to satisfy their needs. Lost goodwill can be an expensive price to pay for not having the right item at the right time.

**IN ACTION** Implementing Speed and Quality in the Production Run at Milton Bradley

Milton Bradley, a division of Hasbro, Inc., has been manufacturing toys for more than 100 years. Founded by Milton Bradley in 1860, the company started by making a lithograph of Abraham Lincoln. Using his printing skills, Bradley developed games, including the Game of Life, Chutes and Ladders, Candy Land, Scrabble, and Lite Brite. Today, the company produces hundreds of games, requiring billions of plastic parts.

When Milton Bradley has determined the optimal quantities for its production run, it must implement these quantities. Some games require literally hundreds of plastic parts, including spinners, hotels, people, animals, cars, and so on. According to Gary Brennan, director of manufacturing, getting the right number of pieces to the right toys and production lines is the most important issue for the credibility of the company. Some companies, including Wal-Mart, can require 20,000 or more perfectly assembled games delivered to their warehouses in a matter of days.

Not getting the correct number of parts and pieces is very frustrating for customers. It can also be time-consuming, expensive, and frustrating for Milton Bradley to supply the extra parts or get returned toys or games. If shortages are found during the assembly stage, the entire production run can be stopped until the problem is corrected. Counting parts by hand or machine was always problematic and not always accurate. As a result, Milton Bradley decided to weigh the pieces and complete games to determine if the correct number of parts had been included. If the weight is not exactly correct, there is a problem that needs to be resolved before the game or toy is packaged or shipped. Using highly accurate digital scales, Milton Bradley has been able to get the right parts to the right production line at the right time. Without this simple implementation approach, the most sophisticated production run results would be meaningless.

**Source:** D. Smock. "Games Tip the Scale at Milton Bradley," *Plastics World* (March 1997): 22–26.

## 12.3  INVENTORY CONTROL DECISIONS

Even though there are literally millions of different types of products manufactured in our society, there are only two fundamental decisions that you have to make when controlling inventory:

1. How much to order
2. When to order

*The purpose of all inventory models is to minimize inventory costs.*

The purpose of all inventory models is to determine how much to order and when to order. As you know, inventory fulfills many important functions within an organization. But as the inventory levels go up to provide these functions, the cost of storing and holding inventory also increases. Thus, we must reach a fine balance in establishing inventory levels.

**TABLE 12.1**     **Inventory Cost Factors**

| ORDERING COST FACTORS | CARRYING COST FACTORS |
|---|---|
| Developing and sending purchase orders | Cost of capital |
| Processing and inspecting incoming inventory | Taxes |
| Bill paying | Insurance |
| Inventory inquiries | Spoilage |
| Utilities, phone bills, and so on, for the purchasing department | Theft |
| Salaries and wages for purchasing department employees | Obsolescence |
| Supplies such as forms and paper for the purchasing department | Salaries and wages for warehouse employees |
|  | Utilities and building costs for the warehouse |
|  | Supplies such as forms and papers for the warehouse |

A major objective in controlling inventory is to minimize total inventory costs. Some of the most significant inventory costs follow:

*Components of total cost*

1. Cost of the items
2. Cost of ordering
3. Cost of carrying, or holding, inventory
4. Cost of stockouts
5. Cost of safety stock, the additional inventory that may be held to help avoid stockouts

The inventory models discussed in the first part of this chapter assume that demand and the time it takes to receive an order are known and constant, and that no quantity discounts are given. When this is the case, the most significant costs are the cost of placing an order and the cost of holding inventory items over a period of time. Table 12.1 provides a list of important factors making up these costs. Later in this chapter we discuss several more sophisticated inventory models.

## 12.4   ECONOMIC ORDER QUANTITY: DETERMINING HOW MUCH TO ORDER

The *economic order quantity* (EOQ) model is one of the oldest and most commonly known inventory control techniques. Research on its use dates back to a 1915 publication by Ford W. Harris. This model is still used by a large number of organizations today. This technique is relatively easy to use, but it does make a number of assumptions. Some of the more important assumptions follow:

*Assumptions of the EOQ model*

1. Demand is known and constant.
2. The *lead time*, that is, the time between the placement of the order and the receipt of the order, is known and constant.
3. The receipt of inventory is instantaneous. In other words, the inventory from an order arrives in one batch, at one point in time.
4. Quantity discounts are not possible.
5. The only variable costs are the cost of placing an order, *ordering cost*, and the cost of holding or storing inventory over time, *holding* or *carrying cost*.
6. If orders are placed at the right time, stockouts or shortages can be avoided completely.

*The inventory usage curve has a sawtooth shape in the EOQ model.*

With these assumptions, inventory usage has a sawtooth shape, as in Figure 12.2. Here, $Q$ represents the amount that is ordered. If this amount is 500 units, all 500 units arrive at

**FIGURE 12.2**

**Inventory Usage over Time**

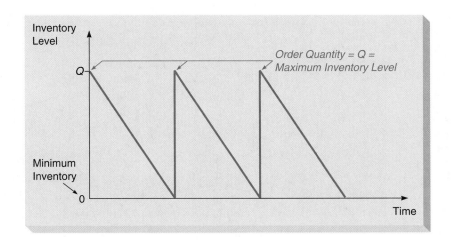

one time when an order is received. Thus, the inventory level jumps from 0 to 500 units. In general, an inventory level increases from 0 to $Q$ units when an order arrives.

Because demand is constant over time, inventory drops at a uniform rate over time. (Refer to the sloped line in Figure 12.2.) Another order is placed such that when the inventory level reaches 0, the new order is received and the inventory level again jumps to $Q$ units, represented by the vertical lines. This process continues indefinitely over time.

## Ordering and Inventory Costs

*The objective of the simple EOQ model is to minimize ordering and carrying costs.*

The objective of most inventory models is to minimize the total costs. With the assumptions just given, the significant costs are the ordering cost and the carrying, or holding, cost. All other costs, such as the cost of the inventory itself, are constant. Thus, if we minimize the sum of the ordering and carrying costs, we are also minimizing the total costs.

To help visualize this, Figure 12.3 graphs total costs as a function of the order quantity, $Q$. As the value of $Q$ increases, the total number of orders placed per year decreases. Hence, the total ordering cost decreases. However, as the value of $Q$ increases, the carrying cost increases due to larger average inventories that the firm has to maintain.

The optimal order size, $Q^*$, is the quantity that minimizes the total costs. Note in Figure 12.3 that $Q^*$ occurs at the point where the ordering cost curve and the carrying cost curve intersect. This is not by chance. With this particular type of cost function, the optimal quantity always occurs at a point where the ordering cost is equal to the carrying cost.

Now that we have a better understanding of inventory costs, let us see how we can determine the value of $Q^*$ that minimizes these costs. In determining the *annual* carrying cost, it is convenient to use the *average* on-hand inventory. Referring back to Figure 12.2, we see that the on-hand inventory ranges from a high of $Q$ units to a low of zero units, with a uniform rate of decrease between these levels. Thus, the average inventory can be calculated as the average of the minimum and maximum inventory levels. That is,

*The average inventory level is one-half the maximum level.*

$$\text{Average inventory level} = (0 + Q)/2 = Q/2 \qquad (12\text{-}1)$$

We multiply this average inventory by a factor called the *annual inventory carrying cost per unit* to determine the annual inventory cost.

## FIGURE 12.3

**Total Cost as a Function of Order Quantity**

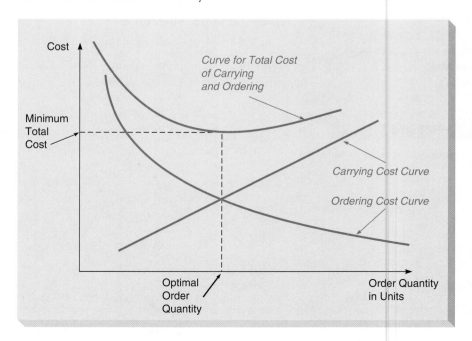

## Finding the Economic Order Quantity

We pointed out that the optimal order quantity, $Q^*$, is the point that minimizes the total cost, where total cost is the sum of ordering cost and carrying cost. We also indicated graphically that the optimal order quantity was at the point where the ordering cost was equal to the carrying cost. Let us first define the following parameters:

- $Q^*$ = Optimal order quantity (i.e., the EOQ)
- $D$  = Annual demand in units for the inventory item
- $C_o$ = Ordering cost *per order*
- $C_h$ = Holding or carrying cost *per unit per year*
- $P$  = *Purchase cost per unit* of the inventory item

The unit carrying cost $C_h$ is usually expressed in one of two ways, as follows:

1. As a fixed cost. For example, $C_h$ is $0.50 per unit per year.
2. As a percentage (typically denoted by $I$) of the item's unit cost or price. For example, $C_h$ is 20% of the item's unit cost. In general,

$$C_h = I \times P \tag{12-2}$$

*I is the annual carrying cost as a percentage of the cost per unit.*

For a given order quantity $Q$, the ordering, holding, and total costs can be computed using the following formulas[2]:

$$\text{Total ordering cost} = (D/Q) \times C_o \tag{12-3}$$

$$\text{Total carrying cost} = (Q/2) \times C_h \tag{12-4}$$

$$\begin{aligned}\text{Total cost} &= \text{Total ordering cost} + \text{Total carrying cost} + \text{Total purchase cost}\\ &= (D/Q) \times C_o \quad\quad + (Q/2) \times C_h \quad\quad + P \times D\end{aligned} \tag{12-5}$$

Observe that the total purchase cost (i.e., $P \times D$) does not depend on the value of $Q$. This is so because regardless of how many orders are placed each year, or how many units we order each time, we will still incur the same annual purchase cost.

*Total cost is a nonlinear function of Q.*

The presence of $Q$ in the denominator of the first term makes Equation 12-5 a *nonlinear* equation with respect to $Q$. Nevertheless, since the total ordering cost is equal to the total carrying cost at the optimal value of $Q$, we can use Equations 12-3 and 12-4 to calculate the EOQ as

*We determine Q\* by setting ordering cost equal to carrying cost.*

$$Q^* = \sqrt{(2DC_o/C_h)} \tag{12-6}$$

## Sumco Pump Company Example

We now apply these formulas to the case of Sumco, a company that distributes pump housings which it buys from a manufacturer. Sumco would like to reduce its inventory cost by determining the optimal number of pump housings to obtain per order. The annual demand is 1,000 units, the ordering cost is $10 per order, and the carrying cost per unit per year is $0.50. Each pump housing has a purchase cost of $5. How many pump housings should Sumco order? To answer these and other questions, we use the ExcelModules program, which is discussed next.

---

[2] See a recent Operations Management textbook such as J. Heizer and B. Render. *Operations Management*, 6/e. Upper Saddle River, NJ: Prentice Hall, 2001, for more details of these formulas (and other formulas in this chapter).

## Using ExcelModules for Inventory Model Computations

### Excel Notes

- ■ The CD-ROM that accompanies this textbook contains a set of Excel worksheets, bundled together in a software package called ExcelModules. The procedure for installing and running this program, as well as a brief description of its contents, is given in Appendix A.
- ■ The CD-ROM also contains the Excel file for each example problem discussed here. The relevant file name is shown in the margin next to each example.
- ■ For clarity, all worksheets for inventory models in ExcelModules are color coded as follows:
  - ■ *input cells*, where we enter the problem data, are shaded yellow.
  - ■ *output cells* showing results are shaded green.
- ■ Although these colors are not apparent in the screen captures shown in the textbook, they are seen in the Excel files in your CD-ROM.

*We use Excel worksheets to do all inventory model computations.*

When we run the ExcelModules program, we see a menu option titled ExcelModules in the main menu bar of Excel. We click on ExcelModules and then click on Inventory Models. The choices shown in Program 12.1A are displayed. From these choices, we select the appropriate model.

When we select any of the inventory models in ExcelModules, we are first presented with a window that allows us to specify several options. Some of these options are common for all models, whereas others are specific to the inventory model selected. For example, Program 12.1B shows the options window seen when we select the *EOQ* inventory model. The options here include the following:

1. Title of the problem. Default value is *Problem Title.*
2. Graph. Checking this box results in graphs of inventory costs versus order quantity.
3. Holding Cost. Fixed amount or percent of unit cost.
4. Reorder Point. Checking this box results in the calculation of the reorder point, for a given lead time between placement of the order and receipt of the order. We discuss the reorder point in Section 12.5. This option is available only for the *EOQ* model.

---

**PROGRAM 12.1A**    **Inventory Models Submenu in ExcelModules**

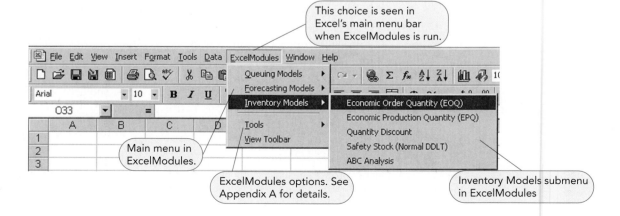

**PROGRAM 12.1B**

**Samples Options Window for Inventory Models in ExcelModules**

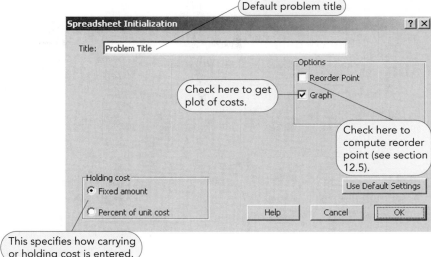

**Using ExcelModules for the EOQ Model**  We first show, in Program 12.2A, the options we select for the Sumco Pump Company example.

When we click OK on this screen, we get the worksheet shown in Program 12.2B. We now enter the values for the annual demand $D$, ordering cost $C_o$, carrying cost $C_h$, and unit purchase cost $P$, in cells B6 to B9, respectively.

**File: 12-2.xls**

---

### Excel Notes

- The worksheets in ExcelModules contain formulas to compute the results for different inventory models. The default value of zero for the input data cause the results of these formulas to initially appear as #N/A, #VALUE!, or #DIV/0!. However, as soon as we enter valid values for these input data, the worksheets will display the formula results.

- Once ExcelModules has been used to create the Excel worksheet for a particular inventory model (e.g., EOQ), the resulting worksheet can be used to compute the results with several different input data. For example, we can enter different input data in cells B6:B9 of Program 12.2B and compute the results without having to create a new EOQ worksheet each time.

---

**PROGRAM 12.2A**

**Options Window for EOQ Model in ExcelModules**

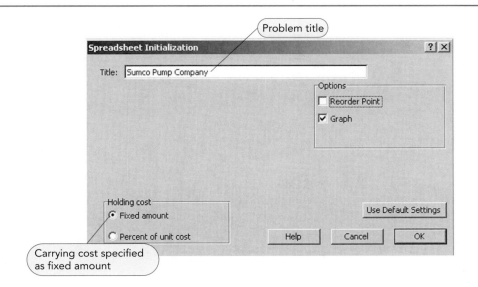

**PROGRAM 12.2B**   EOQ Model for Sumco Pump Company

| | A | B | C | D | E |
|---|---|---|---|---|---|
| 1 | **Sumco Pump Company** | | | | |
| 2 | Inventory | EOQ Model | | | |
| 3 | Enter the input data in the cells shaded YELLOW. | | | | |
| 4 | | | | | |
| 5 | **Input Data** | | | | |
| 6 | Demand rate, D | 1000 | | Input data | |
| 7 | Ordering cost, $C_o$ | $10.00 | | | |
| 8 | Carrying cost, $C_h$ | $0.50 | (fixed amount) | | |
| 9 | Unit purchase cost, P | $5.00 | | | |
| 10 | | | | | |
| 11 | **Results** | | | EOQ is 200 units. | |
| 12 | Economic order quantity, Q* | 200.00 | | | |
| 13 | Maximum inventory | 200.00 | | | |
| 14 | Average inventory | 100.00 | | Average inventory = ½ Maximum inventory | |
| 15 | Number of orders | 5.00 | | | |
| 16 | | | | | |
| 17 | Total holding cost | $50.00 | | Holding cost = ordering cost | |
| 18 | Total ordering cost | $50.00 | | | |
| 19 | Total purchase cost | $5,000.00 | | | |
| 20 | Total cost | $5,100.00 | | | |
| 21 | | | | | |
| 22 | | | | | |
| 23 | | | | | |
| 24 | | | | | |
| 25 | | | | | |
| 26 | **Cost Table for Graph** | Start at | 50.000 | Increment by | 16.667 |
| 27 | | | | | |
| 28 | | Q | Order cost | Holding cost | Total cost |
| 29 | | 50.00 | 200.00 | 12.50 | 212.50 |
| 30 | | 66.67 | 150.00 | 16.67 | 166.67 |
| 31 | | 83.33 | 120.00 | 20.83 | 140.83 |

Data for graph, generated and used by ExcelModules

The worksheet calculates the EOQ (shown in cell B12 of Program 12.2B). In addition, the following output measures are calculated and reported:

- Maximum inventory ($= Q^*$), in cell B13
- Average inventory ($= Q^*/2$) in cell B14
- Number of orders ($= D/Q^*$) in cell B15
- Total holding cost ($= C_h \times Q^*/2$) in cell B17
- Total ordering cost ($= C_o \times D/Q^*$) in cell B18
- Total purchase cost ($= P \times D$) in cell B19
- Total cost ($= C_h \times Q^*/2 + C_o \times D/Q^* + P \times D$) in cell B20

As you might expect, the total ordering cost of $50 is equal to the total carrying cost. (Refer to Figure 12.3 on page 524 again to see why.) You may wish to try different values for the order quantity Q, such as 100 or 300 pump housings. (Plug these values in one at a time in cell B12.) You will find that the total cost (in cell B20) has the lowest value when Q is 200 units. That is, the EOQ, $Q^*$, for Sumco is 200 pump housings. The total cost, including the purchase cost of $5,000, is $5,100.

If requested, a plot of the total ordering cost, total holding cost, and total cost, for different values of Q is drawn by ExcelModules. The graph, shown in Program 12.2C, is drawn on a separate worksheet.

**Plot of Costs Versus Order Quantity for Sumco Pump Company**

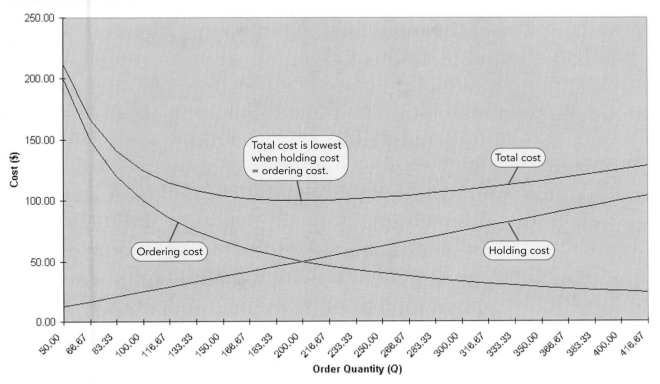

## Purchase Cost of Inventory Items

*We can calculate the average inventory value in $ terms.*

It is often useful to know the value of the average inventory level in dollar terms. We know from Equation 12-1 that the average inventory level is $Q/2$, where $Q$ is the order quantity. If we order $Q^*$ (the EOQ) units each time, the value of the average inventory can be computed by multiplying the average inventory by the unit purchase cost $P$. That is,

$$\text{Average dollar value of inventory} = P \times (Q^*/2) \qquad (12\text{-}7)$$

## Calculating the Ordering and Carrying Costs for a Given Value of Q

Recall that the EOQ formula is given by Equation 12-6 as

$$Q^* = \sqrt{(2DC_o/C_h)}$$

In using this formula, we assumed that the values of the ordering cost $C_o$ and carrying cost $C_h$ are *known* constants. In some situations, however, these costs may be difficult to estimate precisely. For example, if the firm orders several items simultaneously from a supplier, it may be difficult to identify the ordering cost separately for each item. In such cases, we can use the EOQ formula to compute the value of $C_o$ or $C_h$ that would make a given order quantity the optimal order quantity.

*For given Q, we compute $C_o$*
*or $C_h$ that makes Q optimal.*

To compute these $C_o$ or $C_h$ values, we can manipulate the EOQ formula algebraically and rewrite it as follows:

$$C_o = Q^2 \times C_h / (2D) \tag{12-8}$$

and

$$C_h = 2DC_o / Q^2 \tag{12-9}$$

where $Q$ is the given order quantity. We illustrate the use of these formulas in Solved Problem 12-1 at the end of this chapter.

## Sensitivity of the EOQ Formula

*If any of the input data values*
*change, EOQ also changes.*

The EOQ formula in Equation 12-6 assumes that all input data are known with certainty. What would happen if one of the input values is incorrect? If any of the values used in the formula changes, the optimal value of $Q^*$ would also change. Determining the magnitude and effect of these changes on $Q^*$ is called *sensitivity analysis*. This type of analysis is important in practice since the input values for the EOQ model are usually *estimated* and hence subject to error or change.

Let us use the Sumco example again to illustrate this issue. Suppose the ordering cost $C_o$ is actually $15, instead of $10. Assume the annual demand for pump housings is still the same, namely, $D = 1,000$ units and that the carrying cost $C_h$ is $0.50 per unit per year.

*Due to the nonlinear formula*
*for EOQ, changes in $Q^*$ are*
*less severe than change in*
*input data value.*

If we use these new values in the EOQ worksheet (as in Program 12.2B), the revised EOQ turns out to be 245 units. (See if you can verify this for yourself.) That is, when the ordering cost increases by 50% (from $10 to $15), the optimal order quantity increases only by 22.5% (from 200 to 245). This is because the EOQ formula involves a square root and is, therefore, *nonlinear*.

We observe a similar occurrence when the carrying cost $C_h$ changes. Suppose Sumco's annual carrying cost is $0.80 per unit, instead of $0.50. Assume the annual demand is still 1,000 units, and the ordering cost is $10 per order. Using the EOQ worksheet in ExcelModules, we can calculate the revised EOQ as 158 units. That is, when the carrying

---

  **IN ACTION**    Inland Steel Uses Systems Contracts to Control Inventory Costs

Sound inventory control involves much more than computing the economic order quantity. In most cases, other practical and financial considerations must be taken into account to minimize total inventory costs and to provide tighter control on inventory levels. Both practical and financial considerations led Inland Steel to consider several inventory policies, including systems contracts.

Inland Steel produces approximately 5.5 million tons of steel each year. The steel mill has two blast furnaces that supply steel to four casting operations. Yet, steel inventory is not the company's only inventory concern. For many large corporations, office equipment such as scanners, printers, and fax machines can represent a substantial investment. Furthermore, all steel-processing facilities are controlled through computers, which are considered office equipment by Inland Steel.

Tricia Wynn, a project buyer for Inland Steel, was concerned about high costs and a lack of standardization for office equipment. To overcome these problems, she developed a comprehensive inventory ordering system that took advantage of standardization and contract buying. The result was a contract ordering system that provided superior equipment at substantial savings. Most of the equipment was leased or rented. The new system provided low monthly rates for office equipment, free installation, and a 30-day free trial. Another advantage was a floating systems contract. With this type of contract, there is no termination date, which helps reduce the time and costs of maintaining leasing agreements. The bottom line is that a systems contract approach allowed Inland Steel to order good-quality office equipment for fewer dollars.

**Source:** K. Evans-Correia. "All Systems Go," *Purchasing* (March 23, 1989): 106–107.

cost increases by 60% (from $0.50 to $0.80), the EOQ decreases by only 21%. Note that the order quantity decreases here since a higher carrying cost makes holding inventory more expensive.

## REORDER POINT: DETERMINING WHEN TO ORDER

Now that we have decided how much to order, we look at the second inventory question: when to order. In most simple inventory models, it is assumed that receipt of an order is instantaneous. That is, we assume that a firm waits until its inventory level for a particular item reaches zero, places an order, and receives the items in stock immediately.

In many cases, however, the time between the placing and receipt of an order, called the *lead time* or delivery time, is often a few days or even a few weeks. Thus, the when to order decision is usually expressed in terms of a *reorder point* (ROP), the inventory level at which an order should be placed. The ROP is given as

*The ROP determines when to order inventory. It is found by multiplying the daily demand times the lead time in days.*

$$\text{ROP} = (\text{demand per day}) \times (\text{lead time in days})$$

$$= d \times L \tag{12-10}$$

Figure 12.4 shows the reorder point graphically. The slope of the graph is the daily inventory usage. This is expressed in units demanded per day, $d$. The *lead time*, $L$, is the time that it takes to receive an order. Thus, if an order is placed when the inventory level reaches the ROP, the new inventory arrives at the same instant the inventory is reaching zero. Let's look at an example.

### Sumco Pump Company Example Revisited

Recall that we calculated an EOQ value of 200 and total cost of $5,100 for Sumco (see Program 12.2B on page 528). These calculations were based on an annual demand of 1,000 units, ordering cost of $10 per order, annual carrying cost of $0.50 per unit, and a purchase cost of $5 per pump housing.

**FIGURE 12.4**

**Reorder Point (ROP) Curve**

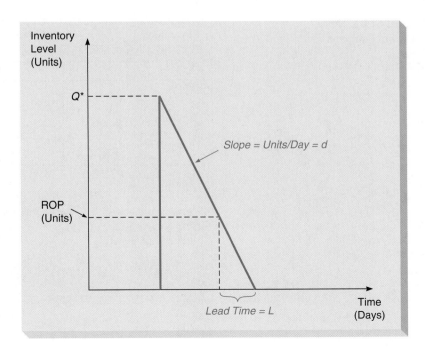

Now assume that there is a lead time of 3 business days between the time Sumco places an order and the time the order is received. Further, assume there are 250 business days in a year.

*To compute the ROP, we need to know the demand rate per period.*

To calculate the reorder point (ROP), we must first determine the daily demand rate, $d$. In Sumco's case, since there are 250 business days in a year, and the annual demand is 1,000, the daily demand rate is 4 (= 1,000/250) pump housings.

**File: 12-3.xls**

**Using ExcelModules to Compute the ROP**  We can include the ROP computation in the EOQ worksheet provided in ExcelModules. To do so for Sumco's problem, we once again choose the EOQ option from the Inventory Models submenu in ExcelModules (see (Program 12.1A). The only change in the options window (see Program 12.2A) is that we now check the box labeled Reorder Point. The worksheet shown in Program 12.3 is now displayed. We enter the input data as before (see Program 12.2B). Note the additional input entries for the daily demand rate in cell B10, and the lead time in cell B11. In addition to all the computations shown in Program 12.2B, the worksheet now calculates and reports the ROP of 12 units (shown in cell B24).

Hence, when the inventory stock of pump housing drops to 12, an order should be placed. The order will arrive three days later, just as the firm's stock is depleted to zero. It should be mentioned that this calculation assumes that all of the assumptions listed earlier for EOQ are valid. When demand is not known with complete certainty, these calculations must be modified. This is discussed later in this chapter.

## 12.6  ECONOMIC ORDER QUANTITY WITH NONINSTANTANEOUS RECEIPT

In the EOQ model, we assumed that the receipt of inventory is instantaneous. In other words, the entire order arrives in one batch, at a single point in time. In many cases, however, a firm may build up its inventory gradually over a period of time. For example, a firm

**PROGRAM 12.3**

**EOQ Model with ROP for Sumco Pump Company**

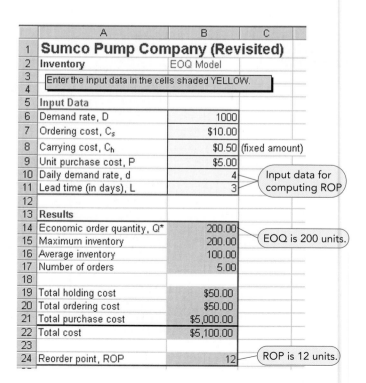

| | A | B | C |
|---|---|---|---|
| 1 | **Sumco Pump Company (Revisited)** | | |
| 2 | Inventory | EOQ Model | |
| 3 | Enter the input data in the cells shaded YELLOW. | | |
| 4 | | | |
| 5 | Input Data | | |
| 6 | Demand rate, D | 1000 | |
| 7 | Ordering cost, $C_s$ | $10.00 | |
| 8 | Carrying cost, $C_h$ | $0.50 | (fixed amount) |
| 9 | Unit purchase cost, P | $5.00 | |
| 10 | Daily demand rate, d | 4 | Input data for computing ROP |
| 11 | Lead time (in days), L | 3 | |
| 12 | | | |
| 13 | Results | | |
| 14 | Economic order quantity, Q* | 200.00 | EOQ is 200 units. |
| 15 | Maximum inventory | 200.00 | |
| 16 | Average inventory | 100.00 | |
| 17 | Number of orders | 5.00 | |
| 18 | | | |
| 19 | Total holding cost | $50.00 | |
| 20 | Total ordering cost | $50.00 | |
| 21 | Total purchase cost | $5,000.00 | |
| 22 | Total cost | $5,100.00 | |
| 23 | | | |
| 24 | Reorder point, ROP | 12 | ROP is 12 units. |

*The EPQ model eliminates the instantaneous receipt assumption.*

may receive shipments from its supplier uniformly over a period of time. Or, a firm may be producing at a rate of $p$ per day *and* simultaneously selling at a rate of $d$ per day (where $p > d$). Figure 12.5 shows inventory levels as a function of time in these situations. Clearly, the EOQ model is no longer applicable here, and we need a new model to calculate the optimal order (or production) quantity. Because this model is especially suited to the production environment, it is also commonly known as the *production lot size* model or the *economic production quantity* (EPQ) model. We refer to this model as the EPQ model in the remainder of this chapter.

In the production process, instead of having an ordering cost, there will be a *setup cost*. This is the cost of setting up the production facility to manufacture the desired product. It normally includes the salaries and wages of employees who are responsible for setting up the equipment, engineering and design costs of making the setup, paperwork, supplies, utilities, and so on. The carrying cost per unit is composed of the same factors as the traditional EOQ model, although the annual carrying cost equation changes.

In determining the annual carrying cost for the EPQ model, it is again convenient to use the *average* on-hand inventory. Referring back to Figure 12.5, we can show that the maximum on-hand inventory is $Q \times (1 - d/p)$ units, where $d$ is the daily demand rate and $p$ is the daily production rate. The minimum on-hand inventory is again zero units, and the inventory decreases at a uniform rate between the maximum and minimum levels. Thus, the average inventory can be calculated as the average of the minimum and maximum inventory levels. That is,

*Formula for average inventory in the EPQ model.*

$$\text{Average inventory level} = [0 + Q \times (1 - d/p)]/2 = Q \times (1 - d/p)/2 \qquad \text{(12-11)}$$

Analogous to the EOQ model, it turns out that the optimal order quantity in the EPQ model also occurs when the total setup cost equals the total carrying cost. You should note, however, that making the total setup cost equal to the total carrying cost does not always guarantee optimal solutions for models more complex than the EPQ model.

### Finding the Economic Production Quantity

Let us first define the following additional parameters:

- $Q^* = $ Optimal order or production quantity (i.e., the EPQ)
- $C_s = $ Setup cost per setup

FIGURE 12.5

**Inventory Control and the Production Process**

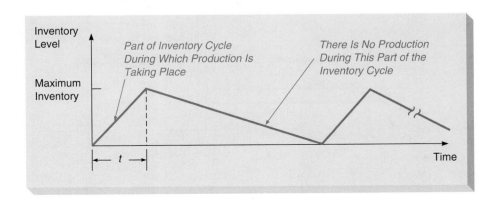

For a given order quantity $Q$, the setup, holding, and total costs can now be computed using the following formulas:

$$\text{Total setup cost} = (D/Q) \times C_s \tag{12-12}$$

$$\text{Total carrying cost} = [Q(1 - d/p)/2] \times C_h \tag{12-13}$$

$$\begin{aligned}
\text{Total cost} &= \text{Total setup cost} + \text{Total carrying cost} + \text{Total production cost} \\
&= (D/Q) \times C_s \quad + [Q(1 - d/p)/2] \times C_h + P \times D
\end{aligned} \tag{12-14}$$

*Here is the formula for the optimal production quantity. Notice the similarity to the basic EOQ model.*

As in the EOQ model, the total production (or purchase, if the item is purchased) cost does not depend on the value of $Q$. Further, the presence of $Q$ in the denominator of the first term makes the total cost function nonlinear. Nevertheless, since the total setup cost should equal the total ordering cost at the optimal value of $Q$, we can use Equations 12-12 and 12-13 to calculate the EPQ as

$$Q^\star = \sqrt{2DC_s/[C_h(1 - d/p)]} \tag{12-15}$$

## Brown Manufacturing Example

Brown Manufacturing produces mini-sized refrigeration packs in batches. The firm's estimated demand for the year is 10,000 units. Since Brown operates for 167 business days each year, this annual demand translates to a daily demand rate of about 60 units per day. It costs

**PROGRAM 12.4A**  **EPQ Model for Brown Manufacturing**

|  | A | B | C | D | E |
|---|---|---|---|---|---|
| 1 | **Brown Manufacturing** | | | | |
| 2 | Inventory | Economic Production Quantity Model | | | |
| 3 | Enter the data in the cells shaded YELLOW. You may have to do some | | | | |
| 4 | work to compute the daily production and demand rates. | | | | |
| 5 | | | | | |
| 6 | **Input Data** | | | | |
| 7 | Demand rate, D | 10000 | | | |
| 8 | Setup cost, $C_s$ | $100.00 | | | |
| 9 | Carrying cost, $C_h$ | $0.50 | (fixed amount) | | |
| 10 | Daily production rate, p | 80 | | | |
| 11 | Daily demand rate, d | 60 | | | |
| 12 | Unit purchase cost, P | $5.00 | Carrying cost is specified as a fixed amount. | | |
| 13 | | | | | |
| 14 | **Results** | | | | |
| 15 | Economic production quantity, $Q^\star$ | 4000.00 | EPQ is 4,000 units. | | |
| 16 | Maximum inventory | 1000.00 | | | |
| 17 | Average inventory | 500.00 | | | |
| 18 | Number of setups | 2.50 | | | |
| 19 | | | | | |
| 20 | Total holding cost | $250.00 | Holding cost = setup cost | | |
| 21 | Total setup cost | $250.00 | | | |
| 22 | Total production cost | $50,000.00 | | | |
| 23 | Total cost, TC | $50,500.00 | | | |
| 24 | | | | | |
| 25 | | | | | |
| 26 | **Cost Table for Graph** | Start at | 1000.00 | Increment by | 333.33 |
| 27 | | | | | |
| 28 | | Q | Setup cost | Holding cost | Total cost |
| 29 | | 1000.00 | 1000.00 | 62.50 | 1062.50 |
| 30 | | 1333.33 | 750.00 | 83.33 | 833.33 |
| 31 | | 1666.67 | 600.00 | 104.17 | 704.17 |

Data for graph, generated and used by ExcelModules

about $100 to set up the manufacturing process, and the carrying cost is about $0.50 per unit per year. When the production process has been set up, 80 refrigeration packs can be manufactured daily. Each pack costs $5 to produce. How many packs should Brown produce in each batch? As discussed next, we determine this value, as well as values for the associated costs, using the ExcelModules program.

**File: 12-4.xls**

**Using *ExcelModules* for the EPQ Model**  We select the Economic Production Quantity (EPQ) option from the Inventory Models submenu in ExcelModules. (Refer back to Program 12.1A.) The options for this procedure are similar to that for the EOQ model (see Program 12.2A). The only change is that the ROP option is no longer available here. After we enter the title and other options for this problem, we get the worksheet shown in Program 12.4A. We now enter the values for the annual demand $D$, setup cost $C_s$, carrying cost $C_h$, daily production rate $p$, daily demand rate $d$, and unit production (or purchase) cost $P$, in cells B7 to B12, respectively.

The worksheet calculates and reports the EPQ (shown in cell B15), as well as the following output measures:

- Maximum inventory $(= Q^*[1 - d/p])$, in cell B16
- Average inventory $(= Q^*[1 - d/p]/2)$ in cell B17
- Number of setups $(= D/Q^*)$ in cell B18
- Total holding cost $(= C_h \times Q^*[1 - d/p]/2)$ in cell B20
- Total setup cost $(= C_s \times D/Q^*)$ in cell B21
- Total purchase cost $(= P \times D)$ in cell B22
- Total cost $(= C_h \times Q^*[1 - d/p]/2 + C_s \times D/Q^* + P \times D)$ in cell B23

**PROGRAM 12.4B**    **Plot of Costs Versus Order Quantity for Brown Manufacturing**

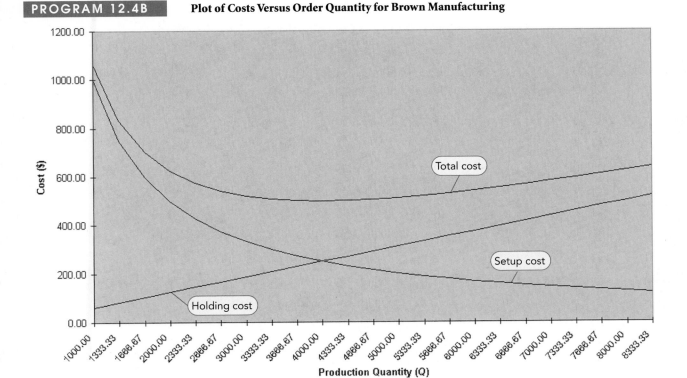

Here again, as you might expect, the total setup cost is equal to the total carrying cost ($250 each). You may wish to try different values for Q, such as 3,000 or 5,000 pumps. (Plug these values one at a time in cell B15.) You will find that the minimum total cost occurs when Q is 4,000 units. That is, the EPQ, Q*, for Brown is 4,000 units. The total cost, including the production cost of $50,000, is $50,500.

If requested, a plot of the total setup cost, holding cost, and total cost, for different values of Q is drawn by ExcelModules. The graph, shown in Program 12.4B, is drawn on a separate worksheet.

### Length of the Production Cycle

*Production cycle is the length of each manufacturing run.*

Referring back to Figure 12.5 on page 533, we see that the inventory buildup occurs over a period $t$ during which Brown is both producing as well as selling refrigeration packs. We refer to this period $t$ as the *production cycle*. In Brown's case, if $Q^*$ = 4,000 units and we know that 80 units can be produced daily, the length of each production cycle will be $Q^*/p$ = 4,000/80 = 50 days. Thus, when Brown decides to produce refrigeration packs, the equipment will be set up to manufacture the units for a 50-day time span.

## 12.7  QUANTITY DISCOUNT MODELS

*A discount is a reduced price for the item when it is purchased in large quantities.*

To increase sales, many companies offer quantity discounts to their customers. A *quantity discount* is simply a reduced cost for the item when it is purchased in larger quantities. It is not uncommon to have a discount schedule with several discounts for large orders. A typical quantity discount schedule is shown in Table 12.2.

As can be seen in Table 12.2, the normal cost for the item is $5. When 1,000 to 1,999 units are ordered at one time, the cost per unit drops to $4.80, and when the quantity ordered at one time is 2,000 units or more, the cost is $4.75 per unit. As always, management must decide when and how much to order. But with quantity discounts, how does the manager make these decisions?

As with other inventory models discussed so far, the overall objective is to minimize the total cost. Because the unit cost for the third discount in Table 12.2 is lowest, you might be tempted to order 2,000 units or more to take advantage of this discount. Placing an order for that many units, however, might not minimize the total inventory cost. As the discount quantity goes up, the item cost goes down, but the carrying cost increases because the order sizes are large. Thus, the major trade-off when considering quantity discounts is between the reduced item cost and the increased carrying cost.

Recall that we computed the total cost (including the total purchase cost) for the EOQ model as follows (see Equation 12-5):

$$\text{Total cost} = \text{Total ordering cost} + \text{Total carrying cost} + \text{Total purchase cost}$$
$$= (D/Q) \times C_o + (Q/2) \times C_h + P \times D$$

| TABLE 12.2 | DISCOUNT NUMBER | DISCOUNT QUANTITY | DISCOUNT (%) | DISCOUNT COST ($) |
|---|---|---|---|---|
| **Quantity Discount Schedule** | 1 | 0 to 999 | 0 | 5.00 |
| | 2 | 1,000 to 1,999 | 4 | 4.80 |
| | 3 | 2,000 and over | 5 | 4.75 |

In what follows, we illustrate the four-step process to determine the quantity that minimizes the total cost. We will, however, use a worksheet included in ExcelModules to actually compute the optimal order quantity, and associated costs, in our example.

### Four Steps to Analyze Quantity Discount Models

*Calculate Q\* values for each discount.*

1. For each discount price, calculate a $Q^*$ value using the EOQ formula (Equation 12-6). In quantity discount EOQ models, the unit carrying cost $C_h$ is typically expressed as a percentage ($I$) of the unit purchase cost ($P$). That is, $C_h = I \times P$, as discussed in Equation 12-2. As a result, the value of $Q^*$ will be different for each discounted price.

*Next, we adjust the Q\* values.*

2. For any discount level, if the $Q^*$ computed in step 1 is too low to qualify for the discount, adjust $Q^*$ upward to the *lowest* quantity that qualifies for the discount. For example, if $Q^*$ for discount 2 in Table 12.2 turns out to be 500 units, adjust this value up to 1,000 units. The reason for this step is illustrated in Figure 12.6.

*The total cost curve is broken into parts.*

   As seen in Figure 12.6, the total cost curve for the discounts shown in Table 12.2 is broken into three different curves. There are separate cost curves for the first ($0 \le Q \le 999$), second ($1,000 \le Q \le 1,999$), and third ($Q \ge 2,000$) discounts. Look at the total cost curve for discount 2. The $Q^*$ for discount 2 is less than the allowable discount range of 1,000 to 1,999 units. However, the total cost at 1,000 units (which is the minimum quantity needed to get this discount) is still less than the lowest total cost for discount 1. Thus, step 2 is needed to ensure that we do not discard any discount level that may indeed produce the minimum total cost. Note that an order quantity computed in step 1 that is *greater* than the range that would qualify it for a discount may be discarded.

*Next, we compute total cost.*

3. Using the total cost equation (Equation 12-5), compute a total cost for every $Q^*$ determined in steps 1 and 2. If a $Q^*$ had to be adjusted upward because it was below the allowable quantity range, be sure to use the adjusted $Q^*$ value.

*We select Q\* with lowest total cost.*

4. Select that $Q^*$ that has the lowest total cost as computed in step 3. It will be the order quantity that minimizes the total cost.

### FIGURE 12.6

**Total Cost Curve for the Quantity Discount Model**

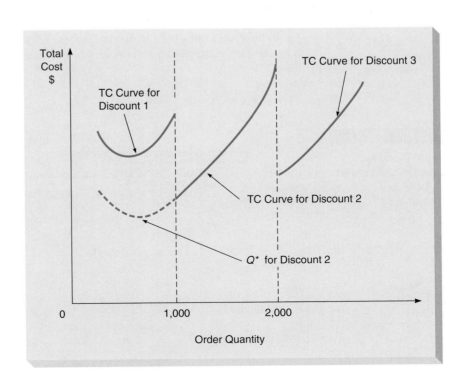

# Brass Department Store Example

*Example of the quantity discount model*

Brass Department Store stocks toy cars. Recently, the store was given a quantity discount schedule for the cars, as shown in Table 12.2 on page 536. Thus, the normal cost for the cars is $5. For orders between 1,000 and 1,999 units, the unit cost is $4.80, and for orders of 2,000 or more units, the unit cost is $4.75. Furthermore, the ordering cost is $49 per order, the annual demand is 5,000 race cars, and the inventory carrying charge as a percentage of cost, $I$, is 20% or 0.2. What order quantity will minimize the total cost? We use the ExcelModules program to answer this question.

**File: 12-5.xls**

**Using *ExcelModules* for the Quantity Discount Model**  We select the Quantity Discount option from the Inventory Models submenu in ExcelModules (see Program 12.1A). The window shown in Program 12.5A is displayed. The option entries in this window are similar to that for the EOQ model (see Program 12.2A). The only additional choice is the box labeled Number of price ranges. The specific entries for Brass Department Store's problem are shown in Program 12.5A.

When we click OK on this screen, we get the worksheet shown in Program 12.5B. We now enter the values for the annual demand $D$, ordering cost $C_o$, and holding cost percentage $I$ in cells B7 to B9, respectively. Note that $I$ is entered as a percentage value (e.g., enter 20 for the Brass Store example). Then, for each of the three discount ranges, we enter the minimum quantity needed to get the discount, and the discounted unit price $P$. These entries are shown in cells B12:D13 of Program 12.5B.

The worksheet works through the four-step process and reports the following output measures for each discount range:

- EOQ value (shown in cells B17:D17), computed using Equation 12-6
- Adjusted EOQ value (shown in cells B18:D18), as discussed in Step 2 of the four-step process
- Total holding cost, total ordering cost, total purchase cost, and overall total cost, shown in cells B20:D23

In the Brass Store example, observe that the $Q^*$ values for discounts 2 and 3 are too low to be eligible for the discounted prices. They are, therefore, adjusted upward to 1,000 and

---

**PROGRAM 12.5A**

**Options Window for Quantity Discount Model in ExcelModules**

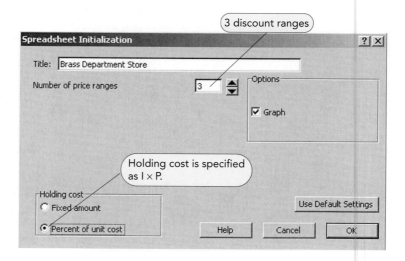

**PROGRAM 12.5B**    **Quantity Discount Model for Brass Department Store**

|     | A | B | C | D | E | F | G |
|-----|---|---|---|---|---|---|---|
| 1 | **Brass Department Store** | | | | | | |
| 2 | Inventory | Quantity Discount Model | | | | | |
| 3 | Enter the data in the cells shaded YELLOW.  The minimum quantity is the minimum amount | | | | | | |
| 4 | that needs to be ordered in order to get the price for that range. | | | | | | |
| 5 | | | | | | | |
| 6 | **Input Data** | | | | | | |
| 7 | Demand rate, D | 5000 | | | 20% is entered as 20 here. | | |
| 8 | Ordering cost, C₀ | 49 | | | | | |
| 9 | Carrying cost %, I | 20.00% | (percentage) | | | | |
| 10 | | | | | | | |
| 11 | | **Range 1** | **Range 2** | **Range 3** | | | |
| 12 | Minimum quantity | 0 | 1000 | 2000 | | | |
| 13 | Unit purchase cost, P | $5.00 | $4.80 | $4.75 | | | |
| 14 | | | | | | | |
| 15 | **Results** | | | | | | |
| 16 | | **Range 1** | **Range 2** | **Range 3** | Q* for each price range | | |
| 17 | Economic order quantity, Q* | 700.00 | 714.43 | 718.18 | | | |
| 18 | Adjusted order quantity | 700.00 | 1000.00 | 2000.00 | Adjusted Q* value | | |
| 19 | | | | | | | |
| 20 | Total holding cost | 350.00 | 480.00 | 950.00 | | | |
| 21 | Total ordering cost | 350.00 | 245.00 | 122.50 | | | |
| 22 | Total purchase cost | 25,000.00 | 24,000.00 | 23,750.00 | | | |
| 23 | Total cost | 25,700.00 | 24,725.00 | 24,822.50 | | | |
| 24 | | | | Lowest cost option | | | |
| 25 | | | | | | | |
| 26 | **Cost Table for Graph** | Start at | 525.00 | Increment by | 86.00 | | |
| 27 | | Q | Unit cost | Setup cost | Holding cost | Total unit cost | Total Cost |
| 28 | Data for graph, generated and used by ExcelModules | 1 | 525.00 | 5.00 | 466.67 | 262.50 | 25000.00 | 25729.17 |
| 29 | | 2 | 611.00 | 5.00 | 400.98 | 305.50 | 25000.00 | 25706.48 |
| 30 | | 3 | 697.00 | 5.00 | 351.51 | 348.50 | 25000.00 | 25700.01 |
| 31 | | 4 | 783.00 | 5.00 | 312.90 | 391.50 | 25000.00 | 25704.40 |

**PROGRAM 12.5C**    **Plot of Total Cost Versus Order Quantity for Brass Department Store**

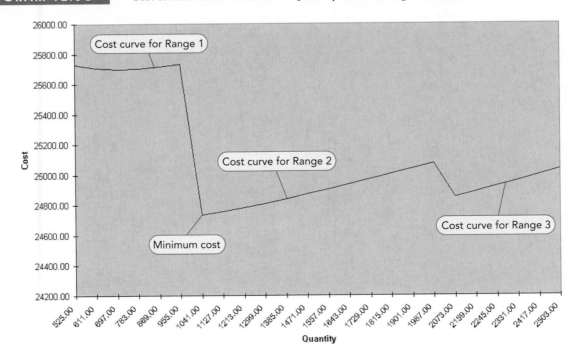

2,000, respectively. With these adjusted $Q^*$ values, we find that the lowest total cost of $24,725 results when we use an order quantity of 1,000 units.

If requested, ExcelModules will also draw a plot of the total cost for different values of $Q$. The graph, shown in Program 12.5C, is drawn on a separate worksheet.

## 12.8   USE OF SAFETY STOCK

*Safety stock* is additional stock that is kept on hand.[3] If, for example, the safety stock for an item is 50 units, you are carrying an average of 50 units more of inventory during the year. When demand is unusually high, you dip into the safety stock instead of encountering a *stockout*. Thus, the main purpose of safety stock is to avoid stockouts when the demand is higher than expected. Its use is shown in Figure 12.7. Note that although stockouts can often be avoided by using safety stock, there is still a chance that they may occur. The demand may be so high that all the safety stock is used up, and thus there is still a stockout.

*Safety stock helps in avoiding stockouts. It is extra stock kept on hand.*

One of the best ways of maintaining a safety stock level is to use the ROP. This can be accomplished by adding the number of units of safety stock as a buffer to the reorder point. Recall that

$$\text{Reorder point (ROP)} = d \times L$$

*Safety stock is included in the ROP.*

where $d$ is the daily demand rate, and $L$ is the order lead time. With the inclusion of safety stock ($SS$), the reorder point becomes

$$\text{ROP} = d \times L + SS \tag{12-16}$$

How to determine the correct amount of safety stock is the only remaining question. The answer to this question depends on whether or not we know the cost of a stockout. We discuss both of these situations next.

---

**IN ACTION**   Telephone Companies Analyze Price Quotations and Quantity Discounts

In many cases, companies buy inventory supplies from several suppliers. This was the case with Bellcore, formed in 1984 to allow the regional Bell operating companies to share common resources. The operating companies, which included Ameritech, Bell Atlantic, BellSouth Telecommunications, NYNEX, Pacific Bell, Southwestern Bell, and US West are often referred to as Bell client companies.

By pooling their resources, the Bell client companies have considerable power over their suppliers. As a result, they decided to select suppliers of required raw materials and inventory based on the availability and amount of quantity discounts and business volume discounts. Whereas a traditional quantity discount is based on the amount of a particular inventory item that is ordered, a business volume discount is based on the total dollar value of all items purchased. With a business volume discount, the supplier typically discounts each item by the same amount in an order.

One major inventory item needed by the Bell client companies is modular circuit boards, so managers of these firms inquired how they could purchase the boards from Bellcore under business volume discounts. The result was a quantitative model, called the Procurement Decision Support System (PDSS), that determines the optimal ordering policy based on the most economical purchase of items under business volume discounts. PDSS was written to run on personal computers. The program allowed Bell client companies to move away from quantity discounts toward business volume discounts.

What is the result of using business volume discounts? PDSS now controls inventory and products worth more than $600 million. The savings for Bell client companies have ranged from about $5 million to $15 million per year.

**Source:** P. Katz et al. "Telephone Companies Analyze Price Quotations with Bellcore's PDSS Software," *Interfaces* 24 (January–February 1994): 50–63.

---

[3] Safety stock is used only when demand is uncertain, and models under uncertainty are generally much harder to deal with than models under certainty.

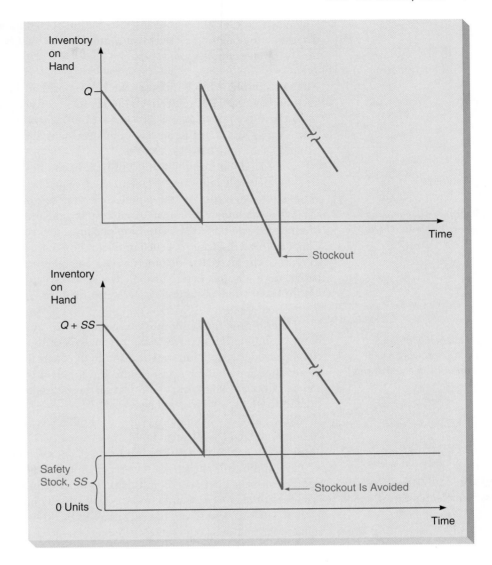

**FIGURE 12.7**

**Use of Safety Stock**

## Safety Stock with Known Stockout Costs

When the EOQ is fixed and the ROP is used to place orders, the only time a stockout can occur is during the lead time. Recall that the lead time is the time between when an order is placed and when it is received. In the procedure discussed here, it is necessary to know the probability of *demand during lead time* (denoted as *DDLT*) and the cost of a stockout. In what follows, we assume that DDLT follows a discrete probability distribution. This approach, however, can be easily modified when DDLT follows a continuous probability distribution.

What factors should we include in computing the stockout cost per unit? In general, we should include all costs that are a direct or indirect result of a stockout. For example, assume that if a stockout occurs, we lose that specific sale forever. Thus, if there is a profit margin of $1 per unit, we have lost this amount. Furthermore, we may end up losing future business from customers who are upset about the stockout. An estimate of this cost must also be included in the stockout cost.

*Loss of goodwill must be included in stockout costs.*

When we know the probability distribution of DDLT and the cost of a stockout, we can determine the safety stock level that minimizes the total cost. We illustrate this computation using an example.

**ABCO Example**  ABCO, Inc. uses the EOQ model and ROP analysis (which we saw in Section 12.4 and 12.5, respectively) to set its inventory policy. The company has determined that its optimal ROP is 50 (= $d \times L$) units, and the optimal number of orders per year is 6. ABCO's DDLT is, however, not a constant. Instead, it follows the probability distribution shown in Table 12.3.[4]

Since DDLT is uncertain, ABCO would like to find the revised ROP, including safety stock, which will minimize total expected cost. The total expected cost is the sum of expected stockout cost and the expected carrying cost of the *additional* inventory.

*We use a decision making under risk approach here.*

When we know the unit stockout cost and the probability distribution of DDLT, the inventory problem becomes a decision making under risk problem. (Refer to Section 8.5 in Chapter 8 for a discussion of such problems if necessary.) For ABCO, the decision alternatives are to use an ROP of 30 (alternative 1), 40 (alternative 2), 50 (alternative 3), 60 (alternative 4), or 70 units (alternative 5). The states of nature are DDLT values of 30 (state of nature 1), 40 (state of nature 2), 50 (state of nature 3), 60 (state of nature 4), or 70 units (state of nature 5).

*Stockout and additional carrying costs will be zero when ROP = demand during lead time.*

Determining the economic consequences for any decision alternative and state of nature combination involves a careful analysis of the stockout and additional carrying costs. Consider a situation in which the ROP equals the DDLT (say, 30 units each). This means that there will be no stockouts and no extra units on hand when the new order arrives. Thus, stockouts and additional carrying costs will be 0. In general, when the ROP equals the DDLT, total cost will be 0.

*If ROP < DDLT, total cost = total stockout cost.*

Now consider what happens when the ROP is less than the DDLT. For example, ROP is 30 units and DDLT is 40 units. In this case we will be 10 units short. The cost of this stockout situation is $2,400 (= 10 units short $\times$ $40 per stockout $\times$ 6 orders per year). Note that we have to multiply the stockout cost per unit and the number of units short times the number of orders per year (6 in this case) to determine annual expected stockout cost. Likewise, if the ROP is 30 units and the DDLT is 50 units, the stockout cost will be $4,800 (= 20 $\times$ $40 $\times$ 6), and so on. In general, when the ROP is less than the DDLT, total cost is equal to the total stockout cost.

**TABLE 12.3**

**Probability of Demand During Lead Time for ABCO, Inc.**

| NUMBER OF UNITS | PROBABILITY |
|---|---|
| 30 | 0.2 |
| 40 | 0.2 |
| ROP ⟶ 50 | 0.3 |
| 60 | 0.2 |
| 70 | 0.1 |
| | 1.0 |

---

[4] Note that we have assumed we already know the values of $Q^*$ and ROP. If this is not true, the values of $Q^*$, ROP, and safety stock would have to be determined simultaneously. This requires a more complex solution.

Finally, consider what happens when the ROP exceeds the DDLT. For example, ROP is 70 units and DDLT is 60 units. In this case, we will have 10 additional units on hand when the new inventory is received. If this situation continues during the year, we will have 10 additional units on hand, on average. The additional carrying cost is $50 (= 10 additional units × $5 carrying cost per unit per year). Likewise, if the DDLT is 50 units, we will have 20 additional units on hand when the new inventory arrives, and the additional carrying cost will be $100 (= 20 × $5). In general, when the ROP is greater than the DDLT, total cost will be equal to the total additional carrying cost.

Using the procedures described previously, we can easily set up a spreadsheet to compute the total cost for every alternative and state of nature combination. The formula view for this spreadsheet is shown in Program 12.6A, and the values are shown in Program 12.6B.

*If ROP > DDLT, total cost = total additional inventory carrying cost.*

**File: 12-6.xls**

---

**PROGRAM 12.6A**    **Formula View of Safety Stock Computation for ABCO, Inc.**

| | A | B | C | D | E | F | G |
|---|---|---|---|---|---|---|---|
| 1 | ABCO Stockout Costs | | | | | | |
| 2 | | | | | | | |
| 3 | Stockout cost per unit = | | | 40 | | | |
| 4 | Carrying cost per unit per year = | | | 5 | | | |
| 5 | Number of orders per year = | | | 6 | | | |
| 6 | | | | | | | |
| 7 | | | | State of nature (DDLT) | | | |
| 8 | Alternative (ROP) | 30 | 40 | 50 | 60 | 70 | EMV |
| 9 | 30 | =0 | =$D$3*(C$8-$A9)*$D$5 | =$D$3*(D$8-$A9)*$D$5 | =$D$3*(E$8-$A9)*$D$5 | =$D$3*(F$8-$A9)*$D$5 | =SUMPRODUCT(B9:F9,B$14:F$14) |
| 10 | 40 | =$D$4*($A10-B$8) | =0 | =$D$3*(D$8-$A10)*$D$5 | =$D$3*(E$8-$A10)*$D$5 | =$D$3*(F$8-$A10)*$D$5 | =SUMPRODUCT(B10:F10,B$14:F$14) |
| 11 | 50 | =$D$4*($A11-B$8) | =$D$4*($A11-C$8) | =0 | =$D$3*(E$8-$A11)*$D$5 | =$D$3*(F$8-$A11)*$D$5 | =SUMPRODUCT(B11:F11,B$14:F$14) |
| 12 | 60 | =$D$4*($A12-B$8) | =$D$4*($A12-C$8) | =$D$4*($A12-D$8) | =0 | =$D$3*(F$8-$A12)*$D$5 | =SUMPRODUCT(B12:F12,B$14:F$14) |
| 13 | 70 | =$D$4*($A13-B$8) | =$D$4*($A13-C$8) | =$D$4*($A13-D$8) | =$D$4*($A13-E$8) | =0 | =SUMPRODUCT(B13:F13,B$14:F$14) |
| 14 | Probability | 0.2 | 0.2 | 0.3 | 0.2 | 0.1 | |

Cost = stockout cost, if ROP < DDLT

Cost = Additional holding cost if ROP > DDLT

Cost = 0 if ROP = DDLT

Expected monetary value of each decision alternative

---

**PROGRAM 12.6B**

**Safety Stock Computation for ABCO, Inc.**

| | A | B | C | D | E | F | G |
|---|---|---|---|---|---|---|---|
| 1 | **ABCO Stockout Costs** | | | | | | |
| 2 | | | | | | | |
| 3 | Stockout cost per unit = | | | $40 | | | |
| 4 | Carrying cost per unit per year = | | | $5 | | | |
| 5 | Number of orders per year = | | | 6 | | | |
| 6 | | | | | | | |
| 7 | | | | State of nature (DDLT) | | | |
| 8 | Alternative (ROP) | 30 | 40 | 50 | 60 | 70 | EMV |
| 9 | 30 | $0 | $2,400 | $4,800 | $7,200 | $9,600 | $4,320 |
| 10 | 40 | $50 | $0 | $2,400 | $4,800 | $7,200 | $2,410 |
| 11 | 50 | $100 | $50 | $0 | $2,400 | $4,800 | $990 |
| 12 | 60 | $150 | $100 | $50 | $0 | $2,400 | $305 |
| 13 | 70 | $200 | $150 | $100 | $50 | $0 | **$110** |
| 14 | Probability | 0.2 | 0.2 | 0.3 | 0.2 | 0.1 | |

Input data

Probability of each DDLT value

Best alternative is ROP = 70.

The expected monetary values (EMV) in column G show that the best reorder point for ABCO is 70 units, with an expected total cost of $110. Recall that ABCO had determined its optimal ROP to be 50 units if DDLT was a constant. Hence, the results in Program 12.6B imply that due to the uncertain nature of DDLT, ABCO should carry a safety stock of 20 (= 70 − 50) units.

## Safety Stock with Unknown Stockout Costs

*Determining stockout costs may be difficult or impossible.*

When stockout costs are not available or if they are not relevant, the preceding type of analysis cannot be used. Actually, there are many situations where stockout costs are unknown or extremely difficult to determine. For example, let's assume that you run a small bicycle shop that sells mopeds and bicycles with a one-year service warranty. Any adjustments made within the year are done at no charge to the customer. If the customer comes in for maintenance under the warranty, and you do not have the necessary part, what is the stockout cost? It cannot be lost profit because the maintenance is done free of charge. Thus, the major stockout cost is the loss of goodwill. The customer may not buy another bicycle from your shop if you have a poor service record. In this situation, it could be very difficult to determine the stockout cost. In other cases, a stockout cost may simply not apply. What is the stockout cost for lifesaving drugs in a hospital? The drugs may only cost $10 per bottle. Is the stockout cost $10? Is it $100 or $10,000? Perhaps the stockout cost should be $1 million. What is the cost when a life may be lost as a result of not having the drug?

*An alternative to determining safety stock is to use service level and the normal distribution.*

In such cases, an alternative approach to determining safety stock levels is to use a *service level*. In general, a service level is the percent of the time that you will have the item in stock. In other words, the probability of having a stockout is 1 minus the service level. That is,

$$\text{Service level} = 1 - \text{probability of a stockout}$$

or

$$\text{Probability of a stockout} = 1 - \text{service level} \tag{12-17}$$

**IN ACTION**   Inventory Modeling at the Philippines San Miguel Corporation

In a typical manufacturing firm, inventories comprise a big part of assets. At the San Miguel Corporation (SMC), which produces and distributes more than 300 products to every corner of the Philippine archipelago, raw material accounts for about 10% of total assets. The significant amount of money tied up in inventory encouraged the company's Operations Research Department to develop a series of cost minimizing inventory models.

One major SMC product, ice cream, uses dairy and cheese curd imported from Australia, New Zealand and Europe. The normal mode of delivery is sea, and delivery frequencies are limited by supplier schedules. Stockouts, however, are avoidable through airfreight expediting. SMC's inventory model for ice cream balances ordering, carrying, and stockout costs while considering delivery frequency constraints and minimum order quantities. Results showed that current safety stocks of 30–51 days could be cut in half for dairy and cheese curd. Even with the increased use of expensive airfreight, SMC saved $170,000 per year through the new policy.

Another SMC product, beer, consists of three major ingredients: malt, hops, and chemicals. Since these ingredients are characterized by low expediting costs and high unit costs, inventory modeling pointed to optimal policies that reduced safety stock levels, saving another $180,000 per year.

**Source:** E. Del Rosario. "Logistical Nightmare," *OR/MS Today* (April 1999): 44–45.

FIGURE 12.8

Safety Stock and the
Normal Distribution

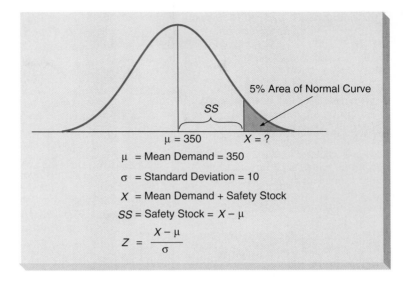

5% Area of Normal Curve

$SS$

$\mu = 350$     $X = ?$

$\mu$ = Mean Demand = 350

$\sigma$ = Standard Deviation = 10

$X$ = Mean Demand + Safety Stock

$SS$ = Safety Stock = $X - \mu$

$$Z = \frac{X - \mu}{\sigma}$$

To determine the safety stock level, it is only necessary to know the probability of DDLT, and the *desired* service level. Here is an example of how the safety stock level can be determined when the DDLT follows a normal probability distribution.

**Hinsdale Company Example**  The Hinsdale Company carries an item whose DDLT follows a normal distribution with a mean of 350 units and a standard deviation of 10 units. Hinsdale wants to follow a policy that results in a service level of 95%. How much safety stock should Hinsdale maintain for this item?

*We find the Z value for the desired service level.*

Figure 12.8 may help you to visualize the example. We use the properties of a standardized normal curve to get a $Z$ value for an area under the normal curve of 0.95 = (1 − 0.05). Using the normal table in Appendix C, we find this $Z$ value to be 1.645.

As shown in Figure 12.8, $Z$ is equal to $(X - \mu)/\sigma$, or SS/$\sigma$. Hence, SS is equal to $Z \times \sigma$. That is, Hinsdale's safety stock for a service level of 95% is (1.645 × 10) = 16.45 units (which can be rounded off to 17 units if necessary). We can calculate the safety stocks for different service levels in a similar fashion.

*A safety stock level is determined for each service level.*

Let's assume that Hinsdale has a carrying cost of $1 per unit per year. What is the carrying cost for service levels that range from 90% to 99.99%? To compute this cost, we first compute the safety stock for each service level (as discussed earlier), and then multiply the safety stock by the unit carrying cost. The $Z$ value, safety stock, and total carrying cost for different service levels for Hinsdale are summarized in Table 12.4. A graph of the total carrying cost as a function of the service level is given in Figure 12.9.

*Relationship between service level and carrying cost is nonlinear.*

Note from Figure 12.9 that the relationship between service level and carrying cost is nonlinear. As the service level increases, the carrying cost increases at an increasing rate. Indeed, at very high service levels, the carrying cost becomes very large. Therefore, as you are setting service levels, you should be aware of the additional carrying cost that you will encounter. Although Figure 12.9 was developed for a specific case, the general shape of the curve is the same for all service-level problems.

**File: 12-7.xls**

**Using ExcelModules to Compute the Safety Stock**  We select the Safety Stock (Normal DDLT) option from the Inventory Models submenu in ExcelModules (refer back to Program 12.1A). The options for this procedure include the problem title and a box to specify if we want a graph of carrying cost versus service level. After we specify these options, we get the worksheet shown in Program 12.7A. We now enter the values for the

| TABLE 12.4 | SERVICE LEVEL (%) | Z VALUE FROM NORMAL CURVE TABLE | SAFETY STOCK (UNITS) | CARRYING COST ($) |
|---|---|---|---|---|
| **Cost of Different Service Levels** | 90 | 1.28 | 12.8 | 12.80 |
| | 91 | 1.34 | 13.4 | 13.40 |
| | 92 | 1.41 | 14.1 | 14.10 |
| | 93 | 1.48 | 14.8 | 14.80 |
| | 94 | 1.55 | 15.5 | 15.50 |
| | 95 | 1.65 | 16.5 | 16.50 |
| | 96 | 1.75 | 17.5 | 17.50 |
| | 97 | 1.88 | 18.8 | 18.80 |
| | 98 | 2.05 | 20.5 | 20.50 |
| | 99 | 2.33 | 23.3 | 23.20 |
| | 99.99 | 3.72 | 37.2 | 37.20 |

**PROGRAM 12.7A**   **Safety Stock (Normal DDLT) Model for Hinsdale Company**

|  | A | B | C | D | E |
|---|---|---|---|---|---|
| 1 | **Hinsdale Company** | | | | |
| 2 | Inventory | Safety Stock (Normal DDLT) | | | |
| 3 | Enter the input data in the cells shaded YELLOW. | | | | |
| 4 | | | | | |
| 5 | **Input Data** | | | | |
| 6 | Mean DDLT, $\mu$ | 350 | | | |
| 7 | Std deviation of DDLT, $\sigma$ | 10 | | | |
| 8 | Service level desired | 95.00% | (percentage) | | |
| 9 | Carrying cost, $C_h$ | $1.00 | | | |
| 10 | | | 95% is entered as 95 here. | | |
| 11 | **Results** | | | | |
| 12 | Safety stock, SS | 16.45 | | | |
| 13 | Reorder point, ROP | 366.45 | ROP = $\mu$ + SS | | |
| 14 | | | | | |
| 15 | SS carrying cost | $16.45 | | | |
| 16 | | | | | |
| 17 | | | | | |
| 18 | **Cost Table for Graph** | Start at | 89.00% | Increment by | 1.00% |
| 19 | | | | | |
| 20 | | Service level | SS carrying cost | | |
| 21 | | 89.00% | 12.27 | | |
| 22 | | 90.00% | 12.82 | | |
| 23 | | 91.00% | 13.41 | Data for graph, generated and used by ExcelModules | |
| 24 | | 92.00% | 14.05 | | |
| 25 | | 93.00% | 14.76 | | |
| 26 | | 94.00% | 15.55 | | |
| 27 | | 95.00% | 16.45 | | |
| 28 | | 96.00% | 17.51 | | |
| 29 | | 97.00% | 18.81 | | |

## FIGURE 12.9

**Service Level Versus
Annual Carrying Costs**

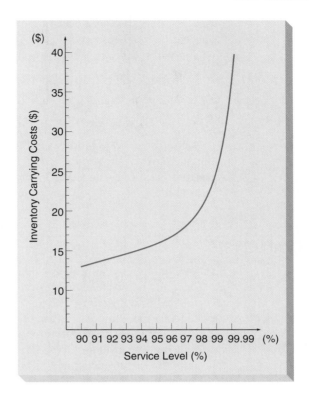

## PROGRAM 12.7B

**Plot of Safety Stock Cost Versus Service Level for Hinsdale Company**

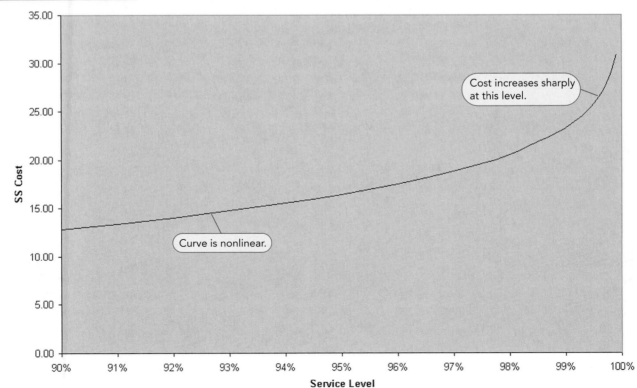

mean DDLT ($\mu$), standard deviation of DDLT ($\sigma$), service level desired, and carrying cost $C_h$ in cells B6 to B9, respectively.

The worksheet calculates and displays the following output measures:

■ Safety stock SS ($= Z \times \sigma$), in cell B12
■ Reorder point ($= \mu + Z \times \sigma$) in cell B13
■ Safety stock carrying cost ($= C_h \times Z \times \sigma$) in cell B15

If requested, ExcelModules will draw a plot of the safety stock carrying cost for different values of the service level. The graph, shown in Program 12.7B, is drawn on a separate worksheet. As expected, the shape of this graph is the same as that shown in Figure 12.9.

## 12.9 ABC ANALYSIS

So far, we have shown how to develop inventory policies using quantitative decision models. There are, however, some very practical issues, such as *ABC analysis*, that should be incorporated into inventory decisions. ABC analysis recognizes the fact that some inventory items are more important than others. The purpose of this analysis is to divide all of a company's inventory items into three groups: A, B, and C. Then, depending on the group, we decide how the inventory levels should be controlled. A brief description of each group follows, with general guidelines as to which items are A, B, and C.

*The items in the A group are critical.*

The inventory items in the A group are critical to the functioning of the company. As a result, their inventory levels must be closely monitored. These items typically make up more than 70% of the company's business in dollars, but only about 10% of all inventory items. That is, a few inventory items are very important to the company. As a result, the inventory control techniques discussed in this chapter should be used where appropriate for every item in the A group (refer to Table 12.5).

*The B group items are important.*

The items in the B group are important to the firm but not critical. Thus, it may not be necessary to monitor all these items closely. These items typically represent about 20% of the company's business in dollars and constitute about 20% of the items in inventory. Quantitative inventory models should be used only on some of the B items. The cost of implementing and using these models must be carefully balanced with the benefits of better inventory control. Usually, less than half of the B group items are controlled through the use of inventory control models.

*The C group items are not as important in terms of annual dollar value.*

The items in the C group are not as important to the operation of the company. These items typically represent only about 10% of the company's business in dollars but may constitute 70% of the items in inventory. Group C could include inexpensive items such as bolts, washers, screws, and so on. They are usually not controlled using inventory control

| TABLE 12.5 | | | | |
|---|---|---|---|---|
| **Summary of ABC Analysis** | INVENTORY GROUP | DOLLAR USAGE (%) | INVENTORY ITEMS (%) | ARE QUANTITATIVE INVENTORY CONTROL TECHNIQUES USED? |
| | A | 70 | 10 | Yes |
| | B | 20 | 20 | In some cases |
| | C | 10 | 70 | No |

models since the cost of implementing and using such models would far exceed the value gained.

We illustrate the use of ABC analysis using the example of Silicon Chips, Inc.

## Silicon Chips, Inc., Example

Silicon Chips, Inc., maker of super-fast DRAM chips, has organized its 10 inventory items on an annual dollar-volume basis. Table 12.6 shows the items (identified by the item number and part number), their annual demands, and unit costs. How should the company classify these items into groups A, B, and C? As discussed next, we use the worksheet provided in ExcelModules to answer this question.

**File: 12-8.xls**

*Items are sorted in descending order of percentage $ volume.*

**Using *ExcelModules* for ABC Analysis** We select the ABC Analysis option from the Inventory Models submenu in ExcelModules (refer back to Program 12.1A). The options for this procedure include the problem title and boxes to specify the number and names of the items we want to classify. After we specify these options for the Silicon Chips example, we get the worksheet shown in Program 12.8. We now enter the volume and unit cost for each item in cells B7:C16 of this worksheet.

When we enter the input data, the worksheet computes the $ volume and percentage $ volume (computed as a percentage of the total $ volume) for each item. These values are shown in cells E7:F16 of Program 12.8. After entering the data for *all* items, we click the button marked Analyze. The worksheet now sorts the items in descending order of percentage $ volume. These values are shown in descending order in cells F21:F30 of Program 12.8.

The sorted results for Silicon Chips, Inc.'s problem are shown in cells A21:C30 of Program 12.8. Items 3 and 7, which constitute only 20% (= 2/10) of the total number of items, account for 71.97% of the total $ volume of all items. These two items should therefore be classified as group A items.

Items 9, 6, and 4, which constitute 30% (= 3/10) of the total number of items, account for 23.20% (= 95.17 − 71.97) of the total $ volume of all items. These three items should therefore be classified as group B items.

The remaining items constitute 50% (= 5/10) of the total number of items. However, they account for only 4.83% (= 100 − 95.17) of the total $ volume of all items. These five items should therefore be classified as group C items.

**TABLE 12.6**

**Inventory Data for Silicon Chips, Inc.**

| ITEM NUMBER | PART NUMBER | ANNUAL VOLUME (UNITS) | UNIT COST ($) |
|---|---|---|---|
| Item 1 | 01036 | 100 | $8.50 |
| Item 2 | 01307 | 1,200 | $0.42 |
| Item 3 | 10286 | 1,000 | $90.00 |
| Item 4 | 10500 | 1,000 | $12.50 |
| Item 5 | 10572 | 250 | $0.60 |
| Item 6 | 10867 | 350 | $42.86 |
| Item 7 | 11526 | 500 | $154.00 |
| Item 8 | 12572 | 600 | $14.17 |
| Item 9 | 12760 | 1,550 | $17.00 |
| Item 10 | 14075 | 2,000 | $0.60 |

**PROGRAM 12.8**    **ABC Analysis for Silicon Chips, Inc.**

Click this button *after* entering all input data.

| | A | B | C | D | E | F | G | H |
|---|---|---|---|---|---|---|---|---|
| 1 | **Silicon Chips, Inc.** | | | | | | | |
| 2 | Inventory | ABC Analysis | | | | | | |
| 3 | Analyze | Enter the volume and the costs into the data table. Then click the **Analyze** button. | | | | | | |
| 4 | | | | | | | | |
| 5 | Input Data | | | | | | | |
| 6 | | Volume | Unit cost | | Dollar volume | % Dollar volume | Cumulative $-vol % | |
| 7 | Item 1 | 100 | $8.50 | | $850.00 | 0.37% | 0.37% | |
| 8 | Item 2 | 1200 | $0.42 | | $504.00 | 0.22% | 0.58% | |
| 9 | Item 3 | 1000 | $90.00 | | $90,000.00 | 38.78% | 39.37% | |
| 10 | Item 4 | 1000 | $12.50 | | $12,500.00 | 5.39% | 44.75% | |
| 11 | Item 5 | 250 | $0.60 | | $150.00 | 0.06% | 44.82% | |
| 12 | Item 6 | 350 | $42.86 | | $15,001.00 | 6.46% | 51.28% | |
| 13 | Item 7 | 500 | $154.00 | | $77,000.00 | 33.18% | 84.46% | |
| 14 | Item 8 | 600 | $14.17 | | $8,502.00 | 3.66% | 88.13% | |
| 15 | Item 9 | 1550 | $17.00 | | $26,350.00 | 11.35% | 99.48% | |
| 16 | Item 10 | 2000 | $0.60 | | $1,200.00 | 0.52% | 100.00% | |
| 17 | | | | Total | $232,057.00 | | | |
| 18 | Input data | | | | | | | |
| 19 | **ABC Analysis: Items sorted in descending order by dollar volume** | | | | | | | |
| 20 | | Volume | Unit cost | | Dollar volume | % Dollar volume | Cumulative $-vol % | |
| 21 | Item 3 | 1000.000 | 90.000 | A | $90,000.00 | 38.78% | 38.78% | |
| 22 | Item 7 | 500.000 | 154.000 | | $77,000.00 | 33.18% | 71.97% | 2 items |
| 23 | Item 9 | 1550.000 | 17.000 | | $26,350.00 | 11.35% | 83.32% | |
| 24 | Item 6 | 350.000 | 42.860 | B | $15,001.00 | 6.46% | 89.78% | 3 items |
| 25 | Item 4 | 1000.000 | 12.500 | | $12,500.00 | 5.39% | 95.17% | |
| 26 | Item 8 | 600.000 | 14.170 | | $8,502.00 | 3.66% | 98.83% | |
| 27 | Item 10 | 2000.000 | 0.600 | | $1,200.00 | 0.52% | 99.35% | |
| 28 | Item 1 | 100.000 | 8.500 | C | $850.00 | 0.37% | 99.72% | 5 items |
| 29 | Item 2 | 1200.000 | 0.420 | | $504.00 | 0.22% | 99.94% | |
| 30 | Item 5 | 250.000 | 0.600 | | $150.00 | 0.06% | 100.00% | |
| 31 | | | | Total | $232,057.00 | | | |

Items are sorted in descending order of percentage $ volume.

Sorted values of percentage $ volume

# SUMMARY

This chapter presents several inventory models and discusses how we can use ExcelModules to analyze these models. The focus of all models is to answer the same two primary questions in inventory planning: (1) how much to order and (2) when to order. The basic EOQ inventory model makes a number of assumptions: (1) known and constant demand and lead times, (2) instantaneous receipt of inventory, (3) no quantity discounts, (4) no stockouts or shortages, and (5) the only variable costs are ordering costs and carrying costs. If these assumptions are valid, the EOQ inventory model provides optimal solutions. If these assumptions do not hold, more complex models are needed. For such cases the economic production quantity and quantity discount models are necessary. We also discuss the computation of safety stocks when demand during lead time was unknown for two cases: (1) cost of stockout is known and (2) cost of stockout is unknown. Finally, we present ABC analysis to determine how inventory items should be classified based on their importance and value. For all models discussed in this chapter, we show how Excel worksheets could be used to perform the computations.

# GLOSSARY

**ABC Analysis.** An analysis that divides inventory into three groups: Group A is more important than group B, which is more important than group C.

**Average Inventory.** The average inventory on hand. Computed as (maximum inventory and minimum inventory)/2.

**Carrying Cost.** The cost of holding one unit of an item in inventory for one period (typically a year).

**Demand During Lead Time (DDLT).** The demand for an item during the lead time between order placement and order receipt.

**Economic Order Quantity (EOQ).** The amount of inventory ordered that will minimize the total inventory cost. It is also called the optimal order quantity, or $Q^*$.

**Economic Production Quantity (EPQ) Model.** An inventory model in which the instantaneous receipt assumption has been eliminated. The inventory buildup, therefore, occurs over a period of time.

**Instantaneous Inventory Receipt.** A system in which inventory is received or obtained at one point in time and not over a period of time.

**Lead Time.** The time it takes to receive an order after it is placed.

**Ordering Cost.** The cost of placing an order.

**Purchase Cost.** The cost of purchasing one unit of an inventory item.

**Quantity Discount.** The cost per unit when large orders of an inventory item are placed.

**Reorder Point (ROP).** The number of units on hand when an order for more inventory is placed.

**Safety Stock.** Extra inventory that is used to help avoid stock-outs.

**Safety Stock with Known Stockout Costs.** An inventory model in which the probability distribution of DDLT and the unit stockout cost are known.

**Safety Stock with Unknown Stockout Costs.** An inventory model in which the probability distribution of DDLT is known. The stockout cost is, however, not known.

**Service Level.** The chance, expressed as a percent, that there will not be a stockout. Service level = 1 – probability of a stockout.

**Setup Cost.** The cost to set up the manufacturing or production process.

**Stockout.** A situation that occurs when there is no inventory on hand.

**Total Cost.** The sum of the total ordering, total carrying, and total purchasing costs.

# KEY EQUATIONS

**(12-1)**  Average inventory level = $(0 + Q)/2 = Q/2$

Average inventory for EOQ model.

**(12-2)**  $C_h = I \times P$

Carrying cost expressed as a percentage of unit purchase cost.

**(12-3)**  Total ordering cost = $(D/Q) \times C_o$

Total ordering cost for EOQ model.

**(12-4)**  Total carrying cost = $(Q/2) \times C_h$

Total carrying cost for EOQ model.

**(12-5)**  Total cost = Total ordering cost + Total carrying cost + Total purchase cost = $(D/Q) \times C_o + (Q/2) \times C_h + P \times D$

Total cost for EOQ model.

**(12-6)**  $Q^* = \sqrt{2DC_o/C_h}$

Formula to compute the economic order quantity.

**(12-7)**  Average dollar value of inventory = $P \times (Q^*/2)$

**(12-8)**  $C_o = Q^2 \times C_h/(2D)$

Formula to compute the ordering cost that would make a given order quantity the optimal order quantity.

**(12-9)**  $C_h = 2DC_o/Q^2$

Formula to compute the carrying that would make a given order quantity the optimal order quantity.

**(12-10)**  ROP = (demand per day) × (lead time for a new order in days) = $d \times L$

Formula to compute the reorder point.

**(12-11)**  Average inventory level = $[0 + Q(1 - d/p)]/2 = Q(1 - d/p)/2$

Average inventory for EPQ model.

**(12-12)**  Total setup cost = $(D/Q) \times C_s$

Total setup cost for EPQ model.

**(12-13)**  Total carrying cost = $[Q(1 - d/p)/2] \times C_h$

Total carrying cost for EPQ model.

**(12-14)**   Total cost = Total setup cost + Total carrying cost + Total production cost = $(D/Q) \times C_s + [Q(1 - d/p)/2] \times C_h + P \times D$

Total cost for EPQ model.

**(12-15)**   $Q^* = \sqrt{2DC_s/[C_h(1 - d/p)]}$

Formula to compute the economic production quantity.

**(12-16)**   Reorder point (ROP) = $d \times L + SS$

Reorder point including safety stock.

**(12-17)**   Probability of a stockout = 1 − service level

Relationship between probability of a stockout and service level.

# SOLVED PROBLEMS

## Solved Problem 12-1

Patterson Electronics supplies microcomputer circuitry to a company that incorporates microprocessors into refrigerators and other home appliances. Currently, Patterson orders a particular component in batches of 300 units from one of its suppliers. The annual demand for this component is 2,000.

a. If the carrying cost is estimated at $1 per unit per year, what would the ordering cost have to be to make the order quantity optimal?
b. If the ordering cost is estimated to be $50 per order, what would the carrying cost have to be to make the order quantity optimal?

### Solution

a. Recall from Equation 12-8 that the ordering cost can be computed as

$$C_o = Q^2 \times C_h/(2D)$$

In Patterson's case, $D = 2,000$, $Q = 300$, and $C_h = \$1$. Substituting these values, we get an ordering cost $C_o$ of $22.50 per order.

b. Recall from Equation 12-9 that the carrying cost can be computed as

$$C_h = 2DC_o/Q^2$$

In Patterson's case, $D = 2,000$, $Q = 300$, and $C_o = \$50$. Substituting these values, we get a carrying cost $C_h$ of $2.22 per unit per year.

## Solved Problem 12-2

Flemming Accessories produces paper slicers used in offices and in art stores. The minislicer has been one of its most popular items: Annual demand is 6,750 units. Kristen Flemming, owner of the firm, produces the minislicers in batches. On average, Kristen can manufacture 125 minislicers per day. Demand for these slicers during the production process is 30 per day. The setup cost for the equipment necessary to produce the minislicers is $150. Carrying costs are $1 per minislicer per year. How many minislicers should Kristen manufacture in each batch? Assume minislicers cost $10 each to produce.

### Solution

**File: 12-9.xls**

To solve this problem, we use the *Economic Production Quantity* (EPQ) option in the *Inventory Models* submenu of ExcelModules. The input entries, as well as the resulting computations, are shown in Program 12.9.

The results show that Flemming Accessories has an EPQ of 1,632 units. The annual total setup and carrying costs are $620.28 each. The annual total cost, including the cost of production, is $68,740.56.

## PROGRAM 12.9

**EPQ Model for Solved Problem 12-2**

|     | A | B | C | D |
|-----|---|---|---|---|
| 1 | **Solved Problem 12-2** | | | |
| 2 | Inventory | | Economic Production Quantity Model | |
| 3 | Enter the data in the cells shaded YELLOW. You may have to do some | | | |
| 4 | work to compute the daily production and demand rates. | | | |
| 5 | | | | |
| 6 | Input Data | | | |
| 7 | Demand rate, D | 6750 | | |
| 8 | Setup cost, $C_s$ | $150.00 | *Input data* | |
| 9 | Carrying cost, $C_h$ | $1.00 | (fixed amount) | |
| 10 | Daily production rate, p | 125 | | |
| 11 | Daily demand rate, d | 30 | | |
| 12 | Unit purchase cost, P | $10.00 | | |
| 13 | | | | |
| 14 | Results | | | |
| 15 | Economic production quantity, Q* | 1632.32 | *EPQ is 1632 units.* | |
| 16 | Maximum inventory | 1240.56 | | |
| 17 | Average inventory | 620.28 | | |
| 18 | Number of setups | 4.14 | | |
| 19 | | | | |
| 20 | Total holding cost | $620.28 | | |
| 21 | Total setup cost | $620.28 | | |
| 22 | Total production cost | $67,500.00 | | |
| 23 | Total cost, TC | $68,740.56 | *Total cost is $68,740.56.* | |

---

## Solved Problem 12-3

Dorsey Distributors has an annual demand for a metal detector of 1,400. The cost of a typical detector to Dorsey is $400. Carrying cost is estimated to be 20% of the unit cost, and the ordering cost is $25 per order. If Dorsey orders in quantities of 300 or more, it can get a 5% discount on the cost of the detectors. Should Dorsey take the quantity discount?

### Solution

**File: 12-10.xls**

To solve this problem, we use the *Quantity Discount* option in the *Inventory Models* submenu of ExcelModules. There are two discount levels in this case. The input entries, as well as the resulting computations, are shown in Program 12.10. The results show that Dorsey should order 300 units each time at a discounted unit cost of $380. The annual total ordering cost is $116.67, and the annual total carrying cost is $11,400. The annual total cost, including the total purchase cost, is $543,516.57.

## PROGRAM 12.10

**Quantity Discount Model for Solved Problem 12-3**

|     | A | B | C | D | E |
|-----|---|---|---|---|---|
| 1 | **Solved Problem 12-3** | | | | |
| 2 | Inventory | Quantity Discount Model | | | |
| 3 | Enter the data in the cells shaded YELLOW. The minimum quantity is the minimum amount | | | | |
| 4 | that needs to be ordered in order to get the price for that range. | | | | |
| 5 | | | | | |
| 6 | Input Data | | | | |
| 7 | Demand rate, D | 1400 | | | |
| 8 | Ordering cost, $C_o$ | 25 | | | |
| 9 | Carrying cost %, I | 20.00% | (percentage) | | |
| 10 | | | | *Carrying cost entered as a* | |
| 11 | | Range 1 | Range 2 | *percentage of unit price* | |
| 12 | Minimum quantity | 0 | 300 | | |
| 13 | Unit purchase cost, P | $400.00 | $380.00 | | |
| 14 | | | | | |
| 15 | Results | | | | |
| 16 | | Range 1 | Range 2 | | |
| 17 | Economic order quantity, Q* | 29.58 | 30.35 | | |
| 18 | Adjusted order quantity | 29.58 | 300.00 | *Adjusted Q* values* | |
| 19 | | | | | |
| 20 | Total holding cost | 1,183.22 | 11,400.00 | | |
| 21 | Total ordering cost | 1,183.22 | 116.67 | | |
| 22 | Total purchase cost | 560,000.00 | 532,000.00 | | |
| 23 | Total cost | 562,366.43 | 543,516.67 | *Minimum cost option* | |

## ⟱ SELF-TEST

■ Before taking the self-test, refer back to the learning objectives at the beginning of the chapter, the notes in the margins, and the glossary at the end of the chapter.

■ Use the key at the back of the book to correct your answers.

■ Restudy pages that correspond to any questions that you answered incorrectly or material you feel uncertain about.

1. The following is not a basic component of an inventory control system:
   a. planning what inventory to stock and how to acquire it
   b. forecasting the demand for parts and products
   c. organizing the internal inventory users and explaining how they can help control inventory costs
   d. controlling inventory levels
   e. developing and implementing feedback measurements for revising plans and forecasts

2. The following is not a valid use of inventory:
   a. the decoupling function
   b. an inflation hedge
   c. smooth out irregular (cyclical) supply and demand
   d. the interlocutory function
   e. to achieve quantity discounts

3. The inventory decision may be summarized by two questions:
   a. to make or buy and how much
   b. how much and when to order
   c. how much to pay and when to order
   d. to make or buy and when to take quantity discounts
   e. none of the above

4. The economic order quantity (EOQ)
   a. has been around since 1915.
   b. is the same as the optimum order quantity ($Q^*$).
   c. is designed to minimize the total of carrying costs and ordering costs per year (or similar time period).
   d. is that order quantity where the absolute value of the slopes of the ordering and the carrying cost curves are equal.
   e. all of the above.

5. The average inventory level in the basic EOQ model used in this chapter is
   a. one-half of the order quantity.
   b. that quantity on hand one-half of the way between order receipts.
   c. one-half way between the maximum inventory level and the minimum inventory level.
   d. all of the above.

6. For the EPQ model
   a. the quantity in inventory is presumed never to equal the order size.

   b. inventory is assumed to grow at a rate equal to the daily production rate minus the daily usage rate while the product is being produced.
   c. a different optimum order size is computed from that which would have been calculated if the order were purchased from an outside supplier.
   d. all of the above.
   e. none of the above.

7. For both the basic economic order quantity model and for the EPQ model
   a. the average inventory is equal to one-half of the maximum inventory.
   b. the average inventory is equal to one-half of the order size.
   c. the total annual carrying cost will be identical if the optimum order size is identical.
   d. all of the above.
   e. none of the above.

8. The quantity discount model
   a. requires the minimization of the annual costs of the product and the annual ordering cost and the annual carrying cost.
   b. indicates that quantity at which it would be worthwhile taking advantage of the discount.
   c. indicates how much of a discount is necessary to save money by ordering enough to achieve the next quantity discount.
   d. can be used for only one or two quantity discount amounts.

9. The carrying cost per unit
   a. is calculated in the same manner (per unit cost times the number of units per year) for both the basic optimum order quantity model and for the production run model.
   b. is calculated as a percentage of the cost of the item in the quantity discount model.
   c. is calculated at zero for the stockout *periods* of time in the stockout model computation.
   d. all of the above.

10. _____ is additional stock that is kept on hand in case demand is greater than expected.

11. _____ is 1 minus the probability of a stockout.

12. The purpose of _____ is to divide all of a company's stock into three groups.

## DISCUSSION QUESTIONS AND PROBLEMS

### Discussion Questions

12-1  Why is inventory an important consideration for managers?

12-2  What is the purpose of inventory control?

12-3  Under what circumstances can inventory be used as a hedge against inflation?

**12-4** Why wouldn't a company always store large quantities of inventory to eliminate shortages and stockouts?

**12-5** Describe the major decisions that must be made in inventory control.

**12-6** What are some of the assumptions made in using the economic order quantity?

**12-7** Discuss the major inventory costs that are used in determining the EOQ.

**12-8** What are some of the methods that are used in actually determining the equation for the EOQ?

**12-9** What is the ROP? How is it determined?

**12-10** What is the purpose of sensitivity analysis?

**12-11** What assumptions are made in the EPQ model?

**12-12** What happens to the EPQ model when the daily production rate becomes very large?

**12-13** In the quantity discount model, why is the carrying cost expressed as a percentage of the unit cost, $I$, instead of the cost per unit per year, $C_h$?

**12-14** Briefly describe what is involved in solving a quantity discount model.

**12-15** Discuss the methods that are used in determining safety stock when the stockout cost is known and when the stockout cost is unknown.

**12-16** Briefly describe what is meant by ABC analysis. What is the purpose of this inventory technique?

## Problems

**12-17** Lila Battle has determined that the annual demand for number 6 screws is 100,000 screws. Lila, who works in her brother's hardware store, is in charge of purchasing. She estimates that it costs $10 every time an order is placed. This cost includes her wages, the cost of the forms used in placing the order, and so on. Furthermore, she estimates that the cost of carrying one screw in inventory for a year is one-half of 1 cent. How many number 6 screws should Lila order at a time?

**12-18** It takes approximately 8 working days for an order of number 6 screws to arrive once the order has been placed. (Refer to Problem 12-17.) The demand for number 6 screws is fairly constant, and on the average, Lila has observed that her brother's hardware store sells 500 of these screws each day. Because the demand is fairly constant, Lila believes that she can avoid stockouts completely if she only orders the number 6 screws at the correct time. What is the ROP?

**12-19** Lila's brother believes that she places too many orders for screws per year. He believes that an order should be placed only twice per year. If Lila follows her brother's policy, how much more would this cost every year over the ordering policy that she developed in Problem 12-17? If only two orders were placed each year, what effect would this have on the ROP?

**12-20** Barbara Bright is the purchasing agent for West Valve Company. West Valve sells industrial valves and fluid control devices. One of the most popular valves is the Western, which has an annual demand of 4,000 units.

The cost of each valve is $90, and the inventory carrying cost is estimated to be 10% of the cost of each valve. Barbara has made a study of the costs involved in placing an order for any of the valves that West Valve stocks, and she has concluded that the average ordering cost is $25 per order. Furthermore, it takes about two weeks for an order to arrive from the supplier, and during this time the demand per week for West valves is approximately 80.

(a) What is the EOQ?
(b) What is the ROP?
(c) What is the total annual inventory cost (carrying cost + ordering cost)?

**12-21** Ken Ramsing has been in the lumber business for most of his life. Ken's biggest competitor is Pacific Woods. Through many years of experience, Ken knows that the ordering cost for an order of plywood is $25 and that the carrying cost is 25% of the unit cost. Both Ken and Pacific Woods receive plywood in loads that cost $100 per load. Furthermore, Ken and Pacific Woods use the same supplier of plywood, and Ken was able to find out that Pacific Woods orders in quantities of 4,000 loads at a time. Ken also knows that 4,000 loads is the EOQ for Pacific Woods. What is the annual demand in loads of plywood for Pacific Woods?

**12-22** Shoe Shine is a local retail shoe store located on the north side of Centerville. Annual demand for a popular sandal is 500 sandals, and John Dirk, the owner of Shoe Shine, has been in the habit of ordering 100 sandals at a time. John estimates that the ordering cost is $10 per order. The cost of the sandal is $5. For John's ordering policy to be correct, what would the carrying cost as a percentage of the unit cost have to be? If the carrying cost was 10% of the cost, what would the optimal order quantity be?

**12-23** In Problem 12-17 you helped Lila Battle determine the optimal order quantity for number 6 screws. She had estimated that the ordering cost was $10 per order. At this time, though, she believes that this estimate was too low. Although she does not know the exact ordering cost, she believes that it could be as high as $40 per order. How would the optimal order quantity change if the ordering cost were $20, $30, or $40?

**12-24** Annual demand for the Doll two-drawer filing cabinet is 50,000 units. Bill Doll, president of Doll Office Suppliers, controls one of the largest office supply stores in Nevada. He estimates that the ordering cost is $10 per order. The carrying cost is $4 per unit per year. It takes 25 days between the time that Bill places an order for the two-drawer filing cabinets and the time when they are received at his warehouse. During this time, the daily demand is estimated to be 250 units.

(a) What is the EOQ?
(b) What is the ROP?
(c) What is the optimal number of orders per year?

**12-25** Pampered Pet, Inc., is a large pet store located in Eastwood Mall. Although the store specializes in dogs, it also sells fish, turtle, and bird supplies. Everlast Leader, which is a leather lead for dogs, costs Pampered Pet $7 each. There is an annual demand for

**Table for Problem 12-29**

| Cost Factor | Cost ($) | Cost Factor | Cost ($) |
|---|---|---|---|
| Taxes | 2,000 | Inventory inquiries | 450 |
| Processing and inspection | 1,500 | Warehouse supplies | 280 |
| New product development | 2,500 | Research and development | 2,750 |
| Bill paying | 500 | Purchasing salaries | 3,000 |
| Ordering supplies | 50 | Warehouse salaries | 2,800 |
| Inventory insurance | 600 | Inventory theft | 800 |
| Product advertising | 800 | Purchase order supplies | 500 |
| Spoilage | 750 | Inventory obsolescence | 300 |
| Sending purchasing orders | 800 | | |

6,000 Everlast Leaders. The manager of Pampered Pet has determined that the ordering cost is $10 per order, and the carrying cost as a percent of the unit cost is 15%. Pampered Pet is now considering a new supplier of Everlast Leaders. Each lead would cost only $6.65, but to get this discount, Pampered Pet would have to buy shipments of 3,000 Everlast Leaders at a time. Should Pampered Pet use the new supplier and take this discount for quantity buying?

**12-26** Douglas Boats is a supplier of boating equipment for the states of Oregon and Washington. It sells 5,000 White Marine WM-4 diesel engines every year. These engines are shipped to Douglas in a shipping container of 100 cubic feet, and Douglas Boats keeps the warehouse full of these WM-4 motors. The warehouse can hold 5,000 cubic feet of boating supplies. Douglas estimates that the ordering cost is $10 per order, and the carrying cost is estimated to be $10 per motor per year. Douglas Boats is considering the possibility of expanding the warehouse for the WM-4 motors. How much should Douglas Boats expand, and how much would it be worth for the company to make the expansion?

**12-27** Bill Doll (see Problem 12-24) now believes that the carrying cost may be as high as $16 per unit per year. Furthermore, Bill estimates that the lead time is 35 days instead of 25 days. Resolve Problem 12-24 using $16 for the carrying cost with a lead time of 35 days.

**12-28** Northern Distributors is a wholesale organization that supplies retail stores with lawn care and household products. One building is used to store Neverfail lawn mowers. The building is 25 feet wide by 40 feet deep by 8 feet high. Anna Young, manager of the warehouse, estimates that about 60% of the warehouse can be used to store the Neverfail lawn mowers. The remaining 40% is used for walkways and a small office. Each Neverfail lawn mower comes in a box that is 5 feet by 4 feet by 2 feet high. The annual demand for these lawn mowers is 12,000, and the ordering cost for Northern Distributors is $30 per order. It is estimated that it costs Northern $2 per lawn mower per year for storage. Northern Distributors is thinking about increasing the size of the warehouse. The company can only do this by making the warehouse

deeper. At the present time, the warehouse is 40 feet deep. How many feet of depth should be added on to the warehouse to minimize the annual inventory costs? How much should the company be willing to pay for this addition? Remember that only 60% of the total area can be used to store Neverfail lawn mowers.

**12-29** Lisa Surowsky was asked to help in determining the best ordering policy for a new product. Currently, the demand for the new product has been projected to be about 1,000 units annually. To get a handle on the carrying and ordering costs, Lisa prepared a series of average inventory costs. Lisa thought that these costs would be appropriate for the new product. The results are summarized in the table at the top of this page. These data were compiled for 10,000 inventory items that were carried or held during the year and were ordered 100 times during the last year. Help Lisa determine the economic order quantity.

**12-30** Melinda Sholer has spent the past few weeks determining inventory costs for Toco, a toy manufacturer located near Taos, New Mexico. She knows that annual demand will be 20,000 units per year and that carrying cost will be $0.50 per unit per year. Ordering cost, on the other hand, can vary from $40 per order to $50 per order. During the past 486 working days, Melinda has observed the following frequency distribution for the ordering cost. Melinda's boss would like Melinda to determine an EOQ value for each possible ordering cost and to determine an EOQ value for the expected ordering cost.

| Ordering Cost ($) | Frequency | Ordering Cost ($) | Frequency |
|---|---|---|---|
| 40 | 24 | 46 | 64 |
| 41 | 34 | 47 | 45 |
| 42 | 44 | 48 | 44 |
| 43 | 56 | 49 | 23 |
| 44 | 76 | 50 | 10 |
| 45 | 66 | | |

• **12-31** Jan Gentry is the owner of a small company that produces electric scissors used to cut fabric. The annual demand is for 8,000 scissors, and Jan produces the scissors in batches. On the average, Jan can produce 150 scissors per day during the production process. Demand for scissors has been about 40 scissors per day. The cost to set up the production process is $100, and it costs Jan 30 cents to carry one pair of scissors for one year. How many scissors should Jan produce in each batch?

• **12-32** Jim Overstreet, inventory control manager for Itex, receives wheel bearings from Wheel-Rite, a small producer of metal parts. Unfortunately, Wheel-Rite can only produce 500 wheel bearings per day. Itex receives 10,000 wheel bearings from Wheel-Rite each year. Since Itex operates 200 working days each year, the average daily demand of wheel bearings by Itex is 50. The ordering cost for Itex is $40 per order, and the carrying cost is 60 cents per wheel bearing per year. How many wheel bearings should Itex order from Wheel-Rite at one time? Wheel-Rite has agreed to ship the maximum number of wheel bearings that it produces each day to Itex when an order has been received.

⦂ **12-33** North Manufacturing has a demand for 1,000 pumps each year. The cost of a pump is $50. It costs North Manufacturing $40 to place an order, and the carrying cost is 25% of the unit cost. If pumps are ordered in quantities of 200, North Manufacturing can get a 3% discount on the cost of the pumps. Should North Manufacturing order 200 pumps at a time and take the 3% discount?

⦂ **12-34** Mr. Beautiful, an organization that sells weight training sets, has an ordering cost of $40 for the BB-1 set. (BB-1 stands for Body Beautiful Number 1.) The carrying cost for BB-1 is $5 per set per year. To meet demand, Mr. Beautiful orders large quantities of BB-1 seven times a year. The stockout cost for BB-1 is estimated to be $50 per set. Over the past several years, Mr. Beautiful has observed the following demand during the lead time for BB-1:

| DEMAND DURING LEAD TIME | PROBABILITY |
|---|---|
| 40 | 0.1 |
| 50 | 0.2 |
| 60 | 0.2 |
| 70 | 0.2 |
| 80 | 0.2 |
| 90 | 0.1 |

The reorder point for BB-1 is 60 units. What level of safety stock should be maintained for BB-1?

⦂ **12-35** Linder Lechner is in charge of maintaining hospital supplies at General Hospital. During the past year, the mean lead time demand for bandage BX-5 was 60. Furthermore, the standard deviation for BX-5 was 7. Ms. Lechner would like to maintain a 90% service level. What safety stock level do you recommend for BX-5?

⦂ **12-36** Ralph Janaro simply does not have time to analyze all of the items in his company's inventory. As a young manager, he has more important things to do. The following is a table of six items in inventory along with the unit cost and the demand in units.

| IDENTIFICATION CODE | UNIT COST ($) | DEMAND IN UNITS |
|---|---|---|
| XX1 | 5.84 | 1,200 |
| B66 | 5.40 | 1,110 |
| 3CPO | 1.12 | 896 |
| 33CP | 74.54 | 1,104 |
| R2D2 | 2.00 | 1,110 |
| RMS | 2.08 | 961 |

Which item(s) should be carefully controlled using a quantitative inventory technique, and what item(s) should not be closely controlled?

⦂ **12-37** The demand for barbeque grills has been fairly large in the past several years, and Home Supplies, Inc., usually orders new barbeque grills five times a year. It is estimated that the ordering cost is $60 per order. The carrying cost is $10 per grill per year. Furthermore, Home Supplies, Inc., has estimated that the stockout cost is $50 per unit. The reorder point is 650 units. Although the demand each year is high, it varies considerably. The demand during the lead time appears in the following table:

| DEMAND DURING LEAD TIME | PROBABILITY |
|---|---|
| 600 | 0.3 |
| 650 | 0.2 |
| 700 | 0.1 |
| 750 | 0.1 |
| 800 | 0.05 |
| 850 | 0.05 |
| 900 | 0.05 |
| 950 | 0.05 |
| 1,000 | 0.05 |
| 1,050 | 0.03 |
| 1,100 | 0.02 |
| | Total 1.00 |

The lead time is 12 working days. How much safety stock should Home Supplies, Inc., maintain?

⦂ **12-38** Dillard Travey receives 5,000 tripods annually from Quality Suppliers to meet his annual demand. Dillard runs a large photographic outlet, and the tripods are used primarily with 35-mm cameras. The ordering cost is $15 per order, and the carrying cost is 50 cents per unit per year. Quality is starting a new option for its customers. When an order is placed, Quality will ship one-third of the order every week for three weeks instead of shipping the entire order at one time. Weekly demand over the lead time is 100 tripods.

   (a) What is the order quantity if Dillard has the entire order shipped at one time?
   (b) What is the order quantity if Dillard has the order shipped over three weeks using the new option from Quality Suppliers, Inc.? To simplify your calculations, assume that the average inventory is equal to one-half of the maximum inventory level for Quality's new option.
   (c) Calculate the total cost for each option. What do you recommend?

**12-39** Linda Lechner has just been severely chastised for her inventory policy. See Problem 12-35. Sue Surrowski, her boss, believes that the service level should be either 95% or 98%. Compute the safety stock levels for a 95% and a 98% service level. Linda knows that the carrying cost of BX-5 is 50 cents per unit per year. Compute the carrying cost that is associated with a 90%, a 95%, and a 98% service level.

**12-40** Quality Suppliers, Inc., has decided to extend its shipping option. Refer to Problem 12-38 for details. Now, Quality Suppliers is offering to ship the amount ordered in five equal shipments once each week. It will take five weeks for this entire order to be received. What are the order quantity and total cost of this new shipping option?

**12-41** The inventory data for the six items that Xemex stocks is shown in the table at the bottom of this page. Lynn Robinson, Xemex's inventory manager, does not feel that all of the items can be controlled. What ordered quantities do you recommend for which inventory product(s)?

**12-42** Georgia Products offers the following discount schedule for its 4- by 8-foot sheets of good-quality plywood:

| ORDER | UNIT COST ($) |
|-------|---------------|
| 9 sheets or less | 18.00 |
| 10 to 50 sheets | 17.50 |
| More than 50 sheets | 17.25 |

Home Sweet Home Company orders plywood from Georgia Products. Home Sweet Home has an ordering cost of $45. The carrying cost is 20%, and the annual demand is 100 sheets. What do you recommend?

**12-43** Sunbright Citrus Products produces orange juice, grapefruit juice, and other citrus-related items. Sunbright obtains fruit concentrate from a cooperative in Orlando consisting of approximately 50 citrus growers. The cooperative will sell a minimum of 100 cans of fruit concentrate to citrus processors such as Sunbright. The cost per can is $9.90.

   Last year, a cooperative developed the Incentive Bonus Program (IBP) to give an incentive to their large customers to buy in quantity. Here is how it works: If 200 cans of concentrate are purchased, 10 cans of free concentrate are included in the deal. In addition, the names of the companies purchasing the concentrate are added to a drawing for a new personal computer. The personal computer has a value of about $3,000, and currently about 1,000 companies are eligible for this drawing. At 300 cans of concentrate, the cooperative will give away 30 free cans and will also place the company name in the drawing for the personal computer. When the quantity goes up to 400 cans of concentrate, 40 cans of concentrate will be given away free with the order. In addition, the company is also placed in a drawing for the personal computer and a free trip for two. The value of the trip for two is approximately $5,000. About 800 companies are expected to qualify and to be in the running for this trip.

   Sunbright estimates that its annual demand for fruit concentrate is 1,000 cans. In addition, the ordering cost is estimated to be $10.00, and the carrying cost is estimated to be 10%, or about $1.00 per unit. The firm is intrigued with the incentive bonus plan. If the company decides that it will keep the trip or the computer if they are won, what should it do?

**12-44** George Grim used to be an accounting professor at a state university. Several years ago, he started to develop seminars and programs for the CPA review course. The CPA review course is a course to help accounting students and others interested in passing the CPA exam. To develop an effective seminar, George developed a number of books and other related materials to help.

**Table for Problem 12-41**

| ITEM CODE | UNIT COST ($) | ANNUAL DEMAND (UNITS) | ORDERING COST ($) | CARRYING COST AS A PERCENTAGE OF UNIT COST |
|-----------|---------------|------------------------|--------------------|---------------------------------------------|
| 1 | 10.60 | 600 | 40 | 20 |
| 2 | 11.00 | 450 | 30 | 25 |
| 3 | 2.25 | 500 | 50 | 15 |
| 4 | 150.00 | 560 | 40 | 15 |
| 5 | 4.00 | 540 | 35 | 16 |
| 6 | 4.10 | 490 | 40 | 17 |

The main product was the CPA review manual developed by George. The manual was an instant success for his seminars and other seminars and courses across the country. Today, George spends most of his time refining and distributing this CPA review manual. The price of the manual is $45.95. George's total cost to manufacture and produce the manual is $32.90. George wants to avoid stockouts or develop a stockout policy that would be cost-effective. If there is a stockout on the CPA review manual, George loses the profit from the sale of the manual.

George has determined from past experience that the ROP from his printer is 400 units, assuming no safety stock. The question that George must answer is how much safety stock he should have as a buffer. On average, George places one order per year for the CPA review manual. The frequency of demand for the CPA review manuals during lead time is as follows:

| DEMAND | FREQUENCY | DEMAND | FREQUENCY |
|--------|-----------|--------|-----------|
| 300 | 1 | 600 | 4 |
| 350 | 2 | 650 | 4 |
| 400 | 2 | 700 | 3 |
| 450 | 3 | 750 | 2 |
| 500 | 4 | 800 | 2 |
| 550 | 5 | | |

George estimates that his carrying cost per unit per year is $7. What level of safety stock should George carry to minimize total inventory costs?

**: 12-45** George Lindsay sells disks that contain 25 software packages that perform a variety of financial functions, including net present value, internal rate of return, and other financial programs typically used by business students majoring in finance. Depending on the quantity ordered, George offers the following price discounts.

| QUANTITY ORDERED | | |
|------|------|------|
| FROM | TO | PRICE |
| 1 | 500 | $10.00 |
| 501 | 1,000 | 9.95 |
| 1,001 | 1,500 | 9.90 |
| 1,501 | 2,000 | 9.85 |

The annual demand is 2,000 units on average. His setup cost to produce the disks is $250. He estimates holding costs to be 10% of the price or about $1 per unit per year.

(a) What is the optimal number of disks to produce at a time?

(b) What is the impact of the following quantity-price schedule on the optimal order quantity?

| QUANTITY ORDERED | | |
|------|------|------|
| FROM | TO | PRICE |
| 1 | 500 | $10.00 |
| 501 | 1,000 | 9.99 |
| 1,001 | 1,500 | 9.98 |
| 1,501 | 2,000 | 9.97 |

**: 12-46** Demand during lead time for one brand of TV is normally distributed with a mean of 36 TVs and a standard deviation of 15 TVs. What safety stock should be carried for a 90% service level? What is the appropriate ROP?

**: 12-47** Based on available information, lead time demand for CD-ROM drives averages 50 units (normally distributed), with a standard deviation of 5 drives. Management wants a 97% service level.

(a) What value of $Z$ should be applied?
(b) How many drives should be carried as safety stock?
(c) What is the appropriate ROP?

**: 12-48** A product is delivered to Sridhar Garla's company once a year. The ROP, without safety stock, is 200 units. Carrying cost is $15 per unit per year, and the cost of a stockout is $70 per unit per year. Given the following demand probabilities during the reorder period, how much safety stock should be carried?

| DEMAND DURING REORDER PERIOD | PROBABILITY |
|--------|-----------|
| 0 | 0.2 |
| 100 | 0.2 |
| 200 | 0.2 |
| 300 | 0.2 |
| 400 | 0.2 |

**• 12-49** Barbara Flynn's company has compiled the following data on a small set of products:

| ITEM | ANNUAL DEMAND | UNIT COST |
|------|---------------|-----------|
| A | 100 | $300 |
| B | 75 | 100 |
| C | 50 | 50 |
| D | 200 | 100 |
| E | 150 | 75 |

Perform an ABC analysis on her data.

**: 12-50** Boreki Enterprise has 10 items in inventory as shown in the table on the next page. Theodore Boreki asks you, the recent operations management graduate, to divide these items into ABC classifications. What do you report back?

| ITEM | ANNUAL DEMAND | COST/UNIT |
|------|---------------|-----------|
| A2 | 3,000 | $50 |
| B8 | 4,000 | 12 |
| C7 | 1,500 | 45 |
| D1 | 6,000 | 10 |
| E9 | 1,000 | 20 |
| F3 | 500 | 500 |
| G2 | 300 | 1,500 |
| H2 | 600 | 20 |
| I5 | 1,750 | 10 |
| J8 | 2,500 | 5 |

**12-51** Judy Stamm opened a new beauty products retail store. There are numerous items in inventory, and Judy knows that there are costs associated with inventory. However, because her time is limited, she cannot carefully evaluate the inventory policy for all products. Judy wants to classify the items according to dollars invested in them. The following table provides information about the 10 items that she carries:

| ITEM NUMBER | UNIT COST | DEMAND (UNITS) |
|-------------|-----------|----------------|
| E102 | $4.00 | 800 |
| D23 | 8.00 | 1,200 |
| D27 | 3.00 | 700 |
| R02 | 2.00 | 1,000 |
| R19 | 8.00 | 200 |
| S107 | 6.00 | 500 |
| S123 | 1.00 | 1,200 |
| U11 | 7.00 | 800 |
| U23 | 1.00 | 1,500 |
| V75 | 4.00 | 1,500 |

Use ABC analysis to classify these items into categories A, B, and C.

## CASE STUDY

### Sturdivant Sound Systems

Sturdivant Sound Systems manufactures and sells stereo and CD sound systems in both console and component styles. All parts of the sound systems, with the exception of speakers, are produced in the Rochester, New York, plant. Speakers used in the assembly of Sturdivant's systems are purchased from Morris Electronics of Concord, New Hampshire.

Jason Pierce, purchasing agent for Sturdivant Sound Systems, submits a purchase requisition for the speakers once every four weeks. The company's annual requirements total 5,000 units (20 per working day), and the cost per unit is $60. (Sturdivant does not purchase in greater quantities because Morris Electronics, the supplier, does not offer quantity discounts.) Rarely does a shortage of speakers occur because Morris promises delivery within one week following receipt of a purchase requisition. (Total time between date of order and date of receipt is 10 days.)

Associated with the purchase of each shipment are procurement costs. These costs, which amount to $20 per order, include the costs of preparing the requisition, inspecting and storing the delivered goods, updating inventory records, and issuing a voucher and a check for payment. In addition to procurement costs, Sturdivant Sound Systems incurs inventory carrying costs, which include insurance, storage, handling, taxes, and so on. These costs equal $6 per unit per year.

Beginning in August of this year, management of Sturdivant Sound Systems will embark on a companywide cost control program in an attempt to improve its profits. One of the areas to be scrutinized closely for possible cost savings is inventory procurement.

### Discussion Questions

1. Compute the optimal order quantity.
2. Determine the appropriate ROP (in units).
3. Compute the cost savings that the company will realize if it implements the optimal inventory procurement decision.
4. Should procurement costs be considered a linear function of the number of orders?

*Source:* Professor Jerry Kinard, Western Carolina University.

## CASE STUDY

### Martin-Pullin Bicycle Corporation

Martin-Pullin Bicycle Corp. (MPBC), located in Dallas, is a wholesale distributor of bicycles and bicycle parts. Formed in 1981 by cousins Ray Martin and Jim Pullin, the firm's primary retail outlets are located within a 400-mile radius of the distribution center. These retail outlets receive the order from Martin-Pullin within two days after notifying the distribution center, provided that the stock is available. However, if an order is not fulfilled by the company, no backorder is placed; the retailers arrange to get their shipment from other distributors, and MPBC loses that amount of business.

The company distributes a wide variety of bicycles. The most popular mode, and the major source of revenue to the company, is the AirWing. MPBC receives all the models from a

**Demands for AirWing Model**

| MONTH | 2000 | 2001 | FORECAST FOR 2002 |
|-------|------|------|-------------------|
| January | 6 | 7 | 8 |
| February | 12 | 14 | 15 |
| March | 24 | 27 | 31 |
| April | 46 | 53 | 59 |
| May | 75 | 86 | 97 |
| June | 47 | 54 | 60 |
| July | 30 | 34 | 39 |
| August | 18 | 21 | 24 |
| September | 13 | 15 | 16 |
| October | 12 | 13 | 15 |
| November | 22 | 25 | 28 |
| December | 38 | 42 | 47 |
| Total | 343 | 391 | 439 |

single manufacturer overseas, and shipment takes as long as four weeks from the time an order is placed. With the cost of communication, paperwork, and customs clearance included, MPBC estimates that each time an order is placed, it incurs a cost of $65. The purchase price paid by MPBC, per bicycle, is roughly 60% of the suggested retail price for all the styles available, and the inventory carrying cost is 1% per month (12% per year) of the purchase price paid by MPBC. The retail price (paid by the customers) for the AirWing is $170 per bicycle.

MPBC is interested in making the inventory plan for 2002. The firm wants to maintain a 95% service level with its customers to minimize the losses on the lost orders. The data collected for the past two years are summarized in the table on the left. A forecast for AirWing model sales in the upcoming year 2002 has been developed and will be used to make an inventory plan for MPBC.

### Discussion Questions

1. Develop an inventory plan to help MPBC.
2. Discuss ROPs and total costs.
3. How can you address demand that is not at the level of the planning horizon?

***Source:*** Professor Kala Chand Seal, Loyola Marymount University .

## INTERNET CASE STUDIES

See our Internet home page at **www.prenhall.com/render** for these additional case studies: (1) Professional Video Management; (2) Drake Radio; (3) La Place Power; and (4) Western Ranchman Outfitters.

## BIBLIOGRAPHY

Bernard, Paul. "Are Your Customers Getting Better Service Than You Planned to Provide?" *APICS—The Performance Advantage* (July 1997): 30–32.

Bowers, Melissa R. and Anurag Agarwal. "Lower In-Process Inventories and Better on Time Performance at Tanner Companies, Inc," *Interfaces* 25, 4 (July–August 1995): 30–43.

Denton, D. Keith. "Top Management's Role in Inventory Control," *Industrial Engineering* (August 1994): 26–27.

Edds, Daniel. "The Real Costs of Quantity Discounts," *School Planning and Management* (March 1998): 14.

Emmons, Hamilton et al. "The Role of Return Policies in Pricing and Inventory Decisions for Catalogue Goods," *Management Science* (February 1998): 276–283.

Gould, Eppen et al. "Backup Agreements in Fashion Buying," *Management Science* (November 1997): 1469–1484.

Greis, Noel. "Assessing Service Level Targets in Production and Inventory Planning," *Decision Sciences* 25, 1 (January–February 1994): 15–40.

Katok, E., T. Serrander, and M. Wennstrom. "Setup Reduction Through Process Improvement in Aluminum Can Manufacturing,"

*Production and Inventory Management Journal* 29, 4 (fourth quarter 1998): 77–82.

Landvater, D. V. *World Class Production and Inventory Management.* Newburg, NH: Oliver Wight Publications (1997).

Lieberman, M. B., S. Helper, and L. Demeester. "The Empirical Determinants of Inventory Levels in High-Volume Manufacturing," *Production and Operations Management*, 1 (spring 1999): 44–55.

Millet, Ido. "How to Find Inventory by Not Looking," *Interfaces* (March 1994): 69–75.

Sandvig, J. C. "Calculating Safety Stock," *IIE Solutions* 30, 12 (December 1998): 28–29.

Smock, Doug. "Games Tip the Scale at Milton Bradley," *Plastics World* (March 1997): 22–26.

Sox, Charles et al. "Coordinating Production and Inventory to Improve Service," *Management Science* (September 1997): 1189–1197.

van der Duyn Schouten, Frank et al. "The Value of Supplier Information to Improve Management of a Retailer's Inventory," *Decision Sciences* 25, 1 (January–February 1994): 1–14.

# APPENDICES

# APPENDIX A: USEFUL EXCEL COMMANDS AND PROCEDURES FOR INSTALLING EXCELMODULES

## A.1   INTRODUCTION

Excel is Microsoft Office's spreadsheet application program. A *spreadsheet* lets you embed hidden formulas that perform calculations on visible data. The main document (or file) used in Excel to store and manipulate data is called a *workbook*. A workbook can consist of a number of worksheets, each of which can be used to list and analyze data. Excel allows you to enter and modify data on several worksheets simultaneously. You can also perform calculations based on data from multiple worksheets and/or workbooks.

This appendix provides a brief overview of some basic Excel commands and procedures. It also discusses how add-ins, such as Solver and Data Analysis, can be installed and enabled in Excel. Finally, it describes the installation and usage procedures for ExcelModules, a software package included in the CD-ROM that accompanies this text. We use ExcelModules to develop and solve decision models for queuing (Chapter 9), forecasting (Chapter 11), and inventory control (Chapter 12).

In addition to the extensive help features built into Excel, there are thousands of online tutorials available to help you learn Excel. Many of these are quite comprehensive in their content. To get a current listing of these online tutorials, simply type in "Excel Tutorial" in the search box of your browser.

## A.2   GETTING STARTED

Once Excel has been installed, you can start the program by either clicking Start|Programs|Microsoft Excel (in Microsoft Windows 95 or later) or double-clicking any Excel workbook that already exists in your computer. Depending on how you start Excel, it either opens the existing workbook or automatically creates an empty workbook named Book1. The number of worksheets in the new workbook is set in the options (click Tools|Options| General to change this number). You can easily add more worksheets (click Insert| Worksheet) or remove existing ones (click Edit|Delete|Sheet). The maximum number of worksheets in a workbook is 255. The sheet tabs at the bottom of each worksheet help you identify and move to each worksheet in your workbook. You can rename any sheet by double-clicking on its tab and typing in the new name.

### Organization of a Worksheet

A worksheet consists of columns and rows, as shown in Program A.1. Columns are identified by letters (e.g., A, B, C), and rows are identified by numbers (e.g., 1, 2, 3). Where a row and a column intersect is known as a cell. Each cell has a reference, based on the intersection of the row and column. For example, the reference of the cell at the intersection of column B and row 7 is referred to as cell B7 (as shown in Program A.1).

A *cell* is the fundamental storage unit for Excel data, including both values and labels. A *value* is a number or a hidden formula that performs a calculation, and a *label* is a heading or some explanatory text. We can enter different types of entries (e.g., text, numbers, formulas, dates, and times) into cells.

### Navigating Through a Worksheet

You can navigate through a worksheet using either the mouse or the keys on your keyboard. To select a cell using the mouse, click the cell (e.g., B7, as shown in Program A.1). To move anywhere on a worksheet, you can also use the arrow keys, or the Page Up and Page Down keys, on the keyboard.

**PROGRAM A.1**    **General Layout of an Excel Worksheet**

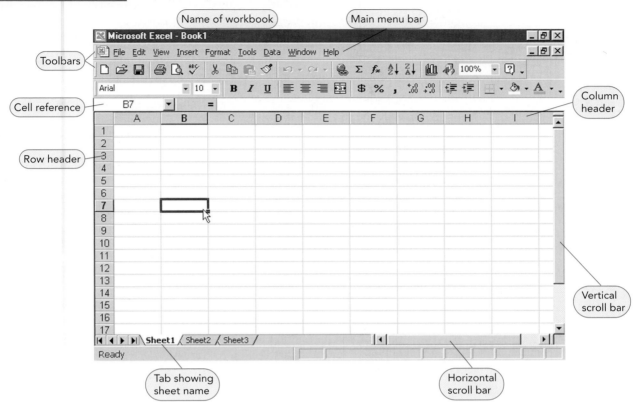

You can also use the Go To menu option to navigate between cells. This option is useful if you want to modify the contents of a cell. To go to a specific cell, click Edit|Go To. In the Go To dialog box, you can even click the Special button to go to cells with special features. For example, you can choose to go to cells with comments, to blank cells, or to the last cell in the worksheet.

## Toolbars

A toolbar consists of icons that provide shortcuts to common tasks. Excel has several tool-bars built in for your use. By default, the Standard and Formatting toolbars are visible when you open Excel. To view other toolbars (e.g., Drawing, Charts), click View|Toolbars and then select the desired toolbar(s). Most of the icons in Excel's toolbars are similar to the ones in other Microsoft Office programs (e.g., PowerPoint, Word). You can customize any toolbar by clicking View|Toolbars|Customize.

**Standard Toolbar**  The Standard toolbar, shown in Program A.2, includes shortcuts to many common file-related tasks, such as saving or printing.

**PROGRAM A.2**    **Standard Toolbar in Excel**

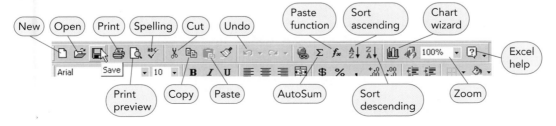

The following list indicates the tasks associated with some of the icons on this toolbar, along with the corresponding command to use in Excel's main menu bar. To see the specific task associated with an icon, you can move the cursor briefly over that icon to see an on-screen description of that icon (as shown in Program A.2 for the Save icon).

1. *New.* Open a file (File|New).
2. *Open.* Open an existing file (File|Open).
3. *Save.* Save the current file (File|Save).
4. *Print.* Print the current worksheet (File|Print).
5. *Print Preview.* View the current worksheet as it would appear when printed (File|Print Preview).
6. *Spelling.* Check the spelling of the contents in the selected cells.
7. *Cut.* Cut the contents of the selected set of cells (Edit|Cut).
8. *Copy.* Copy the contents of the selected set of cells to the clipboard (Edit|Copy).
9. *Paste.* Paste the cut or copied contents to the cells starting with the current location of the cursor (Edit|Paste).
10. *Undo.* Undo the last change made on a worksheet (Edit|Undo). You can access and undo the last 16 actions that you have done.
11. *AutoSum.* Add the values in a range of cells. (Excel guesses the range based on the current location of the cursor.) You can edit the selected range if necessary.
12. *Paste Function.* Provides a list of functions available in Excel and descriptions of each function (Insert|Function). See Section A.4 for more details.
13. *Sort Ascending.* Sorts a selected series of numbers from least to greatest or a selected series of words in alphabetical order (Data|Sort).
14. *Sort Descending.* Sorts a selected series of numbers from greatest to least or a selected series of words in reverse alphabetical order (Data|Sort).
15. *Chart Wizard.* Takes you through a step-by-step procedure for creating different types of charts using the data in a workbook (Insert|Chart).
16. *Zoom.* Vary the zoom level of the current worksheet to make cell entries appear bigger or smaller (View|Zoom).
17. *Microsoft Excel Help.* Invoke the Office Assistant for help (Help|Microsoft Excel Help).

**Formatting Toolbar**  The Formatting toolbar, shown in Program A.3, includes shortcuts to many frequently used formatting operations, such as font sizes and cell alignment.

**PROGRAM A.3**    **Formatting Toolbar in Excel**

The following list indicates the tasks associated with some of the main icons on this toolbar, along with the corresponding command in Excel's main menu bar. To see the specific task associated with an icon, you can move the cursor briefly over that icon to see an on-screen description of that icon (as shown in Program A.3 for the Bold icon).

1. *Font.* Gives a list of available fonts (Format|Cells|Font).

2. *Font Size.* Gives a list of available font sizes (Format|Cells|Font).

3. *Bold.* Toggles the entries in the selected cell between bold and nonbold (Format|Cells|Font).

4. *Italics.* Toggles the entries in the selected cells between italics and nonitalics (Format|Cells|Font).

5. *Underline.* Toggles the entries in the selected cells between underlined and nonunderlined (Format|Cells|Font).

6. *Align Left.* Left justifies the contents of the selected cells.

7. *Center.* Centers the contents of the selected cells.

8. *Align Right.* Right justifies the contents of the selected cells.

9. *Merge and Center.* Select the group of cells you want to merge and center, and then click the icon. Note that if you merge several cells in a row, only the data in the first cell will be retained. The same is true for columns.

10. *Currency Style.* Converts the numerical values of the selected cells to appear in currency format.

11. *Percent Style.* Converts the numerical values of the selected cell to appear in percentage format.

12. *Increase Decimal.* Increases the number of decimal points shown for the numerical values in the selected cells.

13. *Decrease Decimal.* Decreases the number of decimal points shown for the numerical values in the selected cells.

14. *Borders.* Opens a box that can be used to place different types of borders around the selected cells.

15. *Fill Color.* Fills the selected cells with the selected color. (Default is no fill.)

16. *Font Color.* Converts the color of the font to the selected color. (Default is black.)

## Office Assistant

If you are unsure about how to perform any action in Excel (or any other Microsoft Office program), you can use the Office Assistant to help you. The Office Assistant can display tips on how to use different Excel features or provide help on the specific task you are performing.

To open the Office Assistant, click the Help icon on the Standard toolbar (or click Help|Microsoft Excel Help). The Office Assistant is a cartoon character selected during the installation process. You can change settings for the Office Assistant by clicking the Options button. For example, you can specify that the Office Assistant displays tips when you launch an application.

You can use common constructions to query the Office Assistant. For example, you can type, "How do I format a cell?" and click the Search button. The Office Assistant then responds with links to various help topics. If none of the suggestions match your query, click See more. When you have located the response that best matches your query, click the item. The help text is then displayed.

## A.3 WORKING WITH WORKSHEETS

To enter data or information in a worksheet, first click on the cell in which you want to enter the data. Then, simply type in the data. You can enter numbers, text, dates, times, or formulas. (These are discussed in Section A.4.) When you are done, hit enter, and the next cell in the column is automatically selected.

**Selecting a Group of Adjacent Cells** Click the first cell to be selected. Hold down the Shift key and click the last cell to be selected. All cells in between these two cells will automatically be selected. Alternatively, after clicking the first cell, hold the left mouse button down and drag until you have selected all the cells you need.

**Selecting a Group of Nonadjacent Cells** Left-click the first cell to be selected. Hold down the Ctrl key and click each of the other cells to be selected. Only the cells you clicked will be selected.

**Selecting an Entire Row or Column** Click the header (number) of the row that you want to select in its entirety. To select more than one entire row, keep either the Shift or the Ctrl key pressed (as discussed in the preceding item for selecting cells), depending on whether the rows are adjacent or nonadjacent. You can use a similar procedure to select one or more columns in their entirety.

**Editing Data** To edit the existing information in a cell, double-click the cell to be edited (or click once on the cell and press the F2 function button on your keyboard). You can now simply type over or modify the contents as desired.

**Clearing Data** To clear the data in selected cells, first select the cells that you want to clear. Next, hit the Delete button on your keyboard.

### Working with Rows and Columns

There are several operations that you can perform with the rows and columns in a worksheet. Some of these are as follows.

**Inserting Rows or Columns** To insert a new row, click on the row header above where you want the new row to be. Then, click Insert|Row. To insert a column, click on the column header to the left of where you want the new column to be. Then, click Insert|Column. To insert multiple rows or columns, select multiple row or column headers before clicking Insert.

**Deleting Rows or Columns** To delete a row or column, select the row(s) or column(s) that you want to delete. Then click Edit|Delete.

**Changing Column Width** To change the width of a column, place the cursor on the right edge of the column header that you want to change. The cursor will change to a plus sign with arrows pointing to the left and right. Click and hold the left mouse button and drag to the desired width. Double-clicking will automatically adjust the column width to the widest entry in the column.

**Changing Row Height** To change the height of a row, move the mouse to the bottom edge of the row heading. The cursor will change to a plus sign with arrows on the top and bottom. Click and drag to the new desired height. Double-clicking will automatically adjust the row height to the tallest entry in the row.

**Hiding Columns or Rows** To hide a row (or a set of rows), first select the rows to hide. Then, click Format|Row|Hide (or right-click the mouse and select the Hide option). You can use a similar procedure to hide columns (click Format|Column|Hide).

**PROGRAM A.4**

**Options for the Paste
Special Feature in Excel**

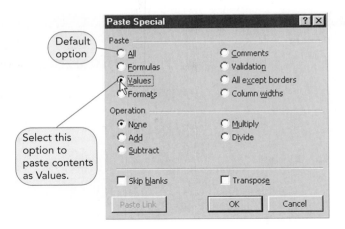

Default option

Select this option to paste contents as Values.

**Unhiding Columns or Rows**  To unhide a hidden row (or a set of hidden rows), first select the row before and after the hidden row. Then, click Format|Row|Unhide (or right-click the mouse and select the Unhide option). You can use a similar procedure to unhide hidden columns (click Format|Column|Unhide).

## Formatting Worksheets

Once you have created a worksheet, Excel has an extensive set of options you can use to format the appearance of various cells. Some of these options follow.

**Changing Appearance of Numbers in Cells**  To change the appearance of numbers in cells, first select the cells that you want to format. Then, click on Format|Cells|Number and select the desired format (e.g., currency, numerical, percentage, fraction).

**Alignment and Text Control**  You can adjust how an entry is positioned within a cell. To do so, select the cells that you want to align and then click Format|Cells|Alignment. You can now select the desired options (e.g., word wrap, cell orientation).

**Paste Special**  A useful feature of the paste operation in Excel is the Paste Special operation. After cutting or copying the content of selected cells, you can invoke this feature by clicking Edit|Paste Special. The window shown in Program A.4 is displayed. You can now select any of the choices including the following:

1.  *All.* The formulas and formats are pasted in the new locations.
2.  *Formulas.* Only the formula is pasted in the new locations (i.e., without the formats). The values in the new cells depend on the cell references in the formulas.
3.  *Values.* Only the values of the selected cells are pasted in the new locations (i.e., without the formulas or formats).
4.  *Formats.* Only the formats of the selected cells are pasted in the new location.

You can also use the Paste Special feature to perform mathematical operations (e.g., adding the contents of selected cells) before pasting.

## A.4  USING FORMULAS AND FUNCTIONS

Formulas allow you to perform calculations on your worksheet data. A formula must start with an "equal to" (=) sign in Excel. To enter a formula, click the cell where you want to enter the formula. Next type an "=" sign, followed by the formula. A formula can consist of

**PROGRAM A.5**

**Functions Available in Excel**

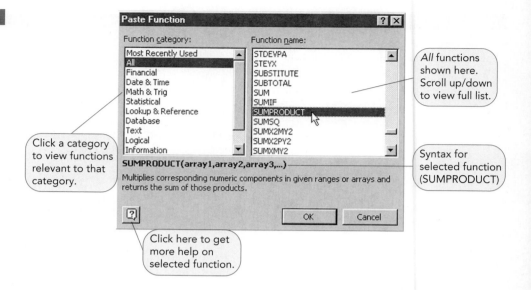

mathematical operations involving numbers or cell references that point to cells with numerical values. After typing in a formula, press Enter to perform the calculation. By default, Excel will automatically recalculate the formula if you change any of the input values used in the formula.

Functions are formulas that are already built into Excel. To see the full list of built-in functions in Excel, click Insert|Function (or the Paste Function icon on the Standard toolbar shown on page 565). The list is shown in Program A.5. You can view subsets of these functions by selecting the category (e.g., Statistical, Financial) in the left pane. The functions relevant for that category then appear in the right pane.

When you select a specific function, the syntax for that function is displayed at the bottom of the window. For example, Program A.5 shows the syntax for the SUMPRODUCT function. For more detailed help on the selected function, click the Help button (shown as a "?") in the bottom left of the window.

When using functions in Excel, you can prefix the function with an "=" sign and directly type in the function using the required syntax. Alternatively, you can select the cell in which you want to use a particular function. Then, you can call up the list of available functions (as described previously) and select the desired function. A window that shows the required input entries for the selected function is now displayed to guide you through the creation of the cell entry using the function.

## Errors in Using Formulas and Functions

Sometimes, when you use a function or formula, the resulting output indicates an error in your entry. The following is a list of common errors when using formulas or functions, and their possible causes:

1. #DIV/0! indicates that the formula or function involves division by zero.

2. #Name? indicates that the formula or function is not recognized by Excel. This is usually caused by a typographical error.

3. #VALUE indicates that one or more cell references used in a formula or function are invalid.

4. #### indicates that the cell is not wide enough to display the number. This can be easily remedied by increasing the width of the cell.

## A.5 PRINTING WORKSHEETS

If you wish to print the entire worksheet using the print defaults, you can go directly to the print menu by clicking either File|Print or the Print icon on the Standard toolbar. Alternatively, you can make modifications to your printed output, as discussed in the following sections.

**Setting the Print Area** If you wish to print only a portion of the current worksheet, first select the desired region of cells to print. Then click Print|Print Area|Set Print Area. You can clear a selected print area by clicking Print|Print Area|Clear Print Area.

**Print Preview** Before printing a worksheet, it is a good idea to preview what your printer output would look like. To preview a worksheet, click on Print|Print Preview (or click the Print Preview icon on the Standard toolbar). Program A.6 shows the options available in the Print Preview window.

**Setting Print Margins** To change the print margins, go into Print Preview and then click Margins. Position the mouse over the margin handle (i.e., the lines indicating the margins). Click and drag the margins to the desired position. Or click File|Page Setup|Margins and type in the desired margins.

**Page Breaks** To insert a page break, first click on the row or column where you want the page break to be. For rows, the break will be above the selected row. For columns, it will be to the left of the selected column. Then, click Insert|Page Break. To remove an existing page break, first select the rows (or columns) on either side of the page break. Then, click Insert|Remove Page Break.

**Centering Data on a Page** To center data on a page, click File|Page Setup|Margins (or click Setup|Margins from within the Print Preview options). Check the boxes corresponding to whether you want the data centered horizontally, vertically, or both.

### PROGRAM A.6

**Options Available in the Print Preview Window**

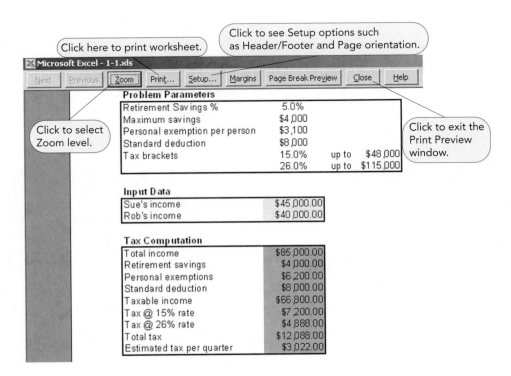

**Inserting a Header or Footer** To add a header and/or a footer, click File|Page Setup|Header/Footer (or click Setup|Header/Footer from within the Print Preview option). To add a header, click on Custom Header. To add a footer, click on Custom Footer. When you have selected either option, you get another screen where you can enter the text and format the header or footer.

**Printing the Worksheet** After making all adjustments, to print a worksheet you can do one of two things: You can either click File|Print or you can click Print from within the Print Preview option.

## A.6 INSTALLING AND ENABLING EXCEL ADD-INS

Add-ins are special programs that are designed to perform specific tasks in Excel. Although Excel includes several add-ins, we focus here on only two add-ins, Solver and Data Analysis, that are useful in decision modeling.

Both Solver and Data Analysis are included with all recent versions of Excel. However, if you choose to install Excel using the default options, only Data Analysis is installed during the installation process. To install Solver, you need to change the installation defaults for Excel by clicking on the Excel options during the installation process and then choosing Add-Ins. Make sure the box next to the Solver option is checked. Note that the option to install the Analysis ToolPak (i.e., Data Analysis) is already checked by default.

Even after these add-ins have been installed, they need to be enabled (or switched on) in order for them to be available in Excel. To check if these add-ins have been enabled, start Excel and click Tools. If you see Data Analysis and/or Solver as menu options, the add-in has been enabled on that personal computer. However, if you do not see either (or both) add-ins, click Tools|Add-Ins.

The list of available add-ins is now displayed, as shown in Program A.7. To enable Data Analysis, make sure the boxes next to Analysis ToolPak and Analysis ToolPak—VBA are both checked. Likewise, to enable Solver, make sure the box next to Solver Add-In is checked.

Depending on the boxes you checked, the corresponding add-in should now be shown as an option under the Tools menu in Excel. For example, Program A.8 shows that both Data Analysis and Solver add-ins have been enabled. From here onward, these add-ins will be available each time you start Excel on that personal computer. To access either add-in, simply click Tools and select the appropriate choice in the menu.

**List of Available Add-Ins**

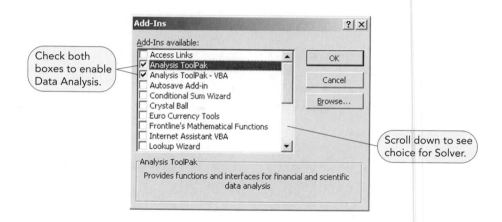

**PROGRAM A.8**

**Tools Submenu Showing
Enabled Add-Ins**

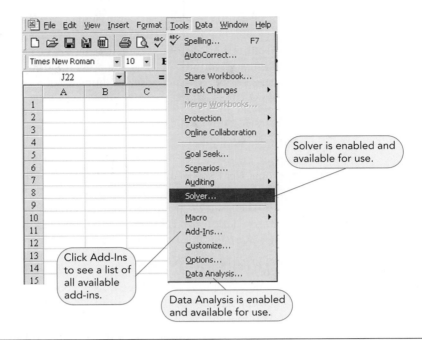

Solver is enabled and available for use.

Click Add-Ins to see a list of all available add-ins.

Data Analysis is enabled and available for use.

## A.7  INSTALLING AND USING EXCELMODULES

Your CD-ROM includes a customized Excel add-in called ExcelModules. This program has been designed to help you to better learn and understand decision models in queuing (Chapter 9), forecasting (Chapter 11), and inventory control (Chapter 12). Program A.9 shows the modules available for each topic, as well as the submodules available for forecasting models. Instructions for using each submodule in ExcelModules are provided at appropriate places in Chapters 9, 11, and 12 of this book.

To run ExcelModules on your personal computer, you must have Excel version 5 or better installed. To install ExcelModules, follow these steps:

1. Insert the CD into the CD-ROM drive.
2. Click Start|Run|Browse in Windows 95/98/Me/2000/XP.
3. Change to the ExcelModules folder on the CD-ROM.
4. Run the file ExcelModules.exe (by double-clicking the file).
5. Follow the setup instructions on the screen.

**PROGRAM A.9**       **Modules and Forecasting Models Submodules in ExcelModules**

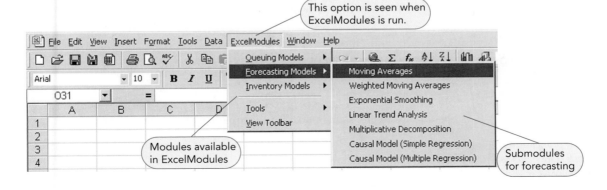

This option is seen when ExcelModules is run.

Modules available in ExcelModules

Submodules for forecasting

Default values have been assigned for most installation parameters in the setup program, but you can change them if you like. For example, the default values are that the program will be installed to a directory on the C: drive named C:\Program Files\ExcelModules and that the program group will be named ExcelModules. Generally speaking, it is only necessary to simply click Next each time that the installation program asks you a question.

### The Program Group

Under Windows 95/98/Me/2000/XP, a program group with three options is added to the Start menu. You can start the program by clicking the ExcelModules icon in the program group. Help is available from within the program, but if you want to read some information about the program without starting it first, use the ExcelModules Help icon.

The program group also contains an icon named Prentice-Hall Web Page. If you have an association for HTM files with a Web browser (e.g., Microsoft Internet Explorer, Netscape), this link will point you to program upgrades.

### Starting the Program

If you do not have Excel already open, you can click on Start|Programs|ExcelModules and then the ExcelModules icon in order to start the program. Alternatively, the installation program would have created a shortcut and placed it on your desktop. This shortcut can be used to start ExcelModules directly by double-clicking on it. When ExcelModules is started, it automatically starts Excel also.

If you already have Excel open, then simply load the file ExcelModules.xla, which is in the directory where the software was installed. (The default is C:\Program Files\ExcelModules if you did not change this at the time of installation.)

It is also possible to install ExcelModules as an add-in. This will load the program each time that you start Excel. To do this, start Excel first. Then, go to Tools|Add-Ins|Browse and select the file named ExcelModules.xla.

ExcelModules serves two purposes in the learning process. First, it can help you solve homework problems. You enter the appropriate data, and the program provides numerical solutions. In addition, ExcelModules allows you to note the Excel formulas used to develop solutions and modify them to deal with a wider variety of problems. This "open" approach allows you to observe, understand, and even change the formulas underlying the Excel calculations, conveying Excel's power as a decision modeling tool.

### Technical Support

If you have technical problems with ExcelModules that your instructor cannot answer, send an e-mail message to Professor Howard Weiss at hweiss@sbm.temple.edu. Be sure to include the name of the program (ExcelModules), the version of the program (click Tools|About to check the version number), the module in which the problem is occurring, and a detailed explanation of the problem. Attach the data file for which the problem occurs (if appropriate).

## APPENDIX B: PROBABILITY CONCEPTS AND APPLICATIONS

 **FUNDAMENTAL CONCEPTS**

*People often misuse the two basic rules of probabilities by making such statements as "I'm 110% sure we're going to win the big game."*

There are two basic statements about the mathematics of *probability*:

1.  The probability, $P$, of any event or state of nature occurring is greater than or equal to 0 and less than or equal to 1. That is,

$$0 \leq P(\text{event}) \leq 1$$

(B-1)

A probability of 0 indicates that an event is never expected to occur. A probability of 1 means that an event is always expected to occur.

2.  The sum of the simple probabilities for all possible outcomes of an activity must equal 1. Both of these concepts are illustrated in Example 1.

**Example 1: Two Laws of Probability**  Demand for white latex paint at Diversey Paint and Supply has always been 0, 1, 2, 3, or 4 gallons per day. (There are no other possible outcomes and when one occurs, no other can.) Over the past 200 working days, the owner notes the following frequencies of demand:

| QUANTITY DEMANDED (GALLONS) | NUMBER OF DAYS |
|:---:|:---:|
| 0 | 40 |
| 1 | 80 |
| 2 | 50 |
| 3 | 20 |
| 4 | 10 |
| | Total 200 |

If this past distribution is a good indicator of future sales, we can find the probability of each possible outcome occurring in the future by converting the data into percentages of the total:

| QUANTITY DEMANDED | PROBABILITY |
|:---:|:---:|
| 0 | 0.20 (= 40/200) |
| 1 | 0.40 (= 80/200) |
| 2 | 0.25 (= 50/200) |
| 3 | 0.10 (= 20/200) |
| 4 | 0.05 (= 10/200) |
| | Total 1.00 (= 200/200) |

Thus the probability that sales are 2 gallons of paint on any given day is $P(2 \text{ gallons}) = 0.25 = 25\%$. The probability of any level of sales must be greater than or equal to 0 and less than or equal to 1. Since 0, 1, 2, 3, and 4 gallons exhaust all possible events or outcomes, the sum of their probability values must equal 1.

## Types of Probability

There are two different ways to determine probability: the *objective approach* and the *subjective approach.*

**Objective Probability**  Example 1 provides us with an illustration of objective probability assessment. The probability of any paint demand level is the *relative frequency* of occurrence of that demand in a large number of trial observations (200 days in this case). In general:

$$P(\text{event}) = \frac{\text{number of occurrences of the event}}{\text{total number of trials or outcomes}}$$

Objective probability can also be set using what is called the *classical* or *logical* method. Without performing a series of trials, we can often logically determine what the probabilities of various events should be. For example, the probability of tossing a fair coin once and getting a head is

$$P(\text{head}) = \frac{1}{2} \quad \begin{array}{l} \longleftarrow \textit{number of ways of getting a head} \\ \longleftarrow \textit{number of possible outcomes (head or tail)} \end{array}$$

Similarly, the probability of drawing a spade out of a deck of 52 playing cards can be logically set as

$$P(\text{spade}) = \frac{13}{52} \quad \begin{array}{l} \longleftarrow \textit{number of chances of drawing a spade} \\ \longleftarrow \textit{number of possible outcomes} \end{array}$$

$$= \frac{1}{4} = 0.25 = 25\%$$

*Where do probabilities come from? Sometimes they are subjective and based on personal experiences. Other times they are objectively based on logical observations such as the roll of a die. Often, probabilities are derived from historical data.*

**Subjective Probability**  When logic and past history are not appropriate, probability values can be assessed *subjectively*. The accuracy of subjective probabilities depends on the experience and judgment of the person making the estimates. A number of probability values cannot be determined unless the subjective approach is used. What is the probability that the price of gasoline will be more than $4 in the next few years? What is the probability that our economy will be in a severe depression in 2007? What is the probability that you will be president of a major corporation within 20 years?

There are several methods for making subjective probability assessments. Opinion polls can be used to help in determining subjective probabilities for possible election returns and potential political candidates. In some cases, experience and judgment must be used in making subjective assessments of probability values. A production manager, for example, might believe that the probability of manufacturing a new product without a single defect is 0.85. In the Delphi method, a panel of experts is assembled to make their predictions of the future. This approach is discussed in Chapter 11.

## B.2    MUTUALLY EXCLUSIVE AND COLLECTIVELY EXHAUSTIVE EVENTS

Events are said to be *mutually exclusive* if only one of the events can occur on any one trial. They are called *collectively exhaustive* if the list of outcomes includes every possible outcome. Many common experiences involve events that have both of these properties. In tossing a coin, for example, the possible outcomes are a head or a tail. Since both of them cannot occur on any one toss, the outcomes head and tail are mutually exclusive. Since obtaining a head and a tail represent every possible outcome, they are also collectively exhaustive.

**Example 2: Rolling a Die**  Rolling a die is a simple experiment that has six possible outcomes, each listed in the following table with its corresponding probability:

| OUTCOME OF ROLL | PROBABILITY |
|:---:|:---:|
| 1 | $\frac{1}{6}$ |
| 2 | $\frac{1}{6}$ |
| 3 | $\frac{1}{6}$ |
| 4 | $\frac{1}{6}$ |
| 5 | $\frac{1}{6}$ |
| 6 | $\frac{1}{6}$ |
| | Total 1 |

These events are both mutually exclusive (on any roll, only one of the six events can occur) and are also collectively exhaustive (one of them must occur and hence they total in probability to 1).

**Example 3: Drawing a Card**  You are asked to draw one card from a deck of 52 playing cards. Using a logical probability assessment, it is easy to set some of the relationships, such as

$$P(\text{drawing a 7}) = \frac{4}{52} = \frac{1}{13}$$

$$P(\text{drawing a heart}) = \frac{13}{52} = \frac{1}{4}$$

We also see that these events (drawing a 7 and drawing a heart) are *not* mutually exclusive since a 7 of hearts can be drawn. They are also *not* collectively exhaustive since there are other cards in the deck besides 7s and hearts.

You can test your understanding of these concepts by going through the following cases:

*This table is especially useful in helping to understand the difference between mutually exclusive and collectively exhaustive.*

| DRAWS | MUTUALLY EXCLUSIVE? | COLLECTIVELY EXHAUSTIVE? |
|---|---|---|
| 1. Draw a spade and a club | Yes | No |
| 2. Draw a face card and a number card | Yes | Yes |
| 3. Draw an ace and a 3 | Yes | No |
| 4. Draw a club and a nonclub | Yes | Yes |
| 5. Draw a 5 and a diamond | No | No |
| 6. Draw a red card and a diamond | No | No |

## Adding Mutually Exclusive Events

Often we are interested in whether one event *or* a second event will occur. When these two events are mutually exclusive, the law of addition is simply as follows:

$$P(\text{event } A \text{ or event } B) = P(\text{event } A) + P(\text{event } B)$$

or more briefly,

$$P(A \text{ or } B) = P(A) + P(B) \tag{B-2}$$

For example, we just saw that the events of drawing a spade or drawing a club out of a deck of cards are mutually exclusive. Since $P(\text{spade}) = \frac{13}{52}$ and $P(\text{club}) = \frac{13}{52}$, the probability of drawing either a spade or a club is

$$P(\text{spade or club}) = P(\text{spade}) + P(\text{club})$$
$$= \frac{13}{52} + \frac{13}{52}$$
$$= \frac{26}{52} = \frac{1}{2} = 0.50 = 50\%$$

The *Venn diagram* in Figure B.1 depicts the probability of the occurrence of mutually exclusive events.

## Law of Addition for Events That Are Not Mutually Exclusive

When two events are not mutually exclusive, Equation B-2 must be modified to account for double counting. The correct equation reduces the probability by subtracting the chance of both events occurring together:

$$P(\text{event } A \text{ or event } B) = P(\text{event } A) + P(\text{event } B)$$
$$- P(\text{event } A \text{ and event } B \text{ both occurring})$$

**FIGURE B.1**

**Addition Law for Events that Are Mutually Exclusive**

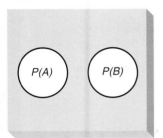

$P(A \text{ or } B) = P(A) + P(B)$

*The formula for adding events that are not mutually exclusive is $P(A \text{ or } B) = P(A) + P(B) - P(A \text{ and } B)$. Do you understand why we subtract $P(A \text{ and } B)$?*

**Addition Law for Events that Are Not Mutually Exclusive**

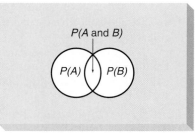

$$P(A \text{ or } B) = P(A) + P(B) - P(A \text{ and } B)$$

This can be expressed in shorter form as

$$P(A \text{ or } B) = P(A) + P(B) - P(A \text{ and } B) \tag{B-3}$$

Figure B.2 illustrates this concept of subtracting the probability of outcomes that are common to both events. When events are mutually exclusive, the area of overlap, called the *intersection*, is 0, as shown in Figure B.1.

Let us consider the events drawing a 5 and drawing a diamond out of the card deck. These events are not mutually exclusive, so Equation B-3 must be applied to compute the probability of either a 5 or a diamond being drawn:

$$\begin{aligned}
P(\text{five } or \text{ diamond}) &= P(\text{five}) + P(\text{diamond}) \\
&\quad - P(\text{five } and \text{ diamond}) \\
&= \tfrac{4}{52} + \tfrac{13}{52} - \tfrac{1}{52} \\
&= \tfrac{16}{52} = \tfrac{4}{13}
\end{aligned}$$

## B.3   STATISTICALLY INDEPENDENT EVENTS

Events can either be *independent* or *dependent*. When they are *independent*, the occurrence of one event has no effect on the probability of occurrence of the second event. Let us examine four sets of events and determine which are independent:

1.   **(a)** Your education   ⎫  *Dependent events.*
     **(b)** Your income level ⎭  Can you explain why?

2.   **(a)** Draw a jack of hearts from a full 52-card deck ⎫  *Independent events*
     **(b)** Draw a jack of clubs from a full 52-card deck ⎭

3.   **(a)** Chicago Cubs win the National League pennant ⎫  *Dependent events*
     **(b)** Chicago Cubs win the World Series ⎭

4.   **(a)** Snow in Santiago, Chile ⎫  *Independent events*
     **(b)** Rain in Tel Aviv, Israel ⎭

The three types of probability under both statistical independence and statistical dependence are (1) marginal, (2) joint, and (3) conditional. When events are independent, these three are very easy to compute, as we shall see.

A *marginal* (or a *simple*) *probability* is just the probability of an event occurring. For example, if we toss a fair die, the marginal probability of a 2 landing face up is $P(\text{die is a } 2) = \tfrac{1}{6} = 0.166$. Because each separate toss is an independent event (i.e., what we get on the first toss has absolutely no effect on any later tosses), the marginal probability for each possible outcome is $\tfrac{1}{6}$.

*A marginal probability is the probability of an event occurring.*

*A joint probability is the product of marginal probabilities.*

The *joint probability* of two or more independent events occurring is the product of their marginal or simple probabilities. This can be written as

$$P(AB) = P(A) \times P(B) \tag{B-4}$$

*where*

$P(AB)$ = joint probability or events $A$ and $B$ occurring together, or one after the other

$P(A)$ = marginal probability of event $A$

$P(B)$ = marginal probability of event $B$

The probability, for example, of tossing a 6 on the first roll of a die and a 2 on the second roll is

$$P(\text{6 on first and 2 on second roll})$$

$$= P(\text{tossing a 6}) \times P(\text{tossing a 2})$$

$$= \frac{1}{6} \times \frac{1}{6} = \frac{1}{36}$$

$$= 0.028$$

*A conditional probability is the probability of an event occurring given that another event has taken place.*

The third type, *conditional probability*, is expressed as $P(B|A)$, or "the probability of event $B$, given that event $A$ has occurred." Similarly, $P(A|B)$ would mean "the conditional probability of event $A$, given that event $B$ has taken place." Since events are independent, the occurrence of one in no way affects the outcome of another, $P(A|B) = P(A)$ and $P(B|A) = P(B)$.

**Example 4: Probabilities When Events Are Independent**  A bucket contains 3 black balls and 7 green balls. We draw a ball from the bucket, replace it, and draw a second ball. We can determine the probability of each of the following events occurring:

1.  A black ball is drawn on the first draw.

$$P(B) = 0.30$$

*(This is a marginal probability.)*

2.  Two green balls are drawn.

$$P(GG) = P(G) \times P(G) = (0.7)(0.7) = 0.49$$

*(This is a joint probability for two independent events.)*

3.  A black ball is drawn on the second draw if the first draw is green.

$$P(B \mid G) = P(B) = 0.30$$

*(This is a conditional probability but equal to the marginal because the two draws are independent events.)*

4.  A green ball is drawn on the second draw if the first draw was green.

$$P(G \mid G) = P(G) = 0.70$$

*(This is a conditional probability as above.)*

## B.4  STATISTICALLY DEPENDENT EVENTS

When events are statistically dependent, the occurrence of one event affects the probability of occurrence of some other event. Marginal, conditional, and joint probabilities exist under dependence as they did under independence, but the form of the latter two are changed.

A marginal probability is computed exactly as it was for independent events. Again, the marginal probability of the event $A$ occurring is denoted $P(A)$.

Calculating a conditional probability under dependence is somewhat more involved than it is under independence. The formula for the conditional probability of $A$, given that event $B$ has taken place, is now stated as

$$P(A \mid B) = \frac{P(AB)}{P(B)} \tag{B-5}$$

*A Presbyterian minister, Thomas Bayes (1702–1761), did the work leading to this theorem.*

The use of this important formula, often referred to as *Bayes' law* or *Bayes' theorem*, is best defined by an example.

**Example 5: Probabilities When Events Are Dependent**  Assume that we have an urn containing 10 balls of the following descriptions:

4 are white ($W$) and lettered ($L$).

2 are white ($W$) and numbered ($N$).

3 are yellow ($Y$) and lettered ($L$).

1 is yellow ($Y$) and numbered ($N$).

You randomly draw a ball from the urn and see that it is yellow. What, then, we may ask, is the probability that the ball is lettered? (See Figure B.3.)

Since there are 10 balls, it is a simple matter to tabulate a series of useful probabilities:

$$P(WL) = \frac{4}{10} = 0.4 \qquad P(YL) = \frac{3}{10} = 0.3$$

$$P(WN) = \frac{2}{10} = 0.2 \qquad P(YN) = \frac{1}{10} = 0.1$$

$$P(W) = \frac{6}{10} = 0.6, \text{ or } P(W) = P(WL) + P(WN) = 0.4 + 0.2 = 0.6$$

$$P(L) = \frac{7}{10} = 0.7, \text{ or } P(L) = P(WL) + P(YL) = 0.4 + 0.3 = 0.7$$

$$P(Y) = \frac{4}{10} = 0.4, \text{ or } P(Y) = P(YL) + P(YN) = 0.3 + 0.1 = 0.4$$

$$P(N) = \frac{3}{10} = 0.3, \text{ or } P(N) = P(WN) + P(YN) = 0.2 + 0.1 = 0.3$$

**FIGURE B.3**

**Dependent Events of Example 5**

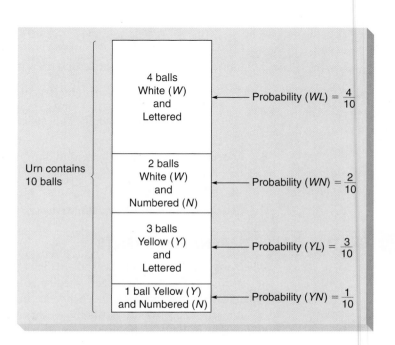

We can now apply Bayes' law to calculate the conditional probability that the ball drawn is lettered, given that it is yellow.

$$P(L \mid Y) = \frac{P(YL)}{P(Y)} = \frac{0.3}{0.4} = 0.75$$

This equation shows that we divided the probability of yellow and lettered balls (3 out of 10) by the probability of yellow balls (4 out of 10). There is a 0.75 probability that the yellow ball that you drew is lettered.

Recall that the formula for a joint probability under statistical independence was simply $P(AB) = P(A) \times P(B)$. When events are *dependent*, however, the joint probability is derived from Bayes' conditional formula. Equation B-6 reads "the joint probability of events $A$ and $B$ occurring is equal to the conditional probability of event $A$, given that $B$ occurred, multiplied by the probability of event $B$."

$$P(AB) = P(A \mid B) \times P(B) \tag{B-6}$$

We can use this formula to verify the joint probability that $P(YL) = 0.3$, which was obtained by inspection in Example 5 by multiplying $P(L|Y)$ times $P(Y)$:

$$P(YL) = P(L \mid Y) \times P(Y) = (0.75)(0.4) = 0.3$$

**Example 6: Joint Probabilities When Events Are Dependent**   Your stockbroker informs you that if the stock market reaches the 12,500-point level by January, there is a 70% probability that Tubeless Electronics will go up in value. Your own feeling is that there is only a 40% chance of the market average reaching 12,500 points by January. Can you calculate the probability that *both* the stock market will reach 12,500 points *and* the price of Tubeless Electronics will go up?

Let $M$ represent the event of the stock market reaching the 12,500 level, and let $T$ be the event that Tubeless goes up in value. Then

$$P(MT) = P(T \mid M) \times P(M) = (0.70)(0.40) = 0.28$$

Thus, there is only a 28% chance that *both* events will occur.

## B.5   REVISING PROBABILITIES WITH BAYES' THEOREM

Bayes' theorem can also be used to incorporate additional information as it is made available and help create *revised* or *posterior probabilities*. This means that we can take new or recent data and then revise and improve upon our old probability estimates for an event (see Figure B.4). Let us consider the following example.

**FIGURE B.4**

**Using Bayes' Process**

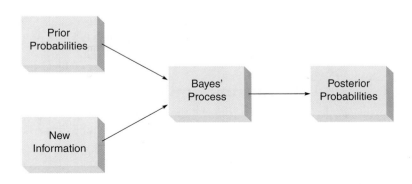

**Example 7: Posterior Probabilities**  A cup contains two dice identical in appearance. One, however, is fair (unbiased) and the other is loaded (biased). The probability of rolling a 3 on the fair die is $\frac{1}{6}$ or 0.166. The probability of tossing the same number on the loaded die is 0.60.

We have no idea which die is which but select one by chance and toss it. The result is a 3. Given this additional piece of information, can we find the (revised) probability that the die rolled was fair? Can we determine the probability that it was the loaded die that was rolled?

The answer to these questions is yes, and we do so by using the formula for joint probability under statistical dependence and Bayes' theorem. First, we take stock of the information and probabilities available. We know, for example, that since we randomly selected the die to roll, the probability of it being fair or loaded is 0.50:

$$P(\text{fair}) = 0.50 \qquad\qquad P(\text{loaded}) = 0.50$$

We also know that

$$P(3 \mid \text{fair}) = 0.166 \qquad\qquad P(3 \mid \text{loaded}) = 0.60$$

Next, we compute joint probabilities $P(3 \text{ and fair})$ and $P(3 \text{ and loaded})$ using the formula $P(AB) = P(A|B) \times P(B)$:

$$P(3 \text{ and fair}) = P(3 \,|\, \text{fair}) \times P(\text{fair})$$

$$= (0.166)(0.50) = 0.083$$

$$P(3 \text{ and loaded}) = P(3 \,|\, \text{loaded}) \times P(\text{loaded})$$

$$= (0.60)(0.50) = 0.300$$

A 3 can occur in combination with the state "fair die" or in combination with the state "loaded die." The sum of their probabilities gives the unconditional or marginal probability of a 3 on the toss, namely, $P(3) = 0.083 + 0.300 = 0.383$.

If a 3 does occur, and if we do not know which die it came from, the probability that the die rolled was the fair one is

$$P(\text{fair} \,|\, 3) = \frac{P(\text{fair and } 3)}{P(3)} = \frac{0.083}{0.383} = 0.22$$

The probability that the die rolled was loaded is

$$P(\text{loaded} \,|\, 3) = \frac{P(\text{loaded and } 3)}{P(3)} = \frac{0.300}{0.383} = 0.78$$

These two conditional probabilities are called the *revised* or *posterior probabilities* for the next roll of the die.

Before the die was rolled in the preceding example, the best we could say was that there was a 50–50 chance that it was fair (0.50 probability) and a 50–50 chance that it was loaded. After one roll of the die, however, we are able to revise our prior probability estimates. The new posterior estimate is that there is a 0.78 probability that the die rolled was loaded and only a 0.22 probability that it was not.

## General Form of Bayes' Theorem

*Another way to compute revised probabilities is with Bayes' theorem.*

Revised probabilities can also be computed in a more direct way using a general form for Bayes' theorem. Recall from Equation B-5 that Bayes' law for the conditional probability of event $A$, given event $B$, is

$$P(A \,|\, B) = \frac{P(AB)}{P(B)}$$

However, we can show that

$$P(A \mid B) = \frac{P(B \mid A)P(A)}{P(B \mid A)P(A) + P(B \mid \overline{A})P(\overline{A})} \qquad \text{(B-7)}$$

*where*

$$\overline{A} = \text{the complement of the event } A; \text{ for example,}$$
$$\text{if } A \text{ is the event "fair die," then } \overline{A} \text{ is "unfair" or "loaded die"}$$

Now let's return to Example 7.

Although it may not be obvious to you at first glance, we used this basic equation to compute the revised probabilities. For example, if we want the probability that the fair die was rolled given the first toss was a 3, namely, $P(\text{fair die}|3 \text{ rolled})$, we can let

event "fair die" replace $A$ in Equation B-7.

event "loaded die" replace $\overline{A}$ in Equation B-7.

event "3 rolled" replace $B$ in Equation B-7.

We can then rewrite Equation B-7 and solve as follows:

$$P(\text{fair die} \mid 3 \text{ rolled})$$

$$= \frac{P(3 \mid \text{fair})P(\text{fair})}{P(3 \mid \text{fair})P(\text{fair}) + P(3 \mid \text{loaded})P(\text{loaded})}$$

$$= \frac{(0.166)(0.50)}{(0.166)(0.50) + (0.60)(0.50)}$$

$$= \frac{0.083}{0.383} = 0.22$$

This is the same answer that we computed in Example 7. Can you use this alternative approach to show the $P(\text{loaded die}|3 \text{ rolled}) = 0.78$? Either method is perfectly acceptable, but when we deal with probability revisions in Chapter 8, you may find that Equation B-7 is easier to apply.

## B.6  FURTHER PROBABILITY REVISIONS

Although one revision of prior probabilities can provide useful posterior probability estimates, additional information can be gained from performing the experiment a second time. If it is financially worthwhile, a decision maker may even decide to make several more revisions.

**Example 8: A Second Probability Revision**  Returning to Example 7, we now attempt to obtain further information about the posterior probabilities as to whether the die just rolled is fair or loaded. To do so, let us toss the die a second time. Again, we roll a 3. What are the further revised probabilities?

To answer this question, we proceed as before, with only one exception. The probabilities $P(\text{fair}) = 0.50$ and $P(\text{loaded}) = 0.50$ remain the same, but now we must compute $P(3,3|\text{fair}) = (0.166)(0.166) = 0.027$ and $P(3,3|\text{loaded}) = (0.6)(0.6) = 0.36$. With these joint probabilities of two 3s on successive rolls, given the two types of dice, we can revise the probabilities:

$$P(3,3 \text{ and fair}) = P(3,3 \mid \text{fair}) \times P(\text{fair})$$

$$= (0.027)(0.5) = 0.013$$

$$P(3,3 \text{ and loaded}) = P(3,3 \mid \text{loaded}) \times P(\text{loaded})$$

$$= (0.36)(0.5) = 0.18$$

Thus, the probability of rolling two 3s, a marginal probability, is $0.013 + 0.18 = 0.193$, the sum of the two joint probabilities.

$$P(\text{fair} \mid 3,3) = \frac{P(3,3 \text{ and fair})}{P(3,3)}$$

$$= \frac{0.013}{0.193} = 0.067$$

$$P(\text{loaded} \mid 3,3) = \frac{P(3,3 \text{ and loaded})}{P(3,3)}$$

$$= \frac{0.18}{0.193} = 0.933$$

What has this second roll accomplished? Before we rolled the die the first time, we knew only that there was a 0.50 probability that it was either fair or loaded. When the first die was rolled in Example 7, we were able to revise these probabilities:

probability the die is fair $= 0.22$

probability the die is loaded $= 0.78$

Now, after the second roll in Example 8, our refined revisions tell us that

probability the die is fair $= 0.067$

probability the die is loaded $= 0.933$

This type of information can be extremely valuable in business decision making.

## B.7    RANDOM VARIABLES

The preceding section discusses various ways of assigning probability values to the outcomes of an experiment. Let us now use this probability information to compute the expected outcome, variance, and standard deviation of the experiment. This can help select the best decision among a number of alternatives.

A *random variable* assigns a real number to every possible outcome or event in an experiment. It is normally represented by a letter such as $X$ or $Y$. When the outcome itself is numerical or quantitative, the outcome numbers can be the random variable. For example,

**TABLE B.1**    **Examples of Random Variables**

| EXPERIMENT | OUTCOME | RANDOM VARIABLES | RANGE OF RANDOM VARIABLES |
|---|---|---|---|
| Stock 50 Christmas trees | Number of Christmas trees sold | $X$ = number of Christmas trees sold | $0, 1, 2, \ldots, 50$ |
| Inspect 600 items | Number of acceptable items | $Y$ = number of acceptable items | $0, 1, 2, \ldots, 600$ |
| Send out 5,000 sales letters | Number of people responding to the letters | $Z$ = number of people responding to the letters | $0, 1, 2, \ldots, 5,000$ |
| Build an apartment building | Percent of building completed after 4 months | $R$ = percent of building completed after 4 months | $0 \leq R \leq 100$ |
| Test the lifetime of a lightbulb (minutes) | Length of time the bulb lasts up to 80,000 minutes | $S$ = time the bulb burns | $0 \leq S \leq 80,000$ |

| | | | RANGE OF |
| | | RANDOM | RANDOM |
| EXPERIMENT | OUTCOME | VARIABLES | VARIABLES |
|---|---|---|---|
| Students respond to a questionnaire | Strongly agree (SA) Agree (A) Neutral (N) Disagree (D) Strongly disagree (SD) | $X = \begin{cases} 5 \text{ if SA} \\ 4 \text{ if A} \\ 3 \text{ if N} \\ 2 \text{ if D} \\ 1 \text{ if SD} \end{cases}$ | 1, 2, 3, 4, 5 |
| One machine is inspected | Defective Not defective | $Y = \begin{cases} 0 \text{ if defective} \\ 1 \text{ if not defective} \end{cases}$ | 0, 1 |
| Consumers respond to how they like a product | Good Average Poor | $Z = \begin{cases} 3 \text{ if good} \\ 2 \text{ if average} \\ 1 \text{ if poor} \end{cases}$ | 1, 2, 3 |

**TABLE B.2**

Random Variables for Outcomes That Are Not Numbers

consider refrigerator sales at an appliance store. The number of refrigerators sold during a given day can be the random variable. Using $X$ to represent this random variable, we can express this relationship as follows:

$$X = \text{number of refigerators sold during the day}$$

In general, whenever the experiment has quantifiable outcomes, it is beneficial to define these quantitative outcomes as the random variable. Examples are given in Table B.1.

When the outcome itself is not numerical or quantitative, it is necessary to define a random variable that associates each outcome with a unique real number. Several examples are given in Table B.2.

There are two types of random variables: *discrete random variables* and *continuous random variables*. Developing probability distributions and making computations based on these distributions depends on the type of random variable.

*Try to develop a few more examples of discrete random variables to be sure you understand this concept.*

A random variable is a *discrete random variable* if it can assume only a finite or limited set of values. Which of the random variables in Table B.1 are discrete random variables? Looking at Table B.1, we can see that stocking 50 Christmas trees, inspecting 600 items, and sending out 5,000 letters are all examples of discrete random variables. Each of these random variables can assume only a finite or limited set of values. The number of Christmas trees sold, for example, can only be integer numbers from 0 to 50. There are 51 values that the random variable $X$ can assume in this example.

A *continuous random variable* is a random variable that has an infinite or an unlimited set of values. Are there any examples of continuous random variables in Tables B.1 or B.2? Looking at Table B.1, we can see that testing the lifetime of a lightbulb is an experiment that can be described with a continuous random variable. In this case, the random variable, $S$, is the time the bulb burns. It can last for 3,206 minutes, 6,500.7 minutes, 251.726 minutes, or any other value between 0 and 80,000 minutes. In most cases, the range of a continuous random variable is stated as: lower value $\leq S \leq$ upper value, such as $0 \leq S \leq 80,000$. The random variable $R$ in Table B.1 is also continuous. Can you explain why?

## B.8  PROBABILITY DISTRIBUTIONS

Earlier we discussed the probability values of an event. We now explore the properties of *probability distributions*. We see how popular distributions, such as the normal, Poisson, and exponential probability distributions, can save us time and effort. Since selection of the appropriate probability distribution depends partially on whether the random variable is *discrete* or *continuous*, we consider each of these types separately.

## Probability Distribution of a Discrete Random Variable

When we have a *discrete random variable*, there is a probability value assigned to each event. These values must be between 0 and 1, and they must sum to 1. Let's look at an example.

The 100 students in Pat Shannon's statistics class have just completed the instructor evaluations at the end of the course. Dr. Shannon is particularly interested in student response to the textbook because he is in the process of writing a competing statistics book. One of the questions on the evaluation survey was: "The textbook was well written and helped me acquire the necessary information."

5. Strongly agree
4. Agree
3. Neutral
2. Disagree
1. Strongly disagree

The students' response to this question in the survey is summarized in Table B.3. Also shown is the random variable $X$ and the corresponding probability for each possible outcome. This discrete probability distribution was computed using the relative frequency approach presented previously.

The distribution follows the three rules required of all probability distributions: (1) the events are mutually exclusive and collectively exhaustive, (2) the individual probability values are between 0 and 1 inclusive, and (3) the total of the probability values sum to 1.

Although listing the probability distribution as we did in Table B.3 is adequate, it can be difficult to get an idea about characteristics of the distribution. To overcome this problem, the probability values are often presented in graph form. The graph of the distribution in Table B.3 is shown in Figure B.5.

The graph of this probability distribution gives us a picture of its shape. It helps us identify the central tendency of the distribution, called the *expected value*, and the amount of variability or spread of the distribution, called the *variance*.

## Expected Value of a Discrete Probability Distribution

Once we have established a probability distribution, the first characteristic that is usually of interest is the *central tendency*, or average of the distribution. The *expected value*, a measure of central tendency, is computed as a weighted average of the values of the random variable:

*The expected value of a discrete distribution is a weighted average of the values of the random variable.*

$$E(X) = \sum_{i=1}^{n} X_i P(X_i)$$

$$= X_1 P(X_1) + X_2 P(X_2) + \cdots + X_n P(X_n) \tag{B-8}$$

| TABLE B.3 | | | |
|---|---|---|---|
| **Probability Distribution for Textbook Question** | | | |
| OUTCOME | RANDOM VARIABLE ($X$) | NUMBER RESPONDING | PROBABILITY $P(X)$ |
| Strongly agree | 5 | 10 | 0.1 = 10/100 |
| Agree | 4 | 20 | 0.2 = 20/100 |
| Neutral | 3 | 30 | 0.3 = 30/100 |
| Disagree | 2 | 30 | 0.3 = 30/100 |
| Strongly disagree | 1 | 10 | 0.1 = 10/100 |
|  |  | Total 100 | 1.0 = 100/100 |

**Probability Function for
Dr. Shannon's Class**

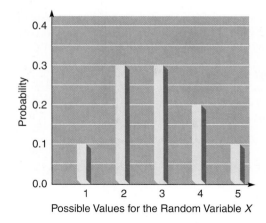

*where*

$X_i$ = random variable's possible values

$P(X_i)$ = probability of each of the random variable's possible values

$\displaystyle\sum_{i=1}^{n}$ = summation sign indicating we are adding all $n$ possible values

$E(X)$ = expected value of the random variable

The expected value of any discrete probability distribution can be computed by multiplying each possible value of the random variable, $X_i$, times the probability, $P(X_i)$, that outcome will occur, and summing the results, $\Sigma$. Here is how the expected value can be computed for the textbook question:

$$
\begin{aligned}
E(X) &= \sum_{i=1}^{5} X_i P(X_i) \\
&= X_1 P(X_1) + X_2 P(X_2) + X_3 P(X_3) \\
&\quad + X_4 P(X_4) + X_5 P(X_5) \\
&= (5)(0.1) + (4)(0.2) + (3)(0.3) \\
&\quad + (2)(0.3) + (1)(0.1) \\
&= 2.9
\end{aligned}
$$

The expected value of 2.9 implies that the mean response is between disagree (2) and neutral (3), and that the average response is closer to neutral, which is 3. Looking at Figure B.5, this is consistent with the shape of the probability function.

## Variance of a Discrete Probability Distribution

In addition to the central tendency of a probability distribution, most people are interested in the variability or the spread of the distribution. If the variability is low, it is much more likely that the outcome of an experiment will be close to the average or expected value. On the other hand, if the variability of the distribution is high, which means that the probability is spread out over the various random variable values, there is less chance that the outcome of an experiment will be close to the expected value.

The *variance* of a probability distribution is a number that reveals the overall spread or dispersion of the distribution. For a discrete probability distribution, it can be computed using the following equation:

$$\text{variance} = \sum_{i=1}^{n} [X_i - E(X)]^2 \, P(X_i) \tag{B-9}$$

where

$$X_i = \text{random variable's possible values}$$

$$E(X) = \text{expected value of the random variable}$$

$$[X_i - E(X)] = \text{difference between each value of the random variable and the expected value}$$

$$P(X_i) = \text{probability of each possible value of the random variable}$$

To compute the variance, each value of the random variable is subtracted from the expected value, squared, and multiplied times the probability of occurrence of that value. The results are then summed to obtain the variance. Here is how this procedure is done for Dr. Shannon's textbook question:

$$\text{variance} = \sum_{i=1}^{5} [X_i - E(X)]^2 P(X_i)$$

$$\text{variance} = (5 - 2.9)^2(0.1) + (4 - 2.9)^2(0.2) + (3 - 2.9)^2(0.3) + (2 - 2.9)^2(0.3) + (1 - 2.9)^2(0.1)$$

$$= (2.1)^2(0.1) + (1.1)^2(0.2) + (0.1)^2(0.3) + (-0.9)^2(0.3) + (-1.9)^2(0.1)$$

$$= 0.441 + 0.242 + 0.003 + 0.243 + 0.361$$

$$= 1.29$$

A related measure of dispersion or spread is the *standard deviation*. This quantity is also used in many computations involved with probability distributions. The standard deviation is just the square root of the variance.

$$\sigma = \sqrt{\text{variance}} \tag{B-10}$$

where

$$\sqrt{\phantom{x}} = \text{square root}$$

$$\sigma = \text{standard deviation}$$

The standard deviation for the textbook question is

$$\sigma = \sqrt{\text{variance}}$$

$$= \sqrt{1.29} = 1.14$$

## Probability Distribution of a Continuous Random Variable

There are many examples of *continuous random variables*. The time it takes to finish a project, the number of ounces in a barrel of butter, the high temperature during a given day, the exact length of a given type of lumber, and the weight of a railroad car of coal are all examples of continuous random variables. Since random variables can take on an infinite num-

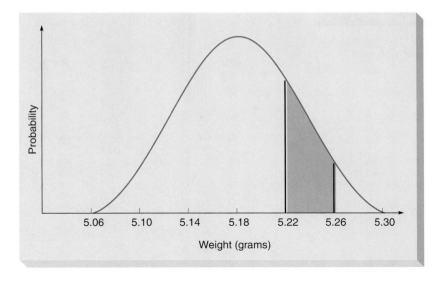

**FIGURE B.6**

**Sample Density Function**

*A probability density function, f(X), is a mathematical way of describing the probability distribution.*

ber of values, the fundamental probability rules for continuous random variables must be modified.

As with discrete probability distributions, the sum of the probability values must equal 1. Because there are an infinite number of values of the random variables, however, the probability of each value of the random variable must be 0. If the probability values for the random variable values were greater than 0, the sum would be infinitely large.

With a continuous probability distribution, there is a continuous mathematical function that describes the probability distribution. This function is called the *probability density function* or simply the *probability function*. It is usually represented by $f(X)$.

We now look at the sketch of a sample density function in Figure B.6. This curve represents the probability density function for the weight of a particular machined part. The weight could vary from 5.06 to 5.30 grams, with weights around 5.18 grams being the most likely. The shaded area represents the probability the weight is between 5.22 and 5.26 grams.

If we wanted to know the probability of a part weighing exactly 5.1300000 grams, for example, we would have to compute the area of a slice of width 0. Of course, this would be 0. This result may seem strange, but if we insist on enough decimal places of accuracy, we are bound to find that the weight differs from 5.1300000 grams *exactly*, be the difference ever so slight.

In this section we investigate the fundamental characteristics and properties of probability distributions in general. In the next three sections we introduce two important continuous distributions—the normal distribution and the exponential distribution—and a useful discrete probability distribution—the Poisson distribution.

## B.9  THE NORMAL DISTRIBUTION

*The normal distribution affects a large number of processes in our lives (e.g., filling boxes of cereal with 32 ounces of corn flakes). Each normal distribution depends on the mean and standard deviation.*

One of the most popular and useful continuous probability distributions is the *normal distribution*. The probability density function of this distribution is given by the rather complex formula

$$f(X) = \frac{1}{\sigma\sqrt{2\pi}}\; e^{\left[\dfrac{-\frac{1}{2}(X-\mu)^2}{\sigma^2}\right]} \tag{B-11}$$

The normal distribution is specified completely when values for the mean, $\mu$, and the standard deviation, $\sigma$, are known. Figure B.7 shows several different normal distributions

**Normal Distribution with Different Values for μ**

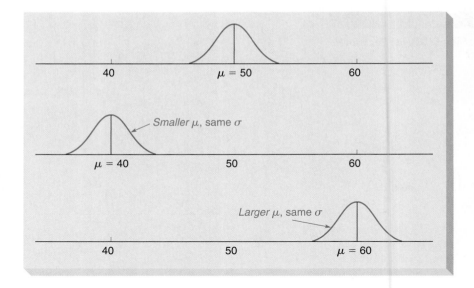

with the same standard deviation and different means. As shown, differing values of μ will shift the average or center of the normal distribution. The overall shape of the distribution remains the same. On the other hand, when the standard deviation is varied, the normal curve either flattens out or becomes steeper. This is shown in Figure B.8.

As the standard deviation, σ, becomes smaller, the normal distribution becomes steeper. When the standard deviation becomes larger, the normal distribution has a tendency to flatten out or become broader.

## Area Under the Normal Curve

Because the normal distribution is symmetrical, its midpoint (and highest point) is at the mean. Values on the X axis are then measured in terms of how many standard deviations they lie from the mean. Recall that the area under the curve (in a continuous distribution) describes the probability that a random variable has a value in a specified interval. The normal distribution requires mathematical calculations beyond the scope of this book,

**Normal Distribution with Different Values for σ**

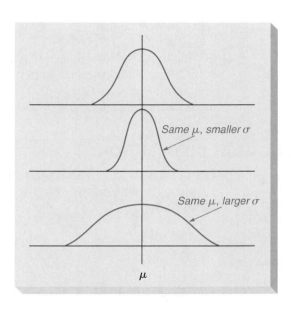

**FIGURE B.9**

**Three Common Areas Under Normal Curves**

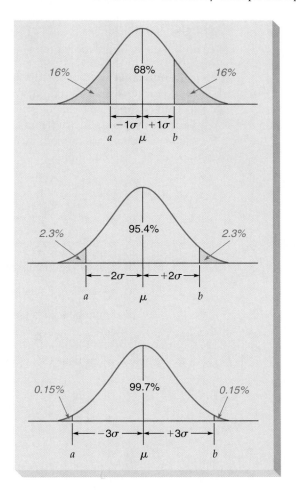

*Figure B.9 is very important, and you should comprehend the meanings of ±1, 2, and 3 standard deviation symmetrical areas. Managers often speak of 95% and 99% confidence interval, which roughly refer to ±2 and 3 standard deviation graphs.*

*95% confidence is actually ±1.96 standard deviations, whereas ±3 standard deviations is actually a 99.7% spread.*

but tables that provide areas or probabilities are readily available. For example, Figure B.9 illustrates three commonly used relationships that have been derived from standard normal tables (discussed in the next section). The area from point $a$ to point $b$ in the first drawing represents the probability, 68%, that the random variable will be within 1 standard deviation of the mean. In the middle graph, we see that about 95.4% of the area lies within ±2 standard deviations of the mean. The third figure shows that 99.7% lies between ±3$\sigma$.

Translating Figure B.9 into an application implies that if the mean IQ in the United States is $\mu = 100$ points and if the standard deviation is $\sigma = 15$ points, we can make the following statements:

1.  68% of the population have IQs between 85 and 115 points (i.e., ±1$\sigma$).

2.  95.4% of the people have IQs between 70 and 130 points (±2$\sigma$).

3.  99.7% of the population have IQs in the range from 55 to 145 points (±3$\sigma$).

4.  Only 16% of the people have IQs greater than 115 points (from first graph, the area to the right of +1$\sigma$).

Many more interesting remarks could be drawn from these data. Can you tell the probability that a person selected at random has an IQ of less than 70? Greater than 145? Less than 130?

## Using the Standard Normal Table

To use a table to find normal probability values, we follow two steps.

**Step 1** Convert the normal distribution to what we call a *standard normal distribution*. A standard normal distribution is one that has a mean of 0 and a standard deviation of 1. All normal tables are set up to handle random variables with $\mu = 0$ and $\sigma = 1$. Without a standard normal distribution, a different table would be needed for each pair of $\mu$ and $\sigma$ values. We call the new standard random variable $Z$. The value for $Z$ for any normal distribution is computed from this equation:

$$Z = \frac{X - \mu}{\sigma} \tag{B-12}$$

*where*

$X$ = value of the random variable we want to measure

$\mu$ = mean of the distribution

$\sigma$ = standard deviation of the distribution

$Z$ = number of standard deviations from $X$ to the mean, $\mu$

For example, if $\mu = 100$, $\sigma = 15$, and we are interested in finding the probability that the random variable $X$ is less than 130, we want $P(X < 130)$.

$$Z = \frac{X - \mu}{\sigma} = \frac{130 - 100}{15}$$

$$= \frac{30}{15} = 2 \text{ standard deviations}$$

This means that the point $X$ is 2.0 standard deviations to the right of the mean. This is shown in Figure B.10.

**FIGURE B.10**

**Normal Distribution Showing the Relationship between Z Values and X Values**

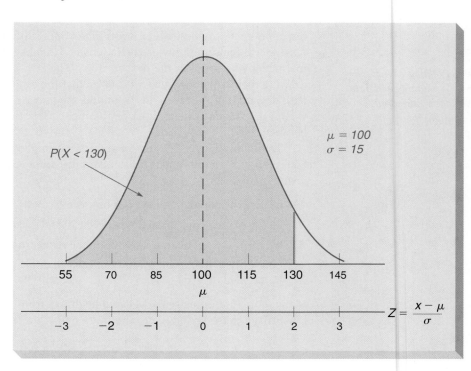

**Step 2**  Look up the probability from a table of normal curve areas. Appendix C on page 602 is such a table of areas for the standard normal distribution. It is set up to provide the area under the curve to the left of any specified value of $Z$.

Let's see how Appendix C can be used. The column of the left lists values of $Z$, with the second decimal place of $Z$ appearing in the top row. For example, for a value of $Z = 2.00$ as just computed, find 2.0 in the left-hand column and 0.00 in the top row. In the body of the table, we find that the area sought is 0.97725, or 97.7%. Thus,

$$P(X < 130) = P(Z < 2.00) = 97.7\%$$

This suggests that if the mean IQ score is 100, with a standard deviation of 15 points, the probability that a randomly selected person's IQ is less than 130 is 97.7%. By referring back to Figure B.9, we see that this probability could also have been derived from the middle graph. (Note that $1.0 - 0.977 = 0.023 = 2.3\%$, which is the area in the right-hand tail of the curve.)

To feel comfortable with the use of the standard normal probability table, we need to work a few more examples. We now use the Haynes Construction Company as a case in point.

## Haynes Construction Company Example

Haynes Construction Company builds primarily three- and four-unit apartment buildings (called triplexes and quadraplexes) for investors, and it is believed that the total construction time in days follows a normal distribution. The mean time to construct a triplex is 100 days, and the standard deviation is 20 days. Recently, the president of Haynes Construction signed a contract to complete a triplex in 125 days. Failure to complete the triplex in 125 days would result in severe penalty fees. What is the probability that Haynes Construction will not be in violation of their construction contract? The normal distribution for the construction of triplexes is shown in Figure B.11.

To compute this probability, we need to find the shaded area under the curve. We begin by computing $Z$ for this problem:

$$Z = \frac{X - \mu}{\sigma}$$

$$= \frac{125 - 100}{20}$$

$$= \frac{25}{20} = 1.25$$

Looking in Appendix C for a $Z$ value of 1.25, we find an area under the curve of 0.89435. (We do this by looking up 1.2 in the left-hand column of the table and then moving to the 0.05 column to find the value of $Z = 1.25$.) Therefore, the probability of not violating the contract is 0.89435, or about an 89% chance.

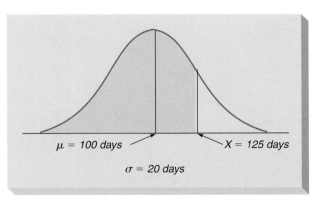

$\mu = 100$ days          $X = 125$ days

$\sigma = 20$ days

**Probability That Haynes Will Receive the Bonus by Finishing in 75 Days**

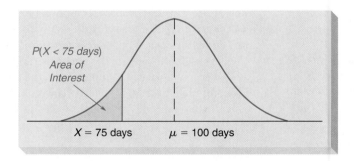

Now let us look at the Haynes problem from another perspective. If the firm finishes this triplex in 75 days or less, it will be awarded a bonus payment of $5,000. What is the probability that Haynes will receive the bonus?

Figure B.12 illustrates the probability we are looking for in the shaded area. The first step is again to compute the $Z$ value:

$$Z = \frac{X - \mu}{\sigma}$$

$$= \frac{75 - 100}{20}$$

$$= \frac{-25}{20} = -1.25$$

This $Z$ value indicates that 75 days is $-1.25$ standard deviations to the left of the mean. But the standard normal table is structured to handle only positive $Z$ values. To solve this problem, we observe that the curve is symmetric. The probability that Haynes will finish in *less than 75 days is equivalent* to the probability that it will finish in *more than 125 days*. In Figure B.11 we found the probability that Haynes will finish in less than 125 days was 0.89435. So the probability it takes more than 125 days is

$$P(X > 125) = 1.0 - P(X < 125)$$

$$= 1.0 - 0.89435 = 0.10565$$

Thus, the probability of completing the triplex in 75 days or less is 0.10565, or about 10%.

One final example: What is the probability that the triplex will take between 110 and 125 days? We see in Figure B.13 that

$$P(110 < X < 125) = P(X < 125) - P(X < 110)$$

**Probability of Haynes' Completion between 110 and 125 Days**

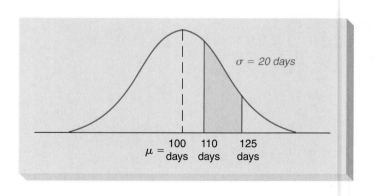

That is, the shaded area in the graph can be computed by finding the probability of completing the building in 125 days or less *minus* the probability of completing it in 110 days or less.

Recall that $P(X < 125$ days$)$ is equal to 0.89435. To find $P(X < 110$ days$)$, we follow the two steps developed earlier:

1. $$Z = \frac{X - \mu}{\sigma} = \frac{110 - 100}{20} = \frac{10}{20}$$

   $$= 0.5 \text{ standard deviations}$$

2. From Appendix C, the area for $Z = 0.50$ is 0.69146. So the probability the triplex can be completed in less than 110 days is 0.69146. Finally,

$$P(110 < X < 125) = 0.89435 - 0.69146 = 0.20289$$

The probability that it will take between 110 and 125 days is about 20%.

---

### B.10  THE EXPONENTIAL DISTRIBUTION

The *exponential distribution*, also called the *negative exponential distribution*, is used in dealing with queuing models. The exponential distribution describes the number of customers serviced in a time interval. The exponential distribution is a continuous distribution. Its probability function is given by

$$f(X) = \mu e^{-\mu x} \tag{B-13}$$

*where*

$X$ = random variable (service times)

$\mu$ = average number of units the service facility can handle in a specific period of time

$e$ = 2.718,  the base of natural logarithms

**FIGURE B.14**

**Negative Exponential Distribution**

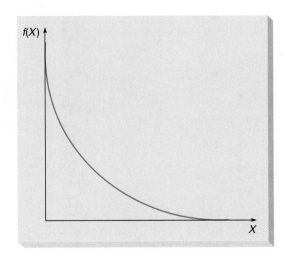

The general shape of the exponential distribution is shown in Figure B.14. Its expected value and variance can be shown to be

$$\text{expected value} = \frac{1}{\mu} \qquad (B\text{-}14)$$

$$\text{variance} = \frac{1}{\mu^2} \qquad (B\text{-}15)$$

The exponential distribution will be illustrated again in Chapter 9.

## B.11 THE POISSON DISTRIBUTION

An important *discrete* probability distribution is the *Poisson distribution.*[1] We examine it because of its key role in complementing the exponential distribution in queuing models in Chapter 9. The distribution describes situations in which customers arrive independently during a certain time interval, and the number of arrivals depends on the length of the time interval. Examples are patients arriving at a health clinic, customers arriving at a bank window, passengers arriving at an airport, and telephone calls going through a central exchange.

The formula for the Poisson distribution is

$$P(X) = \frac{\lambda^x e^{-\lambda}}{X!} \qquad (B\text{-}16)$$

*where*

$P(X)$ = probability of exactly $X$ arrivals or occurrences

$\lambda$ = average number of arrivals per unit of time (the mean arrival rate), pronounced "lambda"

$e$ = 2.718, the base of the natural logarithms

$X$ = specific value (0, 1, 2, 3, and so on) of the random variable

**FIGURE B.15**

**Sample Poisson Distribution with $\lambda = 2$**

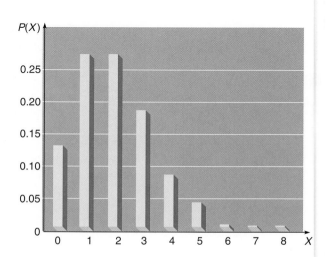

---

[1] This distribution, derived by Simeon Poisson in 1837, is pronounced "pwah-sahn."

The mean and variance of the Poisson distribution are equal and are computed simply as

$$\text{expected value} = \lambda \tag{B-17}$$

$$\text{variance} = \lambda \tag{B-18}$$

A sample distribution for $\lambda = 2$ arrivals is shown in Figure B.15.

# GLOSSARY

**Bayes' Theorem.**  A formula that allows us to compute conditional probabilities when dealing with statistically dependent events.

**Classical or Logical Approach.**  An objective way of assessing probabilities based on logic.

**Collectively Exhaustive Events.**  A collection of all possible outcomes of an experiment.

**Conditional Probability.**  The probability of one event occurring given that another has taken place.

**Continuous Probability Distribution.**  A probability distribution with a continuous random variable.

**Continuous Random Variable.**  A random variable that can assume an infinite or unlimited set of values.

**Dependent Events.**  The situation in which the occurrence of one event affects the probability of occurrence of some other event.

**Discrete Probability Distribution.**  A probability distribution with a discrete random variable.

**Discrete Random Variable.**  A random variable that can only assume a finite or limited set of values.

**Expected Value.**  The (weighted) average of a probability distribution.

**Independent Events.**  The situation in which the occurrence of one event has no effect on the probability of occurrence of a second event.

**Joint Probability.**  The probability of events occurring together (or one after the other).

**Marginal Probability.**  The simple probability of an event occurring.

**Mutually Exclusive Events.**  A situation in which only one event can occur on any given trial or experiment.

**Negative Exponential Distribution.**  A continuous probability distribution that describes the time between customer arrivals in a queuing situation.

**Normal Distribution.**  A continuous bell-shaped distribution that is a function of two parameters, the mean and standard deviation of the distribution.

**Poisson Distribution.**  A discrete probability distribution used in queuing theory.

**Prior Probability.**  A probability value determined before new or additional information is obtained. It is sometimes called an *a priori* probability estimate.

**Probability.**  A statement about the likelihood of an event occurring. It is expressed as a numerical value between 0 and 1, inclusive.

**Probability Density Function.**  The mathematical function that describes a continuous probability distribution. It is represented by $f(X)$.

**Probability Distribution.**  The set of all possible values of a random variable and their associated probabilities.

**Random Variable.**  A variable that assigns a number to every possible outcome of an experiment.

**Relative Frequency Approach.**  An objective way of determining probabilities based on observing frequencies over a number of trials.

**Revised or Posterior Probability.**  A probability value that results from new or revised information and prior probabilities.

**Standard Deviation.**  The square root of the variance.

**Subjective Approach.**  A method of determining probability values based on experience or judgment.

**Variance.**  A measure of dispersion or spread of the probability distribution.

# KEY EQUATIONS

**(B-1)**  $0 \leq P(\text{event}) \leq 1$

A basic statement of probability.

**(B-2)**  $P(A \text{ or } B) = P(A) + P(B)$

Law of addition for mutually exclusive events.

**(B-3)**  $P(A \text{ or } B) = P(A) + P(B) - P(A \text{ and } B)$

Law of addition for events that are not mutually exclusive.

**(B-4)**  $P(AB) = P(A) \times P(B)$

Joint probability for independent events.

**(B-5)**  $P(A \mid B) = \dfrac{P(AB)}{P(B)}$

Bayes' law for conditional probabilities.

**(B-6)** $P(AB) = P(A|B) \times P(B)$

Joint probability for dependent events: a restatement of Bayes' law.

**(B-7)** $P(A|B) = \dfrac{P(B|A)P(A)}{P(B|A)P(A) + P(B|\overline{A})P(\overline{A})}$

A restatement of Bayes' law in general form.

**(B-8)** $E(X) = \displaystyle\sum_{i=1}^{n} X_i P(X_i)$

Computes the expected value of a discrete probability distribution.

**(B-9)** Variance $= \displaystyle\sum_{i=1}^{n} [X_i - E(X)]^2 P(X_i)$

Computes the variance of a discrete probability distribution.

**(B-10)** $\sigma = \sqrt{\text{variance}}$

Computes the standard deviation from the variance.

**(B-11)** $f(X) = \dfrac{1}{\sigma\sqrt{2\pi}} e^{\left[\dfrac{-\frac{1}{2}(X - \mu)^2}{\sigma^2}\right]}$

The density function for the normal probability distribution.

**(B-12)** $Z = \dfrac{X - \mu}{\sigma}$

Computes the number of standard deviations, $Z$, the point $X$ is from the mean $\mu$.

**(B-13)** $f(X) = \mu e^{-\mu x}$

The exponential distribution.

**(B-14)** Expected value $= \dfrac{1}{\mu}$

The expected value of an exponential distribution.

**(B-15)** Variance $= \dfrac{1}{\mu^2}$

The variance of an exponential distribution.

**(B-16)** $P(X) = \dfrac{\lambda^x e^{-\lambda}}{X!}$

The Poisson distribution.

**(B-17)** Expected value $= \lambda$

The mean of a Poisson distribution.

**(B-18)** Variance $= \lambda$

The variance of a Poisson distribution.

# DISCUSSION QUESTIONS AND PROBLEMS

## Discussion Questions

**B-1**   What are the two basic laws of probability?

**B-2**   What is the meaning of mutually exclusive events? What is meant by collectively exhaustive? Give an example of each.

**B-3**   Describe the various approaches used in determining probability values.

**B-4**   Why is the probability of the intersection of two events subtracted in the sum of the probability of two events?

**B-5**   What is the difference between events that are dependent and events that are independent?

**B-6**   What is Bayes' theorem, and when can it be used?

**B-7**   How can probability revisions assist in managerial decision making?

**B-8**   What is a random variable? What are the various types of random variables?

**B-9**   What is the difference between a discrete probability distribution and a continuous probability distribution? Give your own example of each.

**B-10**  What is the expected value, and what does it measure? How is it computed for a discrete probability distribution?

**B-11**  What is the variance, and what does it measure? How is it computed for a discrete probability distribution?

**B-12**  Name three business processes that can be described by the normal distribution.

**B-13**  After evaluating student response to a question about a case used in class, the instructor constructed the following probability distribution. What kind of probability distribution is it?

| RESPONSE | RANDOM VARIABLE X | PROBABILITY |
|----------|-------------------|-------------|
| Excellent | 5 | 0.05 |
| Good | 4 | 0.25 |
| Average | 3 | 0.40 |
| Fair | 2 | 0.15 |
| Poor | 1 | 0.15 |

## Problems

• **B-14** A student taking Management Science 301 at East Haven University will receive one of five possible grades for the course: A, B, C, D, or F. The distribution of grades over the past two years is as follows:

| Grade | Number of Students |
|-------|--------------------|
| A | 80 |
| B | 75 |
| C | 90 |
| D | 30 |
| F | 25 |
| | Total 300 |

If this past distribution is a good indicator of future grades, what is the probability of a student receiving a C in the course?

• **B-15** A silver dollar is flipped twice. Calculate the probability of each of the following occurring.
  - (a) A head on the first flip
  - (b) A tail on the second flip given that the first toss was a head
  - (c) Two tails
  - (d) A tail on the first and a head on the second
  - (e) A tail on the first and a head on the second or a head on the first and a tail on the second
  - (f) At least one head on the two flips

• **B-16** An urn contains 8 red chips, 10 green chips, and 2 white chips. A chip is drawn and replaced, and then a second chip drawn. What is the probability of
  - (a) a white chip on the first draw?
  - (b) a white chip on the first draw and a red on the second?
  - (c) two green chips being drawn?
  - (d) a red chip on the second, given that a white chip was drawn on the first?

• **B-17** Evertight, a leading manufacturer of quality nails, produces 1-, 2-, 3-, 4-, and 5-inch nails for various uses. In the production process, if there is an overrun or if the nails are slightly defective, they are placed in a common bin. Yesterday, 651 of the 1-inch nails, 243 of the 2-inch nails, 41 of the 3-inch nails, 451 of the 4-inch nails, and 333 of the 5-inch nails were placed in the bin.
  - (a) What is the probability of reaching into the bin and getting a 4-inch nail?
  - (b) What is the probability of getting a 5-inch nail?
  - (c) If a particular application requires a nail that is 3 inches or shorter, what is the probability of getting a nail that will satisfy the requirements of the application?

⁞ **B-18** Last year, at Northern Manufacturing Company, 200 people had colds during the year. One hundred fifty-five people who did no exercising had colds, whereas the remainder of the people with colds were involved in a weekly exercise program. Half of the 1,000 employees were involved in some type of exercise.
  - (a) What is the probability that an employee will have a cold next year?
  - (b) Given that an employee is involved in an exercise program, what is the probability that he or she will get a cold?
  - (c) What is the probability that an employee who is not involved in an exercise program will get a cold next year?
  - (d) Are exercising and getting a cold independent events? Explain your answer.

⁞ **B-19** The Springfield Kings, a professional basketball team, has won 12 of its last 20 games and is expected to continue winning at the same percentage rate. The team's ticket manager is anxious to attract a large crowd to tomorrow's game but believes that depends on how well the Kings perform tonight against the Galveston Comets. He assesses the probability of drawing a large crowd to be 0.90 should the team win tonight. What is the probability that the team wins tonight and that there will be a large crowd at tomorrow's game?

⁞ **B-20** David Mashley teaches two undergraduate statistics courses at Kansas College. The class for Statistics 201 consists of 7 sophomores and 3 juniors. The more advanced course, Statistics 301, has 2 sophomores and 8 juniors enrolled. As an example of a business sampling technique, Professor Mashley randomly selects, from the stack of Statistics 201 registration cards, the class card of one student and then places that card back in the stack. If that student was a sophomore, Mashley draws another card from the Statistics 201 stack; if not, he randomly draws a card from the Statistics 301 group. Are these two draws independent events? What is the probability of
  - (a) a junior's name on the first draw?
  - (b) a junior's name on the second draw, given that a sophomore's name was drawn first?
  - (c) a junior's name on the second draw, given that a junior's name was drawn first?
  - (d) a sophomores' name on both draws?
  - (e) a junior's name on both draws?
  - (f) one sophomore's name and one junior's name on the two draws, regardless of order drawn?

⁞ **B-21** The oasis outpost of Abu Ilan, in the heart of the Negev desert, has a population of 20 Bedouin tribesmen and 20 Farima tribesmen. El Kamin, a nearby oasis, has a population of 32 Bedouins and 8 Farima. A lost Israeli soldier, accidentally separated from his army unit, is wandering through the desert and arrives at the edge of one of the oases. The soldier has no idea which oasis he has found, but the first person he spots at a distance is a Bedouin. What is the probability that he wandered into Abu Ilan? What is the probability that he is in El Kamin?

⁞ **B-22** The lost Israeli soldier mentioned in Problem B-21 decides to rest for a few minutes before entering the desert oasis he has just found. Closing his eyes, he dozes off for 15 minutes, wakes, and walks toward the center of the oasis. The first person he spots this time he again recognizes as a Bedouin. What is the posterior probability that he is in El Kamin?

**B-23** Ace Machine Works estimates that the probability their lathe tool is properly adjusted is 0.8. When the lathe is properly adjusted, there is a 0.9 probability that the parts produced pass inspection. If the lathe is out of adjustment, however, the probability of a good part being produced is only 0.2. A part randomly chosen is inspected and found to be acceptable. At this point, what is the posterior probability that the lathe tool is properly adjusted?

**B-24** The Boston South Fifth Street Softball League consists of three teams: Mama's Boys, team 1; the Killers, team 2; and the Machos, team 3. Each team plays the other teams just once during the season. The win–loss record for the past five years is as follows:

| WINNER | (1) | (2) | (3) |
|---|---|---|---|
| Mama's Boys (1) | X | 3 | 4 |
| The Killers (2) | 2 | X | 1 |
| The Machos (3) | 1 | 4 | X |

Each row represents the number of wins over the past five years. Mama's Boys beat the Killers three times, beat the Machos four times, and so on.

(a) What is the probability that the Killers will win every game next year?
(b) What is the probability that the Machos will win at least one game next year?
(c) What is the probability that Mama's Boys will win exactly one game next year?
(d) What is the probability that the Killers will win less than two games next year?

**B-25** The schedule for the Killers next year is as follows (refer to Problem B-24):

Game 1: The Machos
Game 2: Mama's Boys

(a) What is the probability that the Killers will win their first game?
(b) What is the probability that the Killers will win their last game?
(c) What is the probability that the Killers will break even—win exactly one game?
(d) What is the probability that the Killers will win every game?
(e) What is the probability that the Killers will lose every game?
(f) Would you want to be the coach of the Killers?

**B-26** The Northside Rifle team has two markspersons, Dick and Sally. Dick hits a bull's-eye 90% of the time, and Sally hits a bull's-eye 95% of the time.

(a) What is the probability that either Dick or Sally or both will hit the bull's-eye if each takes one shot?

(b) What is the probability that Dick and Sally will both hit the bull's-eye?
(c) Did you make any assumptions in answering the preceding questions? If you answered yes, do you think that you are justified in making the assumption(s)?

**B-27** In a sample of 1,000 representing a survey from the entire population, 650 people were from Laketown, and the rest of the people were from River City. Out of the sample, 19 people had some form of cancer. Thirteen of these people were from Laketown.

(a) Are the events of living in Laketown and having some sort of cancer independent?
(b) Which city would you prefer to live in, assuming that your main objective was to avoid having cancer?

**B-28** Compute the probability of "loaded die, given that a 3 was rolled," as shown in Example 7, this time using the general form of Bayes' theorem from Equation B-7.

**B-29** Which of the following are probability distributions? Why?

(a)

| RANDOM VARIABLE X | PROBABILITY |
|---|---|
| −2 | 0.1 |
| −1 | 0.2 |
| 0 | 0.3 |
| 1 | 0.25 |
| 2 | 0.15 |

(b)

| RANDOM VARIABLE Y | PROBABILITY |
|---|---|
| 1 | 1.1 |
| 1.5 | 0.2 |
| 2 | 0.3 |
| 2.5 | 0.25 |
| 3 | −1.25 |

(c)

| RANDOM VARIABLE Z | PROBABILITY |
|---|---|
| 1 | 0.1 |
| 2 | 0.2 |
| 3 | 0.3 |
| 4 | 0.4 |
| 5 | 0.0 |

**B-30** Harrington Health Food stocks 5 loaves of Neutro-Bread. The probability distribution for the sales of Neutro-Bread is listed in the following table. How many loaves will Harrington sell on average?

| Number of Loaves Sold | Probability |
|---|---|
| 0 | 0.05 |
| 1 | 0.15 |
| 2 | 0.20 |
| 3 | 0.25 |
| 4 | 0.20 |
| 5 | 0.15 |

- **B-31** What are the expected value and variance of the following probability distribution?

| Random Variable X | Probability |
|---|---|
| 1 | 0.05 |
| 2 | 0.05 |
| 3 | 0.10 |
| 4 | 0.10 |
| 5 | 0.15 |
| 6 | 0.15 |
| 7 | 0.25 |
| 8 | 0.15 |

- **B-32** Sales for Fast Kat, a 16-foot catamaran sailboat, have averaged 250 boats per month over the past five years, with a standard deviation of 25 boats. Assuming that the demand is about the same as past years and follows a normal curve, what is the probability sales will be less than 280 boats?

- **B-33** Refer to Problem B-32. What is the probability that sales will be more than 265 boats during the next month? What is the probability that sales will be less than 250 boats next month?

- **B-34** Precision Parts is a job shop that specializes in producing electric motor shafts. The average shaft size for the E300 electric motor is 0.55 inch, with a standard deviation of 0.10 inch. It is normally distributed. What is the probability that a shaft selected at random will be between 0.55 and 0.65 inch?

- **B-35** Refer to Problem B-34. What is the probability that a shaft size will be greater than 0.65 inch? What is the probability that a shaft size will be between 0.53 and 0.59 inch? What is the probability that a shaft size will be under 0.45 inch?

- **B-36** An industrial oven used to cure sand cores for a factory manufacturing engine blocks for small cars is able to maintain fairly constant temperatures. The temperature range of the oven follows a normal distribution with a mean of 450°F and a standard deviation of 25°F. Leslie Larsen, president of the factory, is concerned about the large number of defective cores that have been produced in the last several months. If

the oven gets hotter than 475°F, the core is defective. What is the probability that the oven will cause a core to be defective? What is the probability that the temperature of the oven will range from 460 to 470°F?

- **B-37** Steve Goodman, production foreman for the Florida Gold Fruit Company, estimates that the average sale of oranges is 4,700 and the standard deviation is 500 oranges. Sales follow a normal distribution.

  (a) What is the probability that sales will be greater than 5,500 oranges?
  (b) What is the probability that sales will be greater than 4,500 oranges?
  (c) What is the probability that sales will be less than 4,900 oranges?
  (d) What is the probability that sales will be less than 4,300 oranges?

- **B-38** Susan Williams has been the production manager of Medical Suppliers, Inc., for the past 17 years. Medical Suppliers, Inc., is a producer of bandages and arm slings. During the past 5 years, the demand for No-Stick bandages has been fairly constant. On the average, sales have been about 87,000 packages of No-Stick. Susan has reason to believe that the distribution of No-Stick follows a normal curve, with a standard deviation of 4,000 packages. What is the probability that sales will be less than 81,000 packages?

- **B-39** Armstrong Faber produces a standard number two pencil called Ultra-Lite. Since Chuck Armstrong started Armstrong Faber, sales had grown steadily. With the increase in the price of wood products, however, Chuck has been forced to increase the price of the Ultra-Lite pencils. As a result, the demand for Ultra-Lite has been fairly stable over the past six years. On the average, Armstrong Faber has sold 457,000 pencils each year. Furthermore, 90% of the time sales have been between 454,000 and 460,000 pencils. It is expected that the sales follow a normal distribution with a mean of 457,000 pencils. Estimate the standard deviation of this distribution. (*Hint:* Work backward from the normal table to find Z. Then apply Equation B-12.)

- **B-40** Patients arrive at the emergency room of Costa Valley Hospital at an average of 5 per day. The demand for emergency room treatment at Costa Valley follows a Poisson distribution.

  (a) Compute the probability of exactly 0, 1, 2, 3, 4, and 5 arrivals per day.
  (b) What is the sum of these probabilities, and why is the number less than 1?

- **B-41** Using the data in Problem B-40, determine the probability of more than 3 visits for emergency room service on any given day.

- **B-42** Cars arrive at Carla's Muffler shop for repair work at an average of 3 per hour, following an exponential distribution.

  (a) What is the expected time between arrivals?
  (b) What is the variance of the time between arrivals?

# APPENDIX C: AREAS UNDER THE STANDARD NORMAL CURVE

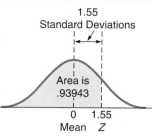

1.55
Standard Deviations

Area is
.93943

0    1.55
Mean  Z

**Example:** To find the area under the normal curve, you must know how many standard deviations that point is to the right of the mean. Then the area under the normal curve can be read directly from the normal table. For example, the total area under the normal curve for a point that is 1.55 standard deviations to the right of the mean is .93943.

| Z | .00 | .01 | .02 | .03 | .04 | .05 | .06 | .07 | .08 | .09 |
|---|------|------|------|------|------|------|------|------|------|------|
| 0.0 | .50000 | .50399 | .50798 | .51197 | .51595 | .51994 | .52392 | .52790 | .53188 | .53586 |
| 0.1 | .53983 | .54380 | .54776 | .55172 | .55567 | .55962 | .56356 | .56749 | .57142 | .57535 |
| 0.2 | .57926 | .58317 | .58706 | .59095 | .59483 | .59871 | .60257 | .60642 | .61026 | .61409 |
| 0.3 | .61791 | .62172 | .62552 | .62930 | .63307 | .63683 | .64058 | .64431 | .64803 | .65173 |
| 0.4 | .65542 | .65910 | .66276 | .66640 | .67003 | .67364 | .67724 | .68082 | .68439 | .68793 |
| 0.5 | .69146 | .69497 | .69847 | .70194 | .70540 | .70884 | .71226 | .71566 | .71904 | .72240 |
| 0.6 | .72575 | .72907 | .73237 | .73536 | .73891 | .74215 | .74537 | .74857 | .75175 | .75490 |
| 0.7 | .75804 | .76115 | .76424 | .76730 | .77035 | .77337 | .77637 | .77935 | .78230 | .78524 |
| 0.8 | .78814 | .79103 | .79389 | .79673 | .79955 | .80234 | .80511 | .80785 | .81057 | .81327 |
| 0.9 | .81594 | .81859 | .82121 | .82381 | .82639 | .82894 | .83147 | .83398 | .83646 | .83891 |
| 1.0 | .84134 | .84375 | .84614 | .84849 | .85083 | .85314 | .85543 | .85769 | .85993 | .86214 |
| 1.1 | .86433 | .86650 | .86864 | .87076 | .87286 | .87493 | .87698 | .87900 | .88100 | .88298 |
| 1.2 | .88493 | .88686 | .88877 | .89065 | .89251 | .89435 | .89617 | .89796 | .89973 | .90147 |
| 1.3 | .90320 | .90490 | .90658 | .90824 | .90988 | .91149 | .91309 | .91466 | .91621 | .91774 |
| 1.4 | .91924 | .92073 | .92220 | .92364 | .92507 | .92647 | .92785 | .92922 | .93056 | .93189 |
| 1.5 | .93319 | .93448 | .93574 | .93699 | .93822 | .93943 | .94062 | .94179 | .94295 | .94408 |
| 1.6 | .94520 | .94630 | .94738 | .94845 | .94950 | .95053 | .95154 | .95254 | .95352 | .95449 |
| 1.7 | .95543 | .95637 | .95728 | .95818 | .95907 | .95994 | .96080 | .96164 | .96246 | .96327 |
| 1.8 | .96407 | .96485 | .96562 | .96638 | .96712 | .96784 | .96856 | .96926 | .96995 | .97062 |
| 1.9 | .97128 | .97193 | .97257 | .97320 | .97381 | .97441 | .97500 | .97558 | .97615 | .97670 |
| 2.0 | .97725 | .97784 | .97831 | .97882 | .97932 | .97982 | .98030 | .98077 | .98124 | .98169 |
| 2.1 | .98214 | .98257 | .98300 | .98341 | .98382 | .98422 | .98461 | .98500 | .98537 | .98574 |
| 2.2 | .98610 | .98645 | .98679 | .99713 | .98745 | .98778 | .98809 | .98840 | .98870 | .98899 |
| 2.3 | .98928 | .98956 | .98983 | .99010 | .99036 | .99061 | .99086 | .99111 | .99134 | .99158 |
| 2.4 | .99180 | .99202 | .99224 | .99245 | .99266 | .99286 | .99305 | .99324 | .99343 | .99361 |
| 2.5 | .99379 | .99396 | .99413 | .99430 | .99446 | .99461 | .99477 | .99492 | .99506 | .99520 |
| 2.6 | .99534 | .99547 | .99560 | .99573 | .99585 | .99598 | .99609 | .99621 | .99632 | .99643 |
| 2.7 | .99653 | .99664 | .99674 | .99683 | .99693 | .99702 | .99711 | .99720 | .99728 | .99736 |
| 2.8 | .99744 | .99752 | .99760 | .99767 | .99774 | .99781 | .99788 | .99795 | .99801 | .99807 |
| 2.9 | .99813 | .99819 | .99825 | .99831 | .99836 | .99841 | .99846 | .99851 | .99856 | .99861 |
| 3.0 | .99865 | .99869 | .99874 | .99878 | .99882 | .99886 | .99899 | .99893 | .99896 | .99900 |
| 3.1 | .99903 | .99906 | .99910 | .99913 | .99916 | .99918 | .99921 | .99924 | .99926 | .99929 |
| 3.2 | .99931 | .99934 | .99936 | .99938 | .99940 | .99942 | .99944 | .99946 | .99948 | .99950 |
| 3.3 | .99952 | .99953 | .99955 | .99957 | .99958 | .99960 | .99961 | .99962 | .99964 | .99965 |
| 3.4 | .99966 | .99968 | .99969 | .99970 | .99971 | .99972 | .99973 | .99974 | .99975 | .99976 |
| 3.5 | .99977 | .99978 | .99978 | .99979 | .99980 | .99981 | .99981 | .99982 | .99983 | .99983 |
| 3.6 | .99984 | .99985 | .99985 | .99986 | .99986 | .99987 | .99987 | .99988 | .99988 | .99989 |
| 3.7 | .99989 | .99990 | .99990 | .99990 | .99991 | .99991 | .99992 | .99992 | .99992 | .99992 |
| 3.8 | .99993 | .99993 | .99993 | .99994 | .99994 | .99994 | .99994 | .99995 | .99995 | .99995 |
| 3.9 | .99995 | .99995 | .99996 | .99996 | .99996 | .99996 | .99996 | .99996 | .99997 | .99997 |

**Source:** Reprinted from Robert O. Schlaifer. *Introduction to Statistics for Business Decisions,* published by McGraw-Hill Book Company, 1961, by permission of the copyright holder, the President and Fellows of Harvard College.

# APPENDIX D: SOLUTIONS TO SELECTED PROBLEMS

## Chapter 1

**1-19** (a) 6,250 units    (b) 7,000 units    (c) $125,000
(d) $140,000    (e) Proposal A    (f) Proposal B

**1-20** (a) 12,500 units    (b) $100,000    (c) $350,000

**1-22** (a) 25,000 books    (b) $750,000

**1-23** (a) 30,000 books    (b) $900,000

**1-26** 6,881 units

## Chapter 2

**2-14** $X = 33.33, Y = 33.33$, Profit = $66.66

**2-16** $X = 2, Y = 3$, Profit = $26

**2-18** $X = 25.71, Y = 21.43$, Cost = $68.57

**2-22** 5 TV spots, 68 ads, exposure of 1,535,000

**2-23** 40 air conditioners, 60 fans. Profit = $1,900.

**2-25** 200 model A tubs, 0 model B tubs. Profit = $18,000.

**2-27** 40 undergraduate, 20 graduate. Cost = $160,000.

**2-28** 10 Alpha 4s, 24 Beta 5s. Profit = $55,200.

**2-31** 24 coconuts, 12 skins. Wealth = 5,040 rupees.

**2-35** Make only MCA regular modems (27,747.75 of them). Profit = $629,041.

## Chapter 3

**3-1** (a) Let $F$ = number of French provincial produced; $D$ = number of Danish modern produced

$$\text{Max Revenue} = \$28F + \$25D$$

$$3F + 2D \leq 360$$

$$1.5F + 1D \leq 200$$

$$0.75F + 0.75D \leq 125$$

$$F \geq 60$$

$$D \geq 60$$

(b) $F = 60, D = 90$, Revenue = $3,930

**3-5** (a) Let $N$ = number of newspaper ads; $T$ = number of TV spots

$$\text{Min Cost} = \$925N + \$2,000T$$

$$0.04N + 0.05T \geq 0.40$$

$$0.03N + 0.03T \geq 0.60$$

$$N, T \geq 0$$

(b) $N = 20, T = 0$, Cost = $18,500

**3-7** (b) Chauncey = 26, Sweet Italian = 5, Bourbon = 6.5, Russian Martinis = 14.25, Total = 51.75 drinks

**3-8** (a) Let $A$ = Adv $, $S$ = Store display $, $I$ = Inventory $, $M$ = % markup

$$\text{Max Rolls} = 20A + 6.8S + 12I - 65,000M$$

$$A + S + I \leq 17,000$$

$$A \geq 3,000$$

$$S - 0.05I \geq 0$$

$$M \geq 0.20$$

$$M \leq 0.45$$

$$A, S, I, M \geq 0$$

(b) $A = \$17,000, M = 0.20$, Rolls = 327,000

**3-10** (b) Internal modems = 496.55, External modems = 1,241.38, Profit = $195,504.83

**3-12** (b) 1,762.5 acres wheat in SE, 437.5 acres wheat in N, 131.03 acres, alfalfa in SE, 771.43 acres barley in N, 228.57 acres barley in NW, Profit = $337,862.07. *Note:* This problem has multiple optimal solutions.

**3-14** 2,791 medical patients (= 61 medical beds) and 2,105 surgical patients (= 29 surgical beds). Revenue = $9,551,659 per year.

## Chapter 4

**4-10** (a) Solution changes to $X = 50, Y = 0$, Profit = $150.    (b) Solution remains at $X = 33.33, Y = 33.33$, Profit changes to $75.    (c) Solution stays at same corner point, but now $X = 42.86, Y = 14.28$, Profit = $57.14.

**4-12** (a) Solution changes to $X = 2.86, Y = 1.71$, Profit = $21.71.    (b) Solution changes to $X = 5, Y = 1.5$, Profit = $29.

**4-13** (a) Total audience would increase by 406.    (b) No. They are already over this contract level.    (c) No. Need to increase exposure to at least 3,144.83. (d) 0 to 6,620.69

**4-15** (a) Total cost decreases by $0.0038.    (b) 100% rule satisfied, same mix; Total cost is $0.0529. (c) 100% rule satisfied; total cost decreases by $0.0038.

**4-18** (a) Each circuit board produced will decrease total profit by $138.64. Similar interpretations for floppy drives, hard drives, and memory boards.    (b) No impact. There are 37.93 hours of slack on device 3. (c) Yes. Total profit increases by $25,490.40. (d) 100% rule satisfied. Total profit decreases by $11,902.80. Not a good deal.

**4-20** (a) Profit increases by $1.    (b) Profit increases by $1.50.    (c) 100% rule satisfied. Profit decreases by $0.25.    (d) 100% rule satisfied. Profit increases by $0.50.    (e) New product will be included in the revised product mix.

**4-23** Compact model not attractive; Kiddo model is attractive.

**4-25**  (a) $0 to $7.33   (b) No

**4-27**  No. Profit would decrease by $3.225 for each TwinTote made (if TwinTotes are not included in the 40% limit for ToddleTotes. Profit would decrease by $1.685 if it is included).

## Chapter 5

**5-12**  Total distance = 5,400 "student miles"

**5-13**  (a) Total cost = $31,750   (b) Total cost with trans-shipment = $27,500

**5-14**  Morgantown–Coaltown = 35, Youngstown–Coal Valley = 30, Youngstown–Coaltown = 5, Youngstown–Coal Junction = 25, Pittsburgh–Coaltown = 5, Pittsburgh–Coalsburg = 20, Total distance = 3,100 miles

**5-17**  Cost with New Orleans = $20,000, Cost with Houston = $19,500. Houston should be selected

**5-21**  A12 to W, A15 to Z, B2 to Y, B9 to X, Time = 50 hours

**5-23**  Total "cost scale" = 86

**5-24**  Stand 1 to C, Stand 2 to B, Stand 3 to A, Stand 4 to D, Total distance = 18 miles

**5-26**  Total rating = 335

**5-27**  One solution is 1-2, 1-3, 1-4, 3-6, 4-5, 6-7, 7-9, 8-9, 9-12, 9-10, 10-11, 11-13, and 12-14. Total distance = 4,500 feet.

**5-29**  1-3-5-7-10-13, Distance = 430 miles.

**5-34**  Maximal flow is 17.

**5-36**  Maximal flow is 2,000 gallons.

**5-37**  Shortest distance is 74. The path is 1-3-7-11-14-16.

**5-40**  Total length is 21. One solution is 1-2, 1-3, 3-7, 4-5, 5-6, 6-8, 6-7, and 8-9.

## Chapter 6

**6-13**  3 large posters, 4 small posters, Profit = $17

**6-15**  Build in Mt. Auburn, Mt. Adams, Norwood, Covington, and Eden Park, Profit = $37,000

**6-19**  500 two-drawer cabinets, 400 three-drawer cabinets, and two-drawer sales goal underachieved by 100.

**6-23**  $X_1 = 15$, $X_2 = 20$, first 3 priority goals fully satisfied, $d_1^+ = 30$

**6-24**  (b) $X_1 = 49$, $X_2 = 69$, $X_3 = 30$, $X_4 = 20$. All goals are fully met. *Note:* To get this solution, we need to restrict social time to 20 hours.

**6-25**  $X_1 = 2.93$, $X_2 = 6.36$, $X_3 = 3.61$, Objective value = 424.88

**6-28**  (b) 18.3 XJ6s, 10.8 XJ8s, Revenue = $70,420

## Chapter 7

**7-13**  26 days; critical path is B-D-E-G.

**7-15**  19 weeks; there are two critical paths: A-C-G and B-E-G.

**7-17**  36.33 days; critical path is C-D-E-F-H-K.

**7-18**  0.9463

**7-20**  (a) 0.0228   (b) 0.3085   (c) 0.8413   (d) 0.9772

**7-21**  $181,600; cost underrun = $9,600; behind schedule.

**7-25**  44 weeks, time increases to 47.83 weeks.

**7-26**  34 weeks; critical path activities are 11, 13, 14, 16, 17, 18, 19, 21, and 23.

**7-29**  (a) Project completion = 38.33 weeks   (b) D is still on the critical path. Project completion time is 29.167 weeks.   (c) Project completion time is 25.667 weeks. Critical path changes.   (d) Project completion time is 22.833 weeks. Critical path changes.

## Chapter 8

**8-14**  Maximin criterion: best alternative is Texan. −$18,000.

**8-18**  (b) Large wing   (c) No

**8-21**  (b) Back roads   (c) Time saved is 3.33 minutes.

**8-22**  Construct clinic. EMV = $30,000.

**8-23**  (b) Survey should be taken. EMV = $36,140. (c) EVSI = $11,140

**8-25**  Conduct survey. If survey is favorable, build large shop. Otherwise, do not build.

**8-27**  (b) Use supplier A.   (c) $60 less than supplier A

**8-29**  Do not conduct survey. Build medium-sized facility. EMV = $670,000.

**8-31**  Do not conduct survey and do not construct clinic. They are risk avoiders.

**8-32**  Jon's decision would change. He would not conduct the survey. He would build the large plant.

**8-33**  (a) Broad Street, 27.5 minutes   (b) Expressway (c) Lynn is a risk avoider.

**8-35**  Jack should accept his kids' bet.

## Chapter 9

**9-11**  (a) 0.375   (b) 0.2 days or 1.6 hours   (c) 0.225 (d) 0.141, 0.053, 0.020, 0.007

**9-12**  (a) 4.167 cars   (b) 0.4167 hours   (c) 0.5 hours (d) 0.8333   (e) 0.1667

**9-15**  (a) 6 trucks   (b) 12 minutes   (c) 0.857   (d) 0.54 (e) $1,728/day   (f) Yes. Savings = $3,096

**9-18**  (a) 3 doctors   (b) 2 doctors   (c) 4 doctors

**9-21**  $36 with 1 loader, $18 with 2 loaders, Savings = $18 with 2 loaders

**9-22**  Do not recommend a second gate.

**9-24**  L = 0.8125, W = 0.8125, Probability of waiting = 0.5

**9-25**  Service rate should be 2.63 per hour. Service time should average 22.8 minutes per customer.

**9-27**  L = 5.9625, W = 6.625, Worth about $158

**9-30**  4 entrances, 2 exits

## Chapter 10

*Note:* Answers in this chapter will vary based on number of replications used. All answers shown here are based on 3,000 replications using *Crystal Ball*.

**10-15** Expected ending balance = $47, Probability of negative balance = 0.148

**10-16** (a) Cost/hour is generally more expensive if we replace 1 pen each time.    (b) Expected cost/hour with 1 pen policy = $1.38 (or $58/breakdown). Expected cost/hour with 4-pen policy = $1.12 (or $132/breakdown).

**10-19** (b) About 5.5% of patients visit the x-ray department more than once.

**10-22** Expected stockout per month = 3.72

**10-23** Expected total cost per month = $17,562

**10-26** Probability of getting more than $250 = 0.15

**10-28** Ann should order 170 hot dogs, expected profit = $107.42, percentage of unsold hot dogs = 11.2%

## Chapter 11

**11-13** (a) 337    (b) 380    (c) 423

**11-14** MAPE for 3-period MA = 22.92%, MAPE for 3-period WMA = 21.17%.

**11-16** The 3-period WMA has the lowest MAPE (= 21.17%).

**11-18** Year 2 = 422, year 3 = 443.9, year 4 = 466.1, year 5 = 495.2, year 6 = 521.8

**11-20** MAPE = 7.05% when $\alpha = 0.9$. MAPE = 10.20% when $\alpha = 0.6$.

**11-22** $Y = 421.2 + 33.6X$ if years are coded 1 to 5. Next year's sales = 622.8

**11-24** (b) $Y = 1.0 + 1.0X$    (c) 10

**11-27** (a) Forecast for 25th week with $\alpha$ of 0.1 = 47
(b) Forecast for 25th week with $\alpha$ of 0.6 = 58
(c) $\alpha$ of 0.6 seems to be better.

**11-28** Forecast for 25th week with $\alpha$ of 0.9 = 62.6. $\alpha$ of 0.6 is optimal.

**11-32** (b) $Y = 5.06 + 1.593X$    (c) 2,099,000 people

**11-34** $Y = 1.229 + 0.545X$, 73 patients if rate is 131.2, 51 patients if rate is 90.6.

**11-35** $130,000, $108,000, $98,000, $184,000

**11-37** $Y = 1.028 + 0.003X$, $r^2 = 0.479$, $Y = 2.227$, $Y = 3.77$

**11-39** Quarter 1 = 59.4, Quarter 2 = 66.1, Quarter 3 = 72.8, Quarter 4 = 98.3

## Chapter 12

**12-17** 20,000 screws

**12-18** 4,000 screws

**12-21** 8 million loads of plywood

**12-25** Use the new supplier and take the discount. Total cost = $41,416.25.

**12-26** Expand to 10,000 cu ft to hold 100 motors, Expansion worth $250 per year

**12-28** Add 160 feet, pay up to $1,920 per year.

**12-31** 2,697 scissors

**12-32** 1,217 wheel bearings

**12-33** Take the discount; Total cost = $49,912.50.

**12-34** Lowest EMV is $125 with ROP of 90. Keep 30 units of safety stock.

**12-36** Item 33CP needs strict control, no strict control for the others.

**12-37** Lowest EMV is $3,425 with ROP of 1,050. Keep 400 units of safety stock.

**12-40** Order quantity = 852, Total cost = $176

**12-42** Order quantity = 51, Total cost = $1,901.21

**12-46** Safety stock = 19.22 (rounded to 20) units, ROP = 56 units

**12-50** G2 and F3 are Group A items, A2, C7, and D1 are Group B items, Rest are Group C items

## Appendix B

**B-14**  0.30

**B-16**  (a) 0.10    (b) 0.04    (c) 0.25    (d) 0.40

**B-18**  (a) 0.20    (b) 0.09    (c) 0.31    (d) dependent

**B-19**  0.54

**B-23**  0.947

**B-28**  0.78

**B-30**  2.85

**B-31**  $E(X) = 5.45$, Variance = 4.047

**B-32**  0.8849

**B-34**  0.3413

**B-38**  0.0668

**B-39**  1829.27

**B-40**  (b) 0.6125

**B-41**  0.7365

# APPENDIX E: SOLUTIONS TO SELF-TESTS

## Chapter 1

1.  c
2.  d
3.  b
4.  c

5.  a
6.  a
7.  a
8.  a
9.  b

10.  a
11.  c
12.  Decision modeling
13.  Defining the problem
14.  schematic model

15. algorithm
16. Decision modeling
17. quantitative analysis, management science
18. probabilities
19. parameter
20. formulation, solution, interpretation

## Chapter 2

1. b
2. b
3. a
4. b
5. c
6. d
7. b
8. a
9. b
10. c
11. a
12. b
13. b
14. b
15. a
16. d
17. b

## Chapter 3

1. a
2. b
3. b
4. b
5. b
6. d
7. e
8. e
9. d
10. c
11. c
12. c
13. b

## Chapter 4

1. a
2. b
3. a
4. b
5. b
6. a
7. b
8. a

9. b
10. c
11. a
12. b
13. a
14. b
15. b

## Chapter 5

1. c
2. e
3. e
4. b
5. c
6. a
7. a
8. b
9. shortest path
10. maximal flow
11. minimal-spanning tree
12. c
13. a

## Chapter 6

1. a
2. c
3. b
4. d
5. a
6. a
7. a
8. b
9. b
10. a
11. a
12. b
13. e

## Chapter 7

1. d
2. b
3. a
4. e
5. c
6. b
7. a
8. d
9. critical
10. optimistic, most likely, pessimistic
11. c
12. b

13. a
14. c
15. b

## Chapter 8

1. a
2. d
3. e
4. b
5. e
6. b
7. c
8. c
9. e
10. e
11. d
12. d
13. decision trees
14. posterior probabilities
15. standard gamble

## Chapter 9

1. a
2. a
3. b
4. e
5. e
6. c
7. c
8. a
9. b
10. b
11. c
12. first-come, first served
13. exponentially distributed
14. simulation
15. unlimited

## Chapter 10

1. b
2. b
3. a
4. b
5. a
6. b
7. (1) define the problem, (2) introduce the variables associated with the problem, (3) construct a numerical model, (4) set up possible courses of action for testing, (5) run the experiment, (6) con-

sider the results, and (7) decide what course of action to take

**8.** (1) it is relatively straightforward and flexible, (2) it can be used to analyze large and complex real-world situations that cannot be solved by conventional decision models, (3) it allows what-if types of questions, (4) it does not interfere with the real-world system, (5) it allows us to study the interactive effects of individual components or variables to determine which ones are important, (6) it allows time compression, and (7) it allows for the inclusion of real-world complications that most decision models cannot permit

**9.** (1) it can be very expensive, (2) it does not generate optimal solutions to problems, (3) managers must generate all of the conditions and constraints for solutions that they want to examine, and (4) each simulation model is unique

**10.** b
**11.** d
**12.** c
**13.** e
**14.** c
**15.** b
**16.** d
**17.** b
**18.** a

## Chapter 11

**1.** d
**2.** c
**3.** b
**4.** b
**5.** b
**6.** trend × seasonality × cycles × random variations
**7.** b
**8.** a
**9.** d
**10.** b
**11.** b
**12.** a
**13.** a
**14.** a
**15.** a
**16.** independent variable is said to cause variations in the dependent variable
**17.** (1) moving averages, (2) weighted moving averages, (3) exponential smoothing, (4) linear trend projection, (5) decomposition
**18.** (1) trend, (2) seasonality, (3) cycles, (4) random variations
**19.** c
**20.** Simple regression has one independent variable and multiple regression has many independent variables.
**21.** Exponential smoothing is a weighted moving average model in which all previous values are weighted with a set of exponentially declining weights.
**22.** Study the shape of the relationship between the dependent and the independent variables.

## Chapter 12

**1.** c
**2.** d
**3.** b
**4.** e
**5.** d
**6.** d
**7.** a
**8.** b
**9.** d
**10.** Safety stock
**11.** Service level
**12.** ABC analysis

# INDEX

Note: Any page number with an "n" after it means that topic can be found in a footnote.